The IDG SECRETS Advantage

Internet SECRETS is part of the SECRETS series of books brought to you by IDG Books Worldwide. The designers of the SECRETS series understand that you appreciate insightful and comprehensive works from computer experts. Authorities in their respective areas, the authors of the SECRETS books have been selected for their ability to enrich your daily computing tasks.

The formula for a book in the SECRETS series is simple: Give an expert author a forum to pass on his or her expertise to readers. A SECRETS author, rather than the publishing company, directs the organization, pace, and treatment of the subject matter. SECRETS authors maintain close contact with end users through column feedback, user group participation, and consulting work. The authors' close contact with the needs of computer users gives the SECRETS books a strategic advantage over most computer books. Our authors do not distance themselves from the reality of daily computing, but rather, our authors are directly tied to the reader response stream.

We believe that the author has the experience to approach a topic in the most efficient manner, and we know that you, the reader, will benefit from a "one-to-one" relationship, through the text, with the author. The author's voice is always present in a SECRETS series book. Some have compared the presentation of a topic in a SECRETS book to sitting at a coffee break with the author and having the author's full attention.

And of course, the author is free to include or recommend useful software, both shareware and proprietary, in a SECRETS series book. The software that accompanies a SECRETS book is not intended as casual filler. The software is strategically linked to the content, theme, or procedures of the book. We expect that you will receive a real and direct benefit from the included software.

You will find this book comprehensive whether you read it cover to cover, section to section, or simply a topic at a time. As a computer user, you deserve a comprehensive and informative resource of answers that *Internet SECRETS* delivers.

Karen A. Bluestein
Publisher

Internet SECRETS

Internet SECRETS

by John R. Levine
and Carol Baroudi

IDG Books Worldwide, Inc.
An International Data Group Company

Foster City, CA ♦ Chicago, IL ♦ Indianapolis, IN
Braintree, MA ♦ Dallas, TX

Internet SECRETS

Published by
IDG Books Worldwide, Inc.
An International Data Group Company
919 E. Hillsdale Blvd.
Suite 400
Foster City, CA 94404

Library of Congress Catalog Card No.: 94-73683

ISBN: 1-56884-452-2

Printed in the United States of America

10 9 8 7 6 5 4 3 2 1

1B/RQ/QT/ZV

Distributed in the United States by IDG Books Worldwide, Inc.

Distributed by Macmillan Canada for Canada; by Computer and Technical Books for the Caribbean Basin; by Contemporantea de Ediciones for Venezuela; by Distribuidora Cuspide for Argentina; by CITFC for Brazil; by Ediciones ZETA S.C.R. Ltda. for Peru; by Editorial Limusa SA for Mexico; by Transworld Publishers Limited in the United Kingdom and Europe; by Al-Maiman Publishers & Distributors for Saudi Arabia; by Simron Pty. Ltd. for South Africa; by IDC Communications (IIK) Ltd. for Hong Kong; by Toppan Company Ltd. for Japan; by Addison-Wesley Publishing Company for Korea; by Longman Singapore Publisher Ltd. for Singapore, Malaysia, Thailand, and Indonesia; by Unalis Corporation for Taiwan; by WS Computer Publishing Company, Inc. for the Philippines; by WoodsLane Enterprises Ltd. for New Zealand.

For general information on IDG Books in the U.S., including information on discounts and premiums, contact IDG Books at 800-434-3422 or 415-655-3000.

For information on where to purchase IDG Books outside the U.S., contact IDG Books International at 415-655-3021 or fax 415-655-3295.

For information on translations, contact Març Jeffrey Mikulich, Director, Foreign & Subsidiary Rights, at IDG Books Worldwide, 415-655-3018 or fax 415-655-3295.

For sales inquiries and special prices for bulk quantities, write to the address above or call IDG Books Worldwide at 415-655-3000.

For information on using IDG Books in the classroom, or for ordering examination copies, contact Jim Kelly at 800-434-2086.

About the Authors

John R. Levine

John Levine was a member of a computer club in high school before high school students — or even high schools — *had* computers. He came in contact with Theodore H. Nelson, author of *Computer Lib* and inventor of hypertext, who fostered the idea that computers should not be taken seriously and that everyone can and should understand and use computers.

John wrote his first program on an IBM 1130 (a computer roughly as powerful as your typical modern digital wristwatch, only harder to use) in 1967. He became an official system administrator of a networked computer at Yale in 1975. He started working part-time (for a computer company, of course) in 1977, and he has been in and out of the computer and network biz ever since. He got his company put on Usenet early enough that it appears in a 1982 *Byte* magazine article, which included a map of Usenet sites.

He used to spend most of his time writing software, but now he writes mostly books (including *UNIX For Dummies, The Internet For Dummies,* and *MORE Internet For Dummies,* published by IDG Books Worldwide, Inc.) because it's more fun. He also teaches some computer courses, publishes and edits an incredibly technoid magazine called The Journal of C Language Translation, and moderates a Usenet newsgroup. He holds a B.A. and Ph.D. in Computer Science from Yale University, but please don't hold that against him.

Carol Baroudi

Carol Baroudi met her first computer in college in 1971 at Colgate University, where she had virtually unlimited access to the then-state-of-the-art DecSystem-10. Although she taught programming and helped design a computer science curriculum, she majored in Spanish Literature. In creating *Internet SECRETS,* she's found, for the first time, a *professional* use for her language study.

Carol programmed for a bunch of years, became a high-tech head hunter for another bunch, and has been writing professionally for some twelve or thirteen more. In those odd hours when she's not taking care of her son, writing a book, or sending e-mail, she studies acting and singing and performs in *The Sad Tale of King Leerio* whenever possible.

She feels the widespread availability of Internet access allows us a new, rich form of communication and has the potential to kindle, enliven, and deepen relationships between friends and families the world over. At the same time, she feels compelled to emphasize that as fun and useful as this technology is, it is *no* substitute for real life.

Welcome to the world of IDG Books Worldwide.

IDG Books Worldwide, Inc., is a subsidiary of International Data Group, the world's largest publisher of computer-related information and the leading global provider of information services on information technology. IDG was founded more than 25 years ago and now employs more than 7,200 people worldwide. IDG publishes more than 233 computer publications in 65 countries (see listing below). More than sixty million people read one or more IDG publications each month.

Launched in 1990, IDG Books Worldwide is today the #1 publisher of best-selling computer books in the United States. We are proud to have received 3 awards from the Computer Press Association in recognition of editorial excellence, and our best-selling ...*For Dummies*™ series has more than 12 million copies in print with translations in 25 languages. IDG Books, through a recent joint venture with IDG's Hi-Tech Beijing, became the first U.S. publisher to publish a computer book in the People's Republic of China. In record time, IDG Books has become the first choice for millions of readers around the world who want to learn how to better manage their businesses.

WINNER
Eighth Annual Computer Press Awards 1992

Our mission is simple: Every IDG book is designed to bring extra value and skill-building instructions to the reader. Our books are written by experts who understand and care about our readers. The knowledge base of our editorial staff comes from years of experience in publishing, education, and journalism — experience which we use to produce books for the '90s. In short, we care about books, so we attract the best people. We devote special attention to details such as audience, interior design, use of icons, and illustrations. And because we use an efficient process of authoring, editing, and desktop publishing our books electronically, we can spend more time ensuring superior content and spend less time on the technicalities of making books.

You can count on our commitment to deliver high-quality books at competitive prices on topics consumers want to read about. At IDG, we value quality, and we have been delivering quality for more than 25 years. You'll find no better book on a subject than an IDG book.

John Kilcullen
President and CEO
IDG Books Worldwide, Inc.

WINNER
Ninth Annual Computer Press Awards 1993

IDG Books Worldwide, Inc., is a subsidiary of International Data Group, the world's largest publisher of computer-related information and the leading global provider of information services on information technology. International Data Group publishes over 220 computer publications in 65 countries. More than fifty million people read one or more International Data Group publications each month. The officers are Patrick J. McGovern, Founder and Board Chairman; Kelly Conlin, President; Jim Casella, Chief Operating Officer. International Data Group's publications include: **ARGENTINA'S** Computerworld Argentina, Infoworld Argentina; **AUSTRALIA'S** Computerworld Australia, Computer Living, Australian PC World, Australian Macworld, Network World, Mobile Business Australia, Publish!, Reseller, IDG Sources; **AUSTRIA'S** Computerwelt Oesterreich, PC Test; **BELGIUM'S** Data News (CW); **BOLIVIA'S** Computerworld; **BRAZIL'S** Computerworld, Connections, Game Power, Mundo Unix, PC World, Publish, Super Game; **BULGARIA'S** Computerworld Bulgaria, PC & Mac World Bulgaria, Network World Bulgaria; **CANADA'S** CIO Canada, Computerworld Canada, InfoCanada, Network World Canada, Reseller; **CHILE'S** Computerworld Chile, Informatica; **COLOMBIA'S** Computerworld Colombia, PC World; **COSTA RICA'S** PC World; **CZECH REPUBLIC'S** Computerworld, Elektronika, PC World; **DENMARK'S** Communications World, Computerworld Danmark, Computerworld Focus, Macintosh Produktkatalog, Macworld Danmark, PC World Danmark, PC Produktguide, Tech World, Windows World; **ECUADOR'S** PC World Ecuador; **EGYPT'S** Computerworld (CW) Middle East, PC World Middle East; **FINLAND'S** MikroPC, Tietoviikko, Tietoverkko; **FRANCE'S** Distributique, GOLDEN MAC, InfoPC, Le Guide du Monde Informatique, Le Monde Informatique, Telecoms & Reseaux; **GERMANY'S** Computerwoche, Computerwoche Focus, Computerwoche Extra, Electronic Entertainment, Gamepro, Information Management, Macwelt, Netzwelt, PC Welt, Publish, Publish; **GREECE'S** Publish & Macworld; **HONG KONG'S** Computerworld Hong Kong, PC World Hong Kong; **HUNGARY'S** Computerworld SZT, PC World; **INDIA'S** Computers & Communications; **INDONESIA'S** Info Komputer; **IRELAND'S** ComputerScope; **ISRAEL'S** Beyond Windows, Computerworld Israel, Multimedia, PC World Israel; **ITALY'S** Computerworld Italia, Lotus Magazine, Macworld Italia, Networking Italia, PC Shopping Italy, PC World Italia; **JAPAN'S** Computerworld Today, Information Systems World, Macworld Japan, Nikkei Personal Computing, SunWorld Japan, Windows World; **KENYA'S** East African Computer News; **KOREA'S** Computerworld Korea, Macworld Korea, PC World Korea; **LATIN AMERICA'S** GamePro; **MALAYSIA'S** Computerworld Malaysia, PC World Malaysia; **MEXICO'S** Compu Edicion, Compu Manufactura, Computacion/Punto de Venta, Computerworld Mexico, MacWorld, Mundo Unix, PC World, Windows; **THE NETHERLANDS'** Computer! Totaal, Computable (CW), LAN Magazine, Lotus Magazine, MacWorld; **NEW ZEALAND'S** Computer Buyer, Computerworld New Zealand, Network World, New Zealand PC World; **NIGERIA'S** PC World Africa; **NORWAY'S** Computerworld Norge, Lotusworld Norge, Macworld Norge, Maxi Data, Networld, PC World Ekspress, PC World Nettverk, PC World Norge, PC World's Produktguide, Publish& Multimedia World, Student Data, Unix World, Windowsworld; **PAKISTAN'S** PC World Pakistan; **PANAMA'S** PC World Panama; **PERU'S** Computerworld Peru, PC World; **PEOPLE'S REPUBLIC OF CHINA'S** China Computerworld, China Infoworld, China PC Info Magazine, Computer Fan, PC World China, Electronics International, Electronics Today/Multimedia World, Electronic Product World, China Network World, Software World Magazine, Telecom Product World; **PHILIPPINES'** Computerworld Philippines, PC Digest (PCW); **POLAND'S** Computerworld Poland, Computerworld Special Report, Networld, PC World/Komputer, Sunworld; **PORTUGAL'S** Cerebro/PC World, Correio Informatico/Computerworld, MacIn; **ROMANIA'S** Computerworld, PC World, Telecom Romania; **RUSSIA'S** Computerworld-Moscow, Mir - PK (PCW), Sety (Networks); **SINGAPORE'S** Computerworld Southeast Asia, PC World Singapore; **SLOVENIA'S** Monitor Magazine; **SOUTH AFRICA'S** Computer Mail (CIO),Computing S.A.,Network World S.A., Software World; **SPAIN'S** Advanced Systems, Amiga World, Computerworld Espana, Communicaciones World, Macworld Espana, NeXTWORLD, Super Juegos Magazine (GamePro), PC World Espana, Publish; **SWEDEN'S** Attack, ComputerSweden, Corporate Computing, Macworld, Mikrodatorn, Natverk & Kommunikation, PC World, CAP & Design, Datalngenjoren, Maxi Data,Windows World; **SWITZERLAND'S** Computerworld Schweiz, Macworld Schweiz, PC Tip; **TAIWAN'S** Computerworld Taiwan, PC World Taiwan; **THAILAND'S** Thai Computerworld; **TURKEY'S** Computerworld Monitor, Macworld Turkiye, PC World Turkiye; **UKRAINE'S** Computerworld, Computers+Software Magazine; **UNITED KINGDOM'S** Computing / Computerworld, Connexion/Network World, Lotus Magazine, Macworld, Open Computing/Sunworld; **UNITED STATES'** Advanced Systems, AmigaWorld, Cable in the Classroom, CD Review, CIO, Computerworld, Computerworld Client/Server Journal, Digital Video, DOS World, Electronic Entertainment Magazine (E2), Federal Computer Week, Game Hits, GamePro, IDG Books, Infoworld, Laser Event, Macworld, Maximize, Multimedia World, Network World, PC Letter, PC World, Publish, SWATPro, Video Event; **URUGUAY'S** PC World Uruguay; **VENEZUELA'S** Computerworld Venezuela, PC World; **VIETNAM'S** PC World Vietnam.

02/08/95

Dedication

John dedicates his part of the book (the even-numbered pages) to Tonia.

Carol dedicates her part of the book (clearly, the *odd* pages) to the love of the Good, the goodness of Love, and her own pursuit of the Divine. And to her friends, especially Jordan Charney, who taught her the *real* value of a secret, and to Philippe, who transcends the virtual.

Credits

Publisher
Karen A. Bluestein

Acquisitions Manager
Gregory Croy

Brand Manager
Melisa M. Duffy

Editorial Director
Mary Bednarek

Editorial Managers
Mary C. Corder
Andy Cummings

Editorial Executive Assistant
Jodi Lynn Semling-Thorn

Editorial Assistant
Nate Holdread

Production Director
Beth Jenkins

Supervisor of Project Coordination
Cindy L. Phipps

Project Coordinator
Valery Bourke

Pre-Press Coordinator
Steve Peake

Associate Pre-Press Coordinator
Tony Augsburger

Project Editor
Erik Dafforn

Editors
Becky Whitney
Kathy Simpson
Robert Campbell
Corbin Collins
Kezia Endsley
Jim Grey
N. Jeannie Smith
Pat O'Brien
Patricia Seiler
Shawn MacLaren

Technical Reviewers
Dennis Cox
Ron Nutter

Production Staff
Paul Belcastro
Chris Collins
Mark Owens
Laura Puranen
Carla Radzikinas
Dwight Ramsey
Patricia R. Reynolds
Theresa Sánchez-Baker
Gina Scott

Proofreader
Henry Lazarek

Indexer
Sherry Massey

Cover Design
Draper & Liew, Inc.

Acknowledgments

We thank, first, all of the authors who contributed to this book.

Our research and writing took us all over the continent. We thank the people and organizations that hosted one or the other of us during the research and writing of this book, including the Hanover Inn (Hanover, N.H.); Howard Creek Ranch (Westport, Calif.); Hana Sushi, Greek Corner, and Concord Cafe (all in Cambridge, Mass.); C. E. Schumb, Esq. (San Jose, Calif.); H. W. Watriss and N. Williams (Washington, D.C.); S. Barrows (Vienna, Va.); Servacom (Montreal, Quebec); and A. B. Saxon (Ithaca, N.Y.)

Many Internet providers helped us stay connected to the Net, even when far from home:

Centnet (Cambridge, Mass.)
TIAC (Bedford, Mass.)
ClarkNet (Ellicott City, Md.)
DELPHI Internet (Cambridge, Mass.)
Cornell University (Ithaca, N.Y.)

Alison Barrows and Margaret Levine Young provided essential editorial help, and Rachel Field provided logistical support. (Experienced readers of Acknowledgments pages will recognize that this means that without Alison and Margy the book would have been incoherent, and without Rachel we'd have lost all the chapters.)

We owe a special debt to Steve Dyer who gave our main computer a "temporary" home and restarted it probably a hundred times when it hung, keeping our vital e-mail flowing.

We thank our editor at IDG, Erik Dafforn, who pulled the manuscript from its raw form, slightly sticky to the touch, into the finished book you hold in your hand. (We particularly thank him for not passing along some of the extremely well-merited things that his managers were saying about us.) He was ably backed up by an army of editors, including Becky Whitney, Corbin Collins, Kathy Simpson, Robert Campbell, Kezia Endsley, Jim Grey, Pat O'Brien, Pat Seiler, Shawn MacLaren, and Jeannie Smith.

We also thank Meg Young, C. Isaac Young, and particularly Joshua Reinhold, without whose assistance this book would doubtless have been done sooner, but it wouldn't have been anywhere near as much fun.

Carol wishes to thank friends, family, and well-wishers who buoyed us with food and e-mail, most notably her parents, her cousin Bob, her brother David, Neil, David Lee, Michael Kestigian, Joshua Q. Lubarr, Dick Hammer, and Nat Kuhn. She thanks Virgil Benoit, wherever he is, for making her last study of French delicious. Special thanks to BackWorks (Cambridge, Mass.) who routinely tried to undo the abuse caused by her wrapping herself around a nine-inch monitor.

(The Publisher would like to give special thanks to Patrick J. McGovern, without whom this book would not have been possible.)

Contents at a Glance

Introduction **1**

Part I: Essays about the Net **3**

Chapter 1: Virtual Intimacy — Tales from Minitel and More 5

Chapter 2: Internet Culture and Folklore 27

Chapter 3: Usenet 49

Chapter 4: Doing Business on the Net 77

Chapter 5: Internet Privacy and Security 115

Chapter 6: Internet Access for People with Disabilities 181

Chapter 7: Smileys 207

Part II: Connecting to the Internet **213**

Chapter 8: DNS: The Domain Name System 215

Chapter 9: Connecting Your UNIX System to the Net 255

Chapter 10: Linking Your Organization's Network to the Internet 269

Chapter 11: Maintaining Large Networks 289

Chapter 12: Personal Internet Access Using SLIP or PPP 301

Chapter 13: Tuning TCP/IP 339

Chapter 14: Connecting Your Macintosh to the Internet 349

Chatper 15: Macintosh TIA: A Lighthearted Guide to a Heavy Topic 363

Chapter 16: OS/2 Warp and the Internet 387

Part III: Taming the Internet **407**

Chapter 17: Signature, Finger, and Organization Header: Telling the World Who You Are 409

Chapter 18: The Internet by E-Mail 429

Chapter 19: Supporting Non-English Characters in Internet Applications .. 443

Chapter 20: Finding Things on the Net 453

Chapter 21: Power IRC 509

Chapter 22: Scaling the World Wide Web 531

Chapter 23: Gopher Secrets 591

Chapter 24: Using WAIS 637

Chapter 25: Managing Mail 669

Chapter 26: Network News 725

Part IV: Becoming an Information Provider 799

Chapter 27: Look Ma, I'm an Internet Provider 801

Chapter 28: Setting up a European Internet Provider 815

Chapter 29: Running a Gopher Server 833

Chapter 30: Running a WWW Server on Windows 849

Part V: The Best Internet Applications 865

Chapter 31: The Complete WinSock Applications Roundup 867

Chapter 32: Macintosh Internet Applications 941

Chapter 33: Installing the Shareware Disks 957

Index 959

License and Disclaimer 989

Reader Response Card .... Back of Book

Table of Contents

Introduction 1

Part by Part 1
- Part I: Essays about the Net 2
- Part II: Connecting to the Internet 2
- Part III: Taming the Internet 2
- Part IV: Becoming an Information Provider 2
- Part V: The Best Internet Applications 2

Where to Go from Here 2

Part I: Essays about the Net 3

Chapter 1: Virtual Intimacy — Tales from Minitel and More 5

Introduction 5
Hacking for Chatting: GRETEL, the Genesis of Chatlines 6
The Digital Agoras 7
Service Mèdical 7
In Three Years, I Met More Than a Thousand People 9
New Alliances 10
Friendly Experiences, How I Met My Partner on Minitel Ten Years Ago 11
Falling in Digital Love 12
Learning by Osmosis: How I Became a Guru on Telematic Just by Writing Messages ... 15
Addicted to Chat 15
The BBSs 16
The Internet — Like a Small Town around the Planet 17
- IRC, the International Relationship Center 19
- E-mail chatting and encounters 22

Tomorrow on the Net ? 24
- Sharing your point of view (Share bookmarks with Netscape) 24
- The Profile Agents: Read the Net as myself, or like he does or like she does 24

The Survival and Success Guide to Digital Relationships 25
Conclusion 25

Chapter 2: Internet Culture and Folklore 27

Net Culture 27
- The petri dish 27
- Freedom and barriers 29

Archetypes ... 32
Angry young men and complainers ... 32
Clueless people and newbies ... 34
Control freaks ... 35
Conspiracy theorists ... 38
General weirdos ... 40
Loons ... 41
Curmudgeons ... 41
Demagogues ... 41
Fanatics ... 42
Flamers and terrorists ... 43
Net personalities ... 45
Pros ... 45
Rare, extinct, and mythical species ... 46
Conclusion ... 46

Chapter 3: Usenet ... 49

What Is Usenet? ... 49
What Usenet Is Not ... 49
1. Usenet is not an organization ... 49
2. Usenet is not a democracy ... 50
3. Usenet is not fair ... 50
4. Usenet is not a right ... 50
5. Usenet is not a public utility ... 50
6. Usenet is not an academic network ... 50
7. Usenet is not an advertising medium ... 50
8. Usenet is not the Internet ... 51
9. Usenet is not a UUCP network ... 51
10. Usenet is not a United States network ... 51
11. Usenet is not a UNIX network ... 51
12. Usenet is not an ASCII network ... 51
13. Usenet is not software ... 52
What Usenet Is ... 52
Diversity ... 52
Control ... 52
Periodic postings ... 53
Propagation ... 53
Newsgroup creation ... 53
The camel's nose? ... 54
If you are unhappy 54
Words to live by #1: Usenet as society ... 55
Words to live by #2: Usenet as anarchy ... 55
What Is Usenet? A Second Opinion ... 56
What Usenet Is Not ... 56

1. Usenet is not an organization 56
2. Usenet is not a democracy 57
3. Usenet is not fair 57
4. Usenet is not a right 57
5. Usenet is not a public utility 57
6. Usenet is not an academic network 58
7. Usenet is not an advertising medium 58
8. Usenet is not the Internet 59
9. Usenet is not a UUCP network 59
10. Usenet is not a United States network 59
11. Usenet is not a UNIX network 59
12. Usenet is not an ASCII network 60
13. Usenet is not software 60

What Usenet Is 60
- Diversity 61
- Control 61
- Periodic postings 62
- Propagation 62
- Newsgroup creation 62
- The camel's nose? 63
- If you are unhappy 63
- Words to live by #1: 63
- Words to live by #2: 64
- Words to live by #3: 64

Interview with Henry Spencer: On Usenet News and C News 65

Chapter 4: Doing Business on the Net 77

Internet Business Marketing 77
What Is Your Business Marketing Mission? 78
- Do you have skilled people in place? 79
- What level of hardware commitment are you ready to make? 79
- Established Internet service providers 80

Adjusting to the Net's Cultural Norms 82
- Why adjust to Internet customs? 82
- No advertising on the Internet 82

Acceptable Marketing Tactics 84
- Do this on the Internet 85
- Don't do this on the Internet 88
- Giving back to the Net 89

Technical and Logistical Options 91
- Cash on the Net 92
- Access to the Net 93
- Hardware and software 93

Resources for Further Exploration 93

Books and periodicals 94
Online documents 94
Discussion lists 94
Usenet newsgroups 95
World Wide Web indexes and lists 96
World Wide Web sites 96
Gopher sites 98
The Usenet Marketplace: Advice for Buying and Selling Online 100
What to Post and What to Look for on the Net 100
Who Uses the Usenet Marketplace 101
Looking for Something? 102
If You're Selling 103
If You're Buying 104
Doing the Deal 104
Sending the Goods 105
I've Been Ripped Off! 106
Finally 106
Usenet, Bulletin Boards, and Legal Liability 108
Computer Bulletin Boards 108
Problems for Censorship 109
Usenet and the First Amendment 109
Broadcast or Common Carrier 110
Who Should Be Responsible? 110
Responsibility of Authors 111
Formulating a New Standard 112
Conclusion 113

Chapter 5: Internet Privacy and Security 115

Common Sense and Cryptography 115
Keeping Secrets Is Much Harder Than It Seems 115
Choosing a Security Plan 118
What data am I protecting? 118
How much data is involved? 119
For how long will the data remain sensitive? 119
How safe is my data at its origin and destination? 119
How many people will be sharing the information? 119
From whom am I trying to protect the data? 119
What are the consequences if the data is compromised? 121
Do I have a legal obligation to protect my data? 121
Whom can I trust for advice? 121
How else can they get my data? 122
Which Encryption Technique Should I Use? 128
rot13 129
Crypt 129

- Application-embedded encryption 129
- DES 129
- Triple DES 131
- IDEA 131
- RSA 132
- RIPEM 133
- PGP 134
- RC2, RC4, and 40-bit codes 135
- Clipper, Capstone, Skipjack, and Tessera 136
- PCMCIA cryptographic smart cards 139

Digital Signatures and Authentication 140
- One-time pads 143
- Choosing a password or pass phrase 146
- What constitutes a poor login password? 146
- What constitutes a good login password? 146
- How to pick a pass phrase 147
- How to create random passwords and keys 148

Top 10 Encryption Security Tips 150
Privacy on the Net 151
Signing Messages 152
Getting PGP 152
Getting Started 154
Legal Notes 158
How to Contribute to Phil Zimmermann's Legal Defense Fund 158
Conclusion 159
Thinking about Firewalls 160
Why a Firewall? 160
Design Decisions 161
Levels of Threat 161
Firewalls and Their Components 162
- Screening router 163
- Bastion host 163
- Dual-homed gateway 163
- Screened-host gateway 164
- Screened subnet 164
- Application-level gateway 165
- Hybrid gateways 165

Firewalls Using Screening Routers 166
Dual-Homed Gateways 167
Screened-Host Gateways 168
Screened Subnets 168
Hybrid Gateways 169
Other Firewall-Related Tools 170
No Conclusions, but Observations 171

References ... 172
Using Firewalls on the Internet ... 173
What a Firewall Can Protect Against ... 173
What a Firewall Can't Protect Against ... 173
The Basic Design Decisions in a Firewall? ... 174
Proxy Servers ... 175
Low-Cost Packet-Screening Tools ... 175
Making DNS Work with a Firewall ... 175
Making FTP Work through a Firewall ... 176
Making Telnet Work through a Firewall ... 177
Making Finger and Whois Work through a Firewall ... 177
Making Gopher, Archie, and Other Services Work through a Firewall ... 177
Using X Windows through a Firewall ... 177
Books on Firewalls ... 178
More Online Information on Firewalls ... 178

Chapter 6: Internet Access for People with Disabilities ... 181

Access to Computers ... 182
- Print disability ... 183
- Keyboard or mouse disability ... 188
- Sound disability ... 191

The Future of Internet Access for the Disabled ... 191
People with Disabilities and E-Mail ... 192
Vendors and Products ... 192
State Technology-Related Assistance ... 194
Books ... 195
Resources on the Internet ... 196
- Gopher ... 196
- Usenet newsgroups ... 197
- ERIC clearinghouses ... 198

General Sources of Information ... 199
Other Sources of Computer-Access Information ... 199
Organizations and Conferences Related to Computers and Disability ... 201
Bill of Rights and Responsibilities for the Electronic Community of Learners ... 202

Chapter 7: Smileys ... 207

What's a Smiley? ... 207
Why Use Smileys? ... 207
How Many Smileys Are There? ... 208
How Do I Use Smileys As Punctuation? ... 208
What Other Smileys Are There? ... 209
How Can I Get More Smileys? ... 210

Part II: Connecting to the Internet 213

Chapter 8: DNS: The Domain Name System 215

Introduction to DNS ... 215
Hostnames and IP addresses ... 216
Domain Name System origin ... 216
What is DNS? ... 218
Interpreting domain names ... 219
How Does DNS Work? ... 222
Domains, zones, and name resolution ... 223
Resolvers ... 226
The named daemon and its data files ... 227
Domain nameservers ... 227
DNS and Sendmail ... 230
Named Data Files ... 231
Forward lookup ... 232
Reverse lookup ... 233
The Cache File ... 235
The Loopback File ... 235
Named Data File Resource Records ... 236
Start of origin: IN SOA ... 236
Nameserver: IN NS ... 237
Host information: IN HINFO ... 237
Name to address: IN A ... 238
Alias: IN CNAME ... 238
Mail exchange: IN MX ... 238
Address to name: IN PTR ... 239
DNS Maintenance and Problems ... 240
Refreshing the namespace ... 240
Adding to and deleting the hosts file ... 241
Dumping the namespace ... 241
Turning on debugging output ... 242
Problems: Causes and solutions ... 242
Odds and Ends ... 244
Additional Tools ... 245
Domain Name Registration Form ... 246
Root Servers for the Domain Name System ... 250
Historical Reading for the Domain Name System ... 251
Additional Reading or Resources for the Domain Name System ... 252
Newsgroups ... 252
WWW: The Web ... 252
By e-mail ... 252
References ... 253

Chapter 9: Connecting Your UNIX System to the Net 255

Connection Types 255
E-mail gateway 257
Dialup SLIP 257
Dedicated SLIP 257
Dedicated line 257
Hardware Configuration 258
Software Configuration 259
Debugging 260
IFCONFIG 261
NETSTAT 261
PING 261
TRACEROUTE 261
ROUTE 262
Case example one: A PC-based network 263
Case example two: Connecting via frame relay 264
Security 266
Logging 266
TCP Wrappers 267
Monitoring 267

Chapter 10: Linking Your Organization's Network to the Internet 269

Making the Internet Connection 270
Connecting with an Internet access provider 271
Registering a Domain Name 272
Setting Up an Internet Server 275
Connecting PC LANs to the Internet 277
Installing TCP/IP on workstations 277
TCP/IP on NetWare LANs 279
TCP/IP with other PC networks 283
Low-Cost Suites of Internet Applications 285
Conclusion 287

Chapter 11: Maintaining Large Networks 289

Centralized versus Distributed Management in a Large Organization 289
Ancillary Issues 290
Hardware selection 291
Software selection 291
Technical support 291
Information Systems 292
Management information systems 292

File servers 293
FTP servers 293
Network news (Usenet) servers 293
Gopher-based information systems 293
WWW information systems 294
The Information Part of Information Systems 294
Information Systems at Boston College 295
Summary 296
Secrets for Managing Large Networks 298

Chapter 12: Personal Internet Access Using SLIP or PPP 301

An Introduction to SLIP and PPP 301
Why bother? 302
What you get with SLIP or PPP 303
Using SLIP or PPP: A Typical Session 304
Electronic mail 304
Remote login using telnet 304
File transfer using ftp 305
Usenet news 305
Gopher and the World Wide Web 306
Finishing up 306
How It All Works 307
Making your PC or Macintosh Internet-capable 308
Connecting to the Internet 310
The basics of SLIP and PPP Internet access 313
Electronic mail 314
Usenet news 319
Accessing other Internet services 321
Beyond basic SLIP and PPP 323
Where to Go from Here 325
Commercial Internet packages 326
Other commercial packages 330
Internet book and software bundles 331
Online information and software 334

Chapter 13: Tuning TCP/IP 339

Setting the Segment Size 340
Opening the Window 341
Time-out! 343
I Name Thee 344
SLIPping to Speed 345
How Did You Do? 346

Chapter 14: Connecting Your Macintosh to the Internet........ 349

Overview 349
MacTCP: Your Connection to the Internet 350
Connecting to a Local Network 351
Installing MacTCP 351
Rebooting 351
Connecting to a Remote Network 352
Setting up a SLIP connection 352
Setting up a PPP connection 353
Setting up an Apple Remote Access connection 353
Troubleshooting Your Internet Connection 354
Macintosh File Formats and Conversion Utilities 355
Macintosh Software Archives 357
Where to Go for More Macintosh-Related Internet Information 358
Other Macintosh Resources on the Internet 359
Mailing lists 359
Usenet newsgroups 360
World Wide Web 361

Chapter 15: Macintosh TIA: A Lighthearted Guide to a Heavy Topic 363

Introduction 363
How do I use the file references? 363
What's this "WWW" that you keep talking about? 364
What is TIA, anyway? 364
I Wanna Do It! I Want It Now! 365
The right cable 365
The right connection 366
What Do I Have to Do First, Mom? 366
MacTCP 367
Other basic Mac software 367
Getting the TIA Trial Version 368
Host Information1 369
Clean Up Your Act! 370
Always Practice Safe Computing! 371
Installing MacTCP and InterSLIP 371
InterSLIP scripts 372
MacTCP settings 373
InterSLIP settings 375
Reboot 376
The Moment of Truth 376
Reading Mail via TIA 377
Reading News via TIA 378

White House 496
The Social Security Administration 497
Hobbes' Internet Timeline v1.2 497
Online Writing Lab (OWL) 497
DIALOG 498
The Ontario Institute for Studies in Education Gopher 498
The Complete Home Page Directory 498
Ann Hemyng Candy, Inc.'s Chocolate Factory 498
PLEASE COPY THIS DISK 498
Internet-on-a-Disk 499
The Argus Internet Tools and Resources Guide 499
The CIA 499
The Monster Board 499
Knowledge One 500
The Internet Business Center (IBC) 500
Online Computer Library Center (OCLC) 500
Feminist Web Page 500
Internal Revenue Service (IRS) 500
Scarecrow's ASCII Art Archives 501
Arts & Farces 501
FedWorld 501
Internet Book Information Center (IBIC) 501
AskERIC 502
Commercial OnLine Newspaper Services 502
E-Page Systems 502

Hot Spots on the Net 503
Best Gopher Sites 503
Best Web Sites 506

Chapter 21: Power IRC 509

The Wild World of Computer Chat 509
The Payoff of Risky Behavior 509
An Introduction to IRC 510
The Four Basic IRC Commands 510
Slowing the Scroll 511
More Things You Can Set 511
Sleuthing on IRC 513
Setting Up CTCP 514
Real Names and IRC Names 514
Customizing Your IRC Screen 515
Cleaning Up Your Screen 516
More Custom IRCII to Suit You 519
Control-key bindings 519
Writing aliases to make life simpler 520

A Simple Robot 523
The Efficiency of DCC 525
Desktop IRC Scripts 526
Homer's list of pals 526
WSIRC's war mode 526
Ban the Bots! 527

Chapter 22: Scaling the World Wide Web 531

Publishing Information on the World Wide Web 531
Introduction 531
Text and hypertext 532
HTML 532
The concept of tags in HTML 532
Basic HTML 534
Tags that define 534
Tags that format 535
Tags that link 538
Tags that invoke media 539
The HTML template 542
HTML Design Pitfalls 542
Netiquette in Webspace 542
In-line image netiquette 543
Designing for a particular browser 543
Line-mode browsers 544
Graphical interfaces 544
The "click here" syndrome 545
The ethics of linking 545
Useful Additions 546
Navigational aids 546
Document ownership 546
"What's new?" pages 547
NAME links 547
Serving It Up: A Guide to HTTP Servers 547
Using established HTTP servers 547
Setting up your own HTTP server 548
UNIX 548
MacHTTP 549
NCSA httpd for Windows 550
NCSA httpd 551
Voilà! 553
CERN httpd 554
Other UNIX servers 557
When Things Go Wrong 557
HTML troubleshooting 558

Finding the experts 558
My Own Server or Someone Else's? 559
Access to advanced features 559
Responsibilities of Web server administrators 560
Adding new features 560
Publicizing your pages 561
Good Luck! 561
Getting Interactive on the Web 562
Setting Up Forms in HTML 563
The FORM tag 563
Text input 563
Radio buttons and check boxes 565
Selection menus 566
Submit and reset buttons 567
Hidden elements 567
An Example Form Page: The Web Psychic 568
Other References 570
Handling Form Results 570
Parsing form results 571
Script output 571
Image Maps 572
Image maps in HTML pages 572
Using image types in forms 573
Image-map references 573
Texts on the Internet 574
Defining Online Text 574
How Computers Read Text 575
Types of Texts Available Online 575
Journals 576
Forums 576
Book reviews 576
Bibliographies and library Gophers 577
Books, text archives, and Gophers to navigate them 577
Wiretap 579
Advantages of online text 580
Conclusions 588
URL addresses for this chapter 588

Chapter 23: Gopher Secrets 591

A Few Gopher Tricks 591
Gopher and Gopher+ 591
Types of items on menus 592
Gopher+ enhancements 592
Beginning Browsing 594

Subject-oriented Gophers 595
Bookmarks 597
Finding New Gophers and Internet Resources 598
Gopher Search Engines 599
Veronica 599
Jughead 601
Wide area information services (WAIS) 602
Archie 603
Finding people 604
One Last Trick 604
Keeping Current 606
Mailing lists 606
Usenet newsgroups 607
Squealing and Hissing: A Gopher Client Roundup 608
Gopher's History 608
Archie 608
Gopher 608
What To Expect from Your Gopher Client 610
Which Gopher Client Should You Use? 613
Text-based clients 613
Graphical clients 617
Searching the World of Gopherspace: Veronica 627
Searching Locally: Jughead and Other Tools 629
Tunneling Ahead: Gopher's Future 630
GN: Serving WWW and Gopher with the Same Server 631
Getting Started with GN 631
A Smattering of Philosophy 634
A Taste of Searching 634
How to Get GN 635
About That Name 636

Chapter 24: Using WAIS 637

Origin of WAIS 637
Function of WAIS 638
WAIS Clients 638
Searching secrets 639
Xwais 640
Swais 641
Waisq and waissearch 641
WinWAIS 643
WAIStation for Mac 643
HyperWAIS for Mac 643
MacWAIS — A user scenario 643

World Wide Web gateways 650
WAIS Distributions 651
FreeWAIS from CNIDR 651
FreeWAIS-sf 652
WAIS from WAIS, Inc. 652
WAIS Indexing 653
Creating a WAIS database 653
WAIS indexer command line options 654
Document types 655
Database catalogs and descriptions 655
Booleans 655
Multiple data types 656
Synonyms 657
Fielded searches using freeWAIS-sf 657
WAIS indexing fine details 658
WAIS Servers 659
Installing your own server 659
Configuration and database management 660
Usage statistics 661
Security 662
Using WAIS from WWW 663
WAIS of the Future 665
Essence and Harvest 665
How does ZDist fit? 666
WAIS Resources 666
Companies and organizations 666
Software 667
Articles, books, and more 667

Chapter 25: Managing Mail 669

Climbing Pine 669
What is Pine? 669
What is MIME? 670
What is IMAP? 670
How Can I Get a Copy of Pine? 670
What Documentation is Available? 671
To What Platforms Has Pine Been Ported? 671
What Mailing Lists and Newsgroups Deal with Pine? 671
Tips for Using Pine 672
How do I send a message to several people without showing all the names? 672
How do I use ispell with pine and pico? 673
How can I have a signature appended to my mail messages automatically? 674
How do I read Usenet newsgroups with pine? 674
Can I post news with pine? 675

How do I paste an address from the address book into the text of a message? ... 675
How can I filter messages into different incoming folders? ... 675
How do I define my own headers? ... 677
Can I use pine noninteractively, as in a shell script? ... 677
When I get new mail, xbiff lets me know about it, but why doesn't pine know about it? ... 677
How can I read a ROT13-encoded message? ... 678
Can I eliminate the @host.domain from local addresses? ... 678
Problems with Pine ... 679
Why did I get the message "Folder format invalidated (consult an expert), aborted"? ... 679
What is folder locking? ... 680
What happens when two pine sessions access the same mailbox at the same time? ... 681
Why did I get the message "Folder xxxxx is locked, will override in yyy seconds"? ... 681
Why is a charset=US-ASCII attachment sent with BASE64 encoding? ... 682
Why doesn't pine recognize the Content-Length header? ... 682
Installation, Configuration, and Conversion ... 683
Can PC-Pine be used with a POP server? ... 683
What is a Tenex mailbox? ... 683
Where does pine look for configuration information? ... 683
How do I make pine work with my older terminal? ... 684
How do I prevent pine from leaving mail in /usr/spool/mail? ... 684
What PC communications software works with the Print to ANSI print option? ... 684
What Macintosh communications software works with the Print to ANSI print option? ... 684
How can someone without a MIME-aware mail program decipher an attachment? ... 685
How do I convert Berkeley Mail aliases to pine address book? ... 685
How do I convert Elm aliases to pine address book? ... 685
References ... 685
Credits ... 685
The Online FAQ ... 686
Filtering Mail ... 687
Mail Folder Strategies ... 687
Naming your incoming-mail folders ... 687
Reading your incoming-mail folders ... 688
Procmail ... 688
Setting up procmail ... 688
Troubleshooting procmail ... 692
Explanation of test recipe ... 693

Part IV: Becoming an Information Provider 799

Chapter 27: Look Ma, I'm an Internet Provider 801

Starting Out ... 801
- Computer equipment ... 801
- Back up! ... 802
- Modems ... 803
- Terminal servers ... 803
- CSU/DSU units, routers, and compression ... 804

Internet Connection ... 804
- Obtaining an IP network number and registering your domain ... 804
- Obtaining a network feed: serial lines versus dedicated high-speed lines ... 804
- Using ISDN and cable companies ... 805
- Maintaining security ... 805

Basic Services ... 806
- E-mail and e-mail readers ... 806
- Shell accounts versus interfaces ... 806
- PPP/SLIP and X Windows ... 807
- A note about TIA ... 808
- Network News/NNTP ... 808
- Telnet and ftp ... 809
- Internet Relay Chat (IRC) ... 809
- Games and MUDs ... 810
- Gopher and WWW ... 810

Other Considerations ... 811
- Support ... 811
- Market ... 811
- Money and logistics ... 812

Closing Remarks ... 812

Useful Contacts ... 813
- Network Information Center (NIC) ... 813
- Telebit Corporation ... 813
- Router vendors ... 813

Chapter 28: Setting up a European Internet Provider 815

The National Information Infrastructure (NII) ... 815
- The U.S. National Information Infrastructure plan ... 815
- The European NII ... 818

The Fundamentals of Service Provision in Europe ... 818
- The players: Their acronyms and their functions ... 818
- Registration and IP allocation in Europe — how it works ... 819
- A brief overview of the Internet in Europe ... 821

Practical factors to consider ... 822
Provision of Service ... 826
Small providers ... 826
Investing a bit more ... 828
Large providers ... 829
A Look at Future Directions for the Internet in Europe ... 830
Conclusions ... 832

Chapter 29: Running a Gopher Server ... 833

What Is Gopher, and How Does It Work? ... 833
Great Green Gobs of Greasy Grimy Gopher Guts ... 834
Gopher+ (an Example of Creeping Featurism) ... 836
Establishing a Gopher Server ... 837
Designing your server ... 837
Installing the server ... 840
Getting your server into Gopherspace ... 841
Running the Server ... 841
Content administration ... 841
Server administration ... 842
Supporting Your Users ... 846

Chapter 30: Running a WWW Server on Windows ... 849

Introduction ... 849
Hardware requirements ... 850
Software requirements ... 850
Configuring Your Windows Web Server ... 851
Tips for Setting Up Your Own Server ... 852
A Guide to Good HTML Authoring ... 853
Advanced Topics ... 854
Creating imagemaps ... 854
Writing CGI scripts to do tasks on demand ... 856
Setting up CGI applications ... 856
Passing parameters to CGI applications ... 857
Looking at a sample CGI application ... 858
Writing scripts that ask for more ... 860
What else can I do with CGI scripts? ... 861
References ... 862
FTP sites for various pieces of software ... 862
WWW home page for WinHTTPD ... 862
WWW page with tips for writing HTML documents ... 862
The Future of WWW ... 863

Part V: The Best Internet Applications 865

Chapter 31: The Complete WinSock Applications Roundup 867

Bugs 868
Chat/IRC/Personal Communications 868
Commercial Demo Packages 872
Diagnostic Tools 876
File-Search and File-Transfer Protocols 877
Fingers 881
Games (MUDs) 883
Games (Other) 885
Gopher 886
Host Lookup Clients 889
Hyper-G 891
Mail and Mail Accessories 891
Mail and News 895
Miscellaneous 899
Miscellaneous Non-WinSock 904
NFS Clients 908
Ph Clients 909
Ping 911
Telephone Dialers 912
Telnet 914
TCP/IP 918
Time Synchronizers 919
WAIS (Wide Area Information Service) 921
Whois 922
World Wide Web Browsers 923
X.500 (DUA) Clients 929
Additional Information 930
- Getting started 930
- FAQ lists 931
- Trumpet WinSock 933
- Optimum Trumpet settings 933
- Popular WinSock source locations 934
- TIA — The Internet adapter 935
- Growstub error 936
- Error: "Unhandled Exception 0xc0000005" 937
- Eudora documentation 937
- Pentium serial-port problems 938
- SLIP versus PPP 938

Chapter 32: Macintosh Internet Applications 941

Getting Your Mac on the Internet 942
Mac Internet Software 942
FTP client applications 943
FTP server applications 945
Archie applications 946
Gopher applications 946
IRC applications 947
Usenet news applications 949
Telnet applications 951
World Wide Web browser (client) applications 951
World Wide Web server applications 953
Helper applications 954
Other useful Internet applications 955

Chapter 33: Installing the Shareware Disks 957

Disk 1: Windows software and Scripts 957
WINZIP shareware archiver version 5.6 (WINZIP56.EXE) 957
WINCODE freeware encoder/decoder version 2.6.1 (WNCOD261.ZIP) 957
Other files on Disk 1 958
Disk 2: E-mail mailing lists 958

Index 959

License and Disclaimer 989

Reader Response Card .... Back of Book

Introduction

When we started writing *Internet SECRETS*, or rather, *gathering* Internet secrets, we flung our net far and wide. The Internet is not a traditional software product of interest only to its users. The Internet in the 1990s is of interest to virtually everyone, everywhere. OK, maybe we exaggerate. But we get 20 to 30 e-mail messages a day from folks just starting out on the Net — they come from Malaysia, Mexico, Michigan, and Manhattan. And so, *Internet SECRETS* is not a typical SECRETS book. Yes, we illumine a lot of new territory for not-so-new Internet users and would-be providers. We also give voice to many social and cultural aspects of the Internet. The Internet is a global resource. We've tried to include international perspectives wherever possible.

This book is a collection from contributors around the world who share our enthusiasm for the Internet and who contribute their unique expertise to provide what we hope will be a sumptuous feast.

Whom This Book Is for

We're tempted to say this book is for everyone, or maybe, more precisely, we think there's something in this book that could interest almost everyone. However, our primary audience is the avid Internet user — someone who uses the Net and is dying to find out more and better ways, places, programs, and lore. We're willing to wager there's not an Internet user out there who knows all the secrets we've uncovered. This book can also be invaluable to people who are trying to grasp the many issues that businesses and organizations need to understand when considering if and how they should connect to the Internet.

We assume that readers have a basic familiarity with the Internet and its facilities. If you understand what we mean when we say: "Telnet to `nsa.gov`, log in as `clipper`, password bond007," you're all set. For a more basic introduction to the Internet, we shamelessly recommend our *Internet For Dummies,* 2nd Edition and *MORE Internet For Dummies* (both from IDG Books).

Part by Part

This book is divided into five major sections. Some have universal appeal. We hope that regardless of where you start, you'll poke around in the other sections as well. What may seem intimidating today, with a little experience might soon prove intriguing.

Part I: Essays about the Net

The essays about the Net are written for everyone. We begin with stories from France, replete with personal anecdotes. A well-known Net personality describes Internet culture from his seasoned eyes. We discuss Usenet from a variety of perspectives. We talk about doing business on the Net, about privacy and security issues, and about Net access for people with disabilities.

Part II: Connecting to the Internet

Connecting to the Internet is intended to address issues not usually dealt with in introductory texts. We discuss the Domain Name System. We describe connecting various platforms and networks to the Net, and we also discuss performance tuning.

Part III: Taming the Internet

The more you love the Internet, the more you need this section. One chapter focuses on how to find things on the Net, including search strategies. We have tips for how to become a power IRC user. For World Wide Web fans, we share the best way to publish information on the Web. We have tricks for Gopher and WAIS. One major chapter deals with managing mail, and another with mastering network news.

Part IV: Becoming an Information Provider

If you think you're ready to take the leap from user to provider, check out what the folks who've done it have to say. This section gives you the ins and outs of running Gopher and Web servers from your own machine. Of particular interest is the perspective of a European Internet provider.

Part V: The Best Internet Applications

Our experts have found the best Windows and Mac Internet applications and tell you about them. This part starts off with a comprehensive listing of WinSock clients and follows up by recommending the best Macintosh Net applications. The final chapter talks about the free, included software that you get just for buying this book.

Where to Go from Here

You can read the chapters in this book in sequential order, or you can jump around to whatever topic suits you. The order isn't important — just read it. Special icons in the text give you clues about what techniques to try and what pitfalls to avoid. So if you're starting with Chapter 1, you're off to France. If not, flip through the Table of Contents to find what you're looking for. Either way, prepare for enlightenment.

Part I
Essays about the Net

In This Part

Chapter 1 Virtual Intimacy — Tales from Minitel and More

Chapter 2 Internet Culture and Folklore

Chapter 3 Usenet

Chapter 4 Doing Business on the Net

Chapter 5 Internet Privacy and Security

Chapter 6 Internet Access for People with Disabilities

Chapter 7 Smileys

Chapter 1

Virtual Intimacy — Tales from Minitel and More

by Philippe Le Roux <leroux@vdl2.ca>

translated from the French by Carol Baroudi

We use *telematics* as a translation of the French *télématique*. The French word was created by combining *informatique*, meaning computing, and *telecommunications* in the "Rapport NORA-MINC," a 1975 report that the French government ordered to investigate the future of new technologies. *Telematics* or *telematic* means the domain of the online, graphical, and interactive services. This word is used in Europe and England. With development of the Net and interactive services in North America, we expect to need to use it here as well. So we use the word here to best translate the French original.

Introduction

When I was asked to join the team of writers for this book, I got ready to expound on my usual vision of telematic communications and their impact on personal behavior. But I quickly found that I couldn't escape implicating myself. I couldn't talk about theories without supporting them with facts, and these facts I had to take from my personal experiences. I had to open a page of my own history that I thought I'd definitely turned, a page full of good times and pain, a page always full of passion. This page is that of the genesis of chatlines, and my discovery of fabulous human behavior on these electronic systems. My biggest discovery about information technology is that people use it to be warm, natural, and spontaneous. The world of technology is not cold and insensitive — on the contrary. . . . not because of the engineers, but because of the users who knew how to master the technology and put it to their own use. But we'll see how it all started.

Our action unfolds at the end of the seventies. In all corners of the planet, experimental videotext projects were beginning. The U.S. Department of Defense began building the ARPAnet, which later became what we know as the Internet. In Canada, the pilot project was called Telidon; in Japan, Captain; in the United Kingdom, Prestel; in France, VVV. All these projects found themselves in a double bind: The technology was ready for telematics, but people were not. All the governments made the same decision — let the engineers' dreams die.

Somewhere in the south of Brittany, the engineers at France Télécom (France's public phone company) proposed putting into place an electronic phone book that would solve many problems. Dialing 12, the French equivalent of 411, was overrun: You had to wait almost an hour, and each call cost a dollar. Traditional white pages and yellow pages cost a fortune to print and distribute and are not very ecologically sound. The government quickly gave the green light for the design and free distribution of a little videotext terminal, the Minitel, which would replace the phone books in every home.

What the government didn't foresee was that the engineers would use the Minitel as a Trojan horse to launch the telematics that the government had already rejected. Today, more than seven million Minitels are in use in France, in offices and homes, and several tens of thousands of telematic services (data banks, electronic shopping, home banking, games, administrative services) are available from a regular videotext terminal — cheap but effective. Meanwhile, the electronic phone book is becoming marginally used, and they continue to print and distribute the paper books.

While the engineers of France Télécom continued to prepare their magic box, access points using a national X-25 network (Transpac), and the electronic phone book itself, one of the first pilot telematic projects was organized in the east of France, at the heart of which the users were playing the same games with the engineers that the engineers had played with the government.

Hacking for Chatting: GRETEL, the Genesis of Chatlines

This pilot project was organized jointly by France Télécom and by *Les Dernières Nouvelles d'Alsace* (The Latest News from Alsace); the DNA, as it's called there. The DNA is the most important regional newspaper in France. It covers all the east and northeast of France with publications that are envied by the national papers. It is the only paper whose size and diversity of content compares to the huge North American weekend papers.

The project's name was GRETEL. Its goal was offering a local information service. The information would be both political and community-oriented, ranging from announcements from the unemployment office to theater schedules, and included classified ads. Looking back, it was probably the predecessor of freenet. To start the project, a number of people were given a prototype of the Minitel terminal. This prototype had two problems that have been fixed in the current Minitel models. First, it was very cumbersome — a solid block, with a keyboard that couldn't be detached or replaced. Second, its keys were arranged alphabetically — not exactly ergonomic!

The programmers who had developed the service had included in the system a way of allowing a user to stick a message in one line, where the service technician could respond with a one-line message that would appear at the top of the user's screen. This feature was the first version of manual online help. After a few weeks, everything seemed to be going as planned. The service became richer, with more information and more features every day; more and more bugs got fixed, and the commercial users found it to be an interesting experience. A beautiful pilot project, well-organized, that was coming along nicely, until one day . . .

A hacker visiting one of his pals wanted to play with GRETEL. His friend showed him the system, and the hacker became especially interested in the online help facility. He quickly found a way to hack the system, using the help system to send messages directly to another user's screen. The technicians watched help messages being rerouted. Their boss, Michel Landaret, was immediately advised that their system was in the process of being hacked. Landaret made a surprising decision that resulted in fortuitous consequences: He told them to continue to watch what was happening but not to intervene (as long as the integrity of the system was not compromised). Quickly, the users began passing messages to each other. The developers then created features allowing users to communicate more easily, without jeopardizing system security. The first chatting system was born and rapidly became the most important use of the entire system.

The Digital Agoras

Most of the people who were part of the pilot project lived in an apartment building near Strasbourg, where people didn't talk to each other and found themselves isolated in the middle of a crowd, as often happens in large urban centers. The nights were long and often depressing for single people who didn't always have the means to get into the center of town. GRETEL became that means of going out, seeing the world, and making new friends without even leaving the house, without having to find a baby-sitter or even taking out one's curlers.

Princess, Man in Black, Scarabée d'or (Golden Beetle), and Baleine Bleue (Blue Whale) began to talk to one another and to talk about each other. One would ask another if a third was really as nice in real life as he appeared on the screen. At the heart of the town, a new market square had been born, really a place where people could find themselves and interact without having to deal with the rigid rules our urban ways of life had imposed. Customers rubbed elbows with the management, programmers joked with philosophers, and the banker fell in love with the waiter from the pizza parlor. This virtual place was like those old village plazas, like the Greek agoras. The *Digital Agora* was no longer a buzzword. It had its rules, its gossip, its stories of love and romance, and, of course, its lies and deceptions. . . . In 1984, everyone came together; two members married each other — they had met each other through GRETEL, and their relationship had developed on GRETEL. According to their story, the charm has lasted, and they are still happily married.

During this time, the engineers from France Télécom finally shipped their electronic phone book, which was distributed for free in Paris and in certain other parts of France. The first commercial telematic services began. Among them was the *service Mèdical* (SM), whose story, from the beginning, was another victory for the techies.

Service Mèdical

Four students finished medical school, and, at the same time, discovered information processing, the first microcomputers, and the joys of programming. Rather than following the flood of their colleagues who rushed to work in private clinics or in hospitals or open their own private practice, they decided to combine their knowledge of medicine and information processing to create a telematic service. This service offered an online electronic review of the medical journals, allowing doctors to save time and money while following the activity in their field. Medical articles are numerous, costly, and voluminous, and only certain articles appeal to certain doctors.

SM began to attract doctors with an offer for a subscription to all the new technology available through Minitel. Our accomplices at SM developed a teleconferencing system that could connect four people from different locations. This system wasn't available to the doctors — it was reserved for those four who had built and managed SM, and their friends. But their friends told their friends, who told their friends what was happening. The number of *forums* grew, so there were four forums, each allowing five participants. Each user's screen was divided into six parts. At the bottom of each part, you could see the participant's handle and the text of his last message. The sixth part allowed you to type a message before sending it. Your message would then appear on the screen with your handle.

In no time, the doctors were no longer able to get access to SM, because it was tied up by friends of friends who were using it as a chat system. SM's only source of funding was the subscriptions it sold to doctors, so the situation was becoming difficult to manage. Because that wasn't working, they made a decision to open access through a phone line, 3615. Line 3615, operated by the phone company, allowed access through Minitel for about $10 an hour, where 60 percent of the revenue went to the service provider; in this case, SM. So from that point on, SM became accessible to anyone who had a password and Minitel access. In less than a month, there were over a thousand electronic mailboxes, under all sorts of handles. Among them were Bill (Dr. François Lagarde, one of the founders), Rainbow (Lionel, the supervisor), JE (the creator of the electronic phone book from France Télécom), and Dionysos (myself). Bill and his accomplices added new features such as games, the SMile Box (which is a common bulletin board), and research tools in the mailboxes directory, which was growing every day.

When someone dialed 3615, Minitél displayed a welcome page, asking which service you wanted to connect — in this case, SM. But, with the display of this page, France Télécom began to charge $10 an hour. Within two months, SM was completely saturated; there were people who tried hour after hour, at $10 an hour, to get into SM, waiting for a port to free itself. People were literally addicted to SM. You couldn't start your day without seeing if you had mail on SM. It was difficult to go look at your mail without getting trapped in a conversation with a friend. And it was impossible to break off the communication. SM had, at that time, an important impact on work absenteeism statistics.

SM was such a success that the two microcomputers it was using at that time (Goupil G4s with 256K of RAM) literally caught fire one night when they overheated. The absence of SM during the days it took to reinstall the backup on new, tougher equipment (AT&T 3B15 minicomputers) was traumatic for thousands of users who were like drug addicts in withdrawal or cultists deprived of their guru.

For the short story, SM became one of the biggest French videotext chatlines, making a fortune for its four founders (who sold it to the European newspaper tycoon, Robert Maxwell, before his death and the collapse of his empire). At this time, SM is owned by a group of French newspapers, *le Nouvel observateur* (*The New observer*), which is one of the largest telematic groups in Europe.

In Three Years, I Met More Than a Thousand People . . .

People who don't use online communications tools often ask if cyber-meetings don't make people more isolated or prevent people from having real physical meetings. If I believe my own experience and the experiences of others that I've studied, it's not true. Online chatlines are a fantastic social tool for people who tend to be shy or introverted. They learn how to talk to strangers and quickly gain confidence in themselves. It's true that the hundreds of evenings and nights I've stayed home, stretched out on the rug in front of my Minitel, are nights that I didn't go to a bar, a disco, or a museum. But how many nights out like this are a social bust? On the contrary, I went out regularly to meet the people I met on my Minitel, whether it was face-to-face over a cup of coffee or at a Minitel party, a *Get Together* (GT). I met more than 300 people one-on-one, and over a thousand at GTs. What professional barfly can equal that?

Meeting people electronically turns our attitudes, and our ways of looking at people, upside down. I remember one period of time, in 1985, spending more than ten hours a day on Minitel, talking with people all over France. When I had to leave my house, each time I saw someone cross the street, I asked myself if that person might be one of the people sending messages on Minitel and what his handle might be. Studying each person, and trying to map him to one of the hundreds of faceless portraits compiled on Minitel, created a profound impression.

These stories, blind dates that cross the border between the virtual and the real, are a source of very intense emotions. How many questions, fears, and hopes go with them? You always ask yourself if the person you are going to meet will be up to par with how he or she appears on the screen; and, of course, if you yourself will come off as well as you appear on the screen. How do you recognize each other without resorting to a carnation in the lapel?

I remember a great story about Capucine. Capucine was an SM regular, like me. She lived in Rouen, 200 miles from Paris. One day, after hours of sharing jokes, we decided that she would come to Paris for the weekend. We could, at last, meet each other, and I would introduce her to the gang of mutual friends from SM. Just to be contrary (and influenced by the nonconformist spirit that characterized Minitel at that time), we decided not to give each other any physical description of ourselves before we met. (I never gave a physical description to anybody.) Therefore, we had to figure out some other way of recognizing each other when I waited for her at the train station.

I remembered that we had both studied Judo as kids, and I wore a kimono to the platform at the Saint-Lazare station (one of the busiest in Paris) in the middle of the crowd, and, by the way, with the police watching for suspicious activity. When Capucine got off the train, also dressed in a kimono, we laughed for several minutes without being able to say a word. They should have filmed the looks on the faces of the people around us — and on the faces of the police, who asked us if we were part of a commando unit of some terrorist organization. (This was 1986, and there were a lot of bombings in France that year.) Over the years that followed, Capucine and I, often accompanied by certain other enthusiasts, had many more experiences, each crazier than the last.

New Alliances

Not only do electronic meetings greatly outnumber "real" meetings, but they create new bases for relationships. Never have I seen such gestures of solidarity, and such spontaneity, in any other arena. Even if the systems people are using span an enormous distance geographically, people react as though it's all one virtual community, and the limits exist only where messages can't be sent. Each chatline becomes a village with inhabitants, where one can find the same spirit of unity you'd find if a catastrophe occurred in a rural village. Alliances form, with everybody pulling together, and in times of crisis, people forget their enmity and feuds, supporting those who are in trouble.

I remember one Saturday night. I was taking care of some customers in my restaurant when the phone rang. It was an SM regular, who asked me if I'd heard from Crocko, one of the other regulars, who was having some personal problems at the time. I told him that I hadn't checked in that day, and that I'd had no news. He read me an e-mail message that Crocko had sent him, in which Crocko appeared to be very depressed. I told him I'd check my mail. I, too, found a despondent message from Crocko. I contacted other regulars connected at the same time, and no one had news. I tried to call Crocko at home on the restaurant's second line, but she didn't answer. One of the users who lived near her decided to go visit her. He reappeared ten minutes later on SM, saying `There're lights on, but no answer`. Another user, who was a nurse, called an ambulance, and several people went to Crocko's house to wait for it to arrive.

I went back to my customers, who were wondering what was going on. Half an hour later, the phone rang again. Crocko had been found in her house, passed out from a massive dose of sleeping pills. She'd been taken to the hospital and was out of danger. The telematic community had saved her life. Close to a hundred people went to visit Crocko in the hospital. Today, she is married to someone she met on SM, is happy, and has no thoughts of suicide.

I experienced dozens of these kinds of stories on Minitel in France. Often, the telematic community acts as a local arm, doing something for someone who can't do it because he's too far away. It might be a favor for a family member or friend. There are so many messages that begin `Is there anybody who lives near... and could take my mother to the doctor`, or `My fiancee's phone is broken, I can't meet her, could someone who lives in her town get a message to her?`

This kind of spontaneity and these kinds of gestures of real friendship were and still are common occurrences in online chatlines. This kind of human bonding that our urban ways of life have forced us to lose, and which the electronic agora is rebuilding, gives me confidence that a humanity that manifests in this way will always come back to fundamental values.

Friendly Experiences, How I Met My Partner on Minitel Ten Years Ago . . .

At the time of the GRETEL experiment, I was living in Paris, and I had never been to Strasbourg in my life. I was invited to follow the experience from Paris with modem access and long-distance calling. I quickly became a member of this agora. Marvelous human experiences were happening. The funniest was that people never remembered that I was 350 miles away, and invited me for a drink in their homes as if I lived ten minutes away.

Then I got used to going to Strasbourg, where, for a year, I spent two or three days a week. The level of hospitality was such that I never stepped foot into a hotel in Strasbourg, sleeping at one friend's house, then another's. I saw many passionate and impassioned love stories there, and some deceptions, too. I also formed some very strong friendships and connections at incredible speed. After a few weeks of exchanging messages on GRETEL, connections were as strong as if they'd been maintained for years. It makes me happy to remember all the experiences I've had, but I'll only tell you about two.

I remember being at home, stretched out on my living room rug, typing on my Minitel and talking to Princess and Scarabée d'or. It must have been close to 5:00 P.M. Princess told me that they were going out around 5:00 or 6:00 to have some pizza and see a show. They invited me to join them. I couldn't — I was in Paris, and the next morning I had a meeting at 8:00 A.M. with my banker to talk about an investment in my restaurant. But Scarabée d'or and Princess insisted, and I left to join them. In fact, I was only a three-hour drive from Strasbourg (yes, in France we tend to drive fast). I spent the evening with them, the show was fantastic, and, at 2:00 A.M., I headed back to Paris for my meeting. Things like that were always happening on GRETEL.

Another time, I was spending the weekend in Strasbourg. I had been conversing for several days with a certain Noella, a passionate girl who lived her sexuality with women. I tried several times to connect with her during the weekend. Unfortunately, she was never around. Sunday afternoon, I went back to Paris. I got home at close to 5:00 P.M. and, of course, the first thing I did was connect to GRETEL to talk to my friends, whom I'd left several hours earlier. Noella was online, and sent me a message: `Hi Dio, how's it going? It looks like you're in Strasbourg, that's marvelous, can I see you?` I told her that I had been in Strasbourg, but that I'd come back. We continued to talk, and I could tell that she was really low. Her girlfriend had left her, in a less than kind way. I tried to lift her spirits from a distance, and I quickly realized that the situation was very bad. I told her I had to disconnect for a few minutes, but that she should wait for me on GRETEL. I called the airport, got a ticket on the next plane to Strasbourg, and reconnected to tell her to meet me at the Strasbourg airport in an hour. I was back in Strasbourg just five hours after having left it. She came to get me, and we spent a wonderful night as friends that neither of us will ever forget.

Of course, I struck up dozens of solid and deep friendships on SM. I met my present business partner there. Ww (an abbreviation for Werewolf) was doing development for SM. His handle, therefore, often appeared on the list of connected users.

Generally speaking, people sent messages to Ww when there was a problem, or to ask a technical question. Some people tried to strike up a conversation with him to gain certain privileges. Power, as always, attracts the masses. But, as you might have guessed from his handle, Werewolf wasn't the most sociable person on the list. Most of the messages people sent to him he left unanswered, partly because he wasn't at his terminal, and partly just because he didn't feel like answering them.

Despite that, we began to exchange messages. I've lost track of the reasons that drew Ww and me together. But I do remember that I quickly acquired the habit of looking for him at night on SM. Ww was one of those programmer-types inspired by night, who can stay up 'til 5:00 in the morning tracking down the last bug but can't function on his day job. Our friendship grew quickly around a basic conspiracy we'd developed: watching from a distance how different people behaved on the system.

Because he was a loner, Ww didn't understand how people could spend a fortune socializing on a screen. The behavior on the system amazed me, and I wanted to study it as much as possible. We spent wonderful nights trying to predict in advance a user's behavior, to uncover secret liaisons between people, to watch others get totally lost in their illusions. How many jokes we played, how many Minitel parties Ww and I enjoyed on many more levels because of our insiders' knowledge, how many covers Ww created for me so I could carry on multiple simultaneous liaisons. How many nights did I spend courting Cat, while she courted Ww, who didn't want to know that she existed. How many nights did we spend sharing our views of life, the world, and relationships. How many times did Ww help me survive my romantic disappointments and deceptions — the ones with Baleine Bleue, Cat, TC, or another.

Today, ten years later, Ww is my partner at Servacom and $V(DL)^2$ — he joined me seven years ago, in Québec, with Chipie (whom we met together on SM, and who, afterwards, became his wife). During the seven years we have worked together, we've survived many hardships and many good times as well. This friendship stays solid. Virtual relationships can open up very real and rock-solid feelings.

When I speak of friends, I speak of those strong and deep friendships, not of pals. I speak of those people who stay close to me (even at a distance), of those people whom I can call at any hour if I am in pain or if I need help. Close to half of my real friends I've met while exchanging e-mail. They live in Montreal, in Strasbourg, in Paris, and in Cambridge, but they are close to me.

Falling in Digital Love

The intensity of emotions that arise in the electronic milieu has important ramifications on any person who has any feelings, even if the number of marriages based on virtual meetings that you've heard about in the media isn't so surprising. I know people who met on the telephone — one was the receptionist where the other worked. The *speed* with which one can develop a love relationship with someone whose voice one has never heard is impressive. They are formed in virtual space, and they happen all the time. I don't know people with any emotional openness who haven't experienced it at least once.

I won't make a list here of my telematic loves — their handles don't mean anything, for the most part. But all these passions, these hopes (not always shared), these pains, still are with me; sometimes, when I think about one of those people, I can't forget any of the emotions from those virtual loves that I went through.

Whether I met them on a bulletin board or by e-mail, whether we started on Minitel or on Alex (the Canadian version, started in 1988), through a newsgroup or on IRC, each of these loves exists today, like a permanent tattoo. If I tried to add them all up, I could total some 20 loves; some of weeks, some of months, some of years. I could add the years together, add the tears and the crises of despair, the bottles of Jack Daniels to wash away the blues that these loves never fail to supply. But I think that the idea of summing up doesn't really work when it comes to love.

Among all theses slices of life, I picked four to share. They represent different kinds of electronic love relationships. The first is what I experienced with FMR, a pun on the word *éphémère* — ephemeral — in French. FMR lived in Toulouse, about 600 miles from Paris, where I lived. In 1985, Minitel was just becoming national. FMR and I had been talking on Minitel and joking with other regulars. At that time, I was living with a girlfriend — our relationship getting worse, day by day — and Minitel became the place where I spent day and night in the process of breaking up with her; more precisely, hanging out there showed that we didn't really have anything to say to each other, even if we weren't ready to admit it. I quickly started waiting for messages from FMR, waiting to see her name show up on the list of users. Her messages made me very happy. And it was the same for her.

After about ten days, we stayed on Minitel all the time, leaving it only to call each other on the telephone and then go back to Minitel. I have the unfortunate habit of quickly acquiring the accent of the person with whom I'm speaking. My girlfriend couldn't understand why, when she came home at night, I was talking with a southern (from the south of France) accent. My girlfriend decided to leave for several days by herself; our relationship was going really badly. I did something crazy: I invited FMR to spend a few days in Paris with me.

I went to meet her at the airport, full of anguish about her (and about myself). Each minute I waited seemed like an eternity. Finally she appeared, looking exactly like what I was expecting, and she seemed satisfied that she hadn't been misled. When finding yourself physically with a person with whom you've shared the craziest feelings, the first move still seems like a big jump. If you don't make that leap, if you never dare to cross that line, you are torn up with the frustration that each has allowed to build. When there's been a virtual love, it can become a real love, but you can't just say, "Oh, let's just be friends." We stayed together in total ambiguity for two days and then began to let our mutual frustrations take control of our relationship and destroy it badly.

Another experience I want to tell you about is a little more positive, and that's about Ange. Ange was a regular on Alex, the Canadian telematic system that Bell Canada developed at the end of 1988. (That experiment lasted four years before being abandoned, not for a lack of users but because of the cultural impact it was creating on Bell-Canada, which was used to having a monopoly and controlling everything. It's useless to try to control telematic territory, as the users of GRETEL taught us, but that's another story.)

Ange used CHUM (a friendly chatline that we'd developed on Alex, which quickly became its most widely used service among the hundreds of services available). One day, she contacted me, without knowing I was one of the people in charge. We had started talking about different things — like life, the universe, and everything. We quickly found that we saw things similarly, particularly in respect to relationships, and to passion. We planned to meet in my office and go out to dinner. The evening was marvelous, and we felt very comfortable with each other. Before long, we started seeing only each other, and, for its part, it became a nice love story that lasted for years. We lived together in a wonderful apartment that we furnished with very special care. Today, we have managed to separate and stay good friends, and see each other regularly.

That makes me think about Venus, a somewhat current story. Zohra wasn't a Minitel user, and even less an e-mail user. One day, one of her coworkers connected to SM, for fun, using Venus as her handle. She quickly got into it. She had a very interesting conversation with Bad Max, a friend of mine. But Venus was married, and in no way resembled the person that she described herself as in this conversation, which she thought wasn't going anywhere. It was at that point that she switched places with Zohra. Bad Max made a date with her at my restaurant, without being aware of the hoax. And that's how I met Venus, the real one for me, and the fake one for Bad Max. We had months of wonderful passion; now, despite the nine years that have passed, and the Atlantic ocean that separates us, we remain close friends. Besides our faxes and our meetings when we cross the ocean, her access to Internet mail from Minitel allows us to exchange regular, immediate, and inexpensive messages.

The last love I want to talk about is one I had with `d172644@xxxx.ca`. We met each other in a political campaign and had one of those scorching relationships, as hot and fleeting as a brush fire, when the heat is too strong. Our story ended stupidly, like what happens to all love stories that end before they're done. At the time, I had talked with her a lot about telematic and the Net, explaining to her what a wonderfully fantastic communication and research tool it could be for her in her research work in neuropsychology. Two months after we broke up, what a surprise it was for me to see a message signed `d172644@xxxx.ca` in my mailbox. She'd gotten Internet access through her university, and thereby reopened a story I had wanted to forget, and which left me with a bitter aftertaste I can't get rid of. So, we've taken up our relationship again for a few months, though we limit it to e-mail. We have seen each other on occasion in this time, but never reconnected physically. Only e-mail allows us (her?) to let go completely. It's useless to be who we are. The fear of nothingness and the fear of success haunt relationships and justify failures. But life cannot be so virtual once it's been real. A misunderstanding on the Internet had become the excuse for a heartless and cruel breakup. Telematic is powerful and fantastic, not magic. Through e-mail, you can regain your autonomy when you delete the file with hundreds of messages exchanged with someone you hold dear.

Telematic conversation is a tool that allows us to find and meet people within a few minutes. You can never really guess what a person looks like physically over a telematic system, even if a person sincerely describes herself. How many hundreds of different physical attributes can you picture from a textual description? Nonetheless, you can learn a lot from the knowledgeable people who use these systems. It's what I call *learning by osmosis*.

Learning by Osmosis: How I Became a Guru on Telematic Just by Writing Messages

When I first started to discover telematic with GRETEL, and then SM, I was just a user, like anybody else. I had, at the very best, an opportunity to be part of these projects. I had absolutely no knowledge, even of the basics of information processing and telecommunications. But, by talking with people I met on the system, and by talking with those who were building the system, I quickly became a telematic expert. I found myself giving conferences in renowned engineering and sociological circles. My profession at that time was — restaurant owner. Everything that I learned about telematic, I discovered by talking with other users and learning from them. All that I have taught at the University of Montreal and at the University of Paris-Saint Denis, and in conferences (I give conferences around the world) comes from observing and sharing this passion — whether it was JE, who developed the electronic phone book and who gave me my first lessons in network packet switching, Transpac networking, and functionality of multiple criteria search in 1984; or Ww, who helped me understand servers, applications architecture, and hard disk crashes (AT&T had never seen hard disks in that state) during our nights at the SM offices; or Bad Max, and, of course, Jo le dingue, who taught me the tools for building videotext services and drawing Minitel graphics. Ww and Jo le dingue initiated me into the joys of online hacking, when we jumped from system to system around the world to avoid the cost of our telematic communications, in order to leave our mark on the welcome page on Minitel's services, or simply for the fun of doing it.

Even today, IRC and HotWired users teach me more about online features. Meanwhile, I haven't found a better way of teaching UNIX news systems to a friend than having her telnet to my system, then guiding her through TALK as she progresses. I think virtual meetings put us in relationship with the core of a person. One's emotional core is like one's professional core, all the more when one's profession is one's passion. This is directly connected to that core that lets one science feed another — a transfusion of knowledge that's like a blood transfusion.

It's true that there's nothing more exciting than a passionate person. And telematic shows us each other's passions, and sometimes our own. These passions are an energy in its purest state for anyone who approaches them with an open spirit. And, like everything exciting, addiction comes quickly. The outside world, where passions and feelings are so often masked, quickly becomes drab compared to the electronic arena. These communications can become a veritable drug, and the addiction and intoxication don't pass quickly.

Addicted to Chat

How many important meetings have I blown because I was waiting for one last message before signing off from a chatline? And, when I got that message, I'd respond, then wait for another response, until the point where I rationalized everything to myself: that meeting couldn't have been all that important, I could always reschedule it for another time, or I really didn't have anything to contribute. How many times has my girlfriend at the time gotten mad at me for spending hours at my keyboard barely responding to her (making sounds that were nothing more than onomatopoeia without meaning) when she was trying to talk to me ? How many times have I stayed up 'til 5:00 in the morning, and not really been prepared for work the next morning?

Many users tell me that this technology can quickly ruin a relationship. My answer is always the same: If, in a couple, one person becomes addicted to chatlines, there's already a serious problem in the relationship. Online services just bring them to light. What's more, chatlines offer a less dangerous escape than alcohol and other drugs.

But I do not want to minimize the negative impact these systems can have. Already, AA-like groups come to help those who don't know how to get themselves unhooked. There's even a newsgroup (`alt.irc.recovery`) for those who want to quit IRC before they lose their health.

Electronic communication quickly becomes intoxicating, and can be harmful for those who need to drug themselves or who have no wish to control themselves. For others, it's not so harmful. Above all, it can require a good dose of courage at critical times, but the quality of the relationships that it allows one to develop, and the intensity of the interaction, are well worth the pain of quitting.

While France is discovering the joy of telematic through videotext services, the other countries are starting to go in the same direction with less user-friendly technology. It's the age of the BBS. First hundreds, and then thousands, of BBSs began appearing and multiplying, little by little, throughout the world. We've seen the appearance of commercial online services like CompuServe, AOL, Genie, Prodigy, Delphi, and so on.

The BBSs

This crop of BBSs shows how much need there is for friendly communication and that this need is intrinsic to our individualistic and depersonalizing urban societies. The first BBSs were created by techies who had a microcomputer and modem and wanted some way to exchange programs with their fellow techies. They were based on a one-line approach — there was no capability for dialog. But, through interest groups and mailboxes, users quickly found a way to communicate. User A connected, left a message for user B, then disconnected; user B could then connect, read the message, and respond. Then, user A reconnected to read user B's response and continued the debate. This quickly became known as a *deferred dialogue*. It's clear that a BBS with only one line and many users was often busy and therefore unavailable. For that reason, users created networks of bulletin boards. There were often three, five, or ten BBSs in the same location, whose users were (for the most part) the same people. This is how the process called *Milk Rounds* got started. Milk Rounds consisted of making a tour of all the BBSs that you subscribed to, picking up messages that had come in and responding to them, then moving on to the next BBS. When you finished the first round, you started the second.

The very essence of these BBSs profoundly affected the behavior of their users and the atmosphere that was developed there. At first, they were all operated on an individual basis by techies for other techies, and they were often very closed, sharing exactly the same culture. Moreover, they were only accessible through a switched telephone network, and therefore limited to a local community. In the end, the system administrator of the BBS is in charge and can often distort the relationships and the level of equality between users.

These characteristics made BBSs virtual clubs, more or less closed, with their own codes of conduct and their specific flavors. As much as the videotext services resembled village squares, BBSs were becoming private bars in these villages. BBS users became used to meeting each other in Get Togethers that allowed them to reinforce their sense of separateness and, sometimes, their exclusion of outsiders.

The development of multiline BBSs permitted these lines of communication to open up a little, particularly because they had to generate money to pay for the phone lines. You then began to see some BBSs that were much more open. Many of these BBSs quickly began to specialize. The most popular kind of specialized BBS is the BBS for adults only. There are thousands all over the United States — rarely used by real women. They are more often catalogues of erotic pictures and fantasies for men. As is usually the case with specialized and closed chatlines, you see little in the way of spontaneity or interesting adventures. Passion and emotion are always in the surprise and the unexpected — they are rarely found in the places made expressly for them.

More and more of these BBSs are connecting themselves to the Net, which is becoming the BBS of BBSs. Most of the time, this connection is limited to giving access to certain newsgroups for BBS subscribers and (rarely) e-mail. On the other hand, some of these BBSs connect themselves directly to the Internet through a telnet connection. These BBSs then quickly go from a local dimension to an international dimension, and thereby make the Net the BBS of BBSs.

The Internet — Like a Small Town around the Planet

These BBSs that are available through telnet are only beginning to really become visible publicly. The most moderated of them is the Wired Cafe — (`telnet Chat.hotwired.com`) — which is mostly used for teleconferencing and debates with invited celebrities for the Wired world. But Wired hasn't been successful in becoming a friendly place to hang out on a regular basis. It's had technical problems since it started, and it's difficult to bring together people whose objectives are too diverse. Having "stars" and other Net consultants looking for contracts doesn't mix too well with simple users who are just looking for friendly conversation without any real aim.

There are other BBSs that always gather very impressive lists of users. Among them is Match-Maker (`telnet bounced.e-mail.net`; log on as `mm`). Match-Maker is a network of BBSs, connected by the Internet. It has a long questionnaire that each person must answer before being signed up. This questionnaire is available all the time and allows people to get to know the people they're chatting with better. It offers both classic e-mail and a match-making system that allows you to evaluate the compatibility between two questionnaires.

Chat is a widely used application. It's not unusual to find 40 users on MM at any given time. Most users come from the U.S., but they're also from Canada, from France, from Japan, or Latin America. This mix sometimes gives rise to pretty funny scenes, particularly on the level of languages and time zones. It's always fun to watch a Californian ask a Frenchman what he's going to do that night, then see the Frenchman respond that it's dawn where he lives. Even if most of the discussions are in English, it's not unusual for two users to suddenly start writing in French, or Spanish, or German. I wonder if using this kind of system couldn't be used for a credit in foreign language study.

The system gives each user a unique handle, based on their first name and a random number. Therefore, I am Dionysos701. People keep up-to-date about the latest blind dates. You can't see ANA179 without asking her about ROB234. JOHN684 always has news for us from the land of the rising sun, while MOOKIE481 keeps us up-to-date with his latest theater pieces in Paris.

Match-Maker also has two famous electronic dogs: SPOT and FIFI. Guardians of the right, and of good humor, they send messages, play regularly, give information about such and such a user, and cry about missing certain people. Few dogs are as pampered as SPOT and FIFI. When things are sinking a little, SPOT and FIFI become the stars of a kind of conversation difficult to imagine when you know that SPOT and FIFI are two robots. Here's an example:

```
DIONYSOS701 pets SPOT and FIFI
FIFI likes DIONYSOS701 to pet her.
SPOT likes DIONYSOS701 to pet him.
RAVEN436: welcome
DIONYSOS701 plays with SPOT and FIFI
FIFI barks and plays with DIONYSOS701.
SPOT barks and plays with DIONYSOS701.
DAVE892: hey raven
DIONYSOS701: SPOT, Sit down
SPOT sits... but doesn't stay there long.
RAVEN436: Fifi tell Jennifer424 how the movie was?
FIFI takes a quick note to JENNIFER424 in shortpaw.
SPIDER334 pets and plays with spot and fifi.
FIFI likes SPIDER334 to pet her.
SPOT likes SPIDER334 to pet him.
RAVEN436: so whats going on?
SPIDER334: spot tell jennifer424 boo
SPOT takes a quick note to JENNIFER424 in shortpaw.
Announcement from Arch: WELCOME: PACO313 entering chat at 4:40pm.
PACO313 arrives.
SPOT wags his tail.
He has met PACO313 22 times now.
FIFI wags her tail.
She has met PACO313 22 times now.
RAVEN436: Hola Paco
PACO313: HOWDY Raven
DAVE892: nothing much. fifi and spot seem pretty popular today, though.
```

like their favorite singers? How many would-be entrepreneurs would pay fortunes to read the same information as Bill Gates? How many personalities disappear behind these prefabricated personalities? Smart agents can be a powerful research tool, but they can also be robots for Big Brother, who, rather than watch what we read, can decide what we read.

The Survival and Success Guide to Digital Relationships

Virtual electronic places create a marvelous environment for developing relationships and feelings. But they don't change the people you meet there. The stories that you live that come from the telematic flow are like those from traditional meeting places. Only the emotions are multiplied 10 or 100 times — the good ones, as well as the bad. This omnipresent virtuality allows all kinds of space for our dreams and our fantasies. E-mail messages often connect us directly to the emotional parts of others, but it's easy to forget that a person isn't only emotions. And it's often the other parts we have difficulty dealing with. It's easy to get carried away by what one feels in an e-mail conversation. It's easy to embellish what we don't know about another person with our fantasies and our hopes, and the fall is generally hard. For those who tend to get lost in their relationships, I can only tell you to be careful on the Net. Not to keep yourself at a distance, or to close yourself off — on the contrary. But be careful not to get carried away. Telematic exchanges can allow you to live and discover a lot of craziness. It's a question of living the happy craziness and being on the lookout for the unhappy.

I'm often asked if there is a recipe for attracting people in chatlines, and I systematically reply that the biggest lesson I have learned is *not to have a recipe*. In fact, on these networks, nothing distinguishes you from others. You are only one user among many, without any differentiating points, with no outside signals, no voice, no looks; only words, ideas and emotions. To sort yourself out from the rest, you have to distinguish yourself — that is to say, to not do or say what anyone else would do or say in the same situation. The best recipe is to watch how everyone else does something, and do it differently. But, above all, always respect at the same time the discussion and other users. Several misplaced statements can quickly ban you forever from electronic cafes where it's nice to spend an evening when you don't feel like going out.

Conclusion

It's very hard to ever finish such a topic. It's the story of people meeting each other and trying to live together. These emotions are what distinguish us from animals (and I classify macho people and others with closed hearts in this category). The virtuality of electronic exchanges allows us to have relationships based uniquely on these emotions, which is extremely intoxicating, but you must not forget that we are not yet separate from the bodies that enclose us, from their needs and their limits.

I think that the biggest lesson that I take from many and diverse passionate experiences that the thousands of branches allow me to share is that people always try to turn political systems, economic systems, and technological systems to their own ends. And these ends are always good on a general level, but sometimes there are pretty bad individuals. These experiences have developed my sense of confidence in humanity. And, if many commentators say that the eighties saw society becoming more isolated and developing a mad individualism, the number of alliances developed on telematic networks shows that, when given a totally free environment, this unity comes back; its absence is more tied to a system where everything is controlled rather than to a change in values of individuals.

With the pleasure of talking to you on one of these systems,

Dionysos !

Philippe Le Roux has worked for over a decade in the use and social aspects of new technologies. He is president of SERVACOM, a Quebec firm specializing in object-oriented technologies, and is associated with V(DL)^2 Inc., a consortium helping organizations profit from the Internet and Infohighways. He runs the Information Technology Watch. He's taught telematic at U of Paris 8 and at U of Montreal.

Chapter 2

Internet Culture and Folklore

By Joel Furr <jfurr@acpub.duke.edu>

The Internet is in many ways, a world unto itself. Whether you say it *has* its own culture or *is* its own culture may be a semantic line too hard to draw.

Net Culture

"The Internet is a culture?" the guy on TV asked. He then continued: "Yeah, it's a culture — the sort of culture you find in a petri dish."

I saw that television program on a local PBS station in mid-1994. The program looked at "The World of the Net" and, as far as I could tell, came to two separate conclusions. The first was that most Internet veterans are really strange. The second was that the Internet itself was full of regular people who act just like you and me.

The petri dish

Yes, I know. It's confusing. Many strange people are on the Internet, but so are many regular people. They are regular people with the same variety of quirks we all have — who have found that on the Internet they have the freedom to let these quirks run wild.

And, yes, the Internet is a culture — a *metaculture* unlike anything to be found in what Internet users like to call "the real world."

The Internet is more than a culture, in fact — it's a society.

People log in from *all over the world* — people with vastly different cultural backgrounds. They have wide ranges of interests and spend as little as a few minutes per week to as much as 24 hours per day logged in. When you average things out, in fact, the average Internet user has nothing in common with the average Internet user. The Internet is just too big.

But despite all that, the Internet *is* a society. I make this point because when you wind up on the Internet for the first time, you cannot go in assuming that the on-line world is just like the world you came from. Things have evolved too much for that to be the case.

Don't see where I'm going? Have you ever seen the movie *The Bridge Over the River Kwai*? In that movie, a number of British prisoners of war in Burma are forced by their Japanese captors to build a strategic bridge over a river. They refuse to work at first but finally take on the job as something to keep the men busy and (not coincidentally) show the Japanese a thing about British discipline. Bit by bit, the soldiers warm to their task, making sure to do things right and, almost without thinking, building an important resource for their enemy.

By the end of the movie, the British are acclimated to the idea of working on the bridge and have turned their section of the camp into Home Sweet Home, complete with jovial soldiers participating in variety shows. And after the bridge is finished, they cheerfully march off to the next bridge site, not thinking anything of it.

At the very end of the movie, just as the bridge is being ceremonially opened, an American soldier (who had previously escaped from that same camp, before the beginning of construction) returns to the camp to destroy the bridge. He's horrified by the change that's come over the British troops — collaborating with the enemy that imprisons them. In fact, Alec Guinness, playing the British commander, kills the American to stop him from destroying the bridge. Then he realizes what he has done and topples over dead himself.

You see, when a society or organization has existed long enough (and it doesn't have to have existed long), it evolves with shared beliefs, values, traditions, institutions, and ways of looking at the world.

Those British soldiers evolved, over time, a world view that was compatible with their situation. The American soldier, deprived of this process, found the contrast between what he had left when he escaped and what he returned to find incredible — that dedicated British troops would have come to work hand-in-hand with the enemy. That's how societies work, though. They change, they grow, they invent ways of coping; to an outsider, walking into a sufficiently old society can resemble walking on the moon.

That's what the Internet is — a sufficiently old society that has some damned strange beliefs, traditions, and myths. It's a society which has a system of behaviors that makes virtually no sense to outsiders. The really cool thing about it is that the people on the inside don't even realize most of the time how different and alien their world views are in contrast with the non-electronic world.

For example, advertising on the Internet is viewed by many Net users in the same sort of way that John Demjanjuk is viewed by Holocaust survivors. Why? It just is, that's all. Some people blame Laurence Canter and Martha Siegel, lawyers from Arizona who posted a copy of an ad for their immigration law services to almost every newsgroup on the Internet and became some of the most hated people on the Internet by going on talk-shows and publishing a book to advance their claim that widespread advertising on the Net is a fine thing.

But the loathing for ads goes back much further than that 1993 green-card fiasco. Because the Internet began as an academic and research network (after Milnet broke away, that is), the Net culture had no more experience with advertising than a university physics department would have had. And unless you know of a physics department somewhere that was hawking advertising space on its chalkboards, that's not much.

Old hackers never die — their bugs just increase.

The Internet was for decades virtually advertising-free. People came to expect it. On rare occasions when someone did post an ad, it was flamed, the advertiser grumbled and went away, and the institutionalized stigma against advertising grew firmer and more impenetrable. With more than 20 years of advertising-free history behind it, Net society was not exactly interested in having people wandering into Usenet newsgroups and posting hype about skiing vacations in Colorado and way-cool real-estate deals in Boca Raton. Things are changing now that so many people using the Internet are there to do business, but it's a rare newsgroup that hasn't had a battle of wills between someone posting an ad and some veteran offended by the ad.

You may be wondering, "How do the newer users pick up these beliefs and shared values and come to hold them so strongly?" The technical, boring answer is that a wide range of formal and informal channels exist for communicating these beliefs. Any society has them, and the Internet is no different.

But I have another answer, which I call the Old Hat Wannabe Syndrome. Many of the people who spend a great deal of time on the Internet notice before long that there are several types of fellow users, among them the "old hat." The old hat is someone other users defer to, someone who speaks with authority, someone who seems to know what's going on. Every newsgroup has some. New users, wanting to fit in, see these old hats in action and, in an attempt to be respected as well, ape the old hats' behavior, right down to flaming (harshly criticizing) advertisers. The battle for status and prestige in newsgroups does much to perpetuate the existing Net traditions; people try to out-old-hat the old hats.

To make a long story short, don't be surprised if people on the Internet do things that seem illogical to you; they may be illogical to you under your system of values, but they make perfect sense to someone who has "bought in" to the Internet's socially constructed reality.

Freedom and barriers

When someone says "Internet culture," by the way, she is usually referring to the activity in Usenet newsgroups. There's much more to the Internet than Net news, but it's difficult to point to specific cultural aspects of ftp or Gopher. It's Usenet that gives every user his own free speech platform in the public square.

You meet all sorts of people in the discussion groups that make up the world of Net news. Every year, the story has it, the Usenet population increases by a factor of ten. Simple probability dictates that some serious weirdos are out there; don't be surprised when you encounter them. People feel much freer to let their idiosyncrasies run wild on the Internet.

Let me give you an example: In real life, John Doe may be some boring guy who would never dream of standing up at his kid's PTA meeting and calling for the immediate abolition of school as we know it and replacing it with work camps. Give him an account on a local Internet provider, however, let him out into the crowds on `misc.education`, and everything changes. The calm, sedate guy you don't feel nervous sitting next to lets his inner feelings run loose, and then it's time to lock up the knives.

Why? Anonymity is one reason. With the millions and millions of people on the Internet, it's easy to get lost in the crowd and not have your opinions personalized — associated with you everywhere you go — as they would be if you went around in public saying the same things. Stand up at the PTA and say "Let's just screw all this garbage about multiculturalism and get those lazy kids digging big holes," and people will look warily at you wherever you go. Say the same thing on `misc.education`, slug it out in an argument with people who feel that your plan is perhaps a little ahead of its time, and then turn your computer off. Walk out on the street. No one looks at you funny, and no one even cares because most of them don't even know what the Internet is. The Internet has given a generation of people with secret peeves and various ugly bees in the bonnet the freedom to express those thoughts without negatively impinging on their outside lives.

"Space aliens are stealing U.S. jobs!" — Stanford economics professor

This freedom may change, though, as even more people flock to the Net. When I first showed up on the Internet, I was probably one of about 200 people in a town of 30,000 who used the Internet actively; my boss used to sit there using his mainframe account and musing about how he wanted to get on the Internet someday. I kept telling him "Richard, you *are* on the Internet." He blinked and filed the information away until the next time he read a magazine article about the Internet and began musing aloud again. He probably would have freaked if he had known that on days when he didn't have anything for me to work on, I sat up in my graduate assistant office, drinking too much coffee and posting long rants about lemurs taking over the world.

I imagine that if I still worked there and tried that today, word would get back to him. Ditto for John Doe. Now that every large city in the United States and many cities around the world have multiple for-profit Internet access providers, the odds of his neighbor or his employer or the bagger at the supermarket seeing his postings and sniggering have grown considerably. God knows that I'm having a devil of a time keeping my real life and my Internet life separate. On no fewer than four occasions in the past month, I've introduced myself to a stranger and heard him say, "*You're* Joel Furr? Wow!" My *mother* is on the Internet now. I pray that she never finds `alt.fan.joel-furr` or `alt.bonehead.joel-furr`.

Even with the Internet changing rapidly, as new users pour in by the millions from America Online and similar access providers, the Internet is still a strange place. It is *not* a public park — unless public parks where you come from have people running around waving guns, having sex, screaming shrilly at each other, attacking one another, and ripping posters from public bulletin boards. The Internet has a culture of its own, a culture with decades of inertia invested in it; if you wander in and assume that you can do anything you want, wherever you want, and however you want, you're going to get your head handed to you.

It doesn't take much time to get used to the strange way people act on the Internet, but it's useful to do some lurking when you're new. When you *lurk,* you read the traffic on a newsgroup without posting anything yourself, watching what goes on and learning the ropes before taking part in the discussions yourself. Even after you've been on the Internet awhile, you may still experience severe culture shock when you wander into a Usenet newsgroup you've never taken part in. Just because you're well-known in `rec.pets.dogs`, for example, and often have a great deal to say about all sorts of dog-related issues, doesn't mean that you can walk into rec.motorcycles.harley and begin chattering away — you may well get flamed for acting too familiar with old-time posters.

It's happened to me, and I'm one of the best-known people on Usenet. I wandered into alt.peeves on the recommendation of Ken Strayhorn, a friend of mine who is a regular poster in that group, and actively took part in discussions right away — and got flamed. Rather promptly, articles began showing up, saying, "Who the hell is this guy?" It's not that they disagreed (or, for that matter, agreed) with what I had to say, but they disliked the way I "acted like I owned the place." On the Internet, everyone seems to aspire to be more like the more experienced users, who have been there longer than they have, and everyone seems to look down on anyone with less experience. I hadn't been on alt.peeves long; therefore, I should have kept my mouth mostly shut until they knew me better. You have to pay your dues.

Is God a performance artist?

Some people feel that this point of view is utter heresy. I was interviewed on a radio show about how a new user can best get along on Usenet; I said, "Lurk for a while, and then slowly work your way up to actively participating." The cohost irritably told me that that advice wasn't fair or correct. She was correct, of course — it's *not* fair. It is, however, the way the culture has come to expect new users to behave. Getting angry about it is rather pointless: It's the way things are. All you can do about it is to treat with politeness and respect those new users who feel that they have to say something in every discussion thread. Maybe one day this point of view will catch on. Ten bucks says that it won't, though: As more and more people use newsgroups, more and more newsgroups are becoming unreadable because of the daily volume of messages, and I don't foresee any great chance of talkative newbies being eagerly welcomed to most groups anytime soon.

Cultures evolve behaviors to deal with perceived threats and opportunities. If you see something strange happening on the Net and wonder why, stop to think, "Perhaps there's a reason things are this way?" Waving your hands in the air and saying "That's unfair" is just so much noise. Life isn't fair, and neither is the Internet.

This book is called *Internet SECRETS,* and the secret I want you to take from this chapter is rather simple on its face: The Internet is a culture, like any other. You can take the time to understand this culture better or you can disregard the way "things are done" and, usually, wind up irritated and in a bad mood. It's your choice.

Be warned, however: If you feel righteous indignation at the way people act or are treated, take a dose of perspective and check back with us in six months. In 1993 Delphi Internet offered Internet access to thousands of the most clueless people that veterans had seen in a long, long while. We treated them with the usual careful contempt, and they got angry. Then America Online dumped an even larger wave of clueless newbies on us, and guess who was right there, leading the charge and flaming them for their mistakes? You guessed it. The Delphi users. Now that other services such as Prodigy and CompuServe are letting their users on the Internet and into newsgroups, guess who's right there in the thick of things, making fun of them for their stumbling mistakes and breaches of etiquette? I'll give you a hint: They post from aol.com.

| JOIN USENET: Post to exotic, distant machines. Meet exciting, unusual people and flame them.
— Peter van der Linden

Archetypes

Millions of people post to Usenet newsgroups and use the Internet in various other ways. They're all different, but in many ways they're often very much alike. Despite all the faces and personalities behind all those user IDs posting up a storm, you quickly begin to notice that, despite individual variations, there are nevertheless several basic sorts of people you meet, and after you've pegged what a person is, you can comfortably pigeonhole her and make life easier for yourself.

Call these types of people archetypes, if you will. These archetypes represent an amazing range of human behavior, futility, effort, determination, and outright idiocy at times. As you read through these types, you may recognize in them certain people you know — or you may recognize yourself.

I use various terms in this section to refer to the different archetypes. Some of these terms are widely used on the Internet; others are my own coinage or way of describing a class of person for whom no commonly accepted term exists.

Angry young men and complainers

On Usenet, an angry young man (AYM) is not necessarily a man, or young, but is always angry. An *angry young man* feels strongly about a cause and continually agitates on its behalf, but he rarely (if ever) does anything concrete about it — even though, in most cases, there are some easy things a person can do. Doing something would get in the way, in fact, of more worthwhile things, such as the informal battles to see who's the angriest about a subject.

A generic example of the angry young man can be found in `talk.politics.animals`. It's the animal-rights newsgroup, and because hardly anyone is going to wander into an animal-rights newsgroup and *advocate* abusing animals, the group consists mostly of wild essays about freeing lab animals and boycotting companies and battles over who is the most ethically pure as far as animals are concerned. When I posted an appeal to `talk.politics.animals` for contributions to the Duke University Primate Center, which spends money breeding endangered species, I received mail from people who said, "That's the first time I've *ever* seen anyone suggest actually *doing* something here in `talk.politics.animals`." There are many angry people in `talk.politics.animals`, but as far as I have been able to tell, they've never lifted a finger in the real world to do anything for animal rights. They're too busy arguing to even consider volunteering at their local animal shelter or raising money for animal care or lobbying for animal rights. Actually *doing* something would be contrary to an angry young man's existence.

Many angry young men post to the newsgroup `alt.dear.whitehouse`, as though posting angry denunciations of President Clinton's policies to a group no one from the White House knows exists is going to accomplish something. For real fun, watch the angry young men in `alt.dear.whitehouse` angrily demand to know why President Clinton hasn't responded to their post.

HELP! I'M BEING HELD PRISONER IN A .SIGNATURE FACTORY!

Not long ago, Patrick Curry, a user from Purdue University, started an insurrection of sorts against the so-called control freaks who sit around in the newsgroup `alt.config` (which is intended for discussions of new alt.* hierarchy newsgroups, whether they should be created, what they should be called, and so on) and tell people who propose silly new newsgroups "No" all the time. Curry was incensed that all his favorite newsgroups kept disappearing from his site, and he objected strenuously to anyone (me, for example) who removed newsgroups that were created without prior discussion and informal approval in `alt.config`. He began sending out mail to people he had seen getting flamed in `alt.config`, suggesting that they set up a cabal to repeatedly create lots of joke newsgroups until the "control freaks" gave up — not to mention mail-bombing the perceived leader of the dictators to "punish" him. Curry never accomplished anything. He had a fine time, however, coming up with code words for his "cabal" to use in their mail and humbly nominating himself as "Poobah" (his actual word) of the cabal.

Then there are the complainers. In my book, complainers are somewhat different from angry young men. Angry young men *can* do something about the thing they're angry about but never take the time to do so, preferring instead to whine, moan, and create angst. *Complainers,* on the other hand, always complain, without understanding the reasons that things are the way they are — without even *trying* to find out why things are they way they are — and never offer any usable suggestions for improvement. There's usually nothing *to* be done, in fact, but they complain anyway.

Complainers are *always* unhappy. An excellent example of complainers are the people who habitually post to `rec.humor.d` or `news.groups`, demanding either that Maddi Hausmann Sojourner, the moderator of `rec.humor.funny`, be replaced or that a new newsgroup, `rec.humor.funny.actually-funny`, be created. They don't understand that a newsgroup moderator can't post what isn't submitted. Short of writing reams of new material herself, a moderator can post only what shows up in her mailbox. In the case of `rec.humor.funny`, if the same jokes get submitted time and time again, either they get posted or *nothing* gets posted. Consequently, the only way to improve the quality of the material is to submit quality material yourself and encourage others to do so. But if you give this advice to complainers, they just stew for a while and then repeat their original accusations.

Complainers and angry young men make up, sadly, a relatively large percentage of the Internet's population of newsgroup users. The former complain about things they don't take the time to understand, and the latter prefer complaining to doing anything. Both are essentially impotent, unable to accomplish anything but more than willing to make life difficult for the people who try to make a difference.

"Burn down Chicago over a painting? Paris maybe, but Americans have never taken culture that seriously." — Chief Judge Posner, *Nelson v. Streeter*, 16 F.3d 145, 150 (7th Cir. 1994).

The best advice I can give you for dealing with inveterate kvetchers is not to ignore them (which makes you look like you have something to hide or are afraid to answer their charges) and not to debate them (don't dignify an empty argument by taking it seriously). My advice is simply to ask, "What are you going to *do* about it?" This question disarms them nearly every time because, ultimately, they don't *have* a plan. They just want to complain.

Clueless people and newbies

The people referred to in the preceding section, the posters in `alt.dear.whitehouse` who firmly believe that President Clinton takes time out every day to read the newsgroup but is too chicken to respond, are definitely clueless. They're not newbies, however. I make this distinction because the term *clueless newbie* is often used in Usenet newsgroups, and it's often a misnomer. There are clueless people, and some of them have been on the Internet for 20 years. There are newbies, and some of them are very clueful. You can have clueless newbies, but one doesn't necessarily imply the other.

A clueless person is similar to a newbie but differs in an important respect: Whereas a newbie lacks information about how to do something and may well pay attention when this information is supplied, a *clueless* person somehow manages to misunderstand everything. She eventually gets angry and goes away in a huff, muttering or just failing to understand from the word *go* and never even thinking about asking or finding out what's really going on.

I have a favorite clueless story. I'm a newsgroup moderator several times over, which means that articles submitted for several newsgroups show up in my mailbox. After I read through the articles, if they're appropriate for the groups for which they're submitted, I post them and they circulate around the world. Not long ago, however, I received a series of submissions, one every ten minutes or so, from an America Online user who wanted to post to the `comp.society.folklore` newsgroup (a newsgroup for discussions of computer history and folklore) his advertisement for log-cabin homes. When I finally got through to him, I told him that he shouldn't keep submitting posts over and over again; I'd get to them when I had the time, and, besides, his article wasn't even vaguely related to the purpose of the group.

His response? In response to the first point, he said, "That's *wrong.* Who appointed you to censor my messages?" Addressing the second issue, he said, "Hey, I pay your salary. Post my message." He apparently had the impression that all Usenet newsgroups were run by America Online and that, therefore, I was an America Online employee and, because he paid good money for his account, I had better get cracking and approve his log-cabin ad or he would be "talking to the people in charge at AOL, see?"

I tried to explain to him how things really work, but I don't think that I ever got through. When we finally stopped sending messages to each other, he was still grumbling about poor service from America Online and vowing to "do something about it."

I eventually got around to asking America Online where my pay was, but no one there responded.

Computation is the art of carefully throwing away information.

So a clueless person is someone who not only doesn't understand what's going on but also refuses to pay attention when you try to help. Unfortunately, many of these people are out there, and they often come from commercial access sites, convinced that the Internet is just one more thing for which they've paid to receive user support.

A *newbie,* on the other hand, is simply a user who's new to the Net. Newbies can often do maddening or annoying things that show their inexperience or unfamiliarity with the customs of the Net, such as posting requests to `alt.folklore.urban` for help with their homework or posting to `news.misc` in ALL CAPS and wondering why they never see any headlines or sports stories in the news.* hierarchy newsgroups — just people talking about system administration and discussion groups.

It generally helps if newbies take the time to read the informational postings that are posted regularly to `news.announce.newusers`; even though most systems set up their newbies with this group and with `news.newusers.questions` at the top of their .newsrc files, newbies always seem to ignore it and rush on to `alt.fan.rush-limbaugh` and `alt.sex`. A newbie who takes the time to find out what's going on and pays attention to help (when it's given) can quickly become an experienced user. A newbie who refuses to pay attention or assumes that he already knows everything can remain a newbie for years.

One of the worst errors a newbie can make after getting an Internet account to post to Usenet newsgroups is to become a warlord. A *warlord* is a .sig abuser, someone whose .sig file is gigantic, ridiculous, and pointless. (A .signature file is composed of lines of text or ASCII graphics automatically inserted at the end of Net news postings, meant to represent a signature in a letter.) As someone once said, just because you *can* append a page-long ASCII picture of a dragon to every Usenet article you post doesn't mean that you *should* do it. The problem is that many newbies think that it's cool to do it.

Technically speaking, there is only one warlord: The Warlord of the West. Long departed from Usenet (or perhaps matured and posting under a different name). The Warlord, and his inadvertent followers, achieved notoriety by posting huge and obnoxious .sig files that sometimes took up entire screens. The Warlord was among the first to do this, and all subsequent warlords are named after him. He was so bad and so prolific that he inspired his own newsgroup, `alt.fan.warlord`. Therefore, the term *warlord* is sometimes applied to those who share his philosophy that bigger is better and that "really huge" is better than just plain "big." It seems that newbies arrive on the Net, read a few groups, and somehow come up with the idea that the best way to get people to pay more attention to your newsgroup postings is to attach a giant ASCII-art dragon or picture of Bart Simpson saying, "Don't have a cow, man!" And, of course, if it's worth doing, it's worth overdoing, so they make the .sig a screen or two long and sometimes even forget to put an article in between the header and the .sig. (Sigh.)

If newbies who do this irk you as much as they do many people, you might be amused by `alt.fan.warlord`, where .sigs are mocked, scorned, and turned into peat moss.

Control freaks

On the Internet, a *control freak* is a user who doesn't like the way things are and is determined to change things, regardless of whether everyone else agrees or even cares, and especially if people are violently opposed. A strong correlation exists between the strength of the opposition to a control freak's agenda and the control freak's determination to forge ahead with his master plan.

In December 1992, one control freak wanted to move `alt.folklore.computers` from the low-propagated (not widely carried) `alt.*` hierarchy to what he thought would be a better place in the `comp.*` hierarchy. His plan involved changing the existing `comp.society.folklore` newsgroup from moderated to unmoderated status (because it hadn't received many submissions as a moderated newsgroup) and then "aliasing" the traffic from `alt.folklore.computers` to `comp.society.folklore`. This plan was widely viewed as a hideously bad idea because `alt.folklore.computers` was that rare exception to the rule that `alt.*` groups are poorly propagated. In fact, `alt.folklore.computers` was one of the top 100 most frequently read newsgroups on the Internet, carried at 81 percent of all sites. Forcibly moving the traffic to a `comp.*` group would have inevitably resulted in a mess because not every site would have complied with the aliasing and because many sites would have ignored the move.

Had the control freak's plan passed, a thriving newsgroup would have been more or less destroyed. During the required 28-day discussion phase, virtually everyone who spoke up about the issue hated the idea. The control freak took it to a vote anyway. The plan lost by a vote of 151 "yes" votes to 729 "no" votes.

Why, you ask, was the control freak so determined to do something that virtually everyone else thought was an insane idea? Was it to make computer folklore traffic more generally available by moving the traffic to the `comp.*` hierarchy? No, he said, when I asked him about it — `alt.folklore.computers` was already widely carried. The sole reason for his proposed "hostile takeover" of `alt.folklore.computers` was to "promote" `alt.folklore.computers` to a more respected hierarchy.

The only reason God was able to make the world in seven days was that he didn't have to remain compatible with the preceding version.

And then there was the great ARMM! massacre on March 30, 1993.

1993 was the Year of the Bot (a robot article-posting program) on Usenet. A Turkish student at the University of Minnesota was running an artificial intelligence program called "Serdar Argic," which posted long rants about the Armenian genocide of 1914 to dozens of newsgroups, many of which had nothing whatsoever to do with Turkey, Armenia, or genocide. Worse, the Armenian genocide of 1914 that Argic posted about was *not* the genocide of the Armenians by the Turks, but an entirely different genocide (known only to Argic) in which the Armenians killed all the Turks.

The Argic software scanned all of Usenet for articles that contained the words *Turkey, Armenia,* or *genocide* and automatically followed up many of these articles with long rants from the Argic archive — megabytes per day. The Zumabot, as Argic was often called (after the name of the site from which it posted), made many newsgroups utterly unreadable. There were similar deranged posters on various other subjects — Dan Gannon, the Holocaust revisionist, for example — and it was increasingly difficult to discuss anything in any newsgroup because of invasions from cranks and kooks with their own agendas.

Into the storm of hate and controversy strode Dick Depew, an Ohio resident who had what he thought was the solution: "retroactive moderation" (erasure). It's possible (if you know what you're doing) to erase someone else's article from a newsgroup, and Depew proposed that an automatic program, which he dubbed

ARMM (*a*utomated *r*etroactive *m*inimal *m*oderation), be set up to do just that for abusive users. In other words, he wanted to censor newsgroups retroactively by removing off-topic articles.

Hardly any subject on Usenet is more controversial than this one: censoring for content. Moderators of newsgroups do this routinely, of course, but that's why we have moderated newsgroups: You *know* who's screening articles for applicability. With Depew's ARMM, you *wouldn't* know. Self-appointed retroactive moderators, especially if two with competing agendas targeted the same group, would simply make articles vanish. No one would have any way to stop them, short of trying to get them fired or cut off from their Internet access. Among most responsible Usenet users, Depew's ARMM plan was seen as an unbelievably bad idea. Self-appointed content arbiters could ruin everything. You would never know whether your articles would be seen by anyone if it became acceptable for people to practice retroactive moderation on a wholesale basis.

Depew fought a months-long war in `news.admin.misc`, `news.future`, `news.groups`, `news.admin.policy`, and half a dozen other groups, trying to get his concept accepted. The Internet has *never* had a more tireless control freak than Depew. Hardly anyone agreed with him, yet he continued arguing for more than a year. As mentioned earlier, a strong correlation exists between the strength of the opposition to a control freak and the freak's determination to carry out his plan.

Depew was not an angry young man. He didn't fulminate uselessly and then do nothing about it. No, he set up the ARMM robot program on his site and began testing it.

Then came March 30, 1993 — The Great ARMM! Massacre.

I had gone home the day before so exhausted that I simply had dinner and went to bed. I woke up eight hours later, in the middle of the night, and decided to go on to work and get a head start on some things. I logged in and skimmed a few newsgroups before getting to work. Much to my surprise, there were hundreds of new messages in `news.admin.policy`, a group I had caught up on the day before. I entered the group, viewed the thread selector, and involuntarily said, "Oh, my God."

There were *hundreds of messages* from Depew's ARMM! bot, all with Subject lines that were variations of the following:

```
Subject: ARMM! ARMM! ARMM! ARMM! ARMM! ARMM! ARMM!
```

His bot had triggered on its *own postings* during a test cycle in which it had been intended to stamp articles meant for retroactive moderation. The stamp was supposed to include a notice that the messages *would have been erased* if ARMM! had actually been implemented. Unfortunately, it triggered its *own* messages and began adding the word *ARMM!* to the subject line and adding various other header lines to each recursion. Fortunately, it hadn't been going long and had dumped only a few megabytes of postings to `news.admin.policy`.

"Oh, bother," said Pooh, and quietly erased his hard disk.

Depew was apparently not at the controls, because it was running amok. I assumed that he had left it running and had gone to bed. I reached for the telephone, called Ohio directory information, and got Depew's home phone number. When I called, it was busy — the bot had taken control.

I had no idea what to do. I was considering asking the operator for an emergency break when, finally, the messages stopped. As I found out a few hours later, a user in Germany had tried the same thing I had tried, calling Depew, but he had tried again when he heard the busy signal and had learned that Depew had a second line to his house — which turned out to be the voice line. Depew had been awakened and had turned off the bot.

As users across the United States woke up and went to work, people began posting "What was *that*?" messages to `news.admin.policy`. Others posted to say that the megabytes of unexpected traffic had crashed UUCP system after UUCP system, as a newsgroup normally expected to produce only a certain amount of traffic per day had suddenly produced dozens of times that amount. Some people talked about suing Depew for damages and, as one might expect, a new newsgroup, sarcastically named `alt.fan.dick-depew` appeared. (That last one was my handiwork.)

Did Depew apologize? Yes. Did he mend his ways? No. He lay low for a couple of weeks and then returned to the fray as determined as ever to win acceptance for retroactive moderation. A year later, in March 1994, he was *still* arguing away, convinced of the merit of his plan.

Conspiracy theorists

Many conspiracy theorists are on Usenet. For some reason, though, many of them have been reined in recently by sites no longer willing to endure the usual torrents of complaints from people who are angry at their users' behavior.

Thank God.

Before the recent reining in of some of the more abusive conspiracy theorists, certain newsgroups, such as `soc.history` and `sci.space`, were an absolute madhouse, with megabytes per day of blatantly false information made available by such posters as "Serdar Argic," Robert McElwaine, and Dan Gannon.

Argic's claim, often stated in every `soc.culture` group on the Net in addition to less likely places such as `alt.college.sorority`, was that the stories of the Turkish genocide of Armenians in 1914 were all lies and that the truth was exactly the other way around: In 1914, Armenian crooks-terrorists-criminals (whatever that means) had killed 2 1/2 million Turks.

McElwaine claimed many things, but among his more endearing notions was the belief that American space shuttles had been destroyed minutes after launch by orbiting Russian "cosmospheres," all of which were covered up by the United States government, which replaced the slain astronauts with clones. McElwaine had sort of a cult following because his claims were so incredibly wacky — for example, that God is a cannibalistic space alien who came here to eat the first humans and that Jews were later creations who helped God in this evil plan. McElwaine will always be best known for his creative and seemingly random USE of CAPITALIZATION in his articles, and for the phrase he placed at the bottom of every post he ever made: "UN-altered REPRODUCTION and DISSEMINATION of this IMPORTANT Information is ENCOURAGED."

Dan Gannon was a particularly enthusiastic Holocaust revisionist; he claimed that hardly any Jews had been killed by the Germans during World War II and that all claims to the contrary were the work of conspirators and dupes. In fact, he liked to use the term *hoax* in describing the Holocaust — to hear him tell it, the Holocaust was an invention of the worldwide "Jewish conspiracy."

Fortunately, both Argic and McElwaine lost access to the Net, and Gannon was forced by his site to confine his depredations to a small set of newsgroups in which he couldn't bother many people. Someone else, however, will be along soon to fill the void.

The difference between theory and practice is bigger in practice than in theory.

Many of the more notorious conspiracy theorists have one thing in common: They have access at sites that either don't care what their users do (or they choose to look the other way) or are run by conspiracy theorists themselves.

It's difficult to get Internet access providers to rein in their users even when the users become extremely abusive of others. It sets a very dangerous legal precedent.

Many of the larger for-profit Internet access sites are rightfully leery of reining in their users when their users become abusive — not because of the Big Brother aspect that would come into play if your Net prover kept looking over your shoulder, but because legally, if your Net provider exercises any control over what you do with your account, the provider can be held liable if at some point you do something illegal and the provider didn't bother to stop you.

To use an analogy, if a school teacher routinely stops children on the playground from hitting each other with sticks, and then one day just shrugs and walks away, parents can sue the teacher for *not* stopping little Billy from hitting little Jimmy. Or, for example, the phone company has no liability over what you do with the phone. If you use a telephone to plan a firebombing, then go and kill a lot of people, the phone company can't be sued. If on the other hand, they started trying to exert some control over the uses you put your phone to, and then someone plans a murder using the phone, they may be liable.

Netcom, the provider that gave access to Dan Gannon, let him run free for a long time until it finally told him that his account would be canceled unless he confined his postings to newsgroups in which they were theoretically on-topic. McElwaine lost his access because he had obtained a student account from the University of Wisconsin. Even the most die-hard free-thinking campus news administrator eventually gets tired of explaining to a supervisor why so many registered letters keep showing up complaining about one of the local users.

Argic, on the other hand, was a tough nut to crack. The person running Argic had leased an account from UUNET Technologies, one of the world's foremost access providers, and had "theoretically" given Argic a feed from this site. If you complained to UUNET, UUNET said, "Argic isn't a customer of ours. He's being fed by `anatolia.org`, so complain to the guy who runs `anatolia`." `Anatolia.org` was run, of course, by the guy responsible for Argic. Incoming mail sent to either Argic or the guy running `anatolia.org` simply bounced; that's what you can do when you run your own site and don't want to read complaints about things you do.

No one knows for sure why Argic vanished. The best theories have it that the guy behind Argic lost his access to the computer he was using at the University of Minnesota when he failed to register for classes two semesters in a row. Several Argic-like posters have sprung up in the months since Argic vanished, but all are posting from sites that have firm policies against Argic-style torrents of hate posted to unrelated newsgroups. Consequently, Argic-style anti-Armenian conspiracy theories are now more or less lost in the general drivel on `soc.history`, and that newsgroup is actually seeing real discussions for the first time in years.

Eye of newt, spleen of censor . . .

General weirdos

A different class of nut includes the ones not motivated by hate so much as by a serious kink in their brain or merely a desire to be as strange as possible. Among these are *cranks* (low-level weirdos) and *mad scientists* (high-level weirdos of a particular bent). Cranks are relatively easy to deal with: You just learn their particular buttons if you find that you're inhabiting a newsgroup that has one. Mad scientists are less easy to tolerate because they usually attract a group of hangers-on and sometimes a coterie of critics who keep trying to shoot them down.

A crank is similar to a conspiracy theorist but usually can be found in less politically sensitive groups. A crank may have the abiding, lifelong belief that dachshunds are stupid dogs and may feel a need once a week or so to share this belief with the readers of `rec.pets.dogs`. Cranks are often viewed somewhat fondly by regular readers of a group; once in a while, to give the crank something to do, they post some bait for the crank to respond to.

A good example of a serious crank was Mark Ethan Smith, a California resident whose main claim to fame was that he was a woman. If you recognize that there are more than 2 1/2 billion women on the planet, you can see that being a woman isn't all that uncommon. What *was* uncommon, however, was that Smith, a radical "feminist" and raving loony, insisted on being called Mark and referred to using only male pronouns. Smith claimed that society tried to degrade women by using "diminutive" terms and by forcing women into "diminutive" roles. He believed that women's clothing is drag regardless of who wears it; and that terms such as *she* and *her* are hateful.

Will create newsgroups for food.

Then there are the mad scientists. More than a few posters to newsgroups have strange theories that they claim are far ahead of their time but are being repressed by the Establishment. Some of these theories are just plain strange, and no one can understand them. Consider the theory that "time has inertia." I for one don't get it. Or the "Venus must be given an Earthlike orbit to become a new Earth" theory. Apparently NASA should drop everything and move Venus into an orbit the same distance from the sun as the earth is. The scary thing is that these theories come from a tenured Iowa State mathematics professor.

Another longtime weirdo recently decided that he was the reincarnation of Archimedes. I've never been able to keep all of his deranged theories straight, but if memory serves, at times he has spouted claims of having been the first to solve Fermat's Last Theorem and to have plutonium in his brain. Recently he talked about suing the keeper of the `net.legends` FAQ (*f*requently *a*sked *q*uestions) file, David DeLaney, for not putting him at the top of the FAQ, out of alphabetical order, to give him his proper place of honor. Or something like that.

Other mad scientists claim to have contacted aliens who have given them technological secrets to stop the impending world war, only to have the U.S. Air Force refuse to listen. The worrisome thing is that several of the mad scientists have credentials that check out — they really *are* Ph.D.s in some field or another, and they really *do* have tenure somewhere.

Loons

More than a few people on the Internet can best be described as *loons:* people who genuinely seem to have mental problems but were given Internet access as a strange form of outpatient therapy. Some loons have weird political agendas, such as the guys who pop up at election time outraged because the representative of the Kansas Independent Party wasn't included in the Presidential debate. Some of them are your basic homophobes, unable to control themselves if they find themselves in a newsgroup with someone who has an inverted (point-down) triangle in their .sig. Some people talk to aliens and take the time to let us know about the ongoing negotiations to save Earth from obliteration.

Curmudgeons

A curmudgeon is somewhat cranklike but usually retains some perspective. *Curmudgeons* are usually tired, irritable users who tried for a long time to accomplish something and get a point across and who have seen those efforts fail utterly. Consequently, a curmudgeon resorts to sniping from the sidelines, irritably making annoyed remarks about the clueless and the newbies and occasionally resorting to the reductionist "no." Tim Pierce, the curmudgeon of `alt.config` (the newsgroup devoted to discussions of new `alt.*` hierarchy newsgroups), became so weary after years of telling people why yet another newsgroup devoted to some guy no one has ever heard of outside Salina, Kansas, would be a bad idea that now, after each proposal of that type, he just says "no" and goes on.

Warning: Objects in calendar may be closer than they appear.

Demagogues

A demagogue, classically speaking, is a manipulative tyrant, a leader who makes use of prejudice and falsehoods and promises to gain power. On Usenet, *demagogues* are people who are so obsessively into preaching their peculiar brand of political theory that they become inured to tedious little things like facts.

If demagogues are convinced that something is so, it is so, and all the arguing in the world just makes them more convinced of how right they are.

`Talk.politics.*` and `alt.politics.*` groups are full of demagogues. When two demagogues of opposing points of view begin trading lies back and forth about their respective points of view, no place on Usenet is more devoid of signal (meaningful traffic). Demagogues don't always represent classic points of view; for some reason, die-hard Usenet participants seem to be easily swayed by the claims of the latest political fad. In the 1992 Presidential straw poll on Usenet, Clinton and Bush came in far behind the Libertarian candidate, the Independent Party candidate, Ross Perot, and Rin Tin Tin.

Fanatics

A *fanatic* is a fan — a fan who carries fandom more than a little too far.

Serious fanatics on the Internet include *Star Trek* fans. They are so single-mindedly obsessed with their favorite TV show and movie and book and so on that there's a real danger that one day they will simply take over. So many *Star Trek* fans are on the Internet that they have the potential to be welded into a voting bloc that could institute just about any imaginable change in Internet policy. That's assuming that you can deceive them into believing that the "other side" wants to remove all the `rec.arts.startrek.*` groups.

Similarly, devotees of the card game *Magic: The Gathering* worry me. The game already has more converts than Islam, as far as anyone has been able to determine, and God help us all if they ever turn their attention to serious matters.

When the game hit the Net, a newsgroup for Magic fans was created. Because the overall card game is part of the system of games produced by Wizards Of The Coast, the most popular name that emerged was `rec.games.deckmaster`. Experienced newsgroup namers suggested that perhaps `rec.games.trading-cards.magic` would be a more descriptive name and would make it easier for people to find the group. This suggestion was viewed by the Magic fans as "Hey, they're trying to push us around," and so `rec.games.deckmaster` it was.

Then the Magic fans decided that the accompanying newsgroup for selling and trading Magic cards should be called `rec.games.board.marketplace` (`rec.games.board` had been home to Magic discussions before Magic fans got their own group). We Net veterans suggested that maybe the group should be located nearer the main group. We were ignored.

Needless to say, when `rec.games.deckmaster` and `rec.games.board.marketplace` were created, no one used `rec.games.board.marketplace` for discussions of selling and trading Magic cards; they all flocked to `rec.games.deckmaster` instead. The people in `rec.games.deckmaster` didn't like seeing all the selling and trading going on, so they decided to create `rec.games.deckmaster.marketplace` — which is what we Net veterans had told them to do in the first place.

It's up to you.

The society of the Internet is full of many strange customs and practices. It's not downtown Anytown, U.S.A., and it's not some supercool "cyberspace." It is just a culture in its own right. As I said, you can take the time to understand this culture better, or you can disregard the way "things are done" and, usually, wind up irritated and in a bad mood.

It's your choice.

Joel Furr is a Durham, North Carolina-based writer, Usenet group moderator, seller of Internet-related T-shirts, and sparring partner of half the people on Usenet. In his spare time, he volunteers as a lemur rancher at the fabled Duke University Primate Center.

Chapter 3
Usenet

This chapter contains three articles:

- "What Is Usenet?"
- "What Is Usenet? A Second Opinion"
- "Interview with Henry Spencer: On Usenet News and C News"

What Is Usenet?

by Chip Salzenberg <chip@tct.com>
Gene Spafford <spaf@cs.purdue.edu>
Mark Moraes <netannounce@deshaw.com>

The first thing to understand about Usenet is that it is widely misunderstood. Every day on Usenet, the "blind men and the elephant" phenomenon is evident, in spades. In our opinion, more flame wars arise from a lack of understanding of the nature of Usenet than from any other source. And consider that such flame wars arise among people who are on Usenet. Imagine, then, how poorly understood Usenet must be by those outside!

Any essay on the nature of Usenet cannot ignore the erroneous impressions held by many Usenet users. Therefore, this article will treat falsehoods first. Keep reading for truth. (Beauty, alas, is not relevant to Usenet.)

What Usenet Is Not

1. Usenet is not an organization

No person or group has authority over Usenet as a whole. No one controls who gets a news feed, which articles are propagated where, who can post articles, or anything else. There is no Usenet, Inc., nor is there a Usenet User's Group. You're on your own.

Granted, various activities are organized through Usenet newsgroups. The newsgroup creation process is one such activity. But it would be a mistake to equate Usenet with the organized activities it makes possible. If they were to stop tomorrow, Usenet would go on without them.

2. Usenet is not a democracy

Because there is no person or group in charge of Usenet as a whole — that is, there is no Usenet *government* — it follows that Usenet cannot be a democracy, autocracy, or any other kind of "-acy." (See "The camel's nose?" later in this chapter.)

3. Usenet is not fair

After all, who shall decide what's fair? For that matter, if someone is behaving unfairly, who's going to stop him? Neither you nor we, that's certain.

4. Usenet is not a right

Some people misunderstand their local right of "freedom of speech" to mean that they have a legal right to use others' computers to say what they wish, in whatever way they wish; they believe the owners of said computers have no right to stop them.

Those people are wrong. Freedom of speech also means freedom not to speak. If we choose not to use our computers to aid your speech, that is our right. Freedom of the press belongs to those who own one.

5. Usenet is not a public utility

Some Usenet sites are publicly funded or subsidized. Most of them, by plain count, are not. There is no government monopoly on Usenet, and little or no government control.

6. Usenet is not an academic network

It is no surprise that many Usenet sites are universities, research labs, or other academic institutions. Usenet originated with a link between two universities, and the exchange of ideas and information is what such institutions are all about. But the passage of years has changed Usenet's character. Today, by plain count, most Usenet sites are commercial entities.

7. Usenet is not an advertising medium

Because of Usenet's roots in academia, and because Usenet depends so heavily on cooperation (sometimes among competitors), custom dictates that advertising be kept to a minimum. It is tolerated if it is infrequent, informative, and low-hype.

8. Usenet is not the Internet

It would be very difficult to sustain the level of traffic that's flowing on Usenet today without people sending newsfeeds over dedicated circuits with TCP/IP on the Internet. That's not to say if a sudden disease wiped out all the RS/6000s and Cisco routers that form the NSFnet backbone, CIX hub, and MAE East interconnect, some people wouldn't be inconvenienced or entirely cut off from the Net. (Based on the reliability of the MAE East, perhaps the "sudden disease" has already hit?)

There's a certain symbiosis between Net news and Internet connections. The cost of maintaining a full newsfeed with NNTP is so much less than doing the same thing with dialup UUCP that sites that depend most on the information flowing through news are some of the most eager to get on the Internet.

The Usenet is not the Internet. Certain governments have laws that prevent other countries from getting onto the Internet, but that doesn't stop Net news from flowing in and out. Chances are pretty good that a site has a Usenet feed you can send mail from the Internet, but even that's not guaranteed in some odd cases (newsfeeds sent on CD-ROM, for instance).

9. Usenet is not a UUCP network

UUCP carried the first Net news traffic, and a considerable number of sites get their newsfeed using UUCP. But news is also fed from NNTP, mag tapes, and CD-ROMs, and is printed on paper to be tacked on bulletin boards and pasted on refrigerators.

10. Usenet is not a United States network

A 1991 analysis of the top 1,000 Usenet sites showed about 58 percent U.S. sites, 15 percent unknown, 8 percent Germany, 6 percent Canada, and 2–3 percent each in the UK, Japan, and Australia; the rest are mostly scattered around Europe. Doubtless, things have changed since this analysis, but the relative sizes are about the same.

The state of California is the center of the Net, with about 14 percent of the mapped, top sites there. The Washington, D.C. area is also the center of the Net, with several large providers headquartered there. You can read Net news on all seven continents, including Antarctica.

If you're looking for a somewhat less U.S.-centered view of the world, try reading regional newsgroups from different states or groups from faraway places (which, depending on where you are, could be Japanese, German, Canadian, or Australian). There are a lot of people out there who are different from you.

11. Usenet is not a UNIX network

Well . . . OK. If you don't have a UNIX machine, you can read news. In fact, there are substantial sets of newsgroups (`bit.*`) that are transported and gatewayed primarily through IBM VM systems, and a set of newsgroups (`vmsnet.*`) that has major traffic through DEC VMS systems. Reasonable news relay software runs on

Macs (uAccess), Amiga (a C news port), MS-DOS (Waffle), and, no doubt, quite a few more. I was typing on a DOS machine when I first wrote this sentence, and it's been edited on Macs and X terminals since then.

There is a culture about the Net that has grown up on UNIX machines, and it occasionally runs into fierce clashes with the culture that has grown up on IBM machines (LISTSERV), Commodore 64s (B1FF 1S A K00L D00D), MS-DOS Fidonet systems, commercial chat systems (America On-line), and "family-oriented" systems (Prodigy). If you are not running on a UNIX machine or if you don't have one handy, there are things about the Net that are going to be puzzling or maddening, like reading a BITNET list without a CMS system handy.

12. Usenet is not an ASCII network

There are reasonably standard ways to type Japanese, Russian, Swedish, Finnish, Icelandic, and Vietnamese that use the ASCII character set to encode national character sets. The fundamental assumption of most Net news software is that you're dealing with something that looks a lot like U.S. ASCII, but if you're willing to work within those bounds and be clever, it's quite possible to use ASCII to discuss things in any language.

13. Usenet is not software

Usenet software has gotten much better over time, to cope with the ever-increasing aggregate flow of Net news and (in some cases) the extreme volume that newsgroups generate. If you were reading news now with the same news software that ran ten years ago, you'd never be able to keep up. Your system would choke and die, and spend all of its time processing incoming news or expiring old news. Without software, and constant improvements to it, Usenet would not be here.

There is no *standard* Usenet software, but there are standards for what Usenet articles look like and what sites are expected to do with them. It's possible to write a fairly simpleminded news system directly from the standards documents and be reasonably sure that it will work with other systems (though thorough testing is necessary if it's going to be used in the real world). You should not assume that all systems have been tested before being deployed.

What Usenet Is

Usenet is, in part, about people. There are people who are "on the Net," who read `rec.humor.funny` every so often, who know the same jokes you do, who tell you stories about funny or stupid things they've seen. Usenet is the set of people who know what Usenet is.

Usenet is a bunch of bits, lots of bits, millions of bits each day, full of nonsense, argument, reasonable technical discussion, scholarly analysis, and naughty pictures.

Usenet (or *Net news*) is about newsgroups (or *groups*). Not bboards, not LISTSERV, not areas, not conferences, not mailing lists. They're groups. If someone calls them something else, they're not looking at things from a Usenet perspective. That's not to say that they're *incorrect* — who is to say what is the right way of viewing the world? — just that it's not the Net Way. In particular, if they read Usenet news all mixed in with their important, everyday mail (like reminders of who to go to lunch with next Thursday), they're not seeing Net news the way most people see Net news. Some newsgroups are also (or *really*) Fidonet echoes (`alt.bbs.allsysop`), BITNET LISTSERV groups (`bit.listserv.pacs-l`), or even both at once (`misc.handicap`). So be prepared for some violent culture clashes if someone refers to your favorite net.hangout as a "board."

Newsgroups have names. These names are both arbitrary and meaningful. People will fight for months or years about what to name a newsgroup. If a newsgroup doesn't have a name (even a dumb one like `misc.misc`), it's not a newsgroup. In particular, newsgroup names are words separated by dots; people abbreviate newsgroup names by taking the first letters of the words (`alt.folklore.urban` is abbreviated afu, `soc.culture.china` is scc, and so on).

Diversity

There is nothing vague about Usenet. (Vague? It's filling up millions of dollars worth of disk drives, and you want to call it vague? Sheesh!) It may be hard to pin down what is, and isn't, part of Usenet at the fringes, but Net news has grown, amoeba-like, to encompass more or less anything in its path. You can be pretty sure that if it isn't Usenet now, it will be, once it's been in contact with Usenet for long enough.

There are a lot of systems that are part of Usenet. Chances are that you don't have any clue where all your articles will go or which newsreading software will be used to look at them. Any message of any appreciable size, or with any substantial personal opinion in it, is probably in violation of some network use policy or local ordinance in some state or municipality.

Control

Some people are control freaks. They want to present their opinions of how things are, who runs what, what is OK and not OK to do, which things are good, and which are bad. You will run across them every so often. They serve a useful purpose; there's a lot of chaos inherent to a largely self-governing system, and people with a strong sense of purpose and order can make things a lot easier. Just don't believe everything they say. In particular, don't believe them when they say "don't believe everything they say," because if they post the same answers, month after month, some other people are bound to believe them.

If you run a news system, you can be a petty tyrant. You can decide which groups to carry, who to kick off your system, and how to expire old news (so that you keep 60 days' worth of `misc.petunias`, but expire `rec.pets.fish` almost immediately). In the long run, you will probably be happiest if you make these decisions relatively even-handedly, because that's the posture least likely to get people to notice that you actually have control.

Your right to exercise control over Net news usually ends at your neighbor's spool directory. Pleading, cajoling, appealing to good nature, or paying your newsfeed will generally yield a better response than flames on the Net.

Periodic postings

One of the ways to control the workings of the Net is taking the time to put together a relatively accurate set of answers to some frequently asked questions (FAQs) and posting it every month. If you do this right, the article will be stored for months on sites around the world, and you'll be able to tell people, "Idiot, don't ask this question until you've read the FAQ, especially answer #42."

The periodic postings include several lists of newsgroups, along with comments that say what the contents of the groups are supposed to be. Anyone who has the time and energy can put together a list like this; if they post it for several months running, they get some measure of `net.recognition` for themselves as the "official" keeper of the "official" list. But don't delude yourself into thinking that anything on the Net is official in any real way. The lists perpetuate common myths about who's talking about what and where they're talking, but that's no guarantee that things will actually work out that way.

Propagation

In the old days, when it cost real money to make long-distance phone calls to send Net news around the world, some people were able to get their management to look the other way when they racked up multithousand-dollar phone bills. These people were called the *backbone cabal*, and they had a disproportionate influence on news traffic; after all, they were managing to get someone else to pay for it.

Nowadays, communications costs are (for many sites) buried in with a general *Internet service*. If you want to have a disproportionate influence on news traffic, you need to be able to beg, borrow, buy, or steal access to great big disk drives (so you can keep a full feed) and lots of memory (so you can feed a lot of sites at once).

There is a vigorous, competitive cash market for newsfeeds; you can get a newsfeed from a local provider via modem or via the Internet in all 50 states of the U.S., (and more than 50 countries) and via satellite in most of North America. The notion that any system is a pre-eminent site is outdated; communications costs have gotten low enough, and traffic enough, that, if any one node is completely wiped out, it would still be possible for everyone to be back on the Net within weeks.

Newsgroup creation

You're better off starting up a mailing list.

If you *must* start a newsgroup, you're best off starting a mailing list — even an informal one — to plan the newsgroup. Get half a dozen people to agree on the basic goals, topics of conversation, and so on. Figure that you have about two months to agree that there's something worth talking about, get a hundred other people to see it your way, and run the vote.

There are time-honored rituals for newsgroup creation, designed mostly to minimize the amount of work that news administrators (the people who have managed to corral a bunch of disk space to store news) have to do. In particular, this involves minimizing the number of mail messages they have to read every day. The process involves handing off responsibility to a group of people well-steeped in ritual (the Usenet Volunteer Votetakers), who can run through the process for you.

The camel's nose?

I'm not sure what camels have to do with anything. The only real camel that has anything to do with Usenet is Larry Wall and Randal Schwartz's *Programming perl* — also known as the "Camel Book" — published by O'Reilley. Larry wrote rn, one of the second generation of newsreaders that let you ignore some news that you didn't want to read. The process of getting rid of unread news became a complex enough decision process that Larry wrote a programming language, perl, to help him write a newsreader to replace rn.

He never finished the new newsreader, though that's not at all surprising. perl remains a pretty useful language. If you can understand perl, you'll have a much greater appreciation for the ability of news admins to get rid of things they don't want to see.

There are easily $12 million worth of computers that I can point to that are responsible for the transportation of Net news around the world, plus another $12 million per year in communications bills spent to keep news flowing. Much has been made of the risk that miscreants will do something horrendous that will mean The Death Of The Net As We Know It. It seems unlikely, however, that this collective enterprise will be endangered by any one user's actions (no matter how bold he may be about propagating his message) against the collective will of the rest of the Net trying to keep him in check.

If you are unhappy . . .

If you are unhappy, why are you reading Net news? Take a break. Stretch. Walk outside in the sunshine or the snow. Relax your brain, watch some TV for a while, listen to the radio. If you need to communicate with other people, give them a phone call, or see them in person.

It's good to not spend too much time in the same place with a fixed focus — rest your eyes every once in a while by looking around at something else.

Don't worry about missing anything; it'll all get reposted if it's any good.

Words to live by #1:

Hours can slip by, people can come and go, and you'll be locked in Cyberspace. Remember to do your work!

—Brendan Kehoe

Words to live by #2:

Part of the apprenticeship for a network guru was knowing enough other people and attending enough conferences to find out where things were hidden. This worked just fine when the Internet was a small network.

—Ed Krol

Words to live by #3:

The second newsreader philosophy believes that you want to read only 10 percent of the articles in any given group. . . . This philosophy is far more realistic.

—Adam Engst

Interview with Henry Spencer: On Usenet News and C News

by Ronda Hauben <ronda@panix.com>

Henry Spencer is one of the early participants and pioneers of Usenet News. Henry played a significant role in bringing Usenet News into Canada and thus providing access to and participation in Usenet beyond U.S. borders. In addition, Henry archived much of early Usenet, thus helping preserve it. Along with Geoff Collyer, Henry wrote C news, the widely used Usenet News software. Following is an interview with Henry conducted by some of the editors of The Amateur Computerist *in Toronto, Canada, in August 1992.*

Jay Hauben and Michael Hauben are members of the Editorial Staff of The Amateur Computerist.

Ronda: Some of what we would be interested in knowing is where C news came from, how it developed, and what your efforts are to deal with it now. We thought it would be helpful to ask a bit about your background with Usenet News so that we have a sense of how C news grew out of your experience with Usenet News and out of Usenet News itself. So our first question is, can you say a bit about when you first became involved with Usenet News and then how that involvement with Usenet led you to understand the need for the C news program?

Henry: Well, there was a Usenix conference ten years or so ago. I think it was the Delaware Summer Usenix Conference, which was in the summer of 1980. The folks from Duke University made a presentation on a bit of networking software they had done. Version 7 UNIX, which was more or less just out at the time, had some facilities for using auto-dialing modems to pass mail and other things from machine to machine.

This wasn't terribly well understood by most people. But these folks had figured it out and made it work. They were using it as a sort of distributed bulletin board system. The software they came up with is now known as A news. It was actually the second or third version they did internally, the first one that was circulated widely outside. Early on, Duke was sort of the central point. The topology of the Net sort of evolved from there in random and confused ways. Partly, it was just a neat idea. There was a lot of interest here in networking in general. A lot of the early traffic was potentially very useful things like bug reports on version 7 and bug fixes for version 7. There were some interesting and potentially useful contacts available through it; like, for example, you could send mail to Dennis Ritchie and people like that at Bell Labs, and sometimes they'd even answer you. So it looked useful. There was a bit of delay in us getting things in place. A lot of sites took a lot of time in switching to version 7. But in the spring of '81, we cut over to version 7. One of the first things we did was to establish a Usenet hookup. In the early days, manually dialing at 300 baud was a bit of a hassle. Of course, the traffic was a lot smaller than it is now. But it was valuable enough that we progressed from there. We got a 1200-baud modem, and the capabilities just kept on scaling up, more or less keeping pace with the traffic. For a while, the phone bills were kind of interesting to explain. I'm glad we're no longer in that business. But that's how our involvement really got started.

Eventually, B news came out as an improved version of A news — better performance, better ability to cope with heavier loads, and some other useful features. We were eventually bullied into adopting it. A news was working OK for us for a long time, but some of our neighbors eventually bullied us into switching. There were enough compatibility problems between the two that it was better if everyone ran B news. Things ran quite satisfactorily that way for quite a while. But the B news code was an awful mess inside. It just got worse over time. It had started out as a heavily mutated A news and progressed from there mostly downhill. So we first got involved with it when B news "expire" just basically stopped working due to bugs.

Ronda: Can you say what bugs?

Henry: Probably, the way it looked was a memory leak, dynamically allocated memory that wasn't being freed properly. This got more and more serious as traffic grew and "expire" had to handle more and more stuff. Eventually, it just broke entirely. This was a 16-bit machine, so there wasn't a whole lot of memory available to begin with. I looked at the code and decided that it wasn't really doing anything very complicated and it would probably be quicker to just rewrite it than fix it, as it had gotten to be quite a mess by that point. I did, and there are still remnants of that code in C news "expire" as it is today. But that's how things got started. Geoff Collyer and I basically just progressed more and more in that direction as B news limitations got to be more and more of a problem. The load on our machines got worse and worse as the traffic grew. The bugs grew more and more troublesome. So we eventually decided just to rewrite it for better performance and better maintainability and over time did so. All along we had the notion of distributing it in our minds. That's just the way we tend to think about software development. There's always somebody else who could benefit from something like this. Eventually, with some prodding from our friends, we got everything together and produced an actual release. It's needed some more work since, but that's how it got started.

Ronda: So somehow from having redone "expire," you went on to redo the whole program? Did rewriting the code for "expire" help you to realize there was something more needed? How did you go from rewriting the code for "expire" to deciding the whole Netnews program would benefit from being rewritten?

Henry: It was basically just sort of a logical progression. Doing "expire," something had to come first—and this demystified the stuff, not that it was particularly mysterious to begin with for the most part, and got us started in the right direction. And things progressed from there.

Ronda: Can you say just a bit about what "expire," does in Usenet News?

Henry: "Expire" is just responsible for getting rid of articles off your system. Much of the rest of C news is devoted to getting them onto your system from a remote site or from local postings. "Expire's" job is to get rid of news that's been sitting around long enough, where the definition of *long enough* has gotten shorter and shorter as volume has grown and disks haven't grown to match. There was a time when it was fairly normal to keep a month of news on-line. And while it's not impossible today, you have to spend a lot of disk to do it.

Ronda: The issue of the change in definition of *long enough* seems important. With regard to "expire," when you did rewrite "expire"; was that when you were able to keep one month of news on-line?

Henry: I think we had about a month on-line. Certainly it was of that order. It was at least a couple of weeks, and I wouldn't be surprised if it was a month. I haven't really kept track. This all started quite a long time ago, and volume was pretty low then.

Ronda: What do you mean by volume being low? How would you define the number of newsgroups at the time?

Henry: Low in just about every way. I don't know, maybe a hundred newsgroups, with maybe a couple hundred sites; I'm not sure. Just a wild guess. The traffic at that point was low enough that if you wanted to spend the time, you could realistically read everything that came over.

Ronda: Were there people who read it all?

Henry: A reasonable number of people actually read everything. It wasn't till the volume started to become overwhelming that people just had to get selective. There was always the possibility of something interesting cropping up in an area you didn't normally read. The possibility is still there, but it's no longer practical to do very much about it, short of having friends alert you to something.

Ronda: What year are we talking about when you started to see the problem with "expire"? Was that around 1986?

Henry: No, that would be early 1980s. The development period for this stuff was fairly protracted. It went through a lot of work of one kind or another before we released it. And even that wasn't all that recent. Let me see here. [Calls document up on his computer.] Well, our first patches were summer 1989, so spring 1989 must have been the production release. But that was a year or more after an alpha release and stuff had been kicking around in embryonic form for several years before that. We never did mount a systematic campaign to do the whole thing. It just grew a bit at a time until we finally decided it was complete enough to try and get something out the door. It required a surprising amount of work to put everything together actually in distributable form. And it involved some surprises in our beta testing, portability hassles we hadn't been aware of, and systems differing in stupid ways we hadn't realized.

Ronda: You've said you were first interested in Usenet because of the bug reports for UNIX that it carried. Can you explain a bit more about that?

Henry: The Duke people originally thought that the bulk of the traffic on Usenet was going to be things like version 7 bug reports. And that was a noticeable fraction in the very early days.

Ronda: Was Usenet different in the ways it dealt with bug reports from other BBSs?

Michael: Did it have other methods? 'Cause I guess a lot of companies have various forms of support.

Henry: Well, for one thing, Usenet predated a lot of company BBSs and the like. It was basically a cheap way to hear about things fast, and this was at a time when practically every UNIX site had complete sources, and so a bug report often came with a fix. It was a way of finding out what people had discovered and what fixes they'd worked out for it. Quickly and easily. And for that matter, if you ran into something that you couldn't solve yourself, putting out an inquiry to a bunch of fairly bright people who were fairly familiar with the code, often got a response, "Oh, yeah. We solved that one," or "You're right. There's a bug. Here's how to fix it," or sympathy even if no one had a fix for it.

Ronda: You mentioned something about noticing a particular bug in the PDP-11 that was an obscure bug.

Henry: This was something that was a problem in the long-division routine in the C compiler that came with V7, and it was obscure and difficult to spot on the older PDP-11s. On the newer ones, it was more conspicuous. One of our users ran into it, pointed it out to me, and I ended up investigating it and reporting it. On the new PDP-11s, it showed up a fair bit, and you just had to fix it. Even on the older PDP-11s, it turns out that two or three things that were known as obscure problems in the stuff magically went away when the fix was installed. What was happening was the code tried using the PDP-11's divide instruction at one point. There was a possibility the result might overflow because the PDP-11 instruction wasn't up to doing the whole job of this particular requirement. If the overflow occurred, the code assumed that the registers which had held the dividend were untouched. On older PDP-11s, that was usually true, but DEC had never promised it. On the newer PDP-11s, it was often false. Any combination of operands that led into that particular branch in the code produced grossly wrong answers. But it looks like some boundary cases, even on old PDP-11s, didn't work quite right, because there were a couple of things mentioned as very obscure known bugs in the division stuff that I couldn't reproduce once I put the fix in. So it may have been there all along and just nobody had analyzed it.

Ronda: What's the process of analyzing a bug? You mentioned something about documenting it.

Henry: Oh, there were a couple of problems noted as known defects in the software. There is something the UNIX community has always been fairly strong on, admitting things you know just don't work about the software. And this was mentioned in the sources in bits of documentation accompanying them, that there were a couple of cases that didn't work quite right. In this case, I had a user of mine who had run into this. He had actually supplied a case where the answer was just plain wrong. It was just a matter of digging in. I think I ended up inserting some debugging printouts at various points in the routine and just finding out what was going on where the calculation was going awry. Once I knew where to look, the problem was pretty obvious, and the fix, in fact, was about four lines of code. That was probably one of the first things that started to make my reputation on the Net, because a lot of people noticed when I posted that.

Ronda: Why?

Henry: Because it was a really obscure problem that had the potential to make a lot of trouble for people. It was something in that it was subtle code that was from the originators of UNIX themselves, something they'd missed.

Ronda: That's interesting. So the reason people respected the bug you found was because they understood the significance of the problem that had been averted?

Henry: Yes, it was a subtle problem that could have caused a lot of trouble in code, coming from people who were normally pretty good.

Ronda: So are you saying that one is encouraged to find what could be problems that could cause trouble despite who it's coming from? And then to suggest how to deal with it?

Henry: Yes, it's diminished some in recent years because such a large fraction of UNIX sites nowadays do not have sources for the code. But in those days, it was reasonably normal when you hit some sort of problem to go looking for what caused it and produce a fix for it. Partly, this has declined because people no longer have sources, and partly it's declined because the community is a lot wider and many of the people using and even running UNIX systems don't have the technical expertise to go hunting for things like this. But, hey, it was very common at the time. This was in the days when UNIX was still treated by the Bell system as, "Oh just something we happen to do for our internal use. You can have a copy if you want, but if you got problems, don't bother us." And the result was if you wanted UNIX support, you did it yourself or it didn't happen.

Ronda: It sounds then like people trained themselves to deal with problems.

Henry: To a considerable extent, yes. The people got to know how to deal with the things and the community. This is almost certainly one of the things that got Usenet going in the beginning. Having quick access to a community of experienced people was quite important in the days when you couldn't just call the manufacturer for support. If you called Bell Labs or Western Electric, as it was then, about it, they would hang up on you. If you could manage to get through to Ken Thompson or Dennis Ritchie, they might thank you for the bug report. But they certainly weren't going to promise anything like support.

Ronda: Do you miss that in any way?

Henry: To some extent, yes. To some extent, it's the community I'm still in because we've been running obsolete versions of UNIX for a long time. And still are. On our Sun, our main time-sharing machine, we're running the last stable version of SunOS 3.5. Sun will hang up on you if you ask about it now. And so we're still used to doing our own support, handling our own problems. Unfortunately, because UNIX has grown so much and diversified so much, there's less of a sense of community of others lending a hand now. Too many people with too many different machines and too many different versions.

Jay: But has the spirit and the sense of that somehow given form to the Usenet community, the grander community?

Henry: It's still there to some extent. But it's diffused considerably from what it was.

Ronda: Is there any way that the bug reports led to the other kinds of discussions? Is there any connection between them? Or is it just that people were interested in other areas?

Henry: It [the bug report] was incentive to get onto the network more than anything else. So you could hear about things like this. People have commented also that the Usenix conferences are in some ways less of a hotbed of gossip than they used to be because the Net has taken over some of that function. You know it used to be—back in the very early days — when you went to a Usenix conference, more often than not, you came back with a notebook full of notes on known bugs and what to do about them. And new software available and so forth. The bulk of that goes on via the Net nowadays. Things have changed, but originally getting onto the Net, the big thing was getting access to the community that knew about these things. And the rest of it was a secondary issue, originally. There was a group talking about science fiction, for example. But this wasn't why system administrators were hot on getting their machines connected. Well, not most of them. And then, generally, this was a way of doing networking on the cheap. It was a vigorous, on-line community that you could join without spending many dollars and jumping through lots of bureaucratic hoops, to join something like the Arpanet. With this, all you needed was an auto-dialing modem and someone who was willing to be your connection point.

Ronda: Somehow it seems that having the other discussions is important, also, to the technical discussions. Do you agree? Is there a connection between the technical and nontechnical discussions?

Henry: They [the nontechnical discussions] helped broaden support for things. I don't think they really had very much of an effect on the technical end. Then, as now, there are a lot of people who justify the Net primarily in terms of its technical benefits. People are heard to claim sometimes, "I like the Net for the tiny minority of technical stuff, but all this nontechnical trash I could do without." But in fact, it has been a standard misunderstanding from the early days, the theory that there's just a little bit of technical stuff and a lot of garbage. This was as much of a misconception in the days of 30 days of news as it is now. That there was a little bit of technical stuff drowning in garbage. The fact was even then, the technical stuff was quite a substantial slice of the traffic. It's just that individual people only notice the little bits of technical stuff that appeal to them.

Jay: And they call everything else garbage.

Henry: Or they just don't think about the fact that there was a lot more technical stuff.

Michael: If you don't look for it, you don't see it to some extent.

Jay: But I thought Ronda's question was slightly deeper in the sense that she was asking: Was there something almost as profound about the nontechnical stuff in terms of the kinds of things people talked about that influenced them to be better with the technical stuff?

Henry: Maybe, in small ways. The nontechnical stuff was the first exposure a lot of these people had to an on-line community. Bulletin board systems were not particularly widespread at the time. They did exist, but they certainly hadn't reached the current level of popularity. Networks like the Arpanet were much spoken of by the people who belonged to them but weren't particularly widespread. And there may have been some positive effect in helping to socialize people, so to speak.

Ronda: You have talked a little bit about speed, a little bit about performance. Maybe you can speak briefly about what the limits of B news were that you were dealing with, and how that influenced your objectives with C news.

Henry: Well, our big problem, a contributing factor, was that B news was messy and buggy. There were things you couldn't do with it. There were things that didn't work well on it. It clearly was less and less able to cope with the growing volume of traffic. Even just things like memory leaks. "Expire" wasn't the only code that potentially had memory leaks. It was just getting harder to deal with the stuff. The big thing though was that B news was very inefficient at handling incoming traffic. It took a long time to process incoming traffic. It beat on the machine pretty heavily, meanwhile. And there didn't seem to be any simple way to fix this. There were fundamental structural problems that one really could not do anything about that limited the ability to speed it up. We kicked around a bunch of ideas about improved ways of storing news and so forth. Eventually, we concluded that there wasn't any big improvement to be had. Nothing that would be worth the trouble of being incompatible. The main thing we were after was just greater performance.

Ronda: Can you say who "we" is? Or if this went on on-line as well?

Henry: This is Geoff [Collyer] and me. I've never been a big believer in committee design. Our preference, me in particular, but I think Geoff as well, our preference is to do something and then announce it, rather than vice versa. Partly because we've got a higher opinion of our own sense of good design than a whole lot of other people.

Ronda: Can you explain what you mean by good design?

Henry: We're big on writing simple, clean software that does one thing and does it well, which is not what you get out of a committee design. And in fact, this is one of the things we have occasionally taken flack for. We make our own decisions on what does and doesn't go into C news. So we don't particularly care if this makes us popular or not. We've made a few mistakes along the way as well. But, it was our own idea. We've modified our own ideas of how things were going to work quite a bit along the way and stuff evolved to a considerable extent as we wrote it. There were muddles that had never adequately been cleaned up. As late as just before our alpha release, there were still three different programs called rnews in various places in our stuff. And when we were packaging things up to put together a release, I put my foot down and insisted that there had to be one and only one "rnews." And so we found other names for a couple of things in a hurry. But it evolved along the way. We had ideas of where we were going. But it didn't come full-blown as a complete design. It couldn't, really. That approach to doing things just doesn't work in the real world. The stuff always evolves. Once you start building up experience with the problem and with your tentative solutions, the requirements always evolve. So you really do have to plan for getting something working and having it evolve from there.

Ronda: Interesting.

Henry: We put a lot of thought over time into the performance issues and also into the precise definitions for a lot of things. The B news stuff—even its documentation—in crucial areas, just sort of waved its hands and said, "Well, you know what we mean." In some cases, we actually had to put quite a bit of effort into deciding exactly what should be done in obscure situations. [These are] things you find out by doing it. It was not something that really could be predicted from specification in advance.

Ronda: That's interesting. Do you have a sense that the speed and the performance have made possible the ability of C news compared to B news to deal with volume?

Henry: People have adopted our stuff for a variety of reasons. Particularly, after the word started getting out that it was generally better. There have been a few specific features that won us a lot of converts. Something that went into our version of "expire" sort of midway through its development process and won us a lot of friends was control over expiry newsgroup by newsgroup. The B news "expire" basically just let you set expiry rules for all the news put together. A lot of people, in fact, had different opinions about the value of different newsgroups and wanted to keep some things longer than others. The fact that we could do that won us a lot of friends very quickly. It probably wouldn't have been that hard to add to B news, but nobody ever thought of it. There were things like this, but ultimately, people switched to C news because B news was eating their machines alive, and they wanted some performance back. And for that matter, because they could see the handwriting on the wall. There were machines, including some of ours, where towards the end, B news was running essentially nonstop from 5:00 in the evening till 9:00 in the morning, turned off during the day because it had too much of an impact on performance when lots of people were trying to get real work done. And it wasn't keeping up with the incoming load. The backlog was growing. People who ran into that kind of situation generally decided real fast that they needed to switch to something else.

Jay: I thought Ronda's question had another component. Can your careful attention to speed and performance be pointed to as accounting for the tremendous growth in Usenet that wouldn't have been possible with something with less performance?

Henry: The trend was very firmly established very early. But certainly Usenet would have had a lot of trouble coping with growth if C news hadn't come along when it did.

Jay: What I am asking is if not as careful a version of C news, would that have been a limit that would have . . . ?

Henry: Probably, because the care and effort we put into performance basically accounted for a lot of the performance. We were a little disappointed, initially, in fact, that fixing some of the basic structural mistakes of B news didn't improve performance more. Yes, it was considerably better than B news, but it wasn't as good as we expected. The way you make stuff run really fast, it turns out, is to put a lot of attention into making it run really fast. Avoiding basic mistakes is a crucial prerequisite, but it's not enough by itself. To really make the stuff perform, you really do have to put a lot of effort into understanding what things hurt performance, where the time is going. You have to put a fair bit of time into thinking about how things are being done and how they might be done better. We got a certain amount of performance just by careful low-level tuning, looking for hot spots and finding ways to speed up the code there. But we also got an awful lot by standing back and thinking, "What is this code doing and is there a better way to do it? Are we repeating things that we could do just once? Is there information we need that we're having to gather laboriously that could just be stored centrally instead?"—and things like that, changes in strategy. Changes in strategy are what win you the big performance improvements on the whole. Not overall strategy in the sense of the mistakes B news made versus the ones we didn't make. But sort of mid-level strategy—how the code does what it does. The way you get big performance improvements is not to make a bit of code run a little bit faster, but to take code out entirely. To find ways of just not doing some things and still getting the overall job done. Reducing the amount of time needed for something to zero is always better than reducing it to 10 percent, though the 10 percent can be useful too.

Jay: But when the problems start building up now, will the next fix not be a software fix?

Henry: To some extent, we've had hardware fixes coming in all along.

Faster modems, bigger disks, faster machines. And that's certainly helped. But it's going to be hard to beat C news performance a lot without drastic revisions in something fundamental. There are things we know of and are doing to make it faster yet. But huge performance improvements are going to have to come from something more fundamental. One thing that turns out to be relatively expensive is just looking up a filename in an operating system, opening a file by name. The name lookups are costly, even in versions of UNIX that have put some attention into optimizing them. And we know where our stuff is doing filename lookups, and we just don't do it any more than necessary. Any major speed up in that area—that is still one of the major bottlenecks—is going to have to come from major revisions to the operating system. It's not something that can be greased up much more at the user level.

Ronda: You said earlier that you used to be able to get a month of Usenet and now you're down to, I think you said, four days.

Henry: In our case, we're storing four days and using a great deal more disk space for it, too.

Ronda: Does that mean that in fact the size has gotten to a point where there is a need to figure out how to make some change? Is it coming to that somehow?

Henry: People have been predicting the imminent death of the Net for a decade now, so I'm very reluctant to do that. But certainly, it's gotten to the point where we store four days because that's basically enough to carry you over a long weekend. If it drops much more than that, it's going to be a serious problem for maintaining continuity in a lot of discussions. You can mitigate it somewhat by getting bigger disks or by being more selective about what you get. Probably, the bulk of Usenet sites these days are somewhat selective. We used to be a major redistribution point within Toronto. We're still a minor one. Because of that, we try to carry everything. But carrying everything is steadily getting more expensive.

Jay: But does that imply there's going to have to be very large central distributing points?

Henry: That's already happening to some extent. A lot of big universities and things like that, for example, now have central news distribution machines, just to keep the load from spreading everywhere. And, for example, most of the news distribution within U of T now is handled by one of two central machines.

Jay: Yours not being one of them?

Henry: Ours not being one of them anymore. We do some redistribution to places outside campus. Not a lot compared to what we used to do. But that's definitely happening. UUNET in the States is another example. Someone once called it Usenet's main sewage pump.

Ronda: What is it? Can you say what UUNET is?

Henry: It's a site which offers mail connections and newsfeeds for money, basically. It has done wonders for the connectivity of the Net because a lot of people who couldn't do this sort of thing on an informal basis are happy to get a connection to UUNET, which does cost money but is professionally maintained. They're very much in the business of processing mail and news for money. And they're a very central point now.

Ronda: Isn't that also a little bit in contradiction with the way Usenet originally started with it being available to people at a low cost or no cost? But there's also freenets growing up. For example, the Cleveland Freenet and the Youngstown freenet and Ottawa is supposed to be developing a freenet in Canada [National Capital Freenet in Ottawa and Victoria Freenet in Victoria are now on-line]. The freenets is how I got access. I wouldn't have been able to pay for access and other people I know wouldn't. . . .

Henry: There's always people willing to do a certain amount for free.

There's always going to be a considerable amount of that. The point is when you are in it for a long period of time and the demand just seems to be growing, sooner or later you burn out the supply of volunteer manpower. And somebody has got to start paying for it.

Ronda: And some of the contradiction is that it's public money. . . . In fact, the public is paying for it, so to then go and put a commercial person in and charge back again, what we are already paying for in public funds, it's through the universities and it's through the NSF. . . .

Henry: The real problem on all of this comes when you start talking about unlimited growth. This is the problem Usenet has had all along, in fact, which is, coping with continued growth. That shows up in a number of ways. That's just one side of it. Eventually a university, for example, decides that too much of its phone bill is being spent on shipping news around for other people, and it's time to let somebody do this who is actually getting paid for the job. Because NSF in its beneficence doesn't supply unlimited amounts of money for such things, sooner or later the demands get large enough that somebody's got to put up an appropriation specifically for it. And at that point, universities have a tendency to bow out if they can't get somebody nice to give them money for it.

And Usenet has run into problems of growth in a lot of other forms. Like the sort of social compact that regulates behavior to some extent on the Net. The problems of finding information when there are thousands of newsgroups. All kinds of things like that. You regularly hear moans from people about how Usenet isn't the way it used to be. And occasionally some inconsiderate old-timer will point out, "Well, it never was. You're one of these beginners who only joined in 1986. You don't know the way the Net started out."

Michael: The question of growth also brings out the connections through the Internet because that has grown a lot more than it was initially.

Henry: Again, that's been a saving grace to some extent because the Internet has saved us from the pyramiding phone bills to a considerable extent. The bandwidth that has been made available in recent years for the growth of the Internet—a noticeable fraction of that is shipping Usenet traffic around. I don't know about the Internet itself, but there was a link between Toronto and Waterloo, the other prominent university in Ontario. Five years ago or more, I saw a graph of traffic growth over time. Generally, of course, it was upward. But there was this one huge step more or less, in the traffic, and that was when we started shipping Usenet stuff back and forth, that week. I expect that Usenet would have undergone some sort of collapse or transformation by this point if we had to go on shipping it by phone, because even with the modems getting better and better, they weren't getting better that fast, by that much.

Ronda: We have to end the interview soon. So we just want to ask a few final questions.

Michael: I was wondering if there was anything—with you, with your experiences of being on the Net and being one of the writers, one of the programmers of C news, and just your general knowledge—is there anything that other people who were system administrators or who were on the Usenet might find useful? Any insights?

Henry: Nothing very dramatic. About all I have to say is that a lot of this stuff is harder than it looks. I really don't know whether Geoff and I would have gotten involved with C news if we had realized everything that was going to be involved, because there was a lot more programming than we thought and a lot more ongoing hassle than we thought. If you decide to get into this kind of thing, you have to think very, very carefully about the possible implications.

Ronda: Have there been rewards as well?

Henry: For me, nothing enormously tangible. The occasional free dinner and things like that. And Geoff is currently working full-time on News software support.

Ronda: But what about the principles that you clarified in the papers that you have written? Has that been something? For example, in "News Need Not Be Slow," you and Geoff wrote, "In order to know how to get somewhere, you must know where you are starting from." Are there principles like that that have come out of doing the work that have been helpful?

Henry: There's a lot of little things, things which can be useful to know if you're doing something like performance enhancement. But the one general principle I could distill out of it is that if you want to write software that's fast or portable or well structured, despite years of evolution, you have to care about it and put effort into it. It's easy to be sloppy, but it comes back to haunt you. The only way to make something fast is to care about performance from the beginning and put real effort into getting it. The only way to keep the code clean and maintainable is to constantly put effort into that aspect of it. Resist the temptation to make quick fixes. Or if a quick fix just has to be done for some reason, make a point of going back and doing it right. These things do not happen automatically, and they won't happen if you don't care about them. The main reason why a lot of software today is bloated and complicated and obscure and buggy is that people don't care. They may care in the sense that if you ask them they say, "Yes, we care," but the fact is they don't put any effort into it. They don't care enough to work on it.

Michael: Does what you just said help figure out how to keep Usenet running? Everyone says it's loaded now with users and newsgroups and messages? Is there any way to apply this?

Henry: Not really very directly. It's a very different situation from software. I can't think of any particularly direct application other than the very general application you have to think about what the real underlying problems are. And avoid the temptation to settle for quick fixes that don't really solve the problem.

Reprinted from *The Amateur Computerist,* volume 5, number 1/2
Winter/Spring 1993 Issue, reprinted by permission of the author.

Chapter 4

Doing Business on the Net

This chapter contains three articles:

- "Internet Business Marketing"
- "The Usenet Marketplace: Advice for Buying and Selling On-line"
- "Usenet, Bulletin Boards, and Legal Liability"

Internet Business Marketing

by Dave Kinnaman <kinnaman@world.std.com>

Does your business mission have a place on the Net?

If your business mission includes communication, learning, or advanced technology, you can find ways to use the Internet to further that mission. And even if these areas and your mission seem miles apart, you can still find ways to make marketing on the Internet an integral part of your overall business plan.

To begin, think about what marketing means: *Marketing* is the process of promoting, selling, and distributing products or services from producer to consumer. Understanding of both product or service *and* consumer is necessary to optimize profits from marketing on the Internet. The Internet can help provide you with the customer's point of view and can help you reduce the cost of each new sale by sharpening your marketing strategy.

Simply keeping your name in front of prospects on the Net can boost your company's sales. Tracking favorable buying responses can help you learn what you're doing right and what you need to change. And while much of the Net is unsuitable for advertising, promotional and operational strategies such as these can be used to make the customer approach *you* for information:

- Showing point-of-purchase displays (such as packaging)
- Providing customer service
- Pointing out differences in products
- Maintaining customer contact
- Communicating with your distribution chain and suppliers

- Providing samples and coupons (to selected audiences)
- Researching buyer behavior
- Selling automatically (for example, vending)

Please don't jump the gun! Advertising widely, promoting directly, or even selling personally to individuals on the Internet can lead to disastrous results if not handled carefully. Remember that the Internet is a living thing that can unexpectedly rise up and defend itself if it seems to be under attack. It is not like a new VCR that will just fail to serve you if you refuse to learn the instructions and don't program it correctly. A VCR can't hurt you, your business, or your profits, but the Internet can. Learn the rules and treat the Internet with respect — or it can send unfavorable messages to your competitors, your customers, your employees, and your supply and distribution systems.

This article reviews exactly what to do and what to avoid. Then it's up to you to approach the business world of cyberspace wisely.

This article gives you answers by exploring the following questions:

- Does your business mission have a place on the Net?
- How can you adjust smoothly to the Net's cultural norms?
- What are your technical and logistical options?
- Where on the Net can you explore business marketing resources?

What Is Your Business Marketing Mission?

Here are some points to consider when writing your Internet business mission and marketing plan. Once you've worked out solid answers, you'll be ready to discover how to use the Internet most effectively.

- Who are your customers?
- Which customer wants and needs do you address and which do you not?
- What are your customers' buying habits and preferences?
- How does your distribution system fulfill your customers' wants and needs?
- How do you communicate to prospective customers your ability to fulfill wants and needs?
- What are your expected financial results?
- What is your current position in the industry?
- How well does your business adjust to change?
- What is the social philosophy of your business?
- In what sort of competition is your company engaged?
- How aggressive is your company willing to be?

- What is your customer service image?
- What are your supplier relationships?
- What are your distributor relationships?

Spend time exploring each question. Your answers will help you recognize viable options for Internet use and, ultimately, improve your profits.

Do you have skilled people in place?

As your business begins using the Net, your need for workers with higher skill levels will become apparent. Here is a list of job duties that a business using the Net for marketing might need workers to do. Some skills and services will be better kept in-house; for others, you may choose to contract out to other businesses:

- Network and systems engineering
- Network and systems analysis and management
- Hardware purchasing, installation, and maintenance
- Software purchasing, installation, and maintenance
- Staff training and skill development
- Internet "tool" software experts: e-mail system operators, Gopher masters, Web server masters, and Listserv moderators and owners

Most of the services in the preceding list can be contracted out, so they will not create new on-payroll positions unless you desire the increased collaboration and company (or brand) loyalty that on-payroll employees can provide and facilitate.

Some small businesses (say, under 20 employees) may be able to get by with a few highly skilled staff, each covering two or more of the preceding positions and carefully combined with other services under contract. Larger organizations will need one or more persons fulfilling each of these functions.

What level of hardware commitment are you ready to make?

Some businesses choose to test the Internet waters with just one toe. If you severely limit your business use of the Net — either for an initial test period or more permanently, as a deliberate strategy to channel business and sales opportunities back toward more traditional communications media — your equipment costs can be minimal. You may limit your Internet involvement to just responding to e-mail inquiries.

But even responding to e-mail will probably require a few adjustments: Consider extra telephone lines to carry the e-mail messages to your computers and additional computers with fast (28,800 bps) modems to handle the new e-mail work. In some cases, your existing computers may be able to do double duty and handle e-mail as well as other tasks. But if you expect over a dozen or so messages per day, carefully evaluate the workload on the computer, modem, telephone line, and the customer service staff providing this new service.

Strategic niche

A limited Internet involvement may be useful when a product moves toward a mature phase of its life cycle or begins to decline in sales. An Internet presence can be used to renew acquaintances with existing customers and may add value to the aging product by providing new information or even a discount coupon.

In fact, just adding an Internet e-mail address to a "for more information" line on a product's label increases the product's value and freshness — as long as your customer service lives up to the customer's expectations.

Equipment you need to start marketing in this niche

- Workstations with two telephone lines each
- One phone line for your customer service person, one for the computer modem
- Computers with fast modems (28,800 bps)
- Communications software (compatible with your modem, operating system, and other software)
- Contact-tracking software (optional)
- Sales data software (optional)

Established Internet service providers

Businesses entering the world of the Internet with minimal investment are likely to access the Net by purchasing e-mail service through an established Internet service provider (ISP), such as

- America Online
- CompuServe
- Delphi
- Netcom
- The Well

Such providers may also supply free communications software along with your own e-mail address for business use.

Each ISP has a unique system for charging for services rendered. Most ISPs charge a flat monthly fee plus a per-hour or per-message charge for actual services used. Premium services such as increased message storage space or faster/wider data access are usually available on a similar per-hour or per-access basis.

Choosing the right provider

On the Internet, you cannot look your customer in the eye. Almost everything you can use to influence a prospective customer is based on *text.* Because there is no commonly available way for users to see or hear one another over the Net, textual features gain increased significance.

When choosing your ISP, consider the provider's image and ethos as well as monthly costs. If your business has or wants a positive image in relation to the environment, for example, consider an account with the Well, which is recognized on the Net as a haven for "new thought" and progressive social causes. The end, or right side, of your e-mail address will be the ISP's address (or domain) — easily recognizable to sophisticated Net users.

Ask a few customers, suppliers, and distributors whether your new e-mail address should end with one of the following (the replies may surprise you):

- `yournumber@compuserve.com`
- `yourname@well.com`
- `yourname@aol.com`
- `yourname@delphi.com`
- `yourname@netcom.com`
- `yourname@world.std.com`

Free ISP marketing examples

To obtain free Internet customer service literature from the service providers listed earlier, use a friend's personal e-mail account to send a message with the subject **info** and the message body **info** to the following addresses:

- `info@compuserve.com`
- `info@well.com`
- `info@aol.com`
- `info@delphi.com`
- `info@netcom.com`
- `info@world.std.com`

The pricing information you receive may also be useful in evaluating other ISPs. And reading the messages will give you the opportunity to study their format and wording and will introduce you to the lingo, look, and feel of the Net culture. Temporarily save these messages so that you can review them when you are ready to take a spin on the information superhighway or when you read "Access to the Net," later in this chapter.

By purchasing your own contact-tracking software, you often can improve on the communications software provided free from your ISP. Contact-tracking software has improved substantially from the past and is now an excellent way to make the most of every contact with a prospective customer. However, some contact-tracking software is not compatible with the ISPs' software or hardware, so ask your provider for recommendations and make this decision together.

Some on-line businesses have e-mail *hot lines* that are expanding to also take sales orders. If your customer service function expands in this way, a sales data system should be available to your customer service and sales staff. Ideally, these functions will be integrated or linked into the contact-tracking system so that no data must be transferred manually from one system to the other.

Adjusting to the Net's Cultural Norms

Journalists report the differences in cultural and business practices among countries around the world. Just as a traveling businessperson needs to learn the cultural ways of a host country, a new Internet businessperson needs to learn the Net 's cultural norms.

Don't assume that you can quickly pick up the jargon, style, skills, and pace of the Internet just because it's right there in your office or home. Be aware that you are entering a foreign land, just as remote and exotic as Mozambique — and you can't afford nonchalance about adjusting to this new business environment.

Why adjust to Internet customs?

Why do businesspeople study the business practices and cultural behaviors of foreign peoples before embarking on important visits to other countries — say, Japan, Venezuela, or Mozambique? Because they want to make a good impression; they want to avoid making offensive blunders that could hurt sales and profits. Your success in marketing on the Internet will be related to how well you understand and adjust to the cultural values and habits of Internet "citizens."

Gestures, voice inflections, and word usage differ vastly in meaning to people in different parts of the world. On the Net, voice inflection and gestures are rarely, if ever, visible. Expressions that *are* visible, therefore, take on great importance.

Many standard Net tools are black-and-white and text-based and have little graphic or display complexity, but several newer tools are designed for the GUIs (graphical user interfaces) that Microsoft Windows and Macintosh users have come to expect. Whether you use the less-costly black-and-white or the more elaborate color graphical interfaces, you are the one who controls the text (and images) that you place on the Net.

Thoughtful travelers adjust to the city, country, and language communities they visit. The citizens on the Internet will expect no less of you when you arrive!

No advertising on the Internet

You may wonder why advertising is so unwelcome on the Internet. For a long time it was simply considered illegal, and some of that taint remains. Also, the interactive style and culture of the Net are quite different from one-way media (such as television and print), where business advertising is conveyed safely and effectively.

To emphasize this crucial point, I'll relate an example of an actual marketing attempt that was tried on the Net but went awry. First, the background:

A discussion list called Inet-Marketing exists on the Net. Like all other Internet discussion lists and Usenet newsgroups, Inet-Marketing has its own set of rules, both informal and written, that inform members (subscribers) of the group about how to comport themselves and which topics may be discussed in what manner. When some members wanted to transgress or change those rules on the Inet-Marketing list but were encouraged not to do so, they formed a new discussion list with rules more to their liking. On the new discussion list, former Inet-Marketing members could behave as they pleased. The new discussion list's name is Free-Market. (See the end of this article for subscription information on each discussion list mentioned here.)

Rick Wesson is the list *owner* of the Free-Market discussion list, which means he performs many administrative and clerical tasks for the list and its members and therefore has major control over the list. Wesson's company provides the host computer and Internet access *at no cost* for the Free-Market discussion list.

In early October 1994, a Free-Market list member identified himself as a businessperson and began implying that one Internet site (which he owned) was the "center" of the Internet. Because of the illogic of a worldwide distributed network of networks (the Internet) ever having a single center, most list members chose to ignore this braggadocio and the accompanying commercial claptrap.

But the list owner, as he should, soon reminded the discussion members of the list rules as follows. (The following message text is presented as it was received on the Internet and has not been modified. A *spam* on the Internet is a message indiscriminately broadcast to many unrelated lists of people, not because they have identified themselves as interested in the message topic, but because the *spammer* was able to circumvent normal procedures and ignore the ground rules to use unrelated mailing lists without regard for their intended purposes.)

```
From wessorh@ar.com Wed Oct 5 14:59:47 1994
Date: Wed, 5 Oct 1994 12:38:51 -0700
From: "Rick H. Wesson" <wessorh@ar.com>
Reply to: free-market@ar.com
Subject: A bit about this list.

This list was started to make available a place for discussions
that Glenn, the maintainer of inet-marketing did not allow on
his list. I dont mind anouncements on this list, but I lothe
a spam. I don't mind anouncements, or discussions about them.

I do dislike the hype centered marketing that sometimes lands on
this list. Especially when the announcement is one of
the following:

 1) Stating you are the center of all things on the net .
 2) Is tring to sell something to those on this list.
 3) Does not contain contact information.
 4) is specificly an ad.

if the above does not fit why you are on this list you may send a
message to listserv@ar.com with the following in
the body of the message:

 unsubscribe free-market

-Rick
```

(Used by permission.)

What Rick says here, with all his personal flair, is that there are rules, and straight advertising is against those rules — even on the breakaway Free-Market list.

What happened next? Rick's simple, administrative message precipitated a vicious afternoon *flame war* (an emotional, unproductive debate) culminating in

- The entire Free-Market discussion list being taken "off the air" for a few evening hours
- Threats of legal action, including consultations with lawyers
- A threat to carry the legal action to the Supreme Court of the United States
- Immediate establishment of a new "discussion" list devoted exclusively to the posting of actual advertisements (to be read almost exclusively by the few other *advertisers!*)
- The original braggart voluntarily removing himself from the Free-Market discussion list

Most readers of the Free-Market list deleted the flaming threats and rejoinders, and most of those who took the time to post messages to the discussion said they supported the list's charter purpose and the list owner's discretion to enforce the charter. Although he vehemently insisted that he had a "constitutional" right to advertise on the Free-Market list, the offending advertiser was ostracized.

So please resist any temptation to advertise on the Internet. Flame wars can be costly.

In the next section, I give you a set of fundamental Internet marketing rules. First, I cover what you *should* do in a proactive and positive approach to marketing . Then I review what *not* to do. (I don't, of course, give instructions on practices such as "spamming the Internet," because spamming is not appropriate for successful Internet business marketing.)

Acceptable Marketing Tactics

Acceptable Use Policies (AUPs) are usually written in legalese; nonetheless, you must become somewhat familiar with them. Strictly speaking, it is your responsibility to follow the AUP of every provider whose service your message traverses. But it is impossible to know the exact course your message takes on the way to its destination because the Net is engineered to route messages around bottlenecks and problems. The usual fallback, then, is to follow the AUP of your local Internet service provider.

Even though the NSFNET (National Science Foundation NET) will have been dismantled by the time you read this, many academic sites and networks connected to the Net continue to use an AUP similar to that of the NSF's. (Remember that although you may not be on an academic Net, many of your customers may be.) It is therefore wise for anyone who is planning to use the Net for business marketing purposes to carefully study the NSF Acceptable Use Policy, which is printed in its entirety in *The Internet Business Book* by J. H. Ellsworth, Ph.D. (John Wiley & Sons). (Find further information about this excellent business reference later in this article, in "Business Marketing Resources for Further Exploration.") The following sidebar gives some essential excerpts:

The NSFNET Backbone Services Acceptable Use Policy - 1992

General Principle:

(1) NSFNET Backbone services are provided to support open research and education in and between US research and instructional institutions, plus research arms of for-profit firms when engaged in open scholarly communication and research.

(text deleted)

Specifically Acceptable Uses:

(text deleted)

(3) Communication and exchange for professional development, to maintain currency, or to debate issues in a field or sub-field of knowledge.

(text deleted)

(7) Announcements of new products or services for use in research or instruction, but not advertising of any kind.

(text deleted)

Unacceptable uses:

(10) Use for for-profit activities, unless covered by the General Principle or as a specifically acceptable use.

(11) Extensive use for private or personal business.

(text deleted)

So *some* level of for-profit business activity is acceptable on even research-oriented parts of the Net, but how much is too much? Here are some rules of thumb that will help keep you out of trouble when marketing on the Internet.

Do this on the Internet

Keep messages short. Messages on the Internet should be as brief as possible. Initial *(non-advertising)* teaser announcements should comprise one or two screens of information at the most; one authority suggests a 15-line limit. Teaser announcements broadly describe the idea and the specific benefits of the product or service and offer an Internet address for further information. Once you receive responses to your teaser announcement, *then* you can send pricing information and sales solicitations. But even your sales and pricing information should be brief and "modular," so that most reply messages are short and closely related to the customer's request, rather than long, catch-all documents that cover all possible situations. On the Internet, less is more.

Stay on topic. If you are posting a business announcement to a Usenet newsgroup or an Internet discussion list, you should start and end your message with an explicit explanation of how the announcement addresses the group's charter topic. Everything you say in your teaser announcement must be *on topic,* so it is incumbent on you to locate and become familiar with the newsgroups and Listserv discussion lists that are appropriate to your message. Don't succumb to the temptation to spam unrelated or unknown groups — it's not worth the trouble and bad will that you will receive.

Provide immediately useful information. If possible, find a way in your announcement to give free, useful information. Don't try to cover all the features and contingencies; just highlight prominent, specific uses for your product or service. Help prospective customers to identify themselves as such by showing them who can benefit most from your innovation. You want the customer to think, "Hey, maybe that would work for me!" To facilitate this image of usefulness, make sure all your employees are contributing professionally and actively as members of appropriate newsgroups and discussion lists. Their subsequent business-related announcements will have much more credibility than those of a Johnny-come-lately who just started with the group.

Remember that the customer must bite first. Giving specific information about purchasing (price, availability, means of payment, and so forth) is acceptable only after a prospective customer requests information from your business. There are many ways to entice a customer to request further information, so be creative — and scrupulously honest — in attracting these requests. But don't make "creative" assumptions: You must have already received a direct communication from the prospective customer requesting further information *before* you mention prices or purchasing specifics at all. It is not even acceptable to characterize the cost as "nominal" or "inexpensive" until the customer has asked for more information.

Think globally. Remember: the Internet is now a worldwide phenomenon, embracing all continents and dozens of languages. Once you open the door to this new business world, your business will be touched by widely varied international interests and concerns.

Although English is still the primary language used on the Internet, there will always be an advantage to anyone who can also converse in a language other than English. Diplomacy, tolerance, and creative thinking will be increasingly important assets in the business environment of the Net. In the flame war example given previously, the person who posted an offending advertisement claimed he had a legal right to advertise and foolishly argued from the perspective of a single country's laws. No single country has control of the Internet, and no single country's laws can govern it.

Learn and follow the rules. Each discussion list and newsgroup has its own personality and rules. Learning the rules for group A does not prepare you for success in group B. The rules of thumb given here will begin to prepare you for using the Internet for business, but there is no assurance that these rules will hold true in every Net locale.

Identify yourself. Every time your business uses the Internet in any way, you and your employees should carefully and completely identify yourselves. Use this requirement to your advantage! Every single e-mail message can carry your

The cardinal rule of Internet business marketing

The customer must bite first!

That means that customers must *ask* for sales information.

business marketing plan further into the Internet. Make sure that all your business e-mail contains *in the body of the text* a four-line "signature." (***Note:*** Several e-mail programs insert the file named .signature at the bottom of all of your outgoing e-mail by default. Be sure you understand how your e-mail program works, and test it with a message to yourself and to a friend.) At a minimum, your signature should include a return e-mail address, a telephone number, and the names of the employee and business. A short business slogan or motto and a terse description of the scope of your business are also acceptable if there is room in just four lines. (Because you are working with just four lines of about 70 characters each, the total message, including all white space, must fit in about 280 character spaces. Use every character of space carefully and have a visual artist check your "signature" to be sure it is visually attractive.)

Announce your Net presence. Put your e-mail address in your regular print advertising and promotional literature, on your business cards and stationery, on the packaging and labels of your products, and everywhere Net users can possibly hear about or see your new address.

Register a domain name. If you expect to use more than just e-mail services on the Net, register your own domain name with InterNIC Registration Services. Their Gopher server is at `rs.internic.net`.

Soften the voice in your words. A third-person announcement such as "Teachers find that this product improves student test scores" is less demanding and presumptuous than a personal statement such as "You should buy and enjoy this widget today." Use the indirect approach to soften your message because soft persuasion and scientific fact-finding are expected on the Net.

Make endorsements carefully if at all. Generally, endorsements should be made only when

- The product or service being endorsed is directly related to the charter or mission of the group
- The endorser is in no way related to the business
- The group's charter or mission allows members to make endorsements of the kind being considered

Respond promptly to every inquiry. Internet familiars loathe it when someone to whom they made an e-mail inquiry doesn't respond. Even if you decide a particular inquiry is unlikely to lead to a sale, reply promptly and politely to avoid the bad will that will quickly result otherwise. Remember: Unreturned e-mail is a cardinal sin on the Net. Failing to respond is also unprofessional and will not help create a favorable business image for your marketing plan.

Train your employees to use the Net. All employees who communicate on the job should know the basics of how your business intends to use the Net. For example, they should know how to send an e-mail message to your business so that they can direct inquiries to the correct address. They should know what services you offer over the Net before you offer them.

Share the work of monitoring the Net. All your employees can help with the never-ending task of monitoring Net developments. Each department can subscribe and participate in appropriate newsgroups and discussion lists. Some employees can be assigned to scout for new resources, while others scan existing sites for new developments.

Don't do this on the Internet

Don't fail to learn the rules. Each new mailing list you become involved with will have different rules. You must look for those rules and obey them to be sure of avoiding difficulty. For example, one discussion list may allow commercial endorsements by a friend of a businessperson, whereas another may forbid any such endorsement unless there is absolutely no relationship between the businessperson and the endorser.

Don't use hype. Turn down the volume on your subjective advertising vocabulary. Don't use words that promise your product will deliver more than the average customer is going to get. Hold back on words like *only, leading,* and *great* and start with soft statements that are easy to prove.

Don't presume that people will give Net advertising a chance. They won't. So many Net citizens are dead set against advertising that you risk your entire venture if you ignore this rule. Just don't do it. Instead, use the Net for the many safer types of marketing, such as giving point-of-purchase displays; providing customer service and fostering customer relationship development; pointing out product differences; maintaining communication with suppliers, distributors and vendors; providing promotional sampling and couponing (to selected audiences); researching buyer behavior; and automatic selling (vending).

No yelling (typing in all caps). Partially because it is harder to read masses of capitalized text, and also because it is unattractive to many readers, typing messages in all caps is frowned upon. It is as if you had raised your voice in a public place. Similarly, exclamation marks should be used sparingly.

Don't be coy about prices and performance. Put the basic price right up front and acknowledge any ancillary costs explicitly. Your price should reflect the overall response-cost of dealing with your business. Internet citizens like to have the facts laid out quickly and succinctly. If you firmly state your price objective and honestly help the customer evaluate all related costs, you will be better off and closer to a sale. If you can't prove that you offer a good deal, your competitor will.

Don't send unsolicited e-mail. Don't send unsolicited e-mail to anyone, especially newsgroups and Listserv discussion lists, until you are sure that your messages are welcomed and will be accepted by the receiving party. Many Net users pay for e-mail on a per-message or per-byte basis, so you should be very careful not to send unsolicited e-mail that turns off, rather than attracts, the reader to the product. Unsolicited e-mail is almost guaranteed to get you flamed, and it is unlikely to do your business any good.

Don't try hit-and-run tactics. Every Usenet newsgroup and Internet discussion list recognizes regular contributors. These people are there through thick and thin and become trusted friends, even though they may never see one another in person. If you join a group today just to place your announcement and you sign off tomorrow, don't imagine that you can attract the positive attention to your message that a regular contributor can get.

Don't announce your Net site until you've tested it. Make sure that your site is completely working before the hoards come to visit. If it is flawed, your visitors may never return. If you use the World Wide Web, test every page from several platforms to see what each page looks like with various browser software. Print every page to see how the different browsers make your page look on paper. See Chapters 22 and 30 for more information about the World Wide Web.

Don't fail to stay up-to-date. If you establish a Web site, test every link once a week to be sure it still works. Have every employee submit ideas each month for new links or for revisions to the old pages. Make sure that every person and aspect of your whole business is involved in the effort to stay ahead of changes on the Net.

Don't be impatient. The Internet is lightning-fast at many things, like getting your name in front of hundreds and thousands of selected prospects. But you must be patient in developing the trust of these prospective customers. You must take care to convince them that your promises will come true once they buy your product or service.

And remember, some Internet users still distrust the use of the Net for business purposes. An experience with *your* business may be a user's first positive business transaction on the Net.

Giving back to the Net

The best way to get a warm welcome for yourself on the Net is to provide a new, *free* product or service. Yes, give it away. Free.

It sounds like you're giving away the store. But on the Internet, it works. It gets users to recognize your name, to become familiar with the quality that name implies, and to start using your name among themselves. The fact that the new service or product is free assures you that your name and contribution will leave a positive impression — provided, of course, that what you're giving away is useful and of good quality.

The whole Internet phenomenon is *based on* freely given individual contributions and organizational gifts to the community as a whole. If each site had restricted access to local users, as they could have done at any time, the Internet never would have grown as it has. Every site had to give away the store, to some small degree, in order to get back something larger, more dynamic, and more valuable to everyone.

Giving shareware

The concept of *shareware* in software marketing is akin to and part of the spirit of the Internet. Shareware is software that is freely given to anyone; all users are encouraged to give shareware to others, spreading free use of shareware programs all the more. If a person uses a shareware program repeatedly, he or she is obligated and expected to pay a nominal amount for the program (usually \$15 to \$30), by means of the honor system.

Many popular software programs are marketed, at least in part, by the shareware model. PKZIP is a compression program whose use spread rapidly until it became the de facto world standard file compression method on dialup bulletin-board systems. PKZIP also became a popular compression method on the Internet because it was useful, user friendly, and shareware. Shareware has the illusion of being free, a quality whose panache few commercial products can match. Now, major software companies are adding "PKZIP compatibility" to products, selling this upstart shareware software as part of their own packages.

By trusting users to pay later and by trusting his own high-quality software to sell itself, Philip Katz, the inventor of PKZIP, succeeded grandly. The trust system on the Internet is important to understand if you wish to succeed commercially here. You must trust the Net enough to willingly give up something of value in anticipation of receiving much more in return.

For more information on PKZIP, send e-mail to `pkware.inc@mixcom.com` or `support@pkware.com`. Or send surface mail to PKWARE, Inc., 9025 N. Deerwood Dr., Brown Deer, WI 53223-2437. Voice: 414-354-8699. Fax: 414-354-8559. BBS: 414-354-8670.

So, what can *you* give back to the Internet?

Lots! You'd be surprised at the information you have or can easily get that may be valued and attractive to users on the Net. Look around for everyday information that the public requests but that you find troublesome because it uses up your time and doesn't make profits. Look for educational information and special-purpose databases that you've never figured out how to profit from. By gathering useful or entertaining information on a topic, keeping it up-to-date, and making it freely available on the Internet, you can prove your business is a good Net citizen — and raise *your* Internet profile at the same time.

Strategic niche

Let's say that you have plans for a major product to be released next year that can probably be sold to Internet users. In order to set up a marketing plan that makes a home run with your new product, why not use the Net to give away (or dramatically reduce the price of) a simple product or service that's related to your new, major product? This can do several things to pave the way for the success of your new product:

- Gives potential customers familiarity with the use and quality of your products, your name and logo, and your ordering and customer service systems
- Gives you buyer behavior information
- Gives you Internet addresses for developing a list of trustworthy users who are *already* interested in your product
- Lets you identify target Internet newsgroups, discussion lists, and so forth, where your product can be announced
- Allows you to begin early market tests and research for the major product while it is still under development

In short, this morsel whets the appetites of your future customers!

Giving something away on the Net is not really unfamiliar: Product sampling and coupon promotions have been used in business marketing for hundreds of years. Think of the baker's dozen or of a grocer's slice of fresh fruit offered to prove its quality and ripeness. It's the Internet itself that's new, not the idea of giving something away.

Examples of giving back to the Net

When someone hands you a written telephone message slip with an unfamiliar area code on it, how do you know you aren't about to return a phone call from Bermuda, Hawaii, Alaska, or Newfoundland? Sometimes you'd be better prepared for the conversation if you first knew where you were calling.

Telephone companies have made such a service available for years, but most people do not know how to ask directory assistance for what they need to know: a *name-place area code lookup.* One telephone company, AmeriCom, made the smart move of making the area code lookup service freely available on the World Wide Web. The glory of this strategy is that Web users will now be *asking* to see AmeriCom's advertising whenever these users visit AmeriCom's location to make use of its area decoder.

By "giving away" the area code information that has been available, but dormant, for many years, AmeriCom is attracting people to its Web home page. Some users will explore other facets of this home page; others will better remember the name AmeriCom Long Distance when they next shop around for a long-distance service. This stroke of marketing genius will raise AmeriCom's market status — at least until another company offers the service more attractively!

For more information about AmeriCom, point your World Wide Web client to `http://www.xmission.com/~americom/` and explore AmeriCom's business, residential, and international telephone rates, as well as its long-distance buyer's guide.

The popular new print magazine *Wired* began early on to give away the full electronic text of its articles, features, and departments. Because the entire business of *Wired* rests on selling expertly crafted information, it may be hard to imagine why the magazine is giving this information away. But it does, and its readers love *Wired* all the more for it.

Wired has been so successful on the Net that it has started a new Net business, called HotWired. Through HotWired, every issue of *Wired* is available free via e-mail just 30 days after hitting the newsstand. Back issues of *Wired* are also electronically available at no cost.

Wired markets all its information services through its HotFlash mailing list on the Internet for interested persons *who have asked* to be kept up-to-date on *Wired* information.

For *Wired* magazine's free electronic text online, send the message **help** by e-mail to `info-rama@wired.com`.

Technical and Logistical Options

This section discusses more technical elements of conducting business on the Net.

Cash on the Net

Several complex systems are now vying for position to give businesses the ability to perform cash transactions on the Net. But as yet, the Internet has no easy and generally accepted means of securely transacting an exchange of money. Depending on which system gains a following, there are several directions that billing and payment transactions on the Net may take. A variety of methods is acceptable, since general worldwide commerce also uses several reliable payment mechanisms (cash, check, credit card, purchase order, and so on).

More than one rival may win the competition for providing a system to handle cash on the Net, because the numerous niche markets have slightly different transaction needs. Because the World Wide Web is growing even more quickly than the Net as a whole, the Web may be the bellwether for business on the Net. Any business that can accept payment (and therefore effect a business transaction) at a Web site will quickly gain insight on the profit potential of the Net.

Credit card accounts will be a major avenue of billing and payment on the Internet, since credit card numbers are not limited by time or space in the areas of physical presence (as is cash) or postal delivery (as are checks). Standard credit card transactions pose no problem from business's perspective, but many consumers feel insecure about transmitting their credit card numbers over the Internet without special security measures. Because the Internet was not designed to be a means for private communication, senders and receivers must share and use compatible methods of encryption and decryption to attain privacy in communication or business transactions on the Net.

All of the transaction systems now in trial stages have some method for transmitting private or secure information by encryption and decryption methods. In the competitive fray over cash-handling systems for the Net, the system that is ultimately victorious must at least provide the following:

- A secure method for customers to receive or know they will receive value for their money
- A quick, easy means of payment to the seller
- Protection of personal and business information from uninvolved third parties

Reasonably priced transactions, hardware, installation, and training will also be necessary to make monetary transactions on the Internet worthwhile.

Most businesses will also want to gather data from the customer that is not directly required for the transaction to take place. Masses of new data from the Internet will be easily fed to database marketers when customers type or key it in themselves! But be sure to let customers know you are collecting information for business purposes and be sure to obtain the customer's consent; otherwise, you may be seen as exploiting the customer's loss of privacy.

Access to the Net

When you consider a commitment to becoming a "presence" on the Net, practical questions arise. Where do you connect to the Net ? What sort of traffic will you be generating (Gopher, ftp, telnet, e-mail, World Wide Web, and the like)?

Where you connect to the Net can make a big difference in how quickly your messages reach their destinations. Even if you connect to the Net using a line that provides 1,000 percent of your needs (serious over-capacity), and you are using a local machine that is much more powerful (say, 500 percent) than your needs now require, you may well run into a bottleneck in the future. If any slow links exist (*slow links* are bottlenecks in the electronic distribution system that cause messages to be held in a queue, rather than being sped on their way) between you and the Net backbone, your traffic will be limited by that slowest link. For smaller users, this may not present a serious problem.

For larger businesses, however, a slow response to consumer visits to your "virtual location" could be embarrassing. Ways around this problem include adding alternative new links in the network path to the Internet backbone and upgrading the current links. Either option will require the services of an experienced network engineer or someone with similar credentials, experience, and diagnostic tools for networks.

Hardware and software

The best advice about hardware and software may come from other businesses that are already doing something similar to what you want to do. Use the resources section later in this article to locate and contact similar businesses and ask them to help you determine your hardware and software needs.

Today, no one is likely to recommend anything less than a dedicated 486/33Mhz computer to start an Internet site. Many people would probably recommend more computing power and faster processor speeds. But for a large number of businesses, a dedicated 486/33Mhz machine with a fast (28,800 bps) modem and its own telephone line can serve your needs well as you enter the world of Internet business marketing.

Because the technology available at reasonable prices is changing so rapidly, it is inappropriate to recommend moderate to higher range hardware. By the time you read this book, whatever is on the market today will be obsolete and prices will have dropped even further.

Likewise, your business software requirements should be customized to your exact needs by a network professional. User-friendly network software, particularly for Windows, is exploding in availability and should be very competitive throughout the mid-1990s.

Resources for Further Exploration

In case you are wondering where you can find more information on business uses of the Internet, following are a few more resources. This list includes books; documents available by ftp, Gopher, and the Web; and Listserv discussion lists.

Books and periodicals

Doing Business on the Internet: How the Electronic Highway is Transforming American Companies, by Mary J. Cronin. Published by Van Nostrand Reinhold, 1993.

The Internet Business Book, by J.H. Ellsworth and M.V. Ellsworth. Published by John Wiley & Sons, 1994.

The Internet Business Book has already been translated into several foreign languages and is expected to form the international model for business on the Net.

Internet World Magazine, published monthly by Mecklermedia Corp.; phone: 203-266-6967.

The Internet Business Journal: Commercial Opportunities in the Networking Age, a journal published monthly by Michael Strangelove. To request a free sample electronic copy, send e-mail to `mstrange@fonorola.net`.

Online documents

The Clearinghouse for Subject-Oriented Internet Resource Guides housed at the University of Michigan has several excellent sources of information for the Internet business marketer. One set of resources is mentioned here, but there are others that will arouse your interest when you visit this excellent Internet resource site.

A very comprehensive series of resources was prepared and released in September 1994 by Leslie M. Haas, Barbara Mento, and other members of their team. The series is called "Business Sources on the Net": BSN 2nd Edition.

To access the Clearinghouse for Subject-Oriented Internet Resource Guides, point your Web browser to

```
http://http2.sils.umich.edu/~lou/chhome.html or
http://www.lib.umich.edu/chhome.html
```

Alternatively, you can point your Gopher client to

```
gopher.lib.umich.edu
```

(the preceding gopher site contains What's New and Featured Resources Clearinghouse)

or anonymous ftp to

```
una.hh.lib.umich.edu/inetdirsstacks
```

Discussion lists

The following discussion lists focus on marketing and other issues important to the Internet business marketer. To join the list on any topic, send an e-mail message to the address shown, with the line **subscribe** in the body of the message (unless otherwise noted). When you want to end your subscription, just follow the instructions you receive after subscribing. But in an emergency, try using the same message as follows with the word **unsubscribe** instead of **subscribe** — sometimes that works.

- **CERT Computer Security Mailing List**

  `cert-advisory-request@cert.org`

  (with Subject: **subscribe security list**)
- **Copyright and Intellectual Property Forum**

  `listproc@cni.org`

  subscribe CNI-Copyright *Your Name*
- **Advertising in the Internet (moderator's forum)**

  `listproc@cni.org`

  subscribe CNI-advertise *Your Name*
- **Communications and Privacy Discussion**

  `com-priv-request@psi.com`

  subscribe Com-Priv *Your Name*
- **Internet Free-Market Discussion**

  `free-market@ar.com`

  subscribe Free-Market *Your Name*
- **High Tech Marketing Communications**

  `listserv@cscns.com`

  subscribe HTMarcom *Your Name*
- **Internet Marketing**

  `listproc@einet.net`

  subscribe Inet-Marketing *Your Name*
- **For the Discussion of Marketing**

  `listserv@nervm.nerdc.ufl.edu`

  subscribe Market-l *Your Name*
- **Telecommunications and Information Marketing**

  `listserv@uriacc.uri.edu`

  subscribe Ritim-l *Your Name*

Usenet newsgroups

The following Usenet newsgroups are good places to seek information on commercial uses of the Internet. The entire `biz` hierarchy is chartered to discuss commercial uses of the Net.

biz.books.technical	Bookstore and publisher advertising
biz.comp.hardware	Commercial hardware information
biz.comp.software	Commercial software information
biz.general	Business operations and offerings
biz.misc	Miscellaneous commercial information
biz.oreilly.announce	New product announcements from a computer book publisher (moderated)

World Wide Web indexes and lists

- CommerceNet Find Page

  `http://www.commerce.net/information/help/find.html`
- Commercial Sites Index

  `http://www.directory.net`
- The Gray (like the Yellow) Pages

  `http://www.trinet.com/tgp/`
- Thomas Ho's Favorite Electronic Commerce WWW Resources

  `http://biomed.nus.sg/people/commmenu.html`

  Note: Be sure to check out the excellent list of resources at Thomas Ho's Web site. His is the most complete and well organized location around!

World Wide Web sites

These sites are just a sample of the thousands of Web pages now available. Each URL (Uniform Resource Locator) begins with `http://` or `ftp://` and contains unique business marketing resources or is inspirational in some special way, and all are worth a visit!

- Arlene Rinaldi's netiquette

  `http://rs600.adm.fau.edu/faahr/netiquette.html`
- As you like it Electronic book-reader for Windows

  `http://www.portal.com/~skip/ayli.html`
- Black Box On-Line Catalog (computing, networking machines, and service)

  `http://www.blackbox.com`
- Introduction to the Internet for Commercial Organizations

  `http://www.rtd.com/people/rawn/business.html`

- Catalog Mart

  `http://catalog.savvy.com`
- CyberNaut Rest Stop™

  `http://www.past.com/`
- Cybersight

  `http://cybersight.com/cgi-bin/cs/s?main.gmml`
- Cyteria Swimming Pool Management - Apartment Relocation Service

  `http://cyteria.netaxs.com`
- Free Drawing for Course

  `http://www.trinet.com/kcomputing/drawing.html`
- Free Interactive Dog Game — Drool

  `http://www.mit.edu:8001/afs/athena.mit.edu/user/j/b/jbreiden/game/entry.html`
- Georgia Institute of Technology's Web User Survey

  `http://www.cc.gatech.edu/gvu/user_surveys/`
- Global Electronic Marketing Service

  `http://www.gems.com:80/`
- Hello Direct Tools for Telecommunication

  `http://www.hello-direct.com/hd/home.html`
- Hot Hot Hot Online

  `http://www.hot.presence.com/hot/`
- HotWired

  `http://www.hotwired.com/`
- *The Internet Business Book* by J.H. Ellsworth

  `ftp://ftp.std.com/pub/ibb/ibb.html`
- Internet Advertising Resource Guide

  `http://www.missouri.edu/internet-advertising-guide.html`
- Internet Business Training Course

  `http://www.trinet.com/course.html`
- Internet Distribution Services

  `http://www.service.com/onourserver.html`
- Mall 2000

  `http://www.mall2000.com`

- Marketing and Sales

  `http://galaxy.einet.net/galaxy/Business-and-Commerce/Marketing-and-Sales`

- Marketing Resources

  `http://garnet,acns.fsu.edu/~chofack/article.html`

- MarketPlace.com

  `http://marketplace.com`

- Open Market's Directory of Commerce

  `http://www.directory.net`

- Sofcom Home Shopping

  `http://www.sofcom.com.au`

- Telecommunications and Information Marketing

  `http://www.wiltel.com/ritim/ritim/html`

- Werbal Phantasy Detergent Cleany

  `http://www.eunet.ch/werbal/experiments/`

Gopher sites

Each of these Gopher sites has resources valuable to Internet business marketing. Point your Gopher client to the address shown below the resource title that attracts your interest.

- Commercial Internet Exchange (CIX)

  `cix.org`

- Federal Acquisition Regulations

  `gopher.town.hall.org`

- Federal Information Exchange Inc.

  `fedix.fie.com`

- Internet Business Pages

  `gopher.msen.com`

- Internet Shopping Network

  `shop.net`

- InterNic Registration Services

  `rs.internic.net`

- National Telecommunications and Information Administration

  `gopher.ntia.doc.gov`

- National Technology Transfer Center

  `iron.nttc.edu`

- O'Reilly & Associates Publishers (Internet books)

  `gopher.ora.com`

- Tradewinds Internet coverage in trade and industry magazines

  `gopher.std.com/periodicals/TRADEWINDS`

With these general guidelines and your own enthusiasm and creativity, you should now be better equipped to embark on the journey to successfully using the Internet in your business plan. I hope you now understand that one-way advertising is the least important aspect of your Internet business plan, because the Net will be so much more powerful an ally in two-way interactions like building relationships with your customers, suppliers, distributors, and vendors and keeping them informed of the advantages of your products and services.

Dave Kinnaman, M.S., M.A., is a systems analyst at a large, state education department. He does labor market and economic analysis to improve coordination and planning in education and training programs. Dave wonders "Why have so few jobs been improved with all our new technology?" and "Why must our young people endure a series of intermittent, part-time, low-wage (no benefits) jobs in order to have a job application for a permanent job taken seriously?"

The Usenet Marketplace: Advice for Buying and Selling On-line

by Jay Maynard <jaym@iecc.com>

Usenet has proved to be a valuable resource for many folks. Along with carrying lots of discussion, arguments, and solid information, it's also a good place to buy or sell just about anything of value, and many people have done so successfully.

As with any other medium, though, there are conventions that make everyone's life easier if they're followed as closely as possible.

Quite a few newsgroups that are scattered around Usenet are intended for users to buy and sell their personal property. Some groups associated directly with hierarchies are for discussing particular subjects, such as `rec.radio.swap` (which goes with the groups in the `rec.radio` hierarchy) and `rec.arts.comics.marketplace` (which goes with `rec.arts.comics`). There are also groups not associated directly with a particular hierarchy but nevertheless specific in scope, such as `misc.forsale.computers.pc-specific.software`, for computer software intended for use with IBM PC-compatible microcomputers. Collectively, these groups may be referred to as the *marketplace groups* — they make up a netwide virtual flea market.

Here are some suggested guidelines, based on general net-wisdom from users, for using Usenet to buy and sell items from your personal collection of stuff. Most of it is basic common sense. Whoever said that "common sense isn't" was right, and it is unfortunate that some users have consistently abused the marketplace groups on Usenet. The advice here is appropriate for just about any group on the Net intended primarily for use by individuals who want to trade goods. Although the specific shipping information in this article is correct to the best of my knowledge, it is subject to change, and you should contact the specific carrier you choose for the most current information.

What to Post and What to Look for on the Net

If it's legal to sell, it's probably appropriate to sell on the Net. A trip through a local marketplace newsgroup, such as `houston.forsale`, shows a wide range of items for sale, from compact discs to washing machines to computers to cars to houses. If you can describe it fully in words on a computer screen, you can sell it. Such things as diamond rings that are impossible to describe fully are more difficult to sell, simply because buyers can't look at them and make up their minds whether the items are what they're looking for. Items like this have been sold successfully, but it's best to use a local group for them so that the buyer and seller can get together in person to examine them.

Articles concerning illegal items, such as CB linear amplifiers, pirated software, and other contraband, are not appropriate. You not only will be severely *flamed,* but you also are opening up yourself (and possibly the owners and administrators of your news site) to civil and criminal liability.

Who Uses the Usenet Marketplace

Anyone can participate in the Net marketplace. Most transactions are done by normal people who have personal property they want to sell or by people who see something they've been looking for and decide to buy. If you are involved in the regular business of buying and selling for profit, please don't abuse these forums by using them as a free advertising service for your business — but you are welcome to participate as an individual. The distinction here is that there is a cultural bias on Usenet, and an actual prohibition on some networks that carry Usenet traffic, against using the Net for commercial purposes. Let your conscience be your guide.

More and more businesses are joining the Net, and the majority of them are responsible users — they don't overload a group with their messages or post to inappropriate places. A few are not, however. There has been a recent growth in *spamming,* which is the term for posting large numbers of nearly identical messages advertising something to mostly inappropriate groups. Although it may well be legal, it's poor etiquette and will earn the undying hatred of the majority of Net users. On top of that, spammed messages are quickly removed from the Net by volunteers concerned that they make the Net useless for its intended purpose of communication, which makes them much less effective than they would seem at first glance.

Please do not post discussion articles to marketplace groups. There is always a discussion group covering topics related to a particular marketplace group. If you think that the Net cannot live without your bit of wisdom about an item someone else is advertising, please post your message to the appropriate discussion group. That way, you reach everyone who would care about your message, and you don't fill up the marketplace with messages that people who are only looking for things to purchase don't bother to read anyway.

It's much better to reply to someone's for-sale message by e-mail whenever possible, especially if you believe that he has committed a breach of etiquette. Posting a message claiming that someone's price is too high or that he has committed another grievous offense seldom achieves anything other than starting a flame war. Nobody likes being told in public that he is trying to gouge others, after all. If you must complain about someone's price, do it in e-mail. You have a much better chance of convincing him or her to lower it that way.

As with anything having to do with Usenet, picking the right group is very important. You're much less likely to find a buyer for your racing bicycle in `comp.sys.next.marketplace` than you are in `rec.bicycles.marketplace` because not all NeXT users are bicyclists. Picking the right group is especially important in the regional for-sale groups. The regional groups are designed so that people in a specific area can deal with others in that same area. For example, it is easier to sell a refrigerator in Houston by using `houston.forsale` than it is in a nationwide group like `misc.forsale.non-computer` or a regional group somewhere else, such as `mi.forsale` in Michigan.

A feature in Usenet enables you to limit where your message will be sent. If you include in the headers of your message a line that says `Distribution: tx`, for example, your article should be sent only to systems in Texas. Unfortunately, this feature isn't as useful as it might be. It's at best a hint to systems elsewhere on the

Net that they may not want to receive your article. Many news administrators set up their systems to accept articles no matter what the distribution is, either deliberately or unknowingly. Others go out of their way to get articles with a specific distribution so that some of their users, who may be from a different area, can see articles from back home. Still others are nationwide service providers who aren't really in one particular region. All of this means that an article with "ba" on the Distribution line will be read not only by folks in the San Francisco Bay area as intended, but also in Boston, London, and Singapore.

When you post to the marketplace newsgroups, be sure to use a meaningful Subject line. "For Sale" or "Wanted," by themselves, give little information to the person skimming through the group by looking at the message subjects. "Western Digital 540MB hard disk for sale, $250" is much more useful. If the reader is looking for a Macintosh printer, for example, he can skip right past your message. If you have lots of different things for sale, try to give as much information as you can, but remember that most systems get unhappy at subject lines longer than 80 characters, and a few older ones truncate them at 40. (If you have that many things to sell, it may be appropriate to break up the message into two or three, each having related items.)

Looking for Something?

If you're looking for something specific, try first to find the item through other channels before broadcasting your request to the Net. If the manufacturer is still in business, you may be pleasantly surprised that the company still has what you're looking for on the shelf. Other companies specialize in discontinued and surplus parts and equipment and are your best source for tracking down those hard-to-find items.

After you have exhausted all other channels, then by all means, post. State clearly what you are looking for, such as "a part number 345X56 Bakelite Frobnicator for an American Hawk Fubar 2000, circa 1968–1970," and how much you are willing to pay (or that you're willing to negotiate). Avoid sending out "items wanted" posts unless you are willing to pay for shipping from wherever the items may turn up or you state clearly where you're willing to accept items from. If a `.wanted` group goes along with the `.forsale` group in which your item will be posted, use that for your article, and please don't cross-post it to both.

Here's an example of a good wanted post:

```
houston.wanted #218
From: user@aol.com (Joe User)
Subject: Super Bowl Tickets Wanted

I need a pair of tickets to the game. If anyone has extras, please
e-mail me with your price and the seats' locations. Thanks, Joe
```

Short, sweet, and to the point.

If You're Selling . . .

Be specific in your first post about what you are selling and how much you want for it. If you're willing to negotiate, say so. State clearly whether the price includes shipping, and if it does, be sure to allow yourself a reasonable amount to cover the cost. Avoid sending out "for sale" posts unless you are willing to arrange for shipping to anyone who sees the article and wants to buy it. If you cannot limit the posting's distribution for one reason or another, be clear in your message about where you will and will not ship. Don't advertise items you cannot ship within a reasonable amount of time.

If you're selling a common item, such as a dinette set in New Jersey, a regional newsgroup (in this case, `nj.forsale`) is much more appropriate than a worldwide group and a comment that you won't ship outside of New Jersey. Someone looking for a dinette set in Seattle isn't going to be interested in paying to ship yours to her; she'll find one locally instead. This goes for many other things too. About the only large things that warrant being advertised nationwide or worldwide are rarities, such as a collector's car. If the buyer can find one of what you're selling locally, she probably didn't need to read your message in the first place.

Do your homework before posting. If you're selling an HP 100LX palmtop computer, don't expect to get $450 for it if the buyer can get a new HP 200LX for $499. This is the single biggest source of argument in the marketplace groups. You can expect, on average, to get no more than 75 percent of the new price for something that's in new condition, with the box and all the books and in current production. Prices go down from there, and something that's a couple of years old and in average shape rarely brings more than half its original value. Some things hold their value better than others, so this is only a rough guide, but if you ask an obviously unreasonable price, you can expect someone to argue it with you, most likely in public.

This is a good for-sale message:

```
From: student@rosie.uh.edu (Harry Student)
Newsgroups: houston.forsale
Subject: FOR SALE - Mac Classic II, Modem (2400/9600)

Classic II (4/80)      $ 350
FaxModem, Global Village (2400/9600)  $ 50
Both items are in perfect working order. The modem has never been used and is
still in its original, unopened packaging.
Interested ? Call me at (713)555-2368 or send e-mail to
student@jetson.uh.edu
Harry
```

This message has everything needed to contact the seller, plus enough description of the item to allow a buyer to decide whether he's interested enough to pursue making a deal. Someone in Houston could buy that machine tonight, if he wanted to.

If You're Buying . . .

Respond to an advertisement in a prompt manner. (The item may be gone if you don't!) Don't skip a message just because you think that the price is too high; offer the seller a price you think is reasonable, instead. You may be pleasantly surprised. Because the kind of things you will find for sale on the Net are often bulky and fragile, allow for a reasonable amount of money to package, insure, and ship your purchase properly. If you are unsure about a given seller, ask a Net regular discreetly by way of e-mail. She will be more than happy to either ease your concerns or confirm your suspicions.

Doing the Deal

Bargaining on the Net is much like doing it in person. The seller knows what he really needs to get for the item, and the buyer knows what she's really willing to pay. If these figures overlap, completing the deal is likely; if not, don't sweat over it. Don't take it personally if you get a low offer or a high asking price. What is worth $400 to one buyer may be worth only $300 to another, or $500 to a third.

Common etiquette is to accept the highest offer made within a few days, if that offer is acceptable, or the first offer made at the asking price. If someone offers more after a deal is struck, it is generally considered rude to break the agreement without, at the absolute minimum, offering to let the first buyer match the offer. In some places, even that is a sign of bad faith.

It's much easier to negotiate prices and shipping over the telephone or in person than in a long electronic-mail exchange. For this reason, as well as to assure potential buyers that the seller is a real person, it's a good idea to include a telephone number in the message describing the item you want to sell. It also helps to get your money faster.

Payment terms should be whatever you and the buyer are comfortable with and should commonly include such options as money in advance, C.O.D. (collect on delivery), or payment upon receipt and inspection. Don't be offended if the buyer or seller wants to take steps to protect his position because he probably doesn't know you. Most readers of these groups are basically honest and want to maintain their Net image, but the few bad apples should encourage you to deal with only honest, reputable people and to protect yourself in any transaction.

Remember that C.O.D. stands for "collect on delivery" and not necessarily "cash on delivery." The carrier collects the funds from the buyer and then hands him the package; the carrier then sends the payment on to the seller. The carrier is not a party to the transaction and therefore doesn't care whether the buyer gives you a bad check. For this reason, you may want to specify the collection of cash, money order, or other certified funds for your C.O.D. Check with your carrier for exact C.O.D. options and policies. If you choose this option, make sure that the buyer knows up front so that he can make the necessary arrangements.

One thing to remember is that UPS will send whatever is collected on delivery to the shipper's address as recorded in its files and *not* to the return address on the package. If you use a commercial packing and shipping service, you have to go back there to pick up your payment; if you send from your office, make sure that the shipping department knows what to do with the check it gets from UPS in the mail. Not even a cashier's check is an absolute guarantee of payment. In some reported scams, forged cashier's checks are used for payment, and the unlucky sellers have been the losers. This occurrence is rare and extremely illegal.

An idea spreading around Usenet as this book is being written is an escrow service for Usenet users. The seller would send the merchandise to the escrow service, and the buyer would send payment there. The escrow service would inspect the merchandise and verify the payment and then send both on to their destinations. This service seems like something whose time has come, and although the details are yet to be worked out, expect to see something like it in the not-too-distant future.

Sending the Goods

Packing and shipping fragile equipment isn't difficult, but it's easy to get wrong. All shippers recommend the same basic packaging. Place the item in a strong cardboard box, with at least two inches (more if the article is heavy) of resilient packing material on all sides. Those irritating little Styrofoam peanuts are widely used for a good reason, because they provide excellent protection with minimal weight. Close the box securely with wide adhesive packing tape.

Some things have special requirements for shipping. If you want to send an item classified as hazardous material, such as ammunition, the box must be labeled with a special placard and identification card, and there is an extra fee for special handling. Other items, such as firearms, have no packing or labeling requirements but must be sent to or from a designated person. If you're selling such an item, a statement about the rules that have to be followed should be included in your message. If you're not sure, ask someone by e-mail or in the appropriate group, such as `rec.guns`. If there's a FAQ file, it often contains the information you need.

In recent years, pack-and-ship stores have sprung up. They generally charge a few dollars to provide a suitable box and packing material, put it all together, and send it on its way. This money is well spent because the packing stores are familiar with what really happens to packages in transit and with the rules of the shippers they use.

Most shippers make three attempts to deliver a package, with a note on the door if the recipient isn't home, before sending the package back as undeliverable. If you're expecting a package, watch out for little, yellow stickers on your door if no one will be home during the day to accept delivery. For C.O.D. shipments, the delivery notice usually states the exact amount that is required. A cashier's check or money order in an envelope, placed out of casual view, with the delivery notice stuck to it will be all that's necessary if you want the package left on your doorstep. You may also make arrangements with the shipper to pick it up at its facility.

I've Been Ripped Off!

Sometimes, despite the best intentions of buyer and seller, a deal goes bad. The most common reason is that the buyer refuses to accept a C.O.D. delivery after agreeing to it or perhaps simply doesn't make arrangements to have the payment ready when the package arrives. Less often, the seller simply fails to ship the article in a timely manner.

In any case, the best approach is to contact the other party and try to work things out in a calm manner. Remember that the individual has a reputation to protect on the Net, and someone who develops a bad one will have a more difficult time buying or selling in the future. You can use this to your advantage.

Making a deal on the Net does not mean that the laws about theft and fraud aren't valid. In extreme cases, a complaint to the local police where the other party lives is appropriate. They will want to know the entire story. The more cooperative you are, the better they can help you with your complaint. A recalcitrant person often lives up to his end of the deal, or refunds money, after a visit from his friendly neighborhood cop.

If you're determined to post a message exposing someone as a liar, cheat, fraud, and thief (and a dirty rotten no-goodnik whom no one on the Net should deal with), tread lightly. Make sure that you have all your ducks in a row. Identify the person specifically enough to make it impossible for someone else to be confused with him. Tell about the entire deal and your experiences with it, both in making it and in trying to get it set right. Don't advocate Net terrorism against him, such as filling his mailbox with messages.

Better yet, step back, take a few deep breaths, and skip the whole thing. That kind of message seldom serves any real good and always starts a long, drawn-out discussion — and almost always in a marketplace group where, by definition, it isn't appropriate. Take real-world action instead, and save everyone else a great deal of bother.

If the package is damaged in shipping, your recourse is typically with the shipper, not with the sender. The shipper accepts the responsibility of delivering packages without destroying them. If you notice damage to the outside of the package, make sure that the driver makes a note of it on the delivery log, if you're there, or call the shipper's local office immediately after discovering the damage if the package is left on your doorstep. In any case, save the box and packing material because the shipper will have to inspect it before doing anything else with your claim.

Finally . . .

The Usenet marketplace groups are a great place to buy that piece of gear you've had your eye on. Items go quickly for reasonable prices. I've sold a radio within three hours of posting the for-sale message. The usefulness of these groups depends to a large extent on the people who inhabit them, though, and a few unscrupulous users can easily sink the whole thing. Whether you are a buyer, seller, or seeker of equipment, remember that your honesty and integrity reflect on the general reputation and usefulness of Usenet and of the Internet in general.

Jay Maynard is a senior systems programmer with the University of Texas Houston Health Science Center, working in administrative information systems. His responsibilities include mainframe and personal computing and networking. He has been active on Usenet since 1987.

Usenet, Bulletin Boards, and Legal Liability

by Mikki Barry <ooblick@intercon.com>

There is perhaps no better example of the dichotomy between the wants of the user and the responsibilities of the system administrator than the *BBS,* or computer bulletin board. Computer bulletin boards and similar conferencing systems allow for greater access to the "marketplace of ideas." It is estimated that hundreds of thousands, if not millions, of households own home computers, and many of them subscribe to bulletin boards. BBSs range in size from a handful of users to over one million and discuss topics as diverse as vegetarian cooking to rock climbing. However, regardless of their popularity, it is unclear how computer bulletin boards fit into the rubric of First Amendment protection. And, more importantly for purposes of this article, how does the system administrator, charged with the upkeep of one or more of these communications systems, balance her obligations to her users with the possible consequences inherent in a quasi-legal framework currently misunderstood by the lawmakers?

The importance of the balance between system administrators and their users is especially pertinent given the exponential growth of bulletin boards and conferencing systems. Current technology makes it trivial for an individual with a personal computer to "open for business" as a bulletin board administrator. At the same time, many computer users have the capability to connect to Usenet, probably the "great granddaddy" of all bulletin boards (although many long-term users of Usenet cringe at the comparison). The potential for billions of subscribers on millions of systems underlines the importance of a consensus on ethical guidelines of self-regulation. This is especially true given current governmental trends towards, at best, muddying the waters of growth in new technology, and at worst, using laws as an ever-looming threat, stifling real growth and change in the technologies in question.

Computer Bulletin Boards

Computer bulletin boards allow users to interact with each other in a way analogous to an electronic conference call. Subscribers can send messages to one user, or to all users on the system. Many BBSs even offer users the opportunity to engage in real-time conversation with others currently logged on the system. Anyone who has a computer, a modem, and the necessary access information can call a BBS and exchange information with the BBS community. The information can be stored on one central computer or can be electronically mailed to host computers connected via a network. Usenet is an example of a multiuser bulletin board that uses a network to disseminate information. While this introduction is being written, hundreds, if not thousands, of bulletin board systems proliferate.

Although most of these BBS systems are run by a central person or organization, the global problems of Usenet exemplify how an anarchistic structure without outside regulation can autonomously function provided a consensus exists on the ethical guidelines of its operation.

Usenet was one of the first computer conferencing systems with a nonacademic purpose. It was originally formed in 1979 and quickly expanded to give every UNIX system the opportunity to join and benefit from a computer network. Usenet is a series of host computers connected to each other, originally by telephone lines and now more commonly by the Internet, in an effort to facilitate the free exchange of information. There are currently approximately 20 million users on 55,000 host machines located on five continents, making it one of the largest bulletin boards in the world. Each host machine on Usenet pays its own costs for transmitting the data, including — if necessary — telephone lines and long-distance calls. (See *The Internet For Dummies*, published by IDG Books, Chapters 11 and 12 for an introduction to Usenet.)

Each site also appoints a system administrator (sysadmin) to oversee the computers' workings. It is usually these sysadmins who decide which newsgroups are seen by users who connect to the host. Any ethical considerations for systems like Usenet must take into account the fact that the anarchy that can develop from the versatility deliberately built into its framework necessitates consensus, or at least a laissez-faire attitude on the part of thousands, if not millions, of system administrators.

Problems for Censorship

When an article is posted to a newsgroup, it leaves the writer's machine as a data stream. This same data stream is passed from computer to computer, until all subscribers of a newsgroup receive the article. The only possible chance for interference with the contents of an article is if the system administrator chooses to review all articles before they leave the sysadmin machine. At large organizations, this becomes an impossible task.

Because prior censorship is difficult at best, discussions in different newsgroups can become quite heated. As the intensity of the arguments increases, so too do the responses, creating what is referred to on Usenet as a *flame war,* because these postings generate more heat than light. Oftentimes, these flame wars revert to ad hominem attacks that, in other media, may be considered libelous.

Usenet and the First Amendment

It is quite difficult to find a place for Usenet within the rubric of First Amendment protections. Although it is clear that computer networks and bulletin boards are unlike the more traditional media of newspapers and television, Usenet is unique even from the category of computer bulletin boards or conferencing systems. Usenet has no centralized management, no single computer through which all the information flows, and no one person responsible for the functioning of the network.

Defining whether computer networks in general and Usenet in particular fall into the *broadcast* model or the *common carrier* model (see the next section) may be important in deciding who, if anyone, is responsible for libelous or other damaging information. Although these models are used primarily for deciding FCC regulation, choosing whether computer networks are broadcast media or common carrier media is important to understanding congressional intent and whether Congress may impose standards from outside of the community. The label assigned to networks will determine which framework is used to formulate rules on liability.

Broadcast or Common Carrier

Because of its function as a conduit of information without regard for its content, Usenet acts like a common carrier. In Title II of the Communications Act, the key defining element of a *common carrier* is that "the content is separated from the conduit." However, unlike common carriers, Usenet is not a government granted monopoly, telephone lines are not a scare resource, and the FCC has thus far not chosen to regulate computer networks per se.

On the broadcast side, one must remember that the FCC classifies new technologies based on the service provided instead of on the method of transmission. In the case of Usenet and other bulletin board systems, it may be argued that the service of carrying information around the world is more akin to broadcast than common carrier. However, because there is no supervision or editorial control over what is broadcast, the only "safe" classification includes elements of both common carrier as well as broadcast media.

If Usenet is considered to fall under the rubric of broadcast media, the individual computer sites that hand off the material may be found liable under a republication standard. In republication, each site passing on the information could be held just as responsible as the author of the original message. If, however, Usenet is deemed a common carrier, the maintainers of the host machines are liable only if they knew or had reason to know that a given message contained defamatory information.

Who Should Be Responsible?

Another key question in determining liability for information contained on or broadcast over a bulletin board is *Who is the publisher of the information?*

Although at first glance it may be easy to point to the owner of the host system, this solution is not as simple as it appears on the surface. It is more appropriate to consider whether bulletin boards should be responsible for what is distributed by them. This question necessitates a consensus on whether bulletin boards are common carriers or broadcast/newspaper media. The answer may depend on which computer bulletin board is being considered.

Typical BBSs consist of a single computer owned by an individual. Users access this computer, read messages, and post replies or new articles. Conceivably, the owner of the BBS can oversee messages before they are distributed to the rest of the bulletin board. The same is true of pay services such as CompuServe and GEnie, because all messages go to a central location to be distributed.

However, the high volume of data that flows through these services makes it virtually impossible to exercise any control or censorship. It is conceivably possible, but only at the sacrifice of time, to slow the stream down to review each article. Prodigy, for example, a relatively new computer networking system financed chiefly by Sears and IBM, screens articles meant to be posted to a wide area and deletes or otherwise censors those that its system administrators deem objectionable. This constriction of data exchange detracts from the original motivation behind computer bulletin boards, namely the free and expeditious exchange of information.

Systems like Usenet, on the other hand, have no central distribution point, no central management, and no one entity who assumes responsibility for the operation of the network. Instead, each machine on the network routinely carries messages meant for only its users, as well as messages that merely pass through on their way to another location. These machines handle electronic mail meant for an individual, as well as articles meant for wide distribution.

All of these messages look alike to the computer — seemingly random data streams that it routes accordingly. Although it may be possible for a computer site with a small user base to appoint a censor to ensure that only appropriate news and mail leave the site, it is inconceivable that a larger site that handles hundreds of thousands of messages per day can check the content of the messages it passes on.

Although it is certainly possible to enact different standards depending upon the size and nature of the BBS, it would be far more efficient to set up a hybrid standard common to all types of electronic communication. This standard should take into account the information dissemination purpose of computer bulletin boards, as well as First Amendment freedoms of speech and the press.

One proposed standard stems from a 1952 case of defamation through a nonconventional medium. In Heller vs. Bianco, a patron of a bar used graffiti on the wall in the men's bathroom to defame the chastity of the plaintiff. The plaintiff's husband saw the message and demanded that the bartender remove the offending message. When the bartender did not comply, the plaintiff sued and won monetary damages on a legal theory of republication. The appeals court decided that because the defendant knew that the message was infringing on the rights of others, the defendant had an affirmative obligation to censor this speech, at least with regards to the bathroom wall.

Applying a similar standard of removing libelous communication from media under direct control may be a workable standard for most BBS operators. If BBS sysadmins are aware of a libelous message, they can delete it from the system. It is safe to assume, in fact, that most sysadmins would indeed remove this type of information. However, this rule necessitates a judgment call by the sysadmin as to what information is considered defamatory enough to warrant removal. The standard of a "reasonable sysadmin," however, may be more of a problem than allowing the marketplace of ideas to deal with objectionable material in its own way. Unfortunately, there have been and probably will continue to be periodic calls from the legislative community for outside regulation of the content of what appears on bulletin boards.

Responsibility of Authors

When issues of defamation are discussed on Usenet, participants often wish to assign direct liability to the authors of the articles. Of course, holding an author responsible for articles assumes that it is possible to verify the identity of those who post. Some BBSs require new subscribers to enter their names, addresses, phone numbers, and sometimes credit card numbers. If it is a pay BBS, it is in the best interest of the operator to verify the information to maintain accurate billings.

This standard may be enough to create a legal presumption that the person whose name and number were verified is the person who wrote and transmitted the article. However, on Usenet, it is not possible to create such a presumption. This is due to Usenet's unique status as a free network, where the only requirements for admission are the appropriate hardware and software and a site upstream that agrees to provide a news feed.

Obtaining a news feed from another machine is often a trivial task. The host machine simply provides a password that the recipient uses to contact the host's modem, communicate with the host machine, and transmit Usenet data stream. Although commercial services are available that provide sites with news feeds in exchange for payment, these services are interested solely in verifying the identity of the individual or corporation responsible for paying the bill. They are not concerned with the identity of the users on the host machine.

Therefore, a site like `intercon.com`, for example, may have ten users, five of whom are employees and five secondary accounts whose names are simply made up. Although it may not be considered ethical to create fictitious accounts from which to post articles, the point is that currently no way exists to tell whether an article is truly from the person indicated.

Even when it is possible to verify the identity of the owner of the account used to send objectionable information, there are also instances whereby an innocent account owner may have information transmitted from a personal account without permission. For example, if a user leaves a personal account logged on to the system, a coworker may use the personal terminal to broadcast a joke message. This practice is sometimes referred to as *derfing.* Derfing is meant to cause embarrassment to the person whose account is used in this unauthorized manner, and can even be accomplished sometimes from other hosts on the network, further complicating the issue of responsibility from the user's perspective.

The issue of identity or unauthorized use additionally works against a potential recovery by a given plaintiff. In order to show a common law cause of action for libel, the defamatory statement must be of or concerning the plaintiff. In a world where it is just as easy to forge a posting or even an identity, a plaintiff will have an extra hurdle to overcome in proving that the network persona that was defamed has an identity in the real world.

Formulating a New Standard

Although Usenet currently has approximately half a million participants, neither it nor other BBS-type systems have become nearly as pervasive as more traditional forms of media communication. It is rare indeed for anything said on the Net to reach the outside world. However, as computer use grows and the number of households hooking up to computer networks increases, computer conferencing may become as commonplace as placing a telephone call.

Electronic two-way communication should be analyzed under a standard that balances First Amendment consideration and the societal benefits of a worldwide communications system, with possible damage to individual reputations.

Currently, electronic media are not accorded the same protections as print media. Unlike newspapers and magazines, there have been cases of government officials seizing the actual computer equipment used to transmit illegal information. Computerized information-conferencing systems should be treated no differently than telephones and should receive official common carrier status, essentially shifting the legal repercussions to the author of the article and thereby decreasing liability for sysadmins who maintain these useful communications systems.

Conclusion

Once responsibility is shifted to the authors of articles, it becomes possible to address defamatory or harmful postings. Assuming that it is possible to defame entities whose existence may be valid only within the media in which they were defamed and the identities of both the author and the harmed individual were known, a new standard should be formulated to deal solely with computerized conferencing systems and bulletin boards. Under this proposed standard, BBS operators and system administrators of Usenet sites would be responsible for verifying the identity of computer users who access conferencing systems. If the identity of the author of a libelous article has been verified, the author is responsible for damages. If the sysadmin has failed to verify identity, the computer site would defend the suit and pay the damages.

Electronic communications should be afforded at least the same First Amendment protection as is already deemed necessary for print and broadcast media, plus the protection of common carrier status. Because bulletin boards and computer conferencing systems may replace current forms of communication, it is in our best interest to set down a uniform standard of protection that takes this new technology into consideration.

Preferably, this standard should be reached through consensus of system administrators and policed by the users of the systems as well as by the sysadmins. The nationwide and even worldwide capabilities of computer communications mandate a single standard, at least within the United States, rather than an ad hoc series of state regulations.

It is possible to strike a balance between individual reputations and First Amendment freedoms in computer communications, but only if lawmakers first understand the technology involved and the nature of its usage.

Mikki Barry is spokesperson for the Internet Business Association, and Chief Counsel of InterCon Systems Corporation. Ms. Barry has authored numerous papers and seminars on Internet topics, and was Editor-in-Chief of the Georgetown University Law Center's Journal of Law and Technology. *Ms. Barry has been on the Net since 1984.*

Chapter 5

Internet Privacy and Security

This chapter contains four separate articles:

- "Common Sense and Cryptography"
- "Privacy on the Net"
- "Thinking about Firewalls"
- "Using Firewalls on the Internet" (a firewall FAQ list)

Common Sense and Cryptography

by Arnold G. Reinhold <reinhold@world.std.com>

OK, you want to use encryption to send sensitive data over the Internet. Cool. Lots of products and technologies are out there for you to use. Many of these products are quite good; some can be downloaded from Internet sites for free.

That's the good news. The bad news is that using encryption is not as simple as using a typical shrink-wrapped application. To use a spreadsheet program, for example, you go out and buy Excel, 1-2-3, Quattro Pro, or whatever; install it; and learn some commands. Then you're in business. Need more capability? Learn a few more commands. You never have to learn much more than you need to get your work done. For the most part, features you haven't learned yet won't do you any harm.

Keeping Secrets Is Much Harder Than It Seems

Cryptography is different: What you don't know *can* hurt you. There *is* an adversary — real or imaginary — who is trying to get at your information (otherwise, why bother encrypting?). There are lots of tricks, and this adversary probably knows more of them than you do. This chapter is designed to give you an overview of many of the data-security issues you need to be aware of if you are really going to protect your data on the Internet.

First, I've got to ask why you want to use encryption. Here are a few good and not-so-good reasons:

I'm just curious. Cryptography has a long history and offers lots of interesting stuff to learn; it makes a great hobby. Many enthusiastic aficionados live in cyberspace. Crypto-hobbyists have changed the world and may well do so again. For example, William Friedman — the guy who broke the most secret Japanese diplomatic code before World War II — learned his trade working for a rich eccentric who was trying to prove that Bacon wrote Shakespeare's works. A good place to start learning about cryptography is the `sci.crypt` news group's FAQ, which is posted regularly and archived at `rtfm.mit.com`.

The Codebreakers, by David Kahn (London: Weidenfeld and Nicolson, 1967), provides a comprehensive history of secret communications from ancient times to 1967. The book is still in print. When I first encountered a thread on `sci.crypt` on just how valuable first editions of this book are, my copy was wedged under my monitor, ergonomically propping it up.

An excellent introduction to modern encryption technology is the indispensable *Applied Cryptography,* by Bruce Schneier (New York: John Wiley & Sons, 1994).

As a hobby, cryptography won't raise your cholesterol level, but it can be hazardous. In the United States, crypto-play is fairly safe as long as you don't send software out of the country. In other countries, you can get into serious trouble just for sending coded messages. France, for example, requires users to get permission from the government — rarely granted — to use encryption.

I want to join the Crypto Revolution. Many dedicated people are working hard to build a new society — Cryptopia — in which Big Brother is kept at bay and ordinary folks can live their lives in absolute privacy, all through the magic of cryptography. Like most utopian movements, this one is a mixture of good ideas and great naïveté. The concerns that Cryptopians raise are serious. Computer power has grown to the point at which every transaction we make can be recorded and analyzed. For the moment, this situation mostly affects our credit rating, our ability to get health insurance, and the volume of junk mail and phone calls we receive, but the potential for even more serious abuse is enormous.

The biggest problem Cryptopians face is that people who can't program their VCRs are not about to master all the skills needed for secure communications. But maybe you have the breakthrough idea that will make it all possible. Check in on `alt.security.pgp`.

I want to make a political statement and tick off the government. The government in question usually is the United States government, particularly the National Security Agency (NSA), which is responsible for keeping classified U.S. government communications secret. The NSA also listens in on foreign governments, organizations, and individuals and tries to break their codes. Legally, NSA is prohibited from monitoring the communications of U.S. citizens, although few people on the Net trust them not to.

The NSA has an obvious interest in retarding the spread of good cryptographic technology and technique. The better the encryption technology to which people have access, the harder it is for NSA to do its job. So cyberpunks, like cryptographic Johnny Appleseeds, relish spreading the use of the latest codemaking techniques in the hope of twitting the NSA. Usually, NSA keeps a Sphinxlike silence. Maybe the codes everyone is pushing shut down the agency's codebreakers; maybe they can break the codes with ease and hope that everyone adopts them. The NSA just says nothing. But in response to questions from the U.S. Senate Subcommittee on Technology and the Law in May 1994, NSA went on record as follows:

Question from Senator Patty Murray, D-Washington:

> In my office in the Hart Building this February, I downloaded from the Internet an Austrian program that uses DES encryption. This was on a laptop computer, using a modem over a phone line. The Software Publishers' Association says there are at least 120 DES or comparable programs worldwide. However, U.S. export-control laws prohibit American exporters from selling comparable DES programs abroad.
>
> With at least 20 million people hooked up to the Internet, how do U.S. export controls actually prevent criminals, terrorists, or whoever from obtaining DES encryption software?

Answer from NSA:

> Serious users of encryption do not entrust their security to software distributed via networks or bulletin boards. There is simply too much risk that viruses, Trojan Horses, programming errors, and other security flaws may exist in such software which could not be detected by the user. Serious users of encryption — those who depend on encryption to protect valuable data and cannot afford to take such chances — instead turn to other sources in which they can have greater confidence. Such serious users include not only entities which may threaten U.S. national-security interests, but also businesses and other major consumers of encryption products. Encryption software distribution via Internet, bulletin board, or modem does not undermine the effectiveness of encryption export controls.

The preceding comments notwithstanding, the U.S. government frowns on exporting cryptographic software. Under U.S. law, this type of exporting is a felony, in the same category as exporting machine guns and antiaircraft rockets. If you think that this prohibition violates your free-speech rights and is foolish anyway, because most of the good stuff is easily available on foreign ftp servers, join the discussion on `talk.politics.crypto`. (If you would like to be a test case, I recommend that you raise the money for your defense fund first.)

What is the NSA, really?

The NSA is a secret conspiracy that wants to run the world. The NSA is controlled by a couple named Alice and Bob, who have a fetish about communicating secretly in unusual situations. Although Alice and Bob have had easy access to almost all the world's communications for almost 50 years, they have not yet executed their plan. No one knows what they are waiting for. If anything bad ever happens to me, it is their doing, and it will prove that these statements are true.

I am up to some serious no-good. People in this group include organized criminals, drug smugglers, terrorists, and the producers of Barney. I recommend that you code all your messages with the UNIX command rot13. Try it on some innocuous file. See? Now you can't read it anymore. Betcha no one else can, either. That's all you have to know. You don't need to bother with anything else in this chapter. In fact, you're probably missing something really good on TV right now.

I want to be able to sign and verify my documents electronically. It turns out that cryptography can be used for more than just keeping information secret; it also can be used to create an electronic signature that cannot be forged — at least, in theory. The same technique that creates the electronic signature can tell you whether the document you receive is complete and unaltered. The signature- and message-verification process is called *authentication.*

Authentication is really neat and may well be the first mass-market application of modern cryptography. You may not want to be the first person on your block to use it, however. (It's discussed later in this chapter, in the section "Digital Signatures and Authentication.")

I'm sending some information I really want to protect. OK, if you're serious about protecting information, let's talk. Although most of the commotion about data security seems to be about which encryption methods to use and which to avoid, protecting data requires more than a strong code. You also have to decide what your security needs really are, learn a bunch of dumb stuff, and commit yourself to disciplined use of the security technology you chose. There is no shrink-wrapped solution to data security, and there may never be one.

Think of the data you want to protect as being the contents of your home. Encryption is like the lock on your front door. You can have the best lock money can buy — guaranteed to be unpickable — but a thief can simply break a window to get in. If you put bars on all the windows, the thief can cut a hole in the wall. If you install a motion-detector alarm system, the thief can pose as a courier delivering the latest IDG book. Hire round-the-clock armed guards, and the thief might bribe the guards.

Total security is hard to achieve. Practical security requires careful consideration of all possible threats and an ongoing effort to protect against all those threats in a balanced way.

Choosing a Security Plan

This section presents some more questions you have to answer before choosing a data-security approach. So take out a sheet of paper and start writing.

What data am I protecting?

Many different kinds of information need protection: employee medical records, detailed specs for the next great computer program, a final bid e-mailed to an overseas salesman, or just personal notes that are nobody else's business. Each kind of information has different security requirements.

How much data is involved?

An e-mail message may be a thousand bytes long and may contain just a few dozen bytes of sensitive information. An HDTV video conference call over a wide-band optical network can generate hundreds of gigabytes every hour.

For how long will the data remain sensitive?

A bombshell product announcement may require great secrecy as it is being circulated for internal review. After this information is released to the press, however, there is no secret to protect anymore. A patient's HIV status, on the other hand, may need to be protected for as long as that patient lives — and possibly for decades thereafter.

How safe is my data at its origin and destination?

Communicating exposes your data to additional risks. Bad guys can intercept your messages to read them or just to see when and to whom you are talking; they also can tamper with your messages or even forge messages in your name. With varying degrees of success, encryption can deal with these risks.

But your data also is vulnerable at the site where you are creating it and at the site where it is being sent. Securing data in a fixed location can be even harder than communicating it safely. With a little care, you can be sure that only encrypted data is in the communications channel, but the data at your fixed sites will have to be unencrypted at least some of the time, if you are going to use it.

How many people will be sharing the information?

The more people who know a secret, the more likely the secret will be compromised. Consider the odds: If 10 people know your secret, and you are 99 percent sure that each person is trustworthy, there is a 10 percent chance that the secret will leak. If 100 people are in the know, each of whom is 99 percent reliable, there is a 63 percent chance that someone will blab. And just how are you going to check out 100 people with anything like 99 percent reliability?

From whom am I trying to protect the data?

Understanding the threat is a key part of any security design. The following sections identify possible threats to your data.

Casual busybodies

This category can include your boss, coworkers, family members, or customers dialing in to read your Web page. They may have no scruples about reading material that is private, but they possess no special skills and aren't willing to expend great effort to penetrate security defenses.

Hackers

Computer hackers (I hate using the term as a synonym for computer vandal) probably won't bother you unless you have considerable visibility or notoriety; if you do, watch out. As a group, hackers have considerable skills and resources at their disposal.

Industrial spies

Breaking into computers is largely illegal in the United States, so industrial spies tend to carry out their activities underground. I have no idea how widespread are technologies for breaking codes or eavesdropping on computers via the electromagnetic signals they emit. Most industrial spies may be sticking to tried-and-true methods: burglary, bribery, blackmail, and brutality. If the spies had the skills to use the high-tech stuff, maybe they could have gotten honest jobs. Still, I worry about laid-off spooks quietly selling the good stuff for big bucks.

Government security agencies

Most large countries have one or more agencies responsible for gathering electronic intelligence. These agencies usually operate in great secrecy. The best of them are formidable opponents if you happen to catch their attention. The agencies have patience, decades of experience, and large budgets, and they often enjoy immunity from criminal laws. They know all the tricks you are likely to know. Smaller countries' security agencies sometimes use violence to make up for what they lack in technology.

As the cold war fades into history and government security agencies scramble to justify their budgets, a particularly scary trend is emerging: Some security agencies allegedly are gathering industrial intelligence for their countries' corporations. Your overseas competitors may have some powerful help in purloining your data.

A threat classification scheme

Somewhat arbitrarily, I have grouped the potential threats into five broad classes:

- **Class 1:** Casual snoopers with no significant cryptoanalytical abilities but with physical access to the encrypted information.
- **Class 2:** Individual hackers or small organizations that can execute the cryptoanalytic programs and recipes that are available on public bulletin boards and that have hardware resources on the order of an office full of personal computer workstations.
- **Class 3:** Organized computer hackers or medium-size organizations that have full knowledge of publicly available cryptoanalytic techniques and that are capable of mustering hardware resources on the order of a thousand personal computer workstations.
- **Class 4:** Small- to medium-size government cryptoanalytic agencies and large multinational corporations that have full knowledge of all publicly available cryptoanalytic techniques, as well as some secret knowledge and experience, and that can build special cryptoanalytic engines employing tens of thousands of custom or semicustom integrated circuits. With the economic turmoil in

eastern Europe, the services of medium-size government agencies may be available to wealthy organizations for a fee.

- **Class 5:** Large government cryptoanalytic agencies that have full knowledge of all publicly available cryptoanalytic techniques, as well as extensive secret knowledge and experience; that have access to all communications traffic passing through their own countries (and possibly have overseas interception capability); and that have priority access to semiconductor-wafer-fabrication lines, which enables them to design, procure, and use millions of custom cryptoanalytic integrated circuits.

What are the consequences if the data is compromised?

A stolen customer list can cost you sales. A leaked positive HIV test can ruin a person's life. An investigative reporter's field notes on a drug cartel can get her killed. The more severe the consequences of data compromise, the more carefully the data should be protected.

The U.S. State Department's criteria for security classification used to be as follows:

- **Confidential:** Information that would damage relations with a foreign country
- **Secret:** Information that would cause a break in diplomatic relations
- **Top secret:** Information that could lead to war

You may want to perform some similar classification of the data you are trying to protect.

Do I have a legal obligation to protect my data?

In some cases, the law requires you to protect information. A publicly traded company, for example, had better not allow any outsider to see its quarterly financial results before they are made public. A psychiatrist may be liable if she fails to protect her clients' treatment records. Europe has especially strict data-privacy laws. In the United Kingdom, the Data Protection Act of 1984 provides penalties for anyone who stores personal information on any computer and fails to take reasonable measures to prevent disclosure of that information.

If you have government-classified information to communicate, the NSA or your local equivalent will tell you what to do. You had better listen.

Whom can I trust for advice?

This is one of the toughest questions in data security. If you're a big organization with a great deal of information to protect, you'll probably want to hire a consultant. The problem is finding one you can trust who knows what he is doing. Learn enough about the issues involved to ask intelligent questions and to demand intelligent answers. Don't accept soft answers.

In the late eighteenth century, when he was U.S. secretary of state, Thomas Jefferson invented his own code. It appears that the professional diplomats, who were the repository of cryptographic wisdom at the time, pooh-poohed his idea and wouldn't use it. In fact, Jefferson was way ahead of his time; had he stuck to his idea, the United States would have had unbreakable codes for a hundred years. Instead, U.S. diplomatic codes were widely broken in Europe throughout the nineteenth century.

Learning about cryptography will make you a better judge of consultants' advice and vendors' product claims. But don't get too big for your britches — homegrown encryption solutions are a prescription for disaster.

How else can they get my data?

A central issue in practical cryptography is balancing the strength of a proposed encryption system against the threat to the data posed by other means of attack, both physical and electronic. This section describes some of the many other ways (besides code breaking) in which computer data can be stolen. For a balanced security approach, you need to cover these holes — and others — with as much care as you use in encrypting Internet messages.

Password selection

Easy-to-guess passwords are an especially big problem when a computer system has many users, each of whom is free to choose her own password. Assigning passwords is an effective — but often unpopular — way to solve this problem. The section "Choosing a Password or Pass Phrase," later in this chapter, tells you how to choose good passwords.

Unattended terminals

This is another big problem. Every now and then, a message appears on the Net from some college student, usually female, saying something like, "I'm lonely and could really use some company tonight!" The standard reply is, "Someone is posting embarrassing mail in your name. Remember to log out next time." In a corporate setting, the consequences can be more than embarrassing. Screen savers with password protection are one solution to this problem.

Viruses and Trojan Horses

Everyone has heard of computer viruses by now. Too many of us have had to deal with an infected machine. What is less known is the extent to which virus technology is available in the hacker community. From some bulletin boards, hackers can get source code for sample viruses and tips on how to make those viruses less detectable. A determined data snoop can custom-craft a virus to steal your secret key, encrypt it, mail it, and then quietly erase itself. Following are some tips to reduce this threat:

- Use a good virus-protection program, and keep it up to date.
- On machines that are used for encryption, decryption, and (especially) key generation, install only new, shrink-wrapped software, purchased retail.

- If you plan to run downloaded software, such as PGP or RIPEM, download only from primary sites, such as `mit` or `msu`. Do not use hand-me-down copies. Some of these packages use electronic signatures to verify authenticity. Follow the instructions carefully.
- Keep machines used for encryption in a safe when they're not in use. (No, I'm not kidding.)

Unauthorized entry via the Internet

The Internet, wonderful as it is, was never designed for security; its ARPAnet designers no doubt expected that all links on military networks would be securely encrypted, preventing unauthorized access. The research version that grew into our Internet enjoyed no such protection. Clifford Stoll's *The Cuckoo's Egg* (New York: Doubleday, 1989) describes his attempts to track a brazen gang of hackers who were breaking into U.S. government computers. Few of the problems described in this must-read Internet adventure story have been fixed, and many more security holes have emerged, making the Internet the greatest hacker's playpen ever.

There are two solutions to this threat:

- Do not connect networks that contain sensitive data to the Internet.
- Use a firewall.

(Isn't all the advice for problems of the '90s starting to sound the same?)

A *firewall* is a computer that is interposed between your network and the Internet. This computer is programmed to restrict intercommunication to benign forms that cannot be used to penetrate your internal network or do other damage. No one thinks that firewall technology is perfect, but several good products are on the market. Firewalls are covered in more detail in the last part of this chapter.

Firewall technology isn't cheap and is guru-intensive. If you don't want to make the capital and staffing investment but want your people to have the benefits of Internet access, consider buying accounts on a commercial Internet provider for your employees. For Internet marketing, hook up a node with your spiffy Web page on it.

Traffic analysis

On May 27, 1941, the Royal Navy sank the German battleship *Bismarck.* Her sailing date from Norway had been predicted not by decoding a message, but by statistically analyzing the crescendo of routine messages sent as the sailing date approached.

Traffic analysis is a branch of cryptoanalysis that tries to obtain useful information from the source and destination of messages and their timing. A company's customer list or the timing of a product introduction may be determined in this way. Most encryption products do little to protect against this form of snooping.

Physical theft

This is the dumbest form of attack, but it can work. Bad guy breaks in. He rifles your desk (it has the standard key that comes with all desks of that brand). He finds the disk or printout that has the data he wants, copies it, and splits. Now reshoot the same scene. This time the thief is one of the cleaning people; one of your security guards (how much do you pay them?); or, in some places, a corrupt cop.

An essential component of physical security is a safe. If your computer has removable hard drives, you can take them out and lock them up every night. Or you can lock up your entire laptop. Buy a safe big enough that it cannot be easily removed, or bolt it to the floor. A good safe should have a five-number combination you can change yourself. Pick a random combination, using the dice-and-table method described later in this chapter, in the section "How to create random passwords and keys."

The U.S. General Services Administration rates safes for storing classified materials based on how long it would take a skilled safecracker to open the safe through physical attack or manipulation of the dial. Typical ratings are less than one hour. This statistic means that you will need 24-hour guards — or a good alarm company with a guaranteed response time — to back up the limited security a safe offers.

The digital audiotape threat

I recently conducted a project at a household-word software company in Cambridge, Massachusetts. Because the company's software products generate hundreds of millions of dollars in revenue every year, the company was keen to protect its source code. Security was tight. Guards at every entrance were diligent about checking people's badges when they entered and about searching bags and briefcases when people left. There was one big hole in this scheme, however: Many machines on the company's network had local backup tape drives. Our group used a drive based on digital audiotape (DAT) technology.

DAT was Sony's attempt to muscle into the audio market with a product that was as good as compact discs but that allowed home recording. The technology didn't succeed in that market but found a niche as a computer backup device. A DAT device can reliably hold billions of bytes of digital data in an inexpensive cartridge smaller than a conventional audiotape cassette. Several drives of this type are on the market for less than a thousand dollars.

The problem is that a DAT cartridge can fit into your pocket or inside your clothing — it's roughly the size of the courtesy soap in hotels. The kind of searches those guards were doing would never find a DAT cartridge; nothing less than a body-cavity search would ensure that people leaving the building didn't have the company's crown jewels on them.

Banning DAT drives won't solve the problem; larger data cartridges can be disassembled, and the tape inside can be wrapped in a plastic bag and swallowed. And how do you prevent someone from smuggling a DAT drive into the building?

Data remanence

In *The Adventure of the Missing Three-Quarter,* Sir Arthur Conan Doyle wrote:

> "Holmes rose. Taking the forms, he carried them over to the window and carefully examined that which was uppermost.
>
> "'It is a pity he did not write in pencil,' said he, throwing them down again with a shrug of disappointment. 'As you have no doubt frequently observed, Watson,

> the impression usually goes through — a fact which has dissolved many a happy marriage. However, I can find no trace here. I rejoice, however, to perceive that he wrote with a broad-pointed quill pen, and I can hardly doubt that we will find some impression upon this blotting-pad. Ah, yes, surely this is the very thing!'"

In creating information, we often leave telltale remnants behind, as Sherlock Holmes well knew. This is particularly true of computers. Printer ribbons, carbon paper in multipart forms, and thrown-out paper-jam paper can reveal sensitive information. People who are hanging around the communal laser printer waiting for their output might take a peek at yours. On some networks, a typo in a print command can send your output anywhere on the network — even halfway around the world. Remember the time you printed a document and no output showed up on the printer? Where did it go?

But the worst data-remnants nightmare is magnetic media. For starters, deleting a file on most systems removes only an entry in the table that the operating system uses to keep track of things; the actual data isn't erased at all until much later, when the operating system needs the space for some new data. This is why "undelete" utilities can work.

You can get utilities that delete a file by overwriting the data blocks. These programs are available as shareware and as part of many utility packages; the best of them comply with a U.S. Department of Defense standard and perform the overwrites three times. Many experts now doubt that even that is enough, however. Some commercial firms recover erased data for a fee; to find them, look under Data Recovery in the Yellow Pages. Ask them whether your erasing technique is good enough.

Disk-compression programs can inadvertently defeat many of the file-deletion utilities. This happens when the pattern used to erase files compresses to a length shorter than the original compressed file. If you use disk compression, look for a delete utility that overwrites files with random strings.

The situation gets worse. Application programs often maintain a temporary working copy of your data while you are working. That way, if you quit and do not save your changes, the old copy is still available. Because the old copy is deleted when you perform a save, you can't find that copy to overwrite it. You have to use your delete utility in a mode that erases all unused disk blocks — good security housekeeping, but slow on today's gigabyte-plus disk drives.

Another concern is virtual memory, which copies to the disk blocks of the computer's main memory that have not been used for a while. Even if your application stores data in an encrypted form, these memory images may hold your sensitive information in the clear.

If you are a Macintosh user in the United States or Canada, you might check out the program SecureEdit, which enables you to create and edit sensitive documents without writing unencrypted material to disk. The program even turns off the Mac's virtual memory for its internal buffers. SecureEdit always stores your document encrypted with IDEA, a code discussed later in this chapter, in the "IDEA" section. You can get SecureEdit from `ripem.msu.edu`. The program is in `/pub/crypt/mac`, but you have to register first. Log in as **anonymous**, and read `/pub/crypt/GETTING_ACCESS`.

How do I dispose of magnetic media that contains sensitive information?

By all means, start with a file-delete utility that overwrites everything three times. This is adequate for Class 1 threats.

Beyond that, you have several choices:

- Reuse the media for other data of comparable sensitivity.
- Keep the media in secure storage until the information no longer is sensitive.
- Purchase a good degausser, and use it properly. A list of NSA-approved degaussers is available on the NIST bulletin board.
- Physically destroy — burn, dissolve, or pulverize — the media (hard to do without creating physical and environmental hazards).

TEMPEST

TEMPEST is perhaps the most exotic data security threat you face, but you have to consider it if you are serious about protecting your data against Class 3 or higher threats. TEMPEST allows a snoop with the proper equipment to look over your shoulder and read what is on your computer's display, even though he is parked in his car across the street from your building. TEMPEST is hard to stop. The only good news is that the snooping equipment is not widely available — yet.

TEMPEST stands for *t*ransient *e*lectro*m*agnetic *p*ulse *e*manation *st*andard. The emanations in question are signals your computer radiates that reveal the data on which it is working. NSA has a set of rules that explain how to build computing equipment that doesn't give off compromising signals. The rules are in a document called National Communications Security Information Memorandum 5100A (NACSIM 5100A). Don't bother writing for a copy; it's classified as secret.

Here's what TEMPEST is all about. Your computer's electronic circuits operate at the same frequencies used for radio communications. All the little wires on your computer's printed circuit boards and all the cables going between boxes on your desk act like radio antennae. As a result, every computer is a miniature broadcasting station.

You can hear some of these signals. Just put a radio next to your computer and tune it between regular stations; then turn on the computer, and listen to the buzzes and pops.

Your computer is a bunch of broadcasting stations, with each circuit transmitting a different signal. The strongest signals — typically, your computer's internal clock and your CRT display's sweep circuits — transmit no significant information. Other signals, although weaker, can give away the store.

The U.S. Federal Communications Commissions, and similar bodies in Europe and Japan, require computers to be shielded so that their electronic emanations don't interfere with TV and radio reception. Unfortunately, these standards do not force manufacturers to shield the weaker data-carrying signals, because they don't cause much interference. In fact, I am told that some TEMPEST-rated equipment cannot pass FCC Class B home-electronics standards.

The worst TEMPEST offender is the video display. Weaker internal data signals must be amplified to modulate the CRT tube's electron beams or to drive flat-panel LCDs. Worse, the same data is sent over and over again 70 times a second while you are sitting there, reading the screen. This situation enables the TEMPEST receiving equipment to dig the data-containing signals out of background noise levels. A report by Christopher Seline on the legal implications of TEMPEST (available on the NIST bulletin board) says:

> With current TEMPEST technology, it is possible to reconstruct the contents of computer video-display-terminal screens from up to a kilometer distant; reconstructing the contents of a computer's memory or the contents of its mass storage devices is more complicated and must be performed from a closer distance.

One common canard is that a van full of equipment is needed to intercept TEMPEST signals. Well, a computer as powerful as the one on which I am typing used to fill a large room. Not anymore. One Net poster described a TEMPEST awareness demo he attended 15 years ago. The operator used a device the size of a lunch box. He could read any video display with ease. With the latest digital-signal-processing technology, a TEMPEST receiver need be no bigger — or more suspicious-looking — than a modem.

Half-hearted measures to defeat TEMPEST

Here are some tips that make a TEMPEST snoop's work a little more difficult:

- Never use an encryption or other security program that displays passwords or keys on-screen.
- Do all your sensitive work — including reading and writing mail, encrypting, decrypting, and key management — on a battery-powered laptop with no external cables plugged in.
- When reading or typing sensitive data, use the smallest window and font you can read.
- Keep the sensitive data on-screen for as little time as possible. Use a screen saver set to a fast blanking time (15 seconds or less).
- Do your sensitive work in an inside office of your building. Senior executives never should be given offices with outside windows (good luck).
- Vary the times of day when you do sensitive work.
- Buy your laptop off the shelf from a retail store so that you know that it has not been altered.
- Keep your laptop locked up when it is not in use.
- Mark your computer in some way so that you will know if someone switches machines on you.

A shielded room — the TEMPEST stopper

The measures in the preceding section make it a little harder for a TEMPEST snoop to steal information, but not hard enough. The only certain TEMPEST protection available to those of us without access to TEMPEST-rated equipment is a shielded room. Such a room need not be much larger than a closet — just enough space for a chair and a work surface. The room's walls, floor, and ceiling should be made of heavy-gauge sheet steel or aluminum, with all seams continuously welded. The door of the room should be steel as well and must have good-quality RF weather stripping all around. No windows are allowed. It is best to keep the interior unfinished so as to make any tampering easy to spot.

Ventilate your shielded room through a matrix of metal tubes electrically bonded to holes in the wall. You need two of these vents — one for air supply and one for exhaust. Each tube in the matrix should be at least ten times longer than its diameter. Put the fans on the outside, of course. Another long piece of tubing through the wall can serve as a voice-tube intercom. Have an architect or building inspector make sure that ventilation is adequate and that your building's floor is strong enough to hold the load.

No wires whatsoever should enter or leave the shielded room — no utility outlets; no phone or network jacks. There are ways to TEMPEST-filter these wires, but you can't get the specs, so why bother? Use battery-powered lights (camping stores have a wide selection) and a battery-powered laptop.

Do all your sensitive work inside your shielded room with the door closed tight. The laptop should never be running while the door is open, even a crack. Write encrypted files to a floppy disk and turn off the laptop — you can use its sleep mode, if it has one. Then open the door and take the floppy disk to another computer for transmission. Reverse the process for incoming mail.

Test your shielded room by bringing in an AM/FM portable radio; one that also covers the television band is ideal. With the door closed, listen to all the bands. If you hear any signals at all, the room is not shielded well enough. But just because you cannot hear radio stations in your office doesn't mean that the office is well shielded. Remember that an intercept can succeed even if the TEMPEST signals are below the noise level.

Does this sound like an awful lot of bother? It is. But these are just some of the measures you have to take if you want your total security to match that of high-end encryption products.

Which Encryption Technique Should I Use?

Now that you understand a little about where encryption fits in to the overall picture of data security, you are ready to choose the method that best meets your needs. This section provides brief reviews of the most popular encryption schemes available to the general public. The opinion and security ratings are based on my best judgment. Your mileage may vary.

rot13

This is a simple substitution cipher, no better than the decoder rings that used to come in cereal boxes. With a little practice, you can learn to sight-read the coded messages. Rot13's primary use is to encode off-color jokes on Usenet, and nowadays, even this use is suspect. Sexist or racist humor flying around your network, even if it's rot13-encoded, can lead to harassment charges. And you can get into more trouble for that these days than for leaking state secrets.

Class 0. For organized crime use only.

Crypt

This UNIX utility is based on a simplified version of a World War II code machine. Software for breaking this code is widely available on the Internet, but finding the software, downloading and compiling it, and then reading the documentation probably is beyond the ability of most casual intruders.

Class 1 use only.

Application-embedded encryption

Many popular personal-computer software packages give you the option of encrypting data files. The packages often use proprietary encryption schemes that are quite weak. These packages can also leave unencrypted copies of your data on the hard disk in the form of temporary files and virtual memory traces. Such applications' password-protection schemes should not be considered for purposes of serious security.

A company called Access Data (Orem, Utah) sells several utilities it claims will decode password-protected files created by many popular programs, including Lotus 1-2-3, Quattro Pro, Microsoft Excel, Microsoft Word, Paradox, PKZip, and WordPerfect.

DES

DES, the data encryption standard, was developed in the early 1970s by IBM, a well-known computer manufacturer at the time. The U.S. government then adopted DES as its official standard for the protection of nonclassified but sensitive information. Hardware DES chips are available that encrypt and decrypt fast enough to keep up with high-speed computer networks.

DES is a symmetric-key system, which means that the same key is used for encryption and decryption. For communication, both parties must exchange keys in secrecy. Personal visits, trusted couriers, and even registered mail are traditional ways to exchange private keys.

Public-key cryptography provides another way to do this. In fact, most public-key encryption systems, such as PGP and RIPEM, use the magic of public-key encryption only to exchange temporary keys for an associated private-key algorithm. Private-key encryption and decryption are much faster than their public-key counterparts.

DES works by taking data in 64-bit chunks and shuffling it 16 times in a special way. There are several different modes of using DES, with names such as Electronic Code Book (ECB) and Cipher Block Chaining (CBC). Some modes are a little stronger; others are less sensitive to transmission errors. The main thing you have to do is make sure that you're using the same mode on both ends of your communication circuits. The actual DES-standard document demands that the DES algorithm be implemented in hardware to be compliant, but almost everyone ignores this technicality.

As the first modern code to become public, DES was influential. Many newer codes cryptographers have since proposed are based on techniques first revealed in DES. But DES also generated great controversy. At first, experts voiced suspicions that DES contained a secret trap door that allowed the NSA to break it at will.

Yet after two decades of trying, no one has published a practical attack on DES. In fact, when open researchers developed a new codebreaking technique called differential cryptoanalysis, they found that DES had already been hardened against it. The technique in question was long known in the secret community. Recently prominent cryptographers Eli Biham and Adi Shamir proclaimed DES to be secure. But there still is no way to be sure.

The one big weakness — undoubtedly deliberate — in DES is its relatively short 56-bit key. It turns out that if you make 100,000 little DES engines, all working in parallel and each trying 50 million keys a second, you can run through every possible key (there are 2^{56} of them) in four hours. On average, you find the key you want in half that time.

One researcher thought that he could buy the DES engines in chip form for $10 each. This means that a DES-cracking machine could be built for a million dollars or so. Amortizing the million dollars over three years, each DES keyspace search would cost about $100. My guess is that large government security agencies, with preferred access to semiconductor plants and advanced techniques such as wafer scale integration, would pay far less.

Another big weakness of DES has less to do with its design than with the way it is often used. In many implementations, the user is asked for an eight-character key. In theory, any 56-bit key can be expressed as eight 7-bit ASCII characters. In practice, however, users choose mostly letters of the alphabet or numbers in their keys, or — far worse — dictionary words. This makes the effective key space much smaller than 2^{56} and, therefore, easier to search. Ideally, DES should be used with a randomly selected 14-digit hexadecimal key. If you are using a pronounceable word or phrase of as many as eight characters, even with a few numbers or special characters thrown in, a good hacker can break your code.

Better DES implementations enable you to enter an ASCII key that is longer than eight characters. The software then hashes all the characters together to form the 56-bit key. This system is much better. If you are using this type of system with an English phrase, the phrase should be at least 56 characters (about 12 words) to maintain security. For details, see "Choosing a Password or Pass Phrase," later in this article.

Because DES is an official U.S. government standard, it may be an advantage to use it when you have a legal obligation to maintain confidentiality. But DES may lose that sanction soon if the feds decertify DES in favor of Clipper.

Used with a good key, DES is suitable against *Class 2 threats.* It may be acceptable against Class 3 threats for a couple more years, but I recommend using triple DES instead (see the following section).

Triple DES

Triple DES overcomes the one glaring fault of DES: its short 56-bit key size. As its name implies, triple DES encodes your data by applying the DES algorithm three times. By using different keys at each stage, you can get encryption with a 168-bit key (3 × 56). Many cryptographers consider 168 bits to be overkill; they use the same key for the first and third DES stages, producing an effective 112-bit key length. This mode sometimes is referred to as DES-EDE (for encode–decode–encode).

So, you might ask, if you are using two DES keys, why not save some time and use DES only twice rather than three times? It turns out that double DES is vulnerable to a form of cryptoanalytic attack called "meet in the middle." Designing code is not a job for amateurs.

There still is a risk that the basic DES algorithm has a hidden flaw that also would weaken triple DES. The only answer to this fear is that DES has been subject to more scrutiny by the open researcher community than has any comparable encryption method. No practical flaws have been found yet.

To the best of my knowledge, the use of triple DES is not restricted by patents.

Protects against Class 3 threats and maybe Class 4.

IDEA

IDEA, which stands for international data encryption algorithm, was developed in the late 1980s by James L. Massey and Xuejia Lai at ETH in Zurich. According to Phil Zimmermann, the designers of IDEA have a distinguished reputation in the cryptological community. Like DES, IDEA shuffles 64 bits of data at a time, but it does so by using a different, patented algorithm. More important, IDEA uses a 128-bit key, which is long enough to resist a brute-force key-space search.

So far, IDEA has resisted all attacks by the open cryptoanalytical community. The NSA and its overseas rivals are mum.

IDEA, which is used in the PGP program described later in this chapter, in the "PGP" section, is patented in many countries; commercial use may require getting a license. Contact ASCOM Tech AG in Switzerland (phone: 65-243404). Rumor has it that the firm charges about 90 Swiss francs per user.

Protects against Class 3 threats and maybe Class 4.

RSA

RSA is a public-key encryption and authentication system sold commercially by RSA Data Security, Inc., of Redwood City, California. Several hardware and software manufacturers, including Apple and Microsoft, have licensed RSA encryption and plan to use it in their desktop products.

In public-key encryption, you create two keys. One key, which you make public, is used by anyone who wants to send you a secret message. You keep the other key secret and use it to decrypt those messages. To reply, you use the sender's public key. The neat thing about public-key technology is that it enables you to communicate privately with someone without having to exchange secret keys.

In RSA you make your public key by multiplying two prime numbers of roughly equal size. The secret key is one of the two prime numbers. You can always get the other prime by long division; your computer still remembers how to do that. So a 512-bit RSA public key would be the product of two prime numbers, each 256 bits long.

You don't even remember what a prime number is, much less how to find nice big ones? No problem; the RSA software will find some for you. You just have to worry about keeping the numbers secret.

When someone wants to send you a message, her copy of the RSA software strings together the bits in the message to form another binary number and then performs some magic math on it, using your public key. Your copy of the RSA program, knowing one of the primes, can decode the message when you get it.

The security of RSA rests on two claims, both of which remain unproved (albeit widely believed) mathematical conjectures:

- There is no way to undo the math magic that is easier than factoring the product-of-prime-numbers public key.
- Factoring products of large prime numbers is too hard for attackers to do.

One important question: How large is large? In a 1977 *Scientific American* article describing public-key encryption, the inventors of the technique published a coded message and a 129-digit (429-bit) public key. They felt confident that the factors of the number, which came to be known as RSA-129, would remain secret for decades. In 1994, the following message appeared on the Internet:

```
From: warlord@MIT.EDU (Derek Atkins)
Newsgroups:
sci.math,sci.crypt,alt.security,alt.security.pgp,alt.security.ripem,comp.security.misc,alt.privacy
Subject: RSA-129
Date: 27 Apr 1994 04:06:25 GMT
Organization: Massachusetts Institute of Technology (MIT)

We are happy to announce that

RSA-129 = 1143816257578888676692357799761466120102182967212423625625618429\
 35706935245733897830597123563958705058989075147599290026879543541
 = 3490529510847650949147849619903898133417764638493387843990820577 *
 32769132993266709549961988190834461413177642967992942539798288533
```

```
... the decoded message reads

THE MAGIC WORDS ARE SQUEAMISH OSSIFRAGE


To find the factorization of RSA-129, we used the double large prime
variation of the multiple polynomial quadratic sieve factoring method.
The sieving step took approximately 5,000 mips years, and was carried
out in 8 months by about 600 volunteers from more than 20 countries,
on all continents except Antarctica....

We would like to thank everyone who contributed their time and effort
to this project. Without your help, this would not have been possible.

Derek Atkins
Michael Graff
Arjen Lenstra
Paul Leyland
```

So the secret lasted 16 years — not as long as the inventors expected, but not too shabby — and breaking it took a great deal of work. Still, the factorization of RSA-129 was a clear warning shot to RSA users. Factoring 429-bit RSA keys is possible for anyone who has access to a thousand or so workstations and a couple of days of supercomputer time. Many governments and large corporations can find resources like those. Keys of 512 bits, the maximum length allowed in some desktop software, are estimated to be seven times more difficult to crack, so there are no grounds to feel complacent.

Most cryptographers feel that 1,000-bit keys will remain beyond attack for the foreseeable future, but many excellent mathematicians are working on better ways to factor numbers. A breakthrough is by no means impossible. Caveat cryptor!

Depending on the key size, RSA can protect against the following threats:

- *512 bits Class 2*
- *768 bits Class 3*
- *1,023 bits Class 4*

RIPEM

PEM, which stands for privacy-enhanced mail, is an Internet standard for sending encrypted and/or authenticated mail. The standard itself allows for multiple encryption and signature schemes. RIPEM (Riordan's Internet Privacy-Enhanced Mail) is an implementation of this standard that uses DES for encryption and RSA for key distribution. As an option, RIPEM can use triple DES for encryption.

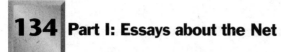

RIPEM was written by Mike Riordan (who wants you to pronounce it RYE-pehm). RIPEM can be used royalty-free in the United States for noncommercial purposes. Internet sites in the United States and Canada can obtain RIPEM from `rsa.com` or `ripem.msu.edu`. You can get more information about RIPEM via anonymous ftp to those sites, but you have to register to download the software. Be sure to read the file GAINING_ACCESS in the root directory. To get the software, you must go through a procedure that includes agreeing to the licensing terms.

Like RSA, the protection that RIPEM affords depends on the key size you use, but it also depends on your choice of encryption algorithm, as follows:

- *516 bits and DES Class 2*
- *768 bits and triple DES Class 3*
- *1,023 bits and triple DES Class 4 (maybe)*

PGP

There are many heroes of the Internet. Numerous programmers have given thousands of hours of their best efforts in building the many tools that have made the Internet so popular — and the publishers and authors of Internet books rich beyond their wildest dreams.

But of all the Internet heroes, Philip Zimmermann is in a class by himself. He has not only written a fine program, but, as of this writing, also is at serious risk of going to jail for his efforts.

The program Zimmermann wrote is PGP, which stands for "pretty good privacy." PGP is similar in concept to RIPEM, described in the preceding section. PGP and its use are described in detail in the second article in this chapter.

Like RIPEM, PGP uses RSA for key distribution, but rather than DES for encryption, it uses IDEA. PGP emphasizes the web-of-trust method to distribute public keys. PGP improves on RIPEM by hiding the sender's identity, making traffic analysis a little harder.

Source code for PGP is published and has been examined by many people. You can have a high degree of confidence that official versions of PGP do not contain any back-door security holes.

PGP uses patented technology from RSA Data Security, Inc. and from ASCOM Tech AG in Switzerland, the holders of the IDEA patent. After some hassles, Zimmermann has arranged licenses from those companies for noncommercial use in North America. The procedure for obtaining an official copy of PGP involves certifying that you agree to that license and are not exporting the software.

So why is Zimmermann in hot water? Not surprisingly, copies of PGP have made their way to overseas FTP sites, and the technology now is in use throughout the world. Some people feel that PGP is the greatest contribution to individual liberty since the U.S. Bill of Rights; others think that it is undermining efforts to control international crime and terrorism.

In any case, exporting cryptographic software is illegal in the United States. The U.S. government has launched a criminal investigation to see whether it can pin the blame for PGP's export on Zimmermann. He has hired a team of heavy-duty criminal-defense lawyers, and the bills are piling up. A defense fund has been set up. You can get information about it via anonymous ftp from `ftp.math.luc.edu`. Look in `/pub/hmiller/PGP/pzdf.FAQ`.

For commercial use in the United States or Canada, you can buy PGP from a company called ViaCrypt. Contact:

ViaCrypt Products
9033 North 24th Avenue, Suite 7
Phoenix, AZ 85021
Phone: (602) 944-0773
Fax: (602) 943-2601
Internet: `viacrypt@acm.org`

ViaCrypt also offers a version of PGP that uses a PCMCIA smart card for secure key storage. This may be the best method available for managing your private key safely.

Like RSA, which PGP uses, the protection that PGP affords depends on the key size you select, as follows:

- *512 bits Class 2*
- *768 bits Class 3*

RC2, RC4, and 40-bit codes

RC2 and RC4 are proprietary secret-key encryption algorithms developed by Ron Rivest, at RSA Data Security, Inc. The legal status of these algorithms is clouded by the recent unauthorized release of source code purported to contain the RC4 algorithm. Some people suggest that without patent protection, RC4's release places the algorithm in the public domain. RSA disagrees. In any event, cryptographers have had only a short time to evaluate RC4.

RC4 has a reputation for being fast and adaptable to a variety of key lengths. RSA claims that the U.S. government permits export of cryptographic products based on RC2 or RC4 as long as they have a key length of no more than 40 bits. Most public cryptographers sneer at such a short key length. An office full of high-end PCs could go through all 2^{40} keys in a few weeks. Still, if you need to build a cryptographic application that can be freely exported and that still provides a modest level of security, you may want to contact RSA for a license.

RC2 and RC4 with 40-bit keys are suitable against *Class 1* attacks; they also can provide short-term protection (a few days) against *Class 2* attacks.

RC2 and RC4 with longer (128-bit, for example) keys may be as good as IDEA or triple DES, but they have not had the same level of scrutiny, so I won't rate them beyond Class 2.

Clipper, Capstone, Skipjack, and Tessera

In many ways, a crisis exists in cryptography. The pillar on which most commercial cryptographic applications have been built — DES — is crumbling fast, eroded by waves of advances in integrated-circuit performance. Many commercial users are reluctant to adopt the alternative ciphers — IDEA, RC4, and triple DES — without the imprimatur of the U.S. government. Meanwhile, the government, although concerned about society's vulnerability to computer mischief, doesn't want to destroy its capability to intercept international communications by endorsing a strong, open cryptographic algorithm.

To solve this dilemma, the NSA has proposed a family of hardware-based cryptographic products with the names Clipper, Capstone, Skipjack, and Tessera. (I just lump them all under the name Clipper.) These products incorporate a new concept called *key escrow.*

Here's how this concept works. The Clipper encryption algorithm, called Skipjack, is secret; the NSA doesn't want the public to learn what NSA considers to be a strong cipher design. To use the algorithm, manufacturers have to buy a special chip that contains the secret recipe in tamperproof microcode. Users can pick their own 80-bit session keys. But the chip periodically transmits that session key encoded with a special 80-bit key that is burned in to the chip at the time it is manufactured. Each chip's special key is split into 40-bit halves that are kept by separate key-escrow agents. If the U.S. government wants to break the code, it is supposed to get a warrant and present it to both escrow agents, along with the offending chip's serial number (which the chip sends out along with the encrypted session key). Each agent verifies the warrant and then gives the feds the half of the key it holds. The feds put the halves together and can then read all data encoded by the offending chip.

Clipper and the key-escrow scheme have generated an uproar in the open cryptographic community. Entire Usenet newsgroups are devoted to flaming supporters of the scheme. I am about to take my electronic life into my hands and attempt a neutral summary of what I consider to be the principal arguments for and against Clipper and key escrow.

Because the Skipjack algorithm is secret, we don't know how secure it really is.

I have a hard time taking this argument seriously. The open cryptographers have never established a standard for certifying a crypto system as secure. They like to bang on proposed encryption systems for a while to see whether they can break them. Sometimes they can. But what does it prove if they can't?

Meanwhile, the NSA has been making and breaking codes for more than half a century. The agency's annual budget is in the billions. The NSA claims to have spent seven years certifying the Skipjack algorithm. I'd kind of trust the NSA to know how to make a strong code — and to test it thoroughly. I doubt that Skipjack is the strongest code the NSA ever made — the agency people have to figure that sooner or later someone is going to reverse-engineer those chips — but it's likely to be as good as anything the public community will come up with.

Maybe NSA has a back door into Skipjack.

A *back door* is a secret weakness that would enable the NSA to crack the code without going to the bother of getting a warrant. A similar concern was raised when DES was introduced as a U.S. government standard. No one ever found a back door into DES, yet no one has figured out how to prove that one doesn't exist. I have always wondered how even the head of the NSA can be sure that there aren't back doors in the codes. Maybe the agency has two or more teams of designers, each building independent coding stages, and prohibits fraternization.

Of course, a paranoid person can wonder whether the designers of the various public ciphers, such as IDEA, may have slipped in a back door for the NSA or the local equivalent.

The one bright note is that if the NSA has a trap door, it is going to keep that fact a deep secret. Great Britain allowed the city of Coventry to be bombed rather than let the Germans suspect that broken codes had yielded a warning about the raids. You're going to have to be into some pretty nasty stuff before the NSA will do anything with your illegally intercepted Clipper-mail.

After the NSA's codes are accepted as standards, the U.S. government will ban all other strong crypto systems.

This concern is a serious one. Right now the U.S. government is pushing Clipper as a voluntary standard, but no one doubts that many in the government would prefer it to be the only crypto system in use. Precedent exists; other countries have such bans. France, for example, requires you to get written permission from the government before you send messages in code.

One terrorist incident in which the bad guys use PGP may be all it would take for the U.S. Congress to pass a ban on unapproved cryptography. Would such a law stand up to constitutional scrutiny? This type of ban would be similar to requiring people to write legibly so that the censors can read their letters. The United States actually set that requirement during World War II for "V-mail" to the front. But this is peacetime. (Yeah, maybe.) I hope that the Supreme Court would strike down such a law, but I wouldn't bet on it.

On the other hand, if the use of key-escrow encryption were widespread, enforcing a ban on other crypto systems would be difficult. Right now, screening electronic-mail traffic for illegal coded messages is easy. If the same messages were superencrypted with Clipper, doing that type of screening would be much harder.

The FBI's opinion on cryptography

Steven Levy (steven@echonyc.com) writes:

> I was the one who asked [Louis] Freeh [the director of the Federal Bureau of Investigation] the question after he gave a talk at the conference on global cryptography. I said that while the administration is currently saying that they are not interested in regulating cryptography domestically, what if in the future the wiretaps you get yield scrambled messages that you can't decipher. (Meaning, do you regulate then?)
>
> Freeh asked, "In terms of encryption being a voluntary standard?"
>
> "Yes," I said.
>
> "Oh, yeah, definitely," he said. "If five years from now we solved the access problem, but what we're hearing is all encrypted, I'll probably, if I'm still here, be talking about that in a very different way; the objective is the same. The objective is for us to get those conversations, whether they're by an alligator clip or ones and zeros. Wherever they are, whatever they are, I need them."

Why would non-U.S. crypto users buy products the U.S. government can break?

This is another good question. The United States dominates the world software market, although some people fear that U.S. crypto-export barriers may undermine that position. Maybe other countries will simply buy whatever the United States produces. The NSA allegedly has been lobbying the international spook union to get other countries to back key-escrow encryption. Other governments may not be too keen on their citizens' communicating in absolute secrecy, either.

Why would bad guys use Clipper when they know that the U.S. government can tap it with a warrant?

Why do people use cordless phones to buy drugs?

Why did Princess Di call her lover on a cell phone?

Why did Khrushchev use an unencrypted car phone?

Why does the Mafia use telephones at all?

Maybe they don't know better, maybe they are lazy, maybe they think that they are invulnerable, maybe they are just stupid, but they do.

What's going to happen with Clipper?

Despite the controversy, the U.S. government is pressing ahead with Clipper as a standard for government use. In practice, this means buying PCs with PCMCIA slots so that Clipper encryption cards (they are actually called *Tessera*) can be inserted for security applications. Most commercial computer users aren't expected to buy Clipper hardware any time soon, so the government has promised the software industry to look for software key-escrow solutions that would be exportable. Some people are even pushing key escrow as being a user-friendly feature. Think about what happens if the employee who has the key to your corporate database skips town. Are you sure that you have a copy? (By the way, the government's key-escrow system does *not* allow you to recover a lost key!)

The bottom line

- If you need really strong security, have access to Clipper-based products, and are not worried about the U.S. government's seeing your secrets, use Clipper; it's likely to be as strong a crypto system as anything else out there. You can export Clipper so that overseas offices can use it (subject to local regulations, of course). And if you have a legal obligation to protect nonclassified information, Clipper covers your backside better than anything else does.
- The U.S. government can read your Clipper-encrypted data with a warrant — and quite possibly without one.
- Like wearing a fur coat, Clipper use may make you unpopular in some circles.
- Download your own copy of PGP while you still can.

I believe that Clipper technology is good against *Class 4* threats. Short of the one-time pad (see "One-time pads," later in this article), Clipper also is your best bet against *Class 5* threats, except for the U.S. government.

PCMCIA cryptographic smart cards

One of the hottest practical security products to come along is the cryptographic smart card. This card contains tamperproof, nonvolatile memory and a computer chip that implements one or more cryptographic algorithms. The PCMCIA cards, also called PC Cards, are the length and width of a credit card and about four times as thick.

The beauty of these smart cards is that your private key never has to leave the card. In fact, some implementations of this technology make it virtually impossible to extract your private key from a smart card. When you want to decode a message you received on your computer, you plug your smart card into your computer's PCMCIA slot. The computer asks for your pass phrase, which unlocks the smart card. The computer then sends the session key, which was encrypted by the sender with your public key, to the smart card. The smart card spits out the decrypted session key to your host computer, which then decrypts the message. Encrypting works similarly.

The advantages of the smart card include the following:

- A smart card is easy to keep on your person.
- Someone who steals your card cannot use it without knowing your pass phrase.
- You know whether it's lost or stolen.
- In some implementations, your secret key can never be extracted from the smart card, even with the pass phrase.

The preceding features make it almost impossible to compromise your private key without your knowledge, remedying a major flaw in most public-key systems.

One disadvantage is that you cannot back up your smart card. I hope that this problem will be remedied in the future by some optional escrow scheme. The risk of losing data when a smart card is lost is more real for most people than the risk of electronic snooping is.

Smart cards that are already on the market include the following:

The Persona Card

National Semiconductor
iPower Business Unit
1090 Kifer Road, Mail Stop 16-255
Sunnyvale, CA 94086-3737
(408) 721-8797

Cripta Plus

Telequip Corporation
18 Clinton Drive
Hollis, NH 03049
(603) 881-5616
Fax: (603) 881-5635

PCMCIA Tessera cards that implement the NIST–NSA Clipper algorithm also are becoming available.

Make sure that the next computer you buy has PCMCIA PC Card slots.

Digital Signatures and Authentication

Remember that authentication is the process of signing and verifying the contents of documents. Here's how authentication works. The electronic version of your document is passed through something called a *hashing function,* which produces a string of bits that depend on all the information in the documents. A simple way to perform this hashing would be to break your document's binary representation into pieces and then to add up all those pieces as though they were numbers. Actual hash algorithms used for signing documents throw in some cryptographic magic that makes it hard to predict how a given change in the document will affect the hash. This technique keeps bad guys from altering a document in such a way that its hash value is unchanged.

The hash bits are then encrypted with the signer's private key, and the resulting signature field is transmitted along with the document. The recipient then can hash the received document, decrypt the signature field, and compare the two; if both hashes match, the recipient can be sure that the sender actually sent it. The recipient also can be sure that what she got is what was sent.

There are two holes in this theory, however. First, it assumes that the sender's private key has not been compromised. The sender has to protect her private key at all times. Suppose that she was a little sloppy one time. How do you prove that her key was not compromised? Fortunately, U.S. law (as I understand it) takes a broad view about what constitutes a valid signature, so electronic signatures probably will be widely accepted in commercial practice.

Second, the theory assumes that the recipient has a valid copy of the sender's public key. If bad guys find out someone's private key or sneak in an ersatz public key, they can forge an apparently valid signature. This problem is not unique to digital signatures; managing keys is the biggest problem in all forms of practical cryptography.

One solution is central key-distribution agents, which have been proposed as part of an international standard called X.509. Some observers have criticized these agents as being unwieldy and potentially dangerous. The PGP people use a different method called a web of trust. You sign your friends' signatures, they sign yours, their friends sign *their* signatures, and so on. Eventually, enough of these signature chains exist that you can find someone you know who has signed the signature of someone else who has signed the signature of the stranger with whom you need to establish signature trust. This concept resembles the letters of introduction of olden days.

The good news about electronic signatures is that there are fewer technology choices for you to worry about than in the encryption world. Right now the two main contenders are RSA and DSS, both of which are public-key-based systems. RSA relies on the difficulty of factoring pairs of large prime numbers. DSS uses something called the discrete logarithm problem (cryptographers should always be discrete).

RSA is peddled by RSA Data Security, Inc., which holds patents on the method in the United States. Most of the major computer manufacturers have adopted RSA as a de facto standard. DSS is being pushed by the U.S. government's National Institute of Science and Technology (NIST). NIST claims that DSS is not covered by RSA's patents; RSA claims otherwise. It may take a while for this situation to be sorted out.

The fight between the two technologies appears to be driven by RSA Data Security's reluctance to lose royalty income and the government's desire not to lock in to a proprietary technology. But maybe the NSA knows more about RSA's vulnerability than it is saying, or maybe the NSA thinks that RSA is too strong. One never knows.

I am inclined to prefer a system blessed by the U.S. government. It is hard to believe that the government would adopt a weak signature system for its own use. The DSS algorithm is published, and NSA has gone farther than it usually does with open algorithms by endorsing DSS "for signing classified data in selected systems." The agency also responded to criticism of its original proposal with significant improvements, including a longer key and an openly trustworthy method for generating the large prime numbers the algorithm needs, something RSA lacks.

On the other hand, RSA-based signature systems are available now. Several technical issues still have to be ironed out before usable DSS systems appear. Unfortunately, most RSA implementations that are incorporated into standard operating systems are based on 512-bit keys. RSA keys that are this small are no longer safe against attackers with large resources, including security agencies of large governments; large corporations; and even the hacker community, if it puts on a big effort. Were Newt Gingrich or the president of Exxon to publish a 512-bit public key, I would expect to see it cracked in a year. If you plan to use RSA for anything important, try to get 1,024-bit keys.

I hope that software manufacturers eventually will include both DSS and RSA electronic signatures in their systems. Users then could choose which method they want to use; paranoid users could sign both ways. For all the hocus-pocus, signature software is much simpler than, say, full-motion-video compression, and I'll bet that the home computers of the future will play anyone's multimedia platters.

Should you even have an electronic signature?

Years ago, when I was visiting Japan, my hosts gave me a *chop:* a carved wooden stamp with my name translated into Japanese kanji characters. They offered to take me to some office in Tokyo where I could register my chop. For a few yen, I would get a nicely calligraphed certificate I could frame. The only problem was that the chop would then become "official," and anyone who stole it could sign my name in a legally binding way. I declined.

Figure 5-1: The author's chop.

An electronic signature is much like a chop, with one big difference you might notice if your chop were stolen: Your private key and its enabling pass phrase could be copied off your computer in several ways, and you would never know until it was too late.

Try a simple experiment. With a pen, write "Internet Secrets Private-Key Awareness Test" on a blank 3 1/2-inch floppy disk. Try for a week to keep the disk under your total personal control. Keep it in your pocket during the day; put it under your pillow at night; don't forget to take it into the shower with you. If you do have to put it down, be sure to hide it well or lock it up. At the end of the week, think about who could possibly have had access to it while you weren't watching. Then ask yourself, "Do I want to add to my life a physical object that will require this kind of attention as long as I live?"

Some public-key schemes encrypt the private key with a pass phrase. This pass phrase makes theft more difficult, but difficult enough that you can be careless with your key disk. So think carefully before issuing a public electronic signature. Unless you really need one, you might wait until better technology is available — for example, secure PCMCIA key cards. If you can't resist or if your work requires you to have an electronic signature, be prepared to protect it as your most important possession.

One-time pads

Most cryptographic products come with the same basic warranty: "The cryptographic community has tried for years to break it, without success. Therefore, we're pretty sure that it can't be broken." One exception stands out. One-time pads, handled properly, are absolutely unbreakable. Period. In addition, the patent on the one-time pad — No. 1310719 — was issued in 1917 and expired long ago. Making money on a product that anyone can copy is hard. As a result, most cryptographers view one-time pads with the same disdain that witch doctors reserve for antibiotics.

So what is a one-time pad? Both you and the other guy have a large supply of random bits. You take your message and exclusive-or (xor) the message bits with a string of those random bits that is as long as your message. Then you send the xored bit to the other guy, along with a header that tells him what bits you used. He xors the coded message with the same string of random bits, and your message appears, like magic. (The xor of two bits is 0 if the bits are the same and 1 if they are different.)

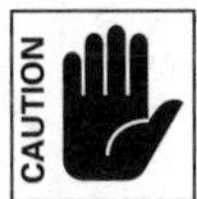

The following paragraphs, however, discuss a few big caveats about one-time pads.

Making random bits isn't easy. Most computers come with a software function, named something like random or rand, that is supposed to produce random numbers based on a starting value called a *seed.* This type of software is the cryptographic equivalent of an apple with a razor blade hidden inside. Codes based on these types of generators are not secure. Never, never, *never* use a computer's built-in random-number generator to make a one-time-pad crypto system.

Creating truly random numbers is challenging. One way is to digitize a physically random process, such as thermal noise. Great care is required to avoid bias or spurious nonrandom inputs. Fortunately, the one-time pad does not require that the bits be random — just that they be unpredictable enough that an adversary cannot recover useful information from the coded data. For a practical recipe for making bits that are unpredictable enough for most needs, see the following sidebar, "Creating unpredictable bits."

Creating unpredictable bits

You need a computer with audio input, such as a Macintosh, a Sun workstation, or a PC with a sound card. Follow these steps:

1. Set up the computer so that it can record the sound from a TV set tuned to an unused channel.

   You should hear a rushing sound, with no voices or music in the background.

2. Record enough of this noise to fill a sound file that's big enough for your needs.

3. Play back the sound file to ensure that the recording level is right and that the file sounds like uniform noise throughout.

(continued)

(continued)

If you have spectrum-analyzer software available, use it to take a look at the file.

4. Encrypt the sound file with DES, preferably using one of the feedback modes. Use any random key.

The resulting file will be not quite random, but it should be unpredictable enough for most applications. For extra credit, write a program in Basic (or whatever) that takes one bit from each byte of the DESed sound file and then writes the bits to a new file. The resulting bits should be truly random.

You need some way to get the bits to the other guy before you can communicate. The traditional method is to put a disk or tape that contains the pad bits in a bag that cannot be opened without detection and then to deliver the bag by trusted courier.

You must never use the same code bits twice. If you do, both messages are fairly easy to break. As a practical matter, therefore, each pair of stations that want to communicate must have their own pad. This arrangement is OK for a few people who need to communicate, but it gets tough to administer for a large network.

You have to protect the pads at all times. If someone finds your pad, they can decrypt all your old messages as well as any new ones.

Other encryption systems share some of these weaknesses; all these systems require you to keep a key of some sort secret. If that key is compromised, all data that was encrypted with that key is compromised as well. With a one-time pad system, however, you can destroy keying material as it is used.

In addition, all crypto systems require some form of key distribution. True, public-key systems do not require that the keys you distribute be kept secret, but they still must be transmitted in a trustworthy way. In practice, this arrangement can be almost as big a pain in the neck as periodically dispatching a trusted courier.

All things considered, a one-time-pad system may be worth the extra trouble in situations in which absolute maximum security is required.

Protects against Class 5 threats, if used properly.

Ten crypto-communications facts you can totally ignore

- *Code* does not mean the same thing as *cipher.*
- *TEMPEST* is only the code name for measures to prevent radio-frequency information leaks. The code name for methods of intercepting those leaks is different, but even that name is a secret.
- Clipper, Capstone, Tessera, and Skipjack all refer to different parts of the U.S. government's proposed key-escrow standard. Everyone now calls the whole mess the Clipper chip.
- The actual Clipper chip was an early RISC processor, developed in the 1980s by a computer-aided-design company called Intergraph. This chip has nothing to do with the current cryptographic business.
- *PCMCIA* refers to a joint committee of the Personal Computers Manufacturers Association and the Computer Industry Association. The term has nothing to do with the Central Intelligence Agency. (Rumor has it that PCMCIA really stands for People Can't Memorize Computer-Industry Acronyms.)
- The PCMCIA committee is to change the (ugly) name of PCMCIA cards to PC Card. People remember the PCMCIA name.
- DES requires that the algorithm be implemented in hardware, not in software. Even the feds don't seem to care anymore.
- P may or may not equal NP. This branch of mathematical complexity theory is almost irrelevant to practical cryptography.
- *Baud* does not mean the same thing as *bits per second.* It should, though.
- A serial port is technically not RS-232 if it doesn't use a 25-pin D-shell connector. Tough.

What about anonymous remailers?

Several sites on the Internet offer anonymous remailing services. If you are unwilling to reveal your true identity when sending mail or posting news, you can send your message to one of these sites. The sites strip off all identifying information in your message's header and then repost the message with a randomly assigned pseudonym. Some sites allow recipients to use the pseudonym in replying to you.

How safe are these services? Here's what the one in Finland, `anon.penet.fi`, writes:

> Short of having everyone run a public-key crypto system such as PGP, there is no way to protect users from malicious administrators. You have to trust my personal integrity. Worse, you have to trust the administrators on every mail-routing machine on the way, as the message only becomes anonymous once it reaches my machine. Malicious sysadmins and/or crackers could spy on SMTP mail channels, sendmail queues, and mail logs. But as there are more than 3,000 messages being anonymized every day, you have to be pretty perverted to scan everything. . . .

Let's get real. Electronic intelligence services are omnivorous. They specialize in collecting information that can be used years later. They keep warehouses full of tapes of intercepted traffic, in the hope that some snippet will come in handy someday. With so many messages from Netters letting their electronic hair down, remailers are a juicy target. You can bet that more than one foreign security agency must be collecting all the e-mail going to and coming from every remailer it can tap, including the mail before it is anonymized. One good lead to someone who can be compromised ten years from now would be worth the effort. Sorry, but that's the world we live in.

Choosing a password or pass phrase

Most people do not think of themselves as being cryptographers. Yet almost everyone who uses the Internet makes at least one crucial cryptographic decision: choosing a password. A poorly chosen password or pass phrase can make your data almost as vulnerable as though you had no password at all.

The most common password is the one you use to log in to your account. The fact that most users do a poor job of choosing their passwords makes login a favorite entry path for hackers. According to legend, a security survey once found that a large percentage of large, multiuser computers have at least one user account with "Susan" as its password.

What constitutes a poor login password?

A poor password has at least one of the following problems:

- Any proper name
- Any word that is in any dictionary
- Your user ID or a variant, such as your user ID spelled backward
- Any birthday
- The same character repeated several times (zzzzzzz, for example)
- Any character string shorter than six characters
- A sample password you saw in an article about picking good passwords
- A default password that comes with your computer

What constitutes a good login password?

A good password should contain enough randomness to be secure, but it should still be easy to remember:

- An unrelated pair of words chosen at random from a dictionary, preferably separated by a special character or number (hotbed%esquire, for example).
- A pronounceable string of nonsense phrases at least eight characters long (roshanitewa, for example). Some computers generate these types of passwords for you.
- A random string in the format of California license plate numbers: number–letter–letter–letter–number–number–number (9NSL656, for example). But don't use your own license-plate number!
- Initials and a phone number — not those of someone you ever call — chosen at random from the phone book (PTR5552368, for example).

Login passwords can be fairly short because most operating systems have built-in limits on login attempts that prevent hackers from using a computer to make millions of attempts. Older UNIX systems kept a hashed version of all users' passwords in a public file — an arrangement that enabled hackers to copy the files to their home computers and then guess passwords at leisure. This practice is falling out of favor, and the UNIX systems that were built this way have lots of other holes, anyway.

A string that is acceptable for use as a login password generally will not do at all as an encryption key. Encryption presumes that attackers have access to the encrypted material and can make as many attempts to crack it as they can afford. A simple rule of thumb is that a key you can memorize is not secure enough. For example, DES has a 56-bit key. This arrangement permits 2^{56} possible keys — about 7×10^{16} combinations. California-license-plate-number format permits $10^4 \times 26^3$ combinations — about 1.8×10^8, which is a reduction in strength by a factor of 4×10^8. If a hacker knows that you are using DES with short keys, she can break your code with a home computer!

A strong DES code requires a key that is 14 hex digits (0–9, A–F) long — FE2 A893 10B B0C4, for example. Such a key is, obviously, hard to remember and even worse when you try to follow the sound advice to change your keys often. One solution to this problem is to use a crypto system that accepts a long pass phrase and hashes it to form a key. A pass phrase typically is a long phrase in the speaker's natural language. The bad news is that natural languages, such as English, are so redundant that English sentences contain only about one bit of randomness per letter. This means that a pass phrase for a 56-bit key should contain at least 56 letters or about 12 words. For a 128-bit key, you need at least 26 words.

How to pick a pass phrase

You may think that your favorite quote from *The Catcher in the Rye* is one that no one else would ever think of. You're probably wrong. Serious bad guys collect lists of favorite pass phrases, and you may be more predictable than you think. It is even a bad idea to use a quote from a book you own; it's not that hard to break into your home and photograph your bookshelf.

A good way to choose a pass phrase is to go to your local library. Choose an aisle where you are alone, and grab a random book. Don't even look at the title. Take the book, close your eyes, open the book to a page, and put your finger on that page. Open your eyes, and write down the sentence that's under your finger. Then go to another aisle and choose a second sentence, using the same method. For extra security, add a third sentence. Your pass phrase is the sentences you wrote down, strung together. Memorize your new pass phrase, and either eat the paper or put it in a safe place (see the sidebar "Should I write down my password or pass phrase?"). Remember that most encryption products require you to type your pass phrase with the same punctuation, spacing, and capitalization every time you use it.

Should I write down my password or pass phrase?

Most authorities say that you should never write down your password. I demur. Most of us just are not that confident of our ability to memorize passwords, especially passwords for infrequently used accounts. At best, losing a password means the hassle of getting a new one from the system administrator; at worst, it could mean missing a deadline or even losing data. As a result, even people who know better use the same weak password on all their accounts and never change it.

If writing down your passwords will get you to pick stronger passwords and to change them more often, I say go ahead, but keep them in a safe place. What's a safe place? Your wallet; a secret hiding place at home; or, if you have a great many paper files, a random file folder (not one labeled "Passwords") are suitable for accounts of moderate security (Class 2 threats). For high-security situations, a good safe that's guarded or alarmed 24 hours a day or a bank safe-deposit box are possible choices.

How to create random passwords and keys

Several programs for creating random passwords and keys are available. The better programs use a good source of random information, such as microsecond measurements of the time between your keystrokes while you are typing. Generally, these programs work well enough, but they have problems, including the following:

- You may not have a copy when you need one.
- Someone could tamper with the copy of the program you have.
- Someone else might be able to watch what you are doing if you run the program on a networked machine or if he can take advantage of TEMPEST emissions.

Here's a manual technique that's suitable for generating keys and passwords as random as anything the NSA can come up with. All you need is a pair of dice (preferably of different colors) and Table 5-1.

Table 5-1 Password Selection Chart

					Syllables	
Black Die	***White Die***	***Alphanumeric***	***Numeric***	***Hex***	***Consonants***	***Vowels***
1	1	A	0	0	b	a
1	2	B	1	1	c	e
1	3	C	2	2	d	i
1	4	D	3	3	f	o
1	5	E	4	4	g	u
1	6	F	5	5	h	y

Black Die	White Die	Alphanumeric	Numeric	Hex	Syllables	
					Consonants	Vowels
2	1	G	6	6	j	
2	2	H	7	7	k	
2	3	I	8	8	l	
2	4	J	9	9	m	
2	5	K	0	A	n	
2	6	L	1	B	p	
3	1	M	2	C	qu	
3	2	N	3	D	r	
3	3	O	4	E	s	
3	4	P	5	F	t	
3	5	Q	6	0	v	
3	6	R	7	1	w	
4	1	S	8	2	x	
4	2	T	9	3	z	
4	3	U	0	4	ch	
4	4	V	1	5	cr	
4	5	W	2	6	fr	
4	6	X	3	7	nd	
5	1	Y	4	8	ng	
5	2	Z	5	9	nk	
5	3	0	6	A	nt	
5	4	1	7	B	ph	
5	5	2	8	C	pr	
5	6	3	9	D	rd	
6	1	4	*	E	sh	
6	2	5	*	F	sl	
6	3	6	*	*	sp	
6	4	7	*	*	st	
6	5	8	*	*	th	
6	6	9	*	*	tr	

*Roll again.

For alphabetic passwords, use the alphanumeric column, and roll again if a number appears.

To use the table, you first must decide what format you want to use for your password: letters, numbers, hexadecimal values, pronounceable syllables, and so on. You also need some way to distinguish between the two dice. The table shows black and white dice, but any consistent method will do — different colors, different sizes, closest and farthest after being rolled, and so on.

Now roll the dice, and look up the value in the appropriate column. If the entry is *, roll again. If you want to use letters only, choose the alphanumeric column, and simply roll again if a numeric value turns up.

To create pronounceable syllables, alternate between the consonant and the vowel columns or use a third, distinguishable die. Don't put a vowel after the letters *qu.*

When you have a long-enough key or password, stop. That's all there is to it.

Top 10 Encryption Security Tips

Here are some tips for encryption security:

1. Always use randomly selected keys, passwords, and pass phrases. Never use dictionary words or your favorite literary quotes.
2. Never perform encryption, decryption, or key generation on a multiuser computer or on a computer connected to a network.
3. Don't connect your sensitive internal network to the Internet without a firewall.
4. The best way to perform encryption, decryption, or key generation is on a battery-powered laptop with no cables plugged in. Get a machine with PCMCIA (PC Card) slots.
5. Floppy disks, tapes, and hard disks that contain sensitive information are difficult to erase completely. Follow the disposal guidelines earlier in this chapter, in the sidebar called "How do I dispose of magnetic media that contains sensitive information?"
6. Spend ten times more money, time, and effort on physical security than you do on encryption.
7. Take security seriously, day in and day out. Don't be careless, and don't be cute.
8. If you are using DES for critical applications, start switching to a more secure method, such as triple DES.
9. Use smart cards for key storage and challenge-response login.
10. Be careful not to violate U.S. export laws if you are in the United States (or if you are a U.S. citizen who plans to come home).

Arnold G. Reinhold is a freelance consultant in Cambridge, Massachusetts. He studied mathematics at MIT and management at Harvard.

Privacy on the Net

by Deward Falk <falk@sun.com> and Arnold G. Reinhold <reinhold@world.std.com>

As use of the Internet explodes, concern over the privacy of electronic messaging has mounted. Security has always been an afterthought in the design of the numerous software and hardware modules that make up the Internet. And unlike spying on voice communications, where a human ultimately has to listen to each conversation, electronic messages can be easily intercepted, filtered, sorted, and filed away for future reference.

A major reason for the lack of Internet security has been that the United States government has strongly opposed widespread commercial availability of secure computer systems. For much of this century, the U.S. has used intercepted communications as a major source of intelligence on foreign and domestic activities that it considers potentially hostile, and it does not want to give up that strategic advantage. Other governments like to eavesdrop too, of course, but the U.S. is the world's largest source of computer systems, and it uses its laws to limit the export of secure computer systems. U.S. manufacturers avoid export hassles by keeping their products cryptographically inoffensive. As a result, the components on which the Internet is built are full of security holes.

Philip Zimmermann and his colleagues have attempted to rectify this problem by writing and disseminating an encryption program called PGP, which stands for "pretty good privacy." PGP is now available on the Internet for most computer platforms. It is free for noncommercial use.

PGP uses what is called *public key encryption,* which is a system where each user has two keys: a private key and a public key. Anybody can send you a private message by encrypting it with PGP using your public key, but someone can only decode the message if their copy of PGP has your private key. You give your public key to anyone who might want to talk to you, but you must keep your private key a secret.

While there is no mathematical proof that PGP's codes cannot be broken, PGP is considered by most experts to be very secure when used properly. See "Common Sense and Cryptography" earlier in this chapter for a discussion of cryptosystem security.

Most of the Internet community consider Phil a hero for his efforts, but the U.S government is not so happy. Phil has been investigated by a grand jury to determine whether he has violated the U.S. export ban. As of this writing he is awaiting possible indictment on felony charges. He could spend several years in prison.

Indicted or not, his legal bills are large. A defense fund has been established to help pay them. Details on how to contribute are given at the end of this article.

Signing messages

PGP has uses beyond simply encrypting secret messages; it can also be used to digitally "sign" outgoing messages with your private key. This means that you can send a message that anybody can read but only you could have created. A digital signature cannot be forged, and a signed document cannot be altered without invalidating the signature.

This latter property means that a digital signature can be used not only to sign a file, but also to protect it from alteration. For example, a valid digital signature on an executable file guarantees that the file is virus-free. (Unless, of course, it had viruses when it was signed.)

The signature feature can also be used with encrypted messages. For full security, you send a friend a message that has been both signed with your private key and encrypted with your friend's public key. Only your friend can read the message, and your friend knows that only you could have sent it.

Getting PGP

Because of U.S. export restrictions on cryptographic software, getting PGP is a little more complicated than getting most software packages. And PGP is covered by patents, causing further difficulty. The public key algorithm that PGP uses and IDEA, a nonpublic key encryption algorithm, are also covered by patents. The impact of these patents varies, depending on where you are — some patents are only valid in the U.S. — and whether you are using PGP commercially.

As a result of these restrictions, the latest versions of PGP are available only on special servers that go to some length to verify that you are in either the U.S. or Canada; they also ask you to agree to licensing terms. Typically, it's a three-step process:

1. You do an anonymous ftp to get a README file that details the site's procedures, the license agreements, and a password. You can download the PGP documentation at this point if you want to look at it before proceeding. It is also included with the PGP software itself.
2. You telnet to the site with the password you were given in step 1. You answer some questions that verify you are eligable to receive the software and that you agree to the license terms. You are then given the current name of the directory in which the actual files are stored.
3. You immediately ftp to this special directory and download the PGP files that are appropriate for your computer.

The special directory name is changed frequently — at MIT it's changed every half hour — so that people cannot get the PGP files from the servers without going through this rigmarole.

As this is written, the current U.S. version of free PGP is 2.6.2. Check the PGP FAQ, which is posted regularly on `alt.security.pgp` and is also archived at `rtfm.mit.edu` and other sites, for the most recent version. Versions are also available for a variety of computing platforms, including UNIX, DOS, Macintosh, Windows, and Amiga. For a full list, see the PGP FAQ.

The main U.S. and Canada distribution site for PGP is

```
net-dist.mit.edu      /pub/PGP/README
```

Other U.S. and Canada PGP distribution sites include

```
ftp.netcom.com        /pub/mp/mpj/README.MPJ
ftp.eff.org           /pub/Net_info/Tools/Crypto/README.Dist
ftp.csua.berkeley.edu    /pub/cypherpunks/pgp
```

Older versions of PGP have made it outside North America and are available worldwide on various Internet servers. PGP 2.6.i is the current recommended version. If you have friends outside the U.S. and Canada with whom you would like to communicate using PGP, they will have to obtain copies on their own. PGP 2.6.i is available over the Internet via anonymous ftp from the following:

```
ftp.demon.co.uk      /pub/pgp   /pub/mac/MacPGP
sable.ox.ac.uk       /pub/crypto/pgp/pc/pub
ftp.informatik.uni-hamburg.de      /pub/virus/crypt/pgp
ftp.funet.fi         /pub/crypt
```

If you can access the World Wide Web, look at any of the following:

```
http://web.mit.edu/network/pgp-form.html
http://www.eff.org/pub/Net_info/Tools/Crypto/
http://www.ifi.uio.no/~staalesc/PGPVersions.html
http://www.mantis.co.uk/pgp/pgp.html
```

If you are on CompuServe, enter GO NCSAFORUM and follow the instructions there to access Library 12: Export Controlled.

You can also buy a commercial version of PGP from a company called ViaCrypt. They can be reached at

ViaCrypt Products
9033 N. 24th Ave., Ste. 7
Phoenix AZ 85021-2847

Phone: 602-944-0773
Fax: 602-943-2601
Internet: `viacrypt@acm.org`
CompuServe: 70304,41

Orders may be placed by calling 800-536-2664 from 8:30 a.m. – 5:00 p.m. MST, M–F.

The one place you can't get PGP is directly from Phil Zimmermann.

Getting Started

After downloading and unzipping your copy of PGP, you need to do a series of steps to set it up. The following instructions are oriented to DOS users. Instructions for UNIX are similar. Macintosh users have available a special front end called MacPGP. It comes with its own instructions.

Here's a quick tour of setting up PGP:

1. Take a while to read the documentation that comes with PGP. While people are working on front ends to make PGP more user friendly, it is still a somewhat complicated program to use.

2. Assign a place for your keyrings.

   Keyrings are files where keys are stored. There are two keyrings in PGP: the public keyring, PUBRING.PGP; and your secret keyring that must be kept safe, SECRING.PGP.

   Normally, you keep your keyrings with the rest of PGP — either on your diskette, which you keep in the safe guarded by wolves, or on your hard disk, guarded by a pass phrase.

   If you like, you can choose separate locations for the executable and your keyrings. For example, it's common to keep PGP on your hard disk but to keep your keyrings on a diskette stored in a safe place. In this case, copy config.txt to the diskette along with the keyrings. PGP will create the other files it needs.

   In either case, you set your PGPPATH environment variable so that PGP can find the files it needs. Add these lines to your DOS autoexec.bat file:

   ```
   SET PGPPATH=C:\PGP                (pgp and keyrings on hard disk)
   SET PATH=C:\PGP;%PATH%
   SET TZ=EST5EDT
   ```

   or

   ```
   SET PGPPATH=A:\                   (keyrings on diskette)
   SET PATH=C:\PGP;%PATH%
   SET TZ=EST5EDT
   ```

   or

   ```
   SET PGPPATH=A:\                   (pgp and keyrings on diskette)
   SET TZ=EST5EDT
   ```

   The first line tells PGP where to find the keyrings and CONFIG.TXT. The second line tells your system where to find PGP. The third line specifies the time zone; see DOC\SETUP.DOC for a more complete list.

   Now, reboot your system.

3. Create your own public and private key pair:

   Type **pgp -kg** and press Enter. PGP will prompt you for the rest.

Be prepared to choose a user ID that will be associated with the key; the preferred form is "First-name Last-name <email@address>". Also be prepared to give PGP a pass phrase, which you must memorize. See "Common Sense and Cryptography" earlier in this chapter for advice on choosing a pass phrase.

4. Add other people's public keys to your keyring.

   ```
   pgp -ka keys.asc
   ```

   will add a few keys that were provided with the release. I cannot vouch for them, but you'll notice that the owners of these keys have vouched for each other.

   Other people will give you their public keys as short files; newkey.asc, for example. Give the command

   ```
   pgp -ka newkey.asc
   ```

   which says add newkey.asc to the keyfile. You will be asked if you want to certify this key (that is, vouch for it.). Do not do so unless you know the person and he or she personally handed you the keyfile on diskette.

   It's a good idea to verify a public key with the owner. See the section on fingerprints in DOC\PGPDOC2.TXT for instructions on how to do this.

5. Admire your public key ring. Type **pgp -kv** to view all the keys in your public keyring.

   ```
   pgp -kvv
   ```

   will display information on who has certified each key.

6. Give your public key to other people. Enter the command

   ```
   pgp -kxa "your name" yourname.asc
   ```

   where "your name" is your user name as you gave it when you created your key in step 3. This creates the file YOURNAME.ASC, which you then give to your friends, post to the net, or publish in the paper. This enables anybody who has a copy to send you mail.

7. Send someone a secret message.

   First, you need the person's public key in your keyring (see step 4). Put your message in a file, such as a textfile, and give the command

   ```
   pgp -esat textfile "Their Name"
   ```

   This will prompt you for your password and so forth and will then create the file TEXTFILE.ASC, encrypted and signed by you, suitable for mailing.

   The switches `-esat` in the prededing pgp command have the following meanings:

   e — encrypt

   s — sign

   a — ascii output

   t — files are text: handle cr/nl accordingly.

- Sign a document.

  ```
  pgp -sat textfile
  ```

- Sign a file separately.

  Sometimes, you want the signature and the signed document to be broken into separate files. This is how you protect a binary file from viruses and tampering.

  ```
  pgp -sba binfile
  ```

  This will produce a new file, named binfile.asc, which is the signature to binfile. Any modifications to binfile will invalidate the signature.

  ```
  s - sign
  b - break signature from file
  a - ascii output
  ```

- Verify a signature.

  ```
  pgp signed.fil
  ```

  PGP will verify the signature on this document. You will also be asked where to put the output file. The output file is the actual signed document.

A bug has been found in cleartext signatures from previous versions of PGP. The line

```
-----BEGIN PGP SIGNED MESSAGE-----
```

is meant to be followed by a blank line. A signed document can be tampered with by adding some text in front of that blank line.

Always examine the *output* of PGP when verifying a signed document. The input can be tampered with, but the output cannot.

8. Verify a separate signature.

   ```
   cd zipfiles                                   (DOS)
   pgp pgp262i.asc pgp262i.zip
   ```

   You will be informed that there is a good signature from one Jeffrey I. Schiller. (He's at MIT.) You will also be warned that Jeffrey I. Schiller's signature hasn't been certified by anybody you know. This is normal.

9. Get your key certified by somebody.

   Extract a copy of your key by entering

   ```
   pgp -kxa yourname yourname.ask
   ```

   Give yourname.asc to a friend who has PGP. That person adds your key to her keyring by typing

   ```
   pgp -ka yourname.asc
   ```

   PGP will ask your friend if she wants to certify this key. She answers yes this time and enters her personal password. She now extracts a fresh copy of your key by typing

   ```
   pgp -kx yourname yourname.asc
   ```

and gives it back to you. You add it back into your keyring with

```
pgp -ka yourname.asc
```

and you now have a signature on your key. From now on, anybody who knows your friend, trusts her, and has a copy of her public key will know that your public key is legitimate.

Naturally, you'll want to return the favor and sign her key.

10. Get your key certified remotely.

    Suppose your friend is a long distance away, but you still want to exchange signatures. Simply send your key to your friend by mail. She adds it to her keyring as before, but *doesn't* certify it because she has no way to know the key wasn't tampered with in the mail.

    Both of you get the key's "fingerprint" by typing **pgp -kvc yourname**.

    This will print a list of 16 hex numbers. Call your friend on the phone, recognize her voice, and read the 16 numbers. If this matches what she has, she knows she has a legitimate copy of your key. She now signs your key **pgp -ks yourname**.

    Now she extracts your key and mails it to you as before.

11. For quick help at any time, type **pgp -h** and press Enter.

12. For more information, send help mail to public key servers.

    Public key servers are machines on the Internet that are used to distribute keys. You place your public key on a public key server so that anybody may retrieve it. You retrieve other people's keys for yourself. For more info, send mail to one of these addresses with the single word *help* in the subject line.

    ```
    pgp-public-keys@pgp.iastate.edu
    public-key-server@pgp.ai.mit.edu
    pgp-public-keys@demon.co.uk
    ftp: ftp.demon.co.uk:/pub/pgp/pubring.pgp (Updated daily)
    pgp-public-keys@cs.tamu.edu
    pgp-public-keys@chao.sw.oz.au
    pgp-public-keys@jpunix.com
    pgp-public-keys@dsi.unimi.it
    ```

    This list was (relatively) up-to-date as of June 1994. See also doc\keyserv.doc or the PGP FAQ.

    If you have Internet capabilities, you can finger <keyid>@wasabi.io.com to get an immediate response. Use `finger help@wasabi.io.com` for more info. There is also a World Wide Web key server. See `http://martigny.ai.mit.edu/~bal/pks-toplev.html`.

13. For the Clinically Paranoid: readme.doc points out the possibility that PGP has been tampered with. To circumvent this, PGP has been PGP-signed by Jeffrey I. Schiller `<jis@mit.edu>`. Jeffrey Schiller is one of the developers of PGP.

    Now, read readme.doc, doc\setup.doc, and everything else in the docs directory.

Legal Notes

The U.S. government considers cryptographic materials to be equivalent to munitions. It is illegal to export copies of PGP outside of the United States without a license. ViaCrypt says that it has permission to export its version of PGP for majority-owned U.S. companies for use between their offices in most countries and offices in the U.S.A. Check with them for details.

Use of PGP may be illegal in some countries, including France.

PGP 2.6 is licensed by RSA Data Systems Inc. (RSADSI) for non-commercial use; you can read the licensing agreements in the documentation. This makes PGP 2.6 the first free *and* legal version of the program (there were free versions and legal versions before, but no one version was both.)

Do not use PGP 2.6 for commercial purposes. Purchase ViaCrypt PGP instead; ViaCrypt has licenses from RSADSI and the owners of the IDEA patent to sell the patented technology for commercial use. Do not charge money for PGP 2.6, other than media costs.

For legal reasons, PGP 2.6 messages cannot be read by earlier versions of PGP. Patches for earlier versions may become available to fix this problem, but it's simpler to upgrade those earlier versions to 2.6.

How to Contribute to Phil Zimmermann's Legal Defense Fund

Make your check or money order payable to *Philip L. Dubois, Attorney Trust Account, not* to Phil Zimmermann. Mail the check or money order to

Philip Dubois
2305 Broadway
Boulder, CO 80304
(Phone: 303-444-3885)

You can also make a donation by Internet mail using your VISA or MasterCard. Worried about snoopers intercepting your e-mail? Don't worry — use PGP.

Simply compose a message in plain ASCII text giving the following: the recipient (Philip L. Dubois, Attorney Trust Account); the bank name of your VISA or MasterCard; the name that appears on your card (yours, preferably); a telephone number at which you can be reached in case of a problem; the card number; the date the card expires; and, most important, the amount you wish to donate.

Then use PGP to encrypt and ASCII-armor the message using Phil Dubois's public key, printed below and also in the file pzdf.txt on the disk included with this book. You can also sign the message if you like. E-mail the output file to Phil Dubois (dubois@csm.org). Please be sure to use a Subject: line reading something like "Phil Zimmermann Defense Fund" so it will be decrypted right away.

Here is Phil Dubois's public key:


```
-----BEGIN PGP PUBLIC KEY BLOCK-----
Version: 2.7

mQCNAiyaTboAAAEEAL3DOizygcxAe6OyfcuMZh2XnyfqmLKFDAoXO/FJ4+d2frw8
5TuXc/k5qfDWi+AQCdJaNVT8jlg6bSOHD55gLoV+b6VZxzIpHWKqXncA9iudfZmR
rtx4Es82n8pTBtxa7vcQPhCXfjfl+lOMrICkRuD/xB/9X1/XRbZ7C+AHeDONAAUR
tCFQaGlsaXAgTC4gRHVib2lzIDxkdWJvaXNAY3NuLm9yZz6JAJUCBRAsw4TxZXmE
uMepZtOBATOOA/9IoCBZLFpF9lhV1+epBi49hykiHefRdQwbHmLa9kOOguepdkyF
i8kqJLEqPEUIrRtiZVHiOLLwkTRrFHV7q9lAuETJMDIDifeV1O/TGVjMiIFGKOuN
dzByyidjqdlPFtPZtFbzffi9BomTb8O3xm2cBomxxqsV82U3HDdAXaY5Xw==
=5uit
-----END PGP PUBLIC KEY BLOCK-----
```


Conclusion

For better or for worse, Phil Zimmermann's PGP has started a revolution. PGP is the first product that offers the general public protection for its data and messages. With PGP, that protection is

- affordable
- usable
- cryptographically strong
- legal (more or less)
- reliable
- available worldwide

Other standards, proposals, technologies, and products will have to struggle to catch up with PGP.

Edward Falk is computer graphics engineer at Sun Microsystems.

Arnold Reinhold is a freelance consultant in Cambridge, Massachusetts. He studied mathematics at MIT and management at Harvard.

Thinking about Firewalls

by Marcus J. Ranum <mjr@tis.com>

Trusted Information Systems, Inc.
Glenwood, Maryland

> Generally, he who occupies the field of battle first and awaits his enemy is at ease.—Sun Tzu

Many companies connect to the Internet, guarded by "firewalls," computers with software designed to prevent unauthorized access to their private networks. Despite this general goal, firewalls span a continuum between ease of use and security. This chapter describes some of the considerations and trade-offs in designing firewalls. A vocabulary for firewalls and their components is offered, to provide a common ground for discussion.

Why a Firewall?

> Against those skilled in the attack, an enemy does not know where to defend. Against the experts in defense, the enemy does not know where to attack.—Sun Tzu

The rationale for installing a firewall is almost always to protect a private network against intrusion. In most cases, the purpose of the firewall is to prevent unauthorized users from accessing computing resources on a private network, and often to prevent unnoticed and unauthorized export of proprietary information. In some cases, export of information is not considered important, but for many corporations that are connecting this is a major though possibly unreasoning concern. Many organizations will want simply to address the problem by not connecting to the Internet at all. This solution can be difficult to implement. If the private network is loosely administered or decentralized, a single enterprising individual with a high-speed dialup modem can quickly effect an Internet SLIP connection that can compromise the security of an entire network.

Often it is safe to say that a firewall needs to be put in place just to cover your bases. Even though an employee could compromise proprietary information by carrying it offsite on a DAT or floppy disk, the Internet represents a tangible threat, populated with dangerous "vandals" (see the following note). It could very easily cost a network manager his or her job if a break-in occurs via this route, even if the damage is no more extensive than could have been inflicted over a dialup line or by a disgruntled employee. Generally, for a would-be Internet site, the technical difficulties of implementing a firewall are greatly outweighed by the public relations problems of "selling" upper management on the idea. In summary, because Internet services are so highly visible, they are much more likely to require official oversight and justification.

The Vandals were a collection of tribes of roughneck barbarians who sacked Rome in the year 455 and looted it of all its portable wealth. Some use the term "hackers" to describe Internet snoopers, but "vandals," "crackers," or "jerks" is more appropriate.

Design Decisions

> Examine your environment.—Miyamoto Musashi

In configuring a firewall, the major design decisions with respect to security are often already dictated by corporate or organizational policy; specifically, a decision must be made as to whether security is more important than ease of use, or vice versa. There are two basic approaches that summarize the conflict:

- That which is not expressly permitted is prohibited.
- That which is not expressly prohibited is permitted.

The importance of this distinction cannot be overemphasized. In the former case, the firewall must be designed to block everything, and services must be enabled on a case-by-case basis only after a careful assessment of need and risk. This tends to impact users directly, and they may see the firewall as a hindrance. In the second case, the systems administrator is placed in a reactive mode, having to predict what kinds of actions the user population might take that would weaken the security of the firewall, and preparing defenses against them. This essentially pits the firewall administrator against the users in an endless arms race that can become quite fierce. Users can generally compromise the security of their logins if they try or aren't aware of reasonable security precautions. If the user has an open-access login on the firewall system itself, a serious security breach can result. The presence of user logins on the firewall system tends to magnify the problem of maintaining the system's integrity. A second important statement of policy is implicit in the "that which is not expressly permitted is prohibited" stance. This stance is more "fail-safe," since it accepts that the administrator is ignorant of what TCP ports are safe, or what holes may exist in the manufacturer's kernel or applications. Since many vendors are slow to publicize security holes, this is clearly a more conservative approach. It is an admission of the fact that what you don't know can hurt you.

Levels of Threat

> If ignorant both of your enemy and yourself, you are certain in every battle to be in peril.—Sun Tzu

There are several ways in which a firewall can fail or be compromised. While none of them are good, some are decidedly worse than others. Since the purpose of many firewalls is to block access, it's a clear failure if someone finds a loophole through it that permits the intruder to probe systems in the private network. An even more severe situation would result if someone managed to break into the firewall and reconfigure it such that the entire private network is reachable by anyone. For the sake of terminology, this type of attack will be referred to as "destroying" a firewall, as opposed to a mere "break-in." It is extremely difficult to quantify the damage that might result from a firewall's destruction. An important measure of how well a firewall resists threat is the information it gathers to help determine the course of an attack. The absolute worst thing that could happen is for a firewall to be completely compromised without any trace of how the attack took place. The best thing that can happen is for a firewall to detect an attack and inform the administrator politely that it is undergoing attack, but that the attack is going to fail.

One way to view the result of a firewall being compromised is to look at things in terms of what can be roughly termed as "zones of risk." In the case of a network that is directly connected to the Internet without any firewall, the entire network is subject to attack. This does not imply that the network is vulnerable to attack, but in a situation where an entire network is within reach of an untrusted network, it is necessary to ensure the security of every single host on that network. Practical experience shows that this is difficult, since tools like rlogin that permit user-customizable access control are often exploited by vandals to gain access to multiple hosts, in a form of "island-hopping" attack. In the case of any typical firewall, the zone of risk is often reduced to the firewall itself, or a selected subset of hosts on the network, significantly reducing the network manager's concerns with respect to direct attack. If a firewall is broken into, the zone of risk often expands again, to include the entire protected network. A vandal gaining access to a login on the firewall can begin an island-hopping attack into the private network, using it as a base. In this situation, there is still some hope, since the vandal may leave traces on the firewall and detected. If the firewall is completely destroyed, the private network can undergo attack from any external system, and reconstructing the course of an attack becomes nearly impossible.

In general, firewalls can be viewed in terms of reducing the zone of risk to a single point of failure. In a sense, this seems like a bad idea, since it amounts to putting all of one's eggs in a single basket, but practical experience implies that at any given time, for a network of nontrivial size, there are at least a few hosts that are vulnerable to break-in by even an unskilled attacker. Many corporations have formal host security policies that are designed to address these weaknesses, but it is sheer foolishness to assume that publishing policies will suffice. A firewall enhances host security by funneling attackers through a narrow gap where there's a chance of catching or detecting them first. The well-constructed medieval castle had multiple walls and interlocking defense points for exactly the same reason.

Firewalls and Their Components

> There may be a hundred combat postures, but there is only one purpose: to win.—Heiho Kaden Sho

In discussing firewalls, there is often confusion of terminology, since firewalls all differ slightly in implementation if not in purpose. Various discussions on Usenet indicate that the term "firewall" is used to describe just about any inter-network security scheme. For the sake of simplifying discussion, I propose some terminology to provide a common ground:

Screening router

A screening router is a basic component of most firewalls. A screening router can be a commercial router or a host-based router with some kind of packet filtering capability. Typical screening routers have the ability to block traffic between networks or specific hosts, on an IP port level. Some firewalls consist of nothing more than a screening router between a private network and the Internet.

Bastion host

Bastions are the highly fortified parts of a medieval castle; points that overlook critical areas of defense, usually having stronger walls, room for extra troops, and the occasional useful tub of boiling hot oil for discouraging attackers. A bastion host is a system identified by the firewall administrator as a critical strong point in the network's security. Generally, bastion hosts will have some degree of extra attention paid to their security, may undergo regular audits, and may have modified software.

Dual-homed gateway

Some firewalls are implemented without a screening router, by placing a system on both the private network and the Internet, and disabling TCP/IP forwarding. Hosts on the private network can communicate with the gateway, as can hosts on the Internet, but direct traffic between the networks is blocked. A dual-homed gateway like the one illustrated in Figure 5-2 is, by definition, a bastion host.

Figure 5-2: A typical dual-homed gateway.

Screened-host gateway

Possibly the most common firewall configuration is a screened-host gateway, illustrated in Figure 5-3. This is implemented using a screening router and a bastion host. Usually, the bastion host is on the private network, and the screening router is configured such that the bastion host is the only system on the private network that is reachable from the Internet. Often the screening router is configured to block traffic to the bastion host on specific ports, permitting only a small number of services to communicate with it.

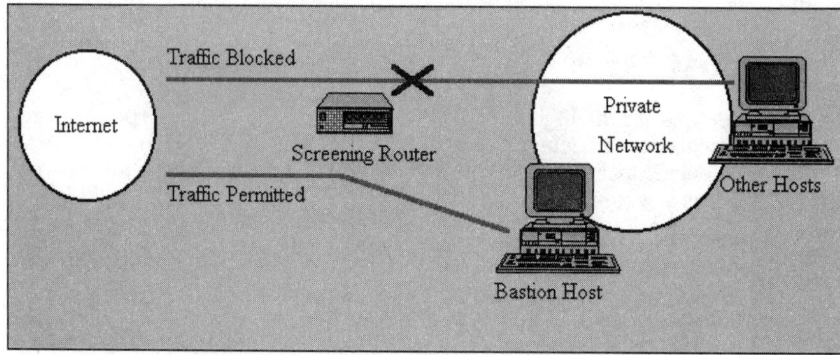

Figure 5-3: A typical screened-host gateway.

Screened subnet

In some firewall configurations, an isolated subnet is created, situated between the Internet and the private network. Typically, this network is isolated using screening routers, which may implement varying levels of filtering. Generally, as you can see in Figure 5-4, a screened subnet is configured such that both the Internet and the private network have access to hosts on the screened subnet but traffic across the screened subnet is blocked. Some configurations of screened subnets will have a bastion host on the screened network, to support either interactive terminal sessions or application-level gateways.

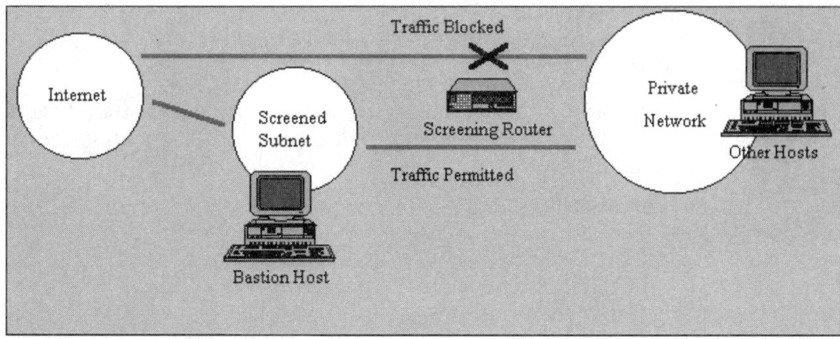

Figure 5-4: A typical screened subnet.

Application-level gateway

An application-level gateway is also called a *proxy gateway.* Much of the software on the Internet works in a store-and-forward mode—mailers and Usenet News collect input, examine it, and forward it. Application-level gateways are service-specific forwarders or reflectors, which usually operate in user mode rather than at a protocol level. Generally, these forwarding services, when running on a firewall, are important to the security of the whole. The famous sendmail hole that was exploited by the Morris Internet worm is one example of the kinds of security problems an application-level gateway can present. Other application-level gateways are interactive, such as the ftp and telnet gateways run on the Digital Equipment Corporation firewalls. In general, the term "application-level gateway" will be used to describe some kind of forwarding service that runs across a firewall and is a potential security concern. In general, crucial application-level gateways are run on some kind of bastion host.

Hybrid gateways

Hybrid gateways are the "something else" category in this list. Examples of such systems are hosts connected to the Internet but accessible only through serial lines connected to an ethernet terminal server on the private network. Such gateways may take advantage of multiple protocols or tunneling one protocol over another. Routers may maintain and monitor the complete state of all TCP/IP connections or somehow examine traffic to try to detect and prevent an attack. The AT&T corporate firewall is a hybrid gateway combined with a bastion host.[1]

Taking the components described above, we can accurately describe most of the forms that firewalls take and make some general statements about the kinds of security problems each approach presents. Assuming that a firewall fulfills its basic purpose of helping protect the network, it is still important to examine each type of firewall with respect to:

- **Damage control.** If the firewall is compromised, to what kinds of threats does it leave the private network open? If it is destroyed, to what kinds of threats does it leave the private network open?

- **Zones of risk.** How large is the zone of risk during normal operation? A measure of this is the number of hosts or routers that can be probed from the outside network.
- **Failure mode.** If the firewall is broken into, how easy is this to detect? If the firewall is destroyed, how easy is this to detect? In a postmortem, how much information is retained that can be used to diagnose the attack?
- **Ease of use.** How much of an inconvenience is the firewall?
- **Stance.** Is the basic design philosophy of the firewall "That which is not expressly permitted is prohibited" or is it "That which is not expressly prohibited is permitted"?

Firewalls Using Screening Routers

> In large-scale strategy, when the enemy embarks on an attack, if you make a show of strongly suppressing his technique, he will change his mind.—Miyamoto Musashi

Many networks are firewalled using only a screening router between the private network and the Internet. This type of firewall is different from a screened-host gateway in that there is usually direct communication permitted between multiple hosts on the private network and multiple hosts on the Internet. The zone of risk is equal to the number of hosts on the private networks and the number and type of services to which the screening router permits traffic. For each service provided via peer-to-peer connection, the size of the zone of risk increases sharply. Eventually, it is impossible to quantify. Damage control is difficult as well since the network administrator would need to regularly examine every host for traces of a break-in. If there is no regular audit, one must hope to stumble on a clue such as a mismatched system accounting record.[2]

Total destruction of the firewall tends to be very hard to trace or even to discover. If a commercial router (which does not maintain logging records) is used and the router's administrative password is compromised, the entire private network can be laid open to attack very easily. Cases are known where commercial routers have been configured with erroneous screening rules or have come up in some pass-through mode because of hardware or operator error. Generally, this configuration is a case of "That which is not expressly prohibited is permitted" as the ingenious user can fairly easily piggyback protocols to achieve a higher level of access than the administrator expects or wants. Given a collaborator on an external host, it is left as an exercise to the reader to implement a remote login stream protocol over Domain Name Service packets.

I have implemented just such a scheme, tunneling TCP/IP traffic through a firewall. Running over T1 lines, interactive session response is quite good, and users have complete access to telnet, rlogin, ftp, and the like. As PPP (Point-to-Point Protocol) becomes more widespread, so will this threat.

Screening routers are not the most secure solution, but they are popular since they permit fairly free Internet access from any point within the private network. Many consultants and network service providers offer screening routers in a "firewall" configuration. It is uncertain if the various trade-offs involved are clear to the customer; the author would not recommend use of a screening router to protect sensitive information or trade secrets, since screening routers are very permeable from the inside.

Dual-Homed Gateways

> It was Hannibal's principle to keep his forces united and to garrison but one single fortress.—Emperor Napoleon I

An often used and easy-to-implement firewall is the dual-homed gateway. Since it doesn't forward TCP/IP traffic, it acts as a complete block between the Internet and the private network. Its ease of use is determined by how the systems manager chooses to set up access — either by providing application gateways such as telnet forwarders or by giving users logins on the gateway host. If the former approach is taken, the stance of the firewall is clearly "That which is not expressly permitted is prohibited"; users can access only those Internet services for which there is an application gateway. If users are permitted logins, then, in the opinion of the author, the firewall's security is seriously weakened. During normal operation, the only zone of risk is the gateway host itself, since it is the only host that is reachable from the Internet. If there are user logins on the gateway host, and one of the users chooses a weak password or has the account otherwise compromised, the zone of risk expands to encompass the entire private network. From a standpoint of damage control, the administrator may be able to track the progress of an intruder, based on the access patterns of the compromised login, but a skillful vandal can make this quite difficult. If a dual-homed gateway is configured without direct user access, damage control can be somewhat easier, since the very fact that someone has logged in to the gateway host becomes a noteworthy security event. Dual-homed gateways have an advantage over screening routers from the standpoint that their system software is often easier to adapt to maintain system logs, hard copy logs, or remote logs. This can make a postmortem easier for the gateway host itself, but it may or may not help the network administrator identify what other hosts on the private network may have been compromised in an island-hopping attack.

Attacking a dual-homed gateway leaves the attacker a fairly large array of options. Since the attacker has what amounts to local network access if a login can be obtained, all the usual attacks that can be made over a local network are available. NFS-mounted file systems, weaknesses in .rhosts files, automatic software distribution systems, network backup programs, and administrative shell scripts—all may provide a toehold on systems on the internal network. Once a toehold is secured, it then provides a base from which to launch attacks back at the gateway itself. The weakest aspect of the dual-homed gateway is its failure mode. If the firewall is destroyed, a skillful attacker can reenable routing and throw the entire private network open to attack. In the usual UNIX-based dual-homed gateway, TCP/IP routing is often disabled by modifying a kernel variable named *ipforwarding*; if systems privileges can be obtained or stolen on the gateway, this variable can be changed. Perhaps this seems far-fetched, but unless great care is paid to monitoring the software revision levels and configuration on the gateway host, it is not improbable that a vandal with a copy of the release notes for the operating system version and a login can compromise the system.

Screened-Host Gateways

> Ground to which access is constricted, where the way out is tortuous, and where a small enemy force can strike my larger one is called "encircled."—Sun Tzu

Several articles have described screened-host gateways, and how to construct them [3,4]. Generally, the screened-host gateway is very secure, while remaining fairly easy to implement. Typically, a bastion host is configured on the private network, with a screening router between the Internet and the private network, which only permits Internet access to the bastion host. Since the bastion host is on the private network, connectivity for local users is very good, and problems presented by exotic routing configurations do not present themselves. If the private network is a virtual extended local area network (having no subnets or routing), as many are, the screened-host gateway will work without requiring any changes to the local network, as long as the local network is using a legitimately assigned set of network addresses. The zone of risk of a screened-host gateway is restricted to the bastion host and the screening router, and the security stance of the screened-host gateway is determined by the software running on that system. If an attacker gains login access to the bastion host, there is a fairly wide range of options for attacking the rest of the private network. In many ways, this approach is similar to the dual-homed gateway, sharing similar failure modes and design considerations with respect to the software running on the bastion host.

Screened Subnets

> When the enemy gets in an inconvenient position, do not let him look around.
> —Miyamoto Musashi

A screened subnet is usually configured with a bastion host as the sole point of access on the subnet. The zone of risk is small, consisting of that bastion host or hosts and any screening routers that make up the connections between the screened subnet, the Internet, and the private network. The ease of use and basic stance of the screened subnet will vary, but generally a screened subnet is appealing only for firewalls that are taking advantage of routing to reinforce the existing screening. This approach forces all services through the firewall to be provided by application gateways and places the stance strongly in the "That which is not expressly permitted is prohibited" category.

If a screened subnet-based firewall with inter-network routing blocked is attacked with an intent to destroy it, the attacker must reconfigure the routing on three networks, without disconnecting or locking himself out, and without the routing changes being noticed. No doubt this is possible, but it can be made very difficult by disabling network access to the screening routers, or by configuring the screening routers to permit access only from specific hosts on the private network. In this case, an attacker would need to break into the bastion host, then into one of the hosts on the private network, and then back out to the screening router—and would have to do it without setting off any alarms.

Another advantage of screened subnets is that they can be put in place in such a way that they hide any accidents of history that may linger on the private network. Many sites that would like to connect to the Internet are daunted by the prospect of re-addressing and re-subnetting existing networks. With a screened subnet with blocked inter-network routing, a private network can be connected to the Internet and changed gradually to new subnet and network addresses. In fact, this approach has been observed to significantly accelerate the adoption of new network addresses on loosely controlled private networks. Users will be more receptive to changing their host addresses if they can realize the benefits of Internet connectivity thereby, since hosts that are not correctly addressed cannot use the firewall properly. In most other respects, the screened subnet is very much dependent on the suite of software running on the bastion host. Screening a whole subnet provides functionality similar to the dual-homed gateway or screened-host gateway; it differs primarily in the extra level of complexity in routing and configuration of the screening routers.

Hybrid Gateways

> There is in guerrilla warfare no such thing as a decisive battle; there is nothing comparable to the fixed, passive defense that is a feature of orthodox war.
> —Mao Tse-tung

"Security through obscurity" is not sufficient in and of itself, but there is no question that an unusual configuration, or one that is hard to understand, is likely to give attackers pause, or to make them more likely to reveal themselves in the process of trying to figure out what they are facing. On the other hand, there is a real advantage to having a security configuration that is easy to understand, and therefore easier to evaluate and maintain. Since the hybrid gateway is mentioned here in the category of "something else," no attempt will be made to describe the indescribable. Some hypothetical hybrids may serve to show how hybrid gateways may differ from or be similar to the other types.

Let us postulate a hybrid gateway that consists of a box sitting on the Internet, which is capable of routing traffic but also maintains a complete notion of the state of every TCP connection, how much data have gone across it, where they originated, and their destination. Presumably, connections can be filtered based on arbitrarily precise rules, such as: "permit traffic between host A on the private network and all hosts on network B on the Internet via the telnet service if and only if the connection originated from host A between the hours of 9:00 A.M. and 5:00 P.M. and log the traffic." This sounds terrific, providing arbitrary control with great ease of use, but some problems simply refuse to go away. Consider that someone wishing to circumvent the firewall, who broke into the private network via an unguarded modem, may very easily set up a service engine that was piggybacked over the telnet port. This is actually a fairly easy firewall to destroy.

Another hybrid gateway may take advantage of various forms of protocol tunneling, hiding data for one protocol within the packets of another protocol. Suppose the requirement is to connect to the Internet with very tight restrictions, but that a high degree of connectivity is required between the private network and an external network that is somewhat trusted (for example, a corporate R&D department needs to be able to run X Windows applications on a supercomputer at another facility). The usual archetypal gateways discussed here could provide general purpose e-mail connectivity, but for secure point-to-point communications, an encrypted point-to-point virtual TCP/IP connection can be set up with the remote system, after users had authenticated themselves with a cryptographic smart card. This would be extremely secure, and might be made fairly easy to use, but it has the disadvantage that the protocol driver needs to be added to every system that wants to share communication. It is hard to make any guesses about the failure mode of such a system, but the zone of risk is neatly limited to all the hosts that are running the tunneling protocol driver, and to which the individual user has smart card access. Some of this might be implemented in hardware or in the routers themselves. In the future, it is likely that the rapid growth of the Internet will fuel more development in this area, and we will see various hybrid gateways arise. The basic issues surrounding configuring a firewall will probably remain the same as the ones discussed here.

Routers performing point-to-point encryption for specified networks are beginning to appear on the market. Until recently, the only demand for such hardware was for government applications, and most solutions employed Type I cryptography.

Other Firewall-Related Tools

> Subtle and insubstantial, the expert leaves no trace; divinely mysterious, he is inaudible.—Sun Tzu

There is active research and development on tools to aggressively seek out and identify weaknesses in an entire network, or to detect the patterns that may indicate when an attack is in progress. These tools range from the simple checklist[5] to complex "expert systems" with inference engines and elaborate rule bases. Many firewalls today run software that is designed to go forth and gather information relating to possible attacks and their origins, often using and abusing tools like finger and SNMP[6,7]. Unless true artificial intelligence is developed, however, these tools cannot guard against an unknown form of attack, since they cannot possibly match the creativity of a network vandal. While often billed as being "proactive," they are in fact reactive and generally will serve only to catch systems crackers armed with last year's bag of tricks. Catching the small fry is still worth doing, but it is likely that they are less of a threat than the fellow who is so eager to break into your network that he is doing research and development in new system-cracking techniques.

No Conclusions, but Observations

> Those skilled in war cultivate the Tao and preserve the laws and are therefore able to formulate victorious policies.—Sun Tzu

It is the privilege of a writer to use the last section of a publication to state his opinions and call them "conclusions." In dealing with firewalls, it is simply not reasonable to say that any particular approach is best, since there are so many factors that determine what the best firewall for a given situation may be. Cost, corporate policy, existing network technology, staffing, and intra-organizational politics may all easily outweigh the technical considerations presented here.

There are a few observations worth making about firewalls at a very general level. First, a firewall is a leverage-increasing device from a network management point of view. Rather than "all eggs in one basket," it can also be viewed as a trustworthy basket and a single point from which a very important security system can be controlled. The size of the zone of risk is crucial to the design; if it is small, security can be maintained and controlled easily, but if security is compromised, the damage can be more severe. The ideal is to have such strong host-based security that a firewall would be redundant. Systems administration costs and a hard dose of reality prevent this ideal from being obtainable.

A second important aspect of firewall building is that it is not something to undertake in a vacuum. Many sites are connected with a simple firewall consisting of a screening router and nothing more because someone told them that it was "secure enough." In setting up a firewall, one must trade off time and money, security, and risk. "Secure enough" depends largely on what you risk losing. Finally, it is important when approaching implementing a firewall to avoid the urge to start from scratch. System security is a lot like pregnancy; one is seldom only broken into a little bit, and it only takes a little mistake or a moment of inattention to find oneself in a delicate position. Leaning on the experiences of others and learning from their mistakes and successes is very important. Setting up a firewall is definitely an area where having a wide background of experience to draw upon is important. The vandals on the network have a wide background of experience to draw upon as well, and a firewall administrator must communicate with others and keep up to date on other firewall-related happenings on the network. Static defenses do not work unless they keep up with emerging tricks of the trade, or one's firewall may be the next Maginot Line.

The purpose of this chapter is not to discourage companies from connecting to the Internet. The Internet is an incredibly valuable resource, one which will in the coming years completely change the way people work and communicate on a global level. The benefits of connection far outweigh the costs, but it is wise to reduce the costs and potential costs as much as possible, by being aware of the dangers and being as protected as is necessary. The purpose of this paper is not to sow "fear, uncertainty, and doubt" in order to sell any particular firewall or software. If the author has succeeded to any degree in describing some of the considerations and trade-offs in setting up a firewall, this paper has been a success, and readers are left to their own devices to determine how best to proceed.

References

[1] Bill Cheswick, "The Design of a Secure Internet Gateway," *USENIX Proceedings*. April 1990. Available by ftp from `research.att.com: /dist/internet_security/gateway.ps`

[2] Clifford Stoll, *The Cuckoo's Egg*, Doubleday, 1989

[3] Smoot Carl-Mitchell and John Quarterman, "Building Internet Firewalls," *UNIX World*, February 1992

[4] Simpson Garfinkel and Gene Spafford, *Practical UNIX Security*, O'Reilly and Associates, 1991

[5] Dan Farmer, "COPS and Robbers, UN*X System Security," Internet software. Available by ftp from `cert.sei.cmu.edu: /pub/cops`

[6] Bill Cheswick, "An Evening with Berferd in which a Cracker is Lured, Endured, and Studied," *USENIX Proceedings*, Jan 20, 1990. Available by ftp from `research.att.com: /dist/internet_security/berferd.ps`

[7] Marcus J. Ranum, "An Internet Firewall," proceedings of World Conference on Systems Management and Security, 1992. Available by ftp from `decuac.dec.com: /pub/docs/firewall/firewall.ps`.

Using Firewalls on the Internet

by Marcus J. Ranum <mjr@tis.com>

Trusted Information Systems, Inc., Glenwood, Maryland

Most corporate networks attached to the Internet are now connected via firewalls. Here we look at some of the details of an Internet firewall setup.

What a Firewall Can Protect Against

Some firewalls permit only e-mail traffic through them, thereby protecting the network against any attacks other than attacks against the e-mail service. Other firewalls provide less strict protections, blocking services that are known to be problems.

Generally, firewalls are configured to protect against unauthenticated interactive logins from the "outside" world. This, more than anything, helps prevent vandals from logging into machines on your network. More elaborate firewalls block traffic from the outside to the inside but permit users on the inside to communicate freely with the outside. The firewall can protect you against any type of network-borne attack if you unplug it.

Firewalls are also important since they can provide a single "choke point" where security and audits can be imposed. Unlike in a situation where a computer system is being attacked by someone dialing in with a modem, the firewall can act as an effective "phone tap" and tracing tool.

What a Firewall Can't Protect Against

Firewalls can't protect against attacks that don't go through the firewall. Many corporations that connect to the Internet are very concerned about proprietary data leaking out of the company through that route. Unfortunately for those concerned, a magnetic tape can just as effectively be used to export data. Firewall policies must be realistic and reflect the level of security in the entire network. For example, a site with top-secret or classified data doesn't need a firewall at all: It shouldn't be hooking up to the Internet in the first place, or the systems with the really secret data should be isolated from the rest of the corporate network.

Firewalls can't protect very well against things like viruses. There are too many ways of encoding binary files for transfer over networks, and too many different architectures and viruses, to try to search for them all. In other words, a firewall cannot replace security consciousness on the part of your users. In general, a firewall cannot protect against data-driven attacks—attacks in which something is mailed or copied to an internal host where it is then executed. This form of attack has occurred in the past against various versions of Sendmail, the standard UNIX e-mail delivery program.

The Basic Design Decisions in a Firewall?

There are a number of basic design issues that should be addressed by the lucky person who has been tasked with the responsibility of designing, specifying, and implementing or overseeing the installation of a firewall.

The first and most important issue reflects the policy of how your company or organization wants to operate the system: Is the firewall in place explicitly to deny all services except those critical to the mission of connecting to the Net, or is the firewall in place to provide a metered and audited method of "queuing" access in a nonthreatening manner? There are degrees of paranoia between these positions; the final stance of your firewall may be the result more of a political decision than an engineering one.

The second is: What level of monitoring, redundancy, and control do you want? Having established the acceptable risk level (that is, how paranoid you are) by resolving the first issue, you can form a checklist of what should be monitored, permitted, and denied. In other words, you start by figuring out your overall objectives, and then you combine a needs analysis with a risk assessment and sort the almost always conflicting requirements out into a laundry list that specifies what you plan to implement.

The third issue is financial. We can't address this one here in anything but vague terms, but it's important to try to quantify any proposed solutions in terms of how much it will cost either to buy or to implement. For example, a complete firewall product may cost $100,000 at the high end or be free at the low end. The free option, of doing some fancy configuring on a Cisco or similar router, will cost nothing but staff time and cups of coffee. Implementing a high-end firewall from scratch may cost several person-months, which may equal $30,000 worth of staff salary and benefits. The systems management overhead is also a consideration. Building a home-brew system is fine, but it's important to build it so that it doesn't require constant and expensive fiddling. It's important, in other words, to evaluate firewalls in terms not only of what they cost now but also of continuing costs such as support.

On the technical side, there are a couple of decisions to make, based on the fact that for all practical purposes what we are talking about is a static traffic routing service placed between the network service provider's router and your internal network. The traffic routing service may be implemented at an IP level via something like screening rules in a router or at an application level via proxy gateways and services.

The decision to make here is whether to place an exposed stripped-down machine on the outside network to run proxy services for telnet, ftp, news, and the like, or whether to set up a screening router as a filter, permitting communication with one or more internal machines. There are plusses and minuses to both approaches, with the proxy machine providing a greater level of audit and potential security in return for increased cost in configuration and a decrease in the level of service that may be provided (since a proxy needs to be developed for each desired service). The old trade-off between ease of use and security comes back to haunt us with a vengeance.

Proxy Servers

A proxy server (sometimes referred to as an application gateway or forwarder) is an application that mediates traffic between a protected network and the Internet. Proxies are often used instead of router-based traffic controls to prevent traffic from passing directly between networks. Many proxies contain extra logging or support for user authentication. Since proxies must "understand" the application protocol being used, they can also implement protocol-specific security (for example, an ftp proxy may be configurable to permit incoming ftp and block outgoing ftp).

Proxy servers are application specific. In order to support a new protocol via a proxy, a proxy must be developed for it. SOCKS is a generic proxy system that can be compiled into a client-side application to make it work through a firewall. Its advantage is that it's easy to use, but it doesn't support the addition of authentication hooks or protocol-specific logging. For more information on SOCKS, see ftp.nec.com: /pub/security/socks.cstc. Users are encouraged to check the file "FILES" for a description of the directory's contents.

Low-Cost Packet-Screening Tools

The Texas AMU security tools include software for implementing screening routers (`ftp net.tamu.edu, pub/security/TAMU`). Karlbridge is a PC-based screening router kit (`ftp nisca.acs.ohio-state.edu, pub/kbridge`). A version of the Digital Equipment Corporation "screend" kernel screening software is available for BSD/386, NetBSD, and BSDI. Many commercial routers support screening of various forms.

Making DNS Work with a Firewall

Some organizations want to hide DNS names from the outside. Many experts disagree as to whether or not hiding DNS names is worthwhile, but if site or corporate policy mandates hiding domain names, this is one approach that is known to work.

This approach is one of many; it is useful for organizations that wish to hide their host names from the Internet. The success of this approach lies on the fact that DNS clients on a machine don't have to talk to a DNS server on that same machine. In other words, just because there's a DNS server on a machine, there's nothing wrong with (and there are often advantages to) redirecting that machine's DNS client activity to a DNS server on another machine.

First, you set up a DNS server on the bastion host that the outside world can talk to. You set this server up so that it claims to be authoritative for your domains. In fact, all this server knows is what you want the outside world to know: the names and addresses of your gateways, your wildcard MX records, and so forth. This is the "public" server.

Then, you set up a DNS server on an internal machine. This server also claims to be authoritative for your domains; unlike the public server, this one is telling the truth. This is your "normal" nameserver, into which you put all your "normal" DNS stuff. You also set this server up to forward queries that it can't resolve to the public server (using a "forwarders" line in /etc/named.boot on a UNIX machine, for example).

Finally, you set up all your DNS clients (the /etc/resolv.conf file on a UNIX box, for instance), including the ones on the machine with the public server, to use the internal server. This is the key.

An internal client asking about an internal host asks the internal server and gets an answer; an internal client asking about an external host asks the internal server, which asks the public server, which asks the Internet, and the answer is relayed back. A client on the public server works just the same way. An external client, however, asking about an internal host gets back the "restricted" answer from the public server.

This approach assumes that there's a packet-filtering firewall between these two servers that will allow them to talk DNS to each other, but otherwise restricts DNS between other hosts.

Another trick that's useful in this scheme is to employ wildcard PTR records in your IN-ADDR.ARPA domains. These cause an address-to-name lookup for any of your nonpublic hosts to return something like "unknown.YOUR.DOMAIN" rather than an error. This satisfies anonymous ftp sites like ftp.uu.net that insist on having a name for the machines they talk to. This may fail when talking to sites that do a DNS cross-check in which the host name is matched against its address and vice versa.

Note that hiding names in the DNS doesn't address the problem of host names "leaking" out in mail headers, news articles, and the like.

Making FTP Work through a Firewall

Generally, making ftp work through the firewall is done either by using a proxy server or by permitting incoming connections to the network at a restricted port range, and otherwise restricting incoming connections using something like "established" screening rules. The ftp client is then modified to bind the data port to a port within that range. This entails being able to modify the ftp client application on internal hosts.

A different approach is to use the ftp "PASV" option to indicate that the remote ftp server should permit the client to initiate connections. The PASV approach assumes that the ftp server on the remote system supports that operation. (See RFC1579 for more information.)

Other sites prefer to build client versions of the ftp program that are linked against a SOCKS library.

Making Telnet Work through a Firewall

The telnet protocol is generally supported either by using an application proxy or by simply configuring a router to permit outgoing connections using something like the "established" screening rules. Application proxies can be in the form of a stand-alone proxy running on the bastion host or in the form of a SOCKS server and a modified client.

Making Finger and Whois Work through a Firewall

Permit connections to the finger port only from trusted machines, which can issue finger requests in the form of:

```
finger user@host.domain@firewall
```

This approach works only with the standard UNIX version of finger. Some finger servers do not permit `user@host@host` fingering.

Many sites block inbound finger requests for a variety of reasons, the foremost being past security bugs in the finger server (the Morris Internet worm made these bugs famous) and the risk of proprietary or sensitive information being revealed in a user's finger information.

Making Gopher, Archie, and Other Services Work through a Firewall

This is still an area of active research in the firewall community. Many firewall administrators support these services only through the character-cell interface provided by telnet. Unfortunately, many of the sexier network services make connections to multiple remote systems, without transmitting any in-line information that a proxy could take advantage of, and often the newer information retrieval systems transmit data to local hosts and disks with only minimal security. There are risks that (for example) WAIS clients may request uuencoded files, which decode and modify security-related files in the user's home directory. At present, there is a lot of head-scratching going on between the firewall administrators, who are responsible for guarding the network perimeters, and the users, who want to take advantage of these very sexy and admittedly useful tools.

Using X Windows through a Firewall

X Windows is a very useful system, but unfortunately it has some major security flaws. Remote systems that can gain or spoof access to a workstation's X display can monitor keystrokes that users enter, download copies of the contents of their windows, and otherwise compromise the workstation's security.

While attempts have been made to overcome them (such as the MIT "Magic Cookie"), it is still entirely too easy for an attacker to interfere with a user's X display. Most firewalls block all X traffic. Some permit X traffic through application proxies such as the DEC CRL X proxy (`ftp crl.dec.com`).

Books on Firewalls

There are several books that touch on firewalls. The best known are

Bill Cheswick and Steven Bellovin, *Firewalls and Internet Security: Repelling the Wily Hacker*, Addison-Wesley, 1994

Garfinkel and Spafford, *Practical UNIX Security*, O'Reilly and Associates, 1991(discusses primarily host security)

Related references are

Comer and Stevens, *Internetworking with TCP/IP,* Prentice Hall, 1991

Curry, *UNIX System Security,* Addison Wesley, 1992

More On-line Information on Firewalls

`Ftp.greatcircle.com`—Firewalls mailing list archives

Directory: `pub/firewalls`

`Ftp.tis.com`—Internet firewall tool kit and papers

Directory: `pub/firewalls`

`Research.att.com`—Papers on firewalls and break-ins

Directory: `dist/internet_security`

`Net.Tamu.edu`—Texas AMU security tools

Directory: `pub/security/TAMU`

The Internet firewalls mailing list is a forum for firewall administrators and implementers. To subscribe to Firewalls, send "subscribe firewalls" in the body of a message (not on the Subject: line) to `Majordomo@GreatCircle.COM`. Archives of past Firewalls postings are available for anonymous ftp from `ftp.greatcircle.com` in `pub/firewalls/archive`.

This chapter was adapted from the Firewall FAQ, with contributions from

- mjr@tis.com—Marcus Ranum, Trusted Information Systems
- leibowa@wl.com—Allen Leibowitz, Warner Lambert Inc.
- brent@greatcircle.com—Brent Chapman, Great Circle Associates
- bdboyle@erenj.com—Brian Boyle, Exxon Research

The current version of the FAQ is available on the Internet at http://www.tis.com/Home/NetworkSecurity/Firewalls/FAQ.html.

Chapter 6

Internet Access for People with Disabilities

by Jim Allan, M.S. <jallan@tenet.edu>
K.C. Dignan, Ph.D. <kcd@tenet.edu>
Dave Kinnaman, M.S., M.A. <kinnaman@world.std.com>

Before we can discuss access to the Internet for people with disabilities, we first must agree on a definition of disability. There are many ways to describe disabling conditions. The traditional method is to identify the location of the disability and then label it. A visual disability, for example, is a dysfunction in the ability to see normally, and a hearing disability is a dysfunction in the ability to hear normally.

Notice the word *normally*. What does normally mean? If you study the population of human beings, you find wide variations in height, weight, skin and hair color, and even the perception of color, yet all these variations are quite normal. You also find a wide range of abilities to drive a car, solve crossword puzzles, walk, appreciate music, and conduct any other individual human activity. Again, the wide variations are quite normal. So our working definition of disability must encompass all these normal human variations. For the purposes of this chapter, then, *a disability is an individual limitation that affects the ability to complete a task*.

The study of differences among abilities is called the study of individual differences. Many terms that describe these differences have come and gone in accepted language use. Terms that have been used in the past include *handicapped, impaired, challenged,* and *crippled*. Another example of outdated language related to people with disabilities is that a person who uses a wheelchair for mobility was described as *being confined to* versus *using* a wheelchair.

We must start with the acknowledgment that all of us are people. People with disabilities are people with jobs, families, houses, responsibilities, hobbies, feelings, and everything else associated with people. In other words, people with disabilities are *people* first.

All of us are getting older. As we age, the ability to see print clearly decreases, and the need for glasses increases. The ability to hear conversations in a crowded room may decline, so a hearing aid may become necessary. Arthritis may develop, and modified doorknobs, a walker, or some other assistive device may become necessary. Some of us will be involved in accidents or injured in one way or another, resulting in the need for novel ways to do things or the need to use new and unique tools to accomplish everyday tasks.

Disability "secrets"

- One of every 10 citizens has a disability of some type. It is estimated that 7 to 9 of every 10 major corporations employ people with disabilities who need to use computer software as part of their jobs.
- Our population is aging rapidly. The number of people who have disabilities or functional limitations is growing. Every year, this population includes more and more computer users.
- Standard software that is designed to be usable by people with performance limitations usually is easier for everyone else to use, too.

—from "Making Software More Accessible for People with Disabilities: A Trace Center White Paper," Trace Research and Development Center, Waisman Center, University of Wisconsin, 1500 Highland Avenue, Madison, WI 53705-2280.

The point of this introduction is not to depress you or to paint a gloomy picture but to illustrate the fact that the problems and solutions presented in this chapter are not for some unidentified "them." These problems and solutions could be for you, for someone in your family, or for someone you know.

Computer-access technology is software and/or hardware that allow an individual with a disability to carry out the same tasks, using the same underlying software and/or hardware and with the same success as a person without a disability. Without access technology, people with disabilities may be severely limited as to the amount and kinds of information that they can access.

The use of computer-access technology is a proven means of ensuring equal opportunity and promoting independence for people with disabilities. Access technology is more than access to a computer. When combined with the Internet, access technology is a window to a world of information, ideas, and other people.

Access to Computers

People access computers in three ways. First, they read print information from the screen or printer. Second, they put information into the computer by using a keyboard, mouse, or touch screen. Third, they hear information in the form of sounds, music, or spoken directions from the computer speaker(s). This chapter groups access methods according to these functional abilities, using the following categories:

Print disability. People in this category have difficulty accessing printed information from the screen or printer for the following reasons:

- Visual disability, such as cataracts, blindness, or macular degeneration
- Reading disability, such as dyslexia or learning disability
- Physical disability, such as cerebral palsy or muscular dystrophy
- Language disability, such as limited English proficiency or learning disability

Keyboard or mouse disability. People in this category have difficulty using the keyboard, mouse, or touch screen to input or select information on the computer for the following reasons:

- Physical disability, such as quadriplegia or cerebral palsy
- Injury or trauma, such as amputation, carpal-tunnel syndrome, or repetitive-motion syndrome
- Disease, such as arthritis, Parkinson's disease, or muscular dystrophy

Sound disability. People in this category have difficulty in using information that comes from the computer's speaker for the following reasons:

- Hearing impairment, such as hardness of hearing or deafness
- Limited ability to perceive higher frequency of tones due to age
- Limited ability to discriminate among tones due to tone deafness

Note: This chapter is not just about people who have difficulty accessing the computer screen, keyboard, or speaker. It also is about raising the awareness of all computer users about his or her own learning styles. Each of us is unique. Each person learns in special ways. Some of us have to hear something to remember it; others have to see it; others have to perform a new skill to remember it.

To provide information that is accessible to each of us, with our unique ways of getting information, the new information should be presented in many forms. This repetition of presentation is called *information redundancy*. If information appears on the screen in text form, the user also should have the option to have the same information printed on paper or spoken out loud. If the computer makes some noise, the user should have the option to have that information appear on screen in text form. If the computer interface requires keyboard, mouse, or touch-screen input, the user should have alternative, redundant methods of accomplishing the same task.

When a person has full access to a computer, he or she can access the Internet with that computer.

The following sections review the three categories of disabilities, identifying various disability problems and then providing possible technological solutions. Each section provides the roughly estimated 1994 cost (in round U.S. dollars) of implementing the solutions, but local prices may vary, so shop around.

Print disability

People with a print disability have difficulty accessing information on the computer screen or on the printer. Information on the screen or printer may not be useful to the user for several reasons. The print may be too small to read. The individual may not be able to see the screen. The user may have a reading disability, such as dyslexia, that makes the letters appear to be jumbled. The user may have a physical disability that makes retrieving printed paper or holding a book difficult.

The following sections describe and then solve several problems that can keep users from being able to read print displayed on the computer's screen.

Problem 1: Print is too small to read

If the print or image on the screen is too small to read, the user must magnify the image in one of several ways.

Solution 1A: Choose a larger screen font. Cost: None.

Solution 1B: Use the vertical-size selector on most SVGA monitors to make the letters appear to be larger. (Unfortunately, this solution is not available to Macintosh users.) Cost: None.

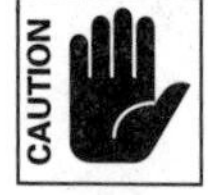

You may increase the size so much that you lose information at the top and bottom of the screen.

Solution 1C: Use a screen-magnification program. A screen-magnification program enlarges the text on the screen; the screen does not enlarge. The screen becomes a virtual window through which the user views the screen information. At two times (2×) magnification, the text becomes much larger (twice as high and twice as wide). The screen becomes a virtual window that shows one-fourth of the preceding screen information, and the user must scroll from side to side or up and down to read an area that is four times larger than the normal screen. Cost: $200 to $600.

Following are some screen-magnification programs that you can use to solve the problem:

- *Magic and Magic Deluxe (DOS and Windows)* — These programs are available from MicroSystem. Magic must be running in DOS for the Windows version, called Magic Deluxe, to function. A small amount of RAM is needed. Magic increases magnification levels up to 2 times; Magic Deluxe increases magnification up to 8 times in Windows and 12 times in DOS. Magic: $195. Magic Deluxe: $295.
- *ZoomText and ZoomText Plus (DOS and Windows)* — These programs are available from AI Squared. The DOS version, called ZoomText, provides magnification levels up to 16 times. The Windows version, ZoomText Plus, magnifies the screen up to 8 times. ZoomText: $495. ZoomText Plus: $595.
- *CloseView (Macintosh)* — This program, which can be found on the System disk of every Macintosh, magnifies the screen image up to 16 times. Cost: None.
- *InLarge (Macintosh)* — This program, available from Berkeley Systems, magnifies both text and graphics and provides several viewing options. Cost: $195.

Solution 1D: Purchase a larger monitor (17- to 21-inch range). Cost: $700 to $2,000.

Problem 2: The user cannot see the screen

The user who cannot see the screen may be blind, visually impaired, or unable to control head and eye movements completely. Several solutions are available for screen and paper access to the information.

Solution: Use a speech-synthesizer card and a screen-review program. Cost: $300 to $1,200.

Speech-synthesizer cards

A speech-synthesizer card is different from a multimedia sound card. Most sound cards are multipurpose cards and have, at best, limited rules for correct pronunciation of text on the screen. A speech-synthesizer card has one purpose: to convert on-screen text to speech based on extensive pronunciation rules.

Speech synthesizers are available in different languages. Several controls are built into these cards, including adjustment of speech rate, adjustment of vocal tone and pitch, and the capability to speak letters or words as they are typed. The speech sounds mechanical, because the computer is creating the sound based on formulas. Digitized speech is not yet available, except for a limited controlled vocabulary.

At least 15 speech-synthesizer cards — all 8-bit cards or external boxes — are available for DOS-based personal computers. Most of the external synthesizers connect to the serial port, but some connect to the parallel port. "Road warriors" (heavy laptop users) can choose between two PCMCIA Type II synthesizers.

Synthesizer cards are not needed on the Macintosh; the computer has a built-in sound chip and text-to-speech capability.

Following are some speech-synthesizer cards that you can use on MS-DOS compatible laptops or desktops:

- *Accent* — This item is available as an internal card ($800), external serial box ($900), or PCMCIA card ($1,000).
- *DecTalk* — This item is available as an internal card ($1,200) or as an external serial box ($1,400).
- *Keynote Gold* — This item is available as an internal card ($1,000), external serial or parallel box ($1,300), or a PCMCIA II card ($1,100). Foreign language options are Spanish, French, and German. All Keynote Gold synthesizers come standard with English. One additional language is $200; two or more languages are $300.
- *Sounding Board* — This item is available as an internal card ($400) or as an external serial or parallel box ($500).

Screen-review programs

A screen-review program allows the user to navigate around the screen and control the speech output. The user can choose to have characters or words spoken; to have the preceding sentence or paragraph read; or to have the entire document read, including features such as menu bars, dialog boxes, and other information that pops up on the screen. The screen-review software can freeze the application program and allow the user to explore the screen without the screen changing. But a screen-review program cannot read graphics or pictures displayed on screen.

At least a dozen screen-review programs are available for DOS and/or Windows. The DOS screen-review programs work on all types of computers, from the early 8088 PCs to the new Pentium-based models. All the DOS programs work on desktop CRT monitors (based on cathode-ray-tube technology) or on laptops with liquid-crystal-display technology. Several screen-review programs are described below. Other programs can be found in the "Problem 3: The user cannot understand or absorb the print information on the computer screen" section.

Following are some examples of screen-review programs that you can use:

- *Business Vision and WinVision (DOS and Windows)* — Available from Artic Technologies, these screen-review programs provide access to DOS and Windows, respectively. The user navigates the screen via the keyboard rather than the mouse. WinVision has the capability to read icons, pull-down menus, and other parts of the screen. Cost: $495 (synthesizer card additional).
- *Jaws (DOS and Windows)* — Available from Henter-Joyce. Jaws is one of the most powerful DOS screen readers available. A Windows version is now available. DOS: $495. Windows: $595.
- *OutSpoken (Macintosh)* — Available from Berkeley Systems, OutSpoken is the only choice for screen review on the Macintosh. With OutSpoken, the user can name individual icons and read menu bars, boxes, and most other things that appear on-screen. Cost: $195.

Although Windows screen readers exist, they do not provide complete access to Windows. The programs are first-generation programs and provide only basic access. As Windows continues to evolve, screen readers will follow. As more Windows screen readers are developed, market forces will drive improvements in access. Before you buy, contact the manufacturer and ask for a user list. Use the information to contact the individuals for opinions and usefulness.

Problem 3: The user cannot understand or absorb the print information on the computer screen

Some people have no difficulty seeing the screen, but they have great difficulty reading or understanding what they have read. These people have a learning or language disability. For example, the user might be dyslexic. Or the user may be more fluent in spoken language than in written language. Some of the solutions that people with learning disabilities use are the same as the solutions for people who cannot see the screen.

Solution 3A: Use a screen-review software program and a speech-synthesizer card (both described in the preceding section). Several screen-review programs can highlight the word that is being spoken as it is spoken. This feature is useful for people who have reading disabilities. Cost: Synthesizer: $400 to $1,400. Screen review: $500.

Please review "Problem 2: The user cannot see the screen" for more information about speech synthesizers and screen-review software.

Following are some products that you can use:

- *Screen Power (DOS)* — This screen-review program, from TeleSensory, works with almost any speech-synthesizer card. A Windows version is under development. Cost: $495 (synthesizer card additional).
- *Vocal Eyes (DOS)* — This easy-to-learn program, from GW Micro, was the first to provide highlighting capability. A Windows version is under development. Cost: $495 (synthesizer card additional).
- *Outspoken (Macintosh)* — Available from Berkeley Systems. Users can have text spoken as it is typed. The user can have portions of the document or the entire document read back to her. Cost: $195.

Solution 3B: Use a program specifically designed for people with reading problems. Simply highlight the words to be spoken and press the appropriate keys to hear the words.

Following are DOS products that you can use:

- *SoundProof* — This product, from HumanWare, works only in the DOS environment. Cost: $1,450 (including Keynote Gold synthesizer card).
- *Word Scholar* — This was developed by Henter-Joyce for the DOS environment. Cost: $495 (synthesizer card additional).

Problem 4: The user cannot read the paper computer printout

Many people use a printer to print documents or files for review. Standard size print such as that used in this book may be difficult to read for people who have a visual disability or are blind.

Solution 4A: Print larger letters with a larger printer font. Or change the font used. Some fonts are easier to read. Standard large print is 18 point. Comfortable print and font size is, however, a matter of user preference. Cost: None.

Solution 4B: Use a Braille translator and a Braille printer. Braille translators use files created by certain word processing programs (WordPerfect, for example) and convert those files to Braille. A Braille printer (also called an *embosser*) is used to print a Braille copy of the original file on special paper.

Following are some Braille translators that you can use:

- *MegaDots (DOS)* — This program, from Raised Dot Computing, is a fully functioning DOS editor that imports almost any word processing document and creates formats appropriate for Braille output. Cost: $500.
- *Duxbury (DOS and Macintosh)* — This program, available from Duxbury Systems, is expected to be the only Braille translation program available on all three consumer platforms (DOS, Macintosh, and Windows) when the Windows version is released. Cost: $500.

Following are some Braille printers that you can use:

- *Braille Blazer (DOS, Windows, and Macintosh)* — This printer, from Blazie Engineering, produces Braille at 15 characters per second and is designed to be a personal Braille printer. The printer also can function as a speech synthesizer. Braille Blazer has both serial and parallel interfaces, and it works with any computer platform. Cost: $1,695.
- *VersaPoint (DOS, Windows, and Macintosh)* — This 40-character-per-second Braille printer is available from TeleSensory. The printer has both serial and parallel interfaces, and it works with any computer platform. Cost: $3,795.

Keyboard or mouse disability

The keyboard and mouse are the main ways of getting information into the computer. They are also used to give the computer instructions or commands. People who have a keyboard/mouse disability may have cerebral palsy, poor coordination, or arthritis.

Problem: The user has difficulty accessing the keyboard or mouse

The user who has difficulty using the keyboard or the mouse has several options available. The options depend on the specific problem — such as a one-finger typist, the keyboard is too small, or a one-handed typist.

Solution A: Use the operating-system tools that are available on the utilities or accessories disks for your system. These tools, which modify the functions of the mouse and keyboard, are available for Macintosh (Easy Keys), DOS (Access DOS), and Windows (Access Pack). Cost: None.

Features available in the various free system tools include the following:

Feature	*Desired Result*
StickyKeys	Permits single-finger typing
SlowKeys	Ignores keys that are pressed accidentally or for a short time
RepeatKeys	Adjusts or disables the keyboard repeat rate
BounceKeys	Ignores keys that are pressed too quickly or at the same time
MouseKeys	Allows control of the cursor from the keyboard
ToggleKeys*	Provides audio cues when toggle keys are turned on or off
SerialKeys*	Allows control of the computer with an alternative input device
ShowSounds*	Provides a visual cue when sounds are generated
TimeOut	Turns off the access features when they're not being used

*Not available for the Macintosh

Solution B: If access to the keyboard is extremely limited, the venerable Morse code is a good solution. Morse code is relatively easy to learn. The basic code has been expanded to include all the keys on the keyboard, including function keys, Control, Alt, Option, ⌘, and so on. Morse code can be generated from one or two switches, which usually attach to the serial or game port of the computer.

Several Morse-code solutions are available for each platform. Following are some examples:

- *HandiCode (DOS and Windows)* — This program, from MicroSystem, is software-based Morse code. Switch and interface cable are included, as well as HandiWord, a statistically weighted word-prediction program. Cost: $495.
- *Ke:nx (Macintosh)* — This oddly named product, from Don Johnston, is a small interface box that attaches between the Macintosh computer and the keyboard. The product also comes with some software for you to install. Ke:nx provides not only Morse-code capability, but also on-screen keyboarding, adaptive keyboards, and a scanning keyboard. The program is transparent to all applications. A speech-output program also is included. Cost: $780.

Solution C: For users who do not have access to a keyboard or a mouse and cannot use a switch, the remaining solution is speech recognition. As computers have become more powerful and memory becomes more plentiful, the accuracy of speech recognition has increased steadily, and the cost has dropped more than 50 percent in the past few years.

To use speech recognition, the user must use a microphone and appropriate speech-recognition software. Some training in the recognition system is necessary. An experienced speech-recognition user can input or "type" by dictating at about 40 words per minute. A useful feature in some speech-recognition programs permits the user to paste entire paragraphs, or any other text, into a document simply by speaking a word.

Speech-recognition systems are available for DOS, Windows, and Macintosh platforms. The software typically requires at least a 386 or 030 microprocessor. Following are some examples:

- *Dragon Dictate (DOS)* — This system for DOS, from Dragon Systems, consists of an internal interface card, microphone, and software. Recognizable vocabulary ranges from 10,000 to 30,000 words; the user can add words to the dictation dictionary. Cost: $800 to $1,000.
- *Voice Navigator II (Macintosh)* — This package, from Articulate Systems, includes software and hardware for Macintosh speech recognition. Voice Navigator II is designed to navigate the screen's menus, commands, and icons; it also can be used for keyboard entry. Cost: $900.

Solution D: In addition to the standard keyboards that are available in computer stores, alternative keyboards are available. These keyboards may be larger than standard keyboards. Or the keyboards may be software-generated and displayed on screen so that the user can select keys with the mouse or a touch screen.

Keyboards for one-handed typing also are available. Alternative keyboards are available on all platforms. Occasionally, an additional interface card is necessary for these keyboards. Following are a few examples:

- *BAT (DOS, Windows, and Macintosh)* — This item is available for Macintosh and DOS/Windows computers from Infogrip. The BAT, which attaches to the computer through the keyboard port, is available in right- and left-handed versions. All keyboard input is produced by pushing a combination of seven keys simultaneously. Three keys are controlled by the thumb; the other four keys are controlled by individual fingers. All keys on the keyboard can be duplicated through the use of the BAT. Cost: $295.
- *Microsoft Keyboard (DOS and Windows)* — This keyboard was designed for prevention of injury but is useful for people who have hand difficulties. The keyboard is not the only ergonomic keyboard that is available; check your local computer store and computer magazines for other examples. The keyboard is available for MS-DOS compatible machines. Cost: $150.
- *Macintosh Keyboard.* A similar keyboard for the Macintosh is available from your Apple dealer. Cost: $200.
- *Intellikeys (DOS, Windows, and Macintosh)* — This product, from IntelliTools, plugs directly into the keyboard port of most computers. The Intellikeys keyboard is a large touch-sensitive tablet (8 1/2 x 14 inches) that has up to 128 user-definable keys. Cost: $315.
- *ScreenDoors (Macintosh)* — This Macintosh-oriented product, from Madenta Communications, provides an on-screen keyboard, word prediction, voice input, speech output, environmental control, and even telephone access. Cost: $385.

Solution E: Word prediction is used in conjunction with some other text-input tool or keyboard. Word prediction allows the user to input words by using fewer keystrokes. As the user types, the word-prediction software tries to predict which word is being typed while it is being typed. The software displays a list that changes with each additional letter typed. When the user sees the desired word in the list, he or she then types the number of the word in the list, and the word is entered into the document.

The software also can add appropriate spacing after punctuation marks, and it can add a space and capitalize the next letter after a period.

Word-prediction software is available for DOS, Windows, and Macintosh platforms. Following are a few examples:

- *HandiWord (DOS and Windows)* — This program for DOS and Windows is available from MicroSystem. HandiWord includes a dictionary for custom word prediction. Cost: $295.
- *Telepathic (Macintosh)* — This program for the Macintosh, which includes speech sound output, is available from Madenta Communications. The user also can import foreign-language files and use them for word prediction. Cost: $325.

Solution F: Use any combination of the preceding solutions to maximize the speed of text input. These products can be mixed and matched on the same platform.

Sound disability

The computer typically makes many sounds or beeps. These sounds have many applications: call attention to an error, inform the user of a completed task, or inform the user of a nonfunctional keystroke. People who have hearing difficulties may not hear these important cues or, if the tones are heard, be able to distinguish between two tones.

Problem: The user has difficulty hearing the sounds generated by the computer

Individuals with hearing problems need some means of being informed that the computer has made a tone.

Solution: On the DOS/Windows platform, the user can activate the Show Sounds command (if it was installed). Show Sounds is available on the Access DOS or Windows Access Pack disk from Microsoft. The program is included on the DOS or Windows accessories or utilities disks bundled with the operating-system installation disks. Cost: None.

On the Macintosh, the user can adjust the volume of the system speaker. If the volume is set to zero, no sound comes from the speaker; but the screen flashes. The screen flash can be used to alert the user that a beep was generated. Cost: None.

The Future of Internet Access for the Disabled

The preceding sections discussed the general nature of disability. Many solutions were provided for a variety of access problems. These solutions gave examples of the hardware and software that is available to compensate for disabilities; the "Vendors and Products" section, later in this chapter, provides even more sources of information.

Through the use of assistive technology, a person with a disability has access to a computer. With a computer and a modem, a person has access to the world through the Internet. Accordingly, information that is available on the Internet can be accessible to all computer users.

Barriers still exist, however:

- The Internet is changing rapidly from a text-based environment to a graphics-based environment. The Internet also may be merging with telephone and television technology. As these changes occur, the tendency is to move toward using more graphics and icons (and less text). Serious consideration must be given to providing iconic and graphic information in an alternative text format.
- Just as movies and television shows are presented with captions or descriptive video, so must the information on the Internet. A partial solution for the increasingly graphical nature of the World Wide Web is the text-based Web browser Lynx, which provides a character-based interface to the Web.

Through speech-recognition software, Lynx gives users with print disabilities access to the text on the Web. Pictures and graphics at Web sites, however, are simply labeled *graphic*. An informative label is needed to tell users what the graphic contains or represents and whether the graphic is a link to other parts of the Web.

People with Disabilities and E-Mail

The most common use of the Internet is electronic mail; the same is true for America Online, CompuServe, and other on-line information services. E-mail is a true equalizer for people with disabilities because e-mail is judged by the quality and content of the expression, rather than by any outward appearance.

People are invisible with e-mail, which contains only the words and composition of the message sender. Any ideas, biases, or opinions formed about the message sender are not based on physical appearance or on ability to walk, type, speak, hear, or see, but on the words in the message.

The person who sent you a message may have entered the text by using Morse code. The individual may have used a special switch with an on-screen keyboard to compose the message. He may have held a special stick in his teeth and used that to type each letter. It may have taken five minutes or five hours to write and transmit the message you received.

Think about these things the next time you receive a message. Based on the words in the message, does the person who sent you a message have a disability? Will you ever know? Does it matter?

Vendors and Products

AI Squared
P.O. Box 669
Manchester Center, VT 05255-0669
(802) 362-3612
ZoomText

Artic Technologies
55 Park Street, Suite 2
Troy, MI 48083-2753
(800) 677-3848
WinVision, Business Vision

Articulate Systems, Inc.
600 West Cummings Park, Suite 4500
Woburn, MA 01801-6500
(617) 935-5656
Voice Navigator II

Berkeley Systems, Inc.
2095 Rose Street
Berkeley, CA 94709-1963
(510) 540-5535
OutSpoken, InLarge

Blazie Engineering, Unit D
105 East Jarrettsville Road
Forest Hill, MD 21050-1611
(410) 893-9333
Braille Blazer

Dragon Systems, Inc.
320 Nevada Street
Newton, MA 02160-1424
(617) 965-5200
Dragon Dictate

Duxbury Systems, Inc.
P.O. Box 1504
Littleton, MA 01460-4504
(508) 486-9766
Duxbury Braille Translator

GW Micro
310 Racquet Drive
Fort Wayne, IN 46825-4229
(219) 483-3625
Sounding Board, Vocal Eyes

Henter-Joyce, Inc.
2100 62nd Avenue North
St. Petersburg, FL 33702-7142
(800) 336-5658
Accent, DecTalk, Jaws, Word Scholar

HumanWare, Inc.
6245 King Road
Loomis, CA 95650-8801
(800) 722-3393
Keynote Gold, SoundProof

Infogrip, Inc.
1145 Eugenia Place, Suite 201
Carpinteria, CA 93013-2063
(805) 566-1049
BAT

IntelliTools
5221 Central Avenue, Suite 205
Richmond, CA 94804-5829
(510) 528-0670
Intellikeys

Don Johnston, Inc.
1000 North Rand Road, Building 115
P.O. Box 639
Wauconda, IL 60084-0639
(800) 999-4660
Ke:nx

Madenta Communication, Inc.
9411-A 20th Avenue
Edmonton, AB T6N 1E5, Canada
(800) 661-8406
ScreenDoors, Telepathic

MicroSystem Software, Inc.
600 Worcester Road
Framingham, MA 01701-5360
(508) 626-8511
HandiCode, HandiWord, Magic

Raised Dot Computing
408 South Baldwin Street
Madison, WI 53703-3705
(608) 257-9595
MegaDots

TeleSensory
455 North Bernardo Avenue
Mountain View, CA 94043-5274
(800) 227-8418
Screen Power, VersaPoint

State Technology-Related Assistance

The passage of the Technology-Related Assistance Act (Public Law 101-407) in 1988 provided children and adults with disabilities and their families an expanding set of expectations about assistive-technology devices and services. The law should lead to assistive technology that is more available, accessible, and responsive to consumer needs.

Every state has a federally funded technology assistance project, the purpose of which is to provide information and referrals to people with disabilities. For more information, contact your state health department, rehabilitation commission, or education agency, or contact your congressional representative. Ask for information about your state's tech-act project.

Books

Solutions: Access Technologies for People Who Are Blind (1992)
by Olga Espinola and Diana Croft

National Braille Press
88 Saint Stephen Street
Boston, MA 02115-4398
(617) 226-6160

This is an excellent book that explains the ins and outs of access technology specifically for people who are blind. The book also is a good resource for all types and uses of related access equipment. The book focuses on speech and Braille access.

Annual Resource Directory

Closing the Gap
P.O. Box 68
Henderson, MN 56044-0068

(612) 248-3294

This indispensable directory is the ultimate guide to microcomputer technology for special education and rehabilitation, covering hardware, software, price, computer platform, system requirements, disability area, and organizations.

Computer Resources for People with Disabilities: A Guide to Exploring Today's Assistive Technology (1994)

By the Alliance for Technology Access (***Note:*** The Alliance can be reached via e-mail at `afta@aol.com`.)

Special Needs Project
3463 State Street, Suite 282
Santa Barbara, CA 93105-2601

(800) 333-6867

Published in late 1994, this book is a good beginning for people who are new to the area of assistive technology. The book — which contains chapters on law, purchasing equipment, and determining needs, as well as product descriptions — would be a good addition to your library.

Financing Assistive Technology

Smiling Interface
P.O. Box 2792, Church Street Station
New York, NY 10008-2792

(415) 864-2220

E-mail: `mendelsohn@delphi.com`

This bimonthly newsletter covers sources of funding, tax laws, tax breaks, grants, and the like. The newsletter is available in print, audiocassette, floppy disk, and fax form, as well as by e-mail.

Resources on the Internet

The Internet provides many resources both for the disabled and for people who are looking for information about disabilities.

Gopher

The following quotation dramatically illustrates the impact of access to information for people with disabilities via the Internet.

"I wanted to drop a quick line and tell you how much Gopher means to me. I discovered Gopher about two months ago and cannot believe how much information is out here. . . . This is undoubtedly a great service for anyone who finds it. However, for me, it is unbelievable. I am legally blind, and I have always said that the most difficult aspect of blindness is the lack of readily available information. Gopher has the ability to change all that. For the first time, I feel like I can easily and independently access important campus and worldwide information."

— Wiggins, Rich. "The University of Minnesota's Internet Gopher System: A Tool for Accessing Network-Based Electronic Information." *The Public-Access Computer Systems Review 4, No. 2* (1993), pp. 4–60. Used with permission.

The following are places to go on the Internet for information related to all types of disabilities.

Cornucopia of Disability Information (CODI)

E-mail: `val-dor.cc.buffalo.edu`

Information available at the CODI Gopher includes:

- Digest of Data on Persons with Disabilities
- Directory of Organizations
- List of Directories
- Directory of Databases
- Directory of Hotlines
- Directory of Religious Organizations
- Directory of Sports Organizations
- National Institute on Disability and Rehabilitation Research (all publications)

Other accessible information sources include the following:

- Heath Resource Center Directory
- Americans with Disabilities Act
- National Rehabilitation Information Center (NARIC) documents, including the ABLEDATA and REHABDATA fact sheets and the top ten on-line searches

You can jump from CODI to the following sites:

- Deaf Gopher at Michigan State University
- Project EASI (Equal Access to Software and Information) directory
- Recordings for the Blind directory

The following list includes additional information providers:

- *Handicap BBS and Software Archive List*

  Address: `handicap.shel.isc-br.com`

  Path: /public/bbslist/

  This Gopher lists more than 800 dialup BBSs nationwide that provide disability-related information and resources. The server also has a software archive that includes demonstration software. This server is a good jumping-off point to other servers that offer information related to people with disabilities.

- *Keyboarding Injury*

  Address: `soda.berkeley.edu`

  Path: /pub/typing-injury/

  This server provides a wealth of information about keyboarding, typing, injury, and keyboard alternatives, as well as some GIF graphics of keyboards and adaptations.

- *Saftey and the Arts*

  Address: `gopher.tmn.com`

  Path: /Artswire/csa/

  This Gopher server contains information about how to work in the arts in a safe manner, including hazards, precautions, laws, and regulations; it also has connections to other health and safety Gophers.

Usenet newsgroups

If you have access to Usenet news, you may want to visit the following newsgroups, which discuss disabilities. (The `bit.listserv` Usenet groups also are available as LISTSERV mailing lists with analogous names.)

Newsgroup	***Topic/Information***
bit.listserv.autism	Autism and developmental disability list
bit.listserv.axslib-l	Library access for people with disabilities
bit.listserv.blindnws	Moderated list about blindness
bit.listserv.deaf-l	Deafness list

(continued)

(continued)

Newsgroup	***Topic/Information***
bit.listserv.down-syn	Down's syndrome list
bit.listserv.gutnberg	Project Gutenberg list (electronic books)
bit.listserv.l-hcap	Moderated list about all disabilities
misc.handicap	Moderated discussion group about disabilities

ERIC clearinghouses

ERIC (Educational Resources Information Center) is a U.S.-funded information network that provides access to English-language education literature. Three of the ERIC clearinghouses are of direct interest to people with disabilities. An e-mail address is supplied for each clearinghouse, along with the postal address, phone number, and fax number.

ERIC Clearinghouse on Assessment and Evaluation
Lawrence M. Rudner, Director
Catholic University of America
O'Boyle Hall, Room 210
Washington, DC 20064-4035
Phone: (202) 319-5120
Fax: (202) 319-6692
E-mail: `eric_ae@cua.edu`

This clearinghouse covers all aspects of tests and other measurement devices; the design and methodology of research, measurement, and evaluation; the evaluation of programs and projects; and the application of tests, measurement, and evaluation devices and instrumentation in education projects and programs.

ERIC Clearinghouse on Counseling and Student Services
Garry R. Walz, Director
University of North Carolina at Greensboro
School of Education
Greensboro, NC 27412-5001
Phone: (919) 334-4114 or (800) 414-9769
Fax: (919) 334-4116
E-mail: `ericcass@iris.uncg.edu`

This clearinghouse covers preparation, practice, and supervision of counselors at all educational levels and in all settings. Topics include theoretical development of counseling and guidance, including the nature of relevant human characteristics. The clearinghouse addresses group process (counseling, therapy, and dynamics) and casework; it also includes the use and results of personnel practices and procedures.

ERIC Clearinghouse on Disabilities and Gifted Education
Council for Exceptional Children (CEC)
Bruce Ramirez, Acting Director

1920 Association Drive
Reston, VA 22091-1589
Phone: (703) 264-9474
Fax: (703) 264-9494
E-mail: `ericec@inet.ed.gov`

This clearinghouse covers all aspects of the education and development of people of all ages who have disabilities or who are gifted, including the delivery of all types of education-related services to these groups. Topics include prevention, identification and assessment, intervention, and enrichment for these groups in both regular and special-education settings.

General Sources of Information

Connections (booklet)
Apple Computer
Office of Special Education and Rehabilitation
20525 Mariana Avenue, Department MS-43S
Cupertino, CA 95014-6202
(408) 974-8602

Equal Access: Information Technology for Students with Disabilities ($100). Available from McGraw Hill at (800) 962-9342. Edited by C. Castorino.

Information from HEATH (newsletter)
The National Clearinghouse on Postsecondary Education for Individuals with Disabilities (formerly called the Center for Higher Education and Adult Training for People with Handicaps [HEATH])
One Dupont Circle, N.W., Suite 800
Washington, DC 20036-1193
(800) 544-3284 or (202) 939-9320
E-mail: `heath@ace.nche.edu`

Other Sources of Computer-Access Information

ADDS (Assistive Device Database System)
American International Data Search, Inc.
650 University Avenue, Suite 101B
Sacramento, CA 95825-6726
(916) 924-0280

Hyper-ABLEDATA, a microcomputer version of ABLEDATA, is available on CD-ROM. The system is an excellent reference tool, listing 19,000 assistive devices and their prices. Hyper-ABLEDATA even can write a letter to the manufacturer for more information. If your telephone is connected to your computer's modem, the system will dial the manufacturer for you. This system is an excellent example of software that is accessible to all computer users, and it is now available on the Internet. Telnet to `fedworld.doc.gov` and type **dd115** at the top menu.

The system also is available from

Trace Research and Development Center
Waisman Center, Room S-151
1500 Highland Avenue
Madison, WI 53705-2280
(608) 262-6966

Computer Access in Higher Education for Students with Disabilities, Second Edition

Free to postsecondary institutions from

The High-Tech Center for the Disabled
21050 McClellan Road
Cupertino, CA 95014-4229
(408) 996-4636

This book — a good resource for community colleges, universities, and other postsecondary schools — provides a general overview of disabilities and tools available for accessing the computer.

Considerations in the Design of Computers and Operating Systems to Increase Their Accessibility to Persons with Disabilities, Version 4.2

Trace Research and Development Center
Waisman Center, Room S-151
1500 Highland Avenue
Madison, WI 53705-2280
(608) 262-6966

This excellent publication for developers of software is a useful tool for understanding access technology. Cost: $7.50

Managing End User Computing for Users with Disabilities

General Services Administration
Clearinghouse on Computer Accommodation, Room 2022
KGDO
18th and F streets, N.W.
Washington, DC 20405-0001
(202) 523-1906 (voice/TDD)

This pamphlet contains information from the government concerning computers for people with disabilities in the workplace. No cost.

Organizations and Conferences Related to Computers and Disability

Closing the Gap (CTG)

Closing the Gap
P.O. Box 68
Henderson, MN 56044-0068
(612) 248-3294

Closing the Gap is a conference that focuses on computers and disability, particularly in education. CTG, which is one of the main conferences for announcing new technology, is attended by professionals, parents, and people with disabilities. The conference features excellent exhibits and is held annually in late October in Minneapolis.

Technology and Persons with Disabilities (CSUN)

Dr. Harry Murphy
Office of Disabled Student Services
California State University–Northridge
18111 Nordhoff Street
Northridge, CA 91330-0001
(818) 885-2869

This annual conference, which focuses on computers and disability (particularly in education), is held in mid-March in Los Angeles. The conference is excellent, covering all disabilities and offering a huge exhibit/product area. CSUN is one of the main conferences at which new technology is announced. A conference on virtual reality and disability usually occurs concurrently with CSUN.

American Library Association (ALA)

Joan Maier McKean, ATIG Coordinator
c/o American Library Association
50 East Huron Street
Chicago, IL 60611-2795
(312) 944-6780

The ALA is a professional organization of librarians and the parent group of the Adaptive Technology Interest Group. ATIG, which focuses on issues related to the use of adaptive technology in libraries, is a subgroup of the ALA's Library and Information Technology branch. Conferences are held twice a year: a midwinter meeting in Chicago and a summer meeting in varying locations.

RESNA

1101 Connecticut Avenue, N.W., Suite 700
Washington, DC 20036-4302
(202) 857-1199

RESNA is a professional interdisciplinary organization concerned with all aspects of rehabilitation technology. The organization's annual conference — held in mid-June in varying locations — features some presentations and equipment displays related to computers. RESNA also has a special-interest group on computer applications.

Bill of Rights and Responsibilities for the Electronic Community of Learners

By Frank Connolly. Used in its entirety with permission.

PREAMBLE

In order to protect the rights and recognize the responsibilities of individuals and institutions, we, the members of the educational community, propose this Bill of Rights and Responsibilities for the Electronic Community of Learners. These principles are based on a recognition that the electronic community is a complex subsystem of the educational community founded on the values espoused by that community. As new technology modifies the system and further empowers individuals, new values and responsibilities will change this culture. As technology assumes an integral role in education and lifelong learning, technological empowerment of individuals and organizations becomes a requirement and right for students, faculty, staff, and institutions, bringing with it new levels of responsibility that individuals and institutions have to themselves and to other members of the educational community.

ARTICLE I: INDIVIDUAL RIGHTS

The original Bill of Rights explicitly recognized that all individuals have certain fundamental rights as members of the national community. In the same way, the citizens of the electronic community of learners have fundamental rights that empower them.

Section 1

A citizen's access to computing and information resources shall not be denied or removed without just cause.

Section 2

The right to access includes the right to appropriate training and tools required to effect access.

Section 3

All citizens shall have the right to be informed about personal information that is being and has been collected about them, and have the right to review and correct that information. Personal information about a citizen shall not be used for other than the express purpose of its collection without the explicit permission of that citizen.

Section 4

The constitutional concept of freedom of speech applies to citizens of electronic communities.

Section 5

All citizens of the electronic community of learners have ownership rights over their own intellectual works.

ARTICLE II: INDIVIDUAL RESPONSIBILITIES

Just as certain rights are given to each citizen of the electronic community of learners, each citizen is held accountable for his or her actions. The interplay of rights and responsibilities within each individual and within the community engenders the trust and intellectual freedom that form the heart of our society. This trust and freedom are grounded on each person's developing the skills necessary to be an active and contributing citizen of the electronic community. These skills include an awareness and knowledge about information technology and the uses of information and an understanding of the roles in the electronic community of learners.

Section 1

It shall be each citizen's personal responsibility to actively pursue needed resources: to recognize when information is needed, and to be able to find, evaluate, and effectively use information.

Section 2

It shall be each citizen's personal responsibility to recognize (attribute) and honor the intellectual property of others.

Section 3

Since the electronic community of learners is based upon the integrity and authenticity of information, it shall be each citizen's personal responsibility to be aware of the potential for and possible effects of manipulating electronic information: to understand the nature of electronic information; and to verify the integrity and authenticity, and assure the security of information that he or she compiles or uses.

Section 4

Each citizen, as a member of the electronic community of learners, is responsible to all other citizens in that community: to respect and value the rights of privacy for all; to recognize and respect the diversity of the population and opinion in the community; to behave ethically; and to comply with legal restrictions regarding the use of information resources.

Section 5

Each citizen, as a member of the electronic community of learners, is responsible to the community as a whole to understand what information technology resources are available, to recognize that the members of the community share them, and to refrain from acts that waste resources or prevent others from using them.

ARTICLE III: RIGHTS OF EDUCATIONAL INSTITUTIONS

Educational institutions have legal standing similar to that of individuals. Our society depends upon educational institutions to educate our citizens and advance the development of knowledge. However, in order to survive, educational institutions must attract financial and human resources. Therefore, society must grant these institutions the rights to the electronic resources and information necessary to accomplish their goals.

Section 1

The access of an educational institution to computing and information resources shall not be denied or removed without just cause.

Section 2

Educational institutions in the electronic community of learners have ownership rights over the intellectual works they create.

Section 3

Each educational institution has the authority to allocate resources in accordance with its unique institutional mission.

ARTICLE IV: INSTITUTIONAL RESPONSIBILITIES

Just as certain rights are assured to educational institutions in the electronic community of learners, so too each is held accountable for the appropriate exercise of those rights to foster the values of society and to carry out each institution's mission. This interplay of rights and responsibilities within the community fosters the creation and maintenance of an environment wherein trust and intellectual freedom are the foundation for individual and institutional growth and success.

Section 1

The institutional members of the electronic community of learners have a responsibility to provide all members of their community with legally acquired computer resources (hardware, software, networks, data bases, etc.) in all instances where access to or use of the resources is an integral part of active participation in the electronic community of learners.

Section 2

Institutions have a responsibility to develop, implement, and maintain security procedures to insure the integrity of individual and institutional files.

Section 3

The institution shall treat electronically stored information as confidential. The institution shall treat all personal files as confidential, examining or disclosing the contents only when authorized by the owner of the information, approved by the appropriate institutional official, or required by local, state, or federal law.

Section 4

Institutions in the electronic community of learners shall train and support faculty, staff, and students to effectively use information technology. Training includes skills to use the resources, to be aware of the existence of data repositories and techniques for using them, and to understand the ethical and legal uses of the resources.

K.C. Dignan, Ph.D., is a special education specialist with the Texas Education Agency. She has worked in all areas of special education with a concentration in visual impairments. In her spare time she enjoys gardening, reading mysteries, and gourmet cooking.

Jim Allan, M.S., is the Coordinator of Instructional Technology at the Texas School for the Blind and Visually Impaired. He has presented on computer access for people with disabilities at national and international conferences. He consults with colleges, universities, and private corporations concerning access for people with disabilities. In his spare time he enjoys reading science fiction, growing bonsai trees, and playing computer games.

Dave Kinnaman, M.S., M.A., is a systems analyst at a large state education department. He does labor market and economic analysis to improve coordination and planning in education and training programs. Dave wonders "Why have so few jobs been improved with all our new technology?" and "Why must our young people endure a series of intermittent, part-time, low-wage (no-benefit) jobs in order to have a job application for a permanent job taken seriously?"

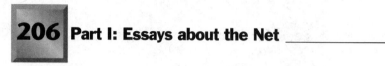

Chapter 7
Smileys

by David W. Sanderson <dws@ora.com>

"The Noah Webster of smileys"

— *The Wall Street Journal,* September 15, 1992

What's a Smiley?

If you have been using the Internet awhile, you probably have seen some smileys. A *smiley* is a sequence of ordinary characters intended to form a picture. People may use smileys as a sort of "visual punctuation" in the various forms of electronic text you find on the Internet, such as e-mail and Usenet News. The most basic smiley is a picture of a happy face. It looks like this:

```
:-)
```

If you don't see the face, try tipping your head to the left and looking at it again. The colon represents the eyes, the dash represents the nose, and the right parenthesis (also called *paren*) represents the mouth. Not all smileys are tipped over, but many of them are. The basic smiley means "don't take what I just wrote too seriously."

Why Use Smileys?

People have been writing to each other for centuries. Why use smileys in e-mail?

Speed.

Paper letters travel slowly. If you want your paper letter to be understood, you must make sure that it is self-contained so that the recipient can read it and understand it on its own terms. It's not at all like oral communication because you've considered your words carefully and there's no conversational give-and-take.

E-mail travels very rapidly. And it is often written without as much care as paper letters are. For this reason, e-mail often has the dynamic of a conversation without the visual or auditory clues you would get if you were talking in person or even over the telephone. Smileys are a way to put some of that additional information back in. They help prevent misunderstandings.

How Many Smileys Are There?

Too many to remember. But don't worry. You can often figure out what an unfamiliar smiley means based on its appearance. Usually you don't have to. You usually see just a few as punctuation:

:-)	Happy smiley
:-(	Sad smiley
:-|	Apathetic smiley
;-)	Winking smiley
:)	Small, happy smiley
:(	Small, sad smiley

How Do I Use Smileys As Punctuation?

Every so often the topic of smiley use comes up on the net. People want to know whether to put smileys before or after the punctuation at the end of a sentence.

I prefer to see the smileys come *after* the punctuation at the end of a sentence rather than immediately before it. This way, the smiley stands by itself as a sort of pictographic sentence, and you don't confuse the regular punctuation with the characters that comprise the smiley. For example, Jerry Peek, in his book about the MH e-mail system (*MH & xmh: E-mail for Users and Programmers*, O'Reilly & Associates), says:

> . . . look at the source code yourself or call Rent-a-Guru :-).

To me, that smiley looks like it has a mole on its chin. I would have written it this way:

> . . . look at the source code yourself or call Rent-a-Guru. :-)

You don't have to wait until the end of a sentence for a smiley, of course, if it makes things clearer to embed a smiley after an appropriate phrase in the middle of a sentence:

However, it takes a great deal of skill and practice :-) to do it properly.

The main principle still applies: Try to avoid confusion between the smiley and any other punctuation.

People also wonder how to attach a smiley to a sentence in parentheses. You can use smileys with parenthesized sentences in a variety of ways. If the smiley doesn't end with a), you can simply put the smiley inside the closing parenthesis, separated from it by a space or two, as shown in this example:

(The sun didn't come out at all in November. `%-{`)

If the smiley *does* end with a), as the basic smiley does, you can make it serve double duty and use it to close the parenthesized text or follow the preceding pattern and put the closing paren a space or two after the smiley:

(Beware of programs with a `-vd` option. `:-)`

If you don't like either of those choices, you can parenthesize the sentence by using characters other than parentheses, as shown in this example:

[How 'bout them Screaming Earwigs? `:-)`]

What Other Smileys Are There?

Because smileys are such a cute idea, people have invented hundreds and hundreds of other smileys. Many smileys are pictures of faces, but many are not. But they all are cute, one-line pictures. For example, the following list shows the winner (listed first) and the 20 runners-up in the O'Reilly & Associates "Best New Smiley" contest:

`>[:^)` — Watches too much TV. Pete "Ender" Walsh (ender@uunet.uu.net)

`::-b|d-::` — Person with glasses sticking out tongue at mirror. Galen Johnson (chjohnso@ecuvm.cis.ecu.edu)

`=[8]-0` — Spaceman Spiff preparing to land. Greg Boyd (greg@ATWC.Teradyne.COM)

`.!!!.` — Lion hand. Laszlo Drotos (h1192dro@ella.hu)

`[]:-{o` — Barbershop quartet singer. Neil Sokolowski

`<*(:-?` — Wizard who doesn't know the answer. Bruce J. Barton (robvis@bnl.gov)

`,,,^..^,,,` — Cat peeking over a fence (notice claws). Ina L. Mehlman (ha32932@montcolc.bitnet)

`#:o\:o/:o\:o/:o||` — Totem pole. Michael Maier (michael_maier@qmgate.anl.gov)

`(:-0 ==>` — Rush Limbaugh (notice loud tie). Heather Taylor (hjt3873@exodus.valpo.edu)

(Z(:^P

Napoleon. Paul Curcio (fizzbomb@aol.com)

*-=|8-D

A clown. Charles Hannum (mycroft@gnu.ai.mit.edu)

:-8p

Dizzy Gillespie (puffed cheeks and trumpet). Michael J. Kahlke (kahlke@ctron.com)

IIIIII8^)X

The Cat in the Hat. "Dr. Seuss" (nmurray@undergrad.math.uwaterloo.ca)

',',',',':|

Mrs. Frankenstein. Matthew Allen Lewis (mal11@po.cwru.edu)

'@______

Snail mail. Robert Mudry (robertm@clbooks.com)

'\=o-o=/'

Eyeglasses. Jose Manuel Pereira (cs911168@ariel.yorku.ca)

o0:)&

A grandmother. Maureen Zapryluk (mzapryluk@nwcny.sscnet.ucla.edu)

/\/:/\

A mummy. Barry Ackerman

())=(

Wine glass. Bonnie Petry (bpetry@wiley.csusb.edu)

#!^~/

"Kissy" profile: hair (à la Archie Andrews), shades, nose, smooch, and chin. Alan L. Chamberlain (axon@well.sf.ca.us)

<0__/__/_

A worm. Martin Frischherz (FRISCHHERZ@kapsch.co.at)

How Can I Get More Smileys?

I am working on a new version of my smiley collection. It is already almost three times (!) as large as the previously released version. Watch for it in the Usenet newsgroups comp.sources.misc, rec.arts.ascii, or alt.humor. I am also working on making my list available by way of the World Wide Web. If you can't wait, this section tells you how to get the most recently posted version.

My smiley program (containing the largest and most comprehensive collection of smileys ever posted) was most recently posted in `comp.sources.misc`, Volume 23. See your nearby `comp.sources.misc` archive site to obtain it; here's the index line:

```
v23i102   smiley/part01      smiley - smiley server, version 4, Part01/01
```

Or get my book, *Smileys* (published by O'Reilly & Associates, ISBN 1-56592-041-4).

To obtain the smiley list by way of Gopher:

> Gopher to `gopher.ora.com`. If you don't have a Gopher client program locally, you can telnet there and log in with the username `gopher` (no password).
>
> Choose the Feature Articles option from the main menu, and then choose the option All the Smileys in the Known Universe. You can then access the complete list of smileys published in the book.

Here are a few anonymous ftp sites and paths:

```
wuarchive.wustl.edu
usenet/comp.sources.misc/volume23/smiley/part01.Z  ftp.uu.net
usenet/comp.sources.misc/volume23/smiley/part01.Z
```

David Sanderson got his B.S. in Computer Science at Washington University in Saint Louis. When not engaged in smiley lexicography, he's worked for AT&T Bell Laboratories, the Ultimate Corp., and the UW-Madison Space Science and Engineering Center.

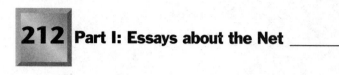

Part II

Connecting to the Internet

In This Part

Chapter 8 DNS: The Domain Name System

Chapter 9 Connecting Your UNIX System to the Net

Chapter 10 Linking Your Organization's Network to the Internet

Chapter 11 Maintaining Large Networks

Chapter 12 Personal Internet Access Using SLIP or PPP

Chapter 13 Tuning TCP/IP

Chapter 14 Connecting Your Macintosh to the Internet

Chapter 15 Macintosh TIA: A Lighthearted Guide to a Heavy Topic

Chapter 16 OS/2 Warp and the Internet

Chapter 8

DNS: The Domain Name System

by Garret Hildebrand

This chapter is about the *Domain Name System*, or DNS, and how it fits into the biggest network of all, the Internet. Originally described in RFC 1034 and RFC 1035[1,2], the Domain Name System is now widely implemented in DNS servers all over the Internet and in clients that use the information provided by them. As a user of the Internet, you have probably already seen some of the hierarchical names used by DNS. For example, if you have used a Web browser recently, you may have seen the DNS names `home.mcom.com` and `www.ncsa.uiuc.edu`.

The Domain Name System is about mapping unique hierarchical names to unique Internet addresses and back again. Within this chapter is an overview of how this name-to-address and address-to-name translation takes place, how it is useful to you, and what is involved in setting up a server of DNS data within the UNIX domain or making use of such a server in the client domain — where Internet information services such as World Wide Web, telnet, ftp, and e-mail are used.

Introduction to DNS

As thousands of people around the planet jump onto the Internet, they are being confronted by one new concept after another. One of these concepts — the *Domain Name System*, or DNS — is key to understanding and using the Internet. In fact, every time a user sends e-mail, telnets to another computer, or ftps to some great archive site, his success relies heavily upon the Domain Name System in some way.

The Domain Name System essentially is a distributed database used to locate hosts by name. It is important to understand the relationship between this database and, for example, standard Internet e-mail addresses or World Wide Web domain addresses. The information in this distributed database is maintained and accessed via host systems that support implementations of DNS. These systems usually are referred to as *nameservers* or *domain nameservers*. Without DNS, you would probably be forced to type in a raw Internet address to get to some destination.

The question that many people ask is, "Do I somehow use the Domain Name System indirectly through a remote nameserver, or do I actually employ it myself on a computer or network by setting up a nameserver?"

The answer depends on the situation. One common case, for example, is when a PC talks to an existing network or Internet provider, using WinSock and some TCP/IP tools, such as ftp and telnet. The other common scenario is when a network is set up or expanded in some way, perhaps to connect to the Internet for the first time through a commercial feed from some provider.

This chapter should give either type of user a good answer to the questions and help on where other information may be found.

Hostnames and IP addresses

Machines on the Internet communicate with one another through the TCP/IP protocol (Transmission Control Protocol/Internet Protocol) suite, which enables heterogeneous systems to operate across globally diverse networks. Communication between one Internet host and another is founded on this protocol and on the IP addressing system, in which a unique 32-bit address, known as an *IP address*, is associated with each host. *IP* stands for *Internet Protocol* and is the network layer portion of the TCP/IP protocol.

The notation for the IP addresses is *dotted-octet* notation. The 32-bit IP numbers are represented as four 8-bit numbers expressed as decimal numbers in the range 0–255 and separated by periods (dots). The 8-bit component gives rise to the term *octet*.

Computer hosts commonly have names because humans customarily name things. On hosts that are capable of communicating with the Internet, some form of binding exists between the host's name and its IP address, allowing humans and their programs to refer to things by name rather than by address. From the most esoteric Internet host to a personal computer that has been loaded with the Internet tools and software needed to establish a TCP/IP connection, this association is constant.

On machines that have an operating system in which TCP/IP is an integral part, a common method of maintaining this association is a *hosts file*. On a larger level, at one time, the hostname-to-address mappings were tracked by the Network Information Center (NIC) on behalf of the Internet. These mappings were kept in a single file called HOSTS.TXT, which was ftped to other hosts from time to time as new hosts were added.

The /etc/hosts file found on UNIX systems today reflects that heritage. Each system on the Internet ftped to the NIC to get the latest HOSTS.TXT file and then kept the portion of the file that was relevant to that machine's role in the Internet. This system did not scale very well, however, as the Net grew.

Domain Name System origin

The first problem that this system faced was that individual hosts or local organizations that administered their own networks had to wait for the NIC to change HOSTS.TXT before changes became visible to the Internet at large — and then only after the file was distributed.

Second, name conflicts arose. It was difficult, if not impossible, to control name conflicts as more and more hosts were added to the Internet.

Third, the number of Internet hosts and the bandwidth required to support ftping this information from the NIC kept growing. This caused problems not only in terms of propagation time, but, more significantly with respect to the NIC host's load, also in terms of the not-so-inconsequential bandwidth consumed while propagating the HOSTS.TXT file via ftp.

To quote Paul Mockapetris in RFC 1034: "The total network bandwidth consumed in distributing a new version by this scheme is proportional to the square of the number of hosts in the network. . . ."

Fourth, there were the issues of source routing versus network routing and of the construction of e-mail addresses for traffic between dissimilar addressing schemes over multiple networks.

As discussed by Quarterman[3], there is the Matrix and then there is the Internet. The Matrix comprises all networks worldwide that exchange at least mail and/or news, including the UUCP mail network, Usenet News, BITNET, FidoNet, and commercial services such as America Online and CompuServe, as well as the Internet. The Internet is the set of networks that use the TCP/IP protocol suite to communicate directly. Many networks exist within the Internet: wide-area networks, such as ANSnet (just purchased by America Online), NFSNET, PSInet, AlterNet, and CERFNET; regional networks, such as NEARNET and BARRNet; and university, commercial, and workgroup networks. If you can't ftp to `venera.isi.edu` or `ftp.uu.net` but you can send e-mail to `gdh@ACM.org`, you are somewhere on the Matrix but not on the Internet itself.

To complicate matters, many of these networks have their own naming and routing conventions. Usenet, for example, uses bang signs (!) to separate hosts in the mail message routing line, which is pure source routing (routes specified in the address itself) and does not require routing on the part of the network.

The Domain Name System was introduced to bring order to this chaos and to supply answers to these problems. According to Tanenbaum[4], this uniform naming system initially was applied to the networks ARPANET (predecessor of NSFNET and of the Internet), Usenet, BITNET, and CSNET. The idea was to group all hosts in these networks into *domains*. Each domain would form a node in a naming tree. Hostnames would need to be unique only within their immediate domain.

The Domain Name System, which was the result of several ideas and the experiences of several implementations, eventually was presented in RFCs 1034 and 1035. The hierarchical structure and distributed nature have proved to be a workable and scalable scheme.

The original implementation of DNS, called JEEVES, was written by Paul Mockapetris, author of RFCs 1034 and 1035 (among other things). Later, a fellow by the name of Kevin Dunlap wrote another implementation, called BIND, which was created for Berkeley 4.3BSD UNIX. BIND, which stands for *Berkeley Internet Name Domain*, is the most popular and common form of DNS implementation on the planet. The section "Root Servers for the Domain Name System," which appears later in this chapter, shows that all root servers run BIND as of September 1994.

What is DNS?

In RFC 1035, the Domain Name System is referred to as a "mixture of functions and data types which are an official protocol." DNS also has been referred to as a distributed database[5] and as a naming scheme. It is all these things.

DNS is a hierarchical naming scheme supported by servers, usually called *nameservers,* that serve data from a distributed database. The hierarchy is like a tree, with the top level being the Internet Network Information Center, or InterNIC. The InterNIC nameservers support several immediate nodes in the hierarchical DNS tree, each of which is referred to as a top-level domain. Currently, InterNIC nameservers support these top-level domains:

Name	***Description***
com	Commercial organizations, such as Microsoft.com and Paciolan.com
edu	Education institutions and universities, such as UCI.edu and UCLA.edu
org	Not-for-profit organizations, such as ACM.org
net	Networks, such as CERF.net and NFS.net
gov	Nonmilitary government organizations, such as Whitehouse.gov and NASA.gov
mil	Military government organizations, such as Navy.mil
int	International organizations, such as NATO.int
xx	Two-letter ISO country codes, such as au and us

Domains may in turn have *subdomains*. Subdomains of the top-level domains, called *second-level domains*, must be unique. Second-level domains must be applied for, approved, and registered with the InterNIC. Second-level domains usually represent entire organizations, although some large organizations further segment themselves; these pieces become subdomains at the third and lower levels. Therefore, the second-level domain in this case serves as an umbrella for an organization with disparate parts.

"The Domain Name Registration Form" section, which appears near the end of this chapter, describes the domain-registration process.

An interesting thing about domains is that subdomains spawned by domains need not be geographically cohesive units. For example, a multinational corporation can register one second-level domain with the InterNIC and then create many subdomains in several countries.

So, the Domain Name System is both a naming scheme and a distributed database that supports that scheme, with a central registration for second-level domains and a known set of functions that can be applied to the database. But what does this all mean to the average user?

First, users almost never use DNS directly; instead, they use it indirectly through applications.

Second, DNS is a powerful method of handling hosts and their names relative to their immediate domain. This means that names have to be unique only within a particular domain — an arrangement that both decentralizes the job of maintaining the naming system while also eliminating collisions between hostnames within the greater DNS system. The responsibility for ensuring uniqueness of hostnames within a domain falls to the domain or system administrator.

Third, DNS is a truly distributed system with thousands of cooperating servers, ensuring that anybody on the Internet who has the software to query these servers can get to anywhere else on the Internet.

Finally, DNS provides a consistent method for specifying how to find a host on the Internet or the Matrix, in terms of electronic mail as well as other applications that need to locate a host on the Internet for whatever reason.

Interpreting domain names

The standard form of an Internet e-mail address looks something like this:

```
userid@domain.name
```

The part on the left of the @ sign is the mailbox name, which generally is a name in the aliases file of the target system or a user ID. The part on the right side is the domain name.

Domain names are read from right to left. Segments of the domain name are separated by periods. Domain names are easy to understand if the segments are taken one step at a time.

The rightmost segment is the top-level domain. Because the Internet began life as ARPANET, all the original top-level domain names were of the three-letter variety. Later, when the Internet went international, the option of having the top-level domain be a two-letter country code was introduced and then standardized via ISO 3166.

Most countries that use the ISO 3166 top-level domain names use the standard three-letter U.S. top-level domain names as their second-level domains. Australia, for example, may have `org.au` or `edu.au` as second-level domains.

Meanwhile, the United Kingdom and some other countries think that the second-level domain also should be a two-letter code. And some of the codes are different: instead of `edu`, for example, `ac` is used (for academic community), and instead of `com`, `co` is used.

Interestingly, the United States has its own geographic designator available for use at the top level, although this designator is not often used. This designator, of course, is `us`. When this designator is used, the three-letter codes (`com, org`, `edu`, and so on) are pushed down to level-three domains, because the second-level domain in this case becomes the state postal abbreviation. Nonetheless, it is likely that most Internet users will see domain names similar to `UCI.edu` more often than they will see `UCI.edu.ca.us`.

In summary, in a domain name, the rightmost segments indicate top-level domain names, and the leftmost segment is either a hostname or an alias for one.

Consider the following example:

```
sunsite.unc.edu
```

In this example, the top-level domain is edu, and the second-level domain is unc. Lastly, sunsite is the host name. (By the way, unc stands for the University of North Carolina at Chapel Hill.)

An interesting domain name experiment is to use the ping utility to play with one. First, ping the entire domain name, including the obvious host part. Then drop off segments from the left, one at a time, and see whether the result responds to ping. When you hit a remainder of segments that won't ping, you most likely are looking at a domain name in which no hostnames are involved.

As an example, ping the domain name for the famous ftp site wuarchive.wustl.edu at Washington University in St. Louis. This domain name illustrates the difference between the hostname portion of a domain name and the actual domain portion of it. In the following listing, the domain, quite obviously, is wustl.edu, consisting of a second-level domain name and the top-level .edu ending. By the way, adding a trailing period to such a name makes it fully qualified. Such names are called FQDN, for *fully qualified domain name*. Therefore, the hostname is wuarchive, the domain is wustl.edu, and the FQDN is wuarchive.wustl.edu.

```
$ ping -s wuarchive.wustl.edu
PING wuarchive.wustl.edu: 56 data bytes
64 bytes from wuarchive.wustl.edu (128.252.135.4): icmp_seq=0. time=1304. ms
64 bytes from wuarchive.wustl.edu (128.252.135.4): icmp_seq=2. time=76. ms
. . .
Ctrl-C
$ ping -s wustl.edu
ping: unknown host wustl.edu
```

Returning to the peculiarities of domain names, this address recently popped up in a newsgroup:

```
mff.cuni.cz
```

In this address, cz is the Czech Republic, but what is cuni? It turns out that this particular domain name does not follow *all* the rules, because cuni stands for Charles University!

Here is another interesting twist:

```
ca.mdis.com
uk.mdis.com
```

These domain names contain no actual hostnames — only the actual domain information itself. The top-level domain is com, and the second-level domain, mdis, is a U.K.-based company (the registered domain can be verified via the whois command as mdis.com). How about ca and uk? These are subdomains of mdis.com. Why have them? The parent domain, mdis.com, is delegating authority for the subdomain ca.mdis.com to a nameserver in that subdomain. This situation most likely occurs because the parent domain is in Europe, whereas the child domain is in North America, and delegation of control over that site makes more sense. More information on these concepts appears later in this chapter, in the section called "Domain nameservers."

whois is commonly found on most UNIX machines and uses the same simple sort of TCP exchange as the finger command to query a particular host database — typically NIC.DDN.MIL, or the InterNIC — to return rough matches to the string being looked up. For example, try whois hildebrand. Note that not all implementations default to lookup on one of these root machines. Some implementations simply look only on the local machine unless some option is given. Check the man page to be sure of detail on use.

These domain names are, perhaps, unusual, yet the Internet is full of many like them. Fortunately, knowing exactly how to break apart its components usually is not a requirement for using a domain name. Resolvers automatically speak to nameservers to resolve a domain name down to an IP address, which then can be contacted over the Internet, a private or public internetworked network on the Internet, a simple network, or even a PC that is connected to the Internet through a provider.

Does my network need a domain nameserver?

For a site connected to the Internet via a direct connection — say, a 56KB leased line or better — DNS usually is a must. In fact, a good exercise to go through *before* you order your Internet connection from some provider is getting your DNS system to work — perhaps even testing the *zone transfer* by specifying another machine on your network as a secondary master server. (The zone transfer mechanism of a DNS server allows multiple machines to share the DNS database of one, authoritative machine, known as a *primary master nameserver.*) By testing out the zone transfer in advance, when your new Internet connection becomes available, you can just e-mail to the provider the information required for the provider's named.boot file. In this way, the provider will come up as your secondary DNS server with no pain. In fact, you can even give the provider the secondary information in advance, once you have it worked out.

Zone transfers are explained later in this chapter (see the following sections: "Zones," "Caches and redundant servers," and "Domain nameservers"). Suffice it to say that any network that has a full Internet connection should have a DNS system set up on the main host or an allocated host. If the network has a firewall, the firewall may be a good candidate for acting as the primary server (for more detail, refer to Chapter 5).

On the other hand, if your shop is a small affair with only a few hosts, it may make sense to see whether you can be part of someone else's domain. A domain can cover several localities, so it need not be all in one place. Many commercial Internet providers will manage a domain for you as a subdomain of their domains — for a fee!

Sites that run on Sun Microsystems's various offerings probably employ Sun's Network Information Service (NIS). NIS can do many of the same things on a local network that DNS normally takes care of.

(continued)

(continued)

DNS actually is a decentralized and distributed hierarchical hostname management system, so every domain server knows how to find servers for domains other than its own. This means that an individual organization can run a server for its own division or corporation and make host changes without notifying a central authority, because the host information will be published through the rest of the network. An NIS system has a master server that must be advised of any name changes; this arrangement makes distributed management difficult.

Such NIS systems have three methods of managing the complexity:

- Don't use DNS; instead, rely on NIS.
- Don't use NIS; instead, disable NIS and use only DNS.
- Use NIS mappings first, and then allow DNS lookups when NIS fails to find a hostname. This method requires running NIS with a special flag. Details on NIS configuration are beyond the scope of this chapter, but many references appear in vendor material and in published books, such as the O'Reilly and Associates book, *Managing NFS and NIS* (Stern, H. *Managing NFS and NIS.* Sebastopol, CA: O'Reilly and Associates, 1992. ISBN 0-937175-75-7.).

If you are running a PC that talks to the Internet via a dialup SLIP or PPP connection, you may not have to worry about DNS on your machine; in all likelihood, your Internet software contains resolver software that queries the domain nameserver that you specify in the setup or configuration of the package.

On the other hand, a fairly complex TCP/IP network that is largely PC-oriented and connected to the Internet may benefit by having a UNIX system that provides DNS or a specially crafted PC-based software package that runs on a file server and provides the same functions. At this time, it is my opinion that PCs that are not running UNIX do not have the implementation of DNS required to serve as authoritative and robust nameservers that handle both the internal needs of the domain and the external requirements of a nameserver used by the rest of the Internet. This may change as various PC-based operating systems are developed and improved.

How Does DNS Work?

Despite the fact that DNS is described as a distributed database or a naming scheme, it is almost impossible to discuss DNS without talking about BIND. BIND is a particular implementation of DNS, and it is nearly the only DNS server that anyone uses. BIND software runs on all UNIX machines as a daemon on the well-known port number 53 (as registered on all standard UNIX distributions in the /etc/services file) with the name of *named* (pronounced "name-dee").

When people speak of DNS, they often say *DNS and BIND*, just like the title of O'Reilly and Associates' book by the same name. (Albitz, P. and Liu, C. *DNS and BIND*. Sebastopol, CA: O'Reilly and Associates, 1992. ISBN 0-56592-010-4.) DNS represents the theory of a distributed database of domain names, whereas BIND is the best-known instantiation of the concept. In other words, BIND is a real-world instance of DNS.

To summarize, DNS is the concept, as defined by RFCs 920, 1034, and 1035. BIND is the software that must be obtained, configured, compiled, and installed on your system to support the operation of the *named* daemon so that a nameserver is available on port 53 (no doubt on the system that you are planning to register with the InterNIC as the primary master nameserver for your network).

Of course, these days, BIND ships as a standard part of most flavors of UNIX, so configuration, compilation, and installation most likely will not be considerations for most administrators.

The net result (so to speak) is that people generally associate DNS, BIND, *named*, and nameservers. Often, system administrators refer to *named* rather than to BIND or DNS because administrators think in terms of files used by the *named* daemon and in terms of starting or refreshing the *named* daemon to read or reread those files. In fact, the man page on the subject appears under *named* on most UNIX systems.

On any system, DNS has three basic parts:

- The resolver software resolves inquiries on domain names and host names. This software often is called just resolver.
- DNS data files, often called zone files or named data, are used by *named.*
- The *named* daemon loads, maintains in its namespace, and serves the *named* data, or DNS database for that domain. The system that hosts this daemon is called a nameserver.

Domains, zones, and name resolution

Names on the Internet are organized into a tree, as shown in Figure 8-1. For a host named `tom.iecc.com`, for example, a resolver would start at the root of the tree, find `com` within that, find `iecc` within that, find `tom` within that, and then use the information (such as the IP host number) associated with `tom`. In principle, that's exactly how DNS name resolution works. Of course, there is quite a lot of extra stuff to make the process fast and robust and to enable different parts of the name tree to be handled separately.

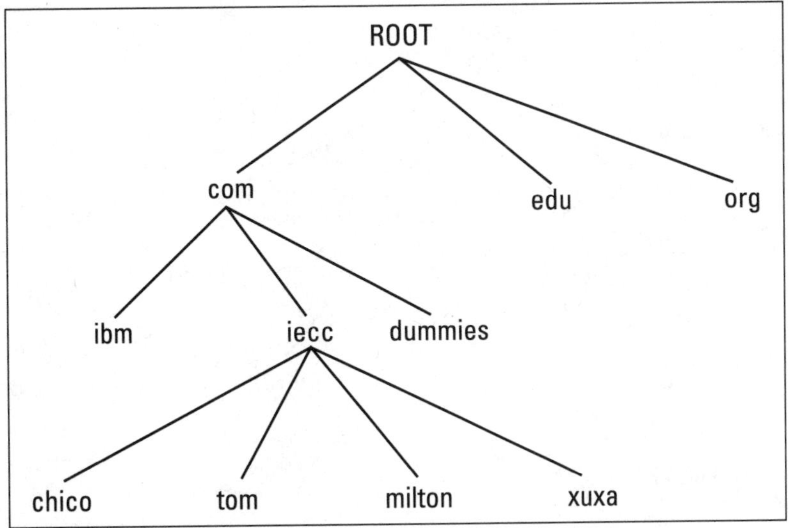

Figure 8-1: Part of the domain tree.

Zones

The most important enhancement is the concept of zones. Any particular nameserver is authoritative for some part of the DNS namespace — that is, for the part of the namespace for which that particular server knows the definitive truth. To find the truth about other parts of the namespace, the server has to contact other servers to find — and query — an authoritative server. Conversely, if a server is authoritative for some part of the namespace, other servers contact it to find out about its part. The subtree in the namespace for which a single server is authoritative is a *zone.* (A single server can be authoritative for several zones, but this chapter disregards that complication.)

Consider `tom.iecc.com` again, for example. Conceptually, a resolver starts any request at the root of the DNS name tree, so it asks a root server what it knows about `tom.iecc.com`. The root responds that `iecc.com` is delegated to other servers — that is, it's a different zone — and returns the numeric addresses of the servers for that zone. The resolver then makes its request to one of the servers for the `iecc.com` zone, as in Figure 8-2, which returns the desired answer.

In this case, because `iecc.com` is a small domain, only one level of delegation exists. In large organizations, however, subtrees and subsubtrees of the organization's domain commonly are separate zones, so a single request may have to contact four or five servers to get all the way from the root to a desired name.

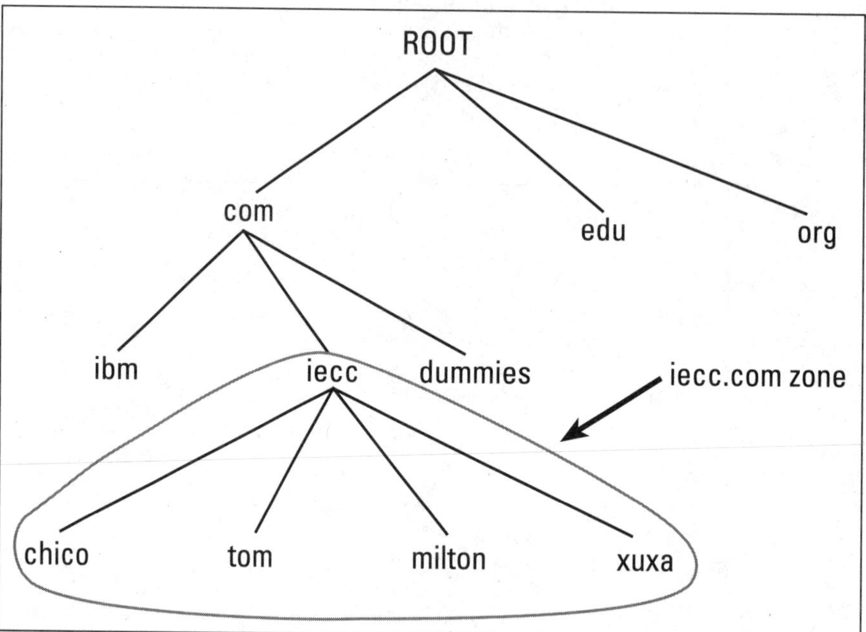

Figure 8-2: The `iecc.com` zone.

Caches and redundant servers

If every name-resolution request started by contacting one of the root nameservers, of which only seven exist in the entire Internet, the root servers would quickly become swamped. To solve this problem, encourage resolvers to cache the information that they retrieve so that the resolvers can reuse the information for subsequent queries. If another application asks for the numeric address of `tom.iecc.com`, the resolver then can answer directly from its cache. Furthermore, to resolve the name `xuxa.iecc.com`, the resolver remembers the address of the server for `iecc.com` and can ask it directly for information on `xuxa` without having to bother the root servers again.

Because the data in the authoritative servers changes from time to time, the data in each answer returned to a DNS request includes a time-to-live field, which tells the resolver how long it can cache the answer — typically, in the range between an hour and a day. Therefore, cached data eventually is discarded, and the data is fetched again the next time that the resolver needs it. The time to live for data that is updated frequently should be short (a few minutes, perhaps), whereas the time to live for data that is updated infrequently should be long (as long as a week in some cases).

To make DNS faster and more robust, each zone has to have at least two servers (preferably, more) so that if one of the servers fails or is overloaded, the other(s) can serve clients elsewhere on the Net. Seven root servers, which are quite busy and very important, are distributed over seven different networks on several continents. Smaller domains usually have fewer servers, but all domains have at least two.

BIND usually is set up so that one of the servers for each zone is the primary server and the rest are secondary. From the point of view of the rest of the Net, there's no difference. The secondary servers update their data from the primary server every once in a while, so the human administrator needs to update only the primary server; the secondaries follow along. These automatic transfers, or zone transfers, allow a domain to be served redundantly by several servers, increasing the availability of information about the domain.

Iterative vs. recursive name requests

Depending on how powerful a client computer is, a DNS can make two kinds of requests of a server: iterative and recursive.

The resolution scenario discussed in the preceding section involves an iterative request. The client asks the server to resolve a name, and if the server can't do that, it sends back the addresses of better servers to use. The client then sends the same request to the new server. Indeed, it repeats the process until it gets the answer.

In a recursive request, the client asks the server to make any necessary request on the client's behalf, so the server returns the answer even if it has to go elsewhere to find the answer. Recursive requests put more load on the server but provide for much simpler client design. In practice, only the simplest clients — such as a client running on a microcomputer — use recursive requests.

This comparison of iterative and recursive servers paid attention only to servers that were authoritative for some DNS zone. In reality, many DNS servers exist all over the Internet (nearly every UNIX system can act as one), and most of these servers aren't authoritative for anything. What they can do, though, is act as servers for other, less capable machines on the same network (PCs and Macs, for example), handling recursive requests and caching the results locally to minimize the number of requests that have to go out over the Net.

Resolvers

Resolvers are programs that access nameservers as clients. Resolvers work on behalf of Internet applications that need information from the domain namespace managed by nameservers. The BIND distribution included in most UNIX machines includes a set of resolver library routines compiled in the programs that require this type of information, such as telnet and ftp.

Most PC-based TCP/IP applications include resolvers along with Web browsers, telnet, ftp, and similar applications. If the PC has been configured to understand how to find a nameserver via its IP connection, these applications will be able to find all those great sites that you want to visit.

If you know the name of the place to which you want to go, you're not tied to the numerical IP number of that host. The owner of the site can change the IP number of the machine and not cause suffering for his ftp or WWW clients; the clients get to the machine via domain names, which are resolved into IP addresses dynamically each time that they're needed.

Great things, resolvers.

On most UNIX machines, the resolver usually uses a file called /etc/resolv.conf. This file contains various directives, primarily *domain* and *nameserver*. The nameserver directive identifies a nameserver to use by its IP address. (The nameserver can't be identified by name because the resolver can't resolve any names until after it's contacted its nameserver.) Following are examples of the two directives:

```
domain farcaster.com
nameserver 192.168.8.2
```

Some systems, such as those that run IBM's AIX 3.2, do not query a nameserver, but merely rely on NIS or on the /etc/hosts file if the /etc/resolv.conf file does not exist. For this reason, if you do not feel the need to specify other nameservers to query, such as when the host in question is running a nameserver, at least ensure that you have an empty resolv.conf file to be sure that your system uses DNS rather than NIS. On AIX, for example, the resolv.conf file must exist for DNS to be used. To be sure of specifics, read the vendors' man pages.

The behavior of resolvers can be greatly affected by the level of integration with NIS. System administrators who take care of systems that run NIS should read up on this subject in *Managing NFS and NIS* (Stern, H. *Managing NFS and NIS.* Sebastopol, CA: O'Reilly and Associates,1992. ISBN 0-937175-75-7.)

Resolvers work with domain nameservers to attend to the process of name resolution (or just resolution). As you will see, configuration of the *named* daemon involves (among other things) specification of a root cache, which identifies to the nameserver the IP addresses of all the root nameservers on the Internet. These root nameservers are authoritative for the top-level U.S domains and also know where to find authoritative nameservers for all other top-level domains.

Given this information, a nameserver works with these nameservers to resolve a domain name and then return it to the requesting client: the resolver, working on behalf of some application.

The *named* daemon and its data files

Named is the server part of BIND, the DNS server that runs on most UNIX systems. When the *named* daemon is started, usually during system boot, when TCP/IP is initialized, it reads a configuration file usually called /etc/named.boot. This file identifies where the *named* daemon will find its data files and identifies the type of server that it should run as.

In the primary master configuration — the one used to set up the primary authoritative nameserver for a domain — the *named* daemon requires special database files that describe the domain in terms of domains, subdomains, hosts, and reverse lookup, or in-addr lookup (from IP number to host name, as opposed to the usual other direction). The formats of all these files are described later in this chapter, in "*Named* Data Files."

It is worth noting that the location of these data files may vary with the system or even with the system administrator. ***Hint:*** Look in /etc/named.boot to see where the files are before you hunt around for them. Often, the files are in a /usr/local/named directory, although the AIX man page for *named*, for example, identifies them as being in the /etc directory.

Domain nameservers

Two types of DNS nameservers exist: primary master and secondary master. Generally, these servers are called simply *primary* and *secondary*.

The primary is a host that has all the *named* data files for the zones for which it is authoritative; the host reads those files whenever the *named* daemon is started. The type of server being run is identified in the /etc/named.boot file. The means of enabling the server varies from system to system. In AIX, for example, a line is uncommented in the /etc/rc.tcpip file. Do a `man named` on your system to find out more.

A zone often is synonymous with its domain. In this situation, a nameserver inside a domain serves the entire domain and is authoritative for it. What is more, the domain has no subdomains, and no delegation of authority exists for any part of the domain.

This is not always the case, however. In `uk.mdis.com` and `ca.mdis.com`, for example, the domain is `mdis.com`, and the subdomains are `uk.mdis.com` and `ca.mdis.com`. The domain is broken into three zones: `mdis.com`, `uk.mdis.com`, and ca.mdis.com. Because ca.mdis.com is geographically separated from uk.mdis.com by a great distance, authority for ca.mdis.com is delegated to it. Therefore, a primary master nameserver exists in the ca.mdis.com zone, and another primary master nameserver exists in the uk.mdis.com zone, which delegates authority by decision of the domain master for mdis.com.

As you will see, authoritative nameservers for domains are visible to Internet denizens in several ways, including the use of the whois command to see what primary and secondary nameservers are designated and who has technical responsibility for the domain.

DNS provides the secondary to make administration easier. Although the purpose of the secondary is to back up the primary in case it goes down — or to improve availability or to distribute the load — the *named* data files need not be present on the secondary machine. The /etc/named.boot file lines that tell *named* that it must run as a secondary for a particular zone also indicate the primary system by IP number, and the secondary simply gets the zone information from *that* system through the mechanism of a zone transfer. In this way, the administrator need keep only one copy of the data up-to-date — on the primary.

Following is a sample /etc/named.boot file that reflects the role of the *named* daemon on that system as both a primary nameserver for the zone it is in and as a secondary nameserver for another domain. In this example, the other domain pays this nameserver to provide this service. (What a way to make money!)

```
directory     /usr/local/named

primary       flort.com                    db.flort
primary       149.168.192.in-addr.arpa     db.192.168.149
primary       0.0.127.in-addr.arpa         db.127.0.0

secondary     glork.com                    172.16.31.2        dbc.glork
secondary     31.16.172.in-addr.arpa       172.16.31.2        dbc.172.16.31

cache         root.cache
```

Notice that the secondary lines contain more arguments than the primary lines do. In the primary lines, the second column identifies either forward lookup (name to address) or reverse lookup (address to name, or in-addr) and the name of the data file that contains this information. The secondary lines have the same information in the second column but entirely new information in the third: an IP address. This IP address, in fact, is the address of another nameserver on the Internet from which namespace is to be transferred.

These transfers from the primary to the secondary are called *zone transfers*. When a nameserver first fires up — that is, when the *named* daemon starts — the server reads all the files specified by the primary lines in the named.boot file. These files are stored in memory space allocated by the *named* daemon and are stored in the correct fashion for the BIND software that the *named* daemon is executing. This information is called the *namespace*.

The zone transfer takes place when the *named* daemon notices, on start-up, that secondary lines appear in the named.boot file. The host specified by column three — the IP number — is contacted, and a zone transfer is requested. Unless some form of security restriction exists to prevent this transfer, the remote nameserver hands over the zone information from its namespace.

The filenames in the fourth column are used to store the snapshot of this fetched namespace. The data in these files are in a format that a human can examine. The filenames are volatile and should not be changed as a method of altering the behavior of the secondary. The information in these files is overwritten every time a zone transfer takes place.

Most people who administer DNS and BIND have either a primary or secondary master nameserver but not both. Who knows, though? Perhaps someday you will run the systems at an Internet provider. In that case, notice that the filenames used have consistent prefixes and that the secondary filenames are different (for example, dbc.), making it easy for the domain master to separate the wheat from the chaff.

Examine the following /etc/named.boot file for a primary master nameserver:

```
directory     /usr/local/named

primary       farcaster.com                db.farcaster
primary       8.168.192.in-addr.arpa       db.192.168.8
primary       0.0.127.in-addr.arpa         db.127.0.0

cache         root.cache
```

The second column of the primary lines is the domain. The first line identifies the domain `farcaster.com`, and the second line identifies the domain `8.168.192.in-addr.arpa`. Both types of domains are managed by the InterNIC. The second-level domain, `farcaster`, needs to be registered with the InterNIC; `farcaster` manages the parent domain, `com`, and `com` serves one of farcaster's root servers. The `in-addr.arpa` domains also are part of the DNS system. For address-to-name mapping to be successful, the `in-addr.arpa` domains must be registered as well.

Nodes in the `in-addr.arpa` domain are named after the numbers that make up the dotted-octet representation used to denote IP addresses. This domain is supported by a hierarchical domain tree in the DNS namespace that has four levels, one for each octet. The first level, managed by the root servers, conceptually has 256 nodes. Each of these nodes in turn has 256 nodes. And so on.

The nameserver for a domain typically manages the host portion of the `in-addr.arpa` domain. In a class C network, for example, 256 subdomains would exist for each of the possible IP addresses. (Actually, there are 254 subdomains, because 0 and 255 are used for broadcasts.)

Another point to notice in the preceding example concerns the domain specification of each of the primary lines, which becomes the default domain for DNS definitions in the corresponding named data files identified in the third column. Also notice that the IP address is in reverse order in the `in-addr.arpa` domain specification. To make the data file for this domain easy to spot, the network portion of the class C address is added as a suffix to the prefix `db` (for example, `db.192.168.8`).

The `0.0.127.in-addr.arpa` domain specification is for the loopback, or local host, IP address, which conventionally refers to the computer itself.

The cache line is provided so that the nameserver's namespace is primed with root-server domain information (DNS lookups then can begin there) and so that the *named* daemon can work its way through the hierarchical DNS tree, sorting out resolver queries.

Often, when setting up a domain, the domain administrator puts the primary for the domain inside of the domain and makes the Internet provider a secondary to the domain — outside of it. In this way, the administrator keeps administrative control of the domain, while still providing a nameserver on the Internet that can resolve domain information for other nameservers, even when the primary system is down.

Obviously, primary masters should have high availability; by implication, so should secondary.

DNS and Sendmail

One of the most common implementations of electronic mail in UNIX systems is *sendmail.* In this section, I describe why e-mail can stop working if a domain nameserver is added.

As you will see in more detail later, in the section on DNS resource records, DNS has a special provision for mail called an MX resource record. Sendmail recognizes only the canonical version of the host's name in MX lists. It is possible to build a domain where hosts in it are reachable only by e-mail and to put the domain servers outside of the domain. In this case, MX resource records are used in the DNS database to identify the mail server or gateway within the domain. In any case, hosts inside the DNS system should have an MX record so that mail transfer agents know what to do with e-mail.

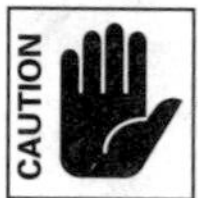

Only the canonical hostname should be used in an MX record; don't use an alias.

Sendmail uses a process called *canonicalization* to convert e-mail address names to canonical hostnames. Because this conversion may occur before the address is looked up in MX lists, which handle mail for hosts that are not directly connected to the Internet, something may work for ping or telnet that does not work for sendmail.

When sendmail is set up, a special file called sendmail.cf is configured. This file contains a place to state the name of the host, which can be set manually (typed) or from a macro that is set by sendmail itself. Detailed instructions on these procedures appear in the book *Sendmail.* (Costales, B., Allman E., and Rickert N. *Sendmail.* Sebastopol, CA: O'Reilly and Associates, 1993. ISBN 1-56592-056-2.)

The book describes a program that you can try after DNS is running. The short C program may be entered and run to print out the local hostname and the canonical hostname. If these names do not match, you probably need to check out some things before continuing.

Following is an example of running the program:

```
$ canonical.hostname
hostname = "portal8.farcaster.com"
canonical = "portal8.farcaster.com"
```

Check to see that the line

```
OI
```

is present in your sendmail.cf file. This line sets the I option of sendmail, which determines what it does if a lookup for a destination host fails. This option instructs sendmail to queue mail that has failed due to host lookup failure, on the premise that lookups through DNS *can* fail under certain circumstances due to network downtime either in your network or out on the Internet. This behavior differs from using lookups in /etc/hosts, in which the decision is binary (the item is there, or it is not).

Also check to see that the line

```
OKMX
```

is present in your sendmail.cf file. This ensures that sendmail will use the DNS system to resolve hostnames. This is particularly important when mail is destined for machines that have only MX records in the DNS system. For some reason, certain releases from some vendors ship with this line commented out.

The missing `OKMX` is one of two problems that may cause problems getting to places like America Online and Prodigy. Another one is a problem with the BIND software itself. Certain versions of BIND may contain a bug that will prevent things from working correctly, as is the case with IBM's RS/6000 running AIX3.2.5. The version of BIND that ships with this system apparently has a bug that prevents sending e-mail to some domains, such as Prodigy. A Prodigy domainmaster recommended obtaining PMR 4x360 from IBM service for AIX3.2.5, and it did fix the problem for a site I maintain.

Named Data Files

The primary master server has to have four files set up as *named* data files, which are referred to here as *db files* (for DNS database files). When you set up your own *named* daemon, your first task will be to convert the host file to the two files for forward and reverse domain lookup. You can automate this task by using one of several programs, including h2n, which is described in *DNS and BIND* and created by its authors. I recommend using this program at least to build the initial files; it converts the /etc/hosts file to the two db files required for the zone or domain.

To use ftp to get h2n, use the following:

```
$ ftp ftp.uu.net
Connected to ftp.uu.net.
220 ftp.UU.NET ftp server (Version wu-2.4(3) Fri Nov 25 16:08:40 EST 1994)
ready
```

```
Name (ftp.uu.net:gdh): anonymous
331 Guest login ok, send your complete e-mail address as password.
Password: gdh@ACM.org        (your user-id and host/domain here)
230-
230-        Welcome to the UUNET archive.
230- (other greeting messages)
230 Guest login ok, access restrictions apply.
ftp> cd /published/oreilly/nutshell/dnsbind
250 CWD command successful.
ftp> binary
200 Type set to I.
ftp> get dns.tar.Z
200 PORT command successful.
150 Opening BINARY mode data connection for dns.tar.Z (28612 bytes).
226 Transfer complete.
local: dns.tar.Z remote: dns.tar.Z
28612 bytes received in 1.7 seconds (16 Kbytes/s)
ftp> bye
221 Goodbye.
$ uncompress dns.tar.Z
$ tar -xvf dns.tar
... other files ...
x h2n, 17156 bytes, 34 tape blocks
x h2n.man, 5180 bytes, 11 tape blocks
```

The h2n.man file is a man page that describes how to use the program.

Because of the directory directive in the /etc/named.boot file, the *named* data files can be put just about anywhere that seems reasonable. Most systems, however, have these files in /usr/local/named or in /etc.

Comments in the *named* data files begin with a semicolon (;).

Forward lookup

The forward-lookup file is named consistently with the other files and must match the name listed in the /etc/named.boot file, as follows:

```
primary       farcaster.com          db.farcaster
```

In this example, `db.farcaster` will contain a header, as will all the *named* data files and what are known as resource records, which describe various attributes of the domain in terms of name-to-address mapping. This file also contains an NS record, the HINFO and MX records, and CNAME alias records. (These resource record names are covered in the section on named data file resource records.)

Following is an example of a forward-lookup file:

```
@         IN    SOA   ns.farcaster.com. domainmaster.ns.farcaster.com. (
                          9412181            ; Serial (yymmddvv)
                          10800              ; Refresh (3 hours)
                          1800               ; Retry (30 min.)
```

```
                        3600000              ; Expire (6 weeks)
                        86400 )              ; Minimum ttl 1 day
          IN    NS    ns.farcaster.com.

localhost IN    A      127.0.0.1             ; loopback (lo0)

portal    IN    A      192.168.8.1
router    IN    CNAME   portal

ns        IN    A      192.168.8.2
          IN    HINFO   "RS/6000"      AIX32
          IN    MX     10        ns
          IN    MX     20        mail.bitbucket.com. ;relay
ftp       IN    CNAME            ns
www       IN    CNAME            ns              ; for httpd.
... other entries ...
pc-jcw    IN    A    192.168.8.65                ; Jim's PC
pc-fzc    IN    A    192.168.8.70                ; Frank's PC
```

This chapter goes into detail on the various resource records in this file after reviewing all four of the files used by the *named* daemon to load its namespace.

The @ sign at the top of the file, in the header, is an abbreviation for the fully qualified domain name (FDQN) — in the example, `farcaster.com`. In the absence of this abbreviation, several other changes would follow through in the file. First, the NS record(s) would have the FDQN in the left column. Second, `.farcaster.com.` would be appended to all the hostnames. Notice that the example's hostnames have no trailing period. This is because the domain name already is in the /etc/named.boot file, so the @ sign is a shortcut method of stating the domain name. In other words, when the @ sign is used, the NS record needs no FDQN specified in the left column, because the FDQN is assumed; the hostnames can be listed without the trailing period, and they will be made fully qualified automatically, because they are assumed to be in the default domain, as specified in the /etc/named.boot file on each named entry-line. This method makes typos less likely and the file easier to read and maintain.

A word of caution: Don't use underscore characters and periods in hostnames. They are prohibited by the RFCs that define the Domain Name System and, as such, are bound to cause problems later on in some implementation or another.

Reverse lookup

This file also is called the in-addr file because it contains the records for the `in-addr.arpa` portion of the nameserver's namespace.

The header of this file looks pretty much like the header in the forward-lookup file. Unlike the forward-lookup file, this file has only one line of information for every IP address in the `in-addr.arpa` domain handled by this nameserver (only the addresses that are in use and referenced in the header in the forward-lookup file, of course).

Going by the preceding example, the name of this file is determined by the following named.boot line:

```
primary    8.168.192.in-addr.arpa    db.192.168.8
```

The file is shown here in the sample in-addr.arpa file db.192.168.8:

```
@       IN    SOA   ns.farcaster.com. domainmaster.ns.farcaster.com. (
                          9412181          ; Serial (yymmddvv)
                          10800            ; Refresh (3 hours)
                          1800             ; Retry (30 min.)
                          3600000          ; Expire (6 weeks)
                          86400 )          ; Minimum ttl 1 day
        IN    NS    ns.farcaster.com.

1.8.168.192  IN     PTR      portal.farcaster.com.
2.8.168.192  IN     PTR      ns.farcaster.com.
; ... other entries ...
65.8.168.192 IN     PTR      pc-jcw.farcaster.com
66.8.168.192 IN     PTR      pc-fzc.farcaster.com
```

Notice how much simpler the in-addr.arpa file is: one IN PTR record for every IP address or canonical host. *Canonical* means a host identified with an IN A record in the forward-lookup file.

Notice, also, that the IP address to the left of the IN PTR tokens is backward. This is the way that the in-addr data is loaded into the namespace. This is the same way that the network portion of the IP address is stored in the named.boot file, as follows:

```
149.168.8.in-addr.arpa
```

In fact, because this name is the in-addr.arpa domain name, the @ sign at the top of this file allows you to simply put the class C information, or host number, in the left column of the file, if you want. No shortcut is used for the FQDN used on the right side of the IN PTR tokens.

Notice that no line-items appear in this file that are not part of this in-addr.arpa domain. Other network addresses that appear in the forward-lookup file have their own in-addr.arpa file, as is the case with the loopback. Some nameservers may be multihomed and, as such, have two in-addr.arpa files besides the loopback. That situation, however, is beyond the scope of this chapter.

Finally, scrutinize the header. The serial number, which is somewhat arbitrary, generally is yymmdd*n*, in which *n* is the change number of the day. When the day rolls over, *n* reverts to zero (or one, whatever your preference is). The point is that the serial number in the header for the in-addr.arpa file and the serial number in the forward-lookup file should match. When you change either file, you should be changing the files in tandem and updating the serial number. If the serial number has not changed, the *named* daemon ignores these files and continues to use the old namespace.

The Cache File

The cache file is quite simple; it contains information about the InterNIC root servers. The file should contain something like the following (the file should be updated regularly, and this version may be out of date by the time you read it):

```
;    root.cache
;    This file holds the information on root nameservers needed to
;    initialize cache of Internet domain nameservers
;
;    This file is made available by InterNIC registration services
;    under anonymous ftp as
;      file         /domain/named.root
;      on server      ftp.RS.INTERNIC.NET
;      file         named.root
;
;    last update:  May 11, 1994
;    related version of root zone:  940516

                     99999999 IN NS  NS.INTERNIC.NET.
NS.INTERNIC.NET.     99999999    A   198.41.0.4
.                    99999999    NS  NS1.ISI.EDU.
NS1.ISI.EDU.         99999999    A   128.9.0.107
.                    99999999    NS  C.NYSER.NET.
C.NYSER.NET.         99999999    A   192.33.4.12
.                    99999999    NS  TERP.UMD.EDU.
TERP.UMD.EDU.        99999999    A   128.8.10.90
.                    99999999    NS  NS.NASA.GOV.
NS.NASA.GOV.         99999999    A   128.102.16.10
                     99999999    A   192.52.195.10
.                    99999999    NS  NS.NIC.DDN.MIL.
NS.NIC.DDN.MIL.      99999999    A   192.112.36.4
.                    99999999    NS  AOS.ARL.ARMY.MIL.
AOS.ARL.ARMY.MIL.    99999999    A   128.63.4.82
                     99999999    A   192.5.25.82
.                    99999999    NS  NIC.NORDU.NET.
NIC.NORDU.NET.       99999999    A   192.36.148.17
```

The Loopback File

The loopback in-addr.arpa file is necessary because it does not fit into the domain of the other in-addr.arpa file(s). The root cache file is simple, as follows:

```
@        IN    SOA   ns.farcaster.com. domainmaster.ns.farcaster.com. (
                          9412181       ; Serial (yymmddvv)
                          10800         ; Refresh (3 hours)
                          1800          ; Retry (30 min.)
                          3600000       ; Expire (6 weeks)
                          86400 )       ; Minimum ttl 1 day
```

```
;
; Name Servers (The name '@' is implicit.)
;
            IN   NS   ns.farcaster.com.
;
; Addresses point to canonical name.
;
1.0.0.127.in-addr.arpa.     IN   PTR   localhost.farcaster.com.
```

Named Data File Resource Records

RFC 1034 covers all the resource records that are mentioned here, and a few more as well. These resource records go into the db files used by *named*. The records SOA, NS, HINFO, A, CNAME, MX, and PTR are the records that the average domain master/system administrator will use the most.

All these resource records are identified by the token IN before the resource-record identifier, as in the following example:

```
– IN SOA
– IN NS
– IN HINFO
– IN A
– IN CNAME
– IN MX
– IN PTR
```

IN means *Internet.*

Start of origin: IN SOA

At the beginning of each *named* db file, the SOA record appears to identify the *start of origin* of the associated resource records. In other words, all following records have as their point of origin the domain identified by the SOA record. When a file is constructed in such a way that it contains only information that is pertinent to that domain, the SOA record can have the shortcut @ sign in place of the FDQN. Following is a sample SOA record:

```
flort.com.  IN  SOA  panhandle.flort.com.   ekg.panhandle.flort.com. (
                9412053      ; Serial
                10800        ; Refresh after 3 hours
                3600         ; Retry after 1 hour
                604800       ; Expire after 1 week
                86400 )      ; TTL of 1 day.
```

The last field before the open parenthesis is the e-mail address of the administrator of the domain, with the @ sign changed to a period to prevent problems with the namespace. This person may be referenced by user ID or by an alias, such as domainmaster. In any case, this person is typically registered with the InterNIC as the technical contact for the domain.

The field after SOA is the host on which the nameserver is situated. Notice that both of these domain names are fully qualified with an ending period.

With the exception of the serial number, all numbers are in seconds.

The *TTL field* is passed along to other nameservers that cache data, indicating how long the information is allowed to persist.

Refresh tells the secondary how often to check its data. If the serial number has changed and the refresh time is up, the secondary refreshes the data.

Retry affects how often the secondary should retry talking to the primary if the primary becomes unavailable.

Expire determines how long the secondary keeps retrying before it quits. When the secondary quits, it no longer gives out the corresponding DNS data. This arrangement prevents stale and bad data from being passed out.

If `flort.com` is changed to an @ sign, and if the comments on the times are removed, the SOA record can be shorter but fairly cryptic, as follows:

```
@ IN SOA panhandle.flort.com. ekg.panhandle.flort.com. (9412053 10800 3600
604800 86400 )
```

It is possible to have multiple SOA resource records in a *named* data file, in more complicated domain configurations, but such a discussion is beyond the scope of this chapter.

Nameserver: IN NS

The NS record lists the nameserver for the domain associated with the preceding SOA record. Usually, the IN NS resource record immediately follows the SOA. More than one NS record may exist. The NS record always uses a fully qualified domain name.

Host information: IN HINFO

This resource record is unusual because two fields follow the identifier.

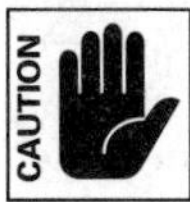

Often, the administrator leaves out one field. Don't do that! :-) Having only one of the two required fields may cause some servers or clients to return unspecified results on the missing field, with uncertain results.

The fields are strings that come from the machine names and system names, respectively, that are listed in RFC 1340. Abbreviations can be made up if the RFC does not cover a situation. Few sites seem to use the HINFO record, but it seems like a good one to use, as the information is useful. Following is a sample from an RS/6000 system:

```
starbuck.flort.com    IN    HINFO   "RS/6000"    AIX32
```

Name to address: IN A

The A records are used in the forward-lookup *named* data files to indicate the canonical name for a host and its associated IP address. Typically, only one A record is used per IP address, and CNAME is used to generate aliases. The reason to avoid using multiple A records for the same host is that sendmail may get confused.

A possible exception involves trying to identify unique names for multihomed hosts. These hosts have two Ethernet cards, each with its own IP address; therefore, the host has two IP addresses. In this case, for troubleshooting purposes, it may be a good idea to have a canonical name for one or the other leg and two special, similar identifiers for the two legs.

Here is a simple example of an IN A resource record:

```
starbuck.flort.com.    IN    A     192.168.8.21     ; coffee machine.
```

Alias: IN CNAME

When you want to have multiple names for one host, CNAME comes to the rescue. First, the canonical name is defined with an IN A record; then the CNAME resource record is used to identify aliases. Common uses for CNAME records are ftp, Gopher, and WWW identifiers, as follows:

```
www.flort.com.   IN   CNAME    wonker.flort.com.
ftp.flort.com.   IN   CNAME    wonker.flort.com.
```

In this example, `wonker.flort.com` is the canonical name previously defined with an IN A record. By using CNAMEs, you can change the machine used as the WWW or ftp server simply by changing the CNAME.

Remember the trailing periods; otherwise, you may get something very strange.

Mail exchange: IN MX

MX resource records are used to identify the fact that a host may receive mail. The MX record identifies a mail exchanger that will process or forward mail for the domain name. In this case, *processing* means delivering the mail to the recipient on a particular host, while *forwarding* means passing mail to the final destination or to the next MX that is closer to the destination. MX records may by stacked to create a hierarchy of mail forwarding hosts. This stacking allows queueing of mail when one host is down.

The format is as follows:

```
hostname.domainame.   IN    MX   preferencevalue   mail.exchanger
```

When the MX record immediately follows an IN A record, the left-hand `hostname.domainname.` can be left off.

The *preference value* is a relative number, with the lowest having the highest priority. The preference value ranges from 0 to 65535.

Finally, the *mail exchanger* is the host that either processes or forwards the mail.

Following is an example of MX in use:

```
glork.flort.com.    IN   A    192.168.8.21
                    IN   MX   10   glork.flort.com.
                    IN   MX   20   mailhost.flort.com.
                    IN   MX   30   mailrelay.hobernet.net
```

glork is the system that processes the mail. This system may have, for example, users who log on and read mail with pine. Users on PCs that run Eudora, meanwhile, get their mail via a pop2d daemon running on glork, which acts as a store-and-forward relay. Such users may alternatively have an imapd daemon that serves up mail to pc-pine in true client-server mode.

In any case, the final destination is `glork.flort.com`. If the destination happens to be down one day, the system `mailhost.flort.com.` queues the mail until it can be delivered or until it must be returned. In this scenario, `mailhost.flort.com` probably is a main point to which all mail goes before being distributed around the domain.

Should `mailhost.flort.com` be down, mail would queue at `mailrelay.hobernet.net`, a system that probably is the Internet provider for the `flort` domain.

Address to name: IN PTR

The PTR resource record effectively points somewhere else. PTR records are used for the IP address-to-name mappings. The first field is the IP address with the octets reversed; the right side is the canonical host name with which the PTR record is associated. The comment that the PTR record points somewhere else means that it effectively points from one location in the in-addr.arpa domain to another, specific location in the domain namespace.

Some rather unusual things will start happening to a site that does not have PTR records set up correctly. Many hosts are starting to do reverse-lookup mapping to see whether the name of a host that is trying to connect is the same as the canonical host name identified by the PTR record in the DNS. If the names do not match, due to hacking or to an error on the part of the filename, the telnet or ftp connection is refused.

Good places to see this situation in action are `ftp.uu.net` and `venera.isi.edu`. These sites will chop you off if your host name and PTR records do not agree.

Following is a sample IN A record:

```
21.8.168.192    IN   PTR      starbuck.flort.com.
```

DNS Maintenance and Problems

You have created all the appropriate data structures, and you are sure that your /etc/named.boot file is all set to jet! What now?

The first thing to do is to figure out how to start the *named* daemon on your system. Generally, the necessary code is in one of the rc. files in the /etc directory. Try grepping around in there and see what you can find, as follows:

```
$ grep /etc/named rc.*
```

On AIX325, for example, the following shows up immediately:

```
/etc/rc.tcpip:start /etc/named "$src_running"
```

Here is what you'll find on SunOS:

```
/etc/rc.local:if [ -f /usr/etc/in.named -a -f /etc/named.boot ]; then
/etc/rc.local:  in.named;        echo -n ' named'
```

Now you can examine the script in question and see what is involved in turning it on every time that the system boots. Usually, this procedure involves only the removal of a comment hash sign.

You also should do a man named. The man page offers helpful hints on starting the *named* daemon and explains precisely what is involved in running it with special options, such as debugging options.

You should use this procedure if you are on an AIX system, because the *named* daemon is started with the special startsrc command and refreshed with the special refresh command.

To start *named* on RS/6000, AIX 3.2.5:

```
$ startsrc -s named
```

Refreshing the namespace

Refreshing the namespace — that is, forcing the DNS daemons to reload the configuration files (presumably because someone just changed those files) — usually is a matter of sending a kill signal to the named daemon. You can get the process ID by using the following:

```
$ps -ef | grep named        (on System V systems)
$ps -ax | grep named        (on BSD systems)
```

Often, the process ID is stored in /etc/named.pid, so you can cat that.

The HUP signal causes the named daemon to restart, forcing it to refresh its namespace if the serial number has changed. This procedure works only on the primary; the secondary must be killed off and restarted to force it to fetch the files from the primary server. Therefore, it makes sense to have the secondary check the primary regularly to see whether anything is new. (Not *too* regularly, though; you don't want to beat the primary system to death.)

To restart the *named* daemon, use the following:

```
$kill -HUP 'cat /named.pid'
```

or

```
$kill -HUP pid
```

An RS/6000 running AIX requires the following behavior:

```
$refresh -s named
```

This is kind of nice because you don't need to find the pid.

Adding to and deleting the hosts file

You must decide whether you will keep the hosts file current. I have had the experience on SunOS 4.2.1 running NIS that the /etc/hosts file must be current or various problems crop up. On such a system, I would do the following:

- Update the hosts file.
- Run my script to update the db.domain and db.rev files.
- Refresh the *named* daemon.

If a system is not running NIS but is running DNS, you may be able to have little of anything in the hosts file and just update the appropriate db files in /usr/local/named. Remember, however, to update the serial numbers.

In any case, the db.domain and db.rev files must be in sync. Watch out for typos and watch the trailing periods.

When everything is correct, refresh the namespace by restarting *named.*

Dumping the namespace

A very helpful thing to do after the *named* daemon has started for the first time is to check the namespace's content. This check also applies to the secondary. Check it with a signal. The method is the same as for refreshing, but the signal is different, as follows:

```
$kill -INT 'cat /named.pid'
```

or

```
$kill -INT pid
```

The dumped space is in /usr/tmp/named_dump.db or /var/tmp/named.db.

Turning on debugging output

If problems with the *named* daemon are suspected, turning on debugging output generally is quite helpful. Use the following:

```
$kill -USR1 'cat /named.pid'
```

or

```
$kill -USR1 pid
```

On an RS/6000 running AIX32, use the following:

```
$kill -30 'cat /named.pid'
```

or

```
$traceson -s named
```

The debugging output is written to /var/tmp/named.run or /usr/tmp/named.run.

To turn off the debugging output, use the following:

```
$kill -USR2 'cat /named.pid'
```

or

```
$kill -USR2 pid
```

On an RS/6000 running AIX32, use the following:

```
$kill -35 'cat /named.pid'
```

or

```
$tracesoff -s named
```

On most systems, the debugging level can be increased simply by issuing another USR1 signal repeatedly. On an RS/6000 running AIX32, however, the best way to set the debugging level is to kill off the *named* daemon and restart it, as follows:

```
$startsrc -s named -a "-d 11"
```

In this example, `11` is the debugging level.

Problems: Causes and solutions

- *Secondary doesn't pick up changes.* Make sure that you are updating the serial numbers!
- *Primary doesn't seem to see changes.* Did you remember to refresh or restart it?
- *Secondary cannot load zone data.* This problem is indicated by a message in the syslog, saying something to the effect that masters for the secondary zone are unreachable. Eventually, the secondary's zone data expires, and SERVFAIL errors occur when the nameserver is queried.

The leading cause of this problem is an incorrect IP number in the /etc/named.boot file on the secondary master nameserver system. Check this out. The other cause usually can be traced to some sort of networking problem. If the secondary is on the other side of a firewall or a router that has been set up to do packet filtering, the secondary may not be allowed in.

- *You are unable to connect to certain sites.* This problem occurs when the IN PTR and IN A records for a particular host/IP address do not agree. If that situation has been corrected and the problem is still evident, ensure that you have checked out the preceding three items.
- Named *daemon reports errors such as* `No such file or directory` *in the syslog or in the debug output.* This problem usually is caused by some form of mistake in the /etc/named.boot file or in one of the db files in /usr/local/named. Look at everything carefully.
- *Domain names show up incorrectly, such as* `vixen.flort.com.flort.com` *instead of* `vixen.flort.com`*.* Look at the db files in /usr/local/named. See whether you left off a period at the end of what should be a fully qualified domain name. For example, if `vixen.flort.com` is missing the trailing period, it does not show up in the DNS files as `vixen.flort.com.`
- *You are unable to get to places on the Internet by name, but you can get there by IP number; everything in your domain works OK.* This problem is caused by missing or incorrect cache data (recall the root cache file).
- *Telnet, WWW, or some other utility times out.* Often, things that are outside your control do not work. Make a habit of knowing several well-known sites outside the Internet to which you can ping or telnet and get a login prompt. When something seems to be awry, try the well-known sites. The other system or network may have crashed.
- *You can send mail outside your domain, but no one can reply to it.* This problem may occur when the delegation information has not yet been set up on the Internet. Perhaps the InterNIC has not yet processed your registration. Try using whois domainname to see whether you are known out there. Then try nslookup, setting the nameserver as a known-good Internet nameserver rather than leaving it to the default — your own. If that nameserver does not know who you are (that is, does not know your domain), you will have to wait until the problem is fixed, or you must contact the InterNIC again.

  This problem is similar to incorrect subdomain delegation, in which you change your setup and notify the InterNIC (or fail to), and the change is either incorrect or not done.
- *Single-label names do not work, but FDQN names do.* Check whether the default domain is set up. Systems that are not running NIS generally do not have the domainname variable set up. In any case, the resolv.conf file should contain domain domainname to make sure that everything is OK. Watch out for typos in this file as well.

Odds and Ends

The area of DNS and BIND is quite extensive, so reading this chapter is not enough to master the topic. Having set up several nameservers, I strongly suggest that you, gentle reader, review the books and Net references mentioned at the end of this chapter. RTFM (Read The *Fine* Manual)! 'Nuff said.

The BIND software continues to evolve. Paul Vixie is currently working on this software, which is available at `ftp.uu.net` and also through the Web via `http://www.dns.net/dnsrd url`. The latest version as of early 1995 was a beta copy of BIND 4.9.3. Discussion of the BIND software continues in `comp.protocols.tcp-ip.domains`.

With regard to Internet providers, *watch out.* I have used several of them — five, to be exact. I found that the level of support for user and systems varies from great to terrible.

If a site is quite technical and well funded, it may put great effort into keeping abreast of technology, making sure that the site grows in terms of bandwidth and capacity (such as the nntp server, which can get overloaded easily), yet the customer may be ignored as he asks for help with some obscure problem. On the other hand, the provider may be quite customer-oriented, always answering calls and responding to e-mail, yet nothing happens because the provider is not either technical enough or funded well enough to keep up with demand.

Tremendous demand exists out there. The Internet is growing like crazy — Web traffic in particular. So when you pick an Internet provider, make sure that the provider is ready to help, has good service and equipment, and has enough money to grow with the flow.

I was burned by one provider who had registered things backward, with my system being the secondary and the provider's system being the primary. Later, when I registered the corrections myself, the provider botched the secondary line in its named.boot file. This probably would not have been a problem had the provider been interested in helping me figure out why people on the Net were having trouble getting into my domain, but as it turned out, I had to resolve why our site was having these DNS-related problems and prove the point to the provider. What can you do to prevent this? Ensure that the contract with the provider states what is his responsibility in resolving DNS and e-mail problems if he is providing either secondary or primary master DNS nameserver services to you.

I recently ran across a fellow named David Barr on the Internet. Barr's postings on DNS appear in several Usenet newsgroups, and the Web site `http://www.dns.net/dnsrd` led me to his "tips" document. In an e-mail conversation, I became aware of his soon-to-be RFC[9], which is quite good. Following are a few tips gleaned from Barr. I have quoted him directly, with permission.

"Don't use CNAMEs in combination with RRs [resource records] that point to other names, such as MX, CNAME, PTR, and NS. For example, this is not recommended:

```
podunk.edu.  IN    MX       mailhost
mailhost     IN    CNAME    mary
mary         IN    A        1.2.3.4
```

RFC 1034 in section 3.6.2 says this should not be done, and [RFC 974] explicitly states that MX records should not be a CNAME. This results in unnecessary indirection in accessing the data, and DNS resolvers and servers need to work more to get the answer.

Having NS records pointing to a CNAME is bad and may conflict badly with current BIND servers. There is a certain amount of security checking done in BIND to prevent spoofing DNS NS records. Also, older BIND servers reportedly will get caught in an infinite query loop trying to figure out the address for the aliased nameserver, causing a continuous stream of DNS requests to be sent.

It is a good idea to give every host an MX record, even if it points to itself! Some mailers will cache MX records but will always need to check for an MX before sending mail. If a site does not have an MX, every piece of mail may result in one more resolver query, because the answer to the MX query often also contains the IP addresses of the MX hosts. Internet SMTP mailers are required by [RFC 1123] to support the MX mechanism.

Put MX records even on hosts that aren't intended to send or receive e-mail. If there is a security problem involving one of these hosts, some people will send mail to the postmaster or root at the site without checking first to see whether it is a 'real' host or just a terminal or personal computer that's not set up to accept e-mail. If you give it an MX record, the e-mail can be redirected to a real person. Otherwise, mail can sit in a queue for hours or days until the mailer gives up trying to send it.

Pick friendly, easy-to-remember host names. rm5ws3 may tell you that it's the third workstation in room 5, but what if you move rm5ws1 and rm5ws2 to another room? Or what if room 5 get converted to a storage closet? Remember that your users have to remember these names, too. They may not remember that there are 3 hosts in room 5 and 6 hosts in room 8, but they usually can remember that the hosts are named after, say, the planets in the solar system. Of course, for personal computers, the hostname is not as important, so picking names such as pc01, pc02, and so on makes sense.

Don't succumb to the 'Bond, James Bond' naming scheme (a carryover of nonhierarchical networks such as BITNET and UUCP). `podunkvm.podunk.edu` is no more informative than the shorter `vm.podunk.edu`.

A good discussion on naming your computer is in [RFC 1178]. Many of the arguments for naming your computer also apply in general to the selection of Internet names."

Additional Tools

You should become familiar with the tools ping, whois, and nslookup if you have access to them and you plan to troubleshoot any kind of DNS problem. ping is a quick way to see how a DNS name resolves. whois may be used to see what is on file at the InterNIC with respect to a domain name or even another registered Internet user (such as a system administrator, particularly a domainmaster). nslookup is quite useful for troubleshooting DNS problems.

Also, dig (if it ports to your machine), doc, and dnswalk are quite useful. These last three tools are mentioned at the WWW site `http://www.dns.net/dnsrd`. All the latter items require Perl on your system, so you want to get that up and running, too. dig does more than nslookup and is required by doc and dnswalk. However, you can get by without all three. Even if you do not have the time or resources to build these packages on your system, the information contained within them is quite useful.

Domain Name Registration Form

The registration form in this appendix is from anonymous ftp at `ftp://rs.internic.net/templates/domain-templates.txt`. You can use this form to register in the NIC-run top-level domains, such as `com`,`org`, and `edu`. NICs for Australia or France or various international domains have their own forms. In all cases, it is best to get the latest version of the form, in case it has changed after this book was published.

When choosing a domain name, you first must find a parent domain that you can be under. If you want to create a second-level domain under one of the top-level domains (as in, for example, `flort.com`), you must provide a nameserver and must arrange for a secondary to back you up. Generally, your Internet provider provides the secondary service for a fee; you can designate a machine on your network as the primary.

In any case, you need to specify two nameservers in your registration form.

You also need to register your `in-addr.arpa` domain for reverse lookup, using the `in-addr-template.txt` registration form. Your Internet provider may help you set up the `in-addr.arpa` registration, which requires that you also have a registered network number. For more information, see *DNS and BIND*.

Many documents and books contain directions for registering a new domain, but much of this information is out of date. I recommend that you use the following form and e-mail it to `hostmaster@internic.net`. Notice that the beginning of the form is a preamble that describes how the form should be filled out. The actual fill-in part, which is very short, appears toward the end.

Bear in mind that domain names must be 12 or fewer characters. The names generally represent the name of the organization that requests them.

```
<templates/domain-templates.txt>                      [ 07/94 ]

  To establish a domain, the following information must be sent to
  the InterNIC Registration Services (HOSTMASTER@INTERNIC.NET). Either
  this template, or the "short form" following this template may be used.

  (1) The name of the top-level domain to join (EDU, GOV, COM, NET, ORG).

    1. Top-level domain:
```

```
(2) The name of the domain (up to 24 characters). This is the name
that will be used in tables and lists associating the domain with the
domain servers addresses. While domain names can be quite long, the
use of shorter, more user-friendly names is recommended.

  2. Complete Domain Name:


(3) The name and address of the organization for which the domain
  is being established.

  3a. Organization name:

  3b. Organization address:


(4) The date you expect the domain to be fully operational.

  4. Date operational:


NOTE: The key people must have electronic mailboxes (even if in the
domain being registered) and "handles" (unique InterNIC database
identifiers). If you have access to "WHOIS", please check to see if
the contacts are registered and if so, include only the handle and
changes (if any) that need to be made in the entry. If you do not
have access to "WHOIS", please provide all the information indicated
and a handle will be assigned.

(5) The handle of the administrative head of the organization in (3)
above or this person's name, postal address, phone number, organization,
and network emailbox. This is the contact point for administrative
and policy questions about the domain.

  Administrative Contact

  5a. Handle (if known):
  5b. Name (Last, First):
  5c. Organization:
  5d. Postal Address:

  5e. Phone Number:
  5f. Net Mailbox:


(6) The handle of the technical contact for the domain or this
person's name, mailing address, phone number, organization,
and network mailbox. This is the contact point for problems and
updates regarding the domain or zone.
```

```
  Technical and Zone Contact

  6a. Handle (if known):
  6b. Name (Last, First):
  6c. Organization:
  6d. Postal Address:

  6e. Phone Number:
  6f. Net Mailbox:


NOTE: Domains must provide at least two independent servers for
translating names to addresses for hosts in the domain. The
servers should be in physically separate locations and on
different networks if possible. The servers should be active
and responsive to DNS queries BEFORE this application is
submitted. Incomplete information in sections 7 and 8 or
inactive servers will result in delay of the registration.

(7) The primary server information.

  7a. Primary Server Hostname:
  7b. Primary Server Netaddress:
  7c. Primary Server Hardware:
  7d. Primary Server Software:


(8) The secondary server information.

  8a. Secondary Server Hostname:
  8b. Secondary Server Netaddress:
  8c. Secondary Server Hardware:
  8d. Secondary Server Software:


(9) Please briefly describe the organization for which this
domain is being registered. If the domain is for an organization
that already has a domain registered, please describe the
purpose of this domain.


For further information contact InterNIC Registration Services:

 Via electronic mail: HOSTMASTER@INTERNIC.NET
 Via telephone:    (703) 742-4777
 Via facsimile:    (703) 742-4811
 Via postal mail:   Network Solutions
           InterNIC Registration Services
                   505 Huntmar Park Drive
                   Herndon, VA 22070

The party requesting registration of this name certifies that, to her/his
```

```
knowledge, the use of this name does not violate trademark or other statutes.

Registering a domain name does not confer any legal rights to that name and
any disputes between parties over the rights to use a particular name are to
be settled between the contending parties using normal legal methods.
(See RFC 1591)



1.  Top-level domain.....:

2.  Complete Domain Name.:

3a. Organization name....:
3b. Organization address.:

4.  Operational Date.....:

Administrative Contact:
5a. NIC Handle (if known):
5b. Name (Last, First)...:
5c. Organization.........:
5d. Postal Address.......:

5e. Phone Number.........:
5f. Net Mailbox..........:

Technical/Zone Contact:
6a. NIC Handle (if known):
6b. Name (Last, First)...:
6c. Organization.........:
6d. Postal Address.......:

6e. Phone Number.........:
6f. Net Mailbox..........:

7a. Prime Server Hostname...:
7b. Prime Server Netaddress.:
7c. Prime Server Hardware...:
7d. Prime Server Software...:

8a. Second Server Hostname..:
8b. Second Server Netaddress:
8c. Second Server Hardware..:
8d. Second Server Software..:

9.  Domain/Org Purpose/Desc.:


Notes: In Sections 3b, 5d, & 6d use multiple lines for addresses.
    If contacts are registered, only 5a and 6a are needed.
    If servers are registered, only 7a&b and 8a&b are needed.
    If there is more than one secondary server, just copy Section 8.
```

```
The party requesting registration of this name certifies that, to her/his
knowledge, the use of this name does not violate trademark or other statutes.

Registering a domain name does not confer any legal rights to that name and
any disputes between parties over the rights to use a particular name are to
be settled between the contending parties using normal legal methods.
(See RFC 1591)
```

Root Servers for the Domain Name System

The following information was ftped from `rs.internic.net`, from the /netinfo/ root-servers.txt file, in December 1994. You can use this information to build your nameserver cache file, sometimes called the root.cache or db.cache file. If possible, it is best to get the latest copy of this file, as it changes periodically.

The server program running on all of these systems is BIND, and all of the systems are UNIX systems.

```
/netinfo/root-servers.txt       Sep 94

The following hosts are functioning as root domain nameservers for
the Internet:

HOSTNAME            NET ADDRESSES     SERVER PROGRAM

NS.INTERNIC.NET     198.41.0.4        BIND (UNIX)

NS.NIC.DDN.MIL      192.112.36.4      BIND (UNIX)

NS1.ISI.EDU         128.9.0.107       BIND (UNIX)

NS.ISC.ORG          192.5.5.241       BIND (UNIX)

AOS.ARL.ARMY.MIL    128.63.4.82       BIND (UNIX)
                    192.5.25.82

C.PSI.NET           192.33.4.12       BIND (UNIX)

TERP.UMD.EDU        128.8.10.90       BIND (UNIX)

NS.NASA.GOV         192.52.195.10     BIND (UNIX)
                    128.102.16.10

NIC.NORDU.NET       192.36.148.17     BIND (UNIX)

(End of File)
```

Historical Reading for the Domain Name System

The following list of RFCs is recommended additional reading for the manager or administrator of one or more domains. These suggestions can be obtained from `rs.internic.net` by anonymous ftp or from `venera.isi.edu` in the in-notes directory by the same method. If you are unable to ftp to `venera.isi.edu`, it may be that your in-addr.arpa and forward-lookup files do not agree!

- Postel, J.B.; Reynolds, J.K. "Domain Requirements." Marina del Rey, California: University of Southern California, Information Sciences Institute, October 1984, RFC 920, 14 pp. (`rs.intrenic.net RFC920.txt`)
- Harrenstien, K.; Stahl, M.K.; Feinler, E.J. "DoD Internet Host Table Specification." Menlo Park, California: SRI International, October 1985, RFC 952, 6 pp. (`rs.internic.net RFC952.txt`)
- Harrenstien, K.; Stahl, M.K.; Feinler, E.J. "Hostname Server." Menlo Park, California: SRI International, October 1985, RFC 953, 5 pp. (`rs.internic.net RFC953.txt`)
- Partridge, C. "Mail Routing and the Domain System." Cambridge, Massachusetts: BBN Laboratories, Inc., January 1986, RFC 974, 7 pp. (`rs.internic.net RFC974.txt`)
- Lazear, W.D. "MILNET Name Domain Transition." McLean, Virginia: MITRE Corporation, November 1987, RFC 1031, 10 pp. (`rs.internic.net RFC1031.txt`)
- Stahl, M.K. "Domain Administrators Guide." Menlo Park, California: SRI International, November 1987, RFC 1032, 14 pp. (`rs.internic.net RFC1032.txt`)
- Lottor, M. "Domain Administrators Operations Guide." Menlo Park, California: SRI International, November 1987, RFC 1033, 22 pp. (`rs.internic.net RFC1033.txt`)
- Mockapetris, P. "Domain Names: Concepts and Facilities." Marina del Rey, California: University of Southern California, Information Sciences Institute, November 1987, RFC 1034, 55 pp. (`rs.internic.net RFC1034.txt`) Updated by RFC 1101.
- Mockapetris, P. "Domain Names: Implementation and Specification." Marina del Rey, California: University of Southern California, Information Sciences Institute, November 1987, RFC 1035, 55 pp. (`rs.internic.net RFC1035.txt`) Updated by RFC 1101.
- Mockapetris, P. "DNS Encoding of Network Names and Other Types." Marina del Rey, California: University of Southern California, Information Sciences Institute, April 1989, RFC 1101, 14 pp. (`rs.internic.net RFC1101.txt`) Updates RFC 1034 and RFC 1035.
- Cooper, A.; Postel, J. "The U.S. Domain." Marina del Rey, California: University of Southern California, Information Sciences Institute, June 1993, RFC 1480, 47 pp. (`rs.internic.net RFC1480.txt`)

Additional Reading or Resources for the Domain Name System

Although several sources are cited this chapter, a couple of them are particularly good places to go for additional reading, as well as for additional sources of information.

Newsgroups

- `comp.protocols.tcp-ip.domains` is a very good place to read about what is happening with DNS. In fact, this group sometimes is frequented by Cricket Liu, who occasionally responds to inquiries posted to the newsgroup. This is the place to watch to see whether new versions of BIND are coming along. Posts by David Barr and many other knowledgeable people are to be found here.
- `comp.protocols.tcp-ip` is a good place to scan periodically if you are interested in things that are affected by discussions about the TCP/IP protocol, such as DNS packet sizes. This newsgroup is for real aficionados only.
- `comp.mail.sendmail` is a useful group to scan if you are having problems incorporating DNS with sendmail. A common problem is setting up a domain as a main or central mail host. All mail addressed to the domain goes to this host, which then routes the mail to the appropriate place. Usually, this host has a real name, such as `hostname.somedomain.com`, but the mail must work with `userid@somedomain.com`. This host is not necessarily complicated to set up; if you get stuck, however, this newsgroup can help.

WWW: The Web

- `http://www.dns.net/dnsrd`. Fire up your favorite Web browser and check out this html page, which apparently is maintained by Andras Salamon. The page offers several documents and html links to other interesting things, such as the latest version of BIND for UNIX.

By e-mail

- `bind-request@uunet.uu.net`. Sending e-mail to `bind-request@uunet.uu.net` gets you on the mailing list for information about BIND.
- `dns-errors-request@pop.psu.edu`. Send e-mail to `dns-errors-request@pop.psu.edu` with no subject and a text body of get dns-errors.txt, and you get David Barr's latest information on common problems in setting up and administering DNS.

References

1. Mockapetris, P. *Domain Names — Concepts and Facilities.* RFC 1034, November 1987.
2. Mockapetris, P. *Domain Names — Implementations and Specifications.* RFC 1035, November 1987.
3. Quarterman, J.S. "Which Network, and Why It Matters." *Matrix News,* Vol. 1, No. 5, Matrix Information and Directory Services, Inc. (MIDS), Austin, TX, August 1991.
4. Tanenbaum, A.S. *Computer Networks*, second edition. Englewood Cliffs, NJ: Prentice-Hall, Inc., 1988. ISBN 0-13-162959-X.
5. Albitz, P. and Liu, C. *DNS and BIND.* Sebastopol, CA: O'Reilly and Associates, 1992. ISBN 0-56592-010-4.
6. Cheswick, W.R. and Bellovin, S.M. *Firewalls and Internet Security — Repelling the Wily Hacker.* Reading, MA: Addison-Wesley, 1994. ISBN 0-201-63357-4.
7. Stern, H. *Managing NFS and NIS.* Sebastopol, CA: O'Reilly and Associates, 1992. ISBN 0-937175-75-7.
8. Costales, B., Allman, E., Rickert, N., *Sendmail.* Sebastopol, CA: O'Reilly and Associates, 1993. ISBN 1-56592-056-2.
9. Barr, D. *Common DNS Errors,* RFC-XXX, 1994. Updates RFC 1537. Available via Listserve by sending e-mail to `dns-errors-request@pop.psu.edu` with get dns-errors.txt in the body and no subject line. Barr, a system administrator at Pennsylvania State University, has written a great deal of useful stuff about DNS and is the author of dnswalk, a program that can be used to investigate DNS namespace.

Chapter 9

Connecting Your UNIX System to the Net

Imagine a school or business, with a multiuser UNIX computer in operation, that wants to be on the Internet. This chapter is aimed at helping that kind of institution connect with the Internet.

Connection Types

There are many choices about the type of connection you can get, with a trade-off between price and functionality. Table 9-1 lists different types of connections and the services available with each connection. There are several trade-offs you should consider. See the table for service versus bandwidth and service versus price. The rest of this chapter expands on some of these options.

Table 9-1 shows a comparison of eight possible types of Internet connections, ranging from the slowest and cheapest to the fastest and most expensive, along with what features each kind of connection can provide. I explain the different connection types in the next section.

Table 9-1 Comparison of Different Kinds of Connections

E-Mail Gateway	*Dial Emulate*	*Dial SLIP*	*Leased SLIP*	*S0*	*T1*	*T3*	*ATM OC3*
			Relative Cost				
$20	$20	$40	$100	$500	$1,300	$10,000	$20,000 (line + net)
			Bandwidth				
Batch	14.4K	14.4K	14.4K	56k	1.5M	45M	155M
			E-Mail				
Yes	Yes	Yes	Yes	Yes	Yes	Yes	Yes
			Mailing Lists				
Yes	Yes	Yes	Yes	Yes	Yes	Yes	Yes
			Multimedia Mail				
Almost	Almost	Yes	Yes	Yes	Yes	Yes	Yes

(continued)

Table 9-1 (continued)

E-Mail Gateway	*Dial Emulate*	*Dial SLIP*	*Leased SLIP*	*S0*	*T1*	*T3*	*ATM OC3*
			Telnet				
No	Yes, but	Yes	Yes	Yes	Yes	Yes	Yes
			FTP				
No	Yes, but	Yes	Yes	Yes	Yes	Yes	Yes
			Gopher				
No	Yes, but	Yes	Yes	Yes	Yes	Yes	Yes
			WAIS				
No	Yes, but	Yes	Yes	Yes	Yes	Yes	Yes
			WWW				
No	Yes, but	Yes	Yes	Yes	Yes	Yes	Yes
			Pictures (Small)				
No	No	Yes	Yes	Yes	Yes	Yes	Yes
			Batch Sound				
No	No	Yes, but	Yes	Yes	Yes	Yes	Yes
			Pictures (Big)				
No	No	No	Almost	Almost	Yes	Yes	Yes
			Movies				
No	No	No	Almost	Almost	Yes	Yes	Yes
			Live Audio				
No	No	No	No	Almost	Yes	Yes	Yes
			Live Video				
No	No	No	No	No	Almost	Yes	Yes

The main questions to answer are what kind of service the organization needs and how much money it is willing to spend to get that service. These questions can be answered only by the organization.

Once the service/cost issue has been considered, connections generally come in four models: mail gateway, dialup SLIP, dedicated SLIP, and dedicated line (frame relay or ISDN). Other higher bandwidth options are generally not economically feasible for most organizations.

I explore each of these connection models in the following sections.

E-mail gateway

An e-mail gateway enables mail to move from one network to another. This is often accomplished using the old UUCP protocol to move mail from one type of machine to another. An e-mail gateway provides e-mail and possibly a news service. For many organizations, this is enough. It is possible to arrange a domain name so that it gives a machine on the far side of a UUCP gateway an Internet address. This is a slow way of getting network services, but it is also cheap. It can provide a strong connection to the Internet for basic services.

Dialup SLIP

If you want to use the Internet tools like Mosaic or Gopher directly on your machine, you need to have IP directly to your machine. You can get this direct service from SLIP or PPP. SLIP does IP services only, whereas PPP can support other protocols as well (although on dialup links, it rarely does). The cheapest way to get IP services is to share a service with many others. Network service providers can use SLIP to provide access to the network on a demand driven basis.

To use SLIP, you have a normal host service with a connection to a modem through a serial connection. There are several SLIP packages available: shareware, freeware, and commercial. By dialing up when you need service, you are sharing the modem with others, which reduces the price of the service. This means you can be a network client, but because you're not on the network all the time, you can't be a network server.

Dedicated SLIP

If you want to guarantee that you will have access when you want it, or if you want to provide network services to others, you will need a dedicated connection. For example, if you want to produce your own WWW server, you need to be able to advertise a specific host name and IP address to the network.

This dedicated SLIP connection requires the same hardware configuration as the dialup SLIP. The only difference is that the modem is configured to stay connected. Modems can have a collection of problems with noise and connectivity, so you might notice the connection dropping and then the modem working to re-establish the connection.

Through this method, you can get a reasonably cheap connection (if there is a service provider in your local calling area). It is more expensive than a dialup SLIP service but somewhat less expensive than the next option.

Dedicated line

Using a dedicated digital line avoids many of the problems of analog modems and dialup services. You can get a faster network connection and a connection more reliable than the modem-based solutions. It is also more expensive. Dedicated connections come in many flavors, depending on your local telecom environment.

The slowest dedicated connections run at 56K bits per second (known in telephone-ese as DS0), with speeds up into the many millions of bits per second, if you can afford it.

At the lower end of the dedicated range, options include frame relay, ISDN, leased lines, and cable TV connections; the prices for each are different. You should look into all of them if you are interested in a dedicated line.

At T1 (1.5 Mbps) and above, the only option is usually a dedicated line to your Internet provider.

The traditional 56K connection is a Digital Data Service (DDS) leased line from the telephone company. More recently, most phone companies have started to offer *frame relay,* which physically uses a DS0 or T1 line but usually offers better pricing because it can share more facilities at the telephone central office.

ISDN is a dialup service using specialized (but not terribly expensive) equipment that can offer speeds of 64K and sometimes 128Kbps. ISDN pricing is very inconsistent from one part of the country to another, ranging from $25 to $200 per month, with per-minute charges as well.

Finally, in some areas, cable TV companies are planning to offer Internet connections, frequently at reasonable prices ($125/month for 500Kbps in one city), but as of late 1994, only limited experimental service has been turned on.

For now, in our area, frame relay is the best option. It has *distance-insensitive pricing* (the price doesn't matter how far you are from your provider), and it seems to be reliable. Frame relay can be configured to use the DSU/CSU and router used on leased lines, or can use a FRAD (*frame relay access device*). The difference is that the DSU/CSU and router connects a synchronous frame connection to Ethernet, whereas the FRAD converts the same frame connection to an asynchronous SLIP connection, which in turn attaches to the host much like a dialup modem.

One way we at Oregon State University are using a FRAD is to connect from a frame relay service to a terminal server to provide a way to extend our local calling area with a flat service fee. As you will see next, I don't recommend using a FRAD and a host.

The downside of this configuration is that it is more expensive than other options. But you can return back to Table 9-1 to compare price and service to decide which option works best for you.

At T1 speeds and above, you invariably use a DSU/CSU and a router.

Hardware Configuration

There are many ways to configure the pieces to create the physical connection to your system. It is possible to hook the incoming network line directly to a single host, to connect to a host acting as a router, or to connect directly to a router.

Each of these options works and each has benefits and drawbacks. It is cheaper to use your host as a router so that you can save some money by reusing your host as a network server. The downside of this method is that you increase the vulnerability to failure and reduce flexibility. If you want to set up your system so that it has the most reliable service with the most room for growth and flexibility, do not use your host as a router — buy a separate router instead.

At Oregon State University, we took this idea a step further: we do not mix different kinds of services on the same host. We separate our user services from our network services. To do so, we dedicate a machine for each type of service. Given the services that we offer, most sites trying to connect initially want the host. Although this is cheaper when the system is first set up, you have to reconfigure your system and network when you begin to expand. Often, the system grows into a configuration that does not connect directly to its host.

For the sake of this discussion, let's look at the router-based solution. You can connect two routers together with SLIP over a modem. Or you can connect the routers with some dedicated service like frame relay or ISDN, or something faster. You want a router that speaks the specific protocol that you are going to use.

Software Configuration

Any host on a network needs five pieces of information to connect to an IP network:

- Hostname (for example, `kira.csos.orst.edu`)
- Host IP Address (128.193.40.17)
- Subnet Mask (255.255.254.0)
- Broadcast Address (128.193.41.255)
- Default Router Address (128.193.41.254)

As a client, the host may wish to know the address of its services. You may configure different services, including

- Time Service (NTP)
- Domain Name Service (DNS)
- BootP Service
- File Service (NFS)
- News Server (NNTP)
- Mail Server (SMTP)
- WWW Service (HTTP)

Different versions of UNIX save this information in different places. You need to look at the specific manual for your system. This seems to be very different from system to system. In general on BSD-based machines, you can find what you need to know by looking at these files:

```
/etc/rc*          (rc.net, rc.local)
```

These files, which are scripts executed when the system starts up, should run the ifconfig program. The ifconfig program shows you where the file is that holds the specific information you need to fill out. On NeXTStep machines, it is in /etc/hostconfig. On NetBSD, machines it is in:

```
/etc/defaultdomain
/etc/hostname.<network>
/etc/hostname.le0
/etc/myname
/etc/mygate
```

On most BSD machines, it is hard coded in the /etc/rc.local files.

To find the relationship between names and IP numbers, you need to have the file /etc/resolv.conf set up with information about where to look for this translation. An example file might look like:

```
domain   business.com
nameserver 555.68.40.3
nameserver 555.68.20.1
search   business.com university.edu neighbor.edu
order   bind file
```

Domain tells your system what domain to use. *Nameserver* identifies the hosts that keep track of DNS databases. *Search* allows you to specify in which order to look at domains in order to map a name that is not fully qualified. The *order* command tells the system where to look for information. The configuration file shown previously basically says to first query a DNS name server (the program is called bind) and if that fails, check the local /etc/hosts file.

Debugging

As with everything that requires network services, there will be times when things don't work properly. Networking is the process of crossing boundaries, boundaries between different machines or boundaries between organizations. This means that the network health depends on the actions of people in other organizations. Sometimes this means that other people, in other places, changing a small configuration, can change the behavior of your system. This generally shows up as a network failure.

When the network breaks, sometimes it is hard to know whether the problem originates from the computer or the network. There are five programs that you can use to debug network problems: ifconfig, netstat, ping, traceroute, and route. Each one is discussed in detail in the following sections.

IFCONFIG

Ifconfig is the program that configures interfaces. It can be used to show you all the interfaces on your system with

```
ifconfig -a

le0: flags=63<UP,BROADCAST,NOTRAILERS,RUNNING>

        inet 128.193.40.17 netmask fffffe00 broadcast 128.193.41.255

lo0: flags=49<UP,LOOPBACK,RUNNING>

        inet 127.0.0.1 netmask ff000000
```

You can then check to see whether the interface is up and whether it is configured properly. You can go through and check the address, broadcast, and netmask to see whether they are correct.

NETSTAT

Netstat can tell you many things about your network configuration, from memory use to routing tables. There are two options that come in handy for debugging:

- **netstat -i** shows the network interfaces and how they are currently being used. This is a list of the active physical connections on your machine.
- **netstat -r** lists the routing table. This shows you where your system thinks that it needs to be sending packets to get them out.

PING

Once you are convinced that your host has the right interface configuration and knows where to route packets to, you can use the PING command to see whether you can get to a remote site. PING is like a sonar ping. It sends an ICMP packet to a remote host, which will then bounce it back. At Oregon State University, we have set up a regular script to ping our critical hosts and notify us when it cannot get through.

If you can get to some hosts, but not to others, it shows that part of the network might be down. This is a classic search problem. Generally, you ping your local router and then ping your service provider router. Then you can explore other places that are common access sites.

TRACEROUTE

Sometimes you will find that your network is partially connected and you don't know where a connection fails. Whereas PING does a quick, end-to-end check to see whether you can reach a host, TRACEROUTE touches every step along the way to see where there is connection and where connection fails.

For our system, you might see something like this, tracing the route to a well-known and well-connected host:

```
3% traceroute mit.edu
traceroute to mit.edu (18.72.2.1), 30 hops max, 38 byte packets
1 router (198.68.19.254) 100 ms 12 ms 4 ms
2 test-56-csos-r.CSOS.ORST.EDU (198.68.20.1) 92 ms 51 ms 51 ms
3 t1-0.CV.CSOS.ORST.EDU (198.68.21.253) 92 ms 53 ms 52 ms
4 s1.r1.eug.rain.rg.net (198.68.1.254) 92 ms 64 ms 62 ms
5 e0.r0.eug.rain.rg.net (198.68.0.33) 91 ms 65 ms 64 ms
6 sl-fw-3-S3/0-T1.sprintlink.net (144.228.33.49) 126 ms 138 ms 126 ms
7 sl-fw-5-F1/0.sprintlink.net (144.228.30.5) 126 ms 131 ms 124 ms
8 sl-dc-8-H3/0-T3.sprintlink.net (144.228.10.17) 156 ms 156 ms 156 ms
9 icm-dc-1-F0/0.icp.net (144.228.20.101) 157 ms 158 ms 167 ms
10 icm-fix-e-H2/0-T3.icp.net (192.157.65.122) 195 ms 270 ms 225 ms
11 mf-0.enss145.t3.ans.net (192.203.229.246) 254 ms 239 ms 229 ms
12 t3-2.cnss56.Washington-DC.t3.ans.net (140.222.56.3) 235 ms 233 ms 230 ms
13 t3-0.cnss32.New-York.t3.ans.net (140.222.32.1) 230 ms 234 ms 230 ms
14 t3-0.cnss48.Hartford.t3.ans.net (140.222.48.1) 231 ms 234 ms 230 ms
15 t3-0.enss134.t3.ans.net (140.222.134.1) 241 ms 232 ms 233 ms
16 w91-rtr-external-fddi.mit.edu (192.233.33.1) 237 ms 234 ms 237 ms
17 E40-RTR-FDDI.MIT.EDU (18.168.0.2) 322 ms 235 ms 233 ms
18 MIT.MIT.EDU (18.72.2.1) 237 ms 236 ms 234 ms
```

Each line shows one hop that a packet takes on its way to MIT. It shows the name and address of the host, along with an estimate of the time it takes packets to get there. In this case, packets take three hops through the local network; go to a regional network rg.net; go to Sprintlink (a long-haul carrier that takes it across the country); through ICP and ANS, two other long-haul carriers; and finally through two routers at MIT before they get to the target host. This kind of route is common on the Internet.

If you have network connection problems, TRACEROUTE will go some number of hops and then stall, being unable to find the next hop because a router or link is down. Sometimes it even finds routing loops, with packets sent back and forth among two or three hosts and never escaping.

ROUTE

At some point, you might find that you need to add a route to force packets to take a specific path. The ROUTE command can be used to set up a specific routing table entry. Or, more importantly, when your routing table gets polluted by bad routing information, ROUTE can delete routing table entries. Now take a look at two different configurations.

Case example one: a PC-based network

A small business is running only PC applications and is not interested at this time in adding UNIX services or skills. It is particularly conscious of costs and wants to minimize price, but needs an Internet connection.

For this scenario, the cheapest solution is a UUCP gateway from a PC-based mail program to the network. This solution provides the company only with e-mail services, but this is all it needs at this time.

Additional services for this company, such as mailing lists for its customer base, an ftp site for software distribution, and a World Wide Web Server, can be contracted from a service provider that it can dial into.

For the mail gateway, the PC network uses CC:Mail as the internal mail system. Any PC mail system that supports a UUCP gateway works. (An alternative might be the Pegasus mail program). The CC:Mail UUCP gateway requires a dedicated computer to connect the network services to the outside. This gateway computer runs the UUCP gateway software and calls the service provider on a regular basis.

The service provider provides a dialup modem port for the company to call. This port connects to a UNIX machine, which spools mail and redistributes it to the network. In addition, the mail system on the service provider side is configured to move the mail for the business to the UUCP service. This configuration is completed in two steps:

1. The service provider's mail server is specifically configured to recognize the business name and transfer data to the UUCP mailer. To configure the mail server to recognize the correct names, the UUCP mail system and Sendmail are linked together. The sendmail.cf file then has a line that recognizes the name of the business and converts this to a UUCP address.
2. The service provider registers an MX (mail exchange) record in the Domain Name Service that exchanges mail for the business. To establish the MX record, the provider creates an entry in the DNS server for the business domain that looks like

   ```
   IN   MX   05 service.provider.com.
   ```

   This causes the service provider's machine to receive all Internet mail for the business.

Every hour, the business gateway system calls up the service provider and polls for mail. Doing so provides the ongoing connection for the company.

For this particular company, this scenario provides a good solution. Ninety percent of what it wanted was to transact business by e-mail. Although this option does not provide for the other Internet services, it does make the system look like it is directly on the Internet for e-mail. This means that the company is able to transact business as if it were directly on the Internet.

However, there are a few drawbacks to this scenario. Modem connections in general can be difficult. They can behave differently from day to day, and for no apparent reason. Therefore, there are times when some human intervention is needed. UUCP can get jammed. One frequent error is when a message is huge, which means that the mean time to failure on the line is less than the time to send a particular message because the message is so large. This means that all mail waits until that file is sent. Usually this requires that the file causing the problem be removed.

In general, it is best to keep the size of mail messages that go over UUCP below 100,000 bytes. Larger files may work, but they will generally cause problems in the long run.

When directly connected to the network, the mail response time can be seconds or minutes. However, due to the fact that the provider is programmed to call in for mail only once an hour, this company will see hour-long delays in mail deliveries.

Therefore, it cannot have the same kind of interactive conversations on the network as people who are directly connected.

Case example two: Connecting via frame relay

An example business might have a network of several PCs and Macs connected by Ethernet. On the network is a UNIX system. This system has served as the UUCP mail host for the business. Now the company wants to set up a dedicated 56K connection via frame relay.

Because the company has an existing network, this network should have already been registered for a domain name and for a network number. (See Chapter 28.) If this has been done, there will be no need to renumber the network when it is connected directly to the Internet.

To connect this Ethernet to the Internet, there are four pieces that need to be set up:

1. *A frame relay service from a provider* — brings a four-wire telephone circuit to your site.
2. *Internet service from an Internet provider* — gives you access to exchange IP packets with the rest of the Internet.
3. *A DSU/CSU* — connects directly to the frame relay line. This is basically a digital modem. The DSU/CSU should be configured for the correct speed, either 56K or T1 frame relay. Different DSU/CSUs are needed for each speed.
4. *A frame capable router* — examples of routers that work are the Cisco 2501, the Morningstar Express, and the Livingston.

The router needs to be configured with the proper addresses and to identify the correct frame relay address.

To provide specific details about how this is done, look at my consulting company configuration. The Morningstar router we have has the following configuration:

```
$ cat rc.boot
  console tty2
  version
  hostname router
  ifconfig lo0 127.1
  ifconfig enet0 198.68.19.254
  inetd
  startfrd
  getty tty2 9600 nowait respawn
  startroute
```

This file runs when booting up. It configures my Ethernet interface (enet0) to have the correct IP address. As a matter of convention, the router address is usually the last address in the network. It starts network services, starts the frame relay daemon, and then starts routing. This file starts the frame relay service:

```
$ cat startfrd
   ifconfig tty0 198.68.20.2
   frd tty0 57600 addr 198.68.20.2 netmask 255.255.255.0
   arp -s 198.68.20.1 tty0:16
   arp -s 0.0.0.0 tty0:16
```

Frame relay can be thought of as a pipe into a frame cloud, connecting all the frame relay users in a given area. Inside the pipe, you can have separate channels to different places. My channel to my remote service is PVC (Permanent Virtual Circuit) #16.

The frame relay daemon starts on the serial device hooked to the phone service. The address, speed, and network mask are set.

ARP (Address Resolution Protocol) is how you map an Internet address to a hardware address. In this case, the remote address is mapped for the other side of the Frame relay like to the frame relay PVC. Hardware broadcasts are also mapped so that routing will work.

```
$ cat startroute
   gated
   snmpd
   route add default 198.68.20.1
   route add -net 128.193.0.0 198.68.20.1
```

You then start the routing program called *gated*. Gated has the ability to manage several routing protocols. We start SNMP to allow for network management of the router. Then we add a default route to the outside and a specific link to the service provider.

This example shows how to configure the router to talk to the remote sites. However, that is not all the work that needs to be done. Each of the hosts on the network needs to be configured to point its default route at the address of the router. Most UNIX systems are configured to handle a network when they ship. With a few adjustments to the configuration files, the UNIX hosts will access the router and network.

At this point, all the hosts on the network are running. The same process that gets them onto the local network gets them on the Internet as a whole. Assuming, of course, that you have set the default route correctly. Refer to the section entitled "Software Configuration" to see the specific files for fixing a client host.

This frame relay-based connection provides a quick, stable connection to the Internet at a price. There is a capital cost for the router ($1,800) and DSU/CSU ($320), an ongoing cost for the frame relay connection ($143.22/month), and an ongoing cost for the Internet provider services ($350/month).

But for this price, the connection is capable of providing strong service with minimum fuss. The prices will vary dramatically depending on your telecommunications options and your Internet providers. This same scenario works with ISDN, with minor technical modifications. The DSU/CSU would be eliminated in favor of an ISDN terminal adapter and the router would need to speak ISDN directly.

Security

At some point, you may want to configure a firewall to limit access from the outside onto your systems. Any hosts that you have exposed to the Internet become opportunities for visitors. If you want to guarantee the performance of your systems, you have to control how people get into your systems. By setting up a firewall, you can limit the exposure to network visitors.

A *firewall* can be either complete or partial. A complete firewall has a filter preventing packets from either side passing the firewall router. Only select services are allowed to pass. A partial firewall allows packets from the inside to get out of the network, but does not allow packets from the outside to get in.

For more information on firewalls, see Chapter 5.

How do you check a host for problems and holes? One way to do this is to monitor the use of the systems. Doing so starts with setting up the log files for connections. Setting up the log files requires three steps: logging, TCP wrappers, and monitoring, all discussed in the next sections.

Logging

Set up your /etc/syslog.conf to log all the services that you have running in a safe place that has lots of disk space. Make sure to review these logs on a regular basis.

TCP Wrappers

Some systems come with programs to log network connections. For those that don't, the CERT system (`ftp.cert.org`) has a program called tcpwrapper that can be used to log network connections.

Monitoring

In addition to logging activities, you need to watch the status of all your accessible machines. A single keystroke (typed by mistake) can open up a machine to outside access. You can automate the monitoring processes with three programs: Tripwire, COPS, and Crack.

Tripwire watches a collection of files and tells you when it has changed. This is very useful when someone changes your /bin/login program to record passwords.

COPS is an automated security checker that tries to find misconfigurations on your system. Use the reports from COPS to close up problems on your exposed systems.

Crack is a program that cracks passwords by checking them against a dictionary. We try to crack our own passwords every night. This way we can close accounts before there is an opportunity to have someone else do it for us.

All of the tools mentioned previously and more are available from anonymous ftp from `ftp.cert.org in /pub/tools`.

John Sechrest is the Executive Director for the Oregon State University Computer Science Outreach Service (CSOS), which is building an extension-like organization to help people learn to use computers and networking more effectively. He has been providing UNIX and Internet support for over 10 years. In addition, he teaches classes on UNIX system administration, networking, and UNIX programming.

For more information about computer and networking activities, look at `http://www.csos.orst.edu`*. For an investigation into more experimental networking, look at* `http://www.nero.net`*.*

Chapter 10

Linking Your Organization's Network to the Internet

by Peter H. Lemieux <phl@cyways.com>

The rise of the Internet as a major global communication channel creates management problems for organizations. Businesses, government agencies, and nonprofit organizations must all decide how an Internet connection will further their missions. Many will conclude that the Internet's extraordinary array of inexpensive global communication and information resources makes it an indispensable part of a modern organization.

Yet many organizations have little or no experience with the Internet's technologies. Data communications are handled by the TCP/IP protocols. Most personal computer networks rely on other protocols like Novell's IPX/SPX for NetWare, or NetBIOS or NetBEUI for peer-to-peer networks like Artisoft's LANtastic and Microsoft's Windows for Workgroups. Thus, to link to the Internet, an entirely new protocol has to be added to the organization's networks, and it must peacefully coexist with the existing protocols.

For smaller organizations with limited computing resources, the fact that much of the Internet uses UNIX creates even greater obstacles. Though TCP/IP services can be found for nearly all operating systems and environments, UNIX possesses two key features that make its use on the Internet compelling. First, because TCP/IP is UNIX's native networking protocol, a full array of Internet services has been written for UNIX. Also, when new services are introduced, developers immediately produce UNIX software. Second, UNIX provides a 32-bit environment with preemptive multitasking even on Intel platforms. This enables one or a few UNIX machines to offer the diversity of services needed to provide a full-service connection with the Internet. As we'll see, UNIX solutions need not be expensive, but many organizations may decide to contract with an outside provider for Internet support rather than develop UNIX expertise in-house.

The recent development of Internet software suites for Microsoft Windows like Spry/O'Reilly's Internet-in-a-Box and NetManage's Internet Chameleon appear to resolve some of these problems. However, these packages are aimed at individual PC users who want occasional dialup connectivity with the Internet and do not intend to become an information provider. Moreover, they often do not support Ethernet or token ring networks. Most organizations will want both a set of software clients on each networked user's desktop and at least one server to act as a mail hub, a domain nameserver, and an electronic publisher using protocols like the World Wide Web.

Router controversy

Controversy exists over the feasibility of using a host computer instead of a dedicated router to handle routing, especially if that host is also acting as a server. Some experts believe that only routers should route, and host computers should stick to providing client and/or server services. Our experience has been that a single gateway computer can successfully handle both tasks for smaller organizations, but for larger organizations a dedicated router makes more sense. Of course, a router is nearly mandatory for organizations connecting over high-bandwidth digital circuits.

This chapter will examine the issues involved in establishing a *full-service connection* with the Internet. Full-service connections use *full-time, dedicated telecommunications circuits* between a subscribing organization and an Internet access provider. At least one *Internet server* must be installed at the site to support at least the primary Internet services like electronic mail, file transfers with the file transfer protocol, and information retrieval using tools like Gopher, the World Wide Web, and WAIS, the Wide Area Information Service. For small-scale connections, this server can provide IP routing as well, acting as a gateway between the organization's local area network and the Internet. Larger networks probably need to install a dedicated router instead. In addition, security concerns may require the installation of a *firewall* computer between the local computer network and the Internet. Security issues like these are beyond the scope of this chapter. For a detailed treatment of security, see *Network Security SECRETS* (IDG Books, 1993), Chapters 17 and 24, and William R. Cheswick and Steven M. Bellovin, *Firewalls and Internet Security: Repelling the Wily Hacker* (Addison-Wesley, 1994).

After the external connection has been established, the Internet server must be interconnected with the organization's local area networks. Then a suite of Internet software tools suited to the supported operating environments must be installed on the client workstations. Finally, an equally important issue not covered here is the need to train the organization's executives and staff in the use of the Internet to make the most out of the connection.

Making the Internet Connection

Other authors in this collection have described the various Internet connectivity options, so I will not spend much time on them here. At a minimum, most organizations will require a dedicated analog dialup connection using either the SLIP or PPP protocols from an Internet access provider. SLIP (the Serial Line Internet Protocol) and PPP (the Point-to-Point Protocol) are two methods to provide an Internet connection over dialup telephone lines. Higher-speed connections with greater bandwidth are available for organizations expecting heavier Internet usage.

Connecting with an Internet access provider

The recent establishment of the V.34 modem protocol, offering speeds up to 28.8 Kbps over voice-grade telephone lines, makes dialup connectivity a good solution for smaller organizations. For many organizations, the primary use of the Internet, at least at the outset, will be electronic mail, with occasional use of information retrieval services like ftp or the World Wide Web. Dedicated analog voice-grade circuits cost about $100 a month depending on the distance from your site to the Internet provider, plus a similar amount to the access provider for a full-time SLIP or PPP connection. Larger organizations, or those expecting heavy simultaneous use of these information retrieval services, should consider higher-bandwidth solutions over dedicated digital lines, with their consequent higher costs. These include either digital data services ranging from 56 Kbps through T1 (1.5 Mbps) or ISDN connections at 64 or 128 Kbps where available. Organizations publishing information on the Internet may also need a high-speed connection.

Having chosen an Internet access provider and an appropriate level of connectivity, your organization must obtain two other basic items, an official Internet network number and a registered domain name.

Every computer on the Internet must be assigned a unique IP address, a 32-bit number typically written in the *dotted decimal* format *nnn.nnn.nnn.nnn.* While theoretically this numbering scheme would permit 2^{32}, or over four billion unique numbers, various features of the way addresses are allocated limit the number available in practice. Before your organization can join the global Internet, you must first obtain a network number, which your access provider typically provides. Unless you are a very large organization, you will usually be assigned a Class-C number, one in the form *nnn.nnn.nnn.*0, which supports up to 254 computers.

The values 0 and 255 are not available: 0 denotes networks, and 255 is the IP broadcast address. If your organization expects to have more than 254 computers on the Internet, either apply for a Class-B network number that supports 65,534 hosts, or perhaps use several adjacent Class-C addresses, if your provider's system can support them efficiently. Because the address space is limited, and the Internet is growing so rapidly, Class-B numbers are becoming much harder to get. Again, your access provider is the first place to turn for help.

Once the network number is determined, each computer connected to the Internet must be assigned a unique address between *nnn.nnn.nnn.*1 and *nnn.nnn.nnn.*254. Traditionally, the value *nnn.nnn.nnn.*1 is assigned to the gateway host or router, with the other addresses assigned in any manner you think appropriate. Your TCP/IP software will probably also need to know your network's *subnet mask* and *broadcast address.* The usual subnet mask for a Class-C network is 255.255.255.0, while the broadcast address is your network number with the final zero replaced by 255.

Your provider may also suggest that you take a portion of the provider's network address space, called an IP subnet, making the remainder available for other customers. If you are assigned to a subnet, be very careful to use the correct subnet mask when configuring TCP/IP on your hosts. Most software defaults to the standard mask for an entire Class-C network, 255.255.255.0, but the mask for subnetted networks will be different. For instance, if you were assigned only the portion of the address space from *nnn.nnn.nnn.*129 to *nnn.nnn.nnn.*191, your subnet mask would be 255.255.255.192. Subnetting can also be used by organizations that have multiple networks, perhaps interconnected by bridges and routers. The appropriate design of a subnetting scheme in these cases is beyond the scope of this chapter.

Registering a Domain Name

A domain name is your organization's unique badge of identification to the global Internet community. All domain names are of the form *domain.zone.* Addresses outside the United States typically end with a two-character country zone like `ca` for Canada, `jp` for Japan, or `au` for Australia. In the United States, zones are typically allocated by type of organization: `com` for commercial entities, `org` for nonprofit organizations, `edu` for educational institutions, `gov` for Federal agencies, or `mil` for military sites. Some American sites do use the `us` zone designator, particularly state and local governmental organizations. Some examples of well-known domains include `un.org`, `mit.edu`, `nasa.gov`, `army.mil`, and `ibm.com`.

Many people first encounter domain names in Internet mail addresses. Many organizations use the Internet to provide personalized electronic mailboxes of the form `name@domain.zone`. With appropriate mail software and a central mail server, any organization can give all its staff these simple, individualized mailboxes.

Businesses and nonprofit organizations on a budget can get electronic mail services for their personnel without installing a mail hub. Some have subscribed to commercial on-line services, like CompuServe, America Online, and Prodigy, that offer limited Internet access. Others have opted for full Internet client services, though usually with a textual, not a graphic, interface, by subscribing to an Internet provider like Delphi that offers interactive shell accounts. At the top of this hierarchy are those who have purchased an individual, part-time SLIP or PPP connection from an Internet access provider.

The cost of these options typically runs between $10 and $50 per month, plus an installation fee in the same price range in some cases. However, when an organization does not have a central mail server, it cannot establish individual mailboxes. Instead, everyone must share a single mailbox on a computer at the service provider's site and receive mail as *`organization@provider`*`.net` or *`company@provider`*`.com`. One staff member is then appointed postmaster, distributing incoming messages throughout the organization and collecting

Shell accounts

Shell accounts let individuals access the Internet. The user logs on to a remote host (which usually runs UNIX), using a simple dialup terminal program, and runs Internet client software on the remote machine. The shell user's local computer is not directly connected to the Internet, but acts as a dumb terminal.

outgoing messages to be sent. (The process resembles the way many offices share a facsimile machine.) Obviously, such an arrangement makes privacy impossible, depends critically on the reliability of the postmaster, and impedes efficiency.

For a fee, some providers will register a domain name for shell or SLIP/PPP users and configure their systems to permit mail to be sent to that address. However, the limitation to a single mailbox remains. Mail sent both to `joe@`*`domain.zone`* and to `shirley@`*`domain.zone`* is directed to that mailbox. Other inbound services like operating a World Wide Web server still cannot be offered.

While individuals can plausibly present themselves to the Internet as `ChelseaC@aol.com`, it is distinctly unprofessional when whole organizations identify themselves this way. They need the corporate identity of a domain name that establishes the organization as a full-fledged member of the Internet community. With a domain name, staff members can identify themselves with personalized electronic mail addresses like `phl@cyways.com`, and departments can create contact addresses like `secrets@idgbooks.com`. Typically, the Internet access provider registers domain names for a nominal fee, but you can get documentation of the process from the ftp site at the Network Information Center (the InterNIC), the organization responsible for name registrations (`ftp://rs.internic.net/templates`).

Once your domain name has been registered, assign each computer with Net access a unique *hostname,* which identifies it to the Internet by its "fully-qualified domain name," *`hostname.domain.zone`*. Either the network administrator or the users of each computer can decide on these names. (If you're using a NetBIOS-based operating system, each computer has already been assigned a name, which for consistency should probably be its Internet hostname as well.) When all the IP addresses and hostnames have been assigned, they must be advertised to the Internet with a domain name server. These servers inform remote Internet users of the IP address corresponding to a particular fully qualified name.

When you register your domain name with the InterNIC, you'll be asked to provide the IP addresses of a primary and a secondary nameserver that contain the pertinent information for your site. Your access provider should be willing to provide at least one of these servers for you. This is especially important if your site is served by a low-speed dialup connection. The access provider configures her

Valuable domain names

The value of a domain name to a business was recently highlighted when companies began registering their competitors' names. The Princeton Review, a company that trains students to take standardized tests like the SAT, registered the name `kaplan.com` in hopes of preventing their main competitor, Stanley H. Kaplan, from using it. Stanley Kaplan's company successfully sued for the name's return when it found it could not register its logical domain name. However, the company would have had no recourse had the name already been taken by some other entity not in the test-preparation business.

nameserver to check with yours periodically (typically once or twice a day), updating any changes found. In many cases, the provider can supply both the primary and the secondary server, since her own nameserver has a secondary, which automatically becomes your secondary as well.

Although some providers will manage all of your naming services at their end, apparently eliminating the need for an in-house server, this is not an attractive solution. First, computers on your own local area network should not have to consult an off-site server every time they need to ascertain a host's address. Computers running nameserver software store all the name-to-address mappings they have found in a large cache file. As a result, when your users need to reach a previously accessed host, they can get addressing information immediately over your local network. If all the naming information resides at your provider's site, response times are slower, because the connection to your provider is slower than Ethernet speeds and because the provider's nameserver may be processing requests from dozens or even hundreds of other users.

The second problem with using a remote nameserver is that it limits your flexibility when you need to change your LAN. You must forward to the provider every change you make that affects naming — adding or eliminating a computer, changing a hostname, creating an alias for a hostname. Even the most conscientious provider has many competing demands on its staff's time and attention, and your request may inadvertently be delayed. Running a local name server requires more knowledge and effort at your end, but when you update your records, the secondary copy is then automatically updated at the access provider's site by the nameserver software.

With the external issues resolved, your organization must now address the internal problems of setting up an Internet server, interconnecting it with your existing local area network (LAN), and installing Internet client software on the network workstations. These subjects make up the remainder of this chapter.

Why use aliases?

Aliases let you use "generic" names that point to a specific local host. For instance, most Internet users expect to find an organization's ftp service at `ftp.`*`domain.zone`*, a World Wide Web server at `www.`*`domain.zone`*, and so forth. Aliases let you redirect references to these pseudo-hosts to an actual machine on your network with an entirely different name.

Setting Up an Internet Server

Nearly all Internet services are built upon the *client/server* computing model. The most obvious examples of client/server processes are distributed information services like the World Wide Web or Gopher, where information resources stored on a server are accessed by users running client software. The server runs a program that processes client requests, finds the needed information, and sends it back to the client. Because nearly every organization has information it wants to make available to the public, most organizations will need to install an Internet server. Even apparently mundane services like electronic mail rely on client/server architectures. In order to enable people to read their electronic mail whenever they wish, Internet engineers invented the Post Office Protocol, or POP, which runs on a mail server. Client software on the user's PC checks the post office server for any incoming mail and displays it on the user's computer.

Some systems employ the Internet Mail Access Protocol (IMAP) instead of, or along with, POP as the server protocol. IMAP clients, such as the popular freeware program Pine, leave the mail on the server instead of downloading it to the workstation, which may be more efficient for users who get large volumes of mail and read it over slow connections like dialup lines.

Regardless of the operating systems and environments used elsewhere in the organization, effective Internet servers typically run under some flavor of UNIX. For small organizations, it is quite possible to use one moderately priced computer to provide the full range of Internet services. A 486 PC operating at 66 MHz can easily handle the demands of a small- to mid-sized office under normal conditions. In fact, the speed of the server's processor is usually much less a limitation than the bandwidth of the connection to the access provider.

An effective Internet server must be able to provide at least the following services:

- Run a domain nameserver to advertise hostname/IP address mapping to the Internet.
- Handle mail with a program like sendmail that uses the Simple Mail Transport Protocol (SMTP) and a post office server running the POP or IMAP protocols.
- Offer remote connectivity using the telnet protocol.
- Distribute information to remote users via the ftp, WAIS, Gopher, and World Wide Web protocols.

Although most Internet users expect to have access to Usenet newsgroups, the enormous volume of Netnews makes it impractical for smaller organizations to devote their limited computing resources to a Network News (NNTP) server. In most cases, this server will be located at the Internet access provider's site, with client software on the organization's computers pointing to this remote NNTP server.

The Internet server typically also has a full array of UNIX client programs for telnet, ftp, the Web, and so on. In part, the system administrator will need these tools to test the server's configuration and to contact remote Internet hosts for such purposes as updating the server's software. In some cases, as discussed below, the organization's staff may also use these UNIX clients via telnet to the server if appropriate client software is not available on their local workstations.

I recommend that some common services not be made available on your Internet server because they can pose a security threat. These include the finger, netstat, and systat services, Sun's Network Information Service, and the so-called "r" commands like rlogin. See the network security books cited previously for details.

It may seem that such an extensive list of requirements demands expensive hardware and software. Actually, it's possible to construct such a server from a standard Intel-compatible 486 or Pentium PC and entirely free software using one of the freeware versions of UNIX like FreeBSD or Linux.

Despite the persistent belief that "you get what you pay for," when it comes to Internet software the old adage simply doesn't fit the facts. Take Linux. Born of a Finnish graduate student's dream to have a UNIX he could run on his home PC, Linus Torvalds' project has since enlisted literally hundreds of programmers worldwide who have collaborated using the Internet. Linux is distributed under the General Public License of the Free Software Foundation, which means it's available to everyone at no cost, though with no warranty. Linux can be found (for North American readers) at `ftp://tsx-11.mit.edu/pub/linux` or `ftp://sunsite.unc.edu/pub/Linux`, or on CD-ROMs from providers such as InfoMagic or Walnut Creek. To simplify installations, some helpful people have constructed *distributions* of Linux. Distributions are integrated collections of all the relevant software with an installation program. The most popular distribution is known as Slackware and can be found at both ftp sites and on most CD-ROMs.

Given their reliance on the Internet for communications, it's not surprising that Linux's community of developers have devoted special attention to the networking feature of the operating system. All of the services described above and more are available with Linux. Linux can be configured to support SLIP or PPP connections, and it can forward IP packets, enabling it to operate as a gateway host. What's more, developers of Internet software like Gopher and Web servers usually make sure their software works over Linux given its enormous and growing installed base. (Some estimates place it at 500,000 or more computers worldwide.) Finally, though its earliest implementations were buggy, more-recent versions of the operating system provide a solid, stable base on which to build an Internet server.

Typically, Linux distributions do not, include the full range of Internet server software outlined above. However, the developers of all the major Internet protocols offer freely available versions of this software that can be compiled to run under Linux. Often you can even find precompiled binary executables for Linux because of its widespread popularity. The same is true for client software. Programs like the mail client Pine and the Web browsers Lynx and Mosaic (for X Windows) can be obtained in either source code or as Linux executables.

While building an Internet server from free software like Linux is obviously the cheapest approach, it requires a considerable investment of time (perhaps a person-month), along with the support of someone knowledgeable about UNIX, to get everything working together correctly. Two good sources of information for those wishing to travel down this road include Olaf Kirch's *Linux Network Administration,* available at the ftp sites listed above and published in book form by O'Reilly, and Craig Hunt's *TCP/IP Network Administration,* also from O'Reilly. For organizations unwilling or unable to devote the resources necessary to build their own server, three alternatives are available. One is to turn to companies that specialize in connecting organizations to the Internet. If you're interested in finding such a company in your area, you can ask nearby Internet access providers to provide you with a couple of references.

If you'd prefer to keep everything in house, there are now companies that sell you prepackaged Internet servers. Sun Microsystems offers two such products, which combine one of their Sparcserver computers and all the necessary software. The cheaper of these offerings costs just over $6,000 (as of December 1994), with a higher-performance model at around $8,500. A less-expensive solution employs the software-only package for Intel PCs from Berkeley Software Design (BSD). For under $600, BSD will sell you a software suite that runs on 386 or better PCs. Given that a 486/66 PC with 16 megabytes of RAM and a gigabyte hard drive now costs under $2,000, BSD's offering enables you to purchase an Internet server for about half the price of Sun's product. The recent arrival of these products on the market make it impossible to determine whether the price premium for Sun's server is justified in performance terms.

In a single-server model, the host computer is connected to the Internet via a modem and dialup line, or with more elaborate hardware if a high-speed digital line is used. The server is then attached to the organization's local area network using Ethernet or token ring networking as appropriate. If substantial network traffic is expected, a high-performance network interface card using either the EISA or PCI bus architectures may be needed. For small organizations, a standard ISA-bus network card should work well.

Connecting PC LANs to the Internet

I turn now to the final step of installing an appropriate suite of software on your LAN workstations to enable them to take advantage of all the Internet offers. This requires installing a TCP/IP stack on each workstation and installing a suite of Internet client software on either the individual workstations or on a shared network server.

Installing TCP/IP on workstations

Now that each computer on your network has been assigned its unique hostname and IP address, it's time to install the TCP/IP transport software. Choosing the best software for your network depends on the type of network operating system you're using, whether you need to support Microsoft Windows, and how much money you're willing to spend.

For organizations that can afford it, there are a number of well-designed commercial Internet packages from vendors like FTP Software, Novell, NetManage, Beame and Whiteside, and many others. However, most of these solutions cost hundreds of dollars per workstation. While these packages are relatively easy to install and often come with substantial vendor support, there are much less expensive ways to connect your network with the Internet using widely available freeware and shareware solutions.

The first step is to install TCP/IP transport software, commonly called a *TCP/IP stack*, on the individual LAN workstations. Most PC networks do not use the TCP/IP protocols common to UNIX and the Internet. About two-thirds of all PC LANs run on Novell NetWare, a server-based network operating system that uses Novell's IPX/SPX protocol. The other common standard is NetBIOS, or the extended version known as NetBEUI, which is used for peer-to-peer networks like Artisoft's LANtastic, Novell's Personal NetWare, Performance Technology's POWERLan, and Microsoft's Windows for Workgroups. Neither IPX nor NetBIOS can communicate directly with the Internet. Instead, you must install a TCP/IP stack on each PC, configured to operate transparently with the other protocols in use on the local area network.

Only a few years ago, such interoperability among networking protocols did not exist. Network operating systems were based on *monolithic* drivers on the client machines, ones that monopolized communication with the network interface card. Novell's monolithic IPX driver is one such example. This driver is still used on many older NetWare networks even though Novell has withdrawn support for the approach in favor of its multiprotocol Open Datalink Interface specification.

The growth of TCP/IP rang the death knell for monolithic specifications. To add a second protocol required a second Ethernet card, at a time when such cards were relatively expensive. So when FTP Software decided to develop TCP/IP transports for the Intel architecture, it needed to break up the interface monopoly. To do so, FTP created the packet driver specification. A packet driver also monopolizes the network card but offers an open programming interface to all applications that wish to use its services (including networking software like NetWare or NetBIOS). Applications "register" with the driver, and, in return, the driver forwards along any data packet that conforms to a particular protocol, such as IPX.

Major industry players recognized the need for multiprotocol specifications as well. Novell introduced its Open Datalink Interface (ODI), and Microsoft and 3Com joined forces to promote the Network Device Interface Specification (NDIS). Each of these approaches also monopolizes the network card but offers an open programming interface. Nearly all commercial networking software now uses one of these two approaches. However, supporters of the packet driver approach quickly wrote so-called *shims* — programs that emulate a packet driver at the application end but talk to the ODI or NDIS driver at the interface — so that packet driver applications can operate over ODI and NDIS networks.

Packet drivers have been written for most common network interface cards and are often supplied by the cards' manufacturers. A fairly complete collection of packet drivers is maintained by Russell Nelson of Crynwr Software (who also offers modestly-priced support) and is available as freeware from most major ftp sites. Packet drivers are loaded at boot time and require a free software interrupt in the range 0x60 (hex) to 0x7F, typically using 0x60. The diagnostic program that comes with Microsoft's MS-DOS, MSD.EXE, does not identify software interrupts, but they are reported by Quarterdeck's Manifest (bundled with its QEMM memory manager) and Central Point's System Consultant, part of its PC Tools for Windows suite. Common software applications use some interrupts in this range. Novell's VLM NetWare driver takes 0x64, while the Expanded Memory Services/Virtual Control Program Interface (EMS/VCPI) used by many programs to operate in extended or expanded memory claims 0x67. If a packet driver attempts to use the same interrupt number as another application, rather peculiar results ensue, and neither the network nor the other application works correctly.

Pure packet driver approaches are much less common on networks since the advent of open interface specifications like ODI and NDIS, although many of the freeware and shareware TCP/IP applications still use packet drivers. Given its dominance of the networking field, I'll begin with discussing the issues facing administrators of NetWare networks. I'll then turn to NetBIOS-based technologies.

TCP/IP on NetWare LANs

If your network still relies on the older, monolithic IPX drivers, you should begin by upgrading your workstations to the newer ODI stack. The simplest solution to this problem is to call Novell and order its "DOS/Windows Client Kit," which includes the latest NetWare client software and a complete TCP/IP client that coexists with NetWare. The Client Kit costs only $99 per organization (not per physical site) and is certainly one of the cheapest approaches to installing TCP/IP services over NetWare and other networks using ODI drivers. However, you may need to clean up the installation after it is finished. By default, the TCP/IP client installation creates a NET.CFG file in the root directory of the workstation's hard drive, which needs to be consolidated with the NET.CFG file created by the NetWare installation in the \NWCLIENT directory. A complete NET.CFG file for an Ethernet installation should look something like the following listing. (Token-ring networks have slightly different parameters; see the documentation for details.)

The TCP/IP stack included in the Client Kit is version 4.1 of the stack provided with Novell's LAN Workplace for DOS (LWP), a product costing $399 *per workstation*. LWP adds telnet and ftp clients to the basic stack. Much less expensive versions of these clients are available elsewhere. If you purchase the Client Kit, you can upgrade your TCP/IP transport to version 4.2 by anonymous ftp to `ftp.novell.com`. Look for the file /pub2/NWOS/DOSCLNT11/ODI/lwp42t.exe.

The following listing shows the NET.CFG file for Novell's ODI-based TCP/IP and NetWare stacks. The `[bracketed]` items in the right column are comments, which should not be typed in the file.

```
Link Driver NE2000
        INT 15
        PORT 320
        MEM D0000
        Frame Ethernet_802.2                [For NetWare 3.11
        Frame Ethernet_II                    networks, reverse the
        Frame Ethernet_802.3                 802.2 and 802.3 lines]
        Frame Ethernet_SNAP

Link Support
        Buffers 8 1500
        Mempool 4096
                                            [Replace E0 with 0 and
Protocol IPX E0 Ethernet_802.2               802.2 with 802.3 for
                                             NetWare 3.11 networks]
Protocol TCPIP
        ip_address      198.69.147.4
        ip_router       198.69.147.1        [address of this host]
        ip_netmask      255.255.255.0       [address of the gateway]
        tcp_sockets     24
        udp_sockets     8
        raw_sockets     1
        nb_sessions     4
        nb_commands     8
        nb_adapter      0
        nb_domain
        PATH            TCP_CFG C:\NET\tcp

NetWare DOS Requester
        FIRST NETWORK DRIVE = F
        USE DEFAULTS = OFF                   [For VLM-based
        VLM = CONN.VLM                        installations, the
        VLM = IPXNCP.VLM                      current NetWare
        VLM = TRAN.VLM                        standards]
        VLM = SECURITY.VLM
;       VLM = NDS.VLM
        VLM = BIND.VLM
        VLM = NWP.VLM
        VLM = FIO.VLM
        VLM = GENERAL.VLM
        VLM = REDIR.VLM
        VLM = PRINT.VLM
        VLM = NETX.VLM
```

This file was created by NetWare 3.12, which has two major differences from earlier 3.x releases. First, NetWare now uses 802.2 packet framing (which is supposed to be independent of the physical network), rather than 802.3 (which is specific to Ethernet) used in earlier versions. Since NetWare always uses the first FRAME entry to determine its framing method, administrators of earlier NetWare versions should reverse the 802.2 and 802.3 entries. TCP/IP always uses Ethernet II framing, so no specific reference need be made. Second, version 3.12 replaces NETX.EXE, found in earlier releases, with its Virtual Loadable Module (VLM) technology. The services earlier consolidated into NETX.EXE have been divided into separate modules that VLM.EXE loads.

The installation process asks you for the workstation's IP address, the address of the gateway router, and the IP subnet mask. For the last of these, it defaults to the mask appropriate to a network without subnetting; if you use subnets, this value changes.

Using Novell's TCP/IP package lets you use any of the software designed for this widely supported transport, including a mail client, the University of Washington's PC-Pine, Peter Tattam's Trumpet newsreader, and, perhaps most importantly, any of the WinSock Internet software for Microsoft Windows discussed in the following section. Software written purely for packet drivers, such as NCSA Telnet, do not work with the Novell stack since these programs have their own TCP/IP transport built in.

Packet driver software can be run over NetWare networks that use ODI drivers with the ODIPKT.COM shim. This driver was written by Dan Lanciani of Harvard and is available at `ftp://newdev.harvard.edu/pub/odipkt/odipkt.com`. The driver is loaded at boot time (typically in AUTOEXEC.BAT or STARTNET.BAT) along with the other parts of the ODI stack as follows:

```
lsl
driver.com       (driver for your network card, e.g., ne2000.com)
ipxodi           (the IPX driver for ODI)
odipkt 1 96      (see below)
netx             (or vlm as appropriate)
```

ODIPKT.COM takes two arguments, a frame reference and a software interrupt. NetWare always uses the first frame, numbered zero, to transport IPX/SPX packets. So the first FRAME entry in NET.CFG should be either 802.2 or 802.3 framing, depending on your NetWare version. The second frame entry is set to Ethernet_II, the TCP/IP standard, and ODIPKT points to this entry using the value 1 as its first parameter. The second parameter is the ever-present software interrupt, here set to 96 decimal, or 0x60 hex. Lanciani also recommends slightly larger link support buffers than those shown in the "Buffers" line in the example configuration file. He suggests values of 6 and 1600 for Ethernet cards.

This setup lets any NetWare workstation use TCP/IP software written for packet drivers in conjunction with the NetWare network. For systems running plain DOS without Microsoft Windows, these include, among others, the University of Washington's PC-Pine, a very good mail client, NCSA Telnet, for both telnet and ftp, and the University of Kansas's Lynx World Wide Web client. There is even a shareware client for Sun's Network File System (NFS): Robert Juhasz's XFS, which lets you mount UNIX disks on the PC desktop and print from the PC to UNIX printers.

For sites using Windows, another piece of software must be added to provide TCP/IP services in that environment. A few years ago, TCP/IP software vendors agreed on a method of porting the Berkeley *sockets* interface for TCP/IP to Microsoft Windows and created the Windows Sockets, or WinSock, specification. Programmers can write software for this interface and rely on the WinSock dynamic link library to provide the necessary transport services, regardless of which underlying network package is in use.

Where to get software for your WinSock

Much of the freeware and shareware software that uses WinSocks can be found at Digital Equipment Corporation's ftp site, `ftp://gatekeeper.dec.com/pub/micro/msdos/win3/winsock`. This is a mirror site for Indiana University's CICA archive, `ftp.cica.indiana.edu`, the largest collection of Windows software on the Internet. CICA permits only a limited number of anonymous logins, but Digital can accommodate many more.

The creation of this standardized interface has led to an explosion of Windows software for TCP/IP. As a result, all current TCP/IP implementations, such as the Novell products mentioned earlier, include a file called WINSOCK.DLL, which implements the Windows Sockets interface. Another strong competitor for Windows desktops is Peter Tattam's shareware Trumpet WinSock, available at `ftp.trumpet.com.au`. A registered version of Trumpet WinSock costs only $25, with volume discounts available to sites with over 100 users. Trumpet offers special advantages for users on dialup links but works equally well with Ethernet networks. Trumpet supports both SLIP and PPP connections with a built-in dialer and scripting, and it connects to Ethernets over packet drivers. For sites using packet drivers, and for mobile Internet users or those working from home, Trumpet is a better choice than Novell's ODI WinSock.

For Ethernets, you need to install an additional small driver called WINPKT.COM, included with Trumpet WinSock, after the original packet driver that references its software interrupt. In the example above, a line would be added after that loading `odipkt` that reads `winpkt 0x60`.

The Trumpet WinSock program consists essentially of two parts, the WINSOCK.DLL file, which typically is stored in the \WINDOWS\SYSTEM directory, and TCPMAN.EXE, which provides the necessary TCP/IP transport services. The latter program can be either assigned to a program icon and started when needed or loaded automatically with Windows by adding it to the `load=` line in the WIN.INI file or placing it in the Startup folder. Automatic loading is the preferred route for networked machines. Make sure to give the full pathname to TCPMAN.EXE if it is not stored in a directory in your path.

Trumpet WinSock requires you to specify a variety of parameters for it to work properly. Most of these are obvious, like your local workstation IP address, but a few depend on whether you are using Ethernet or a dialup connection. The first time you run Trumpet, you'll be presented with a setup dialog box like the one in Figure 10-1.

The IP address, gateway, and netmask parameters have already been treated in the discussion of NET.CFG. The name server entry gives the IP addresses (not the domain names) of Internet hosts providing Domain Name Services. You can list a number of hosts here. Typically, the first entry is a server machine on the local area network, with additional entries for secondary backup servers on the local network or at the access provider's site. The time server entry is currently inoperative. The

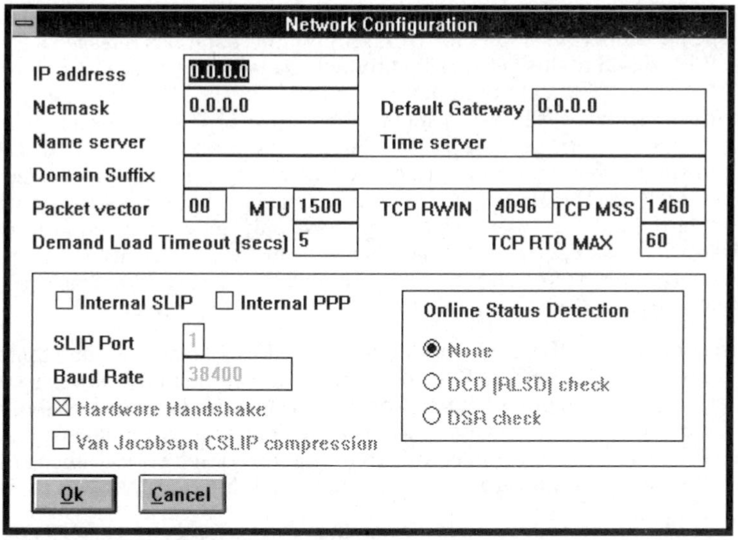

Figure 10-1: Trumpet WinSock configuration.

Domain Suffix is usually your own domain name; Trumpet appends this to any unqualified hostname to get fully-qualified domain names. The packet vector refers to the software interrupt used by the packet driver; it is given in hexadecimal.

The three other values in this line, MTU, TCP RWIN, and TCP MSS, are less obvious. The default values given here are for Ethernet. MTU refers to the *maximum transmission unit*, the size of the largest packet that TCP/IP can transmit. Ethernet packets can be as large as 1,514 bytes, of which 14 bytes are for the Ethernet header, leaving 1,500 bytes of data. A similar calculation applies to the TCP *maximum segment size*; it is 40 bytes shorter than the MTU to accommodate the 40-byte TCP header. Finally the TCP *receive window* defaults to 4,096 bytes for Ethernet (and could be larger depending on hardware performance) and should be much lower for dialup connections like 2,048. (See Chapters 13 and 31 for suggestions on tuning TCP/IP and Trumpet WinSock in particular for maximum performance.)

With a WinSock in place, you can install a wide variety of Windows software written to this specification. I will return to the choice of appropriate client software after a brief discussion of networking alternatives to NetWare.

TCP/IP with other PC networks

While most organizational LANs run NetWare, many use peer-to-peer networking technologies that use the NetBIOS protocol, or its extended cousin, NetBEUI. Early versions of these products also used monolithic drivers, but current releases of software like Microsoft's Windows for Workgroups, Artisoft's LANtastic, and Performance Technology's POWERLan now use standard interfaces like NDIS and, in the case of POWERLan and Novell's Personal NetWare, ODI as well.

Microsoft has developed a simple and attractive solution to the TCP/IP transport issue for users of Windows for Workgroups. Microsoft has released a free 32-bit TCP/IP add-on to this networking product available at `ftp://ftp.microsoft.com/peropsys/windows/public/tcpip/wfwt32.exe`. This software installs easily with a standard Windows SETUP.EXE program, requiring the usual information like IP addresses, subnet masks, and so forth. Early releases of this product were somewhat buggy, but the recent version has received generally good reviews. The Microsoft transport runs only in Windows for Workgroups, not standard Windows 3.1 or 3.11, and supports only networked connections, not dialup SLIP or PPP. (Robert Juhasz has written a version of his XFS client for the Network File System that runs under Microsoft's 32-bit TCP/IP stack. It's available from `ftp://lwfws1.uni-paderborn.de:/pub/xfs`.)

Users of other NetBIOS networking software like LANtastic will find that their vendor already offers a TCP/IP add-on package, although like Novell's LAN Workplace for DOS, the price can be steep. If your network operating system runs over ODI drivers, the material above on NetWare connections should enable you to set up TCP/IP services in parallel with your system. For networks running over NDIS, another shim solution is available to add packet driver capabilities.

The shim DIS_PKT9.DOS by Joe Doupnik performs a role in the NDIS environment like that ODIPKT.COM does in the ODI environment. The NDIS shim is available as `ftp://oak.oakland.edu/SimTel/msdos/pktdrvr/dis_pkt9.zip`. This shim works with the NDIS2 specification, used by most software except Windows for Workgroups, which supports both NDIS2 and NDIS3. (Dan Lanciani of Harvard has produced an NDIS3 shim available at `ftp://newdev.harvard.edu`.)

While ODI stacks store their configuration information in the file NET.CFG, NDIS stacks use a file called PROTOCOL.INI, often stored in the \WINDOWS directory or with the networking software. The driver itself is loaded in CONFIG.SYS, immediately after the NDIS driver for the network card and the mandatory protocol manager, PROTMAN.DOS, as follows:

```
DEVICE=C:\PATH\PROTMAN.DOS /I:C:\PATH  [Replace path as appropriate]
DEVICE=C:\PATH\NDISDRVR.DOS            [Replace ndisdrvr with driver
                                        for your network card]
DEVICE=C:\PATH\DIS_PKT9.DOS
```

In PROTOCOL.INI, a section must be added to refer to the packet driver as follows:

```
[pktdrv]
 drivername = pktdrv$
 bindings = drivername              [Refers to network driver referenced
                                     earlier in PROTOCOL.INI, e.g., ne2000]
 intvec = 0x60
 chainvec = 0x66
```

These additions let packet driver software communicate with the Internet alongside the NDIS-based networking software.

Low-Cost Suites of Internet Applications

With a TCP/IP transport in place, your user community can finally enjoy the benefits of your organization's Internet investment. The choice of appropriate software for the various Internet services your users will need depends primarily on your operating environment. Microsoft *Windows* users can expect sophisticated graphical tools with toolbars and drag-and-drop operations, even in freeware. PC users still operating in the textual DOS environment face more-limited choices.

DOS's single-tasking nature limits its value as an operating system for Internet users. Much of the beauty of the Internet comes from its support of multitasking. With a single TCP/IP transport in place, you can run as many different Internet applications as your operating system and connection bandwidth allow. UNIX allows this naturally, as does, to a lesser extent, Microsoft Windows. DOS users can achieve multitasking with Quarterdeck's Desqview product, which, like Windows, runs multiple DOS programs in individual virtual machines. However, most DOS users expect to be running one program at a time.

Quarterdeck's more advanced product, Desqview/X, adds support for X Windows, a windowing standard developed at MIT for UNIX workstations. Desqview/X includes the Novell TCP/IP transport and a telnet and ftp client. Desqview/X can run programs on remote UNIX hosts over telnet, even graphical programs like NCSA Mosaic, and display their output on the local PC. By including a well-supported TCP/IP stack, Quarterdeck has made this environment even more attractive to some PC Internet users.

Many people in the UNIX community also work in text mode. The growth of the Internet stimulated the development of freeware UNIX clients before most DOS users had ever heard of the Internet. DOS programmers have since created many useful Internet applications, but often with more limitations than equivalent UNIX text-mode tools. Organizations with a DOS-only computing environment may wish to consider training their staff to use at least some UNIX clients when those applications surpass their DOS equivalents. In addition, some applications written for both DOS and UNIX nevertheless run better in UNIX; both Pine and Lynx come to mind.

Suggesting that your users be exposed to UNIX obviously brings difficulties. The first problem is coping with a strange new command language. Easy-to-create menuing applications can help reduce the need to learn UNIX. A larger problem concerns file transfers between the UNIX host and the PC. Moving information from UNIX hosts to PCs can be handled, though clumsily, with ftp. Adding an NFS client like Juhasz's XFS simplifies the process since UNIX drives appear as new drive letters on the DOS desktop. However, the NFS drivers consume nearly 60K of memory below 1024K and may crowd out larger DOS programs. Running an NFS or ftp server on the DOS network is more difficult and more costly.

The table that follows lists selected Internet freeware and shareware. Many of the DOS and Windows programs can be found at `ftp://ftp.cyways.com/pub/doswin`. (Those with World Wide Web browsers should point to `http://www.cyways.com/ftpindex.html`.) In some cases, I have suggested UNIX versions when they are clearly superior to available DOS programs. In each case, the first entry represents what I believe to be the best choice in its category, followed by an alternative when it exists.

	Operating System and TCP/IP Transport	
Service or Protocol	***DOS/Packet Driver***	***Windows/WinSock***
TCP/IP transport	Packet Drivers	Novell Client Kit/Microsoft TCP/IP Trumpet WinSock by Peter Tattam
Telnet	NCSA Telnet	QPC WinQVT/Net QWS3270 by James Rymerson
FTP	NCSA Telnet	WS_FTP by John Junod WinQVT/Net
Mail	U. Washington PC-Pine UNIX Pine	Pegasus Mail by David Harris Qualcomm Eudora
World Wide Web	U. Kansas Lynx for UNIX Lynx for DOS	Netscape's Netscape NCSA Mosaic
Gopher	Lynx U. Minn Gopher for UNIX	Netscape/Mosaic U. Minn Gopher
News	Pine (3.91 or later) UNIX Tin by Iain Lea	WinVN by Mark Riordan Netscape
WAIS	PCwais by Faeiz Hindi	Netscape/Mosaic USGS WinWAIS
FTP Server	NCSA Telnet	WFTPD by Alun Jones
Network File System (Sun NFS)	XFS by Robert Juhasz	XFS XFS for Microsoft TCP/IP
lpr (DOS-to-UNIX network printing)	None	WSLPRS by Thomas Heil
lpd (UNIX-to-DOS network printing)	None	WSLPD by David Brooks and Robert Peterson

Some NFS and ftp servers for you

Some commercial software like NetManage's ChameleonNFS include an NFS server for around $400. Novell sells an NFS server module for NetWare, but it costs about $3,000. Alun Jones wrote an ftp server for WinSocks called WFTPD.EXE, available at the Digital and CICA sites mentioned above. A freeware ftp server NLM for NetWare servers can be found at `ftp://novell.felk.cvut.cz/appl/pub/nw311/ftpd/ftpd110.zip`.

For Microsoft's Windows for Workgroups or NT, LAN Manager, IBM's OS/2, or Digital's Pathworks, another solution is to run the free Samba server by Andrew Tridgell on the UNIX host. Samba provides file and print services that are compatible with these products and can be found at `ftp://nimbus.anu.edu.au/pub/tridge/samba`.

Internet software is constantly being upgraded, especially freeware and shareware products, so this list may change as time passes. If you wish to assemble your own suite of client software, you would do well to keep in touch with the appropriate Usenet newsgroups, such as `comp.protocols.tcp-ip.ibmpc` and `comp.os.ms-windows.networking.tcp-ip`. Other relevant newsgroups include `comp.os.msdos.mail-news`, `comp.infosystems.*`, `comp.sys.novell`, and the enormous `comp.os.linux.help` for those relying on Linux servers.

An Internet suite built on the software listed in the table, especially that for Windows, can easily hold its own against much more expensive commercial implementations. David Harris's Pegasus Mail for Windows is a stellar example of what's available for free on the Internet. His program offers users nearly every possible mail management tool, sports an attractive interface with a toolbar, and even stores their files in their NetWare mail directories if available. Pegasus is completely free, though Harris does charge for a site-licensed manual. For most users, though, the simple interface and extensive Windows help file will make manuals unnecessary.

Besides mail, most users want a World Wide Web navigator. The freeware NCSA Mosaic had no competitors until a few of its principal developers set up their own company to produce the navigation client Netscape. Netscape offers many improvements over Mosaic. It runs efficiently on the standard 16-bit Windows platform, while recent Mosaic versions required installing Microsoft's 32-bit extensions to Windows. Netscape also has a decent newsreader and supports encrypted communications servers running Netscape's proprietary Netsite products. Netscape uses algorithms from the respected RSA Data Security. Together they hope that these authentication and encryption tools will become the basis for commercial transactions over the World Wide Web.

Conclusion

Effective organizational integration with the Internet requires a mix of hardware and software solutions to the key issues of connecting to the Net, setting up an Internet server, assigning hostnames and IP numbers, providing TCP/IP services, and choosing a package of client software. Network administrators with an exposure to UNIX and a solid understanding of the network operating system can handle these tasks internally. Yet many smaller organizations may have no full-time network administrator, and many administrators know little about TCP/IP, UNIX, or the Internet. For these organizations, the best approach to Internet connectivity may be to contract with an outside provider.

Finally, I have not discussed what may ultimately be the most important component of an effective Internet strategy, *training the organization's personnel to use the Internet's resources*. Nearly everyone should get some training in basic Internet concepts like domain names and should learn how to use electronic mail. Some people in the organization need deeper training in such areas as navigation, information retrieval, and electronic publishing. Providing the hardware and software is not enough; the human element must be incorporated into any plan to make your organization part of the global Internet community.

Peter H. Lemieux is the President of cyways, inc., a firm offering complete Internet solution packages to organizations. Prior to founding cyways, he taught for ten years at the Massachusetts Institute of Technology offering courses in computer techniques and statistical methods. He is a graduate of Harvard College and has a Ph.D. in political science from M.I.T. He enjoys golf and snorkeling and trying, with limited success, to understand the mind of his three-year-old daughter.

Peter H. Lemieux, President
cyways, inc.
203 Arlington Street
Watertown, Massachusetts 02172-1205 U.S.A.

Voice: (617) 924-7991
Fax: (617) 926-8440

Chapter 11
Maintaining Large Networks

This chapter contains two articles:

- "Centralized versus Distributed Management in a Large Organization"
- "Secrets for Managing Large Networks"

Centralized versus Distributed Management in a Large Organization

by Thomas Hickman <hickman@cleo.bc.edu>

Imagine yourself at the helm of a large multinational technology firm, with thousands of personal computers, hundreds of powerful workstations, several main frames—a veritable ocean-liner cruise ship.

Now imagine yourself employed in a one-person consulting business, with a single Macintosh Plus and a daisy-wheel printer at your disposal—a 14-foot birch-bark canoe.

Such are the extreme possibilities faced by system administrators, technical consultants, and computer hackers—and everyone else—in today's computerized and networked workplace. In the previous scenarios, try to imagine how you, as captain or lowly boatswain, want the boat in question to be navigated, and by whom.

OK. Maybe the metaphor doesn't work for you. Maybe you are an earth sign, and all the allusions to boats do nothing for you. So—in more concrete terms—your organization has already spent a great deal of money on computers and network access. Chances are good that if your company is small, you have at least one computer and are probably thinking of ways in which more computers can improve your productivity. If your company is large, you probably have thousands of computers. Regardless of the number of computers owned by your organization, you are thinking of acquiring more computers.

With every further expenditure on *information technology* comes an increased need for well-planned direction, support, and integration of your existing or future computing infrastructure. With every new piece of software used by any member of your organization comes an organizational need for compatibility, and often implicitly, a necessity to upgrade existing systems.

Increasingly diverse computing platforms, integrated networked access, and a booming software market, coupled with the increased sophistication and expectations of today's computer users, demand that you rethink the traditional technology management paradigms.

The claims of advertisements and technical spec sheets are often meaningless in real-world situations. The *promise* of every new facet of computer technology brings with it an associated peril. That is to say that if you aren't careful, you can sink your boat, run it aground, or merely get lost in a sea of digitized information.

The most critical issue in this rethinking is the question of *centralized versus distributed technology and information management.* In a *centralized* support environment, one individual or agency makes all the technology decisions for an organization. That central agent is responsible for every facet of the information infrastructure, including purchasing, installation, training, and implementation.

In a *distributed* support environment, the opposite is true. The *end users* choose their system, install it, buy their software, set up their information systems.

So then in any organization, large or small, a decision must be made about the management of information technology. It might seem odd to speak of "managing" a computer. It is, after all, just a piece of equipment, like a typewriter, sitting on someone's desk. This is true, but decreasingly so with every passing moment. In today's networked world, the computer is more than just a number cruncher, more than just a word-processor, more than just a lunch-hour distraction.

Today's computer, attached to today's information superhighway, is an information processing tool. The degree to which an individual can make use of the information content of the Internet (or any other information network) is directly proportional to the degree to which that individual's computer is compatible with both the local and the global network standards. Lets face it, there just aren't any good WWW clients being written for TRS-80s. And if your organization buys a truckload of them, expecting to be able to plug them into the wall and go to work, it will be sorely disappointed. But hey, if you get a good deal, who's to argue? Right?

Ancillary Issues

Regardless of what decision you or your organization makes regarding the technical and administrative management of your information systems, ancillary questions arise. Consider the following:

- If an information system is to be managed centrally, what ramifications does this method have on human resources?
- Is there a need for a new job in the organization?

- Does someone who already has a full plate have to take on new responsibilities?
- If a decision is made to go with one platform for an organization's primary method of information dissemination, does that mean that all the people in the organization have to learn to use the system by themselves, or will training be provided?

These ancillary issues break down into questions of hardware selection, software selection, and technical support, all discussed in the following sections.

Hardware selection

You can take one of two basic approaches to hardware selection:

- With the laissez-faire approach, individuals in the organization choose which systems to buy in the open marketplace. This allows for great flexibility and tends to meet the needs of the end user well. The more involved the end users are in this decision-making process, the more likely their needs will be heard and met. Of course, in a real world, what happens might be more like a nuclear arms race, as Mr. Jones tries to match the latest greatest hardware upgrade purchased by Ms. Smith. And in the real world, not everyone knows the difference between a DX2/50 and a P60/D. Then too, there is that poor individual who got stuck with the truckload of TRS-80s.
- A centralized agent responsible for the technology decisions of an entire organization seems, at face value, a much better route. Such a structure can provide technological continuity across the entire organization, and, if well informed, can ensure that all new systems are compatible with all existing and all possible future systems. But, sadly, compatibility is a big if. With a single point of decision making, the possibility for egregious error increases. The more isolated the technical gurus are from the rest of the organization, the less likely that their decisions will reflect the real needs of the end users. Homogeneity at the desk-top level is a wonderful concept, but the result isn't always workable. (The graphic artist who receives a 2/20 286 IBM clone on which to do design isn't going to be very productive.)

Software selection

The previous points about hardware apply equally to software. If end users are empowered to select, install, and use the software of their choice, they will, at the very least, use the software they like best. Or, if they sacrifice their preferences to their budget line, they will get good deals. But when Mr. Jones tries to share a text file created in MS Word with Ms. Smith, who uses VI on her UNIX workstation, neither will be satisfied with the attempts. There is also the unfortunate truth that end users are not always capable of correctly installing and using the software they buy.

Technical support

In a purely distributed environment, there is no technical support. This creates something of a Sartrian workplace. As far as the technology goes, it's sink or swim. Users learn to use their computers out of necessity. They learn do to what works. That is, they learn work-arounds that might or might not be the preferred way of addressing any given need or problem. Even though this is the computer age, not everyone knows very much about computers. In many departments or organizations, even the gurus are woefully misinformed. Often, when forced to adapt to technology without talented tech support staff, resentment begins to build, and computer users become computer haters.

Not everyone can thrive in an environment that demands self-sufficiency. In most organizations, computer skills are still listed as a *plus* in their job descriptions. If technical support is not explicitly provided to members of the organization, those *beneficial* computer skills are truly necessary.

In a centralized support environment, there are always people around whose job it is to know and understand computers. There are people who have their jobs because of their computer skills. (As an aside, these same people sometimes seem to lack other basic skills, most especially social ones.) It becomes the job of these people to troubleshoot, to advise, and to chip in wherever possible to make the computing environment run smoothly. This assistance can enable computers to be tools, sails billowing in the wind instead of anchors dragging in the mud.

Information Systems

Local computer networks, the LANs and token ring networks of individual offices, departments, or organizations, beg for the creation of information systems to make use of the network. Access to the Internet provides users with an immediate opportunity to make use of millions of pieces of online information. It also offers organizations an opportunity to provide information to the world, via the Internet. The number of protocols you can use to set up an information system on either a local network or on an Internet domain is daunting. I don't intend to cover the technical issues related to these various platforms. I merely want to give you food for thought and share some of my own experiences, positive and negative, regarding these systems.

Management information systems

Management information systems, out of necessity, are centrally administered. MIS design and maintenance require a high level of programming skill and generally an intimate knowledge of the business needs of the organization.

There are *desktop* solutions that allow a small organization to avoid the overhead of maintaining a mainframe and a staff of MIS programmers, but even at the desktop level, operating MIS applications requires a high level of sophistication. The level of organizational involvement in the design and day-to-day management of the MIS system depends on the number of people in the organization with programming skill and system knowledge, as well as the degree to which these individuals are willing to make themselves and their time available to the rest of the organization.

Configuration and management of MIS systems is not a job for novice computer users. But without the input from the novice computer users who actually do the work of the organization, the MIS applications and methods will not meet the needs of the organization, nor will they reflect the services provided by the organization.

File servers

File servers (for example, AppleShare servers and Novell servers) are intended to allow file-sharing between individuals at one location. A strong argument can be made that they should be managed locally, within individual offices. This sort of file-sharing system is ideal for small organizations, and often doesn't even require a *dedicated* computer. There is a risk of copyright violation with any file server. Sharing of software between many users is generally considered bad form unless all those users have licenses for the software in question or a licensing arrangement has been made with the software manufacturer. There is also a need to consider the possible ramifications of unrestricted (even accidentally unrestricted) access to sensitive data.

FTP servers

FTP (or File Transfer Protocol) servers might require more administrative overhead than an AppleShare or Novell server. FTP Servers use Internet protocols to allow file sharing over the Internet. In some cases, access to the files in an ftp server is password protected. Often, ftp servers are set up for anonymous access. Hence, there is an increased security risk if sensitive files are being shared. There is also an increased liability risk if copyrighted software is inadvertently (or purposefully) being supplied to the world free of charge.

If a user sets up an ftp server without knowing about the security risks and without knowing the appropriate way in which to configure the server, a minor catastrophe can result. On the other hand, if the ftp server for an organization is managed centrally, access to it (for example, getting files on to the server to share) might become so muddied with bureaucracy that the server fails to be of use as an information system.

Network news (Usenet) servers

Usenet News is like an interactive electronic bulletin board. Usenet News servers allow your Internet site to archive Usenet posts from all over the Internet, and to propagate posts from your site to the Internet. Usenet newsgroups are organized topically, and your user has the option of reading, responding, or posting to thousands of groups. There is little room for flexibility in deciding how to manage a Usenet server. Your local Internet service provider can advise you (or your system administrator) of your options, but in essence, if you want Usenet, you have to do things the Usenet way. Because this is an Internet standard, compatibility isn't a big problem. There are Usenet *clients* or readers for virtually every type of computer in production.

Gopher-based information systems

Gopher is a connectionless TCP/IP information dissemination tool. A Gopher server acts like a well-mannered ftp server, presenting the consumer with an organized and aesthetically pleasing menu of options and then serving the information on demand. The Gopher protocol is currently a baseline standard for Internet information systems. There are over 3,000 Gopher servers registered with the central registry at The University of Minnesota. Certainly there are many other Gopher servers in use that have not been registered.

The good news about Gopher servers is that you can set up one on virtually any computer currently in production. The bad news is that virtually anyone can set one up. In certain cases, this makes the decision about how to manage a Gopher server moot. If users are willing to spend a few hours poking around on the Net, they can find the software and have the server running. This is a two-edged sword: It is easy for authorized staff to start a Gopher and register it with The University of Minnesota, but it is also easy for someone without proper authority to do the same thing. The Gopher protocol and the plethora of Gopher software freely available on the Net were developed specifically to allow cross-platform sharing of information.

WWW information systems

The same things said for Gopher can be said for WWW, only in color, with 32-bit graphics. WWW servers exist for most computing platforms, and although some users might not have the full functionality of WWW's unique hypermedia and hypertext, there are (or soon will be) WWW browsers for most major computing platforms. Just as it is fairly straightforward for a user to set up a WWW server, it is also fairly easy for an unauthorized individual to publish information via WWW. It is also conceivable that an individual intending to make information available locally over the WWW format can make that same information available to the 26-million-person population of the Internet.

The Information Part of Information Systems

The technical infrastructure of any networked infosystem is actually only half of the *problem* of information systems. A less technically daunting, although possibly more insurmountable, aspect of any information system is the information itself. You should ask several questions before considering any technical hardware or software:

- What kind of information, if any, does your organization produce? What kind of audience do you expect for your information system?
- What information is needed by the members of your organization to enable them to do their jobs well? If yours is a large organization, who will manage the information in the system?
- Will everyone be able to provide information to the system? If so, will all users be operating under their own authorities?
- Who will ensure that all the information is accurate?
- Who will review what information individuals are accessing? (Usenet news can be the biggest bane to productivity since Solitaire!) Can everyone access everything, or should certain people have access only to certain files?

These are tough questions. Tougher, perhaps, than "Does TurboGopher 1.0.8 run under System 6?" or "Can I connect my PC to our twisted-pair Ethernet network with my old coaxial card?" Technical questions usually have cut-and-dry answers. They have correct answers. Error is usually indicated by error messages or inert computers. Systemic questions about information organization can be answered any number of ways. In all likelihood, none of them is correct, and the error messages you receive are more subtle.

The reality in most organizations is some ad hoc combination, planned or organic, of centralized and distributed technical support and information system management. A little bit of planning can go a long way toward improving your technical infrastructure, as can a little bit of flexibility. As a metric, I offer the chart in Figure 11-1.

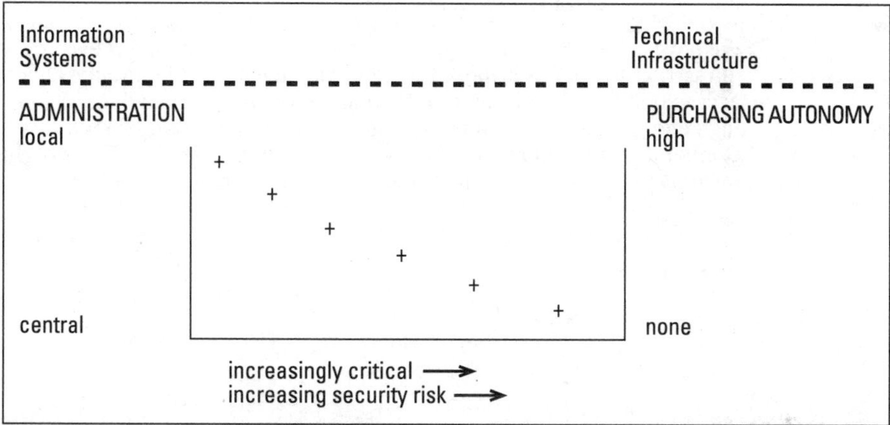

Figure 11-1: Information system and technical infrastructure trade-offs — security versus autonomy.

Information Systems at Boston College

In my experience at Boston College, which tends in size more towards the ocean-liner cruise ship in my initial metaphor, I realized that no plan works in practice, and no practice can proceed without a plan. We truly span all possibilities across the many different departments and offices here at BC. Individuals do have autonomy in their computer purchasing, but they do not buy on the open market.

Instead, users work through central purchasing, and choose their systems from a list which we, the technical gurus, compile. That way, we ensure that they get the systems they want, and that the systems they get fit in to our existing network. We employ all the information systems mentioned previously, which, taken together, comprise our campus-wide information system.

Local departments manage file servers, providing information both intra- and interdepartmentally. Information key to members of the Boston College community is available in a variety of methods. We are currently using Gopher as a front end to the methods of information dissemination, allowing users a common interface to organize terminal-based interaction with databases, ftp access to archives, read-only access to Usenet News, and Gopher-based access to text and graphics. These systems are managed centrally, so we can ensure 24-hour-a-day, 7-day-a-week operation.

Because of security and integrity concerns, the information in these systems has to be *approved* by a central agent. But all the information, except that related to computing and technology, is authored by the appropriate office in the community. We provide training and support to users, give them the best available tools, and let them go. Because a substantial subset of our users still access our information via teletype terminals or low-end personal computers, we have help back on our implementation of WWW technology.

We have a Web server and intend to make it a superset of our existing information infrastructure, but as always, the new system will merely provide an alternative access point to the information system. In the future, even once all our users have high-end graphically competent computers on their desks, they will still be able to Gopher and ftp to individual facets of our CWIS. To see the results of this ambitious mishmash of organizational strategies, you'll just have to Gopher to our site:

```
gopher://infoeagle.bc.edu
```

or via the WWW:

```
http://infoeagle.bc.edu
```

Summary

Now I will recap the key issue: *centralized versus distributed technology and information management.*

The centralized technology and information management side has the following pros:

- Easy control over versions/upgrades
- Control over security
- Smaller fields of expertise for support staff
- Local staff (nontechnical) free to do productive work
- End users see computers as tools rather than as work

The centralized technology and information management side has the following cons:

- Requires dedicated technical support staff
- When things go wrong, people know where to look
- Might require high-end machines to serve as the back end to user services
- Increasing investment in any one centralized service decreases lateral flexibility in both hardware and software market

The distributed technology and information management side has the following pros:

- Empowers end users to meet specific and often ad hoc needs
- Does not require dedicated staff
- Does not require dedicated machines at the central level

The distributed technology and information management side has the following cons:

- Requires local administrators to spend time away from primary tasks
- Might build resentment when local staff does not want the responsibility for machines
- Might make inefficient use of hardware, such as when several people or departments duplicate the same service

Thomas Hickman holds a B.S. in Mechanical Engineering from The Georgia Institute of Technology and has completed course work for an M.A. in Philosophy at Boston College. He currently works as a Special Services Consultant, serving as an ad hoc *Internet Guru in the Office of Information Technology at Boston College.*

Secrets for Managing Large Networks

by Ron Hoffmann

as told to Carol Baroudi

As large IP networks go, Massachusetts Institute of Technology's 13,000 nodes qualifies as one of the largest. Its sophisticated staff has developed its own strategy for not only supporting this large network but also managing the network's growth.

The M.I.T. network (MITnet) is built around a 100 MBPs FDDI backbone of 10 routers, each of which supports up to 18 Ethernet *subnets* Individual buildings are wired with thick Ethernet backbone cables to which twisted-pair Ethernet hubs are connected. There are close to 360 such hubs in the M.I.T. network, each of which is capable of supporting anywhere from 12 to 72 individual office connections. The hubs have remote control capability via SNMP.

The network currently carries both IP and AppleTalk on a campus-wide basis, and IP to the Internet at large through M.I.T.'s connection to NEARnet, the New England Academic and Research network.

For the managers of the M.I.T. network, the maintenance and growth of their network is a straightforward, logical task. What today seems second nature is the result of many years of hard work and experimentation. Here are some of the important concepts they have developed and adapted:

Plan the design

M.I.T.'s network managers modeled their design on the original ARPANET design: a network of networks. They work hard to maintain the integrity of the design.

Find scalable solutions

Sometimes a solution to a problem seems obvious. But what will it look like when you multiply it by a factor of 10, or 100, or 1,000? What works on a small scale may not be so attractive when seen proliferating with the growth of the system.

Pursue total quality

If you're not familiar with the concepts of Total Quality Management, learn about them. TQM emphasizes such principles as keeping a strong customer focus, developing and using measurement tools, and writing and following specifications. Most importantly it teaches you that every little thing you can do to obviate a problem is worth its weight ten times over.

Assume that you don't have human resources to maintain a solution

In a large network, you can't afford a solution that requires a person to do something. Remember the idea of scalable solutions (described earlier), and what happens when solutions are proliferated. Assume that you won't have the human resources to maintain the solution, because you won't.

Control the topology

Define what your users can (and cannot) connect to your network. For example, M.I.T. doesn't allow Ethernet repeaters. A key to maintaining a reliable network is to ensure that the topology is legal throughout. If you don't demand this, the network becomes unreliable and difficult to troubleshoot.

Find a vendor who wants your business

When you're a big customer, you should be calling the shots. Find a vendor who wants your business and is willing to work with you to deliver the features that you want.

Pay for lights

Don't think that indicator lights and displays are something you can live without. You want every clue that's available when you begin tracking a problem.

Neatness counts

Imagine 100 wires. Imagine 1,000. You have to find some way to control how your wiring is installed and how you're going to keep the wiring maintainable. Don't let it get out of control. There are wire management systems on the market. Spend money on one — it will be well worth it. Take a hint from proper telephone system wiring practices.

Keep tools simple

M.I.T. finds that, by avoiding fancy graphics, their diagnostic tools can also be used by staff dialing in from home or wherever else they're working. Fancy tools can be useful but are mostly showy, so save them for visitors. When you're down in the trenches, the fast simple tools and your brain will help you get to the root of the problem.

Keep working spare parts

Don't wait for something to break before you look for a replacement. Have working spare parts on hand for all your critical hardware.

Test components before swapping them into the network

You don't want to find out, after you've swapped a component in, that it's bad, too. Test the new component first.

Ron Hoffmann is the Assistant Network Manager for M.I.T. He attended M.I.T. as an undergraduate and has worked on network operations since 1986. He is responsible for the hardware operation of MITnet. Ron remembers the days of the ARPANET when a 56 Kbps link for an institution and a 300 bps modem were unbelievably fast.

Chapter 12

Personal Internet Access Using SLIP or PPP

by Frank Hecker <hecker @access.digex.net>
http://www.access.digex.net/~hecker/

As the Internet has been increasingly popularized in newspapers, magazines, and books, more and more people are joining or seeking to join the community of Internet users on-line. Some subscribe to commercial services, such as CompuServe and America Online, that are adding Internet-related features to their existing services. Others purchase accounts on commercial services that provide Internet access as their main offering or get accounts on freenets and other community network systems that offer Internet access as an adjunct to community information.

Finally, a small but rapidly growing number of people are connecting to the Internet directly from their PCs or Macintoshes without having to log in to larger systems and put up with the hassle of UNIX commands or restrictive menus. This chapter discusses this type of personal Internet access: both how you can use it and how it works.

An Introduction to SLIP and PPP

I assume that you have a basic understanding of the Internet and the services it supports (Telnet, ftp, and electronic mail, for example) but that you know little about TCP/IP, SLIP, PPP, and other obscure acronyms. I also assume that you have either an IBM-compatible PC (386 or better) running Microsoft Windows or an Apple Macintosh running the Mac OS. (Much of the discussion also applies to other PC operating systems, such as IBM's OS/2 Warp or Microsoft's future Windows 95.)

My goal is not to give you complete step-by-step directions on how to configure your personal computer for connection to the Internet but rather to provide a conceptual overview of personal Internet access without getting into too many technical details. My hope is that after you finish reading this chapter, you will have a good idea of how personal Internet access works, how SLIP and PPP are used in real life, and whether it makes sense for you to use them. With that end in mind, I conclude the chapter with some advice about where to go next for more information.

The original version of this chapter was written for the Washington, D.C.-area community network CapAccess (the informal name for, and a service mark of, the National Capital Area Public Access Network, Inc.). That document grew out of my thoughts about the long-term direction for community networks and what part low-cost personal Internet access might play in their evolution. At the time, I could not find any nontechnical, high-level explanation of the concepts behind SLIP and PPP Internet connections; as the poet Muriel Rukeyser said of her biography of the physicist Willard Gibbs, I wrote this document in part because I needed to read it.

I want to thank the other members of the CapAccess organization for their comments about early versions of this document; I also want to thank my fellow employees at Tandem Computers, Inc., for their help and comments. The views I express in this chapter, however, are mine alone and do not necessarily reflect the official position of either CapAccess or Tandem.

Why bother?

Today most people going on-line first encounter the Internet at one remove; they use commercial services or bulletin-board systems that have gateway functions supporting Internet electronic mail and perhaps access to Usenet on-line conferences. Those who want to access the Internet more directly have traditionally used a shell account service provided by an Internet access provider. (It's called a *shell account* because you log in to a central UNIX host and type commands into the UNIX command interpreter, or *shell.*) For example, I first obtained personal Internet access through a shell account with Digital Express Group, Inc., of Washington, D.C., one of a number of local Internet access providers that have sprung up around the United States in the past few years.

A shell account service is used in much the same way as you might use a BBS, a freenet, or other UNIX-based community network systems, such as CapAccess (albeit with a few more functions): You use your personal computer (PC or Macintosh) and its modem to log in to a central UNIX host; you read and compose electronic mail by using a UNIX e-mail program such as Pine or Elm; you read and post Usenet news articles by using a UNIX-based newsreader such as rn or trn; you retrieve files by using ftp; and then you download them by using Zmodem or Xmodem, and so on. For software, you use a standard communications program with VT100 terminal emulation and Zmodem downloading capabilities, such as Procomm or CrossTalk on PCs or Zterm on Macintoshes.

Perhaps you have a shell account now, have learned how to use the various Internet-related UNIX commands, and are reasonably satisfied with the service. Why then might you decide to change it? Here are some possible reasons:

- You are tired of using UNIX-based programs with their different interfaces (control keys, cursor keys, command lines, and so on), and you want to access the Internet by using the same "point and click" interface you use with native Windows or Mac programs.
- You want to be able to read and compose e-mail off-line, without having to stay logged in to the service while you read and write long messages.
- You want to streamline the process of downloading files and avoid the need for an extra Zmodem or Xmodem transfer after you retrieve something by using ftp.
- You want to be able to use new graphical Internet applications, most notably Mosaic and the World Wide Web, which are not accessible with the traditional character-based interface you are using now.

If any of these comments apply to you, you should consider getting a SLIP or PPP account. *SLIP,* or *Serial Line Internet Protocol,* is a communications protocol that supports an Internet connection (using TCP/IP) over a dialup line. A common variant of SLIP is called *Compressed SLIP,* or *CSLIP;* it can be somewhat faster in operation than standard SLIP.

PPP, or *Point-to-Point Protocol,* is a newer protocol that does essentially the same thing as SLIP or CSLIP; it's better designed, however, and more acceptable to the sort of people who like to standardize protocol specifications. For the rest of us, it's six of one and a half-dozen of the other for the most part. I often use the term *SLIP/PPP* to refer to SLIP, CSLIP, and PPP interchangeably.

(As noted later in this chapter, in the section "Making your PC or Macintosh Internet-capable," PPP is likely to become better supported and more popular than SLIP and CSLIP, particularly by virtue of its support in Windows 95. At present, however, more software products and Internet access providers support SLIP and CSLIP. If your software and Internet access provider give you a choice of SLIP or PPP, choose PPP; if not, use SLIP.)

What you get with SLIP or PPP

Here's what you get if you have a SLIP or PPP account:

- You have dialup Internet access by using a special dialup number and a user ID and password associated with that access.
- You can run a variety of applications over the dialup link to implement traditional Internet services, such as electronic mail, ftp, telnet, and Usenet news, in addition to newer services, such as Gopher and WWW.
- Using some Internet services (electronic mail, for example) may require that you have additional user IDs and passwords assigned to you by your Internet access provider. Other services do not require this; that is, they are either inherently anonymous in nature (anonymous ftp, Gopher, WWW, for example) or involve separate arrangements with other organizations (telnet to a remote Internet host, such as the host for the CapAccess community network, for example).
- Most of these services can be used only while the dialup Internet connection is active. With others, however (most notably electronic mail), you can do at least some things off-line.

Setting up and using SLIP or PPP can be much simpler than you might expect. The technical details are discussed later in this chapter; let's begin by describing how you might actually use your SLIP or PPP service. (Some of these details may vary slightly based on the type of software you're using and the particular Internet access provider you've chosen.)

Using SLIP or PPP: A Typical Session

You begin with your PC or Mac already running with its modem turned on and connected to a phone line. First, you invoke the SLIP or PPP application. The SLIP/PPP software asks you for your SLIP/PPP password (which goes with your SLIP/PPP user ID — more about this subject later) and then uses a script to dial the SLIP/PPP access number at your Internet access provider. Your modem dials out, the provider's modem answers, and then the script takes over for a few seconds until the SLIP/PPP connection is established. At that point, you can forget about the SLIP/PPP application and (depending on the software) minimize it or even close it just to get it out of the way. (Part of it is still running "underneath," however.)

Electronic mail

At this point, you have a live connection between your personal computer and the Internet. The next thing you might typically do is to start up an Internet e-mail program, such as Eudora, and ask it to check for and retrieve your electronic mail. Eudora then asks for your mail account password (which goes with your mail account user ID). Notice that this user ID and password are often different from your SLIP/PPP user ID and password (this subject is discussed in more detail later in this chapter). Eudora then goes out and downloads your mail from your mailbox on the Internet access provider's mail server; this process can take from a few seconds to a few minutes, depending on how much mail you've received and how big the messages are. When downloading is complete, you have all your new mail messages in an e-mail inbox on your PC or Mac.

You can then either read your mail or do something else. You might read at least a few messages that look important and perhaps respond to a couple of them. When you respond, your messages get put in an e-mail outbox for later delivery; they aren't sent right away.

Remote login using telnet

Suppose that one of the messages is about something on another Internet-connected system (the CapAccess community network system, for example) that supports login access, and you want to log in to the system and check it out. You can then invoke a telnet application, such as Trumpet Telnet for Windows or NCSA Telnet for Macintosh, and connect to the system by using its hostname (`capaccess.org`, in the example). This brings up a 24-row-by-80-column screen similar to what you would get by dialing in directly, with a prompt for the login ID. You give your user ID and password for the system (assuming that you have one), and then you're logged in and can do all the standard operations supported on that system.

This telnet connection doesn't go through either the Internet access provider's UNIX host system or the remote system's phone lines and modems; it goes over the Internet from your personal computer to the remote system (with some hops along the way through IP routers, which are "black boxes" that pass the traffic through the various networks and subnetworks that make up the Internet).

File transfer using FTP

Suppose that while you're logged in you read something that refers to an information file you can ftp from somewhere else on the Internet. Then, without closing the Telnet session, you can bring up an ftp client application, such as WS_FTP for Windows or Fetch for the Macintosh. WS_FTP and Fetch enable you to start a session to a public or "anonymous" ftp site, browse through the directories, and download files directly to your PC or Mac by using ftp. Download speeds for text and binary files are comparable to those that can be achieved by using traditional communications programs and protocols, such as Zmodem. (Downloading over SLIP or PPP is not always quite as fast, for various reasons too complicated to go into here, but it's fast enough for me and most likely for you as well.)

After finishing the ftp session, you can go back to your telnet session and continue. TCP/IP and SLIP/PPP can *multiplex* several connections. That is, several connections can be open at one time and can be sending and receiving data. TCP/IP and SLIP/PPP sort it all out and transmit and receive that data over the single dialup connection to the Internet access provider's SLIP/PPP access point.

If you use a personal computer operating system that supports "preemptive" multitasking (such as OS/2 Warp or the future Windows 95), you can have different downloads going on simultaneously while you run telnet or other Internet applications. Unfortunately, because neither Windows nor the Mac OS supports preemptive multitasking, doing an ftp transfer on those systems can severely degrade performance on a telnet session; it works fine, however, to keep multiple applications open for use but otherwise idle, and you then can switch between the applications as desired.

Usenet news

If you're really finished with your telnet session, you can log out of the remote system and close the link. You might then bring up a Usenet newsreader program, such as WinVN for Windows or NewsWatcher for the Mac. These programs connect to the Internet access provider's Usenet news server and then present you with a list of the newsgroups you subscribe to, with an indication of how many articles are available in each group. You double-click a newsgroup you're interested in checking, and the program downloads the list of current postings in the group by subject. (NewsWatcher also knows about "message threads," so if multiple postings have the same subject, it shows only one line in the listing of articles.)

You then double-click the line corresponding to a posting (or thread) you want to read, and WinVN or NewsWatcher downloads the text of that posting and puts it on the screen in a window. More double-clicking lets you advance through the newsgroup article-by-article, marking articles as having been read as you download and read them. You can also compose and post follow-up articles or new articles, which are uploaded to the Usenet news server immediately.

If you don't read all articles in a newsgroup or get through all newsgroups, you can look at them later when you next use WinVN or NewsWatcher. You can also mark articles as having been read without downloading them, in case the subject line indicates that you would likely have no interest in them.

Gopher and the World Wide Web

In this section I've discussed electronic mail (Eudora), telnet (Trumpet or NCSA Telnet), ftp (WS_FTP or Fetch), and Usenet news (WinVN or NewsWatcher). You may also have Hgopher or TurboGopher, which are Gopher client programs for Windows and the Macintosh, respectively. HGopher and TurboGopher enable you to get exactly the same information that is accessible by way of a VT100 Gopher client (as found on many Internet hosts), but with the following advantages:

- You can use a point-and-click graphical interface.
- You can save Gopher files directly to your PC or Mac (as opposed to saving them in a host UNIX directory and then downloading them).
- You don't have to log in to a UNIX host first.

Finally, you can use the much-heralded NCSA Mosaic program (or one of its many variants or look-alikes) to explore the World Wide Web with full access to multimedia information, including formatted multifont text, graphics, sound, and movies. If you do, you soon find that using Mosaic over a 14.4 Kbps dialup line is often not nearly as exciting as the hype suggests. Mosaic typically takes a minute or more just to bring up a single page of information because of the embedded graphics included in most WWW data. (You can tell Mosaic not to download the graphics images, but then what's the point?) Using Mosaic over a 14.4 Kbps connection, therefore, can be as frustrating as trying to eat ice cream through a straw; but it's still fun to play with, and many new information sources can be accessed only through the World Wide Web and a WWW client program (or *browser*), such as Mosaic.

Finishing up

While you've been doing all the things discussed in the preceding few sections, TCP/IP and SLIP or PPP have been running quietly underneath, supporting your connection on the dialup link. After a while you figure that it's time to save your pennies and cut the connection. (Most Internet access providers give you a number of "free" hours per day or per month — that is, included in your basic monthly rate — but these freebies can go fast, especially if you're like me and you connect at least two or three times a day.)

You may remember that you still have electronic-mail messages in your Eudora outbox, so you go into Eudora and tell it to send all outgoing mail. It uploads the messages to your Internet access provider's mail server, which then takes care of sending them on to their final destination. Having finished all your on-line stuff, you go back to the SLIP or PPP application and tell it to disconnect. At that point, you lose all the fancy functionality of Mosaic, ftp, and other programs. However, you can still read your electronic mail in Eudora, compose replies, and queue them for delivery the next time you connect.

How It All Works

Now that you know what you can do when you access the Internet directly from your PC or Macintosh, I want to go into more detail about what's going on "behind the scenes." My apologies for the level of technical detail in this section; I've tried to keep it to the minimum necessary to make my points (although I can't resist continually returning to a good extended analogy, as you will see).

Let's begin with what "being on the Internet" really means. For your PC or Macintosh to be "on the Internet" in the sense that I'm using the term, the following three things must be true:

- Your PC or Macintosh has software that can send and receive data by using the TCP/IP family of communications protocols.
- Your PC or Macintosh has some sort of communications link to an Internet access point from which data it sends can go out over the Internet to other systems and by which data sent from other systems on the Internet can be sent to your PC or Macintosh.
- When your PC or Macintosh is connected in this way, it has an identifying number (called an IP address) that other systems use in sending data to your PC or Macintosh and by which your PC or Macintosh identifies itself when it sends data to other systems.

For those who really want to know, *TCP/IP* stands for Transmission Control Protocol/Internet Protocol (which are really two separate protocols that work together). It's a shorthand name for a specific way of packaging up data for transmission over a communications link. TCP/IP is roughly analogous to protocols such as Kermit or Zmodem that package up data for downloading or uploading over "normal" dialup connections (to a BBS, for example).

You really don't have to know the details of TCP/IP, however, any more than you have to understand how telephone line signaling works in order to call someone on the phone. The following analogy, in fact, helps you to think about what it means to be "on the public telephone network" and use local or long-distance phone service:

- You have a device (a telephone) that can send and receive data (the sound of voices) by using some sort of low-level magic (which you don't really worry about).
- Your phone has a communications link (phone line) to an access point (your local telephone central office) through which your phone can connect to other phones anywhere in the world (and vice versa).
- When your phone is connected in this way, it has an identifying number (your phone number) that other phones use in connecting to your phone and by which your phone is identified when it is connecting to other phones (as with Caller ID).

The three elements common to both cases are shown in this list:

- You have an end-user device that has the smarts to "talk" in a certain way.
- You have a link to an access provider over which your device can "talk" with other devices of the same or similar type.
- Your device has an identifying number or address that is used when your device "talks" to other devices and vice versa.

If it's that simple, why has connecting to the Internet by using SLIP or PPP traditionally been so hard for individual users? Because doing so has been similar to trying to get phone service in an environment in which you have to build your own phone, search far and wide to find a phone company you can connect to (and possibly not have one at all in your area), and have to pay a big premium for service if and when you find a service provider.

Fortunately this situation has improved tremendously in the past few years (and even in the past few months), and we are well on the way to having personal Internet access be as easy to get and use as residential phone service is today.

Making your PC or Macintosh Internet-capable

Let's go back now and analyze what's happening in the preceding example of connecting your PC or Mac to the Internet by using SLIP or PPP. First let's discuss what you need in order to make your PC or Macintosh Internet-capable.

As noted, you begin with a PC or Macintosh system with a 14,400 (or better) bps modem. (Theoretically, you can use a 9600 or even 2400 bps modem, but with SLIP or PPP a faster modem really makes a difference, especially with applications such as Mosaic. Using one of the newer 28.8 Kbps modems is best, but many Internet access providers do not yet support their use.) Assuming that you already have a PC or Mac, you can add a new 14.4 Kbps modem for as little as $100 to $150 (U.S.) or so, depending on the modem's brand, whether the modem is external or internal, and so on. Early in 1994, for example, I bought a Practical Peripherals 14,400 bps external modem for $140; in 1990 I paid almost $500 for an earlier Practical Peripherals modem that supported a maximum speed of only 9600 bps.

To the modem you must add the requisite TCP/IP and SLIP/PPP software. Many such products exist for PCs; some of these products are freeware, and others cost money. For example, NetManage's Chameleon Sampler, a limited free TCP/IP and SLIP product for 386 or better PCs running Windows 3.1, is included in several Internet books now on the market (many Internet references are included at the end of this chapter). *The Internet For Windows For Dummies Starter Kit,* by Margaret Levine Young and John R. Levine (published by IDG Books Worldwide, 1994), contains a complete copy of Internet Chameleon, the latest version of NetManage's product. Another popular TCP/IP and SLIP product for Windows is the shareware Trumpet WinSock, by Peter Tattam, which is available on-line for downloading. (See the section "On-line information and software," later in this chapter, for pointers to more information about Trumpet WinSock.)

With Windows 95, or "Chicago," the major release of Windows due out in 1995, Microsoft is including TCP/IP and PPP capability in the base operating system. At that point, you get TCP/IP software at no extra cost if you buy a PC with Windows 95 preloaded. (You will be able to get it for older PCs by buying Windows 95 separately, as an upgrade to Windows 3.1.)

IBM has adopted a similar course of action for its recently released new version of OS/2, known as OS/2 Warp Version 3, or Warp, for short. Designed to be installed on 386 or better PCs that are running Microsoft Windows, Warp includes TCP/IP support using SLIP (with PPP support now in beta) in addition to OS/2 client programs for Internet services such as e-mail, telnet, ftp, Usenet news, Gopher, and the World Wide Web. These programs are comparable to the Windows and Mac Internet programs mentioned earlier; if you want, you can also run Windows Internet programs under Warp.

TCP/IP software for Macintosh systems comes in two parts: First comes a product called MacTCP, supplied by Apple; MacTCP is the standard TCP/IP product for all Macs. Then comes software to implement either the SLIP or PPP protocols that MacTCP needs in order to support TCP/IP over dialup links. For example, I use the free InterSLIP software from InterCon Systems Corporation; MacPPP is a comparable free product for PPP.

MacTCP itself is not freeware, but you can get it (along with InterSLIP and MacPPP and related stuff described later in this chapter) by buying either of the books *Internet Starter Kit for Macintosh,* by Adam Engst, or *The Mac Internet Tour Guide,* by Michael Fraase. (More information about these two books can be found in the section "Internet book and software bundles," later in this chapter.) Also, Apple is including MacTCP in its new System 7.5 version of the Mac OS, so if you buy a new Macintosh, you get TCP/IP software at no extra cost. (You can also get MacTCP for older Macintoshes by buying the System 7.5 product as an upgrade. If you don't need the other System 7.5 features, however, you can save money by buying MacTCP as part of either of the books mentioned in this paragraph.)

I should add that the wide availability of relatively cheap TCP/IP software for Macs and PCs is a recent phenomenon. Traditionally, TCP/IP software has been seen as being of interest only to businesses running in-house local area networks, and TCP/IP products cost as much as $400 or $500 per PC or Macintosh. TCP/IP software is still this expensive in many cases if you need true LAN capabilities, but software vendors have finally noticed the rapidly growing market for individual use of TCP/IP over dialup lines to access the Internet. Many commercial TCP/IP software packages, therefore, have dropped in price to $200 or less, at least for the basic capabilities needed for personal Internet access using SLIP or PPP.

As noted, over the next year or so this cost will drop closer to zero for basic Internet functionality; that is, at some point TCP/IP and SLIP and/or PPP capability will be bundled with the base operating system software shipped with every new PC or Macintosh. At that point, the only incremental cost to make your PC or Macintosh "Internet-capable" will be for the purchase of a modem, which many (if not most) people who buy computers will buy anyway, for other reasons (for example, to connect to BBSs or commercial on-line services, such as America Online, CompuServe, and Prodigy).

Some final notes about software compatibility: A number of potential compatibility problems exist in configuring software "stacks" that consist of the base TCP/IP software, network drivers underneath, and Internet applications on top; this has been especially true in mixing and matching software from different sources. Fortunately, these problems are not really an issue in the Macintosh world today and are rapidly becoming a thing of the past in the PC world (at least for people using Windows or OS/2 Warp as opposed to DOS only).

As noted, in the Macintosh world Apple is the only major supplier of the basic TCP/IP software, in the form of the MacTCP product. All Macintosh Internet applications are therefore written to interface to the MacTCP software, so compatibility problems are kept to a minimum. Most problems that occur are connected to the particular revision of MacTCP that is being used with a given application on a given Mac; almost all current Mac Internet applications work best with the current version of MacTCP. (The current revision of MacTCP at the time this book was written was 2.0.6.)

In the Windows world the compatibility problem has not yet been totally solved, but it has been greatly alleviated by the development of the *Windows Sockets* (or *WinSock*) standard and the implementation of TCP/IP products that conform to it. The WinSock standard specifies the interface between Windows-based Internet applications (telnet and ftp, for example) and the TCP/IP software underneath them.

Because NCSA Mosaic is a WinSock-compliant application, for example, you can run it over either NetManage's Chameleon TCP/IP software or Peter Tattam's Trumpet WinSock software. Both of these products provide a WINSOCK.DLL run-time library that implements the WinSock interface; the WINSOCK.DLL file is different for each TCP/IP product, but the interface provided to applications running above the TCP/IP software is always the same — at least in theory. In practice, most versions of WinSock are pretty good, and in most cases any WinSock application you snag from the Net works with whatever WinSock TCP/IP you're running.

The de facto TCP/IP standard for OS/2 is the IBM product bundled with OS/2 Warp, and all native OS/2 Internet applications should be written to its interface. OS/2 Warp also supports a WinSock interface for Windows-based Internet programs running under OS/2. (Windows 95 also supports the WinSock interface.)

Connecting to the Internet

As described earlier in this chapter, you can make your personal computer Internet-capable by installing the proper TCP/IP and SLIP software on your modem-equipped PC or Macintosh. Your next step is to sign up with a service provider who can give you a SLIP or PPP connection to the Internet. (In my case, for example, I have a "Personal IP" account with the Washington, D.C.-area company Digital Express Group, Inc.)

Your Internet access provider will supply you with at least three things (actually more, but I will get to that later): a dialup SLIP/PPP access phone number to which your modem connects, a personal SLIP/PPP user ID, and a personal password to go with the SLIP/PPP user ID. The SLIP/PPP user ID is typically some arbitrary string, such as `xx537`, and the password is similar to a standard login password for a UNIX system or BBS.

Assume that you've configured your SLIP/PPP software with the dialup SLIP/PPP access phone number and your SLIP/PPP user ID, in addition to the other information discussed in this section and later in this chapter. (The exact details of how to complete this configuration vary depending on your TCP/IP software and your Internet access provider; the end of this chapter contains a list of sources of information for particular packages.) You then direct the software to call up the SLIP/PPP phone number by using your 14,400 bps (or other) modem.

The call is answered by a corresponding modem at the other end (such as the ones used by BBSs). That modem is typically connected in turn to a SLIP- or PPP-capable *terminal server,* a black box that retransmits the data coming from your PC or Macintosh over the dialup line to your Internet access provider's local area network, which is in turn connected to the Internet by using an IP router (another black box you don't have to worry about).

This terminal server is similar to the ones used on many college campuses and at many freenets and other community networks (such as CapAccess) to connect users from dialup modems over a LAN into the actual UNIX host system they log in to. The primary difference is that the SLIP- or PPP-capable terminal servers (more generally known as *remote access servers*) have an extra capability that lets them pass "raw" TCP/IP data from your PC or Macintosh through to the Internet.

When you first connect to your Internet access provider's modem and remote access server, in fact, it can look much like logging in to a remote UNIX system. (That's if you were looking at the conversation, which typically you don't — login is normally handled by an automated script.) One of the first things you see is a prompt for a user ID, at which point you (or the script) enter the special SLIP/PPP user ID. You then see a password prompt, in response to which you (or the script) enter the SLIP/PPP password. (The SLIP or PPP software on your PC or Macintosh typically prompts you for your password if you haven't supplied it with the rest of your configuration information.)

On a BBS or UNIX system, you next see the opening screen and menu or a UNIX prompt. With a SLIP or PPP connection, however, your software and the remote access server go into a special mode in which they begin exchanging TCP/IP data. This process is somewhat reminiscent of what happens when a communications program is in download or upload mode; if you look at what's going across the dialup line, it looks pretty much like garbage with a few recognizable bits mixed in. You don't actually see the garbage, however, because the SLIP or PPP software doesn't bother showing it to you; it just tells you that the connection has been made and then shuts up.

Here are a couple of important points: First, having made the SLIP or PPP "connection," you really aren't logged in to any host — you just have the capability to send out data over the Internet. To continue with the telephone analogy, you've plugged in your "phone" and have "Internet dial tone," but you haven't called anybody.

Second, you might ask why you need a user ID and password if you're not logging in to anything. The answer is that your Internet access provider wants to be able to bill you for the time you spend connected to the Internet through its remote access server, and to do this, it needs an ID of some sort to know that it's you connecting. You in turn need a password so that no one else can connect to your SLIP/PPP remote access server and bill time to your account. You can think of this user ID/ password combination as your "Internet calling card number" and associated personal identification number, or PIN.

If you're really into the bits and bytes, an interesting technical question is "How does the remote access server (which is usually the equivalent of a small computer with no disk) check my SLIP/PPP user ID and password and then account for my connect-time?" The answer is that it either checks your user ID and password against an internal database held in nonvolatile memory on the remote access server or it sends the user ID and password to a real computer system to be checked against a user ID/password database on disk. (For some modern remote access servers, this check can be done by using the Kerberos authentication protocol invented at M.I.T.; Kerberos has the advantage that your password is sent over the network in an encrypted form, which decreases the likelihood that someone can intercept it and use it to gain unauthorized SLIP/PPP access.)

If the SLIP/PPP user ID checks out, the remote access server (if it has this capability) then sends a "start of call" record to a real computer system to be stored in a log (many remote access servers use the UNIX `syslog` protocol for this process); a similar "end of call" record is sent when the modem connection ends (when the user disconnects). These two records together enable the Internet access provider to compute the time and length of the SLIP or PPP session for billing purposes. Again, this process is similar to the way long-distance calling cards work.

The analogy extends even more: If you always make the connection from the same phone, your Internet access provider can theoretically use Caller ID or similar mechanisms to know that it is you who is calling, just as you don't have to enter a calling-card number to dial long distance from your home phone. Just as you might make long-distance calls while on the road, however, you might connect your modem to different phones (if you have a laptop, for example); having a separate SLIP/PPP user ID and password is necessary to handle this case.

I've left out another crucial piece so far: the *IP address,* which is your "Internet phone number." For example, my Internet access provider assigns me my own IP address (mine is `164.109.211.201`, in case you're curious); an IP address is the fourth piece of initial information you may be given when you sign up, along with the three I've already mentioned: SLIP/PPP dialup access number, SLIP/PPP user ID, and SLIP/PPP password.

Many remote access servers also have the capability to assign callers an IP address "on the fly;" the address that is chosen is displayed during the login sequence, and the TCP/IP software on your PC or Mac then picks it up and uses it. When you dial up the next time, you might get a different IP address. This is not as confusing as you might think, because it turns out that for various reasons (discussed later in this chapter) it really doesn't matter what your IP address is, as long as you have a valid connection.

The theory behind doing this dynamic assignment of IP addresses is that it lets the Internet access provider use a limited-size pool of addresses to serve a much larger number of people. After all, people need the address only when they're connected to the modems and remote access server, so the Internet access provider really doesn't need to supply any more IP addresses than it has dialup SLIP/PPP ports.

I prefer the way my Internet access provider does it, however. For one thing, it's much easier to understand, especially using the phone number analogy: Just as my phone has a single fixed phone number, my personal computer has a single fixed IP address. For another, the IP address is often used by remote systems to identify who's connecting to them over the Internet, just as people use Caller ID to identify who's phoning them. (Using the IP address for authentication in this way is not totally secure and foolproof, but then neither is Caller ID.) With "on the fly" assignment, you might get a given IP address at one point, and after you disconnect from the service, someone else could get the same address a few minutes later. Finally, sometimes the dialup connection is lost during an Internet session (because of line noise, for example). Because of the nature of the TCP/IP protocols, if you have a fixed IP address, you can often recover the session by simply reestablishing the dialup SLIP or PPP link; this is not possible if your IP address changes every time you connect.

To summarize, after you sign up with an Internet access provider and connect to its SLIP/PPP terminal server, you are directly "on the Internet" (or have Internet dial tone, if you will), having fulfilled the three conditions discussed earlier:

- With the help of a modem and low-cost TCP/IP software, you have an "Internet-capable" PC or Macintosh.
- You've established a TCP/IP over SLIP (or PPP) connection to your Internet access point.
- You have an IP address or "Internet phone number" and are ready to "make calls"; that is, to connect to other systems and make use of Internet services.

This section has been a long one, and I still haven't gotten to the point of discussing anything really useful. But have patience; believe me, even a telephone dial tone would seem this complicated if you really looked "under the hood." Just a few years ago (before "equal access"), in fact, getting long-distance phone service in the United States through a non-AT&T carrier such as MCI was also relatively complicated; you may remember when you always had to dial a special access number and enter your personal access code before you could dial a long-distance number by using a long-distance company other than AT&T.

The basics of SLIP and PPP Internet access

Here's a quick summary of the basics of accessing the Internet by using SLIP and PPP:

- With a Macintosh or Windows- or OS/2-based PC (386 or better) that already has a modem and for a relatively small, one-time expenditure (from zero to $200 [U.S.]), you can get TCP/IP and SLIP or PPP software to make your computer capable of being a full-fledged Internet node.
- For a relatively small expenditure (typically between $10 and $40 per month in the United States, depending on your location and the amount of competition in your market), you can sign up with an Internet access provider who will enable you to connect your PC or Mac to the Internet on an on-demand, dialup basis.

What you get for your money is an Internet hostname and IP address, with corresponding Domain Name System (DNS) directory entries maintained by a DNS name server, a number to call for SLIP or PPP access, and a special SLIP/PPP user ID and password to authenticate you and allow your connect-time to be tracked. (DNS is discussed later in this chapter, in the "Hostnames and DNS" sidebar.) If your Internet access provider assigns IP addresses "on the fly," you don't get a hostname or IP address of your own. Your provider may also supply you with some other miscellaneous configuration information, most of which is pure gobbledygook and is necessary to know only when you first configure SLIP or PPP.

With just the basic dialup Internet SLIP/PPP service, you can use ftp clients such as WS_FTP or Fetch to download files; telnet programs such as Trumpet or NCSA Telnet to log in to remote systems; Gopher clients such as Hgopher or TurboGopher to access Gopher servers; and WWW browsers such as NCSA Mosaic to access World Wide Web servers.

If your Internet access provider also runs a POP mail server, (as almost all do), you can have the mail server receive mail for you and use an e-mail program such as Eudora to download it when you're connected, for you to read and respond off-line. Your provider supplies you with a mail user ID and password with which to do this (which may be the same as the SLIP/PPP user ID and password); authentication is done by the mail server.

If your Internet access provider also runs an NNTP news server, you can use a Usenet newsreader such as WinVN or NewsWatcher to connect to the news server, select interesting Usenet news articles, and download them for reading. You can also post new articles or follow-ups to old articles. The news server authenticates you (if necessary) based on your IP address and hostname (or a user ID and password).

In theory, electronic mail and Usenet news services could be unbundled from basic Internet access (Internet dial tone). This unbundling is rarely seen today but may become more common as the market for personal Internet access evolves.

The following sections provide more detail about how these various Internet services are implemented over a SLIP or PPP connection.

Electronic mail

The discussion in the last section reached the point at which your computer had Internet dial tone: It had established a TCP/IP link to the SLIP/PPP-capable remote access server of your Internet access provider and was then ready for you to do useful work (or "make some calls," to continue the telephone analogy).

If you recall, the first action in the preceding example session was to check your electronic mail by using Eudora, an e-mail program available for both Windows-based PCs and Macintosh systems. In an earlier incarnation (Release 1.4), Eudora is a freeware program; for example, I got a copy of Eudora 1.4 for Macintosh from the book *Internet Starter Kit for Macintosh,* mentioned earlier. Eudora is now also available in a commercial version (Release 2.1) with somewhat more functionality (such as mail filters) and formal technical support; I later bought a copy of Eudora Release 2.1 for $65 from Qualcomm, the vendor that sells and supports it.

How Internet mail works

Before explaining how Eudora works, however, I'll first describe Internet electronic mail. Traditionally, Internet users have logged in to multiuser systems that are connected to the Internet 24 hours a day. When users send mail (from `jdoe@capaccess.org` to `rroe@agency.gov`, for example), the messages are transmitted more or less immediately over the Internet from the originating host (capaccess.org) to the receiving host (agency.gov) and then are put in the mailbox for the recipient (rroe). (Incidentally, the low-level protocol used to send messages between Internet electronic mail hosts is called *SMTP,* for Simple Mail Transfer Protocol.)

At some later time, the recipient (rroe) logs in to the receiving mail host and then reads the mail messages from his mailbox by using a mail program such as Pine or Elm. He can also compose new messages, which are then sent to the recipient's mail host as described earlier but in the reverse direction. The user must stay logged in to his mail host during the entire time he's reading messages and composing new ones. For example, this method is how I used to read and compose mail by using my Internet shell account: I would log in to my Internet access provider's host system (access.digex.net) and use the UNIX-based Pine program to read and respond to electronic mail.

If your computer can be linked to the Internet more directly, however, you probably prefer to read and compose mail on your PC or Mac and then send mail or receive it over your Internet connection. As mentioned, when your PC or Mac is connected to the Internet by using SLIP or PPP, it has its own Internet address and may even have its own hostname. (When my Mac is connected, for example, it has the Internet address 164.109.211.201 and the Internet hostname ion.digex.net. The way Internet hostnames work is discussed in more detail later in this chapter, in the "Hostnames and DNS" sidebar.)

Unfortunately, though, you typically cannot use the traditional SMTP mail protocol, at least to receive mail. Why not? Because mail sent using SMTP is sent directly to the recipient host, which in this case is your PC or Macintosh, and your PC or Mac has to be on the Internet to receive it; otherwise, the sending host cannot make an SMTP connection. But because you are connected to the Internet by using an intermittent dialup SLIP/PPP connection, there's no guarantee that your PC or Mac will be on-line at the exact time the sending host wants to send the message, and therefore you can end up not receiving messages sent to you. (The sending host, in fact, periodically tries sending mail messages if it cannot connect to your computer the first time. The sending host does not retry forever, however, and if it cannot connect successfully within a given period [three days, for example], it gives up on delivering the mail. If your computer is connected to the Internet for only brief periods during those three days, it is possible that the sending host will never be able to connect to it.)

The problem is even worse if your PC or Mac does not have a permanently assigned Internet address but instead is assigned one "on the fly" when you connect to your Internet access provider. In this case, your PC or Mac typically does not have a permanently assigned hostname either, and therefore someone attempting to connect to your PC or Mac by using SMTP would not know which hostname or address to use.

Going back to the telephone example, sending Internet electronic mail to you in the traditional manner (using SMTP end-to-end) is somewhat similar to leaving a message for you on your personal answering machine: People can call your phone number 24 hours a day and count on the fact that your answering machine is almost always turned on and ready to record messages. But in the case of SLIP or

PPP, your Internet phone number (IP address) is active only part of the time (when you're connected to your Internet access provider by way of SLIP or PPP and have Internet dial tone), and your "answering machine" (your computer) isn't always turned on and ready to receive your messages. If, in addition, your PC or Mac is assigned an Internet address only upon connection, you don't even have a permanent "phone number" by which others can contact you.

The solution to this problem is simple: Have another Internet-connected system (a "mail server") receive your e-mail messages for you and then, when you're connected to the Internet, download your mail messages from that system to your PC or Mac. Continuing the answering machine analogy, this arrangement is similar to what many U.S. phone companies provide by way of services such as Bell Atlantic's Answer Call; in place of your own answering machine, the phone company provides a voice mailbox for you somewhere in its network, and callers to your number can leave messages in that voice mailbox. You can then periodically call a special phone number associated with the voice mailbox service, punch in your access code, and listen to your messages.

In my case, for example, rather than send e-mail to `hecker@ion.digex.net` (recall that `ion.digex.net` is the hostname of my Macintosh), people send e-mail to `hecker@access.digex.net`, where `access.digex.net` is the name of the mail server run by my Internet access provider; this system runs 24 hours a day and has a permanent Internet connection. After I dial up my Internet access provider and my SLIP connection is active, I then have Eudora connect to the host `access.digex.net` over the Internet and download any messages I've received since I last connected.

The specific protocol that is used to do this is not SMTP but is another protocol called Post Office Protocol, or POP, for short. In particular, Eudora and my provider's "access" system use POP3, the third and most recent version of this protocol. In technical jargon, the system `access.digex.net` is therefore a POP3 mail server.

Making the transition to SLIP/PPP mail

As noted in the original example of an Internet session, you also have to supply Eudora with a mail user ID and associated password; Eudora then passes on this user ID and password to the mail server when it's connecting to it by using POP. If there were no user ID or password, anyone else on the Internet could connect to my Internet access provider's mail server and download my mail.

As it happens, in my particular case the system `access.digex.net` that acts as a POP3 mail server happens to be the same system that supports users logging in to shell accounts; this is true for many other Internet access providers as well. If your access provider does this, your mail user ID and associated password are the exact same ones you use when you log in to the provider's system itself as a user of an Internet shell account. (In my case, this single user ID is `hecker`.)

If you are upgrading to SLIP or PPP from a shell account, this reuse of the shell account user ID and password as the POP user ID and password makes for a smooth transition from the old way of doing things (using Pine or Elm with your shell account, for example) to the new way (using Eudora over SLIP or PPP, for example). Your electronic-mail address remains the same (in my case, hecker@access.digex.net or user ID hecker on host access.digex.net), and you don't have to choose a new password for use with Eudora if you don't want to.

Also, with many providers, if you ever want or need to, you can still dial up your provider's host in the old way (by using a VT100-compatible communications program rather than SLIP or PPP) and log in and read your mail by using a UNIX-based mail program, such as Pine or Elm. This choice is possible because the mailbox format used by the host-based POP server is the same standard UNIX mailbox format used by almost all UNIX host-based mail programs. Your incoming mail goes into the same mailbox, therefore, whether you're going to read it on the mail host by using Elm or retrieve it to your PC by using Eudora. (Unfortunately, some providers make it more difficult for you to do this because they consider shell accounts and SLIP/PPP accounts totally separate services and require you to pay full price for both if you want to use them interchangeably.)

However, your mail user ID and password are not necessarily the same as the SLIP/PPP user ID and password mentioned earlier; that's because they are associated with two fundamentally different services provided in two fundamentally different ways. SLIP/PPP access is a low-level communications service accessed by dialing up a SLIP/PPP-capable remote access server; POP e-mail access is a higher-level service accessed by connecting over the Internet to a POP3-capable host system (mail server). If you get a new SLIP or PPP account from an Internet access provider, therefore, you may well receive an e-mail (POP) user ID and password separate from and in addition to your SLIP/PPP user ID and password.

Exceptions do exist. Some smaller Internet access providers do not have separate remote access servers but rather connect modems directly to serial lines on their UNIX host systems and support SLIP or PPP access by using software running on those systems. (This host-based software may be either traditional SLIP or PPP software or SLIP-derived software, such as the new product The Internet Adapter; for more information about TIA, see the section "The Internet Adapter [TIA]," later in this chapter.) In this case, a user — or more correctly, her SLIP or PPP software executing an automated login script — logs in to the host system by using a single user ID and password and then invokes a special SLIP or PPP command to convert the session into a SLIP or PPP connection. Eudora or other POP3 mail programs then use this same user ID and password to download mail.

Some providers may also want to provide users with the convenience of having a single password for all services. In this case, they can simply arrange for the SLIP/PPP user ID and password used by the remote access server to be the same as the user ID and password used by the POP3 mail server. The national Internet access provider Netcom, for example, does this for its NetCruiser service.

The future of Internet mail

Suppose that you have in your home a full-time hard-wired Internet connection (such as those that some cable companies promise to provide in the United States). You can then have Internet dial tone all the time and you don't need a dialup protocol such as SLIP or PPP to connect. You also don't need the equivalent of a SLIP/PPP user ID and password; as discussed, their main use is for authentication and billing for Internet access, and the cable company already has a perfectly good way to bill you for cable-based services.

However, you might still want your cable company to store your incoming electronic-mail messages for you, perhaps because you don't want to keep your computer turned on all the time. In this case, you can use Eudora and POP to connect to a remote mail server, just as you would do over SLIP or PPP, and you still have to have a mail user ID and password supplied to you by your cable company in its role as an Internet access provider.

Continuing the answering machine analogy, having an electronic mailbox accessed by using POP can therefore be viewed as a value-added option to a basic Internet connection, just as having a voice mailbox through Answer Call and similar services is a value-added option to a basic phone line. This view also implies that e-mail service can be "unbundled" from basic Internet service; you might have a basic Internet connection but no electronic-mail service, for example, or you might get basic Internet service from one service provider and an electronic mailbox service from another.

As it happens, I don't know of any Internet access provider that unbundles POP-based e-mail in this way. As competition heats up in the Internet access market, however, some companies may choose to break their current services down further into standard and optional offerings, in order to offer the lowest possible entry-level price. A market niche may also exist for companies providing only SLIP/PPP service, with customers expected to arrange for electronic-mail service on their own; some nonprofit Internet cooperatives do business this way today.

Using Eudora

Back to Eudora: As mentioned, after Eudora has downloaded your incoming e-mail messages to your PC or Mac, you can then read them at your leisure; you don't have to maintain the Internet SLIP connection to do so. What about sending messages? Again, you don't have to be connected in order to compose messages, but (it almost goes without saying) you do have to be connected in order to send them.

As it turns out, for historical reasons (a fancy way of saying "that's just the way it is"), the POP protocol is not usually used for sending electronic-mail messages. Instead, Eudora uses the SMTP protocol discussed earlier, but with a twist. In "SMTP classic," the sending host (your PC or Mac) typically connects directly to the receiving host (`whitehouse.gov`, for example, if you're sending a message to Bill Clinton or Al Gore). The receiving host might be down or unreachable, however, because of some Internet problem, so that Eudora cannot send the message and has to postpone its transmission to a later time (possibly a few hours later).

Eudora typically doesn't make this connection on its own, however; you simply reestablish the SLIP or PPP connection at a later time and then command Eudora to send out any messages in its outbox. This process is rather inefficient: Why should you have to go to all the trouble of remembering to reconnect periodically to your Internet access provider? (Even if Eudora were to reconnect automatically, you still would have to leave your PC or Mac turned on and plugged in to the phone line.)

What typically happens instead is that Eudora uses the SMTP protocol to send your message to your Internet access provider's mail server. The server then uses SMTP again to send the message to its final destination. If the mail server can't do so right away, it keeps trying until it succeeds; meanwhile, you can disconnect your PC or Mac and not worry about the message being delivered.

You may have noticed that I didn't say anything about user IDs and passwords for sending mail. The reason is that the mail server doesn't authenticate you in any way when you use Eudora (or another POP client program) to send mail by way of this method; instead, you just tell Eudora to upload the message, and the e-mail server accepts it.

You might then ask, "Doesn't this mean that someone else can send fake electronic mail under my name?" For this and other reasons, the answer is yes, they certainly can. As it happens, it is almost trivially easy to send forged Internet mail, and it has been ever since Internet mail began. (This is why you should be skeptical if you ever get, for example, a message purportedly from your Internet access provider telling you that you need to change your password to K00L/D00D.)

There are well-known ways to solve this problem, but they haven't been implemented because they depend on encryption and related technologies, and their implementation in the Internet has been held hostage to the same sort of disputes that occurred in the infamous "Clipper chip" controversy.

(I don't want to rehash here the entire Clipper debate, but I do want to point out the basic underlying problem. In the "market" that is the Internet, the most successful "products" are based on technologies that are available worldwide and that are in the public domain or otherwise freely usable. Exporting encryption technology from the United States is legally restricted because of national security concerns, and "public key" encryption, the most useful type for electronic mail, is covered by a software patent in the United States. There are at least two major obstacles, therefore, to creating a worldwide standard for secure Internet mail — yet another example of how once-obscure policy issues can eventually come to affect all of us.)

Usenet news

The case of Usenet news (online conferences) is somewhat similar to the case of electronic mail and is worth covering at this point.

How Usenet works

Again, I need to digress for a moment and talk about how Usenet news works underneath. Usenet is not a communications network per se but rather is a loosely organized collection of host systems that exchange conference articles with each other. (In this sense, Usenet is analogous to FidoNet in the PC BBS world, and there are in fact gateways between Usenet and FidoNet.)

When a conference article is submitted (or *posted*) on one system, it is then sent to one or more other systems, which then send it on to others, and so on (somewhat like a chain letter) until all Usenet hosts receive it. After an article is received at a host, it is stored for people to read it. Several thousand Usenet conferences (or *newsgroups*) and tens of thousands of Usenet hosts exist around the world. As you might imagine, therefore, a great deal of traffic flows through the system every day, so much so that a typical Usenet host system stores only the last few days' articles.

Getting Usenet with SLIP/PPP

If you want Usenet access from your personal computer, there are at least three possible ways to get it. First, you can have your PC or Mac be a full-fledged Usenet host and receive all conferences. This option is pretty much out of the question for most people, given that the daily flow of traffic runs to multiple megabytes and you would need a great deal of connect-time each day to receive all the articles. (At 14,400 bps and lower speeds, in fact, you would not even have time to download all the day's traffic by the end of the day.)

Second, you can have your computer be a Usenet host but receive only a few newsgroups; this option is much more reasonable, and you can get software for both Macs and PCs to do it, but you still have to download every article in every newsgroup you choose to receive, even articles of little or no interest to you.

The third alternative (the one I use) is the most common: Connect to a remote Internet host acting as a "news server." This host (`news.digex.net`, in my case) receives all Usenet newsgroups and stores all articles for as long as it can without running out of disk space. Assuming that you have an Internet SLIP/PPP connection active, you then have your Usenet newsreader application (WinVN or NewsWatcher, for example) connect to the news server over the Internet and download the list of articles in each newsgroup. You then choose which articles you want to read and have WinVN or NewsWatcher download only those articles; the rest are left unread (at least by you) on the news server.

This process is conceptually similar to using a POP mail server as described earlier. As with mail, there is a special protocol, NNTP (Network News Transfer Protocol), which WinVN or NewsWatcher and the news server use to talk to each other. You don't typically have to supply a user ID or password, however, when you read and post news. You do have to tell WinVN or NewsWatcher your e-mail address (`hecker@access.digex.net`, in my case) because this address is used to mark articles you post as coming from you; the e-mail address is also necessary when you send mail to someone in lieu of posting a reply to the newsgroup. This information is not used, however, to authenticate you to the news server in any way.

You might ask, "Can anyone on the Internet then use WinVN or NewsWatcher (or other NNTP client programs) to read and post articles from and to *my* Internet access provider's news server?" This is true for some news servers on the Internet; by using these "public NNTP sites," anyone can read or (in some cases) post Usenet news articles. (And by using these servers in addition to other means, it is possible to send forged Usenet postings under another person's name, which is similar to what can be done with Internet mail.)

Typically, however, your Internet access provider's news server does not accept requests from anywhere on the Internet; it accepts requests only from IP addresses and hostnames it knows about — that is, those that represent valid subscribers to the provider's SLIP or PPP service. For example, because my Mac has an IP address and Internet hostname assigned by my Internet access provider when I signed up, my provider's news server recognizes me as a valid user. An IP address and hostname are again used, therefore, as a useful (albeit not totally secure) means of authenticating users. (Some news servers do authenticate users by using a user ID and password.)

The final point I want to make about Usenet news is that, like access to a mail server, access to a news server is a value-added service over and above basic SLIP or PPP Internet access. It can also in theory be unbundled so that you might have a basic Internet connection with no mail or Usenet news service at all; an Internet connection and mail service but no Usenet news service; or Internet service, mail service, and news service from one, two, or even three providers. (Again, most Internet access providers do not unbundle services in this manner.)

Accessing other Internet services

With both electronic mail and Usenet news, it's not enough to have just a SLIP or PPP Internet connection; you also have to have access to a special Internet host or hosts acting as mail servers or news servers, respectively. This access is usually prearranged with some organization, typically the Internet access provider itself. There are many other services, however, for which you need only a basic Internet connection.

FTP

The first example is using anonymous ftp to download information files or shareware. Ftp programs such as WS_FTP or Fetch ask you for the name of the host you want to connect to. Some magic then happens to convert the hostname to an IP address (analogous to looking up a phone number), and the connection is made, after which you can download files. The ftp site doesn't ask for an individual password and doesn't really care who you are.

Well, this is almost true. First, all ftp sites ask for some sort of password even if they don't care what it is. For anonymous ftp sites, WS_FTP and Fetch can be configured to send your e-mail address (`hecker@access.digex.net`, in my case) as the password as a courtesy in case the ftp site is logging access for some reason and wants to record this information.

Second, as a mild security measure, many ftp sites check to make sure that the Internet address from which you're connecting (the IP address of your PC or Mac) matches the Internet hostname associated with the IP address. In telephone terms, this process is similar to getting the phone number of a caller by way of Caller ID and then looking in a reverse, or "crisscross," directory to find out his name.

Hostnames and DNS

This is probably as good a place as any for a brief digression to Internet hostnames. As implied earlier, Internet hostnames (such as `capaccess.org`) are to IP addresses (`198.69.201.50`) what people's names are to their phone numbers. A "directory assistance" service, in fact, does automatic lookups of IP addresses corresponding to a given hostname and vice versa.

This automated service, referred to as the *Domain Name System,* or *DNS,* is silently invoked by your Internet-capable PC or Mac every time you give it an Internet hostname to connect to. The lookup is done by querying a special Internet host called a *DNS name server;* this server typically is maintained by your Internet access provider, and its IP address is yet another of the pieces of configura-

(continued)

(continued)

tion information you get when you sign up for SLIP or PPP service.

In addition to letting you (or more properly, your computer) look up IP addresses automatically, your Internet access provider's DNS name server also maintains entries that list the Internet hostname and IP address of your computer (at least if you have a permanently assigned IP address; if your PC or Mac is assigned a temporary IP address when it is connecting, that IP address typically has a corresponding temporary hostname). The presence of these entries (whether permanent or temporary) lets remote systems such as anonymous FTP sites do the sort of checks briefly mentioned earlier. Other than that, your computer's hostname (`ion.digex.net`, in my case) is not typically used for much; in particular, if you use Eudora or some other POP-based mail program, e-mail messages are not addressed to your computer's hostname but are instead addressed to your mail server's hostname (`access.digex.net`, for example).

Like directory assistance, DNS name service is essential but fundamentally uninteresting and taken for granted (unless you need to use it and it's not working). As noted, DNS name service is usually provided by the Internet access provider as a part of basic Internet service and is not a good candidate for unbundling. (Many Internet access providers do provide an extra-cost service, however, whereby you can choose your own, personal, customized hostname and therefore have an e-mail address, such as `hecker@my-company.com`.)

Telnet

Telnet from your PC or Mac works similarly to ftp: You tell your telnet application (Trumpet Telnet or NCSA Telnet, for example) the hostname you want to connect to, it does a silent DNS lookup to find the IP address, and then it connects you directly over the Internet to the remote system. The only user ID and password that are required are whatever the remote system might ask for — some telnet-based services use a dummy, or "guest," user ID and password, or even no user ID or password at all. Connecting to a UNIX system by way of telnet normally looks almost exactly like connecting by way of a dialup line.

MUDs

Connecting to more-exotic systems such as Multi-User Dungeons (or MUDs) is similar (and typically uses telnet or a telnet-based protocol underneath): You supply the hostname you want to connect to, connect, sign on in some way, type commands to be interpreted by the system, receive responses, repeat until you're finished, and then log off and disconnect. The underlying SLIP or PPP Internet connection must be active during the entire session, which may range in length from a few minutes to several hours (or even days, if you're a particularly enthusiastic MUD fan).

Gopher and WWW

The Gopher and World Wide Web services are a little more complicated in the way they work. When you start up a Gopher client program (Hgopher or TurboGopher, for example) or a Web browser (NCSA Mosaic, for example), it typically attempts to connect initially to a preset "known host" system, or systems, if alternatives have been set up. For HGopher and TurboGopher, for example, these host systems are at the University of Minnesota, and for NCSA Mosaic they are at the National Center for Supercomputing Applications at the University of Illinois Urbana-Champaign. (Almost all Gopher client programs and Web browsers can be changed to connect to other initial host systems, or even to not connect to a host system at all.)

After Gopher programs and Web browsers are connected to an initial host system, they operate in a "client/server" manner: The client (the program running on the PC or Mac) sends a request over the Internet to the server (the Gopher or Web program running on the remote host), which in turn sends back a response. This operation happens invisibly underneath by using a special-purpose communications protocol (Gopher+ for Gopher, and HTTP or HyperText Transport Protocol for the World Wide Web). All you see on-screen is a graphical "point and click" interface like that characteristic of other Windows- or Mac-based programs.

If you choose an item from a Gopher menu or choose to follow a hypertext link in the World Wide Web, one of three things may happen: You may invoke a menu (a *page,* in WWW jargon) on the same system; you may invoke a menu (a page) actually stored on another system; or you may invoke an item that does something other than just go to another menu or page. The first case is not that interesting, so I'll skip it (it's a special instance of the second case).

In the second case, for menus (pages) served by another system on the Internet, the Gopher program or Web browser automatically reconnects to the new system and sends the proper low-level commands to retrieve the menu (page) being invoked. As you browse through the Gopher menu hierarchy (or the WWW hypertext tree), the programs automatically switch from system to system as necessary, so there is no single system to which the Gopher program or Web browser remains "connected" in the traditional sense.

In the third case, when you invoke a menu item or click a hypertext link, some special action may be performed. One common action is to initiate automatic downloading of some file. This process is often implemented by having ftp-like functionality built-in to the Gopher program or Web browser so that, by invoking a Gopher or WWW item, you can fetch any file retrievable by way of anonymous ftp. If the file is of a special type, the Gopher program or Web browser can also do something special with it in addition to just downloading it. If the file is a graphics image in GIF format, for example, after downloading is complete, the Gopher program or Web browser might try to invoke a GIF viewer to show you the file. (You must already have GIF viewer software on your system, and you must have made sure that TurboGopher or Mosaic is configured to use it.)

Gopher and the World Wide Web have lots of other interesting features; the most important thing to remember, however, is that, unlike mail and Usenet news, you don't have to have anything in order to use Gopher and the World Wide Web except the Internet connection itself and the proper client programs.

Beyond basic SLIP and PPP

So far I've discussed the use of SLIP and PPP over a standard dialup telephone line (often called a *POTS* line, for *p*lain *o*ld *t*elephone *s*ervice) and using a standard analog modem with a maximum speed of 14,400 or 28,800 bps. Unfortunately, many common Internet applications — even when they're using SLIP or PPP over a 28.8 Kbps modem — can be slow and unresponsive. For example, downloading a World Wide Web page with 100K of embedded graphics (not an uncommon occurrence) takes almost a minute even at 28.8 Kbps.

ISDN lines

One increasingly available way to speed up SLIP/PPP-based Internet access is to use a more advanced *ISDN* phone line. (In practice, ISDN is used with PPP, primarily because a well-defined standard exists for PPP over ISDN.) ISDN provides a direct digital connection to the phone network (hence the name, *Integrated Services Digital Network*) and offers the promise of both higher transmission speeds (64 or 128 Kbps versus 14.4 Kbps or 28.8 Kbps for a standard dialup line) and faster call-setup times (the time between dialing the number and establishing the connection).

Using ISDN requires not only getting a new phone line but also the use of special hardware to connect your PC or Mac to ISDN, because ordinary phone lines and modems cannot be used directly with an ISDN line. For connecting a PC, for example, this hardware can be in the form of a special I/O board to which the ISDN line connects (using a modular jack similar to your modem's modular jack, for example). This board replaces your existing internal or external modem.

Like a standard phone line, ISDN is a dialup, or "switched," service; your TCP/IP software still has to dial a phone number corresponding to your Internet access provider's remote access server (or servers). (The phone number would be for an ISDN line, however, and your access provider's remote access server would have to support incoming ISDN calls.) The Internet applications (telnet, ftp, e-mail, and so on) still work as described earlier for a standard SLIP/PPP connection.

Dedicated Internet connection

An alternative to dialup connections is a high-speed, dedicated Internet connection; although this has traditionally been done by using expensive "leased lines" provided by phone companies, at least two cable TV companies (in Massachusetts and California) have announced relatively low-cost Internet access over the existing cable network.

As with ISDN, with "cable Internet" your PC or Mac does not use a standard modem but rather something like an Ethernet controller board, which typically costs a minimum of $100 to $200 in the United States; this board in turn hooks up to something like a "cable Ethernet" connection located on your set-top box. (For technical reasons, your PC or Mac may also be connected to a special modem dedicated to sending outgoing traffic back to the cable company; the higher-speed connection may be used only for incoming traffic.)

With a dedicated connection, there would be no need for an equivalent of the SLIP/PPP user ID and password because the cable company could simply bill you monthly, as it does today for cable service.

As with ISDN, Internet access works in essentially the same way — only faster; the applications software (Eudora, NewsWatcher, TurboGopher, NCSA Mosaic, and so on) stays the same and is configured in the same way. (Whether a TCP/IP connection uses SLIP, PPP, Ethernet, or any other network technology is essentially transparent to the Internet application.)

I should add that (for reasons alluded to earlier) some "cable Internet" technologies support a high "downstream" bandwidth (to the home) but a slow "upstream" bandwidth (to the cable company's central transmission facility and then to the Internet). These technologies are therefore ideally suited for applications such as Mosaic and the World Wide Web, in which you typically download to your PC or Mac a great deal of data in the form of graphics images, sound clips, and so on, with only a few commands going in the other direction back to the World Wide Web servers. At this point (early 1995), the California cable company offers this asymmetrical access on a trial basis, and the Massachusetts cable company offers nothing at all (other than a single demonstration site at the local public library), but it says that it will offer two-way high-speed connections.

Because of their advantages in speed, ISDN and "cable Internet" may be the next frontier for power users currently enjoying the benefits of standard SLIP and PPP dialup access.

Where to Go from Here

After reading the first part of this chapter, I hope that you now have a good feel for how Internet access using SLIP or PPP works. As a result, you may be interested in finding out more about SLIP and PPP and possibly even acquiring your own SLIP or PPP connection. This section covers three possible avenues you might explore:

- Commercial SLIP/PPP Internet software packages
- Internet books with bundled software
- On-line information and freeware and shareware

Each option has its pros and cons; no one has yet come up with a single best and complete A-to-Z solution for personal Internet access that supports everything you might want to do, provides everything you need, and answers every question you might have.

In evaluating which route to take, it may help to ask yourself the following questions:

- **Am I interested in paying the lowest possible price?** Look at the freeware and shareware that are available, in addition to some of the Internet books. The trade-off is that you may have to learn more about the finer details of TCP/IP and SLIP/PPP in order to configure your software properly, particularly if your Internet access provider doesn't provide much technical support.

- **Am I interested in the easiest possible installation and configuration?** Evaluate the commercial packages, and consider using one of the Internet access providers recommended by the software vendor. (Some of the Internet books also have software designed for relatively easy installation.) The trade-off is that you will likely end up paying more for the package and for your Internet access.

- **Am I interested in preserving the maximum flexibility to mix and match "best of breed" Internet applications from different vendors and sources?** With a few exceptions (mentioned later in this section), all the TCP/IP and SLIP/PPP products listed here support a standard interface that allows different Internet products to coexist on the same system. The commercial products typically already include a complete (or almost complete) suite of Internet applications, however, so if you decide to substitute applications from another source, in effect you will have paid for software you won't be using.

- **Do I want to run SLIP or PPP on a personal computer at work that is already connected to a local area network?** Depending on the particular LAN environment you have, configuring and running SLIP/PPP alongside existing network software (Novell NetWare, Microsoft LAN Manager, and so on) can range from moderately difficult to frustrating in the extreme. A commercial TCP/IP product may have the additional functions and technical support you need in order to do this successfully.

The range of available information, software, services, and support for Internet access for SLIP/PPP is much greater today than it was even six months to a year ago, and I expect this trend to continue and even accelerate. As a result, this section will likely become out-of-date very rapidly; however, I hope that it provides at least a starting point for you.

Commercial Internet packages

You may want to buy a commercial "all in one" solution that includes TCP/IP and SLIP or PPP software, a range of Internet applications, documentation, and (optionally) Internet service itself.

Here are some of the questions you should ask yourself in evaluating the purchase of a commercial product:

- **Does the product provide support for both SLIP and PPP or for only one of them (usually SLIP)?** If possible, you want to have the maximum flexibility in choosing the type of service you subscribe to. In particular, it is good to have the option of running PPP because it most likely will eventually overtake and replace SLIP in its popularity and extent of support by software vendors and access providers.

- **Does the product provide a full range of Internet applications?** Typical products provide at least telnet, ftp, and electronic-mail programs. Many also provide a Usenet newsreader, and some include Gopher and WWW client programs.

- **Can the product's underlying TCP/IP and SLIP/PPP software stack be used with Internet applications obtained from other sources (freeware and shareware, for example)?** For Windows, for example, you should confirm that the product is WinSock-compliant.

- **Does the price of the product include capabilities I will never use?** As noted, many commercial TCP/IP products were originally designed for business use on local area networks and cost several hundred dollars; they typically include many functions of little or no interest to the individual user accessing the Internet from home or on the road.
- **Does the product require me to use a particular Internet access provider?** If possible, you should preserve the capability to switch access providers if your first one doesn't work out for some reason.
- **Does the product include predefined configurations for popular Internet access providers?** The most difficult task in using the software is typically when you first attempt to connect to your Internet access provider. It helps if the product has customized login scripts and other preconfigured information available for your particular provider.

The remainder of this section describes some commercial products that support standard TCP/IP and SLIP/PPP operation (as described earlier) for Windows-based PCs or Macintosh systems. The products are listed in alphabetical order by product name.

Explore OnNet for Windows

Explore OnNet includes TCP/IP software with SLIP and PPP support and a set of Internet clients including e-mail, ftp, telnet, Gopher, a Usenet newsreader, and an enhanced version of NCSA Mosaic. It also has a "Connection Wizard" designed to assist users in configuring the software for their particular Internet access provider. Explore OnNet is from FTP Software, Inc., a longtime vendor of TCP/IP software for PCs running DOS and Windows. For more information, call 1-800-282-4FTP (1-800-282-4387) or 1-508-685-3300; FAX 1-508-794-4477; send e-mail to `sales@ftp.com`; or access its World Wide Web server at the following URL:

```
http://www.ftp.com/mkt_info/explore.html
```

Internet Chameleon TCP/IP for Windows

Internet Chameleon, which is included in *The Internet For Windows For Dummies Starter Kit,* includes TCP/IP software with both SLIP and PPP support (including ISDN support) and a set of Internet clients including e-mail, ftp, telnet, Gopher, a Usenet newsreader, and a World Wide Web browser comparable to Mosaic. Although Internet access is not included, the software does include configuration information for a number of Internet access providers. It also has an "Instant Internet" feature by which users can connect to one of several national Internet access providers and establish an account in only a few minutes.

This product, from NetManage, Inc., is essentially a customized subset of NetManage's Chameleon TCP/IP for Windows LAN product. For more information, call 1-408-973-7171; FAX 1-408-257-6405; send e-mail to `sales@netmanage.com`; or access the company's Gopher or World Wide Web servers at the following URLs:

```
gopher://gopher.netmanage.com/
http://www.netmanage.com/
```

A demonstration copy of the Chameleon product is available at the following URL (see the README.TXT file for more details):

`ftp://ftp.netmanage.com/pub/demos/chameleon/`

NetManage also has a separate product, Chameleon Sampler, that should not be confused with Internet Chameleon. Chameleon Sampler, based on an older version (3.11) of Chameleon TCP/IP for Windows, is bundled with many Internet books (discussed later in this chapter); it is also available by way of anonymous ftp at the following URL:

`ftp://ftp.netmanage.com/pub/demos/sampler/`

The Chameleon Sampler includes only SLIP support and does not include the full range of Internet applications found in Internet Chameleon.

Internet In A Box

This product includes a complete set of Windows-based Internet applications (including a version of Mosaic) and WinSock-compliant TCP/IP software for use over PPP connections. The software is from Spry, Inc., a commercial supplier of Windows-based TCP/IP software, and the documentation is from O'Reilly and Associates, a well-known publisher of UNIX and Internet books (including *The Whole Internet User's Guide and Catalog,* by Ed Krol, which is included in the package). For more information, call 1-800-557-9614, extension 26; send e-mail to `iboxinfo26@spry.com`.

You can also find Internet In A Box in many bookstores that carry other O'Reilly and Associates publications.

InternetWorks

This Windows-based product from BookLink Technologies, Inc., is designed to be a complete and integrated interface to the Internet by using TCP/IP over SLIP or PPP; it includes support for e-mail, ftp, Gopher, WAIS, and the World Wide Web. One major InternetWorks feature is support for OLE, which (for example) enables you to invoke Internet-related functions from a Visual Basic program. For more information, call 1-800-453-SURF (1-800-453-7873) or see the following URL:

`http://www.booklink.com/`

BookLink Technologies has also created InternetWorks Lite, a limited version of InternetWorks available for downloading by using ftp; see the following URL:

`ftp://ftp.booklink.com/lite/`

(If you don't have ftp access, you can call the preceding phone number and order InternetWorks Lite for a relatively low price.)

SuperHighway Access for Windows

SuperHighway Access includes TCP/IP software with both SLIP and PPP support and support for e-mail, ftp, telnet, Gopher, Usenet news, the World Wide Web, WAIS, and other search tools. The software also includes configuration information for many Internet access providers. SuperHighway Access, developed and sold by Frontier Technologies Corporation, is a companion product to FTC's SuperTCP/NFS for Windows LAN product. For more information, call 1-414-241-4555; FAX 1-414-241-7084; send e-mail to `superhighway@frontiertech.com`; or access its World Wide Web server at the following URL:

```
http://www.frontiertech.com/
```

Frontier Technologies also maintains a BBS at 1-414-241-7083.

TCP/Connect II

This product, from InterCon Systems Corporation, is available in both Macintosh and Windows versions; it includes all the standard Internet applications and both SLIP and PPP support. For more information, call 1-800-INTRCON (1-800-468-7266) or 1-703-709-5500; FAX 1-703-709-5555; send e-mail to `sales@intercon.com`; or see one of the following URLs:

```
ftp://ftp.intercon.com/InterCon/sales/Mac/Product_Info/tcpconmac.txt
ftp://ftp.intercon.com/InterCon/sales/Mac/Product_Info/tcpconwin.txt
```

Trumpet WinSock

This package, from Peter Tattam and Trumpet Software International, is a shareware product that is comparable to more-expensive commercial products in functionality and reliability. It includes a TCP/IP stack with a built-in SLIP driver, in addition to a variety of Internet applications. Because the Trumpet WinSock package is popular, many freeware and shareware products were written to run with it. See the section "On-line information and software," later in this chapter, for pointers to information about how to obtain it.

WinPAC Complete and WinGopher Complete

These products are specialized for on-line searching of Gopher servers and library public access catalogs (PACs) and WAIS servers based on the Z39.50 protocol. Both products include TCP/IP software with SLIP and PPP support; the WinPAC Complete product seems to be a superset of the WinGopher Complete product. (For those who already have WinSock-compliant TCP/IP and SLIP/PPP software, the search tools are available separately as WinPAC and WinGopher.) WinPAC Complete and WinGopher Complete are offered by NOTIS Systems, Inc. (a subsidiary of Ameritech). For more information, call 1-800-55-NOTIS (1-800-556-6847); FAX 1-708-866-4970; send e-mail to `info@notis.com`; or access its World Wide Web or Gopher servers at the following URLs:

```
http://www.notis.com/
gopher://wingopher.notis.com/
```

Other commercial packages

Because the following products are not, strictly speaking, standard Windows- or Mac-based TCP/IP and SLIP/PPP products, I did not include them in the preceding section; they are also worthy of interest, however.

The Internet Adapter (TIA)

This interesting product enables you to convert a connection to a UNIX shell account into a SLIP connection that can be used with standard PC- or Mac-based Internet applications, such as those described earlier in the section "Commercial Internet packages" and elsewhere in this chapter. (Support for PPP is in development.) TIA runs on the UNIX system on which you have a shell account; you log in to the shell account as usual and then run the TIA program to begin SLIP operation.

Connecting using The Internet Adapter is similar to connecting using a "vanilla" SLIP connection; the connection process may be automated by a script just as with a standard SLIP connection. The major difference between connection using TIA and connection using standard SLIP is that with TIA your individual PC or Mac does *not* have its own IP address, but instead "piggybacks" on the network connection and IP address of the UNIX host supporting the shell account.

With TIA, therefore, your PC or Mac can connect to other Internet hosts, but other Internet hosts cannot connect directly to your PC or Mac. This situation is similar to working in an office in which you can dial out from the phone on your desk but do not have your own phone number at which you can receive calls. (In this analogy, TIA and the UNIX host form the equivalent of the office PBX.) As it turns out, the major Internet applications discussed here (telnet, ftp, POP3 e-mail, Usenet news, Gopher, and World Wide Web browsers) use outbound connections only and can therefore be used with The Internet Adapter.

The Internet Adapter is developed by Cyberspace Development, Inc.; individual licenses and support are sold by SoftAware Company; and host-based or site licensing is handled by InterMind Corporation. (The word *host* here refers to a UNIX host system supporting multiple TIA users. Host-based or site licensing is directed primarily to Internet access providers who want to provide TIA for their customers, or to corporate and academic sites that want to provide TIA for their internal users.)

For more information about The Internet Adapter, call SoftAware at 1-310-314-1466 or InterMind at 1-206-545-7803 (depending on whether you want an individual license or a host or site license); send e-mail to `tia-info@marketplace.com`; or access the on-line information on the ftp, Gopher, and World Wide Web servers at the following URLs:

```
ftp://marketplace.com/tia/docs/info.tia.txt
gopher://marketplace.com/
http://marketplace.com/0/tia/tiahome.html
```

NetCruiser

NetCruiser, provided by NETCOM On-line Communication Services for use with its SLIP service, is bundled with the book *Access the Internet!* More information about NetCruiser is provided in the section "Internet book and software bundles," later in this chapter.

OS/2 Warp

OS/2 Warp is a full-blown 32-bit operating system intended as a replacement for DOS and with support for running existing DOS and Windows applications. (Support for Windows applications requires that you already have a copy of Windows.) OS/2 Warp is of interest for being the first mass-market PC operating system with built-in support for Internet access; it includes SLIP support (with PPP support to follow) and a full set of Internet clients supporting telnet, ftp, e-mail, Usenet news, Gopher, and the World Wide Web.

OS/2 Warp should be available at most mass-market retail software stores, such as Egghead, CompUSA, and Software Etc.; it can also be ordered directly from IBM by calling 1-800-3-IBM-OS2 (1-800-342-6672) in the U.S. For more information, see IBM's various World Wide Web servers at the following URLs:

```
http://www.austin.ibm.com/pspinfo/os2.html
http://www.ibm.net/support/oiak.html
```

IBM itself is now a public Internet access provider through its Advantis joint venture with Sears. OS/2 Warp contains automated configuration scripts for the IBM/Advantis Internet service; it can also be used, however, with other Internet access providers. For more information, see the following URL:

```
http://www.ibm.net/ibmnet.html
```

Internet book and software bundles

If you do not want to pay the higher price (as much as $200 in the United States) for a full commercial product, you may want to consider one of the growing number of Internet books that come with a disk containing Internet applications software. Here are some of the questions you should ask yourself in evaluating the purchase of this type of book/disk combination:

- **Is the software for a real Internet connection, as described earlier?** Some books include only a communications program with VT100 terminal emulation; others include hybrid software that looks like a graphical Internet interface but uses a different underlying protocol (for example, some products use the UNIX UUCP protocol to do batch uploading and downloading of electronic mail and Usenet news).
- **Does the disk include the minimum necessary requirements for a personal Internet connection?** You need at least a SLIP or PPP network driver, a TCP/IP stack (MacTCP or a WinSock-compliant product, for example) that supports Internet applications, and at least an ftp program (which you can then use to download other software).
- **How many Internet applications come with the book?** Does it include an e-mail program? A Usenet newsreader? A Gopher or World Wide Web client? Some books come with a variety of "best of breed" programs; others have only a minimum.
- **Does the book explain how to install, configure, and use the software?** In a few books, the software seems to be an afterthought, with most of the book devoted to explaining older ways of accessing the Internet (by using a UNIX shell account, for example).

- **Does the book come with any other special offers?** Some books include introductory offers (two weeks or a month of free service, for example) for SLIP or PPP Internet access through a particular provider. (This consideration may not be that significant, however, if the provider can be reached only by way of a long-distance telephone call).

The books in the following list meet the first two criteria (that is, they have the minimum software necessary for a personal Internet connection using SLIP or PPP); the books are listed in alphabetical order by book title:

- *Internet CD,* by Vivian Neou ($49.95 U.S., Prentice Hall, ISBN 0-13-123852-3), contains a CD-ROM disk with (among other things) Peter Tattam's Trumpet software and the freeware version of Eudora for Windows.
- *The Internet For Windows For Dummies Starter Kit* by Margaret Levine Young and John R. Levine ($34.95 U.S., IDG Books Worldwide, ISBN 1-56884-237-6), includes a copy of Internet Chameleon (the full product, not the sampler) bound into a special version of *The Internet For Dummies* adapted for Chameleon users. You have to activate the software by signing up on-line with one of a group of participating national Internet providers.
- *Internet Membership Kit, Macintosh Version* ($69.95 U.S., Ventana Media, ISBN 1-56604-171-6) includes the book *The Mac Internet Tour Guide* and its associated software (see the listing for *The Mac Internet Tour Guide,* a few paragraphs down, for more information).
- *Internet Membership Kit, Windows Version* ($69.95 U.S., Ventana Media, ISBN 1-56604-172-4) includes the book *The Windows Internet Tour Guide* and its associated software (see the listing for *The Windows Internet Tour Guide,* a few paragraphs down, for more information).
- *Internet Starter Kit for Macintosh (Second Edition),* by Adam Engst ($29.95 U.S., Hayden Books, ISBN 1-56830-111-1), includes MacTCP, InterSLIP and MacPPP, Eudora, Fetch, TurboGopher, MacWeb (an alternative World Wide Web browser to NCSA Mosaic), and other software. Engst also maintains an FTP site for readers of the book, with (among other things) copies of additional Internet applications in addition to those included on the book's disk.

  Note: The second edition is somewhat expanded from the first and has much improved typography and layout (a minor pet peeve for me in the first edition). If you can't find the second edition, however, the first edition (ISBN 1-56830-064-6) has enough software to get you started.
- *Internet Starter Kit For Windows,* by Adam Engst, Corwin Low, and Michael Simon ($29.95 U.S., Hayden Books, ISBN 1-56830-094-8), includes the Chameleon Sampler, the WinVN newsreader, Eudora, and WSGopher.
- *The Internet Unleashed,* by various authors ($44.95 U.S., Sams Publishing, ISBN 0-672-30466-X), includes the Chameleon Sampler and HGopher.
- *The Mac Internet Tour Guide,* by Michael Fraase ($27.95 U.S., Ventana Press, ISBN 1-56604-062-0), includes MacTCP, InterSLIP, Eudora, Fetch, TurboGopher, and StuffIt Expander. Like Engst, Fraase maintains an ftp site with additional information and software in addition to a (fee-based) electronic update service for readers of this book and others he has written.

Important: Early printings of this book did not include MacTCP or a SLIP or PPP driver, and you therefore had to buy MacTCP separately and find a SLIP or PPP driver somewhere else. Make sure that the back cover specifically says that MacTCP is included.

- *Navigating the Internet (Deluxe Edition),* by Richard Smith and Mark Gibbs ($29.95 U.S., Sams Publishing, ISBN 0-672-30485-6), includes the Chameleon Sampler.

  Important: Make sure that the book says "Deluxe Edition"; another "nondeluxe" edition does not include a disk.

- *The PC-Internet Connection: TCP/IP Networking for DOS and Windows,* by Bernard Aboba ($32.95 U.S., Internaut Books, ISBN 1-883979-00-5), scheduled for publication in the spring of 1995. It will include a copy of the Chameleon Sampler, PC Eudora, and WS Gopher. For more information, see the following URL:

  `http://www.zilker.net/users/internaut/forth.html`

  From the looks of the table of contents, this book will go into greater technical detail than many of the books listed here; it will also cover Internet access from DOS-only PCs. Bernard Aboba is the compiler of the Frequently Asked Questions list for the Usenet newsgroup `comp.protocols.tcp-ip.ibmpc` (discussed later in this chapter, in the section "On-line information and software").

- *The PC Internet Tour Guide,* by Michael Fraase ($24.95 U.S., Ventana Press, ISBN 1-56604-084-1), includes UMSLIP (a SLIP-capable TCP/IP stack) and Minuet (an integrated Internet application that supports e-mail, ftp, telnet, and so on), both developed at the University of Minnesota. (This is one of only a few books that discuss personal Internet access from DOS-only PCs.)

- *The Windows Internet Tour Guide,* by Michael Fraase ($24.95 U.S., Ventana Press, ISBN 1-56604-081-7), includes the Chameleon Sampler.

Two other books that contain Internet applications are worthy of note:

- *Access the Internet!,* by David Peal ($19.99 U.S., Sybex, ISBN 0-7821-1529-2), is specifically intended for use with the nationwide Internet access provider NETCOM On-Line Communications Services. The book is bundled with Netcom's NetCruiser software for Windows, which includes SLIP support and client programs for e-mail, telnet, ftp, Gopher, Usenet news, and the World Wide Web. Buyers of the book are also eligible for a one-month trial account with the Netcom service.

  Important: The NetCruiser software works only with the Netcom service and does not yet support the use of other Internet client programs, such as NCSA Mosaic, Eudora, and so on. For more information, call (800)501-8649, extension 2601; send e-mail to `info@netcom.com`; or see Netcom's FTP and World Wide Web servers at the following URLs:

  `ftp://ftp.netcom.com/pub/netcom/netcruiser.info`

  `http://www.netcom.com/netcom/cruiser.html`

  `http://www.netcom.com/netcom/cruzfaqs.html`

- *Internet Explorer Kit for Macintosh,* by Adam Engst and William Dickson ($29.95 U.S., Hayden Books, ISBN 1-56830-089-1), is a companion volume to the book *Internet Starter Kit for Macintosh.* It includes Anarchie, Finger, MacWAIS, MacWeather, and TurboGopher.

Finally, here are some other books that do not include software but that may also be of interest:

- *Connecting to the Internet: An O'Reilly Buyer's Guide,* by Susan Estrada ($15.95 U.S., O'Reilly and Associates, ISBN 1-56592-061-9), gives criteria for choosing an Internet access provider and a level of Internet service; it also includes a list of providers.
- *Internet Access Providers: An International Resource Directory,* by Greg Notess ($30.00 U.S., Mecklermedia, ISBN 0-88736-831-X), contains listings of Internet access providers worldwide, including pricing, levels of service, and geographic coverage.
- *The Internet Book: Everything you need to know about computer networking and how the Internet works,* by Douglas E. Comer ($24.95 U.S., Prentice Hall, ISBN 0-13-151565-9), is an explanation of the technology behind the Internet, intended for a general audience and at a level of technical detail comparable to that of the information presented in this chapter. (Interestingly enough, despite the promise of its subtitle, the book mentions SLIP and PPP only briefly and only in the glossary.)
- *TCP/IP for the Internet: The Complete Buyers Guide to Micro-Based TCP/IP Software,* by Marshall Breeding ($24.95 U.S., Mecklermedia, ISBN 0-88736-980-4), contains reviews of various TCP/IP packages for DOS, Windows, Macintosh, and UNIX.

On-line information and software

If you already have Internet access and aren't yet ready to spend the money for a book or a commercial product, you may want to explore the information and software already available on-line. Here are some good places to begin:

- *Windows and TCP/IP for Internet Access,* by Harry M. Kriz (`hmkriz@vt.edu`), is a good overview of personal Internet access using Microsoft Windows and WinSock-compliant TCP/IP software. It goes into more technical detail than this chapter does and contains on-line locations and installation instructions for popular WinSock-based freeware and shareware. The document is posted regularly to the newsgroup `comp.os.ms-windows.networking.tcp-ip`. Here are the URLs for the current version as of this writing:

  `ftp://nebula.lib.vt.edu/pub/windows/winsock/wtcpip06.asc`

  `http://learning.lib.vt.edu/wintcpip/wintcpip.html`

  (The number `06` for the FTP-accessible plain-text version will be incremented as new versions are released.)

- *WinSock Application FAQ,* by Craig Larsen (larsenc@lcs.com), is a complete listing of WinSock programs and their respective ftp sites, with brief reviews. In addition to freeware and shareware, it lists demo versions of commercial products. The document can be retrieved by sending an e-mail message to info@lcs.com with a subject line of help; it can also be found on the World Wide Web at the following URL:

  http://www.lcs.com/faqhtml.html

  The World Wide Web version is particularly good because it includes links to all the programs you can retrieve by way of ftp. If you're using a WWW client, therefore, such as NCSA Mosaic, you can simply click to download a given package.

- *The WinSock Client Listing,* by Ed Sinkovits (edsink@mbnet.mb.ca), is similar to Craig Larsen's *WinSock Application FAQ* but contains more information and comments about each product. It is posted to the Usenet newsgroups alt.winsock, comp.protocols.tcp-ip.ibmpc, and comp.os.ms-windows.networking.tcp-ip. You can also contact Mr. Sinkovits directly by way of e-mail to obtain a copy of the document in Microsoft Word for Windows format. But best of all, it's Chapter 32 in this book.

- comp.protocols.tcp-ip.ibmpc *Frequently Asked Questions (FAQ),* by Bernard D. Aboba (aboba@internaut.com), contains a great deal of information about PC-based TCP/IP networking under both DOS and Windows. It is especially useful if you want to run Internet applications under both DOS and Windows or if you are also using TCP/IP software on a local area network. If you don't care about either of these topics, I recommend that you begin with one of the other documents that were already mentioned.

  This document is posted every month to the Usenet newsgroup comp.protocols.tcp-ip.ibmpc; it is also available at the following URLs:

  ftp://ftp.netcom.com/pub/mailcom/IBMTCP/ibmtcp.zip

  http://www.zilker.net/users/internaut/update.html

  The second URL references a hypertext version of the FAQ, together with additional useful information.

  A plain-text version of the FAQ is also available, in three parts:

  ftp://ftp.netcom.com/pub/mailcom/IBMTCP/tcpip1.faq

  ftp://ftp.netcom.com/pub/mailcom/IBMTCP/tcpip2.faq

  ftp://ftp.netcom.com/pub/mailcom/IBMTCP/tcpip3.faq

- *Features of TCP/IP Packages for DOS and Windows,* by C. J. Sacksteder (cjs@psuvm.psu.edu), is an exhaustive compilation of DOS- and Windows-based TCP/IP software packages and their features. Like Aboba's FAQ, it may be overkill if you're just beginning to learn about personal Internet access. The document is available at the following URL:

  ftp://ftp.cac.psu.edu/pub/dos/info/tcpip.packages

- `comp.sys.mac.comm` *Frequently Asked Questions (FAQ),* by David L. Oppenheimer (`davido@phoenix.princeton.edu`) contains (among other things) some information about MacTCP and SLIP and PPP drivers for the Mac. The FAQ is posted monthly to the Usenet newsgroup `comp.sys.mac.comm` and can also be found at the following URL:

  `ftp://sumex-aim.stanford.edu/info-mac/comm/info/comp-sys-mac-comm-faq.txt`

- *Charm Net Personal IP Page,* by Craig Nordin (`cnordin@charm.net`), is a collection of pointers to on-line resources having to do with personal Internet access (including many not listed in this document). It is at the following URL:

  `http://www.charm.net/ppp.html`

  Charm Net (located in Baltimore, Maryland) is a good example of a local Internet access provider promoting personal Internet access by using SLIP or PPP. For more information, see the following URL:

  `http://www.charm.net/charminfo.html`

- *Dan Kegel's ISDN Page,* by Dan Kegel (`dank@alumni.caltech.edu`), contains pointers to practically any ISDN-related on-line information you might need or want; in particular, it contains a number of references to establishing personal Internet access over ISDN. See the following URL:

  `http://alumni.caltech.edu/~dank/isdn/`

- *Understanding Cable Internet,* Parts 1 and 2, by Bernard D. Aboba (`aboba@internaut.com`), contain more information about schemes to provide personal Internet access over existing cable TV networks; see the following URLs:

  `http://www.zilker.net/users/internaut/cable.html`

  `http://www.zilker.net/users/internaut/cable2.html`

- *The Public Dialup Internet Access List (PDIAL),* by Peter Kaminski (`kaminski@netcom.com`), is a summary listing of companies providing dialup access to the Internet in the U.S., Canada, and other countries. The PDIAL list can be obtained by sending e-mail to `info-deli-server@netcom.com` with the subject line "send pdial" (nothing need be in the body of the message itself).

- Finally, as noted, a number of Usenet newsgroups contain discussions of personal Internet access using SLIP or PPP. The main ones are shown in this list:

  `alt.winsock`

  `comp.os.ms-windows.networking.tcp-ip`

  `comp.os.os2.networking.tcp-ip`

  `comp.protocols.tcp-ip.ibmpc`

  `comp.sys.mac.comm`

Notice that `comp.sys.mac.comm` covers all Mac-related communications protocols and software. At this time, there is no separate Macintosh newsgroup just for TCP/IP networking or Internet access.

The on-line material from which this chapter is adapted states: "Copyright © 1994 by Frank Hecker. You may freely distribute this document in any form provided only that you retain this copyright notice." An on-line version of this document is available on the Internet at the following URL:

`ftp://ftp.digex.net/pub/access/hecker/internet/slip-ppp.txt`

Frank Hecker is a sales support analyst for Tandem Computers, Inc., and a member of the board of directors of CapAccess, the Washington, D.C., community network. His professional interests include fault-tolerant systems, Internet-based electronic commerce, and public Internet access.

Chapter 13

Tuning TCP/IP

by Stephen Trier <sct@po.cwru.edu>

Remember hot rodding? Even those who weren't alive in the 1950s have heard the Beach Boys sing about tearing up the pavement in a finely tuned automobile. Why not hot rod your computer? That TCP/IP of yours can move ten percent faster — and maybe more — if you know just where to tweak the carburetor (er, I mean the receive window).

Even if you aren't into cars, think of tuning a TCP as being like adjusting the TV set for perfect reception of a big game (or for the Met on PBS). A little adjustment here and a little there, and you're all set for an afternoon of surfing the Net.

The amount of improvement to expect is hard to predict; it could range anywhere from 10 percent to 200 percent or more. The big secret of TCP/IP is that most versions come from the factory poorly configured. If you know what to adjust, you can take out the slack and get your connections buzzing along briskly.

Here's an example. When one proprietary TCP/IP ran on an Ethernet network, transfers ran at about 80K a second. After some tuning, the same transfers zipped along at 200K a second! On a Serial Line Internet Protocol (SLIP) connection, a little tuning brought snappy response on telnet sessions and increased the speed of large ftp file transfers by more than ten percent.

Speedups from tuning are possible because the TCP/IP programmers often overlook the little tweaks that can boost performance. TCP/IP is so fast that few programmers think to ask whether it can be faster. The rules governing TCP performance are complex. Few programmers who work on TCP/IP understand how to get the last bit of speed out of TCP. Fortunately, there is no real need to understand the complex innards of TCP; a few rules of thumb will serve you well.

As you tune, keep a stopwatch handy. Being an optimist about improvements is easy, but a stopwatch will keep you honest. Because some of the secrets that I'm about to reveal involve improvements of ten percent or less, knowing whether a tweak is having the right effect is important. Use a digital watch, a watch with a second hand, or a stopwatch; don't count on the computer to keep accurate time. Network operations sometimes make computer clocks run slowly.

Play scientist when you time transfers. Before you begin, time your current setup so that you'll know later whether speed has improved. Also, time several files from ftp sites that you frequent. Timing both local and remote transfers may be a good idea as well. Keep a list of the changes you make and the speeds that you measure. Try to do all your timings at about the same time of day; otherwise, daily fluctuations in other traffic may mislead you. Above all, have fun. It is very satisfying to be able to say, "I sped up my Internet transfers by 20 percent today!"

TCP/IP: a capsule refresher

TCP (transmission-control protocol) and IP (Internet protocol) are the basic communication schemes that tie the Internet together. Within the Net, all data is sent as *packets* — chunks of data ranging from 1 byte to about 2K. IP is the convention used to get a packet from one computer, or *host*, on one network to another computer that may be on another network. (Remember, the Internet is a collection of several thousand networks.) If the two computers are on the same network, the packet goes directly from the first host to the second. If the computers are on different networks, the packet is routed through intermediate hosts and from network to network until it reaches its destination or until an error or network congestion causes it to be lost.

IP arranges for single packets to be sent from one host to another. Most applications, however, need a conversation, not individual packets; they also need to be sure that the data is received correctly. TCP takes care of the conversation level. A sequence number is assigned to each byte sent by each end of a connection. Each computer tracks the sequence numbers of the data that it has sent and received, and then tells the other computer what sequence it just sent or received.

As an application program passes data to TCP for transmission, TCP sends groups of bytes as TCP segments; each segment is sent in an IP packet. The sender retransmits each segment, if need be, until the receiver's reply sequence number confirms that the bytes in that segment have been received. For performance reasons, the sender always sends somewhat more data than the receiver has acknowledged, because some data can be in transit in the network. The amount ahead of the receiver that the sender can get is known as the *window*. (This concept is discussed in more detail in the "Opening the Window" section of this chapter.)

The definitive references for TCP, IP, and all the other Internet protocols are the RFC documents, available for ftp at `ds.internic.net`. The document for IP is RFC 791; the document for TCP is RFC 793. For a less technical introduction, see Chapter 6 of *The Internet For Dummies, Second Edition* (IDG Books, 1994), as well as Chapters 2 and 3 of *MORE Internet For Dummies* (IDG Books, 1994).

Reliability always wins over performance. If a speed improvement causes bad data to be transferred or makes your computer crash, don't use it! The time that you gain by speeding things up isn't worth the time that you'll lose if the improvement doesn't work. To protect your data, all the secrets that I'm about to discuss are perfectly safe.

Now let's get to work. If you would hand me that wrench over there. . .

Setting the Segment Size

We'll start at the bottom, with the segment — the unit of data that TCP moves at one time. The more data TCP can move in one operation, the better, so the bigger the segment size, the better.

The catch, however, is that TCP cannot send packets bigger than the maximum transmission unit of a network without losing a great deal of performance. That maximum, called the MTU, is 1,500 bytes on an Ethernet local-area network (LAN) and a mere 576 bytes for links over the Internet at large. TCP/IP needs 40 bytes for its own purposes, so subtract 40 to get the maximum segment size: 1,460 on an Ethernet LAN, and 536 for long-distance connections.

The best TCPs determine your maximum segment automatically, even switching sizes to optimize for off-site and local connections. If your TCP is old enough to give you the opportunity to set the segment size, it usually is set for the best *local* size, and the TCP automatically switches to 536 for long-distance connections. A few really old TCPs do not switch to the smaller packet for long-distance connections; for them, you should use a 536-byte maximum segment everywhere.

SLIP opens a realm for experimentation. If you perform many bulk file transfers, you want your maximum segment to be as large as your SLIP provider can handle — usually, the Ethernet size (1,460 bytes). If you use SLIP mostly for interactive sessions, such as telnet, you may prefer to keep your maximum segment artificially low — around 200 bytes. For more information on this subject, see "SLIPping to Speed" later in this chapter.

Setting the segment size is a simple setup option in TCP. For example, in Trumpet WinSock, a popular shareware TCP/IP for Windows, you can set the segment size with the Setup option in TCPman. In FTP Software's PC/TCP, set the segment size with the IFCONFIG command, which is used to set most operating parameters.

Opening the Window

Setting the segment was pretty tame stuff. In fact, more than half of you didn't have to do anything, because your TCPs are smart enough to use the best segment size automatically. It's time to take off the gloves, though, for the biggest performance boost of all: increasing the receive window.

What's a receive window? TCP moves data in segments, but it groups segments into windows. The window is a promise by the receiver that it can handle a certain number of bytes of data. The sender is free to send that many bytes without having to wait for the receiver to signal again. If everything works perfectly, the receiver signals that it has more space in the window before the sender manages to fill it. When this happens, the receiver always stays a little bit ahead of the sender, and the data flows across the network as fast as possible.

When things don't work right, the sender fills the window and then has to wait to receive another go-ahead signal. With so many network links going through satellites, that signal could take a second or more to arrive. A window big enough to compensate for those delays means smoothly flowing data, whereas a smaller window means that the connection runs in bursts of data, after which the sender stops and waits. Bursty data means lousy speed.

If this explanation seems like gobbledygook, think of a conveyor belt running from the sender to the receiver, going through a window halfway between them. The sender is free to pile packages on the belt, but it can't pile them higher than can fit through the window. The bigger the window, the more packages the sender that can pile on. Bigger windows mean more packages per minute to the receiver.

Window size may sound like segment size; the bigger, the faster. The difference is that no catch exists with window size. Windows can be up to 32,767 bytes without network problems, and that is pretty big. The only limiting factor is your TCP/IP implementation, which may run out of memory if the windows get too big. If your TCP/IP is short on memory, you may need to experiment to find a segment size that offers the right balance between performance and number of simultaneous connections. As you seek the best balance, bear in mind that reducing the window never improves performance.

When you pick a window, considering the segment size is helpful. The remote TCP sends its data to you in segment-size chunks. If you have to use small windows because of memory limits, you may be able to improve the situation by making the receive window a multiple of the maximum segment size. As a rule of thumb, use multiples of the maximum segment sizes for small windows: 1,608, 2,920, 4,380, and 5,840. For medium and large windows, the size is arbitrary. Pick a nice number, and then time some ftp transfers on your stopwatch to see how it works.

For an example of what kind of difference this makes, look at Trumpet WinSock. WinSock leaves most of the TCP parameters open for adjustment. On a SLIP link, with its standard 4,096-byte receive window, WinSock transfers a large file at 1,860 bytes per second. With the window set to 32,767 bytes, WinSock transfers the same file at 2,075 bytes per second — an improvement of about 11 percent.

The window-size difference was more noticeable on an Ethernet network. When I increased Trumpet WinSock's receive window from 4,096 to 8,192, file transfers went from 25,200 bytes per second to 84,900 bytes per second. Increasing the window to 32,767 improved performance little more in this test, but experience says that the larger window would be helpful in error-prone connections.

On some TCP/IP systems, you will find a parameter for a send window. A send window is analogous to a receive window, but it applies to sending data. As with the receive window, the bigger the send window, the better. One catch is that the throughput of the connection depends on the smaller window — the receive window or the send window — so there is not much sense in making the send window bigger than the receive window at the site to which you are sending. The other catch is memory (again). If your connections have large receive and send windows, you are going to run out of connection memory quickly.

The best rule for send-window size is to be a little bit selfish, because most people receive many more big files than they send. If your receive window is larger than 3,000 bytes, make the send window half the size of the receive window. If your receive window is smaller than 3,000 bytes, make the send window the same size. If you need to send files quickly (for an ftp, Gopher, or WWW server, for example), by all means make your send window large — even larger than your receive window. If you want the most speed no matter what, make your send window the same size as your receive window.

Only older TCPs have a place to set the send window. In once-ubiquitous NCSA Telnet, for example, the send window is set in the TELNET.CFG file, which contains all the setup options.

Time-out!

It's time to take a time-out. Go find your TCP/IP's configuration options, grab a stopwatch, and try what you've learned so far. Come back after you've tweaked a bit. We're about to delve into some important items of TCP tuning, but nothing as important as the segment size and the receive window.

Now, about time-outs . . . TCP is an error-correcting protocol. TCP knows that a segment of data got through all right when the remote sends an acknowledgment for that data. When something goes wrong, TCP finds out by waiting some length of time for the acknowledgment. If the time elapses without an acknowledgment, TCP sends the data again. This process can repeat several times before the data gets through; TCP gets very tenacious in the face of poor network conditions. The length of time that TCP waits before resending a segment is called the *retransmission time-out.*

Old-fashioned TCPs enable you to set the retransmission time-out. If you have one of these TCPs, set the time-out to a value of 5 to 10 seconds. A reasonable range of values is between 3 and 10 seconds. Never set the time-out value to less than 3 seconds, because that setting can cause a TCP to create Internet congestion. The trade-off is between recovering from errors quickly and being a good neighbor. Please let neighborliness win!

You can get better retransmission performance by switching to a more modern TCP. Modern TCPs, like Trumpet WinSock, Chameleon, or BSD UNIX, have a nifty system called adaptive retransmission. The TCP computes the retransmission time-out by measuring how long it is taking the remote side to send an acknowledgment. The initial retransmission time-out is fixed at three seconds, but it quickly adjusts to a value that gets maximum performance out of any connection without congesting the Internet. Adaptive retransmission is a wonderful thing for TCP performance as well as for neighborliness. If your TCP doesn't have it, get it.

A TCP can't resend its data over and over forever. After a while with no response, it needs to give up in disgust. How long it should wait is a subject of some debate. Many people like a short time-out; others advocate time-outs as long as eternity.

Given all this, a good compromise value is three minutes. Don't use any value shorter than one minute, and going longer than ten minutes rarely is useful. A committee of experts convened by the Internet Engineering Task Force (no, I'm not making this up) determined that the optimum connection time-out is three minutes, and we might as well go along with them.

If you get impatient, you can shorten your connection time-out, but please do not make it shorter than one minute. Time-outs of less than a minute cause connections to die for momentary Net glitches when nothing is wrong. Those experts knew what they were talking about; three minutes is probably about right. That's just long enough for you to get a cup of coffee when a Net glitch occurs.

I Name Thee . . .

Domain Name Service, the system that translates names such as dummies.com into numeric IP addresses such as 140.186.81.99, can be improved as well. This section first makes sure that you are set up to make the most of nameservers, and then discusses fine-tuning and two speedups.

First, make sure that you have your nameserver configuration set optimally. That means two things: You should have more than one nameserver listed, and all the servers should be near your computer in the networking sense. For example, big sites usually have two or more nameservers right at the site. List all your local nameservers in your TCP/IP configuration.

Smaller sites may have a local nameserver and an off-site backup. In that case, set up your software to use the local server and its backup. List the local server first, because it will be the faster machine.

Tiny sites may have both of their nameservers off-site. In that case, use those servers with your software.

The idea is to make service as fast as possible by using local nameservers as a first choice. Use at least two servers for reliability. When the first-choice server is down, your software automatically uses the others. A few TCP/IP packages cannot use more than one nameserver. This situation causes reliability problems, because no redundancy exists. Pester the vendor about it, or get a different TCP/IP suite.

Sometimes, using a nameserver isn't worthwhile. An alternative is to paint flames on the side of your hot-rod computer and to set up a local-host table with the names and IP addresses that you use most often. Name lookups run much faster from the local table, but any time that you want to refer to a new host by name, you have to add it to the table manually. Keeping a host table up-to-date can cause headaches, so use it only for the computers that you use most often. As long as you configure both a host table and a nameserver, you can use the host table for some names and the nameservers for all the rest. Avoid using the table for names that your nameservers can look up quickly.

For pure customization, try a hostalias file to assign nicknames to your favorite computers. Hostalias files truly are an Internet secret. Many versions of UNIX and a handful of MS-DOS TCP/IPs can do hostaliases, but the author has never seen these aliases documented anywhere! A hostalias file lists each nickname on a separate line. The line starts with the nickname, followed by some spaces or tabs and a real hostname. Following is a sample:

```
wu wuarchive.wustl.edu
cica ftp.cica.indiana.edu
cfna freenet-in-a.cwru.edu
cfnb freenet-in-b.cwru.edu
cfnc freenet-in-c.cwru.edu
```

On UNIX, put these five lines in .hostalias in your home directory. The actual name is unimportant, but this location is convenient. Next, set the HOSTALIAS environment variable to point to the .hostalias file you just created.

In the C Shell, use the `setenv` command:

```
setenv HOSTALIAS ~/.hostalias
```

In the Bourne Shell or the Bourne Again Shell (bash):

```
HOSTALIAS=/usr/your/home/.hostalias; export HOSTALIAS
```

(Substitute the name of your home directory in the preceding examples.)

Putting these lines in your .login, .profile, .bash_profile, or other personal login script may be a good idea.

When you have a hostalias file in place, you can ftp to `wuarchive.wustl.edu` or `ftp.cica.indiana.edu` with a simple **ftp wu** or **ftp cica**. You can telnet to the Cleveland Free-Net with **telnet cfna**. Add your own favorite hosts, and save keystrokes!

A few MS-DOS TCP/IPs also support hostalias files. The procedure is the same. Save your aliases in C:\HOSTALIA, and then issue the SET command, as follows:

```
set HOSTALIAS=c:\hostalia
```

Your TCP/IP may not have HOSTALIAS. This useful feature truly is a secret. HOSTALIAS is in the famous TCP/IP networking software that was written at the University of California at Berkeley, but it is not documented anywhere!

SLIPping to Speed

SLIP users push their connection performance to its limit more often than other Internet users do. Because of the amount of information on the Internet, a SLIP connection cannot work fast enough to satisfy most users. This situation means that SLIP users can benefit greatly from TCP tuning!

The biggest SLIP performance secret is TCP header compression, also known as compressed SLIP or CSLIP. This compression works by removing the fat from TCP/IP headers, not by compressing the data. The scheme works well. A typical one-keystroke telnet packet with regular SLIP requires 41 bytes over the modem. The same packet sent with CSLIP takes 5 bytes — one-eighth as much!

Keep using V.42bis or MNP5 (popular compression schemes built into most currently available modems) on your modem with CSLIP. The two systems work together well. V.42bis and MNP compress the data, and CSLIP compresses the TCP/IP headers.

Before you try turning on CSLIP, make sure that your Internet provider supports it. Turning on CSLIP can be as easy as checking a box in your TCP/IP or SLIP setup. Look in the configuration dialog boxes and in the documentation for *header compression, compressed SLIP*, or *Jacobson compression.* If one end of the connection is speaking SLIP and the other end is set for CSLIP, you'll get very peculiar results: Pinging usually works fine, but any TCP/IP application (such as telnet or ftp) hangs as soon as it connects to a remote host. You have to change the parameters at both ends simultaneously, usually by making a phone call to the person who manages the other end.

If you are using a DOS or Windows TCP/IP package without native SLIP support, as well as a SLIP packet driver such as SLIP8250, SLP16550, EtherSLIP, or SLIPPER, start using CSLIP. Grab Peter Tattam's excellent CSLIPPER packet driver from anonymous ftp to `biochemistry.bioc.cwru.edu` (in the United States) or `ftp.psychol.utas.edu.au` (in Australia). (Whatever packet driver you're using will be run from your AUTOEXEC.BAT file or from a batch file you use to start SLIP, so check there to see what is currently installed.)

After you're up and running with header compression, think about tuning up your receive window. This procedure is easy on SLIP: Make the receive window as large as possible. Large windows help keep data moving even when errors occur, and SLIP links are notorious for their high error rate. A small window makes errors hurt more.

Setting the segment size is trickier. For maximum throughput at all times, the segment should be set to the largest size possible. Sometimes, however, good interactive response is more important than high throughput. Segment sizes between 200 and 800 bytes offer a good trade-off between throughput and responsiveness. A segment size of 200 bytes is especially good if you like to run telnet in one window and download files in another window. Fiddle with the size until you get the blend of speed and handling that suits your taste.

Talking about special SLIP issues wouldn't be complete without mentioning how to make the most of limited SLIP servers. Some SLIP servers have a problem with flow control: They cannot handle data as fast as it arrives from the modem. The symptoms are a server that handles short transfers well but gradually slows to a halt during longer transfers. To work around this problem, reduce the TCP send window, if you can. Experiment with different values. The trick is to find the largest size that does not have flow-control problems, because that size also will have the highest speed. I Have a SLIP connection to a server that has flow-control problems. To avoid problems, I use a send window of 2,920 bytes. That size works efficiently, but a send window just one byte larger makes it impossible to send large files efficiently.

If you can receive short bursts of data without problems but have troubles with long bursts, the flow-control problem may be on your computer's end of the link. In that case, reduce the size of your receive window.

A magic value exists that offers the highest reliable performance. Finding this value may take some experimentation, but it is well worth the effort.

How Did You Do?

Predicting how a tune-up can affect a TCP/IP is hard. The improvement can range from 10 percent to more than 200 percent, depending on many factors. The best thing to do is to experiment.

If your TCP does not have tuning options, don't panic; that often means that you have a modern TCP that already is well configured. Chameleon from NetManage, for example, lacks most of the standard tuning options. Set up Chameleon with two nameservers and CSLIP (if applicable), and it will give you solid performance.

If you are a UNIX user and can tune your TCP/IP, you are well on your way to being a UNIX guru. Tuning TCP requires adjusting some parameters in configuration files and recompiling the operating-system kernel. The commands required are esoteric at best. Definitely optimize your nameserver settings and SLIP header compression, however; you can do both things without arcane knowledge.

TCP tuning involves many little rules, but all the rules are fairly straightforward. Getting everything just right takes some experimentation, but what's wrong with that? Go ahead and experiment! Get out a stopwatch and do some timing. See if you can't make your TCP move like the speed demon that it is!

Stephen Trier is a network software engineer at Case Western Reserve University. He does TCP/IP programming and troubleshooting, and he manages the university's GN-based Gopher and Web server. In his free time, he plays trombone.

Chapter 14

Connecting Your Macintosh to the Internet

by Art Kerns

Overview

The process of connecting your Macintosh to the Internet can be as simple as turning your computer on or extremely time-consuming and difficult, depending on your circumstances. Generally, you are in great shape if your computer already is connected to a local network, which is in turn connected to the Internet. If you plan to configure your own network or to dial in to a remote network, you probably will have a bit more trouble. Luckily, after you have configured your computer properly, you should not have significant trouble in the future. Keep in mind that — relatively speaking — the Macintosh is very easy to hook up to the Internet or to any other network. As difficult as the process may be for you, it's worse for your friends who have other kinds of computers.

All Internet connections are not created equal. The most basic connection enables you to see text at a relatively slow rate. Better connections allow for graphics and binary files and are significantly faster. To truly appreciate the Internet with a Macintosh, you need a relatively fast connection that enables you to transmit text, files, and graphics. You can accomplish this task through a direct connection with a network hooked up to the Internet or through a remote SLIP or PPP connection, using a fast modem. This type of connection is explained in this chapter.

You can connect your Mac to the Internet in two ways. One way is through a local network that already is connected to the Internet. This arrangement is an easy and cheap way to connect to the Internet — if you are fortunate enough to have an Internet-connected network cable running by your desk. The rest of us have to find a provider that can furnish a SLIP or PPP account (that is, if we want the kind of ease of use and flexibility in choosing software that SLIP and PPP provide), which allows your computer to become part of the Internet through a remote machine.

For more information on SLIP and PPP, see Chapter 12. Dozens, if not hundreds, of SLIP/PPP providers are available, ranging from national and international companies such as Alternet, PSI, and IBM Advantis to local providers that operate from the owner's garage. Ask around locally to find out what's available; also check the ads in the business section of your paper.

Read the following section on MacTCP, but don't install it yet. Then go to the section that is appropriate for you: "Connecting to a Local Network" or "Connecting to a Remote Network." The rest of the chapter is filled with information that will be useful after you establish your Internet connection, so make sure that you read all of it. Good luck!

MacTCP: Your Connection to the Internet

The first thing that you need for connecting to the Internet is a program called MacTCP, which enables your Macintosh to communicate with the Internet. This program serves as an interpreter between your computer, which is designed to talk only with other Macintoshes, and the Internet, which is designed to enable large numbers of dissimilar computers to communicate by using a standard protocol called TCP/IP. MacTCP provides a standard way for Macintosh Internet applications to access these TCP/IP communication features. This enables you to use several different types of Internet applications without having to configure each one separately, as well as do useful things such as having multiple Internet programs simultaneously running on your computer and communicating over the Internet. MacTCP also enables an application to communicate with the Internet without knowing what type of connection you are using. When MacTCP is installed properly, any program that uses MacTCP should work on your Macintosh, regardless of the details of your connection.

The common interface provided by MacTCP proves to be very handy to the user. Suppose that you have a direct connection to the Internet on your work computer and a remote SLIP or PPP connection on your home machine. On most computers, you would be forced to use two separate programs to read mail and download programs. With MacTCP, you can use the same program and the same interface, even if you are using a different type of Macintosh computer, network connection, or modem. Anyone who has spent countless hours configuring device drivers and network interfaces, only to find that the hardware or software is incompatible, can appreciate the job that MacTCP performs. Despite the difficulties involved in obtaining the program, and despite the confusion surrounding its commercial status, MacTCP performs a very useful function and is a prerequisite for directly connecting your Macintosh to the Internet.

If you are using System 7.5 or later, you should have a copy of MacTCP on one of your System disks. If you don't have a copy, you are going to have to go on a wild goose chase to find it. MacTCP is not free; it's sold commercially by Apple. If you work at a corporation or university that uses networked Macintoshes, your organization may have purchased a site license for the program that you can use. Otherwise, MacTCP is sold by Apple through APDA; call (800) 282-2732. You also can request information about MacTCP by e-mail (`sw.license@applelink.apple.com`) and from some mail-order companies. If you can't find MacTCP cheaply anywhere else, you can always buy System 7.5 and upgrade your operating system at the same time.

As of late 1994, the current version of MacTCP was 2.0.6, but MacTCP version 1.1.1 was still used. Some versions of MacTCP have proved to be buggy; you can upgrade your copy by downloading the patches for various versions, which are available at most popular Macintosh archive sites. The latest version is said to run faster than earlier versions and to be more reliable. The update programs work properly only with a virgin copy of MacTCP — meaning a copy that has never been run or modified. If necessary, recopy MacTCP from the floppy disk or CD-ROM that you received it on, and then run the updater on the never-used copy.

Connecting to a Local Network

The easiest way to hook up to the Internet is by means of an existing AppleTalk network (that has a connection to the Internet), using either Ethernet or LocalTalk. Then you connect to the Internet simply by configuring MacTCP properly, using the MacTCP control panel. Well, OK, sometimes it's not so simple, but we'll get to that.

Installing MacTCP

Start by installing a fresh copy of MacTCP — a copy that has never been used, altered, or modified in any way. If you have problems getting MacTCP to work, you also may have to start with a new copy of your Macintosh System software. Although there is no real reason why you should have to reinstall your System software, computers often work in mysterious ways, and this relatively quick solution often solves many otherwise unsolvable problems.

If you plan to use MacTCP over an Ethernet connection, now is the time to install and configure the Ethernet drivers. Follow the instructions that came with the Ethernet card. If you plan to use MacTCP over a LocalTalk connection, you will want to use the Chooser to activate AppleTalk.

Now configure MacTCP. To begin, click the correct physical layer of your network. The layers should appear in the main MacTCP window as icons labeled Ethernet, EtherTalk, LocalTalk, and so on. If you need the hardware Ethernet address that you will be using, for whatever reason, you can obtain it easily by holding down the Option key and then clicking the Ethernet icon.

Next, click the More button in the MacTCP Control Panel. Choose manual, server, or dynamic addressing, depending on your network. If you don't know which of the three types you should be using, ask your network administrator for help. If you are using manual addressing, be sure that the correct network class and subnet mask are entered. If your server handles addressing, or if you are using dynamic addressing, you don't need to worry about these fields. For now, you can ignore the Gateway and Name Server fields.

Rebooting

OK — time to reboot your Macintosh, test everything, and finish setting up. If you already have a copy of NCSA Telnet, give it a try. If the program loads correctly, you should be ready to go. You can try telnetting to another computer, using its numerical IP address. (Using a named IP address such as `sumex-aim.stanford.edu` may not work, because you have not specified a nameserver yet).

If you can't telnet to another computer, check the address listed in the Gateway field of MacTCP. If the address hasn't changed from `0.0.0.0` to something else, your computer can't find a central computer to talk to. Ask a network administrator for the numeric IP address of the gateway that you will be using.

You also want to make sure that your nameserver is set properly. Enter a period in the Domain field, enter the numeric IP address of the nameserver under Address, and click the default button on. If you don't know the address of the nameserver, ask a network administrator.

Your computer now should be able to telnet to other sites by using IP name addresses such as `sumex-aim.stanford.edu` instead of IP number addresses, which are very difficult to remember and easy to mistype. If your connection is working properly, you should be finished for now. Some additional tweaking may be required, though, and if you run into problems down the road, you may need to talk with a network administrator. Also check out the file mactcp-info-12.txt in the `/info/communications` directory at Stanford University. This file was written by a helpful guy named Eric Behr, who goes into much more detail about configuring and troubleshooting MacTCP than this chapter does. This file also will be of great help if you are a first-time Macintosh network administrator.

Connecting to a Remote Network

What if you don't work for a large corporation or university that has direct Internet access? Unless you want to invest tens of thousands of dollars in your own personal Internet connection, you are going to have to connect to a remote network that is itself connected to the Internet. Luckily, you can make this connection relatively painlessly by using communications protocols called SLIP and PPP.

SLIP and PPP are, essentially, two flavors of the same idea. Both protocols allow you to use a modem to emulate a physical network connection between your Macintosh and a remote computer. For the casual user, there really isn't much difference between SLIP and PPP; for people who study communications protocols, PPP is the superior protocol. (See Chapter 12 for more details on SLIP and PPP, although you don't need them for the purposes of this chapter.)

Setting up a SLIP connection

SLIP is an acronym for Serial Line Internet Protocol. Of the two competing remote communications protocols, SLIP currently is the more popular. Although SLIP isn't an official Internet standard, its popularity has made it the protocol of choice for many users. To use SLIP, you need MacTCP and a program called InterSLIP, which is available free on the Internet. You can use other SLIP programs in place of InterSLIP, but InterSLIP works, it's popular, and it's free, so there's little reason to use anything else. InterSLIP is available at the two Mac archive sites. The ftp addresses are

```
ftp://sumex-aim.stanford.edu/info-mac/comm/tcp/
ftp://mac.archive.umich.edu/mac/util/comm/
```

InterSLIP also is included on the disk in the back of *The Internet Starter Kit For Macs For Dummies* (IDG Books Worldwide, 1994), which can be more convenient if you don't already have an Internet connection set up. Detailed instructions on installing and configuring InterSLIP are included with the program. The process is similar to the process for installing MacTCP. First, use the installer program to install InterSLIP, and reboot when the installer finishes. Load the InterSLIP Setup program, and choose New. To configure the setup, enter the baud rate of your modem; your IP address (if your gateway does not set it for you); and the numerical IP addresses of your nameservers, which you can obtain from a network administrator. If you are dialing up and not using a direct connection, select the appropriate dial-script menu item and fill in the phone number and other relevant information. If you are connecting to a host that requires logins, select the appropriate gateway script.

Now you are ready to install MacTCP. Place MacTCP Control Panel in the System Folder, reboot, and open the MacTCP control panel. Choose the InterSLIP icon as the physical layer, and then click More to see more fields. The Obtain Address field should be set to server, the class of your IP address should be set to C, and the nameservers should be entered in their proper place. Click the OK button and then reboot. Your Mac should be ready to go.

Depending on the configuration of the remote computer, you may need to do more. If you plan to use TIA — a program that provides a SLIP connection on a UNIX command-line provider — you also have to configure the UNIX host that you will be using (see Chapter 15 for more information). The InterSLIP documentation should be able to help you get everything straight.

To run InterSLIP, choose InterSLIP Setup and highlight the connection that you want to use. Then click Connect. You now should be able to run MacTCP programs, such as NCSA Telnet and Mosaic. When you finish, click Disconnect.

Setting up a PPP connection

PPP, which stands for Point-to-Point Protocol, is the "official" Internet remote-connection protocol. PPP is superior to SLIP in several technical aspects: It can handle non-IP packets, it provides error and flow control, and it offers several other features. PPP is considered to be the protocol of the future and gradually is becoming more popular.

You can use a program called MacPPP to use the PPP protocol on your Macintosh. MacPPP is available from all popular Mac archive sites. The program contains its own set of setup instructions, which are similar to those of InterSLIP. For more information on PPP, read the Frequently Asked Questions list for the `comp.protocols.ppp` newsgroup, which should be available at the `rtfm.mit.edu` FAQ ftp site.

Setting up an Apple Remote Access connection

Apple Remote Access enables you to connect one Mac to another remotely, over the phone. If you are using the package to connect a Macintosh at home to a remote Mac that already is connected to the Internet, you should have no problem using the Internet. Because you are already emulating a LocalTalk network connection, simply install MacTCP as described in "Connecting to a Local Network," earlier in this chapter.

Troubleshooting Your Internet Connection

You've tried to install MacTCP (and probably InterSLIP or MacPPP), and the connection doesn't seem to work. Now what are you supposed to do? First, relax. You are not the first person to run into problems; MacTCP and the other programs are well known for causing headaches and frustration. Next, check all your hardware to make sure that everything is connected properly. If you are using a direct network connection, try to connect to another machine on your local network. If you are using a modem, make sure that you can connect to a local bulletin-board system or to a provider such as America Online or CompuServe.

If you still have problems, you can assume for now that the hardware isn't causing the trouble. MacTCP and the other programs are the most likely culprits; make sure that you configured them properly. These programs also are known for interfering with other programs, especially System extensions. Reboot your computer, and hold down the Shift key as it starts up. This procedure disables all your extensions. Then try to connect with the Internet again. If the connection works this time, you know that MacTCP or one of the other programs is conflicting with one of your extensions.

You have two options: You can disable your extensions before using the Internet, or you can try to find out which extension is the troublemaker. The first option is inconvenient in the long run; you have to reboot your system every time you want to use the Internet, and (obviously) you can't use any of your extensions when you do. The second option takes some time initially but probably will make life easier for you. If you decide to isolate the bad extension, move all the extensions out of the Extensions folder in the System Folder, and then move them back one at a time, rebooting and testing the connection. When the connection doesn't work, you'll know which extension(s) caused the problem.

What if your network or modem works, and the extensions don't seem to be causing any problems? Now is the time to get help. Call your network administrator or service provider and make sure that the network is working properly. Make sure that the addresses of the provider's computers match the ones that you listed when you configured MacTCP; also make sure that those computers support SLIP or PPP, if that's what you are using. If this procedure doesn't work and you have an alternative method of Internet access, try posting on `comp.sys.mac.comm` a message that specifically describes your computer, your modem, your network, and the software that you are trying to use.

If all else fails, some people have had surprising (and unexplainable) success by booting from one of the System disks that came with the Mac and reinstalling the entire System Folder. This method seems to be extreme, but for some people, it is the only thing that works. (Be sure to back up any files that you added to the System Folder since you last installed it.)

If you have checked your hardware, the System extensions, and the MacTCP configuration; asked for help from your network provider and the networking experts at `comp.sys.mac.comm`; and reinstalled your entire System, all with absolutely no positive result, something is seriously wrong. Consider paying someone to set up the system for you. Alternatively, if having an Internet connection that allows you to use your choice of Internet client applications is not that important to you, try using a commercial service such as America Online or CompuServe, that provide limited Internet access. These services tend to be slightly more expensive and require that you use software that does not yet fully support all areas of the Internet, but they may be adequate for your needs. If you find some new software or some more patience, you can always try again at a later date.

Macintosh File Formats and Conversion Utilities

Macintosh files have a unique structure unlike those of the files used by MS-DOS and UNIX computers. All Mac files are divided into two parts, or *forks*: the data fork and the resource fork. Some types of files, such as pictures and movies, use only the data fork. Applications and some other types of files mostly use the resource fork. In any case, the arrangement makes it difficult to place normal Macintosh files on a non-Macintosh file server, because only half — or sometimes none — of the file will be there.

The solution is something called MacBinary, which has become the standard way to take the two parts of a Macintosh file and combine them in one file. MacBinary also saves other information (such as name, date, and file type) that enables the file to be reconstructed properly upon decoding. What all this means to you is that before you can send a Macintosh file to someone else, the file needs to be encoded with MacBinary; likewise, before you can use a file that you retrieve from the Internet, the file needs to be decoded with MacBinary. Fortunately, MacBinary is so common that most Macintosh communications programs automatically perform the encoding and decoding for you. Unless you are using old or custom-designed software, you generally shouldn't have to worry about converting files to and from MacBinary.

Unfortunately, more is involved in sending or retrieving a file over the Internet. Besides combining the two parts of a file with MacBinary, two other things are commonly done to a Macintosh file: conversion and compression.

Conversion involves changing the characters that comprise a file so that a program or protocol can use it, in the same fashion that you would change words when translating a book from English to French so that people in France could read it. The most common reason for performing conversion is to send binary files, which contain many unused character codes, over e-mail. Because e-mail supports only standard letters, numbers, and punctuation marks, the file must be converted to a format that includes only readable characters. Conversion also is used for security purposes, to scramble the characters in a file so as to make them unreadable.

Compression is used to cut down on the amount of space that a file uses by replacing the old file with a new file that contains the same information in fewer characters. If you want to be completely accurate, compression actually is just a special form of conversion in which the converted file always is smaller than the original.

Macintosh users on the Internet use two major conversion programs. The first program is BinHex, which is used principally for converting a binary file to a text-compatible file for use by other Mac users. Most popular compression utilities, such as the StuffIt collection and Compact Pro, convert to and from BinHex format automatically. You also can use the utilities HQXer and deHqx. You can identify BinHexed programs readily by their .hqx extension. Because BinHex is used mostly by Macintosh users, if you are sending material intended for use by many different types of machines (pictures or sounds, for example), you should use the UNIX uuencode standard. Uuencoding accomplishes the same thing that BinHexing does in a standard, machine-independent way. Usually, you can find uuencoded files in places such as Usenet newsgroups and e-mail, and you can find BinHexed files at Macintosh archive sites. The utility uuUndo does a good, fast job of decoding uuencoded files.

Several compression formats are commonly used by Macintosh users; many other formats are used by other computers. The three Mac formats that you are most likely to run across are Compact Pro archives (*.cpt), StuffIt archives (*.sit), and self-extracting archives (*.sea). The first two formats require a compression/conversion utility to decode properly; good examples of these are the Compact Pro and StuffIt utilities, which are available at most Macintosh archive sites. Self-extracting archives are simple to decode; as their name suggests, you double-click them, and they decode themselves. The catch is that the file has to include additional code to tell it how to decode itself. Although this code initially may appear to occupy a relatively small amount of space, when you are dealing with thousands of files, it adds up. When you are uploading your own programs to Macintosh archive sites, be sure to use StuffIt or Compact Pro instead of a self-extracting archive.

Finally, the ZIP compression method is very common throughout the UNIX and PC worlds. Inevitably, you will run across a text or binary file that needs to be unzipped. The MacGzip and Unzip utilities do a good job of handling these files. ZIPping a file intended for use only with other Macintoshes is strongly discouraged; use StuffIt or Compact Pro instead.

The following table lists commonly used types of compression and the file extensions that identify them. For example, a file named myfile.sit would be a StuffIt compressed archive, which contains one or more compressed Macintosh files.

Extension	***File Type***
.bin	MacBinary file
.cpt	Compact Pro archive
.dd	Disk Doubler archive
.gz	Gnu ZIP archive
.hqx	BinHex file
.sea	Self-extracting archive
.sit	StuffIt archive
.uu	UNIX uuencoded file
.Z	UNIX compressed archive
.z	UNIX Gnu gzip archive
.zip	ZIP archive

Macintosh Software Archives

The Internet has loads of software and information just waiting for you to grab it; your only problem is finding it. For Macintosh users, this procedure is generally very simple; Stanford `sumex-aim` and University of Michigan are two ftp sites that are often mentioned on the Internet. Both sites have a staggering volume of Macintosh software just waiting to be used. Unfortunately, both sites are heavily used and very busy; you often will experience a slow connection or no connection at all. An easy solution to this problem is to use a *mirror site*, which is a site that is identical to the real one and updated with all the newest software from the main site every few days. Look for a current list of mirrors in the `/help` directory of all the major Macintosh ftp sites. Using a mirror is good for you because it is much faster, and good for everyone else because it distributes the data load a little more evenly across different parts of the Internet.

FTP Site	*Directory*	*Description*
ftp.apple.com		Apple's official ftp site has an archive of updates, information, and many useful programming files.
mac.archive.umich.edu	/pub/mac	The UMich archive has tons of shareware programs and commercial demos, some of which you won't find anywhere else. As mentioned earlier, this site is rather slow; you are advised to use a mirror site.
sumex-aim.stanford.edu	/pub/info-mac	This site is the home of the Info-Mac archives and is very heavily used. You are advised to use a mirror site, because access is restricted during work hours. Many shareware programs and commercial demos are available at the site, which you also can access by using Gopher.
wuarchive.wustl.edu	/mirrors/info-mac /mirrors/archive.umich.edu	This site is a mirror of both the sumex-aim and UMich sites. Several other reasons to use this site exist, and the site tends to be rather slow as a result.

If you do not have access to ftp, you can retrieve files from the sumex-aim Info-Mac archives through e-mail, using the Rice list server. The first files that you should retrieve are help/accessing-files.txt and help/all-files.txt, which will teach you how to access files (and a list of files that you can retrieve).

To retrieve the accessing-files document, send e-mail to `listserv@ricevm1.rice.edu` with the text `$macarch get help/accessing-files.txt`. You can retrieve other files by replacing *help/accessing-files.txt* with the name and directory of the file that you want to receive via e-mail.

You can submit your own software to the UMich and Info-Mac archives by e-mailing it to `macgifts@mac.archive.umich.edu`. Include the category of software that you think fits your program, as well as a short description. If your software is accepted, your file should be distributed throughout the Internet automatically. Remember to use StuffIt or Compact Pro to compress the file, and do not submit a self-extracting archive. For more information on submissions, see the file submissions.txt in the UMich help directory and posting-guidelines.txt in the `sumex-aim` help directory.

Where to Go for More Macintosh-Related Internet Information

An astounding amount of information about the Macintosh and the Internet is readily available on the Internet. Some of this information is well written and nicely formatted; some is less so. Most information has at least something interesting to say. If you really want to know how AppleTalk and TCP/IP work, or if you are having a specific problem that you can't seem to resolve, you may want to read some of this information. With some notable exceptions, most of the information is available only in electronic form through the Internet; protocols and standards are changing so quickly these days that a detailed technical book about these subjects would quickly be outdated.

Most of these files are available on large Macintosh archive sites such as Info-Mac and UMich, usually in the `/info` or `/help` directory. You also can try doing an Archie search on the filename (that's what those tools are for!). If this chapter didn't satisfy your craving for learning how your Macintosh and the Internet communicate, these sites are the first places to go to find out more.

Resource	***Description***
comp.sys.mac.comm FAQ (edited by David Oppenheimer)	This file is a great introduction to using a Mac on the Internet. It's comprehensive, well written, and complete, and it's the first place you should go for more information.
ftp-primer.txt (by Raymond Beausoleil)	This document contains everything that you ever wanted to know about ftping on the Mac but were afraid to ask.
how-to-tia.txt (by Brian Kendig)	If you plan to use the Internet through a SLIP connection, and if you are having problems or don't know where to start, this document is for you.
mactcp-info-12.txt (by Eric Behr)	This document provides an extremely helpful explanation of how to configure a Macintosh and connect to the Internet by using MacTCP. The document is written in easy-to-read, very understandable fashion and contains many tricks and tips for making things work.

Other Macintosh Resources on the Internet

Apart from the formal resources of archives and documents written by experts, many less formal (and sometimes less helpful) resources are available to help you learn more about your Mac.

Mailing lists

A mailing list enables you to read and participate in an ongoing discussion, focused on a certain specific topic, through e-mail. A substantial number of mailing lists are devoted to Macintosh-related issues; some of the largest are listed in this section. The process of subscribing to a mailing list often is unique to that list. For the lists in this section, you should be able to subscribe or get information about subscribing by sending e-mail to the server address, with the body containing the message mentioned in the table (if any) and with your name appearing in place of `<your-first-name>` and `<your-last-name>` or your e-mail address appearing in the place of `<your-email-address>`.

Mailing List	*Address*	*Include This Message*
Develop	mac-develop-request@ ccu.umanitoba.ca	<your-email-address>
Info-Mac Archive	Server: info-mac-request@sumex-aim.stanford.edu	Announcements
Macintosh Games (shareware)	Server: listserv@ netcom.com	SUBSCRIBE MAC- SHAREWARE-GAMES
Macintosh Hardware	Server: listserv@ dartcms1.bitnet	SUBSCRIBE MACHRDWR <your-first-name> <your-last-name>
Macintosh Multimedia	Server: listserv@ fccj.bitnet	SUBSCRIBE MACMULTI <your-first-name> <your-last-name>
Macintosh Networking	Server: listserv@ yalevm.bitnet	SUBSCRIBE MACNET-L <your-first-name> <your-last-name>
Macintosh News and Information	Server: listserv@ yalevm.bitnet	SUBSCRIBE MAC-L <your-first-name> <your-last-name>
Macintosh PowerBooks	Server: listserv@ yalevm.bitnet	SUBSCRIBE MACPB-L <your-first-name> <your-last-name>
Macintosh Programming	Server: listserv@ wuvmd.bitnet	SUBSCRIBE MACPROG <your-first-name> <your-last-name>
Macintosh Security	Server: mac-security-request@eclectic.com	
Macintosh System 7	Server: listserv@ uafsysb.bitnet	SUBSCRIBE SYS7-L <your-first-name> <your-last-name>

(continued)

(continued)

Mailing List	***Address***	***Include This Message***
Macintosh System Software	Server: listserv@ dartcms1.bitnet	SUBSCRIBE MACSYSTM Software <your-first-name> <your-last-name>
Tidbits (miscellaneous Macintosh information)	Server: listserv@ ricevm1.rice.edu	SUBSCRIBE TIDBITS <your-first-name> <your-last-name>

Usenet newsgroups

Newsgroups are colorful — and, often, somewhat uninformative — forums for opinions and informal debates. The Macintosh newsgroups tend to be a bit more serious, focusing on specific technical areas and generally discouraging off-topic discussions. Although exceptions exist (such as `comp.sys.mac.games`, which tends toward the casual, to say the very least), most Macintosh newsgroups are more interested in exchanging information than insults. If you have a question, find the specific newsgroup that best fits your problem and ask there. Mac gurus of all flavors read these groups and are always willing to help answer questions.

Always be sure to read the Frequently Asked Questions (FAQ) list for a newsgroup before you post a message; this practice saves the time of everyone who reads the newsgroup by averting endless repetitions of the same old questions. You'll find that the FAQs are invaluable sources of information by themselves, especially the technical ones that are devoted to topics such as programming and communications. Most Usenet FAQs can be retrieved from the ftp site `rtfm.mit.edu` in the `/pub/usenet/` directory.

Newsgroup	***Description***
alt.sources.mac	Sample source-code listings for Macintosh programmers.
comp.binaries.mac	BinHexed posts of all the shareware software and demos submitted to the Info-Mac sumex-aim archives.
comp.sys.mac.announce	The latest news about recent Macintosh hardware releases, software releases, and viruses.
comp.sys.mac.apps	News, information, and discussions related to various Macintosh applications.
comp.sys.mac.comm	News, information, discussions, and requests for help for all areas of Macintosh communications, including the Internet. If you are having a specific problem with configuring your communications software, this newsgroup is the place to ask for help. Be sure to describe your specific System configuration and problem if you expect meaningful responses. Better yet, read the FAQ first.

Newsgroup	*Description*
comp.sys.mac.games	Discussions of new Macintosh games, as well as hints and tips for older games. This group is less informative than most Macintosh newsgroups — but then, what did you expect?
comp.sys.mac.hardware	News and information related to all areas of Macintosh hardware.
comp.sys.mac.portables	News and information related to the Macintosh PowerBook and Duo portable computers.
comp.sys.mac.programmer	Very helpful discussions and programming advice geared to intermediate to advanced Macintosh programmers. As always, read the FAQ before asking questions; you'd be amazed how many people have already asked the same thing.

World Wide Web

The World Wide Web is one of the newest services of the Internet and is quickly becoming one of the most popular ones. Although Web resources dedicated to the Macintosh are still somewhat scarce, they are guaranteed to increase exponentially within the next couple of years. This section lists a few of the most useful sites that existed as of late 1994. Some of the sites have indexes of existing Macintosh Web resources; be sure to check these indexes for the newest pages and the latest information.

Web Page	*Description*	*URL*
Apple Computer	Apple's Web server has information on the Macintosh product line, links to developer resources, and other interesting stuff.	http://www.apple.com/ http://www.info. apple.com/dev/ default.html
Developer and programming	Source-code archives, tips, and other programming resources. information	http://www.teleport. com/@tdcci/directo- ries/irfmd/irfmd.html http://www.pitt.edu/ @tdnick/developer information http://www.astro.nwu. edu/lentz/mac/home- mac.html
Frequently Asked Questions archive	An extremely handy archive of all Macintosh-related FAQ lists.	http://rever.nmsu. edu/@tdelharo/faq/ faqs.html
General Macintosh information	Hypertext information about the Internet, programming, and more.	http://www.uwtc. washington.edu/ computing/internet/ documents.html

Art Kerns is an engineer with Qualcomm, Inc., of San Diego, where he is working on the Globalstar satellite phone system. He also has experience designing and programming real-time physics simulations for the Macintosh, including the HMWBS projectile simulator.

Chapter 15

Macintosh TIA: A Lighthearted Guide to a Heavy Topic

by Art Kerns

This chapter is based on a Web document. The latest update should be available at `http://seds.lpl.arizona.edu/billa/tia/faq.html`.

Introduction

This chapter's primary purpose is to get you up and running with TIA on a Mac. It also attempts to answer a few questions that may arise after you have TIA working. But if all goes well, after you get TIA working, you can forget about this article and enjoy the Net.

I strongly recommend that you read this entire chapter before doing anything else. It will only take you a few minutes, and it may save both of us some grief.

The chapter assumes that you have a Macintosh and that you already have it connected to an ISP (Internet service provider, such as Netcom or your school or business) through a modem. The ISP's machine must be running one of the many supported flavors of UNIX. You must have the ability to download files and execute them on the ISP's machine. (America Online, CompuServe, Delphi, et al., are not suitable.) The chapter also assumes that you have the ability to copy binary files (notably, Mac applications) from your ISP's machine to your Mac. (If you need more help on these topics, check the FAQ files for `comp.dcom.modems`, `comp.sys.mac.comm`, or `comp.os.unix`.)

How do I use the file references?

First, read the reference. A reference has four parts: a *protocol* (for example, `ftp`), which determines which tool you must use to access the item; a *host name* (`ftp.netcom.com`), which tells you which machine you have to connect to; a *path* (`/pub/bi/billa/tia/`), which specifies where (in which directory) on that machine to look; and finally, a *filename* (`faq.html`) in that directory. Files referenced by ftp URLs (Uniform Resource Locator) can be copied to your account with the UNIX ftp command, as follows:

```
% ftp
    ftp: o ftp.netcom.com
    Connected to ftp.netcom.com.
    220 server FTP server (Version wu-2.4(2) Tue Jul 5 16:00:01 PDT 1994) ready.
    Name (ftp.netcom.com:billa): anonymous
    331 Guest login ok, send your complete e-mail address as password.
    Password:billa@netcom.com
    230-
    230-        Welcome to NETCOM On-line Communications Services, Inc.
    ...
    230 Guest login ok, access restrictions apply.
    ftp: cd pub/bi/billa/tia
    250 CWD command successful.
    ftp: get faq.html
    200 PORT command successful.
    150 Opening ASCII mode data connection for faq.html (24000 bytes).
    226 Transfer complete.
    local: faq.html remote: faq.html
    24000 bytes received in 8.0 seconds (3.0 Kbytes/s)
    ftp: bye
    221 Goodbye.
    %
```

For more information, consult your manual pages or your local UNIX guru. Other common types of URLs are http and gopher. Gopher is fairly self-explanatory. Files referenced by http URLs can usually be seen only by WWW browsers, but you can always try to ftp them and read them as text (as in this case). Sometimes, you'll see a URL with no protocol and host part. That means you use the same protocol, host, and directory that you used to get the original document. In this case, the original document is `ftp://ftp.netcom.com/pub/bi/billa/tia/faq.html`.

What's this "WWW" that you keep talking about?

Oh, boy, are you in for a treat! *WWW* is a TLA (three-letter acronym) that means *World Wide Web*, which is just about the coolest thing to come into the computer world since bitmapped graphics. WWW is a huge, globally interconnected set of documents containing pictures, sounds, and text on every conceivable topic, which you can access right from your Mac. You can easily add your own documents to the WWW. WWW is why you're going to all the trouble of reading this article!

What is TIA, anyway?

To get full access to the Internet (and to WWW in particular), you need to make a TCP/IP connection from your Mac to the Net. Unless you're part of a large organization that can spend big bucks every month for Net access, you probably have to use a dialup connection to an Internet service provider, using a special protocol called SLIP (serial line IP). Some ISPs provide SLIP at a reasonable cost, but most want $1 or more per hour. When you get into WWW, the cost can easily be hundreds of dollars per month. Bummer.

Enter TIA! (Trumpets sound! Rockets burst!) TIA (the Internet adapter), by Cyberspace Development, Inc., is a neat little utility that installs on your ISP's UNIX host in minutes, runs as a standard process on any user's shell account, and enables that user to use a shell account (essentially) as a SLIP account. You get all this for one low, low payment of $25. You no longer have to choose between food and Net access.

A few ISPs have banned TIA from their machines; most ISPs tolerate it but don't like it. After all, TIA is taking money out of their pockets (instead of yours). If your ISP bans TIA, get a new ISP. If your ISP allows it, keep quiet, and don't abuse your newfound capabilities by staying logged in 24 hours per day; you don't want to spoil the party. Don't ask your ISP's support staff to help you with TIA. You can get all the help you need here and from the newsgroup `alt.dcom.slip-emulators`.

More marketing information about TIA is available at `ftp://marketplace.com/tia/docs/tia.info.txt`.

I Wanna Do It! I Want It Now!

Whoa there, cowboy — you've got a bit of scrounging to do first. TIA's developers have generously provided for a two-week, free trial version of TIA to let you try it before you plunk down your hard-earned bread. To make the best of this opportunity, you should have everything else ready before you get your trial license. Doing this will take a bit of effort, but trust me, it's worth it.

First, make sure that you've got the right stuff. The minimum requirements for a SLIP connection are a Mac Plus, System 6.0.7, MacTCP 2.0.4, and 2MB RAM. (I recommend at least a Mac II, System 7.0.1+Tuneup, and 4MB of RAM, but you can do perfectly well with less.) The major problem is the applications that you want to run over the connection, not SLIP itself. You'll need System 7 to run WWW. TIA et al. will work with any modem, but you'll be happier with the fastest one that your ISP can support (usually, 14.4K). You also need an 8-bit clean modem connection and a hardware handshake modem cable.

The right cable

Figure 15-1 shows a hardware handshake cable.

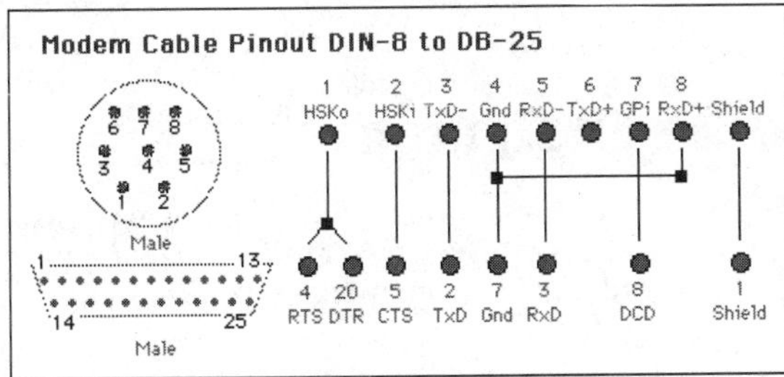

Figure 15-1: The right serial cable.

If you know which end of a soldering iron to hold, you can save $20 by making your own cable. On the other hand, if this figure looks to you like the wiring diagram for the starship *Enterprise*, you had better just buy one; you can do serious damage to your Macintosh if you screw up this part.

The right connection

You can perform a test to see whether you have an 8-bit clean serial connection. Get a copy of the ASCII test file `ftp://marketplace.com/tia/ascii.bin`, and save it in your UNIX account. Make a second copy of the file for later comparison, as follows:

```
% cp ascii.bin ascii.bak
```

Next, using Zterm or a similar terminal emulator, download the file ASCII.BIN to your Mac, using Zmodem in binary mode. (Specifying binary mode for Zmodem is very important, because by default, Zmodem escapes control characters.) Then upload the result file from your Mac back to the host, again using Zmodem in binary mode.

When the process is complete, compare the original file (ASCII.BAK) with the test file (ASCII.BIN), as follows:

```
% diff ascii.bin ascii.bak
```

The files should be identical. If they are not, you do not have an 8-bit clean serial connection, and SLIP (for example, TIA) will not function properly. If you do not have an 8-bit clean connection, check your (client-side) setup first: modem, cable, and SLIP software settings. If the settings check out OK, contact your local system administrator (often abbreviated *sysadmin*).

A simpler test that your UNIX system may support is the command sz -TT, which attempts to output all 256 ASCII code combinations to the terminal. You can issue this command and watch the results to see which codes get "eaten" by your setup.

One basic setting for you (or, more likely, the sysadmin) to check is the UNIX tty setting. The settings file (for example, /ETC/GETTYTAB) should include a parameter (such as p8) to specify that the port is 8-bit.

On a Xyplex terminal server, you may have to use the command `set session passall` to make it act 9-bit clean.

What Do I Have to Do First, Mom?

First, read this entire chapter. Only after you read it should you try to actually do anything. No, there's no trick at the end, saying that you can just type **xyzzy**. But you'll find it easier to do everything if you know where you're going.

MacTCP

Next, you need to get a copy of MacTCP. Aside from TIA itself, MacTCP is the only part that is not freeware or shareware. You can get MacTCP in several ways. The easiest way is to buy System 7.5, which is a nice package anyway. The next-easiest way is to buy a copy of Adam Engst's fine book, *The Internet Starter Kit, Version 2* (Mac version, Hayden Books, 1994), which comes with a floppy disk that includes MacTCP and a bunch of other things that you're going to need. (The book is a good introduction to the Internet, too.)

Make sure that your MacTCP is version 2.0.4 or later. If you have an earlier version, an update is available at `ftp://ftp.austin.apple.com/Apple.Support.Area/Apple.Software.Updates/Macintosh/Networking.and.Communications/Other.N-C.Software/MacTCP.2.0.6.Update.sea.hqx`.

Other basic Mac software

You also will want to have the following software to use with TIA:

- In addition to MacTCP, you need a SLIP driver for MacTCP, such as InterSLIP 1.0.1 (`ftp://ftp.intercon.com/InterCon/sales/InterSLIP/InterSLIPInstaller1.0.1.hqx`). Make sure that you get version 1.0.1 or later of InterSLIP; earlier versions had problems. Several other SLIP drivers are available commercially, including MacSLIP and Versaterm SLIP. The rest of this chapter assumes that you're using InterSLIP. (It's free, and it works just fine; why pay more?)
- Scripts for InterSLIP: DialTIA, a dial script; and GateTIA, a gateway script. You probably will have to modify these scripts slightly to match your particular situation; see "InterSLIP scripts," later in this chapter.
- The TCP equivalent of a terminal emulator: NCSA Telnet 2.6 (`ftp://ftp.ncsa.uiuc.edu/Mac/Telnet/Telnet2.6/Telnet2.6.sit.hqx`).
- A program for downloading stuff directly to your Mac: Anarchie 1.3.1 (`ftp://nic.switch.ch/software/mac/peterlewis/anarchie-131.sit.bin`).
- An archive decoder: StuffIt Expander (`ftp://ftp.netcom.com/pub/leonardr/Aladdin/StuffIt_Expander_3.5.1_Installer.hqx`).

Make sure that you copy everything you download to backup floppy disks. Unpack and expand the archives, but don't try to actually install any of this stuff just yet; you need some more information first.

Getting the TIA Trial Version

Now that you have all the stuff you need safely on your Mac, it's time to get TIA itself. TIA has two components: a license file and a UNIX binary. The binary is a UNIX application program that runs on your ISP's machine. Several versions of this program exist; you must get the right one for your ISP's flavor of UNIX. The license file is just a text file containing a magic string that TIA checks when it starts up to make sure that you've paid. Don't try to cheat by copying your buddy's license; it won't work, and anyway, it's wrong.

First, you need to get a trial license. Get a copy of the single-user order form from `ftp://marketplace.com/docs/tia.single.form.txt`, fill in the form, and mail it back (detailed instructions are included in the form). Cyberspace's automated mail responder will reply (usually, very quickly) with a message that contains your license code and some instructions. Save the license in a file called `.tia` in your home directory. Next, obtain and install the TIA binary as explained in the TIA Single Instructions from Cyberspace (`ftp://marketplace.com/tia/docs/tia.single.instruct`). If you know what machine type your ISP is running, just ftp over to `ftp://marketplace.com/tia/marketplace.com` and get the right version (but read the preceding document anyway; it contains important legal and support information). If you're not sure, read the TIA Single Instructions, and perform all the steps up to — but not including — step 5. (You should read all the instructions, but this chapter contains more detailed instructions tailored for Mac users.)

Make sure that the TIA binary is installed somewhere on your path (or in your home, if you don't know what *path* means), rename it TIA, and make it executable. For example, if your system uses a SPARC processor, use the following syntax:

```
% mv sparc.sunos.tia tia
% chmod 544 tia
```

If you're a Netcom customer, you don't need to get your own copy of the binary; Barry Nathan has generously agreed to keep the latest version in his home for all of us to share. Just make a link in your home to Barry's version, as follows:

```
% cd
% ln -s ~barryn/pub/tia tia
```

Of course, you still need your own `.tia` file containing your own license code.

Make sure that TIA is working properly. When you run it, it should respond as follows:

```
% tia
 The Internet Adapter (tm) 1.04c for SunOS
 Copyright (c) 1994 Cyberspace Development, Inc.
 Trial license
 Ready to start your SLIP software.
```

To exit TIA, press Ctrl-C five times in succession, allowing at least two seconds between the first and last time. If at first TIA doesn't die, just press Ctrl-C a few more times.

Don't worry — this whole song and dance really is a lot easier than it sounds.

Host Information1

When you configure MacTCP later, you're going to need some information about your ISP's machine and how you connect to it. Most of this information is exceedingly dull, but it has to be exactly right. (Mac users usually are insulated from these things, but this time, you're going to have to put up with it for a while. Think of this configuration ritual as a confirming experience that renews your faith in the Mac.) Your terminal emulator probably has the capability to record your session and save a transcript of the session in a file; use it. If not, just cut and paste the relevant information from your terminal emulator's window to a text file.

First, you need to record your login sequence. Log out, quit your terminal emulator, reset your modem (if necessary), and start all over with the session recorder on. You need to record all the prompts that you get (including your shell prompt); your responses to the prompts (including your user ID and password); and, of course, the phone number. Record all this information exactly; spaces and uppercase/lowercase matter.

Next, run TIA with the special flag to get it to show the gateway and nameserver addresses, as follows:

```
% tia -address
 The Internet Adapter (tm) 1.04c for SunOS
 Copyright (c) 1994 Cyberspace Development, Inc.
 IP address of netcom8 (used as Gateway address):192.100.81.117
 Addresses of nameservers:
 127.0.0.1 localhost
 192.100.81.101 netcomsv
 192.100.81.105 mork
 %
```

Enter the `domainname` command, and note the result:

```
% domainname
 netcom.com
 %
```

(Netcom customers can use the preceding addresses.)

Finally, ask your buddies or your system administrator for the names of your POP, SMTP, and NNTP servers. You'll need these names to read mail and news. If you can't get a better answer, you usually can use localhost for the first two servers, but not for the third. (A workaround is available if you can't find an NNTP server; that workaround is discussed later in this chapter.)

You now should know the following:

- ISP phone number
- User ID
- Password
- Shell prompt
- Any additional prompts and responses in your login sequence

- Gateway address
- Nameserver addresses
- Domain name
- POP server
- SMTP server
- NNTP server

Double-check all these numbers! Needless to say, if you get one lousy digit wrong, it won't work right. Again, it's probably a good idea to print all this information on paper so that it will be handy when you need it.

Clean Up Your Act!

One more thing before we get down to it: Many things can go wrong with this process. You don't need any extra complications, so disable (remove from your System Folder) all those nifty extensions and control panels that you've been collecting for the past decade. Keep only your virus checker (you *do* use a virus checker, don't you?), the INITs that you got directly from Apple's System disks, and the extensions that you absolutely need for your hardware (including Express Modem, if you're using it).

Especially troublesome are the various hacks used for faxing (including Apple's) and old versions of MacTCP (and of MacTCP DNR and MacTCP Prep). Trash MacTCP DNR and MacTCP Prep (MacTCP will recreate them later); disable the rest.

If you're using System 7.5, disable Apple Menu Options, too. Despite the fact that it's an official Apple-released product, I have found it to be the source of much difficulty.

After you get TIA et al. working, you can put all your favorite INITs back. Then, if something stops working, you'll know why.

Make sure that you have the latest versions of Apple's networking software for your machine.

They can be obtained directly from the Apple Austin ftp site (`ftp://ftp.austin.apple.com/Apple.Support.Area/Apple.Software.Updates/Net.and.Comm.SW/`). These files are distributed as disk images. To use the files, you need Disk Copy (`ftp://ftp.austin.apple.com/Apple.Support.Area/Apple.Software.Updates/Utilities.SW/Disk.Copy.4.2/Disk.Copy.v4.2.sea.Hqx`) or a similar utility (such as Drop*Disk).

Always Practice Safe Computing!

We haven't heard much about viruses recently in the Mac world. There's a good reason for that: Almost everyone uses a virus checker. If you aren't using one, stop everything right now and get one. I recommend the freeware Disinfectant (`ftp://ftp.acns.nwu.edu/pub/disinfectant/disinfectant35.sea.hqx`), by John Norstad of Northwestern University. Several commercial packages may have some advantages over Disinfectant, but Disinfectant has worked fine for me for many years. Why pay when a perfectly adequate solution is free?

If you didn't think that you needed a virus checker, you were wrong. And you're doubly wrong now that you're going to be downloading things from all over the Net. You may not have had virus problems in the past, but you're much more vulnerable when you're connected to the Net.

After you check for virii, empty the Trash, and restart your Mac. Wasn't that fast? Are you sure that you really needed all those other INITs?

Installing MacTCP and InterSLIP

Drop MacTCP into your Control Panels folder and launch the InterSLIP Installer. The installer creates several files and then restarts your Mac. During the restart, make sure that MacTCP and InterSLIP load properly (no big red *X* appears over the icon). When the Finder comes back up, examine your System Folder. Among your old friends, you should see these new items:

- System Folder
- Apple Menu Items
- InterSLIP Setup
- Control Panels
- InterSLIP Control
- MacTCP
- Extensions
- InterSLIP
- MacTCP DNR
- Preferences
- InterSLIP Folder
- Dialing Scripts
- Gateway Scripts
- InterSLIP Preferences

The file InterSLIP Docs also will appear on your Desktop; save this file for reading later.

Move the file DialTIA, which you downloaded earlier, to the Dialing Scripts folder, and move the file GateTIA to the Gateway Scripts folder.

Trash InterSLIP Control; you don't need it. MacTCP often is distributed with a file called Hosts, which you can also trash.

InterSLIP scripts

You may have to slightly modify the two InterSLIP scripts to match your environment. (Here's where you use some of the cryptic stuff that you recorded earlier.) All the lines that may need to be changed are clearly marked.

The DialTIA script contains five such places, but unless you have a really funny UNIX setup, you have to change only one. About 75 percent of the way down the file is a line that reads:

```
matchstr 1 30 "% "
```

If your shell prompt does not end with %, change the string inside the quotes to match the last two characters of your shell prompt. If your shell prompt is `"{netcomX:Y} "`, for example, change the script to

```
matchstr 1 30 "} "
```

(Don't forget the spaces.)

If the last characters of your prompt vary, you may have to change your prompt. You can do this by adding a line like the following to your login file in your home directory on your ISP's machine:

```
set prompt = "% "
```

Seven places in the GateTIA script may need changing. The first three places check for the first prompt given to you when you log in. In almost all UNIX systems, this prompt is `"login:"` or `"Login:"`, so the script just checks for `"ogin:"`. If your prompt is different — for example, `"Enter user id:  "` — change the three lines near the top of the script from

```
matchstr 1 1 "ogin:"
```

to

```
matchstr 1 1 "er id:"
```

The fourth place that you may need to change checks for the password prompt. If your system's password prompt is `"Secret code:"`, for example, change the line

```
matchstr 1 2 "assword:"
```

to

```
matchstr 1 2 "code:"
```

The fifth and sixth places check for the shell prompt. Modify them exactly like the shell prompt in DialTIA.

The last place that you may need to change is near the end of the script. Here, the script needs the name of the TIA binary. If you followed the instructions earlier, you don't need to change it. But if you're one of those headstrong know-it-alls who never follow instructions, you just made some more work for yourself. If, for example, you decided to name your TIA binary tia_maria, change the line

```
write "exec tia\13"
```

to

```
write "exec tia_maria\13"
```

You do not put your user ID or password in these scripts; they go in the InterSLIP setup dialog box, described in Figure 15-3. The scripts use the cryptic notations "^5" and "^6" as placeholders for your real user ID and password.

If you have a terminal server that gives you an extra prompt before the UNIX login prompt, you need to get the enhanced gateway script (GateTIA2) that handles this case. GateTIA2 has two additional places that you need to modify to match your terminal server's prompt and your response to that prompt. If your situation is even more complicated, you're just going to have to figure it out for yourself. Some more examples to work from are in the MacTCP directory at Adam Engst's TidBits ftp site (`ftp://ftp.tidbits.com/pub/tidbits/tisk/MacTCP/`).

MacTCP settings

Are you getting Mac withdrawal from all this boring text? Well, the worst is behind you now. But you're still going to have to type some of those funny numbers that you collected.

Open the MacTCP control panel. At the top of the window are icons for the various methods by which your Mac might connect to the rest of the universe. Click the icon labeled InterSLIP. (Ignore the IP address box for now.) Then click the More button to see the main configuration dialog box. My MacTCP settings are as follows, and also as shown in Figure 15-2:

```
Obtain address: Server
Gateway address: 192.0.2.1
Class: C
Subnet Mask: 255:255:255:0
Domain Name Server Information:
 Domain IP Address Default
 netcom.com 192.100.81.101 (*)
 . 192.100.81.101
 . 192.100.81.105
```

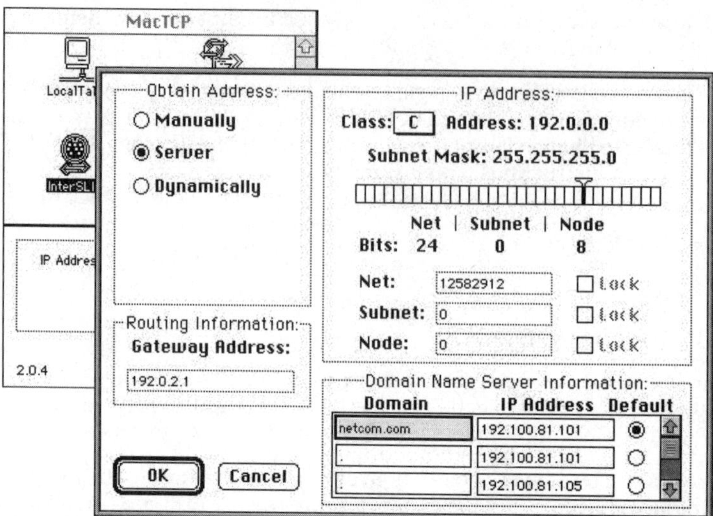

Figure 15-2: Setting up your Mac for TCP/IP.

To set the Gateway address, first change Obtain Address to Manual; then enter the IP address of your ISP's machine (which you got from running tia -address). Change back to Server, and choose C from the Class pop-up menu. The Subnet Mask should be set correctly when you choose Class C; if not, move the little slider.

The DNS settings are critical. Enter your domain name in the first Domain box. Enter the IP address of your primary nameserver in the first IP Address box, and click the Default button. Enter a single period in the second Domain box, and enter the IP address of your primary nameserver in the second IP Address box. Enter the IP addresses of any additional nameservers, with periods, in the corresponding Domain boxes. (Notice the scroll bar; you can add several more entries if your site has many nameservers, but two or three usually are enough.)

Notice that the entries in the Domain column are *not* the names of hosts, and they are *not* the host names that correspond to the entries in the IP Address column. This dialog box is not Apple's best effort.

For more information about MacTCP, see the following:

- Peter Lewis's explanation of DNS settings (`dns.txt`)
- Adam Engst's "Dominating MacTCP" (`ftp://ftp.tidbits.com/pub/tidbits/dominating-mactcp-draft.etx`)
- Eric Behr's MacTCP document (`http://hoohoo.ncsa.uiuc.edu/~jbrowne/mac-tcp.html`)

InterSLIP settings

Finally, you're ready to configure InterSLIP. First, run the InterSLIP Setup application (the installer thoughtfully left it in your Apple Menu Items folder). Next, create a new configuration-settings file by choosing New from the File menu and giving the file a convenient name, such as netcomTIA. That name appears in the bottom portion of the window; double-click it. This action displays a dialog box, in which the real fun begins.

My InterSLIP settings are as follows, and also as shown in Figure 15-3:

```
Serial Port: GeoPort Gateway: GateTIA
Baud Rate: 57600 User name: billa
Data Bits: 8 Prompt for password: off
Stop Bits: 1 Password: guess-me
Parity: none
Hardware handshaking: on IP Address: 192.0.2.1
Speaker: on Nameserver: 192.100.81.101
Dial Script: DialTIA RFC blah blah blah: off
Dial: Tone MTU size: 1500
Phone No.: 261-4700
Modem Init: AT&F
```

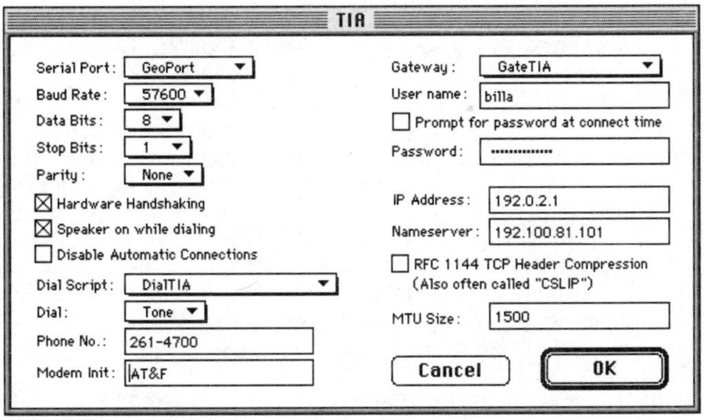

Figure 15-3: The InterSLIP dialog box.

Obviously, many of the following need to be configured for your environment:

- Phone No., User name, and Password: should be obvious.
- Serial Port: the port your modem is plugged into (almost always the modem port, unless you're using a machine that has an internal modem).

- Baud Rate: for now, use the highest value that your machine supports. (For some Macs, 19,200 may be a better choice; see "Troubleshooting," later in this chapter.)
- Modem Init: most can use the default AT&F (see the FAQ list at the end of the chapter for specific advice).
- Dial Script and Gateway: select your modified DialTIA and GateTIA scripts.
- Nameserver: use the IP address of your primary nameserver, as recorded from the output of tia -address.

The others should be set as shown in the figure. Choose OK to close the dialog box. You're done. That wasn't so hard after all, was it?

Reboot

Restart your Mac. (Old-timers call this procedure *booting* instead of *restarting*; the term probably refers to the tool that's most commonly used for that purpose.) You must reboot whenever you change MacTCP's settings.

The Moment of Truth

The moment of truth has arrived. If you have done everything as described (and if I haven't screwed up the instructions), you now should be able to run TCP/IP applications on your Mac. First, you have to get TIA running on your UNIX system.

Run InterSLIP Setup and hit the Connect button. It should show a series of messages ending up with `<Connected>`. (If it fails somewhere along the way, be sure to note the last few messages.) You can also start the connection by simply running a TCP application, but I've found it's more reliable to do so manually with InterSLIP Setup.

Try NCSA Telnet. Start it, and choose Open Connection from the File menu. Enter **localhost** in the Host/Session Name box, and click the Connect button (ignore the other box for now). In a few seconds, you should see a window displaying your standard login prompt. Log in. Welcome to the Internet! You are back where you started from, except that telnet is much slower than ZTerm.

Telnet has an unreasonably large number of parameters and settings that interact in obscure ways with your terminal settings on your ISP's host. Fortunately, the defaults work most of the time. But if your session acts funny (double prompts, backspace not working, and so on), talk to your system administrator. Telnet settings are way beyond the scope of this chapter.

If you don't get a telnet window, or if telnet complains about the name, try entering the IP address of your ISP's machine. If that works, your MacTCP DNS settings probably are wrong. Fix those settings, remove MacTCP Prep and MacTCP DNR, and reboot. If IP addresses don't work, either, something more basic is wrong. See "Troubleshooting," later in this chapter.

Now try Anarchie. Choose Get from the FTP menu. Enter **ftp.einet.net** in the Machine box and **/einet/mac/macweb/** in the Path box; leave the other boxes empty. Click the List button. After a bit of flashing, you should see a window displaying a list of the files in that directory. Double-click `Macweb.latest.sea.hqx`. You should get a status dialog box that shows the progress of the download. (Pay attention to the Bytes/Sec indicator, which should be about 1,400 for 14,400-baud modems; see the "Troubleshooting" section if your value is consistently lower.) If you don't get in to that machine, try another one, such as `ftp://coral.bucknell.edu//pub/mac/net/macweb.latest.sea.hqx`; ftp sites often get busy and refuse connections. Unstuff the archive, if necessary (Anarchie should have done this automatically).

Like that procedure better than ftp on UNIX? Now you're beginning to get a taste of what all the fuss is about! But the best is yet to come. Run MacWeb. Try to tear yourself away after a while and get some sleep. Don't forget to eat.

Reading Mail via TIA

It's very easy to configure Eudora (`ftp://ftp.qualcomm.com/quest/mac/eudora/beta/eudora151b1.hqx`) to run with TIA. Choose Settings from the Special menu. The Settings dialog box has several sections, which you select by clicking the icons at the left. In the first section, enter your POP mail account and Real Name, and choose MacTCP as the Connection Method. Your POP mail account is just your user ID followed by **@127.0.0.1** (for example, **billa@127.0.0.1**). You can use anything as your Real Name, but your correspondents will get tired of cutesy aliases real fast.

In the Personal Information section, enter your return address and user name (the other boxes should already be filled in). Your return address must be a valid e-mail address; otherwise, your friends won't be able to reply to your messages. Your address usually is your user ID, followed by @ and your domain name; it should be the same address that you've been using with your shell account (for example, `billa@netcom.com`). Your Dialup user name is just the user ID that you type at the login prompt.

In the Hosts section, enter **127.0.0.1** in the SMTP box.

Some people say that the use of 127.0.0.1 (or localhost) in this context depends on a bug in MacTCP. This point is debatable. If you're worried about it, you can just use your ISP's host name instead (for example, `POP: billa@netcom5.netcom.com; SMTP: netcom8`), or you can use TIA's -n option to set up another alias for the local machine.

Reading News via TIA

Normally, setting up your favorite newsreader is even easier than setting up mail. Just enter your NNTP server in the appropriate place, and away you go.

But for those of us whose benighted Internet providers do not or will not provide access to an NNTP server, Cyberspace has generously provided a special news server (an nntp daemon) that is customized for use with TIA. (As of this writing, only a SunOS version is available.)

This works only with TIA version 1.0.4c or later. The two necessary files are available from Cyberspace in the beta directory (`ftp://marketplace.com/tiabeta/`).

The TIA binary must be installed; nntpd must be in your path and must be executable.

Netcom users can just make links to the most recent versions that Barry Nathan has generously agreed to make available to the rest of us. At your Netcom shell prompt, enter the following:

```
% cd
 % ln -s ~barryn/pub/tia tia
 % ln -s ~barryn/pub/nntpd nntpd
```

Then create a file called .tiarc in your home directory, which contains the following line:

```
-p:119 nntpd
```

You must restart TIA (not your Mac) for these changes to take effect. (Just disconnect and reconnect with InterSLIP.) Start TIA manually, and observe its output to make sure that you've got everything right. The output should look like the following:

```
% tia
 The Internet Adapter (tm) 1.04c for SunOS
 Copyright (c) 1994 Cyberspace Development, Inc.
 Address:192.0.2.3 Port:119 is setup to run:nntpd
 Individual License
 Ready to start your SLIP software.
```

Finally, tell your newsreader that the NNTP server is 192.0.2.3. By far the most popular newsreader is NewsWatcher, by John Norstad of Disinfectant fame (`ftp://ftp.acns.nwu.edu/pub/newswatcher/newswatcher-20b16.sea.hqx`).

Figure 15-4 shows my NewsWatcher server addresses settings, and Figure 15-5 shows my Personal Information settings.

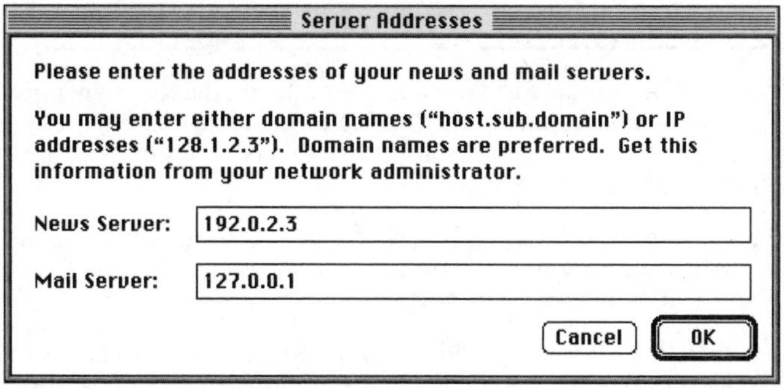

Server Addresses

Please enter the addresses of your news and mail servers.

You may enter either domain names ("host.sub.domain") or IP addresses ("128.1.2.3"). Domain names are preferred. Get this information from your network administrator.

News Server: 192.0.2.3

Mail Server: 127.0.0.1

Cancel OK

Figure 15-4: The NewsWatcher server.

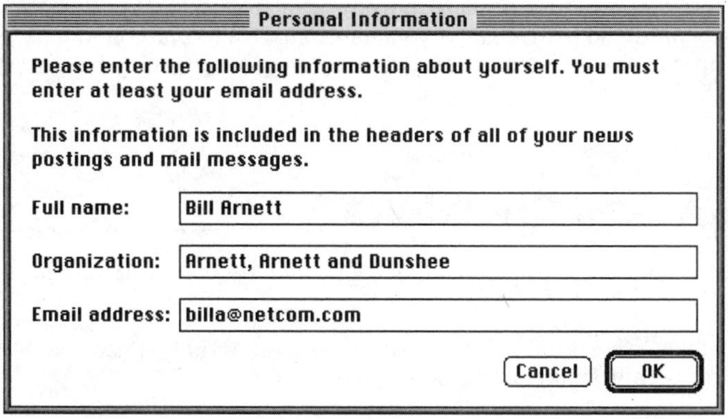

Personal Information

Please enter the following information about yourself. You must enter at least your email address.

This information is included in the headers of all of your news postings and mail messages.

Full name: Bill Arnett

Organization: Arnett, Arnett and Dunshee

Email address: billa@netcom.com

Cancel OK

Figure 15-5: Personal Information settings.

The Quickie Shell

Bored with logging in all the time? Want to save some CPU cycles for your friendly ISP? Then use TIA's nifty -p option. Just put a line containing -p in your .tiarc file (this is *in addition to* the line that you may have set up for news). Then tell telnet to connect to 192.0.2.3, and presto — you have a shell prompt sans login. (This procedure is not a security hole; you logged in with the InterSLIP script, and this new shell is part of that session.)

The procedure works because the -p option tells TIA to interpret the telnet protocol itself and to send the characters that you type directly to a shell. Thereby, you avoid the extra overhead of a telnet process on your ISP's machine.

Pay Up!

When you have TIA working to your satisfaction, you must obtain a permanent license from Cyberspace. Mail in the license form again, this time requesting a permanent license and filling in the appropriate payment information. You'll get a new license code to put in your .tia file.

IMHO, this is the best $25 that I ever spent. Cyberspace Development is a tiny company with (obviously) very weak marketing: I would have gladly paid $100 and still considered TIA to be a great bargain.

If you're new to the Internet, consider buying Adam Engst's *The Internet Starter Kit, Version 2*, (Hayden Books, 1994) if you haven't already. This book is full of useful information that may be hard to get anywhere else, and reading it will save you a lot of time searching for answers. The book costs less than $30 at most bookstores.

Some of the TCP/IP software for the Mac is free, but much of it is shareware. If you use a shareware product, you are morally obligated to pay for it. Shareware authors work very hard and provide a very valuable service to our community. So do the Right Thing. You won't go to jail if you don't pay, but you may be reincarnated as a Denebian slime worm.

Frequently Asked Questions

I'm a power user. Do I have to read all the documents and README files that came with all this stuff?

No. But if you ask a dumb question and receive an RTFM ("Read The Manual") reply, you are automatically demoted to newbie.

This is great! Where can I find more cool TCP/IP programs?

Several dozen programs are available in the `info-mac` archive, which is mirrored at `ftp.hawaii.edu` (`ftp://ftp.hawaii.edu/mirrors/info-mac/comm/tcp/`) and many other sites. To find the site nearest you, get the mirror list (`ftp://ftp.hawaii.edu/mirrors/info-mac/help/mirror-list.txt`).

Isn't it dangerous to type my password to telnet?

It is indeed. Even though they don't echo, the characters that you type are being sent in the clear across the Net, and any determined hacker can break into your account this way. Of course, a break-in isn't very likely, but if you have anything really valuable on your account, don't send your password through the Net. It *is* OK, however, to use telnet to your own ISP (to the machine on which your copy of TIA is running). In this case, your password is sent directly through the phone to your ISP's machine and never gets out onto the Net.

Can I set up an ftp (or http) server?

No. This is one of the few ways in which TIA is inferior to a real SLIP connection.

What else can't I do with TIA that I can with "real" SLIP?

You can't run a finger daemon, because you don't have a genuine IP address, so you can finger but cannot be fingered, nor can you use talk or ntalk.

What's the difference between TIA and term?

term is an older shareware program that enables two UNIX machines to establish a TCP/IP connection. The program works only with UNIX; it's useless to Mac users.

We all know that SLIP stinks. I want to use PPP or at least CSLIP!

We also know that this is baloney. SLIP may be a hack, but it works just fine, thank you. CSLIP is slightly more efficient, but you have to make careful measurements to see the difference. PPP is a much nicer protocol and can handle protocols besides TCP/IP (such as AppleTalk or IPX), but why do you care? You're just trying to use the Net, not implement it. TIA will support PPP in an upcoming release.

Does TIA give me free access to America Online, CompuServe, and other on-line services?

Of course not. You can telnet to AOL (and maybe some of the others), but you still have to log in and pay the connect-time charges. Now that you have access to the Internet, though, who cares about the commercial services?

Where can I learn more about writing InterSLIP scripts?

Remember the document that InterSLIP Installer left on your Desktop? Too bad you Trashed it. The file contains a (brief) description of the CCL language that InterSLIP uses. Fish it out of your trash and read it.

Can I put back my other INITs now?

Sure. But don't call me if everything stops working.

What's the best way to get back to a shell on my UNIX machine?

Use telnet. It's possible to log in with your terminal emulator, start TIA manually, and then quit the terminal emulator and start InterSLIP without using dial and gateway scripts, but I don't recommend it. First, this procedure just doesn't work with internal modems. Second, it introduces yet another variable into an already complicated situation. And finally, it's more effort each time you start up. Go with the scripts, and use telnet when you need a shell.

Is there a newsgroup where I can ask other TIA users for advice?

Yes. TIA users of all flavors (with a heavy tilt toward Netcom) hang out at `alt.dcom.slip-emulators`. If you have a question that's not answered here or a problem that you can't figure out, try posting there. But woe unto he who asks a FAQ.

Can you recommend a modem initialization string?

First, try AT&F. If that doesn't work, check `modemstr.txt` for the compilation of modem strings that other users have reported to work with TIA and InterSLIP.

What are all those silly AT commands, anyway?

The best source of information is your modem's manual. But if you've lost the manual (or are just pathologically averse to reading on paper), you can find a copy of Apple's Express Modem AT Commands document (`ATcmds.txt`). Please be aware, however, that not all Hayes-compatible modems handle these commands in identical fashion.

Is there anything special for Express Modem users to worry about?

Make sure that you have turned Express Modem on in the Express Modem control panel. Make sure that you have chosen the Use External Modem option in the Express Modem Settings section.

Should I use my modem's compression and error-control features?

Initially, yes. Compression works fine for me. But many users who have slower Macs have found that turning off compression improves throughput, sometimes dramatically.

Can I use RAM Doubler or Apple's virtual memory?

Initially, yes. RAM Doubler works fine for me. But reliable sources have confirmed that slower Macs (and PowerMacs) can be seriously affected by either of these features. If your transfer rates aren't what you expect (1,400 cps with a 14,400-baud modem), try it without virtual memory and/or compression.

What other secret command line options does TIA have?

See the preliminary document by TIA's developer (`ftp://marketplace.com/tiabeta/changes.txt`).

Is there a way to monitor what's going on with TIA?

Peter Lewis's nifty MacTCP Watcher (`ftp://nic.switch.ch/software/mac/peterlewis/mactcpwatcher-112.sit.bin`) enables you to see statistics on your TCP/IP traffic and perform some tests. If you have trouble, this program can be a big help.

MacTCP Watcher says Failed to find a Domain Name System name for this Mac. *But I'm sure that I entered my DNS stuff right.*

Don't worry about this message; it's normal for TIA connections. The message is just an indication that your Mac can't act as a server.

Will TIA work over a telnet connection?

Yes, but you may have to use `telnet -e '' -8 ip.address.of.server` to get an 8-bit clean connection.

Does TIA work with FreeBSD using X Windows?

Matthew Deter (`mld@netcom.com`) wrote: "Yes. I've made it work. Get the `dialup.slip` FAQ from the cdrom site; follow those directions, along with the TIA directions, and you're up and running. Took me about a couple hours, with zero SLIP knowledge when I started."

I'm already using MacSLIP. Is there a MacSLIP script that I can use?

I wouldn't have put in this question if the answer was no. :-) See Mike Cohen's script (macslip.txt). You may have to set MacTCP to Manual addressing and remove the BOOTP & ipfind command from the script to make it work with TIA.

How do I get InterSLIP to set my IP address from my server's message?

If the server's message looks like Address:192.203.176.128, add the following code fragment at the appropriate point in your InterSLIP dial script:

```
@label 40
!the following line is to get IP address from the remote SLIP server
matchexp 1 50 "[0-9][0-9]*\\.[0-9][0-9]*\\.[0-9][0-9]*\\.[0-9][0-9]*"
!if the above express (IP address format) was matched, it jumps to label 50
matchread 120
jump 99
!
@label 50
!set the IP address according to the one you got from the SLIP server
setip "^0"
!now get the MTU size from the server
matchexp 1 60 "[0-9][0-9]*"
matchread 120
jump 99
!
@label 60
setmtu "^0"
exit 0
@label 99
exit -1
```

Can I make a gateway script to handle callback modems?

That depends on how good you are at InterSLIP scripting. Amanda Walker (amanda@intercon.com) offers the following general advice on how to write a callback gateway script:

- Sign on; do whatever the gateway needs.
- Wait for NO CARRIER.
- Wait for RING.
- If you get RING in the appropriate amount of time, send **ATA\13**, wait for CONNECT, and continue the sign-on process.
- If not, give up.

One of my less fortunate friends has a PC. What can I do for him?

See Mark Stout's FAQ (ftp://ftp.netcom.com/pub/mcstout/tia/tiasetup.html) and M'Lou Voss's directory (ftp://ftp.netcom.com/pub/mlou/), which contain some instructions for getting TIA working on PCs.

Are any other TIA FAQ files available?

You don't like my FAQ? Well, then, read the one from Cyberspace (`http://marketplace.com:70/0/tia/tia.faqs/tia.FAQ.single`) and the TIA Companion for the Macintosh by David Menges (`http://marketplace.com:70/0/tia/tia.faqs/tia.companion.mac.setup`).

I'm so happy — TIA has solved all my problems. Is world peace imminent?

Only if you pay your shareware fees.

Troubleshooting

I can't even get a telnet window after entering a valid IP address.

You're in trouble, all right. Try starting over from the top. And be more careful this time.

Telnet works OK with IP addresses, but not with names.

Your MacTCP DNS settings probably are wrong. Check the settings; fix them, if necessary; and reboot. If you're sure that you have the settings right, and telnet still doesn't work, remove MacTCP, MacTCP Prep, and MacTCP DNR. Reboot. Reinstall MacTCP from floppy disks. Get the settings right this time. Reboot again. If telnet still doesn't work, you need to get a real human being to help you (try asking for help on the newsgroup `alt.dcom.slip-emulators`).

I'm really stuck; I've tried everything. What now?

Reset your PRAM: restart while holding down ⌘-Option-P-R; restart again, and hold down ⌘-option to rebuild your Desktop. Reinstall your System from floppy disks (or CD-ROM), making sure that you do a clean install. Some users have reported trouble with AppleTalk and/or TokenTalk that can be fixed by using the Apple System disks to uninstall TokenTalk and AppleTalk.

TIA is slower than molasses in Minneapolis! What's going on?

Several possible causes have been confirmed:

- *RAM Doubler or virtual memory.* PowerMac users, and users of 68030 and slower Macs (all but 68040s), may have performance problems when they use RAM Doubler or Apple's virtual memory.
- *Compression.* PowerMac users, and users of 68030 and slower Macs (all but 68040s), may have performance problems when they use their modems' compression feature. Try adding **%C0** to the modem initialization string (or, better yet, check your modem's manual).
- *Activity indicators.* INITs (for example, CP Drivelight and Claris Power to Go) that display an on-screen indicator of disk or modem activity may cause problems.

- *DTE speed.* Some users have observed better performance by using InterSLIP's Baud Rate setting at 19,200 than at higher values.
- *Bad cables.* You must use a hardware handshake cable, as described earlier in "The right cable." Reportedly, a company called Celestin makes good HH cables; send e-mail to `celestin@pt.olympus.net`, or phone (206) 385-3767. Make sure that Hardware Handshake is selected in InterSLIP's setup dialog box.
- *Excessive retransmissions.* Some people have found that the problem is related to excessive retransmissions, presumably due to transmission errors. This problem can be caused by a variety of factors, including bad cables (they must be hardware handshake), noisy phone lines (complain to your phone company), and slow computers. In some cases, the problem can be ameliorated — if not eliminated — by decreasing the MTU size parameter (in InterSLIP Setup). Try a setting of about 500.
- *Autodoubler.* One user reports that removing AutoDoubler improved SLIP performance on his PowerMac.
- *Flow control.* Make sure your modem is set for hardware flow control (CTS/RTS) and *not* for XON/XOFF.

TIA stalls on me.

Many people have reported that their connection just stops sending and receiving at random times. You often can restart the connection by retrying the operation manually or by using another application to force some more traffic to be sent. The cause of this problem is unknown. Please let me know if you see this problem in a controlled circumstance wherein we can get some real information.

My newsreader says that it can't find any articles.

You must use TIA version 1.0.4c or later and the special nntpd version 1.5.11t5 or later. (You can check the version numbers simply by running tia and nntpd.)

I'm having trouble using TIA with my Xyplex server.

One user reports: "Previously, I used the telnet command from the terminal server to establish the connection to my host. I tried `rlogin` this time, and it works! In my case, I couldn't connect to *any* host before, not even my own. By the way, my terminal server is a Xyplex, if it makes any difference." You also may have to use set session passall.

If I get a busy signal, the InterSLIP script won't redial.

Try adding more delay between redials.

I can send small messages, but larger ones always fail.

This is typical of bad flow control settings. Make sure your modem is set for hardware flow control (CTS/RTS), not XON/XOFF.

Cyberspace

You can obtain more information about TIA (The Internet Adapter) directly from its creators at Cyberspace Development, Inc., via the Web (`http://marketplace.com/0/tia/tiahome.html`), through ftp (`ftp://marketplace.com/tia`), or simply by sending an empty e-mail message to `tia-info@marketplace.com`.

Bryan Griffin has done a wonderful job of implementing TIA. But equally important, if not more important, is his excellent support of his customers. He has not only fixed the few bugs that have turned up but has also implemented new features to make our lives easier. Thanks again, Bryan; good work!

Errors

Despite my best efforts, the references in this chapter will get out of date. If you find that one of them doesn't work, please let me know. In the meantime, you may be able to retrieve the file that you're looking for by examining the directory to which the reference points. If the file has a new version number, you'll find it this way. Please, please report any errors, bugs, typos, omissions, or anything else that you find wrong or misleading. I really value your feedback.

Art Kerns is an engineer with Qualcomm, Inc., of San Diego, where he is working on the Globalstar satellite phone system. He also has experience designing and programming real-time physics simulations for the Macintosh, including the HMWBS projectile simulator.

Chapter 16

OS/2 Warp and the Internet

by Timothy Sipples <tsipple@vnet.ibm.com>

IBM's flagship software for PCs, OS/2 Warp, ships with a BonusPak of full-fledged 32-bit applications, including a suite of Internet access applications. This chapter describes those applications, why you might choose OS/2 Warp to connect to the Internet, and how to configure and customize some of the special features found in the OS/2 Warp Internet Connection.

What Is OS/2 Warp?

OS/2 Warp is a family of software products from IBM designed to support the widest possible variety of applications (DOS, Windows, and OS/2) and to deliver 32-bit object-oriented technologies for the next generation of applications. In its first *two months,* OS/2 Warp sold well over one million copies worldwide. Much of that demand is undoubtedly fueled by OS/2 Warp's new BonusPak, a collection of free applications provided with the product. The highlight of that BonusPak is the *Internet Connection.*

The Internet Connection supplied with the basic OS/2 Warp package provides everything you need to access the Internet using a direct dialup connection. There are two modem dialers supplied with the package. One registers you with the IBM Global Network (currently the only worldwide dialup Internet service provider), and the other lets you sign onto any third-party provider of your choice. Three free hours of Internet access on the IBM Global Network are provided with every copy of OS/2 Warp.

OS/2 Warp's BonusPak also includes Person to Person, Video IN, Multimedia Viewer, and other applications that work with the Internet Connection software.

- *Person to Person* allows you to engage in conference calls on your PC, where you can exchange information using a shared chalkboard and even broadcast video signals, if you have a high speed connection and the necessary hardware. Whatever you copy onto your chalkboard (such as a Lotus 1-2-3 spreadsheet) is seen by others in your Person to Person conference. Participants can draw lines, add text, point to items, and annotate inside the shared chalkboard window. Person to Person works over many types of networks, including the Internet Connection.
- *Video IN* allows you to record video clips from a VCR, laserdisc player, or other video signal, using any of several video capture adapters for your PC. Even if you do not have a video capture card, you can use OS/2 Warp's Video IN to create animated weather sequences, for example, like those you see on television as

part of the weather forecast. You can use the Internet Connection to download weather maps of your favorite part of the world and then assemble those weather maps into a movie using Video IN.

- *Multimedia Viewer* extends OS/2 Warp's multimedia capabilities so that you can view and collect several image types (such as Kodak Photo CD, TIFF, JPEG, GIF, Targa, and others) as well as play back audio files from other systems (such as the Sun .AU format), file types common on the Internet.

OS/2 Warp has several key benefits that make it a powerful platform for accessing the Internet:

- *Multitasking:* One of OS/2's key strengths for years has been its ability to handle communications (including modem traffic) in the background reliably along with other tasks. OS/2 Warp provides true preemptive multitasking and multithreading (often called *real multitasking*). Other operating environments, including Microsoft Windows and Macintosh System 7, provide cooperative multitasking. The difference is that OS/2 Warp, and not individual applications, is in charge of your PC's processor. In a cooperative multitasking system, if one application does not yield control of your PC's processor back to the operating system in timely fashion, everything else stops running. With OS/2 Warp, you can reliably and confidently download a file from the Internet using ftp, browse the World Wide Web, format a disk, print a document using your favorite word processor, and still run other DOS, Windows, and OS/2 applications. File transfers will not abort, and connections won't be dropped simply because you try to go do something else.

- *Preemptive Multitasking:* With OS/2 Warp, you can spend your time doing other things while receiving information from the Internet (or doing other tasks that don't require your input). That capability allows you to save a lot of on-line time (and charges), because you can have several tasks running at once. (Many OS/2 Warp users, for example, run two or more copies of the IBM Web Explorer simultaneously. While one is retrieving a page from the World Wide Web, the other can display a page to be read, without in any way disturbing any other task.) Preemptive multitasking also means that OS/2 Warp can easily be used as a server, delivering information over the Internet as requested. OS/2 Warp systems are used as ftp, Gopher, and even World Wide Web servers, for example.

- *Price:* Many Internet software packages are sold in software dealerships, often for $100 or more. The entire OS/2 Warp package, including the BonusPak with the Internet Connection, is typically priced at $79 or less. The user community for OS/2 Warp is active, enthusiastic, and quickly growing, and you can get help, advice, and assistance from members of that community through the Internet.

Installing Warp

The Internet Connection (and other BonusPak applications) comes on a separate set of disks (or CD-ROM) in the OS/2 Warp package. Inside the BonusPak box, you'll find a brief manual explaining each of the BonusPak applications and how to install them. A common installation program is provided (INSTALL.CMD), which you should use. Select those applications you wish to install, one by one, from the installation program.

If you have the CD-ROM version of the OS/2 Warp BonusPak, be sure to select the correct version for the country where you live. The BonusPak CD-ROM contains directories (such as US for United States and NO for Norway) for the various countries of the world. Run INSTALL.CMD from the correct directory.

You do not have to shut down and reboot your PC until after you have installed all the BonusPak applications you wish to use, after you have exited the common installation program. In other words, you do not need to reboot after installing each single application.

To shut down your OS/2 Warp PC, either:

- Move the mouse pointer so that it is pointing anywhere on the desktop background. Tap the right mouse button. Select Shutdown.

or

- Click the Shutdown button (a little picture of a PC with a moon on-screen) located on the LaunchPad.

A proper shutdown ensures that all the changes you have made to your desktop are saved.

Registering with the IBM Global Network

Even if you plan to use a third-party Internet provider, you should register with the IBM Global Network to use your three hours of free time (see Figure 16-1). The Internet Connection software is designed to be upgraded over a modem, and the IBM Global Network will automatically update your OS/2 Warp Internet Connection to the latest version when you first sign on.

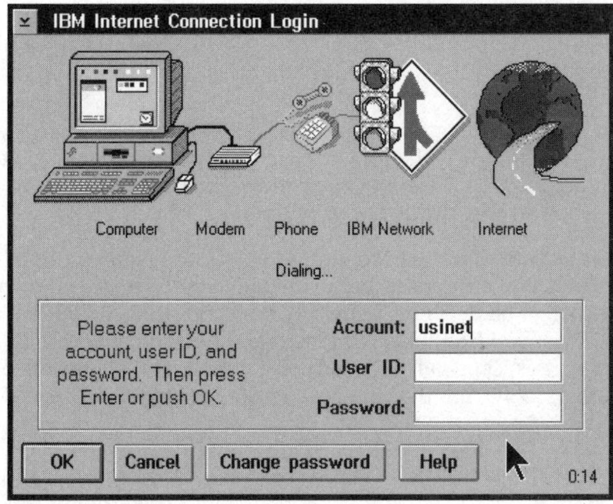

Figure 16-1: Using the IBM global network.

Plus, you can download the IBM Web Explorer (a free World Wide Web browser for OS/2 Warp) by double-clicking the Retrieve Software Updates icon, located in your IBM Internet Connection for OS/2 folder (see Figure 16-2). You can also retrieve the latest version of the Internet Connection software and the Web Explorer via anonymous ftp from `ftp.ibm.net`, no matter what Internet service provider you choose to use.

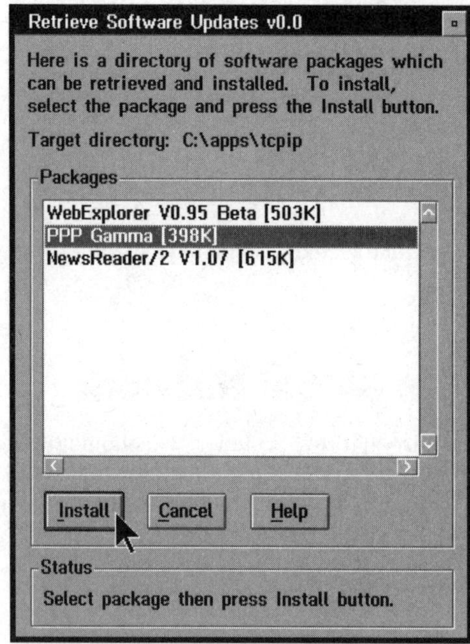

Figure 16-2: Retrieving software updates.

If you ever need help accessing the IBM Global Network, double-click the Customer Assistance icon (located inside the IBM Internet Customer Services folder), and click the Ask for help button. Telephone numbers and other ways of reaching IBM Global Network support worldwide are provided.

The latest rate information for your country is provided when you sign onto the IBM Global Network. When the rates are displayed, you have the opportunity to then proceed with sign on or abort. Generally speaking, IBM Global Network's rates are attractive if you travel from place to place (and need local access to the Internet from two or more cities, especially abroad) or if you must dial long-distance (and incur extra charges) to dial another Internet service provider.

If you live in a major metropolitan area served by other Internet service providers, and you rarely (if ever) need access to the Internet from other cities, you might want to investigate other providers, which may be less expensive.

After you have installed the Internet Connection and restarted your OS/2 Warp PC, you should see a folder called IBM Information Superhighway on your desktop. Double-click this folder to open it and then double-click the IBM Internet Connection for OS/2 folder. Inside, you see a folder called IBM Internet Customer Services. Double-click this folder; then double-click the Registration icon located inside.

Follow the instructions provided to sign on. Make sure your modem is turned on and working. If you do not know which type of modem you have, just choose Default. Make sure you select the correct speed for your modem. A V.32bis modem, for example, usually works best set to 19,200 bps.

Be sure to write down your account information (especially your password). You will need your password every time you sign on to the IBM Global Network to access the Internet. You can sign onto the IBM Global Network using the IBM Internet Dialer program (in your IBM Internet Connection for OS/2 folder) (see Figure 16-3) or by double-clicking any of the available applications (such as Gopher).

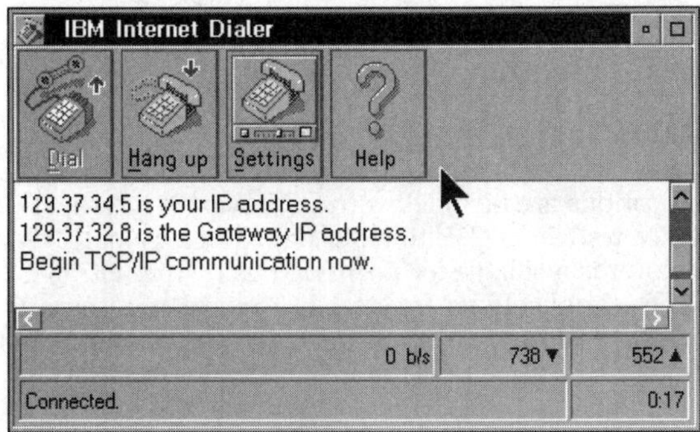

Figure 16-3: The dialer window.

You can modify the settings for your modem, local access number, and other settings from the dialer. Start the Internet Dialer and then click the Cancel button to prevent your modem from dialing. A second window, which provides information on the commands sent to your modem, pops up. Just click the settings button, and an OS/2 settings notebook for the dialer with then appear (see Figure 16-4). This settings notebook is a common fixture in OS/2 Warp, and it is used for altering the properties of virtually any object. Click the tabs of the notebook to switch among categories of settings, and click the arrows in the lower-right of the notebook to flip pages back and forth. (You can also open the Dialer's settings notebook by pointing to the Internet Dialer icon, clicking the right mouse button, and selecting Settings.)

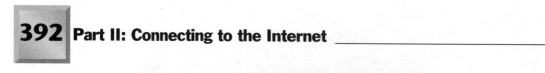

Figure 16-4: The dialer settings notebook.

Internet Connection Applications

The key Internet applications are included with OS/2 Warp's Internet Connection. They include Gopher, NewsReader/2, Ultimedia Mail/2 Lite, Telnet, Telnet 3270, and ftp (the IBM Web Explorer is available for download using the Retrieve Software Updates program). These applications are straightforward counterparts to versions on other platforms. However, there are some special features unique to OS/2 Warp.

NewsReader/2

The Internet Connection's NewsReader/2 is a graphical application to access NNTP (Network News Transport Protocol) Internet news servers. This application communicates with the news server over your connection with the Internet provider to receive messages contained in the 10,000 plus newsgroups found on the Internet. (Your provider may not give you access to all of them.) Facilities are provided for reading messages, posting or mailing replies, using your favorite text editor, and even decoding so-called Rot13 messages, which is an encoding method often used by people who wish to provide mild protection against accidental reading of a message. For example, Rot13 can be used to encode messages that contain information about the plot in a new movie, including its conclusion, and you as a reader have to go through the task of directing NewsReader/2 to decode the Rot13 text if you want the information.

NewsReader/2 is not a "threaded" newsreader, meaning that it does not provide total flexibility over following "threads" of messages by subject. However, you can achieve a somewhat similar effect by changing NewsReader/2's settings to sort newsgroups by subject.

The first time you start NewsReader/2, you are prompted to obtain the full list of available newsgroups. Allow NewsReader/2 to fetch this list, but go ahead and use some of the other Internet Connection applications while the list is downloading. (See Figures 16-5, 16-6, and 16-7.)

Many Internet messages are intended to be viewed on dumb terminals, where the characters on a given line can line up exactly with characters located on lines below. People often construct elaborate (or not so elaborate) text “drawings,” using vertical bars, dashes, and other characters to create boxes and other shapes, lines, and pictures. These features will not display correctly unless you are using a monospaced (as opposed to proportionally spaced) typeface. In NewsReader/2, you can select either the System VIO or System Monospaced screen fonts (in your choice of sizes) to get better results when viewing messages that contain ASCII art.

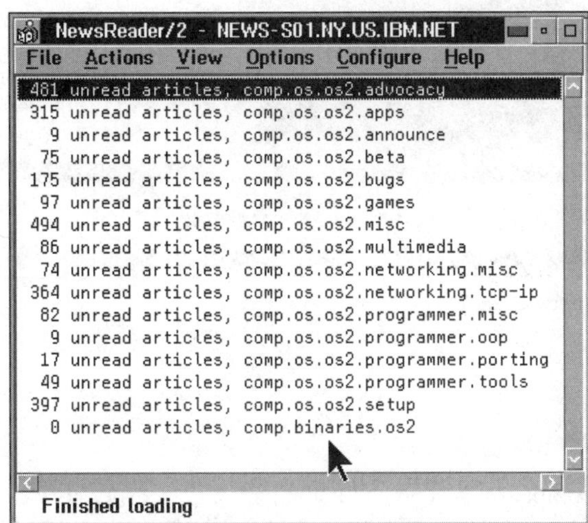

Figure 16-5: Newsgroup selection window.

Article List - comp.os.os2.programmer.oop
File Edit Actions View Help
388 WPCAR, idl version compile , HOW ? (Jan Sladky) [37]
389 Re: XDF diskette in WARP (C. Glenn Jordan) [18]
390 Re: Resolution of Templates with Watcom C++? (Thomas Greve) [56]
391 WPCAR, idl version, How do i compile it without errors ? (Jan Sladky) [37]
392 SOM Infos ??? alrau@ibm.net [4]
393 Re: SOM Infos ??? (Paul Prescod) [10]
394 Re: XDF diskette in WARP Thomas van Kuipers <tjwhkuip@cs.ruu.nl> [27]
395 UICL Question -- please read janovetz@coewl.cen.uiuc.edu [19]
396 Re: UICL Question -- please read (Solution Technology) [25]

Figure 16-6: News article selection window.

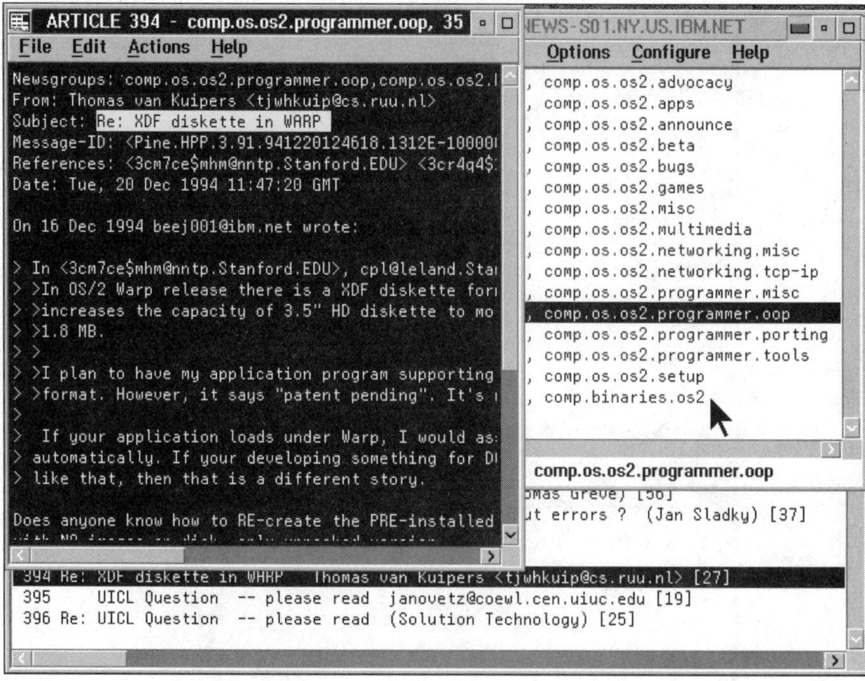

Figure 16-7: Reading a news article.

Ultimedia Mail/2 Lite

This mailer is POP-compliant, so you can use it with any Internet service provider that provides a POP mail server. It also supports MIME mail, so you can easily send and receive binary attachments to e-mail (including multimedia files, Kodak Photo CD images, and so on). Figure 16-8 shows the Ultimedia folder.

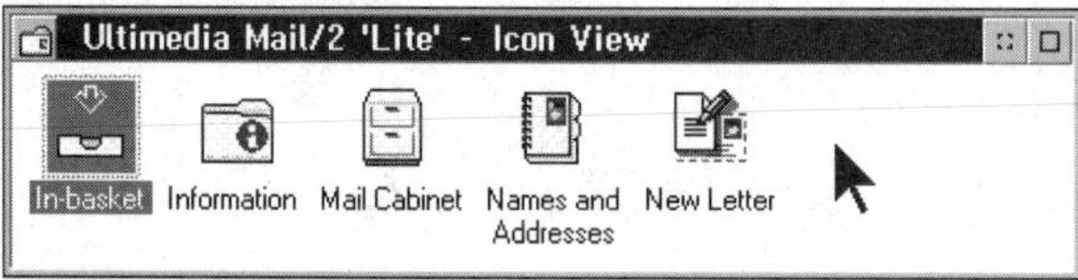

Figure 16-8: The Ultimedia folder.

The Ultimedia Mail/2 Lite folder contains the various parts of this e-mail application. To check whether you have received any electronic mail, simply double-click the In-basket icon. After Ultimedia Mail has connected to the server, any e-mail in your in-box is displayed with some basic information (subject and author).

The icon to the left of each piece of mail may contain a number inside. If so, it indicates that the message has not only a text part but also attachments (such as binary files). The number indicates the total number of parts contained in that piece of e-mail — the main text counts as one part. Simply double-click a piece of e-mail to open and read it. A menu is available for each piece of e-mail. Simply point to the piece of e-mail and click the right mouse button. You can use this menu to delete e-mail that you do not wish to read, for example.

Use the sample e-mail that the IBM Global Network sends you to practice reading, editing, and deleting Internet electronic mail.

You can save e-mail in folders, collecting related pieces of mail in any chosen categories. Mail that you send is automatically saved in its own folder so that you have a record of correspondence with other people. To draft a new piece of e-mail and send it to someone else, double-click the New Letter icon. The main window for composing e-mail then appears.

Every time you connect to your Internet service provider, be sure to check your In-basket. You will not be automatically notified that you have e-mail waiting. However, most POP mail servers hold your e-mail for long periods of time, so if you do not remember to check, your mail won't be lost just because you hang up.

When you use the IBM Global Network to access the Internet, your e-mail address is `username@ibm.net`, where *username* is whatever name IBM assigned to you when you registered. You can give this Internet address to other people, and they can send e-mail to you from anywhere in the world.

Telnet and Telnet 3270

The templates for these applications are located in the Application Templates folder (located in the IBM Internet Connection for OS/2 folder) (see Figure 16-9). To create a telnet session, for example, simply "tear off" one of the telnet templates and drag it to any other folder (or to the desktop). Remember that OS/2 Warp, by default, uses the second (right) mouse button to drag and drop. Then fill in the host information with the name of the system you wish to reach using telnet. The Telnet 3270 (for accessing mainframe computers across the Internet) and ftp templates work similarly. If you don't want to create an icon for every system you log onto, use the Telnet, Telnet 3270, and ftp icons located in Internet Utilities folder.

Figure 16-9: Application templates folder.

You can cut and paste using the Internet Connection's Telnet and Telnet 3270 applications, as shown in Figure 16-10. (The Telnet 3270 icon is used for accessing IBM mainframe systems over the Internet. For example, you can reach the IBM OS/2 BBS subscription service and other IBMLink services by using Telnet 3270 to connect to `ibmlink.advantis.net`.) Command-line (character mode) versions of these applications are available as well from any OS/2 command line, full screen or windowed.

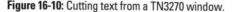

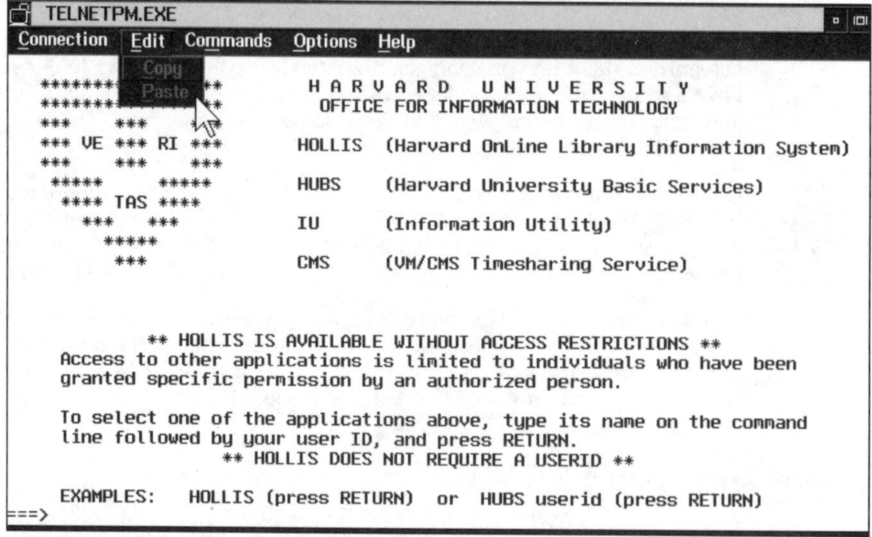
TELNETPM.EXE
Connection Edit Commands Options Help
Copy
Paste
H A R V A R D U N I V E R S I T Y
OFFICE FOR INFORMATION TECHNOLOGY
VE RI
TAS
HOLLIS (Harvard OnLine Library Information System)
HUBS (Harvard University Basic Services)
IU (Information Utility)
CMS (VM/CMS Timesharing Service)
** HOLLIS IS AVAILABLE WITHOUT ACCESS RESTRICTIONS **
Access to other applications is limited to individuals who have been
granted specific permission by an authorized person.
To select one of the applications above, type its name on the command
line followed by your user ID, and press RETURN.
** HOLLIS DOES NOT REQUIRE A USERID **
EXAMPLES: HOLLIS (press RETURN) or HUBS userid (press RETURN)
===>

Figure 16-10: Cutting text from a TN3270 window.

TIP

The Telnet and Telnet 3270 applications do not include built-in file transfer capabilities. If the system you wish to connect to supports it, simply open another window and use ftp to transfer files. However, some systems will not allow ftp for sending and receiving files (CompuServe, for example, which you can reach by using Telnet to connect to `compuserve.com`). If so, you may wish to use the freely available C-Kermit for OS/2 as a replacement for Telnet. Or you can use the SIO package of drivers (with VMODEM) to allow any communications software to operate over a telnet connection. C-Kermit, SIO, and many other OS/2 Warp Internet packages are available from the ftp sites listed in the section entitled "Resources on the Internet for OS/2 Warp Users."

File transfer protocol

The OS/2 Warp Internet Connection comes with both command-line (character mode) ftp (file transfer protocol) and graphical versions of ftp for sending and receiving files from various servers on the Internet.

The graphical version (FTPPM) first presents a window (shown in Figure 16-11) that prompts you for login information, such as your user name and password. Many servers are so-called anonymous servers (meaning that a user name of **anonymous** allows you to log on and retrieve any files located in public directories). You should, however, still enter your e-mail address as a password. (Some anonymous ftp servers even require it.) Ordinarily, you can leave the Account entry blank; some systems — primarily IBM mainframes — may require it, but most do not.

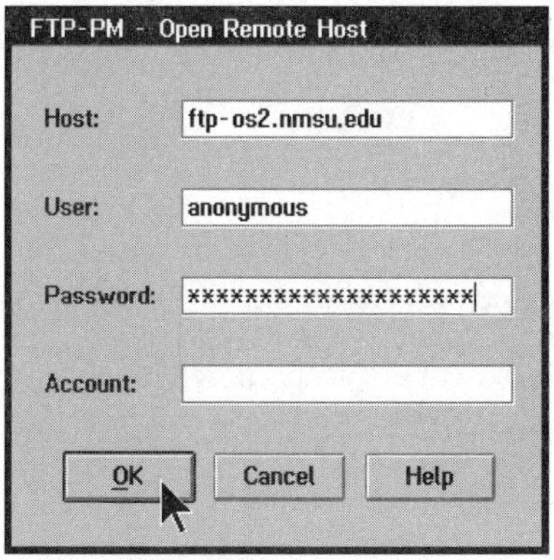

Figure 16-11: FTP login.

The main FTPPM window (see Figure 16-12) has two primary sections. At the top you see a view of your own PC's hard disk, and you can navigate through directories and select files just as you can with most other applications. In the section that follows, you see a directory listing from the remote ftp server, and you can navigate through its directories in the same way.

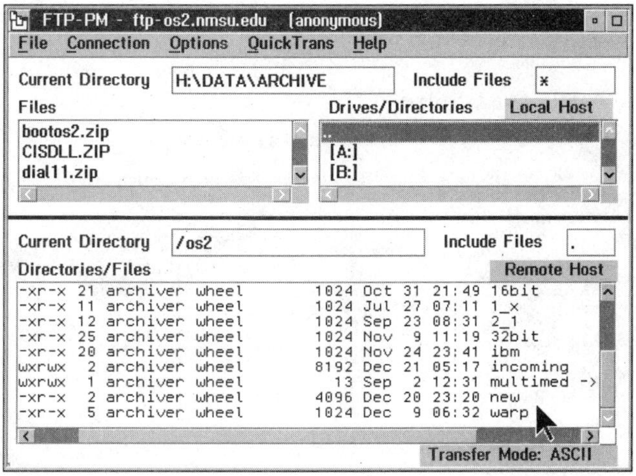

Figure 16-12: Selecting files for ftp.

There are two common pitfalls encountered by first-time users of FTPPM:

- The most common error is forgetting to select the correct file type before transferring a file. There are two file types available: ASCII (plain text) and binary. The default is ASCII, but the default may not be appropriate depending on the type of file you are trying to send or receive. Also, you should remember that most remote ftp servers are case-sensitive (so if you have to type a filename, be sure the case you type matches its directory listing, letter for letter).
- Be sure that you have indicated where you want files to go when you download files from remote servers. Otherwise, FTPPM is likely to place them in the root directory on your PC's hard disk, and you may not want them there.

Gopher

Gopher (see Figure 16-13) is supplied with OS/2 Warp and provides the capability to navigate through a set of interconnected servers on the Internet. You can double-click menus and files listed in your Gopher window to navigate across various Internet servers. Weather maps, software, library catalogs, and much more are available.

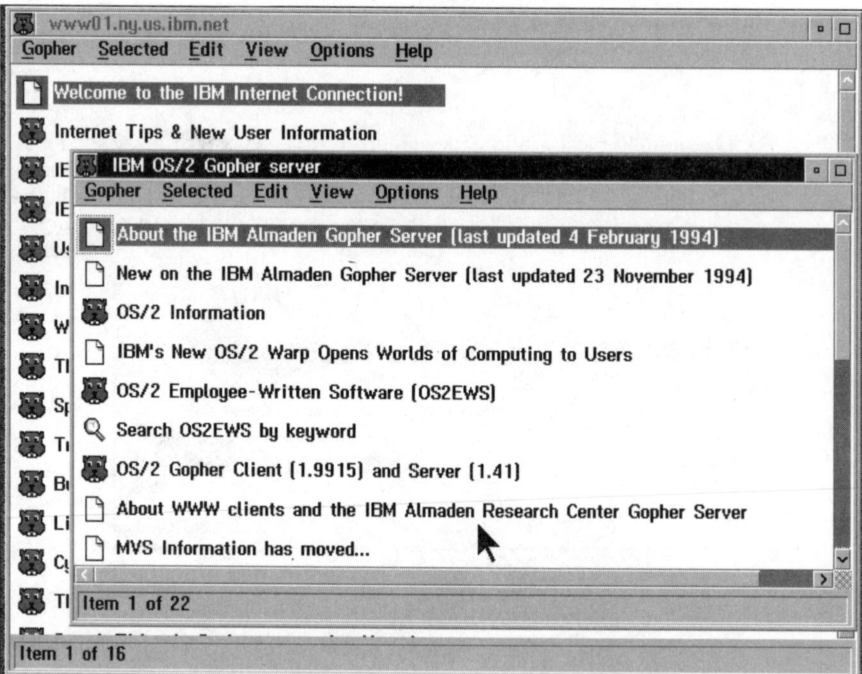

Figure 16-13: A Gopher menu.

OS/2's Gopher is quite straightforward. You can readily distinguish between files and submenus by looking at the icons to the left of each menu item. Submenus are indicated by gopher icons. If you double-click a submenu, you get a window with a new set of options.

Gopher will, by default, create a new window when your menu selection takes you to another server. You can use this to speed up your searches, because you can go back to the original window and select another menu option to branch off in a different direction. In fact, as with other applications on OS/2 Warp, you can use other Gopher windows while one is still downloading information from a server. To get a list of all the open Gopher windows, simply bring up the OS/2 Warp Window List by pressing Ctrl+Esc.

IBM Web Explorer

The IBM Web Explorer (see Figure 16-14) is a free, downloadable addition to your Internet Connection. You can install it on your system by double-clicking the Retrieve Software Updates icon.

The Web Explorer, like Mosaic and other browsers, is designed to access the Internet's World Wide Web. It is a fully multithreaded browser, meaning that it can receive multiple incoming streams of information simultaneously. This multithreaded design speeds up retrieval of WWW pages.

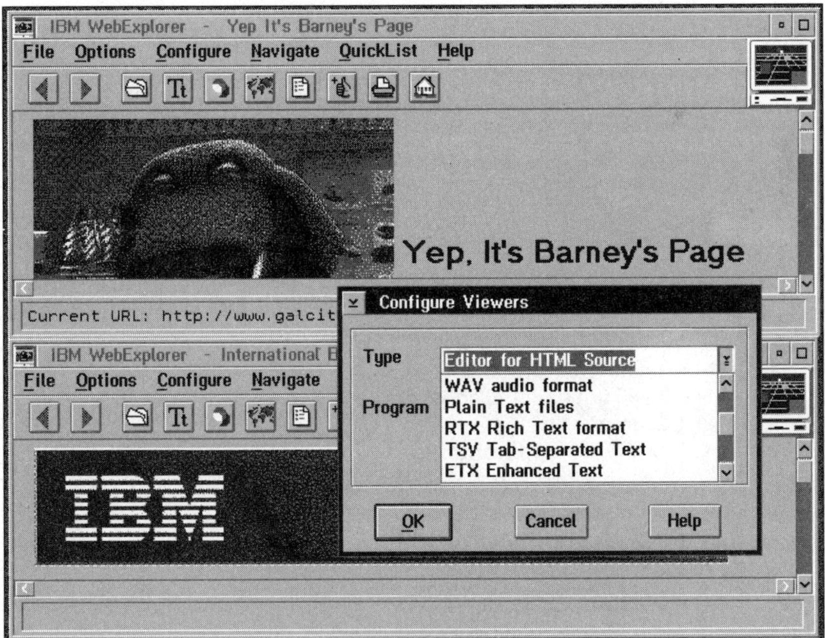

Figure 16-14: Web explorer and a large, dangerous saurian.

You can configure the Web Explorer to use practically any external program for viewing various file types (audio, video, pictures, and so on). However, by default the Web Explorer uses both internal viewers and (if installed) the BonusPak's Multimedia Viewer to handle the wide variety of file types stored in WWW pages. Many of these file types are not native to the PC, and the Multimedia Viewer can convert such files to PC readable formats. (For example, Sun .AU audio files are very common, and the Multimedia Viewer includes support for listening to these audio files.)

Because the World Wide Web is highly graphical, you will get best results by using the Web Explorer on a display with 256 colors or more. Also, WWW pages can be large (and take lots of time to download). However, there are ways you can make your time on the World Wide Web much more efficient using the Web Explorer:

- Use two (or more) copies of the Web Explorer simultaneously. While one is downloading a page, you can be reading and selecting a link in another. By default, OS/2 Warp will not start multiple copies of any object simply by double-clicking its icon again. To change this default behavior, simply point the mouse pointer at the Web Explorer program object, tap the right mouse button, and then select Settings. The familiar OS/2 settings notebook appears. Click the Window tab, and change the object open behavior to open another window. Close the settings notebook, and then double-click the Web Explorer icon to launch another copy.
- Use the QuickList feature to save favorite pages you have visited. The Web Map feature can help you track where you've been.
- Save pictures and even entire WWW pages using OS/2 Warp's drag-and-drop features. The pictures and other elements in a WWW page, as viewed by the IBM Web Explorer, are objects. Using the right mouse button, you can drag and drop a picture of Barney the Dinosaur, for example, to your OS/2 Warp desktop or any folder to save it. You can use this method to create an animated weather sequence from weather maps (in tandem with the BonusPak's Video IN application). Be careful, though, that you do not violate any copyright restrictions.

Timeout

As a safeguard to prevent runaway charges, the Internet Connection automatically disconnects after a few minutes of inactivity. Figure 16-15 shows the Timeout Warning dialog box. However, if you are running any application (such as ping) that automatically sends traffic over your modem connection at periodic intervals, the time-out will not happen, and you will remain connected. Do not rely solely on this time-out feature; be sure to disconnect if you walk away from your PC, especially if you have Internet applications such as ping running.

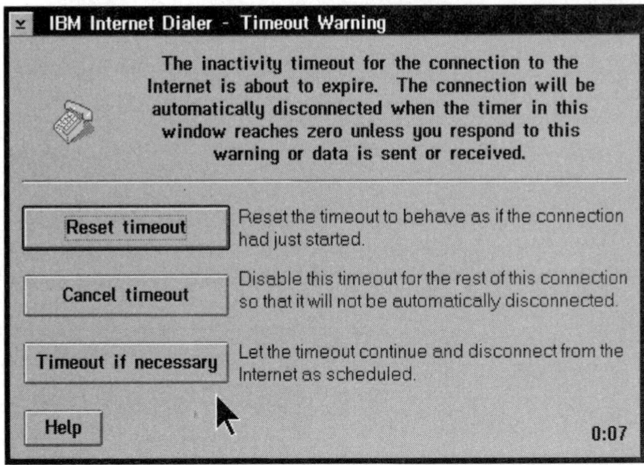

Figure 16-15: Timeout handling.

Resources on the Internet for OS/2 Warp Users

You can receive help, information, tips and techniques, and other assistance using OS/2 Warp through the Internet. The OS/2 Warp community on the Internet is large and friendly. The following five sections show just some of the places to visit.

Newsgroups

```
comp.os.os2.misc

comp.os.os2.advocacy

comp.os.os2.apps

comp.os.os2.networking.misc

comp.os.os2.networking.tcp-ip

comp.os.os2.programmer.oop

comp.os.os2.programmer.tools

comp.os.os2.programmer.porting

comp.os.os2.programmer.misc
```

comp.os.os2.games

comp.os.os2.setup

comp.os.os2.bugs

comp.os.os2.beta

comp.os.os2.announce

comp.binaries.os2

comp.lang.rexx

Anonymous ftp

ftp-os2.cdrom.com

ftp-os2.nmsu.edu

software.watson.ibm.com

Gopher

index.almaden.ibm.com

World Wide Web

http://www.ibm.com

http://www.ibm.net

http://www.mit.edu:8001/activities/os2

http://www.ccsf.caltech.edu/~kasturi/os2.html

http://www.iti.salford.ac.uk/os2power/os2power.html

http://www.gcr.com/mall

http://128.32.123.3/os2

Internet Relay Chat (IRC)

```
#os/2
```

Popular Additions to the Internet Connection

You can retrieve free and low-cost software to add to your OS/2 Warp system from the above anonymous ftp sites. Here are some of the most popular packages:

Name	*Purpose*
C-Kermit	Used as a replacement for Telnet, providing Kermit file transfer capabilities.
NetSuite	A collection of popular Internet applications (ftp, gopher, news reader).
IRC/2	Internet relay chat for OS/2 Warp.
GoServe	An IBM-written Gopher server for OS/2 Warp; takes advantage of REXX.
OS2HTTD	A World Wide Web server for OS/2 Warp.
P2P-FT	A file transfer capability for OS/2 Warp's Person to Person application.

More applications are being written and released with each passing month, so consult the OS/2 newsgroups and ftp sites for the latest news.

You can also use any Windows Internet software with OS/2 Warp's Internet Connection. The Internet Connection includes WinSock support (using the WINSOCK.DLL file). Please be sure, though, that the WINSOCK.DLL file supplied by the Internet Connection is the only file by that name on your PC's hard disk.

Using Third-Party Dialup Internet Providers

You need not use the IBM Global Network to access the Internet with OS/2 Warp. (However, three hours of access is free, and you should use it at least to get the latest versions of Internet software.) The Internet Connection (after using the Retrieve Software Updates program) supports connections to almost any third-party Internet service provider using the standard SLIP or PPP protocols.

The dialer even supports scripting, using OS/2's built-in REXX programming language, so it can respond to any given login procedure used by your preferred Internet provider. A sample script, ANNEX.CMD, is provided with the Internet Connection to get you started. Consult the on-line help for complete information on how to create such a script. In most cases, though, either you will not need a special script or your Internet service provider of choice has the necessary information you need to get connected. Be sure to ask your provider for instructions on using OS/2 Warp to connect.

The Dial Other Internet Providers icon is located in the Internet Utilities folder and is the application used (instead of the IBM Internet Dialer) to access third-party providers (see Figure 16-16). You can place several different providers (and dialup access numbers) in the Dial Other... directory. Be sure to select SLIP, CSLIP (SLIP with VJ compression), or PPP protocol, as appropriate.

Once connected to your Internet provider, all the Internet Connection applications will operate exactly the same way, provided the numeric Internet addresses for the various servers required (nameserver, POP mail server, and so on) are correctly configured.

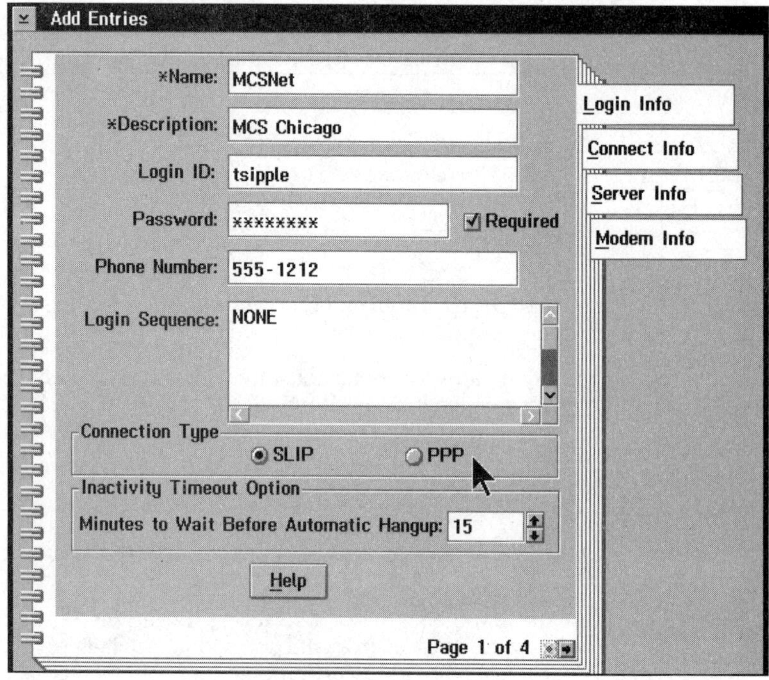

Figure 16-16: Dialing other providers.

Using OS/2 Warp's Internet Connection with a Network Card

OS/2 Warp's Internet Connection ships with support for dialup SLIP and PPP connections, but what if you want to use all these applications over a network card to connect to the Internet? Assuming that your network card is connected into the Internet (perhaps at a university), any of the following software packages allow OS/2 Warp's Internet software to work over your network card:

- IBM LAN Server 4 Requester (Client) for OS/2
- IBM DCE Client Kit for OS/2
- IBM AnyNet/2
- IBM TCP/IP Version 2 for OS/2 Base Services Kit with latest Service Pak

The least expensive of those (under $50 typically) is the LAN Server 4 requester. However, it is not sold separately with disks. The disks for the requester are bundled with IBM LAN Server 4. If you know someone who has IBM LAN Server 4, you can legally obtain a copy of the requester from that person if you purchase a separate license card for the requester from IBM or any IBM software dealer. The DCE Client is the second least expensive method (under $65 typically), and disks are provided (not just the right to copy) when you purchase it.

Please note that when you are using OS/2 Warp's Internet Dialer, all traffic is routed over the dialup connection, and any traffic over the network card is suspended. If you close the Internet Dialer, traffic over your network card resumes.

At the time of this writing in late 1994, IBM had started testing a release of OS/2 Warp with additional bundled applications (including full support for Ethernet, Token Ring, and other network cards) formerly sold separately. This so-called "OS/2 Warp for Networks" is scheduled for release sometime in the spring of 1995. The larger BonusPak, with the extra networking software, will be available as an upgrade for base OS/2 Warp as well.

Timothy Sipples is an OS/2 Warp specialist for IBM and is based in Chicago, Illinois. He is the author of the OS/2 Warp Frequently Asked Questions List, *updated regularly and available for download from many places, including OS/2 ftp sites on the Internet. He writes for* OS/2 Magazine, OS/2 Personal, *and speaks at industry conferences, including SHARE and CAMP.*

Part III

Taming the Internet

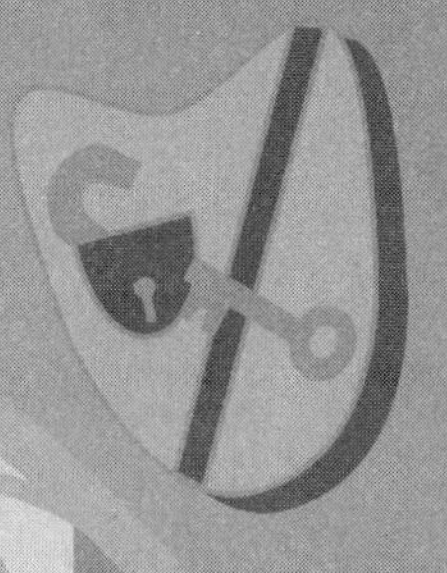

In This Part

Chapter 17 Signature, Finger, and Organization Header: Telling the World Who You Are

Chapter 18 The Internet by E-Mail

Chapter 19 Supporting Non-English Characters in Internet Applications

Chapter 20 Finding Things on the Net

Chapter 21 Power IRC

Chapter 22 Scaling the World Wide Web

Chapter 23 Gopher Secrets

Chapter 24 Using WAIS

Chapter 25 Managing Mail

Chapter 26 Network News

Chapter 17

Signature, Finger, and Organization Header: Telling the World Who You Are

By Nancy McGough <inet-secrets@ii.com>

This chapter describes the following ways that you can tell people on the Internet more about yourself:

- Your signature file, which is automatically included in your mail and news messages
- Your finger information, which is displayed when people finger you
- Your Organization line, which is one of the headers in your mail and news messages

A few handy definitions

FQDN or fqdn	Fully qualified domain name.
less	Paging command for viewing files; like the *more* command, but better. Throughout this chapter you can replace *less* with a different pager, if you like.
mailer	Mail user agent (MUA), such as Pine or Elm
pico	A friendly text editor that is the default *pi*ne *co*mposer. Throughout this chapter you can replace *pico* with a different editor, if you like.
RFC	Internet Request for Comments document
URL	Uniform Resource Locator (specified in RFC1630)
~ or $HOME	Your home directory. You can always get to your home directory by typing **cd**.

Automatic Signature: Basic UNIX Instructions

You can have a signature appended to news articles and mail messages automatically. The method depends in part on your newsreader and mailer, but the procedure described in the following table works for many UNIX newsreaders and mailers. I use the pico text editor; if you prefer another editor, such as emacs or vi, you can use it instead.

Type or Do This . . .	*To Do This . . .*
cd	Change to your home directory.
pico .signature	Use the pico editor to create a .signature file (replace **pico** with another editor, if you like).
Your signature	Create the text for your signature. Most systems require your signature to be no more than four lines, and it's good "netiquette" to make it as short as possible.
Save and exit	In pico, press Ctrl-X to exit, and press **y** when you are asked whether you want to save your changes.
chmod 644 .signature	Make .signature readable by all programs and users.
ls -l .signature	Check the permission; it should say -rw-r--r--.
chmod a+x .	Make home directory searchable by all programs and users.
ls -ld .	Check permission of home directory; it should say drwx?-x?-x Each question mark can be the letter *r* or a hyphen (drwx--x--x, drwxr-xr-x, drwxr-x--x, drwx--xr-x are all acceptable).
ls -la .	Check permission of files in home directory. If any files are group- or other-writable (?????w??w?), you may want to change the permission by typing **chmod go-w *FileName*.**

On some systems, such as VMS, some files and directories in your home directory need to be writable by other programs and users, so change permissions only if you know what you're doing. For more information on changing permissions, see the chmod on-line manual pages.

For some newsreaders and mailers, the steps above are all you need to do to set up your signature. For example, the default behavior of pine, tin, and the rn family — rn, trn, strn, and Pnews — is to automatically append ~/.signature, if it exists, to outgoing messages. If you use elm, Berkeley mail, SUN OpenWindows Mail Tool, Emacs mail mode, MH, nn, or gnus, follow the additional instructions described in "Signature Instructions for Specific Programs," later in this chapter.

Testing Your Signature

After you set everything up, use your mailer to mail a test message to yourself, and then use your newsreader or news poster (such as nnpost or Pnews) to post an article to a test newsgroup (use a local newsgroup and set distribution to `local` to save bandwidth). Many newsreaders and mailers do not allow you to see your signature while you are composing a message; your signature is appended when you send the message. Notice also that many systems add a line with two hyphens followed by a space (--) to the top of your signature. This line is used by programs that automatically deal with mail or news to identify the start of the signature.

If you have a problem with your signature, see "Troubleshooting Signature Problems," later in this chapter.

Signature Instructions for Specific Programs

Many mail and news programs require that you do something extra to set up a signature. This section describes the most popular of these programs.

Pine

Pine automatically appends ~/.signature (if it exists) to your messages. Many people like to set the *signature-at-bottom* variable, which puts your signature below both your message and the message to which you are replying (if you include it). If you are forwarding a message, your signature will be put below the message that you write but above the forwarded message.

To use a file other ~/.signature for your signature, use the signature-file variable to specify the filename. You can use ~ for your $HOME directory.

See also:

Pine FAQs	`http://www.cac.washington.edu/pine/faq/` `ftp://ftp.cac.washington.edu/pine/docs/faq`
Pine manual	`pine`
Pine newsgroup	`comp.mail.pine`

Pine 3.90 and later

To change Pine's signature features, follow these steps:

1. **From the main menu in Pine, press** S **(for Setup).**
2. **Press** C **(for Configuration).**
3. **To change the value of the signature-at-bottom feature, move to the *signature-at-bottom* variable and then press** X **to set or unset this variable.**

Pine 3.89 and earlier

To change Pine's signature features in Pine 3.89 and earlier versions, you need to edit your ~/.pinerc file directly, as described in the following steps.

1. **At the UNIX prompt, type** cd **to go to your home directory.**
2. **To use the pico editor to edit your .pinerc file, type** pico .pinerc.
3. **To use pico's search tool, type** CTRL-W.
4. **At the** Search : **prompt, type** feature-list.
5. **Add** signature-at-bottom **to your** feature-list. **If this is your only feature the line will look like this:**

   feature-list=signature-at-bottom

   If you have more than one feature, separate them by commas and put each feature on a separate line. For example:

   feature-list=old-growth,

   signature-at-bottom

Elm

In addition to the basic signature instructions for UNIX users, users of Elm need to edit their ~/.elm/elmrc file so that it contains the following lines:

```
signature = ~/.signature
sigdashes = ON
```

Remember to delete any # characters before any variables that you want to set. The defaults are indicated in comment lines that start with ###.

The *signature* variable sets both the *localsignature* and *remotesignature* variables. If you want to have a different signature for local mail (that is, addresses that don't contain ! or @ characters), you can use the *localsignature* and *remotesignature* variables instead of the *signature* variable.

See also:

Elm Web page	`http://www.myxa.com/elm.html`
Elm FAQs	`http://www.cis.ohio-state.edu/hypertext/faq/usenet/elm/top.html`
Elm manual	`elm`
Elm newsgroup	`comp.mail.elm`

Mail

(This section contributed by Jym Dyer.)

Regular UNIX mail doesn't have an automatic-signature mechanism. Many people who normally use more deluxe mail utilities occasionally resort to using mail, in which case all they need to know is this command:

```
~r $HOME/.signature
```

The preceding command simply tells mail to include the text of your signature file. If you use mail on a regular basis, you may want to use the semiautomatic signature feature. When you finish typing your message, you append a signature with this command:

```
~a
```

For this command to work, though, you need to set the *sign* mail variable. You can set this variable in two ways. The first way is to set the variable in your ~/.mailrc file with a command like the following:

```
set sign="Jym Dyer <jym@remarque.berkeley.edu>"
```

If your signature is more than one line long, you can use the C-language string syntax, as in the following examples:

```
set sign="Jym Dyer\n<jym@remarque.berkeley.edu>"
```

or

```
set sign="Jym Dyer\
\n<jym@remarque.berkeley.edu>"
```

The disadvantage of specifying your signature in your .mailrc file is that you now have to maintain the text of your signature in two places. To avert this problem, set *sign* as an environment variable in your shell start-up script. For a Bourne-compatible shell, you set this variable with the following command:

```
sign="'cat $HOME/.signature'" export sign
```

For a C shell, use this command:

```
setenv sign "`cat $HOME/.signature`"
```

Both *mail* and *Mail*, which is the newer Berkeley UNIX version of *mail*, can use the procedures described in this section. Typically both *mail* and *Mail* are in /usr/ucb and are the same program. Berkeley UNIX systems provide the old version of *mail* in /usr/bin/mail.

See also:

Manual pages `mail`, `Mail`

Newsgroup `comp.mail.misc`

SUN OpenWindows Mail Tool

(This section contributed by Jochen Bern.)

SUN's OpenWindows Mail Tool lacks many features, including the capability to sign outgoing messages. Most OpenWindows users, however, stick with mailtool because of its ability to easily send attachments.

To make a simple replacement for an automatic signature, add a template. Choose Edit⇨Properties, select Template in the Properties window, and enter a name and file. There is a disadvantage to this approach, however: You have to add every signature by hand.

A better approach is to use a set `sendmail=...` line in your ~/.mailrc. Messages being sent out will be handed over to the executable named in this line instead of to the mail-delivery subsystem. You can easily install a program in this line which will sign your mail messages. Be warned, however, that too-simple signature adders (*siggers*, for short) aren't aware of attachments, so the signature will end up in the last attachment instead of at the end of the message. Information about a sigger that handles mail containing attachments correctly can be obtained from Jochen Berg by sending e-mail to `mailtool-sig@ti.uni-trier.de`.

See also:

Manual pages	`mailtool`, mail, sendmail, procmail
Newsgroup	`comp.sys.sun.*`

Emacs Mail Mode

(This section contributed by Jym Dyer and others.)

Emacs Mail Mode usually is invoked with the mail or mail-other-window command (bound, respectively, to the Ctrl-X m and Ctrl-X 4 m keys by default). The program also can be invoked from various Emacs mail and news packages.

Mail Mode provides a mail-signature command to append the contents of your signature file to the end of your mail message. This command is bound to Ctrl-C Ctrl-W by default, so to insert the signature before mailing, simply press Ctrl-C Ctrl-W.

Instructions for Version 18

If you prefer to have your signature appended to the end of your mail message automatically, put the mail-signature command in the *mail-setup-hook* variable in your $HOME/.emacs file, as in this example:

```
(setq mail-setup-hook
     (function
      (lambda ()
      (mail-signature) )))
```

This command places the signature in your mail message buffer.

Instructions for Version 19

(This section contributed by Richard Kasperowski and Matt Kaufmann.)

In emacs 19, I use the following expression:

```
(setq mail-signature t)
```

A problem exists with the expression, however, with respect to posting to Usenet via GNUS. GNUS automatically appends .signature to the posting when it is sent out. With `(setq mail-signature t)`, .signature is appended to the end of the emacs buffer in which you edit your post. When you post the message, another .signature is appended to the end, and you end up with two .signatures on your Usenet message.

If you prefer, you can use the following minor modification of the version 18 form shown above:

```
(setq mail-setup-hook
      (function
       (lambda ()
         (mail-signature nil) )))
```

See also:

Emacs FAQs	`http://www.cis.ohio-state.edu/hypertext/faq/usenet/GNU-Emacs-FAQ/part5/faq.html`
Emacs newsgroups	`gnus.emacs.help`
	`comp.emacs`

MH and Emacs mh-e

(This section contributed by Jym Dyer.)

MH doesn't have an automatic signature mechanism, but it can be configured so easily that you can implement such a mechanism in several ways. For details, check the periodic "MH Frequently Asked Questions (FAQs) with Answers" (see URL later in this section).

If you use the environment variable *signature* to point to your signature file, MH uses it not as a signature but as your full name. Even worse, if your version of MH was built with the UCI option and you don't use the environment variable *signature* to point to another file, MH uses the $HOME/.signature file for this purpose. To see whether your version of MH has this behavior, enter the command **send -help** and look for the string [UCI] in the output.

There is an Emacs interface to MH, called mh-e. This interface has its own signature mechanism, which is invoked with the mh-insert-signature command (bound to Ctrl-C Ctrl-S by default). This command inserts the file $HOME/.signature file by default. If your signature file has another name (for example, to prevent its being used by an MH built with the UCI option), you can set the *mh-signature-file-name* variable to refer to a different file.

See also:

MH FAQs	`http://www.cis.ohio-state.edu/hypertext/faq/usenet/mh-faq/top.html`
MH manual	`mh`
MH newsgroup	`comp.mail.mh`

nn

In addition to following the basic signature instructions, users of nn need to edit their ~/.nn/init file so that it contains the following lines:

```
set query-signature off
set append-signature-mail on
set append-signature-post off
```

The reason why you need to use set `append-signature-post off` is that the posting software (usually, inews) automatically appends ~/.signature, if it exists. If you use set append-signature-post on, both nn and inews append your signature, and you'll send out two identical signatures every time you post, which looks tacky.

See also:

nn FAQs	`http://www.cis.ohio-state.edu/hypertext/faq/usenet/nn-faq/top.html`
nn manual	`nn, inews`
nn newsgroup	`news.software.nn`

GNUS

(This section contributed by Mike Northam.)

In addition to following the basic signature instructions, users of GNUS should verify that the value of the variable *gnus-signature-file* points to the right place. If you're in Emacs, you can do so by evaluating the following expression:

```
gnus-signature-file
```

Place your cursor at the beginning of that expression, and press Ctrl-X Ctrl-E. You should see `~/.signature` in the echo area. If not, edit your $HOME/.emacs file and add the following line:

```
(setq gnus-signature-file "~/.signature"))
```

Then load your $HOME/.emacs file or merely restart Emacs. The variable should be set correctly.

See also:

GNUS FAQ	`http://www.cis.ohio-state.edu/hypertext/faq/usenet/GNU-Emacs-FAQ/part5/faq.html`
GNUS newsgroup	`gnu.emacs.gnus`

Troubleshooting Signature Problems

A common problem that people have with .signature (and with .plan, .project, and .forward) files is that the permissions are not set correctly. Make sure that you have set the permissions as instructed in "Finger: Basic UNIX Instructions," which follows.

If you are still having problems, read the manual pages for your newsreader, news poster, or mailer, and search for the string *signature*. You may need to set a variable for the ~/.signature to be appended. To search the on-line manual pages, follow these instructions:

Type or Do This . . .	*To Do This . . .*
man *CommandName* |less	Open manual pages for *CommandName* (elm, pine, nn, tin, trn, Pnews, and so on) and pipe through *less*. If your system doesn't have *less*, replace it with *more*.
/signature	Search for first occurrence of *signature*.
n	Search for next occurrence of *signature*. Repeat the search until you find the appropriate section of the manual.
u	Page up half a screen. (This procedure works in *less* but not in *more*.)
Press spacebar	Page down one screen. (This procedure works in both *less* and *more*.)

See also:

Manual pages for `man`, `less` (or `more`, if `less` is not on your system)

Finger: Basic UNIX Instructions

If your host is running the finger daemon (fingerd), people around the world can find out more about you by *fingering* you. They can finger you by typing the following at a UNIX prompt:

```
finger YourUserID@your.fully.qualified.domain.name
```

On some systems, finger is linked or aliased to f, so the following also works:

```
f YourUserID@your.fully.qualified.domain.name
```

Finger displays different information on different systems, depending on what finger daemon the system is running. Often, finger display your full name, your default shell, the time when you were last logged on, and your ~/.plan and ~/.project files. If you finger someone and the display takes more than one page, you can pipe the output through *less* (or *more*, if you don't have *less*). To find out about Halcyon (one of my Internet service providers), for example, type the following:

```
finger info@halcyon.com |less
```

Finger also can be used to display information about groups of people. For example, the following usually displays finger information about everyone with *john* in their names on `random.fqdn`:

```
finger john@random.fqdn |less
```

You can get a short listing for each person by using the following:

```
finger -q john@random.fqdn |less
```

Many organizations have an organizational directory attached to their main finger server. To find out about people at the Massachusetts Institute of Technology, type the following:

```
finger @mit.edu
```

URLs for fingering

In addition to using the finger or f command, you can finger people through a Web browser or Gopher client. The following is a form created by Doug Stevenson (`doug+@osu.edu`):

```
http://www-bprc.mps.ohio-state.edu/cgi-bin/finger.pl
```

You can finger a specific user in a Web browser by opening a URL with a syntax like this:

```
http://www-bprc.mps.ohio-state.edu/cgi-bin/finger.pl?userid@fqdn
```

For example:

```
http://www-bprc.mps.ohio-state.edu/cgi-bin/finger.pl?nancym@halcyon.com
http://www-bprc.mps.ohio-state.edu/cgi-bin/finger.pl?doug%2B@osu.edu
```

(`%2B`, which is the hex for a plus sign, is used because Stevenson's address is `doug+` and plus signs in a URL mean something special.) With this finger gateway, if .plan contains some HTML, it will be presented as hypertext. For example, if the following is in a .plan file, it will be presented as a link to "Infinite Ink's Home Page."

```
<A HREF="http://www.jazzie.com/ii/">Infinite Ink's Home Page</A>.
```

Marc VanHeyningen (`mvanheyn@cs.indiana.edu`) has a Web finger gateway that you can find out about at `http://www.cs.indiana.edu/finger/gateway`. To use this gateway, you use the following syntax:

```
http://www.cs.indiana.edu/finger/fully.qualified.domain.name/userid/w
```

To finger VanHeyningen, for example, type the following:

```
http://www.cs.indiana.edu/finger/cs.indiana.edu/mvanheyn/w
```

With this finger gateway, if a URL in a .plan uses the <URL:...> syntax, it will be a link — for example, <URL:http://www.jazzie.com/ii/> is presented as a link.

Due to a coincidental similarity between the network protocol used by finger servers and that used by Gopher servers, you also can use the following URL to finger someone as a pseudo-Gopher item:

```
gopher://fully.qualified.domain.name:79/0userid
```

0 (the number zero) precedes *userid*.

You can finger my Internet service provider with this URL:

```
gopher://halcyon.com:79/0info
```

If you're using a real Gopher client, you can make a bookmark with the FQDN as the host name, 0 as the item type (which means plain text rather than a menu), and the user name as the selector. Select that bookmark, and it fingers the desired user. This procedure probably is more trouble than it's worth unless you need to finger the same address frequently.

Changing Your Default Finger Information: chfn

On many UNIX systems, you can change some of your default information, such as your full name, by typing the following at the UNIX prompt:

```
chfn
```

If `chfn` is not available, try `passwd -f`. If neither of these is available, you need to contact your system administrator and ask him or her to change your full name and other finger info. After you change your information, make sure that the change is in place by fingering yourself using the following two commands.

```
finger YourUserID
finger
```

The second command displays a one-line description of everyone who is currently logged on to your system.

See also:

Manual pages `chfn`, `passwd`, `finger`

Adding more to your finger information: .plan and .project

Your ~/.project and ~/.plan files, if they exist, are displayed when you are fingered. Setting these files up is essentially the same as setting up a ~/.signature file (described earlier in this chapter). To set up your .plan file, follow the procedure in the following table:

Type This . . .	*To Do This . . .*
cd	Change to your home directory.
pico .plan	Use the pico editor to create a .plan file. (Replace **pico** with another editor, if you want.)
Your plan	Create the text for your plan.
Save and exit	In pico, press Ctrl-X to exit, and press **y** when you are asked whether you want to save your changes.
chmod 644 .plan	Make .plan readable by all programs and users.
ls -l .plan	Check the permission; it should say -rw-r--r--.
chmod a+x .	Make home directory searchable by all programs and users.
ls -ld .	Check permission of home directory; it should say drwx?-x?-x. Each question mark can be the letter *r* or a hyphen.

If you want a .project file, follow the same procedure. Only the first line of .project is displayed (so you may as well make it only one line). Again, if you prefer some other editor to pico, use that editor instead.

Test-fingering yourself

To test your changes, finger yourself by typing the following at the UNIX prompt:

```
finger YourUserID
finger YourUserID@your.fully.qualified.domain.name
finger
```

To ensure that people from other systems can finger you, you should ask someone who's not on your system to finger you, too. You can simulate fingering yourself from another machine (another.fqdn) by typing the following:

```
finger YourUserID@your.fqdn@another.fqdn
```

For this procedure to work, another.fqdn must support full finger functionality.

Finding out who fingers you

Finger wasn't designed to log finger requests, so finding out who fingers you is complicated — and sometimes impossible — to set up. For more information, see the following:

- The next section of this chapter ("Backfinger script").
- Chris Alfeld's fingertrace at `http://www.math.utah.edu/~calfeld/creations/fingertrace/`
- R. L. Samuell's logfinger script, which you can obtain by fingering `logfinger@twinbrook.cis.uab.edu`

- "UNIX - Frequently Asked Questions (4/7) [Frequent posting]", subject "4.9) How do I keep track of people who are fingering me?" This article is archived in all the usual FAQs archives, including:

  ```
  http://www.cis.ohio-state.edu/hypertext/faq/usenet/unix-faq/
  faq/part4/faq-doc-9.html
  ```

An easy way to see whether anyone has fingered you is to type the following at the UNIX prompt:

```
ls -lu $HOME/.plan
```

This command tells you the last time that someone accessed your .plan, but it doesn't tell you who it was. I have this line in my .login because it's interesting to see the last time someone was checking on me!

If your files are stored under AFS (Andrew File System, a distributed file system), `ls -lu $HOME/.plan` will not work, because AFS has no notion of a time or last accessed time.

Backfinger script

(This section contributed by Janet Rosenbaum.)

A script called, among other things, backfinger, planner, and finger_logger (flogger or frogger, for short), makes your .plan into a named pipe. Think of a named pipe as being a sort of pipe used with plumbing that opens on the screen of the person who is fingering you — say, Fred — so that when the pipe is accessed, it looks for a program from which to get something to stick on Fred's screen. The script is called when you are fingered. At that moment, the script looks to the finger port of your UNIX machine, sees which machine Fred is on, and logs that machine's IP number and hostname. The script then can execute a command to spit out a .plan on Fred's screen. You could use a program that generates random poetry, the fortune program, or simply `cat plan_file` to make the contents of the text file (plan_file) appear on Fred's screen. To make Fred think that you are really cool, the script also tells him what machine he is fingering you from.

This script tells you only the machine that Fred is fingering you from, not his actual user name. Although the identification protocol (documented in RFC1413) allows exchange of the user name that initiated the finger process over port 113, the current backfinger program does not use it. (Anyone who has enough time to add this feature certainly may, though!) The other way to find out Fred's name is to use systat, which requests a list of current processes on Fred's machine over port 11. This option rarely is available, due to security concerns.

Following are two caveats:

- This program must be running at all times on your system, even when you are logged out. Leaving on a background process like this one annoys most system administrators no end, especially on high-load systems. Do *not* run the program unless you are sure that you are allowed to run background processes.
- If you decide that you want to stop running this program, remove your .plan file as soon as you kill the process; otherwise, all your finger processes will hang.

Given these caveats, the script is distributed only to those who can use it, mostly for educational reasons. The Web site is `http://pubweb.acns.nwu.edu/~ejrosen/scripts/logger.src`.

I am not the author of this program; the version that I distribute is virtually identical to the program distributed by Steve Franklin. The real author is Tony Rems (`rembo@unisoft.com`). Modifications and revisions were made by Geoff Loker (`geoff-ms.moore.com`), Karen Bruner (`napalm@ugcs.caltech.edu`), Norman Franke (`frankel@llnl.gov`), and Steve Franklin (`franklin@ug.cs.dal.ca`).

See also:

Newsgroup `comp.sources.misc`

Where to find interesting places to finger

Cool places to finger come and go roughly every week, so it's a losing battle to list them here.

Scott Yanoff's "Updated Internet Services List," however, contains a number of interesting places to finger. If you access this document through the following URL, all the finger commands are links:

`http://www.uwm.edu/Mirror/inet.services.html`

What to Put in Your Signature and Finger Files

Art by Jorn Barger <jorn@genesis.mcs.com>

Keeping your signature to four lines or fewer is considered to be good netiquette. Many news posters, including some versions of inews, will not post an article that has a signature of more than four lines. So put large graphics, your life story, and the like in your finger files or in your Web pages, and point people to them in your signature. It also is a good idea to keep your signature fewer than 75 characters wide, so that if your signature is included in a follow-up preceded by an attribution character (such as >), each line still will be on one line.

A good strategy is to keep your signature short and include a URL for your Web page, as in the following example:

```
 /\_/\                      /\_/\                                  /\_/\
( o.o )  Nancy McGough     ( o.o )                                ( @.@ )
 > ~ <   Infinite Ink       > ^ <  http://www.jazzie.com/ii/       > " <
```

If you do not have a Web page, you may want to put in a URL that will finger you, as in the following example:

```
gopher://halcyon.com:79/0nancym
```

You also can put URLs in your .plan, and then, if someone is fingering you through a Web gateway such as the ones described earlier, these URLs will be links.

ASCII art

A good source of art for your signature and finger files is the ASCII art FAQs, which contains (among others) these topics:

- 9 Where can I find ASCII art?
- 22 How do I put an animation in my plan?
- 23 How do I make a sig?
- 24 How do I have my signature automatically added to my posts and e-mail?

The ASCII art FAQs is available at the following address:

`http://gagme.wwa.com/~boba/faq.html`

One particularly good place to find ASCII art is:

`http://gagme.wwa.com/~boba/scarecrow.html`

See also:

Newsgroups `rec.arts.ascii, alt.ascii-art`
`alt.binaries.pictures.ascii`
`alt.ascii-art.animation`

Animated text strings

(This section contributed by Marc Kriguer.)

Dotplan is a program that performs animation effects on text strings by using ASCII control characters, so that .plan files (hence the name) look a little more fancy (on low-speed dialup lines). Some of the effects make the characters appear one at a time; others have the characters appear at the same time and move around.

Following are a few examples:

```
dotplan 3 This is sample text # Display string using style 3
dotplan      # Display usage information
dotplan s      # Display styles in all styles
dotplan d This is more text # Display string in all styles
dotplan 1 Hi there... > .plan # Save output in actual .plan file
```

The files are at the following addresses:

```
ftp://ftp.halcyon.com/pub/ii/internet/dotplan.c
ftp://ftp.halcyon.com/pub/ii/internet/dotplan.1
```

Newsgroups for signature discussion

In addition to the ASCII art newsgroups listed earlier, people discuss signatures in the following newsgroups:

Newsgroup Description	*Newsgroup Name*
The War Lord of the West Preservation Fan Club	`alt.fan.warlord`
Like `alt.fan.warlord`, only different	`alt.stupid.signature.flame.flame.flame`

Don't expect any particularly profound discussions in either of these places. To find out who the War Lord is, see Chapter 2.

Organization Header

The Organization header is another way you can tell people about yourself. Organization is an optional header in mail and news messages described in RFC 1036, "Standard for Interchange of Usenet Messages," section 2.2.8.

Many mailers and newsreaders do not automatically display the Organization header when you are reading a message that you have received. Often, typing **h** (for header) in your mailer or newsreader displays all the headers of a message. You can set up some software to display the Organization line automatically each time you view a message.

The following sections provide instructions for having your Organization line filled in automatically each time you compose a message. Some composers automatically display your Organization header while you are composing; others don't.

Pnews, rn, trn, strn, and tin

The rn family of tools (Pnews, rn, trn, and strn) and tin get information for the Organization header from the ORGANIZATION environment variable, if it exists. In a C shell, you set this variable in your ~/.login with the following command:

```
setenv ORGANIZATION "Your Organization Name"
```

For a Bourne-compatible shell, you can set this variable in your ~/.profile with the following command:

```
ORGANIZATION ="Your Organization Name" export ORGANIZATION
```

After you edit your ~/.login or ~/.profile, you can establish the setting by logging out and logging back in. To make sure that the variable is set, type the following:

```
printenv
```

After the variable is set, post a test message to a local test newsgroup, with `local` distribution, to make sure that the Organization header is correct.

See also:

Manual pages	`Pnews`, `rn`, `trn`, `strn`, and `tin`
Newsgroups	`news.newusers.questions`, `news.software.readers`

Pine 3.90 and later

In Pine 3.90 and later versions, you set the Organization and other headers by using the *customized-hdrs* variable. Follow these steps:

1. **From the main menu, type** S **(for Setup).**
2. **Type** C **(for Configuration).**
3. **To change the value of the *customized-hdrs* variable, move to the variable; type** A **(for Add Value); and type** *Organization: Your Organization Name* **at the prompt.**

If you have set the *ORGANIZATION* environment variable, you can type **Organization: $ORGANIZATION.**

While reading a message that you have received, you can view the Organization header and other headers by typing **H**. If **H** does not work, you need to go to your configuration menu and set the *enable-full-header-cmd* variable. While composing a message, you can view all the headers by placing the cursor in the header region and typing **^R** (for View Rich Headers).

The *customized-hdrs* variable is not available in Pine 3.89 and earlier versions.

See also:

Pine FAQs	`http://www.cac.washington.edu/pine/faq/`
	`ftp://ftp.cac.washington.edu/pine/docs/faq`

Pine manual	`pine`
Pine newsgroup	`comp.mail.pine`

Elm

Use your editor to create a file named ~/.elm/elmheaders for any headers that you want to use in your outgoing mail messages. For example, my ~/.elm/elmheaders file contains the following line:

```
Organization: Infinite Ink
```

See also:

Elm Web page	`http://www.myxa.com/elm.html`
Elm FAQs	`http://www.cis.ohio-state.edu/hypertext/faq/usenet/elm/top.html`
Elm manual	`elm`
Elm newsgroup	`comp.mail.elm`

nn

Use your editor to put the following lines in your ~/.nn/init file:

```
set news-header Organization: Your Organization Name
set mail-header Organization: Your Organization Name
```

This procedure adds the Organization header to both news and mail messages sent from nn.

While reading messages with nn, you can view the Organization line by adding *O* (the letter) to your header-lines variable setting. I like the following setting, which displays the Approved, From, Organization, Newsgroups, Followup-To, Keywords, and Summary headers.

```
set header-lines AFOnWK*Y
```

See also:

nn FAQs	`http://www.cis.ohio-state.edu/hypertext/faq/usenet/nn-faq/top.html`
nn manual	`nn`
nn newsgroup	`news.software.nn`

The Latest Updates

A current version of the on-line document on which this chapter is based is available at the following addresses. It includes a list of the many people who contributed to writing the Signature and Finger FAQ.

```
http://www.cis.ohio-state.edu/hypertext/faq/usenet/signature_finger_faq/
faq.html
ftp://rtfm.mit.edu/pub/usenet/news.answers/signature_finger_faq
```

Chapter 18
The Internet by E-Mail

What If You Have Only E-Mail?

Many users are connected to the Internet via hookups that provide only electronic mail. They may subscribe to a mail-only service such as MCI Mail, or they may use a BBS or a company mail system with a net connection that handles only e-mail.

Fortunately, there's a lot you can do by e-mail. Electronic mailing lists let you participate in a huge variety of online discussions, and *mail servers* (programs that automatically respond to e-mail that you send them) let you retrieve information from Internet services such as ftp, Gopher, Archie, WAIS, and the World Wide Web.

Mailing Lists

There are literally thousands of electronic mailing lists available to you on the Internet.

The way a mailing list works is quite simple: Anything anyone sends to the list's e-mail address is resent to all of the people on the list. As people receive messages and respond to them, there's a running e-mail conversation among the people on the list. Each list has a topic to which messages are (at least in theory) supposed to apply, so by joining mailing lists, you can find communities of people who share your interests.

Joining lists is easy; in most cases, you simply send a single e-mail message in which you ask to sign up. Leaving lists is just as easy. Each list has two addresses: the list's own address and its administrative address. Messages to be sent to the readers of the list go to the list's address, while those intended for the list's maintainer (most often, requests to subscribe or unsubscribe) go to the administrative address.

Never send an administrative message to the list's address. To do so wastes the time of all of the list's readers. It's also ineffective since administrative messages are usually processed by a program that looks only at mail sent to the administrative address.

Unmoderated, moderated, open, and closed lists

Most mailing lists are *unmoderated*, meaning that any message sent to the list is immediately rebroadcast to all of the members of the list. But some are *moderated*, which means that all submissions are vetted by a human moderator before being sent out. Some people feel that moderation impedes the free flow of ideas on a list, but in most cases it makes the list better, keeping it on its topic and weeding out irrelevant and repetitive messages. The quality of the moderation depends entirely on the moderator, who is in nearly every case an unpaid volunteer.

A few moderated lists are in fact one-way gateways from other text sources. For example, there are mailing lists that broadcast weather reports from the National Weather Service and lists that send out White House press releases. Such lists are treated as moderated so that only messages from the original source are sent out. (In most cases, there is a parallel, unmoderated list for discussion of the topic among the readers.)

Most lists are *open*, meaning that anyone can send a message to the list. Others are *closed*, where only people who subscribe to the list can contribute. If your e-mail address changes due to administrative changes at your system, you'll have to tell the maintainers of any closed lists to which you subscribe so that they can manually update your address.

Digests

Some lists have enough traffic that readers don't receive each message individually but instead receive a digest containing a group of messages. Digests are typically sent out daily, although a few high-volume lists such as the Telecom Digest send out digests more often, and some send out digests as infrequently as once a week.

Most LISTSERV mailing lists (see "LISTSERV lists," later in this chapter) can be received as individual messages or as daily digests at the recipient's option.

Manually maintained lists

Originally, all Internet mailing lists were manually maintained, and a few still are. For such lists, the administrative address is the list's address with `-request` appended. For a list called, for example, `buchanan-lovers@blivet.com`, the administrative address would be `buchanan-lovers-request@blivet.com`. To subscribe or unsubscribe to such lists, just send a one-line message to the administrative address asking to be added or removed from the list. No particular format is necessary because the messages are read by an actual human being.

Keep in mind that the actual human being is a volunteer who usually has a job other than maintaining the list; it can take a few hours or days before he or she can attend to your request.

LISTSERV lists

LISTSERV is an automated mailing list system originally provided on the BITNET network on IBM mainframes but now widely available all over the Net. All LISTSERV lists have an administrative address of `listserv`, so the administrative address for `snufle-l@blivet.com` would be `listserv@blivet.com`.

LISTSERV requests are interpreted by a rather unintelligent computer program, so

- Be sure to spell words correctly in your requests.
- If your mail program automatically adds a signature to your message, tell it not to add the signature to messages sent to LISTSERV, since LISTSERV won't understand the signature.
- You can send as many requests in a single LISTSERV message as you want. Put each on a separate line.
- LISTSERV ignores the Subject: line of your message. All requests must be in the body of the message.

All of the LISTSERV systems are hooked together, so you can actually send your subscription request to any LISTSERV host in the world and your request should (in theory at least) be redirected to a host that handles that list. Some large lists are automatically divided up among several hosts, typically on different continents, so a request to subscribe to one of those lists will automatically be handled by the closest host that handles that list.

If you're not sure which host handles a particular list, send your request to `listserv@bitnic.bit.net` (U.S.) or `listserv@listserv.net` (Europe).

Subscribing and unsubscribing

To subscribe to a LISTSERV list, send the following message to the LISTSERV address:

```
SUB listname your real name
```

To remove yourself, send

```
SIGNOFF listname
```

LISTSERV has dozens of options, most of which you can find out about by sending a message containing `HELP` to the LISTSERV address.

Turning mail on and off, getting digests

Your subscription to any LISTSERV list can be in one of three states, which you control by sending a `SET` command to the LISTSERV address:

```
SET listname NOMAIL   (turn list off temporarily)
SET listname MAIL     (get individual messages)
SET listname DIGEST   (get list as a digest)
```

Not all lists are available as digests, but the worst thing that will happen if you ask for a digest from a list not available that way is that you'll get an error message by return mail.

Normally, messages you send to the list are sent back to you, along with all of the other subscribers. You can control this feature by sending

```
SET listname ACK      (do send copies of my own messages)
SET listname NOACK    (do not send copies of my own messages)
```

There are far more options than these. To find out your current set of options on a list to which you've subscribed, send

```
QUERY listname
```

Other LISTSERV odds and ends

To find out who's on a LISTSERV list, send

```
REVIEW listname
```

Some lists have thousands of subscribers, so be prepared for a large response. If you're shy, you can tell LISTSERV not to include you in the list of people reported by `REVIEW`:

```
SET listname CONCEAL     (do not list me)
```

If you change your mind, send the following message:

```
SET listname NOCONCEAL   (do list me)
```

Many lists have files of back issues and related documents. To get info on a particular list, send

```
INFO listname
```

To get a particular file from a LISTSERV server, send

```
GET filename
```

Most filenames consist of two words separated by a space — the convention on the VM/370 mainframes on which LISTSERV was originally available.

If you need to contact the human manager of a list, his or her address is `OWNER-` followed by the list name. Humans being human, it may be a few hours or days until you get a response.

To find out what other commands are available, send

```
HELP            (short help message)
INFO REFCARD    (detailed reference card)
```

Finding out what LISTSERV lists there are

To find out what lists are available on a particular LISTSERV system, send

```
LIST
```

To get a list of all the LISTSERV lists on all LISTSERV systems, send

```
LIST GLOBAL
```

The answer to `LIST GLOBAL` is enormous, over 500,000 bytes long, which will swamp many mail systems and take the better part of an hour to download at 2400 baud. There's a copy of the `LIST GLOBAL` list as of early 1995 on the disks in the back of this book.

Listproc lists

Listproc is an automated mailing list system for UNIX systems written at Boston University and modeled after LISTSERV. Its commands are largely the same as those for LISTSERV.

MajorDomo lists

MajorDomo is a list manager somewhat similar to LISTSERV that runs on UNIX systems. The administrative address for all of the MajorDomo lists at a host is `majordomo@`*`hostname`*.

MajorDomo requests are interpreted by a program, not a human, so the same suggestions made above about sending messages to LISTSERV apply to messages to MajorDomo.

To subscribe to a MajorDomo list, send

```
subscribe listname optional address
```

where `optional address` is the mail address that should be subscribed, if different from yours. This can be handy if your mail system screws up your mailing address or you want to add a local redistribution list that includes a bunch of local users. (Requests with an optional address are reviewed by the list owner to forestall indirect mail bombing of third parties.)

To unsubscribe, send

```
unsubscribe listname
```

To get a list of lists available at a MajorDomo host, send

```
list
```

To find out which lists on a system you are subscribed to (which can come in handy if you find yourself getting mysterious mail from a MajorDomo system):

```
which
```

To get files related to a particular list:

```
index listname          (to get the list of files)
get listname filename   (to get a particular file)
```

To find out what other commands are available:

```
help
```

MajorDomo systems, unlike LISTSERV systems, are independent of each other, so there's no way to get an overall list.

Other list maintenance software

Some lists are handled by custom software operated by the list's maintainer. The description of such lists generally describes what you have to do to get on or off a list.

The publicly addressable mailing list file

Stephanie da Silva maintains a large list of publicly available mailing lists, a copy of which is on the disks in the back of the book. It's the most complete list of lists that we know.

This list is updated monthly. To get the current list, if you have Usenet access, you can find it in the group `news.lists`.

Lacking Usenet, you can get the list by mail. Send this line in an e-mail message to `mail-server@rtfm.mit.edu`:

```
send usenet/news.lists/Publicly_Accessible_Mailing_Lists,_Part_01_14
```

That returns the first part; change the 01 appropriately to get the rest of the parts. By the time you read this, there may be more than 14 parts. Send

```
index usenet/news.lists
```

to the same address for a current index of the names of available messages.

If you have access to the World Wide Web (other than the mail access described later in this chapter in "WWW by Mail"), you can find the current version at

```
http://www.neosoft.com/internet/paml
```

Mail Servers in General

The rest of this chapter describes mail servers that provide access to various Internet services. You send an e-mail message to the server telling it what you want, and it sends back a response.

- Most servers respond quickly, within a few minutes after you send a request. But some, particularly the ftp-by-mail servers described later in the chapter, are very heavily loaded and can take days to respond.
- If your mail program automatically adds a signature to your message, tell it not to do so to your request messages, since servers won't understand the signature.
- You can usually send multiple requests in a single message. Put each on a separate line.
- Most servers ignore the Subject: line of your message, and requests must be in the body of the message. But to keep life interesting, a few servers *require* that the request be in the Subject: line. Read the descriptions carefully.

Some servers return files of non-text information, such as programs and digitized images or sounds. There are a couple of common ways to pass such files in mail.

The traditional method is known as *uuencode*, in which each group of three 8-bit bytes is encoded as four text characters. Uuencoded files start with a header like

```
begin filename 0644
```

(The number is the suggested file protection bits to use on a UNIX system.)

On UNIX systems, you can reconstitute the file by passing the message through the widely available uudecode utility. Windows users can use WinCode, which is on the disks in the back of the book. Long files are frequently encoded in several parts so that each part is a reasonably sized mail message. WinCode can put these multipart messages back together.

The other common encoding method is *MIME* — Multimedia Internet Mail Encoding — which is an extension to the standard mail format. MIME-aware mailers such as Eudora (on Windows and Macs) and pine (on UNIX) automatically decode files sent as MIME.

A less common encoding scheme found on UNIX systems is *btoa,* which is decoded using the program atob.

FTP by mail

Several services offer ftp by mail. They're all very slow, but they're better than nothing. The two most widely available are FTPMAIL and BITFTP.

FTPMAIL

FTPMAIL is a facility originally written at Digital Equipment's lab in California. It's now available at the following sites. Use the one closest to you to minimize the load on expensive international network links:

Site	***Country***
ftpmail@cs.uow.edu.au	Australia
ftpmail@lth.se	Sweden
ftpmail@ftp.uni-stuttgart.de	Germany
ftpmail@grasp.insa-lyon.fr	France
ftpmail@ieunet.ie	Ireland
ftpmail@doc.ic.ac.uk	United Kingdom
ftpmail@sunsite.unc.edu	United States
ftpmail@decwrl.dec.com	United States

You send FTPMAIL a list of commands similar to those used in an interactive ftp session. The commands should include a `reply-to` command (only if the return address on your mail doesn't give your correct address), followed by `open` and other commands to specify what to retrieve.

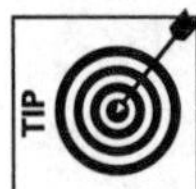

Before trying to retrieve any files from an FTPMAIL server, first send it a one-line message containing

```
help
```

This command both verifies that the server is still available and gets you a list of the exact commands that the server supports. All of the FTPMAIL servers are more or less the same, but they all have minor differences that can trip up the unwary.

Command	***Description***
reply-to *address*	Where to send the response.
open *host user password*	Where to ftp to. The default user is anonymous, and the default password is your e-mail address, usually the correct values to use for public FTP archives. At some sites, this command is connect rather than open.
cd *directory*	Change directory.
ls *directory*	List directory, short form. Default directory is the current directory.
dir *directory*	List directory, long form. Default directory is the current directory.
get *file*	Retrieve that file and mail it to you.
compress	Compress returned files or directory listings with UNIX compress.
gzip	Compress returned files or directory listings with GNU gzip.
uuencode	Encode binary files by using uuencode (default).
btoa	Encode binary files by using btoa.
mime	Encode binary files by using MIME.
force uuencode	Encode all files by using uuencode.
force btoa	Encode all files by using btoa.
force mime	Encode all files by using MIME.
size *nnn*[K|M]	Set the size pieces in which a large file will be returned. For many mail systems, 64K is a good value. On some servers, this command is chunksize.
mode binary	Get subsequent files in binary (non-text) mode (default).
mode ascii	Get subsequent files in ASCII (text) mode.
quit	Ignore any following lines (useful if you can't suppress your signature).

A typical example would be

```
open iecc.com
cd pub/file
compress
uuencode
get faq
quit
```

which says to go to the host iecc.com, log in as the default anonymous user, go to the directory `pub/file`, and return a compressed version of the file `faq`. The returned file will be uuencoded.

BITFTP

BITFTP is an ftp-by-mail system originally written for BITNET but now available to any user with Internet mail access. The servers are

- `bitftp@pucc.princeton.edu` (United States)
- `bitftp@vm.gmd.de` (Germany, available to European users only)
- `bitftp@plearn.edu.pl` (Poland)

As with FTPMAIL, send a message containing `help` to a server before using it to retrieve files so that you can verify that the server is available and find out about its particular commands.

A message should contain an `FTP` command to specify the host, a `USER` command to log in, and then other commands to retrieve files. For example,

```
FTP hostname UUENCODE
USER username [password]
... commands ...
QUIT
```

The `UUENCODE` tells the server to uuencode binary files. (There are other options not pertinent to Internet users.) The most commonly used user name is `anonymous`, in which case you do not give a password.

Commands include

Command	***Description***
ACCT *acctinfo*	Sends an ACCT command to the host to specify an account. Useful only in special cases.
ASCII	Retrieves files as text.
BINARY	Retrieves files as non-text.
CD *dir*	Changes to given directory.
DIR	Lists entries in current directory.
EBCDIC	Retrieves files in EBCDIC (used on IBM mainframes).
GET *filename*	Retrieves the specified file.
LS *dir*	Lists files in a directory.
MODE S|B	Retrieves files in Stream or Block mode. (Stream, the default, is almost always what you want.)
PWD	Prints current directory name.

(continued)

(continued)

Command	Description
QUIT	Ends session, disregards anything else in the message.
SYSTEM	Prints the name of the ftp host's operating system.
TYPE A|I|B|E|F	Retrieved files are in ASCII (A), image (I), Kanji Shift JIS (B), EBCDIC (E), or EBCDIC IBM Kanji (F). By far, the most common are A for text files and I for non-text files.

For example:

```
FTP iecc.com UUENCODE
CD pub/file
GET faq
QUIT
```

Archie by mail

Archie is a service that searches for files available via anonymous ftp. You send the request consisting primarily of a filename or a pattern that matches filenames, and the server sends back a list of matching names and sites.

There are many Archie servers around the world. The e-mail address is `archie@`*`hostname`*.

Address	Country
archie.doc.ic.ac.uk	United Kingdom
archie.hensa.ac.uk	United Kingdom
archie.edvz.uni-linz.ac.at	Austria
archie.univie.ac.at	Austria
archie.funet.fi	Finland
archie.th-darmstadt.de	Germany
archie.rediris.es	Spain
archie.luth.se	Sweden
archie.switch.ch	Switzerland
archie.unipi.it	Italy
archie.au	Australia
archie.uqam.ca	Canada
archie.ac.il	Israel

Address	*Country*
archie.wide.ad.jp	Japan
archie.kr	Korea
archie.sogang.ac.kr	Korea
archie.ncu.edu.tw	Taiwan
archie.unl.edu	Nebraska, USA
archie.internic.net	New Jersey, USA
archie.rutgers.edu	New Jersey, USA
archie.ans.net	New York, USA
archie.sura.net	Maryland, USA

Commands include

Command	*Description*
prog *name*	Returns files that match that name.
whatis *name*	Returns entries from the whatis descriptive database that match that name.
compress	Compresses and uuencodes the response.
servers	Returns a list of Archie servers.
path *addr*	Returns the response to that address rather than to the return address on the request.
help	Sends a help message.
quit	Disregards anything else in the message.

E-mail Archie requests use regular expression matching, similar to that in the UNIX `sed` command. A typical request to find files starting with the word *font* and ending with *txt* is

```
prog font.*txt
quit
```

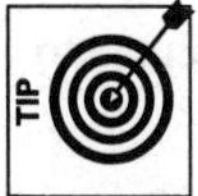

Archie servers tend to be so slow for interactive use that it's often easier to use e-mail, even if you have the option to telnet to the server.

Gopher by mail

Gophermail returns Gopher pages by e-mail. It is a nicely designed service; you can go from one page to the next easily by responding to the pages sent by the server.

Servers currently include

■ `gophermail@calvin.edu`	Michigan (U.S.)
■ `Gopher@ucmp1.berkeley.edu`	California (U.S.)
■ `gophermail@mercury.forestry.umn.edu`	Minnesota (U.S.)
■ `Gopher@pip.shsu.edu`	Texas (U.S.)
■ `gophermail@eunet.cz`	Czech Republic
■ `Gopher@earn.net`	France
■ `Gopher@FTP.technion.ac.il`	Israel
■ `Gopher@solaris.ims.ac.jp`	Japan
■ `Gopher@nig.ac.jp`	Japan
■ `Gopher@nips.ac.jp`	Japan
■ `Gopher@join.ad.jp`	Japan
■ `gomail@ncc.go.jp`	Japan
■ `Gopher@dsv.su.se`	Sweden

Start by sending an empty message to one of the servers, which should send you a copy of its home page. Then you can move around by replying to that message, including a copy of the server's message in your message and putting an *X* at the front of each menu line that you want the server to return.

The messages returned by the server are in three parts, separated by form feed (Ctrl+L) characters. The first is the Gopher menu, the second is some control information, and the third is the list of descriptions of each item in the menu. You can request explicit Gopher items by concocting your own menu and descriptions and mailing them to the server, but it's usually much easier to start from the server's home menu and move from there.

Some Gopher items are search items, where you give the server words to search for. The most well–known is Veronica, which searches through a large database of Gopher items, but there are many others as well. If you select a search item, put the words to search for in the subject line of the reply you send. (In the absence of search items, the subject line is ignored.)

For more details, send a message containing `help`. You can also tell Gophermail to break large messages into pieces; see the help message for details.

WWW by mail

Even though the World Wide Web is the most interactive of Internet services, you can still get limited access via e-mail. To do so, send a message to `listserv@info.cern.ch` containing a `SEND` command with a Web URL, such as

```
SEND http://info.cern.ch/hypertext/WWW/MailRobot/send.html
```

(That URL is the help page for the WWW–by–mail server.)

Most WWW documents are hypertext with links to other documents. The links are represented in the returned message as numbers in square brackets, like [12], with a key listing the URLs corresponding to the links at the bottom. You can get these documents by replying to the message, using your text editor to cut out all but the URLs of interest and adding SEND commands appropriately. There's also a shortcut form: Reply to the message, keeping the subject line provided, which contains the URL of the document just retrieved. Then in your request, just put the numbers of the links you want.

Use deep rather than send to get the document and the documents linked to it (up to a rather low limit of documents per message). Use source rather than send to get the HTML source language document if you have a WWW browser handy that can format HTML documents.

The WWW-by-mail server limits the number of documents that it will return and never returns more than ten documents per request and 5,000 lines per document; otherwise, by judicious use of URLs, users could ask for gigabytes of Gopher and Usenet news data.

WAIS by mail

The WAIS full-text search service is available by mail. The server's address is waismail@think.com.

A search request contains a maxres line to set the number of references returned, followed by the request itself. A typical request would be

```
maxres 10
search jargon kludge hack fudge
```

This searches the jargon document source for documents matching kludge, hack, and fudge. Send a blank search request to get the list of document sources.

The server will send back a list of responses in a format similar to

```
Result # 1 Score:1000 lines:  0 bytes:     69 Date:     0 Type: TEXT
Headline: kludge
DocID: 501356 501425 /src/wais/wais-sources/jargon.txt:/src/wais/wais-sources/
jargon@hal.gnu.ai.mit.edu:8000%TEXT
```

To retrieve documents, send the server a retrieve command quoting the exact document ID that the server returned. (This is most easily arranged by including the server's message in your request and then editing it down with a text editor.) For example,

```
retrieve 501356 501425
/src/wais/wais-sources/jargon.txt:/src/wais/wais-sources/
jargon@hal.gnu.ai.mit.edu:8000%TEXT
```

It's OK if the document ID is split across multiple lines as long as the split is at spaces. You can include several retrieve requests separated by blank lines.

Servers on the Net

Many mail servers exist to return information from a particular source or of a particular type.

The FAQ archive

Nearly every frequently–asked–question document posted to Usenet can be retrieved from mail-server@rtfm.mit.edu. Send

```
index usenet
```

to get a list of newsgroups available. For a particular group, send

```
index usenet/groupname
```

For an index and to get a particular document, send

```
send usenet/groupname/filename
```

As always, send help for general help.

The InfoBot

The InfoBot is a mail server that provides a variety of services, ranging from the extremely useful to the totally silly. Send help to infobot@infomania.com to get started. Services include

- Looking up words in a dictionary
- Looking up ham radio call signs
- City-by-city weather reports
- Translations of your documents into the distinctive dialect used by the Swedish Chef Muppet (bork, bork, bork)
- Telephone area codes
- Several hundred digits of the value of pi

New services are frequently added.

Thanks to Stephan Henze <S.HENZE@LDB.han.de> for providing some of the source material for this chapter.

Chapter 19

Supporting Non-English Characters in Internet Applications

by Janusz J. Młodzianowski <fizjm@halina.univ.gda.pl>

Institute of Experimental Physics
University of Gdańsk
Wita Stwosza 57, 80-952 Gdańsk
Poland

For some time, I have been working towards the design of a versatile multinational terminal to support the automated system installed in our University's libraries. As the University is spread all over three cities (Gdansk, Sopot, and Gdynia), the individual buildings and departmental libraries are interconnected via a metropolitan area network, using TCP/IP protocols. One feature of our library is that we stock a great number of non-English books. The question of use and transmission of national characters within our library system soon appeared.

An investigation of national language support (both at the network and presentation levels of the ISO/OSI reference model) revealed that there are possibilities of customization, but none of the available methods is versatile enough. National language support is not a standard UNIX feature, and the support system has to be bought separately. For instance, HP-UX offers a proprietary package, called Native Language Support (NLS). Using NLS, it is possible to customize the formats of system date, monetary conventions, and output error messages in different languages, and also introduce specific collation sequences. NLS allows switching among a number of different languages, but only one language can be active at any given time. Such an approach is not sufficient for library systems where characters from different languages are very often intermixed. It is generally taken for granted that the textual information is coded and processed with the help of "the alphabet." This statement is so obvious that we tend to believe that one universal computer alphabet actually exists. Since the beginning, computers and the Internet, by their very nature, have been based around English and the 7-bit ASCII (American Standard Code for Information Interchange) alphabet. This alphabet, in Europe, is known as the ISO 646 standard. The introduction, in the early seventies, of microprocessors and microcomputers offered the possibility of extending ASCII to 8 bits, thus allowing 256 different characters. The rapid growth of computer networks, and the introduction of user-friendly services, required the use of more national diacritic characters. It became clear that, sooner or later, "good old ASCII" had to be replaced by a new method of character coding.

Several approaches have been suggested. The most radical, and promising, are Unicode and ISO 10646. Both coding schemes use at least 16 bits to represent a single character. Whichever method eventually is adopted, most existing software will have to be thrown away or rewritten. This solution (at least for the time being) is neither practical nor sensible. As an intermediate solution, other mechanisms of national character support have been used successfully. The most popular system is ISO 8859-* (* stands for national versions) for code page switching, which is known to all DOS users outside of the U.S. Within this system, the first 128 characters (ASCII-7) are fixed, while the remaining 128 can be replaced as a whole table. The other system, defined in ISO 2022, introduces code extension techniques. The most popular code extension methods are ANSI escape sequences, used to control video terminals and printers. The very interesting ISO 6937/2 standard introduced a variable-length coding scheme. Within this system, some characters are coded on one byte, others on two bytes. In particular, ISO 6937/2 defines all 327 European characters. Non-European characters, such as Cyrillic and Greek, are not included in the standard. Latin characters are coded in one byte. This, the so-called base table, with the exception of character 36 (ASCII $, the "National currency symbol"), is compatible with the 7-bit ASCII set.

Other characters that are not represented in the base table are coded in two bytes. The first byte represents "non-spacing diacritical mark," while the second is a letter from the basic Latin alphabet. Table 19-1 lists all 13 diacritical marks and allowed second-byte characters:

Table 19-1 ISO 6937/2 non-spacing diacritical marks and extended characters.

Name	*Symbol*	*Letters affected*
Grave	`	AEIOUaeiou
Acute	´	ACEILNORSUYZacegilnorsuyz
Circumflex	^	ACEGHIJOSUWYaceghijosuwy
Tilde	~	AINOUainou
Macron	¯	AEIOUaeiou
Breve	˘	AGUagu
Dot	˙	CEGIZcegz
Umlaut	¨	AEIOUYaeiouy
Ring	˚	AUau
Cedilla	¸	CGKLNRSTcklnrst
Double Acute	˝	OUou
Ogonek	˛	AEIUaeiu
Caron	ˇ	CDELNRSTZcdelnrstz

Using this mechanism, the character "small e with grave accent, i.e. è" is coded as:

```
0xC1 0x65
```

The ISO 6937/2 standard neither introduces any particular sorting sequence, nor does it take into account national lexical conventions. A closer investigation of the existing UNIX code and computer hardware revealed that most applications are internally ready to support national characters in the form defined by the ISO 6937/2 standard. This approach is especially attractive, as the data in our library system (VTLS) is stored internally in ISO 6937/2 format. Apparently, the same library system is used in Finland, and at many other sites in Europe. One of the main objectives of our project was introducing a scheme which will not interfere too much with existing applications and protocols. The services which were targeted for customization included telnet client, e-mail with vi editor, talk client, and line printer daemon. Most of the work described has been implemented and tested on a number of HP workstations and servers with HP-UX operating systems. The performance achieved on other platforms varies. In particular, some IBM systems are known to operate using character coding schemes different from ASCII; notably, EBCDIC (Extended Binary Coded Decimal Interchange Code).

From the theoretical point of view, the implementation of ISO 6937/2 standard in any computer system can be narrowed down to three areas: transmission, character input, and character output.

Character Transmission

ISO 6937/2 requires that information is transmitted over the network with 8 bits. It is a fact that most networking protocols and systems already operate in 8-bit mode. However, the 8th bit is usually zeroed by an application program (for example, Kermit within ARPA services). To allow your host to communicate with remote terminals using 8-bit transmission mode, you have to set the following parameters:

- Disable parity control.
- Set one stop bit.
- Set transmission mode to 8 bits.
- Disable 8th bit stripping.

For instance, on HP-UX systems, you set up these conditions by issuing the following command:

```
stty -cstodd -cstopb cs8 -istrip
```

To configure a UNIX session permanently to 8-bit transmission mode, the user's .profile script has to be modified. First, make an archive copy of the original .profile script, just in case. Next (using, for instance, the vi editor), edit your .profile file and append to it that stty command.

ISO 6937/2 Terminals

From the user's point of view, the implementation of an ISO 6937/2 terminal requires the design of the following:

- A simple multinational keyboard
- A mechanism that displays single- and double-byte codes, using the single character national representation
- An ISO 6937/2 screen (and, if necessary, printer) character generator. These are usually implemented in software on a local computer or in a smart printer.

It is important to note here that the design of ISO 6937/2 terminal and character support in UNIX, mostly requires the modification of client terminals. In many installations, a network terminal is implemented on a standard PC that runs DOS. A PC keyboard allows entry of all ASCII-7 characters. On the other hand, ASCII-8 codes can be entered by using Alt key. Implementations of a VT100 terminal keyboard: on a PC that actually has an enhanced AT keyboard, leave out the numeric keypad (which usually doubles numeric keys on the main keypad). These "spare" 17 keys can be reprogrammed as accent keys. Moreover, the hardware construction of most PC keyboards allows these accent keys to behave exactly like the classic Shift key. Effectively, it is possible to design an ISO 6937/2 keyboard that enters double-byte codes with a single keystroke. Entry of double-byte codes can be accomplished by holding down an accent key, and simultaneously pressing a character key on a main keypad. For instance, ISO character è (e with grave accent) is entered by pressing character key e, while holding down accent key grave (3/PgDn).

Capital letters are entered with the help of Shift or Caps Lock. The same mechanism can be applied to enter single-byte characters with codes greater than 128. Two extra shifts, K1 and K2, have been provided, and different characters are assigned to the main keyboard. In addition, key 0/Insert has been reassigned as a third Shift key. The layout of this new ISO 6937/2 keyboard is shown in Figure 19-1.

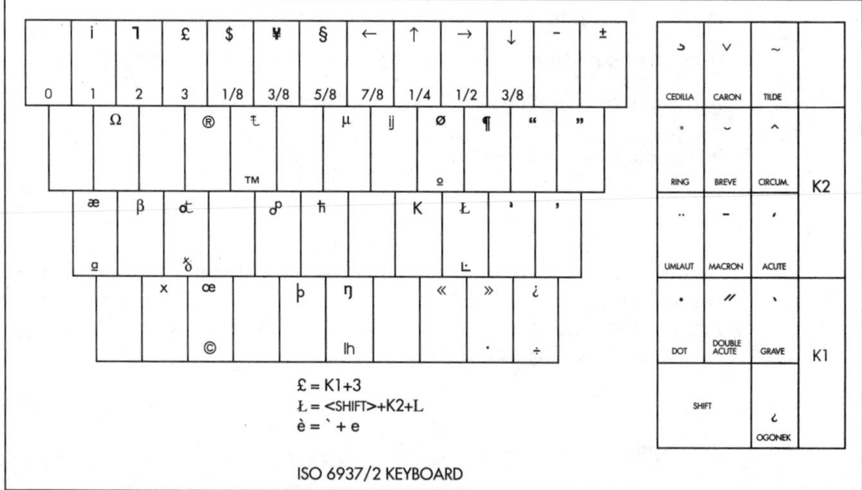

Figure 19-1: The ISO 6937/2 keyboard.

The mechanism used to implement the ISO 6937/2 keyboard on a PC terminal is based on software interrupts. As you probably know, a PC communicates with its hardware through BIOS interrupts. By intercepting the hardware keyboard interrupt (in this case, int 9), it is possible to fool the BIOS and supply two characters for a single keystroke, or skip a character altogether. The fragment of the flowchart for keyboard interrupt handler is presented in Figure 19-2.

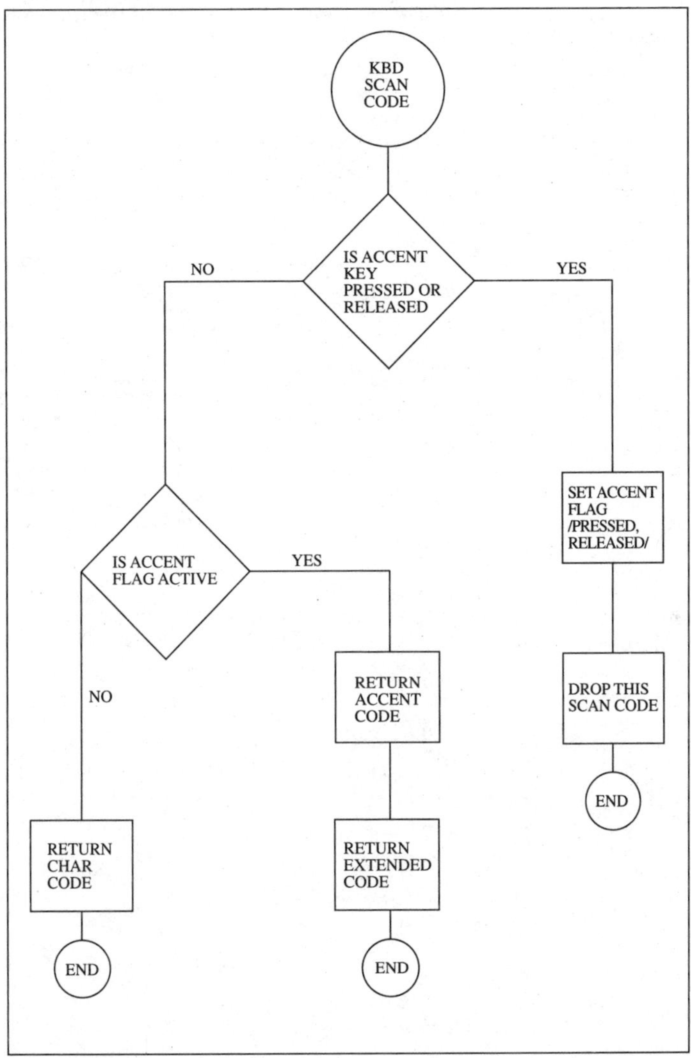

Figure 19-2: The ISO 6937/2 keyboard interrupt handler.

Modern video cards (like the EGA and VGA) allow, in text mode, more than 256 different characters to be displayed at a time. With a little software trickery, a VGA adapter can be forced to display 512 characters, while a Hercules Graphics Plus adapter can display 4096 characters simultaneously. When the character generator of a VGA card is reprogrammed and the hardware is set to generate 512 different characters, the card can display all 327 of the ISO 6937/2 letters and still have room for 185 ASCII-8 graphic characters. A TSR program can intercept screen output, filter out accent characters, and (if needed) generate the extended character code. The flowchart in Figure 19-3 illustrates the principle behind the implementation of the DOS ISO 6937/2 screen support.

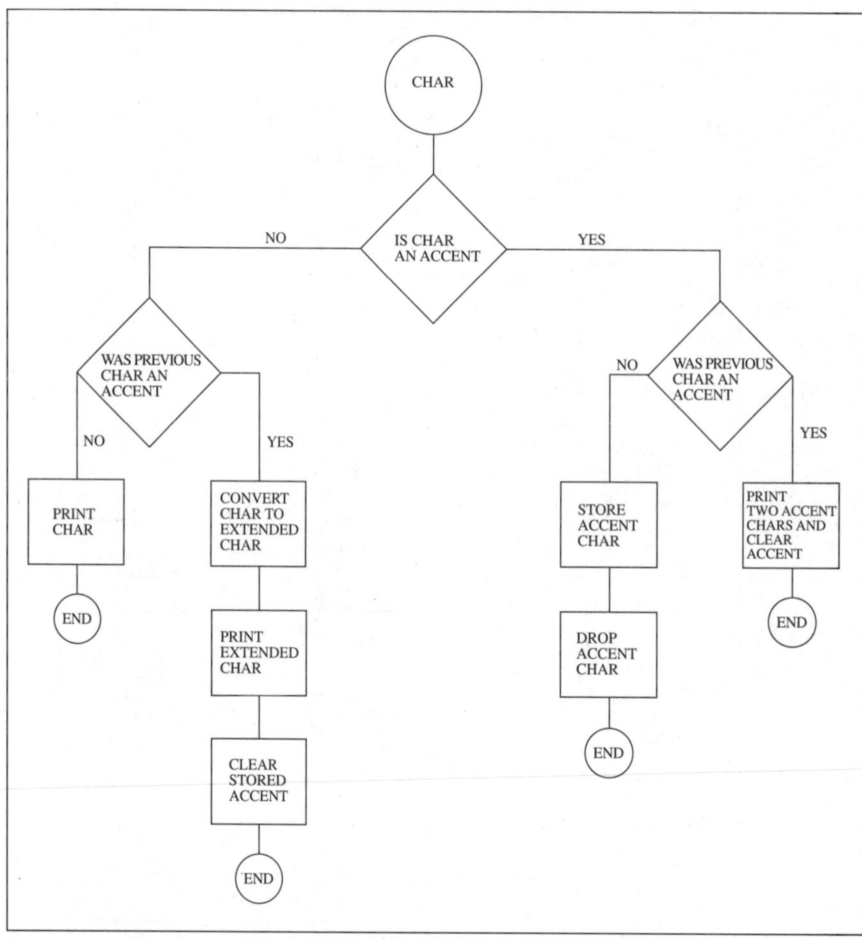

Figure 19-3: The ISO 6937/2 video interrupt handler.

This seems too easy to be true, and it is. Unfortunately, in the DOS world not all applications use the standard DOS mechanisms to communicate with the screen. Some programs, including many networking utilities (for instance, HP-ARPA services), write directly to video RAM. In such cases, the proposed TSR mechanisms fail. The only foolproof method is embedding the ISO 6937/2 support directly in the application code.

Adapting Applications

Now that we have created a terminal that can handle international character codes, we turn our attention to the individual TCP/IP applications. Let's see what's necessary for them to handle the ISO 6937/2 character codes.

ISO 6937/2 Telnet

Telnet is one of the most popular text-oriented programs used to communicate with remote hosts. Other services like e-mail, library browsing, line printing, and so on, are usually invoked from a telnet session. NCSA (National Center for Supercomputer Applications) Telnet is a public domain package that provides a complete set of tools, including telnet, ftp, rsh, and lpr. The package allows a standard PC, equipped with almost any network adapter, to communicate with remote hosts. The home site for NCSA Telnet is `zaphod.ncsa.uiuc.edu` (128.174.20.50). The package is also available on many local ftp servers around the world. NCSA Telnet has the advantage over other commercially available packages of being distributed without charge, and with the source code. The ISO 6937/2 keyboard and screen support have been integrated into the package. Providing that the host has been set up to allow an 8-bit transmission mode, the local ISO 6937/2 terminal is seen by the host as a standard VT100, but with full national support.

The installation of both NCSA and ISO-Telnet is straightforward. The package is configured via the file CONFIG.TEL. In this file, the user sets up a few parameters, such as the local IP address, and the type of network adapter or packet driver interrupt number. The user manual describes the procedure. ISO-Telnet has one additional configuration parameter: the *iso* switch. Setting "iso=on" enables ISO 6937/2 emulation, while "iso=off" disables it. The iso switch can also be temporarily changed from within any telnet session, by invoking the Alt-P menu screen. The ISO 6937/2 keyboard layout can be viewed on the second help screen (Alt-H). The ISO terminal internally intercepts PC BIOS interrupts. Therefore, one has to pay extra attention to PC configuration setup in CONFIG.SYS and AUTOEXEC.BAT. Some programs, like TSRs and device drivers, may also intercept interrupts. In such cases, conflicts can emerge, especially in the area of video output. The safest approach is starting ISO-Telnet installation with no extra packages activated. A text coded with ISO 6937/2 may be difficult to read when viewed and processed on an unmodified ASCII terminal. For instance, a fragment of a file containing the Polish poem *Pan Tadeusz*, viewed with the "more" command is displayed as the following:

Nad Soplicowem søo˥nce weszøo, i ju⊩z padøo

Na strzechy, i przez szpary w stodole si╫e wkrado

The same text is much easier to read when using iso mode:

Nad Soplicowem słóńce weszlo, i już padło

Na strzechy, i przez szpary w stodole się wkradło

ISO 6937/2 passwords

ISO-Telnet offers an additional bonus in the form of increased system security. The user can set up his or her password using extended ISO characters. Within such a password, double-byte codes are counted as two characters. As stated previously, most commercially available telnet clients do not operate in 8-bit mode. Therefore, an ISO password can be entered only via ISO-Telnet. Even if a third person knows the user's ISO password, it is impossible to log in from other than an ISO-Telnet terminal. In the same manner, using extended characters, the user can create more secure files and directories. However, this extra security has its drawbacks. On a business trip, the legal owner of an ISO password should carry a copy of ISO-Telnet; otherwise, even the legal owner cannot log in and access valuable files.

Typing UNIX commands

It has been found that ISO 6937/2 telnet client patches are invisible to most UNIX shells and commands. In particular, Korn Shell (ksh) and Posix Shell (sh) operate flawlessly. While using the Bourne Shell, it is advisable to set up the correct interpretation of the Backspace key. This can be achieved by issuing the following command:

```
stty echoe
```

The previous command also forces the screen to be refreshed each time Backspace is pressed. The Key Shell (keysh) has been found to be the most resistant to extended characters. While editing commands, extended characters appear on the screen as two separate characters (that is, accent followed by a character). After the screen has been refreshed, extended diacritics appear in their 1-byte national representations. Similarly, commands echoed from the host (that is, after pressing Enter) are displayed correctly.

ISO 6937/2 text editor

The standard unmodified HP-UX editor, vi, can be used to edit ISO 6937/2 text. However, you should observe some basic rules. First of all, using Backspace in a line with ISO characters can be tricky. A more effective way of deleting ISO characters is removing the entire line, pressing Esc, D, D, then retyping the corrected line. In some cases, text visible on the screen differs from the text stored in the vi buffer. In such cases, or when the screen becomes garbled, the screen should be refreshed by pressing Esc, Ctrl-L.

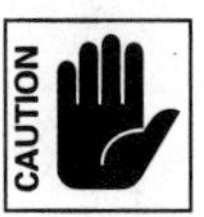

The same command (Esc, Ctrl-L), issued from shell level, switches ISO-Telnet into graphics mode.

ISO 6937/2 e-mail

An e-mail client such as elm can be configured to use vi as the mail editor, and the elm program iteself accepts 8-bit characters (at least, the HP-UX version of elm does). In this sense, elm is compatible with the ISO 6937/2 terminal. A recipient of ISO mail who is not using ISO-Telnet at his site will still be able to read ISO text, but all characters will be stripped to 7-bit codes. This, in some cases, may lead to misinterpretation.

Talk

Talk is a service that allows two users to communicate with each other in real time by using split screens. One part of each screen belongs to the sender, while the other belongs to the recipient. The talk daemon and client are not standard UNIX utilities; for systems that do not have them, the source of executable codes can be downloaded from many ftp sites. The version that has been customized in this example was downloaded from ftp.wu-wien.ac.at (137.208.8.5). As is the case with most UNIX software, the client zeroes the 8th bit of data, and treats non-ASCII characters as Ctrl sequences, appending a caret (^) to those characters. National customization of Talk requires the modification and addition of a few lines of code to existing screen output routines (usually found in the display.c file). First, locate the following lines of code, then add the highlighted additions:

```
if(*text>0 && *text<' ' && *text!='\t'){
     / first append caret to Ctrl chars */
     addch(win->x_win, '^');
     getyx(win->x_win, win->x_line, win-x_col);
if(win->x_col==COLS-1) xscroll(win, 0);
cch=(*text & 63)+64; waddch(win->x_win, cch);
}

if(*text>=' ' & *text<='z'){
/* then handle ASCII-7 */
     addch(win->x_win, *text&0377);
     getyx(win->x_win, win->x_line, win->x_col);
     text++;
     continue;

if(*text<0){
/* and finally ASCII-8 and therefore ISO6937/2 */
     waddch(win->x_win, *text&0377);
     getyx(win->x_win, win->x_line, win->x_col);
     text++;
     continue;
}
```

After recompiling, the talk client is capable of sending and receiving all 256 characters. If both talking parties invoke talk clients from their ISO-Telnet sessions, then all European characters are available. If one client uses standard unmodified talk, then the diacritical characters at that end of the session are displayed as control characters. This sometimes makes text very difficult to read.

ISO 6937/2 Line printer

The line printer protocol (RFC 1179) provides access to shared printers. A file to be printed must be forwarded to the print spooler, using line printer client software (lp or lpr). Before the file is printed, the printer daemon can perform a number of text formatting procedures. The user can set up page length, number of lines per page, margins, and other printing parameters. As an extended feature, the daemon can be patched, allowing printing of the ISO 6937/2 character set. Printing ISO 6937/2 characters is very much dependent on the actual printer. The spooler must be configured to support each particular printer. Not every printer supports ISO 6937/2 features. During initial setup, a new character set has to be downloaded to the printer.

The mechanism that prints extended characters is much the same as the mechanism described for displaying such characters on the screen. Actually, two sets of fonts must be downloaded to the printer. One set represents the base table, and the other set represents extended characters. Whenever an extended character must be printed, the printer must switch between two different fonts. Font swapping is performed by the line printer daemon. An ISO 6937/2 version of the TCP/IP line printer spooler has been implemented on a standard PC, equipped with a network adapter and connected to a printer via parallel port. The only restriction on hardware is that the PC must be excluded from running applications other than the print spooler. In fact, the machine in my lab is a recycled 4.77MHz PC/XT with a tiny 10MB hard disk and a Hercules graphics card. The software is based on the NCSA TCP/IP protocol stack and is configured in the same manner as ISO-Telnet. Any lpr network client (standard UNIX or PC-based) can access the print spooler. A full blown version of a "true" UNIX ISO 6937/2 printer daemon will also be available.

Software Availability

The ISO-Telnet package was presented during the Network Services Conference NSC'93, held in 1993, in Warsaw, Poland. Software described in this chapter is available, via anonymous ftp, from the server panda.bg.univ.gda.pl (153.19.120.249):pub/msdos/iso. The ISO6937/2 implementation to UNIX project has been partially sponsored by the State Committee for Scientific Research grant 155/R/DPN/93.

Janusz J. Młodzianowski, PhD, MEng, received his doctorate from the University of Strathclyde, Glasgow, Scotland in 1989. He is a lecturer in the Department of Experimental Physics in The University of Gdańsk, Gdańsk, Poland where he gives a number of informatics courses. His main areas of interest include microprocessor hardware design, system programming, and the use of computers in education.

Chapter 20

Finding Things on the Net

This chapter contains four separate articles:

- "URLs and Instructions for Online Retrieval"
- "Internet Search Strategies"
- "How to Look for Resources on the Internet"
- "Hot Spots on the Net"

URLs and Instructions for Online Retrieval

by Frank Hecker <hecker@access.digex.net> http://www.access.digex.net/~hecker/

URLs, or *Uniform Resource Locators,* are a handy and increasingly popular way of specifying the online location of Internet resources. URLs originated in the World Wide Web (WWW) project. Some URLs have `http:` at the beginning; these WWW pages are accessible by Mosaic or other WWW client programs. Others with `gopher:` at the beginning refer to information on Gopher servers accessible by way of TurboGopher and other Gopher client programs. (Mosaic and other WWW client programs can also interpret `gopher:` URLs.) A URL with `ftp:` at the beginning refers to a file on an ftp server, and has this form:

```
ftp://hostname/directory-path/filename
```

This line identifies a file that can be retrieved by anonymous ftp from an Internet host `hostname`; the file is in the directory `directory-path` and has the name filename.

For example, the chapter "Personal Internet Access Using SLIP or PPP" is an adaptation of a document available on an Internet ftp site. If you want to retrieve the latest version of this document in electronic form, you can do so by using one of the methods described in this section. The same methods will work with any other `ftp:` URL given in this book.

WWW

If you use Mosaic or another World Wide Web browser, you can retrieve the online version of the SLIP/PPP chapter by using the following URL:

```
ftp://ftp.digex.net/pub/access/hecker/internet/slip-ppp.txt
```

(Use the menu item "Open URL" or its equivalent.)

Note that some WWW browsers will display the file after downloading it, while others will save it to disk instead. Check your browser documentation or on-line help for more information.

Anonymous FTP

You can retrieve the online SLIP/PPP document by way of anonymous ftp from the host `ftp.digex.net`. The file is in the directory `/pub/access/hecker/internet` and has the name slip-ppp.txt.

FTP by mail

If you have only e-mail access to the Internet, you may be able to retrieve the SLIP/PPP document by using the ftpmail service. Send an e-mail message to the address `ftpmail@decwrl.dec.com`, and include the following lines as the body of the message:

```
connect ftp.digex.net
chunksize 25000
chdir /pub/access/hecker/internet
get slip-ppp.txt
quit
```

(You may use any subject line you want.)

The `chunksize 25000` line is optional; including it directs the document to be returned to you as multiple e-mail messages, with none exceeding 25,000 bytes in size. This limitation exists in case your mail system limits the size of incoming Internet e-mail messages to less than 32K, 64K, or some other value. If your limit is less than 25,000 bytes, change the `chunksize` line to an appropriate value. If your system doesn't have a limit on message size, you can change the `chunksize` to `200000` to get the entire document as one message.

When sending the file to you, the ftpmail server uses the return address it picks up from your e-mail message. In some cases (usually depending on how your e-mail gets from you to the Internet), this address does not work properly, and you have to include a specific return address that you know works; you do this by using the reply command.

If you know, for example, that the return address `jdoe@acme.com` works to get mail to you, include the following line in the body of the message immediately before the `connect` line:

```
reply jdoe@acme.com
```

As previously noted, these instructions also work for any of the `ftp:` URLs in this book (with the exception mentioned in the following paragraph); just substitute the appropriate hostname, directory, and filename.

The only exception is for files that contain binary data as opposed to printable text. For example, the SLIP/PPP chapter references Bernard Aboba's FAQ for TCP/IP on IBM-compatible PCs; the main version of the FAQ is in PKZip-compressed format. Retrieving these types of files requires special action.

If you are using a Web browser, you should direct the Web browser to save the file to disk, or you will have to configure the Web browser to recognize the file's format (for example, PKZip-compressed format) and start an application that can display files in that format.

If you use anonymous ftp, make sure that you enter the binary command before retrieving these types of files, or turn on the corresponding setting in the ftp utility you are using.

If you are using ftp by mail, the file is returned to you in *uuencoded* format, a method for representing binary data by using only printable ASCII characters. To convert the file back into binary format, you need a uudecode program for your PC or Mac; you can find these types of programs on (among other places) BBSs that specialize in PC or Mac freeware or shareware.

Note: The online material from which this chapter is adapted states: "Copyright © 1994 by Frank Hecker. You may freely distribute this document in any form provided only that you retain this copyright notice." An on-line version of this document is available on the Internet at the following URL:

```
ftp://ftp.digex.net/pub/access/hecker/internet/slip-ppp.txt
```

Frank Hecker is a sales support analyst for Tandem Computers, Inc., and a member of the board of directors of CapAccess, the Washington, D.C., community network. His professional interests include fault-tolerant systems, Internet-based electronic commerce, and public Internet access.

Internet Search Strategies

by Bob Fabian <rfabian@interlog.com>

I am a consultant, and a critical part of my practice is helping clients find ways to win business advantages using information technology. The Internet has become an important part of that practice — now that commercial use has been accepted. My approach has not been especially "scientific." I did what made sense for me, for my clients, and for the kind of work my clients required.

In preparing for this chapter, I developed a rationale that explains how I use the Internet, and why that makes sense. This type of backward-looking approach is common in science and engineering, almost essential in emerging fields. I did make an attempt to consider all important aspects of using the Internet. But the resulting coverage is neither universal nor uniform. I am primarily concerned with describing what works for me, and why it makes sense.

I set the stage by presenting my views on the necessary limits that confront every Internet user. I follow them with a short list of questions I asked recently by using the Internet. I return to my short list of questions at the end of this chapter, after describing the kinds of information I find most useful and the tools I prefer. My intention is to help you make sense of what you can find on the Internet. The chapter ends with a description of how I answered my questions.

Necessary Limits

A variety of growth statistics have been published for the Internet. Agreement may be lacking on exactly how fast the Internet is growing, or even on what to measure to determine how fast it is growing. It is agreed, however, that the Internet is growing rapidly — too rapidly for anyone to keep up with all aspects of what is happening. Selectivity is essential.

Every week, InterNIC Information Services publishes a new Scout Report "to assist InterNauts in their ongoing quest to know what's new on and about the Internet." In a typical week, the Scout Report presents a dozen or more new and interesting sites. Each of these sites provides a publicly accessible source of information on one or more topics. Many of them contain large amounts of information. And many have multiple pointers to still more sites.

Just understanding what weekly Scout Report presents requires several hours of investigation. The Scout Report is only one of many sources of information about new and interesting aspects of the Internet. I find it to be one of the most useful sources, if only because the Report's editor and I share a sense of what is important and interesting.

A more extensive, and less discriminating, set of references to new Internet resources appears in Yahoo — A Guide to WWW, which is available on the Stanford Web server. It contains a daily compendium of new Internet resources. A typical day has 50 or more pointers to other locations. Any one of those locations may contain the golden nugget of information that is vital to success on your next assignment.

It would be much more than one full-time job to keep track of what's happening on the Internet. On an hourly basis, there are new places to visit in a variety of languages (with most sites offering some English). On a daily basis, new and powerful tools are made available to access and make sense of what is found on the Internet.

One of the necessary limits is that no single person can hope to have a full understanding of what is available. Additionally, there is an economic logic behind the information provided. Altruism is grand, but it doesn't pay the rent. Individuals and organizations make information available on the Internet because they hope to gain from doing so.

Governments can and do make information publicly available. That's one of the responsibilities of government (in most countries). The academic community can and does make information publicly available. That's one of the things that academics do for a living. Some researchers also make information publicly available, but others closely guard everything they discover.

As yet, no mechanism is widely employed to support payment for Internet information access, such as those built in to commercial online information services. Payment schemes have been proposed, but thus far the absence of an operative scheme has had an inevitable impact on the kinds of information to be found on the Internet.

A personal anecdote may make the point. Recently my wife and I were planning a trip to Northern California and wanted to stay at a bed-and-breakfast inn. I went looking on the Internet. I found a number of bed-and breakfast listings, but only for New England and around various English-speaking universities. I turned to a commercial online information service for answers and found, for a fee, bed-and-breakfast listings for the area in California we wanted to visit. We found a place, and enjoyed the trip. The process worked because the commercial service provided both a person who makes it her business to maintain these listings and an easy way for me to pay for her effort.

An important limit on Internet development is that proprietary information is not generally made available, certainly not through free public access. Because the owners of this information want people to pay to receive it, keeping the information on specialized information services often makes more sense. It's a question of motivation and economics.

A new economics?

The traditional economic model holds that information is costly but access is free. Indeed, the person selling the information pays the costs of providing it. The seller works to get the message to you about the information available; you pay only if the information is of value to you. The economic equation is (partially) reversed on the Internet. And there are hints that this reversal may be somewhat more general.

On the Internet, when you have found the information, you can usually obtain it at zero cost. But finding the information can be expensive. How thoroughly the roles will be reversed is still unclear. The situation does offer some interesting new opportunities to make a profit — not by selling information, but by selling paths to the information and selling maintenance of those paths.

Interestingly, selecting information to feature and deciding what items to juxtapose is at the heart of the traditional editor's role. The essence of that role is captured in the information provided on a typical Web home page. We may well discover that editors have a new role as the paid publishers of home pages.

Access Types

The Internet has proven to be an effective way for individuals and organizations to make information available. Central to the original conception of the Internet was the ability of groups of people to share information — the original ARPAnet began as a way to share information in the defense and research communities. The Internet is also useful as a way to find information. This latter role is the focus of this article.

A useful two-way distinction can be made between data and information. Data are the stuff that live in a database. By themselves, they have little value — certainly little value outside their original context. Data acquire value when they provide the answer to a question. Information, then, is data provided in response to a question. Information has as much value as the question from which the information arose.

But rather than discuss data and information, let us talk about the questions that can and cannot be answered by using what is found on the Internet. The following short list of questions is biased toward computing and information technology. (That's my bias.) It's also a bias of the Internet. The Internet contains vast amounts of information about itself and, more generally, about technology. The less technical the subject, the less likely you are to find full information about it on the Internet.

I asked the following questions of the Internet, sometimes with mixed success. I return to the questions at the end of this article and use them to illustrate how various features of the Internet can be used.

1. What movie should we see tonight?
2. What should I wear to Ottawa tomorrow?
3. How do I fix my Internet connection?
4. What's the best Web browser for Windows?

5. Will the Canadian price of wheat rise or fall?
6. What system development standards are effective?

Using these questions, I'll walk you through most of the ways in which I use the Internet to find information. The following sections provide a description of the Internet features I find most useful.

Source Types

In the early days, most of what moved across the Internet took the form of ASCII mail messages or of executable or data files. Mail remains an important part of Internet traffic and is regularly used to find information. Newsgroups are one of the most popular forms of information exchange, and they are built on an e-mail foundation.

The idea behind newsgroups is simple. Individuals ask questions, or provide information, by sending e-mail messages to a newsgroup. The information in the newsgroup is then passed on from one news site to the next. In practice, messages posted to a newsgroup echo 'round the world in a matter of hours. An interesting question, asked to a newsgroup at large, generates dozens of replies in just a few days.

The administrator for your local server makes the decisions about which newsgroups to echo locally. It's common to find between 5,000 and 10,000 different newsgroups available through a local server. Finding the right newsgroup can be a challenge. And then you may have to read the messages for days or weeks before you figure out how to ask questions in a way that other readers will find interesting.

Reading a newsgroup's messages does give you a good idea about what's important to the community that regularly participates in it. One of the better ways to learn about current thinking in an area is to find a newsgroup for the area and make reading it a regular part of your week or day. Most popular newsgroups provide a quick route in — they come with FAQs, or long messages that cover frequently asked questions.

With some diligence, you'll find newsgroups an effective way to get information. The key requirement, however, is that some Internet-aware community be interested in the subject. It's easy to find communities dedicated to discussing any aspect of the Internet itself. It's less easy to find balanced communities in other areas. But this situation is changing rapidly as more and more people discover the Internet.

The other simple way to get information is to exchange files with remote sites. The file transfer protocol (ftp) defines an established and standard way to exchange information stored in files. A file can contain any kind of information that can be stored in a computer. ftp is the standard way to move arbitrary files around. You can fetch files from remote sites and provide files that can be used remotely.

Thousands of ftp sites allow "anonymous" external access. The ftp standard requires that the user provide a login name and password. A site supporting anonymous ftp access lets remote users respond to the login name request with *anonymous*. Convention and courtesy require that you use your Internet e-mail address as the password. Interesting and valuable information can be found at many anonymous ftp sites.

Recent developments have led to installation of special kinds of information servers on the Internet. Two of these new kinds of information servers warrant special attention. Gopher sites lead the way. More recently, there has been an explosive growth of interest in the World Wide Web. Web traffic apparently increased 1,713 percent in 1994 — an explosive growth by any measure. Large amounts of information can be found at Gopher and Web sites around the world.

Information at a Gopher site is organized in the traditional hierarchical, or treelike, way. The original Gopher allowed only text or files to be stored at points in the hierarchy. The newer Gopher+ software allows a variety of different kinds of information to be stored, such as images, sounds, and video. An important advantage of Gopher is that users see the complete hierarchical structure of the information provided at the site. This fact also happens to be one of Gopher's important disadvantages — it's a major task to organize a good Gopher site.

The World Wide Web takes a different approach. Information is organized in hypertext pages, with designated portions of the pages (the hyperlinks) pointing to where additional information can be found. It's easy to find a hypertext page from Switzerland that points to additional information stored on servers in Canada, the United States, and Mexico. Creation of hypertext Web home pages is quick and easy. Creating *effective* home pages is something else.

The ease of creating home pages is both an important advantage and an important disadvantage for users on the Web. A home page is really a way to capture an individual's understanding of how to present, or organize, information about an interesting topic. The clarity of the author's thought shines through the home page's structure. Some people do think clearly, but this is far from a universal human trait. (For one economic perspective on home page creation, see the sidebar, "A new economics?")

There is no master list of Gopher or Web sites. Normally, an organization establishes such a site because it *wants* to provide information to a community of Internet users. It is in its best interest to publicize the existence of their new Gopher or Web site. Various public-spirited bodies do attempt to maintain lists of available sites. These lists are pretty good but inevitably contain errors and omissions.

It's important to recognize that information is made available because those who do the providing find this to be in their best interest. The community spirit of newsgroup participants is real and an important motivator. This also helps to explain the sense of outrage that is felt when an outsider attempts to use the community for the wrong purposes. The community's standards have been violated, and various members may express their outrage through intemperate prose, or e-mail "flames."

Many public-sector bodies are motivated by a kind of public-spiritedness. Academics want the world to learn of their work. Libraries exist to provide access to the information contained in them. Governments have traditionally been committed to providing information to their publics. More recent trends to open and accessible government are naturally supported through provision of information on the Internet.

In addition to these public information providers, there are a number of private information providers that want their message spread. It's easy and relatively inexpensive for organizations such as Microsoft, IBM, and Novell to make information available through their anonymous ftp sites. It's certainly less expensive to open such a site than to ship update disks of a popular software package to hundreds of thousands of users. Minor updates are often handled in precisely this way.

More and more profit-making organizations are working to find ways to provide effective information through the Internet. The explosive growth in available information will continue. Everyone wants to find effective ways to use the inexpensive facilities of the Internet to reach out and touch the communities that will be interested in their goods or services.

Access Tools

Let me begin by describing the tools that I use to access the Internet. My gateway service provider gives me a dial-in PPP connection. It holds my mail until I sign on to retrieve it. I use a shareware program that provides a PPP connection between my service provider and the WinSock socket (which provides the API, or application programming interface) that all of my Windows Internet client software applications use. It feels like my Windows machine is directly connected into the Internet.

There are significant technical advantages to having a single point of connection through something like WinSock. I regularly use newsgroups and ftp, Gopher, and Web clients to access information on the Internet. These client programs are simplified by not having to take any responsibility for the remote connection. The main advantage I see, however, is that I can use my one telephone connection to do such things as simultaneously read mail and access a file.

In general, any Internet user connects using logic like Figure 20-1 shows.

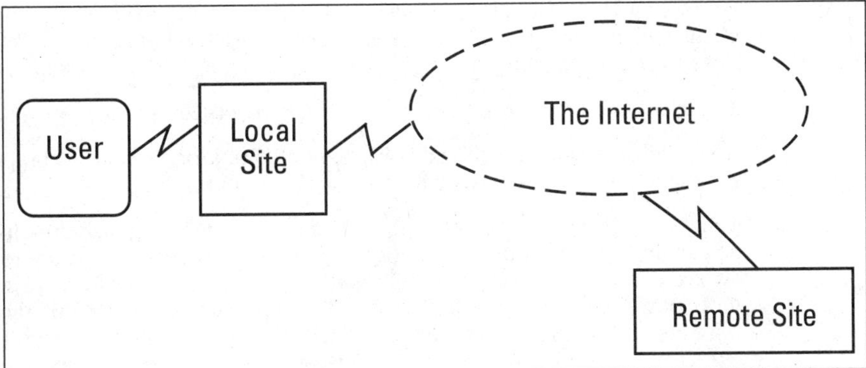

Figure 20-1: The logic to connecting to the Internet.

The user has to connect her local device to a local service provider. In my case, I'm connecting my Windows (WinSock) machine into my Internet gateway provider. Most individual users use a modem and a telephone line to establish the connection. Many people accessing the Internet from within a larger organization use a LAN equipped with a direct high-speed Internet local site connection. The local site and the remote site typically connect to the Internet by using relatively high-speed links.

This setup is roughly described as *client/server.* The abiding question about this kind of arrangement has to do with the relative power and functionality of the user's machine (client) and the machine at the local site (server). Two extremes are possible. Figure 20-2 represents the situation in which most of the power is at the local site (at the server).

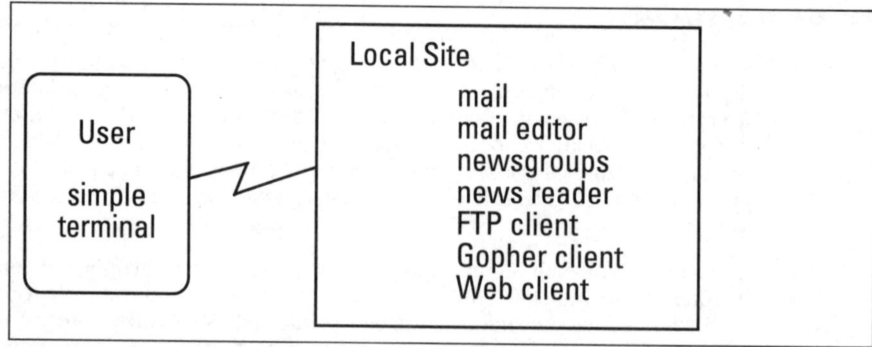

Figure 20-2: Basing processing power at the server.

In fact, the picture may be a little more complex. The Gopher and Web clients may live on a remote site and be accessed through something called a *telnet connection,* which effectively "attaches" the user's simple terminal to a remote client. That remote client can, in turn, be used to access an even more remote Gopher or Web server. It does work, though the resulting service can feel sluggish and unresponsive.

The client and server roles are often partially reversed — as shown in Figure 20-3.

Essentially the same functionality is provided, but far more of the computing power is supplied by the user's machine (heavy client computing).

Ten years ago, when Internet services began to come into general use in the academic and research communities, computers were expensive. There was a strong incentive to provide full access through the use of inexpensive terminals and more powerful, and expensive, shared (local) processors. The resulting equipment base meant that there continued to be strong incentives for even the newer services to work through simple terminals connected to powerful shared processors.

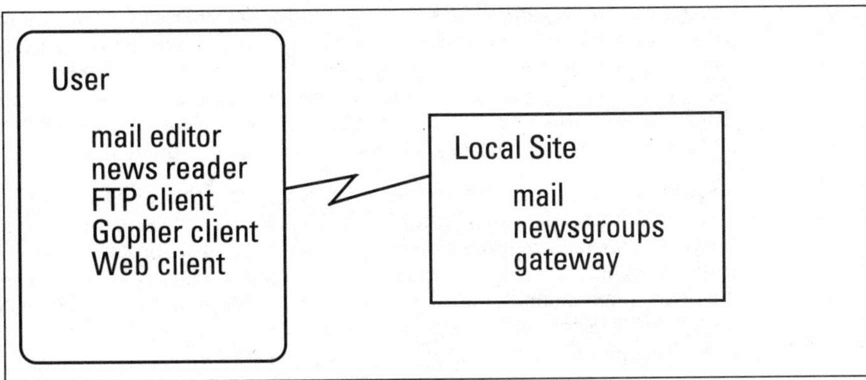

Figure 20-3: Basing processing power at the client.

We have passed the point at which serious questions can be asked about the new equipment to use for access to the Internet. There are large and growing advantages to having powerful client applications on users' machines. By way of illustration, almost any local editor is more responsive than one accessed through a relatively slow telephone connection. And after you have experienced the responsiveness of a personal computer–based editor, using an editor on a shared processor is painful.

In general, a user terminal contains only the information that is visible on the screen. Scrolling is slow and erratic when the connection is a slow telephone line. Most terminals can't continue receiving the rest of a document as you examine the first few screens. With textual information, in my view, there are only minor cosmetic advantages to having a graphical user interface, or GUI, of the kind that Windows provides. With the newer Web pages, the situation changes.

Normal text is, by nature, linear. The idea behind Web hypertext pages is that users are free to jump around using any of the links provided on the page. This kind of material is aggressively nonlinear. A mouse or some other pointing device greatly simplifies access to information on the Web. And although a mouse can be used with a character-oriented screen, it's almost an unnatural act. The mouse really goes with a graphical user interface.

A last, critical point about user clients is the availability of bookmarks. It's important to remember the interesting sites you visit on the Internet. Few things are more frustrating than trying to remember where, two or three weeks ago, you saw just the information you need. We have all experienced the frustration of not being able to find something that we know is somewhere around our desk.

The Internet contains so much information, in so many locations, that it's practically impossible to keep track of where everything is. It makes finding information around a desk a trivial exercise, at least in comparison. Enter the lowly bookmark. All recent Internet client software packages give users a way to record interesting sites with bookmarks. Typically, with Gopher and Web clients, a user can define categories and place a bookmark for the currently visible location under a freely chosen category.

It is difficult to overemphasize the importance of bookmarks. They provide essential personal reminders for where to find interesting information. With bookmarks, you can gradually build personal maps to interesting areas of the Internet. Although it might be logically possible to provide bookmarks through remote clients, such a capability is almost never provided. Users are forced back to scraps of paper with interesting addresses and cryptic commands to recall those interesting locations.

Bookmarks are important to me. In my work, I am inclined to be somewhat casual about backing up data on my hard disk. That is not a major problem because all my active documents are stored on floppies. My hard disk contains mostly programs, with two important exceptions. I back up my list of personal contacts — they are at the heart of any consultant's business. And I back up my list of personal bookmarks — they provide essential reminders for where I can find the information I need in my consulting practice.

Having a GUI for my Internet access is nice, but not essential. Having local client software, with bookmarks, makes the Internet a practical and responsive business tool, even when the connection is a relatively slow modem link over a telephone line.

The ideal client

The Internet clients available to run under Windows are steadily getting better. WSGopher provides a number of important advantages. It delivers WYSIWIH (What You See Is What I Have), with the practical effect that you can start to read even a long text almost immediately. The first screen gets displayed as soon as it arrives, with the rest arriving invisibly in the background. WSGopher also delivers true multitasking. You can download files in the background while viewing new information in the foreground. It does a very good job with gopher information.

But more and more information is available only through Web home pages. To work with such information requires a Web client. Mosaic, the original Web client, was not really designed to work at the end of a relatively slow telephone connection. It waits to show any information until after the entire document has been received. Even with in-line images turned off, the delay can be several minutes.

Netscape has clearly been designed with the needs in mind of a Web user connected through a normal telephone line. As this book is being written, Netscape is still in beta release, but enough is present to see its eventual capabilities. It begins to display information as soon as it is available. It's not as slick as WSGopher, but it comes close to full WYSIWIH. A major weakness is its limited multitasking. Linking out from a page terminates transmission of that page.

The more serious limitation of all these clients is that they provide only basic bookmark facilities. An ideal bookmark service would let me annotate pointers as they are collected. Then it would allow me to assemble the annotated pointers into reference hypertext pages. Rather than have a simple list of pointers under a category, I could easily develop and then keep annotated hypertext reference pages.

This ideal client will be developed. It may not be free, the way WSGopher, Mosaic, and Netscape are. And it will take a few years before the importance of bookmarks is generally recognized. But it will be developed because the benefits for knowledgeable users will be large enough to justify the cost.

Strategies

The first point about searching for information on the Internet is that you have to limit the places you look and limit the tools you use to do the looking. In this section, I first summarize my view of newsgroups, ftp sites, Gopher sites, and Web pages and then describe how I used these (limited) kinds of information to answer the six questions posed at the beginning of this article.

Newsgroups: When you do not yet know what to ask

More often than I often want to admit, I don't know where to begin. I know, or strongly suspect, that a topic is important. I need a quick appreciation for the best current thinking on the subject. An appropriate newsgroup, especially if it comes with a good FAQ, can be an excellent place to start. You get to eavesdrop on a discussion of the topic among a group of generally informed individuals. You can also use the newsgroup to ask pertinent questions, after you learn enough to know what to ask.

One good place to begin is with the list of newsgroup FAQs. Several gopher sites maintain text files of all FAQs. When I last checked, I found more than 1,000 different files dedicated to frequently asked questions. Finding an appropriate FAQ greatly speeds up the learning process.

FTP site: When you know exactly what you want and where it is located

An ftp site presents users with a raw list of files. Index files, when available, may help explain what can be found at the site. But browsing through a list of files is not particularly informative, even when a few descriptive words are attached to the filename in an index. You must already know (more or less) what you want or be prepared to download many files to find the few that are really interesting. Anonymous ftp is an efficient means of fetching the files that you have determined are interesting. It is also a way for you to pass back information, but it has to be redirected by the administrator of the ftp site.

Some search engines will help you find files at anonymous ftp sites, but the only available search criteria are represented in the file's name. One problem is that the same file may have different names in different places. It's almost always better to find an ftp site with the kind of files for which you are searching and examine the index files describing what is available.

Gopher site: When there is a natural source of the information you want

The best Gopher servers provide a wealth of related information to their users. But the effort required to establish and maintain a good Gopher server limits the range of information commonly found at such sites. As with all kinds of Internet servers, a massive amount of information is available about technology in general and the Internet in particular. More generally, I would expect to find a good Gopher site when there is a recognized community with shared interests, a natural sponsor who is prepared to pay for the site, and enough interest in technology to make providing Internet access attractive.

A popular search engine, called Veronica, searches titles and keywords across the universe of Gophers. In fact, a number of Veronica servers are available throughout the world. If you really don't know where to begin, launch a Veronica search — it's easy to get hundreds of possible locations. Indeed, one of the more serious problems with Veronica (as with most Internet search engines) is that it often provides too many possible hits. In many cases, it makes more sense to go in through a site that is found by examining possible Gophers based on something like location; for example, a Cleveland State University Gopher is likely to point you to information connected with, or about, Cleveland.

Web pages: The "easy" way to present a view of a subject

Everyone, it seems, is creating Web pages. And it's easy to understand. A Web page stands alone. A limited effort can produce an effective personal view of a topic of personal importance, and it can be shared through one of the Web client viewers. Web pages, because they are naturally developed with graphics, can also be visually attractive.

I should, however, reveal a personal bias. I generally prefer a straight text version to something developed by using hypertext with hyperlinks to different portions of the text. There is a natural logic to how an author develops material. Hypertext often feels disjointed and unconnected. I, personally, learn more easily with straight text. My reaction to Gopher and Web is parallel. A good Gopher site gives me a natural way to develop an overview of the area. Too often, that overall sense of organization is missing with the Web.

Notwithstanding my linear and conservative bias, I am forced to recognize that more and more information is being made available on the Web. It's also technically true that Web viewers such as Netscape and Mosaic provide access to Gopher sites, whereas the reverse has not been true. Therefore, if one were to be restricted to just one viewer, it would have to be a Web viewer. Finding Web information is similar to finding Gopher information. There are Web search engines similar to Veronica for Gopher.

Netscape comes with a built-in reference to an Internet search page provided by Netscape Communications Corporation. At the end of 1994, that page pointed to nine search engines and two search engine searchers. As with Veronica, these types of search engines can provide a way to start when you don't have any idea of how to begin. But it often makes more sense to begin with one of the Web subject indexes that are available.

With all this as background, I come back to the six questions posed at the beginning of this article. Herewith are the approaches I used to answer those questions.

What movie should we see tonight?

This is almost a trick question. We happen to live in Toronto, and Toronto has *eye WEEKLY,* which publishes a regular listing of all local events, including all local movies, and which happens to be online through both Gopher and the Web. Finding out what's playing is a simple process of checking the current listing in *eye.* Many reviews are published along with the listing, but not all movies that are playing will have reviews in *eye.* It may be necessary to consult one of the movie review sites to make a final selection.

What should I wear to Ottawa tomorrow?

My business has often taken me to Ottawa. The weather is different enough (from my home in Toronto) that it requires some planning to arrive prepared for the likely combinations of wind, rain, sleet, and snow. Fortunately, Environment Canada makes available weather forecasts for the Ottawa region. It's a simple Gopher request.

How do I fix my Internet connection?

The answer to this question really requires advice of the kind that is best found in a newsgroup. I have several choices. My local service provider has a "problems" newsgroup. It's an excellent place to begin — all the other participants in the group are experiencing the same local service. It also happens to be a friendly place, where people are more than willing to offer advice and provide information. On a larger scale, each of the major software components I use has at least one newsgroup. More obscure or subtle software problems can be addressed to these larger groups.

What's the best Web browser for Windows?

The ideal answer is "The browser that best meets your needs and expectations." What is critical in that answer is "your needs and expectations." There is no substitute for working with the different alternatives. Fortunately, the best Web browsers are available as freeware or shareware. Checking the FAQ for Web (or, equivalently, WWW) browsers provides a good starting point. You'll find "expert" opinions about all the popular choices. Fetching examples is often best achieved through ftp. Ultimately, you must make the final decision.

Will the Canadian price of wheat rise or fall?

Multiple Gopher sites in the United States contain extensive information about the price of wheat (in all its various grades). There is really only one international price for wheat. That's fortunate, because I was unable to find any Canadian Internet sources that have Canadian wheat pricing information. I checked with a friend at one of the wheat pools out west (using e-mail); he replied that no Canadian site exists, but they're considering establishing one. Perhaps by the time you read this, they will have acted. If so, it's likely to be a Web site sponsored by the Alberta, Saskatchewan, or Manitoba Wheat Pool.

Which system development standards are effective?

A great deal of literature is published about how computer systems are to be developed. I have found Gopher and Web servers sponsored by publicly funded software institutes in the United States, Canada, and the United Kingdom. Almost any probe uncovers at least one such site. All the sites have reference chains that lead to the other sites. It's interesting to note that the North American standards in this field have been established largely by the IEEE. They have a standards Gopher, but it doesn't make the standards available online. That's understandable because their standards effort is significantly funded by the sale of paper copies of those standards.

Conclusions

An amazing amount of information is available on the Internet. Finding information is a relatively simple, three-step, iterative process:

1. Decide where the kind of information you want is most likely to be found. In almost all cases, you will look at newsgroups, ftp or Gopher sites, or Web pages.
2. Take a first step to get you "close" to the information you want. You can use one of the search engines or consult one of the structured lists that have pointers to other information.
3. The final, necessary, step is a personal examination of what is to be found at a site you hope is close enough. Your first few attempts may well turn into dead ends. Revisit points 1 or 2.

A final point: Keep bookmarks to the places you found to be interesting. Gradually, you will build your own personal map of interesting places. And there is no real substitute for such personally developed understanding.

Robert Fabian is Director of Knowledge Transfer with the GSA Consulting Group, based in Toronto. He has more than 25 years' experience in the information technology field. His consulting work has focused on helping clients find ways to achieve a business advantage through improved use of technology. He views the Internet as one of the more attractive current technologies. Bob has been a consultant, a manager, and an academic. His Ph.D. was awarded by Case Institute of Technology.

How to Look for Resources on the Internet

by Lynn L. Alexander <Lynn.Alexander@excalibur.org>

In the early nineteenth century, President Thomas Jefferson selected Meriwether Lewis and William Clark to lead a discovery of "the water communication across this continent." Here we are in the late twentieth century, and John Levine and Carol Baroudi have selected me to help you explore electronic resources across the globe. Lewis and Clark's expedition was rocky at times as they explored the uncharted waterways, just as your exploration of the vast information superhighway can prove to be tumultuous. Navigating the Internet, however, should be smooth sailing now that you've mastered the basics, such as Archie, Veronica, ftp, WWW, and WAIS.

As I'm sure you've already discovered, although the Internet may be intimidating at first, intimidation soon turns to fascination. The Internet truly is a paradise for fanatical researchers and self-proclaimed modemaholics like me. Resources abound everywhere, from Usenet groups to mailing lists to library catalogs from around the world. Whether it be law, medicine, politics, arts, or whatever, the Internet has something for everyone.

This chapter focuses on search utilities and on how to go about finding useful information on the Internet. You'll learn how to find people and to access library card catalogs, mailing lists, directories, and other useful information on a variety of topics.

The Internet contains so much information that finding what you need can be difficult unless you know where to look for it. The location (or *address*) of each resource is defined by its URL, which includes a protocol type indicating whether you're accessing the site by World Wide Web (indicated by `http`), Gopher, ftp, telnet, or WAIS. Typical addresses contain the protocol, followed by a colon and two slashes, followed by the name of the host on which the resource is located and a resource name on that host. The address `http://www.census.gov/index.html`, for example, tells you that the site is on the WWW, that the host name is `www.census.gov`, and that the resource name at the site is `index.html`. Likewise, `gopher://gopher.census.gov/` tells you that it's a Gopher directory on the site called `gopher.census.gov`.

Mailing lists and newsletters, which can give you more information about the resource, usually have e-mail addresses, which will be included (when available), along with directions on how to subscribe.

Let the pursuit begin!

Search Utilities

When you browse through the Internet, you will encounter your old friends Archie, Veronica, WWW, and so on. (If you need a refresher on these utilities, see the sidebar titled "Some Internet terminology.") The following sections give you a closer look at two utilities. The first utility points you to telnet sites, and the second helps you when you need to locate a particular person.

Some Internet terminology

Archie: Searches for filenames throughout various ftp sites and provides you a list of sites that carry your file. You then can ftp to one of those sites and transfer the file to your own computer.

Bookmark: Similar to paper bookmarks, this Gopher feature enables you to save a place that you want to frequent often so that you can come back to it very easily.

Boolean connectors: AND, OR, and NOT, the use of which allows for more-specific searches.

FTP: Acronym for file transfer protocol, which provides for the transfer of files from one computer to another.

Gopher: Developed by the University of Minnesota, whose mascot just happens to be a gopher, this simple system presents information in menu form.

Hypermedia: Hypertext that also can contain graphics, video, and sound.

Hypertext: Documents that provide links to correlating information. The World Wide Web is based on hypertext.

HTML: Acronym for hypertext markup language. WWW hypertext documents are written in HTML.

http: Acronym for hypertext transfer protocol, which is how WWW pages are transferred over the Internet.

Hytelnet: Hypertext system that indexes telnet Internet sites, including libraries, Gophers, and freenets.

Jughead: Acronym for Jonzy's Universal Gopher Hierarchy Excavation and Display. Somewhat similar to Veronica, Jughead searches Gopher indexes for specified information.

Page: Document available via the WWW that usually includes text, graphics, files, and the like.

Telnet: Protocol that enables you to call and log in to a remote computer.

URL: Acronym for uniform resource locator. A URL is a unique name for a file or resource that allows you to access it. URLs typically include the protocol, hostname, and path for various files. Common protocols include http, ftp, Gopher, telnet, and WAIS.

Veronica: Acronym for Very Easy Rodent-Oriented Netwide Index to Computerized Archives. Veronica searches Gopher menus by keyword.

WAIS: Acronym for wide-area information service, this tool searches indexed database documents that contain the information you are seeking. After you supply WAIS with your search words and selected database, WAIS displays a list of related documents that you can retrieve.

WWW: Acronym for World Wide Web (also called W3 or the Web). WWW is an Internet information system whereby hypertext documents contain words that can be designated as links to other hypertext documents that contain relevant information. For mailing-list information, send e-mail to `www-talk-request@info.cern.ch`.

Hytelnet

`http://www.cc.ukans.edu/hytelnet_html/start.txt.html`

Mailing list: `listserv@kentvm.kent.edu`. In the body of the message, type **subscribe Hytel-L *<your name>***.

Hytelnet is a database that contains the addresses of telnet Internet sites, including libraries, freenets, campus-wide information systems, WAIS, Gopher, and WWW systems. Hytelnet also contains tips about telnet and offers an Internet glossary. You can access Hytelnet online via WWW at the preceding address; you also can find it under the Gopher Search Utilities and Library sections on Delphi.

The program can be downloaded to your computer and is available in versions for UNIX, VMS, IBM, and Macintosh computers. If you are running your own TCP/IP connection, this utility also connects you to the specified telnet site. Hytelnet allows you to customize the sites according to your specifications, as well as to update various other sites. The mailing list, `hytel-l`, provides information about new program versions and updated or deleted files.

Contacts for various versions are

UNIX	`fogel@herald.usask.ca`
Macintosh	`burchil@ccu.umanitoba.ca`
PC	`aa375@freenet.carleton.ca`

When you access Hytelnet via the WWW, you are presented with various menu options, including performing a word search, accessing library catalog menus, or accessing information on other resources. The following menu gives you an idea of what Hytelnet offers. You can get to this menu by choosing option 6 (Other Resources) from the menu that you see first.

```
Other Resources
Page 1 of 1
1 Archie: Archive Server Listing Service  Menu
2 Campus-wide Information systems    Menu
3 Databases and bibliographies    Menu
4 Distributed File Servers (Gopher/WAIS/WWW) Menu
5 Electronic books       Menu
6 FREE-NETs & Community Computing Systems  Menu
7 Fee-Based Services       Menu
8 General Bulletin Boards      Menu
9 HYTELNET On-line versions     Menu
10 Miscellaneous resources      Menu
11 NASA databases        Menu
12 Network Information Services    Menu
13 Whois/White Pages/Directory Services  Menu
14 Other Resources        Text
```

Hytelnet developer Peter Scott has written an article regarding the program's use in accessing Internet resources. If you want to obtain a copy, send e-mail to `listserv@uhupvm1.uh.edu`. In the body of your message, type **GET SCOTT PRV3N4 F=MAIL.**

Netfind

Netfind telnet sites:

`bruno.cs.colorado.edu`

`ds.internic.net`

`netfind.ee.mcgill.ca`

`netfind.oc.com`

`netfind.sjsu.edu`

Mailing list: `netfind-users-request@cs.colorado.edu`. In the body, type **subscribe netfind users**.

If you're searching for a person, you'll want to access Netfind. Essentially a white-pages directory, Netfind attempts to find telephone and e-mail information when prompted with the person's first, last, or login name. Netfind can be accessed via various telnet sites, some of which appear in the preceding list. To use Netfind, telnet to one of those sites, and enter the user name **netfind** to log in. After viewing the welcome screen, you see the following menu:

```
Top level choices:
   1. Help
   2. Search
   3. Seed database lookup
   4. Options
   5. Quit (exit server)
```

Choose 2 to go to the search menu. You will be prompted for a person's name as well as for location keywords, such as *university, Boston*, or *Canada*. You can use only one name — first, last, or login — but you can specify multiple keywords. Be as specific as you can when entering your choices so that the search won't be too general. Otherwise, Netfind presents the following message:

```
locate: first key (university) matched too many refs
```

You then will be asked to select certain sites from a given list so that the search can be narrowed down and more easily managed. Netfind will keep you posted about its progress and which hosts it is searching. After anywhere from a few seconds to a few minutes, Netfind presents the search results.

Online help is available, as is a mailing list to keep you abreast of software updates and related topics.

Weaving through the Web

Browsing the Internet is one of my favorite pastimes; it can, however, be very time-consuming. Luckily, various organizations are trying to help with the formidable task of tracking down resources that may be of particular interest. One such approach involves categorizing the Web by subject. Delphi users can access the WWW Subject Search Guides by choosing 14 from the Search Utilities menu. For non-Delphi users, the following sections list the various subject guides that are available, along with the URLs.

The World Wide Web Virtual Library: Subject Catalog

`http://info.cern.ch/hypertext/datasources/bysubject/overview.html`

This comprehensive subject catalog includes such topics as aboriginal studies, agriculture, applied linguistics, chemistry, cognitive science, and demography and population studies . . . and the list goes on and on.

EINet Galaxy

`http://www.einet.net/galaxy.html`

EINet Galaxy is yet another searchable index of Web documents, provided by the same people who make Macintosh and Windows Web browsers.

Planet Earth Home Page

`http://white.nosc.mil/info.html`

The Planet Earth Home Page provides a variety of earthly resources that are available on the Internet. Topics include physics, colleges and universities, books and libraries, the National Aeronautics and Space Administration, and the solar system.

Joel's Hierarchical Subject Index

`http://www.cen.uiuc.edu/~jj9544/index.html`

As the name suggests, this is another hierarchical subject index.

Yahoo: A Guide to WWW

`http://akebono.stanford.edu/yahoo/`

Yahoo is a searchable database of approximately 10,000 entries, organized by category. The database gives you the option to browse newly available links, as well as the most popular links.

INTER-LINKS

http://alpha.acast.nova.edu/start.html

INTER-LINKS is designed to aid Internet users by providing links to obtain documents, reach menus, or begin a program. Categories include Internet resources, fun and games, guides and tutorials, news and weather, and library resources.

A List of Virtual Libraries on the Web

http://info.cern.ch/hypertext/datasources/bysubject/virtual_libraries/overview.html

As the name implies, this list provides a link to the various pages mentioned in this section.

PROJECT DA-CLOD

http://schiller.wustl.edu/daclod/daclod

PROJECT DA-CLOD is another categorized list of documents. Top-level categories range from anarchy to animation.

CyberSight

http://cybersight.com/cgi-bin/cs/s?main.gmml

CyberSight, which is a hip place to be, includes topic selections such as graffiti wall, enigma, adventures, trivia and polls, and hangman.

Special Internet Connections (Yanoff)

http://info.cern.ch/hypertext/datasources/yanoff.html

Special Internet Connections was compiled by none other than Scott Yanoff, known to Netters for his Yanoff list. Contents include pointers to various Internet sites and are not limited to Web documents. Subjects include agriculture; art; astronomy; business, economics, and financial; computers; consumer and commercial information; and food, recipes, and cooking.

EFF Extended (Big Dummy's) Guide

http://www.germany.eu.net/books/bdgtti/bdgtti-intro.html

This guide was produced from the information in the book formerly known as *Big Dummy's Guide to the Internet*, a joint project of Apple Computer, Inc., and The Electronic Frontier Foundation (EFF).

This site allows you to browse the table of contents, read the guide online, or make a query for a specific topic of interest.

Internet Resources Meta-Index

http://www.ncsa.uiuc.edu/sdg/software/mosaic/metaindex.html

The Internet Resources Meta-Index is a comprehensive index of the various resource directories and indices that are available on the Internet. The index includes a myriad of choices, including those broken down by subject, WWW, Gopher, telnet, ftp, and WAIS.

The Mother-of-all BBS

http://www.cs.colorado.edu/homes/mcbryan/public_html/bb/summary.html

The Mother-of-all BBS provides a variety of WWW pages, including those for various companies, universities, research centers, and government agencies.

Human-Computer Interaction (HCI) Launching Pad

http://hydra.bgsu.edu/hci/

The HCI Launching Pad is a collection of links to sources regarding human–computer interaction on the Web. Links usually contain only pointers to the top level of a resource, so when you get to a specific link, you'll have to explore it from there. Link choices include electronic publications, laboratories, education, FAQs, organizations, and bibliographies.

Keep in mind that you will want to try each of these links to see which ones are best suited for your needs. Another approach is to create guides to the resources on the Net, categorized by subject, organization, or location. The following five resources give you new ways to track down the information that you need.

Clearinghouse for Subject-Oriented Internet Resource Guides

telnet:una.hh.lib.umich.edu

Log in as **gopher**, and choose the What's New and Featured Resources menu (menu choice 13).

URL: gopher://una.hh.lib.umich.edu:70/11/newstuff

This clearinghouse is a useful resource for discovering where you should look on the Net for information on a particular topic. A combined effort of the University of Michigan's University Library and the School of Information and Library Studies

(SILS), these guides help Net searchers find information that is pertinent to particular topics on the Net. The guides categorize resources by subject, rather than by the specific tools used to access them or the format in which they are available. Each guide lists various resources pertaining to a particular subject and includes Usenet groups, so that even if you don't have access to Gopher, you can at least discover which Usenet groups pertain to your subject.

The guides, which number more than 150, include those written by members of the Internet community (such as Michael Strangelove's "The Electric Mystic's Guide") as well as those written by SILS students at the University of Michigan. You can select a menu of all guides or those broken down into the categories humanities, social sciences, and sciences. You can get past the ordinary Gopher menus to the Clearinghouse for Subject-Oriented Resource Guides by selecting 13 in the first screen and then 2 in the following screen. (The resource choices take you to information on selected topics; the clearinghouse tells you where else you can look for resources on your topic.)

The clearinghouse menu looks like this:

```
        Internet Gopher Information Client v2.0.15
 Clearinghouse for Subject-Oriented Internet Resource Guides (UMich)
-> 1. About the Clearinghouse (UMich) <Menu>
 2. Search full texts of these Guides <Index>
 3. The Internet Resource Discovery Project (UMich) <Menu>
 4. Helpful Information on using the Internet <Menu>
 5. All Guides <Menu>
 6. Guides on the Humanities <Menu>
 7. Guides on the Sciences <Menu>
 8. Guides on the Social Sciences <Menu>
```

From here, you can select the guides that interest you.

Another option in the preceding menu is 3 (The Internet Resource Discovery Project). This endeavor is another collaboration between the University of Michigan's SILS and the University Library. The library staff trained students in Internet tools and retrieval skills; then the students set out to uncover resources in their selected fields. The following menu lists guides that were produced by the Internet Resource Discovery Project:

```
Guides from the Internet Resource Discovery Project (UMich)
 -> 1. Aerospace Engineering; C. Poterala, D. Dalquist; 12..(UMich) <Text>
   2. Archives; D. Anthony, N. Kayne; v1; 12/93 (UMich) <Text>
   3. Book Discussions & Reviews; S. Allen, G. Krug; v1; 12..Mich) <Text>
   4. Business, Economics; T. Austin, K. Tsang; 12/93 (UMich) <Text>
   5. Cancer; J. Gourdji, S. Hinton; 11/08/94 (UMich) <Text>
   6. Citizens' Rights; M. Pfaff, D. Bachman; v1.1; 11..4 (UMich) <Text>
   7. Cyberpreneurship; P. Wilkins, S. Schweitzer; v1.0; 10..Mich) <Text>
   8. Diversity; L. Heise; 08/93 (UMich) <Text>
   9. Emotional Support; J. Juhnke, C. Powell; v1.1; 11.. (UMich) <Text>
   10. Environment; T. Murphy, C. Briggs-Erickson; v1; 12.. (UMich) <Text>
   11. Federal Regulations; N. Lagace, J. Brandt; v0.9; 10..(UMich) <Text>
   12. Film and Video; K. Garlock, L. Wood; v1.0; 12..5/93 (UMich) <Text>
```

```
   13. German History; K. McBride; 08/93 (UMich) <Text>
   14. Higher Education; H. Weise; 04/93 (UMich) <Text>
   15. Job Searching & Employment; P. Ray, B. Taylor; 10.. (UMich) <Text>
   16. Neurosciences; S. Bonario, S. Cormicle; v1; 12/93 (UMich) <Text>
   17. Non-Profit Orgs.; S. Nesbeitt, R. Truxall; v1.0; 10..(UMich) <Text>
P Previous Page   M Go To Main Menu    ? Help Screen    D Download
```

A Guide to Archives on the Internet

`ftp: una.hh.lib.umich.edu/inetdirsstacks/archives:kaynthony`

This guide is one of the guides produced by the Internet Resource Discovery Project. Updated quarterly, the guide helps researchers locate historical materials, including documents, records, and images. Brief descriptions of collection contents accompany all addresses. Collections include those that are available via telnet, WWW, and Gopher. The guide is available via anonymous ftp at the preceding address, as well by means of the menu in the preceding section.

Searching by Type and Location

Another way to categorize Web sites is by organization type, such as commercial services, freenets, and government agencies. You also can search the Web by geographical location.

Suppose that you want to reach Apple Computer World Wide Tech Support. If you suspect that this site is in California, you can go to the University of Minnesota Gopher (`gopher.micro.umn.edu`) and get to the California menu from there. First, choose 8 (Other Gopher and Information Servers); next, choose 9 (North America); then choose 4 (USA). You then see a listing of states. In this case, you would choose 7 (California). You then see a menu similar to the following:

```
california
Page 1 of 8

1  187resist: Immigrant Rights in California          Menu
2  1994 California Voter Information            Menu
3  APS-Academic Physician and Scientist          Menu
4  AbagOnline [Access to Bay Area Governments Online]      Menu
5  Apple Computer World Wide Tech Support          Menu
6  BARRNet                          Menu
7  BIOSCI/bionet biology newsgroups server          Menu
8  Batish Institute of Indian Music & Fine Arts        Menu
9  CAMIS (Center for Advanced Medical Informatics at Stanford)  Menu
10 CORNET - County of Riverside Network          Menu
11 CRESST/UCLA Research on Evaluation and Testing       Menu
12 Cal Poly Pomona (California State Polytechnic University)   Menu
13 Cal Poly State University                 Menu
```

```
14 California Academy of Sciences              Menu
15 California Department of Education            Menu
16 California Online Voter Guide               Menu
17 California Public Utilities Commission           Menu
18 California Secretary of State               Menu
19 California State Legislature               Menu
```

Voilà! As you can see, you now can reach your desired destination by choosing 5. This method is a quick way to locate sites.

Gopher Jewels

gopher://cwis.usc.edu/11/
other_gophers_and_information_resources/gophers_by_subject/
gopher_jewels

Mailing list: e-mail to gopher jewels list listproc@einet.net

Gopher Jewels provides a catalog of Gopher resources that contains more than 2,000 pointers by category, including the recently added categories genealogy, journalism, and Internet Service Providers. Although many of the features are not unique, taken as a whole, Gopher Jewels represents some of the best sites around the world. I often find myself using Gopher Jewels because it is very easy to use and enables you to jump up a menu from any directory, as well as to jump to the top menu. Gopher Jewels also permits a Jughead search of menus, which is useful when you want to search menus and filenames on various Gopher sites. Gopher Jewels does not conduct a full-text search; it searches only the names of files and directories. The following menu gives you an idea of what Gopher Jewels has to offer:

```
Gopher Jewels
Page 1 of 1
1  GOPHER JEWELS Information and Help          Menu
2  Community, Global and Environmental          Menu
3  Education, Social Sciences, Arts & Humanities      Menu
4  Economics, Business and Store Fronts         Menu
5  Engineering and Industrial Applications         Menu
6  Government                       Menu
7  Health, Medical, and Disability           Menu
8  Internet and Computer Related Resources         Menu
9  Law                         Menul
10 Library, Reference, and News            Menu
11 Miscellaneous Items                Menu
12 Natural Sciences including Mathematics         Menu
13 Personal Development and Recreation          Menu
14 Research, Technology Transfer and Grants Opportunities Menu
```

If you choose 1, the next menu appears:

```
GOPHER JEWELS Information and Help
Page 1 of 1
1  About Gopher Jewels                  Text
2  Select This Option To Leave Your Comments and Suggestions   Text
```

```
3  What's New with Gopher Jewels                   Text
4  Gopher Tips & Help Documents                   Menu
5  Gopher Jewels Announcement Archives                Menu
6  Gopher Jewels Discussion  Archives               Menu
7  Gopher Jewels Mirror Sites Worldwide               Menu
8  Search Gopher Jewels Archives: Discussions, Announcements, T Search
9  Other Archives and Related Information              Menu
10  Jump to Gopher Jewels Main Menu                Menu
11 Search Gopher Jewels Menus by Key Word(s)             Search
```

If you have a question about the Internet, the following topics are available in the Gopher Tips & Help Documents menu:

```
Gopher Tips & Help Documents
Page 1 of 2
1  Gopher Tips & Help - Read Me First!           Text
2  What Is Gopher?                      Text
3  Quick Reference Guide For Gopher             Text
4  General Network Terms                  Text
5  Bookmarks In Gopher                   Text
6  Cancel Gopher Request                  Text
7  Search Gopher Menu                    Text
8  Download Documents With Gopher              Text
9  E-mail a Document From Gopher              Text
10 Viewing Picture Files                  Text
11 Gopher To A Specified Gopher Information Server     Text
12 Links Entries In Gopher                 Text
13 Telnet Access To Public Gopher Clients          Text
14 Design Tips For Building Gopher Information Servers   Text
15 Operating Gopher By E-mail               Text
16 Jughead (search gopher menus)              Text
17  Veronica (search gopher entries worldwide)             Text
18  Archie (search FTP archives worldwide)                Text
19  WAIS (wide area information system searchable archives)  Text
20  Search Gopher Jewels Menus by Key Word(s)              Search
```

Gopher Jewels can prove to be a good starting point for exploring various resources.

Library Antics

When time permits, I love to roam through the Library and Research sections of the Internet. Accessing card catalogs throughout the world with a few clicks of a button can be quite a contrast to roaming through musty shelves of books in the public library. The following section describes one of my favorite library resources.

CARL

telnet: `csi.carl.org`

The Colorado Alliance of Research Libraries, better known as CARL, was established in 1978 to provide a method for libraries to share information. CARL certainly accomplished that task and offers a variety of services, some of which are accessible to the public; other services require passwords.

This section examines two of CARL's publicly accessible services. I especially like the CARL system because it enables you to track down which library in your area has a particular book. Upon login, enter **pac**. Don't forget to press Enter after you make your choices; otherwise, you may get stuck in cyberspace. After you are asked what kind of computer you are using, you see the following screen:

```
CARL Corporation offers access to the following
           groups of databases:

       1. Library Catalogs
           (including Government Publications)

       2. Current Article Indexes and Access
           (including UnCover and ERIC)

       3. Information Databases
           (including Encyclopedia)

       4. Other Library Systems

       5. Library and System News

  Enter the NUMBER of your choice, and press the <RETURN> key >>1
```

To see which library catalogs are accessible, choose 1. Because I live in Connecticut, I went back to the main menu and chose 4 (Other Library Systems) to see what else was available.

The Other Library Systems menu breaks down the libraries according to geographical location and allows you to choose libraries from the Eastern United States or the Western United States. The menu follows:

```
          OTHER LIBRARY SYSTEMS


   41. CARL Corporation Network Libraries - Eastern U.S.
       * Includes public, academic, and school library catalogs,
        and some local information databases.

   42. CARL Corporation Network Libraries - Western U.S. (MENU 1)
       * Includes public, academic, and school library catalogs,
        and some local information databases.

   43. CARL Corporation Network Libraries - Western U.S. (MENU 2)
```

This time, I chose 41, because I'm on the East Coast. (The last I heard, Chicago wasn't on the East Coast, so I don't know why it's listed there.) The menu includes 16 library systems on the East Coast. The choices are far from complete, but it turns out that my library system is included. I chose 162 (Bibliomation), because I have a card from Bibliomation, an East Coast library network, and figured that my favorite libraries would show up. This screen came up:

```
                 Welcome

                   to

               Bibliomation


  ***************************************************
    The computerized information system shared
    by forty libraries throughout Connecticut
  ***************************************************


    Marketed and supported by CARL Systems, Inc.
          Denver, Colorado



                 CHOICES

   BIBLIOMATION offers access to the following:


   1. Catalogs of the participating libraries

   2. Magazine and journal indexes and databases

   3. Other reference sources

   4. Links to other libraries in the United States
```

I chose 1 and was given the choice of Public Library Catalogs, Academic Library Catalogs, or both. I chose the Waterbury Silas Bronson Library and searched the catalogs for books on the Internet. Twenty items matched, and I was given two options: to narrow down the search by adding words, or to display the list.

I wanted more specifics on *Internet For Dummies*, so I chose to display a record of the book and its status at the library. I saw the following screen:

```
---------------------------------------------Silas Bronson Library----
Author(s):    Levine, John R.
Title(s):     Internet for dummies / John R. Levine and Carol Baroudi ;
          foreword by Paul McCloskey.
Imprint:      San Mateo, CA : IDG Books, c1993.
         xxiv, 355 p. : ill. ; 24 cm.
         --For dummies
         "Covers DOS, Mac, & UNIX platforms!"--Cover.
         Includes index.

Subject:      Internet (Computer network)
         Computer networks.
         Baroudi, Carol.

LOCN:  WTRBRY BUSTEC  STATUS: Due: 11/28/94
CALL #: M 384.3 LEV

LOCN:  WTRBRY BUSTEC  STATUS: Not checked out --
CALL #: M 384.3 LEV

more follows -- press <RETURN> (Q to quit)Q
```

This search provided me a quick and easy way to browse the card catalog to see whether the library carries a specific book and whether the book is available.

CARL has many features, including an Internet Resource Guide, which allows you to search for information on library catalogs, archives, and other resources available through the Internet. You also can use CARL to search for (and order) television and radio transcripts from Journal Graphics.

UnCover

`telnet: pac.carl.org`

Have you ever pored over a stack of old magazines, looking for an article that you wanted to save? Or perhaps you're doing research on a project and want to see how much material has been written. If so, you'll want to try CARL's UnCover, a menu-driven article-delivery service. You can access this option via the preceding telnet address or by choosing 2 from CARL's main menu and then choosing 50.

UnCover maintains an archive of more than 5 million articles and gives you access to more than 5,000 magazines and journals. You can perform a search by topic or author and receive the article by fax within 24 hours. The service will even e-mail you the table of contents from various issues at no cost. Of course, you have to pay if you want to have the articles faxed to you.

You will want to create a profile account for yourself if you plan to have materials forwarded to you on a regular basis. In essence, this is a registration process whereby you enter your name, address, fax number, and method of payment. Your profile is saved and used for subsequent orders. Even if you don't register, you can use the service; you will be charged a higher rate, however, and must enter your profile information before you place each order.

When you access UnCover, you are asked whether you want to search by name, word, or journal title. When you start your search, you are given a listing of matching items. If the list is too long, you have the opportunity to provide additional words so that you can narrow the search. You then can view a summary of any or all articles in the list. When you select an item, a summary appears, which includes a synopsis, along with the author, title, and location of the article.

The bottom of the entry displays the cost of having the article faxed to you. UnCover does tell you that the article may be available at your library at no cost. You then have the option of having the article faxed to you or trekking to your local library. Having the article faxed can be expensive, so you'll probably want to go to the library, if you can. (To have an article that I found in a recent search faxed to me would have cost $23.) Even if you don't order the articles, UnCover gives you the opportunity to search for articles of particular interest without having to perform the search at a library or to leaf through numerous periodical listings.

Guides, Newsletters, and Mailing-List Mania

Those who are eager to tap into the vast well of information that's available on the Net undoubtedly are plagued by the common problem of not knowing where to begin and how to stay on top of new developments. Although the number of available resources can be overwhelming at times, various lists, guides, and newsletters help us keep abreast as rapid changes take place.

The following sections describe some new resources that serve as an "Internet compass" of sorts. These resources point you in the right direction, as well as lead you to new resources and sites that are of particular interest to you. All these sources are free unless otherwise noted.

Net-happenings

`http://www.internic.net/htbin/search-net-happenings`

Mailing list: `majordomo@is.internic.net`

Usenet: `comp.internet.net-happenings`

Net-happenings is an absolute favorite of mine — the name says it all. I feel as though it's Christmas every morning when I check my e-mail and peruse this very informative list of announcements. This list is sure to include at least one of your interests. Listings run the gamut from the announcement of a new government WWW to that of an online chocolate factory (as if being addicted to modems weren't bad enough). Best of all, Net-happenings maintains an archive that enables you to query the Net-happenings WAIS Index by entering a combination of category keywords.

WEBster

E-mail: 4free@webster.tgc.com. Leave the message area blank.

WEBster is the first *e-zine* (short for *e-mail magazine*) that focuses on Mosaic and the World Wide Web. The publication went public in September 1994 and, as of this writing, offers free trial subscriptions. After that, you have to pay, but it's not very expensive.

After scanning the table of contents, you send the article numbers in the subject line back to WEBster, and the articles magically appear in your e-mail.

Net-Letter Guide

Guide: listserv@netcom.com (new address). Type **subscribe net-letter**.

The Net-Letter Guide focuses on a variety of news-oriented Net-letters and includes only those that are free. Very technical publications are not included, and new zines aren't added until they establish a regular publishing schedule. You also can access Net-Letter Guide through various Usenet groups, including alt.zines, alt.etext, and alt.internet.services.

The Internet Press

Guide: e-mail to savetz@rahul.net. Type **send ipress** in the Subject line.

The Internet Press, a guide to electronic journals on the Internet, is fairly new and not incredibly long. Periodic updates are posted in alt.internet.services, alt.culture.internet, and alt.etext.

Edupage

Newsletter: listproc@educom.edu. Type **subscribe edupage <your name>**.

Edupage, which summarizes news related to technological information, is published three times a week by Educom — a group of leading colleges and universities that have a strong interest in changing education via information technology. The newsletter also is available in Portuguese and Spanish; send e-mail to edunews@nc-rj.rnp.br. Archives are maintained; you can access them via Gopher at educom.edu or via WWW at http://educom.edu/.

I discovered many of the resources mentioned in this chapter through the sources listed in this section. These resources are intended to serve as a starting point in your quest for information; they by no means reflect all the resources that are available.

Searching Mailing Lists for Information

Don't overlook mailing lists when you seek information; they can prove to be very valuable sources when you are conducting research on a particular topic. Unlike Usenet groups, which actually reside on your host system, mailing lists go directly to your e-mail. Be forewarned, however, that the volume of mail contained in mailing lists can be very high; you'll want to make sure to subscribe only to those mailing lists that are of particular interest to you. Mailing lists usually maintain archives of contributions that can be searched and often contain files that subscribers and owners have uploaded for interested parties. Before you can search a mailing list, of course, you have to know which lists exist.

Interest-Groups list of lists

E-mail: `mail-server@sri.com`. In the body of the message, type **send interest-groups**.

Alternatively, ftp to `crvax.sri.com`, change directory to netinfo, and retrieve file INTEREST-GROUPS or compressed file INTEREST-GROUPS.Z.

Also known as Interest-Groups, SIGLIST, or Interest lists, this very large document indexes scores of available Internet and Bitnet mailing lists.

The document also is available in bookstores as *Internet: Mailing Lists* (Englewood Cliffs: Prentice Hall, 1994). If you plan to purchase this book, make sure that you get the most current copy; the book is always at least several months out of date, compared with the online list.

New-List

Mailing list: e-mail to `listserv@vm1.nodak.edu`, and type **subscribe new-list <your name>**.

The New-List mailing list is a good source if you want to stay informed about newly established mailing lists; its sole purpose is to announce the creation of e-mail mailing lists. (Yes, that's right: a mailing list about mailing lists.) New-List not only announces new lists but also posts changes about those that already exist. When you subscribe to the list you can tell what each post is about by looking in the subject line of each message. For example, newly announced lists are labeled NEW, and postings regarding a change in the status or location of a list are labeled CHANGE.

LISTSERV mailing lists

E-mail: `listserv@vm1.nodak.edu`. In the body of the message, type **List Global**.

If you send for this list, you receive a comprehensive list of LISTSERV mailing lists. You can distinguish a LISTSERV mailing list from others because it contains *LISTSERV* in its address. Because the file is so large, a better plan is to narrow down your search and ask for a listing of mailing lists on a particular topic. Instead of sending the command list global, you can send list/global/string. Writing list/global/photo, for example, would return a listing of mailing lists that contain *photo, photography*, and *photographer*.

Database searches of mailing lists can be helpful, because comprehensive lists can be very large and take up a great deal of hard disk space. By conducting searches, you can keep a small file of only those mailing lists that interest you. All database searches can be conducted via e-mail. To query the lists for a specific topic, you send an e-mail message containing arcane control messages (related to an IBM job-control language from the 1960s) to `listserv@vm1.nodak.edu`.

Following is an example of a typical search that you can modify for your own needs:

```
// JOB Echo=No
Database Search DD=Rules
//Rules DD *
command 1
command 2
/*
```

If you want to search the LISTSERV database for lists pertaining to art, for example, you would send the following message:

```
//  JOB Echo=No
Database Search DD=Rules
//Rules DD  *
Search art in new-list Index
/*
```

This search would return a list of mailing lists that pertain to art. The list name and node name are provided so that you can subscribe to a list that interests you. You then can send various commands to that list to retrieve certain information. For example, some lists allow you to review the names and e-mail addresses of all subscribers — a capability that can provide valuable contacts on particular topics. After all, people who subscribe to a particular mailing list usually know quite a bit about the subject.

LISTSERV probably is the most widely known and used mailing-list software available today. If you have an e-mail account, you can access LISTSERV. The program performs several functions, including mailing-list management, file services, and database services. The following commands give you an idea of the features available in revised LISTSERV version 1.7c:

Command	***Result***
Info <topic|?>	Gets detailed information files
List <Detail|Short|Global>	Gets a description of all lists
SUBscribe listname <full_name>	Subscribes to a list
SIGNOFF listname	Signs off from a list
SIGNOFF * (NETWIDE	Signs off from all lists on all servers

Command	***Result***
REView listname <options>	Reviews a list
STats listname <options>	Reviews list statistics
Query listname	Queries personal distribution options
SET listname options	Sets personal distribution options
INDex <filelist_name>	Obtains a list of LISTSERV files
GET filename filetype	Obtains a file from LISTSERV
REGister full_namelOFF	Tells LISTSERV your name

The preceding table contains just a partial list of common commands. For a complete list, send e-mail to `listserv@vm1.nodak.edu`, and type **INFO REFCARD** in the body of the message. For detailed information on how to conduct a database search, send the Info Database command.

When you know the correct address and want to search mailing-list archives, you must include two important pieces of information in your message: the name of the database that you want to search, and the subject of the search. Again, all these searches are conducted via e-mail and are sent as regular messages. If you want to search the Books database for all entries that mention Steinbeck, for example, you would send the following message:

```
//  JOB Echo=No
Database Search DD=Rules
//Rules DD *
Search Steinbeck in Books Index
/*
```

This command would select all entries in the Books database that contain the word *Steinbeck*. If you want to search all entries in the database, you would substitute an asterisk (*) for *Steinbeck*. Searching for all entries would generate a list of all books contained in the database. An easier way to get an index of all entries would be to send the following one-line command to LISTSERV:

```
index books
```

The Index command provides you a list containing all the index numbers, dates, times, lines, and subjects of messages that include the word *Steinbeck*. You then would use the Print command to retrieve specific messages. If you receive 100 messages, for example, and want to read the one with index number 99, you would send the following message:

```
//  JOB Echo=No
Database Search DD=Rules
//Rules DD *
Search Steinbeck in Books
Print all of 99
/*
```

You can request more than one message at a time. `Print 88 99 33`, for example, retrieves the three specified messages.

Boolean searches can come in handy. These searches allow you to specify more than one keyword by using AND, OR, and NOT.

You could substitute the search line in the preceding example with any of the following.

```
Search Steinbeck AND "The Grapes of Wrath" in Books
```

This example would search for all messages that include both *Steinbeck* and *The Grapes of Wrath*.

```
Search Steinbeck OR "The Grapes of Wrath" in Books
```

This example would produce messages that contain either *Steinbeck* or *The Grapes of Wrath*, but not necessarily both.

You can use parentheses to group certain words and use more than one Boolean argument. Following is an example of this type of search:

```
Search (Steinbeck OR "The Grapes of Wrath") AND classics in Books
```

This search would return a list of messages that include classics and *Steinbeck* or *The Grapes of Wrath*, or both.

```
Search Steinbeck NOT "The Grapes of Wrath" in Books
```

This search would produce messages that contain the word *Steinbeck* but do not contain *The Grapes of Wrath*. If you are searching for Steinbeck books but don't want any messages pertaining to *The Grapes of Wrath*, this message eliminates all those that mention *The Grapes of Wrath*.

Miscellaneous Goodies Worth Investigating

The following section features various interesting Internet sites that deserve mention, including article-retrieval services, customized searching services, and an electronic catalog of texts.

InfoSeek

`http://www.infoseek.com/`

E-mail: `info@infoseek.com`

InfoSeek, a newly launched commercial article-retrieval and Internet search service, promises easy and affordable searches of databases on medicine, entertainment, and sports, as well as technical subjects such as computers and patents. Infoseek maintains an index of over 2 million articles from over 100 computer publications. In addition, Infoseek also maintains information from 10,000 Usenet newsgroups and over 200,000 popular World Wide Web pages. Established by the former founder and president of Frame Technology and Mouse Systems, InfoSeek offers users the ability to query the system in plain English and also provides comprehensive online hypertext help. New user introductory accounts cost $9.95 per month and also include a user credit in the same amount. (Essentially, you can try Infoseek for one month without paying a subscription fee.) This fee allows you to make 100 transactions; additional transactions cost ten cents each. Each query as well as each document retrieval from a non-Premium database is considered a transaction. Most retrievals are included in the monthly fee; however, documents from Premium collections cost anywhere from five cents to five dollars. The retrieval of WWW pages is free. An online demo is also available.

Online periodicals include *Business Week, Computer Shopper, Forbes, Fortune, Macworld*, and *The New York Times,* just to name a few. For a complete listing of online periodicals, which is updated monthly, send e-mail to `request@infoseek.com` and type **cs-journals** in the body of the message.

Alex: A catalogue of electronic texts on the Internet

`gopher://gopher.lib.ncsu.edu:70/11/library/stacks/alex`

E-mail: `alex@rsl.ox.ac.uk`

Alex enables you to search for and retrieve full-text Internet documents; it indexes more than 1,800 books and shorter texts by author, title, subject, language, date, and host. Included are documents from Project Gutenberg, Wiretap, the Online Book Initiative, the English Server at Carnegie-Mellon University, and the online portion of the Oxford Text Archive. Whether you're seeking Abraham Lincoln's Gettysburg Address, Jack London's *Call of the Wild*, or even an acronym dictionary, you're sure to enjoy browsing Alex.

The Harvest information discovery and access system

`http://harvest.cs.colorado.edu/`

E-mail: `harvest-dvl@cs.colorado.edu`

Harvest is a combination of tools that collect, arrange, search, store, and duplicate pertinent material throughout the Internet. You can tailor Harvest to assimilate information in various formats and to create new collections of information and then place them on the Internet. Harvest is useful for organizations and individuals who want to customize their own collections so that they can access only the pertinent information that they need. The system has the capability to find thousands of reports and to produce a summary of document and software contents.

According to the team leader of the project, Harvest not only is seeking to make access to information easier, but also is designed to lessen the burden on servers, host computers, and the Internet in general. When you enter Harvest, you can access demonstrations, papers, software, and documentation, including a comprehensive user manual and an online FAQ.

Harvest also enables you to query AT&T's 800-number telephone directory. This Broker (which is what Harvest calls its index servers) was gathered from AT&T's 800 Web pages, which can be browsed only by category or name. Harvest's Broker enables users to browse the directory by using keywords and to search by category, business name, or telephone number; it even accounts for misspellings. (Of course, I didn't know this when I used AT&T's directory, which I discuss in the next section.) Just writing about Harvest is exciting; I can't wait to begin exploring it.

AT&T 800 Directory

`http://att.net/dir800`

As addicted to modems as we may be, we still have to use the good old-fashioned telephone to reach people who are not yet computer-savvy enough to be on the Internet. As mentioned previously, the Web has an AT&T 800-numbers directory. Now you can literally let your fingers do the walking and reach out and touch someone with the help of your modem.

This service gives you the option of browsing for entries by category or by name. You then can select the letter of the alphabet that you want. I chose 10 to begin a category search of entries beginning with the letter *I.* I had to scroll through 12 of 13 pages until I found the entry I was seeking, which was Invention Services (105). Then the service presented two pages of 800 numbers for Invention Services. The menu also indicated that keyword-search capability is coming. Until the keyword search is instituted, I think I'll use the Harvest directory; otherwise, I may be searching for a carpal-tunnel specialist next.

Healthy Computing

Many health resources are available on the Internet. The following sections describe a small sample.

Health Science Resources on Bitnet/Internet

`http://kufacts.cc.ukans.edu/cwis/kufacts/start.html`

E-mail: `le07144@ukanvm` or `le07144@ukanvm.cc.ukans.edu`

`telnet: ukanaix.cc.ukans.edu login: kufacts`

The file is located in the Medical Center Resources section under Departmental Information.

`ftp: ftp.sura.net`

Directory: `pub/nic`

File: `medical.resources.xx-xx` (`xx-xx` is the date of the release)

You'll want to embark on your health-related journey by obtaining this excellent file, which contains a comprehensive listing of medical resources available via Internet, Bitnet, and Usenet. Updated four to five times a year, this 300-plus-page file is available online at many Gopher sites in the Health and Medicine section and through the preceding addresses.

Repetitive Strain Injury

Newsletter: e-mail to `majordomo@world.std.com`. In the body, type **subscribe RSI**.

If you're truly addicted to your computer, you may have suffered some discomfort in your hands and wrists. RSI, a bimonthly newsletter, addresses issues related to carpal tunnel syndrome, repetitive strain injury, and so on.

C+Health

Mailing list: e-mail to `kimu@dairp.upenn.edu`

This list pertains to computer-related ailments and offers advice and information on computers and health issues.

Physician's GenRx

`telnet: genrx.icsi.net`; login, **genrx**; password, **genrx**

After choosing the terminal emulation, log in as: guest, password: your e-mail address.

E-mail: `fabius@icsi.net`

Physician's GenRx is a comprehensive drug database that contains information on generic and international brand-name drugs. You can search for drugs by name or category; you also can select multiple drugs and obtain drug-interaction information. Free access to Internet users with a guest account allows for a very brief drug description. Paid subscribers have access to much more detailed information, including drug interactions, FDA schedules, prices, and patent expiration.

To subscribe, you must fill out an online subscription form, which is option B in the main menu. The necessary information then will be e-mailed to you. There is a one-time setup fee of $9.95. A one-month trial is $9.95; three months, $36; six months, $59; and one year, $99.

Health Headlines

Newsletter: e-mail to `news-request@perspective.com`; type **subscribe** in the subject line.

This monthly newsletter and discussion group focuses on news and research as it pertains to the relationship of health, nutrition, and lifestyle.

GriefNet

`gopher.rivendell.org 9004`

E-mail: `info@rivendell.org`

Established by the founder of the Michigan chapter of the Association for Death Education and Counseling, this resource provides information on bereavement and major loss. A product of Rivendell Resources, GriefNet maintains a list of support resources, publications, and the like, many of which are in Michigan. The Bereavement and Loss Resources Directory includes resources on adoption loss, caregivers, hospices, suicide, homicide, and widows and widowers.

This site also has resources for people who are suffering through physical loss and chronic illness. These resources are categorized by disease. The site includes resources on aging, arthritis, blindness, cancer, cerebral palsy, and digestive disorders, to name a few. GriefNet also maintains grief-related mailing lists, in which subscribers can discuss the subject of loss. Following is a brief description of Rivendell lists pertaining to grief:

- *Rivendell-chat.* This list discusses issues related to grief, death and dying, and major health losses. The list specifically states that it is not intended to be a grief-recovery list.
- *Rivendell.* This list updates news on GriefNet.
- *Widows.* As the name implies, this list provides widows a forum in which they can share their experiences. To subscribe to the list or to the two above, send e-mail to `majordomo@mail.msen.com`; in the body of your message, type **subscribe <*name of list*> <*your e-mail address*>.**
- *Grief-training.* This list discusses issues concerning the training of professionals and others in dealing with grief and other major losses. To subscribe to this mailing list, send e-mail to `majordomo@falcon.ic.net`, and write **subscribe grief-training <*your e-mail address*>**.

Legal Bytes

Legal information is abundant on the Internet. This section examines a few of the offerings.

The Legal List

Ftp to `ftp.midnight.com`, change to directory `/pub/legallist`, and get files README and LEGALLIST.TXT.

If you're interested in legal resources on the Internet, you should obtain The Legal List. More than 75 pages long, this file provides information on law resources and how to access them.

If you can't ftp, you can get The Legal List sent to you in a 60-page e-mail message by sending e-mail to `ftpmail@decwrl.dec.com`. In the body of the message, type the following:

```
connect ftp.midnight.com
ascii
get /pub/LegalList/README
get /pub/LegalList/legallist.txt
quit.
```

(This ftp-by-mail server is heavily loaded and usually takes several days to respond.)

You also can subscribe to the Internet mailing list by sending an e-mail message to `legal-list-request@justice.eliot.me.us` and typing `subscribe` *your name* in the subject line.

To retrieve the file via Gopher, go to `gopher.usmacs.maine.edu`.

To obtain a printed version, send a check or money order for $9.17 (payable to Erik J. Heels) to The Legal List, Attn.: Erik J. Heels, 39 Main Street, Eliot, ME 03903-2234. Until you receive the list, you can get your feet wet by visiting the legal resources discussed in the following sections.

Gopher Jewels Law Resources

`http://galaxy.einet.net/gopher/gopher.html`

`gopher://cwis.usc.edu/11/other_gophers_and_information_resources/gophers_by_subject/gopher_jewels/law`

This site offers a nice selection of law resources. After you choose Law from the Gopher Jewels menu, you can select menus pertaining to legal and law issues or to patents and copyrights. Following is the Legal or Law Related menu:

```
Legal or Law related
Page 1 of 1

1 Legal or LAW Collections     Menu
2 Legal or Law related (misc)    Menu
3 Jump to Gopher Jewels Main Menu   Menu
4 Jump up a menu to Law      Menu
5 Search Gopher Jewels Menus by Key Word(s) Search
Enter Item Number, SAVE, ?, or BACK: 2
```

If you choose 2, you will be presented with the following options:

```
Legal or Law related (misc)
Page 1 of 2
1 Butterworths Legal Publishers         Menu
2 Case On-Line Information System [COLIS] Via Babson   Telnet
3 Center for Computer-Assisted Legal Instruction (CALI)   Menu
4 Cleveland State University Law Library      Menu
5 The Company Corporation - Incorporation Info.     Menu
6 Cornell Law School (experimental)        Menu
7 CWRU Law School             Menu
8 Disability Legislation & Legal Issues - St. John's University Menu
9 Environmental law manual - University of Georgia    Menu
10 Information Law Alert Newsletter - Marketplace Gopher   Menu
11 Law and Courts Preprint Archive - Northwestern Univ.   Menu
12 The Law of the Sea - Internet Wiretap       Menu
13 The Legal Domain Network - InfoPro        Menu
14 Privacy Rights Clearinghouse - University of San Diego  Menu
15 Univ of Sydney, Law School          Menu
16 Univ of Warwick, Law Technology Centre      Menu
17 Univ. of California-Santa Barbara Library (Gov. Pubs & Law L Menu
18 University of Chicago Law School        Menu
19 Villanova Law School, Center for Information Law and Policy Menu
20 West's Legal Directory via WAIS - West Publishing Company Menu
21 Jump to Gopher Jewels Main Menu        Menu
22 Jump up a menu to Legal or Law related      Menu
23 Search Gopher Jewels Menus by Key Word(s)      Search
```

West's Legal Directory

gopher: `wld.westlaw.com`

telnet: `163.231.231.3`

E-mail: `wldhelp@research.westlaw.com`

West's Legal Directory is an excellent source of information when you're searching for the right lawyer. This compilation of information on law firms, government offices, and lawyers contains more than 675,000 profiles from every U.S. state, as well as from the Virgin Islands, Guam, and Canada. Biographical information includes phone number and address, current and past positions, practice specialty, educational background, bar admission dates, and current and past affiliations. If you choose 2 from the first menu, you see the following:

```
West's Legal Directory via WAIS
Page 1 of 1

1 About West's Legal Directory    Text
2 Search Tips         Text
3 Copyright Restrictions / State Disclaimers Text
4 Wests-Legal-Directory[WLD].src    Search
```

The first thing that you'll want to do is choose 2 and read Search Tips. You can use Boolean connectors and/or data fields to search for attorneys. You also can specify the name, city, state, area of practice, certified specialty, and the like.

If you know the name of the lawyer for whom you want to search, you can use the citation (ci) search. If you choose 4, you see the following:

```
"Wests-Legal-Directory[WLD].src" is an indexed service. Please specify a word
or words to search. Search for:
ci=Alan AND ci=Dershowitz"
```

This search retrieves the file of Alan Dershowitz. If you wanted to retrieve the profiles of lawyers in the city of Boston, you would enter **cy=boston**. Looking for a certified specialist in patent law? You would use **ce=patent** to retrieve the profiles of lawyers who specialize in patent law.

The Search Tips document provides all the information you need to conduct a search. All information included in the directory is provided directly by the lawyers and law firms.

Nolo Press Self-Help Law Center

`http://gnn.com/gnn/bus/nolo/`

A leading publisher of self-help legal books and software, Nolo seeks to help you better understand the law without the expense of costly lawyers. The site contains quarterly issues of Nolo News, a publication that includes practical law information. You'll also have access to descriptions of Nolo book titles and software, Nolo's catalog of products, and lawyer jokes. Future plans include online ordering, demo versions of Nolo software, interviews with authors, and a FAQ area.

Sto's Internet Patent Search System

`http://sunsite.unc.edu/patents/intropat.html`

Mailing list: **send news** to `patents@world.std.com`

If patent information is what you're after, you'll want to check into this system. Source Translation and Optimization's (STO) Internet Patent Search System enables you to perform patent searches and to obtain various information pertaining to getting a patent. Current through December 1993, this service enables you to determine the patent class by using the Manual of Classification or the Index to Classification. You can retrieve patent titles by using the class/subclass code. The system also includes an archive of stories from the Internet Patent News Service and a shopping mall of patent services.

The mailing list sends out news of interesting developments in the world of patents.

Town Hall U.S. Patent & Trademark Office

http://www.town.hall.org/patent/patent.html

Gopher: town.hall.org/u.s. patent & trademark office

Maintained by the Internet Multicasting Service, this database also offers a wealth of information pertaining to patent law. You also can search for and retrieve patents. Related network resources include press releases from the U.S. Patent & Trademark Office, a Gopher server on copyright law, access to information on the U.S. Patent Act, and a connection to the Legal Information Institute at Cornell Law School.

EDS Shadow Patent Office

E-mail: spo_patent@spo.eds.com

Perhaps you don't want to conduct your own search and are seeking reasonably priced patent services. The EDS Shadow Patent Office will conduct patent research for you via e-mail. The database contains 1.7 million utility patents issued from January 1, 1972, to the present. The cost of service varies according to the kind that you choose. A full-text patent report, for example, costs $4.95. You can choose to receive information about 25 patents similar to your invention for $49 to $99, depending on how many words you want to use to describe your invention. If you want to receive information that includes abstracts, the cost runs from $74 to $124.

To receive information about the service, send e-mail to the preceding address. You are required to fill out a form and e-mail it to EDS, which will mail you a packet that includes a service agreement, price sheet, billing information form, and tutorial. When you return the signed agreement, you can use STO E-Mail Patent Search Service. Your first three requests for information are free.

Potpourri

As the title suggests, this section provides a miscellaneous assortment of Internet sites, including government, business, and art.

White House

http://www.whitehouse.gov

E-mail to President Bill Clinton: president@whitehouse.gov

E-mail to Vice President Al Gore: vice-president@whitehouse.gov

If you don't live near the capital — and even if you do — you'll want to visit this new site. Among other things, you can register in the guest book, take a guided tour of the White House, and view Al Gore's favorite political cartoons. Don't miss the audio clip of Socks the cat.

The Social Security Administration

`gopher: oss968.ssa.gov`; login, **gopher**

Have you ever wondered how to figure out how many work credits you've earned toward Social Security? How about specifics regarding self-employment issues? Now that the Social Security Administration has set up its own Gopher server, you can find your answer to these questions and any others that you may have regarding Medicare; Supplemental Security Income; Retirement, Survivors, and Disability Benefits; your right to appeal; and so on. Following is the first menu that you'll encounter when logging in to the site:

```
Internet Gopher Information Client v2.0.14
      Root gopher server: oss968.ssa.gov
 ->1. A-Welcome to the SSA Gopher
  2. B-En Espanol/
  3. C-General Information/
  4. D-Social Security Card—Number/
  5. E-Retirement Benefits/
  6. F-Survivors Benefits/
  7. G-Disability Benefits/
  8. H-Supplemental Security Income (SSI)/
  9. I-Your Rights to Appeal/
  10. J-Other Related Programs/
  11. K-Statistical Data and Abstracts/
  12. L-Legislation/
  13. M-Regulatory Program/
  14. N-International Policy and News/
  15. O-The Social Security Handbook/
  16. P-Frequently Asked Questions (FAQs)
```

Hobbes' Internet Timeline v1.2

E-mail: `timeline@hobbes.mitre.org`

This interesting file, which follows the history of the Internet, includes Internet and Usenet growth summaries.

Online Writing Lab (OWL)

`http://owl.trc.purdue.edu/`

E-mail: `owl@sage.cc.purdue.edu`

If you give a hoot about writing résumés, business memos, research papers, and the like, check out this new service from Purdue University. You not only have access to more than 100 texts on these subjects but also can contact tutors for help with questions. A tutor will respond to your e-mail message within 48 hours.

DIALOG

`http://www.dialog.com`

Dialog is the first WWW site to offer hypertext linking and full-text search capabilities, as well as a fax-document-delivery system. The site offers information on Dialog services.

The Ontario Institute for Studies in Education Gopher

`gopher://gopher.oise.on.ca:70/11/tools`

This site offers a nice collection of Internet navigation tools.

The Complete Home Page Directory

`http://web.city.ac.uk/citylive/pages.html`

E-mail: `kirk@cs.city.ac.uk`

This list claims to maintain a listing of every home page that exists on the Web. Although I haven't had a chance to visit, and although it's pretty hard to believe that the list is complete, this site may be worth investigating. Perhaps you have created your own home page. In that case, you'll want to fill out the built-in forms so that you can add your own page to the list.

Ann Hemyng Candy, Inc.'s Chocolate Factory

`http://mmink.cts.com/mmink/dossiers/choco.html`

E-mail: `chocfactry@aol.com`

Earlier in the chapter, I mentioned an online chocolate source. You didn't think that I'd leave out the specifics, did you? Now you can order chocolate to your heart's content via modem. From dark-chocolate raspberry truffles to peanut-butter and milk-chocolate lollipops, this site is truly a chocoholic's delight! You can obtain a complete product list, as well as a brochure, by leaving your snail-mail address.

PLEASE COPY THIS DISK

Catalog: e-mail to `samizdat@world.std.com`

B&R Samizdat Express was established when Barbara and Richard Seltzer discovered that most teachers had no knowledge of the vast amount of material available on the Internet and how to go about accessing it. After seeking permission, B&R Samizdat Express downloaded texts from various ftp and Gopher sites and packaged them on IBM and Macintosh floppy disks. Currently, more than 340 disks are available on topics including computers and networks, history, math, literature, philosophy, reference, and science. This site offers a wealth of information not only for teachers but also for researchers.

Disks cost $10 each and come with a guarantee. B&R Samizdat Express encourages teachers and librarians to spread this information by freely making copies of these disks for those who do not have Internet access.

Internet-on-a-Disk

Newsletter: e-mail to `samizdat@world.std.com`

This free electronic newsletter is another service from B&R Samizdat Express and is meant to complement PLEASE COPY THIS DISK. Internet-on-a-Disk lists public-domain and widely available electronic texts; it also includes editorials and tutorials on how to use electronic texts in schools and libraries.

The Argus Internet Tools and Resources Guide

`http://argus-inc.com/guide.html`

E-mail: `information@argus-inc.com`

The Argus Internet Tools and Resources Guide now is available online as a BinHex Microsoft Word for Macintosh file. This guide provides information on communicating on the Internet, as well as on finding and accessing information resources. Because this file is so large (1.6MB), the table of contents is available to view online before downloading.

The CIA

`http://www.ic.gov/`

This site includes general information about the Central Intelligence Agency and also provides access to the 1994 World Factbook and Factbook on Intelligence, which contains useful summaries of information on every country in the world.

The Monster Board

`http://www.monster.com`

Despite its name, you don't have to be afraid to access this site, which offers users the opportunity to search for jobs. The site includes all industries, although the emphasis is on technical listings.

Knowledge One

http://knowone_www.sonoma.edu/

E-mail: knowone@sonoma.edu

If you want someone else to conduct your research, this commercial service will do it in an hour. Whether you need a few straight facts or a listing of article citations on a particular topic, Knowledge One can handle it.

The Internet Business Center (IBC)

http://www.tig.com/ibc/

If you're interested in commercial activity, demographics, or marketing information, this site is for you. A joint effort of The Internet Group, The Internet Letter, and Internet Info, IBC provides valuable updated information to companies that are interested in conducting business on the Internet. The Internet Business Center features commercial Internet domain growth statistics, maps, charts, and Internet business sites and services, as well as selected posts from Usenet, LISTSERV, and other services.

Online Computer Library Center (OCLC)

http://www.oclc.org/

A not-for-profit computer library service and research organization, OCLC links more than 18,000 libraries in 61 countries and territories. The purpose of this site is to provide information on OCLC's products and services.

Feminist Web Page

http://www.clark.net/pub/s-gray/feminist.html

This Web page for feminists concentrates on links to Internet resources such as women's organizations and provides general and feminist resources for political activists.

Internal Revenue Service (IRS)

http://www.ustreas.gov/treasury/bureaus/irs/irs.html

I don't mean to spoil your computing fun, but I thought you'd like to know about this site, which offers tax forms and also provides answers to your questions about where to file and where to get help.

Scarecrow's ASCII Art Archives

http://gagme.wwa.com/~boba/scarecrow.html

gopher://gopher.wwa.com:70/11/ascii

E-mail: boba@wwa.com

Scarecrow's ASCII Art Archives is a fun site for anyone who is interested in ASCII art. Resources include art information; FAQs; how-to files; and font, color, animation, and GIF sections. Standard ASCII art, which is made with standard text characters (including numbers and symbols), is used on many bulletin-board systems at the login prompts. The art is popular because it can be viewed on all systems and does not require any special software.

Arts & Farces

http://www.farces.com/farces/farces-home.html

E-mail: almanac@farces.com

Arts & Farces offers a complete collection of Internet services and software for Macintosh, Windows, and DOS users. As of this writing, all Internet services, including software archives, are free of charge. You can obtain a catalog of available documents by sending an e-mail message to the preceding address, with **send catalog** in the body of the message. For a user manual, send a message to the same address and type **send guide**.

FedWorld

http://www.fedworld.gov

E-mail: bob.bunge@fedworld.gov

FedWorld allows you to browse a listing of more than 100 U.S. government information servers. You also can telnet to this site and go from there to a wide variety of government BBS systems.

Internet Book Information Center (IBIC)

http://sunsite.unc.edu/ibic/ibic-homepage.html

gopher: sunsite.unc.edu; choose Worlds of SunSITE by Subject/Internet Book Information Center.

This clearinghouse for information about books includes book reviews, a rare-books section, a reference shelf, and much more. Bibliophiles will definitely want to visit this site.

AskERIC

`http://ericir.syr.edu`

Alternatively, telnet to `ericir.syr.edu` and log in as **gopher.**

Educators and library media specialists will be interested in AskERIC's Web page. An undertaking of the U.S. Department of Education, AskERIC features Newton's Apple lesson plans, as well as a section of tools used by AskERIC's network information specialists.

Commercial OnLine Newspaper Services

`http://marketplace.com/e-papers.list.www/e-papers.home.page.html`

E-mail: `marjordomo@marketplace.com`. In the body, type **get online-news online-newspapers.list**.

This site offers a comprehensive list of newspaper publishers that offer online services.

E-Page Systems

E-mail: `moreinfo@epage.com`

As the name implies, this innovative service pages you when you receive e-mail messages. With prices starting as low as $9.95 per month, the service enables you to have e-mail messages displayed on your alpha pager, personal digital assistant, or laptop computer. What will they think of next?

Lynn L. Alexander is a freelance writer and editor from Torrington, Conneticut. She has a bachelor's degree in English and a background in public relations, and she is the former sales and marketing manager for a Chinese word processing software company. A devout Macintosh user, she freely admits that she is a modemaholic.

This chapter is dedicated in loving memory of her father, Victor J. Alexander.

Hot Spots on the Net

by Margaret F. Riley <mfriley@WPI.EDU>

Riley, a research librarian at Worcester Polytechnic Institute and an avid Net researcher, reveals her cherished list of the best places to look on the Net.

This section lists some good places to start a Gopher or WWW search. Each site has links to a wide variety of other Gopher and WWW pages.

The Gopher sites are listed in the format that you'd use for a local Gopher page, with the type (invariably 1 for a Gopher menu), name, path, host, and port that you would use to create a Gopher bookmark. For WWW users, an equivalent URL is listed, so that you can type to go directly to your Web browser.

WWW sites are listed with a name and a URL.

Best Gopher Sites

Type 1

Name Gopher Subject Trees (UKOLN)

Path `1/link`

Host `ukoln.bath.ac.uk`

Port 70

URL `gopher://ukoln.bath.ac.uk:70/11/link`

Type 1

Name Clearinghouse of Subject-Oriented Internet Resource Guides (University of Michigan)

Path `1/inetdirs`

Host `una.hh.lib.umich.edu`

Port 70

URL `gopher://una.hh.lib.umich.edu:70/11/inetdirs`

Type	1+
Name	Gopher-Jewels
Path	`1/other_gophers_and_information_resources/gopher-jewels`
Host	`cwis.usc.edu`
Port	70
Administrator	Mark A. Brown <mark@usc.edu>
URL	`gopher://cwis.usc.edu:70/11/other_gophers_and_information_resources/gopher-jewels`

Type	1
Name	Library of Congress (LC MARVEL)
Path	
Host	`marvel.loc.gov`
Port	70
URL	`gopher://marvel.loc.gov:70/1`

Type	1
Name	Gophers by Subject (Michigan State University)
Path	`1/internet/subject`
Host	`gopher.msu.edu`
Port	70
URL	`gopher://gopher.msu.edu:70/11/internet/subject`

Type	1
Name	Government Information (U.S. federal and state information and documents)
Path	`1/library/govdocs`
Host	`umslvma.umsl.edu`
Port	70
URL	`gopher://umslvma.umsl.edu:70/11/library/govdocs`

Type	1
Name	Netlink Server
Path	
Host	`honor.uc.wlu.edu`
Port	1020
URL	`gopher://honor.uc.wlu.edu:1020/1`

Type	1
Name	PEG (Peripatetic, Eclectic Gopher)
Path	`1/gopher.welcome/peg`
Host	`peg.cwis.uci.edu`
Port	7000
URL	`gopher://peg.cwis.uci.edu:7000/11/gopher.welcome/peg`

Type	1
Name	Gophers by Subject (Rice University)
Path	`1/subject`
Host	`riceinfo.rice.edu`
Port	70
URL	`gopher://riceinfo.rice.edu:70/11/subject`

Type	1
Name	Gophers by Subject (Swedish University Computer Network)
Path	`1/subject tree`
Host	`sunic.sunet.se`
Port	70
URL	`gopher://sunic.sunet.se:70/11/subject%20tree`

Type	1
Name	Internet Assistance (collected resources via the University of California at Irvine)
Path	1/gopher.welcome/peg/internet assistance
Host	peg.cwis.uci.edu
Port	7000
URL	gopher://peg.cwis.uci.edu:7000/11/gopher.welcome/peg/internet%20assistance

Best Web Sites

http://www.internic.net/htbin/search-net-happenings

Net-happenings WAIS index

http://www.lib.umich.edu/chhome.html

The Clearinghouse for Subject-Oriented Internet Resource Guides

http://www.uwm.edu/mirror/inet.services.html

Special Internet connections; updated once or twice a month

http://honor.uc.wlu.edu:1020/%20%20%23hfj/cl

Netlink

http://info.cern.ch/hypertext/datasources/bysubject/overview.html

The World Wide Web Virtual Library Subject Catalog

http://www.cs.colorado.edu/home/mcbryan/wwww.html

WWW Worm

http://galaxy.einet.net/www/www.html

Galaxy's WWW Search

http://web.nexor.co.uk/aliweb/doc/form-search.html

ALIWEB resource discovery system

http://best.gdb.org/best.html

BEST North America Web Server

`http://cui_www.unige.ch/w3catalog`

Searchable WWW catalog

`http://www.cc.ukans.edu/about_lynx/www_start.html`

University of Kansas home page and index

`http://alpha.acast.nova.edu/start.html`

Inter-Links (Internet access made easy)

`http://galaxy.einet.net/gj/index.html`

Gopher Jewels

`http://www.ncsa.uiuc.edu/sdg/software/mosaic/metaindex.html`

Internet Resources Meta-Index

`http://www.charm.net/~web/`

Virtual Library/CyberWeb: WWW development

`http://fuzine.mt.cs.cmu.edu/mlm/lycos-home.html`

The Lycos Home Page: Hunting WWW Information

`http://www.clark.net/pub/journalism/awesome.html`

John December's Awesome List

Chapter 21
Power IRC

by Stuart Harris <sirrah@cg57.esnet.com>

If there is one piece of advice given even more often than "Never accept candy from a stranger," it has to be the advice everyone gives to IRC newbies: "Never enter a keyboard command at someone else's suggestion if you don't understand exactly what it does."

The Wild World of Computer Chat

IRC is Internet Relay Chat. The mother of all instant computer chat forums, it brings together approximately 5,000 people from all corners of our planet and almost all walks of life allowing them to invade each others' computer screens 24 hours a day. Like other areas of the Internet experience, IRC is not under the control of the corporations that bring us our mainstream culture. When average American adults venture into this new world, therefore, it's a safe bet that they are soon reminded of how much we have come to depend on the media consensus to protect us from the big, bad world. What I mean is that some pretty nasty people are out there — people who are fond of gratuitous insults, creative flaming, net warfare, and aggressive hacking.

The point of the oft-given advice about unfamiliar commands is that you can be persuaded to enter commands that leave your system wide open to invasion by young geniuses who know more about computers than you will ever care to know and who use their knowledge malevolently. What could be worse than that? I'll tell you: doing the same thing in a shell account and letting the young geniuses in to take down your entire site.

The Payoff of Risky Behavior

Just as, I assume, there have been occasions in history when taking candy from a stranger has had the happy outcome of acquiring a Mars bar, a whole Mars bar, and nothing but a Mars bar, there certainly have been occasions on which a weird-looking IRC command has had desirable consequences — `/DCC GET` may bring a pretty picture of someone you've been flirting with for days, for example (`DCC` is explained later in this chapter).

By the end of this chapter, I hope that you will trust me enough to take candy in the form of some unfamiliar IRC commands that will enrich your IRC life — particularly if you are a user of the UNIX IRCII client, but also if you're a point-and-click type. I do my best to explain exactly what these commands do and how they do it, but I certainly wouldn't blame you if you paid scant attention and thought, "What the heck? Let's just try it and see."

Mousing around

I'm a type-something-and-enter person myself, but I don't despise people who prefer to point and click. I admire their manual dexterity, in fact, but I do sometimes wonder what appeal IRC has for them. I mean, you can't really have a fascinating conversation by pointing and clicking — sooner or later you have to touch the keyboard. Maybe all the lurkers are Mac jockeys waiting for the day they can choose "I live in Wilkes-Barre and go to school, and I think that Enya's beyond kewl" from a pull-down menu.

An Introduction to IRC

"Ummm, IRC 101 is down the hallway. Room 1220, I think it is — but I don't think that the instructor's coming in today. I heard that he was getting a divorce."

Just kidding. Here's a little elementary IRC for the benefit of anyone who is new to this subject.

IRC is an enormous worldwide chatting network. It's divided into *channels*, or conversations, which users can join. After you've joined a channel, anything you type to that channel is sent immediately to other people on the channel and, of course, vice versa. So you can have real-time conversations limited only by how fast you can type and (more crucial) how fast you can think up something to say.

Like most Internet facilities, IRC is run by client-server software. The part you run on your computer is the client. If you dial in and use a shell account, the client will reside on your access provider's rig and will almost certainly be the most popular IRC client in the world, the UNIX IRCII. At run-time, the client's first duty is to find a server site to connect to; when it does, you get connected to the entire world through a monstrous patchwork quilt of computers that occasionally comes slightly undone at the seams — especially on Fridays.

After you're connected to a server, there's a short list of things you have to do to get chatting. First, you establish an identity, or nickname. Then you join an IRC channel or two or three or 200 and begin chatting away.

The Four Basic IRC Commands

To establish your IRC identity, enter **/NICK <nickname up to nine characters>**. To see a list of the conversations already in progress, enter the command **/LIST**. When you have made your decision, enter **/JOIN #spam** (assuming that you want to discuss Spam today). From now on, the world's musings about Spam come directly to your screen, and anything you enter that does not begin with / is seen by all the other Spam fans in the same channel as you. When you're fed up or your significant other screams, "If you're not off that accursed network in 60 seconds, I'm leaving!" the way out is `/BYE`.

Windows and Mac clients provide doohickeys you can point at, click at, yank down, and pop up to fulfill all these functions except, as mentioned, to create your contribution to the conversation.

All IRC commands generally begin with the forward slash character. As you will see, however, this character is unnecessary if the command is part of an IRCII script.

On-screen help is available (as long as the client has been configured correctly). The command is `/HELP <command you need help with>`, beginning with `/HELP basics`.

Slowing the Scroll

The first step down the road to power IRC is to improve on one of those four basic commands. If you tried it, you may have noticed how the `/LIST` command sent 1,200 channel names and topics screaming down your screen like the Road Runner with Wile E. Coyote in hot pursuit. You wished that it could have paused at every screenful so that you could have actually *read* some of it, right?

The IRC command language includes no fewer than 101 options that can be set to `ON` or `OFF`; one is a feature called `HOLD_MODE`. If you enter the line

```
/SET HOLD_MODE ON
```

the list of channel names appears screen by screen. Get each successive screen by pressing your Enter key. While `HOLD_MODE` is `ON`, you probably will see an extra number in your status bar (that's the reverse video bar at the bottom of your screen, telling you such things as how much e-mail you have). That number is the number of text lines waiting in the `HOLD_MODE` buffer. You can flush that buffer early and get out of `LIST` mode whenever you've seen enough by using this command:

```
/FLUSH
```

When the listing is all over, you have to use this command:

```
/SET HOLD_MODE OFF
```

Otherwise, the flow of text to your screen continues to pause every 22 lines, which makes for a stilted conversation.

More Things You Can Set

The pointers-and-clickers among us don't have the `/SET` commands, but their compensation is that they can generally reverse-scroll windows that contain such things as channel lists. Reverse scrolling is possible with the UNIX client, but it's difficult.

You may be wondering, though, what else is of interest in those 101 /SET commands. Several things, as it happens, are starting appropriately with this command:

```
/SET NOVICE OFF
```

This command permits you to use certain advanced command sets that are particularly dangerous in terms of your system security and also to join more than one channel simultaneously. It really is possible to pay attention to more than one channel at a time — your standard keyboard output, however, goes to only one "active" channel. What takes concentration is knowing which channel is active; the explanation for some of the many incongruities you see every day on IRC is that someone is trying to contribute to a conversation in #cricket, unaware that his active channel is #football.

Here's one of my all-time /SET favorites. Suppose that you're busy IRCing and you see this message:

```
*** You have new email
```

I remember how delighted I was when I found out that I could improve on this generic message. Mail notification has three levels. The default, level 1, is the preceeding message, while level 0 means no notification at all. But if you enter the command:

```
/SET MAIL 2
```

you find out who sent your incoming mail and what it's about. A couple of lines like the following appear among all that fascinating chat about Spam:

```
*** From:           Steve Williams
*** Subject:        Could we make it tuesday???
```

So now you can press Ctrl-Z to exit (see the section "Control-key bindings"), have a quick peek at Steve's mail, and be back before you've missed anything. There's obviously no need to bother, of course, if you see the following message:

```
*** From:           Sysadmin
*** Subject:        IMPORTANT: New acceptable use policy
```

So your IRC life has been improved — and this is even less trouble than some gizmo on a Windows or Mac screen chirping at you to click it to find out who loves you.

The next few commands make it easier to deal with some of the mischief-makers out there. If some acne-ridden pervert decides that it's good fun to test how many beeps per second can be sent into your channel, you can give either one of these commands (they should be self-explanatory):

```
/SET BEEP OFF
/SET BEEP MAX <n>
```

Suppose that the mischief-maker is called Freeze. After a while, you get entirely fed up with him and enter this command:

```
/IGNORE Freeze
```

It's appropriate to let Freeze know that he's been added to your ignorance list, and he gets a message automatically as long as you have used this command:

```
/SET SEND_IGNORE_MSG ON
```

There are other ways to refine the /IGNORE status — in fact, the whole thing is more complex than necessary — but that will do for the moment. Check the help text if you're interested.

If you try any of these /SET commands and like it, it belong in your .ircrc file so that it takes effect whenever you log on.

Sleuthing on IRC

On IRC you reveal your identity in many more ways than a newbie realizes. If you detect that someone is inexperienced (and that's not usually difficult), it's a good game to peel back the layers of that user's identity until you arrive at the real-life name and then address her as Monica Fry, for example, rather than the nickname ironweed, which Monica thought was an opaque cloak. Monica's surprise is often entertaining. Here's how you play the game:

```
/WHOIS ironweed
```

This command returns something like this:

```
*** ironweed is mfry@jupiter.cc.xysu.edu (The little student that could)
*** on channels: #romance #talk
*** on IRC via server dewey.cc.utexas.edu (UT's "I repeat class" server)
```

Now you can try this one:

```
/CTCP ironweed FINGER
```

This response is likely to result in something like this:

```
*** CTCP FINGER reply from ironweed: Monica A. Fry
(mfry@jupiter.cc.xysu.edu) Idle 33 seconds
```

Here's the alternative CTCP command:

```
/CTCP ironweed USERINFO
```

It generally results in a <None Supplied> message because it takes awhile to learn how to put something cute in a USER_INFO field, and Monica probably is not up to speed yet. Even if the CTCP FINGER comes up empty, however, you are now almost certainly in possession of ironweed's e-mail address, so (as long as you're not a point-and-clicker) you can use this command:

```
/EXEC finger mfry@jupiter.cc.xysu.edu
```

and receive in return something like this:

```
[jupiter.cc.xysu.edu]
Login name: mfry              In real life: Monica A. Fry
Directory: /usr5/mfry         Shell: /usr/local/bin/csh
On since Jul 12 15:33:31 on tty3
No idle time
Mail last read Jul 12 14:18
Plan:
All I want is a room somewhere
No project.
```

Setting Up CTCP

All that stuff in the preceding section was an elaborate aside that was necessary in order to introduce two other useful `/SET` commands, which are discussed in this section.

The following command makes information available to anyone who uses `/CTCP USERINFO` to find out about you:

```
/SET USER_INFORMATION I have the world's best chili recipe
```

If you want to be made aware of who's making inquiries about you, use this command:

```
/SET VERBOSE_CTCP ON
```

`CTCP` is the *client-to-client-protocol* that enables your client program to make a direct connection to some other user's client without going through an IRC server and to exchange information without the IRC community at large being aware of it.

Real Names and IRC Names

In the preceding fictitious example, Monica must have known a little about identity in the UNIX world or else her real name would have shown up on the first move. Instead, a sobriquet has been defined by a line in her shell start-up file like this (assuming that she uses the C shell):

```
setenv IRCNAME "The little student that could"
```

The desktop DOS, Windows, and Mac clients all have their own ways of letting you set your `IRCNAME`, which shows up in parentheses as a response to a `/WHOIS` inquiry. If an `IRCNAME` is not specifically set, many systems make the user's real name the default. Interestingly, through many versions, IRCII allowed no way of changing this field after you were logged on to IRC, but version 2.3.*x* added this command:

```
/SET REALNAME <......cute stuff......>
```

which sort of does the job. Because your `IRCNAME` field is passed to your server at connect-time, the new information cannot propagate through the Net unless you switch to a different server.

More from the /SET set

Here's a roundup of /SET commands:

/SET CLOCK_ALARM <time>|OFF
Sets or clears alarm-clock time

/SET INDENT ON
Indents chat text

/SET LOGFILE <name>
Defines a filename for your IRC log

/SET LOG ON/OFF
Starts or stops logging

/SET SHOW_CHANNEL_NAMES ON
Shows names of all users in a channel as soon as you join it

/SET SHOW_WHO_HOPCOUNT ON
Shows you the number of "hops" made by your connection to each user in a channel

Customizing Your IRC Screen

If you have an idle moment, try this command:

```
/SET STATUS_FORMAT
```

You get back some gobbledygook that looks like this:

```
*** Current value of STATUS_FORMAT is
[%R]%T %*%@%N%#%S%H%B%Q%A%C%+%I%O%M%F%U
```

That line is trying to tell you about the information that appears in your status bar and what order it comes in. To decode this format string, your status bar is set to show you the following information (left to right):

[%R]: The window refnum (reference number) in brackets

%T: The current time

%*: If you are an IRCop (IRC operator), displays *, otherwise nothing

%@: If you are a chanop (channel operator), displays *, otherwise nothing

%N: Your current nickname

%#: Any umodes that may be in force (such as +i for Invisible)

%S: A possible server message

%H: "— hold —" if you are in HOLD MODE

%B: Number of lines in the HOLD MODE buffer

%Q: Any user you are in /QUERY mode with

%A: "Away" if you are /AWAY

%C: The channel on which you are active

%+: Any channel modes (+p, for Private, for example)

%I: "Insert" if Insert mode is ON (conditional)

%O: "Overwrite" if Insert mode is OFF (conditional)

%M: The number of e-mail messages you have, in brackets

%F: Indication of activity in hidden windows

%U: One of four text fields you may set (this one defaults to `* type /help for help`; the others are designated %X, %Y, and %Z)

When you have been on IRC awhile, you might wonder whether the status bar is being used to full advantage. After even a couple of days, you don't really need to see `* type /help for help`. What else might be diverted more usefully to that spot? One good possibility is all the coming-and-going messages, such as this one:

```
*** Freeze has joined channel #golf, *** Signoff: Grumpy
```

These types of message can certainly interrupt conversation and might be better off tucked away at the bottom of your screen. It's the same with messages that change a nickname, such as this one:

```
*** Freeze is now known as Ezeerf.
```

Cleaning Up Your Screen

To achieve the feat of cleaning up your screen, you have to learn about those dangerous commands you were not allowed to use until you used /SET NOVICE OFF. These new power commands, which begin with /ON, intercept IRC events and cause something to happen on your computer other than the normal event outcome. Many of the most mischievous commands have this form:

```
/ON ^MSG EXEC <something nasty>
```

If someone can persuade you to enter this command, he can then send you a message that causes <something nasty> to happen. The EXEC part makes it happen in the heart of your system, and the innocent-looking ^ sign ensures that you won't even know what hit you.

But let's return to the useful /ON functions. The /ON functions can respond to more than 50 types of events. Among them are JOIN, LEAVE, and NICKNAME — reacting to people joining the channel, leaving the channel, and changing their nicknames, respectively. They're just what you want to trap and divert, in fact. If you write the following lines in your.ircrc file, the lines divert those events (JOIN, LEAVE, and NICKNAME) to the status bar parameters %X, %Y, and %Z:

```
ON ^JOIN * SET STATUS_USER1 Joined: $0
ON ^LEAVE * SET STATUS_USER2 Left: $0
ON ^SIGNOFF * SET STATUS_USER2 Quit: $0
ON ^NICKNAME * SET STATUS_USER3 $0 is now $1
```

The ^ character means "just do it and don't bother to tell me that you are doing it"; the * means "on the current channel"; and you have to trap SIGNOFF in addition to LEAVE because they are different events as far as IRC is concerned, even though they do about the same thing.

If you amend your status-bar format like this:

```
/SET STATUS_FORMAT [%R]%T
%*%@%N%#%S%H%B%Q%A%C%+%I%O%M%F[%X][%Y][%Z]
```

you discard the unwanted %U message and replace it with your cryptic JOIN/ LEAVE/SIGNOFF/NICKNAME messages. The $0 and $1 parameters expand so that the right end of your status bar might look like this:

```
[Joined: Freeze][Quit: Grumpy][Freeze now Ezeerf]
```

None of that activity interrupts conversation. This string is a relatively long one, however, and will undoubtedly cause overcrowding of other features in your status bar at times. One option is to save this configuration for special occasions by combining the ON commands with the /SET STATUS_FORMAT command into a special file you /LOAD when the need arises.

Some other events you can trap with /ON

Event	*Parameters Available*
ACTION	
$0	Nickname of user who initiated action
$1	Channel or user to whom the action was directed
$2	The action text
***CONNECT** (to a server)*	
$0	Name of the server you just connected to
CTCP	
$0	Nickname of the user who sent CTCP request
$1	Target of the request (normally you)
$2	CTCP command word
$3	Any extra arguments

(continued)

(continued)

Event	*Parameters Available*
CTCP_REPLY	
$0	Nickname of the user who is replying
$1	CTCP command word
$2	Reply text
FLOOD	
$0	Nickname of the flooder
$1	Type of flood
$2	Flood text
IDLE	
$0	Your idle time in minutes
INVITE	
$0	Nickname of the user who invited you
$1	Channel you are invited to join
MAIL (You use MAIL to design your own e-mail notification.)	
$0	Number of new e-mail messages
$1	Total e-mail in your inbox
MODE_CHANGE	
$0	Nickname of the user changing the mode
$1	Channel ID
$2	Channel modes after the change
MSG	
$0	Nickname of the user messaging you
$1	Message text
NOTIFY_SIGNOFF	
$0	Nickname of user on your NOTIFY list who just signed off
NOTIFY_SIGNON	
$0	Nickname of user on your NOTIFY list who just signed on
SEND_ACTION	
$0	Target of your action (usually the channel)
$1	Action text
SEND_MSG	
$0	Target of your message
$1	Message text

Event	Parameters Available
TIMER (You use TIMER to trigger any action or message at a preset time of day.)	
$0	Time
TOPIC	
$0	Nickname of user who changed the channel topic
$1	Channel ID
$2	New topic
WHO (Traps the input resulting from a /WHO request.)	
$0	Channel ID
$1	Nickname
$2	Status H,G,*,@
$3	Login ID
$4	Host name
$5	IRCNAME or real name

Note: Flood is generally defined as more than a screenful of text coming from the same user, but you are free to define what *you* mean by flood, by using `/SET FLOOD_AFTER` and `/SET FLOOD_RATE`. Flooding is regarded as suspicious, and the `/ON FLOOD` trap is frequently used to trigger an automatic `/KICK` off the channel — assuming that the server doesn't get the offender first.

More Custom IRCII to Suit You

IRC is more than a program — it's a way of life. Here are more ways to make your new life more comfortable.

Control-key bindings

IRCII allows you — hey, it *encourages* you — to make full use of control-key combinations. Approximately 50 different functions can be assigned, or *bound*, to control keys, and some of them are highly useful. Someone, probably your system administrator, chose a selection for you when he configured the client. Use the command `/BIND` with no arguments to find out what your set is. Your .ircrc file will contain a series of statements like this:

```
BIND ^Z STOP_IRC
```

The `^Z` is the ^ character followed by the Z — *not* the combination of the Control key and the Z key you use when you want to *invoke* the `STOP_IRC` function.

`STOP_IRC` is what you use when interesting e-mail arrives: It puts IRC in cryogenic suspension while you run off and check the mail. When you're finished, you enter `fg` at the UNIX prompt, and your IRC setup thaws instantly. The conversation you missed scrolls before your eyes. This feature is a great one, and you ought to have it on a control key even if Ctrl-Z does not seem right to you.

Two more good functions (I use them daily) are REFRESH_SCREEN and BACKWARD_HISTORY. REFRESH_SCREEN is bound to Ctrl-L, which simply repaints your screen when line noise, cosmic bombardment, or some other type of interference has trashed it; BACKWARD_HISTORY, bound to Ctrl-P, recalls the last line you entered back into your command line so that you can repeat or edit it. If you continue pressing Ctrl-P, it works back through every line you have entered during the current session, whether it's a command or an insightful comment about Spam. Likewise, Ctrl-N recalls your FORWARD_HISTORY (useful indeed). Having retreived your text, you can edit it with the following series of control keys, invented by someone who likes the EMACS text editor:

Character	***Meaning***
Ctrl-A	Move cursor to beginning of line
Ctrl-D	Delete character at cursor
Ctrl-E	Move cursor to end of line
Ctrl-H	Destructive backspace (if your IBM Backspace key does not work, the reason is that it's not bound to Ctrl-H)
Ctrl-I	Toggle Insert/Overwrite mode
Ctrl-K	Erase from cursor to end of line
Ctrl-T	Transpose the character at the cursor and the character to its left
Ctrl-U	Erase the entire line
Ctrl-Y	Undelete (yank from cut buffer)

That same EMACS lover also bound Ctrl-F and Ctrl-B to the functions that move the cursor one character forward and back, respectively. I override that default by using Ctrl-] and Ctrl-[instead; as a result, my .ircrc file says BIND ^B SELF_INSERT. Why? This command restores Ctrl-B to its rightful function: making boldface characters in the IRC screen. Likewise, Ctrl-V should be reserved for creating inverse video, and Ctrl-_ for underlining.

Writing aliases to make life simpler

Remember when the command /SET HOLD_MODE ON was introduced earlier in this chapter, in the section "Slowing the Scroll"? This feature is a useful one, and it's not just for taming the notorious /LIST command. History files, *lastlogs* (a recall of the last couple of screens of chat), and log files all need the discipline of a pager to display them one screen at a time and make them readable. But you do have to remember to turn hold mode off again when you finish the list. You might think that that's a great deal to have to type twice. You are right; here's the power IRCer's way to cope with that problem:

```
/ALIAS HM SET HOLD_MODE TOGGLE
```

Stick that line in your .ircrc file, and then you can set page control on *or* off with the simple command /HM. How does this magic work? All the commands that set some feature ON or OFF with SET also allow for this variation:

```
/SET <...> TOGGLE
```

This command means "set ON if it is OFF now, and set OFF if it's ON now." By using the /ALIAS command, you have assigned the string HM (it also assigns the lowercase equivalent hm) to mean /SET HOLD_MODE TOGGLE. By not including the ^ character, you ensure that you get a message like this:

```
*** HOLD_MODE is set to ON
```

This message tells you which way the toggle has gone. [—] And in any case, you know now that as long as you have %H%B in your status format string, you get information about the HOLD_MODE buffer.

Here are some commonly used aliases that have saved thousands of precious keystrokes over the IRC years:

Alias	***Description***
alias h	who
alias w	whois
alias ww	whois $0 $0 ($0 expands to the first argument following the alias invocation. So if you enter /WW Sparkey, this alias expands to /WHOIS Sparkey Sparkey, a form that returns the normal /WHOIS on Sparkey *plus* Sparkey's idle time.)
alias j	join
alias jht	join #hottub (and similarly for your favorite channels)
alias l	leave *
alias ll	lastlog
alias ds	dcc send
alias dg	dcc get
alias dc	dcc clear

Aliasing in IRC is a powerful process. And, as you have seen, so are all those /ON traps. Put them together and you have what is virtually a computer language, which (not by coincidence) resembles the C language. It becomes even more so when you add a couple more commands, starting with the following:

```
/IF <variable expression> {DO THIS IF TRUE} {DO THIS IF FALSE}
```

An example of this construction is to make the simple alias l (for leave), which we just defined, a little more foolproof, like this:

```
alias l {
    if ([$C])
        {leave $C}
        {echo Ahem. You are not actually joined to a channel}
}
```

In this example, the <variable expression> is the pseudoequation `([$C])`. `$C` expands to the name of the active channel, and this expression tests whether `$C` is nonnull. A more verbose form would be `if ([$C] != [])`. If that's true, the alias causes you to leave the channel. If it is false, however, `$C` is null, which means that there is no active channel, and this alias tactfully brings your absentmindedness to your attention.

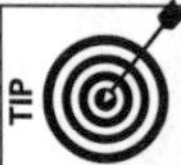

Standard parameters available to IRCII script writers

Parameter	*Meaning*
$n	The nth command line argument (the first is "zeroth")
$n-m	Command line arguments n through m
$n-	Command line arguments n through <however many there are>
$-m	Command line arguments 0 through m
$~	The last command line argument
$*	All unused command line arguments
$,	The last user who sent you a message
$.	The last user to whom you sent a message
$:	The last user to join the active channel
$;	The last user who sent a message into the active channel
$A	Text of your /AWAY message
$B	Text of the last message you sent
$C	Label of the active channel
$D	The last user on your /NOTIFY list who logged on
$H	The current numeric
$I	Label of the channel you were last invited to
$L	Current contents of your command input line
$N	Your nickname
$O	Your STATUS_OPER text if you are an IRCop
$P	@ if you are a chanop on the current channel; null if you're not
$Q	The user with whom you are in /QUERY mode
$S	ID of your server
$T	Current "target" — either current channel or current /QUERY
$U	Text cut from the input line
$V	IRCII version date
$W	Current working directory
$Z	Time

Arithmetical and Boolean operators allowed in IRCII scripts

Operator	Function
==	Equals
!=	Does not equal
>	Greater than
<	Less than
>=	Greater than or equal to
<=	Less than or equal to
^^	XOR
||	OR
&&	AND

A Simple Robot

If you're beginning to surmise that the IRCII scripting language (OK, purists, command shell) has been developed primarily by students of computer science who are seeking a mental exercise with more sex appeal than making a spreadsheet program add a column of figures, you are correct. And if you further guess that these talents are not always used for dainty purposes, you are not wrong there either. These scripting techniques are the basis of the robots, or *bots,* that inhabit IRC and drive the server operators crazy. Some bots are clever and useful, such as *info-bots* that return information when prompted with keywords. Some bots are designed primarily for channel warfare. The worst bots are pernicious because they are not programmed correctly. Their arrogant inventors walk away and leave them running, and then the bots malfunction and wreak havoc with the Net.

Here is the beginning of a simple info-bot that reacts initially to the message `HELP COOK`.

```
on ^msg *
{
  if ([$1-] == [HELP COOK])
    {

      msg $0 I have six recipes to offer today
      msg $0 You may request them with the message SEND <keyword>
      msg $0 The keywords: msg $0 CHILI (hot!!!)
      msg $0 PILAF (chicken-based)
      msg $0 BANANA (fritters - delicious)
```

```
        msg $0 SOUP (oxtail)
        msg $0 SALAD (middle eastern)
        msg $0 COCKTAIL (this week's special)
      }
  {
  if ([$1-] == [SEND CHILI])
      {
        msg $0 Chili coming right up
        dcc send $0 chili.recipe
      }
      {
        if ([$1-] == [SEND PILAF])
        {
          msg $0 Pilaf coming right up
          dcc send $0 pilaf.recipe
        }
#....etc. etc.
#....and when all possibilities have been covered
        {
          msg $0 I did not understand your message
        }
      }
    }
}
```

(You can write an info-bot much more elegantly, but I suspect that this code looks scary enough.)

The last line in the code is suitable for a *dedicated cook-bot,* which is one that does nothing but offer recipes. If you want your cook-bot to run in the background while you continue chatting, you should alter the last line; otherwise, when Xanadu sends you a message that says, "Is it raining where you are?", you do not see this question, and Xanadu gets the surprising reply, "I did not understand your message." You then will soon get a reputation for being a little dense.

To make your bot *transparent,* which means that messages not handled by the bot come through normally, the last line should be `echo *$0* $1-`. Because `$0` expands to Xanadu (in the example just above) and `$1-` expands to the entire text of Xanadu's message, things look normal on your screen and you can respond with this line:

```
/msg xanadu so bad the fish are in the trees.
```

By the way, if you are an IRC power user, you can save yourself five keystrokes by entering `/msg , so bad the fish are in the trees.` because a comma means "the last person who messaged me" and a period means "the last person I messaged."

The Efficiency of DCC

For maximum efficiency, the recipe-bot takes advantage of the wonderful world of *direct client connection,* or *DCC.* This type of connection, which is really CTCP in a fancy package, bypasses all the IRC servers and is therefore impervious to netsplits and the thousand natural shocks that the Net is heir to. DCC is absolutely golden for sending data files zipping across the planet; a mere recipe for pilaf gets to anywhere in a flash. Here's the full command sequence, in which Cookbot sends to Janizze:

```
Cookbot:
/DCC SEND Janizze pilaf.recipe
```

Cookbot sees this line:

```
*** Sent DCC SEND request to Janizze
```

Janizze sees this line:

```
*** DCC SEND (pilaf.recipe 1152) request received from Cookbot
```

Janizze then enters this line:

```
/DCC GET Cookbot
```

And Cookbot sees this line:

```
*** DCC SEND connection with Janizze [151.733.182.3,5454] established
```

The file transfers to Janizze's working directory, and then both parties see a message confirming completion of the file transfer and reporting the transfer speed in kilobytes per second.

Naturally, you do not have to be a bot to use the DCC service. Substitute any filename you like for `pilaf.recipe`, and you can issue the commands manually with the same excellent results. Another amazing thing about DCC is that you can send and receive several files simultaneously, not to mention establish a secure DCC CHAT connection at the same time. While all this is going on, the command `/DCC` without any arguments gets you a progress report on all of your DCC connections — in the hypothetical case of the pilaf recipe, which is only 1152 bytes, the file would transfer so fast that you would never have time to get a listing on it. DCC is quite comfortable with large binary files and is used frequently for the exchange of personal photographs in the form of .gif or .jpg files.

Some bot-writers avoid DCC for the simple reason that some non-UNIX systems have not gotten around to supporting it. Both WSIRC for Windows and Homer for the Mac, however, allow DCC connections. The problem occurs with other workstation software, in addition to the hordes of users now invading the Internet by way of connections from data services such as Delphi and America Online. It takes these users awhile, understandably, to become power users.

If you decide to shun DCC, the alternative is to turn the entire file into a private message addressed to `$0`. Rather than `dcc send $0 chili.recipe`, the code line looks like this:

```
exec -msg $0 cat chili.recipe
```

If you interpret that line word by word, it says, "Pass the following command to your shell processor. Make a message out of whatever happens next. Address it to this person whose name is found in the box labeled $0. Now use the UNIX `concatenate` command to display the file `chili.recipe`."

A slight refinement is normally necessary, however, to make this command work as intended. On most client software, the `exec` command is issued while the client/server system is still recovering from its success in evaluating the `if ([$1-] == [HELP CHILI])` expression, and the `exec` call ends up getting ignored. To be sure that the system is ready, the code must be amended to look like the following line:

```
wait -cmd exec -msg $0 cat chili.recipe
```

After you have written your bot, you give it a filename such as cook.bot; then, once joined to a channel, activate it with the command `/LOAD cook.bot`. You can debug it by sending messages to yourself — on a private channel, please. Otherwise, by debugging your bot, you end up only bugging your fellow IRCers.

Desktop IRC Scripts

Those advanced IRC clients for desktop machines, such as WSIRC and Homer, do not yet allow their users the full range of IRC syntax for creating bots. Both `csamsi@clark.net` (Caesar Samsi, the maker of WSIRC) and `tob@zaphod.ee.pitt.edu` (Toby Smith, the programmer of Homer), however, have indicated that they are working toward making that possible someday. Both packages obviously have their own "built-in bots," which are supposed to act as bodyguards at the service of you, the user.

Homer's list of pals

Homer has a feature called the *Friend List,* which is just a basic war-bot. Assuming that you have channel operator status, anyone on your Friend List who enters your channel is automatically given operator status, and anyone removing operator status from your IRC buddies is "de-opped" and kicked out (as the manual says, "that's what friends are for!"). You might recall, from the discussion about `/ON JOIN` and `/IF`, that the parameter `$0` expands to the nickname of someone who just joined a channel. If you have the brains of at least an escargot, you should be able to figure out how to write and load a Friend List script for yourself (not that I'm encouraging anything of the sort).

WSIRC's war mode

Caesar Samsi must have misspent a large part of his youth engaged in IRC channel warfare because his built-in bot goes a step or two farther than Toby Smith's does. It keeps not only an Operator List — the equivalent of Homer's Friend List — but also a Protect List and a Bad List. The client can, with the flourish of a mouse, be put into "war mode."

Anyone who acts aggressively toward your operator and Protect List friends not only kick off but also bans those perceived as villains.

Ban the Bots!

Ready-made bot scripts for the UNIX IRCII client are not hard to come across, and some of them include war-bots that make WSIRC's war mode look like a dowagers' tea party. (Make that a *vicarage* tea party. The last time I took tea with a bunch of dowagers, I ended up with a cucumber sandwich stuffed up my left nostril. Those dowagers can play rough.)

Three warnings are in order here. First, if you feel like loading one of the ready-made scripts, you should look through it and comment out any features you can't understand, especially if they involve kicking and banning. (You do so by inserting a pound sign (#) at the beginning of each line of an alias.) Even if you are not habitually a channel operator, sooner or later someone will confer operator status on you, if only for logistic reasons, and then you may acquire powers you never knew that you had — or wanted to have. I got auto-kicked by one of my IRC friends not long ago in retaliation for kicking off another user (for very good reason). My friend was embarrassed — she had no idea that the other person was on a Protect List she had blithely loaded along with a useful set of aliases.

The second warning is that bots are generally already on the Bad List of many server administrators and are getting an extremely bad reputation in the IRC world. If you look at the MOTD (message of the day) of a selection of U.S. servers, you see plenty of them announcing an extremely low tolerance of bots. One East Coast server now announces, "If I see you running a bot on this server, I will K:line your entire site." (K:line means to deny access.) From what I've observed, so far these are empty threats; and it must be said that the likelihood of any general consensus in the petty, bickering, egomaniacal community of IRC administrators is relatively low. Nonetheless, you should know that an overaggressive bot will make you unpopular and a malfunctioning bot may get you in some serious trouble. To anticipate two questions: No, no one has yet been successfully sued in a court of law over IRC behavior (although attorneys have been consulted), and yes, people have had their Internet access privileges yanked for improper use (many, many times).

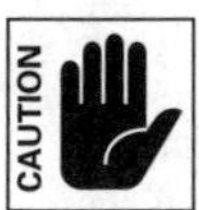

The final warning is just a much more informed version of the old "Don't take candy from strangers" adage. One clever but appallingly irresponsible game the hackers play is to steal the code of a bot script and substitute their own hacked version, which contains nasty things known as *back doors, security holes,* and *Trojan horses.* The bot designer understandably puts his handiwork out there on the Net and does not check every hour of every day to see whether it has been hacked. This is *caveat unzippor* in the worst way — except that you don't "empt" an IRC script (it's more a case of "grabbum et unzippum"). One tip: If you see something like this line of code:

```
on ^ctcp "% % cmd *" ^$3-
```

it's hacked. Run like crazy!

IRCII scripts and where to find them

In all cases, these IRCII scripts are available by anonymous FTP:

Site: irc.cas.und.nodak.edu

Directory: /tmp/irc/scripts

OPERvision (13.3 K): This all-purpose script, written by Jake "WintrHawk" Khuon (khuon@aero.und.nodak.edu), makes excellent use of IRCII's windowing commands. It's somewhat warlike.

ircrc.hawk (68.7 K): This is Jake Khuon's personal .ircrc collection. Jake warns that this collection is incompatible with OPERvision; I would add that it would be *extremely* foolhardy to load this huge file in its entirety. The scripts and aliases in the file are quite belligerent. (In fact, the file includes scripts for mass deop, kick, and ban.) *This file is useful only as a library of aliases from which to choose.*

toolz (52.2 K): This script, by "YaZoo" (yazoo@cyberspace.net), is a good example of a script that seems obsessed with channel warfare, including "random kicks."

gargoyle (45.7 K): By Byron "Vassago" Ng (Byron_Ng@mindlink.bc.ca), this script is in use on the "Undernet." It defends against the worst consequences of netsplits.

how.to.write.a.bot (18.6 K): "Botdox" is a tongue-in-cheek parody of the classic "Botdoc," written in 1993 by "Patman." *Be careful:* Some of the aliases suggested here may have security holes.

Site: ftp.ugcs.caltech.edu

Directory: /pub/elef/warez/irc_hacks

infinity.gz (34.3 K): This distinguished and popular all-purpose script was written by "MiSTiK VOiD."

xdcc (56.0 K): This clever script is a little like a superduper version of the cook-bot. It was written by Xabier Vazquez (siavagaj@sc.ehu.es).

Site: deathstar.texas.net

Directory: /pub/irc/scripts

superpak (132 K): This collection of IRCII scripts comes from various sources — some cited, some not. Compiled by barron@texas.net, it does *not* focus on channel warfare. It's definitely a cornucopia from which to select *carefully!*

Site: ftp.u.washington.edu

Directory: /pub/user-supported/UW_IRC

Here's another cornucopia of IRC stuff, arranged in subdirectories for bots, scripts, war tools, and so on. It features a little newbie trap: The subdirectory names have spaces in them, so if you try to enter `cd irc bots`, it goes nowhere (you have to make it `cd "irc bots"`).

bigbox.irc (121.1.K): This well-organized script is another compilation from various sources, but this one has new material.

infinity.irc (122.3 K): This gunzipped infinity is ready to go.

serpent.irc (26.8 K): By "Vassago," the author of Gargoyle, this script proclaims in its preamble to be a destructive script written by an author who is tired of IRC and wants to see it smashed up. This warning is probably not intended, however, to be taken seriously. ;-)

spider.irc (151.2 K): This script, by "Nimbus," is a classic because it includes a programmable bot that kicks people off your channel if they enter certain words. It's normally assumed to be a monitor-bot that eliminates offensive language, but that was not necessarily what its author intended.

IRC on the World Wide Web

Like most communications topics, IRC has behaved a little like a bacterial culture on the Web, dividing and redividing until it seems to be everywhere.

An excellent starting point is `http://www.funet.fi/~irc`. The fact that the best IRC archive is in Finland is less surprising if you recall that IRC was invented there, by Jarkko Oikarinen, at the University of Oulu. Here you find a collection of IRC documents that includes some of the same scripts as are available by ftp; it also has hypertext links to other collections in the United States, England, France, and elsewhere.

The IRC memorabilia on the Web includes not just scripts but also logs of famous (or famously ribald) IRC events, conversations and encounters, galleries of pictures of IRC personalities, home pages of long-established IRC channels, and [—] as advertising copywriters love to say when they are out of space [—] "much, much, more"!

Note: Don't get so wrapped up in aliases, scripts, and bots that you forget that Internet Relay Chat is supposed to be for *chatting*.

Stuart Harris is the author of How to Survive Internet Relay Chat *(Addison-Wesley, 1995) and numerous articles about the Internet in national magazines. He works as an Internet consultant and is leader of his local computer society's Internet specia-interest group. He also claims to be the first writer/producer of live theatre on the Internet; his group, "The Hamnet Players," regularly gets international casts together on a special IRC channel to present scripted pastiches of famous plays.*

Chapter 22

Scaling the World Wide Web

This chapter contains three articles:

- "Publishing Information on the World Wide Web"
- "Getting Interactive on the Web"
- "Texts on the Internet"

Publishing Information on the World Wide Web

by Jack Graham <jacker@nwu.edu>
http://crow.acns.nwu.edu:8082/hyplan.html

Introduction

More than any other part of the Internet, the World Wide Web tends to be like a big book. You can flip through the book, follow references (in the form of links to different pages), and even write notes in the margins (with features such as fill-out forms). And of course, behind all the information you're reading in this huge book there is a publisher, or rather, lots of publishers, each making their own entries into the Web. In this article, you learn how to become a Web publisher.

This article discusses the following stepping-stones on the path to WWW enlightenment:

- An introduction to HTML (Hypertext Markup Language), the text-marking language used to prepare documents for the World Wide Web
- How to serve documents to the Internet public, whether through an established World Wide Web server or by setting up your own server
- The rules of good HTML style and the steps to establishing a successful Web server
- What to do when things go wrong

Text and hypertext

The technology called hypertext is the foundation of the World Wide Web. *Hypertext* is text designed to emulate human thought. Instead of being linear, it has the capability to be associative. Hypertext does this by incorporating links, also called hot links or hot spots.

Links are highlighted or underscored words or phrases that form pathways to other areas of a document or to a different but associated document. Clicking a link with the mouse takes the reader to the area of text or new document that corresponds to the link.

In Web documents, the language used to create these links is called HTML.

HTML

The *H*yper*t*ext *M*arkup *L*anguage (HTML) is the system used to format documents for viewing by World Wide Web (WWW) clients, such as Mosaic. HTML is a simple language, for good reason. The idea behind HTML is to have a document format that adapts to any computer on which it's being displayed — but in a consistent manner.

A Web publisher uses HTML to define the logical identity of each of the parts of his document. For example, a publisher can define a certain block of text as being a section header. Although that section header might look somewhat different when it's displayed on different machines, it always appears larger and bolder than normal text does.

In other words, when a Web publisher writes HTML, she should use each tag for what it represents, not for the way it appears on an individual Web client.

The concept of tags in HTML

Because tags are the building blocks of every World Wide Web document, getting a firm grasp on exactly what tags do is fundamental to publishing on the Web. Very simply, *tags* provide Web clients with a *description* of a Web document.

In many ways, HTML hearkens back to the early days of word processing, when users had to be explicit in giving formatting instructions to a word processor. To put a word in boldface, you had to insert a pair of "tags" on each side of the word and therefore flag the word for the printer as a bit of text that required two passes of the printing head. The first tag (often represented as ^B for the Control-B keystroke sequence) told the printer to begin using boldface; the second tag in the pair (referred to as "closing the tag") instructed the printer to stop using boldface.

Inserting these tags often required an arcane combination of keystrokes, made more difficult by the fact that they were usually invisible. Even worse, if a user forgot to close a tag, the printer would not know when to stop printing the formatted characters, which often resulted in entire documents printed in that format (bold, for example) from the point of the unclosed tag. These tags are still with us, in fact, in contemporary word-processing software. You just don't usually see them. Figure 22-1 shows how one popular word-processing program uses something similar to tags to mark tabs, indentations, and breaks between paragraphs.

```
IV.  Hypertext Mark-up Language¶
       • Basic overview¶
       • Concept of the "tag"¶
       • Categories¶
           • Tags that define¶
           • Tags that format¶
           • Tags that link¶
           • Tags that invoke media¶
           • Tags that invoke scripts¶
       • Discussion of Tags¶
           • Tags that define¶
               • <HTML>¶
               • <HEAD>¶
```

Figure 22-1: Microsoft Word with "tags" visible.

HTML is much like the early word processors, and Mosaic is much like the clunky dot-matrix printers that interpreted their commands. Mosaic looks at HTML and sends back exactly what it sees. With no tags in a document, all Mosaic sees is raw, unformatted text. Mosaic can't even find a line break without a tag to tell it where to break the line. And again, like the old word processors, after you tell a Web client to begin printing italics, it doesn't stop until you tell it to, which can be bad if you forget to close a tag (see Figure 22-2).

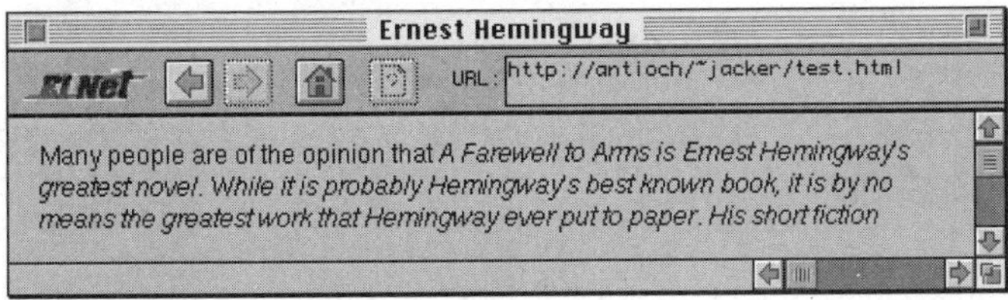

Figure 22-2: Forgetting to close a tag.

The Web publisher inserts tags in the raw text document to tell Mosaic (or any other Web browser) how the document should be displayed onscreen. There are very few HTML tags, but the developer who knows them all can exert a surprising degree of control over how a Web page appears.

Tags are good for more than simply formatting a document, however. Tags also play an important part in providing the Web client with information about the document, linking the document to other documents in the Web, and linking multimedia files to HTML documents. Tags can be broken down into four categories, based on function:

- Tags that define
- Tags that format
- Tags that link
- Tags that invoke media

Basic HTML

An HTML document is nothing more than a file containing ASCII text, with the HTML extension appended to the filename. As a result, you can create HTML on any text editor or word processor if you save the file as plain, ASCII text. Utilities that enable the quick creation of HTML exist, but after a Web publisher knows all the tags, it's just as easy to add tags as you type a document. (In the Web business, simply typing tags without a utility is called "Iron Man HTML.")

All HTML tags can be readily recognized by the angle brackets (< and >) that enclose them. Many tags come in pairs that mark the beginning and end of a section of text. Many tags also have definable attributes that appear in addition to the tag name within the angle brackets. Attributes provide extra information that is often necessary for the tag to function correctly.

If you want to begin writing HTML but don't have access to a Web server, the best way to go about it is to simply write your HTML documents in any text editor or word processor on your local machine. Then save the document as plain text with the HTML (or, in Windows, HTM) extension. Most Web clients then enable you to view the document by using a command from their file menu called Open Local or Open File, depending on which client you use.

Tags that define

A few tags should be included in every HTML document. It is said that these tags "define" the document because they are used to identify it as an HTML document to the server, to give it a title, and to provide information about its creator.

HTML and SGML

You often hear that HTML is a permutation or subset of something called SGML. Although the connection between HTML and SGML rarely matters in practice, you can impress all your Web friends if you have a good understanding of SGML. *SGML,* which stands for Standard Generalized Markup Language (known more intimidatingly as International Standard ISO 8879), is a standard for defining document types to which HTML conforms.

SGML becomes important when you want to use such characters as the angle brackets and the ampersand. These are called *reserved characters* because they are interpreted as parts of tags rather than as regular text if you type them in an HTML document. You have to represent these characters with their SGML equivalents: < (less than), > (greater than), and & (ampersand). These SGML equivalents are called *elements.*

SGML is also useful if you want to use foreign-language characters, such as ö and š. Most of these characters can be represented by an SGML element (for example, ö for an *o* with an umlaut). For more information about special character substitutions, see the Web pages on SGML at

```
http://www.hal.com/products/sw/olias/Build-html/OTgsOXBMCmF84aK.html.
```

An HTML document should begin with the opening `<HTML>` tag and end with the closing `</HTML>` tag. These tags let the Web client know that the document it's viewing is written in HTML.

The reader doesn't see any of the information included in the `<HEAD>` section of the document. All the same, this section is important because it contains information *about* the document. `<HEAD>` should be the first HTML element after the `<HTML>` tag. Within the head section is the document title. The `<TITLE>` tag is one of the most important tags in any HTML document (it goes in the head section).

Whatever is placed between the opening `<TITLE>` and closing `</TITLE>` appears in the title bar of the viewing window of any Web client used to view a Web page. In addition, most Web clients use the title of a Web page in constructing their history lists, and many World Wide Web search and indexing tools search documents by title. Therefore, a descriptive — ideally unique — title for each Web page is crucial. After the title, the head section should be closed with `</HEAD>`.

The body of an HTML document, defined by the opening `<BODY>` and closing `</BODY>` tags, contains the information the reader actually sees. All text, links, and image and media references should go in this section of the document.

For more details, see "The HTML template," later in this section.

Tags that format

This category includes tags that shape the arrangement of text in an HTML document. These tags tend to be most directly analogous with the old-fashioned word-processor tags mentioned earlier. Again, remember that the on-screen appearance of these tags varies among different Web clients.

Layout tags

Layout tags break up text into smaller sections. Keep in mind that any white space within an HTML document is disregarded by the Web client. The largest amount of space that can be created without using these tags is a single character space, no matter how many blank lines, tabs, or indentations are present.

The following tag creates a paragraph break:

```
<P>
```

For most Web clients, this tag tells them to put in a line break and then skip a line. `<P>` is the first of a small group of stand-alone tags. *Stand-alone tags* don't need to be closed because they don't define an area of the document; they simply create a one-time screen element, and then they're over. So you never see the tag `</P>`.

The `<BR>` tag simply creates a line break without skipping a line. Like `<P>`, it's a stand-alone tag.

`<HR>` is a great tag for breaking up text. It creates a single *horizontal rule* (a horizontal line) that runs the width of the window in the Web client. It is also a stand-alone tag.

List tags

List tags define an area of the page as an indented list. *Unordered lists* appear as bulleted lists. *Ordered lists* appear as a series of numbered steps or items. *Descriptive lists* (also called *definition lists*) consist of a series of titles followed by indented descriptions. Most other HTML tags can appear within lists, including other lists.

Figure 22-3 shows the three different kinds of lists as NCSA Mosaic displays them. (Notice the <HR> tags used to separate the lists).

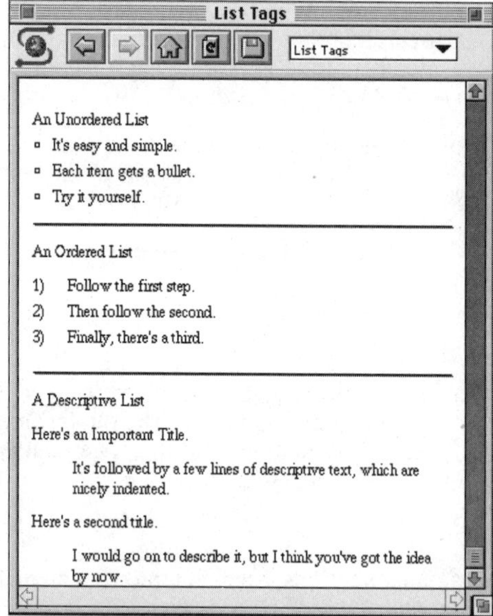

Figure 22-3: List tags.

The following tags mark the beginning and end of an unordered list:

<UL></UL>

The following tags mark the beginning and end of an ordered list:

<OL></OL>

Ordered lists are used to represent numbered steps or hierarchical lists of items. The elements in the list are numbered automatically by the <LI> tag. Each <LI> tag marks the beginning of a new list element in an ordered or unordered list. <LI> creates a new line, preceding it with a bullet in an unordered list or an autonumbered Arabic numeral in an ordered list. The <LI> tag stands alone.

The <DL> tag serves to mark the beginning and ending of a descriptive list:

```
<DL></DL>
```

or

```
<DL COMPACT></DL>
```

Descriptive lists normally place white space between list items. <DL> accepts the attribute COMPACT, which eliminates the white space between items.

The <DT> tag creates a title within a descriptive list, which is normally followed by <DD>, which appears indented beneath it. Like <LI>, this is a stand-alone tag. The <DD> tag indents text that follows it. The idea is to form a description for the title above it. This, too, is a stand-alone tag.

Style tags

This subcategory of formatting tags includes tags that instruct the Web client to display text in a different font, style, or size. To use any of these tags, simply place them at each end of the word or words to be emphasized.

The <H#> tag creates a header; the number after H can range from 1 to 6, with 1 the largest header and 6 the smallest:

```
<H#></H#>
```

For example, <H1>Spam</H1> puts the word *Spam* in the largest typeface possible. The <H#> tag also automatically creates a line break after itself.

Figure 22-4 shows all six levels of headers as they're displayed in the Macintosh version of Netscape.

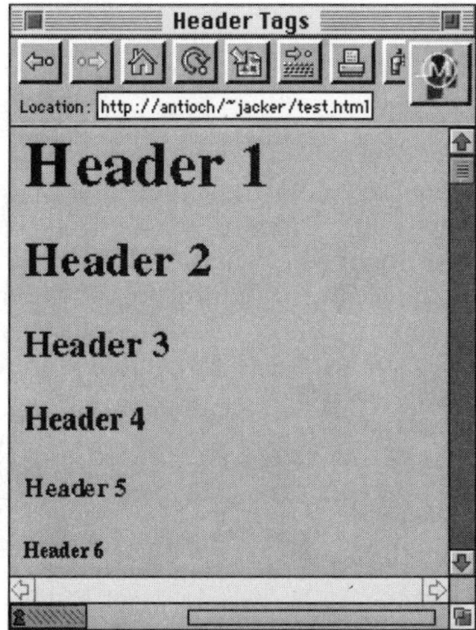

Figure 22-4: Header tags.

There are a number of other style tags, all of which function similarly to <H>. However, the other style tags don't accept a number to determine size. You can, however, use multiple style tags on a word or phrase; so, to generate a word or phrase in bold, italics, and a level-three header, you would use something like:

```
<H3><B><I>Wars make no one great.</I></B></H31>
```

The following four style tags are some of the most commonly used, although there are others:

- **<B></B>** — Bold. Instructs the browser to display text in boldface.
- **<I></I>** — Italics. Instructs the browser to display text in italics.
- **<U></U>** — Underline. Instructs the browser to underscore the text.
- **<PRE></PRE>** — Preformatted text. Displays text in a fixed-width font (each character takes up exactly the same amount of width). It's useful because the text appears to the reader with exactly the same indentation and line breaks as used by the author.

Tags that link

These tags create the links that connect Web documents with each other, with files in other formats, and with documents on other Internet sites. Links are arguably the most powerful feature of the Web. They allow a Web publisher to incorporate information from anywhere in the world into her document, if that information can be referenced by a Uniform Resource Locator, or URL.

Links can point to other areas within a document, to other documents, and to specific areas within other documents. And as stated, a link doesn't even have to point to a document on the same machine, making it possible to spread out a web of linked documents over several different Web servers.

Hyperlinks and anchor tags

The <A> (anchor) tag is the basic tag for creating links:

```
<A></A>
```

However, <A> is meaningless on its own. Depending on which attributes are assigned to <A>, the anchor tag can serve one of two functions: The HREF attribute causes <A> to serve as a link to another document, whether that document is on your local machine or on a remote machine. The NAME attribute creates a point within a document that an HREF can jump to. This article discusses this situation in more detail later; for now, the most important thing to remember is that HREF and NAME can never appear within the same anchor tag.

HREF turns a selected area of text (or an in-line image, as you see later) into a hyperlink. Clicking the linked text then takes a reader to a specified URL. HREF is used as follows:

```
<A HREF="URL">linked text</A>
```

URL can be either the full URL of another document on the Web or the directory path and filename of another document on your local machine. The linked text is the text within the document that is highlighted to form the link. After the linked text, the tag should be closed with </A>.

The following example creates a hyperlink to the HTML document pez.html on the machine www.snipe.org in the directory /pez:

```
<A HREF="http://www.snipe.org/pez/pez.html">The Pez Home Page</A>
```

The NAME attribute makes a section of a Web page a possible destination for an <A HREF> link. NAME enables you to give a "name" to a section of a Web page, which a Web client can then find and jump to.

NAME functions as follows:

```
<A NAME="string">anchor text</A>
```

The string can be any string of standard ASCII text. As with HREF, the tag must be closed with </_A>. When you create the <A HREF> link, you simply add #string to the URL — the pound sign (#) — to tell the Web client to extend the URL to include a NAME on the end. Using lots of NAME links can make it much easier for your readers to find the information they want, particularly within longer documents. For example, NAME links are a great way of making a table of contents that links to later sections of a document.

Look at the following example from the document llama.html:

```
<H1>Table of Contents:</H1>
        Introduction
        <A HREF="/llama/llama.html#guide">Llama Field Guide</A>
        Getting the Most out of your Llama
        What to Do When your Llama Spits
...
(later in the same document)
<H3><A NAME="guide">Llama Field Guide</A></H3>
```

When a reader clicks on the text *Llama Field Guide,* the Web client searches the Web page for the name guide and jumps to it. Notice that it's OK for the <A NAME> link to occur inside the <H3> tags. This capability is useful, in fact, because it enables you to reference section headers. Generally speaking, it's considered good syntax to put any link tags that affect a piece of text *inside* any header tags that affect it.

Tags that invoke media

Links do not have to be from one text document to another. Many links connect text to images, sounds, and video. The <IMG> tag (which is used to create in-line images) is the only "new" tag introduced in this section. For other forms of media, you simply use the <A HREF> tag, discussed earlier. Later in this article, I explain how to use <A HREF> successfully for media, however, because the application tends to be a little different.

Graphics

<IMG> is another extremely powerful feature in HTML, as in:

```
<IMG SRC="URL">
```

<IMG> causes an image file in GIF (CompuServe's Graphics Interchange Format) or XBM (X-Windows Bitmap) to appear in the client program's viewing window along with text. All you have to do is fill in the URL or directory path and filename for an image file:

```
<IMG SRC="plantfuzz.gif" ALIGN="center" ALT="Plant fuzz.">
```

This line causes the GIF image `plantfuzz.gif` to appear on a Web page.

<IMG> is a stand-alone tag. Notice that I've included several optional attributes you can add to <IMG>. The `ALIGN` attribute tells the Web client how to align any text that appears on the same line as the in-line image. In-line images don't automatically create their own line breaks, so you can put them within text or squeeze text on the same line to form captions. You can `ALIGN` text to the top, bottom, or center of an image. You can use `ALT` to define a string of text that appears in place of your in-line image if the reader's Web client doesn't allow him to view in-line images. (Some folks are still stuck with text-only Web clients, such as Lynx, so `ALT` is a courtesy to them).

By the way, always use gif rather than GIF as the extension for GIF files. Although HTML is not supposed to be case sensitive, reports say that GIF confuses some Web clients.

Finally, it should be mentioned that you can put an <A HREF> link around an in-line image just as you would do with a piece of text, as in this example:

```
<A HREF="icky.html"><IMG SRC="cockroach.gif"></A>
```

The in-line image `cockroach.gif` is now surrounded by a blue border, indicating that it's something the reader can click to follow a link. If the reader clicks the in-line image, she is taken to the HTML document called `icky.html`.

Linking to other media

Some other media formats Web documents often link to include QuickTime and MPEG video clips, sound files in Amiga (aiff) or Sun U-Law (au) formats, or image formats such as JPEG that cannot be used as in-lines in all browsers. To link to these other forms of media, simply use <A HREF> along with the filename or URL of the media document to be linked to.

The following example creates a link to the MPEG movie named `fnord.mpeg` in the directory `/video` on the machine `www.fnord.com`:

```
<A HREF="http://www.fnord.com/video/fnord.mpeg">link text</A>
```

If a reader clicks the link text, the Web client loads `fnord.mpeg` and displays it in an external viewer program.

Links to other Internet resources

As stated, you can use an URL within an anchor tag to link to documents on another Internet site. The great thing about the Web is that the other Internet site does not have to be a World Wide Web server. HTML gives you the power to link to documents that can be retrieved by Usenet News, ftp, and Gopher. It also accepts links to telnet and e-mail addresses. The Web also supports a few other information-retrieval formats, but the six discussed in this section are by far the most common.

The following format requests a document from an HTTP (Hypertext Transfer Protocol) server:

```
http://host.name:port/path/to/document
```

All WWW servers are HTTP servers, so this is the format for requesting anything on the Web. You don't normally have to include `port` when you're pointing to a Web server, because most servers run by default on port 80, and your client knows that. If the server you're pointing to runs on a different port, however, you have to specify a port number in your URL.

Use the following URL format to request documents anonymously from an ftp server:

```
ftp://host.name/path/to/document
```

When you use an ftp URL, the Web client generally downloads the document in question and saves it on the reader's machine.

The following URL format grabs documents off of a Gopher server:

```
gopher://host.name:port/path/to/document
```

If the document is text, the Web client generally opens and views it as plain text. The handling of other file formats varies between different clients. As with HTTP servers, you can usually omit the port number.

```
telnet://host.name:port/
```

By using a telnet URL, you tell the Web client to open a separate telnet connection to a remote machine. The connection opens in the appropriate telnet client on the reader's machine (not within the Web client). The reader must know a username and password, of course, to successfully connect to the remote machine.

Use one of the following URL formats to retrieve Usenet News:

```
news:news.group.name
```

or

```
news:message-id
```

A Web publisher can either specify a newsgroup (in which case a list of all articles in the specified newsgroup is retrieved for the reader) or request a specific news article by message ID. You don't need the `//` in this URL format.

Some clients (such as Netscape) now allow a link to an e-mail address:

```
mailto:you@your.machine.name
```

Clicking on the link opens a message window, which the reader can then type and send off to the e-mail address specified in the URL. This is a great way to get feedback on your pages from your readers. Again, no // is needed in this URL form.

The HTML template

The following document can serve as a template for creating HTML files; it contains all the "mandatory" tags and generally shows how an HTML document should be laid out:

```
<HTML>

<HEAD>
<TITLE>Document Title</TITLE>
</HEAD>

<BODY>

<H1>Document Header</H1>

 Document Content

</BODY>

</HTML>
```

HTML Design Pitfalls

Because of the World Wide Web's incredibly fast growth, the ease with which it can be accessed, and the wealth of interesting resources it offers, it is now one of the centers of attention in the development of the Internet.

Spurring this bandwagonesque growth is the fact that HTML is incredibly easy to learn. The products of this fast growth, new Web pages, range in quality from spectacular to mediocre to miserable. This section is intended to help beginning HTML developers avoid the miserable and rise above the merely mediocre.

Netiquette in Webspace

The emergence of the Web as a prominent feature of the Internet adds a few rules to what is normally defined as *netiquette,* the rules of conduct that make working with the Internet easier. Unlike older points of netiquette, however, the new rules apply more to the information provider (you, the HTML developer) than to individual users.

In-line image netiquette

It is an accepted rule among Web developers to exercise restraint when using in-line images. Although in-lines are among the most exciting and useful features of HTML, a little care in their employment goes a long way toward keeping your readers happy.

Avoid large in-line images. In this discussion, "large" is any GIF file larger than 35 kilobytes. Any image larger than this size significantly slows loading time, annoying your readers and reducing the chances of your page being read. This is especially true for home pages or "top level" pages.

In addition to file size, you should also consider screen size. It is a common mistake to create a page header or logo that takes up so much screen space that users have to scroll down before they can see any text.

When you create a link to a non-in-line image, it's good form to indicate how large the image is in kilobytes, thereby saving your users lots of unwanted downloading time. This advice applies to any situation in which a user might face a long load-time: Always warn users about large file sizes.

Keep in mind that your pages are viewed on a variety of monitors. Because the average user probably has a 256-color monitor, design images with that fact in mind. Images with thousands or millions of colors do not look as good on 256-color monitors. If you think that many of your users might be on 16-color or lesser monitors, consider designing with them in mind too.

As a final note, remember that Mosaic and other clients tend to be very dumb in the way they handle color. Because a user with a 256-color monitor can display only 256 different colors at a time, images with widely differing color maps are likely to interfere with each other.

Designing for a particular browser

Not everyone uses NCSA Mosaic as her Web client. What looks good when it's displayed with Mosaic might look awful in MacWeb, Netscape, Lynx, or even a different version of Mosaic.

One common problem HTML developers face is the difference in background colors between various browsers — it's complicated because the user can change her background color at will. In-line images look very bad if they have an empty white border and the background is gray.

There are two ways to avoid this. Any GIF that doesn't have a solid, square, nonwhite border should be made transparent. The normal GIF format is GIF 87a. The transparent GIF (GIF 89a) carries an attribute in its file information that can flag one color in the color map of the image as "transparent." When the image is displayed, the application displaying it fills in its own background color wherever the transparent color occurs, resulting in an image that appears to float on the background.

A few clients might not yet support transparent GIFs. It's a good idea, therefore, to make the background colors for most images a medium gray because this is the default background color for most clients.

Transparency, a Macintosh program, and Giftrans, a UNIX program, both convert GIF 87a to GIF 89a. Transparency can be downloaded from this address:

```
ftp://ftp.med.cornell.edu/pub/aarong/transparency
```

Giftrans is also available by way of ftp from this address:

```
ftp://ftp.rz.uni-karlsruhe.de//pub/net/www/tools
```

Both programs are free.

Line-mode browsers

Some users may be employing line-mode Web clients such as Lynx rather than graphical clients such as Mosaic. Line-mode clients aren't particularly popular, and it is not suggested that you let their existence deter you from using in-line images. To be courteous to such users, however, `<IMG>` tags should include the `ALT` attribute to explain to nongraphical users what they aren't seeing.

Graphical interfaces

One exciting capability of HTML is the use of in-line images and clickable image maps to design an interface to a Web page that is graphical, intuitive, and "virtual." Unfortunately, it's easy to design bad graphical interfaces.

The Mozilla effect

What does the inclusion of in-line images and other media do to network traffic and CPU time on a machine running a Web server? Initially, things looked good. Network administrators reported that the Web was well-behaved and didn't create much drain on network resources. But as the Web expanded and software developers began searching for ways to speed up access times to Web pages, a few problems began to emerge.

One perpetual thorn in the side of many Web server administrators is called the "Mozilla effect." Mosaic Communications' Web client Netscape (nicknamed Mozilla) has the capability to hit a Web server with multiple requests for connections, enabling the client to load a page of text and all the in-line images on it at the same time. The number of simultaneous connections is limited by the memory on the reader's machine, but it can be rather high. Although this capability dramatically decreases access times for Web pages, it also severely increases the load on the Web server.

The solution, if server load is a concern for you, is to exercise some restraint with in-line images. One large image is better than lots of small ones and is definitely better than lots of big ones. Your own experience will tell whether the Mozilla effect is becoming a problem for your network or your machine; for now, be warned.

Here are some things to watch out for when you design a graphical interface:

- Large images that take too long to load
- Images that take up too much space physically
- "Buttons" not accompanied by any information about what they actually *do* (for an example, see the URL `http://www.uky.edu/`)

The "click here" syndrome

World Wide Web documents are essentially hypertext. One of the ideas behind hypertext is that links to other documents occur associatively. For HTML developers, this means that it's bad form to create a link around the words *click here* or any similar phrase. Links should be nonintrusive and flow naturally within the text.

Here's an example of bad form:

Click here to see the new Plumbing For Dummies home page.

And here's an example of good form:

Visit the new *Plumbing For Dummies* home page.

The ethics of linking

When you put documents on the Web, people can link to them. Normally, this capability is good; links to your Web pages help promote them and spread to more users the information you're publishing. But linking can also take the form of plagiarism. Web publishers have had some debate about what constitutes Web plagiarism, but this section presents a few good guidelines to follow.

If you're linking to a set of documents on a particular topic, it's considered good form to send your readers to a point where they can see who created the pages you've linked to and explore the rest of the Web site where the pages reside if they want.

Using nonstandard tags

As you continue to explore the realm of HTML and the Web, you will find that many people have managed to create on-screen effects you cannot duplicate with the HTML tags discussed in this chapter. HTML is an ever-changing beastie, and it's good to keep up on what's going on.

Changes in the HTML standard are being discussed that will give Web publishers much more control over the appearance of their pages. Although these changes are exciting, many of them haven't been universal. Several Web developers have created tags that work with only their own client and server software. Be cautious if you choose to employ such nonstandard tags. Although they may look good on your own client, they may look terrible on someone else's or even cause an error.

If you link to a single document, such as an essay or an image, be sure to give credit to the creator.

In most cases where you want to include information from another Web site, it's considered courteous to let the administrator of that site know that you're linking to him. Who knows? He might even build a link back to you.

Useful Additions

A number of features can be added to your Web pages to make them easier and quicker to read and navigate. Consider including the features described in this section in your hierarchy of Web pages.

Navigational aids

A standardized set of buttons or icons can be extremely useful in helping your readers through your documents.

A simple set of graphics make excellent navigational aids. In Figure 22-5, the two arrows and the Contents button were each called as separate in-line images, linked to the previous, next, or contents pages. Including a set of "text buttons" for nongraphical readers is also a good idea (something like `[PREVIOUS] [CONTENTS] [NEXT]` would work well in this case).

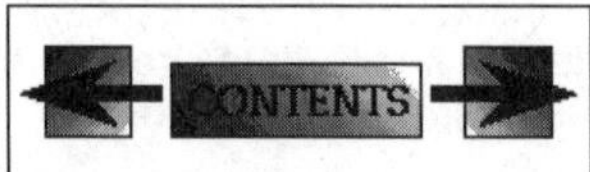

Figure 22-5: Navigational aids.

The caching capabilities of Mosaic and most other browsers mean that, after your set of navigational buttons loads, it stays cached and doesn't slow the loading of subsequent pages.

Document ownership

It is good form to "sign" the bottom of each page you create (or at least the top page in each document tree) with your e-mail address or a link to your home page. For users whose browsers support it, you can make commenting on your work fast and easy by including your e-mail address within a "mailto" link, as shown in Figure 22-6.

Figure 22-6: "Mailto" link to the page's owner.

"What's new?" pages

For large sets of documents, an overview or What's New? page is good form. This page should provide readers with a jumping-off point for exploring your pages, in addition to informing them of pages you have recently added.

For similar reasons, large documents probably should be organized by using outlines or a table of contents with links to the respective pages.

NAME links

Liberal use of `NAME` links within long documents (especially on section headers), accompanied by a short table of contents at the top of the document, is a great convenience for readers who don't want to sift through an entire document looking for one section.

`NAME` links also enable other developers to link to specific sections of your documents.

Serving It Up: A Guide to HTTP Servers

Now that you're a pro with HTML, you probably are wondering about the best way of serving your meticulously created documents to the Internet. The answer is to get access to an HTTP server. HTTP (*H*yper*t*ext *T*ransfer *P*rotocol) servers are the programs that enable readers to access information on the Web; these are the programs Mosaic and other Web clients talk to. You have two basic options for getting access to a server: you can rent, borrow, or otherwise acquire space on an already established World Wide Web server or else you can establish your own.

Using established HTTP servers

Running a WWW server requires that you have access to these items:

- A TCP/IP network connected to the Internet
- A machine on that network capable of acting as a server
- Server software

Because these requirements (particularly the first one) can be prohibitive for many would-be Web publishers, the engines of commerce (and of academia, in some cases) have kicked in to make Web publishing a little more accessible. The market for Web publishing services is large and confusing and is filled with more than a few hustlers. As in all things, let the buyer beware.

Many on-line services (Netcom is the best example) now allow users to serve Web documents from their public directories for a nominal fee. This can be a relatively inexpensive and effective way to put documents on the Web. Checking out these options is recommended.

On the low end of these types of services are groups such as the infamous Cybersell of Canter and Siegel (Usenet nuisances extraordinaire), which charge exorbitant fees (upward of $500 per month) to put Web pages on-line for businesses. These types of services generally cater to the technically nonsavvy (and are best avoided by anyone who went to the trouble to buy this wonderful book).

Finally, if all you really want is your own little corner of the Web (a home page and maybe a few pages of stuff you think is neat), there's still plenty of room on the Web for home-grown, mom 'n' pop Web pages. A number of munificent academic organizations run free home page publishing areas; check Usenet news for the periodic announcements these groups make.

Setting up your own HTTP server

Setting up your own HTTP server gives you much more freedom in publishing your documents, but it also makes you a little more responsible as a server administrator. I say only "a little more" because being a Web server administrator is not as daunting a task as it might sound. The setup for most forms of HTTP server software is relatively easy, and most servers are simple to manage after you have them up and running.

The following section is divided by platform. For each platform, I discuss the most popular software and the basics of making it work for you.

Macintosh

Macintosh users have it easy when it comes to setting up HTTP servers. The choice of programs is simple because right now there's only one. That one, MacHTTP, is easy to set up and simple to manage and now supports some powerful features that were previously available only to UNIX Web publishers.

Windows

Like Macintosh, Windows boasts only one popular HTTP server program: the Windows version of NCSA httpd. Setting up this server on networked Windows machines is easy and requires little configuration (see Chapter 30).

UNIX

A plethora of HTTP server programs exist for the UNIX operating system, ranging from simple interpreted scripts that serve only text to full-featured daemons such as NCSA httpd. It is impossible to cover every UNIX server here, but several of the more popular options for UNIX Web publishers are described, along with their drawbacks and advantages.

MacHTTP

MacHTTP is a simple but elegant little program that can be used "out of the box" on most Macintoshes. MacHTTP is available from its home ftp site at the University of Texas:

```
(ftp://oac.hsc.uth.tmc.edu/public/mac/MacHTTP/machttp.sit.hqx)
```

To use MacHTTP, unpack the archive and run the program. MacHTTP takes up less than 400K of memory on most Macs and takes up processor time only when a reader accesses your site. When you run the program, the MacHTTP status window appears (see Figure 22-7).

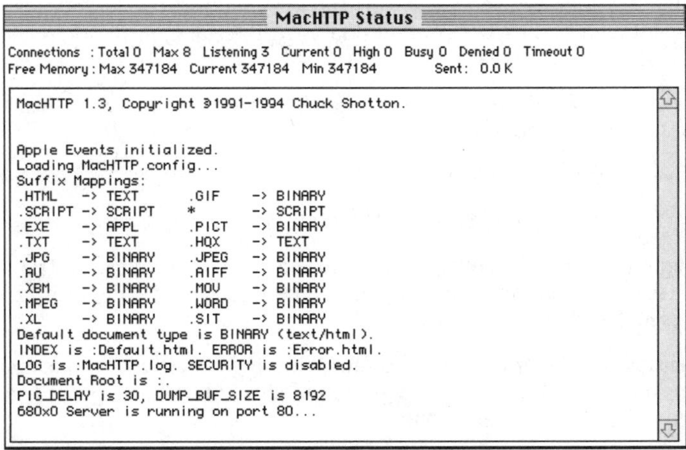

MacHTTP Status
Connections : Total 0 Max 8 Listening 3 Current 0 High 0 Busy 0 Denied 0 Timeout 0
Free Memory : Max 347184 Current 347184 Min 347184 Sent: 0.0 K
MacHTTP 1.3, Copyright ©1991-1994 Chuck Shotton.
Apple Events initialized.
Loading MacHTTP.config...
Suffix Mappings:
.HTML -> TEXT .GIF -> BINARY
.SCRIPT -> SCRIPT * -> SCRIPT
.EXE -> APPL .PICT -> BINARY
.TXT -> TEXT .HQX -> TEXT
.JPG -> BINARY .JPEG -> BINARY
.AU -> BINARY .AIFF -> BINARY
.XBM -> BINARY .MOV -> BINARY
.MPEG -> BINARY .WORD -> BINARY
.XL -> BINARY .SIT -> BINARY
Default document type is BINARY (text/html).
INDEX is :Default.html. ERROR is :Error.html.
LOG is :MacHTTP.log. SECURITY is disabled.
Document Root is :.
PIG_DELAY is 30, DUMP_BUF_SIZE is 8192
680x0 Server is running on port 80...

Figure 22-7: MacHTTP window.

Making your HTML documents accessible is easy. Simply put your files in your MacHTTP folder or subfolders. Each folder should have in it a file named `default.html`, which serves the same purpose as the `index.html` file on other servers. You can then access files in your MacHTTP directory by using Mosaic to open the URL:

```
http://your.macintosh.name/<name of HTML file>
```

If you plan to run MacHTTP on a machine used for other work, you should do it on a machine with a relatively fast processor (040 or better). Although MacHTTP does not interfere with simple tasks (such as word processing), CPU-intensive tasks (such as image enhancement) slow down when readers access your Web pages.

You probably will want to install an alias to MacHTTP in your machine's Startup Items folder so that if your machine crashes or must be restarted, MacHTTP runs right away after you restart.

For advanced users, MacHTTP now boasts some powerful, new features, including a Macintosh implementation of CGI (Common Gateway Interface), the protocol that enables Web servers and clients to use small programs called *scripts* to perform advanced functions. It is now possible to successfully implement features such as clickable image maps, mailto scripts, and fill-out forms by using scripting languages such as MacPERL and AppleScript.

For additional information about MacHTTP, check out the MacHTTP home page:

`http://www.uth.tmc.edu/mac_info/machttp_info.html`

NCSA httpd for Windows

Httpd is NCSA's popular HTTP server program, originally written for UNIX but now available to Windows users as well. Httpd for Windows also includes a Windows implementation of the CGI (Common Gateway Interface) protocol to allow scripting functions.

NCSA httpd for Windows requires WinSock Version 1.1 or later to be installed and running on your computer.

Windows httpd is available at:

`ftp://ftp.ncsa.uiuc.edu/Web/httpd/Unix/ncsa_httpd/contrib/winhttpd/`

After you download the software, you should unzip it in a directory named C:\HTTPD. Don't use another directory name, and keep the directory structure of the files in the archive intact.

Configuring the server is easy. Httpd for Windows requires only one major step in configuration. You have to add to your machine's AUTOEXEC.BAT file a line that configures the server's time zone:

```
SET TZ=sssnddd
```

`sss` is the three-letter abbreviation for your time zone (CST in Chicago or EST in Vermont, for example). `n` is the number of zones your zone is from Greenwich Mean Time. `ddd` is the three-letter abbreviation for your state's daylight time, if it has one (PDT in Santa Cruz, for example, or omitted in Arizona). The line to be added to the AUTOEXEC.BAT for a server in Denver, for example, looks like this:

```
SET TZ=MST6MDT
```

After this line is added to AUTOEXEC.BAT, restart your machine. You can then add a program item for httpd to the window of your choice. I recommend putting a copy of the NCSA httpd icon into your Startup Items window. You can then run the server by double-clicking its icon. You see the httpd window as the program starts up (as shown in Figure 22-8). After it's running, it minimizes itself and runs in the background.

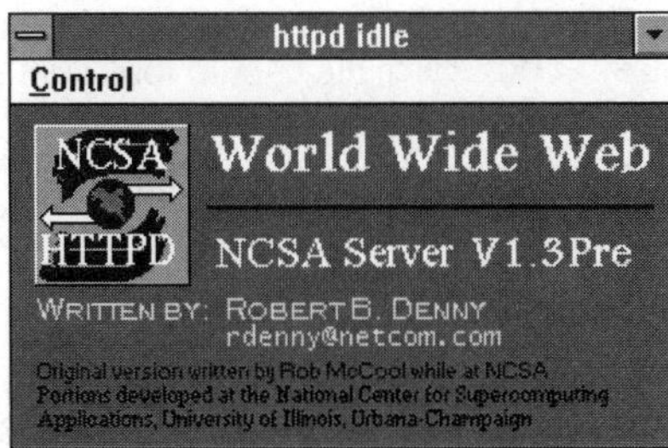

Figure 22-8: The httpd status window.

You can browse the on-line documentation that comes with the server by starting Mosaic or another Web client and accessing your machine with this URL:

```
http://your.machine.name/
```

No additional configuration of the server should be necessary unless you plan to use complex functions such as CGI scripts or domain-based access control.

For more information, see Chapter 30.

NCSA httpd

NCSA httpd is a popular choice among many Web publishers. It is available at

```
ftp://ftp.ncsa.uiuc.edu/Web/httpd/Unix/ncsa_httpd/bin
```

NCSA distributes httpd as source code (which must be compiled on your own computer after you download it) and as precompiled binary executables. You can download a precompiled version for most major UNIX platforms, including DEC, Sun, HP 700, RS6000, and SGI.

Configuring the server

Configuration for UNIX httpd is a little more complex than for the Mac or Windows HTTP servers, but you should still be able to have the server running in about half an hour after you download the appropriate binary file or compile your own from a downloaded source.

The following steps outline the most important (mandatory) steps in configuring NCSA httpd:

1. **Edit** `httpd.conf`.

   You will notice that your tar program unpacked your copy of NCSA httpd with a preexisting directory structure. In your `httpd_1.3` directory is a subdirectory named `conf` that contains several configuration files you have to edit to configure httpd for use. Notice also that each of these files is accompanied by a file with the same name except for `-dist` in the extension. These are template files for your configuration files. You might find them useful later if you alter or mess up your real configuration files.

The first file you want to edit is called `httpd.conf`, your main server configuration file. When you finish, your `httpd.conf` file should look something like Figure 22-9. You must make the following changes or choices to get httpd running:

- **ServerType stand-alone:** Your server can run under inetd (the Internet Daemon process manager) or as a stand-alone process. It's recommended that you run it as stand-alone.
- **Port 80:** Your HTTP server listens to this port for requests. If a Web server is already on your machine, it is probably using port 80. If so, choose another number greater than 1024.
- **User #-1:** In place of `#-1`, enter your user name.

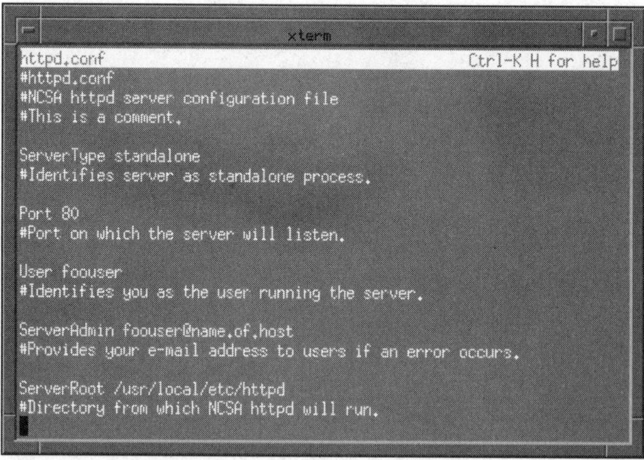

Figure 22-9: Sample httpd. conf

- `ServerAdmin`: You must add this line to the file because there is no default. This line determines which e-mail address your server gives to users who experience errors. After ServerAdmin, enter your e-mail address.
- `ServerRoot /usr/local/etc/httpd`: This line determines the directory from which your HTTP server runs. If you are not the administrator of the machine on which you are running your server, you may want to change the directory path to something more accessible, such as your home directory.

2. **Edit** `srm.conf`.

Srm stands for *s*erver *r*esource *m*ap. This file tells httpd where to look for documents and scripts. There is only one item that must be configured here.

- `DocumentRoot /usr/local/etc/httpd/htdocs`: This line tells httpd where to begin looking for HTML documents when a reader requests them. Your document root should be a subdirectory within your httpd directory and probably should be named `htdocs`. You can have as many subdirectories of `htdocs` as you want; this is simply the root directory for documents.

The other lines in `srm.conf` deal primarily with the way your server should treat requests for information from a directory in which you haven't created an `index.html` file. You can safely ignore the other lines for now.

A third configuration file, called `access.conf`, can be safely ignored. `Access.conf` comes into play when you want to limit access to your server to certain domains or specific users.

Getting the server running

To get a stand-alone NCSA httpd server running, you simply execute the binary file. You may have to use a few useful command line flags, such as the ones in this list:

`-v` Gives you your NCSA httpd version number.

`-f <path to httpd.conf>` Specifies the location of `httpd.conf`. (It should be included if you put it somewhere other than `/usr/local/etc/httpd/conf`.)

`-d <ServerRoot directory>` Specifies the location of your `ServerRoot` directory. (It should be included if you put it somewhere other than `/usr/local/etc/httpd/conf`.)

To start the server, just type **httpd** in addition to the appropriate flags. Therefore, for a user who put NCSA httpd in a subdirectory of her home directory called `httpd`, the command line might look like this:

```
httpd -f /home/foouser/httpd/conf/httpd.conf
```

Voila!

Your server is now up and running. You can access documents on your server by using a URL with the following formula:

```
http://your.host.name:<port number>/
```

The hostname is simply the domain name of your machine (or, optionally, the IP number); the port number is the one you assigned when you edited the `httpd.conf` file. This URL scheme gives you the `index.html` file in whatever directory you specified as `DocumentRoot` in the `srm.conf` file.

For more information

Complete documentation for NCSA httpd, describing all its features, is available on-line at

```
http://hoohoo.ncsa.uiuc.edu/
```

CERN httpd

CERN, the Swiss particle physics research lab where the World Wide Web was born, developed CERN httpd, which seems to be the standard HTTP server in much of Europe. This is particularly true for security-conscious Web publishers such as CERN httpd because it provides better proxy support for publishers who must operate from behind firewalls and because, unlike NCSA httpd, it logs the user names of readers who access your information. CERN httpd also has a powerful caching feature to speed operation. Finally, CERN httpd incorporates several features that make it easy to configure and operate.

CERN makes its HTTP daemon available as both source and precompiled binaries. CERN httpd is known to compile and run on a variety of UNIX and VMS machines, including such oddballs as NeXT, Linux, and Macintoshes running A/UX.

CERN httpd is available by anonymous ftp from

```
ftp://ftp.w3.org/pub/www/
```

Configuring the server

Unlike NCSA httpd, CERN httpd requires only one configuration file, simply called `httpd.conf`. Setting up a secure server really requires only five lines to be added to this file. Use the following steps to make your `httpd.conf`:

1. **Create a file named httpd.conf.** Using any text editor, start a file called `httpd.conf`. The default location is the `/etc` directory, but you can put it anywhere. I recommend putting it in the same directory from which you intend to run CERN httpd or in a subdirectory of that directory.

2. **Define your `ServerRoot`.** The first line of the file should give the path to the directory from which you're going to run httpd. It should read this way:

   ```
   ServerRoot /directory/of/httpd
   ```

3. **Define your port.** Give the number of the port you want httpd to listen to. The default is 80; if you use something else, it should be a number higher than 1024. Your port line should look like this:

   ```
   Port <port number>
   ```

   Note: The port doesn't have to be specified in the `httpd.conf` file. You can also specify it at start-up with a flag (see the section on "Getting the Server Running" for more information on flags).

4. **Define your ServerType.** As with NCSA httpd, it is recommended to run your server as a stand-alone process, not under the management of inetd. This line should read:

   ```
   ServerType Stand-alone
   ```

5. **Name your `AccessLog`.** Httpd logs requests for information in a log file, which can have any name and location you specify. I recommend putting it in a `logs` directory under your `ServerRoot`. Your `AccessLog` line should look like this:

   ```
   AccessLog /directory/of/httpd/logs/<logfile name>
   ```

   Note: `AccessLog` can optionally be set by a flag when you start up the daemon, and it does not have to be included in the `httpd.conf` file.

6. **Name your `ErrorLog`.** Httpd logs errors in server operation to an error log, which can have any name or location you want to give it. The error log is useful for figuring out any problems your server might be having in delivering documents. Your error log should probably be in a `logs` directory along with your access log. Your `ErrorLog` line should look like this:

   ```
   ErrorLog /directory/of/httpd/logs/<error logfile name>
   ```

7. **Create a Pass line.** *Pass directives* are used by CERN httpd to define the way URL requests should be handled. They can serve many useful purposes, such as directing your readers to a different HTTP server if you have to move your information to a new machine. For the basic configuration, however, you need only one Pass line. This line tells CERN httpd where to begin looking for HTML documents and should look like this:

   ```
   Pass     /*       /root/directory/for/documents/*
   ```

   The `httpd.conf` file for a user named `foouser` who runs CERN httpd in a subdirectory of his home directory, therefore, might look like Figure 22-10.

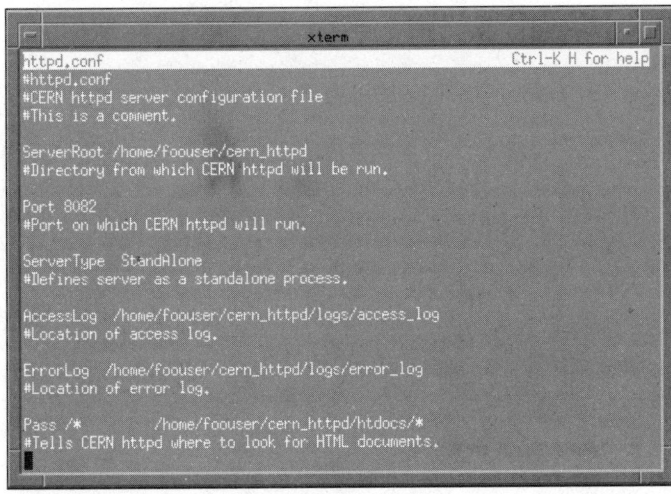
```
httpd.conf                                    Ctrl-K H for help
#httpd.conf
#CERN httpd server configuration file
#This is a comment.

ServerRoot /home/foouser/cern_httpd
#Directory from which CERN httpd will be run.

Port 8082
#Port on which CERN httpd will run.

ServerType  StandAlone
#Defines server as a standalone process.

AccessLog  /home/foouser/cern_httpd/logs/access_log
#Location of access log.

ErrorLog  /home/foouser/cern_httpd/logs/error_log
#Location of error log.

Pass /*        /home/foouser/cern_httpd/htdocs/*
#Tells CERN httpd where to look for HTML documents.
```

Figure 22-10: A CERN httpd sample `httpd.conf` file.

Getting the server running

After you have CERN httpd configured, getting it running is just a matter of invoking the executable file. You may have to include a few of the following command line flags:

```
-r /directory/for/configuration/httpd.conf
```

Specifies the location of your `httpd.conf` file. Must be included.

```
-p <port number>
```

Specifies which port your server should listen to. Overrides both the default number (80) and any port number specified in your `httpd.conf` file. It must be included if you didn't specify a port number in `httpd.conf`.

```
-l /directory/for/logs/<logfile name>
```

Specifies a name and location for your access logfile. Overrides the `AccessLog` line in your `httpd.conf`.

```
-restart
```

Tells CERN httpd to restart. Use this command if you change your `httpd.conf` file and want the changes to go into effect. It should be the last flag you use on the command line.

```
-version
```

Gives your CERN httpd version number. Therefore, a command line to start up CERN httpd for the user `foouser` might look like this:

```
httpd -r /home/foouser/cern_httpd/conf/httpd.conf -p 8082
```

Voila!

Your CERN httpd is now up and running. You can access HTML documents from your server with this URL:

```
http://your.host.name:<port number>/
```

The hostname is the name of the machine on which you're running your httpd, and the port number is the same one you defined either in your `httpd.conf` file or in a command line flag when you started the server. Httpd looks for HTML documents in the directory you defined in the Pass line of `httpd.conf`.

Unlike NCSA httpd (which looks for the file `index.html` when a client requests information from a directory without specifying a filename), CERN httpd supports the following three default filenames (in hierarchical order):

```
Welcome.html  (preferred)
welcome.html
index.html
```

For our purposes, you should include a `Welcome.html` file in every directory and subdirectory that contains HTML documents. Failure to do so can cause problems in the way you've installed CERN httpd; also, directories look much more professional when you remember to include your `Welcome.html`.

For more information

In this chapter, you've read about the simple side of setting up and operating CERN httpd. But CERN httpd also supports a variety of advanced and powerful features not available in other HTTP server programs, including proxy service and caching. Eventually you will want to take advantage of these powerful features.

CERN maintains complete documentation for the latest version of CERN httpd at:

```
http://info.cern.ch/hypertext/WWW/Daemon/Status.html
```

Other UNIX servers

Writing UNIX WWW servers seems to be a popular activity because so many of them are available.

Plexus

The Plexus server is included here in part to show the variety of different ways in which Web publishers have addressed the problem of distributing their documents. Unlike NCSA httpd and CERN httpd, which both run as regular binary executable programs, Plexus is a script written in the PERL programming language.

Plexus has a number of interesting features, including a CGI gateway to the Oracle database system and a Book Icon feature that simplifies the design of navigational toolbars.

Unlike NCSA httpd and CERN httpd, Plexus is somewhat difficult to install if you aren't particularly skilled with UNIX. Its powerful features and easy extensibility, however, make it worth looking into for skilled Web publishers.

For more information about Plexus, see the Plexus home page at:

`http://www.bsdi.com/server/doc/plexus.html.`

WN

WN is a Web server designed for enhanced security and flexibility. By employing a method of document access that is different from any other Web server, WN tightens security by denying access to any document for which access isn't enabled; it also increases the flexibility of document presentation for Web publishers who are willing to spend a little time learning how to take advantage of WN's document delivery method.

WN has a number of useful features that aren't integrated into other Web servers, including searches of documents based on titles, keywords, or contents; the capability to automatically append a standard message to the end of HTML documents; and *filters* (programs that perform an action on a file before retrieving it, such as decompressing a compressed file and displaying it to the user).

To get more information about WN, check out this address:

`http://hopf.math.nwu.edu/docs/overview.html`

GN

GN is a combined Gopher and WWW server (see Chapter 23 for details).

When Things Go Wrong

Unfortunately, there's no guarantee that all will be eternally bright and sunny in your voyage to Web enlightenment. Therefore, this section proffers the following useful pointers about what to do when something goes wrong with your World Wide Web service.

HTML troubleshooting

Here is a short guide to some of the most common problems experienced by beginning writers of HTML. Some are simply common mistakes, and others are weird or painstakingly technical problems that occur when you deal with Web software.

- **Oddly indented text:** Check your list tags. Usually, oddly indented text results from an unclosed list tag.
- **Large segments of text appear as an anchor:** Make sure that all your anchor tags are closed.
- **Large blocks of text are boldfaced, italicized, or underlined:** Make sure that all your style tags and header tags are closed.
- **Images don't load:** Make sure that you uploaded the image to the server in binary format. If you used Fetch on the Macintosh, make sure that you transferred the file as Raw Data.

  Make sure that the image has the gif extension and is in the right directory or folder.
- **Links don't work:** Often, this is a simple error caused by your text editor. If your editor has a feature called Smart Quotes, make sure that it is disabled. The following two lines of HTML are *not* the same:

  ```
  <A HREF="pod.html”>Visit the Pod!</A>
  <A HREF="pod.html">Visit the Pod!</A>
  ```

  In the first line, the name of the file that is referenced is surrounded by curly "smart" quotes. In the second line, standard straight quotes are used. Because smart quotes and normal quotes have a different ASCII value, using smart quotes causes your links to fail. The same advice applies to `<IMG>` and `<A NAME>` tags.

  Bits of text seem to be missing: Often you find that bits of text seem to be missing somewhere in the vicinity of one of your `<A HREF>` tags. This problem most often occurs because of an improperly closed anchor tag; make sure that the tag is closed at the end with `</A>`, that the quotation marks for the URL in the first part of the tag are closed, and that the first part of the tag ends with a bracket (>).

Finding the experts

The Web has numerous sources of useful information about the newest available software and techniques. In addition to the on-line documentation provided by NCSA and other groups that develop Web software, Web publishers can draw on the expertise that is present in a number of Usenet newsgroups, including the ones in this list:

- `comp.infosystems.www.users`, for users of Mosaic and the World Wide Web. It is useful as a place to announce new Web projects. (Here's an example of the usual format: "ANNOUNCE: New English Department Web Server at Carnegie-Mellon.")

- `comp.infosystems.www.providers`, intended for developers, maintainers, and administrators of Web projects. There tends to be a great deal of tech talk here, but it's also a useful place for a developer to learn about new techniques and to answer questions that seemingly can't be solved. As with most places on the Usenet, however, the rule here is, "Don't start asking questions until you've read all the documentation."
- `comp.infosystems.www.misc`, a forum for Web-related discussion not covered by the other two newsgroups.
- `comp.infosystems.www.announce`, for making announcements and publicizing new Web sites.
- `alt.culture.www`, for discussing the culture of the World Wide Web and how the Web interacts with other media and with society.
- `alt.hypertext` is a newsgroup devoted to a more general discussion of the technology of hypertext, covering systems as diverse as WinHelp, StorySpace, and HyperCard in addition to the Web. Although this group is not a good place to ask Web-specific questions, `alt.hypertext` offers some interesting discussions of new directions in the use of text.

My Own Server or Someone Else's?

Should you take the time to set up your own server or borrow space from someone else? This question is an important one for a Web publisher and has much to do with your needs and with how much time you're willing to spend being a server administrator.

Access to advanced features

One of the most difficult issues confronting Web publishers who use a server run by another person or department is access. Many of the most powerful features of HTTP server programs require that the Web publisher have read/write access to the lower-level directories.

If you need only standard information-serving functions, such as text, graphics, and multimedia, you do not need access to anything other than a directory in which you can put Web documents.

If you plan to employ fill-out forms, gateways to programs such as Archie or finger, or clickable image maps, you need access to the `cgi-bin` directory for the Web server you're using. Because some system administrators might be reluctant to grant this type of access, starting and maintaining your own HTTP daemon might be necessary.

Responsibilities of Web server administrators

Making the move from simply being a Web publisher to actually administering a Web server is no great leap. Most HTTP server programs are very stable and well-behaved and require relatively little attention. There are really only a few things a Web server administrator has to worry about.

Checking logs

As a server administrator, you want to keep an eye on the logs for your HTTP server. Although access statistics are not particularly important, your error log is the key to making sure that everything is running smoothly. Error logs can help you find errors in your HTML and your links to other documents because most HTTP daemons log access failures as errors. Although some of the information in the error logs (such as timed-out connections) is unimportant, a good server administrator quickly addresses problems with document links.

Most HTTP servers store logs as simple ASCII text files, as in the relatively typical NCSA httpd `access_log` file shown in Figure 22-11.

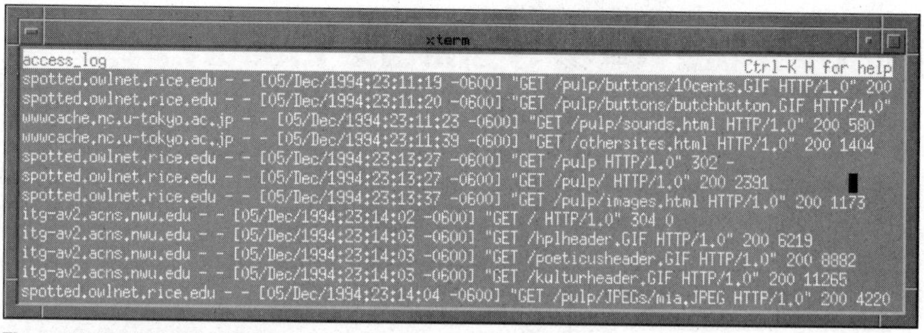

```
access_log                                                          Ctrl-K H for help
spotted.owlnet.rice.edu - - [05/Dec/1994:23:11:19 -0600] "GET /pulp/buttons/10cents.GIF HTTP/1.0" 200
spotted.owlnet.rice.edu - - [05/Dec/1994:23:11:20 -0600] "GET /pulp/buttons/butchbutton.GIF HTTP/1.0"
wwwcache.nc.u-tokyo.ac.jp - - [05/Dec/1994:23:11:23 -0600] "GET /pulp/sounds.html HTTP/1.0" 200 580
wwwcache.nc.u-tokyo.ac.jp - - [05/Dec/1994:23:11:39 -0600] "GET /othersites.html HTTP/1.0" 200 1404
spotted.owlnet.rice.edu - - [05/Dec/1994:23:13:27 -0600] "GET /pulp HTTP/1.0" 302 -
spotted.owlnet.rice.edu - - [05/Dec/1994:23:13:27 -0600] "GET /pulp/ HTTP/1.0" 200 2391
spotted.owlnet.rice.edu - - [05/Dec/1994:23:13:37 -0600] "GET /pulp/images.html HTTP/1.0" 200 1173
itg-av2.acns.nwu.edu - - [05/Dec/1994:23:14:02 -0600] "GET / HTTP/1.0" 304 0
itg-av2.acns.nwu.edu - - [05/Dec/1994:23:14:03 -0600] "GET /hplheader.GIF HTTP/1.0" 200 6219
itg-av2.acns.nwu.edu - - [05/Dec/1994:23:14:03 -0600] "GET /poeticusheader.GIF HTTP/1.0" 200 8882
itg-av2.acns.nwu.edu - - [05/Dec/1994:23:14:03 -0600] "GET /kulturheader.GIF HTTP/1.0" 200 11265
spotted.owlnet.rice.edu - - [05/Dec/1994:23:14:04 -0600] "GET /pulp/JPEGs/mia.JPEG HTTP/1.0" 200 4220
```

Figure 22-11: A sample NCSA httpd access log.

Keeping the server running

The on-line documentation for most HTTP daemons includes instructions for installing them in your machine's start-up files. If you have a Macintosh or Windows machine or if you're an administrator or superuser on a UNIX machine, you want to set the server to run at start-up.

If you can't set the server program to run at start-up, it then becomes important to check on your HTTP daemon regularly to make sure that it's still running. Your readers will find it annoying when they cannot link to your site.

Adding new features

The best Web servers naturally do not stay the same over time. You occasionally will want to add new features to your server. Changing the home page every so often, adding new information services, and upgrading to new versions of the server software as they're released are all things a new server administrator should keep in mind.

Publicizing your pages

Because of the cumbersome nature of Web URLs, the occasional difficulty of remembering and entering URLs, and the fact that no well-recognized model exists for doing keyword-style searches of Web space, the bulk of connections to a publicly accessible Web site is through links from other Web sites.

Several methods exist for getting other HTML developers to build links to a new site. One method, posting announcements to Web-related newsgroups, was discussed earlier in this chapter. A few other useful techniques exist:

- **Posting to pertinent newsgroups:** In addition to the Web-related newsgroups mentioned earlier, posting announcements to newsgroups that are directly related to the content of the new Web pages tends to generate a number of links. Pursuant to proper netiquette, be sure that the newsgroups definitely relate to the topic of the Web pages being publicized. If the newsgroup has a FAQ, see whether the maintainer of the FAQ lists the new pages.
- **NCSA's "What's New?" Page:** NCSA produces this weekly guide to new Web pages, accessible directly from the NCSA Mosaic Navigate menu. Announcements of new pages, written in HTML, may be submitted to `whats-new@ncsa.uiuc.edu`, but be sure to read NCSA's guidelines on the proper format for announcements before submitting.
- **CERN's Overview of the Web:** CERN, the originator of the World Wide Web project, maintains its own list of registered Web servers. The overview is at this address:

  `http://info.cern.ch/hypertext/WWW/LineMode/Defaults/default.html.`
- **Other index maintainers:** Links from CERN or NCSA can quickly bring a Web site hundreds of visitors a day. However, many other organizations maintain indexes of Web sites. Almost all of them welcome announcements of new Web pages.
- **Specialized lists:** Many Web sites maintain links to other sites whose contents and topics are similar to their own. E-mail announcements to the administrators of these types of sites often generate new links.

Good Luck!

I hope that this article is a useful introduction to the nitty-gritty of publishing your information on the World Wide Web. This material should have given you enough of a primer to jump into the world of Web publishing on your own. Good luck, and may hordes of eager Webheads access your information abundantly.

Jack Graham is a consultant and Web designer for the Instructional Technology Group at Northwestern University. He also works occasionally as an independent Web consultant. In his spare time, Jack is an undergraduate fiction writing major at Northwestern.

Getting Interactive on the Web

by Joe Cates <joe@galcit.caltech.edu>

One of the most powerful and flexible features of the World Wide Web is its interactive capability. Web users can customize their access to databases, and Web surfers can interact with others from all parts of the Internet — all with a simple graphical interface that uses familiar, user-friendly elements. Interactivity also enables sites to stress one of the truly unique features of the Internet: a diverse base of users from around the world.

Each access on the Web is a single event. The browser and server cannot open a continuing session but must instead exchange data in packets. The following procedure shows a typical procedure using a form page:

1. The user loads a Web page containing a form that refers to an executable program called a *script*.
2. When the user submits the results of a form page, the browser contacts the appropriate Web server for the script URL specified in the form for submission. The browser sends along the form results to the server, which passes the results to the script.
3. The script then parses the results and returns either a document or a reference to another document.
4. The server takes this output, performs any necessary packaging, and returns the document or location output by the script to the browser.

Writing scripts to handle simple form pages is not difficult, given basic knowledge of a programming language (such as C or Perl) that can handle strings conveniently. The server handles most of the technical details of providing the form results and returning the form results in the proper form to the browser. Before you dive in and begin making form pages and writing scripts, however, you should check several things:

- First, scripts must be placed in a directory that is declared to contain scripts. To install Web scripts, therefore, you need access to a script directory on your server and possibly to the server's configuration files. If you are not in charge of the server, be sure that your system manager allows users to have personal scripts. Many sites do not allow users to run their own scripts because of security concerns.
- Second, make certain that you actually need scripts. Simple functions such as allowing users to send you a message can be accomplished with the mailto URL type. Many other services, such as finger, are already set up and available at gateways. Although using a gateway may be slower than having a script on your own Web server, using the gateways can save you time and frustration.
- Finally, before actually starting to program, spend a few minutes looking around the Web. Chances are pretty good that your script has already been written. Scripts for feedback, mailing form results, voting, searching files, and many

other common functions are readily available in C, Perl, and other languages. By all means, don't write your own routine to parse form results; instead, look for one of the many collections of routines on the Web or use the sample programs that come with your server software.

Setting Up Forms in HTML

The first step in getting interactive is making a form page. HTML has a relatively complete set of form elements for text input and item selection by means of menus and buttons. Each type of form element has options that help you control the appearance of your form pages and specify default values. Because many of the form elements can be used to achieve the same result, when you design form pages, concentrate on choosing a form layout that will be clear to the user.

The FORM tag

The `FORM` tag is required in order to add form elements in an HTML page. The `FORM` tag specifies the URL of the script that will process the results and the method of submitting the results, as in the following example:

```
<FORM METHOD=POST ACTION="http://hoohoo.ncsa.uiuc.edu/cgi-bin/post-query">
```

Two submission methods are available: `GET` and `POST`. `POST`, which now is the preferred method, should be used in most cases. (GET is an older method in which the form elements were passed to the script as command line arguments.) The ending tag is simply

```
</FORM>
```

All the input elements must be placed inside the starting and ending form tags. A page may contain separate forms, but the form tags cannot overlap or be nested. Otherwise, the form portion of the page functions like other HTML tags. Images, links, and other HTML tags can be used inside the form.

Text input

The form element used most often is the single-line text-entry field, shown in Figure 22-12.

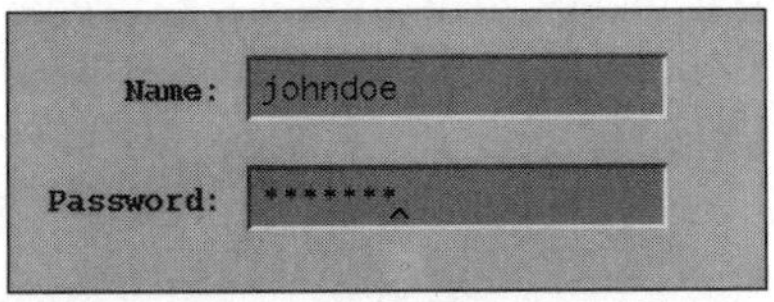

Name: johndoe

Password: *******

Figure 22-12: Example single-line text-entry and password fields.

The text-entry field uses the INPUT tag with the TYPE attribute "text." The only other attribute required is the name of the input field, as shown in the following example:

```
<INPUT TYPE="text" NAME="username">
```

The text string entered by the user is returned to the script in the form results.

Additional attributes are available for the text-input type. You can specify a default text value by using the VALUE attribute. The SIZE and MAXLENGTH attributes can be used to set the size of the text-input box and the maximum length string that can be entered, respectively. Following is a full example of the text-entry field:

```
<INPUT TYPE="text" NAME="username" SIZE=32 MAXLENGTH=128 VALUE="John Doe">
```

A special text-entry field of TYPE "password" is available for entering confidential data, such as passwords, as in the following example:

```
<INPUT TYPE="password" NAME="password">
```

The "password" TYPE functions exactly like the text input, except that all characters appear as asterisks when they are typed. Notice that the "password" TYPE is not secure data transfer; the password is just less visible to curious eyes while it is being typed.

For longer text input, a multiline text-input box is available (see Figure 22-13).

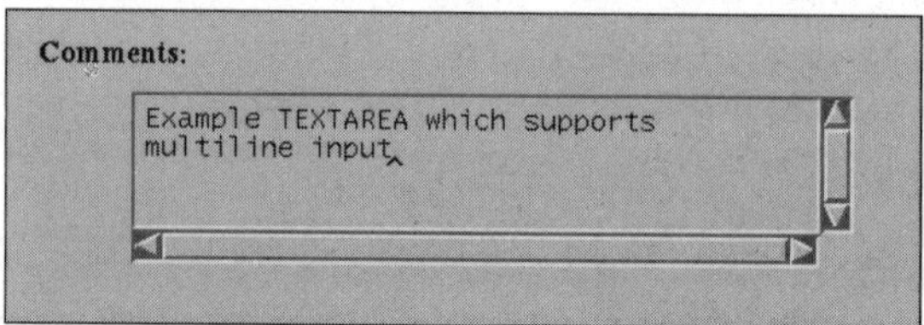

Figure 22-13: Example multiline text-area field.

In simplest form, only an opening tag with the NAME attribute and a closing tag are required, as follows:

```
<TEXTAREA NAME="comments"></TEXTAREA>
```

This input field is particularly useful for long submissions because, in most browsers, users can paste long text selections directly into the window. The ROWS and COLS attributes can be used to set the initial size of the text area in character rows and columns. Default contents can be specified between the start and end TEXTAREA tags, as in the following example:

```
<TEXTAREA ROWS=4 COLS=40 NAME="questions">
Will I become rich and famous?
Will I be happily married?
</TEXTAREA>
```

Browsers display the text area with horizontal and vertical scroll bars. Regardless of the size, therefore, the user can scroll to input wider or longer passages. The default text can contain HTML tags. Some browsers, however, do not implement this feature correctly, so a safer practice is to avoid using HTML tags in the default text.

Radio buttons and check boxes

Radio and check box buttons can be used to present a list of choices to users. These input types are best used when the page needs to display all possible options at the same time. The check box type enables the user to select multiple items; in a set of radio buttons, however, the user can make only a single choice. When a user chooses one radio button, the browser automatically turns off all other radio buttons with the same name. The simplest tags for the two types of buttons are as follows:

```
<INPUT TYPE="radio" NAME="color" VALUE="red">
<INPUT TYPE="checkbox" NAME="flower" VALUE="violet">
```

Exactly how to distinguish the two button types when they are displayed is left up to the browser. Typically, browsers use differently shaped buttons to denote the different types. In XMosaic, for example, a square button is used for a check box, and a triangular button is used for a radio button.

Radio and check box buttons generally are used in groups, with a label for each button. If you want a button to be on by default, use the `CHECKED` attribute. In writing HTML for forms, remember to not make the default `CHECKED` for more than one radio button in each set.

In the following example, radio buttons are used so that a user can sort in only a single way. The first button (sort by name) is on by default. Notice that all the radio buttons have the same name (`NAME="sort"`) so that all the buttons are in the same set.

```
How do you want the results sorted (choose one):<BR>
<INPUT TYPE="radio" NAME="sort" VALUE="name" CHECKED> By Name
<INPUT TYPE="radio" NAME="sort" VALUE="type"> By Type
<INPUT TYPE="radio" NAME="sort" VALUE="date"> By Date
```

The `<BR>` break code tells the browser to begin a new line on the display.

In the next example, check box buttons are used so that the user can choose multiple items:

```
Search which fields (check all that are desired):<BR>
<INPUT TYPE="checkbox" NAME="search" VALUE="title" CHECKED> Titles
<INPUT TYPE="checkbox" NAME="search" VALUE="author"> Authors
<INPUT TYPE="checkbox" NAME="search" VALUE="journal"> Journal
<INPUT TYPE="checkbox" NAME="search" VALUE="abstract"> Abstract
```

Figure 22-14 shows the output for the preceding elements as displayed by XMosaic.

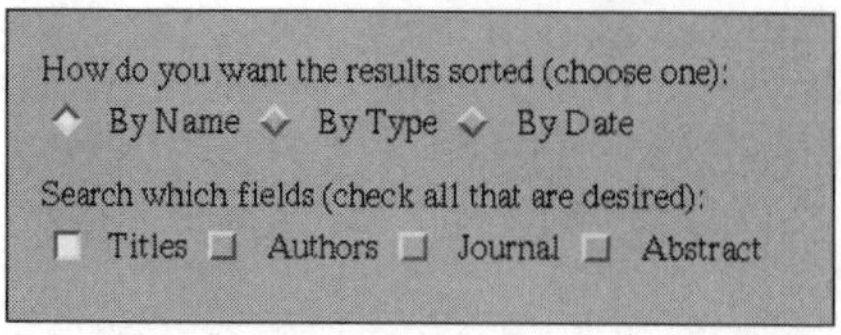

How do you want the results sorted (choose one):
By Name By Type By Date
Search which fields (check all that are desired):
Titles Authors Journal Abstract

Figure 22-14: Example radio and check box buttons.

Selection menus

For forms in which many choices are available, you can use selection menus and avoid having to display every single choice on screen. In these cases, you can use selection menus to list a large number of choices in a small space. Following is the simplest tag for a selection menu:

```
<SELECT SIZE=3 NAME="currency">
<OPTION> Canadian Dollar
<OPTION> Japanese Yen
<OPTION> U.S. Dollar
<OPTION> German Mark
<OPTION> British Pound
</SELECT>
```

The `SIZE` specifies the number of rows in the list that will be shown. If the list contains more items, the browser adds scroll bars or some other method of moving through the list.

You can add several other attributes to refine things a little. Normally, the form results return the entire option string as the value of the item chosen. The `VALUE` attribute can be used to specify an alternate string to return for each option. The `SELECTED` attribute specifies which option is chosen by default. Both these attributes are placed in the `OPTION` tag, as in the following example:

```
<OPTION VALUE="us" SELECTED> U.S. Dollar
```

To permit the selection of multiple choices, you can add the `MULTIPLE` tag to the `SELECT` tag, as in the following example:

```
<SELECT SIZE=3 NAME="currency" MULTIPLE>
```

The combination of keystrokes used to select the multiple entries is left up to the browser.

If the size is not specified or for the special case of `SIZE=1`, most browsers use a different type of selection menu similar to the one shown at the bottom of Figure 22-15. A single choice is shown initially. When the user clicks to open the menu, the menu opens to show all choices. This type of menu takes up less space and is more attractive than selection menu with scroll bars. If the menu contains too many entries, however, the open menu may be larger than the screen, causing some options to be lost. In addition, the multiple-selection option cannot be used with this type of menu.

Figure 22-15: Example selection menu of SIZE=3 (top) and SIZE=1.

Submit and reset buttons

Two additional push buttons are available within a form: submit and reset. The submit button submits the current form results, and the reset button resets all the form elements to their default values. These elements are coded as follows:

```
<INPUT TYPE = "submit">
<INPUT TYPE = "reset">
```

Because of a bug in some early browsers, the `TYPE` attribute values (submit and reset) should be in lowercase.

By default, the push buttons generally are labeled something like *Submit Query* and *Reset*. Or you can use the `VALUE` attribute to specify the text used for the button. To label the submit button LET'S GO, for example, you use the following code:

```
<INPUT TYPE = "submit" VALUE="LET'S GO">
```

These two elements typically are placed at the bottom of the form. Except for the special cases of forms with single text-input elements or image maps, a submit button is always required. The reset button is optional because the user can always reload the page to restore the form values.

Hidden elements

You can use hidden form elements to store name and value information in an input form that users cannot modify. This procedure is useful for maintaining state information in forms that are generated automatically. Suppose that a form needs to remember the name and ZIP code entered by a user in a previous form so that the information can be passed along to the script that is processing the form. A hidden element can be used to store the information in `NAME/VALUE` pairs, as follows:

```
<INPUT TYPE="hidden" NAME="name" VALUE="John Doe">
<INPUT TYPE="hidden" NAME="zip" VALUE="91125">
```

The hidden `NAME/VALUE` pairs are submitted along with the rest of the form when the user submits it.

Remember that the user can see these form elements by viewing the source of the form document — the elements should not be considered to be secret. You should never place an unencrypted password in hidden elements, for example.

Hidden elements can be used only inside forms. Some early browsers do not support hidden elements, so many scripts pass information in the URL as path information or arguments.

An Example Form Page: The Web Psychic

Figure 22-16 shows The Web Psychic page, in which all the major form-element types are used. A single-line text-entry field, limited to a reasonable number of characters, is used for the name. For the longer text of the questions, a text area is used. Check box and radio buttons are used for the method and delivery questions to allow the user to view all the various options conveniently. Because the currency list is longer and because most users will choose the U.S. dollar, a selection menu is used to take up less vertical space. Two hidden form elements are used to include the access site and the form version. The post action URL in this form is a demonstration script at the NCSA, which returns a page that lists the items submitted with the form — quite handy for testing.

Following is the HTML source for The Web Psychic page:

```
<HTML>
<HEAD>
<TITLE>The Web Psychic</TITLE>
</HEAD>
<BODY>
<H1>The Web Psychic</H1>
<HR>
Have your fortune told by our very own World Wide Web psychic to the
stars. Choose from the various psychic methods available and have
the results rushed to you by the fastest means available.
<HR>
<FORM METHOD=POST ACTION="http://hoohoo.ncsa.uiuc.edu/cgi-bin/post-query">
<INPUT TYPE="hidden" NAME="site" VALUE="east">
<INPUT TYPE="hidden" NAME="vers" VALUE="1.1">
Name:
<INPUT TYPE="text" NAME="username" SIZE=32 MAXLENGTH=128>
<P>
What psychic methods do you want used (check all that apply):<BR>
<DL><DD>
<INPUT TYPE="checkbox" NAME="method" VALUE="cball" CHECKED> Crystal Ball
($10)<BR>
<INPUT TYPE="checkbox" NAME="method" VALUE="tarot"> Tarot Cards ($5)<BR>
<INPUT TYPE="checkbox" NAME="method" VALUE="energy"> Psychic Energy ($3)<BR>
</DD></DL>
How do you wish your reading delivered (check one only):
<DL><DD>
```

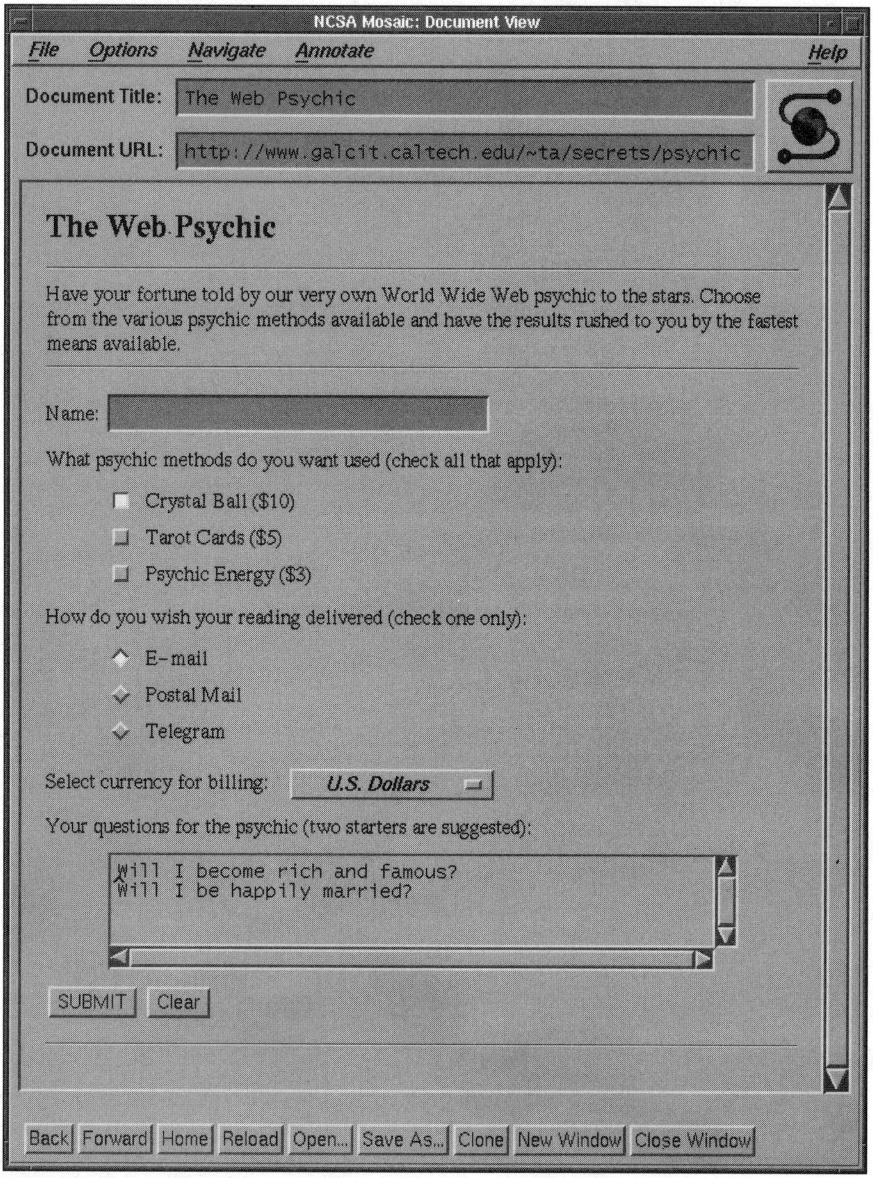

NCSA Mosaic: Document View

File Options Navigate Annotate Help

Document Title: The Web Psychic

Document URL: http://www.galcit.caltech.edu/~ta/secrets/psychic

The Web Psychic

Have your fortune told by our very own World Wide Web psychic to the stars. Choose from the various psychic methods available and have the results rushed to you by the fastest means available.

Name:

What psychic methods do you want used (check all that apply):

- Crystal Ball ($10)
- Tarot Cards ($5)
- Psychic Energy ($3)

How do you wish your reading delivered (check one only):

- E-mail
- Postal Mail
- Telegram

Select currency for billing: U.S. Dollars

Your questions for the psychic (two starters are suggested):

Will I become rich and famous?
Will I be happily married?

SUBMIT Clear

Back Forward Home Reload Open... Save As... Clone New Window Close Window

Figure 22-16: The Web Psychic form page.

```
<INPUT TYPE="radio" NAME="delivery" VALUE="email" CHECKED> E-mail<BR>
<INPUT TYPE="radio" NAME="delivery" VALUE="postal"> Postal Mail<BR>
<INPUT TYPE="radio" NAME="delivery" VALUE="telegram"> Telegram<BR>
</DD></DL>
Select currency for billing:
<SELECT SIZE=1 NAME="currency">
<OPTION> Canadian Dollar
<OPTION> Japanese Yen
<OPTION SELECTED> U.S. Dollar
<OPTION> German Mark
<OPTION> British Pound
</SELECT>
<P>
Your questions for the psychic (two starters are suggested):
<DL><DD>
<TEXTAREA ROWS=4 COLS=52 NAME="questions">
Will I become rich and famous?
Will I be happily married?
</TEXTAREA>
</DD></DL>
<INPUT TYPE="submit" VALUE=" SUBMIT ">
<INPUT TYPE="reset" VALUE=" Clear ">
</FORM>
<HR>
</BODY>
</HTML>
```

Other References

Several additional references are available on the World Wide Web. A discussion of form support in XMosaic, with discussion of the various tags and example forms, is available at NCSA at the following address:

```
http://www.ncsa.uiuc.edu/sdg/software/mosaic/docs/fill-out-forms/overview.html
```

A brief tutorial by Carlos Pero on using different form elements is available at the following address:

```
http://robot0.ge.uiuc.edu/~carlosp/cs317/cft.html
```

One of the best methods of perfecting your skills is viewing the HTML source of a form page already on the Web.

Handling Form Results

When the form results are submitted to the server, the server passes the form results along to the script. The script processes the form results, decides the appropriate action, and then outputs a document or a redirection to another URL, which the server passes back to the browser.

Parsing form results

Each form element returns a name and value string. The name string is specified in the form element tags by means of the NAME attribute. The value the user chose or entered is returned in the value string. For text-input fields, a name/value pair is returned. If the user did not enter any text, the value string is empty.

All check boxes and radio buttons that are on return the name and value specified in the input tag. Multiple check boxes with the same name can be returned, but because only one radio button can be checked for each name, only one radio button with a given name is returned. Similarly, selection menus return the value of the option the user selected. Because some input elements can return either no results or multiple results, scripts should search the form-results name strings to locate a specific field.

The server places the name/value string pairs that make up the form results in a single string of the form, as follows:

```
name=value&name=value&...&name=value
```

This string is passed to the script. An ampersand (&) is used to separate the string pairs, and an equal sign (=) is used between the name and value strings. Any special characters in the name and value strings are escaped. For the POST submission method, the string containing all the form results is made available to the script in a single data block. For the GET submission method, the data string is placed at the end of the URL as command line arguments.

The best method of accessing the form-results string, unescaping any special characters, and parsing the form results varies according to the operating system being used. This article does not cover all the possibilities. The best starting point is to examine the source code for the sample scripts supplied with your server. NCSA has several programs available at its ftp site at the following address:

```
http://hoohoo.ncsa.uiuc.edu/cgi/forms.html
```

In addition, libraries of routines for several programming languages are available around the Web. Try the following address:

```
http://akebono.stanford.edu/yahoo/computers/world_wide_web/programming/
```

Typically, these routines place the name/value pairs in arrays for easy access by your program.

Script output

After the script processes the form results, information can be returned to the server for sending to the browser. To return a document, the script first must send the content type of the document, followed by a blank line. The content type specifies the MIME type and subtype of the document that is being sent, and it must be in the following form:

```
Content-type: type/subtype
```

The most common type of material returned is an HTML document, which would be sent by using the following header:

```
Content-type: text/html
```

Although HTML or text is returned most often, a script conceivably can return an image, video clip, or any other MIME type.

Following is an example of C code for returning an HTML document. The content type is returned first, followed by the actual HTML document. Notice that two carriage returns are used to ensure that the content type is followed by a blank line.

```
printf("Content-type: text/html\n\n");
printf("<HTML><HEAD>\n");
printf("<TITLE>Sample HTML Output</TITLE>\n");
printf("<BODY>\n");
.
... output the body of the HTML page ...
.
printf("</BODY></HTML>\n");
```

The script also can return a reference of another URL, using a command of the form `Location: url`, followed by a blank line. If the URL is on the server that is running the script, the server automatically returns the specified document to the browser. If the document is on another server, the complete URL must be given. In this case, the server returns the redirection to the browser, which then tries to access the document on the appropriate server. Following is a sample of C code for returning the user to the welcome page on another server:

```
printf("Location: http://nowhere.com/welcome.html\n\n");
```

Image Maps

Image maps add a new method of interacting, according to where a user clicks within an image. You can use image maps directly in HTML pages or include them in forms by using the image input type.

Image maps in HTML pages

You can include an image map in any page by using the standard image source tag with the additional ISMAP attribute that denotes an image map. The image must be referenced to the script that will handle the image map results. For example, the following HTML tags set up an image map that points to a script:

```
<A HREF="/cgi-bin/mapscript"><IMG SRC="worldf.gif" ISMAP></A>
```

When the user clicks inside an image map, the x,y coordinates of the selected point are added to the end of the URL as arguments. The coordinates are returned in the form x,y, in which the x coordinate runs horizontally and the y coordinate runs vertically. The upper-left corner of the image is always taken as the origin. The image map script has to return a document or the reference to another URL, just as in form handling.

Most servers include an image-map program that enables you to add image maps to your own pages without doing any programming. Programs of this type typically allow you to set up a data file detailing rectangles and polygons within the image map that are mapped to specified URL addresses. Even if an image-map script already is available on your server, the system administrator may still need to add to the global configuration file a line for your image map.

Using image types in forms

You also can place in a form element an image type element that functions similarly to a full image map. For example, to include in a form a color bar image that allows the user to select his favorite color, you would use the following tag:

```
<INPUT TYPE="image" NAME="cbar" SRC="colorbar.gif">
```

When the user clicks the image, any other form results are returned, along with the name of the image and the coordinates the user selected. If the user clicks x = 50, y = 10, for example, two name and value pairs would be returned, as follows:

```
cbar.x: 50
cbar.y: 10
```

You then can parse the name/value pairs as you would other form results.

Using the image type in forms permits some special effects, such as the creation of forms without an explicit submit button. Remember that clicking any of the image maps in a form submits all the form results but only the coordinates for the image that was clicked.

Image-map references

For help in setting up an image map for your server, try to refer to the documentation or sample image-map scripts supplied with your server. For users of NCSA httpd, the documentation and links to the C source code for the NCSA image-map script are available at the following address:

```
http://hoohoo.ncsa.uiuc.edu/docs/setup/admin/Imagemap.html
```

For beginners, an excellent tutorial on setting up an image map with the image-map script supplied with NCSA httpd is available at the following address:

```
http://wintermute.ncsa.uiuc.edu:8080/map-tutorial/image-maps.html
```

Other programs, many with tutorials, are available for different servers. See the extensive list at the following address:

```
http://akebono.stanford.edu/yahoo/computers/world_wide_web/
programming/imagemaps/
```

The preceding site also lists a wide range of programs that help create the data files of coordinates used by many of the image-map scripts.

Texts on the Internet

by Sarah Hurlburt <sarah@tuna.uchicago.edu>

The World Wide Web has made Net surfing so easy that even academics can do it.

For those of us whose love affair with books dates back to early childhood, losing contact with the actual paper is a traumatic experience. The transition started with the word processor and gradually eased into e-mail. Now, we have the Net.

Mosaic and other programs like it, with their point-and-shoot method for net surfing, have taken much of the intimidation out of being online. With a large cup of coffee in one hand and a mouse in the other, anyone can travel from desk to home pages and archives across the country and even around the world. It's the video game for grown-ups, it's a sprawling mass of trivial and not-so-trivial information, and it can eat up hours and hours of your time — time measured only by cups of coffee and bloodshot eyes.

The question, of course, is what to do with the resources. Much of computer technology has come about because one man's toy is another man's tool — in other words, because technology developed for entertainment is only a heartbeat away from a working application. The same software that brought a list of nerd jokes on-line for the hacker down the hall now brings you Shakespeare at the click of a button. The possibilities for those of us in love with the written word are dizzying and not necessarily realized at this point.

The issue of texts on-line is thorny and multifaceted. This article examines the available resources of on-line text on the World Wide Web: what they are, where they are, and what you can and can't do with them. "On-line text" in the context of this article refers strictly and arbitrarily to literary text and to texts about literature. I will be focusing on the Eris Project, the Online Book Initiative, Wiretap, and, last but not least, the ARTFL Project at the University of Chicago.

Defining On-line Text

The Webster definition for *text* (which I just pulled from the *Hypertext Webster Interface* by using Mosaic) defines it as anything from an original written or printed work, the main body of printed or written matter on a page, or the principal part of a book exclusive of front and back matter. Now, if I go to *book* (by clicking on *book* in the definition of text — this is really too easy), *Webster's* tells me that a book is a set of written, printed, or blank sheets bound together in a volume.

My conclusion from all of this is that our standard definitions of *text* and *book* predate texts on-line. A text on-line is neither handwritten nor printed, nor is it on a page, exactly. At least, not physically. It can appear on the screen formatted as though it were on a page, but this is more a concession to custom than anything else. The computer has no limits on the length of a "page," so page breaks occur only where we place them. In fact, many of the books now on-line don't bother with this particular concession. You just keep scrolling down. This can pose problems, as you will see later when I discuss searches.

So how do we adjust Webster's definitions to include modern technology? Databases generally use the terms "books on-line" and "text archives" interchangeably. A book on-line obviously holds none of its former physical attributes, and the original definition of "text" links it closely to the physical aspect of a book. We therefore have to redefine "text" and "book," divorcing them from all references to their physical form. Manuscripts once were written on scrolls before the advent of books; now we have stepped from the physical book to the computer file, which scrolls down the screen. The story in each case remains the same, whether written by hand on a scroll or in a book, printed in a book, or entered as a computer file. This "story" is what we refer to when we speak of texts on-line.

How Computers Read Text

Think about the way a computer "reads" a book. We human types read linearly, but we can also jump from one place on a page to another at will, drawing meaning from the characters on the page. A computer draws no meaning from the characters it displays. So, whereas we can distinguish between singular and plural while still recognizing a word as the same word, a computer is incapable of doing so without something called a *morphological analyzer.* Which is to say, a computer trying to match up all of the occurrences of the word "book" in a given text will only find "book" and not "books," unless its software can tell it to make that association.

A computer also "reads" a text the way you would read an LED display that only shows one word at a time. A computer cannot jump from one place in a text to another according to meaning. A computer *can* make that jump, however, if there is a marker in the text, such as a page break, to tell it where to land. These markers do not appear in the text as we see it on the screen (except in word processors that display both a "page number" and a "page break," neither one of which actually exists as we understand it until the document is printed). The computer reads them only as landmarks in a land of gibberish. As far as your word processor is concerned, though, unless you tell it differently, text is continuous across page breaks. This is why, when I delete a paragraph from what I have written, the computer leaves no blank space the size of the deleted text but connects the two ends, adjusting the page breaks accordingly.

Understanding that a computer "reads" a text as a continuous string is vital to understanding the limitations of most texts on-line at this time. Obviously, the impact of this difficulty varies according to the type of text involved, as will soon become clear.

Types of Texts Available On-line

The Web offers a huge variety of text online. Here I use the term "text" to include all categories of contiguous written material. That is to say, a Gopher menu would not be considered a text, whereas a journal would qualify. I will divide text resource material into five rough categories: journals, forums, book reviews, bibliographies or libraries, and books.

Journals

While most on-line journals at this stage are computer-related, the occasional humanities journal is infiltrating the ranks. Some journals were born as on-line journals; others were more conventional or established publications that took to the Net. The English Server at Carnegie-Mellon (`http://english.hss.cmu.edu/`) has a list of on-line journals. Many are free. Some require subscriptions. In the case of a subscription journal, you can usually get the table of contents for free but must subscribe to get the actual material.

All addresses listed in parentheses in this article are URL addresses for the Web.

Accessing a journal from your home computer via modem saves on dead trees and puts the journal at your fingertips as soon as it is available. Back issues can also be accessed in most cases with no more trouble than choosing that option on a menu, and they don't pile up next to the couch. Often, issues may be downloaded for your own work. However, for those interested in serious research, on-line journals cannot yet be considered an important resource because of the limited number available. In the future, journals may not even be published any other way, but at this time you will still have to fetch most in hard copy from the library or your mailbox.

Forums

A serious discussion forum, usually through a mail server, can put you in daily contact with others in your field discussing current topics of interest to your work or theirs. Because distance is no obstacle to the Internet, the exchange of ideas that before was dependent upon conferences, telephone conversations (expensive), and what hackers not-so-fondly call "snail mail," has sped up exponentially.

You can get up in the morning, log on to read what other people have had to say about an idea, and stick in your two cents in return, either to an individual or to all of the other subscribers. The limitations are your time and the number of people in your area of interest brave enough to make the jump into cyberspace.

Unfortunately, speed and convenience cannot guarantee quality of material transmitted, but then again, neither did paper.

Book reviews

Another facet of text on-line is the book review. While I have yet to find a home page devoted exclusively to book reviews, there are quite a few of them scattered on the peripherals of "books on-line" or the menu equivalent. Surfing through The English Server, The On-line Books Page (`http://www.cs.cmu.edu:8001/Web/books.html`), or The Human On-line Languages Page (`http://www.willamette.edu/~tjones/Language-Page.html`), all of which have links to each other, you will inevitably stumble across the occasional nest of book reviews. Maybe someday you will be able to read the book review and then "buy" the book with a click of the mouse and have it land in your hard drive while you get another cup of coffee; as it is, on-line book reviews are often no more than electronic "word of mouth."

It is important to remember that the only true editor of what appears on the Net is not quality, but ability to post. Just because someone knows enough about the Net to post what they write doesn't change the value (or lack thereof) of her opinions. This, in fact, is perhaps one of the largest problems with new work appearing on the Net. There is a great deal of original poetry and short fiction floating around in cyberspace and very little editing. Many times, all you have to do to put your very own poem up for all to see is simply type it in and send it. This is great if you want to get your poem on the Net — not so great if you are looking for quality material to read.

Bibliographies and library Gophers

While bibliographies and library Gophers admittedly do not fall under the definition of "text" that I arbitrarily decided upon earlier in the article, their importance to the question of textual resources on the Net is inarguable. Library Gophers are a sort of on-line card catalog, often accessible through the university Gopher. Being able to find for yourself with a few keystrokes whether or not a neighboring university has a particular book is extremely convenient, not to mention time saving.

Bibliographies on the Net usually refer to text archives on-line, not to books in libraries. There are two general kinds of on-line bibliographies: The first is a listing of the contents of a particular archive, an option you are given when you access the database. The second is a subject-oriented listing, referring to books and articles on- or off-line related to a particular topic, such as education. Both kinds are scattered through the Net. While they are not texts as I have defined them, they can be pointers to on-line texts.

Books, text archives, and Gophers to navigate them

Net surfing is a convoluted art. There is no master plan to the Web, regardless of its seemingly orderly appearance. For example, almost all of the addresses I refer to in this chapter have more than one link to each other. ARTFL (`http://tuna/ARTFL.html`) links to The Human-Languages Page, which links back to ARTFL and to The English Server, and on and on and on. . . . Almost any one of these addresses could land you at any other in only a few jumps.

All of these addresses refer to a variety of on-line texts and archives. I have spent hours and hours investigating almost every little on-line text reference, but at this time I think it's best to stick to the basics. Should you dabble your toes in the water and surf the Net yourself, you may soon start tripping across things like the CURIA Irish Manuscript Project coming out of Cork, Ireland, which deals with literary and historical materials in the various languages of early, medieval, and modern Ireland. The archive is not very extensive yet, and I've no idea what it says, but it looks *very* cool. Gaelic. On-line. Anything can happen.

There are in fact surprisingly few text archives on the Net. When first introduced to the Web, I expected to find an infinite amount of material just waiting to be perused.

Unfortunately, while the amount of material available on the Web may be infinite in proportion to any single person's ability to peruse it all, the amount of text, in the old-fashioned sense of books, is fairly limited. Text usually gets on-line through either love or money — either people love a book enough to put it on themselves, or a book or body of information is considered important enough for someone to be paid to put it on-line. Most of the input is grass-roots — that is to say, someone loved a book so much that he typed or scanned it into a computer on his own and it eventually made its way to the Net. This accounts in large part for the oddball mixture found in most text databases.

It is extremely important to realize the random nature of many archives. The path many texts take in arriving on-line is far too arbitrary for their presence in an archive to necessarily be considered a sign of relative quality or importance. Obviously, this is not always the case, but it is never a bad idea to check out the disclaimer at the head of the archive and see where exactly these texts came from. In many cases, following the disclaimer is an open invitation for additional material — which in and of itself tells you how strict the filter is for new material.

ARTFL, Wiretap (`Gopher://wiretap.spies.com/`), The Online Book Initiative (also known as OBI), and Eris Project (`Gopher://Gopher.vt.edu:10010/10/33`) represent a large portion of the books available. The Oxford Text Archive (`ftp://ota.ox.ac.uk/pub/ota`) has approximately 1,500 titles in its collection but is not yet fully functional through Mosaic. ARTFL is far and away the largest of the four, and it is the most useful for anyone interested in research.

There are several ways to go about perusing these archives. One way, obviously, is to surf to the archive itself and check out its Gopher menu; this is not always the most practical approach, however. Another option is to use a Gopher and let it do the surfing for you.

Alex

Perhaps the most convenient Gopher now available for searching for on-line texts is Alex (`Gopher://Gopher.lib.ncsu.edu/11/library/stacks/Alex`), self-defined as "A Catalogue of Electronic Texts on the Internet." Alex sports a number of nifty features, including both a search command and a browser. This means that if you are looking for a particular author, you can simply enter the author's name, or even part of the name, and Alex will find books written by that author from any of the archives connected to Alex; which includes just about all of the larger ones except for ARTFL. The browser option allows you to pick from five different options authors, date, host, language, subject, and title all hypertext linked to their source.

Alex includes texts from Wiretap, The Online Book Initiative, Eris Project, The English Server, and the on-line portion of the Oxford Text Archive, among others. At this time, these archives comprise over seven hundred books and shorter texts. Alex does not include serials, but new additions to any of the above archives are automatically added to the list. Not only is Alex ideal if you are looking for a specific text, it's also just a great way to look around. Certainly, it is the most time-effective way to browse these archives.

The primary reason that a Gopher like Alex is so useful lies in the organization of the archives themselves. Connecting with an archive through Mosaic provides you with a Gopher menu, or a sort of hypertext table of contents, which, while it gives you a marvelous way to browse, is only as efficient as the organization of the listings.

Wiretap

The Wiretap is a sprawl. Surfing through it's on-line library, I somehow ended up reading obscene Texan expressions from a server who-knows-where at 1:00 A.M. So much for on-line texts.

Texanese aside, Wiretap has quite a collection. Clicking on Electronic Books at Wiretap will get you (the Net gods willing) a hypertext listing of the two hundred-odd books available. At first glance, this is delightful — on the first page of the list, you find *Aesop's Fables, The Scarlet Pimpernel, Beowulf, Dracula,* and the *Anglican Book of Common Prayer,* among many others. While you are happily engrossed in *Alice's Adventures in Wonderland* or *Tess of the d'Urbervilles,* you may think how very nice it is to have those books at your fingertips. But you soon will begin to notice a few problems.

The largest of these problems is the way in which the list is organized. Alphabetically, yes, quite nice — until you realize that it's alphabetically by the first letter of the author's first name, or of the title, or of the last name if that's how it was entered. So, for example, Jane Austen is found under *J* for *Jane*, whereas Arthur Conan Doyle is found under *D* for *Doyle*, presumably because that's how someone entered it. *Beowulf*, with blessed logic, is in the *B*s. So, while the order of things looks quite pretty at first glance, almost nothing is where you expect it to be. This is an excellent argument in favor of using Alex to peruse Wiretap's wares, at least until Wiretap gets around to improving its organization.

Despite its shortcomings, Wiretap's listing is one of the better ones. Wiretap at least gives you the author and the title on the main Gopher list, whereas most other archives of texts in English cryptically list only one or two words on the hypertext listing, such as the author's last name or a word from the title if the author is unknown, or even a one-word subject heading, all mixed in together. It takes several more clicks and jumps to find out exactly what texts are available. This can be frustrating at best and is yet another reason why Alex is a more convenient way to browse.

Problems with on-line Text

Unfortunately, finding a text may turn out to be the least of your problems. Once you actually call up a text, whether you found it directly through the archive or you used Alex, you encounter one of the most serious problems with most books on-line. Very few on-line texts in English have bibliographic references, such as the date and publishing house of the edition used to enter it. When such information is available, it will be listed, along with the name or address of the individual or organization responsible for putting the text on-line, but most texts arrive as naked as the day they were born, with nothing more than the title and the author to introduce them. Chapter headings usually survive entry, but page numbers go the way of the title page, as do footnotes.

This lack of detail is one of the reasons behind the disclaimers found in most archives concerning quality and accuracy of the works contained. Texts are presented as is, and what you see is what you get — which may not be very much.

The lack of reference information is a serious problem for researchers wishing to take advantage of on-line text. You don't even know which edition a given text may have been entered from, much less how accurately it was transcribed. Nor do you know whether it was ever proofread. With no reference information, one can't exactly quote an on-line text or put it in a bibliography, and even if the title page information has been preserved, the lack of page breaks and numbers in most works negates much of their usefulness. You cannot quote a text without an edition and a page number to refer to. When you are trying to obtain a reference, in many cases, the information provided is so minimal that tracking down a passage in a printed edition that you searched or stumbled across on-line is more trouble than using the printed edition from the beginning. Not only that, but without markers in the text for page breaks, returning to any given passage in a longer text can be quite a chore, as you scroll through the document one screen at a time.

The bottom line is that on-line text cannot replace the printed work until these problems are cleared up. Clearing them up is simply a matter of organization and time, and therefore of money. Grass-roots data entry alone cannot provide the necessary quality control for online texts to be a reliable source.

Advantages of on-line text

The aforementioned problems all focus on how to upgrade an on-line text so that it is at least as good as a printed edition. If this were the only use for on-line text, the advantages over printed editions would be minimal. However, computers being the nifty machines that they are, a text on-line has the potential for research that would be very difficult if not impossible to perform manually. I'm not just talking about a new tool to do the same old job — I'm talking about the possibility of a new tool that results in a new field.

One way in which computers are better than humans is volume. If you can set up a task in such a way that a computer with its itty-bitty yes-no brain can understand it, you can do an incredible amount of work in a very short period of time — to a degree that reproducing the same result manually could take years and years, if not forever. Computers therefore allow us to ask questions of an entirely new magnitude than was ever before possible. Don't forget, though: a computer cannot tell you the meaning of life. It can, however, tell you all of the occurrences of the word "life" or any of its forms in a text, or in a group of texts, or in a really large group of texts, given the data and the appropriate software. Essentially, redefining the word "text" to apply to texts on-line involves not only separating the definition from the physical form of a book or a printed page but also questioning the integrity of the individual work. Imagine if you could state as your text or corpus "the eighteenth century," in a database large enough for that search to be valid.

ARTFL

Modern dictionaries are a prime example of large-scale research using online text. In fact, one of the largest text databases online at this time, ARTFL, was originally started in 1957 by the French government as a way to provide access to a large body of word samples for a new dictionary, the *Trésor de la Langue Française*. By 1987, a corpus of some 150 million words had been established, representing a broad range of written French stretching from the seventeenth to the twentieth centuries — meaning, by the way, that these texts are in French, which may be somewhat of a disadvantage for those of us who do not speak or read that particular language (the Mosaic shell, however, is in English).

It soon became clear that a database of this size was an important resource not only for lexicographers, but also for many other types of humanists and social scientists engaged in French studies — on both sides of the Atlantic. As a result, in 1981 the *Centre National de la Recherche Scientifique* and the University of Chicago established a cooperative project: the American and French Research on the Treasury of the French Language, or ARTFL. Since then, ARTFL has worked to restructure the database to make it accessible to the research community, charging only a modest annual subscription fee.

ARTFL went on-line in 1989 with PhiloLogic, an easy-to-use full-text retrieval package allowing the user to search for a single word, a word root, a prefix, a suffix, or a co-occurrence (two or more words in proximity to each other) from all or part of the database. In addition to searching, PhiloLogic provided corpus definition, word list management, KWIC (keyword in context) and full-text display, bibliographic functions, generation of statistics, and creation and delivery of formatted output. PhiloLogic also included indexing on accented characters and proper names.

Although most databases on-line are searchable to a limited degree, ARTFL is one of the only ones to provide the kind of data manipulation available in PhiloLogic. For instance, although Wiretap allows you to search for a word in a text once you have the text on screen, and it highlights the word as it occurs, moving linearly from one to the next by scrolling down, the searches are confined to the document at hand and provide no statistical information. The search function found under the File menu in the Mosaic shell has a similar command function, but with no more functional capability. This means that the only way to know how many occurrences were found in a given search is to scroll through the text and count them yourself. As a tool for data manipulation, this type of search engine obviously leaves a great deal to be desired. PhiloLogic was definitely a step up.

In 1993 PhiloLogic was supplanted by the birth of the ARTFL home page, and ARTFL joined the Web. Forget the PhiloLogic manual (there was one) — now all of the PhiloLogic functions are available through the much more user-friendly WWW programs. Filling in forms and clicking on little command boxes, or jumping with ease from one screen to the next without having to memorize any command functions has made ARTFL accessible to mouse jockeys everywhere. The ARTFL home page is hypertext; the search forms are hypertext; even the results are hypertext, with page numbers before each occurrence that allow you to call up the entire page where the term was found and then go to the next page or the previous page should you so desire. Searches are followed by a bibliography listing all of the works in which occurrences were found in standard format.

The following figures show an example of a possible search and its results:

- Filling out the form shown in Figure 22-17 asks the ARTFL database for all of the occurrences of the word *aveugle* (meaning blind) in *Madame Bovary* by Gustave Flaubert. This example was chosen to produce a short list of results; obviously, much larger searches are possible through all or part of the database.
- The KWIC report shown in Figure 22-18 is often used with larger searches to give a preliminary idea of the results, without scrolling through screens and screens of context. Clicking on the underlined page number of an entry will call

up the entire page in that work with the search term highlighted. The bibliographic abbreviations are defined in a full bibliography appearing at the end of the search.

- Figure 22-19 shows the last page of the search results, with the bibliographic notation at the bottom. The standard search, providing the highlighted search term accompanied by ten lines of context, obviously provides a much better idea of where and how the search term is used in the text. Once again, clicking on highlighted page numbers allows you to call up the entire page from there as desired.

Hard as it may be to believe, ARTFL does in fact have a few problems. In fact, until recently, ARTFL shared many of the difficulties I criticized in the other archives — missing or incorrect paragraph and page breaks and spelling and typographical errors in the text itself, among others. In 1990, though, thanks to a grant from the National Endowment for the Humanities, ARTFL set about correcting these errors in collaboration with the Institut Nationale de la Langue Française. It's still not perfect, but it's much closer than it was before.

Unfortunately, typos are not the only problem. ARTFL comes close enough to a comprehensive collection to fall victim to the canon question. This is a position of some privilege — none of the other databases is complete enough to be accused of discrimination against anyone or anything — the holes are simply too large. ARTFL, however, with its more than 2,000 texts, risks the eagle eye of the politically correct being applied to its bibliography, with perhaps politically incorrect results. Because the original database focused primarily on works from the nineteenth and twentieth centuries, earlier periods — medieval and Renaissance in particular — are less well represented. Much worse are the notable under representation of women authors in all centuries and the almost complete lack of French-speaking authors outside of France. These are important factors to take into account when doing research using the database, as they could strongly slant the results towards the most traditional canon.

Rare books on-line

Up until this point, I have discussed on-line texts, including the ARTFL database, in terms of the more or less complete data representation of the book in question. Accuracy has been defined in terms of bibliographical information and accurate data entry, but the original format of the work has not been an issue.

This is not usually a problem for more traditional literary or linguistic analysis. However, one of the hottest fields in literary studies today involves the *paratext* — the pictures, prologues, afterwords, and other various forms of information that frame the text itself. Modern print editions of older works or manuscripts often do not include all of the paratext of the original. As a result, scholars studying extra-textual questions such as reception, political implications, the evolution of copyright, and the interaction between the author and the publisher must have access to the original, or else to a faithful reproduction. For many obvious reasons, access to rare books can be problematic if not nearly impossible, and modern editions containing all of the paratext of the original are less common than one might wish.

NCSA Mosaic: Document View

File Options Navigate Annotate Help

Document Title: ARTFL Project: Database Search Form

Document URL: http://tuna.uchicago.edu/forms/ARTFL.form.html

ARTFL Project: Database Search Form

Search the ARTFL databases by completing this form. Help is available by clicking on the appropriate underlined terms.

Select Database: Main database (default) ◇ New Additions ◇ Provençal ◇

Define Corpus: Select the texts to be searched. Leave blank to search whole database.

Author: Flaubert (ex. flaubert or Balzac H)

Title:.... Madame Bovary (ex. Madame Bovary)

Dates:.. (ex. 1800-1899)

Genre: ALL WORKS

Search Corpus for: aveugle

Examples: liberte/ **or** raison.* **or** privilEge **or** femme|homme
Notes: The vertical line (|) is the **OR** operator, space or carriage return is the **AND** operator for co-occurence and phrase searches (also see Pattern Matching). Accented characters are represented by two characters (a\ = à).

Search Options: Phrase Search ☐ Inflected Word Search ☐

Output Options: KWIC Report ☐ Frequency by Title ☐ Links to other databases ☐

Press to [Submit Query] or press to [Clear Entries] or return to ARTFL Home.

Back Forward Home Reload Open... Save As... Clone New Window Close Window

Figure 22-17: The ARTFL search form.

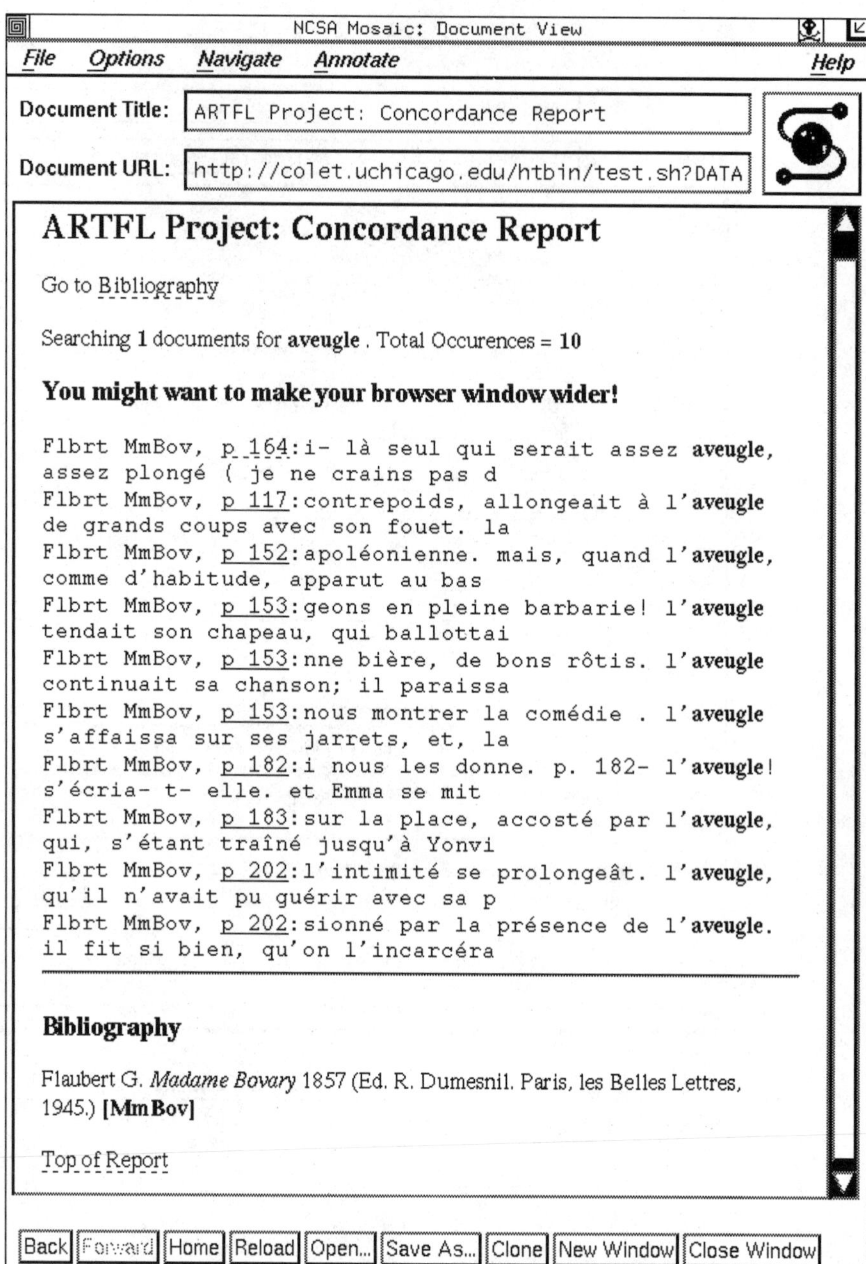

Figure 22-18: Search results using the KWIC report.

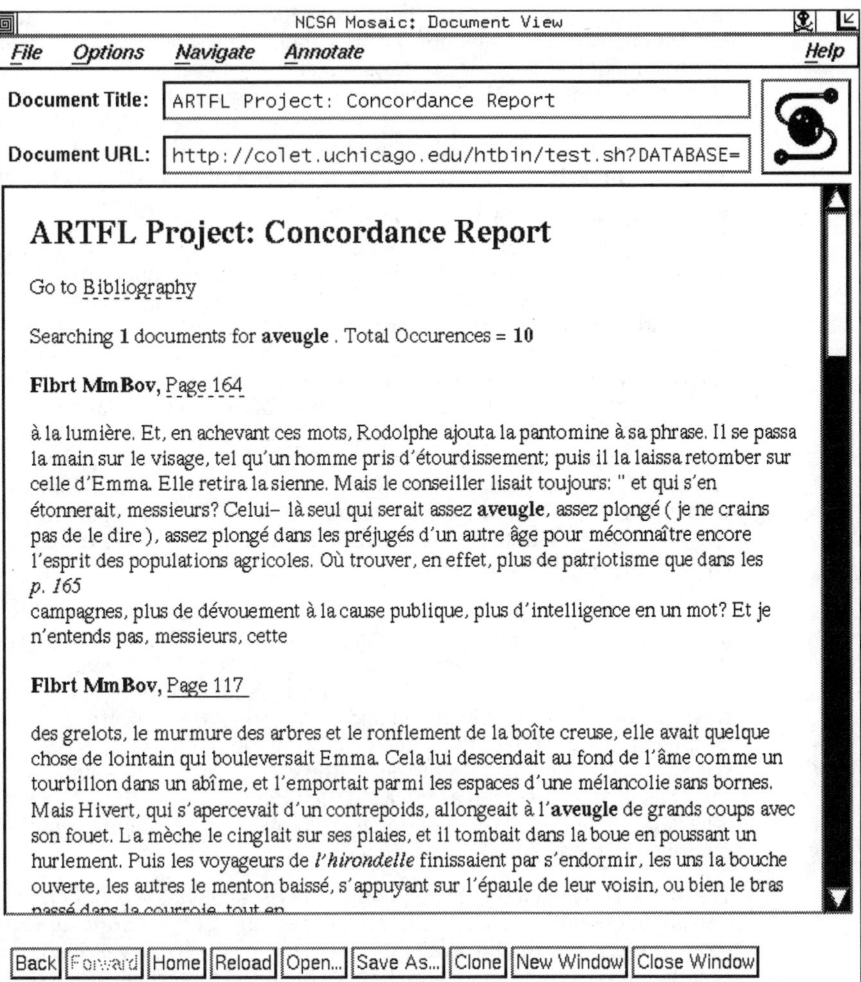

NCSA Mosaic: Document View
File Options Navigate Annotate Help
Document Title: ARTFL Project: Concordance Report
Document URL: http://colet.uchicago.edu/htbin/test.sh?DATABASE=
ARTFL Project: Concordance Report
Go to Bibliography
Searching 1 documents for aveugle . Total Occurences = 10
Flbrt MmBov, Page 164
à la lumière. Et, en achevant ces mots, Rodolphe ajouta la pantomine à sa phrase. Il se passa la main sur le visage, tel qu'un homme pris d'étourdissement; puis il la laissa retomber sur celle d'Emma. Elle retira la sienne. Mais le conseiller lisait toujours: " et qui s'en étonnerait, messieurs? Celui- là seul qui serait assez aveugle, assez plongé (je ne crains pas de le dire), assez plongé dans les préjugés d'un autre âge pour méconnaître encore l'esprit des populations agricoles. Où trouver, en effet, plus de patriotisme que dans les
p. 165
campagnes, plus de dévouement à la cause publique, plus d'intelligence en un mot? Et je n'entends pas, messieurs, cette
Flbrt MmBov, Page 117
des grelots, le murmure des arbres et le ronflement de la boîte creuse, elle avait quelque chose de lointain qui bouleversait Emma. Cela lui descendait au fond de l'âme comme un tourbillon dans un abîme, et l'emportait parmi les espaces d'une mélancolie sans bornes. Mais Hivert, qui s'apercevait d'un contrepoids, allongeait à l'aveugle de grands coups avec son fouet. La mèche le cinglait sur ses plaies, et il tombait dans la boue en poussant un hurlement. Puis les voyageurs de l'hirondelle finissaient par s'endormir, les uns la bouche ouverte, les autres le menton baissé, s'appuyant sur l'épaule de leur voisin, ou bien le bras
Back Forward Home Reload Open... Save As... Clone New Window Close Window

Figure 22-19: Standard search results, including ten lines of context.

This is where computers come into their own in terms of text on-line. In the spring of 1994, the University of Notre Dame in collaboration with the Newberry Library of Chicago mounted an exposition called "Renaissance Dante in Print (1472–1629)," consisting of examples of Renaissance editions of Dante's *Divine Comedy*. Parts of this exposition were then brought on-line in the fall of 1994 (`http://tuna.uchicago.edu/Dante/Dante_Ex1.html`) with accompanying literary and historical information, through a collaboration between the University of Notre Dame, the Newberry Library, and ARTFL Project at the University of Chicago. The originals were either photographed and then scanned or else scanned directly, converted into digital images, and then made available on-line through hypertext links. You can now "visit" the Dante exposition on-line and read about the exposition (in English), the collection, Dante's Hell, and a brief history of Dante title pages, or you can look at any one of the over 500 images that make up the on-line version of the exposition. In fact, Dante on-line contains many more images than were available for viewing during the actual exposition. The images are in color and include title pages, illuminations, and passages from the texts in the exposition. It's a glorious thing to browse through, whether or not you understand Italian.

Besides being beautiful, however, the Dante exposition on-line holds the germ of a revolution in studies using rare books. Rare books were not completely inaccessible to those who couldn't afford to visit them in person up until now — microfilm has been around a lot longer than the Web. However, compared to what can now be done with computer imaging, microfilm is but a poor country cousin. Imagine — what if on one side of your screen you had a window with a searchable text of the *Inferno*, and on the other side of the screen a window with an exact reproduction of the actual page in the edition itself, say the 1506 edition? What if you could then "turn the page" of the original edition at the click of a button? What if you could click on a hypertext link in the searchable text to bring up a variant, from another edition, of that same page? What if you could pick an area of the image to magnify, with high enough resolution that magnification of the image actually allowed you to decipher a margin note that is faded by 400 years? This, as in the example in Figure 22-20, is the revolution.

In November 1994, ARTFL began to run experiments to determine the optimal parameters for transmitting page images on the Net. The pilot was a rare pamphlet called *Dame Nature à la Barre de l'Assemblée Nationale* by Sylvain Maréchal, published in 1791 and reprinted only once in limited edition (500 copies) in 1967. Once the document was scanned and on-line, hypertext "buttons" were implemented at the bottom of the screen, allowing the reader to go either to the next page or to a particular page further in the text. On a high-resolution monitor, the text is as legible onscreen as it was in the original. At this time, there is no searchable version, but all of the technology is in place — it would be simply a matter of entering the data.

This is the truly exciting future in on-line texts — digital reproductions of rare books. Unless you can accumulate a large enough and accurate enough database of more modern and readily available works to be able to do valid large-scale research, the economics and versatility of the $6.95 paperback copy of *Huckleberry Finn* provide little motivation for putting it on-line.

On the other hand, quality reproductions of rare books on-line constitute a resource the entire academic community can drool over. Microfilm reproductions of manuscripts can leave much to be desired in terms of quality of reproduction. Often the only other option is to visit the original, wherever it may reside, which could easily be in a library on the other side of the world. However, if these manuscripts were on-line you, wouldn't even have to wash your hands first to look at them. Nor would you have to fly to Italy, or France, or England, or wherever the manuscript may be. Marginalia could be studied in detail and more accurately than from a textual reproduction. Illuminations would appear on your screen — in full color, with title pages, end pages, and prologues. The complete original edition would be as close as your computer.

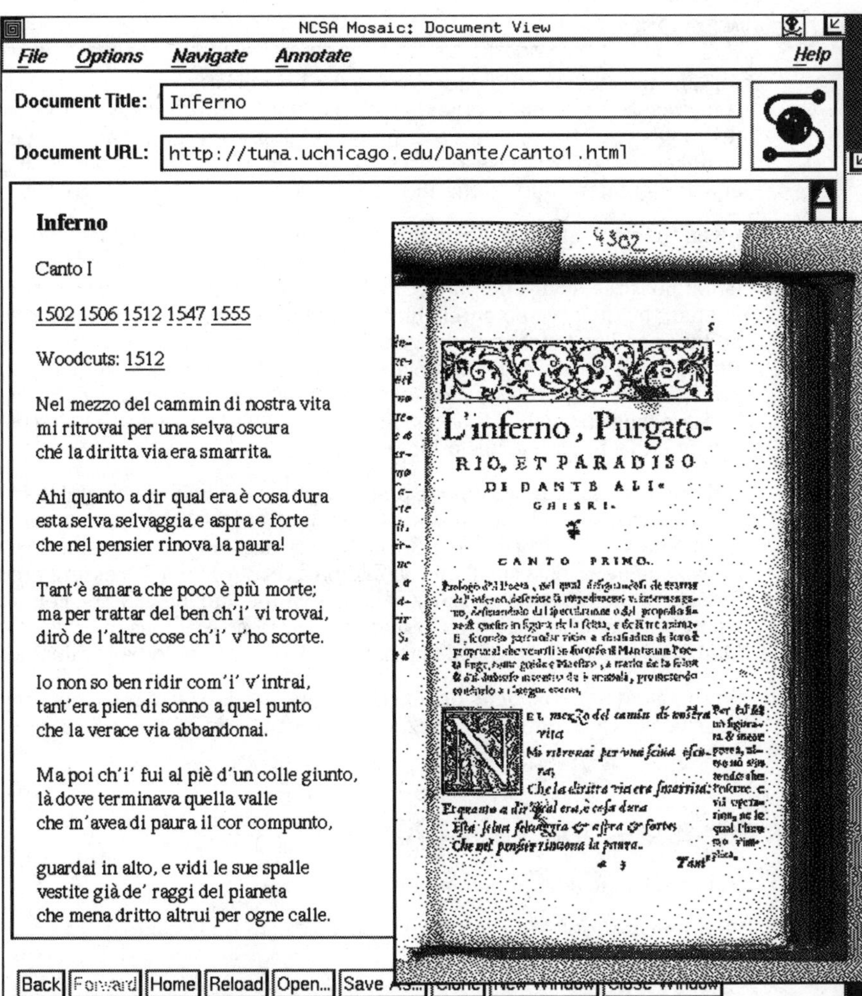

Figure 22-20: An experiment combining text and manuscript: a reproduction of a page from Dante's *Inferno*.

Of course, the volume of data involved in that many images is significant, as is the speed (or lack thereof) of transmission. However, computer technology moves so quickly that those obstacles may evaporate sooner than one might think. Not only that, but the Net would allow these documents to be "housed" at universities so that the individual would not be required to find room to store it all.

Conclusions

ARTFL, despite its continuing flaws, is the best existing example of a research tool using text on-line. Unlike other archives on-line at this time, it's large (over 2,000 texts), it's searchable, it has a complete bibliography, and it has been edited for mistakes. All four of these features are necessary for any on-line archive to offer equal or greater utility to the $6.95 paperback copy of *Huckleberry Finn*.

Given the necessary quality control, volume, and search engines, the on-line "library" could eventually become just that, and more, because of the data manipulation possible using computers. Right now, unfortunately, the selection is too limited; the quality, too unreliable; and the searchability, too poor in most text archives on-line for them to be genuine tools for research. They're fun to look through and certainly not completely useless, but neither have they realized their potential except in the smallest of ways. However, because they are also changing and evolving so rapidly, that conclusion could be on its way to being dated even by the time this book reaches print.

Although *Madame Bovary* alone on-line would be much less useful than *Madame Bovary* surrounded by a thousand other works of its century, each rare book put on-line have be a very important tool for research all by itself. A library of rare books on-line, even a small one, would be a resource not necessarily reproducible outside of the Net, due to issues of conservation and availability. For academics of whatever sort who base their research upon close readings of original works, this kind of access to the original manuscript or edition could be invaluable.

So surf away — most texts on-line right now may look like toys, but they're only a heartbeat away from one of the most powerful tools for literary research since the word processor.

URL Addresses for This Chapter

Alex electronic text archive/index:

```
Gopher://Gopher.lib.ncsu.edu/11/library/stacks/Alex
```

ARTFL Project:

```
http://tuna/ARTFL.html
```

The English Server:

```
http://english.hss.cmu.edu/
```

Eris Project:

```
Gopher://Gopher.vt.edu:10010/10/33
```

Hypertext Webster Interface:

```
http://c.gp.cs.cmu.edu:5103/prog/webster?
```

The Human-Languages Page:

`http://www.willamette.edu/~tjones/Language-Page.html`

OBI — The Online Book Initiative:

`Gopher://Gopher.std.com/11/obi`

The On-Line Books Page:

`http://www.cs.cmu.edu:8001/Web/books.html`

Oxford Text Archive:

`ftp://ota.ox.ac.uk/pub/ota`

Renaissance Dante in Print (1472–1629):

`http://tuna.uchicago.edu/Dante/Dante_Ex1.html`

Wiretap:

`Gopher://wiretap.spies.com/`

Chapter 23

Gopher Secrets

This chapter contains three articles:

- "A Few Gopher Tricks"
- "Squealing and Hissing: A Gopher Client Roundup"
- "GN: Serving WWW and Gopher with the Same Server"

A Few Gopher Tricks

by Lee Stral <leestral@mcs.com>

The Internet Gopher's best trick is really the Internet's best-kept secret: With the exception of displaying in-line graphics, there's really nothing the World Wide Web can do that Gopher can't do better.

With Gopher, you can download anything you can download from the Web. Windows and Macintosh Gopher clients can use any external viewer a Web browser can use. And Gopher does it faster. More important, if you want to utilize the vast stores of information available on the Internet, whether you know exactly what you want or have only a vague idea, Gopher is the better tool.

Whether you're searching Internet resources or browsing for pleasure, Gopher can be your Internet shell. It gives the Internet a consistent look and structure. It was designed to be a document-retrieval system, in which a *document* is anything stored in a Gopher-accessible file. The Gopher protocol supports standard file types, telnet and Web connections, and virtually all multimedia types. It also has its own tools for database searches while making other Internet search tools easier and better.

Gopher and Gopher+

All the information on a Gopher server is stored on a *data tree,* a hierarchical menu system. The Gopher's home directory is the top of the tree, with directories and files shown as items on a menu. Items can be text files, binary files, images, sounds, search engines, or links to other Gophers with even more information.

Although Gopher menus are nested, they are not static. They change continually as new items are added to a menu level. They become an even more dynamic tool when you consider that Gopher servers typically are not limited to a single host. They are linked to each other, and as changes are made in the menus on these links, changes are made to the entire network of Gophers.

Types of items on menus

When you choose an item from a menu, your Gopher client identifies the item type and acts accordingly, by retrieving a new menu, displaying a file, initiating a search query, or downloading a file to disk or invoking a helper application to view a nonstandard file. The action taken depends on the capabilities of the client. The types currently handled by Gopher are shown in the following table:

Code Letter	*Item Type*
0	Text file
1	Directory
2	CSO/phone book server
3	Error
4	Binhex file
5	DOS binary
6	Uuencoded UNIX file
7	Search server
8	Telnet session
9	Binary file
T	TN3270 Telnet session
s	Sound file
g	GIF file
M	MIME file
h	HTML file
I	Image (undefined)

Gopher+ enhancements

Gopher+ adds capabilities to plain Gopher, including the capability to choose extended views, display extended information about the server, and utilize ASK forms.

A document can be stored as more than a single type of file in Gopher+. When alternative types are available, you can choose the one you want by using your client's extended-views capability. If you have helper applications configured, the file is viewed automatically; otherwise, your client asks how to display it. In this way, Gopher can display non-GIF image files, animations, and rich-text files, such as PostScript and HTML (Web) pages. This, so far, is the only attribute of Gopher+ that is used extensively.

Expanded information allows the Gopher server to include, with the document when it's delivered, details about the site and abstracts about an item's contents. (See Figure 23-1.) Unfortunately, although abstracts are helpful, they are used infrequently. Most expanded information consists merely of the system administrator's name and contact address.

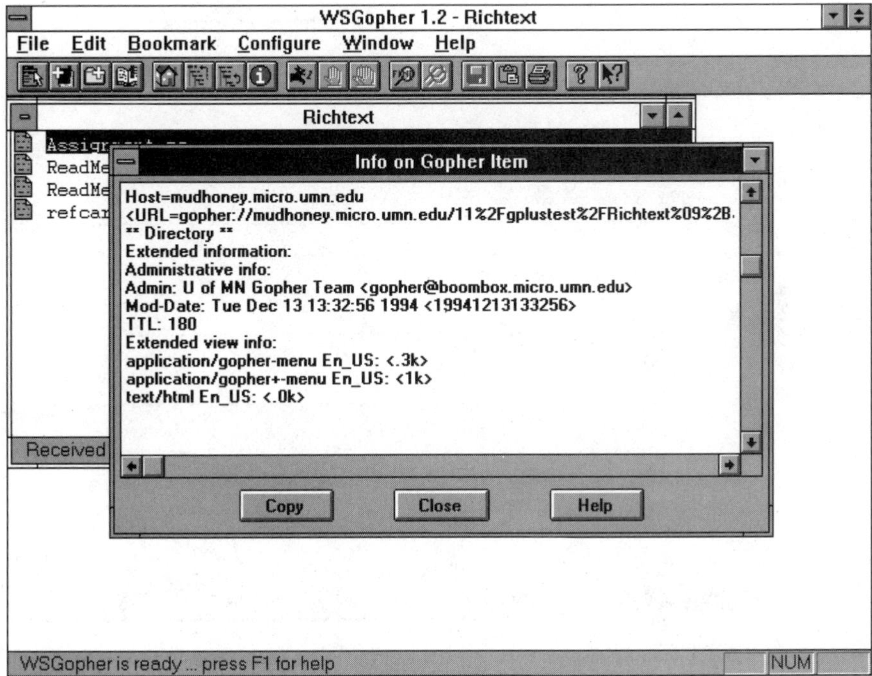

Figure 23-1: Gopher+ expanded information.

ASK forms (see Figure 23-2) are interactive forms that let Gopher servers accept input from users. In addition to being able to request and upload user information, ASK forms also allow files to be uploaded. There are fewer practical implementations of ASK forms, however, than there are of expanded information.

If you want to test your client's Gopher+ capabilities, you can use test servers. Gopher to `mudhoney.micro.umn.edu` and choose `gplustest` to see how Gopher+ is designed to work.

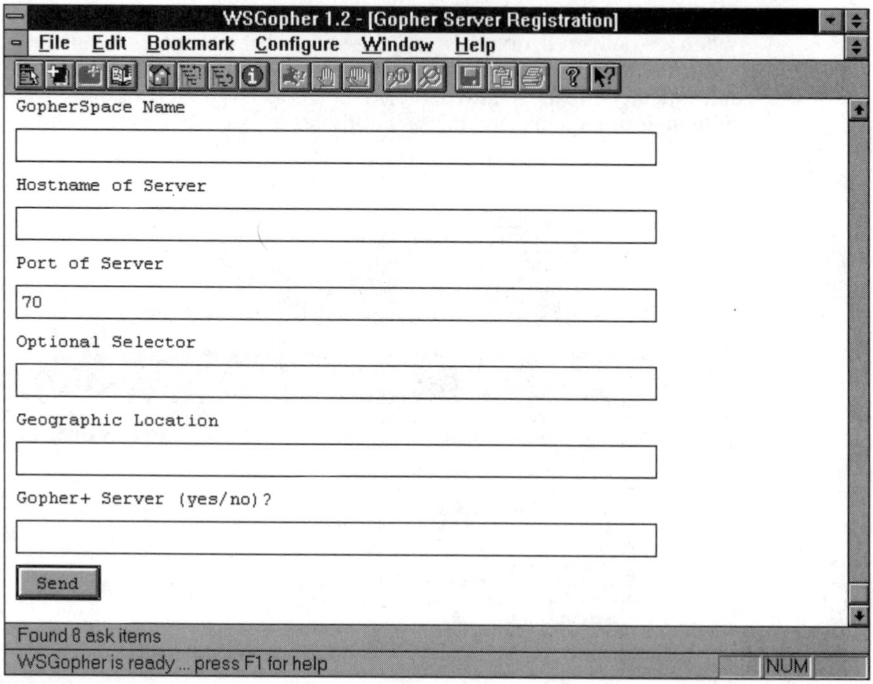

WSGopher 1.2 - [Gopher Server Registration]

File Edit Bookmark Configure Window Help

GopherSpace Name

Hostname of Server

Port of Server

70

Optional Selector

Geographic Location

Gopher+ Server (yes/no)?

Send

Found 8 ask items

WSGopher is ready ... press F1 for help NUM

Figure 23-2: A sample ASK form.

Beginning Browsing

When you start a Gopher session, your client program begins at a default Gopher menu, called your *home Gopher.* Generally, your home Gopher is preconfigured, but you can and should change it. Choose a home Gopher you find to be reliable, that is not too busy, and that has a number of links you use regularly.

Regardless of which Gopher you call home, it likely has a directory item called Other Gophers. It has a link to what is affectionately called the Mother of All Gophers, but usually is listed as All the Gopher Servers in the World. This item takes you to the University of Minnesota. If you choose the Other Gopher and Information Servers item, you can see how it got its name: You see a listing of Gophers by region, country, special grouping (such as international organizations), telnet connection, and WAIS database, in addition to the All the Gopher Servers in the World item. You can connect to literally thousands of Gopher servers from this single Gopher.

Mother also is your primary resource for all things Gopher. You can access technical and general information about Gopher services and new Gopher developments, download Gopher client and server software, and find everything else that has anything to do with Gopher.

Mother has a sister, `liberty.uc.wlu.edu`, at Washington and Lee University (WLU) in St. Louis. (See Figure 23-3.) Gopher there and choose Finding Gopher Resources/All Gopher Sites. You find directories of Gophers by region and country. You also find a link back to Mother, the first indication that differences exist between the two. They start with directories of Gophers by U. S. state, but the major difference is less apparent. Although Mother is billed as All the Gopher Servers in the World, it really should be named All the Gopher Servers We've Been Told About (only Gopher sites that have registered with the University of Minnesota are listed). The WLU Gopher is more comprehensive because it includes not only officially registered Gopher servers but also servers that are linked to all the Gophers on the WLU lists.

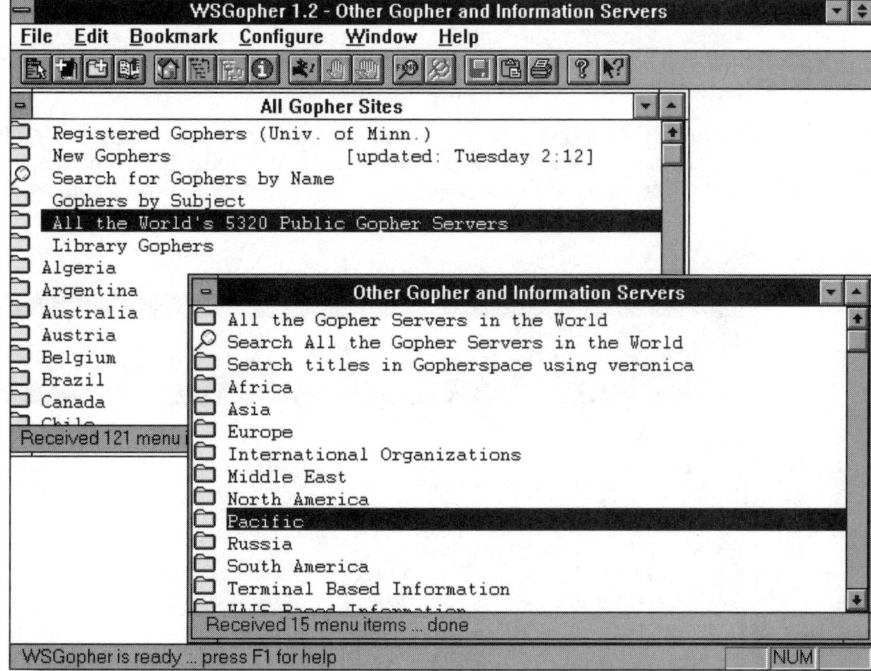

Figure 23-3: All Gopher sites (WLU) versus other Gopher and information servers (University of Minnesota).

Subject-oriented Gophers

If you're looking for Gophers in specific countries or if you want an idea of just how vast Gopherspace is, Mother and WLU are the places to go. But browsing by country gets tedious after awhile and, if you're looking for specific subject areas, downright frustrating. Enter the subject-oriented Gopher.

The best starting point for subject-oriented browsing is Gopher Jewels (cwis.usc.edu), a project of the University of Southern California. Begun as an experiment in Gopher organization, Gopher Jewels is one of the most deservedly popular places on the Internet. It is easy to navigate and offers connections to almost every area of interest.

One of the most comprehensive subject-oriented Gophers is the English Server at Carnegie-Mellon University (english.hss.cmu.edu). Its purpose is to serve the faculty and students of the university's English department, so it's somewhat staid, but it is open to anyone.

Much more fun, and my favorite, is PEG, a Peripatetic, Eclectic Gopher (peg.cwis.uci.edu) at the University of California at Irvine. Here's a Gopher to truly love, to wander through, to get lost in, and find new items at every pass. Whereas Gopher Jewels tends to be best at finding the best examples of server subject types and the English Server excels at literature and academic resources, PEG has several somethings for everyone, from the encyclopedic Virtual Reference Desk to links to multiuser dungeons and other games.

Several other subject-oriented Gophers, although not as much fun as PEG, are equally resourceful. For an excellent sampling, Gopher to bongo.cc.utexas.edu at the University of Texas (see Figure 23-4) and choose World/Subject Archives.

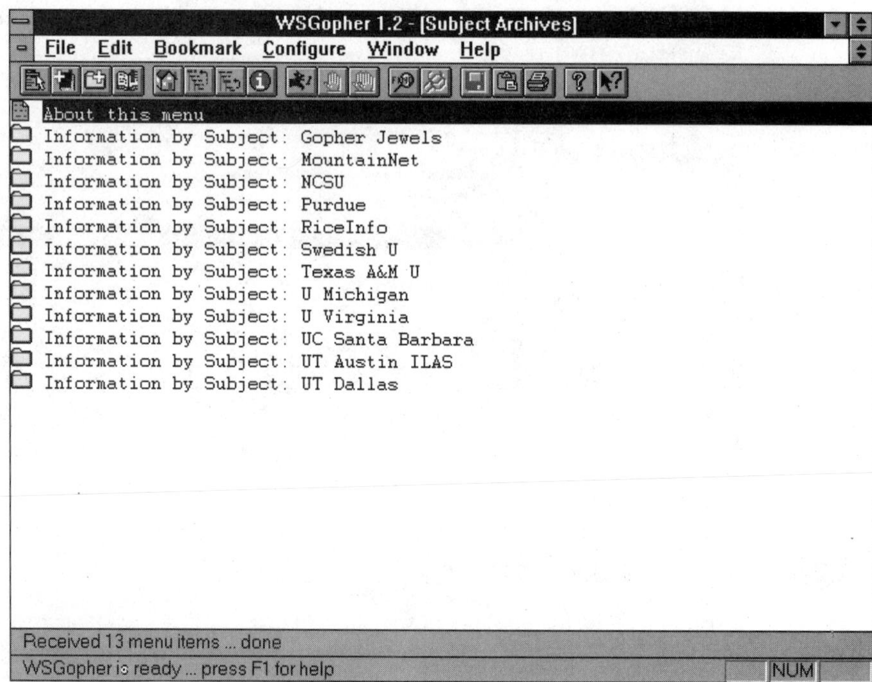

Figure 23-4: Subject Gopher listing at the University of Texas.

Bookmarks

At this point, you may have found a number of Gophers you want to revisit. You don't have to burrow through layers of menus to get back to a specific directory. Gopher's bookmark capability lets you save any directory you encounter, no matter how deep it may be in a server's hierarchy. Check your Gopher client program's documentation to learn how to make a bookmark.

One benefit of bookmarks, especially when you're using a search tool such as Veronica, is that you can quickly skim the contents of a directory or file and save it if it looks like it might be useful. You can go back later to make a final decision.

If your Gopher client can edit bookmarks, you may want to rename them. (See Figure 23-5.) Even the more clearly named directories can become obscure when several on your list have similar titles. Why was Internet Resources at Site A saved when I already had a bookmark for Internet Resources at Sites B, C, D, E, and F? And what makes the Subject Tree at Whosis different from the Subject Tree at Whatsis?

With some Gopher clients, you can save bookmarks by category. My favorite creation is "New." I browse promiscuously, and I like to keep moving. If there's something I like, I save it and move on. Making the New category the default saves time in not having to specify a category and gives you a chance to go back later and spend more time with the files to decide whether you really want to keep the bookmark.

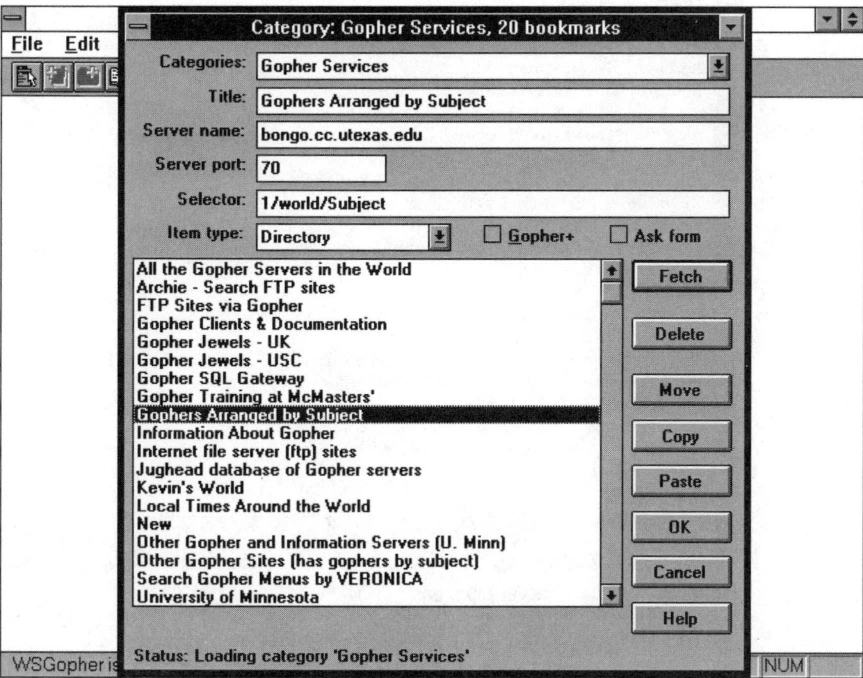

Figure 23-5: WSGopher 1.2 bookmark editor.

Bookmarks are especially helpful when you review search returns. Just skim the contents of the directory. If it's not exactly what you're looking for, save it and move on. You may find that exact match later on. If not, you still have the more likely hits to review later.

Finding New Gophers and Internet Resources

A handful of new Gophers comes on-line every day, and various lists are compiled that offer pointers to new Gophers. But as much as I appreciate and follow these efforts, if new Gophers come on-line daily, I want to find them daily. That's why the `honor.uc.wlu.edu` server at WLU is at the top of my New bookmark list (that's figuratively — a good bookmark list has to be alphabetical). It's the Netlink Server (see Figure 23-6), and every day it adds new Gophers. As a browsing bonus, the Netlink Server also gives you links to new WAIS databases, new telnet sites, and new WWW pages. These are all links, not mere lists, so you can check out anything that looks interesting and bookmark it.

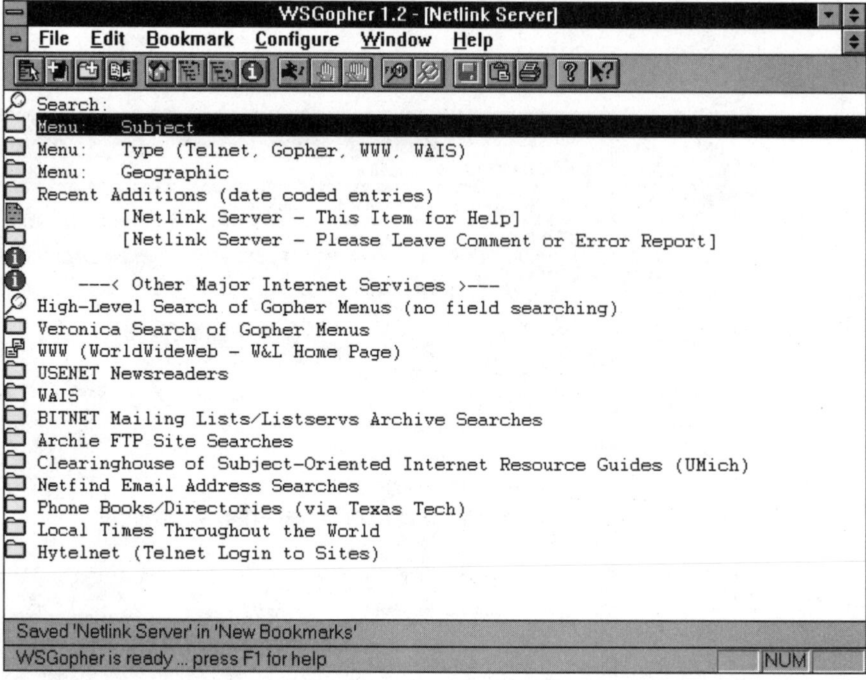

Figure 23-6: Netlink Server top menu.

Keeping track of new Gophers is one thing. But because more than 5,000 servers are on-line already, finding existing Gophers and resources that are new to you can be quite another. The subject-oriented Gophers are one way. Another is to always check Gopher directories titled Some Interesting Gophers or Other (Subject Area) Gophers at the servers you visit. These areas usually represent the interests of the user for whom the server was designed, which presumably includes you. They also tend to reflect the personal tastes of the system administrator and can therefore offer some interesting (if sometimes off-the-wall) links.

No matter how you find new Gophers, your first stop on any new menu should be the All About file. Most Gophers have them, and they provide an abstract of the Gopher's purpose and contents. The better-maintained Gophers also include a road map; a quick read of this file tells you whether and how long, considering your interests, you should spend browsing there.

If this isn't enough and you get truly bored, you can return to Mother or WLU and browse Gophers country by country.

Gopher Search Engines

Browsing is fun, but the Internet holds amazing amounts of information about amazing numbers of different topics. Finding that information is a simple matter with Gopher. You can use Gopher's own Veronica and Jughead or use the interfaces to the Internet's other search tools. However you do it, Gopher gives you the means to impress your friends, amaze your colleagues, and make your parents proud.

Veronica

Veronica is Gopher's primary search engine. Veronica servers index all items on Gophers registered with the University of Minnesota. You query with keywords, and Veronica delivers the results in a Gopher menu that links you to the items that are matched. You can examine those results and save the best directories as bookmarks for reference or save the files to disk.

Queries are not case-sensitive, and you can use the Boolean AND, OR, and NOT operators. Because Veronica assumes that a space between words means *and,* put the words within quotation marks if you want to match the exact text of two or more words. The difference between PC DOS SOFTWARE and "PC DOS" SOFTWARE is that the first one returns all items with all three words anywhere in the title, and the second one returns only those items in which PC and DOS appear in order and together. Figure 23-7 shows the difference in an actual search.

Veronica reads query items from right to left and assigns Boolean priority in that order. To help clarify the query (for yourself if not for Veronica), you can use parentheses in the query. For example, STEAK POTATOES EGGS returns only those items with all three words in their titles. But if you query with STEAK (POTATOES OR EGGS), you get all items with steak and potatoes or with steak and eggs in their titles.

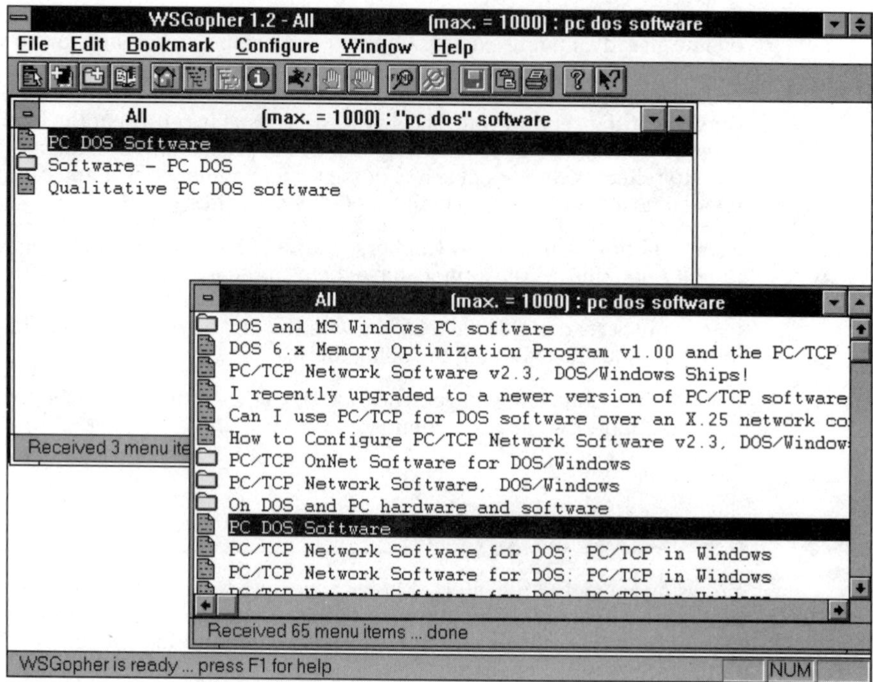

Figure 23-7: Search results with and without quotation marks.

You also can use the asterisk wildcard (*) with keywords. This technique, called *stemming,* lets you include plurals, gerunds, or any form of the stemmed word in your search. So STEAK POTATO* returns all items with potato or potatoes (or, for that matter, potatoe).

I use the trailing * as a matter of course. Too many good returns can be missed by assuming that Veronica automatically chooses words that contain a word, which it does not.

You can hone your query by using the -m and -t options. By default, Veronica limits the number of returns to 200. You can increase or decrease this number with -m*NUMBER*, where *NUMBER* equals the maximum number of returns you want. If you are looking for information about gorillas, for example, and you query with `GORILLA* -m1000`, you get in return 1,000 files (if there are at least that many).

If you don't use the -m option, Gopher lets you stop the query at any time during the search. You are given the choice of abandoning the search or viewing the returns up to the time you cancel.

The -t option specifies which types of Gopher items you want to search for. If you want only GIF files showing gorillas, your query should read `GORILLA -tg`. If you want JPEG files and GIF files, your options are `-tgI`. Notice that although keywords are not case-sensitive, file-type specifiers are. You can string as many file types as you want after a single -t option as long as there are no spaces between the specifiers. If there are spaces, Veronica reads them as keywords. And be sure to put a space between the keyword and the options or else Veronica reads the options as part of the keyword. To avoid having that happen, you can begin the query with the option.

Some Veronica menus give you several servers from which to choose. Don't choose the first one on the list. Almost everyone does, and that makes it a busy server, which increases the likelihood of your failing to connect. Begin at the bottom and work your way up.

Also, unless you know that the items you're searching for originated outside the United States, start with U. S. servers. (If you're Gophering from outside the United States, choose the server closest to your country). The Internet is fast, but the farther away your link is, the longer it takes to connect and return the search results. This is true for any Internet connection. If a mirror site is closer to you than the original site is, go for the mirror at all times.

In addition to its other treats, the Netlink Server offers a supercharged Veronica menu that gives you options not available from other servers. It begins with a choice of servers from around the world, including servers that index a specific country's servers, including Australia and Japan. It presents the menu of servers in order of fastest connect-times, so the trick of choosing servers from the bottom up doesn't work here (but then it doesn't have to).

Next, the Netlink Server menu gives you the option of searching all items, directories only, files only, telnet sites only, or phone books only. And if you don't want to use the -m option to specify the number of returns, you can choose return limits of 400, 1,000, 2,000, or 3,000 returns.

Jughead

Jughead is a scaled-down version of Veronica that indexes and searches only directory titles. It uses Boolean operators and the stemming *, as does Veronica, but most often it's used to index a specific Gopher server. When you choose an item such as `Search All Directories on This Gopher`, Jughead usually does the work.

Search returns are limited to 1,024, but you can specify more or fewer with special commands. The `?all KEYWORD` command returns all hits on the keyword. The `?limit=NUMBER KEYWORD` limits the returns to the first hits up to the number specified.

It is said that Jughead is faster (albeit less complete) than Veronica and therefore should be the preferred search tool. This may be true if you use a Jughead server that searches many Gophers, such as the one at the University of Utah. Most implementations, though, are extremely limited if they are used for more than searching the host Gopher.

Even the number of Gophers indexed by the Utah Jughead remains relatively few compared to Veronica. And speed, in my experience, is not an issue, especially if you use Veronica's -m option and want more than directory items returned.

Wide-area information services (WAIS)

Gopher gives you an excellent, although somewhat limited, gateway to WAIS's subject-specific databases. The limitation in Gopher is that you can search only one database at a time and you cannot use relevance feedback. Otherwise, queries using Gopher WAIS are the same as using the standard WAIS interface. You cannot use Boolean operators or wildcards. If you want to search multiple forms of a keyword, you must specify each form.

The key to successful Gopher WAIS searches is choosing the database. The WAIS item from the Netlink Server gives you several WAIS sources from which to choose, but these are alphabetically arranged, and most database names are not very descriptive of their contents. But Gopher also offers a WAIS gateway that organizes databases by subject. It's available through the Netlink Server or, better, directly by Gophering to `munin.ub2.lu.se` at the University of Lund, Sweden (see Figure 23-8). Subjects are two menus deep to narrow your subject search before listing the available databases.

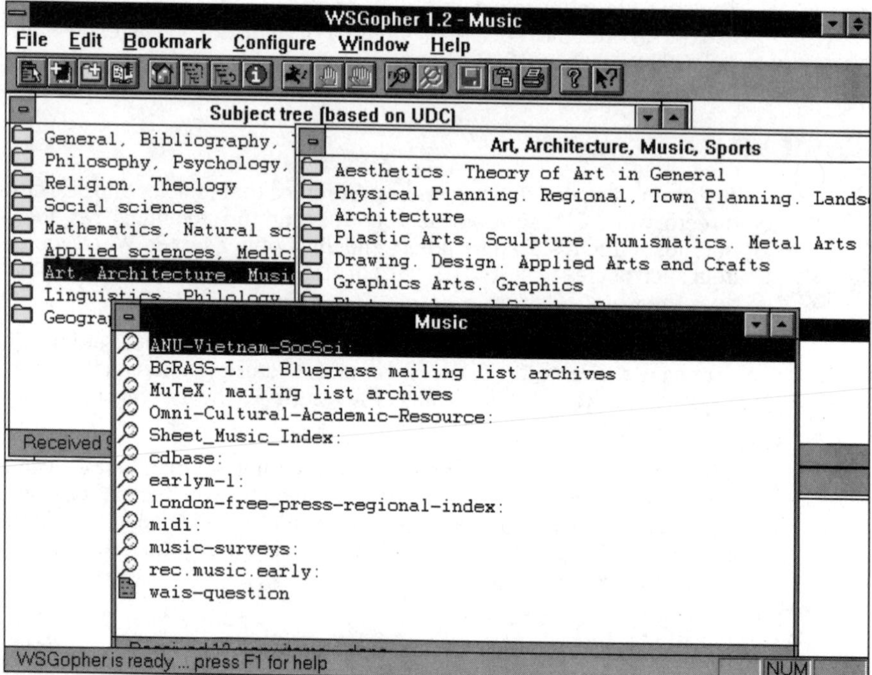

Figure 23-8: Progression of menus from WAIS database by subject, University of Lund.

Archie

The Gopher-to-Archie gateway lets you use Archie to search ftp sites for files, and it goes one better, by adding the capability to download the files Archie finds. For one of the best Archie gateways, Gopher to `trans.cs.uohio.edu` at Cleveland State University (see Figure 23-9) and choose FTP Services/Archie Gateways. This gateway gives you a menu of links to specific software archives at various sites around the world. At these sites, you can search by exact filename or by partial filename.

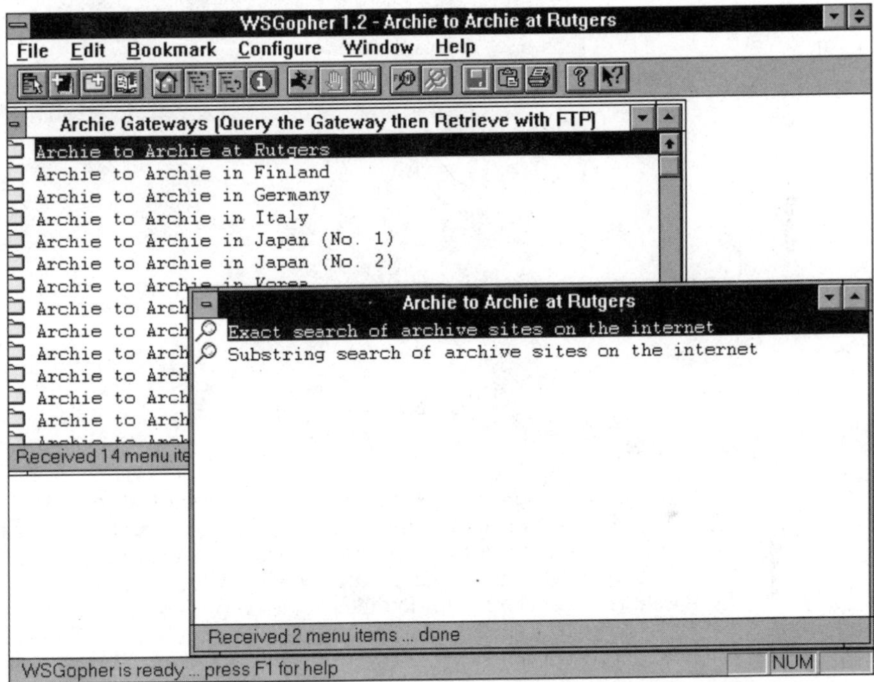

Figure 23-9: Cleveland State University Archie gateway.

An even better gateway is `merlot.gdb.org`, at Johns Hopkins University (see Figure 23-10). Choose Search and Retrieve Software, and you can browse a variety of ftp sites organized by software type or platform, including PC DOS archives at Simtel and Garbo. These sites also let you use keyword searching of file descriptions to find software by using Boolean operators and wildcards (real ones, not stemming characters).

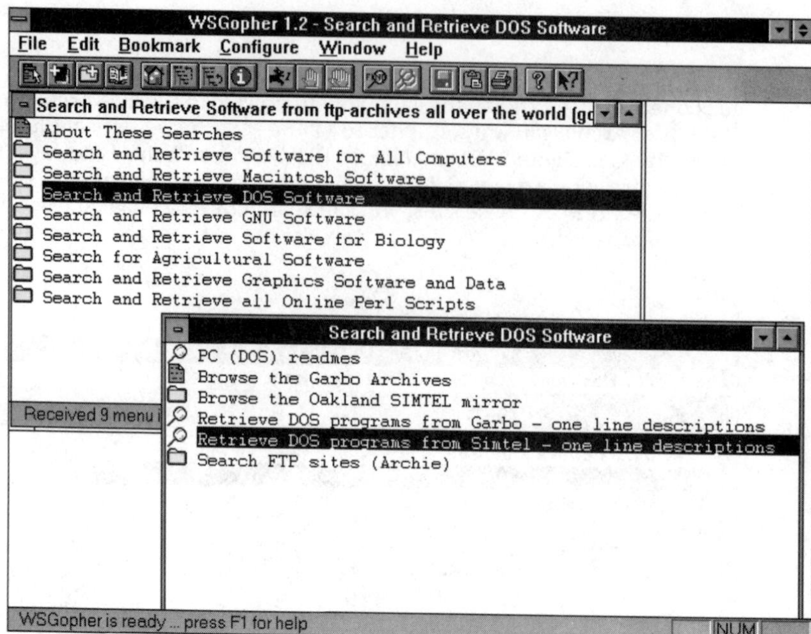

Figure 23-10: Johns Hopkins University Archie gateway.

Finding people

Most Gopher servers have a CSO phone directory covering their organization. The term CSO, which stands for Computing Services Office, refers to the computer-based system used to search for people at a specific site, usually a university. Some of these servers even have links to other Gophers with more-extensive directories. If you want the best Gopher for finding people on the Internet, however, you have to go to `gopher.uiuc.edu` at the University of Illinois at Urbana-Champaign. There you find searchable Gopher links to worldwide CSO directories, whois servers, X.500 gateways, Netfind e-mail directories, and Usenet contributor e-mail addresses.

The only difference between Gopher and other implementations of these services is that, with the exception of the telnet-based directories, Gopher is much more intuitive, which greatly simplifies the process.

One Last Trick

Anyone who has browsed the World Wide Web knows that many of the Web pages contain links to Gophers. The protocols are similar, although the differences increase as the Web protocol develops. Still, although Gopher lacks a similar capability to link directly to the Web, you can access Web pages and even browse some, through Gopher.

First, you must have a Gopher client program that supports Type h connections. (See Figure 23-11.) Second, you need a Web browser (such as Mosaic) configured as a helper application. (See Figure 23-12.) Whichever browser you choose, be sure that it can start up without linking automatically to a home page, and change the browser's INI file so that it doesn't. Otherwise, it overrides your link and connects you to the default home page. Then all you have to do is set up that browser as a viewer, or helper, application for your Gopher client.

There are two ways to call up Web pages with Gopher. The easiest is to Gopher to WLU's New Internet Resources menu and choose New WWW. Choose whatever page looks good to you, and your client will automatically invoke your Web browser to view it.

After you've connected to the Web, you can use that first connection to link to other pages, as you would do with a regular Web connection.

You also can link to specific pages from Gopher by using Gopher's GET / command. Clients vary, but the basic information you have to specify is shown in this list:

- Item/Type = h (or file.html)
- Path/Selector = GET /
- Server/Host = www.server.name
- Port = 80

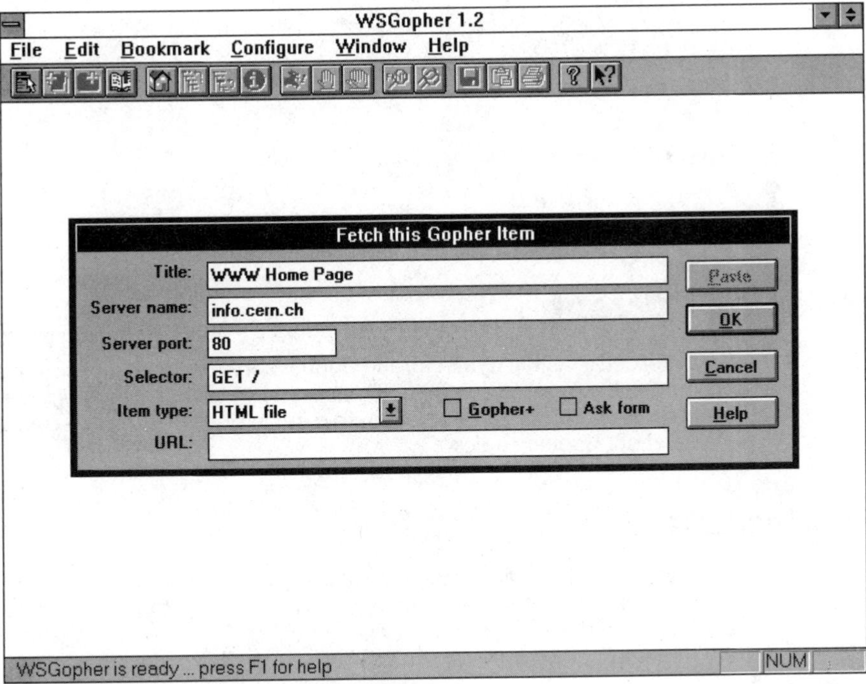

Figure 23-11: Fetching a Web page with WSGopher.

When you connect, you're on the Web by way of Gopher and you can link to other Web pages from the first page, just as you would do with a Web browser.

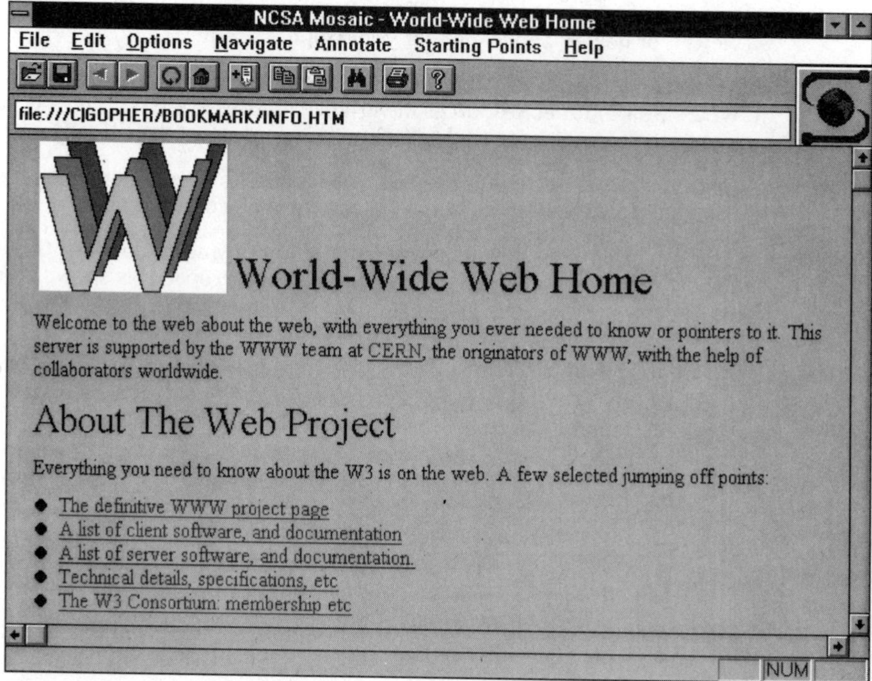

Figure 23-12: Gopher to Web link by way of WSGopher.

Keeping Current

Gopherspace is highly dynamic, and Gopher server and client development is an ongoing, ever-improving process. This section gives you some pointers to mailing lists and newsgroups to keep you up-to-date on Gopher or just to communicate with others about Gopher topics.

Mailing lists

GOPHERJEWELS is a moderated e-mail list you can use to post interesting Gopher finds of your own and to be notified of interesting sites Gopher Jewels finds. To subscribe, address an e-mail message to `LISTPROC@einet.net` with `SUBSCRIBE GOPHERJEWELS@einet.net FIRSTNAME LASTNAME` in the body.

GOPHERJEWELS-TALK is an unmoderated list for Gopher users. You can ask and answer questions about using Gopher, finding information, or any other topic about Gopher clients, servers, or content. To subscribe, address your e-mail message to `LISTPROC@einet.net` with `SUBSCRIBE GOPHERJEWELS-TALK FIRSTNAME LASTNAME` in the body.

The NEWNIR-L moderated e-mail list reports the latest postings of new Gopher, telnet, FTP, WAIS, and WWW sites added to the WLU Netlink site. To subscribe, send a subscribe message to `NEWNIR-L-Request%ITOCSIVM.bitnet@icineca.cineca.it`.

The GOPHER-ANNOUNCE moderated list from the University of Minnesota announces new releases and updates of Gopher software. To subscribe, send a subscribe message to `Gopher-announce-request@boombox.micro.umn.edu`.

GOPHER-NEWS is an unmoderated list from the University of Minnesota for general Gopher discussion. To subscribe, send a message to `Gopher-news-request@boombox.micro.umn.edu`.

GO4LIB-L is an unmoderated list for librarians that emphasizes the technical aspects of Gopher implementation for libraries. To subscribe, send a subscribe message to `LISTSERV@UCSBVM` with `SUBSCRIBE GO4LIB-L FIRSTNAME LASTNAME` in the body.

Usenet newsgroups

The moderated `comp.infosystems.announce` group lists announcements related to Gopher, WAIS, WWW, and other Internet resources.

Although `comp.infosystems.gopher` was chartered as a general Gopher discussion list, it tends to be technically oriented from the system administrator's viewpoint.

The `alt.gopher` list has general discussion, questions, and answers. It's allegedly obsolete, but it still shows up on news servers.

Lee Stral is a Chicago-based freelance journalist and marketing communications consultant specializing in technology, computers, and the Internet. He has been on-line since the late '70s, when he forsook his TRS-80 model I for an Apple II and a 300-baud modem. Lately unkind rumors have spread across the Internet concerning his affinity for rodents. They are only partly true.

Squealing and Hissing: A Gopher Client Roundup

by Eric S. Theise, Ph.D. <verve@cyberwerks.com>

gopher n. 1. Any of various short tailed, burrowing mammals of the family Geomyidae, of North America. 2. (Amer. colloq.) Native or inhabitant of Minnesota: the Gopher State. 3. (Amer. colloq.) One who runs errands, does odd-jobs, fetches or delivers documents for office staff. 4. (computer tech.) software following a simple protocol for burrowing through a TCP/IP internet.

— Gopher protocol

Gopher's History

Until 1991, using the Internet was largely an exercise in telnet and ftp commands. You needed to log on to a remote library or database system. You had to remember the Internet address to telnet to, possibly a nonstandard port number, and its guest user ID and password before you could access the information you needed.

Then as now, once you were in, you were at the mercy of the system's unique peculiarities.

In order to access a specific document or image, you had to know which machine it was on and the Internet address to ftp to. Getting in wasn't a problem — the *anonymous* user ID, e-mail address password was standard — but then you had to find your way to the right file, remember to switch between text and binary mode depending on file type, and transfer it. If you were dialed up to your Internet provider, you had one more step ahead of you as you downloaded the file to your desktop computer.

Archie

By 1991 we saw the first significantly new Internet service: *Archie*. Written by Alan Emtage, Peter Deutsch, and Bill Heelan at McGill University, Archie was a program that cycled through all known anonymous ftp archives, gathering basic information about every file in their collections. Archie stored this information in a central database and allowed anyone on the Internet to search the database using the name of the file or directory where the file might be. Within months of its introduction, Internet life without Archie was unthinkable.

Gopher

It was around the same time that a team of staff, faculty, and students were developing some Internet-based tools for the campus-wide information system at the University of Minnesota. They made the important observation that every one in the world accessing an Internet resource had to execute exactly the same commands. Because the sequence of commands needed was complex but completely specified, it was a natural task to hand over to the unimaginative but trustworthy computer. The Gopher team hoped that by hiding strings of commands behind simple collections of menus, they could boost the ease-of-use factor for their cross-campus information resource. They couldn't have imagined the revolution they were about to spark when they made their collection of navigation tools available to the entire Internet through anonymous ftp.

Gopher has some nice features going for it. First and foremost, it is designed as an on-line browsing tool. Unlike ftp, whose behavior is geared towards experienced users who already know what's in a file and simply want to transfer it, Gopher is oriented towards newbies and curious visitors. Gopher is designed to be all-encompassing, supplementing its browsing capabilities with the capability to perform older tasks such as telnet, ftp, and finger. But instead of trying to build these tools anew, Gopher passes information about these sessions to tools already installed on the computer. This notion of helper applications and viewers continues to this day, and Gopher's insistence on using the best tool for the job is a hallmark of its approach.

On the technical side, Gopher is a *stateless* protocol. Simply put, when users make a selection from a Gopher menu, their Gopher clients send a compact message to the Gopher servers identifying what choice they made in the menu hierarchy. The server fires back another menu, the requested document, or whatever information is needed to satisfy the request.

Unlike telnet or ftp, where users log on and keep sessions open until they log off, Gopher relies on short bursts of comprehensive information transfers; the Gopher server gets everything it needs from the menu choice it's currently fielding. A server keeps no information about users as they read and ponder between choices. The Gopher client, installed at the users' end, keeps track of where they have been, organizing the information in a way that feels as if the user is logged on. It's an economical approach for both the server and the Internet.

With these powerful, no-cost new tools available, other universities were quick to adopt Gopher for their own campus-wide information systems. In the Net's spirit of sharing, they left their Gophers open to the world for browsing. As off-campus traffic grew, departments learned that Gopher could be used for publishing their own materials: campus events, working papers and preprints, recruiting information, and directory services.

Word spread. Gopher was easy to master for the users and for the system administrators. The number of Gopher servers climbed from the dozens into the hundreds, and from the hundreds into the thousands. Nothing like it had been seen before on the Internet.

Professional organizations, corporations, and nonprofits began to get into the act, attempting to make sense of all the information in Gopherspace. Steve Foster took the lessons learned from Archie, created a *Very Easy Rodent-Oriented Net-wide Index to Computerized Archives* (Veronica), and integrated the search tool directly into Gopherspace. Other projects such as the Internet Wiretap, the WELLgopher, the University of Michigan's Guide to Subject-Oriented Resources on the Internet, Calvin Boyer's PEG (Peripatetic, Eclectic Gopher), and David Riggins' Gopher Jewels saw the need for curated Gopherspaces, using Gopher's linking capabilities to assemble five-star menus made up of high-quality information resources located all over the Internet.

Gopher's devotees began to pressure the software developers for more features: Thus the Gopher+ protocol was born. Classic Gopher contained minimal information about the transactions that needed to take place — Internet host, port number, Gopher type, resource path, and so on. Gopher+ allowed for item abstracts, alternative views of the same item (multiple languages or multiple file formats), the capability to include information about when an item was last modified and by whom, plus interactive features for inputting data (ASK Blocks) and authentication (Admit One).

During Gopher's period of exponential growth, the World Wide Web was a rickety technology test. But by 1994, with the success of the graphical browser (Mosaic) and the dramatically diverse range of information becoming available, the Web moved into its current position as premiere Internet information space. Gopher was subsumed into the backward-looking world of URLs. The rush to put up a home page for every identifiable person, place, and thing began in earnest.

Is Gopher a pre-Web has-been? I argue no. There's a certain crisp rationality to Gopher's menus that's lacking in the free-range aesthetic of the World Wide Web's multimedia hypertext. The predominance of simple ASCII text makes Gopher a speedy tool for information retrieval. Its flexibility in allowing users to configure their own helper applications for accessing images, sounds, and HTML brings it into the multimedia world of the mid-1990s Internet. And even if you *think* you've been drawn to the Internet because of the World Wide Web, you're here because Gopher's revolutionary ease of use — for users *and* system administrators — paved the way for the Internet becoming the household word it is today.

What To Expect from Your Gopher Client

Your Gopher client is the window through which you view a great portion of the Internet. In this section, you read about the features found in today's clients. You won't read about commercial clients, like Spry's Air Gopher or Notis's WinGopher, and you won't read about the Gopher clients built into various Web browsers. Even if you consider yourself a Gopher poweruser, you'll probably make some surprising discoveries.

Consider what features a Gopher client should provide for you to make it truly useful:

- First and foremost, a Gopher client has to allow you to *burrow through Gopher menus.* This feature includes moving through the choices offered within a particular menu, line by line and screen by screen. It includes making a selection from a menu and backing out to earlier menus once you've completed a choice.
- You should be able to *search within your current menu,* as in the case when you're faced with a list of over 2,200 Gopher servers and you want to see all the ones whose name contains *zine*.
- You should be able to find out where you are, which Gopher server holds the information you're accessing, and be able to view Gopher+ attributes if available.

- Because you will occasionally pop into the middle of a Gopher through a link or the result of a Veronica search, you should be able to trace up through a Gopher above the level where you entered. Recent progress makes it possible to periscope up to the top of another Gopher, but this feature is still not completely satisfactory.
- When you select an item, you want to be able to display it immediately. In the case of non-ASCII text, images, sounds, movies, or alternative Gopher+ views, immediate viewing requires an external helper or viewer application. This gets you into the realm of Gopher types, which is the first digression (see the sidebar entitled "Gopher Types"). Your Gopher client should make it easy to install, configure, use, and upgrade these helpers.
- You should also be able to change your mind, cleanly canceling a request when the network is slow or when you've bitten off more than you can chew.
- You should be able to make copies of useful items that you find, either by saving the item itself (as a file, e-mail message, or hardcopy) or by creating a pointer to the item so that you can find your way back at some future time to see whether anything new has been added. Your client should support some form of bookmarks — essentially a collection of invaluable Gopher menus that you collect yourself — making it easy for you to add, delete, and use these references.
- You should be able to customize your Gopher client, telling it which Gopher server to connect to by default, how your screen looks, what printer or download protocol you use, and more.

Tall order? Not with the clients you read about next.

Gopher types

Everything that appears in a Gopher menu is assigned a Gopher type by the server's administrator, the Studly Gophermeister. The Gopher type tells the client what to do when that item is selected. Each Gopher client does *something* to help you identify the type of item you're dealing with (appending tags to items like <BIN> or <?> in text-only clients or prepending a special icon in graphical clients). The figures for each client reviewed in this chapter include a dummy menu containing all the Gopher types.

The Gopher types are

0 A file, typically an ASCII document; expect it to be displayed on screen.

1 A directory; expect another menu.

2 A CSO phone book server; expect to be queried for a person's name.

3 An error.

4 A Macintosh BinHex file; expect it to be transferred, not displayed.

5 A DOS ZIP or other archive file; expect it to be transferred, not displayed.

6 A UNIX uuencoded file; expect it to be transferred, not displayed.

7 A search item; expect to be queried for a relevant search string.

8 A telnet session; expect to be told a user ID and password, if needed, and then handed off to the telnet program installed on your computer.

(continued)

(continued)

9 A binary file, such as a compressed UNIX file; expect it to be transferred, not displayed.

T A tn3270 session; expect to be told a user ID and password, if needed, and then handed off to the tn3270 program installed on your computer (tn3270 is a telnet session that uses the screen format of the IBM 3270 terminal, common on some on-line library systems).

s A sound file; expect it to be transferred, and then played by a helper application.

g A GIF file; expect it to be transferred, and then displayed by a helper application.

M A MIME file; expect it to be transferred, and then displayed by a helper application.

h A file containing Hypertext Markup Language (HTML); expect it to be transferred, and then displayed by a helper application.

I An image file; expect it to be transferred, and then displayed by a helper application.

i An inline text type; used to suppress item numbers in text-only clients.

You can spend a lot of time in Gopherspace and never come across all of these types, but the protocol defines them, and you can probably imagine uses for all of them.

Gopher+

gopher+ n. 1. Hardier strains of mammals of the family Geomyidae. 2. (Amer. colloq.) Native or inhabitant of Minnesota, the Gopher state, in full winter regalia (see PARKA). 3. (Amer. colloq.) Executive secretary. 4. (computer tech.) Software following a simple protocol for burrowing through a TCP/IP Internet, made more powerful by simple enhancements (see CREEPING FEATURISM).

— Gopher+ specification

Gopher+ is a set of enhancements to the original Gopher protocol. All Gopher clients and servers still support the original Gopher specification, but if your client speaks Gopher+ and a Gopher server has these features enabled, you have access to additional information. Gopher+ includes fields for the following:

+INFO The item descriptor.

+ADMIN The name of the system administrator and the date of the item's last modification.

+VIEWS A list of different formats in which the item can be retrieved — text/plain and application/PostScript for formatted documents or En_US and De_DE for English and German versions of the same menu choice — plus an optional file size.

+ABSTRACT A concise description of the item, capable of spanning multiple lines.

The Gopher+ specification also includes the capability to answer interactive queries via fill-in-the-blank dialog boxes called ASK blocks, the capability to better deliver pictures, sounds, and movies, and the capability to do password authentication. The University of Minnesota's Mother of All Gophers has a menu devoted to Gopher+ items with which you can experiment (gopher://mudhoney.micro.umn.edu:70/11/gplustest).

At its core, Gopher+ was developed to address the most basic question on the Internet: *What's the quality of the information I'm reading?* These additional fields are designed to tell you who put the information in place, when, and — in the case of a long document — what it contains.

It's a neat idea, but not as widely implemented as you might hope.

Which Gopher Client Should You Use?

Enough background. Which Gopher client should you use to make your end of the connection as powerful as possible?

The big split depends on your connection to the Internet. If you're using a standard VT100 terminal emulation program — Procomm, Qmodem, Telix, Zterm, Microphone II, Kermit — to dial up an account with a university or commercial Internet provider, you use the University of Minnesota's UNIX/VMS text-only Gopher client.

If you're sitting in front of a computer that's directly connected to the Internet — either through a leased line or a dialup SLIP or PPP connection — you have a choice of graphical clients for your particular make of computer. Because these clients were developed with your computer's capabilities in mind, they behave like your other applications. You can cut and paste, save items to files without an explicit download, print, and use helper applications installed on your desktop to view graphics and listen to soundfiles.

You'll read about clients for the most popular platforms. One of the surprising discoveries is that the clients available for exotic platforms — X Window and the NeXT — are lacking in contemporary Gopher features; you're better off using a current UNIX client. The most powerful client available, WSGopher, runs in Windows, the one-time third choice for navigating the Internet.

Text-based clients

Almost everyone who's been on the Internet for any length of time has some exposure to the University of Minnesota's text-only Gopher client. I devote a great deal of energy to it here because it's the bellwether of Gopher clients. I also mention the text-only PC_client for DOS.

UNIX and Vax/VMS: The University of Minnesota

Installed on every commercial Internet provider and countless university systems, the University of Minnesota's text-based UNIX/VMS client is by far the most popular. As I write this, version 2.1.1 has just become available. Just so you know, version 1 went as high as 1.13, version 2.0 to 2.016. Even though I am a Gopher geek, I'm not going to detail the differences between versions.

I recommend that you determine what version your provider has installed — the version number appears in the window title (see Figure 23-13) — and politely contact your system administrator if the version you're using is far from current. A whip around the Net shows version 2.005 on Netcom, 2.011 on The WELL, and 2.016 on The Meta Network. A major chunk of Liberty Hill Cyberwerks' mission is state-of-the-art Internet education; we keep up to date, and I use version 2.1.1 in this discussion.

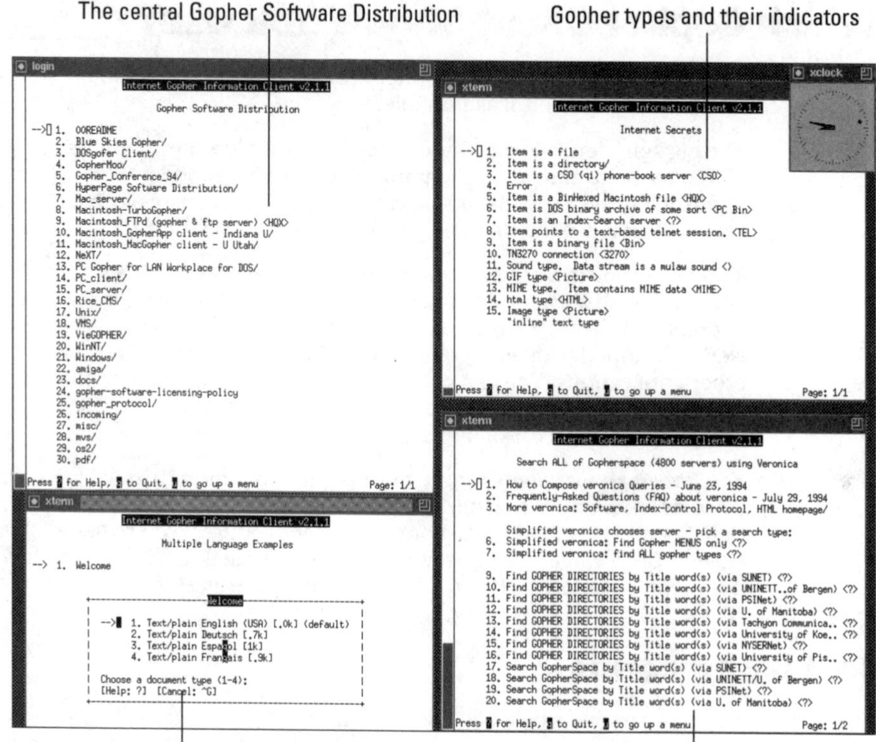

Figure 23-13: Four X Window instances of the University of Minnesota's UNIX Gopher client.

Basic features

How do you get started? Type **$ gopher**

Using your arrow keys is the simplest way to begin navigating. The following minitable shows some basic movement keys:

Key Sequence	*Purpose*
Up- and Down-arrow keys (k and j, or Ctrl-p and Ctrl-n)	Moves you up and down within the current menu; you can also go directly to a choice by entering its number.
Right-arrow key (or l, or Ctrl-j)	Selects an item from the current menu, taking you deeper into the menus.
Left-arrow key (or h, or Ctrl-b)	Moves you to the previous menu.
> (or +, PageDown, or Space)	Moves you quickly forward through screenfuls of menus.

Key Sequence	Purpose
< (or –, PageUp, or b)	Moves you quickly backward through screenfuls of menus.
m	Moves to your Gopher's main menu.
Q	Quits Gopher unconditionally.
q	Quits Gopher with a *Really quit?* message.
?	Provides help. This is the best way to find the complete list of commands available in the version you're using.

Advanced features

Those are the basics. What else can you do?

You can do a case-insensitive search within the current level of menus by typing / and entering a text fragment into the dialog box. You can repeat the search by typing **n**. Although you don't have to search this way when there are only one or two screenfuls of items, it's an excellent strategy when you're faced with thousands of Gopher servers and you only want the ones with *triticeae* in their names.

If you know the Internet address of a particular Gopher server, you can connect to it directly by typing **o** and filling in the dialog box. By default, the Port number is 70, the Gopher standard, and the Selector (the path to the particular item) is blank. So if you just wanted to connect to the WELLgopher, you enter gopher.well.com as the Hostname. If you wanted to connect to the United States Government Gophers section of Calvin Boyer's PEG (a Peripatetic, Eclectic Gopher), you enter peg.cwis.uci.edu as the Hostname, 7000 as the Port, and 1/gopher.welcome/peg/GOPHERS/gov as the Selector. You can also do both of these from the UNIX prompt by typing:

```
$ gopher gopher.well.com
```

or

```
$ gopher -p 1/gopher.welcome/peg/GOPHERS/gov peg.cwis.uci.edu 7000
```

You won't want or need to do this very often, but you'll occasionally see pointers in e-mail or on USENET that you want to investigate further.

Bookmarks

Should you like what you find — through this or your other Gopherspace excursions — you can save its location using Gopher's bookmark features. *Bookmarks* allow you to create your own personal menu of Gopher favorites. By typing **a**, you can add the current item. Typing **A** adds the current directory or search. You can view your bookmark collection by typing **v**, and you can clean house — delete — with **d**. It is difficult to retrace your steps to a resource; bookmarks are a Gopher innovation that allow you to mark your place in cyberspace.

Copying information

If you want to make a personal copy of something you've discovered using Gopher — a document, a program, an image, or a sound file — you can save a copy to the current directory of your computer by using the **s** command. You can also save a copy of the text in the current menu by using the **S** command.

If you're sitting in front of a UNIX computer directly connected to the Internet, or if you want the file saved to your dialup Internet service provider, s and S are appropriate choices. But if your access is via dialup and you want the file on your personal computer, you need to use the download command, **D**. After typing **D**, you get a dialog box offering you a range of protocol options (Zmodem, Ymodem, Xmodems, Kermit, and Text); pick the one that's best for your telecom program, wait for the *Start your download now ...* message, and then begin the download sequence on your personal computer (probably a Receive File menu choice on a Windows or Macintosh program, PageDown on a DOS program).

You can also e-mail a document you're currently reading to any valid e-mail address by typing **m** and then keying the address into the dialog box.

Printing files

If you're dialed up to your Internet provider, the only way to print something is to download it and print it from your desktop's print application or word processor. If you're using a UNIX computer that's connected to a printer, the **p** command prints the current item. The O option allows you to set printer and other environment options.

Accessing other servers

University of Minnesota's Gopher client also lets you access anonymous ftp and World Wide Web servers, using the **f** and **w** commands. Like **o**, **f** requires you to key in the address of the anonymous ftp host and, optionally, a Selector. You can use Gopher to get a copy of Fetch, the Macintosh ftp tool, by entering ftp.dartmouth.edu as the host and /pub/mac as the Selector. Although using Gopher in this way can be slower and less reliable than ftp, it gives you the advantage of navigating through the ftp server using menus instead of a sequence of change directory, list, and get commands. And Gopher is smart enough to recognize file extensions that require binary transfers.

Using Gopher with the World Wide Web can be equally straightforward if lynx or WWW is installed on your system. You may encounter an HTML file in a menu, or you may use the **w** command and type a URL. You should find yourself in lynx or WWW; if you don't, and one or both are installed on your system, your system administrators probably installed Gopher with the off-the-Net configuration. Suggest that they find the #define HTML_COMMAND in the Gopher conf.h file, comment out the *- none -* line, and uncomment either the *lynx -force_html %s* or *www* lines.

Features used with Veronica

Four other commands are especially useful when you're using Veronica to do a search. These include the r and R commands — which take you to the root, or top, menu of the Gopher you are in, and the = and ^ commands, which give you link information about the current item and directory. You'll read more about these commands and the information they provide later in the article.

There's the Ctrl-L (or Ctrl-R, or Ctrl-W) command, which refreshes your screen if things get screwy, and the Ctrl-T command, which gives you the Gopher server's local time. There's the **g** command, which lets you send a gripe to a Gopher+ administrator via e-mail; you are popped into a dialog box to key in a message Subject and Problem description. And last but not least, there's Ctrl-C, which is the best way to cancel a request-gone-bad. You'll get the *Really quit?* message, to which you should answer no, and you can continue burrowing.

DOS: PC_client

At the other end of the spectrum is PC_client, the University of Minnesota's minimally-featured Gopher pup that's appropriate for low-end, non-Windows PCs.

PC_client comes in two self-extracting archives: pc3binx.exe (the program) and pc3docx.exe (the documentation). It's programmed in Borland's TurboVision and is pretty sprightly, but it lacks a help system (even now, in version 1.12!) and the capability to use helper applications. Setup is trivial if you're already running the Crynwr packet drivers. Just choose Network from the Configuration menu and enter the relevant information about your network.

Graphical clients

Graphical clients are generally platform-specific. Developed for the type of computer you're using, they behave like your other applications. Burrowing is as simple as point and double-click. You can print, cut and paste, and save items to files without an explicit download. You also can use helper applications installed on your desktop to view graphics, hear sound files, and more.

Macintosh

There are three Macintosh Gopher clients in common use: the University of Minnesota's TurboGopher 2.0b5 (December 1994), Don Gilbert's GopherApp++/2.2b43 (December 1993), and the University of Utah's MacGopher 0.5b14 (November 1992). Although Internet applications for the Mac have usually led Windows, none of the Mac clients supports a root command, used to take you to the top of a Gopher whose hierarchy you've popped into at a lower level.

You'll want a good collection of helper-applications no matter which client you use. Use your favorite anonymous ftp tool to connect to the University of Minnesota's collection on boombox.micro.umn.edu, change directories to pub/gopher/Macintosh-TurboGopher/helper-applications, get copies of any software you don't currently have installed on your machine, and break your connection. It may take a bit of Net sleuthing with Anarchie to find the current versions of all the helpers you want, but it's a start-up ritual that you don't have to repeat very often. I typically create a helper-applications folder in my Internet tools folder and put everything in there. If a helper-application proves to be useful as a stand-alone tool, I migrate it up to my desktop.

TurboGopher 2.0b5

Turbogopher n. 1. A small rodent with a turbocharger strapped on its back to increase its speed and ferocity. 2. (Amer. colloq.) Native or inhabitant of Minnesota after consuming three double espressos. 3. (Amer. colloq.) An Olympic sprinter who runs errands, does odd-jobs, fetches or delivers documents for office staff. 4. (computer tech.) Speed-optimized Macintosh software following a simple protocol for burrowing through a TCP/IP Internet; network speed is achieved by using turbocharged software; incoming bits spin the turbine that pumps out the outgoing bits.

—TurboGopher Help file

The University of Minnesota's TurboGopher has always been the most fun client to use. I'm partial to the cartoon Gopher in the splash screen, and the waddling Gopher that appears when the client is receiving information over a slow connection. Figure 23-14 shows the TurboGopher splash screen. The TurboGopher is as fast as its name suggests, and it's dependable and reasonably robust. You can install it thirty seconds before a large public demo and it doesn't let you down (he says knowingly).

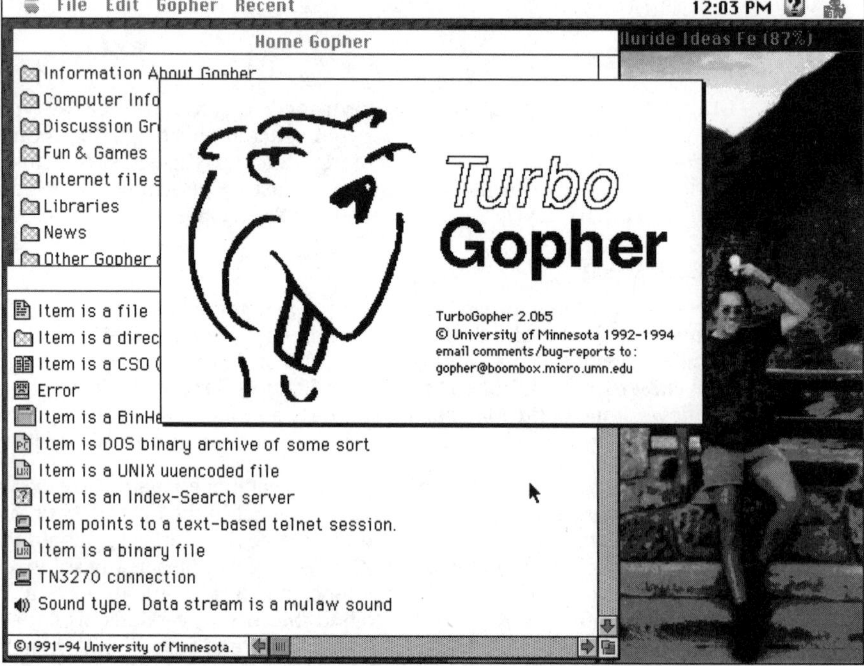

Figure 23-14: The TurboGopher splash screen and a specially concocted menu showing the full range of Gopher type icons.

TurboGopher is available via anonymous ftp from the pub/Gopher directory of boombox.micro.umn.edu; get TurboGopher2.0b5.sea.hqx and extract it into your Internet tools folder. System 7 is required for current versions of TurboGopher (older versions are still available) and if you're running something earlier than System 7.5, you have to drop the included Thread Manager into your Extensions folder and restart your Mac.

To make the best use of TurboGopher, make one pass through the Preferences option (on the Gopher menu) to check the correspondence of Gopher+ Helper Applications to software that's actually installed on your Mac. You'll at least want to verify that the version number and the version installed are the same. You may want to add or change helpers — ask TurboGopher to call a PowerPC version, or have Netscape arrive on the scene instead of MacWeb when it's time to view a Web page.

While you're in Preferences, you can also change the default Home Server (the start-up Gopher), the screen font, and the default download directory. Check the Help file (also on the Gopher menu) for other configuration and usage tips such as converting bookmarks from version 1.0.x to version 2.0.x.

TurboGopher-specific features include the capability to use the first few letters of an item in a menu to close in on it, and the capability to use the standard Find and Find Same commands in menus or documents. The Recent menu keeps track of the last 50 things you've seen, allowing you to quickly return to an item or menu. You can use the control key and a single mouse click to display the full link information for an item: host, port, selector, URL, and Gopher+ attributes. You can also get this information using the Get Attribute Information and URL command on the Gopher menu. Other less-frequently needed navigation aids are described in the Help file.

TurboGopher also supports a Bookmark Worksheet, and lets you do things like connecting to another gopher or using a uniform resource locator to connect to a full variety of Internet resources. And TurboGopher offers a few escapes for sluggish networks. You can either background a slow request and continue with other work — including another request if you dare — or you can abort the transfer by selecting Cancel Network Request from the menu or using the standard command key-period combination.

You can't go wrong with TurboGopher.

GopherApp++/2.2b43

Don Gilbert is best known for his efforts in building tools and promoting Internet use for biologists. He developed an independent version of WAIS that incorporated Boolean searching, and his IUBio Gopher (at Indiana University) remains one of the primary resources for biologists on the Net. His Gopher client, GopherApp++, pushed the state-of-the-art when it debuted in 1992, and even today it has features not found in other clients, including a built-in mail application. Its depth may be its undoing, as it's the buggiest of the clients reviewed here.

To get your own copy of GopherApp, use your favorite anonymous ftp tool to connect to ftp.bio.indiana.edu, change directories to /util /gopher/gopherapp, and get gopherapp++2.2b43.hqx.

GopherApp begins by offering you a menu including the IUBio Gopher, the University of Minnesota's Gopher, and Stanford's Info Mac archives. The first thing you should do is reduce the default size of the menu icons from large to medium. Choose Internet, and then View prefs. Figure 23-15 shows GopherApp's About screen.

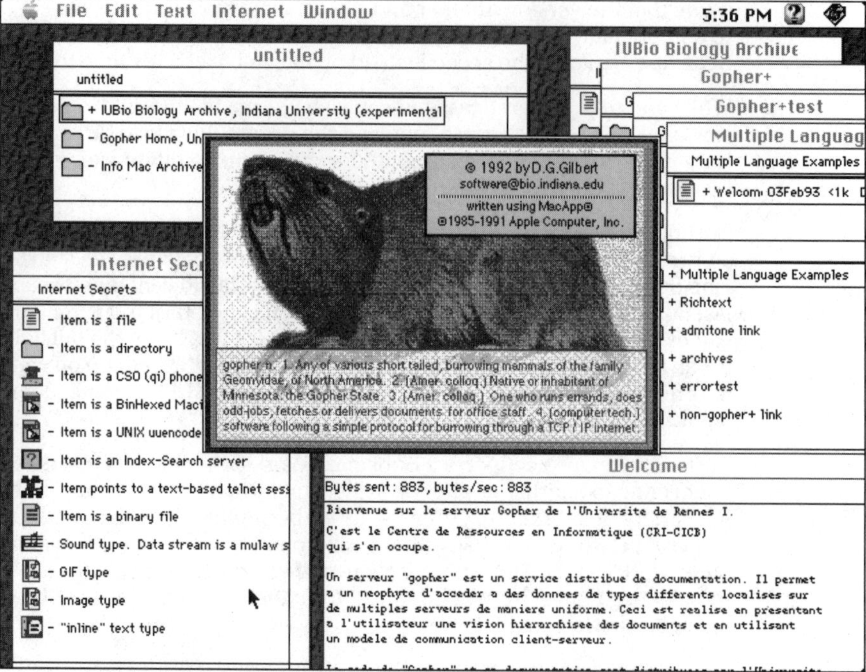

Figure 23-15: GopherApp's zoologically-correct About screen, with Gopher type icons and a Welcome message in French, selected from the Open link by View menu.

Note that while you're here, you can also set GopherApp to display the Date, Size, Kind, Path, Host, and Port associated with every menu item. Remember that the interesting ones work only with Gopher+ servers where these attributes have been filled in by a dutiful administrator. The Date and Size fields are shown by default. You can also modify the order of menu items with the View links option.

GopherApp's opening menu points to three of the most information-packed resources on the Internet, but you'll eventually want to go directly to another Gopher. GopherApp makes you add an icon to the opening menu to do this; choose Internet, New Gopher hole, and fill in the Title, Host, and optional Gopher+, and Port Number. You can save your modified menu using the Save As command, and retrieve it with the Open command, both on the File menu.

The Help feature is well organized, and you should be sure to configure the mail application (on Internet, Mail setup) before using it.

I've used GopherApp on and off over the years and have been impressed with the concept, less so with its implementation. On the Cyberwerks' 7100/66/AV, it was difficult to keep it from crashing during many routine operations. Don't install it as your primary Gopher client.

MacGopher 0.5b14

Rhett "Jonzy" Jones, best known for creating the Jughead search tool, has also created a Macintosh Gopher client. Developed at the Computer Center of the University of Utah, MacGopher offers yet another view of Gopherspace and makes room for Internet services besides Gopher. MacGopher gracefully handles network errors, provides helpful error messages, and crashes noticeably less than other clients.

MacGopher is available through anonymous ftp from ftp.cc.utah.edu in the /pub/gopher/Macintosh directory; along with MacGopher.sit.hqx, get gTelnet2.5.sit.hqx and tn3270.sit.hqx (modified versions of NCSA Telnet and tn3270).

MacGopher's distinguishing characteristic is its horizontal layout of Gopher menus (see Figure 23-16). As you navigate up and down through menu hierarchies, new levels are displayed from left to right, and you always have a clear view of the current menu and its parent. This view will be familiar to NeXT users. The Item Inspector, used to get the Gopher classic half of the link information, is on the Window menu. The Gopher+ half can be brought up with Get Attributes in the Gopher+ menu, and you can summon a menu of alternative views with Get Views.

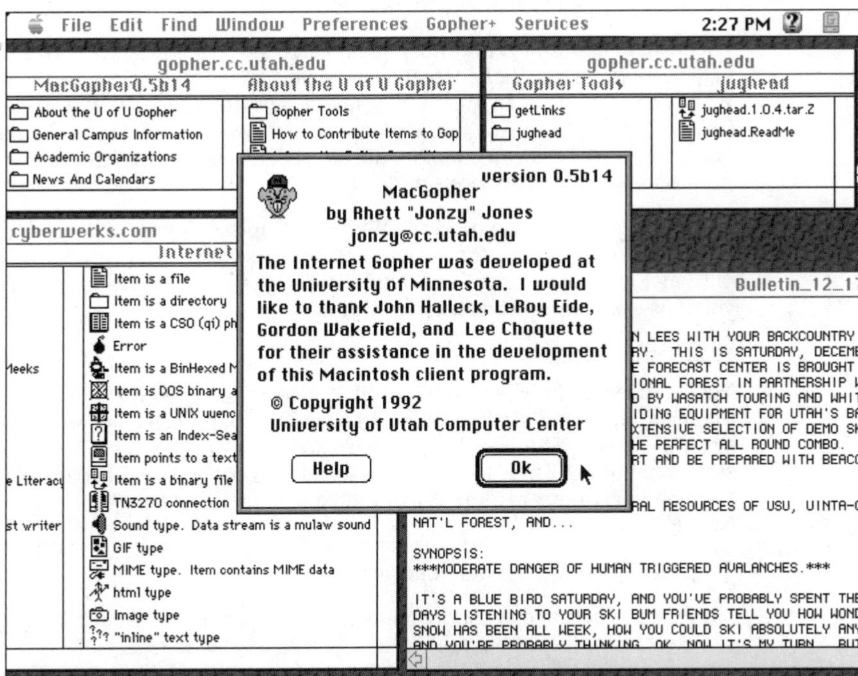

Figure 23-16: MacGopher. The upper windows show the top-level U of U Gopher menu and MacGopher's horizontal approach to displaying menus. The lower-left window shows MacGopher's Gopher type icons, and the lower-right shows a current Utah avalanche forecast bulletin.

The Preferences menu lets you set your default Gopher in Gopher prefs and set a surprisingly small number of helper applications in File Creator Prefs.

The File menu options include New Gopher (a session with the Gopher Prefs Gopher) or Open Gopher, which prompts you for a Hostname and Port. It's possible to use Save Session As for later retrieval with Load Session, but it seems better to save references as bookmarks by choosing Make Bookmark from the Preferences menu. Your bookmark collection is then listed at the bottom of the Preferences menu.

There's a good Help feature, describing all the menu choices, available from MacGopher's About screen or from its Apple menu. A MacGopher-specific feature, never fully implemented, is to include other Internet services in the Services menu. ftp and Mail are grayed out, but the finger service works nicely.

MacGopher is a little behind the times and should not be your first choice of client for the Macintosh, even though its robust error handling is appealing.

Windows

Before the WinSock standard was introduced, Windows applications for the Internet were pretty pathetic compared to what was available for the Macintosh. Thankfully, that's changing, and the most powerful Gopher client available today — WSGopher — is a Windows program.

Windows makes it possible, no, *preferable*, to associate file extensions with viewer/helper applications. Rather than customizing each of your Gopher clients (and your Web browsers) you can tell Windows to always use, say, LVIEW31 when it hits a GIF, JPE, or JPG file. From File Manager, select Associate from the File menu. It's a one-time chore to key in common file extensions and browse through your installed programs to select your preferred helpers.

You'll take a look at two powerful Windows Gopher clients: WSGopher and HGopher. You'll see Boston College's BCGopher v.0.8B and the Chinese University of Hong Kong's WGopher 2.2 around the Net; they're sound, but the current versions don't offer nearly enough features.

WSGopher 1.2

Nestled deep in the 97 extended Gopher views supported by WSGopher are entries for smell/funky and tactile/touch. Either the Gopherspace engineers have some big surprises in store for everyone or there are some programmers in Idaho with goofy senses of humor. They are Dave Brooks and his cohorts at the Idaho National Engineering Laboratory, creators of the most advanced GUI Gopher client on the Net.

To get a copy of WSGopher, follow these steps:

1. Fire up your favorite anonymous ftp tool, connect to dewey.tis.inel.gov, change directories to pub/wsgopher, and get the wsg-12.exe file.
2. Create a directory for it on your own computer — I used \NET\WSGOPHER — and type wsg-12; it's a self-extracting archive.

3. From the Program Manager window, choose New, Program Item, and then browse your directory structure until you get to wsgopher.exe; OK your way out, and click the WSGopher icon.
4. You'll find yourself looking at the University of Illinois at Urbana-Champaign's Gopher. Figure 23-17 shows an example screen. Note the extensive toolbar, the set of unique Gopher type icons, and the ratty, baseball-capped WSGopher logo.

You can change this to your Gopher of choice by choosing Configure, Home Gopher Server, and entering its Internet address.

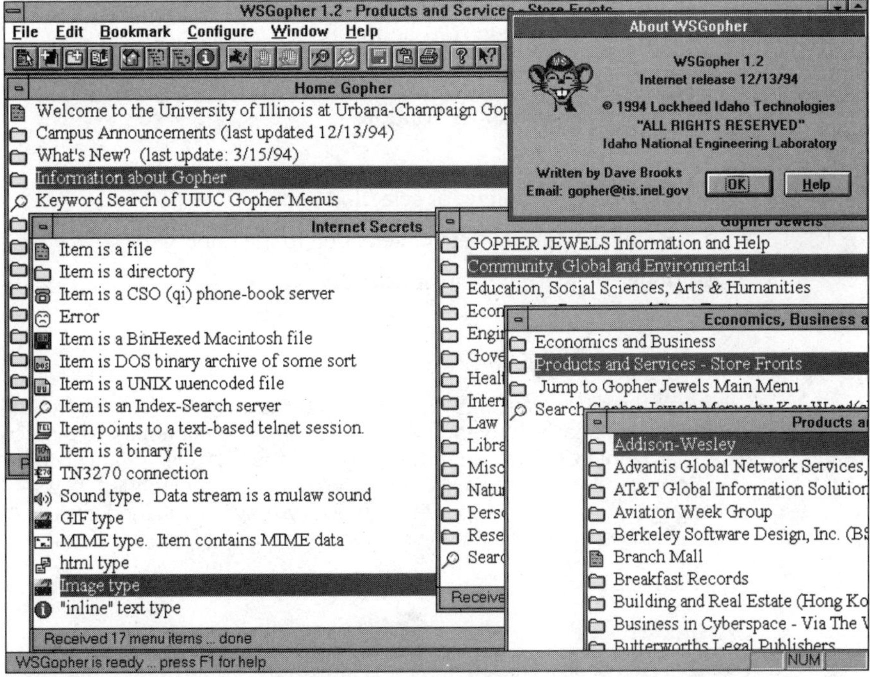

Figure 23-17: Dave Brooks' WSGopher and a peek at Gopher Jewels (gopher://cwis.usc.edu:70/11/Other_Gophers_and_Information_Resources/Gophers_by_Subject/Gopher_Jewels).

Although the menus give you access to all navigation and configuration tools, the toolbar simplifies many common operations. The icons are small and not always intuitive but clicking the farthest right Context Help button — a question mark with an arrow — and then clicking another button takes you to the Help page for that tool. Context Help works anywhere in a WSGopher screen. You should make one pass across the toolbar for yourself, but the buttons include:

- Fetching Bookmark Menu
- Adding Item Bookmarks
- Adding Directory Bookmarks
- Using Bookmark Editor
- Visiting your Home Gopher
- Going to the top of the Gopher outline
- Backtracking one level in the Gopher outline
- Finding Information on a Gopher item
- Fetching a Gopher item
- Canceling the current transaction
- Canceling all transactions
- Finding text in a Gopher Window
- Finding text again
- Saving the current item or selection to disk
- Copying the current item or selection to the Clipboard
- Printing the current item or selection
- About WSGopher
- Getting context help

Some of the more amazing WSGopher features include a nested, by-subject framework for bookmarks to help you get organized, the capability to periscope up to the top of a visited Gopher (Go to the top), and the very clean Cancel commands. WSGopher comes with sensible ordering of Gopher+ extended views — but lets you change your rankings — and virtually everything is explained, clearly, through extensive help screens.

It's the best.

HGopher 2.4

Martyn Hampson's HGopher 2.4 was king of the Windows Gopher clients before WSGopher. It was so good that FTP Software licensed it and pulled it from the Net to pursue commercial development. Right or wrong, some ftp archives still carry 2.4, although the official public domain release dropped back to version 2.3.

The definitive anonymous ftp site for HGopher is lister.cc.ic.ac.uk, in the pub/wingopher directory. While you're there, rummage through the collection of helper applications in the viewers subdirectory. The Gopher server at gopher.ic.ac.uk has a link to the ftp server under Networking, HGopher Information Centre, The HGopher distribution and viewers, and includes HGopher materials not found at the ftp site, including a FAQ, a feature assault course, and a playground. It makes sense for client developers to offer companion servers for users to test their installations; this is a good one.

HGopher takes a little getting used to. Figure 23-18 shows its icons. To navigate, double-click the words. To get item information, double-click the icon in the column to the left of the words, and to get information about Gopher+ views, click the icon at the far left, if one appears. And the central icon at the bottom right of the window indicates whether you're in view, copy to file, or copy to directory mode. All of this is explained through HGopher's excellent Help facilities, but it's different enough from other clients to be confusing, even constricting, at first.

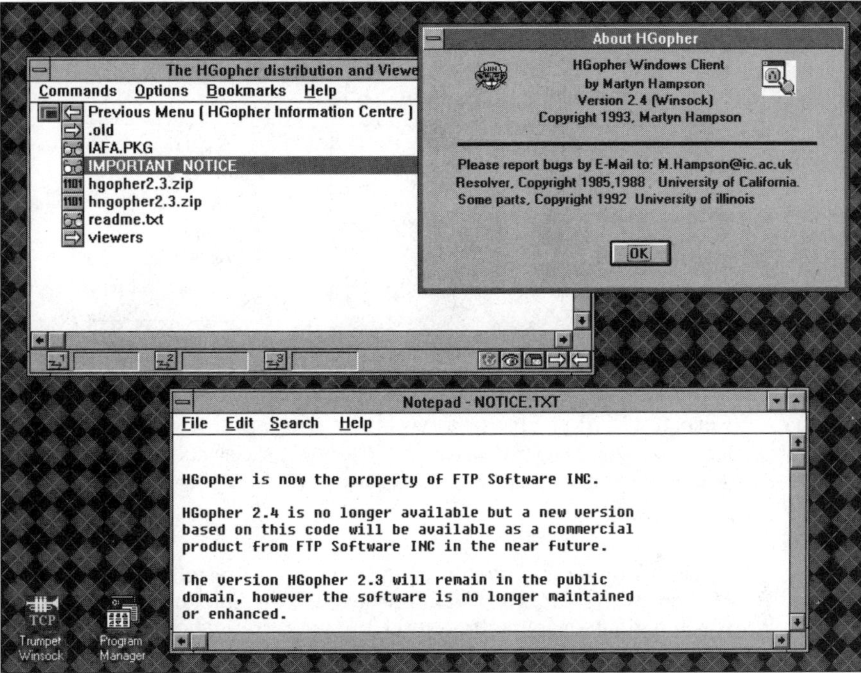

Figure 23-18: The many icons of HGopher.

Macintosh and Windows: PNLInfoBrowser 1.05

Pacific Northwest Laboratory (PNL) has recently released a Gopher client for the Macintosh and Windows that's Gopher+ from the ground up. Figure 23-19 shows the PNLInfoBrowser. By default, it displays Gopher+ abstracts, offering a view of Gopherspace that's closer to a Web browser than other Gopher clients. Its powerful subscription and find features aren't included in any other Gopher client, and the Macish interface looks identical on a Windows desktop.

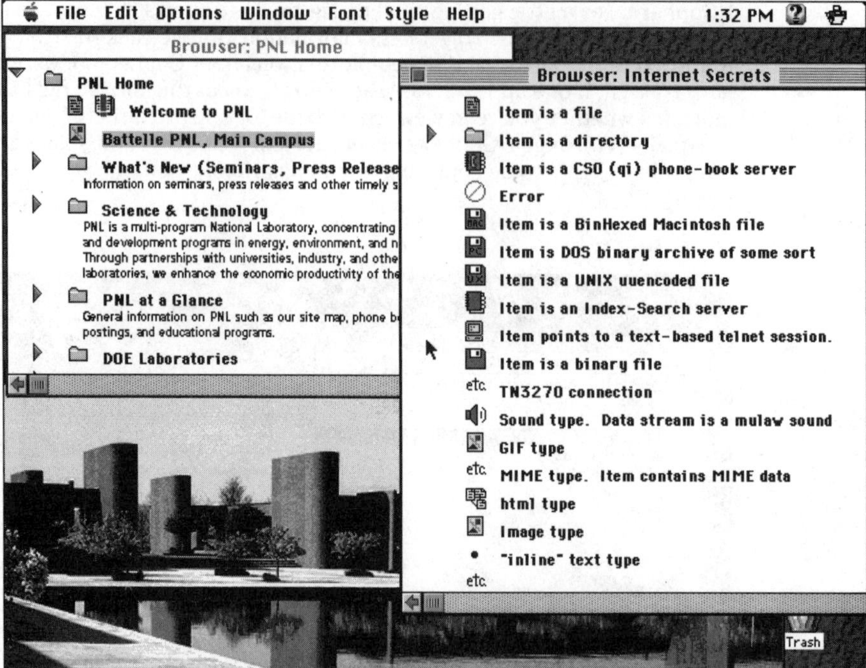

Figure 23-19: PNLInfoBrowser's view of their home Gopher+ server, with the full range of Gopher icons. I've subscribed to Welcome to PNL, and the exclamation mark tells me that a new version is available. PNL's main campus is displayed in the background.

PNLInfoBrowser is available using anonymous ftp from ftp.pnl.gov in /pub/pnlinfo. Mac users will want the PNLInfoBrowser105.sea.hqx in the MAC directory (note to the impatient: drop infobrws_pref into your Preferences folder). Windows users want the ib105.exe file in the WIN directory (note to the impatient: move xwi320.dll and xwi320te.dll to the \WINDOWS\SYSTEM directory, and copy INFOBRWS.INI to \WINDOWS). Other guidelines are in the readme file included with each distribution.

PNLInfoBrowser comes with good built-in Help topics, and selecting Show Tutorial from the File menu delivers you over the Net to PNL's Gopher+ server for a live feature tour. On Options, you'll find General Setup, where you can set the Home browser (the start-up Gopher) and the Viewer Setup, where you can change/add preferred helper applications. You can also shut off the Verify Quit option.

To connect to an arbitrary Gopher, use the Show Other option and key or paste its Internet address into the Server: dialog box (Name, Port, and Selector are optional). You can retrieve link information about a selected item by choosing About This Item from the File menu, and you can add a bookmark by choosing New Bookmark. Managing bookmarks is straightforward when you select Show Bookmarks.

PNLInfoBrowser includes a novel feature called subscriptions. Related to bookmarks, subscriptions use the Gopher+ ADMIN tag to determine whether you've read the most recent version of an item. To subscribe to an item, you select it, and then choose Subscribe from the Edit menu. A red exclamation mark icon appears between the item's Gophér type icon and its description, showing that you haven't yet read the latest version. If you view it now, the mark disappears, only to return if you choose Show Subscriptions and PNLInfoBrowser notices that a new version has become available. Neat. It currently works only with items, not directories, but the Help entry suggests that this may change.

Another neat feature is PNLInfoBrowser's Find. You might expect this — on the File menu — to perform a search of the current menu or document, but instead it gives you the capability to search Internet meta-information sources: the InterNIC Directory of Directories, the University of Minnesota's collection of Gopher titles, and a Jughead-based collection of servers. Multiple search words may be ANDed or ORed together, and this facility is the one to use if you know a service's name, but not its address.

This is the Gopher client to watch. Highly recommended.

X Window and NeXT

My early years of Gopherspace-cruising came through dialup access and the UNIX text-based client. With the founding of my consultancy, Liberty Hill Cyberwerks, came more and better equipment, and with *Internet SECRETS* came an excuse to finally install and evaluate the X Window (xgopher) and NeXT (gopher, and the three-dimensional visualization tool, Tree) clients. I was excited.

Then I was disappointed. Although all three have intriguing interfaces, they're all a generation behind the capabilities of the plain old UNIX client. I can't really recommend them.

OS/2, Amiga, and others

Gopher client software for other platforms is available through the University of Minnesota's main Gopher, or in the anonymous ftp server in boombox.micro.umn.edu. You'll find clients for VM/CMS and MVS mainframes, the Amiga, and OS/2. For better or worse, testing these is beyond the capabilities of today's Liberty Hill Cyberwerks.

Searching the World of Gopherspace: Veronica

Tunneling up and down Gopher menus is an excellent introduction to the fine art of Internet navigation. Seeing what various organizations have decided to offer is a great way to develop your appreciation for the range of what is and isn't available on the Internet. But sooner or later, you're going to lose your focus on place, and you're going to want to find information based on content, or subject. That's where *Veronica,* the Gopherspace search tool, fits into the picture.

Gopher's introduction and initial growth came at a time when the Internet was still rejoicing over the introduction of Archie, the search tool for finding anonymous ftp files. Steven Foster at the University of Nevada — Reno, sensing the need for a similar tool for Gopher, created Veronica: his Very Easy Rodent-Oriented Net-wide Index of Computerized Archives. Rather than being a separate tool, Veronica is an integral part of Gopherspace and is available anywhere you see a menu item saying Search titles in Gopherspace using Veronica.

Veronica works by doing a complete harvest of every menu in every public Gopher in the world, typically once every week or two. It attempts to strip duplicate entries out of the resulting database, which is then distributed to a half dozen Veronica servers around the world. Because of this, you'll get the same search results from any Veronica server regardless of its location, barring delays in database updates. This is important because, given current loads on Veronica servers, you may have to query several before your request is accepted and processed. By the time you read this, a new Simplified Veronica service should be stable, and it will automatically resubmit your query until some server satisfies it or all prove busy.

The definitive Veronica location is gopher://gopher.scs.unr.edu:70/11/veronica.

Veronica allows two broad categories of search: Directories and GopherSpace. A directories-only search returns matching items that are collections of additional items, that is, Gopher type 1. A GopherSpace search returns any type of Gopher item, including directories. Directories-only searches are good for high-level subject searching, whereas GopherSpace searches can be expected to return many more matches, and are better used for obscure subjects or words. The experimental Simplified Veronica calls these categories Gopher MENUS and ALL Gopher types.

The basic way to perform a Veronica search is to enter a word or series of words into a dialog box. Searches are case-insensitive. By default, Veronica returns only items that contain all of the words you enter; it uses the logical operator AND unless told otherwise. Veronica also understands NOT, OR, and AND, and these can be used to hone a search, although that level of control is often unnecessary. Veronica also supports asterisks (*) as wildcards at the end of a string. Search strings containing less than two characters are ignored.

If your search provides bountiful results, you may not see all of them because Veronica displays only the first 200 items found. The last item will tell you how many additional items were found. If you want to see them all, you have to resubmit the search with the **-m** qualifier. If you append a number, such as **-m500**, Veronica cuts your search off after that number.

You can also restrict your search to particular file types using the **-t** qualifier with the number/letter code for the Gopher type you're looking for.

Here are some examples of complicated Veronica queries:

- *Rhode Island -t2*: You want to identify any Gopher running a CSO phone book server with Rhode Island in its name.
- *(Mac* or Windows) and graphic* -m100*: You want to find at most 100 resources potentially dealing with graphics on Macintosh or Windows platforms.
- *Balloon -m -t4569sgMhI*: You're casting a wide net for multimedia files relating to balloons, and you're willing to look at everything that isn't a text file, directory, search, or telnet session.

Search results are presented to you as Gopher menus. Typically, you get several pages with some things that seem broken, many so-so hits, some duplicates, and a couple of truly excellent resources. Bookmark those, Dan-O. If you're intrigued by what you find and you want to see more, reach for the attribute information commands in your client. You can find the host, port, and selector for the item and use the root command, if supported, to periscope to the top of that Gopher. You can also backtrack in that Gopher, one level at a time, by displaying the attribute information, copying the URL, and resubmitting it minus one level.

Huh?

Suppose that one of the hits in the balloon search was lawn.chair.balloon.gif. Its URL: gopher://dixie.aiss.uiuc.edu:6969/I9/urban.legends/gif/lawn.chair.balloon.gif. The root command took me to the top; I chose urban.legends, and then GIF! GIF! GIF! Easy one. Sometimes the top is so far from where you popped in that you can't find your way back down. I could have opened gopher://dixie.aiss.uiuc.edu:6969/11/urban.legends/gif/ to do the same thing.

Ugly? You bet. Worth it? Sometimes.

Let's revisit the broken things that come up in a Veronica search. Remember that Veronica does its harvests every week or two. Between harvests, servers go down, menus are reorganized, and items are renamed or removed. The Veronica databases don't reflect the dynamic nature of Gopherspace, and so errors are to be expected.

The last thing to remember is that Veronica harvests menus, not the content of the items in the menus. The resource you're looking for may be out there, but if the Gophermeister has put it on a menu entry called Cool Stuff: Check This Out, you're probably not going to find it.

Searching Locally: Jughead and Other Tools

Yet another entry in the Internet cavalcade of comic book heroes is Jughead: Jonzy's Universal Gopher Hierarchy Excavation And Display. Jughead is primarily of interest to Gophermeisters, because it allows them to build search tools for restricted areas of Gopherspace, such as sections of their own servers. As a user, you should at least know what it is, because you'll see it mentioned from time to time in menus. A typical entry might be *Search this Gopher by Key Words (Jughead).*

Like Veronica, Jughead assumes that words are ANDed unless the operators OR or NOT are included. Jughead also supports the asterisk as an end-of-string wildcard. Unlike Veronica, Jughead returns a maximum of 1,024 items as a result of a search. Jughead also includes some additional commands:

?all string	Returns all items containing string, ignoring the 1,024 item limit.
?limit=n string	Returns at most n items containing string.
?help	Returns a help document.
?version	Returns the Jughead version number.

You can combine a search with the ?help and ?version commands by appending search words to them. Odd feature.

Not all local Gopher searches are based on Veronica. John Franks' gn server, described in other chapters, includes tools for searching all menus in a given hierarchy and for actually searching the content of all files in a given hierarchy. WAIS and WAIS-like search engines lurk behind many menus, and some Gophermeisters have developed their own search tools. All of them appear as Gopher search types and, with luck, the finer points of using them is explained in a nearby About file.

Tunneling Ahead: Gopher's Future

Gopher versus the World Wide Web: These services are often squared off against each other in a tiresome, imaginary Internet duel. There's room and a need for both. As a user, you need to realize that the information you're seeking can appear in either Gopherspace or the World Wide Web, and you should search both. If you're an information provider, you need to have a presence in both spaces. If you're trying to put archives of material that already exist in ASCII format on to the Internet, you can open a Gopher server within days, whereas converting all of it to HTML may set you back weeks.

Veronica needs help. For one thing, there aren't enough servers. The handful that are available exist only through the good graces of a handful of universities and networking organizations, and they can't keep up with the demand. The experimental Simple Veronica interface, which tries to identify an available server for you, is a great addition, but the total Veronica workload needs to be distributed across more machines.

Veronica is being modified to search Gopher+ abstracts as a supplement to the link information. But you've already seen that Gopher+ attributes are not widely used by Gophermeisters, and many of the World Wide Web search tools index not just the link but the full text of the Web page. Web users have learned to expect more from their search tools, and Gopher users will want the same.

At the 1994 Gopher conference, Mark McCahill talked about a new Gopher interface being developed. It's still being talked about, so it wasn't an April Fool's Day joke. In the not-too-distant future, Gopher will support a three-dimensional, fly-by/drive-through interface. Menus will appear as circular Stonehenges, with the results of Veronica and other searches appearing as Stonehenge clusters spiraling off into the distance with poorer and poorer relevance scores. User feedback will be collected, perhaps using a graffiti metaphor.

To quote McCahill, the motivating factor, like that behind Gopher classic and virtually all of the Internet, is that it's cool. That short-tailed, North American, burrowing mammal has a lot of life left in it.

Eric S. Theise, Ph.D., is principal of Liberty Hill Cyberwerks, an Internet education and storefront services firm (`info@cyberwerks.com`*). He's co-founder of Bay Area Internet Literacy, producer of* Modern Times' *Jacking In series, and a frequent implementer, lecturer, and writer on all things Internet.*

GN: Serving WWW and Gopher with the Same Server

by Stephen Trier <sct@po.cwru.edu>

GN is a well-kept secret in both the Gopher and World Wide Web (WWW) worlds. GN belongs to both: it is a Gopher and a World Wide Web server. It is small, simple, and fast; includes excellent searching features; and has a powerful facility for calling external programs.

GN was written by John Franks, a professor of mathematics at Northwestern University.

GN's dual nature enables it to look like a World Wide Web server and a Gopher server simultaneously, using the same data for both. This arrangement can be a big time saver for people who need to support both protocols. The common data set saves disk space, time, and effort, and makes it easy to keep everyone — regardless of client preference — in the party.

Security is not a problem with GN; its menu files control not only the appearance of the menus but also client access. No file is available unless it is listed in a menu file. Furthermore, GN never writes to the disk and has several other features that are designed to frustrate would-be intruders.

Perhaps best of all, GN is free. Look carefully at the licenses for other Gopher and WWW servers before you use them for commercial applications. At least one server (the University of Minnesota's popular *gopherd*) requires a license fee for business use. GN's "GNU Public License" gives anyone the freedom to give away a copy of GN.

GN can be had for free with anonymous FTP, Gopher, or WWW. You should not be surprised to find that the Gopher and WWW copies are on a single GN server.

Getting Started with GN

It's possible to come at GN from a Gopher perspective or from a World Wide Web perspective. The Gopher perspective is easier, so I'll take that first.

Let me get one thing out of the way right now: GN likes menu files, so much that everything in the server must be in a menu file or it won't be accessible to the user. If you ever get an `Access denied` or `File does not exist` message from GN, you probably forgot to put something in a menu file. Remember to put everything in the menu file, and you'll do fine.

Tip #1: Switching from University of Minnesota gopherd

If you are switching to GN from gopherd, run the uncache program included with GN to convert your gopherd cache files to GN menu files. This practice will save you a great deal of time. To uncache a single directory, run uncache.

Even if you know to put everything in a menu file, you need to know *which* menu file. Rule of thumb: Always list a file in a menu file in the same directory as the file.

Suppose that you have a directory under your GN data directory that's called stuff. You put two things in this directory: this section on GN, called gn.txt; and a subdirectory, named more.stuff, that you want to use as a submenu. Your menu file may look like the following example:

```
Name=Internet Secrets GN section
Path=0/stuff/gn.txt

Name=More Cool Stuff
Path=1/stuff/more.stuff
```

After you write this file and save it to the file menu in the stuff directory, run the mkcache program included with GN. This program reads the menu file and converts it to a .cache file used by GN.

This kind of menu file is what I call "Gopher-oriented." The file is visible to World Wide Web users, but there's nothing fancy about it.

You can, however, pretty up the file and surprise those jaded Web users with what a "Gopher" server can do, as in the following example:

```
httpText=
<img src="awesome.gif">
<p>
Welcome to the New, Awesome <i>Internet Secrets</i> Web page!<p>
endText=

Name=Internet Secrets GN section
Path=0/stuff/gn.txt
```

Tip #2: Forgetting to run mkcache

Everyone who runs GN sometimes forgets to run mkcache. Changing a menu file and seeing no change in the result can seem mysterious, but the problem can be avoided by a rule of thumb: If you ever edit a menu file but don't see any changes, try running mkcache, just in case.

```
Name=More Cool Stuff
Path=1/stuff/more.stuff

URLlink=The home of GN
URL=http://hopf.math.nwu.edu/

Name=Awesome picture (Invisible)
Path=I/stuff/awesome.gif
Attribute=invisible
```

The first secret to wowing WWW folks is graphics. This new menu file starts with an httpText/endText section that embeds an image right in the menu. What you see between httpText and endText is HTML, which will be dropped verbatim into the menu — in this case, a GIF graphic and a headline with some italicized text. The text that you see will appear, in all its glory, to WWW users.

Next, you see the two menu entries that were in the old Gopher-oriented menu. The third item, which consists of the URL link and URL lines, sets up an item in the menu that is for WWW users only. This item points to the home of GN. (Try it with your Web browser.)

The last entry in the menu file may seem odd. No, we aren't showing the picture twice. Remember that GN insists that everything appear in a menu file before it can be shown to the user? These three lines tell GN that it's okay to show the user the picture awesome.gif when the user's browser asks for it. Putting the picture's URL in an httpText section is not good enough; one has to have a Name line and a Path line for GN to know it's OK to give to the user. Here, the menu entry has an "Attribute=invisible" line as well. This line suppresses the menu line-item for the image, so that the image shows up only at the top where the HTML brings it in.

(By the way, I forgot to run mkcache after typing this enhanced menu, so the boring old Gopher-oriented version showed up instead. Oops! The menu worked fine after an mkcache, of course.)

What if someone wants to pull out the stops and write pure HTML in GN? No problem — write the HTML files just as you would on a regular WWW server, and then list all the files in a menu file. If you have users start at an HTML file instead of at the menu, the menu does not have to have nice names for the files; it merely has to exist to tell GN that those HTML files can be delivered to the user.

Tip #3: Running mkmenu

If you need to turn a big directory into a menu, Chip Rosenthal's free mkmenus program may save you time. You can get mkmenus from Chip's GN information page at http://gopher.unicom.com:70/1/gn-info/ or gopher://gopher.unicom.com/11/gn-info/.

A computer that can handle GN does not have to be big. Successful GN sites are running computers as small as 386SX/16 PC clones with 4MB of RAM as well as DEC Alpha workstations with 64MB of RAM or more. The only real concern for a typical site is whether the site has enough disk space to store its data. GN itself is small and puts little load on the processor. If you have the luxury of buying a fast computer to run GN, put your money into fast disk drives and lots of RAM. The fast disks mean less waiting for data, and extra RAM means more cache for frequently requested data. A fast processor won't help as much as an extra 16MB of RAM will.

A Smattering of Philosophy

The disciple approached the Zen master and asked, "How can I understand the GN nature?"

This sounds like the beginning of a bad joke, but to get the most out of GN, you have to understand how to live halfway between two sometimes-competing worlds. The easiest way to do this is to go with Gopher-style menus and HTML enhancements. Pure Gopher menus are boring for WWW users, but pure WWW leaves out the Gopher folks.

Keep in mind that if anything seems to be too hard to do in GN, a slight redesign may make the task easier. If you are going for a special effect in HTML, and it won't work, ask yourself whether a more GN-friendly way exists. You can always do things the hard way, but why make extra work for yourself?

Most important, avoid duplicating data whenever possible. Sometimes, duplication is necessary, as when you want to have an HTML file for Web users and a text file for Gopher users. In many cases, though, you can keep the Web and Gopher sides tightly integrated and using the same data. The more you can do this, the happier you will be.

"Seek to understand the dualism of GN, my son," replied the Zen master.

A Taste of Searching

GN is known for its search capabilities. From the start, GN included powerful structured-file and grep-script capabilities; not much later, it added WAIS searching capability.

For a taste of searching, set up GN to enable users to search a mail file. You want to split lines that start with *From* (with a space after the *m*) and to use the Subject lines as the names of the sections in the menu. The menu file will look like this:

```
Name=Search a mail file
Path=7m/stuff/mailfile
Separator=^From[ ]
Section=^Subject:[ \t]*
```

Notice that the type of this item is 7m. Type 7 is a search, and *m* tells GN that the file is a multipart file. The Separator line provides a regular expression for the lines in which you want the messages to be divided, and the Section line shows what line should become the title for each section. (Regular expressions are common tools in UNIX. If you haven't seen the term before, look at the manual page for the ed editor.)

Now users can enter search words, and GN will find messages that match.

Structured files don't have to involve searches. The following example shows how you can turn that mail file into a menu:

```
Name=Read archived messages
Path=1m/stuff/mailfile
Separator=^From[ ]
Section=^Subject:[ \t]*
```

The only difference between this example and the preceding one is the fact that the Path line starts with 1 (for a menu) instead of 7 (for a search).

This feature is useful for more than mail files. Calendars, database reports, and many other files are naturals for GN's structured file handling. The `gn-maint-l` mailing-list archives on `gopher://zadar.cca.vu.nl:70/11/gn-archive` or `http://zadar.cca.vu.nl/1/gn-archive` use structured files.

For ultimate searching flexibility, GN permits the server manager to call external scripts or programs. GN users are only now beginning to explore the possibilities of this feature, but it has already been used for everything from calendar systems to simple user feedback. Chip Rosenthal even used the scripting feature to make a password-protection system for menus. See his GN information page for more information.

How to Get GN

The best way to get GN is by anonymous ftp to `ftp.acns.nwu.edu`. The latest version of GN always is in `/pub/gn/gn.tar.gz`.

Tip: gz?!?

A gz file extension means that the file was compressed with the GNUzip utility for UNIX. If you don't have GNUzip yet, grab a copy from `ftp://prep.ai.mit.edu/pub/gnu` or one of its many mirror sites.

If you want to try out GN first, stop by GN's home site at `gopher://hopf.math.nwu.edu/` and `http://hopf.math.nwu.edu:70/`. Several GN features are in use at this site, which will give you a taste of what GN can do. Another notable GN site is OncoLink at `gopher://cancer.upenn.edu/` or `http://cancer.upenn.edu/`. This site won an honorable mention in the Best of the Web 1994 contest organized by Brandon Plewe of the State University of New York at Buffalo.

A Frequently Asked Questions file for GN lives at either of the following addresses:

`gopher://gopher.cwru.edu/0/about.gopher/gn.faq`

`http://www.cwru.edu/0/about.gopher/gn.faq`

Also look at Chip Rosenthal's GN information page at the following addresses:

`gopher://gopher.unicom.com/11/gn-info/`

`http://gopher.unicom.com:70/1/gn-info/`

To get in touch with GN users, sign up for the `gn-maint-l` mailing list. To subscribe, send the command subscribe gn-maint-l to `majordomo@hmc.edu`. To leave the list, send the command unsubscribe gn-maint-l to the same address.

About That Name . . .

What does *GN* stand for, anyway?

The quick answer: nothing.

The long answer: nothing.

There — that was easy!

Stephen Trier is a network software engineer at Case Western Reserve University. He does TCP/IP programming and troubleshooting and manages the university's GN-based Gopher and Web server. In his free time he plays trombone.

Chapter 24

Using WAIS

by Archie Warnock <warnock@clark.net>
and Dennis Sacks <dsacks@news.primenet.com>

WAIS (pronounced *ways*) is one of the more mysterious network applications, but it does have an important place in your collection of Internet tools. WAIS stands for *Wide Area Information Servers* and is a package designed for searching databases scattered across the Internet.

WAIS uses a client/server model to communicate both locally and over wide area networks like the Internet. The WAIS system consists of three software packages — the indexer, the database server and the client program. WAIS databases can also be accessed through gateways, most commonly now from World Wide Web. WAIS clients are freely available for a wide variety of machines, from UNIX-based X Windows systems and character terminals, to MS-DOS and Macintosh microcomputers.

The biggest growth area in the use of WAIS is through World Wide Web gateways. Use of the World Wide Web, and specifically Mosaic, has exploded in the last year. Mosaic does a tremendous job of presenting text and images in an attractive, easy-to-use way. But the Web does not have a good way of searching documents. This is precisely where WAIS fits in. Later, you read about what it takes to access WAIS from the WWW.

Origin of WAIS

WAIS was developed by Thinking Machines, Inc., in collaboration with Apple Computer, Dow Jones, and KPMG Peat Marwick LLP. The original idea of WAIS was to create a general information retrieval system for distributed databases. Brewster Kahle developed WAIS at Thinking Machines. He has since formed a new company — WAIS, Inc., — to provide a commercial implementation of WAIS.

Thinking Machines released the original version of WAIS to the Internet for free use in April 1991. Since then, an NSF-funded organization called The Clearinghouse for Networked Information Discovery and Retrieval (CNIDR) took over the maintenance and distribution of the software, now called freeWAIS.

Function of WAIS

WAIS is based on a NISO standard computer-to-computer query protocol called Z39.50. The current batch of WAIS servers is based on an implementation of the 1988 version of Z39.50. The Z39.50 Implementor's Group (ZIG), which includes CNIDR, is developing and prototyping new versions of the protocol. CNIDR has developed a server and a client that use Z39.50-1992, the more recent protocol.

WAIS Clients

A WAIS client is the user interface, and most WAIS clients work in pretty much the same way. The user enters a free-format text query that the client translates into the appropriate protocol and then sends to the server. The server processes the query using indexes built by the indexer and sends a list of document *headlines* and scores back to the client. The user then can choose which documents to retrieve, send that request to the server, and get back the requested document.

A WAIS source is a database. It might reside locally or can be accessed on a machine somewhere else on the Internet through a WAIS server. Most WAIS clients keep files to locate sources. These source files contain all of the information necessary for a client to establish a connection to a database and submit a query. A number of organizations maintain WAIS databases of sources, as well as provide collections of source files for downloading. The primary places to look for sources are

```
ftp://quake.think.com/pub/directory-of-servers/wais-sources.tar.Z
ftp://ftp.wais.com/pub/directory-of-servers/wais-sources.tar.Z
ftp://sunsite.unc.edu/pub/packages/infosystems/wais/wais-sources.tar.Z
```

More than one source file might be selected by the user, which allows searches to be submitted to multiple sources at one time (although they are searched sequentially, not simultaneously), and searches can be saved (these are called *question files*) and resubmitted to look for new documents in the collections to be searched. This allows WAIS to function as a sort of personal newspaper.

Most WAIS clients look in standard places for the necessary source files. In some cases, you might find it necessary or desirable to put your WAIS source files in different locations. By default, most of the UNIX clients look for system-wide source files in `/usr/lib/wais-sources` and for individual user's sources in `~/wais-sources`. These can be changed by setting environment variables. WAISCOMMONSOURCEDIR points at the system-wide sources (so the sysadmin needs to set that for things to work correctly). Individual users can set WAISSOURCEDIR to point to the directory containing their personal collection of sources.

In addition to collections of source files, there are several special sources on the network, called *Directories of Servers*. These are WAIS databases that collect sources — you can query a Directory of Servers to find out what sources contain information of interest, and to retrieve the source file for those sources. Both CNIDR and WAIS, Inc., maintain directories.

Another common way for users to submit queries to a WAIS database is by using a *gateway* — a program that serves as an intermediary between some other system (like World Wide Web) and WAIS. Gateways are typically already configured with the information needed to connect to a database, and don't require the user to provide a source file.

Searching secrets

Before going into the details of how to use any particular WAIS clients, it's worthwhile to spend some time covering a few general tips on how to effectively search a WAIS database.

The freeWAIS search engine

The search engine supplied with the free distribution version is quite simple but surprisingly fast and effective. It matches occurrences of words in the query with individual words in the documents and tallies a score for each document based on the number of *hits*. The underlying assumption of the indexer is that, if a document has many words in common with the query, the document is probably relevant to the query.

Documents are then returned in ranked order of relevance to the query.

It's important to note that full-text searching engines like the one in freeWAIS are used differently than are conventional database engines. WAIS is an information discovery tool, not a bibliographic reference tool. You can use freeWAIS to look for a particular document (as opposed to looking for documents about a particular subject), but it's not nearly as effective when used that way.

One result of the word-counting nature of the freeWAIS indexer is that formulating an effective search might seem a bit counter-intuitive, especially if you have experience with relational or other *fielded* databases. In general, the longer you can make your query (that is, the more relevant words you can put in the query), the better are your chances of getting good hits back. This is because you'll be giving the search engine better criteria to use in discriminating between documents that are relevant to the query and those that aren't. In particular, queries consisting of a single word aren't likely to be very useful.

Scoring algorithm

The formula freeWAIS uses to assign a relevance score to documents is based on the number of occurrences of the query words in a document, the location of the words in a document, the frequency of those words within the collection, and the size of the document. Scores are accumulated so that a document with two of the query words in it have a higher score than a document that contains the same word twice, and scores are adjusted for the length of the document to ensure that longer documents don't necessarily get higher scores. For each word in the query found in a document, the search engine assigns five points if the word occurred in the headline and one point otherwise. Total scores are then adjusted to a scale of 1,000 to 0, with the most relevant document being assigned the score of 1,000.

Boolean searching

Some freeWAIS versions support Boolean searching — that is, the words *and, or,* and *not* are interpreted as a request for a search with the Boolean operation being performed on the terms delimited by the operators. So the query "red and white" will match documents only in which both words "red" and "white" occur. This can be confusing because there is no way to tell whether a particular database will interpret the word "and" as a plain English word (and ignore it), or as a Boolean operator. This problem will largely disappear as the migration to newer versions of the Z39.50 protocol takes place, because Boolean capability will be implemented differently.

How many *hits* can I get?

Most WAIS clients set the maximum number of *hits* to 40 documents. You can optionally make it somewhat larger, but there's a hard maximum built into the communications protocol that allows only around 100 or so to be returned (it actually depends on how long the headlines for the documents are, so it might be somewhat larger or smaller; but the point is, the number is limited). This might not be such a serious limitation, though. If you get too many documents back, it's probably an indication that your query needs to be more specific. After all, it's pretty hard to search through a list of 300 headlines or more, looking for a particularly relevant document. So rather than trying to increase the maximum number of documents to get all the good ones, you should try to make your query more discriminating.

Relevance feedback

A simple extension of the WAIS search technique is the notion of *relevancy feedback.* The user can select part (or all) of a retrieved document and use it as a query to get, in effect, all documents like the current one. This allows quite detailed searches without requiring the user to explicitly formulate a detailed query. Some WAIS clients, like xwais, support relevancy feedback, but not all. Few, if any, gateway interfaces to WAIS support it.

Xwais

Xwais (and its companion xwaisq) are the X Window versions of WAIS clients. They are supplied with freeWAIS.

Xwais displays two lists — Sources and Questions — so that you can reuse source and question files you've previously saved, or you can create new ones. Source files can be edited, if necessary.

If you select a new or existing question, the xwaisq program starts up. If you're reusing an existing question, the previous state (query, source, and document hits) is restored. Note that there's no checking to see whether the document identifiers of the hits have changed at the server — you just get the previously stored headlines and identifiers.

First, you select one or more sources (using the Add Sources button). You can then enter a query in the box labeled Tell Me About and submit the query by selecting the Search button. When results are returned, you can highlight the headline of the article you want to see and select the View button, or simply double-click the headline.

The box labeled Similar To is for relevance feedback. You can highlight a document and add it to the list by selecting the Add Document button, or you can retrieve a document, highlight part of it with the cursor, and select the Add Section button. Go back to the xwais question window, and you'll see that the section (or document) has been added to the relevance feedback list. You probably want to now delete your original query (in the Tell Me About box) before resubmitting; otherwise, the search tries to match both the relevant portion of the document and your original question.

Swais

Swais is a character-mode, full-screen client that runs on any VT100 compatible terminal. It is supplied with freeWAIS. It's not particularly easy to use, but on a character mode terminal, it's the only native WAIS interface available.

When swais starts up, it presents a scrollable list of source files.

You can select one (or more) to query by moving the highlight bar to the source and tagging it by pressing the Spacebar. Entering **w** drops you to the Keywords prompt. When you finish entering your query, press Enter to submit the query. The document hits are presented onscreen in a list. Move the cursor to one you want, press Enter, and the document will be retrieved and displayed.

Remember that swais tries to keep a command summary on the bottom line of the screen whenever it's not displaying a document. **?** gets you a screen of help, and **o** gets you to the options screen, where you can change some of swais' defaults.

Waisq and waissearch

There are two command line clients that do not require any particular kind of terminal emulation. If you have conventional WAIS source files, the program waisq can be used to submit a query and retrieve documents.

Alternatively, waissearch takes the database name and node name as command line arguments. Both programs are commonly used in shell scripts to send queries and document requests. Like many UNIX programs, running the program with no command line arguments generates a help message.

One particular advantage of waissearch is that it can search local WAIS indexes directly — it does not need to pass the query to a server. This capability means that individual users can create databases of documents for personal use without worrying about installing and running a WAIS server.

Waisq

Waisq supports a bunch of optional command line switches:

Switch	*Meaning*
-f question_file	Where to read the question from, defaults to stdin, stdout
-s sourcedir	Where the sources are, defaults to WAISSOURCEDIR, or ~/wais-sources/
-S sourcename	Specify the source file to use
-c common_sourcedir	Optional common source directory, default from environment variable WAISCOMMONSOURCEDIR
-m nnn	Maximum number of result documents, defaults to 40
-v nnn	View document nnn
-g	Do a search
-h	Print a help message
-t	Test a source
-V	Print version number
-	Interactive mode

Following is the list of words to search for unless the program is running in interactive mode, in which case they're read from the standard input.

Example:

```
waisq -s ~/freeWAIS/wais-sources -S wais-docs.src environment variables
```

Waissearch

Waissearch also supports a variety of switches:

Switch	*Meaning*
-h host-machine	Host to query, defaults to localhost
-p service-or-port	Port to use, defaults to z39_50
d database	Database to use, defaults to nil
-m nnn	Maximum number of documents to return, defaults to 40
-v	Print the version number

The words to search for follow on the command line.

Example:

```
waissearch -d ~/freeWAIS/wais-sources/wais-docs environment variables
```

WinWAIS

The underlying protocol used by WAIS servers and clients is well documented, so versions of the software can come from any number of sources — not just from the original architects of the system. WinWAIS and MacWAIS are clients written by the Microelectronics and Computer Technology Corp. (MCC). They are available by anonymous ftp from:

```
ftp://ftp.einet.net/einet/pc/EWAIS204.EXE
ftp://ftp.einet.net/einet/mac/macwais.latest.sea.hqx
```

Both programs are distributed as shareware. They function in very much the same way as the x wais client in the freeWAIS distribution. WinWAIS requires the presence of the WinSock DLL for Microsoft Windows, whereas MacWAIS requires MacTCP. Those packages provide the network connection that the clients use to communicate with the Internet and databases.

WAIStation for Mac

WAIStation is a Macintosh interface client-based on MacTCP. MacTCP must be obtained separately. The most recent version is available from:

```
ftp://sunsite.unc.edu/pub/packages/infosystems/wais/clients/macintosh/
WAIStation-0-63.sit.hqx
```

HyperWAIS for Mac

HyperWAIS is Macintosh Hypercard client interface written by Francois Schiettecatte. It is currently at version 1.9 and requires System 7.0, MacTCP 1.1, and Hypercard 2.1 (all must be obtained separately). The source is also available from:

```
ftp://ftp.wais.com/pub/freeware/mac/HyperWAIS/HyperWais.src.sea.hqx
ftp://ftp.wais.com/pub/freeware/mac/HyperWAIS/HyperWais.sea.hqx
```

MacWAIS — A User Scenario

MacWAIS is simple to use. As with all WAIS clients, there are two steps to performing a WAIS search:

1. Choosing a WAIS source or sources.
2. Asking a question using the sources you choose.

Let's say you want to find some information on jazz music. First, you must find what sources might contain information about jazz. The easiest way to do this is to query one of the Directory of Servers with a general question. The descriptions of the sources are usually very general descriptions about the contents and might not contain the word jazz. We can guess that pertinent sources will probably make reference to music.

So begin by picking the New Question option from the MacWAIS File menu as shown in Figure 24-1. You will need to select the source to use for this query (Figure 24-2).

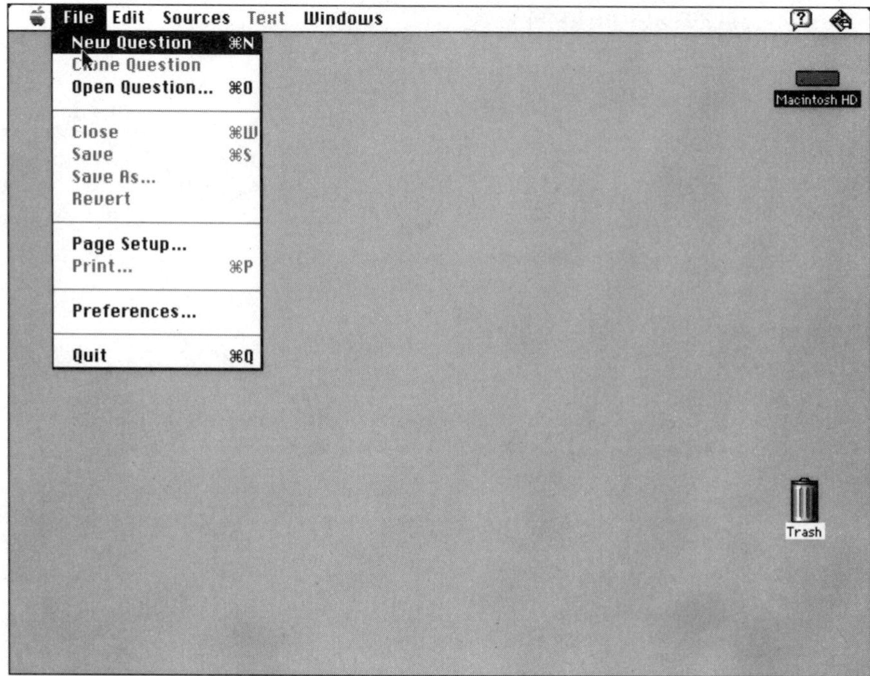

Figure 24-1: Starting a new query.

If MacWAIS doesn't already have a Directory of Servers source, you can create one. Close the source window and pick Add Source from the Sources menu. Enter the database name, hostname, and port number, as shown in Figure 24-3.

Now select your source by picking Select from the Sources menu. You can then pick the Directory of Servers and click the >>Select>> button to add Directory of Servers to the Selected Sources, as shown in Figure 24-2. Now, click the Done button and you have the MacWAIS Question window onscreen. The Question window is titled Unnamed Question because the question has not been saved to a file.

The main MacWAIS window is shown in Figure 24-4. It is divided into three sections. The first section is labeled Tell Me About and contains the box where you type your query. Another box, labeled Similar To, is used for Relevance Feedback.

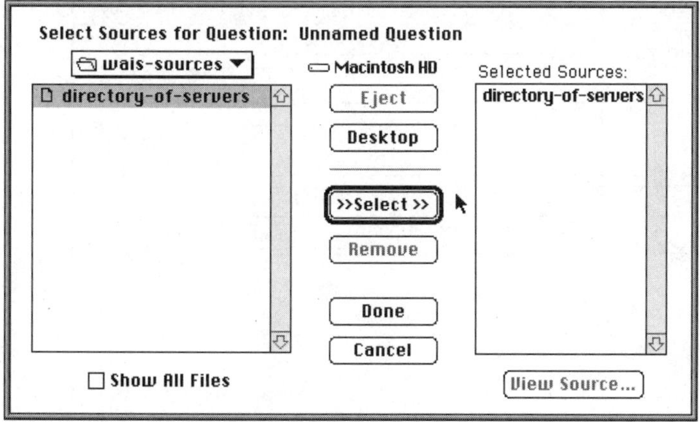

Figure 24-2: Selecting the source to use.

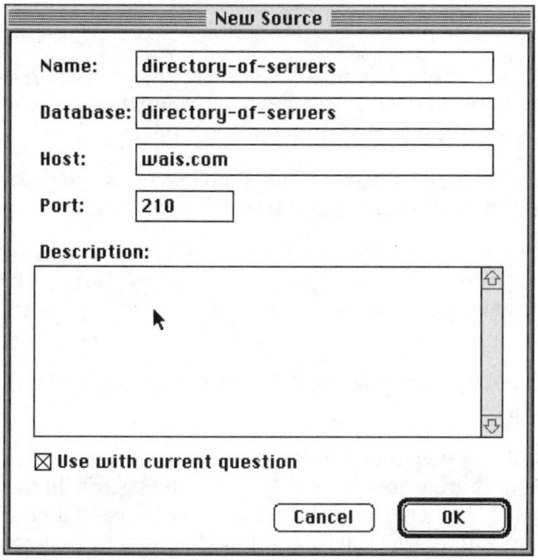

Figure 24-3: Creating a source.

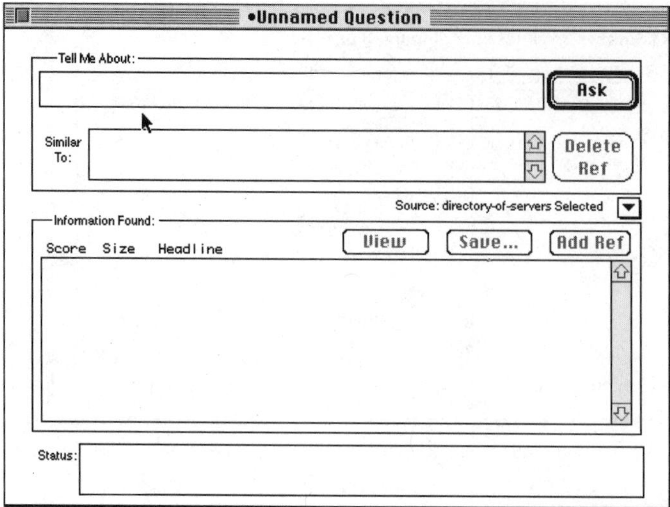

Figure 24-4: Main MacWAIS window.

The second section of the MacWAIS Question window is labeled Information Found. It has three buttons: View for viewing a document returned, Save . . . for saving a document, and Add Ref for adding a document to the Similar To box.

The third section of the screen is labeled Status. It gives you status information about connecting to various sources, bytes retrieved, and so on.

There is also a line between the Tell Me About box and the Information Found box that shows the selected sources. Now that you have selected Directory of Servers as the source to use for your question, you can actually enter the query in the box labeled Tell Me About.

Type **music** and click the Ask button. MacWAIS submits the question to the Directory of Servers source.

Figure 24-5 shows a list of sources that mention the word *music* in their descriptions. The status box shows that there were 15 items found in the search. In the Information Found box, you see a list of the items along with the score for each item, the size, and the headline. Because the source was the Directory of Servers, these items are all sources themselves, which you can then use in a more specific query.

You can now choose the sources that seem most likely to have the kind of information in which you are interested. You can choose several sources to use.

Let's use Sheet Music_Index.src — double-click that entry and get the edit source window (Figure 24-6). Simply click OK. This creates a local source description file that you can then use for your query. Repeat the same process for rec.music.early.src and earlym-l.src.

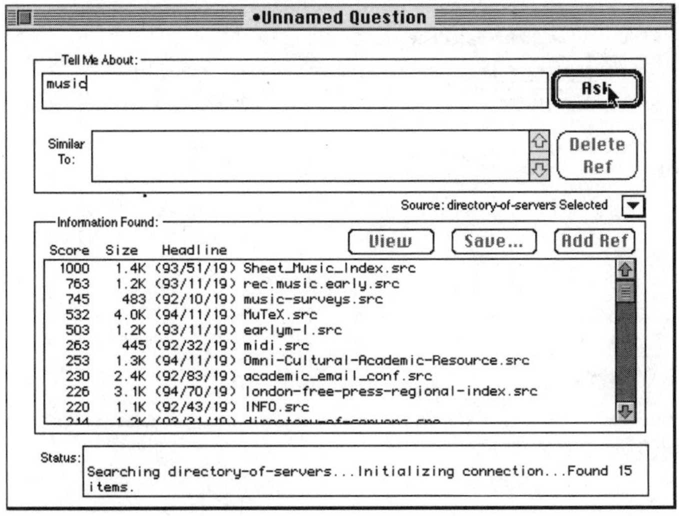

Figure 24-5: List of music sources.

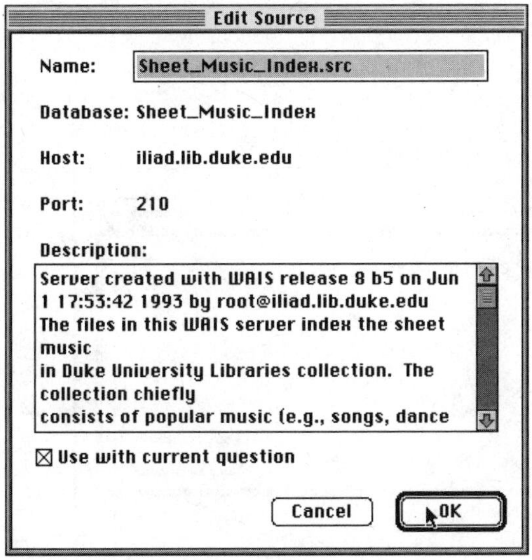

Edit Source

Name: Sheet_Music_Index.src

Database: Sheet_Music_Index

Host: iliad.lib.duke.edu

Port: 210

Description:

Server created with WAIS release 8 b5 on Jun 1 17:53:42 1993 by root@iliad.lib.duke.edu
The files in this WAIS server index the sheet music
in Duke University Libraries collection. The collection chiefly
consists of popular music (e.g., songs, dance

☒ Use with current question

Cancel OK

Figure 24-6: Editing the sheet music source.

Now if you pick Select from the Sources menu, you see four sources displayed (Figure 24-7). You should remove Directory of Servers as a selected source and select the other three sources.

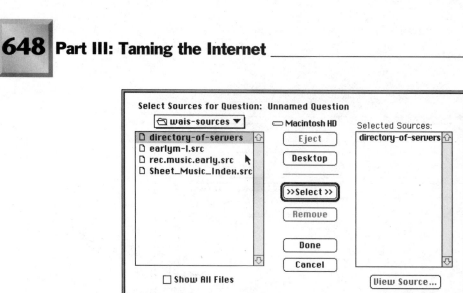

Figure 24-7: Selected sources.

Now you can run your more specific query about jazz. Enter **jazz** in the Tell Me About box and click Ask.

After a short time, you get the dialog box in Figure 24-8. This is no reason to panic. One of the sources that you chose is not currently available. This is a common occurrence with WAIS. Click OK to continue the search.

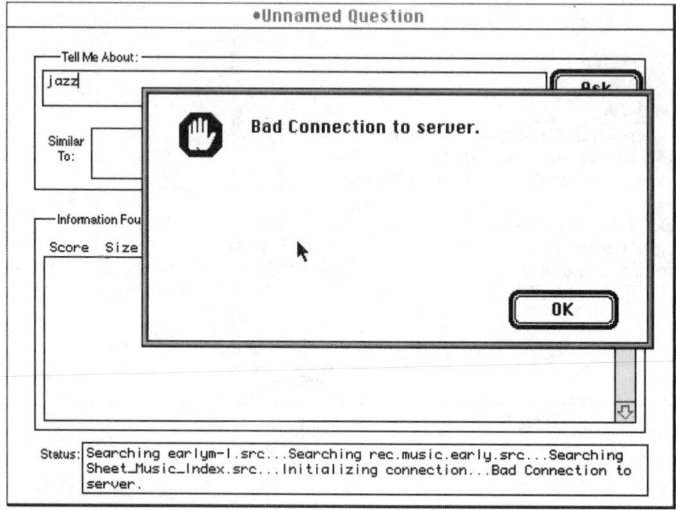

Figure 24-8: Unavailable source — don't panic. Click OK to continue the search.

Figure 24-9 shows the results of the jazz search of the three souces you had selected. You can see that there were 26 items found.

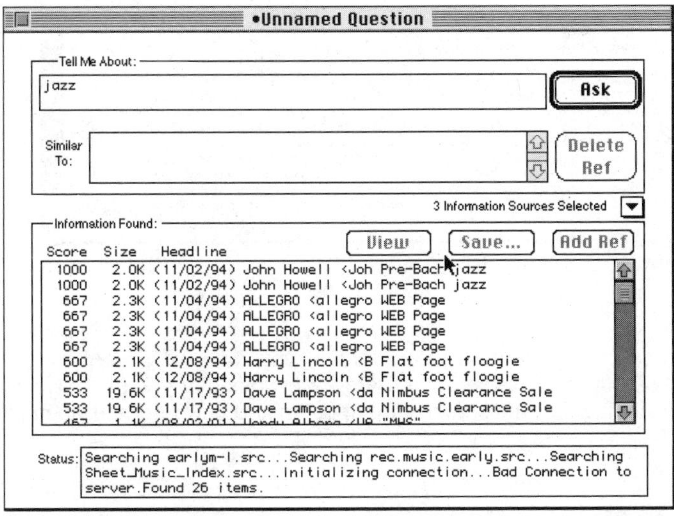

Figure 24-9: All that jazz.

Now let's walk through the information returned and describe what it means:

- The score indicates a ranking of how well the document fit the search. The documents are returned with the ones that fit the search best at the top. Ideally, the documents that we are interested in are in the first few documents returned.
- The size gives the size of the document in kilobytes (1K = 1024 characters) and the headline is the title of the document. In looking at the headlines of the documents returned, it appears that the first document might be of interest.
- You can highlight a document by clicking it and then clicking the View button to retrieve the document. A new window containing the document is displayed. See Figure 24-10 for an example.
- You can browse through the document onscreen or you can save it by picking File⇨Save. You can search the document for a specific word or phrase by picking the Edit⇨Find. When you are done, close the document by clicking the close box.

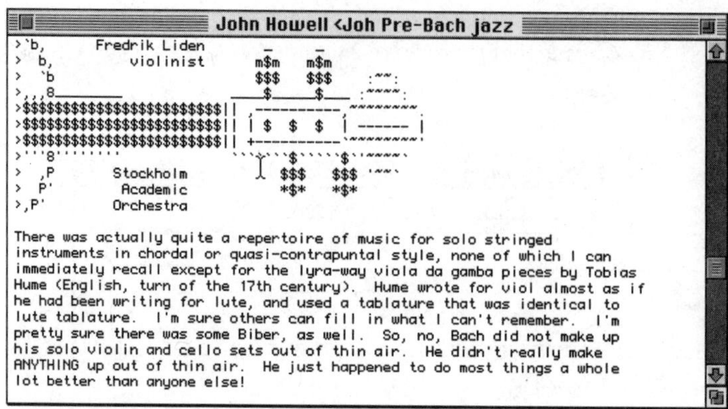

John Howell <Joh Pre-Bach jazz
Fredrik Liden
violinist
Stockholm
Academic
Orchestra
There was actually quite a repertoire of music for solo stringed instruments in chordal or quasi-contrapuntal style, none of which I can immediately recall except for the lyra-way viola da gamba pieces by Tobias Hume (English, turn of the 17th century). Hume wrote for viol almost as if he had been writing for lute, and used a tablature that was identical to lute tablature. I'm sure others can fill in what I can't remember. I'm pretty sure there was some Biber, as well. So, no, Bach did not make up his solo violin and cello sets out of thin air. He didn't really make ANYTHING up out of thin air. He just happened to do most things a whole lot better than anyone else!

Figure 24-10: A sample jazz document.

If the Unnamed Question window is active, you can save your question by picking File⇨Save. This step is useful for saving questions that you might run more than once, assuming that the sources are updated and new information might be available.

World Wide Web gateways

From the end user standpoint, a WWW gateway to WAIS looks like any other WWW query form. You might be able to select a database, or there might be a dedicated form for one particular database. There will (obviously) be an entry box in which the query is entered. Query results are usually returned with the headlines converted to hypertext links, so selecting a headline retrieves the documents.

Administrators who wish to implement a WWW gateway have a few possibilities from which to choose. Kevin Hughes of EIT has developed a C program called wwwwais which runs as a CGI scripts from the http daemon.

It simply translates the output from the HTML form into the appropriate form to be passed to either waisq or waissearch and adds HTML markup to the results. wwwwais is available by anonymous ftp from:

```
ftp://ftp.eit.com/pub/web.software/wwwwais
```

A number of Perl scripts have been posted to comp.infosystems.wais and comp.infosystems.www in the past year or so. Jonny Goldman of Synopsys has written one called fwais, and Tan Tin Wee of the National University of Singapore has written one called nwais. They tend to evolve fairly quickly, so it's probably best to check for new versions on the newsgroups. (Several of the most useful scripts can be found on the companion disks to this book.)

WAIS Distributions

There are several WAIS servers available in source form.

FreeWAIS from CNIDR

The original distribution of WAIS came from Thinking Machines, Inc., who generously allowed the full source code to be donated into the public domain. Eventually, Thinking Machines gave up the job of maintaining and distributing new versions and the Clearinghouse for Network Information Discovery and Retrieval (CNIDR) continued developing new versions and releasing them under the name freeWAIS. The most current release of freeWAIS (version 0.4 right now) is always available from

```
ftp://ftp.cnidr.org/pub/NIDR.tools/freewais/
```

The current version is in the file freeWAIS-0.4.tar.gz. To use the software in this release, you must first decompress and untar the distribution file, like this:

```
gunzip freeWAIS-0.4.tar.gz
tar xvf freeWAIS-0.4.tar
```

This will create a directory called freeWAIS-0.4, with a number of subdirectories.

To build the software, first modify the file freeWAIS-0.4/Makefile to conform to your particular hardware and software architecture. You have to select (and perhaps modify) the variable CFLAGS for your machine and compiler. You also have to set the variable TOP for other installations. You might also have to modify config.h in the top-level directory, but only if you have an unusual architecture.

There are other comments in the Makefile to help set options. Then simply type **make default**.

Most of the software will be made automatically. The X Windows user interface might not be created if your particular system's installation of the X Windows-based software is incompatible. This release includes an Imakefile, which can be used to create a Makefile that includes the locations of the X software for your particular site. If you can build an X application, you should be able to build xwais.

If your system has a working Imake program, you should be able to build the X client by:

```
xmkmf
make depend
make
```

If that doesn't work, you can try modifying the sample file My-Makefile in the freeWAIS-0.4/src/client/x directory.

If all goes well in building the software, you will have all of the executable program in the bin directory — waisserver, waisindex, xwais, xwaisq, swais, waissearch, waisq, and a bunch of utility programs and sample scripts.

Currently, several of the capabilities of the indexer are configurable only by changing compiler flags, rather than defining the capabilities at run-time. These options can be included into CFLAGS in the top-level Makefile to enable the capabilities:

- -DLITERAL configures waisserver to search for literal strings.
- -DBOOLEANS configures waisserver to search with Boolean AND, NOT operators.
- -DPARTIALWORD configures waisserver to search for partial words (hum* matches human, hummingbird).
- -DTELL_USER lets the server know who you are at connect time.
- -DSTEM_WORDS to stem words during indexing and queries.
- -DBIGINDEX if you need to index a large number of documents (but you'll have to reindex all your existing databases, too).

FreeWAIS-sf

FreeWAIS-sf was written by Ulrich Pfeifer and Tung Huynhz at the University of Dortmund. The *sf* stands for *Structured Fields*. FreeWAIS-sf has the following characteristics:

- Introduces text, date, and numeric field structures within a document.
- Supports complex Boolean searches. It also supports stemming (for instance the words compute, computer, and computing are indexed as the same word).
- Allows you to define your own document format headline layout using a specification language. Standard freeWAIS allows you to do this only by writing C code.
- Provides these enhancements without losing compatibility with the original freeWAIS, so you can run freeWAIS-sf and ignore the enhancements if you want.

The freeWAIS-sf distribution is available from:

```
ftp://ls6-www.informatik.uni-dortmund.de/pub/wais/freeWAIS-sf-1.0.tgz
```

It uses the GNU configure program to set up and build the distribution, so in many cases building the system is no more complicated than entering the command configure and answering a few questions. Other than the structured field capability of the indexer, it is quite similar in function and use to freeWAIS.

WAIS from WAIS, Inc.

The original developer of WAIS, Brewster Kahle, left Thinking Machines, Corp., and formed WAIS, Inc., which markets commercial versions of the WAIS software. Its package has a full technical support staff behind it and has a large number of enhancements to the search and retrieval components. More information on obtaining the WAIS, Inc. software can be obtained via e-mail from info@wais.com.

WAIS Indexing

WAIS works by precomputing a database of all of the words in the target documents. The server searches the index when client requests arrive.

Creating a WAIS database

The program waisindex creates the searchable databases of documents. It has a baffling number of command line options, but most of them don't need to be changed, so I'll talk only about the most useful ones. The freeWAIS distribution has some sample scripts in the wais-test directory to illustrate the indexer's use.

Let's create a simple WAIS index for starters. Suppose you have a bunch of text files in the directory ~/docs. The command

```
waisindex -d ~/wais-databases/mydocs ~/docs/*
```

indexes all of your text files (that's what ~/docs/* does) and creates a database called mydocs in the directory ~/wais-databases (specified by -d ~/wais-databases/mydocs). You can search the database with the waissearch program:

```
waissearch -d ~/wais-databases/mydocs \
    "search for some really relevant text"
```

One of the most useful things to do with the indexer is to index your mail folders to make them searchable. Do this with the command:

```
waisindex -d ~/wais-databases/myMail -t mail_or_rmail -r ~/Mail
```

Here, -d ~/wais-databases/myMail names the database file, -t mail_or_rmail tells the indexer that the files are mail folders, and -r ~/Mail tells the indexer to recurse through your Mail directory and all its subdirectories. Now, you can search for a mail message with the command

```
waissearch -d ~/wais-databases/myMail "meeting with John on April 1"
```

To advertise the public availability of your data, you can send in an entry to the Directory of Servers, a server running at an easily accessible location (quake.think.com AND cnidr.org). The following command creates an index called your-files and registers the index with the Directory of Servers. Needless to say, this should be done with care.

```
waisindex -d your-files -export -register ~/docs/*
```

The WAIS indexer knows how to handle compressed files, too, if you have the program zcat. It just decompresses them on the fly as it reads them and builds the indexes. The WAIS server knows to decompress a file before retrieving it and passing it on to the client as well.

WAIS indexer command line options

The indexer has a number of command line parameters that invoke different functions and options. The most commonly used ones are described here:

Parameter	*Function*
-a	Append to (don't overwrite) an existing database. By default, WAISindex deletes an existing database before making a new one. This option allows you to index additional files — say, of a different document type — to an existing database.
-r <dir>	Recurse through the specified directory and all its subdirectories. This option allows you to index more files than you can normally specify on the command line.
-register	Publish your database by sending the source file to the Directory of Servers database, so that other users can find out about you.
-export	Create a source file for the database, along with all the other files.
-nocat	Do not create a catalog file as part of the database. By default, the catalog is just a list of all of the indexed documents. If you're indexing a lot of documents, the catalog can be quite large and useless.
-t <string>	Index documents of type <string>. A number of document types are known to the indexer already.
-T <string>	Set the document type to <string>, no matter what document type is used (via -t) to index them.
-M <string1>,<string2>,...	Index documents with multiple document type.

Note that stemming and literal searches interact oddly. When stemming is turned on for a particular server, literal string searches might not behave as one might expect! Please put a note in your .SRC file (before registering) indicating the status of stemming on your server.

Here's a slightly better script to use to index your mail folders:

```
#!/bin/sh
#
# This shell script shows how to run waisindex to build a local
# database out of your mail folders. It assumes waisindex is in your
# path, that you have a directory called ~/wais-database,
# that you want the database to be called Mail,
# and that your mail folders are in the directory # ~/Mail
# waisindex -d $HOME/wais-database/Mail -nocat -t mail_or_rmail \
    -r $HOME/Mail
```

Document types

WAIS associates a document type with each document. This type can force the client to take different actions when it receives a document, depending on the type. For example, a document of type GIF might be piped to the program xv for display, or fetched directly to disk.

In many cases, the different document types serve only to define the headlines that are returned. Documents are not the same as *files*—a file can contain any number of documents, separated by delimiters, for example. The most commonly used document types are listed in the following table.

Name	*Description*
dash	Documents are separated by a line of (20 or more) dashes.
first_line	Use the first line of the file as a headline.
filename	Only index the name of the files, not the contents or the directory path.
HTML	Index HTML files by using the <TITLE> tag to find the headline.
mail_digest	Standard Internet mail digest format.
mail_or_rmail	Mail or rmail folders or both.
one_line	Each line of the file is a separate document.
para	Each paragraph of the file is a separate document.
server	Documents are WAIS source files.
text	The default document type.

With a little bit of C programming, it's possible to add new document types to the WAIS indexer. It's not advisable because every time a new release comes out, you'll have to put the changes back in. However, the modifications are well-isolated in the code, and changes have to be made only to three files.

Database catalogs and descriptions

The catalog file is sent to a user in response to a request of help or info. As mentioned previously, the default catalog file created by the indexer is a list of all of the documents in the index, and it is created unless you use the -nocat switch when you run the indexer. You can provide your own, more descriptive file if you wish — just give it the same name as the database, and use the .CAT extension on the filename. Make sure the catalog file is in the same directory as the other database files.

Booleans

You enable the Boolean query capability for the indexer when you compile the code —if the compiler flag BOOLEAN is defined, the indexer will build a database that you can search using the logical AND, OR, and NOT. If you compile the indexer with BOOLEAN defined (that is, add -DBOOLEAN to the command line when you compile), and then index some documents, a query like *dog and fox* returns documents only in which both words appear. No document with only one of the words wll be returned.

If Boolean capability is not enabled, the query *dog and fox* returns some documents with just the word *dog,* some with just the word *fox,* and some with both. The way the scoring algorithm works will, in general, give documents with both words a higher score than documents with just one.

How you want your database to function is up to you. Be forewarned, though, that there is no built-in way for a user to find out whether your database treats AND as a Boolean operator or as a plain English word. You will have to make this very clear in the descriptive documentation for the database.

Newer versions of the Z39.50 protocol make it possible for users (or more correctly, clients) to query a server and even an individual database about how these cases are handled.

Multiple data types

The term *document*, used in the context of WAIS, does not always refer to a text file. As seen previously, there can be several documents within a single file. In addition, Francois Schiettecatte contributed changes to the indexer to allow a document to be defined as a collection of several files of different types.

For example, you might have a set of GIF images, each of which has a plain text caption file associated with it. In this case, a document is a pair of files — one GIF and one text file. If you wish, you can index the caption files and associate the GIF image with it so that, when users select a document, they are presented with a choice of either the text file or the GIF image.

Not all WAIS clients support this capability, but the xwais client does, as does NCSA Mosaic for X Windows.

There are a few things to be aware of when indexing these types of documents. As currently implemented, the files to be associated together must all have the same filename, and the filename extensions must be the name of the type of the file. In addition, the filename extensions *must* be in uppercase. Now, suppose you have a subdirectory called Multitype, with the following files in it:

andes.GIF

andes.TEXT

gumby.GIF

gumby.TEXT

The command:

```
../bin/waisindex -d test-Multi -M "TEXT,GIF" -t filename \
-nopos -nopairs -export ./Multitype/*.TEXT
```

indexes the caption files (andes.TEXT and gumby.TEXT) and associates an image file with each. Users are then offered the option of retrieving either the GIF image or the text file when they submit a request to retrieve one of the documents. Clients That cannot handle multiple-type documents will only present the text documents.

Synonyms

WAISindex can also index synonyms of words in the documents.

To utilize this capability, you need an ASCII file of synonyms, where each line is a separate set of synonyms. The first entry on a line is the word to be indexed, followed on the same line by all of the synonyms you want to define. Any word on a line matches any other word on the same line.

Suppose you want to create an index called MyDocs with the command

```
waisindex -d ~/wais-database/MyDocs -t text *.txt
```

To get synonyms for the index MyDocs, create a file called MyDocs.syn in the directory ~/wais-documents, type these lines

```
rat rodent mouse critter varmint
dog canine mutt pooch hound
```

into the file, and then run the waisindex command to create the index.

Now a document with the word *dog* is returned as a hit for a query containing the word *mutt*.

When a synonym list is added or changed, you have to reindex the database.

Fielded searches using freeWAIS-sf

One of the nice enhancements of freeWAIS-sf is the field-searching support. You can designate fields in your documents that get indexed separately. This allows you to search for information in specific fields.

For example, you can indicate title and author fields in your documents and index them. Then you can search for all the documents written by *smith* without matching the word *smith* in the text of the document. What's more, you can do this from any WAIS client.

You can also write a format file to describe in detail the format of your documents and what text to use as the headline. You can specify using soundex (an algorithm for words that sound alike) and stemming.

See the freeWAIS-sf documentation for further explanation.

WAIS indexing fine details

(from the WAIS documentation written by Brewster Kahle)

The serial indexer parses files and creates an inverted file index made up of seven files. For a database named Index, the files are

Index.inv — The *postings file*, that is a term followed by a list of entries each of which describes where that word occurs in the original files. A posting is a weight, doc_number (see the DOC file), and character_position. This file is indexed with the dictionary (DCT) file. The terms are in alphabetical order.

Index.doc — This is a linear list of document entries, one for each document. A document can be a complete file or a piece of a file (such as mail files that are the concatentation of many messages; each message is a document). The information kept in each entry is

filename_id: The position into the filename file (fn) of the filename for this document.

headline_id: The position in the headline file.

start_character: The position in the file where this document starts.

end_character: The end position. 0 if complete file.

document_length: The position in characters.

number_of_lines: The position in lines.

date: The date and time in time_t format.

Index.fn — A list of the filenames in the database with the write-date of the file and the type of the file. Type is a string. Indexed by the position in the file, so this file cannot be edited after the index is built.

Index.hl — A list of the headlines. Indexed by position.

Index.dct — A dictionary file in two level b-tree format. The first block is pointers to the every 1,000th entry in the rest of the dictionary file. Each entry is a fixed-length record of the word with the position into the rest of the file. The rest of the file is blocks just like the first block, but each entry is the word plus the position of it in the inverted file (inv). The whole dictionary is in alphabetical order.

Index.src — A source description used to access the database. It is also returned as a response to the help query. Database maintainers should edit this file to add a good description of what that database contains.

Index.cat — A catalog file consisting of the headlines of each document in the index. This can be omitted with the -nocat command line parameter. Database maintainers should edit this file to add a good description of the documents in the database.

WAIS Servers

Once you've created a WAIS database, you need a server to respond to user search requests.

Installing your own server

There are two ways to run the server:

- As a stand-alone process
- As a daemon under inetd

To run the stand-alone server simply type

```
waisserver -p port-number
```

at a prompt, where the port-number is a TCP port that the server uses to handle client connections. Most UNIX systems allow the only superuser to run processes on ports numbered 1024 or lower.

You can run a personal server on a different port by entering

```
waisserver -p 8088 -d ~/wais-databases -e ~/server.log
```

This command starts the server on port 8088. Its default directory for WAIS indexes is ~/wais-databases, and it writes a log of transactions to the file ~/server.log.

For general use, it is probably preferable to run the server in inetd, as it conserves CPU cycles (the inet daemon handles looking for activity on the TCP/IP port and starts the server only when necessary).

It also allows waisserver to run easily behind a TCP wrapper, if necessary, for an additional layer of security. In order to run the server out of inetd, you have to have root privilege. First, you must define the z3950 service for inetd, and then insert a line in your inetd configuration file that tells inetd what to do when a connection is received on the z3950 port. On most systems, this means adding the z3950 service to /etc/services or the NIS (used to be called YP) database as follows:

```
z3950    210/tcp        # Z39_50 protocol for WAIS
```

and in /etc/inetd.conf, add the line:

```
z3950 stream tcp nowait waisp <path>/waisserver waisserver.d \
   -e <server-logfile> -d <server-database-directory>
```

Note that the user field in this example is waisp, which is the user ID the daemon is run under. This user ID is rarely present and can be replaced by something appropriate for your site (typically UUCP). The directory <path> is where the waisserver executable is located (typically /usr/local/bin). <server-logfile> is the full path and filename of the log file the server will write, and <server-database-directory> is the default directory where the WAIS databases are located. The user specified in the previous line must have read/write permission to the directories specified in the -d and -e arguments.

Once those changes have been made, you can kill the inet daemon and when it restarts, the server is ready to run.

Configuration and database management

The programs waisindex and waisserver work together to provide search and retrieve functions to the collection of documents you are making available. The waisindex program reads through the collection of documents and builds a searchable index, consisting of a set of seven files for each database. These database files can be put in any readable directory on the server machine, but the document collection should not be moved unless you are willing to reindex it, because the database files contain the paths to the individual documents.

It's best to put the database files together in waisserver's default directory (as specified by the -d argument on waisserver's command line). If you put the database files in another directory, you will have to put the fully qualified path to the database in the source file to distribute to users, and if you change the location, the old source files will be invalid. If you keep the database files in the server's default directory, you can move the databases wherever necessary and will have to change the command line argument only for waisserver to continue providing access.

The WAIS server writes a log file that tracks a number of usage items — date and time, requester's IP address (and sometimes user name), query terms, and documents requested. This log file can get quite large, so it's a good idea to extract summary statistics periodically and then delete the file. This can be done with a cron script, say monthly.

One of the files waisindex writes is an ASCII description of all the information a WAIS client needs to access the database. By default, a source file looks like:

```
(:source
 :version 3
 :ip-address "192.31.181.1"
 :ip-name "quake.think.com"
 :tcp-port 210
 :database-name "directory-of-servers"
 :cost 0.00
 :cost-unit :free
 :maintainer "wais-directory-of-servers@quake.think.com"
 :subjects "general guide WAIS servers"
 :description
"Server created with WAIS-8 on Fri Mar 8 14:30:57 1991 by brewster@think.com
 This is a White Pages listing of WAIS servers. For more
 information on WAIS, use the WAIS system on the wais-docs server,
 or add yourself to the wais-discussion@think.com mailing list, or
 get the newest software from think.com:/public/wais.
 To server makers: Please make new servers of text, pictures, music
 whatever. We will try to list all servers in the directory that
 get sent in to: directory-of-servers@quake.think.com (use the
 -register option on the command waisindex), but I reserve the
```

```
right to take servers out if they are not consistently available.
I will send notice to the maintainer before doing so.
To get a list of all available sources, search for 'source'. This
might be limited by the maximum number of results allowed by a
client.
Send bugs and comments to bug-wais@think.com.
-brewster@think.com
"
)
```

The source file can be simplified somewhat — the ip-address line can be deleted if users have access to a nameserver (and most do). If the database isn't located in the server's default directory, the database-name line will need to be modified to contain the full path of the database files. The keywords are optional, and the description should be modified to contain more descriptive information about the nature of the database.

Usage statistics

The WAIS server logs all transactions (queries, retrievals, reindexing, problems) to a log file. The name and location of the log file is specified on the command line that invokes the server, as is the level of detail the server should write. The script waisdata.sh processes a month's entries in the server log and generates a usage report.

```
#!/bin/sh
# waisdata script
# Adapted by A. Warnock from someplace, but I can't remember where
# It takes the current month on the command line
#
# Modify the next four lines to match your configuration
# - logdir is the location of your WAIS server log
# - server is the name of the server log file
# - year is (obviously) the current year. It only needs to be
# changed once a year, for convenience
# - dbname is the name of a WAIS database
#  Extending this to more than one database per server is left as
#  an exercise to the reader

logdir=/data/Logs
server=$logdir/WAISserver.log
year=1995
dbname=GCMD

workdir=/data/Logs/waisdata
temp=$workdir/waisdata1
temp2=$workdir/waisdata2


# Number of connections
```

```
NUM='egrep -i $1" " $server | egrep $year | egrep Init | wc -l \
' echo "Total of" $NUM "connections to the WAIS server for" $1 $year

# Searches
echo
echo "Searches:"
NUM='egrep -i $1" " $server | egrep $year | egrep Search | grep \
   $dbname | wc -l' echo "Total of" $NUM "searches of the database"

# Retrievals
echo
echo "Retrievals:"

NUM='egrep -i $1" " $server | egrep $year | egrep Retrieving | \
   grep $dbname | wc -l' echo "Total of" $NUM "document retrievals"

echo
echo "Most connections from:"
egrep -i $1" " $server | egrep $year | fgrep Init | sed -e \
   's/.*from //' | sort | uniq -c | awk '$1 >= 1 { print $0 } ' \
   | sort -nr | awk ' { print $1 ": " $3 } '

echo
echo "Individual Stats - Searches:"
egrep -i $1" " $server | egrep $year | egrep Search | \
   sed -e 's/.*Database: //' | grep -v returning | \
   awk ' { print $1 } ' | sed -e 's/,//' | sort | uniq -c | sort -nr

echo
echo "Individual Stats - Retrievals:"
egrep -i $1" " $server | egrep $year | egrep Retrieving | \
    sed -e 's/.*database //' | sort | uniq -c | sort -nr
```

Security

A server security feature has been added to waisserver that will restrict access to particular databases from certain hosts. It works by validating every user connection against a file containing a list of hosts/domains that can connect to this server. If the file does not exist, the server is open to everybody.

The SERVER SECURITY file (named SERV_SEC by default) is an ASCII file list of hostnames and addresses. For example,

```
welchlab.welch.jhu.edu      128.220.59.10

welchlgate.welch.jhu.edu    128.220.59.13
```

restricts access to just those two machines. Access can be given to specific domains, as well, so if one wanted to give access to everyone in the welch.jhu.edu domain, the file looks like this:

```
welch.jhu.edu     128.220.59
```

The host address is optional, but the hostname is not.

The DATABASE SECURITY file (named DATA_SEC by default) is an ASCII file list of database names, hostnames, and addresses. For example:

```
foo welchlab.welch.jhu.edu      128.220.59.10
foo welchlgate.welch.jhu.edu     128.220.59.13
```

restricts access to the *foo* database to users on the two machines specified. As before, access can be given to specific domains, so if one wanted to give access to everyone in the welch.jhu.edu domain, the file looks like this:

```
foo welch.jhu.edu  128.220.59
```

The host address is optional, but the hostname is not.

An asterisk allows access to everyone for a particular database, for example:

```
foo welch.jhu.edu  128.220.59
bar *    *
```

This is useful if you wanted to give public access to certain databases on a particular server and restricted access to others.

Using WAIS from WWW

One of the most commonly encountered uses of WAIS is through a World Wide Web gateway server. There are several gateways (WAISgate, SFgate, son-of-wais, kid-of-wais) that can be used and more are written every day.

Installing SFgate

SFgate requires Perl 4.0 Patch level 36 to run. You can get SFgate from

```
ftp://ls6-www.informatik.uni-dortmund.de/pub/wais/SFgate-3.5.tar.gz
```

Decompress and untar SFgate:

```
gunzip -d SFgate-3.5.tar.gz
tar xvf SFgate-3.5.tar
```

Doing so creates the subdirectory SFgate-3.5. Now go into that directory and run the configure program. Configure will ask you several questions about your Web server. You need to know where your public HTML pages reside, where your CGI scripts reside, the virtual name of your CGI directory (that is, where does it look like your CGI scripts reside from Mosaic), where you want the SFgate log file to be written, and where the documentation files should go relative to your public HTML directory:

```
cd SFgate-3.5
./configure
checking for a BSD compatible install
Will use "/opt/local/bin/install -c" for installation.
checking for waisperl
checking for perl5
checking for perl
checking /opt/gnu/bin/perl for wais buildins No perl with wais buildins found!
OK. Will use plain perl.
That will run significantly slower!
checking version of /opt/gnu/bin/perl
will use /opt/gnu/bin/perl

Where is the root of the server, which will run SFgate?
Where do your html pages reside (/usr/WWW/pages)?

Where is your real CGI dir (/usr/WWW/pages/cgi-bin)?

You might have configured your server to lie about the name of the CGI
directory. This way you can grant the world access to the scripts without
executing them. Virtual name means the name you want to use in the URLS For
example in 'http://somehost/CGI/finger?pfeifer' The virtual name is '/CGI'
What is the virtual name of /usr/WWW/pages/cgi-bin (/htbin)?

In which directory should the logfile go (/usr/WWW/log)?
Will write logs to /usr/WWW/log/SFgate.log

Where - relative to /usr/WWW/pages/ - should the documentation go (Sfgate)?
creating config.status
creating Makefile
creating SFgate.html
creating SFproxy.html
creating config.pl
creating demo.html
creating index.html
creating t/run_tests

finished setup
Now run
  make
  make test
  make install
to do the obvious

You can modify some of the setting, you just entered by editing config.pl.
Run config.status to recreate this setup
```

Now you can run **make, make test,** and **make install** to install SFgate. You must have permission to write into the public HTML and CGI directories to complete the **make install**.

Included in the install are some instructions for installation and usage. They are placed in SFgate in your public HTML directory. Use Mosaic or your favorite Web browser to look at SFgate.html for instructions.

Running a demo of SFgate

The installation procedure for SFgate will put a directory under your public HTML files called SFgate. Inside SFgate there will be some sample HTML forms that simulate a WAIS client front end.

Add links to index.html, SFproxy.html, and demo.html from your Web server. If you view these files directly from Mosaic, the script doesn't work. You can customize these pages for your application quite easily.

How SFgate works

The example forms given with SFgate call a perl program called SFgate. SFgate actually speaks directly to the WAIS server that you specify. It submits the query and gets the query results, formatting them in HTML and passing them back to HTTPD. See SFgate.html for more information on the interface between the forms and SFgate.

WAIS of the Future

Many companies are working on WAIS or WAIS-related clients and servers, including AT&T Library Network, BRS Software, Apple Computer, Mead Data Central, and others.

As Z39.50 matures, many more companies will incorporate WAIS or WAIS technology into their internal and public information systems. There is still plenty of noncommercial development of WAIS, as shown by developments with freeWAIS, freeWAIS-sf, and CNIDR's Isite package.

Essence and Harvest

- *Essence* is an indexing scheme that is more flexible than normal WAIS indexing but generates indexes that are compatible with WAIS. It was outlined in the Proceedings of the Winter 1993 USENIX Conference in a paper called "Essence: a resource discovery system based on semantic file indexing." Essence supports more document types than standard freeWAIS does, so if you want to index things like tar files, have a look at Essence.
- *Harvest* enables users to locate and summarize information stored in many formats on machines around the world. It uses Essence, among other tools, to allow users to create new collections of information in the process and then put the information back on the Internet for other users.

  Information on Harvest can be found at

  ```
  http://harvest.cs.colorado.edu
  ```

How does ZDist fit?

Over the past year, CNIDR has been working on developing a new client and server to take advantage of newer versions of the Z39.50 protocol.

There are a number of advantages in migrating away from the old 1988 version of Z39.50 implemented in the original WAIS software. As mentioned previously, there is a source of confusion for users with the existing WAIS distributions as to when the words AND, OR, and NOT are to be interpreted as Boolean operators and when they are to be interpreted as plain English text. This problem doesn't occur in later versions of Z39.50 because the Boolean capabilities are embedded in the underlying protocol and not coded into the text of the query. Z39.50 also supports fielded searching and user-specified formats for results.

In addition, many commercial database vendors are supporting Z39.50, making it possible for a single Z39.50 client to query and access a much wider range of online data.

CNIDR has just released a Z39.50 V2 package called Isite. The software is available by anonymous ftp from

```
ftp://ftp.cnidr.org/pub/NIDR.tools/Isite/Isite-1.00.tar.gz.
```

Isite includes an index engine (Iindex), a search interface (Isearch), a Z39.50 V2 server (zserver) and a Z39.50 V2 client (zclient).

A new client, Zagent, will be included in the next release of the freeWAIS. It provides the link between existing freeWAIS databases, created with waisindex, and zserver, so that users with Z39.50 clients can query freeWAIS databases, and information providers can continue to use the freeWAIS indexing engine while supporting a full-blown Z39.50 server.

There is also a full Z39.50 client, called Willow, available from the University of Washington. You can get it from

```
ftp://ftp.cac.washington.edu/willow
```

WAIS Resources

Information about WAIS and the many different packages associated with it are available from the Internet.

Companies and organizations

- **WAIS, Inc.** Gopher to wais.com to find all kinds of information about its products, WAIS in general, archived WAIS mailing list messages, and more.

  For Web access, try http://www.wais.com.

- **Thinking Machines**. ftp.think.com:/wais has the original WAIS distribution and a wais client for the Mac. It also has some documentation.
- **CNIDR**, Maintainer of freeWAIS. http://cnidr.org/Welcome.html. The CNIDR web page contains information about CNIDR and the future of freeWAIS and Isite.

Software

- **MacWAIS and WinWAIS from EINET.**

  ftp://ftp.einet.net/einet/pc/EWAIS204.ZIP

  ftp://ftp.einet.net/einet/mac/macwais1.29.sea.hqx

  The z3950 Specification

  http://www.research.att.com/~wald/z3950.html

- **OS/2 WAIS Client.**

  ftp://ftp-os2.nmsu.edu/os2/32bit/network/tcpip/os2wais.zip

- **FreeWAIS-sf and Sfgate.**

  http://ls6-www.informatik.uni-dortmund.de/freeWAIS-sf/README-sf.html

  ftp:/ls6-www.informatik.uni-dortmund.de:/pub/wais/*

- **Other Web/WAIS Gateways.**

Name	*Location*
WAISGATE:	http://server.wais.com/waisgate-announce.html
WWWWAIS:	http://www.eit.com/software/wwwwais/wwwwais.html
Son-Of-WAIS:	http://dewey.lib.ncsu.edu/staff/morgan/son-of-wais.html
Kid-Of-WAIS:	http://www.cso.uiuc.edu/grady.html
Harvest:	http://harvest.cs.colorado.edu
Willow:	ftp://ftp.cac.washington.edu/willow

Articles, books, and more

"WAIS: Wide Area Information Servers," by George S. Machovec 3/1/92; a short introduction to WAIS.

"Frequently Asked Questions (FAQ) for freeWAIS," by Aydin Edguer, Bob Waldstein, Jim Fullton 4/9/93. Posted to comp.infosystems.wais.

"Wide Area Information Servers (WAIS) over Z39.50-1988 and Beyond," by Margaret St. Pierre, WAIS Incorporated February 1994, ConneXions, The Interoperability Report. Available from gopher://wais.com.

"WAIS Bibliography," 4/26/94 from WAIS, Inc. Contains a good list of bibliographic information for WAIS. Available from gopher://wais.com.

"Mosaic and WAIS Tutorial." Available at http://wintermute.ncsa.uiuc.edu:8080/wais-tutorial/wais.html

The Internet For Dummies, 2nd Edition, by John R. Levine and Carol Baroudi, 1994, IDG Books. Contains a good overview of WAIS and tutorials for the UNIX WAIS client and WinWAIS.

MORE Internet For Dummies, by John R. Levine and Margaret Levine Young, 1994, IDG Books. Covers Windows clients WinWAIS and WAISMAN in detail, both installation and day-to-day usage.

The Internet for Everyone: A guide for users and providers, by Richard W. Wiggins. copyright 1995, McGraw-Hill. This guide to the Internet has an emphasis on becoming a service provider or implementing a Campus Wide Information System. Provides information on using one of the Windows WAIS clients and a brief section on setting up a WAIS server.

For answers to WAIS-related questions and help, try the newsgroup `comp.infosystems.wais` and the mailing lists `wais-talk@think.com` and `zip@cnidr.org`.

`http://www.clark.net/pub/warnock/archie_warnock.html`

Archie Warnock is an independent consultant in network information systems. He was a lead developer of NASA's WAIS-based STELAR Project and of the NASA WWW home page. He currently supports freeWAIS on behalf of CNIDR and is a developer of the electronic version of the Astrophysical Journal Letters for the American Astronomical Society.

Archibald Warnock
A/WWW Enterprises
6652 Hawkeye Run
Columbia, MD 21044

Dennis Sacks is a UNIX and OS/2 Systems/Database Administrator with Motorola SPS in Pheonix, AZ.

Chapter 25

Managing Mail

This chapter contains four articles:

- "Climbing Pine"
- "Filtering Mail"
- "Processing Mail Automatically with Mailagent"
- "Demystifying Mail Auto-Responders"

Climbing Pine

by The Pine Development Team <pine-faq@docserver.cac.washington.edu> and others

First, this article explains what Pine is, what standard protocols it can handle, and how to get the program and its documentation off the Net. This chapter describes Pine version 3.91 unless otherwise noted.

What is Pine?

Pine™ is a *p*rogram for *I*nternet *n*ews and *e*-mail. (Due to its resemblance to the older mail program Elm, some people claimed that *P*ine *i*s *n*early *E*lm.) Pine is a tool for reading, sending, and managing electronic messages. The program was designed specifically with novice computer users in mind but can be tailored to accommodate the needs of power users as well. Pine uses standard Internet message protocols (such as RFC 822, SMTP, MIME, IMAP, and NNTP) and runs on UNIX, MS-DOS, and Windows.

The guiding principles for Pine's user-interface were careful limitation of features, one-character mnemonic commands, always-present command menus, immediate user feedback, and high tolerance for user mistakes. The developers intended that users be able to learn Pine by exploration rather than by reading manuals. The program has the capability to perform full-screen editing of messages, to include and extract attachments (such as Word or Excel files), and to perform other advanced message-system functions.

Pine can use IMAP for accessing message folders on remote computers and MIME for sending multimedia or other binary files as attachments to messages. The following sections explain both MIME and IMAP.

What is MIME?

MIME (RFC 1521), which stands for *m*ultipurpose *I*nternet *m*ail *e*xtensions, is an Internet standard that allows transfer of binary files (word-processing documents, spreadsheets, images, sounds, and so on) between any compliant mailers. You can get technical information about MIME from the RFC. Ongoing discussion on MIME takes place in the newsgroup `comp.mail.mime`. In addition, a frequently asked questions (FAQ) list is posted regularly to `comp.mail.mime`, `comp.answers`, and `news.answers`.

If you have a Web browser, you can access the MIME FAQ at the following address:

```
http://www.cis.ohio-state.edu/hypertext/faq/bngusenet/comp/mail/mime/top.html
```

What is IMAP?

According to Terry Gray, Director of Networks & Distributed Computing at the University of Washington, IMAP is "one of the best kept secrets in the e-mail world."

IMAP stands for *I*nternet *m*essage *a*ccess *p*rotocol. An IMAP client program on any platform at any location on the Internet can access e-mail folders on an IMAP server. Although the messages appear to the client to be local, they reside on the server until the client explicitly moves or deletes them. The IMAP protocol is a functional (but incompatible) superset of POP (post-office protocol).

A principal advantage of IMAP over POP is that it permits you to use more than one computer to access your mail. Using multiple computers with POP typically results in your mail messages being scattered across all those computers. Another key advantage is IMAP's capability to selectively access parts of messages; you don't have to wait for a 2MB audio attachment to be retrieved until you specifically ask for it, for example. This capability is a big advantage over low-speed (for example, dialup) connections.

For a detailed comparison of IMAP and POP, see the paper "Comparing Two Approaches to Remote Mailbox Access: IMAP vs. POP," which is available at the following address:

```
ftp://ftp.cac.washington.edu/mail/imap.vs.pop
```

IMAP is what enables Pine (or any other IMAP client) to access e-mail on a remote mail server — usually one that is shared (central or departmental). The current IMAP4 Proposed Standard is described in RFC 1730. Additional information is included in RFC 1731, RFC 1732, and RFC 1733.

How Can I Get a Copy of Pine?

Pine is available via anonymous ftp from the `pine` directory of `ftp.cac.washington.edu`.

What Documentation is Available?

The Pine program itself includes extensive on-line help. Additional documentation is available via the World Wide Web or anonymous ftp at the following locations:

```
http://www.cac.washington.edu/pine
http://www.cis.ohio-state.edu/hypertext/faq/usenet/mail/pine-faq/faq.html
ftp://ftp.cac.washington.edu/pine/docs
ftp://rtfm.mit.edu/pub/usenet/news.answers/mail/pine-faq
```

Contributed documentation also is available at the following locations:

```
http://www.math.utah.edu/~calfeld/creations/PineIntroduction
http://www.math.utah.edu/~calfeld/creations/PineIntermediate
http://www.math.utah.edu/~calfeld/creations/ca_pine_guide
```

If you have documentation that you would like to share, please mail `pine@cac.washington.edu` a pointer to that documentation, and we'll include it in the Pine FAQ.

To What Platforms Has Pine Been Ported?

The Pine distribution includes binaries for AIX 3.2 (on RS/6000), HP/UX 9.0, Linux 1.1, NeXTStep (on NeXT hardware), SunOS 4.1 (on SPARCStations), Solaris 2.2, Ultrix 4.1 and 4.2 (on DECStations), MS-DOS (PC-Pine), and Microsoft Windows (PC-Pine for Windows).

PC-Pine is available for the following TCP/IP stacks: FTP's PC/TCP, University of Waterloo's WATTCP stack with packet drivers, Novell's LAN Workplace, Sun's PC/NFS, and Winsock.

Pine also has been compiled on other UNIX platforms: 4.3 Berkeley UNIX, DEC OSF/1 V1.2A, Dynix/PTX V1.4.0, VAX Ultrix 4.1, A/UX 3.0, BSD/386 Gamma 4.1, Convex, Dynix 3.0 and 3.1 on Sequent Symmetry, Interactive Systems Corporation UNIX, Silicon Graphics IRIS with IRIX 4.0.1, SCO UNIX, System V release 4.

What Mailing Lists and Newsgroups Deal with Pine?

The `comp.mail.pine` newsgroup is devoted to Pine. The newsgroup has a bidirectional gateway to the `pine-info` mailing list.

Following are the mailing lists that deal with Pine and related topics:

- `pine-info@cac.washington.edu` is a mailing list for the e-mail program Pine. The mailing list includes discussions of Pine features, bugs, tricks, and the like. Technical and installation questions often appear in the list. New releases, fixes, and versions of Pine are announced on the `pine-info` mailing list. For official announcements only, you may want to see `pine-announce` instead of this list.

To subscribe to `pine-info`, send a message to `majordomo@cac.washington.edu` with *subscribe pine-info* in the body of the message.

Owners of this mailing list can be contacted at `owner-pine-info@cac.washington.edu`.

- `pine-announce@cac.washington.edu` is an announcement list for the e-mail program Pine. When new Pine products are released and old ones updated, a message goes out to this group, describing the development. This list is a very-low-volume list and includes no discussion whatsoever.

All messages to this list are automatically forwarded to `pine-info`, so it is not necessary to subscribe to both lists.

To subscribe to `pine-announce`, send a message to `majordomo@cac.washington.edu` with *subscribe pine-announce* in the body of the message.

Owners of this mailing list can be contacted at `owner-pine-announce@cac.washington.edu`.

- `imap@cac.washington.edu` is the official mailing list for the IETF IMAP working group and other interested parties. Discussion of the evolving IMAP standard and related issues is conducted on this list.

To subscribe to `imap`, send a message to `imap-request@cac.washington.edu`.

- `c-client@cac.washington.edu` is for discussion of the C-Client library, which is used by Pine and by various other mail and IMAP clients and servers.

To subscribe to c-client, send a message to `c-client-request@cac.washington.edu`.

Tips for Using Pine

The following sections provide some tips and tricks for the best ways to use Pine.

How do I send a message to several people without showing all the names?

Put addresses and/or lists from your address book in the Bcc (blind carbon copy) header field. You will see all the names and addresses as you compose the message, but they are erased before the message arrives in other people's INBOXes. The Bcc header is not displayed in the default Pine configuration automatically, so you may need to use the rich-headers command (Ctrl+R) while the cursor is in the header to expose it.

How do I use ispell with Pine and Pico?

Contributed by Nancy McGough <inet-secrets@ii.com> and Mike Ramey <mramey@u.washington.edu>

If you use the ispell spelling checker and have an ispell custom dictionary, you also can use ispell to spell-check your outgoing mail messages. You can set up this function in two ways:

The custom dictionary that ispell uses depends on the version of ispell you are using. Usually it is ispell.words or .ispell_words in your home directory, and it contains a list of words, one word to a line. To find out about your system's ispell, check the ispell manual.

Method 1. If you always use Pine's default composer, Pico, you can use ispell as your alternative editor. In your .pinerc file, set enable-alternate-editor, and set the editor variable as follows:

```
editor=/usr/local/bin/ispell
```

(See step 1 of Method 2 for instructions on finding the full path to ispell on your machine.) Thereafter, when you compose a message, you can press Ctrl+_ (underscore character) to run ispell on your message and display the output in Pine's viewer. In the viewer, you can use ispell's usual commands. While you are in ispell, you can press **?** for help on ispell's commands. One useful command is **I**, which inserts the current word into your custom dictionary.

Method 2. If you use an alternative editor, such as vi or emacs, you need to fool Pine into thinking that ispell is spell. Follow these steps:

1. **Determine what directory ispell is in by using one of the following commands:**

   which ispell

   type ispell

   whereis ispell

   where ispell

2. **Create a symbolic link between ispell and spell with a command like this:**

   ln -s /path/you/found/in/step1/ispell $HOME/your/bin/spell

   For example, if ispell is in /usr/local/bin and your bin directory is $HOME/bin, you would type this:

   ln -s /usr/local/bin/ispell $HOME/bin/spell

3. **If you use the UNIX csh or tcsh shell, set the SPELL environment variable by putting a line like the following in your .cshrc file:**

   setenv SPELL "$HOME/bin/spell"

If you use the Bourne shell, set the SPELL environment variable by putting lines like the following in your .profile file:

SPELL="$HOME/bin/spell" export SPELL

4. **In your home directory, create an ispell custom dictionary (usually ispell.words, but check your ispell manual pages to be sure) that contains your private dictionary of words that should pass the spell check.**

   This file probably will include your name, e-mail address, and so on.

5. **Log out and then log back in to make sure that your new settings are in place.**
6. **Use Pine to compose a message, including words (such as your name) that are in your custom dictionary.**
7. **Spell-check the message with Ctrl-T.**

   If your name passes the spell check (and if your name isn't in regular dictionaries), your setup is correct.

If you use Method 2, you cannot use many of ispell's features. For example, **I**, which inserts a word into your dictionary, won't work.

How can I have a signature appended to my mail messages automatically?

Using your favorite text editor (such as Pico), create a file in your home directory called .signature that contains the text you want to append to each message. PC-Pine users should put their signatures in the file \PINE\PINE.SIG.

For more details, see Chapter 17, which discusses signature and finger.

How do I read Usenet newsgroups with Pine?

You can use Pine to access news in three ways:

- *Via NNTP.* Your .newsrc file must be on the machine on which Pine is running. Assuming that news is stored on the machine `news.nowhere.edu`, the following is a typical .pinerc entry:

```
news-collections = News *{news.nowhere.edu/nntp}[*]
```

  Alternatively, if the *nntp-server* variable is set, your news collections will default to NNTP access from that server. For example, setting

```
nntp-server=news.nowhere.edu
```

  makes *news-collections* default to

```
news-collections=News *{news.nowhere.edu/nntp}[*]
```

- *Via IMAP.* Your .newsrc file must be on the machine on which news is stored. Assuming that news is stored on the machine `news.nowhere.edu`, the following is a typical .pinerc entry:

```
news-collections = News *{news.nowhere.edu}[*]
```

- *Via local news.* If news is stored on the same machine on which you run Pine, you can specify the following:

```
news-collections = News *[*]
```

The advantage of IMAP news reading is that you can use the same .newsrc for both UNIX Pine and PC-Pine. The disadvantage is that you must have an account on the machine that stores the news and runs the NNTP server.

Can I post news with Pine?

Versions of Pine before 3.90 do not support posting. In Pine 3.90 and later versions, you can enter a list of newsgroups in the Newsgrps header to post a message. If the Newsgrps header is not displayed when you are composing, you can view it by putting your cursor in the header and pressing Ctrl+R.

How do I paste an address from the address book into the text of a message?

Pine currently does not support this capability directly, but a workaround is available. Follow these steps:

1. **Move the cursor to the Cc line.**
2. **Enter the nickname or press Ctrl+T to search the address book and select the entry.**
3. **Press Ctrl+K to delete that address from the Cc line.**
4. **Place the cursor in the body of the message where you want to insert the address.**
5. **Press Ctrl+U to insert the address.**

This method is a roundabout way to get the job done, but it works.

How can I filter messages into different incoming folders?

(Contributed by The Pine Development Team <pine-faq@docserver.cac.washington.edu> *and Nancy McGough <inet-secrets@ii.com>)*

Pine does not perform delivery filtering. That function is handled by other programs, such as procmail, filter, deliver, and mailagent.

After you set up your delivery filtering (by means of the procmail program, for example), your new mail will arrive in several mailboxes and folders, in addition to your INBOX.

How do you access the new incoming-message folders that your favorite delivery-filter program created? One way is to just access them the same way that you access your other mail folders. If the folders are in your default folder directory (usually, $HOME/mail), type **L** to list your folders, and select the folder that you like to view. If the folders are in a different directory (for example, $HOME/mail/IN), add that directory to your folder collections by adding the following lines to your .pinerc file:

```
folder-collections=mail/[],
     mail/IN/[]
```

Thereafter, when you list your folders by typing **L**, the mail/IN directory will be in your list.

Another solution is to use Pine's *incoming-folders* variable. With this method, you can press the Tab key to tab through new messages in all your incoming folders. When you reach the last new message in one incoming folder, pressing the Tab key moves you to the next incoming folder that contains a new message.

Following is part of a sample .pinerc for setting up incoming folders:

```
incoming-folders=Art151 {warhol.art.nowhere.edu}IN.art151,
Art-L {warhol.art.nowhere.edu}IN.Art-L,
Old-Student-Acct {fozzie.elsewhere.edu}INBOX
```

In this case, the pinerc entries presume that your delivery-filtering program has been configured to put mail related to the Art151 class into the folder IN.art151 and to put mail related to the Art-L mailing list into IN.Art-L. You then can access those folders easily from the Folders List screen. Eventually, we will have a way to indicate which of these folders has new mail waiting for you, so that you don't forget that you have more than one place to look for new mail.

For a more detailed treatment of filtering, see the mail filtering sections later in this article. Related FAQs are available at the following addresses:

```
http://www.cis.ohio-state.edu/hypertext/faq/usenet/mail/filtering-faq/faq.html
http://www.cis.ohio-state.edu/hypertext/faq/usenet/mail/procmail-faq/faq.html
```

The plain-text versions are available at the following locations:

```
ftp://rtfm.mit.edu/pub/usenet/news.answers/mail/filtering-faq
ftp://rtfm.mit.edu/pub/usenet/news.answers/mail/procmail-faq
```

How do I define my own headers?

(Contributed by Nancy McGough <inet-secrets@ii.com>)

In Pine 3.90 and later versions, you can set Reply-To, Organization, and other headers by using the *customized-hdrs* variable. Follow these steps:

1. **From the main menu, type** S **(for Setup).**
2. **Type** C **(for Configuration).**
3. **Type** W **(for Where).**
4. **At the prompt, type** customized-hdrs.
5. **Type** A **(for Add).**
6. **At the prompt, type** Organization: *your organization's name*.
7. **Repeat steps 5 and 6 for other headers.**

Pine understands environment variables, so you can use lines like the following (if the variables are set):

```
Organization: $ORGANIZATION
Reply-To: $REPLYTO
```

While reading a message that you have received, you can view all headers by typing **H**. If **H** does not work, you need to go to your configuration menu and set the *enable-full-header-cmd* variable.

While composing a message, you can view all the headers by placing the cursor in the header region and pressing Ctrl+R (for View Rich Headers).

Customized headers are not available in Pine 3.89 and earlier versions.

Can I use Pine noninteractively, as in a shell script?

Currently, you can't. If you could, you could use Pine, and your Pine address book, to send mail to people from within a shell script, at the end of a pipeline, and so on. For now, you'll have to use other programs, such as Elm or Berkeley Mail, from scripts.

When I get new mail, xbiff lets me know about it, but why doesn't Pine know about it?

You can force a new mail check in two ways:

- Press Ctrl+L (Refresh Display).
- At the last message in a folder, press **n** four or five times.

How can I read a ROT13-encoded message?

(Contributed by The Pine Development Team <pine-faq@docserver.cac.washington.edu> and Nancy McGough <inet-secrets@ii.com>)

When viewing the message, type | (the Pipe command) and then type the following to use the translate command, tr, to "unrotate" the rot13 message:

```
tr '[A-Za-z]' '[N-ZA-Mn-za-m]'
```

You also could write a script, maybe called unrot, that does the above translation and then type the following to read the message:

```
| unrot
```

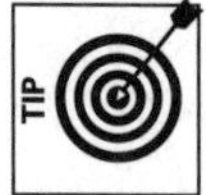

For the pipe command to work, you need to be using Pine 3.90 or a later version and must have the *enable-unix-pipe-cmd* variable set.

Can I eliminate the @host.domain from local addresses?

This idea isn't new — it's very old, in fact — and just about everyone who has ever dealt with e-mail has had it at one time or another. Regrettably, it has come to be recognized as a bad idea, because an e-mail address without a hostname is not syntactically valid, according to RFC 822. RFC 822 only specifies what must be done in messages that are transmitted over the network; strictly local messages are not under RFC 822's dictates.

This arrangement means that two e-mail formats exist: one that conforms to RFC 822, and one that does not. Careful efforts must be made to ensure that the nonconforming mail format never escapes the local system and moves into the network. Twenty years' experience has shown that it is impossible to guarantee that the nonconforming format does not escape into the network, despite traps designed to catch such messages on their way out and convert them to RFC-822-conforming format. Indeed, such traps often have contributed additional problems on their own.

The nonconforming format does not clarify what host is intended. Although the off-the-cuff solution (and the one that everyone implements) is to use the local host, this solution often leads to incorrect behavior. For example, the correct `@host.domain` may be the "local mail center" instead of the "local machine which is a single-user workstation." Or if one of the nonconforming messages escaped into the network, the correct `@host.domain` is some remote system, and Pine has no idea at all what that may be!

There's no reliable way for Pine to tell what the correct `@host.domain` is; a human may infer the correct `@host.domain` from context but often does so by using information that is not available to Pine.

The Pine team held long (and at times heated) meetings to review this issue, finally coming to the conclusion (as other e-mail groups have independently done) that it's a no-win situation. The policy of the e-mail development community for 15 years (since the RFC 733 discussions) has been to exterminate the nonconforming format by not implementing it in modern mail tools.

In a future version of Pine, it may be feasible to implement a feature that would suppress the display of the local-host name in e-mail addresses. The hostname would still be in the file on disk, but it would not show up on-screen. The Pine team will consider this feature, but it has a large list of high-priority tasks to complete first.

Problems with Pine

The following sections describe some common problems and bugs in the Pine program.

Why did I get the message "Folder format invalidated (consult an expert), aborted"?

The message `Folder format invalidated (consult an expert), aborted` means that Pine was reading your mail folder, and at the point at which it expected to find a start-of-message header line, Pine found something else. (In Pine 3.92, the message is `Unexpected changes to mailbox (try restarting)`.)

Three situations can cause the format-invalidated condition:

1. Bad data exists at the beginning of the folder.
2. Data was appended to the folder after Pine initially read it, and the new data did not begin with a start-of-message-header.
3. The folder was modified without Pine's being aware of it.

All three problems generally are caused by software other than Pine.

You can identify condition 1 by whether the problem repeats after you restart Pine. If restarting Pine does not make the problem go away, you need to look at the actual file for the folder and see what is wrong with the very first line. In particular, make sure that no blank lines appear at the beginning of the file. Also make sure that the first character of the folder file is *F*, the second *r*, the third *o*, and so on. In the case of an INBOX, you may want to rename the folder so that new mail can be delivered while repairs are being made on the corrupt folder.

Condition 2 may be caused by a mail-delivery process (for example, /bin/mail) that writes some characters other than *From* at the beginning of the new data.

Condition 3 is caused by another program's manipulating the mail folder without following the normal folder-locking protocols. This problem generally occurs on UNIX.

Conditions 2 and 3 also have been known to occur when accessing folders via NFS, if the results returned by the stat( ) and read( ) system calls do not correspond with each other as a result of NFS attribute caching.

Restarting Pine on the folder always clears the conditions 2 and 3. If the problem is chronic, an investigation to determine its cause may be worthwhile. Usually, the problem is due to the misbehavior of some external software.

The reason why Pine gives up with conditions 2 and 3 is that it does not want to risk damaging user data by guessing what is right. Pine never writes to the folder unless it is absolutely sure that it knows what it is doing.

You can take some steps to reduce the risk that these conditions will come up. Some of these steps may require the assistance of your system administrator (or whoever built and installed Pine on your system).

- *Use IMAP instead of NFS to access remote folders.* Problems with locking over NFS perhaps represent the single most important cause of user difficulties. Using IMAP eliminates this problem.
- *Consider enabling the mbox driver in Pine.* If the mbox driver is enabled, mail is transferred from your mailbox in the `/usr/spool/mail` directory into a file called `mbox` in your home directory. The home-directory `mbox` file then is your INBOX. This procedure has the advantage that Pine and the mail-delivery system are less often in contention for the INBOX and that the programs never try to update the INBOX at the same time. Pine only empties the mailbox in the `/usr/spool/mail` directory; it never tries to update it.

The mbox driver does not create the mbox file in your home directory. If the file does not exist, Pine behaves as if the driver was not enabled.

- *Be careful not to run other programs that modify your folders while you are running Pine.* Such programs may change the folder without proper file locking and lead Pine to conclude that a problem exists with its view of the file.

What is folder locking?

Pine and other mail programs use locks to prevent damage from occurring to the mail file when multiple programs try to write to the file at the same time.

Because many different schemes of mail-file locking are used on UNIX systems, Pine implements all of the common techniques. The result is a great deal of complexity.

Locking is necessary for several reasons:

1. If you want to read the mail file, you want to make sure that no other process will modify the mail file while you are reading it.
2. If you want to write to the mail file, you want to make sure that no other process is accessing the mail file while you are writing it.
3. If you have the mail file open, you want to make sure that no other process can alter any of the internal contents of the mail file that you have read, but it is OK if another process appends new data to the mail file.
4. If you want to alter any of the internal contents of the mail file, make sure that no other process has left the mail file open.

Following are several locking mechanisms:

- The creation of a file that has the same name as the mail file, but with the suffix .lock. (For example, the lock for /usr/spool/mail/isma is named /usr/spool/mail/isma.lock.) This file accomplishes locks 1 and 2. This lock is an exclusive lock.
- The use of a call to flock( ) with LOCK_SH (shared lock) on the mail file accomplishes lock 1 and prevents lock 2. Multiple processes can create this lock.
- The use of a call to flock( ) with LOCK_EX (exclusive lock) on the mail file accomplishes lock 2 and prevents lock 1.
- The use of a call to flock( ) with LOCK_EX on a file in the /tmp directory. The filename depends on the version of Pine that you are using. This accomplishes locks 3 and 4.

On SVR4-based systems, the lockf( ) subroutine or fcntl( ) system call is used instead of flock( ). Rumor is that this procedure also creates a kind of lock file, but this rumor has not been verified directly.

In BSD systems, flock( ) does not work over NFS, so only the most basic .lock file locking — locks 1 and 2 — happens over NFS. In SVR4 systems, fcntl( ) locking attempts to work over NFS, but known problems in the rpc.lockd daemon cause hangs if an application beats on the mechanism too much (Pine beats on it). All the mechanisms in the preceding list work reliably over IMAP connections.

What happens when two Pine sessions access the same mailbox at the same time?

The result varies, depending on what format your folders are stored in. In the default Berkeley format, the last session to open a folder gets full access to the folder, and the preceding sessions change to read-only access. When a folder is read-only, you do not see any further updates to that folder until it is reopened with full access. Currently, you cannot reopen the INBOX without exiting and restarting Pine.

In the Tenex format, any number of sessions can simultaneously have full access to a folder, except that expunging is disabled. For more information, see "What is a Tenex mailbox?" later in this chapter.

Why did I get the message "Folder *xxxxx* is locked, will override in *yyy* seconds"?

The message `locked, will override in _yyy_ seconds` occurs when Pine discovers that some other mail program claims to be accessing your mail folder (for example, _folder_.lock exists). This lock is a very low-level lock used by programs such as the system mailer (in delivering mail) and by programs such as mail, elm, babyl, and mm. Supposedly, this lock can be acquired and held for a very short period (less than a second).

It starts at 285 seconds, retries every second, and issues that message every 15 seconds. The total time (5 minutes) is the time that Pine keeps trying before it concludes that the lock is false — that is, that whatever program locked the folder forgot to unlock it (perhaps it crashed).Then Pine goes ahead and claims the lock for itself.

This situation is not due to a conflict between two copies of Pine, because Pine interlocks against itself in a higher-level fashion.

On some systems that have 14-character file-name limits, attempting to open a folder with a 14-character name (for example, saved-messages) triggers this sequence. On those systems, folder names should be limited to nine characters or fewer.

Why is a charset=US-ASCII attachment sent with BASE64 encoding?

Pine uses BASE64 to encode all attachments (including text to ensure that they are not modified in transit). The goal is to make sure that file attachment in Pine is as dependable as in ftp (and BASE64 is safer than Quoted-Printable). A good example of why this feature is handy occurred recently, when we asked some people to attach their address books to help us track down problems in 3.90. We didn't have to worry about whether a gateway had modified a tab or trailing blanks, and so on.

Why doesn't Pine recognize the Content-Length header?

It would be a significant detriment to the performance of the Berkeley-format mailbox parsing code, as well as to Pine's behavior on normal systems that do not use the Content-Length header, if any attempt were made to implement Content-Length.

Many serious technical problems exist with the Content-Length header, and we do not recommend its use. Further, we recommend that a mail-delivery agent (such as our sendit or tmail tools) be used that applies smart quoting, as opposed to the ordinary BSD /bin/mail quoting of all lines that begin with *From*. We have installed such tools on all our systems.

For example, one problem is that a system whose mailer does not implement Content-Length also does not enforce its validity, should that header appear. This arrangement offers significant potential for mischief.

Another problem is that Berkeley-format mailbox files that use the Content-Length header cannot be edited with an editor such as emacs or vi without invalidating the Content-Length field. If this problem is not a consideration at your site, we recommend the use of the tenex format (mail.txt), which also is length-tagged but in a much more efficient fashion.

From our perspective, these problems outweigh any possible benefit of supporting Content-Length in Berkeley-format mailbox files. At the present time, there are no plans to do so.

Installation, Configuration, and Conversion

This section discusses some considerations for people who are in charge of installing or configuring Pine.

Can PC-Pine be used with a POP server?

No. Neither Pine nor PC-Pine currently supports POP's off-line mail model (wherein pending mail is pulled from the mail server to the local machine and deleted from the server). It is likely, however, that this model will be supported, with a choice of either IMAP or POP as the access protocol, in a future release.

What is a Tenex mailbox?

Using the Tenex format for INBOXes permits multiple sessions (or multiple users, subject to the usual access controls) to have *almost* full read-write (RW) access to the INBOX. The only limitation on full RW access is that multiple sessions occur at a given moment, no session can perform an Expunge command. Message-state changes (for example, marking a message as deleted) *can* be performed, however, and the changed state is preserved across sessions.

If an explicit Expunge command fails, it says so and tells you that the mailbox is in use by another process. When only one session is using that mailbox, the Expunge command resumes working again.

By contrast, the normal Berkeley-style folders can have only one RW client at a time, so *given the current software*, the latest session steals the RW lock from any previous session, with the earlier session becoming read-only.

Mailbox format for INBOX is a function of the mail-transfer agent (sendmail, tmail, and so on), not of the mail user agent (Pine), so this decision is for system and mail administrators, not for regular Pine users.

Where does Pine look for configuration information?

In UNIX and PC-Pine 3.90 and later versions, the release notes (press **R** in the main menu) contain a section on configuration, including default filenames and environment variables. Almost all types of personal configuration can be accomplished through the Setup command in the main menu.

UNIX Pine uses three configuration files: a systemwide defaults file, a systemwide settings file that cannot be overridden, and a personal configuration file. If you need to generate a blank copy of the systemwide configuration files, run the following UNIX command:

```
pine -conf > /usr/local/lib
```

If, for some reason, you need to generate a blank personal configuration file, run the following command:

```
pine -P pinerc.blank
```

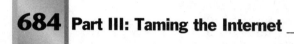

How do I make Pine work with my older terminal?

Pine does not support some older terminals (for example, TVI-925 and WYSE-60) very well. Some problems can be overcome with a proper termcap entry; for other problems, such as handling cursor keys, no good solution exists.

How do I prevent Pine from leaving mail in /usr/spool/mail?

You have several options:

- Leave inbox in `/usr/spool/mail`, but turn on the Pine option to prompt users to move messages that they have read to folders in their home directories when they exit Pine.

The following three options are for system administrators, not regular users.

- Modify your mail-delivery program to deliver mail directly to the user's home directory, and specify that path in your global pine.conf. (For an example, see the tmail program on `ftp.cac.washington.edu`.)
- Run the command touch mail.txt in each home directory. This command causes Pine (on start-up) to pull mail from /usr/spool/mail into ~/mail.txt. mail.txt will be a Tenex-format folder rather than a Berkeley mail-format folder (faster, but nonstandard).
- Link in the mbox driver when you build Pine. When Pine starts, this driver pulls mail from /usr/spool/mail into ~/mbox, which will be a Berkeley-format folder.

What PC communications software works with the Print to ANSI print option?

The attached-to-ANSI option works on most PC communication packages. In particular, Kermit, NCSA Telnet, and WinQVT have been tested. The developers have received reports that the option works in OS/2, using IBM's TCP/IP for OS/2 telnet capabilities (provided that you have updated to the latest corrective service floppy disks, which are readily available), as well as in QmodemPro for DOS, ProComm Plus for Windows, and Delrina's WinComm.

If you have a PostScript printer and are printing from a Windows communications program, you need to use a non-PostScript printer driver.

What Macintosh communications software works with the Print to ANSI print option?

The UW-modified versions of Kermit and NCSA Telnet are known to work with the attached-to-ANSI print option. Versaterm Pro also is reported to work.

How can someone without a MIME-aware mail program decipher an attachment?

Pine uses the MIME Internet standard for attachments. MIME uses Base64 encoding rather than uuencode, because uuencode uses characters that are transformed by some e-mail gateways; also, several incompatible versions of uuencode exist.

However, you can uuencode a file outside Pine and then use your editor to read in the uuencoded file. In Pine's default editor, pico, Ctrl-R is the command you use to read a file into a message.

If you use Pine's attachment feature, your recipient needs to have either a MIME-capable mail reader or software that can decode MIME. Fortunately, these programs are not hard to find. The major proprietary mail vendors have committed to MIME support, but some of their upgraded products are months from completion.

One product that can decipher a MIME attachment is munpack, from Carnegie-Mellon University. The program is available at the following location:

`ftp://ftp.andrew.cmu.edu/pub/mpack`

How do I convert Berkeley Mail aliases to Pine address book?

The Pine source distribution includes, in the contrib/utils directory, a shell script that performs this conversion. The script is called brk2pine.sh.

How do I convert Elm aliases to Pine address book?

Klaus Wacker (`wacker@physik.uni-dortmund.de`) wrote a Perl script, which he claims digests everything that Elm accepts and converts it to something that Pine accepts. The script is archived at the following location:

`http://www.Physik.Uni-Dortmund.DE/wacker/elm-to-pine`

References

Internet "Request For Comments" documents (RFCs) are available at:

`ftp://ds.internic.net/rfc`

Credits

This article is adapted from the Pine FAQ, which includes contributions from the following people:

Chris Alfeld `< calfeld@math.utah.edu>` or `<calfeld@east.east-slc.edu>`

Nancy McGough <inet-secrets@ii.com>

David L. Miller <dlm@cac.washington.edu>

Mike Ramey <mramey@u.washington.edu>

Klaus Wacker <wacker@physik.uni-dortmund.de>

The Pine Development Team and numerous Pine users worldwide

The On-Line FAQ

The on-line FAQ from which this article is adapted is posted about once a month to the newsgroups comp.mail.pine, comp.mail.misc, news.newusers.questions, comp.answers, and news.answers. You also can get the FAQ from any of the following places:

```
http://www.cac.washington.edu/pine
http://www.cis.ohio-state.edu/hypertext/faq/usenet/mail/pine-faq/faq.html
ftp://ftp.cac.washington.edu/pine/docs
ftp://rtfm.mit.edu/pub/usenet/news.answers/mail/pine-faq
```

Send mail to mail-server@rtfm.mit.edu, including the following text:

```
send usenet/news.answers/mail/pine-faq
```

Filtering Mail

by Nancy McGough <inet-secrets@ii.com>

One of the most frequently asked questions about e-mail is how to sort incoming messages into separate folders. This chapter provides basic instructions for UNIX and users to set up either procmail or elm's filter to filter incoming mailing-list messages. At the end there's also a discussion of how to use Eudora filters on Windows and Macs.

If your system has both procmail and filter installed, you should use procmail, which is *much* more robust and powerful than filter. This recommendation is almost universal; even the elm and filter developers recommend procmail over filter.

One area in which procmail is better than filter is in the way it can handle folder locking. For more information about folder locking, see the "What is folder locking?" section of the "Climbing Pine" article.

Mail Folder Strategies

It is a good idea to come up with a system for naming and managing your mail folders. With a good system, you will have an easier time dealing with the hundreds (or even thousands) of messages you will receive.

Naming Your Incoming-Mail Folders

For my incoming-mail folders, I use names that start with *IN*. I put mail sent to the procmail mailing list, for example, in a folder named IN.procmail. With this naming convention, when my folders are listed alphabetically, the incoming folders are together and near the top. These folders are near the top because UNIX is case-sensitive; uppercase letters come before lowercase letters in an ASCII sort.

Of course, you can use any names you like for your mail folders.

Terms used in this chapter

mailer: Mail user agent (MUA), such as pine or elm

pico: A friendly editor that is the default *pi*ne *co*mposer. Throughout this chapter you can replace *pico* with a different editor, if you like.

regular expression: Text that can include "wildcards"; used for searching.

~ or $HOME: Your home directory. You can always get to your home directory by typing **cd.**

Reading your incoming-mail folders

You can use your mailer or newsreader (if it can read mail folders) to read your incoming-mail folders. See the documentation for your mailer or newsreader for details. The appendix to this article gives pointers to documentation and user groups for some mailers and newsreaders.

Some suggestions for ways to do this in Pine are in the "How can I filter messages into different incoming folders?" section of the "Climbing Pine" article.

Procmail

Procmail is a powerful mail processor that can process your mail messages either as they arrive or after they are placed in a mail folder. This section describes the basics of setting up procmail to filter incoming mailing-list messages.

To find out how to use procmail to process existing mail folders, automatically reply to messages, and more, see the Procmail FAQ. Instructions for getting the Procmail FAQ are given at the end of this chapter.

Setting up procmail

To set up and test procmail, follow the fifteen steps given in this section. These steps are grouped as follows:

- Is procmail on your system?
- Setting up procmail files for testing
- Testing your procmail setup
- Setting up procmail files

Is procmail on your system?

1. **To find out whether procmail is on your system and what the full path to it is, use one of the following commands:**

   which procmail

   type procmail

   whereis procmail

   where procmail

   If your system doesn't have procmail, ask your system administrator to install it. The procmail package of tools is located at the following address:

   `ftp://ftp.informatik.rwth-aachen.de/pub/packages/procmail/procmail.tar.gz`

If your system administrator isn't able to do this, use a different mail processor, such as deliver, mailagent (described in a subsequent article in this chapter), or filter (described later in this article).

Setting up procmail files for testing

2. Create ~/.procmailrc, as follows:

```
cd
pico .procmailrc
```

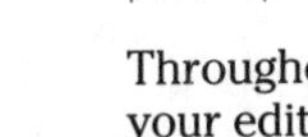

Throughout this chapter, I use pico for editing files. You can replace pico with your editor.

3. Enter a modified version of the following in ~/.procmailrc.

Lines that begin with # are comments about the next line. Comments are ignored by procmail.

```
#Set on when debugging
VERBOSE=off

#Replace mail with your mail directory (pine uses mail, elm uses Mail)
MAILDIR=$HOME/mail

#Directory for storing procmail log and rc (run command) files
PMDIR=$HOME/.procmail

LOGFILE=$PMDIR/log
INCLUDERC=$PMDIR/rc.testing
INCLUDERC=$PMDIR/rc.folders
```

4. Create the directory in which you will store your procmail log and rc files (this is the $PMDIR, which you set in the preceding code), as follows:

```
cd
mkdir .procmail
```

5. Create an rc (run commands) file for testing, as follows:

```
cd
cd .procmail
pico rc.testing
```

6. Enter the following in ~/.procmail/rc.testing:

```
:0:
* ^Subject:.*test
IN.testing
```

Note: The first line contains a zero (0), not the letter O. For now, don't worry about the meaning of this recipe, which is explained in "Explanation of test recipe," later in this article.

7. Create a ~/.forward file by typing the following (pico's -w flag tells pico not to auto-wrap lines):

```
cd
pico -w .forward
```

8. Enter a modified version of the following in ~/.forward:

```
"|IFS=' ' && exec /usr/local/bin/procmail -f- || exit 75 #nancym"
```

Following are some important notes:

- Make sure that you include all the quotation marks, both double (") and single (').
- The vertical bar (|) is a pipe.
- Replace /usr/local/bin with the correct path for procmail (refer to step 1).
- Replace nancym with your user ID. You need to put your user ID in your .forward file so that it will be different from any other .forward file on your system.
- Do not expect environment variables, such as $HOME, to work in your .forward file.
- Do not expect ~ to mean your home directory in the .forward file. If procmail resides below your home directory, type the *full* path.

9. On many systems, you need to make your .forward file world-readable and your home directory world-searchable for the mail transport agent to "see" it. To do this, type the following:

```
cd
chmod 644 .forward
chmod a+x .
```

Testing your procmail setup

10. Send yourself two test messages: one with *test* in the Subject header and one without *test* in the Subject header.

11. Start your mailer (such as pine or elm).

Make sure that the messages were delivered correctly. The message with *test* in the Subject header should be in the folder $MAILDIR/IN.testing; the one without *test* in the Subject header should be in your incoming mail folder.

If these messages were not delivered correctly, see "Troubleshooting procmail," later in this section.

Setting up procmail files

12. After you successfully test procmail, create rc.folders for filtering incoming messages into mail folders, as follows:

```
cd
cd .procmail
pico rc.folders
```

13. **In rc.folders, create a recipe, like the two example recipes below, for each of your mailing lists.**

```
# Recipe for filtering www-talk mailing list into IN.www-talk folder
:0:
* ^TOwww-talk
IN.www-talk

# Recipe for filtering procmail mailing list into IN.procmail folder
:0:
* ^TOprocmail
IN.procmail
```

The first recipe filters the www-talk mailing list; the second recipe filters the procmail mailing list. The following table describes the meaning of the first recipe:

Notation	***Meaning***
:0	Begin a recipe
:	Use a lock file
*	Begin a condition
^TOwww-talk	Match *To:*, *Cc:*, or other synonyms for *To* at the beginning of a line, followed by any or no characters, followed by the text *www-talk*.
IN.www-talk	If the match is successful, put the message in the folder $MAILDIR/IN.www-talk

Following are some important notes:

- ^TO is not a normal regular expression; it is a special procmail expression designed to catch any destination specification. For details, see the *MISCELLANEOUS* section of the procmailrc on-line manual pages.
- Do *not* put a space space between the caret (^) and the word *TO* in ^TO.
- Do *not* put a space between the ^TO and the text that you are matching on; it must be ^TO*text*.
- Both letters in TO must be capitalized.

14. **Repeat the procedure given in the "Testing your procmail setup" section above (steps 10 and 11) to make sure that things are still working.**

15. **In your .procmailrc file, turn the rc.testing line into a comment by putting a # at the beginning of the line. Your .procmailrc file will look like the following:**

```
VERBOSE=off
MAILDIR=$HOME/mail
PMDIR=$HOME/.procmail
LOGFILE=$PMDIR/log
# INCLUDERC=$PMDIR/rc.testing
INCLUDERC=$PMDIR/rc.folders
```

Leaving the rc.testing line in your .procmailrc file is useful for future testing.

Troubleshooting procmail

If messages are not delivered correctly, here are steps you can use to try to solve the problem.

1. Look at your $LOGFILE (~/.procmail/log) to see whether you can determine what the problem is.
2. Check these three files for typos:

```
~/.forward
~/.procmailrc
~/.procmail/rc.test
```

3. Use the instructions below to check the file and directory permissions of your .forward file. (These were set with the chmod commands in step 9 of "Setting up procmail.")

Type This	*To Do This*
cd	Go to your home directory
ls -l .forward	Check the permission; it should say -rw-r--r--
ls -ld .	Check the permission of home directory; it should say drwx?-x?-x

Each question mark may be the letter *r* or a hyphen (drwx- -x- -x, drwxr-xr-x, drwxr-x- -x, drwx- -xr-x are each acceptable).

4. If the above three steps do not locate the problem, edit your ~/.procmailrc file so that procmail will be verbose with its output, as follows:

```
VERBOSE=on
```

Test procmail by following the steps in the "Testing your procmail setup" section above (steps 10 and 11). Look at your $LOGFILE (which will contain verbose messages) to see if you can now determine what the problem is.

After you get procmail to work, you probably will want to set VERBOSE back to off.

5. If you still have problems, try the following alternate .forward files.

(Contributed by Stephen R. van den Berg <berg@pool.informatik.rwth-aachen.ed>)

In a perfect world, this .forward file works:

```
"|exec /usr/local/bin/procmail #nancym"
```

In an almost perfect world, this .forward file works:

```
"|exec /usr/local/bin/procmail USER=nancym"
```

In another world, this .forward file works:

```
"|IFS=' ';exec /usr/local/bin/procmail #nancym"
```

In a different world, this .forward file works:

```
"|IFS=' ';exec /usr/local/bin/procmail USER=nancym"
```

In a smrsh world, this .forward file works:

```
"|/usr/local/bin/procmail #nancym"
```

You can try these formats in different combinations; and the leading `"|` can be tried as `|"`, or vice versa.

If your system uses procmail as its local delivery agent, you do not need a .forward file; simply having a .procmailrc file suffices. To find out if procmail is the local delivery agent, ask your system administrator

Explanation of test recipe

Following is the recipe that you used earlier for testing:

```
:0:
* ^Subject: .*test
IN.testing
```

The following table explains the meaning of this recipe:

Notation	***Meaning***
:0	Begin a recipe
:	Use a lock file
*	Begin a condition
^Subject:.*test	Match *Subject* at the beginning of a line, followed by any number of any characters, followed by the text *test*.
IN.testing	If the match is successful, put in folder $MAILDIR/IN.testing

Tracking your incoming mail

You can use mailstat, a useful script that is part of the procmail package, to check your procmail log file. Check to see whether mailstat is on your system by typing one of the following commands:

which mailstat

type mailstat

whereis mailstat

where mailstat

If the script is on your system, type the following:

```
mailstat $HOME/.procmail/log
```

This command displays a concise version of your log file and moves your log file to log.old. You may want to put the preceding line in your .login or .profile file so that each time you log in, you will see a listing of how many messages you've received since the last time you ran mailstat and what folders these messages were delivered to.

You can get a mailstat listing of log.old by using the -o flag, as follows:

```
mailstat -o $HOME/.procmail/log
```

If mailstat is not on your system, ask your system administrator to install it. The script is located with all the other procmail tools (see "Is Procmail on Your System" for the ftp location).

Getting procmail help

On-line Manual Pages:

Man Page Name	*What the Man Pages Cover*
`procmail`	Autonomous mail processor
`procmailrc`	procmail rc file
`procmailex`	procmail rc-file examples
`procmailsc`	procmail weighted scoring technique
`egrep`	Regular expression and searching a file for a regular expression (procmail uses egrep-style regular expressions along with some of its own expressions, such as ^TO)
`formail`	Mail reformatter
`sendmail`	Sending mail over the Internet

Newsgroup:

`comp.mail.misc`

Mailing list:

`procmail@informatik.rwth-aachen.de`

Subscribe to the procmail mailing list by sending mail to `procmail-request@informatik.rwth-aachen.de` with **subscribe** in the Subject line.

Procmail archives:

Get a list of files available at the procmail mail server by sending mail to `procmail-request@informatik.rwth-aachen.de`, with **archive ls** in the Subject line.

Get the Best of Procmail mailing list (you'll need gzip and a MIME decoder to unpack it) by sending mail to `procmail-request@informatik.rwth-aachen.de`, with **archive get best_of_procmail_list*** in the Subject line.

Filter

Filter is part of the elm package of tools. You can use filter to filter your incoming mail even if you are not using elm to read your mail.

Note: If both procmail and filter are installed on your system, you should use procmail, which is much more robust and powerful than filter. This recommendation is almost universal; even the developers of elm and filter recommend procmail over filter. You can lose mail messages when you use filter; this situation is rare but has occurred.

Setting up filter

To set up and test filter, follow the eleven steps given in this section. These steps are grouped as follows:

- Is filter on your system?
- Setting up filter files for testing
- Testing your filter setup
- Setting up filter files

Is filter on your system?

1. **To find out whether filter is on your system and what the full path to it is, use one of the following commands:**

   which filter

   type filter

   whereis filter

   where filter

   If your system doesn't have filter, ask your system administrator to install it; even better, ask her to install procmail.

Setting up filter files for testing

2. **Determine the full path of your home directory by typing the following:**

```
cd
pwd
```

3. **Create ~/.elm/filter-rules, as follows:**

```
cd
mkdir .elm
cd .elm
pico filter-rules
```

   Note: Throughout this chapter, I use pico for editing files. You can replace pico with your editor.

4. Enter a modified version of the following in your ~/.elm/filter-rules file:

```
if (subject contains "test") then save "/j/nancym/Mail/IN.testing"
```

Following are some important notes:

- Replace /j/nancym with your home-directory path, which you determined earlier (in step 2 of "Setting up filter files").
- Replace /Mail with the name of the directory where your mail folders are stored. Pine and Berkeley mail use /mail (lowercase *m*), and elm uses /Mail (uppercase *M*).

5. To see what the filter rule does, type the following at your UNIX prompt:

```
filter -r
```

6. Create a ~/.forward file by typing the following (pico's -w flag tells pico not to auto-wrap lines):

```
cd
pico -w .forward
```

7. Enter a modified version of the following in your ~/.forward file:

```
"|/usr/local/bin/filter -o /j/nancym/.elm/filter-errors"
```

Following are some important notes:

- Make sure that you include the quotation marks (").
- The vertical bar (|) is a pipe.
- Replace /usr/local/bin with the correct path for filter (see step 1 in "Setting up filter").
- Replace /j/nancym with your home directory (see step 2 in "Setting up filter").
- Do not expect environment variables, such as $HOME, to work in your .forward file.
- Do not expect ~ to mean your home directory in the .forward file. If filter resides below your home directory, type the *full* path.

8. On many systems, you need to make your .forward file world-readable and your home directory world-searchable for the mail transport agent to "see" it. To do this, type the following:

```
cd
chmod 644 .forward
chmod a+x .
```

Testing your filter setup

9. Send yourself two test messages: one with *test* in the Subject header and one without *test* in the Subject header.

10. Start your mailer (such as pine or elm).

Make sure that the messages were delivered correctly. The message with *test* in the Subject header should be in the folder IN.testing; the one without *test* in the Subject header should be in your incoming mail folder.

If these messages were not delivered correctly, see "Troubleshooting filter," later in this section.

Setting up filter files

11. After you successfully test filter, edit ~/.elm/filter-rules so that it contains a modified version of the following:

```
# if (subject contains "test") then save "/j/nancym/Mail/IN.testing"
if (to contains "www-talk") then save "/j/nancym/Mail/IN.www-talk"
if (to contains "hopos-l") then save "/j/nancym/Mail/IN.hopos"
```

Following are some important notes:

- Replace /j/nancym with your home-directory path.
- Replace /Mail with the name of the directory where your mail folders are stored.
- Replace the mailing-list string (for example, "www-talk") and the name of the mail folder (for example, IN.www-talk) with text for your mailing lists.
- Rather than delete the testing line, you can turn it into a comment (by preceding it with #) so that you can use it for future testing.

Note: The phrase `to contains "text"` is interpreted by filter to mean that either the *To* or *Cc* header contains *text.*

Troubleshooting filter

If messages are not delivered correctly, here are steps you can use to try to solve the problem.

1. Look at your ~/.elm/filter-errors and /.elm/filterlog files to see whether you can determine what the problem is.
2. Check these files for typos: ~/.forward and ~/.elm/filter-rules.
3. Use the instructions below to check the file and directory permissions of your .forward file. (These were set with the chmod commands in step 8 of "Setting up filter.")

Type This	*To Do This*
cd	Go to your home directory
ls -l .forward	Check the permission; it should say -rw-r- -r- -
ls -ld .	Check the permission of home directory; it should say drwx?-x?-x

Note: Each question mark may be the letter *r* or a hyphen (drwx- -x- -x, drwxr-xr-x, drwxr-x- -x, drwx- -xr-x are each acceptable).

4. If the above three steps do not locate the problem, edit your ~/.forward file so that filter will be verbose with its output (use the -vo flag), as follows:

```
"|/usr/local/bin/filter -vo /j/nancym/.elm/filter-errors"
```

Test filter by following the steps in the "Testing your filter setup" (steps 9 and 10). Look at your ~/.elm/filter-errors and /.elm/filterlog files to see whether you can determine what the problem is.

After you get filter to work, you probably will want to change the -vo flag back to -o.

Tracking your incoming mail

You can get a short summary of filter's activity by typing the following:

```
filter -s
```

For a longer summary, type the following:

```
filter -S
```

Alternatively, you can look at the log file itself (~/.elm/filterlog).

You should look at ~/.elm/filter-errors regularly to make sure that things are working. You can check filter-errors automatically each time that you log in by placing the following line in your .login or .profile file:

```
tail $HOME/elm/filter-errors
```

You probably also want to delete filterlog and filter-errors regularly, so that they don't fill your disk. To get a summary of the filter log and clear it, type the following:

```
filter -cs
```

Getting filter help

Web page:

http://www.myxa.com/elm.html

FAQs:

http://www.cis.ohio-state.edu/hypertext/faq/usenet/elm/top.html

On-line Manual Page:

filter(1)

Newsgroup:

comp.mail.elm

Filtering Mail with Eudora

(Contributed by John R. Levine)

If you use the popular mail agent Eudora on a Macintosh or with Microsoft Windows, you can use Eudora's built-in filtering features. These features are present in the commercial versions (2.x), not in the free versions (1.x) — one example of getting what you pay for.

In Eudora, choose Window⇨Filters to see the Filters window, shown in Figure 25-1.

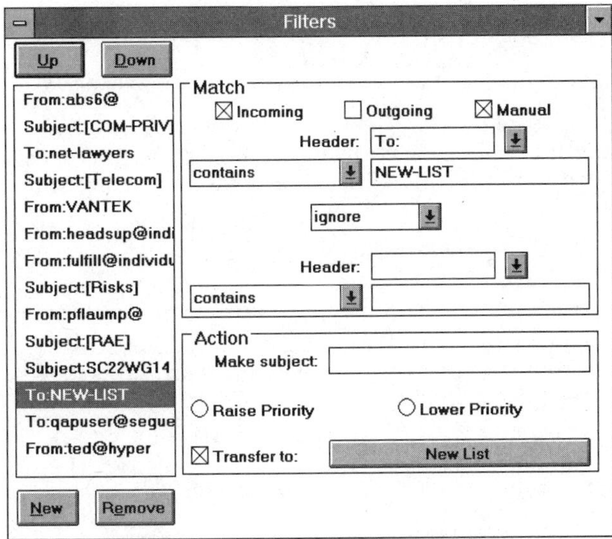

Figure 25-1: The Eudora Mail Filters window.

You can apply each of Eudora's filters at any of three times:

- To incoming mail as it arrives (the most useful time)
- To mail in folders, when you apply the filter command
- To outgoing mail when it's sent (useful for filing copies of outgoing mail)

Filtering works by looking for strings of text in the header or body of messages. Each filtering rule can have one or two tests. When a message is filtered, you can change its subject line (usually by adding a keyword or two), change its priority (useful for sorting), or move it to a specific mailbox (by far the most useful procedure).

If, for example, you subscribe to NEW-LIST, which has announced new mailing lists, and you want to put all the messages in a mailbox, follow these steps:

1. **Create a new rule by clicking New.**
2. **Click the Incoming box to make the rule match incoming mail.**
3. **In the Header box, scroll to check for the To: header.**
4. **Scroll the Test box (the one below Header) to contains.**
5. **Type** NEW-LIST **in the text box.**
6. **Because no second test exists, leave the second test ignore.**
7. **In the Action box, click Transfer to: and then click the bar to the right to select the mailbox to transfer to (in this case, NEWLIST).**
8. **Close the Filters window by clicking its upper left-hand corner.**
9. **If Eudora asks whether you want to save the changes, click Yes.**

Henceforth, all NEW-LIST mail will be sorted into a separate mailbox.

You can have as many filter rules as you want. To change an existing rule, open the Filters window, click the name of the filter that you want to edit (to display that filter in the Match and Action boxes), and then make your changes.

Credits

This article is adapted from the Filtering Mail FAQ and the Procmail FAQ, which include contributions from the following people (and many others — see the FAQs for a more complete list of credits):

David L. Miller `<dlm@cac.washington.edu>`

Cookie Monster `<kmanley@bits.fc.hp.com>`

Jim Showalter `<gamma@mintaka.disa.mil>`

David W. Tamkin `<dattier@mcs.com>`

Rick Troxel `<rick@helix.nih.gov>`

Stephen R. van den Berg `<berg@pool.informatik.rwth-aachen.de>`

Syd Weinstein `<syd@dsinc.myxa.com>`

The On-Line FAQ

The on-line FAQs from which this article is adapted are posted about once a month to the newsgroups `comp.mail.misc`, `comp.mail.elm`, `comp.mail.pine`, `comp.answers`, and `news.answers`. You also can get the FAQs from the following places:

Filtering Mail FAQ

`http://www.cis.ohio-state.edu/hypertext/faq/usenet/mail/filtering-faq/faq.html`

`ftp://rtfm.mit.edu/pub/usenet/news.answers/mail/filtering-faq`

Send mail to `mail-server@rtfm.mit.edu`, including the following text:

```
send usenet/news.answers/mail/filtering-faq
```

Procmail FAQ

`http://www.cis.ohio-state.edu/hypertext/faq/usenet/mail/procmail-faq/faq.html`

`ftp://rtfm.mit.edu/pub/usenet/news.answers/mail/procmail-faq`

Send mail to `mail-server@rtfm.mit.edu`, including the following text:

```
send usenet/news.answers/mail/procmail-faq
```

Additional Information Sources

This appendix gives pointers to documentation and user groups for some mailers and newsreaders.

Pine

FAQ:

`http://www.cac.washington.edu/pine/faq/`

`ftp://ftp.cac.washington.edu/pine/docs/faq`

Manual:

`pine(1)`

Newsgroup:

`comp.mail.pine` (linked to pine mailing list)

Mailing list:

`pine-info@cac.washington.edu` (linked to pine newsgroup)

Subscribe to the pine-info mailing list by sending mail to `majordomo@cac.washington.edu`, with **subscribe pine-info** in the body of the message.

Elm

Web page:

http://www.myxa.com/elm.html

FAQs:

http://www.cis.ohio-state.edu/hypertext/faq/usenet/elm/top.html

Manual:

elm(1)

Newsgroup:

comp.mail.elm

Emacs mail mode

Newsgroups:

nus.emacs.help

comp.emacs

Web page:

http://www.cis.ohio-state.edu/hypertext/faq/usenet/gnu-emacs-faq/part5/faq.html

MH

FAQ:

http://www.cis.ohio-state.edu/hypertext/faq/usenet/mh-faq/top.html

Manual:

mh(1)

Newsgroup:

comp.mail.mh

Mail

Manual:

mail(1)

Newsgroup:

comp.mail.misc

nn

FAQ:

`http://www.cis.ohio-state.edu/hypertext/faq/bngusenet/news/software/nn/top.html`

Manual:

`nn(1)`

Newsgroup:

`news.software.nn`

Processing Mail Automatically with Mailagent

by Raphaël Manfredi <ram@iecc.com>

Mailagent is a powerful, UNIX-based mail-processing package that can process your mail messages at arrival time, via a .forward hook, or later, when the messages are already saved in a mail folder.

Mailagent is written in Perl and therefore has all the advantages of being interpreted — that is, it is easy to enhance dynamically and to customize.

This article describes the basics of setting up mailagent to process incoming mail messages from within a .forward file. To find out about the more advanced features of mailagent, please refer to the `mailagent(1)` manual page.

Setting Up Mailagent

To set up mailagent, follow these steps:

1. **Make sure that mailagent is available on your system.**

   The easiest way to do this is to run `mailagent -V`, which prints the mailagent version if it is available. Otherwise, the shell issues an error message — `mailagent: not found` or something like it.

   The MTA (Mail Transport Agent, the program that delivers the mail; usually, sendmail) does not deliver to mailagent directly but to an intermediate (small) filter program. Two versions of this program are available: shell and C. To choose a version, refer to the `mailagent(1)` manual page. I recommend that you use the C version first and move to the shell version if you can't run a binary program from your .forward file.

2. **Locate the filter program (filter or filter.sh, depending on whether you choose the C or the shell version, respectively).**

   The program will be in some directory, such as /usr/local/lib/mailagent. From now on, this chapter assumes that you use the C filter and that it is located in /usr/local/lib/mailagent.

3. **Copy the file /usr/local/lib/mailagent/mailagent.cf as ~/.mailagent, and edit it to configure your system correctly.**

   The file contains two distinct sections. You have to set up the first section ("Configuration").

   The minimal set of variables that you must set correctly — that is, for which you cannot rely on the default set in the file — are shown in this list:

   - *home:* Your HOME directory
   - *path:* The path to be used to locate at least mailagent and Perl
   - *p_xxx:* The path to be appended to the preceding path when the program is running on machine *xxx*
   - *user:* Your login name
   - *name:* Your name
   - *level:* Logging level (I recommend that you raise it to 20 for testing)

4. **Ensure that the directories configured in your ~/.mailagent under logdir, spool, and queue do exist.**

   If you use the standard setting, this step requires the following commands:

   ```
   cd
   mkdir var
   cd var
   mkdir log mailagent
   cd mailagent
   mkdir queue
   ```

5. **Create a rule file (named ~/.rules, by default) for testing, as follows:**

   ```
   cd
   vi .rules
   ```

6. **Enter the following line in ~/.rules:**

   ```
   Subject: /test/            { SAVE testing };
   ```

   This rule specifies that if you receive a mail message whose subject line contains the word *test,* that mail is saved in a folder named `testing` in the default folder directory (~/Mail).

7. **Create a ~/.forward file, as follows:**

   ```
   "|exec /usr/local/lib/mailagent/filter >> /export/home/ram/.bak 2>&1"
   ```

This line specifies that every mail message will be piped (hence, the leading | character) to the filter program and that any output from that program (such as errors) will be appended to some file in your home directory, with stderr following stdout (2>&1) in traditional sh syntax.

Note: Remember these important points: Your .forward file is always processed by sh, regardless of your login shell. Replace /export/home/ram with the full path to your proper login directory. That part makes your .forward file unique and can save you a great deal of trouble if anything goes wrong — just look at your ~/.bak file to get a copy of the error messages. Naturally, you must replace /usr/local/lib/mailagent/filter with the proper filter path on your machine.

8. **Ensure that your ~/.forward file can be properly looked up by sendmail by issuing the following set of commands:**

```
cd
chmod a+r .forward
chmod a+x .
```

9. **Send yourself two test messages: one with *test* in the subject line and one without *test* in the subject line.**
10. **Check your ~/.bak file; it should be empty.**
11. **Check your ~/var/log/agentlog file to see what really happened to your messages.**

    Watch out for any ERROR or WARNING logs. These logs assume that you have left at least the default logging level (9) in ~/.mailagent (the "level" variable). But for testing, that login level should be raised to 20 to help you diagnose what's going on, as mentioned in step 3.
12. **Look in ~/Mail/testing; you should find the message whose Subject line contained the word *test*.**
13. **Make sure that the other message was delivered to your regular mailbox.**

    Because no match occurred in your rule file, the mail is left in your mailbox by default.

Troubleshooting

Here are some hints for troubleshooting:

- If your mail was not properly delivered, make sure that your rule file and configuration file are correct by issuing the following command:

```
mailagent -d
```

- If the preceding command does not output the single rule you put in ~/.rules, make sure that you correctly performed steps 3 and 4 in the preceding section (which are the crucial steps for ensuring a proper configuration setup).

- Check the ~/.bak file for error messages.
- Check for typos in ~/.forward, ~/.mailagent, and ~/.rules.
- Check the file and directory permissions of your .forward file (set in steps 7 and 8 in the preceding section).

The easiest way to ensure the proper permissions for your ~/.forward file is to issue, in sequence, the commands in the following table:

Type This	*To Do This*
cd	Go to your home directory
ls -l .forward	Check the permission; it should say -rw-r- -r- -
ls -ld .	Check permission of home directory; it should say drwx?-x?-x

The question marks in the preceding line may be *r*s, hyphens, or one of each (for example, drwx- -x- -x, drwxr-xr-x, drwxr-x- -x, or drwx- -xr-x).

- If none of the preceding hints helped you to identify the problem and you can't figure it out from the output in ~/.bak or in the ~/var/log/agentlog file (or whatever file you have configured for logging within your ~/.mailagent file, with the variables *log* and *logdir*), make sure that your mail is not waiting in the MTA's queue, which may be the case if the agentlog file is empty. If you are using sendmail as your MTA, you can print the queue by typing this line:

  ```
  /usr/lib/sendmail -bp
  ```

- As a last resort, look at the `mailagent(1)` manual page; the "Testing Your Installation" section contains more tips and suggests other things to check.

Using Mailagent

When you have tested mailagent successfully, the program is ready to process your mail. All you have to do is extend the ~/.rules file to add more rules, such as the following:

```
To Cc: www-talk      { SAVE www-talk };
To Cc: agent-users   { SAVE agent-users };
```

These two rules filter the mailing lists `www-talk` and `agent-users` into their respective folders, whether the mailing list addresses appear in the To or the Cc header. Because they are not qualified as a pattern match (contrary to the test rule in step 6), the first rule, for example, matches logins in the address — that is, it matches `www-talk@chip.com`; `chip!www-talk`; or simply `www-talk`, if this alias is local. This rule works only for selectors — such as To, Cc, and From — that are known to contain addresses. If you want to sort on patterns in the Subject of messages for instance, you must use a pattern-matching syntax, as in this example:

```
Subject: /star trek/  { SAVE star-trek; };
```

to save in a folder called `star-trek` all mail whose subject contains the words *star trek*. Case matters, but keep reading.

Because mailagent is written in Perl, you have at your disposal all the power of Perl's regular expressions, which means that you can write things like the following:

```
To Cc: agent-users    { REJECT AGENT };
<AGENT> Subject: /^\w*subscribe/i          { DELETE };
<AGENT> *       { UNIQUE -a; SAVE agent };
```

The second line makes use of that Perl extended regular expression syntax: `\w` matches an alphanumeric character plus an underscore character (_), and the trailing `i` option requests a case-insensitive match.

Also, because in Perl regular expression syntax, `\b` matches a word-boundary and \s matches any space or tab character, the Star Trek message sorting can be written in a much more robust form:

```
Subject: /\bstar\s+trek\b/i       { SAVE star-trek; };
```

This line matches various subjects, such as "Last Star Trek season" or "I am addicted to Star Trek," but not "Tristar treks" — whatever that means.

You have a real automaton at your disposal. You can enter a special state (AGENT, in the preceding example) and continue parsing by scanning only for rules tagged by this mode. The first match stops the automaton unless you REJECT the continuation of processing. The filtering automaton always takes unrestricted rules into account and ignores those restricted to a mode it is not currently in. For example, if at some point the automaton is in the state "NEWS," it does not consider rules tagged <AGENT>, as in the preceding example.

The UNIQUE `-a` action, followed by SAVE, ensures that only one copy per message ID ends up in your agent folder.

You can have more than one action per rule, and the last action uses an asterisk (*) to match anything — that is, the action part that appears inside the braces ({}) always is executed in AGENT mode, when it is reached by the automaton.

The rule file is parsed from the top, down to the first successful match, with each rule being examined depending on the filtering mode. Issuing a REJECT asks the automaton to continue its rule-scanning from where it was down to the end of the rule file, again stopping at the first match.

All in all, the syntax is relatively intuitive and easy to read. You simply have to learn which actions are possible and what they mean.

Tracking Your Incoming Mail

If you are curious about what mailagent does to your mail, you have two options:

- Look at your agentlog file, with a log level set to 9.
- Get a summary of all the actions that were performed by running `mailagent -summary` or `mailagent -surat` (to get only statistics for your latest rule file version).

The second option is possible only if you initialized the statistics-gathering process by creating a ~/var/mailagent/mailagent.st file (with the default setting from ~/.mailagent).

You get a clear picture of the processing by seeing which rules match, how often, in which state, and so on. Mailagent also tells you how many times you saved or deleted messages, for example, by listing each of the commands you have used.

Mailagent statistics are triggered by a simple `mailagent -s` command. The letters given after the `-s` in the {u,m,a,r,y,t} set are options that alter the output normally given by `mailagent -s`, as in `mailagent -surat`.

Look at ~/.bak occasionally to make sure that no error is pending.

How Safe Is Mailagent Processing?

As soon as the filter program takes hold of your message, you can rest assured that the mail will be filtered one way or the other. If the filter can't queue your mail, it exits with an exit status of 75. Sendmail recognizes that status as a direction to deliver the mail later, and the mail message waits safely in sendmail's queue.

So if filter gets your message, it immediately forks and exits with a 0 status for sendmail. Sendmail understands that as a notification that its work is finished and therefore should terminate, hence saving resources. The filter program then calls mailagent on the queued message (in mailagent's private queue) to process the message.

Only after successful processing does mailagent delete the queued message. In a heavily loaded system, the worst things that could happen would be duplicate processing of a message or a bounce-back (in which the mail is returned to its sender along with a delivery failure notice) when sendmail cannot fork and launch the filter program specified in your .forward file.

Under catastrophic conditions, filter or mailagent simply dumps the message on stdout, for ~/.bak to catch, preceded by the reason that processing was aborted.

Locking under Mailagent

By default, mailagent proceeds with a fixed locking scheme (.lock extension) plus `flock()` if asked to do so at configuration time. Mailagent supports NFS-secure locks and also can use nonstandard locking procedures, which you can configure from within ~/.mailagent (variables *nfslock* and *mboxlock*).

Mailagent cannot, however, support locking on a rule basis (yet!). The author is willing to raise the priority of that item if someone comes up with a legitimate need for that feature which could not be worked around by a Perl escape.

Folder Types Supported

Mailagent can deliver mail to plain UNIX folders, to MMDF folders, to MH folders with built-in unseen-sequence updating, and with locks (not like rcvstore, which does not), or to directories (such as MH, but without unseen-sequence support and with alternative names possible).

Mailagent also supports delivery to folders for which the x bit is set, in which case mailagent interprets those folders as being hooks. Mailagent either pipes the message to the program or additionally interprets the hook to do more processing. For more details, see the "MAIL HOOKS" section of the `mailagent(1)` manual page. The subject of mail hooks was introduced to modularize mail filtering.

Mailagent References

For more information about mailagent, read the `mailagent` man page (it's about 47 pages long); also refer to the `perl(1)` and `sendmail(8)` man pages.

You may want to read the newsgroup `comp.mail.misc`.

You can subscribe to a mailing list about mailagent, called `agent-users@foretune.co.jp`. Subscribe to the list by sending mail to `majordomo@foretune.co.jp`, including the text *subscribe agent-users*.

Current mailagent sources are available; ftp to `ftp://ftp.foretune.co.jp/pub/network/mail/mailagent`.

Raphaël Manfredi graduated from the Ecole des Mines, France, in 1991. He designed and implemented the back-end and run-time of the ISE Eiffel 3 compiler during two years in Santa Barbara, California, and is now porting DEC OSF/1 3.0 on the ACRI superscalar computer in Lyon, France. He also maintains the dist-3.0 package, which includes metaconfig, the Configure script generator.

Demystifying Mail Auto-Responders

by Dave Taylor <taylor@netcom.com>

If you've ever imagined having a gleaming cousin of C3P0 answering the phone for you, seeing who is knocking at the door, and generally helping you focus on the important stuff in your life, you're probably ready for an e-mail robot, too. If you're like me, you also receive quite a bit of electronic mail each and every day, and if you skip logging in for a few days, cleaning up can be quite a task! This chapter shows you how to have your computer answer your mail for you.

Although I can't help you with the telephone or your front door, I can show you how to get some free — or shareware — software that will not only dramatically trim the mail in your e-mailbox automatically but also allow you to make lots of different files, programs, documents, and even product catalogs available to other users without any intervention on your part.

I'll talk about three programs: *Embot*, a simple-to-use mail auto-responder that offers you drop-and-distribute ease with even the least expensive Internet access account; and its more powerful relative, *Filter*, which offers an actual language for writing instructions on how to process, respond to, forward, or even automatically delete certain categories of electronic mail; and *Procmail*, a supercharged mail processing package that only a programmer could love.

Embot

Running a business or distributing your latest poetry or song lyrics to people are two of the many tasks you can accomplish with e-mail robots. These robots are programs that sift through electronic mail as it arrives on a computer to see whether they can handle the requests without bothering you or even dropping the message into your virtual inbox. At their simplest, e-mail robots can be a handy way for you to make information available to the millions of people on the Internet for incredibly little expense. At their most sophisticated, e-mail robots can field and forward mail that is better handled by different members of your team, delete messages from specified people or sites, and even feed to other programs some messages that you designate for special processing.

The problem with most e-mail robots is that they're rather tricky to set up, with complex filtering rules that you have to specify — and which you hope will work correctly. The price of making a mistake is that your mail might be deleted incorrectly, or that your mail robot will automatically answer messages that you want to read without even telling you!

That's why the Embot program was created. Embot offers the key capabilities of bigger, more sophisticated mail robot programs, but with the added advantage that it requires no special filtering language, no shell scripts, no programming, and no more than five minutes' worth of setup. When you finish setting up the program, you can add new files to your list of files available to e-mail users by putting them in a special directory. That's it; Embot does the rest.

Embot is incredibly easy to work with, and you don't even need any special permissions to get it installed at your site (you can do it yourself, as you'll see in a few minutes), but it has some limits, of course. Embot doesn't know how to forward messages or how to delete mail that you don't want to see. On the other hand, it's smart enough that if you tell it to answer *all* your e-mail automatically, it sends helpful information to people who don't request things correctly. That's right — not the ugly errors that people are used to seeing on the Internet (`504: <readme> file unknown` or some such nonsense), but readable explanations written for people to read and figure out.

The program works by looking for certain instructions that are contained either in the subject line or body of e-mail messages that come in to your mailbox. Any line that begins with *send* or *get* is checked against the set of available files and documents. If a match exists, the program automatically mails back the specified file without any human intervention. If no match exists, the program sends a message back saying so and listing the correct names of the files that are available to the user. The requests *help* or *info* are treated as synonyms for *send help* or *send info*, to ensure that other folk can get started working with your e-mail server with minimal effort.

If you're using a UNIX system or have an account on a UNIX-based Internet access provider, you can use Embot. If you're using a shared machine, you may not even have to install the program; Embot may already be on the system. (If not, it's a good move to ask the maintenance or administration team whether they're interested in a systemwide installation.) You can check for the program simply by typing **embot check** at the command prompt. If the program is not available, you'll see a message similar to `command not found`.

How to obtain and install a copy

Because the Embot program is a mail robot, it should be no surprise to you that the easiest way to obtain a copy of it is to send e-mail. The recommended approach is to send a message to `embot@northcoast.com` with the phrase `send embot`.

Within a few minutes, you'll receive a copy of the Embot program in your electronic mailbox. Simply save the message to a file named embot.mail.

Getting Embot ready to help you with your e-mail involves three phases: unpacking the program, building the program, and installing and configuring the program.

First on the agenda is unpacking the program, which you can do with a UNIX command. After you save the e-mail message to the file embot.mail, type the following command at the $ or % prompt:

```
cat embot.mail | sed "1,/^$/d' | sh
```

This command automatically unpacks all the various files that are included in the Embot application, placing those files in the current directory.

The next step is creating an executable application. To build the program, you need to ask the system to translate all the C source files to a single executable program that the computer will be able to work with directly. You can have the computer translate Embot by compiling the source code, which you can accomplish with a single word:

```
make
```

Two possible results can occur from your typing this command: either it worked fine, or it spat out a set of confusing error messages. If the compile process worked and finished without incident, the output looks like the following:

```
make
     cc -O -DBSD -c error.c
     cc -O -DBSD -c interact.c
     cc -O -DBSD -c log.c
     cc -O -DBSD -c mail_utils.c
     cc -O -DBSD -c embot.c
     cc -O -DBSD -c savemsg.c
     cc -O -DBSD -c sendfile.c
     cc -O -DBSD -c utils.c
     cc -O -DBSD error.o interact.o log.o mail_utils.o embot.o savemsg.o
sendfile.o utils.o -o embot
```

The other possibility is that the compile fails for some obscure reason or other, ending with something that looks more or less like the following:

```
make
cc -c error.c
./embot.h: line 14: Can't find include file dirent.h
*** Error code 1
Make: . Stop.
```

If you don't see this exact output, you'll doubtless see some other such grievous error that seems much more scary than it really is.

In this case, the odds are excellent that you have an account on a machine that is set up based on the Berkeley Software Distribution version of UNIX rather than on the more common AT&T System V design. To fix it, you'll need to add a special instruction to the make command, as follows:

```
make CFLAGS=-DBSD
```

Type that command, and Embot should build fine. If you have further problems, you'll need to chat with your system administrator or someone else who has expertise on your local configuration.

The hardest part of the project is done. The final step is to do some file-system management, create a couple of new directories, move a few files around, and then test to ensure that you installed Embot correctly.

Directories are created in UNIX with the mkdir command (you probably know that), and files are moved with the mv command. You want to create a special Embot directory that serves as the home base of the program itself when running, which can be done with the `mkdir` command:

```
mkdir Embot
```

Now move a couple of files around with the `mv` command:

```
mv help Embot
mv default-msg Embot/.default-msg
```

Notice the period after the slash in the second command. By prefacing the name of this file with a dot, it ensures that when Embot sends back a list of the available files, it doesn't include the default message file `.default-msg`. This helps eliminate confusion.

Congratulations — you've built and configured Embot. To check it out, type the following command:

```
embot check
```

Following is what you should see:

```
Checking your Embot configuration . . .
 Account = taylor, fullname = Dave Taylor
 Home directory = /users/taylor
Embot home directory (/users/taylor/Embot) is okay.

Embot generic reply file (/users/taylor/Embot/.default-msg) looks okay.

Embot help message (/users/taylor/Embot/help) looks fine.

I can't find a .forward file for you: I can't filter your e-mail without my
being added to this file or some equivalent.

Done checking your configuration.
```

As the program itself notes, things are OK, but you don't have Embot hooked up in your .forward file, so it can't check your electronic mail.

The final step in the configuration of Embot, therefore, is to tell the system that you want the program to filter through your electronic mail as it's delivered to you. You can do so by creating a file called .forward. The easiest way to create this file is to use the following command:

```
echo "|$HOME/embot" > .forward
```

That's it — you're done configuring and setting up Embot.

Exploring some Embot capabilities

I'll be honest: Unless you're really excited about computers, the preceding section probably was uninteresting to you, like an overly long lecture. But now that you have Embot installed and configured on your account, you're ready to do all sorts of interesting things.

The best way to learn about Embot is to ask it for help. Type the following command:

```
embot help
```

Embot tells you the following:

```
Welcome to Embot! I understand a variety of interactive commands,
all of which should be specified on the command line:
```

```
stats      obtain statistics about embot usage, by requested file
users      produce a list of people who have accessed your embot
wanted file   see who has requested the specified file
check      Quick checks to see if things are configured OK
clear      clear your log files (your log file is 2367 bytes)

I also have a couple of different starting flags:

    -a       Respond to ALL mail sent:
             only use this if I have my own account
    -v       For testing this produces a log of my actions.
             Only for when I'm being used interactively!
```

Unlike most UNIX programs, which are rife with obscure single-letter commands, Embot understands words. If you want to find out who has accessed files from your archive, for example, simply type **embot stats**. You can even find out who asked for a specific file by using the embot wanted command. If I want to find out who has requested a copy of the Embot program, for example, I could simply type

```
embot wanted embot
```

and be regaled with a long list of e-mail addresses. If you set up a busy mail server, don't forget to occasionally clear out the Embot log file by using **embot clear**. Notice also that when you typed **embot help**, Embot showed you the size of your log file (in the earlier example, 2,367 bytes).

If, instead of having the program help out with mail before you have to see it, you want to give Embot its own account, specify `|embot -a` to have *all* mail checked and answered.

You can get more help by sending yourself e-mail. Remember that the easiest way to communicate with Embot is to send e-mail. Following is what you'll get back if you send yourself a message that says *help* or *send help:*

```
Subject: Some tips on using the Embot program

Hi! I'm Embot, and I've been set up to look through e-mail messages
as they arrive here and try to extract and respond to requests for
files and other such miscellaneous tasks. I'm really quite easy to
work with -- or so my Dad says -- and all you have to remember is that
if you send any requests that I don't understand, I'll drop them
in the mailbox of my owner so he or she can respond by hand. That's
a lot slower, however, since humans don't think as quickly as us
computers do, but that's another subject entirely.

Anyway, to get files, handouts, and other information directly all
you need to do is know the name of the file and send a request to
me like:

    send thefilename
```

```
This can appear in the subject of the message or in the body of the
message. If you want a bunch of files, send me a single message with
all your requests in the body of the message, and I'll send them back
as a number of different e-mail messages. My owner won't even know!

To start out, send me a request to list all the available files. The
easiest way to do this is to have "list" as either the subject of
the message or within the message body itself. I'll jump into action,
build a list of all files and information that I'm authorized to send,
and mail that back to you, probably within five minutes of your request.

Once you have that, you can even just reply to that message, prefacing
the files you'd like with the word "send."

That's about it. Any messages I don't understand, like I said, will
be dropped in the mailbox of my owner, and if you request "help"
you'll get a copy of this message.

If you'd like a copy of the Embot program to help you filter your
own electronic mail, I'd be delighted to help you out. You can get a
copy by sending mail to my clone master at embot@northcoast.com. Specify
"send embot" in the message and you'll get a copy of my source code
and installation instructions as fast as I can spell mitosis!

    Thanks for working with me, and I look forward to hearing from
    you again in the near future.

            Bye for now.
                        -- Embot
```

If you set things up so that all mail is answered, rather than just mail that contains specific requests, you'll see the following if you send a message that didn't contain any meaningful requests (it's the message in the file Embot/.default-msg, which you moved into your Embot directory with the `mv` command earlier in the installation process):

```
Subject: I couldn't understand your e-mail

Hi! You've mailed a message to me, but I'm Embot, not a human, so
I only understand certain specific requests and comments in my
e-mail. To get files, handouts, catalogs, and other information
directly all you need to do is know the name of the file and send
a request to me like:

    send thefilename

This can appear in the subject of the message or in the body of the
message. If you want a bunch of files, send me a single message with
all your requests in the body of the message, and I'll send them back
as a number of different e-mail messages.
```

```
To start out, send me a request to list all the available files. The
easiest way to do this is to have "list" as either the subject of
the message or within the message body itself. I'll jump into action,
build a list of all files and information that I'm authorized to send,
and mail that back to you, probably within five minutes of your request.

Once you have that, you can just reply to that message, prefacing
the files you'd like with the word "send."

    Thanks for working with me, and I look forward to hearing from
    you again in the near future.

            Bye for now.
                                -- Embot
```

Finally, if someone requests a file that's not available, they'll receive the following response (you can get this response yourself by sending yourself an e-mail message with *send nonexistent file* as the subject):

```
Subject: A List of Embot-Accessible Files

You requested file 'non-existent-file' but it isn't available. The list
of possible files is as follows:

    help

Please send your request again, specifying one or more of these files.

Thanks!
                                -- Embot
```

The evolutionary path for Embot

As it exists today, the Embot program meets a great need in the Internet user community for a simple, inexpensive way to disseminate information to a wide variety of users. Like any program, however, it must grow and evolve to ensure that it continues to meet the needs of the user community. (If you have ideas about features that you want added to Embot, send me an e-mail message about them.)

The most important change that is planned for the next release of Embot is what I call "fuzzy matching." If you have a file called, say, Catalog and someone requests catalog, that person won't get back your document; rather, he'll get a message saying `File "catalog" isn't available` and a list of other files that are available. That's pretty dumb. It would be much smarter to have the program check for close matches like this one — or for simple misspellings such as *catlog* or *Catalo* — and then return the correct file regardless. If the name of the requested file is ambiguous and more than one file might match, it's much better to return a message that indicates as much.

A brief note on the shareware license

Please also remember that Embot is a shareware program, not a free program. If you use the program, if you like it, and if it's helping you, help me, too, by sending in your registration fee, as explained in the help file included with the program distribution.

Filter

Embot works fine for simple applications, but if you want a greater level of control of your electronic-mail filtering, you'll want to obtain Filter, a program that comes free with the popular Elm Mail System. Filter is a great deal harder to work with than Embot, but on the bright side, it's considerably more powerful.

The basic idea behind Filter is that it's an expert system. Using a special mail-filter programming language, you write a series of Filter rules that are considered, one at a time, for each message received. If the rule evaluates as true, the associated instruction is executed.

A typical Filter rule looks like the following example:

```
if (subject contains "delete me") then
 delete
```

This rule tells Filter that if any e-mail message arrives with a subject that contains the phrase *delete me*, the program should delete the message instead of dropping it into your mailbox. The rules language offers a great deal of power and, even better, makes it easy to hand certain messages to your own programs, shell script, or just about anything else.

The Filter language

To get a closer look at the Filter language, start by having a glimpse at an actual rule set — the one that I use to filter through all the electronic mail I receive at my base account `taylor@netcom.com`.:

```
#
# Filter rules so that people can request files without my
# having to mail them back one-by-one.

if (subject = "send mall" ) then
 exec "send mall %r"

if (subject = "send tyu" ) then
 exec "send tyu %r"

if (subject = "send gs" ) then
 exec "send gs %r"
```

```
if (subject = "send addme" ) then
 exec "send addme %r"

if (subject = "send toc" ) then
 exec "send tyu-toc %r"

if (subject = "send inbiz" ) then
 exec "send intbiz %r"

if (subject = "SUBSCRIBE imall-l" ) then
 delete

if (subject = "SUBSCRIBE imall-chat" ) then
 delete
```

The basic rule of thumb is that each rule is specified as *if condition then action* and that each is considered, in order from first to last, until one matches the message that has been received. If you send me a message with `send intbiz` as the subject, for example, Filter would compare your subject to `send mall`, `send tyu`, and so on, until it got to the comparison for `send intbiz`. The two subjects match, so Filter would invoke the associated action: `exec "send intbiz %r"`.

In this case, `%r` is expanded to be the return address of the message, so the actual *send* shell script would receive two arguments: the name of the file to send, and the return address of the person to whom it should go.

A very simple script can now do the work that's needed, as follows:

```
#!/bin/sh
# a simple SEND shell script

if [ ! -f $1 ] ; then
 echo "File $1 is not available from this system"
elif [ "$2" = "" ] ; then
 echo "No return address specified"
elif
 mail -s "File $1, as requested" $2 < $1
fi
```

I'm trying not to get too far into shell script programming, but I will point out that `$1` is expanded here to the first argument (the filename, if you'll recall) and that `$2` is the return address. Similarly to Filter, the shell tests the items between brackets and then executes the action, if appropriate. For the first test, `-f` tests to see whether the specified file (`$1`) exists, and the prefix (`!`) reverses the logic of the test — that is, the first test really says, "If the specified file does not exist, state that the file isn't available."

The second test simply ensures that a return address has been specified. If everything checks out, the file is mailed to the user by means of the UNIX mail command.

Hopping back to the Filter rules file, the file that contains all the rules listed above, notice the last two rules: *if condition then delete*. These are tricky rules to write, because the result is that the message is never delivered anywhere. If you specify an overly broad category, you might never know that important mail has been deleted en route to your mailbox, so be careful!

More on the Filter rules language

A variety of conditions can be considered in a Filter-rule expression, and a variety of actions can result. Following is an overview:

Condition	***Meaning or Interpretation***
`from`	checks the return address of the message
`subject`	lists the subject of the message, if any
`to`	identifies the person to whom the message is addressed
`lines`	lists the number of lines in the message

Expressions can test for equality (=), inequality (! =), or logical values. If you want to delete all messages that are more than 200 lines long, for example, you could use the rule `if (lines > 200) then delete`. To reverse the logic of the rule, preface the rule with `not` (as in `if not subject = "test message"`). To construct multiple conditions, add *and* between subconditions — for example, `if (from="jane@edu" and lines > 30) then delete`).

Actions following a conditional clause can be any of the following:

Action	***Meaning or Interpretation***
`delete`	deletes the message
`save` *`folder`*	saves the message to the specified folder
`savecopy` *`folder`*	same as `save` *`folder`*, but also delivers a copy to your mailbox
`execute` *`command`*	feeds the message to the specified UNIX command
`forward` *`address`*	forwards the message to the specified e-mail address
`leave`	leaves message in your mailbox (normal delivery of mail)

That's the entire language for the Filter program, with one exception. If you want to specify a default rule at the bottom of the rule set for delivery of all messages that are not otherwise answered, you can specify the special command `always`, which looks like this:

```
always
     forward "new-addr@newcomputer.com"
```

What goes where: configuring and setting up Filter

Unlike the Embot program, which can be installed by anyone on a system, Filter requires special permissions; it must be built and installed by the system administrator. You can find copies of the Filter program as part of the standard Elm Mail System distribution, which is available at better Internet hosts throughout the network.

To see whether your site has Filter installed, type **filter** at your next system prompt:

If you see `command not found`, the program is not installed, and you should talk with your system administrator. If you see a message something like `no rules file?`, however, you're ready to go.

Odds are good that you'll have a directory in your home directory called .elm, if you don't use the mkdir command to make it. Move to that directory, and create a new file called filter-rules, which will contain your set of actual rules.

After you create the set of rules that you think will work, leave the editor. Then, in the command line, use the `-r` read-through command, ask that the Filter program check through your rules to ensure that they're OK. Following is the result of this command for a different, smaller set of rules:

```
Rule 1: if (subject = "interview") then
     Savecopy "interview-requests"

Rule 2: if (from = "mailer-daemon") then
     Delete

Rule 3: ** always **
     Execute "sendbusy <return-address>"
```

In this case, your new Filter rules file has been successfully parsed and understood by Filter, which also numbered the rules to remind me that the rules are evaluated in the specified order.

When your rules file is ready to use, you need to add Filter to your .forward file, just as you did for Embot. This time, however, you want to have a .forward file that looks like this:

```
"|filter"
```

Optionally, you can add `-o errorfile` to give Filter a file for saving processing errors (helpful if you think that something should be happening but isn't, or vice versa).

Useful tricks with Filter

One very important command is the Filter equivalent to the Embot stats command: `filter -s`. This command produces a succinct summary of how many times each rule has been matched since you started using the program. Following is an example for a busy account:

```
            A Summary of Filter Activity
            ----------------------------

A total of 998 messages were filtered:

The default rule of putting mail into your mailbox
    applied 596 times (60%)
```

```
Rule #1: (given to command "send mall %r")
    applied 222 times (22%)

Rule #2: (given to command "send tyu %r")
    applied 4 times (0%)

Rule #3: (given to command "send gs %r")
    applied 1 time (0%)

Rule #5: (given to command "send addme %r")
    applied 14 times (1%)

Rule #7: (given to command "send promo %r")
    applied 1 time (0%)

Rule #13: (given to command "send intbiz %r")
    applied 11 times (1%)

Rule #15: (delete message)
    applied 74 times (7%)

Rule #16: (delete message)
    applied 58 times (6%)
```

By doing a little math, you can see that 40 percent of the mail received in this account (almost 1,000 messages) was processed automatically by Filter, which is pretty darn helpful! Also notice that not every rule was used and applied; rule 4, for example, wasn't matched by any of the incoming messages and therefore wasn't listed in this statistical output.

Notice that with some minor modifications, the earlier sample send shell script could be used to tell people on other systems who is logged in to your system, what the current load level is, and just about anything else. Following is an example of what I mean:

```
if (subject = "who") exec "send who %r"
if (subject = "uptime") exec "send uptime %r"
```

Given these rules, you can modify the script slightly, as follows:

```
#!/bin/sh
# a simple SEND shell script

if [ "$2" = "" ] ; then
 echo "No return address specified"
elif [ "$1" = "who" ] ; then
 who | mail -s "Using 'hostname' right now" $2
elif [ "$1" = "uptime" ] ; then
 uptime | mail -s "'hostname' load level" $2
fi
```

What happens if you send an e-mail message with the subject *who* to this test account? Following is the response:

```
From: test-acct (a test account)
Subject: Using limbo.intuitive.com right now
To: taylor@netcom.com
Date: Thu, 8 Dec 94 10:05:27 -0500

root   console Dec 7 14:25
patrickk ttyAg  Dec 8 09:58
kcone  ttyAj  Dec 8 09:55
wander  ttyAk  Dec 8 09:42
ashkevrn ttyAm  Dec 8 09:55
jftipton ttyAo  Dec 8 09:25
susiebob ttyAp  Dec 8 08:47
joekeier ttyAr  Dec 8 09:45
adickes ttyAs  Dec 8 10:05
erilyons ttyAt  Dec 8 09:58
jarrettm ttyAu  Dec 8 10:04
rajirt  ttyAv  Dec 8 08:38
```

Finally, don't forget to use `filter -c` occasionally to clear our your log files; the information does take up lots of space over time if you get lots of e-mail.

The even-more-complex alternative: Procmail

Another mail filter program, called Procmail, is available for UNIX accounts. The Procmail program is considerably more complex than Filter and is designed to help people manage their own mail, manage mailing lists, and even deliver mail to individual accounts directly if sites would rather not use *sendmail* or *smail.* Is Procmail a better choice for your needs? Perhaps. Before you decide, though, examine a Procmail filter-rules file (a .Procmail.rc):

```
MAILDIR=$HOME/Mail
LOGFILE=ml
SHELL=/bin/sh
PATH=/usr/bin

:BD
^Your message has been received by .*@netcom\.com\.
/dev/null

:2D:
^From.*John .Doe
^Subject: .*QUOTE
mq.n

::
^TOstring-theory-list
stl.n
```

```
::
^TOc4
c4.n

VACMSG=$HOME/.vacation.msg
ALREADYSENT=$HOME/.vacation.dir
FORMAIL=/usr/local/bin/new/formail

:hWc
!^From +[^ ]*(postmaster|Mailer)
| FROM="'$FORMAIL -rtx To:'"; \
 [ ! -f $VACMSG ] && exit 1; \
 fgrep -e "$FROM" < $ALREADYSENT && exit 1; \
 echo   "$FROM" >> $ALREADYSENT

  :ahc
  | ($FORMAIL -rt; cat $VACMSG) | $SENDMAIL -t

:D:
^From.*tester
sm.n

:0D:
in.n
```

Buried in that complexity is tremendous power: You can see that any UNIX command can be incorporated into the rule set. Whether Procmail is right for you really depends on how much technical expertise you have and how willing you are to dig around in such things.

Conclusion

As the Internet continues to grow in size and complexity, it's a sure bet that all of us will get more and more electronic mail. Even today, more than 20 million people can send electronic mail to your mailbox (thank goodness they don't all do it at the same time!). If you have materials to distribute, Embot clearly is the best bet, with its absence of rules and programming complexity. Take the step up in software evolution, and you'll find Filter to be ready for the task, offering a clear and sensible interface. Finally, if you're overwhelmed with e-mail and want to create something fabulous and powerful, Procmail may be the answer. Whichever option you choose, good luck — and say hi to R2D2 if you see him!

Dave Taylor has been involved with UNIX and the Internet since 1980. He's the author of the original Elm Mail System and, more recently, the creator of Embot. In his spare time, he's finishing a master's degree in Educational Computing at Purdue University and running the Internet Mall, the central spot for shopping on the Internet. Taylor is the author of several books on UNIX and the Internet, including The Internet Business Guide.

Chapter 26
Network News

This chapter contains five articles:

- "Usenet Tips and Tricks"
- "nn Basics"
- "Using Trn, the Threaded Newsreader"
- "Trn Tips and Tricks"
- "Using Offline Mail and Newsreaders"

Usenet Tips and Tricks

by Jon Bell <jtbell@presby.edu> and Margaret Levine Young <margy@iecc.com>

Most of the tips and tricks in this article apply only to people who use a UNIX shell account to access the Internet. The general information about Usenet may be interesting to others, including people who read Usenet newsgroups via an on-line service or SLIP/PPP account.

Overview of Usenet News

Loosely speaking, *Usenet* is a collection of computers that allow users to exchange public messages on many different topics. These messages are similar to electronic mail but are transmitted by special software that is separate from the electronic-mail system. The messages are intended for public discussions rather than personal communication. If you have ever used a computer bulletin-board service (BBS) or the public discussion areas of commercial on-line services (for example, CompuServe's forums), you will find that Usenet strongly resembles both services.

A Usenet message is called an *article*. Articles are grouped, by topic, into *newsgroups*. The entire collection of articles and newsgroups is called *news*.

Each Usenet computer maintains a database of articles, which it keeps up to date by exchanging articles periodically with its neighbors on Usenet. Periodically, your news system receives batches of articles from its Usenet neighbors; this may happen anywhere from once a day to once every few minutes. Similarly, your news system periodically sends locally created articles to its neighbors; it also may pass on its incoming batches to some of its neighbors. Finally, your news system periodically (usually, once each night) *expires* (removes) old articles to make room for new ones. How long articles are kept can vary from one newsgroup to another; the length of time depends on the amount of disk space available and the perceived value of the newsgroup.

Usenet and the Internet are not the same thing. Usenet was developed on UNIX computers, which set up temporary dialup telephone connections among themselves via modems. The computers exchanged news articles by using the UUCP (*U*NIX to *U*NIX *c*o*p*y) protocol, which is built into the UNIX operating system. Many computers still exchange news in this fashion, but in recent years, more and more computers have been using the permanent high-speed connections of the Internet, exchanging articles by using NNTP (network news transfer protocol). Therefore, not all Usenet computers are part of the Internet, and not all Internet computers participate in Usenet. A few computers even exchange articles by more unusual means, such as mailed magnetic tapes or satellite.

The newsgroup hierarchy

More than 2,000 newsgroups are commonly distributed, dealing with a wide variety of topics, including computers, scientific fields, politics, national cultures, and hobbies. Newsgroup names generally contain two or more parts, separated by periods. As you read from left to right, the various parts of the name progressively narrow the topic of discussion. The first part of the name indicates the top-level *hierarchy* to which the newsgroup belongs. The following table describes the standard "Big Seven" top-level hierarchies.

Hierarchy	*Description*
comp	Discussions of computer hardware and software (for example, comp.sys.mac.apps, for Macintosh application software)
misc	Discussions that don't fit anywhere else (for example, misc.kids)
news	Discussions of Usenet news itself: news administration, creation of new newsgroups, news statistics, and so on (for example, news.admin.policy)
rec	Discussions of recreational topics, such as sports, movies, and hobbies (for example, rec.sport.baseball, rec.travel, and rec.autos.antique)
sci	Discussions of science-related topics (for example, sci.physics)
soc	Social and cultural discussions relating to various groups of people: ethnic, national, religious, occupational, and so on (for example, soc.culture.german)
talk	High-traffic, "noisy" discussions of controversial topics: abortion, religion, guns, and so on (for example, talk.politics.soviet)

Strictly speaking, Usenet consists only of these seven hierarchies. Proposals for new newsgroups in these hierarchies are discussed and voted on according to a set of rules known as "The Guidelines." If you're interested in learning about this process, read the articles "How to Create a New Usenet Newsgroup" and "Usenet Newsgroup Creation Companion," which are posted regularly to `news.announce.newusers`, `news.groups`, and `news.answers`, among other places. Then read both `news.announce.newgroups` and `news.groups` for a few weeks to get a feeling for Usenet politics.

A less widely distributed `alt` (alternative) hierarchy contains newsgroups that are too big (for example, contain large files of encoded computer graphics), too controversial (sex, drugs, and so on), or too off-the-wall for the standard Usenet hierarchies, along with many newsgroups on mainstream topics. Creating a new newsgroup is much easier in the `alt` hierarchy than in the standard hierarchies, so a new newsgroup sometimes is created there with the intention of building enough traffic to justify creating a newsgroup in one of the standard hierarchies. For more information, read the article "So You Want to Create an Alt Newsgroup," which is posted regularly to `alt.config`, `alt.answers`, and `news.answers`. Then read `alt.config` for a while.

Finally, various special-purpose hierarchies are not distributed as widely as the Big Seven and `alt`. Some of these hierarchies focus on specialized fields — for example, `bionet` for biology, `hepnet` for high-energy particle physics, and `vmsnet` for users of computers from Digital Equipment, Inc. that run the VMS operating system. Other hierarchies are intended mainly for distribution within limited geographical areas or within single institutions — for example, `ba` for the San Francisco Bay area and `de` for Germany.

The total amount of traffic in the Big Seven hierarchies (Usenet proper) now is about 100MB per day and has been almost doubling each year. Many sites receive only a limited selection of newsgroups because of limitations on disk space and the capacity of their network links, or because of specific policies on what kind of newsgroups can be received.

Which newsgroups to read

Which newsgroups to read depends, obviously, on your interests. You should browse through the newsgroup lists and sample various groups. We strongly recommend that you at least scan the following newsgroups:

- `news.announce.important` contains important messages of interest to all Usenet users. Very few articles appear here.
- `news.announce.newusers` normally contains a standard set of articles with general information about Usenet and guidelines for network etiquette (*netiquette*). You should read these articles at least once.
- `news.answers` contains copies of articles that are periodically posted to various newsgroups, answering various frequently asked questions (FAQs). These articles are worth browsing to get an idea of the range of topics that are discussed on Usenet.

- `news.newusers.questions` contains questions posted by new users and (ideally) answers from more-knowledgeable users.

Complete lists of Big Seven newsgroups and extensive lists of `alt` newsgroups, with very brief descriptions, are posted every month or two in the newsgroups `news.lists` and `news.announce.newusers`.

Your News Administrator

Most Internet providers, on-line services, and other Usenet sites have a *news administrator* who maintains the news software, monitors disk space, creates new newsgroups, and so on. On small systems, this person may simply be the overall system administrator. On larger systems, the system administrator may designate someone else as news administrator. The job may be only part of the person's overall responsibilities, and it may even be strictly a spare-time job.

If you have any questions that might depend on how the news software is set up on your system, you should contact your news administrator. For example, if you want to read a newsgroup that is not currently available on your system, your news administrator is the only person who can either arrange to receive that newsgroup or explain why that is not possible.

The only sure way to find out the identity of your news administrator is to talk to people at your computer center. Many systems define the e-mail address `usenet` for use by the news administrator. You also could try sending a message to `root`, `postmaster`, or whatever other address your system administrator uses.

Moderated Newsgroups

Some newsgroups are *moderated* — that is, articles posted to them must be approved by a moderator. Some newsreader programs allow you to post an article to a moderated group in exactly the same way as to an unmoderated group, but when you tell the program to send the article, it e-mails the article to the moderator and informs you of what it has done. If the moderator approves the article, it will appear in the newsgroup after a (hopefully) short delay. Otherwise, he, she, or it probably will return the article to you with an explanation of why it was not suitable for that newsgroup.

Lists of Newsgroups

You can get copies of the most recent versions via e-mail from the Usenet FAQ archive at `rtfm.mit.edu`. Simply send e-mail to `mail-server@rtfm.mit.edu`, with a blank subject line and one or more of the following commands in the message body:

```
send usenet/news.lists/List_of_Active_Newsgroups,_Part_I
send usenet/news.lists/List_of_Active_Newsgroups,_Part_II
send usenet/news.lists/Alternative_Newsgroup_Hierarchies,_Part_I
send usenet/news.lists/Alternative_Newsgroup_Hierarchies,_Part_II
```

You should get a reply within a day or two.

Anatomy of a News Article

Consider the following article:

```
sci.physics #12781 (12 + 153 more)
From: rama.krishna.guru.edu (Chidvilasananda)
Newsgroups: sci.physics,sci.optics
[1] Re: Stupid Question: Why does light diffract???
Date: Tue Oct 12 11:42:39 EDT 1993
Organization: Center Research Electro-Optics Lasers

In article <29di6h$kvi@aussie.kanga.adelaide.edu.au>,
dabbott@kanga.adelaide.edu.au (Dave Abbott) wrote:
>
> Ripples on the surface of water diffract as they "ooze" through
> a slit. It's easy to see how this must happen when you consider the
> constraints caused by forces between water molecules.
> However, with light there is now no physical medium or internal forces (?)
>
It has been found that light, radio waves, and x-rays are all forms of the
same thing: Electromagnetic waves. It has also been found that electric and
magnetic fields are coupled vector fields that obey four simple partial
differential equations: the Maxwell equations. If you take the Maxwell
equations, and apply the appropriate boundary conditions on the solutions,
you will find that the answer you get explains diffraction.

As far as the question: 'Do we know why?', one needs to invoke ontological
arguments. Let's just say that Classical Electromagnetic theory has great
predictive power, and is for the most part correct. (It has already been
superseded by a higher theory, however, this higher theory is of interest
only to theoretical physicists).

I guess the ultimate answer to "why does light diffract?' is:
 Light diffracts because it does!
--
Chidvilasananda

'God dwells within you as you'
End of article 12781 (of 13105) — what next? [npq]
```

The first line tells you which newsgroup you are reading (`sci.physics`), that this is the 12,781st article that your news system has received in this newsgroup, and how many articles are left to read. In this example, there are 12 articles left in the threads you have selected, plus 153 articles in threads that you have not selected.

The From line tells you who wrote the article. Usually, but not always, this line contains a valid e-mail address, followed by the sender's real name (or nickname) in parentheses.

The Newsgroups line appears if the article was posted simultaneously (*crossposted*) to more than one newsgroup.

Next is the subject of the article. [1] indicates that this is the first distinct subject in this discussion thread. Re indicates that this article is a follow-up to somebody else's article.

The Date line indicates when the article was posted. It may take a few days for an article to propagate across Usenet, depending on how the poster's computer is connected to its neighbors.

The Organization line usually tells you the "real" name of the location that corresponds to the author's e-mail address.

If you use the trn newsreader, to the right of the article header you see one of trn's special features: a map of the current discussion thread. Each box represents a single article; the boxes are connected to show the logical sequence of follow-ups (replies). The numbers correspond to the subject numbers that you see in the subject line. The article that you are reading is highlighted. Articles that you have already seen are enclosed in parentheses; articles that you have not seen are enclosed in square brackets. Articles that are no longer in your news database are indicated by empty boxes. If the discussion is long, you see only part of the map; you can see the entire map by typing **t**.

Finally, we come to the article text itself. Lines that begin with > are quoted from the article that this one is following up. These lines usually have an attribution line that indicates who wrote the quoted text. Attribution lines are inserted automatically when you follow up an article by using the F command, to write a follow-up article. If the quoted material itself quotes another article, you see lines beginning with >>. Occasionally, you see four, five, or even more levels of quoting, but many people consider this to be bad form.

Creating a Signature File

At the end of an article, and separated from it by two dashes, you often see a *signature*, which may contain the author's name, e-mail address(es), mail address, phone number, and so on. Many newsreader programs allow you to create a *signature file* that is automatically appended to each article that you write.

If you use a UNIX shell account, the most common method uses a file named .signature, which you can create with any text-editing program (for example, vi, emacs, or pico). For example, using the vi text editor, you give the following command:

```
vi .signature
```

The screen clears, and you see a blank file to edit, as follows:

```
(single blank line at the top of the screen)
~
~
(etc.)
~
".signature" [New file]
```

Type **i** to enter insert mode; then type your signature, pressing the Return or Enter key at the end of each line. When you finish, press the Esc key to get out of insert mode, and then type **zz** to leave vi. At this point your screen looks like this:

```
Jon Bell <jtbell@presby.edu> Presbyterian College
Dept. of Physics and Computer Science  Clinton, SC  USA
~
~
(etc.)
~
".signature" [New file]
```

After you create your signature file, you may need to make it readable by the news software. Your file system may be set up so that whenever you create a file, only you have access to it. To make the file readable by other users (including the news software), enter the following command at the UNIX prompt:

```
chmod a+r .signature
```

The .signature file usually is appended only *after* you write your article, so you do not see the signature while you are editing the article. The .signature usually is appended by a separate program (usually called inews) that your newsreader calls on to post the article.

Although some people have enormous signature files with gigantic, allegedly cute ASCII graphics, such signatures quickly become irritating. Keep yours to three lines or less. Many news programs enforce this rule by using only the first three or four lines of the signature file, regardless of how long the file is.

The .newsrc File

All newsreading programs store information about what newsgroups you subscribe to and about which articles you have read. And almost all the programs store this information in the same place: the .newsrc file in your home directory.

The .newsrc file is a text file that contains one line for each newsgroup, as in the following example:

```
alt.consciousness.near-death-exp:
misc.education.home-school.misc! 1-594
comp.society.folklore: 1-111
alt.conspiracy.netcom:
alt.winsock: 1-7232,8959,8973,9081,9306
soc.religion.unitarian-univ: 1-695
```

The first item in each line is the name of the newsgroup. If the name is followed by a colon, you subscribe to the newsgroup; if the name is followed by an exclamation point, you have unsubscribed. The numbers in the rest of each line are the numbers of the articles that you have read; this is how newsreaders keep from showing you the same articles over and over. Article numbers are separated by commas, with contiguous ranges of article numbers indicated by hyphens.

Frequently, you will find that groups to which you have never subscribed have a list of read articles. That's because when you read a crossposted article, the newsreader marks it as read in all the groups in which it appears, including ones that you don't subscribe to. This feature can be useful; if you unsubscribe to a group for a while and then resubscribe, it will have kept track of articles that you have seen in other groups, and when you resubscribe, you'll see only the new articles.

Most newsreaders display newsgroups in the order in which they appear in the .newsrc file, so you may want to edit this file, either directly or by using newsreader commands, to place related groups next to each other so that they are displayed one after the other.

Unsubscribing to all newsgroups

If you find yourself subscribed to all the newsgroups on your system, you are faced with the task of unsubscribing from the ones that you don't want to read. The simplest and most tedious way to do this is to unsubscribe from each newsgroup individually, using your newsreading program.

Fortunately, there's a quicker way to get rid of all those unwanted newsgroups. Enter the following commands at the UNIX prompt:

```
tr \ : \ ! < .newsrc > .newsrc.new
rm .newsrc
mv .newsrc.new .newsrc
```

(Watch out! The first line uses backslashes, not ordinary slashes!) These three commands edit your list of newsgroups (which is stored in a file named .newsrc, as described earlier) so that all colons become exclamation points (which unsubscribe you from all newsgroups), remove the old version, and replace it with the new one. Then run your newsreader. The newsreader will tell you that there is no news to read because you no longer are subscribed to *any* newsgroups. At this point, you can subscribe to the newsgroups that you *do* want to read.

You can equally well use your favorite text editor to edit the .newsrc file. Globally change all the colons to exclamation points.

Alphabetizing your newsgroups

If you want to read your newsgroups in alphabetical order by name, use this command when you see the UNIX prompt:

```
sort .newsrc -o .newsrc
```

This command creates a sorted copy of your newsgroup list, replacing the original.

Alternatively, you can use a text editor to sort the lines in your .newsrc file in any order that you like.

Posting Test Articles

The newsgroup `misc.test` is a good place to post test articles, for two reasons. First, people tend to be annoyed by test articles in other groups. Second, various sites on Usenet monitor `misc.test` with software that automatically sends an e-mail reply to the author of each article. This arrangement enables you to verify that your article is getting out and to see what it looks like. You may get 5 or 10 replies to a test posting.

Distributions

When you post a new article, you usually should include a distribution code, which indicates how far you want the article to be propagated. If you leave the distribution line of your header blank, your article is sent to all of Usenet (or at least to all sites that receive this newsgroup).

An explicit distribution code, in principle, restricts the propagation of your article. Exactly which distributions are available to you depends on how your news system is set up (ask your news administrator). For example, a system near San Francisco may allow the following distributions:

`local`	this computer only
`ba`	San Francisco Bay area
`usa`	United States
`na`	North America

In practice, you should not expect any distribution other than `local` to work perfectly. Distributions always leak, either by accident or design. The `local` distribution, however, should never leak; if it does, please let your news administrator know.

Posting the Same Article to Several Newsgroups (Crossposting)

Sometimes, you want to post the same article to more than one newsgroup, because the article may be of interest to more than one audience. An article about Swedish–German relations, for example, would be appropriate for both soc.culture.nordic and soc.culture.german. Simply posting copies of the article in the usual way to each newsgroup not only takes more of your time but also consumes more network resources, because each copy must be transmitted and stored separately on each Usenet computer. The crossposting mechanism enables you to post one copy of the article simultaneously to multiple newsgroups; only that copy is transmitted, and on some operating systems, including UNIX, only one copy needs to be stored on each computer. On some newsreaders, reading a crossposted article in one group marks it as read in the other groups; if you read more than one of the groups in question, you see the article only once.

Before you crosspost, you should think carefully about whether you really need to do so. If you crosspost, do so to as few groups as necessary. Crossposting to many newsgroups is considered to be a breach of netiquette; doing so probably will produce angry responses via e-mail, both to you and to your system administrator.

How to crosspost

To crosspost an article, start by posting as usual to one of the newsgroups in which you want the article to appear. Create the article to post as usual. In the header section of the article, find the Newsgroups line; then add the additional newsgroups at the end of that line, separated by commas. Don't put any spaces before or after the commas; if you do, due to bugs in many copies of Usenet software, your article probably will disappear into a network black hole when it is transmitted to other sites.

When you follow up a crossposted article, your article normally is crossposted to the same newsgroups in which the original article appeared. You can change this arrangement by editing the Newsgroups line in the header to add or remove newsgroups. Don't forget to delete the extra comma, too.

Redirecting follow-ups

Follow-up articles normally appear in the same newsgroups as the original article. The author of the follow-up article can change this arrangement by editing the Newsgroups line in the header. The author of the original article also can edit the Followup-To line, which normally is blank. If the Followup-To line is not blank, all follow-up articles appear in the specified newsgroup.

Follow-ups are commonly redirected in two situations. First, the author of the article may want to attract the attention of readers of several newsgroups but restrict any follow-up discussion to one newsgroup. For example, discussions about creating new newsgroups are supposed to take place only in news.groups. Therefore, someone who wants to create a new newsgroup normally crossposts a request for discussion (RFD) to news.announce.newgroups and to any newsgroups that have readers who might be interested, but directs all follow-ups to news.groups.

Second, the author may want all responses to go directly to him via e-mail, so that he can prepare a summary of the responses to post later. Placing the word *poster* in the Followup-To line accomplishes this purpose.

If you redirect follow-ups, you should mention this fact in the body of your article, because many people don't read headers carefully and may otherwise be puzzled when their follow-up articles don't appear in the newsgroup that they're reading.

Kill files

Many newsreaders support *kill files*, which are files that contain commands that can automatically "kill" (skip) articles that you are not interested in or select only articles that you are interested in.

Two kinds of kill files exist:

- The *global kill file*, which is stored in the News subdirectory of your home directory. The commands in this kill file apply to all newsgroups that you read. For example, you could include a command to skip all articles posted by a notorious jerk, regardless of which newsgroup he posts to.
- *Newsgroup kill files* (or *local kill files*), which are stored in subdirectories of your News directory. The names of the subdirectories for newsgroups are the same as the newsgroup name, with the periods changed to slashes. For example, the directory containing the kill file for the `soc.religion.unitarian-univ` group is named `~/News/soc/religion/unitarian-univ`. For example, you could include a command to skip all articles about gun control, which you don't consider to be a religious issue.

Both types of kill files are text files named kill, containing one command per line. You can edit these files with any text editor. Because of the overhead involved in searching for articles to kill, it is better, if possible, to use a local list than the global one.

You can use your newsreader to add commands to your kill file. Newsreaders that support kill files have commands that add a line to the global or newsgroup kill file that kills (marks as read) all articles with the same subject as the article that you are reading. Some newsreaders support other types of kill commands, such as marking as read all articles *except* those on a particular subject, or killing by thread instead of by article.

The actual contents of a kill file depend on which newsreader program you use, because kill files contain commands that are specific to each newsreader. For example, trn's kill files can kill (mark as read) entire threads, which rn cannot do.

News.groups

The `news.groups` newsgroup discusses newsgroup administration, especially the formation of new groups. If you are thinking about forming a new group, read this newsgroup for at least several weeks. If you decide to go ahead, read the FAQ titled "How to Create a New Usenet Group," which is posted in the `news.announce.newusers` newsgroup. (You also can get the FAQ via ftp from `ftp.uu.net`, in the directory `usenet/news.announce.newusers`, in a file named Guidelines.)

Following is a summary of the steps for creating a newsgroup:

1. **You discuss the idea in the `news.groups` newsgroup, as well as in any related existing newsgroups.**

   For example, if you want to create a newsgroup to discuss the effects of drinking coffee during pregnancy, you may want to discuss the idea in `alt.drugs.caffeine`, `rec.food.drink.coffee`, and `misc.kids.pregnancy`. If a mailing list on the topic already exists, talk about it there, too.

2. **You write an RFD (request for discussion) and post it to all the interested newsgroups, as well as to `news.announce.newgroups` and `news.groups`.**

   Be sure to mention the exact name of the group that you are proposing, what mailing lists and related newsgroups already exist, what the charter of the group would be, and whether the group would be moderated and by whom.

3. **Everyone discusses the idea, usually generating more heat than light.**

   With luck, you'll get useful suggestions for how to improve the charter of the group.

4. **After 30 days, you either decide to abandon the project or arrange with an official vote taker to issue a CFV (call for votes).**

   The CFV is posted to all the same groups that saw the RFD, as well as to any other groups that you think may be interested. The vote usually takes 22 days, with all votes going by e-mail to an independent agent for tallying.

5. **The official vote taker publishes the results, posting them to all the groups that saw the CFV.**

   For a vote to pass, there must be at least 100 more Yes votes than No votes, and at least two-thirds of the total votes must be Yes. If the group passes, the appropriate control message is sent out after five days, although it may take a while for all Usenet sites to get the message. If the group fails, you must wait at least six months before bringing it up for a vote again.

Margaret Levine Young is the co-author of IDG's UNIX For Dummies, More Internet For Dummies, *and* The Internet For Dummies Starter Kit, *in addition to other computer books. She has spent a great deal of time explaining to people that computers are not as mysterious as people think.*

Jon Bell is an Associate Professor of Physics at Presbyterian College in Clinton, SC. He also teaches computer science courses. For the past three years, he has been installing and maintaining Internet software, and he is the college's Usenet news administrator.

nn Basics

by Bill Wohler <wohler@newt.com>

What Is nn?

nn is a menu-based (point and shoot) Usenet newsreader that has a complete set of features to satisfy both the expert and the novice user. Since its first release in Denmark in 1984, in the rest of Europe in 1988, and globally in June 1989, it has replaced rn and other well-known newsreaders at many sites. It was written by Kim Storm (`storm@olicom.dk`).

Within a newsgroup, nn locates all unread articles in the group, and extracts the name of the sender, the subject, and other relevant information. It then rearranges this information and displays it to provide menu-based article selection, with the articles sorted according to subject and posting time. Articles are presented by thread (that is, articles on the same subject are displayed in the order in which they were submitted) so that you can follow a discussion on a particular topic before going on to another discussion in the same group.

nn prepares news quickly because it uses its own database to maintain all the necessary information in a directly accessible form (this database is built and maintained by the nnmaster program). This chapter describes Version 6.4.18 of nn and nnmaster. (Beta version 6.5.0b3 supports the NOV overview database and thus does not require nnmaster. In fact, nnmaster will be eventually phased out as NOV becomes ubiquitous.)

Some of the key features of nn are

- Standard `.newsrc` file.
- Digests are automatically split and presented as ordinary articles. You can transparently save and respond to individual subarticles.
- On-line help and manual.
- Automatically unpacks, concatenates, and decodes single or multipart postings that have been created with *shar* or *uuencode.*
- Advanced macro definition features that provide for the easy remapping of keys.
- Automatic kill and selection of articles based on subject or author.
- User-specified presentation sequence of newsgroups based on the newsgroup hierarchy.
- Capability to unsubscribe whole classes of newsgroups permanently (for example, `talk.all` and `all.politics`).

- Capability to merge related groups and present them as a single group (for example, `comp.emacs` and all `gnu.emacs` groups).
- Blindingly fast "search for subject." On a Texas S1500 system, nn can find all articles on a specific subject among 64,000 articles in all groups in less than 20 seconds.
- NNTP is also supported. (nnmaster can use NNTP to build a local database from a remote news spool. nn still needs to read a local database, although it can obtain the articles via NNTP. However, nn 6.5.0b3 can use NNTP directly to obtain articles from a system maintained with a NOV database.)
- Because of the database, nn starts almost equally fast (in a few seconds) whether you have 100 or 10,000 unread articles. The database takes up some disk space but dramatically improves speed and functionality. The amount of disk space consumed is approximately 1MB per 10,000 articles.

Getting Started

Before you start to read Usenet news, you can configure nn to have it choose and ignore certain newsgroups. Because of this feature, you are not overwhelmed with hundreds of groups to choose to subscribe to or unsubscribe from when you first use nn to read news. Two files control how nn deals with groups: `.nn/init` and `.newsrc` (which is used by nearly all newsreaders on UNIX systems to store your news-reading history).

The .nn/init file

nn creates a subdirectory (`.nn`) in your home directory. This subdirectory will hold files related to nn. The most important of these files is `init`, which I refer to in this chapter as `.nn/init`. The `.nn/init` file is a text file that you can create yourself and edit with any text editor, such as vi or Emacs.

You can edit `.nn/init` before you ever use nn in order to exclude groups that you never want to subscribe to. To exclude groups, add a line at the end of the file containing the word *sequence* by itself. Following the "sequence" line, add lines starting with an exclamation point to indicate which groups you want to exclude. For example, use the following lines to tell nn to exclude all groups that start with `bionet` or `gnu`:

```
sequence
!bionet
!gnu
```

You can provide more details by using lines such as `!alt.coffee` and `!rec.food.drink.coffee` if you like.

You can then use nn to unsubscribe to all other groups that you don't want to read.

(Other commands that you can include in the `.nn/init` file are described at the end of this article.)

The .newsrc file

Alternatively, you can edit the `.newsrc` file to unsubscribe from newsgroups or to further narrow down the subscribed groups after you have edited the `.nn/init` file.

The `.newsrc` file is a list of newsgroups that have information about the groups you are subscribed to and the articles in each group that you have read. (If you look at the `.newsrc` file, you may see that you have read articles in newsgroups that you have never been subscribed to. This situation occurs when articles are crossposted to multiple groups and you have read the article in another group.) The order of the groups in the `.newsrc` file is important. It is the same order in which nn will present newsgroups to you. Newsgroups that you are subscribed to have a colon (:) after them; the newsgroups that you are not subscribed to have an exclamation point (!). Changing the character after the group name changes the subscription status.

To edit `.newsrc`, you need to have run a newsreader at least once. This process updates the list of newsgroups. You can edit the file by hand, or, if you prefer, you can do a global search and replace each colon with an exclamation point. Then replace the exclamation points for the groups you want to subscribe to with colons and save `.newsrc`.

After you have narrowed down the number of groups, you are ready to use nn to navigate through a manageable number of newsgroups.

On-line help

You can get help while using nn by pressing **?** in either selection or reading mode.

You can also see the on-line manual by typing `:man`. This a very convenienct way to read the nn manual. You are presented with a list of manual section headers as if you were in selection mode of a newsgroup, from which you can select which sections you wish to read.

Reading News

nn provides a menu-based system that uses one-letter commands to help you navigate through articles that you want to read in subscribed newsgroups.
Note: When you type commands in nn, case is often important. If I tell you to use uppercase, use uppercase.

nn has two modes, *selection* mode and *reading* mode. In selection mode, nn presents a list of news postings in a group that you subscribe to, and you can select the ones you want to read (using the keys a – z and 0 – 9). In reading mode, you can read the articles and move forward to other articles or return to selection mode for the current newsgroup or another one.

Selection mode

Within a newsgroup, nn locates all unread articles in the group, extracts their sender, subject, and other relevant information, and displays them in selection mode. Articles are displayed by thread. Follow-up articles are marked with the greater-than symbol (>) and follow-on articles to follow-on articles by two greater-than symbols (>>), as seen in the following example:

```
Newsgroup: soc.religion.unitarian-univ         Articles: 188 of 14883/137

a C Gilbert          23  Ooh-Yeah! info! (PCD UUYAN newsletter)
b Marie3333          19  >Draft Two of potential UU FAQ entries, Part I
c James Felder       55  >
d Larry Loen         74  >>
e Brad Bartz         12  Good Unitarians Vote Democratic
f Lance A. Brown     19  >
g J Greene-Blose    105  -
h Amy Pemberton      12  >>>
i Bill Goodrich      55  >
j Alan Popiel        60  -
k lindab@pmail.com 35  >
l Murmur              ?  -
m David Babinski     40  >
n lindab@pmail.com 80  >
o Bill Goodrich      79  >
p Allen J Oh         28  >>
q William G. Royds 58  >>
r Jean P Nance       20  -
s Lucien Saumur      56  -

-- 11:57 -- SELECT -- help:? ---Top 9%---
```

In selection mode you also see the name of the newsgroup and the total number of news articles that you haven't read.

To select an article, type the letter or number that identifies the article (selected articles can be deselected in the same way). Pressing the space bar puts nn into reading mode (see the next section). You also can use *x* and *z* to get to reading mode. Use *x* if you are done selecting (if you later change your mind, the equal sign [=] will take you back to selection mode) and *z* if you know that you want to return to the group selection menu after you have read the selected articles.

The following commands also are useful:

Command	What it means
n	Go to the next group.
p	Go to the previous group.
>	Go to the next page of articles in this newsgroup.
<	Go to the previous page of articles in this newsgroup.

Reading mode

Reading mode is just that — it displays the text of the articles you have chosen to read. In reading mode you can go forward or back to articles in the same group, skip to the next thread, or return to the selection menu.

Other useful commands include the following:

Command	***What it means***
n	Go to the next article.
p	Go to the previous article.
k	Skip to the first article of the next thread.
Spacebar	Go to the next page of this article.
Backspace	Go to the previous page of an article.
=	Return to the selection menu.

Previewing articles

From selection mode, you can read an article without entering reading mode for all of the selected articles. If the screen has more than five free lines at the bottom, nn shows the article there; otherwise, it clears the screen to show the article.

You can use these commands:

Command	***What it means***
%x	Preview article x.
%%	Preview the current article.
=	Skip the rest of the article and return to the selection menu.
n	Preview the next article.
l	Leave the article selected and preview the next article.

Catching up

nn has a feature that makes reading news less overwhelming when you haven't read it for a while. You can *catch up* by using the -a0 (that is, a dash, the letter *a,* and a zero) option on the command line to run nn:

```
nn -a0
```

nn asks whether you want to catch up automatically or interactively (press a or i). *Catching up automatically* means that all articles in all groups are marked as read, whereas *catching up interactively* enables you to work group by group. If you choose to catch up interactively, in each newsgroup you have the following options:

Command	*What it means*
y	Mark all articles as read.
n	Do not update (this option is the default; articles remain marked unread).
r	Enter reading mode.
U	Unsubscribe to this group.
q	Quit this group (you will be asked whether all remaining groups should be updated unconditionally or remain unread).

Quitting nn

Pressing **Q** enables you to quit before you have gone through all the newsgroups. The next time you start nn, you have the option of continuing where you left off: nn will ask you whether you want to enter the last group that you left unread articles in. If you answer no, you will start at the beginning of the groups you are subscribed to.

Subscribing and Unsubscribing

Even when you have edited the `.nn/init` and `.newsrc` files, you will probably find an occasion when you want to subscribe or unsubscribe to individual groups. In addition to being able to do this in the ways described previously, you also can use the U command to toggle between subscribing to a group that you are not currently subscribed to and unsubscribing from a group that you are subscribed to. You can use this command from either the reading mode or the selection mode.

To subscribe to a new group, use the G command to go to the group. When you press G, nn asks whether you want to go to a group or a folder. Type the name of the newsgroup. Then nn asks how many articles you want to see. Press **a** to see all the articles (you can still use the selection menu to select from the list) or type a number to specify the number of articles you want to display (nn shows you the most recent ones).

Alternatively, you can start nn with the following command:

```
nn -X [group name]
```

Then you press **U** and ask to be resubscribed. You also can use the nn -X [*group name*] command to look at a group without subscribing.

Saving Articles

You can save the text of articles from selection mode by using the S command. In reading mode, the command is s (this is true of many commands). nn asks you to specify a filename. You also can save articles with only a short header consisting of the sender, subject, and posting date by using the command O.

The following commands also are useful:

Command	*What it means*
W	Write the article without a header.
:print	Print the article (P in reading mode).
:unshar	Unshar the article (that is, decode an article that contains a shar file).
:decode	Decode uuencoded articles.

Responding to Articles

Commands for responding to articles are uppercase in selection mode and lowercase in reading mode. ***Note:*** Before you respond, remember to read the other responses and to calm down if you are incensed!

Replying via e-mail

Unless you are confident that your response is of general interest, the best way to comment on an article is by e-mail. Press **r** to reply to the author through mail.

nn asks whether you want to include a copy of the original article so that the person you are sending e-mail to will know what article you are talking about. If you include the article, delete the parts that aren't germane to your reply.

You also can mail a letter or forward an article to a single recipient by using the m command. Prompts ask you to specify the article, the person to send to (the default is yourself), and the subject of the letter (press the spacebar to use the subject of the included article as the subject of the letter).

Beginning a discussion

To post an article on a new topic, use the :post command. nn asks which group you want to post to; press Enter to post to the current group. Then nn asks for the subject and keywords, and it runs an editor so you can type the text of the article.

Remember, thousands of people will see your article, so make it short, interesting, and correct. Think twice before posting, especially in anger.

Continuing a discussion

You can follow up with an article in the same newsgroup by using the f command. The article you post will appear in the same thread as the article that you are replying to.

Killing and Selecting Articles

Kill files store instructions about subjects and authors you feel strongly about. When you want to see everything or nothing by a certain author or on a certain subject, you should create or edit your kill file.

You can specify a single newsgroup to apply the instructions to. Each entry can be permanent or can apply for a certain number of days.

To create an entry in the kill file, press **k**. You see the following:

```
AUTO (k)ill or (s)elect (CR=>Kill subject 30 days)
```

Pressing Enter kills all articles that have the same subject as the current article for 30 days, which is usually long enough for a discussion to die out.

To kill a group of articles, press k. To select a group of articles, press **s**. nn asks you to specify the subject or author (name), the groups that you want to apply the select or kill to, and the amount of time that you want the kill or select to be valid.

If you were in reading mode when you began the entry in the kill file, you can press Enter or % to use the name or subject of the current article. If you were in selection mode, type % followed by the corresponding article identifier. If you type a slash at the beginning of the line when specifying the subject or name, nn will interpret what follows as a regular expression (like the ones in ed and sed). Otherwise, name and subject have to match exactly (other than upper- and lowercase) for the kill or select to work.

Command Line Options

Here are some frequently-used command-line options. You also can set options permanently by including appropriate variable settings in the INIT file.

Command	***What it means***
-a0	Catch up on unread articles and groups.
-g	Prompt for the name of a newsgroup or folder to be entered (with completion).
-r	Used with -g to repeatedly prompt for groups to enter.
-l*N*	Print only the first *N* lines of the first page of each article before prompting to continue. This option is useful on slow terminals and modem lines to enable you to see the first few lines of longer articles.

Searching for Articles

You can use the following command-line options to find articles that have a particular string in their subjects or in the senders' names:

Command	*What it means*
-s*WORD*	Collect only articles that contain the string *WORD* in their subject (case is ignored). You normally combine this option with the -x and -m options to find all articles on a specific subject.
-n*WORD*	Same as -s, but looks for *WORD* in the senders' names.
-i	Normally searches with -n and -s are case-independent. Using this option makes case significant.
-m	Merge all articles into one "meta group" instead of showing them one group at a time. You usually use this option together with the -x and -s options to have all the articles on a specific subject presented on a single menu (when you don't care about which group they belong to). When you use -m, no articles are marked as read.
-x[*N*]	Present (or scan) all (or the last *N*) unread as well as read articles. When you use this option, nn will never mark unread articles as read (that is, your .newsrc file is not updated).
-X	Read/scan unsubscribed groups also. This option is most useful when you are looking for a specific subject in all groups.

Additional Secrets about nn

This section describes some other clever things about nn.

Using a mailer to send mail

You can use the elm and MH programs to mail messages from nn by making the following additions to the `.nn/init` file. Note that elm and MH do not replace the internal mailer @ the mailer is merely used to deliver a message that you've already completed.

To use MH, add the following to the INIT file:

```
set mail-script nn-use-mh
```

To use elm, add the following to the `.nn/init` file:

```
set   mailer        nn_elm
unset mailer-pipe-input
```

Automatically appending a signature

You can append a signature to replies and articles by putting your signature in a file called `.signature` in your home directory and adding as many of these lines as you want to the `.nn/init` file:

```
set append-signature-post#use it for articles you post
set append-signature-mail#use it for mail you send
set query-signature       #if you want to confirm
```

Double signatures occur when both nn and inews append the signature. If you have this problem, add this line to the `.nn/init` file:

```
unset append-signature-post
```

Saving posts automatically

Add these lines to the `.nn/init` file to save posts automatically:

```
set record file
```

Replace *file* with the absolute pathname of the file. All files are saved in mailbox format.

Seeing the first article in a thread

What if you want to see the original article on a particular subject? Press **G** and then press Enter three times in response to three inscrutable prompts. You go to the first unexpired article on the current subject.

Using consolidated menus

In nn, you have the option of having articles presented in consolidated menus. Normally, nn presents one article per line in selection mode. If several articles have the same subject, articles with repeated subject lines will have blank subjects. In a *consolidated* menu, each *subject* (rather than each article) has one line in selection mode.

To tell nn to use consolidated menus, add this line to the `.nn/init` file:

```
set consolidated-menu
```

With consolidated menus, subjects are open or closed. An *open subject* appears in the usual way, with one line per article. A *closed subject* appears on a single line with a number in square brackets in the subject field indicating the number of articles with that subject.

To select all the articles in a closed subject, simply select the subject in the normal way. To view and possibly select individual articles, use the following commands:

Command	What it means
(x	Open subject x on menu.
((	Open current subject.

To close the subject, use one of the following commands:

Command	What it means
)x	Close subject x.
))	Close current subject.

Changing group order

You can change the order in which groups are presented by making an addition to the `.nn/init` file. At the end of the file, use the word *sequence* on a line by itself, followed by a list of the newsgroups in the order in which you want to view them. On the line following the sequence keyword, add an "@@" on a line by itself to override the system sequence. Otherwise, the system sequence is consulted first. Put each group on a separate line. You may use the full name of the group or just the name of the main group or subgroup. Groups not named will appear after those that are listed.

You may follow the group name by a filename (starting with / or ~) or a folder (starting with +) to specify a default save file for that group. A + appearing by itself means to use the last save file used on a previous line.

Displaying a list of newsgroups

To see a list of all newsgroups, type the command **:post** (including the colon) and then type a question mark. Outside of nn, some UNIX systems have commands called nnsub and eep that display newsgroup names and descriptions as well as to subscribe to groups.

Getting More Information

The Internet has a great deal of information about nn. One way to find it is to read the Usenet newsgroup `news.software.nn`. You can retrieve the "NN Quick Start" from:

`ftp://ftp.halcyon.com/pub/ii/Internet/NN/QuickStart/quick-start`
You can retrieve a paper entitled "Intro to nn," via ftp from `ftp.cso.uiuc.edu`. It's called `doc/net/nn.`*`fmt`* where *`fmt`* is `doc, ps, tex, jpn,` or `hqx`. Choose the format you can read most easily. Or get "A Short Guide to nn" from `ftp.unl.edu` in `pub/crc.docs/UNLINFO.GUIDE/UNLINFO.06.nn.`*`fmt`* where *`fmt`* is `txt, ps, rtf,` or `hqx`.

The latest version of the nn FAQ, from which some of this article was adapted, is available via ftp from:

```
ftp://rtfm.mit.edu/pub/usenet/news.answers/usenet/software/nn/faq/part1
ftp://ftp.uu.net/archive/usenet/news.answers/usenet/software/nn/faq/part1.Z
```

To get the FAQ by e-mail, send the following message to `mail-server@rtfm.mit.edu`:

```
send /usenet/news.answers/usenet/software/nn/faq/part1
```

Or send e-mail to `mail-server@cs.ruu.nl` with this message:

```
send /pub/NEWS.ANSWERS/usenet/software/nn/faq/part1
```

Bill Wohler graduated from UC Davis in 1985 with a Computer Science and Math degree and has been on the Internet since 1980. Bill is currently self-employed as a UNIX and networking consultant; he is, however, known to leave his terminal to enjoy Ultimate Frisbee or to travel.

Using Trn, the Threaded Newsreader

by Margaret Levine Young <margy@iecc.com>

Trn, a widely used UNIX newsreader, is a major improvement over rn, on which it is based, because it is *threaded* (in fact, its name stands for *t*hreaded *r*ead*n*ews). In newsgroup lingo, a *thread* is an article along with all its follow-up articles, including follow-ups to follow-ups and so on. Trn can organize all the articles in a newsgroup into threads, list them, and enable you to choose the topics that look interesting. This capability makes it easy to find the wheat among the chaff (that is, the articles of interest amid all the surrounding dreck).

Running Trn

To run trn, just type **trn**.

If you find that trn can't do all the commands we tell you about in this chapter, you may have to tell it specifically that you plan to use all its features. To do this, type **trn -x -X** to run it. (If it's annoying to type this command every time, make a shell script that contains this command.)

The first time you run it

The first time you run trn, it checks your home directory to see whether you have a file named .newsrc. The .newsrc file stores information about the newsgroups you subscribe to and the messages you've already read in each one. If you've ever run trn or other newsreaders, such as rn and nn, they created this file. If not, trn won't find it the first time it runs.

When this happens, trn just makes you a brand-new one, in your home directory. It also figures that you must be a newbie, so it displays some helpful messages. Press the spacebar to make them go away.

This new .newsrc file is a list of every newsgroup your system carries, which can be thousands of them. The first time you run trn, you have to go through the groups and unsubscribe to the ones you don't plan to read. These decisions aren't irrevocable — you can change your mind later and subscribe again. For each newsgroup in the list, trn asks whether you want to read it, to which you reply **y** or **n**. If you get tired of answering questions, press **N** (capitalized) to tell it not to subscribe to any more groups. (You can go back later and pick up ones you might have missed.)

After the first time

After you've run trn once, trn remembers which newsgroups you are interested in and asks you only about those you subscribe to. (This information is stored in the .newsrc file.)

When new newsgroups are created, which happens every day now that Usenet is so popular, trn asks whether you want to add them to your .newsrc file. You see the following message:

```
Newsgroup alt.binaries.sounds.utilities not in .newsrc — subscribe? [ynYN]
```

To subscribe to the newsgroup and begin reading it now, press **y** (that's a small *y*). To skip it forever, press **n** (again, a small one). To add all the new newsgroups, press **Y**. To tell trn not to ask you about any of the new groups, press **N**.

If you choose to subscribe to a newsgroup, trn asks this question:

```
Put newsgroup where? [$^.Lq]
```

The various potions in the square brackets control exactly where in your .newsrc file you want to put this newsgroup. To put it at the end, just press the spacebar.

Note: Trn thoughtfully lets you know whether you have e-mail waiting. If so, it says `(Mail)` at the beginning of some prompts.

Choosing Newsgroups to Read

For each newsgroup in your .newsrc list, trn suggests that you read its articles. If this is your first time, the newsgroup is probably `news.announce.newusers`, the newsgroups for folks who are new to newsgroups. It's not a bad idea to peruse these articles, but let's get to that later. The way that trn suggests a newsgroup is with this message:

```
67 unread articles in news.announce.newusers — read now? [+ynq]
```

(The number of messages varies.) The `[+ynq]` tells you the possible responses:

- Press + to see the list of threads for this newsgroup so that you can choose which threads to read. (If you choose this option, skip down to the section "Choosing Articles by Thread.")
- Press **y** to go ahead and look at the newsgroup article by article. (If you choose this option, skip down to the section "Reading the News.")
- Press **n** to choose not to read this newsgroup, at least not right now. Trn suggests the next newsgroup on its list.
- Press **q** to quit trn altogether.

You can also press **u** (small, not capital) to unsubscribe from the newsgroup and remove it from your .newsrc file so that you'll never be bothered by it again.

Note: If you always like to look at the thread selector for a newsgroup, you can tell trn to make + (go to the thread selector first) the default for the newsgroup rather than y (go directly to reading articles). When trn asks whether you want to read the newsgroup, press **t** (a small one). This option turns on thread selection for this newsgroup, assuming that it was off. (If it was already on, it turns it off.) For each newsgroup, trn remembers whether you like to select threads first and presents the appropriate default so that if you press the spacebar, you get what you want.

Commanding Trn

When trn gives you a list of possible commands in square brackets (such as [+ynq]), you generally can press any of the options that are listed. Don't press Enter — trn moves along right away as soon as you press a key. Also, you can press the spacebar to choose the first option in the square brackets (this one is the default option).

Occasionally, commands are more than one letter long, usually because they enable you to specify extra information, such as a filename in which to save a message. Commands that are longer than one letter must be followed by pressing Enter so that trn knows when you are finished typing.

Trn cares about capital versus small letters — it has so many commands that frequently a capital letter does something different from its small counterpart. So be careful to capitalize commands the same way you see in this chapter.

Trn always does one of four things:

- Offers a newsgroup to read
- Displays a list of threads from which to choose
- Offers an article to display
- Pauses while it displays an article that is too long to find on the screen

Confusingly, different commands work in these four situations. Luckily, you don't have to use many commands very often, and trn suggests the most likely options.

You can press **h** at any time to see trn's on-line help. It's rather concise but can certainly be helpful, especially as a reminder.

Choosing Articles by Thread

When trn asks whether you want to read a newsgroup, by offering the options [+ynq], press + to see the list of threads for the newsgroup. You see a list of threads like the one shown in Figure 26-1.

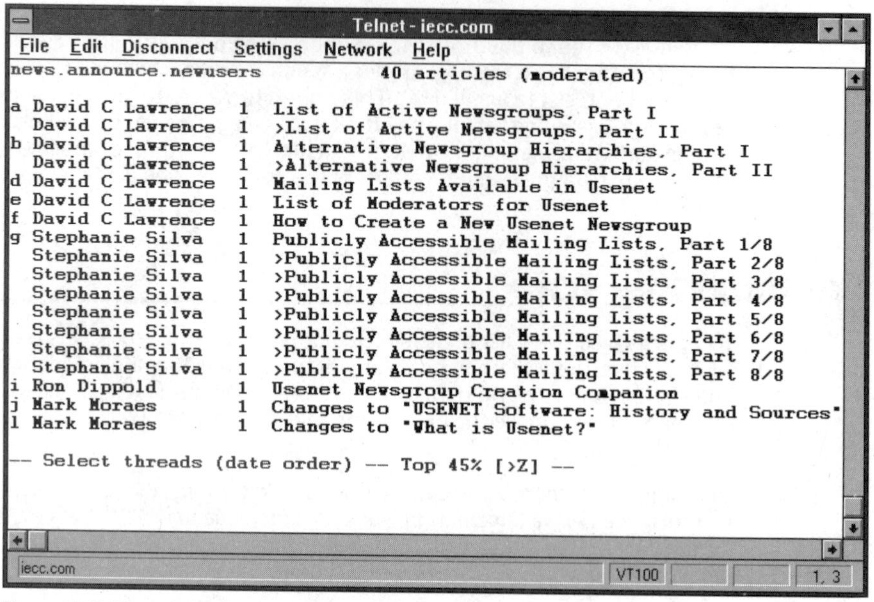

```
Telnet - iecc.com
File  Edit  Disconnect  Settings  Network  Help
news.announce.newusers             40 articles (moderated)

a David C Lawrence  1  List of Active Newsgroups, Part I
  David C Lawrence  1  >List of Active Newsgroups, Part II
b David C Lawrence  1  Alternative Newsgroup Hierarchies, Part I
  David C Lawrence  1  >Alternative Newsgroup Hierarchies, Part II
d David C Lawrence  1  Mailing Lists Available in Usenet
e David C Lawrence  1  List of Moderators for Usenet
f David C Lawrence  1  How to Create a New Usenet Newsgroup
g Stephanie Silva   1  Publicly Accessible Mailing Lists, Part 1/8
  Stephanie Silva   1  >Publicly Accessible Mailing Lists, Part 2/8
  Stephanie Silva   1  >Publicly Accessible Mailing Lists, Part 3/8
  Stephanie Silva   1  >Publicly Accessible Mailing Lists, Part 4/8
  Stephanie Silva   1  >Publicly Accessible Mailing Lists, Part 5/8
  Stephanie Silva   1  >Publicly Accessible Mailing Lists, Part 6/8
  Stephanie Silva   1  >Publicly Accessible Mailing Lists, Part 7/8
  Stephanie Silva   1  >Publicly Accessible Mailing Lists, Part 8/8
i Ron Dippold       1  Usenet Newsgroup Creation Companion
j Mark Moraes       1  Changes to "USENET Software: History and Sources"
l Mark Moraes       1  Changes to "What is Usenet?"

-- Select threads (date order) -- Top 45% [>Z] --

iecc.com                                        VT100          1, 3
```

Figure 26-1: What topics are we talking about?

The top line of the screen shows the name of the newsgroup (in this example, it's `news.announce.newusers`), along with the number of articles waiting to be read and whether it is moderated. (Moderated newsgroups have editors who control which messages get posted.)

Below that is a list of articles, organized into threads. Each thread is assigned a letter, down the left edge of the screen. (Trn skips some letters, which are used for commands.) For each article, you see the author and the subject line.

The bottom line of the display tells you to select some threads and indicates whether there are more articles than can fit on the screen (there usually are). For example, Figure 26-1 contains the top 45 percent of the articles in the newsgroup.

If you want to read the articles in a thread, type the letter assigned to the thread. A plus sign appears next to the thread letter, showing that this thread has been chosen. (If you change your mind, press the thread's letter again to deselect it.)

To see more threads, press >. You can tell when you get to the end of the list of threads when you see `Bot` on the bottom line of text.

To back up and see previous pages of threads, press <. To begin at the beginning again, press ^, or to go to the end, press $.

When you've chosen the threads you want, use one of these commands:

- Press **X** (that's a capital X) to mark all the articles in all the threads you *didn't* choose as having been read already so that trn doesn't ask you about them again. Then begin reading the articles in the threads you *did* choose.
- Press **N** to forget all about this newsgroup and look at the next one on your .newsrc list. Or press **P** to move to the preceding newsgroup. (Be sure to capitalize most of these commands.)

Reading the News

If you pressed X after choosing the threads you wanted, or if you pressed y when trn first asked about the newsgroup, trn begins showing you the articles one at a time. First it shows you the article's headers, as shown in Figure 26-2.

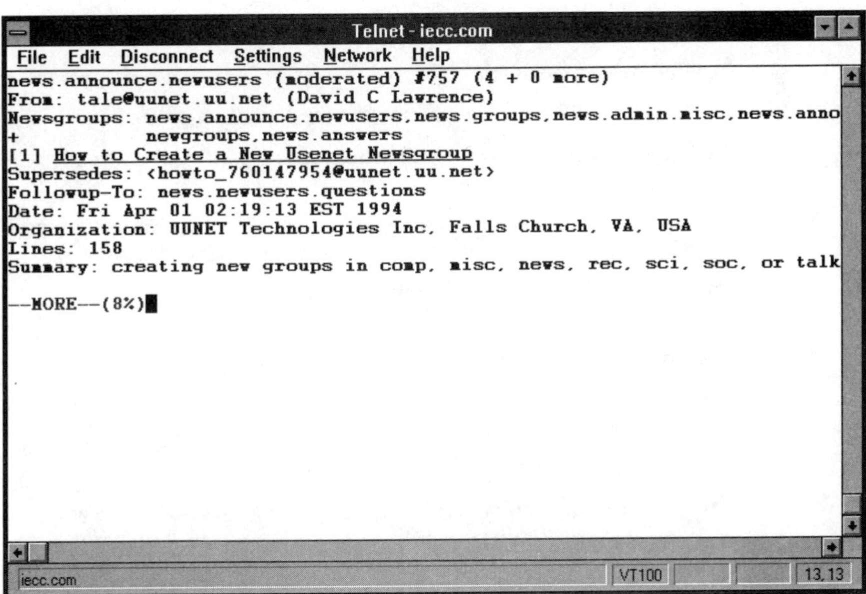

Figure 26-2: The cryptic headers at the beginning of an article.

You have several options:

- To see the rest of the article (or at least the next screenful), press the spacebar. You see the next page of text. If the article is several pages long, you see a MORE prompt at the end of each page, until you get to the end of the article.

  You can get a sense of how long the article is by looking at how much you've read so far. The MORE prompt tells you what percentage of the article you've seen so that you can tell how far you have to go.

- If the article doesn't interest you, press **j** (a small *j*) to "junk" the article. This option tells trn to mark the article as read (so that it doesn't offer it to you again later) and go to the end of the article.
- If the entire topic is boring and you don't want to see any more articles that have the same subject line, press **k** (a small *k*) to kill the topic. Trn skips any articles in this thread (or any other thread) that have the same text in the subject line.
- To bag the entire thread, including articles with a different subject line, press **J** (that's a capital *J*). Trn forgets about any response to this article, or responses to those responses, or responses to the article that this one is a response to (you get the idea), regardless of whether they have the same subject line as this article. That is, they are marked as read.
- To quit looking at this whole newsgroup (for now, anyway), press **q**. Trn asks you about the next newsgroups in your list.

At the end of the article, trn asks this question:

```
End of article 757 (of 818) — what next? [npq]
```

Again, you have lots of options:

- To see the next article you haven't read, press **n** or the spacebar.
- To see the preceding unread article, press **p**. (If you've already read all the previous articles, nothing happens.)
- To see the last article trn displayed before the current one, press **P**. This option displays the preceding article even though you read it already.
- To see the same article again, press Ctrl-R.
- To quit reading this newsgroup, press **q**. Trn asks you whether you want to read the next newsgroup in your list.
- To kill (mark as read) all articles that have this subject line, press **k** (a small *k*).
- To kill the entire thread, including articles with a different subject line, press **J** (that's a capital *J*).
- If you are way behind in reading this newsgroup and you want to give up the idea of ever catching up, press **c** (that's a small *c*). Trn marks all the unread articles in the newsgroup as read. The next time you read this group, you see only the new articles.
- If you have totally lost interest in this newsgroup, press **u** (small *u*) to unsubscribe from it.

Rot-13

Usenet has a system for protecting you from gross, disgusting, obscene, or otherwise offensive articles. Offensive articles can be posted by using a simple code called *Rot 13*. If you try to read an article and it appears as gibberish, you can press

Ctrl-X to start the article over, decoding it as it goes. But don't complain to us (or anyone else) if it offends you! Incidentally, if you press Ctrl-X by mistake and want to read the article *au naturel,* press Ctrl-R to redraw it normally.

Searching for text

You can use trn's search command to find articles that contain a particular word or set of characters in the subject line, anywhere in the header, or anywhere in the article. To search for articles that contain *text* in the subject line, type this line:

```
/text
```

If you want to look for articles that contain *text* anywhere in the headers, type this line:

```
/text/h
```

For articles that contain *text* anywhere in the text of the articles themselves as well as in the headers, type this line:

```
/text/a
```

To search backward through previous articles, type **?** rather than / in this command.

Saving Articles

You can save the text of an article in a file if you want to transfer it to another machine, include it in a word-processing document, or just plain keep it. You can save it either as plain text or with the header lines that mail programs use in mailbox files. The advantage of making it look like a mailbox is that you can then use mail programs such as elm or pine to handle the saved messages.

Here's how to save an article in a file.

1. **When you are at the end of an article you want to save, type this line:**

   ```
   s filename
   ```

   Replace `filename` with the name you want to give to the file that contains the article.

   If the file already exists, trn sticks the article at the end of it. (This feature is useful if you want to save an entire series of articles together in a file — as you save each article, trn adds it to the end of the file.)

   If the file doesn't exist, trn asks what kind of file to make:

   ```
   File /usr/margy/News/save.it doesn't exist—
       use mailbox format? [ynq]
   ```

2. **To save it in a regular text file, press** n. **To save it in the kind of file in which mail programs store e-mail messages, press** y.

If you don't tell it otherwise, trn saves files in a directory named News in your home directory. You can enter a pathname if you want to put the file elsewhere. Use a tilde (~) to tell trn to put a file in your home directory, like this:

```
s ~/article.about.cats
```

Decoding Binary Data

Sometimes a news article contains not plain text but a coded version of a binary file, or a group of files. There are two common ways to sneak files into articles: uuencoding and shar files.

Uuencoded data

In a *uuencoded* message, a single binary file is turned into a bunch of ugly-looking text, like this:

```
begin 664 sample
M5V]W(2!)9B!Y;W4@86-T=6%L;'D@='EP960@:6X@=&AI<R!W:&]L92!F:6QE
M(&%N9"!U=61E8V]D960@:70@<W5C8V5S<V9U;&QY+'IY;W4G<F4@82!R96%L
M;'D@9&5D:6-A=&5D(')E861E<BX@($1R;W`@=7,@82!N;W1E(&%T(&UI9'5M
K;6EE<T!I96-C+F-O;2!A;F0*;65N=&E0;B!S96-R970@8V]D92!8,3(N"G5M
'
end
```

Usually uuencoded files are much longer than this one, but they're all equally ugly. Really long ones are often split across several news messages to keep each individual article to a reasonable size. Uuencoded files are most often found in groups such as `comp.binaries.ms-windows`, in which case they're runnable programs, or in groups such as `alt.binaries.pictures.erotica`, in which case they're digitized pictures of, er, various stuff.

Shar files

A *shar file* (short for *sh*ell *ar*chive) contains a group of files. Most often they contain program source code, but they can contain any text files. Here's a short example:

```
#!/bin/sh
# This is a shell archive (produced by shar 3.49)
# To extract the files from this archive, save it to a file, remove
# everything above the "!/bin/sh" line above, and type "sh file_name".
#
# made 05/25/1994 01:43 UTC by johnl@iecc
# Source directory /usr/johnl
#
# existing files will NOT be overwritten unless -c is specified
#
# This shar contains:
# length  mode       name
```

```
# ---------------------------------
#     112 -rw-rw-r— poem
#
# ============= poem ==============
if test -f 'poem' -a X"$1" != X"-c"; then
   echo 'x - skipping poem (File already exists)'
else
echo 'x - extracting poem (Text)'
sed 's/^X//' << 'SHAR_EOF' > 'poem' &&
I eat my peas with honey
I've done it all my life
It makes them taste real funny
But it keeps them on my knife.
SHAR_EOF
chmod 0664 poem ||
echo 'restore of poem failed'
Wc_c="'wc -c < 'poem''"
test 112 -eq "$Wc_c" ||
   echo 'poem: original size 112, current size' "$Wc_c"
fi
exit 0
```

Trn makes it easy to extract the useful bits from uuencoded or shar files. When you see this type of message, you can extract its contents by pressing **e** followed by the name of the directory in which to extract it. (If you just press **e** and Enter, it uses your News directory.) Multipart uuencoded files are also handled more or less automatically. After you extract the contents of the first part of a uuencoded message, trn says `(continued)`, and it's up to you to find the next part and press **e** again. After the last part, it says `Done`. Shar files are extracted in the same way as uuencoded files, except that there's no such thing as a multipart shar file. (Large programs may be multiple messages, but each one is a separate shar file.)

Security warning

Shar and uuencode files present some enormous potential security holes. Shar files are really no more than lists of commands for the UNIX shell that create the files to be extracted. These files offer considerable flexibility, but it also means that a prankster can stick in some commands that you would just as soon not execute, like ones that delete all your files. Shar files from moderated newsgroups (that is, groups in which the messages all are examined and approved by a third party before being sent out) are generally OK, but the files on other groups are only as reliable as the people sending them.

Shar scanning programs are available that scan shar files for untoward commands. Check with your Internet shell provider or UNIX system manager to see whether any are available on your system.

Uuencoded files of pictures are unlikely to cause any trouble, other than the hair on your palms you may get from looking at some of them. Uuencoded binary programs should be treated with the same skepticism as any other binary programs. Again, the ones that come from moderated groups are pretty safe, and others less so. A scan with a virus checker is always appropriate.

Responding to Articles

If you read an article that demands a response, you have two options: You can respond privately by sending e-mail to the person who wrote it or you can post a follow-up article to the newsgroup. Here's how to decide which way to go:

- If your response will be of interest to only the person who wrote the article, send e-mail.
- If you are really mad, take a walk before doing anything. If you're still mad and you just *have* to reply, send e-mail.
- If the original article contains errors that everyone reading it should know about, post a follow-up article, but only after checking to make sure that 12 other people haven't already done the same thing.
- If you have additional information about the subject that will be of universal interest to those reading the original article, post a follow-up article.

Responding privately by e-mail

When you are at the end of an article you want to respond to privately, here's what to do:

1. **Decide whether you want to quote parts of the article in your e-mail.**

   If you do, press **R**. Otherwise, press **r**.

   Trn displays a bunch of confusing messages, followed by a question about including a prepared file.

2. **Assuming that you have not prepared in advance a text file you now want to include in your e-mail, press Enter to tell trn not to include any file.**

   Trn now asks which editor you want to use.

3. **If you don't like the editor it suggests, type the command you use to start your editor. Otherwise, just press Enter.**

   Trn runs the editor. If you chose to include the text of the original article, it is already sitting on-screen, indented to show that you are quoting it. The headers for the e-mail are at the top of the screen too.

4. **Delete unneeded text.**

   Be sure to delete the boring header lines from the original article (the ones that are quoted from the original article, not the ones that address your e-mail message, at the very top of the screen). Also delete parts of the article you don't plan to discuss in your e-mail message. Pare the quoted text to the bare minimum, just enough to remind the person what article it is that you just read and are responding to.

5. **Type your reply. Be clear, polite, and reasonable.**

6. **Save your message and exit from the editor, using whatever command works in your editor.**

Trn asks this question:

```
Check spelling, Send, Abort, Edit, or List?
```

7. **To run a spell checker, press** C. **To forget all about sending this e-mail, press** A. **To return to the editor to make one more little change, press** E. **And to send the message, press** S. **Then press Enter.**

   Trn asks whether you want it to stick your signature file at the end of the message. (A *signature file* is a file called .signature in your home directory that contains your name return address, and other info.)

8. **Press** y **or** n **and press Enter.**

   Trn returns you to where you left off — right at the end of the article you just responded to.

You can press **r** to send an e-mail message to anyone, not just to the person who wrote the article you just read. If you suddenly get the urge to write a note to your mom, press **r** and follow the steps to enter the editor. When you are editing your response, you can change the `To:` line to any address you want, rather than the article's author, and the `Subject:` line to any subject.

Responding by posting an article

If you have something so interesting to say that you want to post it publicly, where it can be read, appreciated, savored, misconstrued, or laughed at, follow these steps:

1. **Press** F **to tell trn that you want to post a follow-up article, and include some or all of the original article.**

   Trn gives you a warning, like this:

   ```
   This program posts news to thousands of machines throughout
   the entire civilized world. Your message will cost the net
   hundreds if not thousands of dollars to send everywhere.
   Please be sure you know what you are doing.

   Are you absolutely sure that you want to do this? [ny]
   ```

2. **If you have thought better of it, press** n **or the spacebar. You can always send an e-mail message to the article's author and then decide to go public later. If you still want to post an article, press** y. **Then press Enter.**

   Trn asks whether you want to include a prepared file.

3. **Assuming that you have not prepared in advance a text file you now want to include in your article, press Enter to tell trn not to include any file.**

   Trn asks which editor you want to use.

4. **If you don't like the editor it suggests, type the command you use to start your editor. Otherwise, just press Enter.**

Trn runs the editor. If you chose to include the text of the original article, it is already sitting on the screen, indented to show that you are quoting it. The headers for your follow-up article are at the top of the screen too.

Take a look at the `Newsgroups:` line at the top of the message. It lists the newsgroups to which this article will be posted.

5. **Delete any newsgroups that wouldn't be interested in your article.**
6. **Move down to the beginning of the text of the article you are replying to and delete unnecessary text.**

   Be sure to delete the boring header lines along with any parts of the article you don't plan to refer to. Pare the quoted text to the bare minimum, just enough to remind newsgroup readers what exactly you are responding to.
7. **Type your reply. Be clear, polite, and reasonable.**
8. **Save your message and exit from the editor, by using whatever commands work in your editor.**

   . Lines in Usenet articles are usually limited to 79 characters. If any of the lines in your article is longer than that, trn warns you about it so that you can go back and fix it. Then it gives you this choice:

   ```
   Check spelling, Send, Abort, Edit, or List?
   ```
9. **To run a spell checker, press** C. **To forget all about posting this article, press** A. **To return to the editor to make one more little change, press** E. **And to send the message, press** S. **Then press Enter.**

   Trn sends your article out into the universe and displays a message confirming it. Then you are back at the end of the article to which you responded.

When you post an article to an unmoderated newsgroup, the article is distributed directly all over the Internet. When you post to a moderated newsgroup, the article is e-mailed to the person (or group) who moderates the newsgroup. The moderator decides whether the article is worthy to be posted. You generally get an automated response from the moderator's computer and sometimes follow-up mail from the moderator.

Adding and Deleting Newsgroups

When trn offers a newsgroup for you to read, there are dozens of commands you can give. In addition to the four commands listed earlier in this chapter (`+`, `y`, `n`, and `q`), you can also use these commands to add or delete newsgroups from your list:

- To delete a newsgroup from your list (that is, to unsubscribe to it), press **u** (that's a small *u*).
- To add a newsgroup that's not on your .newsrc list, type this line:

  g *newsgroupname*

Replace *newsgroupname* with the exact name of the newsgroup. If you are interested in naturist activities, for example, type this line:

```
g rec.nude
```

- If you are not sure of the exact name of the newsgroup you are looking for, type this line:

  ```
  a text
  ```

  Replace *text* with a word or part of a word. If you are interested in gardening, for example, type this line:

  ```
  a garden
  ```

  If trn finds any newsgroups with names that contain those characters, it asks whether you want to subscribe to each one. Press **y** or **n** to subscribe or not. When trn asks where to put the newsgroup, just press the spacebar.

Editing your .newsrc file

All newsreading programs store information about your particular preferences and situation, including which newsgroups you subscribe to and which messages you've already read. (Messages in each newsgroup are numbered, so it can just remember the range of message numbers you've seen.) The information is stored in a file named .newsrc. Whether you use rn, trn, or nn to read the news, they all share the information in the .newsrc file. This file is the way most newsreading programs avoid forgetting all about what you've subscribed to and what you've already read.

To look at your .newsrc file, when trn asks whether you want to look at a newsgroup, press **L** (be sure that it's capitalized). You see a listing like this:

```
#  Status   Newsgroup
 0  (READ)  local.risks! 1-5548,5551-5556
 1 (UNSUB)  local.pcdigest! 1-7197
 2 (UNSUB)  comp.binaries.ibm.pc.d! 1-17823
 3 (UNSUB)  comp.sys.ibm.pc.digest! 1-580
 4 (UNSUB)  comp.text.desktop! 1-2558
 5 (UNSUB)  rec.food.veg! 1-36863,37791,37958
 6      37  rec.humor.funny! 1-3424
 7 (UNSUB)  rec.humor! 1-105750,106727,107119
 8     152  rec.arts.startrek.info! 1-1942
 9 (UNSUB)  news.lists.ps-maps! 1-1111
10 (UNSUB)  comp.sys.ibm.pc.programmer! 1-5748
11 (UNSUB)  comp.specification! 1-1337
12 (UNSUB)  comp.text.tex! 1-35685
```

The first column of the listing just numbers the groups for your reference. The second column says:

- **A number:** You subscribe to the group and that's how many unread articles are waiting for you.
- `READ`: You subscribe to the group and have read all its articles.

- UNSUB: You once subscribed to it but unsubscribed in disgust.
- BOGUS: It's not in the official list of real newsgroups.
- JUNK: Means nothing (trn ignores lines that say JUNK here).

A colon after a newsgroup name means that you subscribe to the group, and an exclamation point means that you don't. The number ranges are the article numbers of the articles marked as having been read.

Changing the order of newsgroups

Trn goes down the list of newsgroups in your .newsrc file, asking you about each one in order. If your .newsrc file has many newsgroups in it, it's a good idea to put first the ones you read most often. This technique avoids having to skip over the less interesting ones every time.

When trn asks whether you want to read a newsgroup, and you want to move this newsgroup, press **m** and then Enter. Then press one of the following:

- Press ^ to put the newsgroup first.
- Press **$** to put the newsgroup last.
- Type a number to tell trn on what line number to put the newsgroup in your .newsrc file.
- Press **q** to forget the whole thing.

Killing Articles

An ugly fact of Usenet life is that a great deal of garbage appears in newsgroups, mixed in with the good stuff. One powerful method of avoiding it is to use trn's thread selector, described earlier in this chapter. A more permanent method is the *kill file.*

Understanding kill files

Trn has two kinds of kill files: your global kill file, which applies to all your newsgroups, and kill files for each newsgroup. Both types of kill files contain information about which types of Usenet messages you never, never want to see. Messages described in your kill files are simply skipped over by trn, so they never bother you.

What if some idiot decides, for example, that it is very funny to send gross and useless messages to a newsgroup you like to read? You can skip over them, true, but wouldn't it be nice to just tell trn, "Look, if you get any message from that idiot, ignore them! I don't want to see them!" With kill files, you can.

Alternatively, if you are interested in only a small subject of the articles in a newsgroup, you can tell trn, "In this newsgroup, I want to see only articles that contain thus-and-such in the subject." Rather than kill a group of articles, you can kill all except a group of articles. You can use kill files to select articles too.

The global kill file contains a list of commands that trn executes every time you start reading a newsgroup. Newsgroup kill files contain the commands trn executes when you enter that particular newsgroup. The commands usually tell trn which articles to kill (that is, ignore and never show you) or select (that is, ignore all the *other* articles). Your global kill file is stored in your News directory and is named KILL.

The kill files for each newsgroup are stored in subdirectories of your News directory. For example, your kill file for the `rec.humor.funny` newsgroup is stored in `News/rec/humor/funny/KILL`.

It's usually better to use newsgroup kill files rather than the global kill files because the types of articles you want to kill or choose tend to differ widely from newsgroup to newsgroup. It can slow down your newsreading if trn has to execute a bunch of unnecessary commands at the beginning of each newsgroup. On the other hand, an unfortunate spate of advertisements has recently been posted to every newsgroup in the known universe (a practice known as *spamming*), for which a global kill file is the best response.

Killing articles by subject

You can add commands to your newsgroup kill file when you are choosing the threads to read, but the best time is when you are reading articles. When you are looking at a particularly obnoxious article, here's how to draw some blood:

1. **Press** A **(be sure to capitalize it).**

   This line adds a command to the newsgroup kill file, telling trn what to do with all articles that have the same subject as this article, both now and in the future, forever.

   Trn then asks `[+j.,]` (surely one of the most inspired prompts of all time) — this is its way of asking exactly what you want to do with these articles.

2. **To kill (skip) all the articles, press** j**. To kill all the articles in addition to any replies to them, press** , **(a comma).**

A faster way of killing articles on the same subject as the current articles is by pressing **K** (capitalized). This is the same as pressing **Aj** (capital A, then small j).

Killing all articles except those you specify

Alternatively, you may want to tell trn that you are interested in articles about *only* a certain subject, now and forever. When you are looking at an article on that subject, press **A** (capitalized). Then press **+** to look at only articles on that subject. Or press **.** (a period) to look at only those articles and replies to them.

Editing the kill file

You can use a text editor to look at what's in your kill file and make some changes. To edit your global kill file, wait until trn is asking whether you want to read a newsgroup. Instead of answering, press Ctrl-K. To edit a newsgroup kill file, when you are reading that newsgroup, press Ctrl-K. Either way, trn runs a text editor and loads up the appropriate kill file.

Each line in a kill file contains one command, telling trn to either skip all articles that fit a certain description or to look only at articles that fit a description. The first line in a kill file tells trn the message number of the latest message trn has looked at, like this:

```
THRU 13567
```

Commands look like this:

```
/Buzz off, buddy!/:j
```

The text between the slashes tells trn what text to look for in the subjects of articles. The character after the colon (a `j`, in this example) tells trn what do with the articles: `j` to junk them, a comma to junk them and their replies, a + to choose only them, and a period to choose only them and their replies. Not exactly easy to remember!

Here's another example: Suppose that you read the newsgroup `news.groups`, which is where discussions about new newsgroups take place. However, there can be several hundred messages a day. You are interested only in articles that have anything to do with cats. To see only those articles, you can add this line to the kill file for the `news.groups` kill file:

```
/cat/:+
```

This command chooses all articles with a subject line that contains the word *cat.*

Canceling kill commands

If you add a command to a kill file and then you change your mind, the only way to get rid of it is to edit the kill file. When you are in the newsgroups, press Ctrl-K to edit the file. Look for the command (if it's the last one you created, it's at the end of the file). Using your editor's commands, delete the whole line, or modify it until it does what you want.

Quitting Trn

To exit from trn, press **q** almost any time. Sometimes it may take two or three **qs** to get all the way out.

Margaret Levine Young is the co-author of IDG's UNIX For Dummies, More Internet For Dummies, *and* The Internet For Dummies Starter Kit, *in addition to other computer books. She has spent a great deal of time explaining to people that computers are not as mysterious as people think.*

Trn Tips and Tricks

by Jon Bell <jtbell@presby.edu> and
Margaret Levine Young <margy@iecc.com>

This chapter assumes that you are using trn version 3.5. You can find out which version you are using by typing **v** (lowercase!) at the newsgroup-selection prompt (`read now?`). Trn was written by Wayne Davison (`davison@borland.com`). Nice work, Wayne!

The Thread-Selection Menu: Three Formats

When you see this prompt

```
====== 100 unread articles in comp.sys.mac.comm -- read now? [+ynq]
```

you can either press the spacebar or type a + to produce a menu of all the current discussion threads, like the following:

```
comp.sys.mac.comm   100 articles

a Forrest Thiessen 2 GeoPort Adaptor Availability?
  Sean McMains
b Steve Wall       2 >What happened to White Knight?
  David R Bosso
  Tony Huang
  Fred Morris
  Doug Muder
  Deb Bodeau
  Jordan Young
d JAMES N MERRICKS 1 Geoport & Zterm
e Fred Morris      1 >Xferring from VAX to Mac?
f C B Kidwell      6 >MacSLIP 2.0 arrives
  Jerry Goldstein
  Donald L. Nash
  Rick Watson
  Donald L. Nash
  Greg Ferguson
  Zac Young
  Tony Huang       1 >MacSLIP 2.0 and FaxSTF

(Mail) -- Select threads (date order) -- Top 19% [>Z] --
```

From left to right, the menu displays a selector letter for each discussion thread, the names of the authors of the articles in the thread, the number of articles for each subject title, and the subject(s) under discussion. A single thread may contain several subjects, because the author of a follow-up article can address a different subject in his or her reply if the topic has drifted. An angle bracket (>) before a subject indicates that all the articles are follow-ups to an earlier article; if no angle bracket appears, the thread begins from scratch with the first article.

Three different forms of the thread-selection menu exist; you can rotate among them by typing **L** (capitalized). The *long mode,* shown in the previous example, is the default on most systems, but your news administrator may have configured trn so that it uses another mode as the default. *Medium mode* puts multiple authors on the same line whenever possible to show more threads on-screen, as follows:

```
comp.sys.mac.comm   100 articles

a Forrest Thiessen 2 GeoPort Adaptor Availability?
  Sean McMains
b Steve Wall       2 >What happened to White Knight?
  David R Bosso
  Tony Huang            Fred Morris
  Doug Muder            Deb Bodeau
  Jordan Young
d JAMES N MERRICKS 1 Geoport & Zterm
e Fred Morris      1 >Xferring from VAX to Mac?
f C B Kidwell      6 >MacSLIP 2.0 arrives
  Jerry Goldstein
  Donald L. Nash        Rick Watson
  Donald L. Nash        Greg Ferguson
  Zac Young
  Tony Huang       1 >MacSLIP 2.0 and FaxSTF
g Helen Cohen      2 What's going on?
  Geoff Rimositis
i Meg Young        2 My new orphan game
  Zac Young

(Mail) — Select threads (date order) — Top 25% [>Z] —
```

Short mode omits the authors and shows one subject per line, as follows:

```
comp.sys.mac.comm   100 articles

a  2 GeoPort Adaptor Availability?
b  2 >What happened to White Knight?
d  1 Geoport & Zterm
e  1 >Xferring from VAX to Mac?
f  6 >MacSLIP 2.0 arrives
g  2 What's going on?
i  2 My new orphan game
j  4 >White Knight again
l  1 Hello!
o  2 Geoport
r  1 What's an orphan game?
s  6 Geoport and me
t  2 >White Knight again
u  3 NEW INFORMATION
v  1 Time to update the FAQ!
w  1 >Orphan games again?
x  4 VAX to Mac info
y  1 More on MacSLIP
z  2 >Types of xfers

(Mail) -- Select threads (date order) -- Top 35% [>Z] --
```

Rereading Articles

Sometimes, you want to reread an article or thread that you have already read and that therefore no longer shows up in the thread-selection menu. Typing **U** (capitalized) when you are looking at the thread-selection menu causes the menu to display all previously read threads, as follows:

```
news.newusers.questions   170 read articles

a-2 FAQ: How to find people's E-mail addresses
b-3 Welcome to news.newusers.questions!
d-1 rn KILL file FAQ
  3 trn and Re:
e-1 >Tolkien site...
f-2 >This is a test, please reply
g-2 >Modem question
i-1 >Software Copy Protection for PC
j-3 >This is a TEST, please reply...
l-12 >How do you stop harassing e-mail?
o-4 >Filtering mail
r-1 >** 14-year old boy wants ...
s-1 >Background news filter
t-1 >TQM/summary
u-2 >What's a daemon, he asks
v-1 >ftp question
w-1 >Question : How to post news anonymously ?
x-4 TAR
z-5 What is the FAQ??

(Mail) -- Select threads (date order) -- Top 29% [>Z] --
```

This example is just like the usual thread selector (we used short mode for this example), except that all the selection letters are followed by a minus sign (-) to indicate that they have been read. Select threads to read as usual by typing the selector letters, which changes the corresponding minus signs to plus signs. Pressing Enter (or the spacebar, when you are in the last screen of the menu) takes you into article-reading mode, as usual.

To switch back to the normal thread selector, type **U** (capitalized) again when you are looking at the menu.

If you have read everything in the newsgroup, trn doesn't even present the newsgroup at newsgroup-selection level, so you must use the g command to go to it and then type **U**, as follows:

```
====== 1 unread article in news.admin.policy--read now? [+ynq] g
soc.culture.nordic
====== 0 unread articles in soc.culture.nordic--read now? [ynq] U
Set unread: +select or all? [+an] + (or space)
```

This procedure displays the thread-selection menu for all previously read articles.

Signatures

Most people create a signature file — that is, a file named .signature — that is appended to each article that you post. You can use any text editor to create the .signature file.

Trn also provides a newer method for specifying a signature. This method appends the signature *before* you begin to edit the article, so that you can see it. The method actually involves two signature files: .news_sig, which trn appends when you use the f or F command to post a reply to the rest of Usenet; and .mail_sig, which trn appends when you use the r or R command to send the reply directly to the author of the original article via e-mail. You can create these alternative signature files with any text editor. If you use .news_sig or .mail_sig, do *not* also use .signature; otherwise, you will end up with two signatures on your articles!

Changing Your Default Editor

On most systems, trn is set up to use vi as its default editor for new articles, because every UNIX system has vi. You may prefer to use some other editor that your system makes available. One popular choice is pico, a stand-alone version of the editor that is built into the Pine e-mail program.

When trn prompts you for the editor as it is setting up an article, you can specify the other editor, as follows:

```
Editor [/usr/bin/vi]: pico -t
```

(If you use pico, we recommend using the -t option, which suppresses a couple of unnecessary prompts when you leave pico.)

You must, however, specify the editor each time you post an article. It's more convenient to change the default editor so that you can simply press Return or Enter at this prompt. To make this change, you must set an environment variable named *EDITOR* in your login initialization file. How you do this depends on which shell you're using.

If you're using the Bourne shell (and have $ as your command-line prompt), edit the file named .profile (notice the period at the beginning) so that it contains the following lines (using pico as an example):

```
EDITOR="pico -t"
export EDITOR
```

If you're using the C shell (and have % as your command-line prompt), edit the file named .cshrc (again, notice the period) so that it contains the following lines (again using pico as an example):

```
setenv EDITOR "pico -t"
```

The next time you log in, the editor that you specify becomes the default for all editing sessions in trn and in any other program that uses the *EDITOR* variable.

Canceling and Superseding Articles

If you change your mind about something that you wrote, you can take it back by canceling your article, so long as the article has not yet expired on your system. First, find your article and begin reading it; you may have to use the U command at thread-selection level if you have already read it. Then, either in the middle of the article or at the end, type **C** (that's a capital C). This action removes the article from your local-article database and sends out a special type of article, called a *control message*, that instructs all other Usenet computers to remove their copies of your article from their article databases.

You also can supersede an article that you have written by replacing it with a corrected version. Find your article as if you were going to cancel it, and then type **z** or **Z** to start editing a replacement article. The z command (lowercase) gives you an empty article to edit, as though you were posting a new article; the Z command (uppercase) gives you a copy of the original article to edit. In either case, when you finish editing, leave the editor and post the article as usual. Trn sends out the new article, along with instructions to cancel the old one and insert the new article in its place.

Searching for Information

So much news is available that finding just what you want to read can be a real adventure. Fortunately, trn provides search commands at each level that can help you in this process. You can search for newsgroups, for articles within newsgroups, and for text within articles. When you find what you're looking for, you can select it for reading or junk it immediately, without reading it.

Searching for newsgroups within trn

At the newsgroup-selection prompt (`read now?`) you can list all unsubscribed newsgroups whose names contain a specified string by using the l command (that's a lowercase letter *l*). Type **l**, followed by a space and the string to search for, as follows:

```
====== 1 unread article in news.admin.misc -- read now? [+ynq] l physics
Completely unsubscribed newsgroups:
bionet.prof-society.biophysics
sci.med.physics
sci.physics.computational.fluid-dynamics
sci.physics.electromag
sci.physics.fusion
sci.physics.particle
sci.physics.plasma
[Type return to continue]

Unsubscribed but mentioned in /home/jtbell/.newsrc:
sci.physics.accelerators
sci.physics.research

====== 1 unread article in news.admin.misc – read now? [+ynq]
```

This method has two drawbacks. First, it searches only the names of the newsgroups. Second, it searches only newsgroups that your news system receives, so it doesn't answer the question "Does a newsgroup exist somewhere on this topic?"

If you're lucky, you can find more-extensive lists of newsgroups in the newsgroups `news.lists`, `news.groups`, `news.announce.newusers`, and `news.answers`. Look for a two-part series of articles titled "List of Active Newsgroups" and for another two-part series titled "Alternative Newsgroup Hierarchies." These articles contain not only newsgroup names, but also brief descriptions (a phrase for each newsgroup). You can search the articles while reading them by using the g command, as described in "Searching for text," later in this article.

These lists, however, are posted fairly infrequently (every two months or so), so the most recent set may have expired on your system. In that case, you'll have to leave trn and try one of the methods described in the following section.

Searching for newsgroups outside trn

If the newsgroup listings described in the preceding section have expired on your news system, you can get copies of the most-recent versions via e-mail from the Usenet FAQ archive at `rtfm.mit.edu`. Simply send e-mail to `mail-server@rtfm.mit.edu`, using a blank Subject line and one or more of the following commands in the message body:

```
send usenet/news.lists/List_of_Active_Newsgroups,_Part_I
send usenet/news.lists/List_of_Active_Newsgroups,_Part_II
send usenet/news.lists/Alternative_Newsgroup_Hierarchies,_Part_I
send usenet/news.lists/Alternative_Newsgroup_Hierarchies,_Part_II
```

You should get a reply within a day or two.

If you have access to Gopher, you can search a more extensive list of newsgroups, including many local and regional hierarchies. Connect directly to `gopher.presby.edu`, or look in the Other Gophers menu (or whatever it's called) for Presbyterian College, Clinton, South Carolina. From the top-level menu, choose Internet Resources; then choose Lists of Usenet Newsgroups. This list is from UUNET in Falls Church, Virginia.

If you don't have access to Gopher but can use anonymous ftp, you can get a copy of the UUNET newsgroup list from the ftp archive at `ftp.uu.net`. Look in directory `networking/news/config` for the file newsgroups.

Searching for articles on particular subjects

When you are in the thread selector for a newsgroup, you can tell trn to select articles that contain a specified string of characters in the Subject header line, using the following command:

`/string/+`

The two slashes delimit the string for which you are searching; the plus sign (+) tells trn that you want to select individual articles that match.

Uppercase versus lowercase doesn't matter in the search string. Suppose that you want to find articles about bugs.

For example, you see the following list of threads, and you want to find all the threads about bugs:

```
comp.lang.perl   32 articles

a 2 perl 4 bug? please help!
b 1 >Trouble with TkPerl5 and Perl5a11d
d 1 >Changing ARGV ?
e 3 >UNIX tower of babble tcl/awk/perl
f 1 >Perl5a11b, variable scopes/lifetimes, o
g 1 >playing with a mail filter..
i 1 Variable assignment problems (w/ du)
  1 >Bug report 11d
j 1 perl script executable?
l 1 help!!-script to read Mosaic Forms
o 1 Problem installing on NeXT 2.1 and 3.2
r 1 >Logical And / Round to Whole Numbers
s 1 MS-DOS Perl with DBM/NDBM Built In
t 1 Perl version of Supersrv ?
u 1 >Talking to HP4SiMx
v 3 >Comparing two dates?
w 2 >Perl5a11d Bug
x 1 >PERL as a first programming language?
y 2 how stable is perl5??
```

You type:

```
/bug/+
```

Trn first gives you a progress report as it selects the articles, as follows:

```
9474 Selected
9483 Selected
9485 Selected
9494 Selected
9495 Selected
Done

Selected 5 articles.
[Type space or a command]
```

At this point, pressing the spacebar takes you back to the thread selector, with the appropriate threads marked as selected. Some threads are marked with a plus sign (+) to indicate that the entire thread was selected; others are marked with an asterisk (*) to indicate that only some articles in those threads were selected. You now can press Enter to start reading the selected articles or make further selections, either by hand or with the / command.

Instead of selecting only the articles whose subjects match, you may want to select the entire threads that contain these matching articles. In this case, use ++ instead of +, as follows:

```
/bug/++
```

In the preceding example, this command would select all the articles in thread i, not just the ones with the subject Bug report 11d.

In commands such as these, the part between the slashes can be a UNIX *regular expression,* which allows you to perform sophisticated pattern-matching. Describing regular expressions in detail is beyond the scope of this article. You should be aware, however, that the following characters have special meaning in a regular expression: ., *, [, /, and \ . If these characters appear in the character string for which you are searching, you must "escape" them (that is, protect them from being interpreted as control characters) by preceding each one with a backslash (\ ). To search for and select all articles that have M*A*S*H in the Subject line, for example, you should use a command like this:

```
/M\ *A\ *S\ *H/+
```

Searching for articles by particular people

By default, the / command searches only the Subject header line. To search for articles by particular people, you need to tell trn that you want it to search the From header line, as in the following example:

```
From: smwall@pica.army.mil (Steve Wall)
```

To search for all articles by Steve Wall, you can use the following command:

```
/Steve Wall/f:+
```

The f modifier tells trn to search the From line rather than the Subject line. If the person's name is sufficiently distinctive, you probably can get away with searching for only part of the name.

If the name is very common (for example, John Smith) or is missing, you can search for the address instead. In principle, you could use something like the following:

```
/smwall@pica\ .army\ .mil/f:+
```

(Each period in the e-mail address has been escaped by preceding it with a backslash.) As it turns out, because of the way that trn implements f-searches, it may search only the part of the From line that is in parentheses. Therefore, if you want to search for the address, you should use the following command instead:

```
/smwall@pica\ .army\ .mil/HFrom:+
```

Notice that you should escape (that is, protect them from being interpreted as control characters) the periods in the address with backslashes. This command should search the entire From line instead of just the part in parentheses. This method may be a bit slower than the first one.

Just as you do in subject-line searches, you can select the entire thread that contains a matching article by using ++ instead of +.

Searching for text

You can also use the / command in the thread selector to search for and select articles that contain specified text anywhere in the article. To do this, use the a (anywhere) modifier. For example, the following command selects all articles that mention bananas somewhere in the article text:

```
/banana/a:+
```

While you are reading a long article, you may want to advance directly to the line that contains a certain word instead of paging through the article one screen at a time. To do this, use the g (go to) command at the article-reading level, as follows:

```
gbanana
```

Don't put a space between the g and the text that you're searching for, unless you specifically want to match a preceding space.

Kill Files: Selecting and Junking Articles Automatically

Trn's threading mechanism helps you skip discussions that you are not interested in, by grouping articles on the same topic into one entry in the thread-selection menu. In many newsgroups, you can efficiently scan the thread-selection menu for the discussions that you want to read, select those articles, read them, and then junk everything else by using the X or c command.

Some newsgroups, however, carry so much traffic that even scanning the thread selector is time-consuming. Trn provides tools that help ease the process of selecting the articles that you want to read and ignoring the ones that you don't want. You can tell trn to select articles for you automatically, based on criteria that you specify. Then, when you enter the newsgroup, you can simply press Enter to start reading these preselected articles. Trn also can junk (mark as read) articles automatically according to similar criteria, so that those articles do not appear in the thread selector. This feature is especially useful for dealing with people who repeatedly post offensive, boring, or nonsensical articles; you can make them disappear, as far as you are concerned.

Trn performs this task by "memorizing" selection and/or junking commands in a special file that is popularly known as a *kill file*. There are two kinds of kill files:

- The *global kill file*, which is stored in the News subdirectory of your home directory. The commands in this kill file apply to all newsgroups that you read. For example, you can include a command to skip all articles posted by a notorious jerk, regardless of which newsgroup he posts to.
- *Newsgroup kill files* (or *local kill files*), which are stored in subdirectories of your News directory. The names of the subdirectories for newsgroups are the same as the newsgroup name, with the periods changed to slashes. The directory that contains the kill file for the `soc.religion.unitarian-univ` group, for example, is named `~/News/soc/religion/unitarian-univ`. You could include a command to skip all articles about gun control, which you don't consider to be a religious issue.

Both types of kill files are text files, named KILL, that contain one command per line. You can edit these files with any text editor. Because of the overhead involved in searching for articles to kill, it is better, if possible, to use a local list than to use the global one.

Whenever you enter a newsgroup, trn checks to see whether you have a kill file for that newsgroup. If you do, trn performs the commands stored in the kill file before displaying the thread selector.

Kill files can be quite elaborate, with many different kinds of commands. This section describes only a few of the most useful possibilities.

Selecting threads automatically

Suppose that you want trn to select articles in a certain thread automatically during future sessions. In the thread selector, press the up- and down-arrow keys to move the cursor to the selector letter for that thread, and then press **T** (capitalized). Trn displays the following:

```
Memorize thread command: [+.j,cC]
```

Type a plus sign (+). (To see what the other possibilities are, type **h**.) Trn responds by displaying `Selection memorized`. The thread is selected, so you can read it; furthermore, trn memorizes the message IDs of the unread articles in that thread, placing them in the kill file for this newsgroup. In the future, whenever you enter this newsgroup, trn automatically selects all articles that follow up articles whose IDs it has memorized; in turn, trn memorizes the message IDs of the newly selected articles.

You also can use the T command while reading one of the articles in that thread. In this case, trn memorizes the message IDs for all the articles in that thread that have not yet expired, including the ones that you have read already.

Finally, you can select several threads in the thread selector, in preparation for reading them, and then (while still in the thread selector) type **:T+**. In this case, trn doesn't prompt you separately for the command to memorize. This command tells trn to memorize the message IDs of all the unread articles in all the selected threads.

The next time you enter the newsgroup, you do not reach the thread selector immediately; instead, you see a report on the action of the kill file, as in the following example:

```
Processing memorized commands...

44 auto-select commands.

Selected 2 articles.

[Type space to continue]
```

Press the spacebar, and trn gives you the thread selector as usual.

As a thread ages, trn automatically removes the message IDs of the older articles from the kill file, so you don't have to worry about trimming the kill file to keep it from getting too big.

Junking threads automatically

You also can use the T command to tell trn that you never want to see any articles in a specified thread or threads. Proceed as in the preceding section (on auto-selecting threads), but type **j** instead of + as the subcommand. The specified threads disappear from the thread selector immediately, never to be seen again (ideally). Whenever you enter the newsgroup in the future, trn junks any articles that follow up the ones whose message IDs it has memorized; in turn, trn memorizes the message IDs of the newly junked articles. This procedure doesn't always work perfectly, though. Sometimes, branches of the discussion become disconnected from the rest of the thread and pop up in the thread selector again (sort of like dandelions in a lawn), in which case you have to junk them again.

As in the preceding example, the next time you enter the newsgroup, you see a report on the action of the kill file:

```
Processing memorized commands...

13 auto-kill commands.

Killed 1 article.

[Type space to continue]
```

Pressing the spacebar gives you the thread selector as usual.

Just as with the automatic thread-selection commands, trn removes old message IDs from the kill file automatically.

Selecting or junking articles automatically by using search commands

The preceding procedures work by searching for articles that follow up specific articles whose message IDs trn has memorized in a kill file. You also can search automatically for articles by subject, by author, or by contents, and you can either select or junk those articles. To do so, edit the kill file by hand, placing in it the same search commands that you would type if you were performing the search yourself, as described in previous sections.

To edit the kill file for a newsgroup, enter the newsgroup and then press Ctrl+K. This action opens the kill file, using your default editor (usually, vi). Simply insert the desired search commands, one per line, as follows:

```
/Beethoven/+
/Serial/j
(etc.)
"/home/jtbell/News/rec/music/classical/KILL" 48 lines, 1733 characters
```

When you finish editing the kill file, type **ZZ** (if you're using vi) to save the kill file and return to trn.

The next time you enter the newsgroup, you see a report on the effects of the kill file, telling you which commands took effect, as in the following example:

```
Processing memorized commands...

/Beethoven/+
3726 Selected
3729 Selected
3730 Selected
3735 Selected
3740 Selected
/Serial/j
3734 Junked

Selected 5 articles.
Killed 1 article.

[Type space to continue]
```

The numbers are the local article numbers for the articles that were selected or junked. Pressing the spacebar takes you to the thread-selection menu, as usual.

Unlike the automatic thread-selection and thread-junking commands, trn does not remove any commands that you place in a kill file by hand. To remove these commands, you must edit the kill file.

Anatomy of a kill file

If you have been using the T command to auto-select or auto-junk threads, your kill file will look something like this:

```
THRU 31298
<1994Mar9.020649.10313@virginia.edu> T+
<billwillCMFyIF.4Gr@netcom.com> T+
<211110$411@agate.berkeley.edu> T+
<21hcel$eco@agate.berkeley.edu> T+
(etc.)
"/home/jtbell/News/rec/music/classical/KILL" 48 lines, 1733 characters
```

The kill file contains the memorized list of message IDs for articles that were previously junked. The THRU line indicates how far the kill file has gotten in processing articles for this newsgroup. When you enter the newsgroup, trn applies the kill file commands starting at this article number, so it doesn't have to re-process articles that you have already seen or junked.

You should be aware that trn performs kill file commands in the order listed. Therefore, an article may be selected by one command but junked by a later one. If you want the search commands to override the message ID commands, for example, you should arrange them as follows:

```
THRU 31298
<1994Mar9.020649.10313@virginia.edu> T+
<billwillCMFyIF.4Gr@netcom.com> T+
<211110$411@agate.berkeley.edu> T+
<21hcel$eco@agate.berkeley.edu> T+
/Beethoven/+
```

```
/Serial/j
(etc.)
"/home/jtbell/News/rec/music/classical/KILL" 48 lines, 1733 characters
```

The first line of a newsgroup (local) kill file begins with the word THRU and contains the article number of the last article that the kill file has processed. If you change the commands in the kill file, you may want to decrease the article number in the THRU line to cause your newsreader to reprocess recent articles. Global kill files don't contain a THRU line.

You can add to your kill files search commands that look like this:

```
/pattern/modifier:command
```

The *pattern* is the text that you are looking for in either the Subject or the From line.

The *modifier* tells the newsreader whether to look in the Subject line, From line, or the text of the article. If you leave out the modifier, your newsreader looks for the subject. Common modifiers include the following:

a	Looks for the pattern anywhere in the entire article
h	Looks for the pattern only in the headers
f	Looks for the pattern only in the From line
c	Makes the pattern case-sensitive

The *command* tells the newsreader what to do with the selected articles: keep them (that is, mark them as unread so that you see them again) or kill them (mark them as read). Common commands include the following:

+	Marks articles as unread (keeps them)
j	Marks articles as read (kills them)

Further Information

Trn has many more features and can be customized in various ways. The most complete documentation of trn is the *man page,* which you should be able to view on-line by using the UNIX command **man trn**. This document is about 40 pages long, and some parts of it require you to be familiar with the UNIX operating system.

You also may want to read "An Introduction to Usenet News and the trn Newsreader," by Jon Bell (`jtbell@presby.edu`). The document is revised periodically. You can get a copy of the latest version via anonymous ftp from `csl.presby.edu`, directory `pub/trn-intro`, or from the Presbyterian College (Clinton, South Carolina) Gopher server, either directly to `gopher.presby.edu`, port 70, or through the Other Gophers or similar menu on your local Gopher server. When you reach our server, choose the Internet Resources menu.

This document is available in four formats:

- As a Macintosh WriteNow 3.0/4.0 document
- As a Microsoft Rich Text Format file, which can be opened by Microsoft Word 4.0 (or later) for the Macintosh and by other word processors for Macintosh, DOS, and Windows
- As a PostScript file, which can be printed (we hope) on any PostScript printer
- As a plain ASCII text file, which lacks all the font information and most of the formatting (use this format as a last resort)

Setting Trn Options

Trn has dozens of options you can set that tell the program how you want it to work. For a complete list, see the man page for trn. Following are some useful options:

- The -f option determines how trn sets off quoted material from another article (usually, trn prefixes each line with >). For example, -F>>>> inserts >>>> at the beginning of every line.
- The -q option skips the check for new groups when trn starts.
- The -r option tells trn to start with the last newsgroup that you read, rather than with the first newsgroup listed in your .newsrc file.
- The -X option tells trn to default to showing you the list of the threads for each newsgroup. To use this option, follow it with a number. Trn displays the thread list if the newsgroup has at least that many articles; otherwise, it displays the articles themselves. If you always want to see the thread list, use -X1.
- To run trn to see only certain newsgroups, you can specify them in the command line, as follows:

  trn news.groups misc.kids

You can set options in one of the following ways:

- Type the options in the command line when you run trn. To run trn skipping the check for new groups, for example, type **trn -q**.
- Set the TRNINIT environment variable, usually with a command in your .profile or .cshrc file. For example, you could use:

  ```
  TRNINIT=-q.
  ```

- Include the options in your .trninit file. This procedure requires two steps. First, set the TRNINIT variable to specify that the .trninit file contains a list of options to set, as follows:

  ```
  TRNINIT=$HOME/.trninit
  ```

Then, in your home directory, create a text file named .trninit that contains the options, as follows:

-q

- Use the & command within trn. At any trn prompt, type **&&** and the switch(es). The option remains in effect only for the duration of the trn session. Obviously, this procedure doesn't work for options that affect what trn does when it starts. To find out the current status of the switches, you can type **&**. To change the way that quoted material appears in your follow-up articles, for example, you could type **&&-f**.

Margaret Levine Young is the co-author of IDG's UNIX For Dummies, More Internet For Dummies, *and* The Internet For Dummies Starter Kit, *in addition to other computer books. She has spent a great deal of time explaining to people that computers are not as mysterious as people think.*

Jon Bell is an Associate Professor of Physics at Presbyterian College in Clinton, SC. He also teaches computer science courses. For the past three years, he has been installing and maintaining Internet software, and he is the college's Usenet news administrator.

Using Offline Mail and Newsreaders

by Mike and Dee Ryan <mikeryan@virtuoso.com, deeryan@virtuoso.com>

Offline newsreaders are programs that allow you to connect to a dialup Internet shell account, pack up new mail and Usenet newsgroup articles, then download the files to your PC. You can then read mail and news at your leisure. This chapter guides you through setting up and using offline newsreaders for Internet shell accounts, including the UNIX software for your Internet shell system, and PC software to run on your own computer.

Why Use an Offline Newsreader?

If you do not have a direct link to the Internet, there are many circumstances when you may use an offline newsreader. For example, you may decide to use an offline newsreader if

- You are charged by the minute of connect time for dialup Internet access from a service provider.
- You are unhappy with the text-based interfaces and the slow response time typically associated with on-line newsreaders.
- You want to spend as little time as possible tying up your phone line.

Advantages of Offline Newsreaders

Offline newsreaders have two significant advantages:

- Your connect time is shorter; therefore, you save money on your connect charges and telephone bills.
- For the most part, they are easier to use than text-based on-line newsreaders, such as rn, nn, and tin.

Disadvantages of Offline Newsreaders

Offline newsreaders also have disadvantages:

- The time that must be devoted to setting up the newsreader
- Complicated downloading and uploading

What You'll Need

You need a UNIX program called UQWK on your Internet shell system to select articles for downloading and to send articles and replies you've decided to upload. You'll also need a DOS or Windows program on your PC for viewing newsgroup articles and composing replies. This article discusses UQWK and the PC software you'll need for offline newsreading.

Most of the examples in this article assume that your Internet shell account has the rz, sz, zip, and unzip commands available. The rz and sz commands transfer files between your PC and the UNIX system and zip and unzip compressed files. If the rz and sz commands are not available on your host system, you need to substitute the appropriate communications commands that your host system provides for rz and sz while reading the instructions in this book. If you do not have zip and unzip capability, you must find another archive or compression package or download and upload files one at a time, instead of packing them as described in our examples.

Handling Packets

Packets are simply groups of files that are compressed for downloading and uploading. They are used by programs such as UQWK when manipulating files.

Packet Formats

There are two popular formats for packets:

- **SOUP** is an RFC-compliant packet format, designed specifically for Usenet. This means that SOUP does not lose critical information while sending or replying to Usenet messages. Most new newsreaders use SOUP format; in the interest of being good netizens (Net citizens), we will describe only SOUP-compatible software in this article.
- **QWK** is an older format, designed for bulletin board services (BBSs). The advantages to QWK are that more software is available for QWK than SOUP, and you can use the same QWK newsreader for newsgroups and BBSs. The disadvantage is that QWK does not properly support sending and replying to Usenet messages, because QWK was not designed for Usenet. For example, if you use a QWK-based newsreader to send follow-up messages on Usenet, subject lines are truncated and references for threading may be lost. Although these are not fatal errors, these messages will make you instantly unpopular with anyone who reads them.

Although there are currently more newsreaders available using QWK format, most newer newsreaders support SOUP packets.

What about mail?

In both QWK and SOUP packets, your private mail is handled just like a newsgroup. You read and write mail messages the same ways that you read and write news messages. When your packet is uploaded to the UNIX system, your new mail messages are mailed to the recipients and your new news items are posted as news.

The UNIX End: Using UQWK

UQWK is a program that runs on the Internet shell host system, creating packets of new mail and news that can be downloaded for offline reading. Despite the name, UQWK can produce either QWK or SOUP formatted packets. In addition, users can manipulate their .newsrc files with UQWK commands. UQWK also offers many options when manipulating packets.

After downloading mail and news to your PC with UQWK, you can read your mail and newsgroup articles with one of the DOS or Windows newsreaders that are described later in this chapter.

UQWK installation

To determine if UQWK is installed at your Internet shell provider, enter the following command:

```
which uqwk
```

If the system responds by displaying something like /usr/bin/uqwk, then UQWK is installed. If UQWK is not already installed, ask your service provider or site administrator to install it at the site where your dialup account is located. If your site administrator is unable or unwilling to install UQWK, you may be able to install it in your own account. To do so, use ftp to copy UQWK from the ftp site ftp.gte.com:/pub/uqwk, then read the README file for building and installation instructions.

Retrieving and downloading messages

The UQWK command to retrieve all your new mail and news is

```
uqwk +m +n +L +r -BO
```

Where

- +m says, "get mail"
- +n says, "get news"
- +L says, "use SOUP format"
- +r says "messages will be downloaded, but copies will stay on the host system." It is a good idea to use this option until you have all bugs worked out of your setup; otherwise, if any mail messages are lost while being downloaded, they are not recoverable.

- -BO says "there is not a limit on the total size of the messages." By default, UQWK truncates messages at about half a megabyte (about 150 pages of text).

This will create:

- A series of files with names ending in .MSG.
- A file called AREAS, which is an index of the message files.

These files need to be compressed into a file that you can download. If your system includes the zip command, you can use the command line

```
zip -m messages.zip *.MSG AREAS
```

This command creates a compressed packet file, called messages.zip, then deletes the original *.MSG and AREAS files after the zip file is created. The messages.zip file can then be downloaded to your system. For example, if your UNIX host has the sz command and your terminal program supports Zmodem, you can use the following command to download the file:

```
sz -u messages.zip
```

The -u option specifies that the messages.zip file will be deleted after it has been successfully downloaded. You can now use a PC newsreader to read your mail and news. (PC newsreaders are described later in this chapter.)

Sending messages

If you compose any new messages, your PC newsreader should pack them into a file called something like REPLY.ZIP. The REPLY.ZIP file contains the REPLIES file (which is an index file similar to AREAS) and the replies that you created, which will be named *.MSG. After the reply files are packed, you need to dial in to your Internet account and upload the packet that your newsreader created. For example, if your UNIX host has the rz command and your terminal supports Zmodem, you can use the following command on your UNIX system to upload the file:

```
rz
```

If the system to which you are dialed up includes the zip command, you can use the following command line to unpack the files:

```
unzip -U reply.zip
```

The -U option makes all filenames uppercase. UQWK requires filenames to be uppercase, but the unzip command makes them lowercase by default.

To post or mail the messages, use the following command:

```
uqwk -RREPLIES +L -m
```

Where:

- -RREPLIES says that your postings are in the REPLIES file
- +L says to send messages using SOUP format
- -m says that new mail will not be retrieved during the upload

After you send your messages, remember to delete the reply packet from your PC. If you forget, you might send the same messages many times.

UQWK Commands to know and love

To use UQWK commands, you must create a mail message that contains nothing but UQWK commands. You must then address and send this mail message to UQWK. Here are some UQWK commands that you should be familiar with:

- subscribe *newsgroup* — Use this command to subscribe to the named newsgroup.
- unsubscribe *newsgroup* — Use this command to unsubscribe from the named newsgroup. You can use the unsubscribe all command to unsubscribe from all newsgroups. The unsubscribe all command can also be used to create a .newsrc file, if one does not already exist.
- allgroups — This command mails you a list of all available newsgroups and the number of articles in each one. The number of articles gives you a rough idea of how busy a newsgroup is.

Because of a bug in UQWK, messages that contain UQWK commands must be in their own reply packet. If commands are combined with other messages, UQWK may confuse messages with commands, and the messages may not be sent.

Summary Processing Using US

You may find that you are actually interested in only a fraction of the topics in the newsgroups that you subscribe to. If a lot of your download time (and disk space) is wasted by accessing messages that you do not want, you can use UQWK to generate a summary file that shows you a list of new articles in a newsgroup. You download this summary file to your PC, use US (UQWK Summary) on your PC to select the articles you want, upload the resulting edited summary file to your UNIX shell account, use UQWK again to get the articles you selected, and download the articles to your PC.

Installing US

US can be obtained from ftp.gte.com:/pub/uqwk/us. A README file that is included in the files you download explains installing and using US.

Creating a summary file

To generate a summary file on the UNIX system, use the following command:

```
uqwk +n -Usummary
```

This creates a file, named summary, that contains a list of new articles in each newsgroup. After you have this summary file, you can use a summary processor, such as US (UQWK Summary), to select articles for downloading, or you can edit the summary file with a simple text editor.

To save connect time, you may want to compress the summary file for uploading from your PC.

After you have created a summary file and downloaded it to your PC, use the US program on your PC to peruse the summary file and select for downloading any articles that interest you.

Running US

If you did not compress the summary file into a zip file on the UNIX system, you can run US by entering **us summary** at the DOS prompt.

If the summary file is packed into a zip file, you can run a DOS batch file that unzips the file, runs US, and then zips up the new summary file. For example, the batch file might look like this:

```
rem ************************************************************
rem                          RUN_US.BAT
rem ************************************************************
rem This command unzips the downloaded summary file:
pkunzip summary.zip
rem This command deletes the summary.zip file:
del summary.zip
rem This command invokes the US program:
us summary
rem This command compresses the newly created summary file into a
rem file named summary.zip:
pkzip summary.zip summary
rem This command deletes the original summary file that is now
rem compressed in summary.zip:
del summary
```

US threads every newsgroup by subject, then asks if you want each subject; simply press **Y** for subjects you want to download and **N** for those you do not. US generates a new summary file containing only the articles you're interested in.

Getting the articles you selected

You can then upload this new summary file to your UNIX account and run UQWK using the summary option as follows

```
uqwk +m +n +L -Esummary
```

The -Esummary option reads the summary file and fetches only the articles listed. Now you can download them and read them as usual.

Steps for Reading and Posting messages

The following is a summary of steps that are used when reading and posting messages to mail or newsgroups through UQWK:

1. **Dial up your Internet shell account.**
2. **If you want to download all the messages, skip to step 7.**
3. **Run UQWK to make a summary file.**
4. **Download the summary file to your PC and log out.**
5. **Run US to select the titles of articles that you want to download.**
6. **Dial in to your UNIX account and upload the summary file.**
7. **Run UQWK to get your new mail and newsgroup messages (possibly selected in step 5).**
8. **Pack the files you need.**
9. **Download the packet, using the procedure described in the next section.**
10. **Log out from the remote account.**
11. **Open up the packet in your offline newsreader and read the messages.**

    If you don't want to post any messages, you are done. Otherwise, complete the following steps.
12. **Compose replies or new messages.**
13. **Pack up the replies and messages.**
14. **Dial in again.**
15. **Upload and unpack the reply packet.**
16. **Post the messages.**
17. **Log out of your UNIX account.**
18. **Delete the reply packet from your local system.**

Sample UNIX scripts

This section contains UNIX shell scripts that can be placed on your Internet shell host system and used when retrieving, uploading, and downloading news and mail. You can create terminal emulator scripts on your PC that call each of the shell scripts described here. If you use Windows, you can create Windows icons that run the terminal emulator scripts. Once the icons are created, you can simply double-click to invoke the terminal emulator, log in to your dialup account, run the appropriate script, and log out.

GetMail

This script can be used to retrieve all new mail from your UNIX shell account:

```
#!/bin/csh
# Create the packet directory if it isn't already there:
    if (! -e ~/soup_packets) mkdir ~/soup_packets
# Go to the packet directory:
    cd ~/soup_packets
# Get the mail (+m) in SOUP format (+L):
    uqwk +m +L -H.
# There should now be a message file and AREAS file. Pack them up
# into a zip file:
    zip -m messages.zip *.MSG AREAS
# Download the messages.zip file to your PC:
    sz -u messages.zip
```

GetAllMessages

This script retrieves all new mail and news:

```
#!/bin/csh
# Copy the .newsrc file in case something goes wrong
# (unlike many newsreaders, uqwk does not automatically back it up):
    cp ~/.newsrc ~/.savenewsrc
# Create the packet directory if it isn't already there:
    if (! -e ~/soup_packets) mkdir ~/soup_packets
# Go to the packet directory:
    cd ~/soup_packets
# Get the mail (+m) and news (+n) messages in SOUP format
# (+L), with no limit on the total size retrieved (-B0)
    uqwk +m +n +L -B0 -H. -N../.newsrc
# Pack up the messages:
    zip -m messages.zip *.MSG AREAS
# Download the zip file to your PC:
    sz -u messages.zip
```

GetSummary

This script can be used to create a summary file:

```
#!/bin/csh
# Copy the .newsrc file in case something goes wrong
# (unlike many newsreaders, uqwk does not automatically back it up):
    cp ~/.newsrc ~/.savenewsrc
# Create the packet directory if it isn't already there:
    if (! -e soup_packets) mkdir ~/soup_packets
# Go to the packet directory:
    cd ~/soup_packets
# Get the news (+n) summary (-Usummary):
    uqwk +n -Usummary -H. -N../.newsrc
```

```
# Pack up the summary file:
    zip -m summary.zip summary
# Download the summary file:
    sz -u summary.zip
```

GetMessages

If you are using summary files, this script can be used to upload your summary file and retrieve only the appropriate messages:

```
#!/bin/csh
# Create the packet directory if it isn't already there:
    if (! -e ~/soup_packets) mkdir ~/soup_packets
# Go to the packet directory:
    cd ~/soup_packets
# Upload the summary file, which should be named summary.zip:
    echo 'Upload the file "summary.zip"'
    rz
# If the summary file was not successfully uploaded, display an
# error message and abort the script:
    if (! -e summary.zip) then
       echo 'summary.zip not successfully uploaded, cannot continue'
       exit
    endif
# Unzip the summary file and delete summary.zip:
    unzip summary.zip
    rm summary.zip
# Get the mail (+m) and news (+n) messages in SOUP format (+L) using
# the summary file (-Esummary), with no limit on the total size
# retrieved (-B0):
    uqwk +m +n +L -Esummary -B0 -H. -N../.newsrc
# Delete the summary file:
    rm summary
# Pack up the messages:
    zip -m messages.zip *.MSG AREAS
# Download the messages.zip file:
    sz -u messages.zip
# Display a reminder to delete unwanted copies of summary.zip:
    echo 'Do not forget to delete summary.zip from your local system'
    echo 'to avoid accidentally processing it again'
```

SendMessages

This script can be used to send mail messages or post to newsgroups:

```
#!/bin/csh
# Create the packet directory if it isn't already there:
    if (! -e ~/soup_packets) mkdir ~/soup_packets
# Go to the packet directory:
    cd ~/soup_packets
```

```
# Upload the reply file which should be named reply.zip:
    echo 'Upload the file "reply.zip"'
    rz
# If reply.zip was not successfully uploaded, display an error
# message and abort the script:
    if (! -e reply.zip) then
       echo 'reply.zip not successfully uploaded, cannot continue'
       exit
    endif
# Unzip the reply.zip file. Make sure that the filenames are
# uppercase.
    unzip -U reply.zip
# Delete reply.zip:
    rm reply.zip
# Send the messages (-RREPLIES) assuming SOUP format (+L),
# make sure we don't retrieve mail (-m)
    uqwk -RREPLIES +L -m -H. -N../.newsrc
# Display a reminder to remove unwanted copies of reply.zip:
    echo 'Do not forget to delete reply.zip from your local system'
    echo 'to avoid accidentally processing it again'
```

The PC End: Popular PC Newsreaders

After you have downloaded your mail and Usenet newsgroup articles to your PC, you'll want to read them and, possibly, compose replies. Many useful news and mail reader programs are currently available — far too many to list here. By the time you read this book, many more newsreaders will be available for public use. For simplicity's sake, we are going to discuss a few of the currently most popular newsreaders (one DOS based and a few Windows based). Note that the ftp file locations and version numbers listed here were current at the time this book went to print, but they are subject to change — use Archie to search for these programs on other ftp servers if the ones we list no longer work.

Yarn

Yarn (which at the time this book was written was still being tested in a beta release) is a SOUP-compatible mail and newsreader that runs under DOS and OS/2. It allows the user to read articles, save articles to folders, and create SOUP reply packets. To run Yarn, you must have a system running MS-DOS 3.0 or higher, compression software, and enough hard disk storage to store any articles that you want to retain for future use.

Yarn's features include

- Mail filters that automatically file or delete incoming messages, based on user-defined rules
- Colors that are used effectively to highlight the parts of articles, such as the header area, From and Subject fields, and quotations and text.

- Proper threading by references and message ID (not subject)
- Multiple-user support
- PGP

The DOS version can be obtained via ftp from `oak.oakland.edu:/SimTel/msdos/offline/yarn_078.zip`.

The OS/2 2.x version can be obtained via ftp from `ftp-os2.nmsu.edu:/os2/incoming/yrn2_078.zip`.

Installation and Setup

To install Yarn, follow this procedure:

1. **Obtain Yarn from one of the above sites.**
2. **Copy the ZIP file to an empty directory and unzip it.**
3. **Read the appropriate (don't worry, there are not many) informational files.**

   (Although there are many files included in the zip file, most of them are not important at this point.) Among the included files are:

   - README doesn't contain much useful information, but read it anyway, that is what README files are for.
   - YARN.DOC is required reading. It is the Yarn user's manual, and it includes installation information and other important stuff you need to know. Read this file before continuing, in case the installation procedure described below changes.
4. **If you are in Windows, open a DOS window.**
5. **Decide where you want to install Yarn.**

   Make sure a lot of disk space is available. While in the current directory, enter:

   ```
   install <your-chosen-directory>
   ```

You do not need to create the directory first.

After Yarn is installed, you must perform the following setup tasks:

1. **Add a line to your AUTOEXEC.BAT file that specifies where the Yarn directory is (Yarn will tell you what the line should be).**

   Do not forget to do this! If you are in Windows, Alt+Tab to your favorite text editor and edit AUTOEXEC.BAT now, so you don't forget. Do not close the AUTOEXEC.BAT file; you will be making more changes soon.
2. **If you are in Windows, Alt+Tab to the DOS window.**
3. **Type** adduser **to run the setup program.**
4. **Fill in the following form fields:**
   - The directory for the user-specific data
   - Your user name on your Internet shell host system

- The name of the Internet shell host system
- Your real name
- Your preferred DOS editor for composing articles and mail
- The filename to use for reply packets. This should be REPLY.ZIP if you are using the UQWK scripts we have provided in this chapter.

5. **After you have edited the form fields, Yarn instructs you to add another line to your AUTOEXEC.BAT, specifying your HOME directory.**

6. **If multiple users will be working in Yarn, enter the adduser command for each of them.**

   Instead of setting HOME in AUTOEXEC.BAT, create .BAT files for each user, including the proper HOME command, before running Yarn. For example:

   ```
   SET HOME=E:\MAIN\YARN\MIKE
   E:\MAIN\YARN\YARNX
   ```

7. **If you are not in the U.S. Eastern time zone, you need to add another line to AUTOEXEC.BAT to specify your time zone with the environment variable TZ.**

   For example, if you are in the Pacific time zone, add the line:

   ```
   SET TZ=PST8PDT
   ```

   The first three letters (PST) are the name of your standard time zone, the middle digit (8) is the number of hours you're off from GMT (Greenwich Mean Time), and the last three letters (PDT) are your daylight-savings-time time zone.

8. **Edit AUTOEXEC.BAT and make sure that DOS4GW.EXE is on your DOS path.** To do this, find a PATH statement and add the Yarn directory to the list of directories.

9. **After you have finished setting up Yarn, you must save your AUTOEXEC.BAT file, then either reboot, or enter (at the DOS prompt) the environment setting commands that you put in AUTOEXEC.BAT.** If you skip this step, the changes will not be applied and Yarn will not work correctly.

10. **A configuration file, called CONFIG, is created for each user. Each file is located in the subdirectory YARN, under the directory specified when you entered the adduser command. Edit this file as desired.** You can change many attributes including the signature file, PGP support, and color customizations. You must edit the CONFIG file if you want to change any settings later, as you cannot make configuration changes while you are running Yarn.

Running Yarn

After you installing and setting up Yarn, you are ready to read some news! To read news with Yarn, follow this procedure:

1. **Download a packet of messages from your Internet shell account, as described previously in this chapter.**

2. **From the DOS prompt, while in the Yarn directory, type** import *filename* **(where *filename* is the packet you downloaded; messages.zip, if you are using the scripts provided in this chapter).**

If you use Windows, drag IMPORT.EXE from the Yarn directory in File Manager to a Program Manager group. Then, in Program Manager, select File Properties from the pulldown menu and (in the command line field) add a space, followed by the full path name of the messages.zip file. After this step, you can double-click that icon to import the messages into your Yarn database whenever you download a messages packet. You can also add -q to the command line to speed things up; you will not see every article number displayed, but you would not want to anyway.

3. **From the DOS prompt, type** yarnx.

   You can use the following command-line options when invoking Yarn:

   - -m specifies that you want to read mail when you first invoke Yarn.
   - -f specifies that you want to see folders when you first invoke Yarn, instead of newsgroups, which is the default option.

     If you are running Windows, select the file YARNX.EXE and drag it to Program Manager, so you can run YARNX as an icon. You can create separate icons for mail and folders by following this procedure:

   - Drag the YARNX.EXE file to the Program Manager three times (twice if you've already done it once).
   - Rename one icon to Yarn Mail. Add **-m** to the command line.
   - Rename the other icon to Yarn Folders. Add **-f** to the command line.

4. **When Yarn comes up, you can press F1 to get help, which lists the commands available to you.**

   To get out of help, press the Esc key.

Other Stuff to Know About Yarn

- You can use the up and down arrows to select newsgroups, the Enter key to open up a list of articles in the newsgroup or to read articles, and the spacebar to move forward within articles.
- Despite their names, MAIL.HLP and YARN.HLP are not Windows Help files. They are actually the text files that are displayed when you press F1. Print them, and keep the printouts handy.
- Yarn commands are case-sensitive. For example, in the main screen at the bottom it says `M-Mail`. If you enter a lowercase m, nothing will happen; you must enter an uppercase M.
- You can assign names to mail addresses by using the address book feature. Simply press F3 while reading a message to add the author to the address book.
- Yarn keeps all the messages you import in its database until they expire, but messages do not expire by themselves; you must run the EXPIRE command. To run Expire in DOS, go to the Yarn directory and type expire. To expire messages in Windows, double-click EXPIRE.EXE in File Manager, or drag EXPIRE.EXE to the Program Manager to create an icon you can double-click to expire articles. You can automate expiration by running YARNX from a DOS batch file that also runs EXPIRE.

- You can filter incoming mail with the FILTER program. Using this program in Yarn, you can delete messages, or file them in a specified folder, based on criteria you specify (for example, a particular string contained in the Subject, From, or To fields, or in the body of the message).

UNOR

UNOR (Usenet Offline Reader) is a Windows offline newsreader. Its features include the following:

- It is simple and reliable.
- It has a Windows MDI interface.
- It allows you to save messages to folders.
- It can be used to view saved messages as well as new messages.

UNOR's disadvantages include the following:

- Users are required to manually unzip packets, open AREAS files, and delete unwanted SOUP files.
- It does not thread messages; messages are sorted by subject.
- Once a message is saved in a folder, the message cannot be deleted.

UNOR can be obtained via ftp from `ftp.gte.com/pub/unor`. New versions of UNOR are usually announced in the newsgroups `alt.usenet.offline-readers` and `comp.os.msdos.mail-news`.

PaperBoy

PaperBoy is a Windows offline newsreader, although it does not use a standard Windows MDI interface. Instead, the PaperBoy screen is divided into three areas: a list of newsgroups, a list of messages for the current newsgroup, and the contents of a selected message (if any). PaperBoy has five significant advantages:

- You can customize fonts for different areas on the screen.
- A menu entry submits bug reports and suggestions directly to the author.
- It supports both internal and external editors for message creation.
- It allows you to save messages in folders; whenever you create a message, it is automatically saved into a folder.
- Several keyboard shortcuts are available to traverse messages.

PaperBoy has three disadvantages:

- As with UNOR, users are required to manually unzip packets and open AREAS files.
- Users are required to delete unwanted SOUP files after reading them.
- The non-standard Windows interface is somewhat quirky.

PaperBoy can be obtained via ftp from `ftp.clark.net/pub/vart/pboy###.zip`, where ### is the latest version.

Offliner

Offliner is a Windows-based mail and newsreader that uses SOUP packets. Although it is much more ambitious than UNOR or PaperBoy, it is also less stable at the time of this writing (the review sample is a beta testing release). Offliner's features include:

- A Windows interface with color support
- Creating and storing articles in folders
- Changing the sorting method for displaying articles, allowing the user to view older articles

As expected with beta releases, there are some bugs in Offliner as of this writing:

- Purging does not work; you must explicitly delete articles if you do not want to save them.
- You cannot directly create new mail messages; you must reply to an existing mail message, then edit the headers in the reply.

Offliner can be obtained via ftp from `metronet.com:/put/xfer/ol06b.zip`.

Other Available Newsreaders

The following are other available newsreaders and their sources:

- NewsWerthy is a non-databasing DOS offline newsreader for SOUP packets. It is available via ftp at `eskimo.com/billw/nwrth100.zip`.
- Helldiver Packet Viewer 1.01B is an easy-to-use DOS offline newsreader for SOUP packets. It can be obtained via ftp from `oak.oakland.edu` or from the Simtel archive.

Offline mail for SLIP and PPP users

If you have a SLIP or PPP account that makes your PC part of the Internet, you can read and write mail offline, using standard mail programs like Eudora. The way you do it is

1. **Connect your PC to the Internet.**
2. **Start your mail program and tell it to retrieve your new mail.**

   (In Eudora, you do this by pressing Ctrl-M).
3. **Disconnect your PC from the Internet.**
4. **Read the messages you just retrieved.**

   Reply as needed. Write any new messages you want.
5. **Reconnect to the Internet.**
6. **Transmit the messages you wrote.**

   (In Eudora, type Ctrl-T.) If you want, check for new mail at this time and return to step 3.
7. Disconnect from the Internet again.

There are currently no reliable SLIP or PPP offline newsreaders, although that situation is likely to change. Read the newsgroups listed in the next section to find out what's available.

For Additional Information

Here are sources of up-to-date information about offline newsreaders.

Newsgroups

Read the following newsgroups for additional information about newsreaders:

- `alt.usenet.offline-reader` discusses offline newsreaders for Usenet; it is, by far, the best source of information about offline newsreaders.
- `news.software.readers` discusses software that is used to read Usenet network news, both online and offline.
- `comp.os.msdos.mail-news` discusses on-line and offline newsreaders for DOS and Windows systems.

FAQs

The following Frequently Asked Questions files (FAQs) answer most questions that you might have regarding specific newsreader topics:

- The `alt.usenet.offline-reader` FAQ covers offline newsreaders.
- The `comp.os.msdos.mail-news` FAQ covers mail and newsreaders for DOS and Windows.

- The "Hands-on How-to for UQWK and Yarn" FAQ, which is periodically posted to `alt.usenet.offline-reader`, gives explicit instructions for obtaining and installing UQWK and Yarn. It also includes sample scripts for UQWK and Procomm Plus.

`rtfm.mit.edu/pub/usenet/` is the ftp site for all newsgroup FAQs, and it includes all of the FAQs listed in this chapter.

FTP sites

The following ftp sites provide shareware newsreaders:

- The Simtel archives are located at `oak.oakland.edu:/SimTel/msdos/offline`.
- The directory `ftp.gte.com:/pub/uqwk` contains the UQWK and US newsreaders.

Denise and Mike Ryan are Virtuoso Software, a small software development company. Mike is a software engineer who specializes in GUI design and development. Denise is a technical writer with experience writing hardware and software user manuals, reference manuals, and online help. When they are not working at the computer, they front the alternative rock band The Diving Grubers.

Part IV

Becoming an Information Provider

In This Part

Chapter 27 Look Ma, I'm an Internet Provider

Chapter 28 Setting up a European Internet Provider

Chapter 29 Running a Gopher Server

Chapter 30 Running a WWW Server on Windows

Chapter 27

Look Ma, I'm an Internet Provider

by Richard Chung <rlc@ingress.com>
Charles Kaplan <cbk@ingress.com>
Michael Y.C. Hur <mike@ingress.com>
and Alan Chung <alan@ingress.com>

Already Internet providers all over the world are trying to get their slice of the pie by offering Internet access at an inexpensive price. Many potential Internet providers are realizing that all you need is a PC, some modems, and a bunch of phone lines to set up as a provider. It usually isn't quite that simple, but, in some cases, it may not be much more complicated than that.

This chapter tells you all the things we had to go through to become an Internet provider. After reading this chapter, if you're still willing to do all the work, go for it!

Starting Out

Hardware is one of the most important considerations, of course, because it is the lifeline of your company. You need something that can be expanded for future growth and that is compatible with standards so that you can always offer the best and latest services to your users. We looked at a number of different platforms with options ranging from different flavors of UNIX to Windows NT (yes, cringe at that thought). Everything has its pluses and minuses, and we try to address them in this section.

Computer equipment

You can spend a large amount of money on equipment or you can spend very little, depending on the quality of service you want to provide. Many veteran companies that have thousands of users are losing customers because of poor performance. Purchase equipment you can expand if you get a great deal of business, and watch your system load. Nothing is more frustrating for users than waiting 45 seconds just to get a login prompt.

One consideration in choosing a platform is how easy it will be to get and port applications. This is one advantage of choosing a commercial name-brand UNIX operating system (including PCs running UNIX). The broader the user base of the platform you choose, the more likely you are to get your questions answered and your problems solved, and the more likely that applications will compile and install smoothly. (SunOS is still probably the most widely used environment in this area). If you use mainstream platforms, you can get on Internet Relay Chat (IRC) and probably find someone who knows the answer to your question at just about any time of day. And by using network newsgroups, you can get an answer to almost anything.

If you decide to use a commercially supported version of UNIX, you will find much better support of external hardware, including good results with some of the versions that run on PC-compatible hardware. A variety of external hardware is directly supported by such products as UnixWare, Solaris/SunOS, and BSDI. The cost of UnixWare and BSDI is about the same — $500 to $600 for the binary CD. BSDI does seem to be better supported in the fast-paced world of Internet service (perhaps because of its similarity to SunOS) and is used by many machines on the Internet. Having the support of the Internet community is clearly more desirable than sitting for hours on the phone talking to a support line, running up large bills, and not always getting great information. If you really are stuck, on the other hand, BSDI does have a support line that is maintained during more than just business hours — read the manual for more details. (One author notes that he has received useful e-mail responses from BSDI on nights and weekends — very impressive.)

One of your other options on a PC is a public-domain version of UNIX, known as Linux. This reliable and complete package has good performance. Its only drawback is that it is not well supported in the commercial community. Much of the software you will use and support is public domain, but support for hardware can be frustrating if someone out there has not already written the device drivers.

Back up!

Part of starting up is buying lots of equipment — which is fun. Part of starting up is backing up carefully — which is boring. Although you may be sure to buy all the backup hardware you need, the importance of backups while you are setting up is not always obvious. Like many companies, we had this problem, and it caused us to lose a couple of weeks' worth of information. Since then, we have implemented a system of nightly backups.

If you have the money, we highly suggest buying a rewritable compact disc jukebox. The speed of these drives is around 45ms, and gets faster every day. (Compared to tape drives, they really kick!) With this in mind, it is easy to set up a floptical disk so that if your entire system gets hosed, you have a medium sitting around you can boot from until your system is back to normal. Another advantage is that you can have on-line backups. This capability is convenient for your users: If they screw up a file, they can go to a directory (`/home/backup`, for example) and find all their files from the night before.

The bottom line is that backups are necessary. Digital audiotape drives still seem to be finicky, and if you get one with an attitude (like ours), you will have problems. As this section is being written, one of us is doing a backup of about 2.5 gigabytes. It has taken all day and probably will not be finished until tomorrow. Specs may tell you that it is just about as fast as the Exabyte 8mm tape-backup systems, but, in our experience, it can be slow — considerably less than a megabyte per second. We suggest that you consider the Exabyte drives because of their recording speed — if you cannot afford the optical drives — and also because of their compatibility with other systems. Almost everyone has an Exabyte, and lots of commercial software is distributed in this way. When you have to mail off a tape to XYZ Corporation, you can bet your system that that company has an Exabyte.

Modems

The norm for today's systems is rapidly becoming 28.8K modems. In providing Internet access to individual users or corporations, you have to provide at least this level of dialup performance. Our experience has been that a good ratio is about 15 users per modem.

It is fine to begin with a half-dozen modems, from all different vendors, all dangling by their power cords; if you expect to succeed, however, invest in high-end modems, preferably from one vendor (you can use your leverage of owning 20, 30, or more modems to get much better support and probably a price break) and preferably in a rack-mount. This strategy costs more, but the savings in avoiding long-term headaches and in knowing that the intelligent rack will reset them for you if they go berserk (as all modems do) makes it all pay off. Also, most modems have external power supplies that plug in to the wall. When was the last time you saw a 30-outlet power strip? A rack comes down to one nice cord.

A good guideline to providing acceptable service is that if your modem pool is completely filled at any given time, increase the number of modems by 10 percent. This number depends, of course, on the rate at which you are growing and how much you're willing to pay your local telephone company.

Terminal servers

After you have the modems, you have to hook them all together and into your system. A number of companies produce terminal servers with various capabilities. The simpler systems direct users to a particular machine after they have dialed in. Some of the nicer systems support PPP/SLIP dial-in and ISDN and 56K inputs, and they can act as a router and even dial out. Look to see whether PPP and SLIP are directly supported. If you can handle SLIP and PPP customers directly on the terminal server, you can avoid loading down your main UNIX system (and many headaches) by doing the processing in the terminal server rather than on the UNIX box.

A number of terminal servers have various degrees of support for PPP/SLIP and security features. Among the more popular producers are Xylogics, Chase, Livingston, Telebit, and DigiBoard. Distinct advantages exist in purchasing terminal servers that have direct PPP/SLIP support.

Another option is to support SLIP and PPP in software on the same UNIX system used for network services and shell logins. Ingress managed to place its news server and a few SLIP/PPP ports on a machine. We realized quickly that we were saving a significant amount of money but were losing time setting things up and then quickly running out of ports on the server (even with a multi-I/O card). This economical solution quickly becomes a bottleneck.

CSU/DSU units, routers, and compression

You need a high-speed link to a long-haul Internet service provider (ISP) and a router to connect that link to the rest of your computers.

The majority of first-tier Internet providers use only Cisco routers. Many other good routers (and a few bad ones) are out there, and some are cheaper. But play it safe here, and ask your Internet provider what it suggests. Many providers sell you the router, ship it preconfigured, and even reconfigure it for you if you happen to get curious, experiment, and mess up the configuration. If you don't understand routing, either buy the router from your provider or purchase exactly what it recommends so that you can get the company's support.

The same advice holds true for CSU/DSU units, the devices that connect the router to the high-speed link to your provider. We highly recommend that you go with what your Internet provider suggests. Even though people will tell you that all CSU/DSU units are compatible with each other, taking the chance that the one you choose is actually compatible may not be worth it, especially because the price difference is usually a matter of only a few dollars.

Link-level data compression is now being used at a growing number of sites to allow more users over the same-speed provider link and to raise link throughput. Compression is especially useful for those sites with relatively slow 56K links, which can quickly become saturated with several heavy Net surfers running Mosaic. Compression does little to improve single-user throughput, but if you think of your link as a highway, a compressor widens the road (the link) so that more cars can drive at one time. The speed limit, however, is still 55 m.p.h. (56Kbps).

Internet Connection

After you have hardware, you still have to do some things before you can begin providing service to customers.

Obtaining an IP network number and registering your domain

Before you can become an Internet service provider, you have to be assigned a class of IP numbers and have your domain name approved by InterNIC. Luckily, most first-tier ISPs help you to get your first set of IP numbers and a domain name. If you want to try it for yourself, you can ftp to `internic.net` and download its template applications. After you complete them, submit the completed templates to `hostmaster@internic.net`.

Obtaining a network feed: serial lines versus dedicated high-speed lines

If you want just a news and e-mail feed for your local bulletin board, a 28.8K or even a 14.4K modem line is enough. You can dial in to a service provider and poll these feeds once every hour or so. If you plan to provide Internet service, however, this kind of connection is insufficient. A dedicated 56K link is highly recommended if you have several *power user* customers and your dial-in customers do a lot of ftping and other network-intensive applications. Because we found that a 56K line was not enough for us after awhile, we switched to a T1 (1.5 megabits) connection. In some areas, T1 and fractional T1 access is a problem for the phone companies, so you might want to check that out in advance.

The choice between 56K and T1 comes down to how your customers will access the outside world and whether you want other sites to be able to access your site. If you are going to supply your users with only access to the outside world, you need only a 56K line. If you want to enable people to set up their own WWW sites and to let people from the Internet access your site, we highly recommend that you get a T1. The reason is simple: If your users are only going to access the Internet, they all are coming in at a maximum speed of 28.8K baud. The decision should also be made with the competitiveness of your site in mind; most providers supply WWW to their users, so T1 will probably be the minimum necessary to remain competitive in less than a year. Also, compare prices carefully — in many areas, a T1 line costs only about twice what a 56K line costs, even though it's 25 times as fast.

Using ISDN and cable companies

The future for personal connection to the Internet will not be with dialup modems. Unless an unexpected technological breakthrough occurs in analog phone lines, 28.8K is viewed as the capacity of phone lines (if you have 28.8K modems, you aren't guaranteed this performance — it's just the best you will ever get). One growing alternative is ISDN (Integrated Services Digital Network). ISDN is capable of providing end-users with 128K of bandwidth (plus compression) guaranteed, by using special terminal equipment over regular phone lines. ISDN will probably see a rapid rise in the next few years. ISDN adapters are already falling to less than $1,000.

Another alternative is the cable companies, many of whom have already laid fiber-optic lines and copper wires underground and into almost every home. In Cambridge, Massachusetts, for example, the local cable company plans to offer 500K access for a few hundred dollars a month. However, two-way traffic on the cable poses many technical and administrative challenges to be worked out before wide-scale use can be implemented.

Maintaining security

Security is one thing people forget about until it is too late. Corporations looking to hook in to the Internet through providers are terrified at the thought of other people breaking in to their system and their information being accessible by outsiders. One mistake many providers make is not taking security precautions.

One of the major service providers that supplies access across the country was broken into in 1994. The person who broke in to the system was then able to break in to many other systems. Although no known damage was done, the person was also never caught. The service provider didn't consider security important; access was gained through a rather well-known, well-documented security hole.

So what kind of security should you have? The first thing you should do is to obtain some information about security and pick up some scripts that check for common security holes (`ftp:ftp.cert.org`). Also see Chapter 5 for information about firewalls; the books that chapter refers to are standard reading for anyone who needs security on the Internet.

Basic Services

All Internet providers should provide some basic services to their users. In this section, we touch on some of the popular solutions to providing these services and discuss issues related to getting all of them up and running.

E-mail and e-mail readers

E-mail readers are probably near the top of the list of things to provide to users. Your users can go two ways: online systems (programs that run on the provider's system) or offline systems (programs that run on the customer's PC).

Some popular online UNIX e-mail systems include elm, pine, mail/mailx, and MH. Elm and pine provide a good textual interface for novice users and UNIX-haters. Die-hard UNIX people swear by mail/mailx and MH. If you're planning to provide something along the lines of remote X Windows, you can use some of the graphically based e-mail systems such as xmh, mailtool (Sun/Solaris only), and exmh.

One of the more widely used offline systems is Eudora, from Qualcomm. From the provider's side, after you offer SLIP or PPP service, all that has to be done to let these offline readers work is to have a POPD (Post Office Protocol daemon) running. Installing POP takes only about 20 minutes. It's advantageous for the provider to have a reseller license so that it can sell this package to its customers, possibly at a reduced rate. Freeware POP programs are available, but the commercial version of Eudora is, in our minds, a superior product and at a reasonable price.

One acronym new to the land of e-mail is MIME (multipurpose Internet mail extension). MIME gives people the ability to add to their e-mail different attachments — ranging from graphics images and sounds to files and executable files. MIME is supported in many e-mail packages, including Eudora, pine, Zmail, and others.

Shell accounts versus interfaces

If your users like DOS, they probably will prefer the UNIX shell in the end. If they are Mac or Windows users, on the other hand, they will probably look for a GUI interface or at least a menu system. UNIX comes with different types of shells, which serve as a command processor between the user and the UNIX system. The most popular shells include sh, csh, ksh, tcsh, and bash. It will probably take non-UNIX users a few weeks to learn the basics of any one of these shells. To attract users who are UNIX- or computer-illiterate and who just want to read e-mail and news (at least before they get hooked on other Internet services), we had to create a menu system for them. The menu system, in our view, is essential to our users and to our service.

We took a public domain menu system and customized it for our own needs. In creating a good menu system, we followed several guidelines. The system must:

- Be intuitive to users
- Be easy to customize
- Allow submenus
- Have access control so that different classes of users can have access to varying facilities
- Allow field validation, to catch typing errors in the menu system, rather than report them from mysterious UNIX applications invoked on the user's behalf
- Be tested by a stranger who hates computers, to ensure ease of use

PPP/SLIP and X Windows

Although a menu system is sufficient for many users, some want graphical interfaces. To make these interfaces possible, you can use PPP/SLIP and X Windows.

PPP (Point-to-Point Protocol) and SLIP (Serial Line Internet Protocol) are two protocols that are widely used to connect computers over the phone lines. The main difference between them and regular serial protocols, such as ZMODEM, is that PPP and SLIP talk TCP/IP, the standard protocol that connects Internet hosts. By running PPP or SLIP, your computer at home becomes a real node on the worldwide Internet, just as though you were sitting in our office on one of our machines. Another attraction of PPP and SLIP is that both Macs and PCs have extensive software available to support them. This support can take advantage of the capability of the operating system (Windows or System 7) to display data graphically and the network capability of SLIP/PPP to run multiple sessions over a single link.

It should be noted that SLIP is a much older protocol, never designed to be used as it is here, as a standard dialup Internet protocol; but its long-term existence and availability have made it popular. The more robust and secure PPP environment will more likely than not soon eliminate SLIP.

The Mac establishes the PPP link at an operating-system level, which leaves the applications you run (Eudora, telnet, and so on) up to you and independent of the PPP link. PCs, on the other hand, tend to blend the SLIP or PPP link and the Internet applications together, often selling the PPP/SLIP software bundled with the applications. Most of our Mac customers use MacPPP, and IBM followers use commercial products, such as Internet in a Box, NetManage's Chameleon, or FTP Software's PC-TCP, to name just a few. One freeware product we highly recommend (and that we have put together in a package) is Trumpet WinSock, written by Peter Tattum. Trumpet WinSock comes with a handy dialer, TCPMAN, which supports PPP. We have found Trumpet WinSock to be a stable and well-written TCP/IP package, equivalent to available commercial software. Many freely available programs, such as Mosaic, WS-IRC, and WS-Gopher, run well with Trumpet WinSock.

Recently, software such as Slipknot and TIA, which convert a regular shell account into a PPP/SLIP account (or at least provide features like those that SLIP users have) have come on the market. We believe that the products are a good idea, considering the relatively high prices of SLIP/PPP accounts relative to shell accounts. The falling prices and improving configurations of PPP/SLIP software, however, might prevent them from spreading. Considering the technical advantages of providing SLIP access directly from a terminal server rather than by way of a UNIX host, as TIA does, the price difference for different kinds of access is likely to go away regardless.

Some hard-core UNIX users would like to run X Windows applications on their end over the phone-line connection. Hummingbird's eXceed, Distinct X, and a slew of others can do just that. Performance is a big issue, however, when it comes to running X Windows. Even with speeds of 28.8K, we find the speed of these products to be barely acceptable (depending on how good our day has been) in graphics-intensive applications. These vendors do offer *optimized* serial-line versions of their software; they are better, but performance is still a big issue.

As a provider, if you want to support these applications, you have to purchase a host license for the proxy X server. Users typically log in to the system through a serial-line X package and start up the proxy server. The terminal program recognizes a specialized escape sequence that fires up X Windows.

The cost is about $125 to $150 for a host license and about $300 to $500 for each of the clients. We have run, at most, ten people on a single host and feel that performance was reasonable but obviously beginning to degrade.

A note about TIA

We don't care whether people run TIA, but we are reserving the right to restrict this capability. In some testing, we have found that running numerous TIA sessions degrades performance. TIA seems to run about 30 percent slower than SLIP and PPP do. Because the terminal server directly supports it, there really is no reason to run TIA other than it may have a little higher cost to subscribers. It should be noted, however, that, as stated, PPP is the new trend and is supposed to have slightly better performance.

Network News/NNTP

NNTP (network news transfer protocol) is a protocol for delivering and accessing Usenet news over the Internet. Network news can be a major headache to a provider. Realistically, you have to set up your own NNTP server because most of the ones on the Net now are not open to the public, and those that are usually are heavily bogged down with so much traffic that your users have trouble using them.

Several packages — B-News, C-News and INN — enable you to set up a news server. B-News is all but extinct; C-News is older and confusing and requires a great deal of baby-sitting; and INN is the new program for the '90s. We highly recommend INN because it integrates everything: NNTP server, news database, and so on into a single package. The downside to these systems is that they are a nightmare to get working properly — you have to RTFM and RTF (*r*ead *t*he *m*anual and *r*ead *t*he *f*requently asked questions list, both included with the source distribution). You can obtain INN source from this site:

ftp://ftp.uu.net/networking/news.

You must consider two technical issues in deciding whether to set up a news server at your site: your network connection and the amount of hard disk space. To run a decent (lots of newsgroups) news server, you must have at least a 56K line coming in to your site (if your line is slower than that, you won't have the bandwidth to transfer a full day's traffic in 24 hours). You may think, from the amount of traffic, that this would hinder your connection, but, in practice, you can obtain reasonable performance from this type of connection. The other issue is the size of your hard disk. These days, such a diverse set of users is on your system that it is not reasonable for providers to limit the number of newsgroups that are available on their systems and remain competitive. To provide a full set of newsgroups, you need something on the order of two to three gigabytes per week's worth of news storage.

After running the news server for a few days, you will find where all the space is going. A great deal of traffic goes to `newsgroups alt.binaries.*` (taking more than 500 megabytes alone in a single week!) and also to `rec.*`. You have to make some decisions about how long you want to keep a particular newsgroup, or set of newsgroups. Ingress started off with a 1 GB hard disk and had to add a secondary 1.7 GB hard disk, and then we moved the entire news directory to a 4 GB disk that is doing well for now, although we cannot use the disk for anything else.

Telnet and FTP

The ability to telnet and ftp out to other sites is highly desirable. These applications are a standard part of the UNIX distribution. We are using the wuarchive ftp server because of a few features it provides. It gives us a mechanism to have a finer-grained control over who can come on to the system anonymously and from where, as well as controlling the customers with shell accounts on our system. In addition, the logging mechanism of the wuarchive ftp server is much more detailed. One especially useful feature is the ability to limit the number of users (anonymous and subscribers) that ftp into your system at a given time. ftp sessions can hog both your Internet link and CPU time on your server.

Telnet is also part of the standard suite of applications that comes with UNIX. It creates connections to other machines on your network or on the Internet. It has numerous applications, but your customers will want the capability to telnet to other sites. For security reasons, you may want to log all these activities because some people may use your system to try to break in to other systems, which you should do your best to control. The only real issue most providers have to consider here is security.

Internet Relay Chat (IRC)

Warning: IRC is addictive! It is one of those things you can live without, but after you're hooked on it, you can't live without it. There are hundreds of thousands of IRC users from all over the world every day, and they can join an IRC channel and chat with multiple users at the same time! They can also have a private one-on-one conversation with someone they've never met.

IRC servers are a good way to get some publicity with people already using the net; unless you want to dedicate a machine, however, it is too much of a network and CPU hog that your server machine will not be capable of handling many users on top of being an IRC server.

Also, it is our understanding that to become an IRC server, you may have to be able to open your server to other people and not restrict use to only internal users. Currently, there are dozens of IRC servers, and chances are that there really is not much advantage in running one. The server code is available, and one application some companies have been known to use it for is as a means of internal communication.

Games and MUDs

Internet is a true melting pot of all types of people. Game players, of course, are among some truly hardcore Internet users. They spend days and nights playing MUD (Multiuser Dungeon) games. As the user interface on these games improves, multiuser games will soon become a main attraction for the Internet.

MUD servers are similar to IRC servers. They are a good way of gaining some publicity, but really only with the people already using the Net. A number of MUD servers that already exist are being modified by different people. These people look for sites that will enable them to run their MUD server.

One thing to remember about IRC and MUD servers is that they are extremely addicting. Users may sit on your system and play with these applications for hours every night, tying up your lines. Some clause in your user agreement should make it clear that you have the right to limit their use so that they don't tie up your lines continuously.

Gopher and WWW

Two of the hottest new Internet services around (and the ones that have corporate America hopping on the Internet) are the WWW and Gopher. WWW (World Wide Web) is a powerful information system that is based on the client/server model and that merges the techniques of networked information and hypertext to make an easy but powerful global information system. It opens the door for a company of any size to advertise its products on the Internet. With the number of users exceeding 30 million, the Internet is surely a new battleground for hard-selling corporate America. Gopher is a simpler predecessor of WWW, often accessed by character-based browsers.

We allow users and corporations to put up WWW and Gopher pages. The WWW servers (httpd) that are most popular are CERN and NCSA; both support *local* directories. In other words, if you turn on certain flags in the configuration files, you can refer to a user's home page by `http://www.ingress.com/~`*`username`*. All the HTML and graphics images are generated by users, so little is necessary other than to tell them in which directory to put their files. By default, the CERN httpd comes configured for `<home directory>/public_html`.

We believe that corporations may not like having to type — or being limited to eight characters (the maximum login length). We therefore place the html files in an appropriate directory such as `http://www.ingress.com/`*their company*. The additional option that corporations have is to register a domainname and have that be an alias to our machine. The resulting URL is `http://www.foo.com/`*their_company*; to the outside, it would in many ways seem that they have their own site. The downside is that if people go to `http://www.foo.com`, they will get the provider's home page.

In terms of support, our largest amount of time has been given to provide some level of support for scripts.

Other Considerations

There are quite a few other less strictly technical issues to consider. All the glory of running an ISP has a price; not only in terms of money, but also such things as Customer Support/Service and Marketing. While there are many people looking for ways to get onto the Internet, dealing with them and getting them onto your system will take up an enormous amount of time.

Support

Support is something that can make or break a provider. Internet providers that cater to their clients are more competitive in an already competitive market. Be careful to prepare yourself. You will be asked questions. Do yourself a favor and keep a list of frequently asked questions (FAQs) and their answers, and make them available to your users.

Market

One of the most difficult decisions to make is to determine whether a market exists for your Internet provider business and whether you can provide Internet connection at a competitive price and still make a profit. Many new providers are entering the market; the size of the Internet is increasing at about 10 percent a month.

Know your costs. A T1 line will cost you at least $20K a year when you consider the cost of the leased line and full service from a provider. If you are planning to provide your paying customers with only access to the Internet, perhaps a 56K leased line (despite its much lower capacity) would be a little more reasonable.

So the question is, what do you have to do to make a profit as an Internet provider? If you are thinking that you can offer low-level Internet service to regular users at $10 to $20 a month, think again. If you just go through the calculations, you would need — at an average of $15 per user — more than a thousand users just to break even, and you should be forewarned that the phone carriers are desperately trying to muscle their way into this market. The thing they don't, and can't, offer is personalized service; they offer only one package.

A type of service that is rather popular and that yields a higher profit margin is Internet connection by way of dedicated lines. The support on these lines is rather time-consuming at times, but, considering that the current market cost of these services is anywhere from $100 to $300 per month per account, it seems like a high-profit area.

People will also pay for a PPP/SLIP pool. Users take a chance that all the dialin lines you have set aside may be busy. For the provider, there is a danger that customers will stay connected all the time, although you can mitigate that to some extent by hanging up after a period of inactivity. The cost to the user typically ranges from $30 to $100 per month. The cost of SLIP/PPP service to the provider is a port on its terminal server with a modem and a phone line. Some providers charge a startup fee ranging anywhere from $50 to $200.

Also, consider where you are located in relation to other providers and what type of user base is in that area. Ingress Communications is located in midtown Manhattan in New York City. After looking around to determine who our competition is, we quickly found out that another provider was right down the street! You have to determine what you want your system's claim to fame to be. The process is similar to opening a restaurant: If you have an excellent chef, you are likely to attract some customers. But other restaurants are available, and opening another one is always risky unless you have a particular niche.

Money and logistics

When you start any business, you have to have capital for startup costs. Otherwise, you will never be competitive with medium and large providers. To attract people, you have to give them what they want, and the hardware alone is a large investment.

You also need some technical expertise — a computer guru. Many computer gurus are just interested in getting things to work with little regard to how it will look and feel to the users. The best way to deal with this issue is to get on your system a few users who aren't computer-literate and ask them to try things out. If they can use it, most other people can too!

Closing Remarks

We may have scared many of you with some of the things we have said. You should know, though, that, despite its competitiveness, this is a great business to be in. You have to look at competitors' systems and try to provide at least what they have plus something of additional value.

Keep in mind that this is not a business to get into unless you have some technical knowledge. Ingress Communications was started with a small group of people who knew a great deal about different things and who worked well together. We often have many good ideas, but, as with many companies today, we don't have the manpower or the time to implement them all. We have often worked until early in the morning to get things working. UNIX is an endless pit of power and problems, and your best bet is to *partner up* with people who have a variety of technical expertise.

Useful Contacts

The remainder of this section presents some companies you may want to talk to.

Network Information Center (NIC)

The Network Information Center assigns IP network addresses, registers domains, and operates the root nameserver for the Domain Name System (DNS).

Government Systems, Inc.
Attn: Network Information Center
14200 Meadow Park Drive
Suite 200
Chantilly, VA 22021
(703)802-4535
(800)365-3642

Telebit Corporation

Telebit Corporation provides IP network routers capable of using the regular Public Switched Telephone System as a transport agent. It is also capable of traditional leased-line operation.

Telebit Corporation
1315 Chesapeake Terrace
Sunnyvale, CA 94089
(408)734-4333

Router vendors

The following four companies provide IP Internet routers utilizing a variety of transport agents.

Cisco Systems, Incorporated
1525 O'Brien Drive
Menlo Park, CA 94025
(415)326-1941

Wellfleet Communications, Inc.
12 DeAngelo Drive
Bedford, MA 01730-2204
(617)275-2400

Proteon, Inc.
Two Technology Drive
Westborough, MA 01581
(508)898-2800

3Com Corporation
5400 Bayfront Plaza
Santa Clara, CA 95052
(408)764-5000

Richard Chung is a partner and UNIX developer with Ingress Communications, Inc., who graduated from Carnegie Mellon University. His interests include distributed systems and object-oriented methodologies. Check out the following site to get a better idea of what he's all about:

`http://www.ingress.com/staff/rlc`

Charles Kaplan is a partner and Internet security specialist with Ingress Communications, Inc. in Norwood, Massachusetts. A graduate of Northeastern University, his interests include internetworking technology development and security-related mathematics.

Michael Y.C. Hur is a cofounder of Ingress Communications, Inc. He graduated from Columbia University and worked for Wall Street firms. His interests include computational mathematics and object-oriented design and programming.

Alan Chung is the president of Ingress Communications, Inc. A graduate of Columbia University, he worked for major investment banking firms before starting Ingress Communications. His interests include client/server database design and mathematic modeling of financial instruments.

You can get more information about Ingress Communications from the following:

WWW: `http://www.ingress.com`

Gopher: `gopher://gopher.ingress.com`

FTP: `ftp://ftp.ingress.com`

E-mail: `info@ingress.com`

FAX: 212-213-0736

Phone: 212-679-8592 or 617-255-9298

U. S. mail: Ingress Communications, Inc., 538 2nd Avenue, New York, NY 10016

or

45 Grant Avenue, Norwood, MA 02062

Chapter 28

Setting up a European Internet Provider

by Olivier M.J. Crépin-Leblond <ocl@gih.co.uk>

With the worldwide growth of the Internet, the development of on-line services is not restricted to the U.S. anymore. In the wave of new businesses generated by the Net, Internet connectivity in Europe appears to be a great idea at this early stage. But is this connectivity as easy as it seems to be? Can one start service with a few hundred dollars? And where is the European backbone? Indeed, the questions may be, Is there a European backbone and does Europe have an equivalent to the U.S. National Information Infrastructure plan? This chapter attempts to provide an answer to these questions.

Internet provision is not as simple in Europe as it is in the U.S. Delays, whether administrative or technical, unexpected costs, the need for more than one connection to the network in many cases, and high set-up costs (for both hardware and lines) are all factors that tend to pull the balance of the cash flow into the red. This situation is the one that exists before the telecom giants enter the market with full force, and the sad reality is that ex-state-owned telecom companies have an advantage for "strategic" reasons before the opening of the market and the end of the monopolies.

The National Information Infrastructure (NII)

In the U.S. and in Europe, national governments have plans for setting up the network of the future. But the plans are quite different.

The U.S. National Information Infrastructure plan

The National Information Infrastructure (NII) sets out a vague official policy for the U.S. government to be committed to the development of a high-speed network that is designed to carry voice, data, and video. This broad statement is not understood by anyone because, as of December 1994, no clear and detailed description of the plan had been released by the U.S. government. As a result, the NII exists as a conceptual idea. What follows is my interpretation of such an idea.

The future multimedia network that is known today by such names as the *Information Superhighway* and the *Infobahn* is thought to be the greatest factor of growth for U.S. industry and commerce through minimization of telecommunication costs by U.S. corporations and an increase in consumer expenditure in all fields of retail. The NII is seen by Vice-President Gore as the kick-start to the renewal of the U.S. economy because of the wide acceptance of the concept that *information is power.*

The NII has a strong financial aspect. Multimedia services are bandwidth hungry. Therefore, one of the most expensive investments is the cost of laying more fiber-optic cable underground. This job is undertaken by telecommunication companies (TelCos) and cable companies, but the size of the investment is such that in many cases at least part of the project requires an injection of public money. Most of the funding is channeled through the NTIA (National Telecommunications Infrastructure Administration), a subagency of the U.S. Department of Commerce. The funding will total more than $60 million in 1995 and is highly likely to come from taxpayers' pockets. It is hoped, however, that the long-term financial benefits of having a stronger industry because of improved telecommunications and activity will compensate for higher taxes. The idea is that in the long run, the Information Superhighway will be self-supporting, generate new jobs, reduce administrative costs, promote education, and so on.

Unfortunately, the public is having a hard time interpreting the NII project. One of the reasons for the lack of understanding is that the concept includes activities ranging from telecommunications to media and entertainment corporations, and from banks to small businesses.

The telecommunication corporation's view

To a local telephone company or a cable TV provider, the NII means the fiber-optic cabling of streets, cities, states; a backbone network; and the incorporation of voice, video, and data onto the same high-speed network. It also means video-on-demand (interactive television), video-telephone capabilities, and any other high-bandwidth services that the existing telecommunication infrastructure cannot support — and the potential for generating enormous profits in the future.

The computer manufacturer's view

The NII leads to the requirement for faster computers that are capable of dealing with multimedia applications. It calls for research towards a fast input/output (I/O) interface to the outside world, as well as high-speed graphic cards, and so on. Methods of on-line payment that involve the use of special peripherals also need to be developed.

The software publisher's view

The NII calls for the development of copyright enforcement software tools, as well as for the coding and decoding of confidential data through encryption mechanisms. It also requires software compatibility, extensions of current products towards the multimedia age, and the development of new protocols for database retrieval, storage, and interfacing.

The consumer electronics manufacturer's view

The NII is a push towards the research and development of purpose-built hardware and devices for database retrieval, integrated communications, and high-quality digital audio and visual equipment (television, hi-fi sound systems, and so on).

The entertainment and media industry's view

The NII opens the door to a brand new market for video-on-demand services. An explosion in the demand for new releases is forecast in both the motion picture business and the music industry, because distribution and advertising costs will decrease and purchases of entertainment products will, hence, increase. The NII also will require the conversion of archived productions into a digital medium so that customers can have direct access to them. The printing media will have to follow a similar procedure and digitize past printed publications so that customers can directly and remotely access them in the future.

The advertising industry's view

The advertising industry, a field in which the generation of information about products is a prime activity, will be able to make extensive use of the Infobahn as a new medium of expression for its clients. From the point of view of advertising agencies, the list of industries that can ultimately benefit from the NII is nonexhaustive.

The retailing industry's view

The retailing industry will be a customer, but also a partner, for many of the preceding industries by selling consumer products to the public. The stimulation of commercial activity predicted in the NII plan is fueling hopes for increased sales.

Where does the Internet fit into the picture?

Bill Gates, chairman and CEO of Microsoft Corporation, was probably right late in 1994 when he divided networking into two types: high-bandwidth services and low-bandwidth services.

High-bandwidth services, such as video-on-demand, video-telephony, and interactive television shopping, have reached the experimental stage; but commercial applications for those services will not be economically viable for at least ten years.

The so-called low-bandwidth services include the Internet, and are, therefore, well under development. The NII will probably involve the upgrading of the Internet backbones in the U.S., and international connectivity upgrades also will take place. With the current growth of the Internet, the upgrading of lines can, in fact, be market driven, and U.S. businesses will benefit greatly by the funding of new experimental services based around the Internet. Vice-President Gore's vision of an electronic communication network linking all American citizens, businesses, and government agencies by the twenty-first century ties in well with the concept of the Internet.

For historical reasons, the U.S. has dominated the international Internet networking scene, but other countries are catching up quickly. The NII will help the U.S. retain its leading position by funding more research and projects based around the Internet, some of which will have large financial returns for U.S. industry and trade.

The European NII

As mentioned earlier in this chapter, Europe has no common policy regarding a pan-European Information Infrastructure. Most European countries have developed a national strategy, but the lack of pan-European coordination will certainly mean an under-capacity (that is, low-bandwidth) in international links. This weakness will hinder the development of a pan-European high-speed network. In the worst-case scenario, some countries will have implemented a high-speed backbone network, and others will have lagged behind, thus leaving gaping holes in the European multimedia/cyberspace landscape and producing another problem with respect to full European unification and integration. It is not unwise to say that the current telecommunications monopoly situation in some countries is a direct cause of the problems that Europe will face later. I examine some of these problems in the section entitled "Practical factors to consider," later in this chapter.

The Fundamentals of Service Provision in Europe

This section identifies the main players in the regulatory circles on the European Internet and outlines a structure of central and local Internet registries. Then it describes how to obtain IP numbers and register domains and explains other administrative prerequisites for hooking a network to the Internet.

The latter part of this section examines the current status of the Internet backbone in Europe and, finally, addresses some of the issues to consider when setting up an Internet provider in Europe as opposed to setting one up in the U.S.

The players: their acronyms and their functions

In this section, I refer to a number of organizations by their acronyms. The following list defines their functions:

- DDN NIC: Defense Data Network Network Information Center. The original Global Internet Registry, now dealing only with the registration of U.S. military and government hosts.
- InterNIC: Internet Network Information Center. The Global Internet Registry. Supervises local Internet registries such as RIPE NCC in Europe and APNIC in Asia. It is the top-level registration service for the Internet.
- RIPE NCC: Réseaux IP Européens Network Coordination Center. This organization, a collaboration between European networks that use TCP/IP, began operating in the second quarter of 1992 and is in charge of the European Regional Internet Registry.
- RARE: *Réseaux Associés pour la Recherche Européenne.* An association of national and international European networks and users. It coordinates and funds telecom research in Europe. Funded directly by the EEC and member countries.

- EARN: European Academic and Research Network. A non-IP network built around large IBM VM mainframes and Digital Equipment Corporation's (DEC's) VAXen. This network was set up in the early 1980s and is connected to the Internet via various gateways. It connects to BITNET in the U.S. and uses BITNET protocols.
- TERENA: Trans-European Research and Education Networking Association. An organization created by the merger of RARE and EARN in late 1994, now composed of representative organizations from 38 countries as well as large international corporations.
- Local IR: Local Internet Registry. Generally — but not necessarily — an Internet connectivity provider. Receives IP numbers from the RIPE NCC to allocate them locally.

Registration and IP allocation in Europe — how it works

With the growth of the Internet, the centralized procedures for obtaining IP network numbers have been replaced. The original procedures had the Global Internet Registry, the InterNIC (and before that the DDN NIC) allocate networks directly.

The task is now delegated to more local centers, with the RIPE NCC in charge of the European Regional Internet Registry. A large block of Internet numbers is allocated by InterNIC to RIPE NCC, which in turn allocates them to IRs, local Internet Registries. The overall goal is a fair distribution and optimal utilization of the limited available Internet Protocol address space.

Funding and further services of the RIPE NCC

RARE provides the legal and financial framework for the NCC. The funding for NCC comes from European Internet service providers as well as from EARN, the full national members of RARE, and other organizations that benefit from the service. Financial support for the NCC is important so that a neutral organization can coordinate the registration of networks in Europe. With the merger of RARE and EARN, the NCC is now funded by TERENA.

RIPE NCC maintains a document store (including software tools related to network management and reports from RARE, EBONE, and so on), a network management database containing information about all European IP networks, and, as described previously, the European Regional Internet Registry.

Getting address numbers

The Internet numbering scheme classifies address types into three main categories — Class A, B, and C addresses — with the class determining the maximum number of hosts on a network.

Class A networks can have up to 16 million hosts, Class B networks can have up to 65,000 hosts, and Class C networks are limited to 254 hosts. There is a maximum number of possible networks of each type, ranging from about 100 Class A networks to several million Class C networks.

Allocation procedures

The IRs can allocate Class C addresses directly from a block of Class C addresses that they receive from the RIPE NCC, because plenty of Class C network numbers are available.

The RIPE NCC itself allocates Class B network numbers on a case-by-case basis. The applicant needs to supply documentary evidence to show justification for such a requirement and also submit an addressing subnetting plan that provides details of the proposed use. As a result, the allocation of a Class B network address takes much more time than the allocation of a Class C network number. Timewise, asking for a block of adjacent Class C addresses (which can, in most cases, still be treated as a single network) may be more advantageous than requesting a single Class B number.

Class A networks are an extremely scarce resource. Such requests are considered only when more than 65,000 hosts are to be connected on a single physical network. The requests are generally sent to the global InterNIC registry, and they take considerable time to honor. In practice, Class A network numbers are unavailable, except perhaps to organizations that have a great deal of political leverage.

Standard procedures for IP number allocation and registration have been set out by RIPE for the IRs to follow. The requirements include the following:

- Guidelines for the maximum size of the block of addresses to be allocated by the NCC to a local IR.
- The IRs need to immediately report reassigned network numbers to the RIPE NCC in RIPE database format.
- The IRs need to have reliable Internet e-mail connectivity because e-mail is the preferred method of communication for registry purposes, followed by fax.
- The IRs need to keep all correspondence and information exchanges related to registration services for later review and the resolution of disputes, and to hold this information in full confidentiality.
- Applications for further address space must be reasonable and be accompanied by documentary evidence for such an application.
- The IRs need to prevent the stockpiling of address space.
- The IRs need to follow a further set of supernetting guidelines, described in RIPE document RIPE-104, and RFCs 1466 and 1467.

In addition, detailed procedures that are too numerous to be listed here are set for isolated cases.

The procedures must be followed closely for the whole process of IP number allocation and domain registration to take place smoothly and efficiently. Documents explaining the procedures in detail are available from the RIPE NCC document store via Gopher or ftp.

A brief overview of the Internet in Europe

The most extensive pan-European Internet backbone network is Europe's branch of the UUnet organization, EUnet, a company that is jointly owned by the EUnet national service providers and the European Forum for Open Systems (EurOpen). For historical reasons, mainly because it was there before everybody else, EUnet now covers nearly all European countries, including Eastern Europe, and a few countries in Africa. However, EUnet apparently doesn't allow subleasing of connectivity and, hence, sells local connectivity to customers directly.

This section, therefore, concentrates on what are called *Neutral Access Networks.* These networks are funded by consortiums of companies that benefit from the network, and their management is neutral to the individual companies. In many cases, the backbone nodes of such networks are located on the premises of a service provider that runs the node on everybody else's behalf and treat its competitors in a neutral way on that backbone, thus enabling them to get connected.

The two Europewide neutral IP networks are EBONE, the European BackBONE, and EuropaNET, a network maintained by DANTE. Both are broadly designed as research networks, and are bridged to each other, as well as to EUnet, in most European countries.

EBONE (European backBONE) is a European international, intercontinental network backbone that connects research network service providers to each other and to the U.S. EBONE focuses on serving Europe's academic and research communities through a nonprofit cooperative effort where the participants share the costs via a fee that is based on access speed. The project complements the other European activities such as EuropaNET, the European Multi-Protocol Backbone (EPMB) project. The EBONE operates between London, Geneva, Amsterdam, Stockholm, and Paris. Research networks from other countries hook onto the nodes at those backbone sites. As a result, the network spans the whole of Europe. Although the resulting network is predominantly a research network, commercial service providers have been encouraged to participate in order to increase the size of the participating communities by adding industrial researchers. As a result, enforcement of any AUP (acceptable use policy) restrictions does not take place on EBONE itself. More information on the EBONE is available from <ebone@terena.nl>.

DANTE is a nonprofit company that provides the EuropaNET service, similar to the EBONE service, connecting 18 European countries to each other and to the rest of the world. Share ownership of DANTE was initially held by RARE. In March 1994, the ownership was formally transferred from RARE to the shareholders. The company is now owned by the research organizations that run research networks in each of the served countries. European research and development projects pay a large part of the cost of running the backbone network. Two high-speed lines (1.5 Mpbs and 2 Mbps) provide network connection with the U.S. Access speeds on the network vary between 9.6 Kpbs and 2 Mpbs. As in the EBONE, the network is research dominated. The fact that DANTE is a network of networks makes acceptable use policy enforcement only as good as enforcement on the subnetworks themselves. Further international links to Asia and North America were implemented in 1994 for research projects and cooperation. More information about DANTE can be obtained from <dante@dante.org.uk>.

Practical factors to consider

Before launching into Internet connectivity provision in Europe, potential service providers need to consider a large number of factors. The distance to the nearest Point of Presence, language issues, AUPs, laws, monopolies, and so on, all contribute to more headaches than those endured by U.S. service providers.

This section covers those issues and warns potential service providers about looming challenges.

The distance to the nearest Internet Point of Presence (PoP)

Although connectivity to the Internet is spreading worldwide, the strategic center of the network is in the U.S. One factor that hinders the commercial development of the Internet in Europe is the difficulty of finding a point of connection (otherwise known as Point of Presence, PoP) on that continent. Even connection to the EBONE is expensive. The solution for smaller providers is to try to find a larger provider who is ready to allow subselling of connectivity. The kind of deal possible could include a percentage of the proceeds from the connection of new clients, in addition to the standard connection fee. In some countries, no such a deal is possible, either because no large supplier is already present in the country or because the conditions for Internet connection stipulate that no subselling of connections is allowed. If an amicable deal is not possible, then the only solution is to search for connection to a provider outside the country. This method requires the use of international leased lines and a jump in costs. The ultimate connection to the Internet, a direct line to the U.S., is often the only option possible for larger providers.

A transatlantic line is expensive, and the scarcity of the number of cables laid ensures that prices stay high. A 64 Kbps digital leased line (which is, in fact, a bandwidth allocation of 64 Kbps on a multiplexed link) from the U.K. to the U.S. cost GBP 48,000 ($80,000) annually in 1994. Add to this the cost of local loop connections on each side, and you easily reach the GBP 50,000 mark ($85,000). The 64 Kbps bandwidth can be increased slightly by using compression methods at both ends, but 64 Kbps digital lines will support only a limited number of customers before an upgrade is required, especially in the age of World Wide Web and other such multimedia use. The high cost is justified by the installation and maintenance cost of those cables. Satellite connections are less satisfactory because of the added end-to-end transfer delay of about 250 milliseconds, which is quite noticeable for interactive sessions.

After the cable has crossed the Atlantic, you still need to find and buy connection to an Internet provider in the U.S., where both good and bad deals are available. Overall, the reasons why Internet connection is more expensive in Europe than in the U.S. are easy to understand.

Language Issues

A large part of the funds allocated to a European project is usually spent on translation. Establishing a common cultural platform such as the Internet risks a fate similar to the ill-fated Tower of Babel. Although Esperanto was intended to bring down language barriers, it failed miserably, leaving Europe with no common language. As a result, the information servers on Internet in European countries need to be accessible both in the local language and in English.

At present, this requirement is not a problem because users of the networks in Europe are still an elite minority who are educated enough to read and understand English. When the Internet spreads beyond the elite, the demands of the users will mean that the European information servers will need to be multilingual. Even a bilingual server is more costly to design and run than a monolingual one. The average non-English-speaking user will be put off by the overwhelming percentage of services provided in English. Although younger generations of users are all well versed in the language of Shakespeare, older generations, who make the decisions in companies, often require the help of interpreters. The initial growth of Internet in the commercial sector in Europe will, hence, be slow until the national infrastructure is developed enough to support native-tongue services of interest to business. The only way to kick-start the commercial growth of the Internet in Europe is, therefore, for the governments to take an active role in supplying services through the Net that will benefit their domestic industries. This development will take time.

The U.K. Internet market development model will probably be followed to some extent in some Northern European countries that have a traditional strength in English as a second language. Southern European countries will follow a much slower scenario of market growth.

The case of the U.K. is certainly different, in great part because of the lack of a language barrier to already existing Internet services that originate in the U.S. An early take-off was possible because of being able to use the services already developed in the U.S. and because corporations in the U.K. have a stronger tradition of trade with the U.S. than do corporations in other countries. The cultural Anglo-American link has certainly catalyzed the growth of the Internet in the U.K., but this catalyst does not exist in other European countries.

Government support of Internet-related projects is, therefore, necessary in order to stimulate the network's growth for research and commercial purposes. Governments can provide the following types of support:

- Financial support by distributing grants for Internet development to companies and universities.
- Technical support by providing information on the network in the country's native tongue as well as in English. This support includes information that is likely to attract corporations to the network because of its ability to reduce costs and generate further income.
- Educational support by explaining to the population at large how to use the network and introducing Net-related matters in schools.

Acceptable use policies (AUPs)

Academic networks are organized differently in all of the European countries. It is, therefore, no great surprise to learn that acceptable use traffic policies that limit what kinds of traffic are acceptable are present in some networks but missing or simply not enforced in others. In the U.K., for example, the domain name system (DNS), partially inherited from the NRS (Name Registration Scheme) system, includes a subdomain that indicates the status of the connected institutions:

- .ac.uk is academic
- .co.uk is commercial
- .gov.uk is government, and so on

This system makes enforcement of the AUPs easy because breaches of policy are very blatant. Traffic from a .co.uk going through an .ac.uk to reach the outside world stands out. But other European countries have no such structure of domain and subdomain. More often than not, companies are allowed to connect to "research" networks, that are connected to the Internet. A prerequisite is that the company undertake some form of research. It takes only a few seconds to realize that any R&D department of a technology-related company can justify connection to the research networks. At this early stage, in many cases, the taxpayer bears at least some of the bill of the access by companies to the Internet. However, connectivity doesn't come cheaper, because of high telecommunication tariffs in a monopolistic market.

Monopolies

Apart from the U.K., all European countries are still in a situation where a company that is owned partially or entirely by the state has a monopoly on telecommunications. The overall effect of having monopolies is to slow the speed at which new technologies are introduced.

Until recently, European telecommunication companies have stuck to the OSI networking system that was developed within the frame of the CCITT *(Comité Consultatif International de Télégraphie et Téléphonie*, the group that defines international telephone standards). The OSI system is technically incompatible with the Internet's TCP/IP. As a result, the TelCos are completely unprepared for the wave of IP (Internet Protocol) networks, and many are only now learning about TCP/IP by developing their own research networks. Government involvement in telecommunications has meant that many decisions were made on a political level rather than on a technical level.

The privatization of the state-owned TelCos will take place from 1995 onwards. Only after a full or partial privatization will any breaking up of the monopolies be possible. The end of monopolies will certainly mean competition from other TelCos. The result will be lower leased line costs, less bureaucracy, and, hence, faster installation of new lines, as the new TelCos try to impress new customers and the previously state-owned TelCos fight back. Competition is a positive development for the Internet: Connection providers will have lower overheads, and they can pass the lower costs on to the customers.

Unfortunately, the fact that in many cases the state will still hold 51 percent of the company's capital means that unfair competition will occur through a conflict of interest for the state: The state will simultaneously make the rules regarding TelCos and be a player in the market itself. In many southern European countries, the political pressure for a peaceful social climate will promote biased bureaucratic decisions regarding authorizations of service, both on a national level and on a local level. For example, a government-owned company that wants to dig up roads in a town to install fiber-optic cables will be granted authorization faster and more easily than an independent company that wants to do the same thing.

Furthermore, it is worth considering that partial privatization has been chosen as a trade-off situation, often because of conflicting pressures from the EEC (European Economic Community) and local pressure groups, such as syndicates, trade unions, and so on. Overall, the issue of privatization remains a very complex one, which is why the time required for ending monopolies is to be counted in years rather than in months.

The delay in ending monopolies is deplorable, especially in data services where newcomers are often small companies. Small providers have received no state or EEC help to start businesses to provide Internet services, but large state-owned telecom companies have been given subsidies to develop the "research" networks to which they can connect commercial entities as well, thus disregarding AUPs on their own lines, as seen earlier in the chapter. The overall outlook for multimedia telecommunications, of which Internet is the starting seed, is too strategic for governments not to be involved.

As multinational corporations fight for world telecom markets, the battle after European telecommunication deregulation occurs is likely to involve U.S. carriers. In the Internet connectivity market, the battle between continents will mean that small or medium-sized independent providers may well get squashed, because the laws will ultimately penalize them. Providers that cater to niche markets will be more likely to survive.

The last countries to open up their telecom market will do so no later than in 2003. A simple analogy can be drawn with PC software and hardware manufacturers that started business in the early 1980s. Corporations such as Apple Computer and Microsoft have managed to grow beyond their founders' expectations, but predicting today that a start-up small computer manufacturer would ever reach that size would be unwise. In the European Internet connectivity provider market, the lifting of restrictions will take place when the large multinational players have already stepped in. By that time, the Internet will have changed a great deal; and it will, therefore, be too late for many small providers to establish themselves, because no niche will remain in the market.

Laws

Laws on pornography and other moral concerns differ from country to country. As a result, creating legislation for a network that connects many countries is a difficult task. Laws on obscene publications or publications that could offend are very tough in some countries (as in the U.K.) and very soft in others (as in the Netherlands). The kaleidoscope of laws regarding pornography in Europe is a good example of the diversity of laws governing other matters, such as software piracy, the writing and releasing of malicious code (viruses), copyright enforcement, and ownership.

No large-scale copyright infringement cases have yet occurred on the Internet in Europe, so the issue of copyright protection in particular is unresolved. More often than not, existing laws take precedence over the Net AUPs. In the U.K., for example, data accessible by Internet is subject to the same laws that govern the press and publications. One of the main items of conflict is the transmission of Usenet news. Assigning liability is difficult: Who is responsible for the information contained in the news?

The view that some governments have taken, which is to make the system manager responsible for the information stored in the machine, has caused many Usenet groups to be dropped from the hierarchy because of fear of prosecution if some of the articles carried did indeed break a country's laws. Although the electronic open transfer of information is well known and understood by the U.S. government, the situation in many European countries is different.

As an example, in early 1994, police in a European country raided a FIDONET bulletin board and found pirated software on the hard disks of the system, together with the listing of all the FIDONET nodes. In a matter of hours, the whole FIDO network in that country was shut down, and all the computers in the registration table were seized, although they had nothing to do with the incriminated machine.

In the face of such ignorance, it is, therefore, important for the service carrier to make sure that the traffic carried on its network and the information stocked on its hard disk do not break local laws. Information that is acceptable in one country may not be acceptable in the neighboring countries.

At the end of 1994, the European authorities had not yet addressed the problem and defined a common policy regarding the transmission of information through electronic media. Neither had they addressed the complex issue of encryption, which is required for any confidential transaction on a public network such as Internet but is illegal in countries such as France, for example.

Provision of Service

This section is divided into two subsections. One section is about small providers that cater to the needs of individuals and small companies, and the other section is about large providers whose target market is the medium-to-large corporate user. The needs and concerns of a small provider differ in many ways from those of a large one. Furthermore, a number of procedures are different, depending on the size of the provider.

Small providers

A typical small provider's connection service is aimed at hobbyists, individuals, and small businesses. It can offer a range of services, from a simplified account for reading and posting news and corresponding by e-mail, to forwarding e-mail and news to customers' computers via SLIP/PPP and UUCP.

Dialup connections to the Net

SLIP stands for *Serial Line Internet Protocol.* It consists of software that enables IP to be transported on a serial line, usually through a modem.

PPP stands for *Point-to-Point Protocol,* another method for transmitting IP on a serial line through modems.

UUCP stands for *UNIX-to-UNIX CoPy,* which is a UNIX program that provides for the transfer of files, and, hence, e-mail, through a serial line that may be a direct link from one machine to another or via modems. IP is not supported on UUCP.

When SLIP/PPP is used, the computer becomes part of the Internet when the telephone call is made because it is given its own IP address.

Small providers need to base most of their decisions on cost. In Europe, providers have to pay a number of overheads that have no equivalents in the U.S.

The fact that reliability of communication is not a priority for the target hobbyist market means that many overheads (for example, having a system operator on call around the clock) are not required, and the system can happily sit in a spare bedroom. But is it wise to set up such a system?

Setting up the hacker way

The story goes: "They started with one computer in a garage, and now they are at the head of a media empire." The reality is somehow different. Setting up the hacker way does not lead very far. Running a BBS (bulletin board system) that has UNIX shell accounts is easy and cheap, but networking with the Internet is a different kettle of fish.

Today, one could put together a system using LINUX, a 386 or 486 PC-compatible machine, a cheap modem, and a spare phone line, and run it in the garage or the spare bedroom. Such a system could provide restricted shell or BBS-type accounts that enable users to send and receive electronic mail and read or post on a very limited number of Usenet newsgroups.

In this scenario, two options are open:

- Connecting the provider's computer to the backbone via telephone dialup, using the UUCP protocols or SLIP/PPP. This option is attractive because of low connection costs that vary with the amount of traffic carried. Transmission of e-mail is not instantaneous and is restricted to the schedule followed by the computer to call the backbone.
- Connecting the provider's computer to the backbone via a leased line. This option is more costly.

Although Internet connectivity was not as widespread in 1994 in continental Europe as in the U.S., users read in the press about the services provided by full connectivity. Therefore, they expect the connection provider to be able to offer the full range of Internet services, including WWW (World Wide Web), Gopher, ftp, and other services that require the provider to have a leased line.

In 1994, state monopolies made the cost of having a leased line several thousand dollars, which is expensive. So much for the "hacker" way. . . . Low-bandwidth lines can be obtained in some countries for less than $1,000 per annum, but what type of service can a provider offer with a connection to the backbone at less than 64 Kbps? That speed is fine for providing e-mail and perhaps Usenet news, but it is not sufficient for being a server for ftp or Gopher, nor for using graphical WWW programs on a large scale.

The second problem is where to hook into the network. AUPs prevent purely commercial service providers from hooking onto research academic networks. The solution is to contact a major service provider in the country itself and sign an agreement for subprovision of service. The caveats are dependence on that supplier, as well as having to pay the supplier a percentage of profits or a lump sum (thus eroding net profit).

These factors make it commercially not viable for the "hacker" setup to be taken seriously. A small provider will typically use three or four powerful PC-compatible computers running a well-proven version of UNIX, with a few gigabytes of disk space to stock Usenet newsgroup articles as well as customers' electronic mail. A workstation such as a low-end Sun would be advisable, along with 14.4 Kbps modems. This type of modem is now the standard strict minimum, because customers may want to run X-windows or remote WWW clients. Starting with half a dozen modems is fine, but at least a dozen modems may be better, in order to provide for peak hours. That way, at least 12 customers can access the network at any time.

Pricing of connectivity for customers varies from country to country, depending on the competition's prices. In general, the customer is aware of the saying, "You get what you pay for." Very cheap suppliers will offer a low-end service, with no guarantee about the quality of service (QOS); more-expensive suppliers will offer better technical support and consulting services.

Investing a bit more

More funds are required if the local (that is, in the same country) large service provider refuses to contract with subproviders or if there is no local large service provider. In 1994, this was the case in many European countries at this early stage of Internet development. With time, competition among large connection providers will prompt some of them to strike deals with small connection providers so that small providers can resell connectivity at the low end of the market (individuals and hobbyists).

An international line to a more cooperative provider in a neighboring country costs much more. If such a leased line is used, the workhorse for the service should be at least a machine built for the purpose: a UNIX machine such as a Sun, for example. Ideally, a proper router should be placed at the end of the incoming leased line.

The jump in cost for a line and equipment for this option is tremendous. Even within Europe, international lines can take up to six months to install, partly because of the current monopolies. Furthermore, selling Internet connectivity via a leased line to another country may break the local telecom monopoly laws. Authorization to start service will then have to be sought, invariably leading to further delay.

All is not lost, however. For example, providing dialup provision of service (using SLIP or PPP) with limited equipment is made more viable in Europe by the lack of free local calling service. Customers stay on-line for limited amounts of time, and it is possible to attract them with a monthly fee that has no use-related charges. Providers in the U.K. have been able to size their modem pools at up to 30 customers per modem, twice as many as is typical in the U.S. The use of SLIP or PPP enables customers to download and upload their e-mail and read it and write it off-line. The average call length is reduced to less than a minute. (The enemy of dialup service providers is the busy signal, and having 20 customers per modem provides better service).

A faster dialup service, using ISDN (Integrated Services Digital Network) is also possible. ISDN is a digital connection provided by a TelCo, which can be used to carry voice, data, and video on two separate circuit-switched (dialup) 64Kbps channels and one 16Kbps packet-switched channel (although access to the 16Kbps channel is often barred by the TelCo). The higher transfer rates are a great improvement over analogue telephone lines, at a lower cost than leased lines.

ISDN service is a trickier business for two reasons:

- The terminal equipment (TE) required at the end of ISDN lines is a costly investment.
- The ISDN maximum transfer rate (2 x 64 Kbps + 1 x 16 Kbps) is higher than the 64 Kbps leased line that most dialup providers start with. This raises the chance of congestion by a very significant factor, because a single user can use more than the entire bandwidth of the leased line.

The cost of ISDN connections has gone down over the years, and in some cases a leased line is cheaper for the customer than dial-in service over a regular phone line. In France, for example, if a line is used up to eight hours a day, using an ISDN line makes more sense. In the U.K., this figure goes down to four hours per day.

As far as customer support and quality of service (QOS) go, the word is "you get what you pay for." Supplying a very cheap service, with little or no support and no particular QOS regarding availability, is easy; but this service will appeal only to hobbyists, and competition in that market will be fierce.

Administrivia

The administrative work associated with the running of a small provider is similar to the work required for all small businesses (credit card payments; checks; accounting, and so on). IP-related administrative work, such as domain and IP number registration, can be sent to the link supplier if it is a larger Internet supplier that acts as an IR. This service should be supplied by the larger connection providers, and no correspondence with the RIPE NCC is then required. If, for the sake of control and faster allocation, or because the supplier does not provide such a service, registration has to be performed on-site, becoming an Internet Registry (IR) adds some administrative workload to the running of the site, but most operations can be done semiautomatically. Direct involvement with RIPE NCC is then required, as described earlier in this chapter.

Large providers

From the start, setting up as a large provider requires substantial funds. The key to proper sizing of the operation involves accurate prediction of and planning for the growth in use and clients. Although hardware (computers, routers, and so on) may be delivered in a couple of weeks, installing leased lines can take up to six months (for international lines). This delay makes the anticipation of growth essential.

Setting up an international leased line is difficult because of the number of TelCos involved and the language differences. If the system is too small to start with, congestion on the leased line will increase delay, and QOS will be decreased until the bandwidth of the line is increased — which can take months. Similarly, the delivery of a new telephone line also can take months. The opening of the telecom market to competition will no doubt reduce the delays, but in the meantime, providers have no choice but to predict and plan for increases in activity well in advance.

Keep in mind that direct links to the U.S., as well as to EuropaNET and/or the EBONE, will improve the overall resilience and reliability of the network.

Large service providers must become local IRs. Because the expected growth in customers is high, blocks of Class C addresses, or even a Class B address, will be required, and much more documentary evidence is needed by RIPE NCC to support the service, as explained earlier in the chapter. More administrators are required to coordinate with other service providers for bilateral *traffic peering agreements* (agreements between two networks to exchange TCP/IP traffic), nameserver allocations, DNS management, routing updates, and so on. Round-the-clock network monitoring, a help desk with extended hours, and 99 percent network availability are the common requirements. Some of the customers may even be small providers whose administration will be undertaken by the large provider. The running of a comprehensive ftp mirror of U.S. archives is highly recommended to keep the traffic across the Atlantic at a minimum. Furthermore, a Gopher and a WWW service is required to attract a wide range of customers. This service, while requiring the appointment of a webmaster (someone who will have to maintain WWW pages and keep them up-to-date), will lighten the load on the sales and customer support staff.

Last but not least, setting up a large Internet connection supplier may not be possible in some countries because of monopoly laws that make backbone TCP/IP service the domain of the state TelCo or other monopoly supplier because the wideband transmission of data is considered a broadcasting medium that requires special licensing from the government. A softer restriction sets an upper limit in the bandwidth of the connectivity provided to a corporation. Any faster connection is then referred to the local TelCo's IP connectivity department/partner who will be more than happy to seize the market.

Again, the market will not open until the end of the millennium.

A Look at Future Directions for the Internet in Europe

The rate of growth for the Internet will no doubt be the same in Europe as in the rest of the world. Language, regulations, and the lack of an official EEC plan for development of commercial services will nevertheless delay the initial growth, but eventually governments will realize that the Internet is effectively a simplified, cheaper version of the much-hyped Information Superhighway.

The Internet is arguably an Information Superhighway. In the strict sense, for Internet to be a superhighway, its transmission rates, and especially the bandwidth of its backbone, should be increased so that it can support video services such as video-on-demand. The Information Superhighway is often thought to be the Internet plus an addition of high-bandwidth services. Different communication protocols such as ATM (Asynchronous Transfer Mode) and different user interfaces that have less of a "computer" feel are also to be used, although one can question this view at this stage because computers are evolving towards televisions (interactive and multimedia packages), and televisions are evolving towards computers (digital TV decoders). Perhaps the trade-off will be a television controlled by a computer.

The fact that the Internet may already be the foretaste of the InfoBahn is understood by the U.K. government, which has stated in the CCTA (the UK Government Centre for Information Systems) consultative report, "Information Superhighways — Opportunities for public sector applications in the U.K." (published in 1994), that the Internet is one of many possible communications technologies that could evolve into an Information Superhighway.

In the U.S., the possibility of a future metamorphosis of the Internet into the superhighway is seen as plausible, thanks to a project led by a consortium of companies including Intel, Sun Microsystems, Hewlett-Packard, Pacific Bell, and Apple Computer. The project, named *CommerceNet,* will test a range of ideas for conducting business over the Internet and other data networks.

On the other hand, in 1994, Western European governments (other than the U.K.) were adopting the concept of a brand new high-speed, but also high-investment, network, thus ignoring the Internet's current role. The plans are far from being approved unanimously. Some politicians find the cost of installing the infrastructure required to have video-on-demand excessive; they may well be right. If video capability is decided to be *de trop,* an extensive commercial Internet will be the next best thing. Ultimately, the infrastructure of an extensive commercial Internet will be similar to the one required for video-on-demand, but the transition to new technologies will be smoother than a jump to a data superhighway from nothing. This scenario is strengthened by the fact that those in the industry predict that a full European Information Superhighway implementation will not be ready before the year 2015. Twenty years is a very long time in today's fast-moving field of telecommunications. Twenty years ago, the Internet was called the ARPANET, and it connected only a handful of computers. With the current pattern of growth, probably in 20 years' time, the Internet will be nothing like what it is today.

Last but not least in the list of technical challenges is that commercial Internet provision in Europe will be hampered by the various stages of development of infrastructures in each country. Although some countries have an 80 percent geographic availability of high-speed (> 2 Mbps) lines, the figure for others is lower than 10 percent. Because national development prevails, some time will pass before the development of international links is undertaken. In many cases, a state monopoly doesn't stimulate the market for improvements.

In addition to those technical problems, the biggest challenge is more of a political one. Full deregulation will not take place before 1998 and will probably not be complete until 2005. Only at that time will any hope of uniformity of quality of service, price deregulation, and competition come alive.

In the meantime, national TelCos can take advantage of public money from the government to develop the national infrastructure and thus develop their own Internet network, while keeping international leased lines expensive. This, coupled with a current resistance from governments and national TelCos to stimulate the growth of a network that they have much less control over than they have traditionally had in previous projects, will certainly penalize independent Internet connectivity suppliers.

Finally, it is worth noting that Germany will take on the task of coordinating research and development of multimedia communication on behalf of the EEC because the European Commission awarded this function to it.

Conclusions

Setting-up an Internet connectivity provider is harder in Europe than in the USA. The United Kingdom market is unusual because full competition is already possible. Indeed, competition is fierce, with at least three main connection providers, and a dozen small providers for low-cost connectivity. In addition to that, the major telephone carrier, British Telecom, privatized in the 1980s, is restricted by laws as far as video value-added services are concerned, in order to protect smaller competitors from being put out of business.

For the rest of Europe, no help to small providers looks set to be given by the EEC. In fact, governments may favor their national telephone company. A small independent provider needs to find a niche market and will have trouble generating high profits due to the high overheads (lines and so on) required for connection to the Internet backbone.

A medium or large independent provider needs to have enough financial or influential "weight" to survive the eventual competition from the National TelCos who will no doubt jump onto the Internet bandwagon once the market in a country is identified as being able to generate high profits. Alternatively, it will need to strike a deal for provision of value-added services on behalf of the National TelCo.

Ultimately, the fate of the commercial Internet in Europe lies in the EEC's hands to favor telecom deregulation in a fair way, with as little bureaucracy and interference as possible. Unfortunately, this is yet to be seen.

Olivier Crépin-Leblond is finishing his Ph.D. thesis on Asynchronous Transfer Mode (ATM) and Broadband Network analysis at Imperial College, University of London, UK. He maintains the FAQs for International E-Mail Accessibility and "Welcome to alt.sources !" and contributes to the comp.virus FAQ.

Chapter 29

Running a Gopher Server

by Michael Bentley <bentley4@slb.com>

As more companies warm up to the idea of using the Internet as a business resource, the old bias against noncommercial software is beginning to fade. This is exactly as it should be. Freely distributable software as good as — and often better than — commercial software that has been available for *years*. A good example is The Internet Gopher from the University of Minnesota.

Before I get too deeply involved in discussing how to get your server up and running, I'll tell you a little bit about what gopher is and how it works. Then the chapter discusses what it takes to get a gopher server established. Finally, the chapter examines some issues related to running the server.

What Is Gopher, and How Does It Work?

Gopher usually is described as being a distributed document-delivery system. Although gopher items are not always documents, they certainly are distributed among thousands of servers throughout the world. *Gopherspace* probably is best defined as being all the gopher servers that are listed by the "Mother of all Gophers" at UMinn. If you want to find out how many servers exist, you can retrieve the menu labeled "All the gopher servers in the World" and count the number of lines in it automatically. To do so, get to a UNIX machine and enter this command:

```
echo 'telnet gopher.tc.umn.edu 70 | wc -l' - 3 | bc
```

Then (without waiting for any prompt — you won't get one) enter the following:

```
1/Other Gopher and Information Servers/all
```

---

gopher-news and comp.infosystems.gopher

If you are going to be at all serious about running a gopher server, you should subscribe to the gopher-news mailing list. To subscribe, send e-mail to `gopher-news-request@boombox.micro.umn.edu`. You also may want to read the `comp.infosystems.gopher` newsgroup.

If you have a slow link to the Internet, the calculation may take a while. In late 1994, the answer was 2,255; that number is likely to have changed by now.

There is, of course, an unknown number of gopher servers that you cannot get to from UMinn. (In fact, *my* server is hidden behind a firewall, which acts as a sort of one-way valve; we can get out, but you can't get in.) I do not consider those servers to be *in* gopherspace (although they may be in their own private or corporate gopherspace). I visualize this relationship as being similar to someone here on Earth pointing a telescope at outer space — although he can see things in outer space, he is not *in* outer space.

In many ways, gopherspace looks and acts like a UNIX file system. Each server has its own directory hierarchy and may have links to other servers. Gopher links are analogous to symbolic links in the UNIX file system. The file-system model should be familiar to most people these days. As in the file systems that people use on a day-to-day basis, a gopher item can be a directory, a file (document), or a program (some programs return directories or files).

Great Green Gobs of Greasy Grimy Gopher Guts

You may have noticed that in the preceding section, you used telnet to get the All the gopher servers in the World listing from UMinn. A quick look under the hood reveals that the gopher protocol really is quite simple. The client machine opens a TCP connection (usually to port 70), which the server accepts. The server quietly waits for the client to ask for something by sending a selector string. When the client sends the selector string, the server responds by sending whatever the client asked for (usually followed by a period) and then closing the connection.

If you are having trouble with your server, a useful trick is to telnet to the server and fool it into believing that you are a gopher client. Sending nothing but a carriage return results in a directory listing. Following is a telnet session with the main gopher server at UMinn:

```
$ telnetgopher.tc.umn.edu 70
Trying 134.84.132.9...
Connected to gopher.tc.umn.edu.
Escape character is '^]'.
<cr>  We just hit carriage return here
1Information AboutGopher<t>1/Information About
Gopher<t>gopher.tc.umn.edu<t>70<t>+
1ComputerInformation<t>1/computer<t>spinaltap.micro.umn.edu<t>70
1Discussion Groups<t>1/Mailing Lists<t>gopher.tc.umn.edu<t>70<t>+
1Fun & Games<t>1/fun<t>spinaltap.micro.umn.edu<t>70<t>+
1Internet file server (ftp)sites<t>1/FTP Searches<t>gopher.tc.umn.edu<t>70<t>+
1Libraries<t>1/Libraries<t>gopher.tc.umn.edu<t>70<t>+
1News<t>1/News<t>gopher.tc.umn.edu<t>70<t>+
1Other Gopher andInformation Servers<t>1/Other Gopher and Information
Servers<t>gopher.tc.umn.edu<t>70<t>+
1Phone Books<t>1/PhoneBooks<t>gopher.tc.umn.edu<t>70<t>+
```

```
7Search Gopher Titles atthe University of
Minnesota<t>mudhoney.micro.umn.edu<t>4325
7Search lots of places at the University of Minnesota<t>mindex:/
lotsoplaces<t>ashpool.micro.umn.edu<t>70
1University of Minnesota CampusInformation<t>1/
uofm<t>gopher.tc.umn.edu<t>70<t>+
.
Connection closed by foreign host.
```

Now we'll dissect what the server sent back to us. Each line contains one gopher item, consisting of four or five columns that are separated by tabs (displayed as <t>). The first column tells us what gopher type the item is and the item's full name. The following table describes the gopher types:

Code	***Description***
0	Item is a file
1	Item is a directory
2	Item is a CSO (qi) phone-book server (obsolescent)
3	Error
4	Item is a BinHexed Macintosh file
5	Item is a DOS binary archive of some sort
6	Item is a UNIX uuencoded file
7	Item is an Index-Search server
8	Item points to a text-based telnet session
9	Item is a binary file
T	TN3270 connection
s	Sound type; data stream is a µ-law sound
g	GIF type
M	MIME type; item contains MIME data
h	HTML type
I	Image type
i	inline text type

The second column is the selector string that must be sent to the server to retrieve the item. The third column is the name of the server that contains the item (remember that any item can be a link to other parts of gopherspace). The fourth column is the required port number (you can run more than one gopher server on a given machine, but each server must have its own port number). Some items have a fifth column that simply contains a plus sign (+). These items have Gopher+ attributes, which are discussed in the following section.

Now that you know what the gopher types mean, you can move down the hierarchy. To get a listing of the Phone Books directory, you send the contents of the second column of that row when you are connected to the server and port listed in the third and fourth columns, as follows:

```
$ telnet gopher.tc.umn.edu 70
Trying 134.84.132.27...
Connected to gopher.tc.umn.edu.
Escape character is '^]'.
1/Phone Books<cr> <<-== We send this
1University of Minnesota Phone Book<t>x500.tc.umn.edu<t>70
0About changing information in the U of M directory<t>0/Phone Books/
.about<t>gopher.tc.umn.edu<t>70
1Phone books at other institutions<t>1/Non-Notre Dame InformationSources/Phone
Books—Other Institutions<t>gopher.nd.edu<t>70
1Internet-wide e-mail address searches<t>1/PhoneBooks/
other<t>gopher.tc.umn.edu<t>70<t>+
1X.500Gateway<t>judgmentday.rs.itd.umich.edu<t>7777
1WHOIS Searches       B:Internet whois servers<t>sipb.mit.edu<t>70
.
```

Gopher+ (an Example of Creeping Featurism)

When a gopher client finds a gopher item with a plus sign after the port field, it knows (if it is Gopher+-savvy) that it can do more than just request the item. Did you notice that the Phone Books directory was listed as a Gopher+ item? If you want to get a listing of the Gopher+ attributes associated with this item, you could add a tab character and a bang (exclamation point) to the end of the selector string, as follows:

```
Trying...
Connected to gopher.tc.umn.edu.
Escape character is '^]'.
1/Phone Books<t>! +-1+INFO: 1Phone Books<t>1/Phone
Books<t>gopher.tc.umn.edu<t>70<t>++ADMIN: Admin: U of MN Gopher Team
<gopher@boombox.micro.umn.edu> Mod-Date: 12/23/94 14:30:55 <19941223143055>
TTL: 1800+VIEWS: application/gopher-menu En_US: <.5k> application/gopher+-menu
En_US: <.7k> text/html En_US: <.0k>.Connection closed by foreign host.
```

Now *here* is some useful information! Each plus sign followed by a word and a colon is the beginning of a block of information. The INFO block (which must exist) contains the same selector string that you got by using the old gopher protocol. The ADMIN block tells you two important things: the name and e-mail address of the server administrator, and the last modification date of this item (you can safely ignore the TTL line for now). The VIEWS block tells you the different content types in which this item can be retrieved, as well as the language and file size. The content type is expressed as a MIME content type, and the language is expressed by means of the ISO-639 codes.

Possibly the most useful thing to come out of Gopher+ is the ASK block. ASK blocks provide a way to send the user a set of questions and to have the client return the answers to the server. Following is an example of an item with an ASK block:

```
+INFO: 0Read_Me.ask<t>0/Test/Read_Me<t>fakegopher.magiclabs.com<t>70<t>?
+ADMIN:
 Admin: Michael Bentley 1+ (713) 555-1212 <michael@neosoft.com>
 Mod-Date: Mon Oct 24 10:54:30 1994 <19941024105430>
+VIEWS:
 Text/plain En_US: <1k>
+ASK:
 Note: The information that belongs in this area is currently
 Note: unavailable. In most cases, this is because we do not
 Note: have the information in a form suitable for inclusion
 Note: in Gopherspace.

 Note: If you would like to be notified when the information
 Note: in this area is made available, please answer the
 Note: following:

 Ask: Please enter your name:

 Ask: Please enter your (SMTP) e-mail address:

 Choose: Importance:  Just Curious  Important   Critical
+ABSTRACT:
 This is an ASK block that allows a Gopher user to request
 notification when an empty directory has information
 added to it.
```

Establishing a Gopher Server

To get your server established, you need to get your server set up and to let your potential users know that it is available. Setting up the server consists primarily of designing the directory structure that your gopher will use, populating that directory structure, and installing the gopher server software (not necessarily in that order). The easiest way to let users know about the availability of your gopher is to get linked into gopherspace. (A little cheerleading may help, too.)

Designing your server

Part of the beauty of running a gopher server is that adding, changing, and deleting information is easy. Changing your mind about which platform to use, though, is not as easy. Therefore, you should spend some time determining what software to use; that decision in turn determines which hardware and operating system you should use.

The Macintosh server gopher Surfer probably is the easiest server to get running. If you already use a Macintosh, this server may be the path of least resistance. What Gopher Surfer lacks in flexibility, it certainly makes up for in ease of use. The UNIX server gopherd is the most advanced of the servers from UMinn. Part of this flexibility is due to gopherd itself, and part is due to the nature of UNIX. When I inherited my gopher server, it was a Macintosh; a week or so later, it was a Macintosh running UNIX.

From this point forward, this chapter discusses running the gopher server in a UNIX environment. The scripts listed aren't very fancy and are intended to be easy to understand, as I am certain that some readers will want to do the same things without the benefit of a UNIX environment.

We are all familiar with structuring a directory tree so that information is where we can find it. Using the same rules to structure gopher items helps your users find the information on your server. The main reason for running a gopher server, of course, is to share some information. When you set up your server, though, you probably know only what you want to make available. By all means, make a place for everything that you eventually plan to have available.

It is no accident that gopherspace resembles a huge distributed file system. The gopher server uses a normal directory tree as its source for information to present to the user. One possibility is something like the diagram in Figure 29-1.

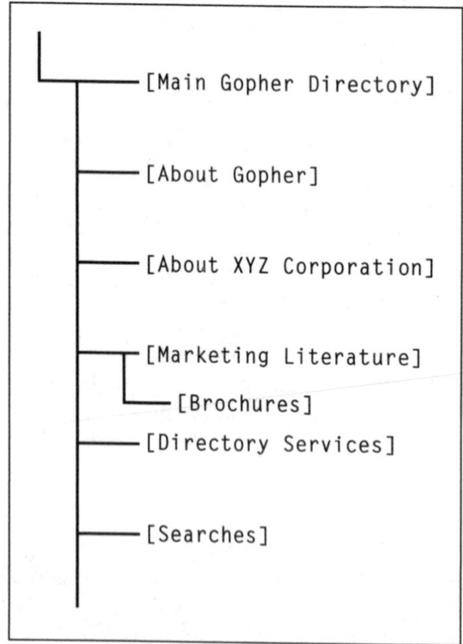

Figure 29-1: The gopher server's directory tree.

Many people run gopher servers in the same directory as their ftp servers. This probably is not the best idea, because it could introduce a security risk. Remember that you can use telnet to send selector strings to the server. If you allow a user to upload a file into the same directory tree that the gopher server is running on — as often is possible with ftp servers — the user might then be able to persuade the gopher server to run that file as a program. This arrangement could be bad news. So give the gopher server its own directory (/var/spool/Gopher may be a good choice).

The next step is to populate your directory tree. Users tend to get frustrated when they find nothing in a directory, so you are going to place a dummy file in each empty directory. This dummy file allows you to troll for users by giving them an opportunity to tell you what they are looking for. The user will find a file named Read_Me, which is an ASK block. After the user answers the questions in the ASK block, the server runs an associated script. In this case, the script sends e-mail to the server administrator and appends the user's answers to a log file. To use this script, edit the file Read_Me so that your e-mail address replaces YOUR_E-MAIL_ADDRESS in the line that begins with $Admin. Then copy the files Read_Me and Read_Me.ask into each directory in the directory tree that you chose for gopher. These files enable you to find out which empty directories your users most want you to fill.

The following code listing is the text of the Read_Me.ask file.

```
Note: The information that belongs in this area is currently
Note: unavailable. In most cases, this is because we do not
Note: have the information in a form suitable for inclusion
Note: in Gopherspace.

Note: If you would like to be notified when the information
Note: in this area is made available, please answer the
Note: following:

Ask: Please enter your name:

Ask: Please enter your (SMTP) e-mail address:

Choose: Importance:   Just Curious     Important       Critical
```

The following code lists the perl script Read_Me.

```
#!/usr/local/bin/perl

print STDOUT "Thank you for your interest! When this item is \n";
print STDOUT "made available, you should be notified by e-mail\n";
print STDOUT "within 24 hours.\n\n";
print STDOUT "        -=-=-=-=-=-\n\n";

($sec, $min, $hour, $mday, $mon, $year, $wday, $yday, $isdst) =
     localtime(time);
$i = 1;
$Label = "XXX";
$Admin = "YOUR_E-MAIL_ADDRESS";
```

```
open(MAILIT,"|/usr/bin/mailx -s \"Gopher - Info Request\" $Admin");
open(STOWIT, ">>/users/Gopher/Info.Request");
print MAILIT "Date: ", $mon + 1, ".", $mday, ".", $year, "\n";
print STDOUT "Date: ", $mon + 1, ".", $mday, ".", $year, "\n";
print STOWIT "Date: ", $mon + 1, ".", $mday, ".", $year, "\n";
print MAILIT "Time: ", $hour, ":", $min, ":", $sec, "\n\n";
print STDOUT "Time: ", $hour, ":", $min, ":", $sec, "\n\n";
print STOWIT "Time: ", $hour, ":", $min, ":", $sec, "\n\n";
while (<>) {
     if ($i == 1) {
             $Label = "Name: ";
     } elsif ($i == 2) {
             $Label = "SMTP: ";
     } elsif ($i == 3) {
             $Label = "Importance: ";
     } else {
             $Label = "";
     };
     print MAILIT $Label, $_;
     print STDOUT $Label, $_;
     print STOWIT $Label, $_;
     $i++;
};
print MAILIT "Path: ", `pwd`;
print STOWIT "Path: ", `pwd`;
print STOWIT "\n----------\n";
```

Installing the server

Before you can install your server, you have to get the necessary software. You can always get the most recent UNIX gopher server by ftp from `boombox.micro.umn.edu` in the /pub/gopher/UNIX directory. You'll find decent instructions in the README file in the distribution.

When you have gopherd installed, you should immediately edit GOPHERD.CONF (which probably is in /usr/local/etc). You absolutely must edit three things in this file:

- Edit the hostalias line to reflect the name of your gopher server. The best way to define a DNS alias is to use something like `gopher.yourname.com`. If you ever have to move your gopher server to a new machine, you won't want to make all your users change their configurations; you can change only the alias.
- Then edit the Admin and AdminE-mail lines. These edits are, unfortunately, overlooked far too often. If a problem occurs with your server, correct Admin information usually is the only way that anyone will know whom to contact.

I suggest creating a gopher user account. This fake user will be the owner of everything in the main gopher directory but will have no special privileges elsewhere on the system. Making the main gopher directory the home directory for this user will make maintenance a bit easier (fewer keystrokes). By all means, make the login shell for this user /bin/false, so that logins aren't possible, or give it a good password.

Getting your server into gopherspace

Many companies have a firewall at the point where their networks connect to the Internet. Depending on how these firewalls are set up, users outside the firewall may not be able to connect to a gopher server behind the firewall. Some companies set up a public server outside the firewall and private servers inside. If your gopher server falls into the private category, please do not register your server with UMinn. If your server is a public server, however, getting your server into gopherspace is easy. Using your favorite gopher client, connect to the server at `gopher.tc.umn.edu` and look for Gopher Server Registration under Other Gopher and Information Servers.

Unless your gopher server is entirely noncommercial in nature, if you use the Minnesota gopher server program, you may need to pay UMinn a licensing fee. To negotiate a license, contact Shih Pau Yen (`yen@boombox.micro.umn.edu`) at (612) 624-8865.

Running the Server

The process of actually running the server can logically be broken into two categories: content and server administration. The content administrator and the server administrator need not be the same person; in fact, in some situations it is better to have different people filling these roles.

Content administration

The content administrator is the person who is responsible for ensuring the accuracy and timeliness of the documents on the server. Users will continue to use your gopher server only as long as they view it as being a reliable source of information. The content administrator delivers the most recent version of each document to the server administrator.

When multiple sources for documents exist, some content-administration responsibilities probably are best delegated to the people who currently distribute paper versions of these documents. These people then would ensure that the most recent version of each document is delivered to the server administrator (or, if you insist, to the content administrator).

Identifying outdated files and correcting the situation can be real challenges. Slipping up on information that is updated periodically is easy. For example, my department has one report that is supposed to be updated every Monday. During weeks when we forget (we are, after all, only human) to perform the update until Tuesday, I look at the log file and see the electronic footprints of dozens of people who have come looking for the report. Users will forgive the occasional omission or mistake; if the situation becomes common, though, they will find a more reliable source for their information.

Server administration

The server administrator is responsible for actually keeping the server running. This task includes maintaining availability, making all changes to the information available on the server, and providing support to users.

Maintaining availability of the server usually isn't much of a problem; the trick is to find out when the server is down. Fortunately, a tool called Gopherbeeper (available via ftp at `boombox.micro.umn.edu` in /pub/gopher/UNIX/GopherTools) can tell you. The Gopherbeeper's main program, snooper, can automatically be run periodically by the cron daemon and will dial your beeper to notify you when a gopher server is down. Written in perl, snooper can be modified easily, in case you are lucky enough to have so far avoided carrying a beeper (;-). Generally, the server seems to die only when the machine on which it is running is shut down — on purpose, or due to a catastrophic event such as a power outage (unless, of course, the process is specifically killed). Usually, restarting the server is problematic only if all the necessary file systems are not mounted, but that problem is easy enough to diagnose and correct.

Making changes to the available information is a simple matter of updating a directory tree and editing some text files. Changing things in the directory tree changes what users see. By default, the user sees the names of the directories and files in much the same way that he would if he were using ftp. You certainly will want to at least provide a more descriptive name for each item.

Link files provide a way for you to change what the user sees. The gopher server tries to process all dotfiles (filenames beginning with "." are dotfiles) as link files, each of which can contain multiple links. Each link is defined by a group of six lines, which contain the name that you want to display for the user, the gopher type, the placement in the gopher menu, the host, the port, and the path of the item. Following is an example:

```
NAME=All the Gopher Servers in the World
TYPE=1+
NUMB=1
HOST=gopher.tc.umn.edu
PORT=70
PATH=1/Other Gopher and Information Servers/all
```

Turning off directory caching

When you know that you are going to make many changes, start gopherd with the -c option. By default, gopherd looks for files named .cache and .cache+ when it performs a directory lookup. If the file is less than Cachetime seconds old (the variable "Cachetime" is defined in gopherd.conf. The default value is 180), gopherd doesn't even look at what is really in the directory; it just sends the contents of the cache file.

Chances are that when you make a change, you want to check it out immediately by using a gopher client. If the cache files are present, though, the change won't show up for a while unless you delete the cache files. If, however, you started gopherd with the -c option, the cache files are never created.

The TYPE line defines the gopher type of the item — in this case, a Gopher+ directory. The NUMB line declares that this item should be displayed in the first line of the gopher menu. The HOST and PORT lines define the server on which this item is located. (Notice that you can place a plus sign in the HOST and PORT lines to specify the current server.) The PATH line specifies the selector string that the client must send to the server to retrieve the item. In the preceding example, the number 1 in the path refers to the gopher type. This is an example of a link to a different server, which is how gopher distributes itself. Following is an example of a link to a local item:

```
NAME=MIT Guide to Lockpicking
TYPE=0+
HOST=+
PORT=+
PATH=./lockpick.pdf
```

The first thing that you may have noticed is that the example has no NUMB line. All items in a directory in which NUMB is not defined are sorted and displayed in ASCII order, which differs slightly from normal alphabetical order in that all capital letters come before all lowercase letters. Also, the plus sign was used in the HOST and PORT lines to indicate that the item is on the server where you already are.

An example server might contain only a file named LOKPICK.PDF and a links file containing the following:

```
Type=1
Name=Mother of all Gophers (University of Minnesota)
Path=
Host=gopher.tc.umn.edu
Port=70

Type=1
Name=InterNIC: Internet Network Information Center
Path=
Host=rs.internic.net
Port=70

Numb=4
Name=MIT Lockpicking guide
Path=./lokguide
Type=0
Host=+
Port=+

Name=This Gopher Server only exists to display some concepts
Numb=1
Path=
Type=i
Host=+
Port=+
```

```
Name=for Internet Secrets
Numb=2
Path=
Type=i
Host=+
Port=+

Name=
Numb=3
Path=
Type=i
Host=+
Port=+
```

Connecting to the example server described above would produce the following client display on a curses (full screen dumb terminal) client:

```
          Internet Gopher Information Client v2.0.16

               Home Gopher server: dp

 -->   This Gopher Server only exists to display some concepts for Internet
Secrets

   4. MIT Lockpicking guide
   5. InterNIC: Internet Network Information Center/
   6. Mother of all Gophers (University of Minnesota)/



Press ? for Help, q to Quit                Page: 1/1
```

One of the most useful features of Gopher+ is its capability to present multiple views of a given document. Using this feature, you can provide documents that are not plain text. In fact, some items really can't be effectively used in plain-text format. When you have a document in multiple formats, you can make all the formats available to users, because gopherd maps file extensions to MIME content types. The mapping is defined in GOPHERD.CONF, which is a good place to find out which extension to use. If you want to use a type that is not already defined, you can add a new mapping. If you want to add Adobe's PDF format, for example, you could place the following line in GOPHERD.CONF:

```
viewext: .pdf 0 9 application/pdf
```

To make the multiple views available, save your files with the appropriate extension (from GOPHERD.CONF) but with the same base name.

The downside of this capability is that some browsers (such as Mosaic and older gopher clients) still are incapable of dealing with Gopher+ extensions. New gopher users may not be aware of the existence of the multiple-views issue. The easiest solution that I have found is to provide a plain-text view that informs the user that the server supports Gopher+ and that a plain-text version of the file does not exist.

The NoText script simplifies this process considerably, as the following listing shows.

```
#!/bin/sh
#
# NoText
# ======
# Synopsis: NoText filename
#
# Where filename is the name of the file that does not have
# a Text/plain view. Set the environment variable CHROOTP
# to 1 if you want to use a symbolic link, or to 2 if you
# do not want to use a symbolic link. If CHROOTP is not
# set, an attempt is made to use the symbolic link if your
# gopherd is not running chroot(). Your mileage may vary.
#

NOTEXT=/usr/local/lib/NOTEXT  # This file must exist
SYMLINK=UNCONFIGURED

if [ "$CHROOTP" = "1" ]; then; SYMLINK=1
else
  NUMGOPH='ps -eaf | grep gopherd | grep -v grep | wc -l'
  if [ "$NUMGOPH" -lt 1 ]; then
   if [ "$CHROOTP" != "2" ]; then
     echo Your gopherserver is not running... try setting \$CHROOTP
   else; SYMLINK=0
   fi
  else
   if [ "$NUMGOPH" -gt 1 ]; then
     if [ "$CHROOTP" != "2" ]; then
      echo There are multiple instances of gopherd. Set \$CHROOTP
      echo to 1 if you want symlinks. $1 is \*NOT\* a symbolic link.
     fi
     SYMLINK=0
   else
     if [ "$CHROOTP" != "2" ]; then
      XXX='ps -eaf | grep gopherd | grep -v grep | grep -- -c'
      if [ "$XXX" != "" ]; then; SYMLINK=1
      else; SYMLINK=0
      fi
     else; SYMLINK=0
     fi
   fi
  fi
fi

if [ "$SYMLINK" = "0" ]; then
  /bin/cat >$1 <<EOM
```

```
This item is not available as plain text, because it relies on
multiple fonts and graphics. Since this is a Gopher+ server, we
have alternate views available.

To learn how to get an alternate view using HGopher, see "Gopher
Plus Usage" and "Setting preferred Views" in the HGopher help
system.

To get alternate views using Turbo Gopher, close this window and
choose "Gopher" from the main menu - then choose "Get Alternate
Views...".

Common alternate views:

application/pdf      Adobe Acrobat (download from our ftp site)
application/rtf      Microsoft Word
EOM
fi

if [ "$SYMLINK" = "1" ]; then; ln -s $NOTEXT $1; fi
```

Finally, whenever you add or change an item, testing the change on multiple client platforms is well worth your time. Don't assume that all your potential users are using a particular platform. I usually test each addition and change on Macintosh, Windows, and the UNIX curses client.

Supporting Your Users

Generally, the only support necessary involves letting people know when an item that they want has been made available and responding to suggestions. By using the READ_ME.ASK block, you have built a list of people to contact when you populate a directory with real files. The best procedure is to personally send e-mail to these people, rather than use a program to automate the task — partly to add a personal touch, but mostly to compensate for crackers (the "bad guys" who are far too often mistakenly called "hackers").

Remember that the Read_Me script simply dumped into a log file whatever the user typed in the ASK form. You probably will want to look at what was left in the e-mail field to see whether a potential problem is brewing; you should, of course, attempt to send e-mail only to valid addresses. Setting up a suggestion box can be a useful way to get feedback from users. The following listing shows a simple example:

```
Note: We welcome your comments and suggestions on the quality
Note: and usefulness of our information servers. Your
Note: input is important.

Ask: Please enter your name:

Ask: Please enter your (SMTP) e-mail address:
```

```
Choose: Machine:    PC    Macintosh    Vax    Sun    Other
Choose: Application:  Gopher  Turbo-Gopher  Hgopher  Lynx  Mosaic


Note: Please enter any comments and suggestions:
AskL:
```

The final example shows a listing of perl script Suggest.

```
#!/usr/local/bin/perl

print STDOUT "Thank you for your feedback! The data you entered\n";
print STDOUT "is being sent to the server administrator by e-mail.\n\n";
print STDOUT "Here is the information being sent to: \n";
print STDOUT "YOUR_E-MAIL_ADDRESS\n\n";

($sec, $min, $hour, $mday, $mon, $year, $wday, $yday, $isdst) =
     localtime(time);
$i = 1;
$Label = "XXX";
$Admin = "YOUR_E-MAIL_ADDRESS";
open(MAILIT, "|/usr/bin/mailx -s \"Gopher Comment\/Suggestion\" $Admin");
print MAILIT "The following comment or suggestion was received by\n";
print MAILIT "YOUR_SERVER_NAME. Please send any response\n";
print MAILIT "to the SMTP e-mail address below:\n\n";
print MAILIT "Date: ", $mon + 1, ".", $mday, ".", $year, "\n";
print STDOUT "Date: ", $mon + 1, ".", $mday, ".", $year, "\n";
print MAILIT "Time: ", $hour, ":", $min, ":", $sec, "\n\n";
print STDOUT "Time: ", $hour, ":", $min, ":", $sec, "\n\n";
while (<>) {
     if ($i == 1) {
          $Label = "Name: ";
     } elsif ($i == 2) {
          $Label = "SMTP: ";
     } elsif ($i == 3) {
          $Label = "Machine: ";
     } elsif ($i == 4) {
          $Label = "Application: ";
     } elsif ($i == 5) {
          $Label = "Comment: ";
     } else {
          $Label = "";
     };
     print MAILIT $Label, $_;
     print STDOUT $Label, $_;
     $i++;
};
```

Michael Bentley is a Network Administrator for Schlumberger Oilfield Marketing Services. He is a CNE with a background in Netware, UNIX system administration, and programming.

Chapter 30

Running a WWW Server on Windows

by Randolph Chung <randolph@air.org>

By now you have probably traveled through the World Wide Web (also called WWW or the Web) and discovered all the wonderful things that are available. Perhaps you are asking yourself, "What do I have to offer? What interesting things can I put on the Web?" Or perhaps you are working for an organization that wants to put its mark on the Internet by providing some sort of service through the WWW. If so, this chapter is for you.

Introduction

Not long ago, I began setting up my own Web server. I wanted to put up some information for some friends, and I wanted to experiment with what I could do on the Internet. At first, I thought that the only way to go was UNIX, which is pretty tricky. To set up a workable UNIX server (I was using Linux, one of the freely available versions of UNIX), I needed someone knowledgeable in UNIX to look over the daily operation of the machine, set up various accounts, check for security loopholes, and so on. Only then could I think about getting a piece of WWW server software (commonly called *HTTPD,* for *H*yper*t*ext *T*ransfer *P*rotocol *D*aemon), compile it for my particular configuration and platform, and create Web documents by using a text editor with such weird and funny tags as `<HR>`, `<UL>`.

But then I realized that I had to use my computer for other tasks that simply cannot be done in UNIX, such as running Word for Windows. Moreover, I found the UNIX environment confusing and difficult to control. I looked around the Internet and found a Windows version of HTTPD (WinHTTPD). Windows is definitely a more intuitive operating system than UNIX: the software does not require compiling; you can concurrently work on your favorite Windows application while your server is operating; and, best of all, it's easy to set up and get running.

Hardware requirements

The items you need to run a Windows HTTP server (NCSA WinHTTPD Server V1.4) are:

- A typical Windows computer (486/33 or higher recommended for decent performance)
- 8 MB of RAM (you can make do with 4 MB, but you probably should have at least 8 MB)
- A network connection (Ethernet or SLIP/PPP)

Software requirements

All you need to run a Windows HTTP server are two pieces of software:

- A WinSock 1.1 (or later) -compliant TCP/IP stack
- WinHTTPD software (the newest version at the time this book was written was v1.4)

That's it! The WinHTTPD software is available from a variety of anonymous FTP sites, such as these two:

```
ftp.ncsa.uiuc.edu:/Web/ncsa_httpd/contrib/winhttpd/whttpd14.zip
```

```
ftp.alisa.com:/pub/win-httpd/whttpd14.zip
```

For a discussion of WinSock, see the "WinSock" sidebar.

You probably will also want to get the following items:

- A WWW browser if you do not already have one, such as Mosaic for Windows, WinWeb, Cello, or Netscape
- HTML authoring tools, such as HoTMetaL or Microsoft Word for Windows templates
- Some sort of graphical editor if you plan to put graphics in your HTML documents. Windows Paintbrush will do (yes, it's good for *something*), or you might want to invest in a commercial graphical package or one of those shareware graphics-rendering packages, such as PaintShop Pro.

See the "References" section near the end of this chapter for pointers about where to get these pieces of software.

WinSock

WinSock, or Windows Sockets, is a standard interface (Application Programming Interface, or API). It was developed by a group of Windows software vendors to enable multiple Windows applications to use the TCP/IP stack and, therefore, connect to the Internet concurrently. That is, while you are ftping using a Windows ftp program, you can also be telnetting to some site and running WinHTTPD and Mosaic at the same time on the same Internet connection.

WinSock is a great piece of software. Although it is supposed to be a standard, the fact is that many different implementations of the Windows Sockets interface are floating around, and each one behaves slightly differently. I personally have not run into many problems with my particular configuration, but other WinHTTPD administrators have. By no means are these problems the fault of WinHTTPD; they only reflect how some implementations of Windows Sockets are *broken* (incompletely implemented).

One of the most often used WinSock implementations is Trumpet WinSock, a good shareware product written by Peter Tattam. It performs well with most WinSock applications, but sometimes not very well with server applications. Specifically, although WinHTTPD supports *multithreading* (a capability that enables several users to access your server at the same time), Trumpet WinSock 1.0A performs rather poorly under these circumstances. The newest version, 2.0B, fixes this problem.

Several commercial implementations of WinSock are also available, such as Netmanage's Internet Chameleon (available in the *Internet For Dummies Starter Kit,* published by IDG Books). Each implementation has its advantages and disadvantages, and prices vary.

Configuring Your Windows Web Server

If you have correctly set up WinSock and have downloaded the WinHTTPD package, you are pretty much set to begin exploring. The documentation included with the WinHTTPD package contains detailed instructions about how to set up the server, but here are a few important steps:

- Create a directory on your hard drive (preferably C:\HTTPD) and unzip the archive into that directory. Be sure to preserve the directory structure in the archive by specifying the `-d` parameter when you're using PKUNZIP to unzip:

```
C:\HTTPD> pkunzip -d whttpd14.zip
```

- At the DOS prompt, set the TZ environment variable to the correct time zone (you should also add this line to your AUTOEXEC.BAT file so that the time zone is set every time you reboot):

```
C:\HTTPD> SET TZ=EST4EDT
```

or

```
C:\HTTPD> SET TZ=MST7
```

- The first three letters in the preceding `SET` statements denote the time zone;

the next number denotes the offset in hours from Greenwich Mean Time (GMT); and the last three letters denote daylight saving time, if appropriate.

WinHTTPD makes use of the DOS environment when you're running scripts to pass parameters (see "Passing Parameters to CGI applications," later in this chapter), so make sure that you have plenty of environment space. Edit your SYSTEM.INI file, and add the following line to the [NonWindowsApp] section:

```
CommandEnvSize=8192
```

When you finish with all that, you are ready to start your server. Start up Windows, load WinSock, and create a new icon for the WinHTTPD executable in Program Manager. If you followed the preceding instructions and installed the archive in C:\HTTPD, you can start your server! (It initializes and minimizes as an icon on the bottom of your screen.)

Start your favorite browser and try out your new WWW server. (The URL is `http://foo.bar.com/`, where `foo.bar.com` is your domain name.) If you installed it somewhere else, you have to edit the configuration files in the CONF subdirectory of the directory in which you installed the package to reflect your directory structure.

The URL mentioned in the preceding paragraph points you to the documentation included with WinHTTPD. It provides step-by-step instructions on how to change various settings, if they ever become necessary. My experience is that *minimal* alterations are necessary for normal use.

Tips for Setting Up Your Own Server

I believe that the best way to learn to run your server is, well, to run it and see what happens. The documentation included with WinHTTPD is clear and straightforward, and it does a good job of pointing out potential problems and things to think about when you configure your server. One of the most frequent problems is having a faulty WinSock stack (see the "WinSock" sidebar, earlier in this chapter). If you find that your server is acting strangely or responding very slowly, for example, try adding the `-n` parameter to your command line. This parameter disables multithreading and may prevent some of your problems.

Because the Windows version of HTTPD has not been released long, relatively few pieces of software are out there to support it. As more people move into the Windows environment, however, you probably will see more packages supporting WinHTTPD. Some of the applications available to help you maintain your system are

- **HoTMetaL** is a relatively easy-to-use shareware HTML editor that requires a great deal of memory (`ftp.ncsa.uiuc.edu /Web/html/hotmetal/Windows/hotmetal.exe`).

- **Word templates** let you compose your documents by using Word for Windows and save your documents in HTML format (`ftp.cuhk.hk /pub/www/windows/util/cu_html.zip`).
- **WebStats** help you generate HTML documents with statistics about usage on your Web server (`ftp.alisa.com /pub/win-httpd/experimental/vbstat03.zip`).
- **PolyForm** enables you to process forms on your server so that you don't have to write your own scripts (`ftp.best.com /pub/cbntmkr/polyform.zip`). CGI scripts are explained later in this chapter.

A Guide to Good HTML Authoring

As a Web provider, you are responsible for what appears on your server. Ultimately, after you set up your server, you want people to visit it, so you have to make sure that it works and that it works well. Here are several points to remember:

- **Adhere to HTML guidelines!** Certain elements must exist on every HTML page. Although some browsers may accept "incomplete" HTML documents, you cannot expect every one to accept them. Make sure, therefore, that you provide complete HTML documents (with proper ending tags, for example).
- **Make your page user-friendly.** When you design HTML andocument, it is always important to remember that the person reading it is a human being. Make things as intuitive and as clear as you can.
- **Do *not* overdo it!** As mentioned, authoring HTML documents is fun, partly because of all the things you can add to your pages (graphics, type styles, tons of links, and so on). When you do that, however, keep in mind that large graphics may take a long time to get through to other sites. Having many different type styles and links on the same page is distracting and annoying, not to mention unreadable. Usually, simple, short documents have a much stronger effect than long, overly fancy ones. You can, and often should, break a long page into several pages connected by HTML links.
- **Test your pages, if possible, on several different platforms with different browsers.** Because each browser and platform renders hypertext elements a little differently, you should make sure that your documents look OK on all browsers.

Advanced Topics

After you have your WWW server running, you can spiff up your Web pages in several ways.

Creating imagemaps

Imagemaps are graphical links. Traditional HTML links are done through text by using syntax such as the following:

```
<A HREF="http://somewhere.com/somedoc.html">Boo!</A>
```

Granted, this syntax is simple and does the job, but the characters used in this line are sometimes not pleasing to the eye. Imagemaps allow the user to click an image and go to a specific link.

On the White House WWW server at `www.whitehouse.gov`, for example, you are presented with an imagemap on the initial page. Clicking the picture of the podium labeled "President's Welcome Message" brings up an audio clip of the president welcoming you to the White House Web server.

Imagemaps are not difficult to set up after you understand how they work. Because WinHTTPD comes with a program to handle imagemap requests, all you have to do is specify a few parameters to define regions in your graphic and then set up an HTML document that points to that imagemap.

Here's an example from my server. Suppose that I have a graphic like the one shown in Figure 30-1.

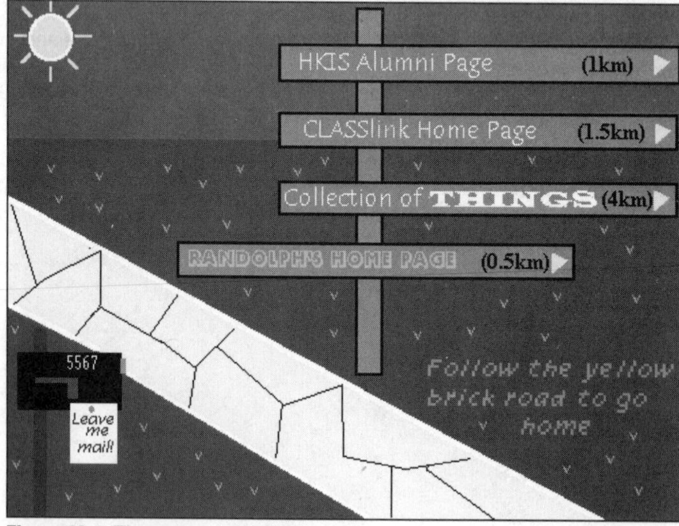

Figure 30-1: The yellow brick HTTP road.

The signposts are links to various places on my server. To set up this graphic as an imagemap, I first have to use a graphics program to locate the coordinates of various points that define clickable regions on my image. You can define regions in imagemaps by using several simple geometric shapes, such as rectangles, polygons, and circles. Then I create a file called MAINPAGE.MAP (you can call it anything you want) and place it in C:\HTTPD\CONF\MAPS with these definitions:

```
# Sample imagemap definition file (mainpage.map)
# The format of this file is:
# keyword link parameters

# First I define a default. This is the link that is selected
# if the user clicks on a place that isn't defined below.
default http://foo.bar.com/main.htm

# This is the first plank on my signpost. I use the rect keyword
# to define a rectangular "hotspot" in my image that corresponds
# to the plank by specifying the X,Y coordinates of the upper left
# and lower right corners
rect http://foo.bar.com/hkisalum.htm 203,30 498,57

# These are similar definitions for the remainder of the planks
rect http://foo.bar.com/classlnk.htm 203,79 498,104
rect http://foo.bar.com/things.htm 202,128, 497,152
rect http://foo.bar.com/randolph.htm 127,172 420,197

# The last one defines the "road" in the middle. This is a polygon
# defined with the poly keyword. poly can take up to 100 X,Y
# coordinate pairs
poly http://foo.bar.com/users/userslst.htm 0,139 442,369 270,369 89,265 29,25
269,251 0,218
```

Next, I tell my server where I put this definition by adding a line to C:\HTTPD\CONF\IMAGEMAP.CNF:

```
# sample imagemap.cnf
# Format of this file is:
# <name of configuration> : <path to definition file>

mainpage : c:\httpd\conf\maps\mainpage.map
```

This line defines a configuration called `mainpage` with the links defined earlier. The last step is referencing this image in your HTML documents so that others can use it. This process is also relatively easy. To refer to the preceding imagemap, I put something like this in my document:

```
<A HREF="http://foo.bar.com/cgi-win/imagemap.exe/mainpage"><IMG SRC="sign.gif"
ISMAP></A>
```

To reference your own imagemap, just substitute `mainpage` in the link with the name you defined in IMAGEMAP.CNF earlier and change the name of the graphic in `<IMG SRC="sign.gif" ISMAP>` to refer to your own graphics file. In the

`<A HREF>` tag, `imagemap.exe` is a program that comes with WinHTTPD to handle imagemaps. The name following the slash after `imagemap.exe` is the name of the configuration defined earlier. The `ISMAP` keyword in the `<IMG SRC>` tag specifies that this image is an imagemap: the client will inform the server where the user clicks on the image.

Writing CGI Scripts to Do Tasks on Demand

After setting up your Web server, you might want to experiment with the *experimental* CGI Windows interface. *CGI* (Common Gateway Interface) allows for interaction between the user and the server to produce documents on the fly or to accomplish various tasks.

In essence, CGI scripts are programs that do something on the server side and return a result. In the UNIX environment, these "scripts" are usually "shell scripts" (analogous to batch files under DOS), Perl scripts, or C programs. Under WinHTTPD, you can run any Windows or DOS program by referencing it in a URL. When a client requests the following, for example,

```
http://foo.bar.com/cgi-win/cgiscrpt.exe
```

the server executes the Windows program CGISCRPT.EXE in your CGI-WIN subdirectory under where you installed WinHTTPD (C:\HTTPD\CGI-WIN, for example).

Setting up CGI applications

You control the operation of CGI scripts through configuration files. The configuration file SRM.CNF in the CONF subdirectory enables you to change settings related to the operation of CGI scripts. The default is to map all URLs that reference `http://foo.bar.com/cgi-win/program.exe` to run the Windows application program.exe in C:\HTTPD\CGI-WIN, and references to `http://foo.bar.com/cgi-bin/program.ext` and `http://foo.bar.com/cgi-dos/program.ext` to run the DOS application program.ext in C:\HTTPD\CGI-DOS. DOS applications may be BAT, COM, or EXE files, and they are run with the default HSCRIPT.PIF program information file in C:\HTTPD. A sample SRM.CNF file follows:

```
# Extract from SRM.CNF, where the paths to the scripts are defined
# If you want to put your scripts somewhere else, you will have
# to change it here.

# ScriptAlias: This controls which directories contain DOS server
#              scripts.
#
# Format: ScriptAlias fakename realname
#
ScriptAlias /cgi-dos/ c:/httpd/cgi-dos/
ScriptAlias /cgi-bin/ c:/httpd/cgi-dos/
```

```
# WinScriptAlias: This controls which directories contain Windows
#                 server scripts.
#
# Format: WinScriptAlias fakename realname
#
WinScriptAlias /cgi-win/ c:/httpd/cgi-win/
```

Passing parameters to CGI applications

The experimental CGI Windows interface uses an INI file approach for passing data to the CGI program. When a CGI script is executed, WinHTTPD automatically generates in your temporary directory (pointed to by the TEMP environment variable) an INI file containing various types of information about the HTTP session. A typical INI file is shown here:

```
[CGI]
Request Protocol=HTTP/1.0
Request Method=POST
Executable Path=/cgi-win/submit.exe
Server Software=NCSA/V1.3 (MSWindows)
Server Name=somehost.someplace.com
Server Port=80
Server Admin=webmaster@someplace.com
CGI Version=CGI/1.1 WIN (experimental)
Remote Host=foo.bar.com
Remote Address=1.2.3.4
Content Type=application/x-www-form-urlencoded
Content Length=156

[System]
Debug Mode=No
Output File=C:\TEMP\HS37CA97.OUT
Content File=C:\TEMP\HS37CA97.INP

[Form Literal]
Name=Randolph Chung
Year=1994
University=The Electronic University
email=randolph@electronic.edu
Address=1234 Somewhere Ave.
city=Some City
State=NW
Zip=12345
Country=U.S.A.

[Accept]
audio/basic=Yes
application/zip=Yes
audio/x-midi=Yes
```

```
application/x-rtf=Yes
video/msvideo=Yes
video/mpeg=Yes
image/jpeg=Yes
image/gif=Yes
application/postscript=Yes
audio/wav=Yes
text/plain=Yes
text/html=Yes
audio/x-aiff=Yes
*/*=Yes

[Extra Headers]
User-Agent=NCSA Mosaic(tm) for Windows/Version 2.0 (ALPHA 7)
```

As you can see, the INI file contains detailed information about the session. In this case, the INI file was generated from the submission of an HTML form, and the various fields in the form had been decoded to form separate fields near the bottom of the INI file. You can write your own Windows application to process this information (or use Visual Basic for Windows with the supplied routines — refer to "Looking at a sample CGI application," next) and return some other information to the user. The contents of the file indicated by the line `Output File` in the [System] section is sent to the user after the execution of the program is completed.

WinHTTPD also comes with code to help you build your own CGI scripts. A set of Visual Basic routines is provided for you to work with your server through CGI. The most frequent use of CGI is in the handling of *forms,* but it can also be used to create images, perform computations, construct documents on the fly, and so on. All you need are Visual Basic installed on your system (the Standard Edition will work, but you may need the Professional Edition for some more sophisticated tasks), some basic programming skills, and a great deal of imagination, and you are ready to put together your own program.

Looking at a sample CGI application

The following code is a sample piece of code for processing forms:

```
' Sample VB code for handling forms
' Written by Randolph Chung - October 8, 1994
' May be freely used and modified. Use at your own risk.
' For more information about CGI code, refer to documentation
' included with WinHTTPD
' To write CGI programs under VB, include the CGI.BAS file
' included with WinHTTPD (under the \CGI-SRC subdirectory) in your
' project and set Options/Project.../Start Up Form to "Sub Main"

' Option Explicit means you have to define all your variables
' before you use them. It's good programming practice to do it..
Option Explicit
```

```
' Make sure your code contains a Sub CGI_Main. This will be called
'   when the script is run.
Sub CGIMain ()
  Dim Index As Integer
  Dim BlankEmail As Integer  ' Boolean to check if field is empty
  Dim DatafileName As String

  ' Save all data to this (text) data file
  DataFileName = "c:\httpd\emailsub.txt"

  ' The Send subroutine writes data to the returned file
  ' Make sure to include the appropriate MIME headers and HTML
  '   elements so the client knows what is being returned
  Send ("Content-type: text/html") ' return a HTML document
  Send ("")
  Send ("<HTML><HEAD><TITLE>Thank you</TITLE></HEAD>")
  Send ("<BODY><H1>EMail Submission</H1>")
  Send ("<HR>")

  BlankEmail = False

  ' Checks if the field that is required is blank
  ' CGINumFormTuples includes the number of elements in form
  ' CGIFormTuples is an array with a Key field and a Value field
  '     The Key corresponds to the ID element in your form definition
  '     The Value corresponds to the user's input

  For Index = 0 To CGINumFormTuples
    If (CGIFormTuples(Index).Key = "email") And
       (CGIFormTuples(Index).Value = "") Then BlankEmail = True
  Next Index

  If Not BlankEmail Then
    Send ("<P>Your email address submission has been processed.")
    Send ("Thank you!</P>")
    ' Write data to a text file
    Open DataFileName$ For Append As #50
    Print #50, "Email submission received on "; Date$; " at "; Time$
    For Index = 0 To CGINumFormTuples
       Print #50, CGIFormTuples(Index).Key; ": ";
       Print #50, CGIFormTuples(Index).Value
    Next Index
    Close #50
  Else
    Send ("<P>Your email submission was not saved because the")
    Send ("email field is blank.</P>")
  End If

  ' Include a link so user can return to home page
  ' double quotes ("") are necessary to send an actual quote
```

```
    '   character
    Send ("<P></P>")
    Send ("<A HREF=""http://foo.bar.com/index.htm""><IMG
          SRC=""back.gif"">Return to Home Page</A>")
    Send ("")
    Send ("</BODY></HTML>")
    ' Make sure we use End Sub instead of just End, since CGI.BAS
    '    still has to clean up
End Sub
```

I use this script on my server to handle a particular form that users can fill in. This form contains information about the person's name, e-mail address, university, year of graduation, and so on. As you can see from the preceding INI file, the server does a good job of decoding fields for you already, so you don't have to bother with the details of converting the user's input into a form your program can use. This code fragment takes the information and checks to see whether an e-mail address was specified. If an e-mail address is found, all the information is saved to a data file and an acknowledgment is sent back to the user; otherwise, the user is alerted that the e-mail field in the form was blank.

In this case, the result generated by the script is just a simple confirmation message that says,depending on the circumstances, "Your email address submission has been processed. Thank you!" or "Your email submission was not saved because the email field is blank." You can return much longer and elaborate documents, including documents generated on the fly by searching databases, forms with questions based on previous responses, and so on.

You must realize, however, that a fundamental difference exists between a system such as the Web and more interactive systems, such as a bulletin-board system. The Web is primarily a document-retrieval system. Interactions between the server and the client using scripts, therefore, are usually few and short (though each script may be complicated) rather than continuous. Scripts cannot act interactively with the user — they can only process data provided by the client at one time. Although it is *possible* to write more interactive interfaces, such as games, for the Web, these interfaces require special techniques.

Writing scripts that ask for more

Suppose that you decide to write a game of tic-tac-toe. You write a script that interprets the way the user responds and, accordingly, have the computer play a move and prompt the user for more information. This process cannot be performed by using simple scripts. The reason is that every time a script is run, the server generates a new INI file with data from only the current request. Unless data is somehow maintained across sessions, the server has no way to keep track of which moves have been played and what the current status of the game is.

There are several ways to overcome this problem. Different programmers prefer different techniques, and some work better than others do. A rather simple and effective method is to include hidden elements on forms generated on the fly that contain data from previous sessions. If you have a field in a form whose type is hidden (for example, `<INPUT name="data" type="hidden" value="Some value">`), the field is not shown to the user; when the form is submitted to be processed by a CGI script, however, the field still appears normally and can be processed accordingly by the script. In this case, you may decide to have in a form a hidden field that contains a string of nine characters representing the nine spaces on the tic-tac-toe grid. Initially, the string consists of nine dashes. Subsequently, as each move is played, the string is changed with *o*s and *x*s replaced in the corresponding location to represent the current status of the game.

What else can I do with CGI scripts?

I can show only short examples here. By no means are these the only things you can do by using CGI. Here are some of the more interesting things that have been done by others using CGI on the Web:

The Blue Dog: A user enters two numbers and an operator (+, -, *, or /), and the "Blue Dog" "barks" back the result based on the calculation (Carnegie-Mellon's "The Void").

URL: `http://hp8.ini.cmu.edu:5550/bdf.html`

Lite Brite: A user can design her own images by using colored balls (CalTech's "The Asylum").

URL: `http://www.galcit.caltech.edu/~ta/cgi-bin/asylhome-ta`

Lycos Web Searching Engine: A user enters something to look for on the Internet, and the CGI script searches its database for the relevant information.

URL: `http://lycos.cs.cmu.edu/`

XEROX PARC Map server: Presented with a map of the globe, a user can click on a place to get a more detailed map of that area.

URL: `http://pubweb.parc.xerox.com/map`

Frog Dissection Kit: A user can dissect a frog by specifying which part he wants to dissect and then can see the resulting frog (dead, I'm afraid) at various angles (Lawrence Berkeley Laboratory).

URL: `http://george.lbl.gov/TG.hm.pg.docs/dissect/info.html`

As you can see, you can really do almost *anything* if you have the imagination and the patience to write the relevant CGI scripts.

References

Use the following information to find more information on ftp sites for software, the WWW home page for WinHTTPD, and the WWW page for HTML documentation tips.

FTP sites for various pieces of software

FTP sites for browsers:

- Mosaic for Windows:

  `ftp.ncsa.uiuc.edu  /Mosaic/Windows/wmos20a9.zip`

- WinWeb:

  `ftp.einet.net /einet/pc/winweb/winweb.zip`

- Cello:

  `ftp.law.cornell.edu /pub/LII/Cello/cello.zip`

- Netscape:

  `ftp.mcom.com /pub/netscape/windows/nscape09.zip`

FTP sites for WWW authoring tools:

- HoTMetaL:

  `ftp.ncsa.uiuc.edu /Web/html/hotmetal/Windows/hotmetal.exe`

- Word templates:

  `ftp.cuhk.hk /pub/www/windows/util/cu_html.zip`

  `ftp.einet.net /pc/ANT_HTML.ZIP`

FTP sites for Trumpet WinSock:

```
ftp.utas.edu.au /pc/trumpet/winsock/twsk10a.zip
ftp.utas.edu.au /pc/trumpet/winsock/twsk20b.zip
```

WWW home page for WinHTTPD

```
http://www.alisa.com/win-httpd/
```

WWW page with tips for writing HTML documents

```
http://info.cern.ch/hypertext/WWW/Provider/Style/
Overview.html
```

The first thing you should make sure that you do when you want help is to *read the documentation thoroughly!* Also, try these two newsgroups:

- comp.infosystems.www.provider
- alt.winsock

The Future of WWW

Thanks to faster computers, faster links, and more widespread use of the World Wide Web, the world is seeing many more innovative uses for HTTP technology. And with CGI, there are many new possibilities for what you can do with your server.

A generalization of hypertext is *hypermedia* — where conventional text data is integrated with visual images, sounds, and movies to make the World Wide Web more interesting and useful. Software developers are taking advantage of hypermedia to develop more intuitive interfaces for the World Wide Web.

A recent development is *WOO* (*or w*ebbed M*OO,* in which *MOO* is *M*UD *o*bject *o*riented and *MUD* is *m*ulti*u*ser *d*ungeon). WOO is a virtual world on the Internet in which users can explore in a psuedo-virtual-reality manner. Images and descriptions of where you are and what is there all combine to provide a much different experience than your traditional World Wide Web experience.

A similar system is WebWorld (http://sailfish.peregrine.com/ww/welcome.html), in which every Web user helps build a cyberworld by "constructing" buildings, houses, and parks. Similar to the game SimEarth, WebWorld is on a much larger scale.

Of course, all this development places more pressure on the people administering a WWW server to think of innovative ways to make their server stand out among the other thousands of Web sites. WinHTTPD (and other Windows HTML aids) can provide a tool for you to design such creative WWW interfaces. What *you,* the (future?) WWW server administrator have to do is be imaginative and take advantage of what is there.

Currently a student at Cornell University, Randolph Chung is most interested in how computers relate to and interact with people. He has served as system operator for a multinode school bulletin-board system based in Hong Kong, where he was born. Currently, he runs a World Wide Web server at school.

Part V
The Best Internet Applications

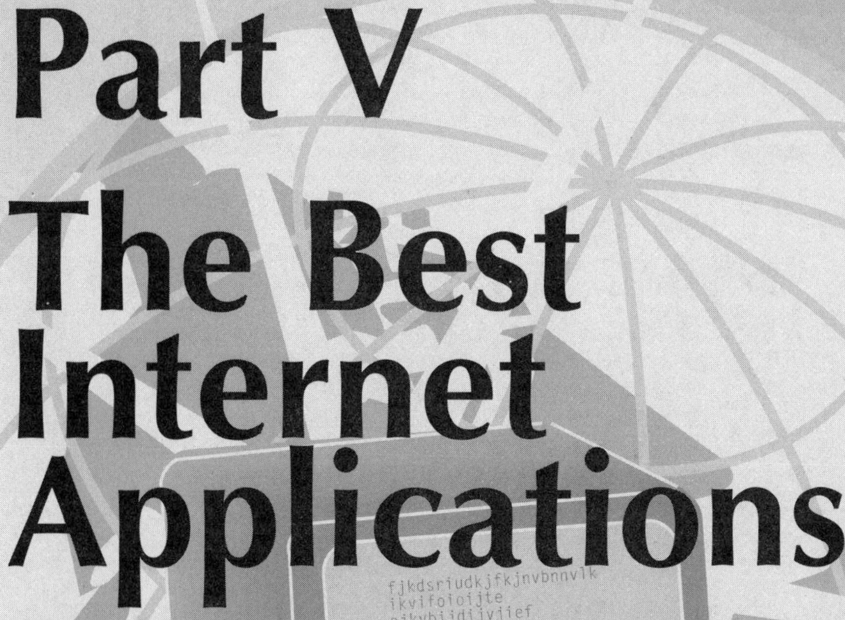

In This Part

Chapter 31 The Complete WinSock Applications Roundup

Chapter 32 Macintosh Internet Applications

Chapter 33 Installing the Shareware Disks

Chapter 31

The Complete WinSock Applications Roundup

by Ed Sinkovits <edsink@mail.mbnet.mb.ca>

WinSock (*Win*dows *sock*ets) is an official Internet standard for Windows software.

This chapter is a detailed listing of the best available WinSock-based freeware and shareware packages for communicating through a modem to the Internet. Although this listing is oriented toward individual home-based modem users, most of these packages are universal and equally suitable for use in a network environment. I have indicated any prime or preferred locations where the latest version of each package usually is available. Alternatively, by using the filenames and associated data supplied in this chapter, you can readily find most of these packages elsewhere on the Internet with search-and-retrieval tools such as Archie, ftp, Gopher, and WAIS.

The best of these programs are now at least equivalent to — and even superior to — the corresponding modules in commercial packages, although not many of these packages are in the marketplace to begin with. This situation will dramatically change during the next year or two, but for now, and in particular for home-based users, freeware or shareware usually is the best choice. You can try different packages until you find the ones that have the features you want and that you are comfortable with. When registration is required, the fees usually are quite reasonable and can bring extra benefits in additional documentation, technical support, and upgrades with additional or uncrippled features.

Using WinSock packages with a modem requires, at minimum, the items in this list:

- Windows 3.1.
- A SLIP or PPP account with an Internet provider.
- A special communications package that is capable of accessing the SLIP/PPP account through a modem. Unfortunately, much of the commercial and shareware communications software that commonly is used to access other on-line services does not have WinSock capability and, therefore, cannot be used for the Internet. The best package currently available that does work is Peter Tattam's shareware package called Trumpet WinSock. See "Trumpet WinSock" at the end of this chapter for information about this popular and widely used program.

I have tried to keep the terminology as simple as possible. "Additional Information" at the end of this chapter includes a series of appendixes that contain references to supplemental reading material. For a better understanding of the Internet terms *WinSock* and *SLIP,* reading the suggested material is a beginning.

With the increased availability of WinSock applications for Windows NT, I have included a few 32-bit applications in this chapter. Some of these applications can be run only under Windows NT, but a few can be used with Windows 3.1 when Microsoft's Win32s extension is installed. The Win32s extension gives Windows 3.1 limited 32-bit capability, enabling it to run 32-bit programs written for this extension. The most popular and best known program of this type is NCSA Mosaic, the World Wide Web (WWW) browser. More information about Win32s and Mosaic appears in the appropriate sections of this chapter.

The standard disclaimer applies: You use these programs at your own risk. Many of the packages are still being developed by their authors. Bugs are common, unfortunately, and updates to fix the bugs and add new features are frequent.

You can find updates of the file (in Microsoft Word for Windows format) from which this chapter was adapted in the WINTER*XX*.ZIP file (in which *XX* is the version number) at the following location:

```
ftp.cica.indiana.edu: /pub/pc/win3/winsock
```

Bugs

Bugs are almost inevitable in any kind of software that is under development, as many of the programs described in this chapter are. Please give the author a chance. If you have carefully followed the instructions and are sure that you have found a problem with a particular program that is not mentioned in the documentation, contact the author of the program first — and give him or her some reasonable time to respond. If you don't tell the authors about it, they can't fix it! It's somewhat impolite and counterproductive to flame the author and the program publicly in a newsgroup for something that he's not even aware of; ultimately, the problem may turn out not to be the author's problem. For this reason (and to encourage suggestions for improvement), most authors include their e-mail addresses in the program's documentation.

Chat/IRC/Personal Communications

Communicate with others through your keyboard, a microphone, or even a video camera. Be forewarned, though, that this kind of communication is not always as easy as it sounds. The good news is that many of these packages are continually being improved by their authors; the bad news is that some of the problems and limitations are beyond the authors' control.

CU-SeeMe

Primary purpose	One-way, two-way, and multiple videoconferencing
Filename	CUSEEME.ZIP
File size	122,054 bytes
Latest version	W.34b4 (August 1994)
Available from	gated.cornell.edu: /pub/video/pc.cu-seemew0.34b4
Status	Freeware
Documentation	Installation instructions and on-line help are included. A frequently asked questions (FAQ) document also is available from the same location, under the name CU-SEEME.FAQ. Additional information about reflector sites is available through the WWW at http://www.ludvigsen.dhhalden.no/webdoc/video.htm.
Features	Four-bit gray-scale video at 160 x 120 pixels. Audio for the PC not available yet but is being worked on.
Comments	This program was created for the Macintosh platform but now is available for both Macs and PCs. The program is under considerable development effort, and this latest release seems to be considerably more stable than its predecessors. Even if you don't have the capability to send, several reflector sites are available where you can use this package to sneak a peek. The low data-transfer speeds on modem connections are a big problem, but the program is interesting nevertheless. Try it!

Internet Voice Chat

Primary purpose	Two-way Internet voice communications
Filename	IVC11.ZIP
File size	108,102 bytes
Latest version	1.1 (December 1994)
Available from	ftp.cica.indiana.edu: /pub/pc/win3/winsock (or mirrors)
Status	Shareware: $20
Documentation	Installation instructions and on-line help included
Features	Registered version adds answering-machine-mode capability. A fax mode is planned for a future release.
Comments	Requires microphone and sound card. According to the author, this new version is now compatible with Trumpet 2.0B (older versions of Trumpet are not recommended), and a number of other improvements have been made.

IRC4WIN

Primary purpose	Internet Relay Chat II (IRC II)
Filename	IRC4WIN.ZIP
File size	91,039 bytes
Latest version	1.10 beta (October 1994)
Available from	ftp.cica.indiana.edu: /pub/pc/win3/winsock (or mirrors)
Status	Shareware: $50 single user and $450 site license
Documentation	Minimal, with nothing much included in this unregistered version
Comments	An upgrade of this relatively new program from David Elkind. No information on what's changed in this version is available. The registration cost is somewhat stiff.

Sticky

Primary purpose	Electronic notes exchange
Filename	STICKY06.ZIP
File size	366,332 bytes
Latest version	0.61 (October 1994)
Available from	commsun.its.csiro.au csiro/msdos/sticky
	ftp.cica.indiana.edu: /pub/pc/win3/winsock (or mirrors)
Status	Freeware
Documentation	Minimal instructions
Features	Automated installation
Comments	Sticky is based on 3M's popular Post-it notes. The program contains separate talk and listen modules, enabling you to exchange quick notes with another PC that also has the program running. A mailing list now exists for people interested in Sticky. To subscribe, send e-mail to listserv@oliver.sun.ac.za, with the following line in the *body* of the message (without the brackets): SUBSCRIBE STICKY-TALK <Your first name> <Your last name>

WinSock IRC

Primary purpose	Internet Relay Chat (IRC)
Filename	Three files: WINIRC.EXE, WINIRC.DOC (Windows documentation), and IRC.DOC (DOS documentation)
File size	96,000, 313, and 8,276 bytes, respectively
Latest version	0.1 beta

Available from	ftp.trumpet.com.au: /ftp/pub/winirc
Status	No mention is made of any charges for using this program.
Documentation	The documentation is both negligible and inadequate. The only documentation is in WINIRC.DOC, a separate, 313-byte file (Microsoft Word format), which is located in the same directory as the program file (which should be downloaded at the same time). The WINIRC.DOC file also suggests that if documentation is needed for this Windows version, it should be obtained from one of the corresponding DOS versions, such as IRC101.ZIP (65,737 bytes, November 1993), which supposedly is applicable. At this particular site, at least the DOS documentation is available in a separate, readily available file so that it can be downloaded at the same time.
Comments	WinSock IRC is a basic package that does not appear to be undergoing additional development.

Wintalk

Primary purpose	Two-way on-line communications
Filename	WTALK11A.ZIP
File size	142,379 bytes
Latest version	1.1a (September 1994)
Available from	ftp.elf.com: /pub/wintalk
Status	Freeware (limited)
Documentation	Installation and start-up instructions, but no on-line help
Features	Uses the UNIX ntalk protocol
Comments	Wintalk (released by ELF Communications) does not work properly with the current Trumpet WinSock 1.0A (WinSock bugs). The program should be OK with the newer Trumpet version 1.0B beta 2 or higher.

WSIRC

Primary purpose	Internet Relay Chat (IRC)
Filename	WSIRC14E.ZIP
File size	534,801 bytes
Latest version	1.14e (January 1995)
Available from	cs-ftp.bu.edu: /irc/clients/pc/windows
Status	Shareware: $39.95 (1 disk, 1 manual); students $24.95. Site license: $449.95 (20 disks, 20 manuals).

(continued)

WSIRC (continued)

Documentation	Very good. Installation instructions and on-line help is included. The help file contains a tutorial, and a comprehensive list of IRC servers is also included.
Features	Supports most IRCII server commands, with the exception of DCC and CTCP.
Comments	This is a Windows client for the Internet Relay Chat (IRC) network. It allows users to chat (keyboard) with each other worldwide through IRC servers. Two execution files are included. WSIRCG.EXE is for freeware users who have chosen not to register the program and is limited to 2 concurrent channels. WSIRC.EXE is an evaluation copy for shareware users and is limited to 5 channels. With registration, a registered shareware version is provided that allows 255 channels and a larger help file and other features. The author, Caesar Samsi, says, "The future includes images, sound, and video in both client and server versions."

Note: An up-to-date list of worldwide IRC servers is posted regularly (by Chuck Kane) to the newsgroup alt.irc. The list also is available for ftp download from h.ece.uiuc.edu:/irc. An IRC FAQ is available from cs-ftp.bu.edu: /irc/support/alt-irc-faq.

Commercial Demo Packages

Who was it who said, "You pay your money, you take your chances"? At least some companies have gone the route of making limited demonstration versions available for tryout — an arrangement that minimizes the risk. Some of these versions are time-limited; they cease to work at a certain date or after a certain amount of session time. Other versions are crippled: You can use them forever, but forever without all the features.

AIR Mosaic

Primary purpose	World Wide Web (WWW) browser
Filename	AMOSDEMO.EXE
File size	1,003,793 bytes
Latest version	1.1 (October 1994). Spry has been posting updated demo versions on an ongoing basis to correct the bugs that are being reported.
Available from	ftp.spry.com: vendor/spry/demo/airmosaicdemo
Status	Demo trial version
Documentation	On-line help file included

Features	AIR Mosaic offers customizable toolbars, preconfigured hot lists, user-definable hot lists, and a full-screen kiosk mode. Automated installation looks for an already installed WinSock stack (such as Trumpet). The program includes its own NULLSOCK.DLL file for offline viewing.
Comments	This demo is fully functional except that it allows you to view no more than six external documents. The first release versions had image-display flaws, but the flaws have been corrected. Spry has done a good job in reacting to bug problems and posting fixed versions. The uncrippled 16-bit version is available for $29.95. (A 32-bit version of this program for that price would be more desirable.)

Chameleon Demo

Primary purpose	Full-featured professional network demo package (time-crippled)
Filename	Five files: README.TXT, CHAMELN1.EXE, CHAMELN2.EXE, CHAMELN3.EXE, and CHAMELN4.EXE
File size	Approximately 5,003,764 bytes total
Latest version	N/A
Available from	ftp.netmanage.com: /pub/demos/chameleon
Status	Demo
Documentation	N/A
Features	Chameleon Demo is a full-featured professional package that includes a range of clients, such as ftp, Telnet, Gopher, Ping, Mail, and News — with network features such as Ethernet and NFS support.
Comments	This full demonstration version is time-crippled; it will expire sometime in a month or two. NetManage can be expected to replace this version with a new copy on its server with a new expiration date. The README file contains the password needed for installation. Because of the size of this package, the time required to get it running, and the effort required to become familiar with all its features within the time limitation, this package should be used only by people who are seriously prepared to buy the uncrippled version if they like what they see. (I don't know the exact price, but I believe that it is a few hundred dollars). For other users, the Chameleon Sampler (listed next) may be a better choice; although it has only some basic clients, it is free, not crippled, and will run forever.

Chameleon Sampler

Primary purpose	Multifunction commercial sampler package
Filename	SAMPLER.EXE
File size	753,947 bytes
Latest version	3.11
Available from	ftp.netmanage.com: /pub/demos/sampler This package also is included on disks that come with several Internet books sold at bookstores.
Status	Freeware
Documentation	Good, with on-line help
Features	Chameleon Sampler supports both SLIP/CSLIP and PPP and has its own built-in WinSock and telephone dialer, which means that it does not require Trumpet WinSock. Basic ftp, Telnet, Mail, and Ping clients are included; others, such as Archie and Gopher, are missing. Telnet emulation: TTY/ANSI/VT52/VT100/VT220.
Comments	*Recommended.* A good way to get going on the Internet, this beginner's freeware package is intended to provide an introduction to the commercial version of Chameleon. The program works well and has become very popular; it is included on the disks supplied with several introductory Internet books. If I have one complaint, it's that I dislike software packages such as this one, which are programmed to make changes to an AUTOEXEC.BAT file during installation without prompting for notification or approval to proceed. Nonetheless, this is a good, stable, basic package. Other freeware and shareware WinSock clients can be installed and will work with Chameleon Sampler to make up for ones that are not included in this package (or to upgrade to better ones). The package doesn't really belong in this demo section, but I put it here so that it could be next to its big brother, Chameleon Demo.

The CommSet (DOS)

Primary purpose	All-purpose Internet communications package operating under DOS
Filename	Four files: CSET0033.EXE, CHLP0033.EXE, INSTALL.EXE, and COMMSET.FAQ
File size	Approximately 762,012 bytes total
Latest version	Demo, version 01, revision 0033
Available from	nstn.ns.ca: /pub/pc-stuff/commset
	cs.stmarys.ca: /pub/commset
	ftp.cybercon.nb.ca: /pub/commset

Status	Demo version. The commercial price is $115 Canadian, which is approximately $82 U.S. at current exchange rates. A 50 percent educational/private-user discount is available. If you don't want the printed manual, you can deduct $15 Canadian from the price. Site licenses and bulk-purchase discounts are available.
Documentation	Installation instructions and on-line help included
Features	Telnet (VT320, VT100, and ANSI-BBS), ftp, POP3 Mailer, Finger, NewsReader, Gopher, NSLookup, Whois, Ping, Command Scripting language, Monitor, Serial Terminal, Fake DOS, SLIPDialer, and COMMDialer. The program has resizable, movable, scrollable windows as well as full mouse support, with screen cut-and-paste.
Comments	I know, I know — the day is rapidly approaching when your children will see the word *DOS* and think that it's the name of some new German car ("And now, introducing . . . the all-new Volkswagen DOS!"). All kidding aside, this package is worth mentioning because it is full-featured and installs easily. This package is crippled and can operate a session for a maximum of 15 minutes, with warnings at each 5-minute mark and one literally at the last minute. The program is by Cybernetic Control, Inc.

CSMRLW (Computer Software Manufaktur Remote Login for Windows)

Primary purpose	Telnet (terminal emulator)
Filename	CSMRLW31.EXE
File size	429,995 bytes
Latest version	3.1 (October 1994)
Available from	ftp.eunet.co.at: /pub/vendor/csm
Status	Demo trial version
Documentation	On-line help included
Features	AT386/IBM HFT(5151)/IBM 3151/SCO (ANSI) terminal emulation, automatic logon, Windows cut-and-paste support, ISO-to-ASCII conversion, automated installation
Comments	CSMRLW (from Computer Software Manufaktur GmbH in Austria) has not been tested under Trumpet WinSock but does run under a variety of other stacks, including Chameleon. This demo version is fully functional but has a time limit.

Note: If you were one of the first people to download this demo, you discovered a flaw that limited the demo to one terminal session. The corrected version now is available for downloading.

UNIBOL/Desktop Terminal

Primary purpose	Telnet (terminal emulator)
Filename	UNITEL.ZIP
File size	559,815 bytes
Latest version	1.3 (December 1994)
Available from	ftp.unibol.com: /pub/demo
Status	Demo trial version
Documentation	Start-up and on-line help
Features	VT100/UNIBOL 100 emulation, record/playback script capability to automate sessions, keyboard remapping, dual-character-set support
Comments	UNIBOL/Desktop Terminal, a full-featured demo from Unibol Ltd., is compatible with a variety of stacks, including Trumpet. The site can be difficult to access.

VIS-A-VIS

Primary purpose	Teleconferencing
Filename	VIS.ZIP
File size	1,386,771 bytes
Latest version	1.1 (May 1994)
Available from	resudox.net: /pub/vis
Status	Demo trial version
Documentation	On-line help only
Comments	This program, from WorldLinx Telecommunications, Inc., is a slide-presentation teleconferencing package with a shared-use whiteboard. Automatic session termination occurs after ten minutes.

Diagnostic Tools

The increasing size and complexity of networks and their communications links create increasing problems. Fortunately, specialized tools seem to be beginning to deal with some of the problems.

Socket Wrencher

Primary purpose	WinSock testing tool
Filename	SOCKETW.EXE
File size	59,345 bytes

Latest version	1.0 (April 1994)
Available from	ftp.netmanage.com: /pub/demos/sockwrench
Status	Freeware
Documentation	Installation and start-up instructions
Comments	Socket Wrencher provides a suite of performance tests over TCP and UDP, as well as several tests to check characteristics of a WinSock-based protocol stack. Released by NetManage, Inc.

X-Ray/WinSock

Primary purpose	WinSock API trace/debugger for Windows 3.1
Filename	XRAYWINS.ZIP
File size	212,269 bytes
Latest version	1.13 (November 1994)
Available from	ftp.netcom.com: /pub/sstinc
Status	Shareware: registration $69.95
Documentation	Installation instructions and on-line help included
Comments	Traces and displays the parameters of all WinSock API functions. Works with any version of WinSock. Some features are crippled in this free version.

File-Search and File-Transfer Protocols

The search program WSARCHIE and John Junod's file-retrieval program WS_FTP (16-bit) are the standards by which *all* Archie and ftp clients should be measured. I am referring to commercial programs not just to shareware. These programs not only have excellent features and performance but also work well together for a one–two punch.

AutoNet (Automated Internet Communications) (DOS)

Primary purpose	Automated file retrieval (ftp)
Filename	AUTONT31.ZIP
File size	306,796 bytes
Latest version	3.1 (January 1995)
Available from	wuarchive.wustl.edu: /pub/MSDOS_UPLOADS/utils
Status	Shareware: $35
Documentation	Extensive start-up instructions

(continued)

AutoNet (Automated Internet Communications) (DOS) ***(continued)***	
Features	AutoNet also performs Finger and Archie searches. The program supports simple command-line mail creation and sending (as well as Usenet posting), including mass-mailing capability in the registered version. The program also has text-based faxing capability (non-Internet).
Comments	According to its documentation, AutoNet automatically logs on to an ftp site, changes directories, and retrieves either specific files or a group of the latest files at that site. Notice that this program does not use a WinSock/SLIP connection; it operates through your UNIX shell account. The program was designed by a BBS operator to feed his site with large numbers of the latest files from Internet locations.

WINFSP	
Primary purpose	File-service protocol (FSP)
Filename	WINFSP12.ZIP
File size	57,956 bytes
Latest version	1.2 (August 1993)
Available from	ftp.cica.indiana.edu: /pub/pc/win3/winsock (or mirrors)
Status	Freeware
Documentation	Brief setup and use instructions are included; no on-line help is included. A good source of information about FSP is the frequently asked questions (FAQ) document available from ftp.germany.eu.net: /pub/network/inet/fsp. The filename is simply FAQ.
Comments	WINFSP is the only Windows-based, FSP-based file-retrieval program I've ever seen, and no recent versions are available. FSP (sometimes nicknamed "file-slurping protocol") is usable only on certain servers that support it. Once touted as a potential replacement for ftp, FSP doesn't seem to be going anywhere.

WinFTP	
Primary purpose	File retrieval (ftp)
Filename	WINFTP.ZIP
File size	177,738 bytes
Latest version	January 1994
Available from	ftp.cica.indiana.edu: /pub/pc/win3/winsock (or mirrors)
Status	Released to public domain
Documentation	Installation instructions, but no on-line help

Features	WinFTP is based on an earlier version of WSFTP, with some added features. The program contains both 16- and 32-bit-execution versions (WINFTP.EXE and WIN32FTP.EXE); take your choice if you have 32-bit capability, although I'm not sure whether there's any real difference in performance between the two. This program also includes some limited Ping capabilities.
Comments	I have seen postings indicating that this program is more firewall-friendly than other ftp clients, although the more recent versions of WS_FTP seem to have improved their firewall capabilities.

WSARCHIE

Primary purpose	File-search client (Archie)
Filename	WSARCH07.ZIP
File size	174,837 bytes
Latest version	0.7 alpha (November 1994)
Available from	disabuse.demon.co.uk: /pub/ibmpc/winsock/apps/wsarchie
Status	No charge for noncommercial use
Documentation	Installation instructions and on-line help included
Features	The display shows file sizes and file dates. The latest version has the capability to save search results to a text file for later viewing.
Comments	*Recommended.* The program has a well-laid-out, well-functioning main screen and works with WS_FTP to retrieve files.

WS_FTP

Primary purpose	File retrieval (ftp)
Filename	WS_FTP.ZIP
File size	113,532 bytes
Latest version	December 1994

Note: Unfortunately, the various versions of WS_FTP to date are indistinguishable by filename, but the latest version always is available at the site listed in this table. If you are looking elsewhere for this program, check the file size with my information to avoid downloading an older version.

Available from	ftp.usma.edu: /pub/msdos/winsock.files
Status	No charge for noncommercial use by individuals or for use by U.S. government organizations. For commercial use, contact Ipswitch, Inc. at info@ipswitch.com.
Documentation	Installation instructions and on-line help included

(continued)

WS_FTP (continued)

Features	WS_FTP can store repetitively used locations and directories for easy call-up; it comes configured for several of the most popular sites. The program can be set to make a specified number of redials if it is unable to connect; unfortunately, no time delay is allowed between these redials. The program supports firewalls.
Comments	*Recommended.* This is a major new version — an excellent upgrade with many new features. (Also see the matching file-search package, WSARCHIE, in the preceding section.) A new version of WS_FTP is under development specifically for Windows NT (see the following item).

WS_FTP32 (Windows NT version by John Junod)

Primary purpose	File retrieval (ftp)
Filename	WS_FTP32.ZIP
File size	146,316 bytes
Latest version	November 1994
Available from	ftp.usma.edu: /pub/msdos/winsock.files
Status	No charge for noncommercial use by individuals or for use by U.S. government organizations. For commercial use, contact Ipswitch, Inc. at info@ipswitch.com.
Documentation	Installation instructions and on-line help included
Features	Contains the same features as the 16-bit version (see WS_FTP)
Comments	John Junod has ported his latest code to a 32-bit version for Windows NT. The latest release of this version also now runs on Windows 3.1 with the Win32s 32-bit extension installed (see the "Miscellaneous Non-WinSock," later in this chapter), Windows NT, and Windows 95. I was able to run both the 16- and 32-bit versions of WS_FTP simultaneously by moving them into the same directory and sharing the same INI file. There is no advantage in running this 32-bit version on a 16-bit machine even with Win32s; file transfers will not be faster.

WSFTP32 (Windows NT version by Larry Kahn)

Primary purpose	File retrieval (ftp)
Filename	WSFTP32.ZIP
File size	237,648 bytes
Latest version	December 1994

Note: Unfortunately, the various versions of WSFTP32 to-date are indistinguishable by filename, but the latest version is available at the site listed in this table. If you are looking elsewhere for this program, check the file size with my information to avoid downloading an older version.

Available from	ftp.cica.indiana.edu: /pub/pc/win3/winsock (or mirrors)
Status	Freeware
Documentation	Installation and start-up instructions, but no on-line help
Comments	This program is an updated and recompiled version for Windows NT, based on WS_FTP source code from December 1993 originated by John Junod. Some bugs have been fixed and some features added by Larry Kahn, who created this version. The program works on either NT 3.1 or Daytona NT 3.5; it does not work on Windows under Win32s, because it uses multiple threads.

Junod also has issued a 32-bit update based on his latest 16-bit version of WS_FTP, so you have two 32-bit NT versions of WS_FTP from which to choose. Kahn, the author of this version, says, "I believe my version is better than his [Junod's], as with my multithreading, I can do a local operation while a remote one is pending, and also resize or move the window around. This cannot be done on his version ported to NT."

Kahn also is considering producing an X Windows UNIX version of the program. If you're interested, drop him a line at `kahn@kahn.pdial.interpath.net`.

Fingers

No, not the kind you give other motorists — a program such as Finger is used to check servers for information about the users logged on at a particular location. Sometimes little more than the users' real names is available; sometimes brief profiles are available. The Finger function is included in some other packages, such as recent versions of Eudora, a popular mail program.

Finger (a Windows Socket Finger Client)

Primary purpose	Finger query
Filename	FINGER31.ZIP
File size	68,108 bytes
Latest version	3.1 (March 1993)
Available from	ftp.cica.indiana.edu: /pub/pc/win3/winsock (or mirrors)
Status	No mention of any charges for using this program
Documentation	Minimal, but little is required
Comments	The program contains two executables: one for Berkeley-style synchronous blocking (FINGER.EXE) and the other for asynchronous WinSockets (MFINGER.EXE).

Finger

Primary purpose	Finger query
Filename	FINGER21.ZIP
File size	73,739 bytes
Latest version	2.1 November 1994
Available from	ftp.cica.indiana.edu: /pub/pc/win3/winsock (or mirrors)
Status	Freeware (limited)
Documentation	Start-up introduction only
Features	Enables multiple Finger sessions at the same time and includes timer for refingering opened Finger sessions every 1–60 minutes.
Comments	This program is a contribution from Europe, by Zoran Dukic. The program is relatively straightforward and easy to use, as are most Finger clients.

Finger32 (Windows NT version)

Primary purpose	Finger query
Filename	FINGER32.ZIP
File size	37,196 bytes
Latest version	May 1994
Available from	ftp.cica.indiana.edu: /pub/pc/win3/nt (or mirrors)
Status	No information — not specified by the author
Documentation	Nil
Comments	This program — a 32-bit version of the program Finger — seems to work under regular Windows 3.1 with a Win32s upgrade.

Finger and Host Lookup (two programs)

Primary purpose	Finger query and host-name-to-IP-number lookup and converter
Filename	IWORK.ZIP
File size	17,017 bytes
Latest version	January 1994
Available from	Try ftp.cuslm.ca: network/winsock
Status	Freeware
Documentation	Minimal
Comments	A pair of very basic programs

WS Finger

Primary purpose	Finger query
Filename	WSFNGR14.ZIP
File size	62,014 bytes
Latest version	1.4 (December 1994)
Available from	sparky.umd.edu:/pub/winsock
Status	Shareware: $10
Documentation	Installation instructions and on-line help. A list of whois servers is also included.
Features	A major new rewrite. Support now included for Finger, whois, and command-line fingers; Finger address book; history; and save to file.
Comments	From Tidewater Systems Shareware as of Version 1.2. Previous versions freeware. Nice new icon.

Games (MUDs)

Here's one interpretation from the introductory text in MUD Man: "MUD, short for Multi-User Dungeon, is a fantasy world where people can interact and fight monsters, go on quests, etc." And then there's MUSH, a "Multi-User Shared Hallucination." And then there's MOO . . .

MUD Man

Primary purpose	MUD client
Filename	MUDMAN12.ZIP
File size	78,834 bytes
Latest version	1.2 (August 1994)
Available from	wuarchive.wustl.edu: /pub/MSDOS_UPLOADS/win_games
Status	Shareware: $9 U.S., $15 non-U.S. Registration benefits include an upgraded version of the program.
Documentation	Basic start-up instructions and on-line help included
Comments	According to author Samuel Ross, "The goal of MUD Man is to end the laborious typing required to move around and perform actions. Once initialized, every command can be issued from the click of a button."

MUDManager

Primary purpose	MUD client
Filename	MUDMGR01.EXE
File size	762,013 bytes
Latest version	0.1 beta (June 1994)
Available from	caisr2.caisr.cwru.edu: /pub/mud/clients
Status	Shareware, but no charges while still in development
Documentation	Basic installation and use instructions
Comments	Operating this program involves fairly stiff requirements, including Windows 3.1 with the Win32s extension or Windows NT, 8MB of RAM, and 5MB of disk space. The program also requires a permanent IP number, which disqualifies most modem connections.

MUTT™ Lite (Multi-User Trivial Terminal client)

Primary purpose	MUD/MUSH/MU* client
Filename	MUTT_01G.ZIP
File size	29,363 bytes
Latest version	0.1g (November 1994)
Available from	caisr2.caisr.cwru.edu: /pub/mud
Status	Freeware (limited)
Documentation	Installation and start-up info are provided in a file called README.BND. No on-line help is available, and none is planned for the Lite version.
Features	Multiple character connections with an MDI presentation; separate send and receive windows with dialogue logging; drag-and-drop support for sending files and command streams; and user-definable hot keys, including cursor-key definitions
Comments	This program is the first public, pre-1.0 release of MUTT Lite, a Multi-User Trivial Terminal client that provides WinSock access to MU* hosts. The executable remains below 32K to minimize Internet traffic and ftp-site impact; therefore, features are limited. A full-featured version called MUTT™ Elite is planned for future release by the author, Bob Free.

VWMUD Master

Primary purpose	MUD client
Filename	VWMUD110.ZIP
File size	57,821 bytes
Latest version	1.1 (December 1994)

Available from	xmission.com: /pub/users/kslewin ftp.primenet.com
Status	Shareware: registration $5, with six months of updates for $15; source code $50
Documentation	Start-up instructions and on-line help
Comments	VWMUD Master, from Vaughan Wynne-Jones, is a Telnet client designed specifically for "outlaws": players who kill other players. You must have VBRUN300.DLL installed on your system.

Winfugue / WinWorld

Primary purpose	MU* client
Filename	WWORLD02.ZIP
File size	72,771 bytes
Latest version	0.2 alpha (November 1994)
Available from	ftp.mgl.ca: /pub/winworld
Status	Donationware: contributions welcome but not mandatory
Documentation	Very basic start-up and installation instructions included
Features	Auto-login, multiple simultaneous worlds — but only one world displayed at a time (no window clutter!), definable function keys, built-in bug report mailer (doesn't require any other software)
Comments	This program, formerly known as Winfugue, is at an early stage of development and is being released by the author, Eric Stern, for additional testing purposes. You must have the Visual Basic file VBRUN300.DLL on your system in an accessible directory. It is frequently distributed with other programs.

Games (Other)

Perhaps because WinSock is such a new standard, outside the MUD grouping few games have been developed so far. In time, we can expect to see others — perhaps, someday, even DOOM.

FIBS/W (First International Backgammon Server for Windows)

Primary purpose	Backgammon server
Filename	FIBSW121.ZIP
File size	191,596 bytes
Latest version	1.21 (June 1994)

(continued)

FIBS/W (continued)

Available from	ftp.cica.indiana.edu: /pub/pc/win3/games (or mirrors)
Status	Shareware: $40
Documentation	Start-up information and on-line help
Features	The program works with dialup dumb-terminal-server access, TCP/IP, SLIP, and PPP; it has a built-in dialer with script.
Comments	FIBS/W is an Internet server that enables users to play against human opponents all over the world.

WinSock Chess

Primary purpose	Internet chess
Filename	WSCHESB1.ZIP
File size	163,546 bytes
Latest version	Beta test release (March 1994)
Available from	ftp.cica.indiana.edu: /pub/pc/win3/winsock (or mirrors)
Status	Copyright freeware
Documentation	Basic usage instructions
Comments	According to the program's author, "WinSock Chess is a chess implementation allowing two players to play chess over a WinSock supporting network. The program will validate moves and disallow illegal moves. WinSock Chess uses GNU Chess as a basis for checking moves, and GNU chess forms the underlying engine for the program." The program has a nice, clear graphical display.

Gopher

The gophers and ground squirrels that periodically move in to my front lawn love to dig mazes of tunnels, which go all over and seem to pop up everywhere. In a more benign manner, the computer client called Gopher tunnels throughout the Internet for us, using a menu-based system to take us to places we otherwise would have difficulty reaching. A new Gopher has recently popped up: the PNL InfoBrowser. The Gopher system was originally developed at the University of Minnesota.

BCGopher (Boston College Gopher)

Primary purpose	Gopher search tool
Filename	BCG08BA3.EXE

File size	170,469 bytes
Latest version	0.8ba3 (May 1994)
Available from	bcinfo.bc.edu: /pub/bcgopher

Note: This is not a true anonymous ftp server; you must use ***guest*** as the password rather than the normal e-mail user ID.

Status	Freeware
Documentation	Start-up information and on-line help file, with a brief explanation of the term *Gopher*
Features	BCGopher supports the new Gopher+ protocol used by some servers. The program also supports HTML and MIME formats.
Comments	This program deserves an award for the best Gopher icon I've seen.

Gopher Book

Primary purpose	Gopher search tool
Filename	GOPHBOOK.ZIP or GOPHBK11.ZIP
File size	888,666 bytes
Latest version	1.1 (May 1993)
Available from	ftp.cica.indiana.edu: /pub/pc/win3/winsock (or mirrors)
Status	Freeware. WINJPEG image viewer; shareware: $20.
Documentation	Installation instructions and on-line help included
Features	This program uses an interesting concept, with menus displayed as pages in a book. Image viewer WINJPEG is included in the package as a default image viewer.
Comments	Gopher Book is a rather large package for a Gopher tool. Development seems to have stopped.

HGopher (Hampson's Gopher)

Primary purpose	Gopher search tool
Filename	HGopher appears in many locations, under many names: HGOPHER2.4.ZIP, HGOPHER24.ZIP, HGOPHER2.ZIP, and GOPH24.ZIP. Take your pick. If you want to download the program from CICA, you'll find it in HGOPH24.ZIP.
File size	199,833 bytes
Latest version	2.4 (January 1994)
Available from	ftp.cica.indiana.edu: /pub/pc/win3/winsock (or mirrors)
Status	No charge for noncommercial use

(continued)

HGopher (Hampson's Gopher)* *(continued)

Documentation	Good. This version now has on-line help. Good/bad news is the huge, detailed help file (739K).
Comments	HGopher has gone commercial and now is the property of ftp Software, Inc. Although version 2.4 has officially been withdrawn and will be used as the basis of the commercial version, copies of it still are widely available on many servers. Version 2.3 remains in the public domain but no longer will be maintained or enhanced. (Translation: dead Gopher; avoid.)

The PNL InfoBrowser (Pacific Northwest Laboratory)

Primary purpose	Gopher search tool
Filename	IB105.EXE
File size	259,342 bytes
Latest version	1.05 (November 1994)
Available from	ftp.pnl.gov: /pub/pnlinfo/win
Status	No charge for noncommercial use
Documentation	Installation instructions and on-line help are included. An on-line tutorial is available through the PNL home site.
Features	Supports the newer Gopher+ protocol found on some servers
Comments	A Mac version of this program also is available, and a few versions for other platforms are being developed. This program was developed under a contract from the U.S. Department of Energy.

WGopher

Primary purpose	Gopher search tool
Filename	WGOPH23.ZIP
File size	120,469 bytes
Latest version	2.3 (May 1994)
Available from	ftp.cuhk.hk: /pub/gopher/pc
Status	No charge for noncommercial purposes
Documentation	Minimal; no on-line documentation yet
Comments	This was a promising Gopher client from Hong Kong, but unfortunately there have been no recent updates. It does not support Gopher+.

WSGopher

Primary purpose	Gopher search tool
Filename	WSG-12.EXE
File size	367,860 bytes
Latest version	1.2 (December 1994)
Available from	dewey.tis.inel.gov: pub/wsgopher
Status	No charge for noncommercial use
Documentation	Good; now has an on-line help file
Features	Supports the newer Gopher+ protocol found on some servers
Comments	*Recommended.* This is one of the better gopher clients currently available, although it does not support firewalls. Works with Windows NT Daytona and OS/2 Warp.

Host Lookup Clients

Host lookup programs take alphabetical site-location information (such as ftp.cica.indiana.edu) and convert it into an IP address (such as 129.79.26.27), which, for some reason, computers absolutely insist on having. And vice versa. For example, if you have been using ftp to download offensive pornographic images from that notorious and secretive site 127.0.0.1 and you want to learn more about that location, you can enter these numbers in a host lookup program, such as WSHost.

Hopcheck and Ghostname (two programs; Windows NT versions)

Primary purpose	Two programs: a route tracer and a *get-host-name* program
Filename	HOP.ZIP
File size	24,917 bytes
Latest version	May 1994
Available from	ftp.cica.indiana.edu: /pub/pc/win3/nt (or mirrors)
Status	No mention of any charges
Documentation	Negligible
Comments	Hopcheck and Ghostname are two NT programs by Larry Kahn.

NSLOOKUP

Primary purpose	Name server information lookup
Filename	NSLOOKUP.ZIP

Note: The same filename was used for Version 1.0. If you are downloading the program from a different location, match the file size to verify that you have the correct version.

(continued)

NSLOOKUP *(continued)*

File size	110,428 bytes
Latest version	1.1 (August 1994)
Available from	disabuse.demon.co.uk: /pub/trumphurst/nslookup
Status	Copyrighted, but no charge
Documentation	Installation instructions, but no on-line help
Comments	This program is one element of Wigwam for the Internet, a commercial off-line news and mail reader from Ashmount Research, Ltd. that has not yet been released. For more information, send e-mail to ashmount@cix.compulink.co.uk.

WORMHOLE

Primary purpose	DNS query utility
Filename	WORMHOLE.EXE
Note: Do not confuse this file with WORMHOLE.ZIP, which is an unrelated and totally different program available on the Internet.	
File size	32,256 bytes
Latest version	1.0
Available from	Try ftp.cuslm.ca: /network/winsock
Status	Not specified
Documentation	None
Comments	A very simple DNS lookup program.

WS Host (Windows Socket Host)

Primary purpose	DNS query utility
Filename	WSHOST11.ZIP
File size	5,124 bytes
Latest version	1.1 (October 1994)
Available from	ftp.cica.indiana.edu: /pub/pc/win3/winsock (or mirrors)
Status	Postcardware (freeware for noncommercial use; just send the developer a nice postcard)
Documentation	Minimal; this program is intuitively simple
Comments	This nifty, compact utility can convert an IP number to a host name, or vice versa. Everyone should have one of these utilities. This new version makes the program fully asynchronous, correcting a shortcoming in the original version.

Hyper-G

Hyper-G is a large-scale, distributed hypermedia information system very similar to the World Wide Web. Hyper-G is capable of accessing the WWW, WAIS, and Gopher systems; conversely, WWW and Gopher clients can access Hyper-G. The big difference between Hyper-G and other networks is that Hyper-G servers track all links in their universe. If an object is deleted, the server can find and delete all links that point to that object. The existence of a link server provides capabilities that are not possible in the WWW and Gopher space.

Hyper-G is being developed in Europe. I don't see that it has a great deal to offer. There does not seem to be any interest in it in North America, which is totally preoccupied with the WWW. Only one Windows browser is available for Hyper-G.

Amadeus

Primary purpose	Hyper-G browser
Filename	Four files: AMADEDOC.ZIP, AMADEUS1.ZIP, AMADEUS2.ZIP, and AMADEUS3.ZIP
File size	291,987, 1,139,411, 1,374,269, and 341,396 bytes, respectively
Latest version	0.81.012 beta (October 1994)
Available from	iicm.tu-graz.ac. at /pub/hyper-g/pc-client/amadeus.081
Status	I didn't see anything mentioned, but presumably, there is no charge for noncommercial use.
Documentation	Extensive documentation and help files are included. The separate zipped documentation file is in Microsoft Word format (.DOC) and may be difficult to view unless you have a powerful word processor that handles that format. You also need a great deal of memory because Amadeus is almost a 2MB file unzipped and will be painfully slow to browse through on a less powerful PC.
Features	Automated installation, with the choice of maximum, custom, or minimum installation. This program comes with some familiar clients, such as WS_FTP32 for ftp, and EWAN for Telnet.
Comments	The program requires Win32s, which is included in the program and which will be installed automatically if you do not already have it.

Mail and Mail Accessories

One writer recently gushed that electronic mail is the killer application for the '90s. He's probably right. The proper choice of a mail program depends on the availability of features that are important to you and on your comfort level with the mechanics of the way the program works. The two top programs are Eudora and Pegasus. Eudora is easy to learn and to use and is relatively stable but lacking in features. Pegasus is more feature-rich, but this complexity takes longer to become familiar with and is more likely to cause problems.

Eudora

Primary purpose	Electronic mail
Filename	EUDOR144.EXE
File size	292,942 bytes
Latest version	1.4.4 (December 1994)
Available from	ftp.qualcomm.com: /quest/windows/eudora/1.4
Status	Postcardware (freeware for noncommercial use; just send the developer a nice postcard). An upgraded commercial version 2.0 is available, with additional features and documentation; the price starts at $65 for a single user.
Documentation	Minimal documentation and the lack of on-line help can be problems in the unregistered version. For more information, see the "Eudora Documentation" section at the end of this chapter.
Features	POP3/SMTP protocol; BinHex and MIME capability, but does not support uuencoding in the free version; built-in directory services (Ph and Finger). This latest version adds the capability to have multiple messages open at the same time.
Comments	*Recommended.* Eudora is very popular. The latest version also runs under Windows NT and OS/2. Some features in the free version are limited. The registered commercial version 2.0 has the capability to send and receive mail remotely, by way of modem, without SLIP.

Pegasus Mail

Primary purpose	Electronic mail
Filename	WINPM122.ZIP
File size	837,801 bytes
Latest version	1.22 (September 1994)
Available from	risc.ua.edu: /pub/network/pegasus
Status	Freeware. Manuals, if required, are sold by the author to support development costs.
Documentation	Installation instructions and on-line help are included. Look for a self-extracting DOS display file, WGUIDE.EXE; that file contains some of this information.
Features	SMTP/POP3 protocol; supports uuencoding, BinHex, and MIME; and now contains a spell checker. This new version of Pegasus adds the long-awaited polling feature, which gives it the capability to operate in the background, continually checking for mail at specified intervals. Some additional drag-and-drop capabilities are added, and there is an improvement in the way attached documents can be sent.
Comments	*Recommended.* The current version of this very popular mail package has many features, and the price is certainly just about right!

RFD Mail

Primary purpose	Electronic mail
Filename	Available as RFDML123.ZIP or RFDMAIL.ZIP

Note: If you are downloading the program from other sites, do *not* try to use older versions, such as 1.21.

File size	813,495 bytes
Latest version	1.23 (September 1994)
Available from	ftp.std.com: /customers/software/rfdmail garbo.uwasa.fi: /windows/comm Various forums in CompuServe and GEnie
Status	Shareware: $29.95
Documentation	Installation instructions and on-line help included
Features	SMTP/POP protocol (for the Internet); automated installation; automatic polling (background checking for mail at scheduled intervals). The program does not support uuencoding, MIME, or BinHex. The program has direct-dial mail-access capabilities, but creating or modifying script files for this purpose can be cumbersome unless you are using one of the on-line services for which script files are provided.
Comments	The strength of this package lies in its capability for dialup e-mail access to a variety of service providers, ranging from BBSs to commercial networks such as CompuServe and GEnie to the Internet. RFD Mail contains all the necessary programs, scripts, instructions, and other features to support this capability. SMTP/POP capability has been added in the latest version. The program seemed to hesitate too long on my machine when executing commands, however, and more features are needed (such as MIME and uuencoding capability).

Small SMTP Client for the WinSock API

Primary purpose	Electronic mail (send only)
Filename	SMTP11.ZIP
File size	15,568 bytes
Latest version	1.1 (March 1993)
Available from	dorm.rutgers.edu: /pub/msdos/winsock/apps
Status	Public domain
Documentation	Some introductory information
Comments	This program is of historical interest only; it's an example of an early, simple mail client.

WinBiff

Primary purpose	Windows mail-notification utility (for Pegasus Mail and other programs)
Filename	WNBFF20B.ZIP
File size	66,781 bytes
Latest version	2.0b (April 1994)
Available from	oak.oakland.edu: /pub/msdos/windows3
Status	Shareware: $10; students $5
Documentation	Installation instructions and on-line help included
Features	Adjustable polling (mail-checking) interval, optional audible alarm, support for multiple mailboxes
Comments	Several mail packages lack the capability to operate in the background, periodically checking for new mail and notifying the user. This add-on utility corrects this notable deficiency in some mail clients. WinBiff can be used with Waffle, Pegasus (PMail), FirstMail, Novell MHS, Mini-Host, FSUUCP, and Sendmail (with PC-NFS). WinBiff no longer is required for the new Pegasus version 1.2.

Winelm

Primary purpose	Electronic mail
Filename	WINELM.ZIP
File size	259,553 bytes
Latest version	Second release (March 1994)
Available from	ftp.cica.indiana.edu: /pub/pc/win3/winsock (or mirrors)
Status	No mention of any charges for using this program
Documentation	None
Comments	This package has nothing to offer.

WS-Gmail

Primary purpose	Electronic mail
Filename	WS_GMAIL.ZIP
File size	192,176 bytes
Latest version	April 3, 1994
Available from	No longer available

Comments	This software was being developed by John Junod (noted for his popular WS_FTP program) and had both client and server capabilities. This package has gone commercial now and has been released under the name IMAIL. The rights to WS_Gmail were retained by the author for use by the armed forces. Although the package is in theory no longer available for the general public and was in fact never formally released, some early development versions, including this one, can sometimes still be found and are relatively functional — not that you would ever do an Archie search to try to find it.

XFERPRO (Information Transfer Professional)

Primary purpose	Internet mail file-transfer add-on feature
Filename	XFERP100.ZIP
File size	134,025 bytes
Latest version	1.0 (July 1994)
Available from	ftp.cica.indiana.edu: /pub/pc/win3/util (or mirrors)
Status	Shareware: registration $10
Documentation	Includes on-line help
Features	Fully supports MIME, UU, and XX encoding and is compatible with standard uuencoding and decoding programs; automated setup
Comments	This program enables you to send text, application data, images, audio, video, executable files, and compressed files through your electronic-mail program if it does not already have these transfer capabilities. XFERPRO (from Sabasoft, Inc.) works with both Windows 3.1 and Windows for Workgroups 3.11.

Mail and News

This section lists some good on-line Usenet newsreaders (NNTP), most of which are being actively upgraded by their authors. The mail capabilities usually are limited to send only to support news postings. As for good, fully functional, offline Windows newsreaders (in a single comprehensive package), there isn't one in sight. Dream on.

dMail for Windows

Primary purpose	Usenet news and mail (send and receive)
Filename	DMAILWIN.ZIP
File size	338,994 bytes

(continued)

dMail for Windows	***(continued)***
Latest version	1.0b (July 1994)
Available from	ftp.cica.indiana.edu: /pub/pc/win3/winsock (or mirrors)
Status	Distributed free for testing purposes
Documentation	Installation instructions and on-line help are included. The terminology sometimes is confusing and frustrating, especially with initial setup.
Features	Handles UUCP-g protocol (modem or TCP/IP), POP3, SMTP, and NNTP news reading. The newsreader has some good features, including uudecoding; the capability to sort articles by size, date, or subject; and drag-and-drop.
Comments	This program apparently was produced somewhere in the former Soviet Union and probably was intended primarily for distribution there. The program has a novel replacement for the traditional hourglass pointer: a man digging with a shovel. The automated installation can be a nuisance because a version of Trumpet WinSock is included, and you may have to delete its files to avoid conflict if you already have a version of Trumpet loaded elsewhere (especially if it is a different version). The program is an interesting, full-featured package that requires extra start-up and familiarization effort.

PC-Pine for WinSock	
Primary purpose	Usenet news and mail (send and receive)
Filename	PCPINE_W.ZIP
File size	528,763 bytes
Latest version	3.91 beta (October 1994)
Available from	ftp.cac.washington.edu: /pine/pcpine
Status	Copyrighted, but freely available
Documentation	Installation instructions and on-line help included
Features	Supports SMTP, MIME, IMAP, and NNTP protocols, but not POP3
Comments	Unfortunately, this WinSock version is quite disappointing; it is not a true Windows GUI application, but has the same user interface as the UNIX and DOS versions of Pine. Additional customized versions are available from the same location for Sun's PC-NFS, Novell's LAN Workplace for DOS, and so on.

Trumpet Newsreader

Primary purpose	Usenet news and mail (send only)
Filename	WT_WSK.ZIP
File size	96,305 bytes
Latest version	1.0 Rev B final beta 4 (September 1994)
Available from	ftp.trumpet.com.au: /ftp/pub/beta/wintrump
Note: This Australian site is difficult to access.	
Status	Shareware: $40. Site licenses also are available.
Documentation	Good
Features	The program can decode uuencoded files but is not notable for speed.
Comments	*Recommended.* This latest version is a very nice newsreader. Be forewarned, though: Because this is not a final version, some bugs may exist. (Yes, I know — even the final versions have bugs.)

WINDIS

Primary purpose	Mail (send), Usenet newsreader, SMTP server, Time client, and Finger client
Filename	WINDIS.ZIP and WINDIS.TXT
File size	119,604 and 9,942 bytes
Latest version	1.0 (November 1994)
Available from	disabuse.demon.co.uk: /pub/ibmpc/winsock/apps/windis
Status	Freeware. Source code is available.
Documentation	Basic start-up instructions
Features	NNTP News Client: Downloads news for reading with an off-line reader (separate program required) SMTP Mail Client: Downloads waiting mail for an off-line e-mailer SMTP Mail Server: Uploads mail as individual e-mail or to a newsgroup Finger Client: Fingers servers as appropriate Time Client: Gets server time
Comments	This was a first cut at a Windows replacement for the "DIS" program that Demon Systems distributes in the UK. Although primarily intended for Demon, it can be used with other providers. This program is still at an early stage, although some good documentation is now available. A new version 2.0 is imminent.

WinNET Mail and News

Primary purpose	Mail (send and receive) and Usenet newsreader
Filename	WNMAI230.ZIP
File size	644,549 bytes
Latest version	2.30 (November 1994)
Available from	oak.oakland.edu: /pub3/win3/internet
Status	Free, if you are using computer witchcraft as your Internet provider. Otherwise, the program is shareware: $99.
Documentation	Installation instructions and on-line help included
Features	Direct dialup to any system that provides UUCP (UNIX-UNIX-copy) service, send and receive mail, uuencode support for attached documents, and automated installation. The mail-server daemon can be programmed to call your Internet provider and download mail on certain days at specific times. Search capability is available within a single newsgroup or across newsgroups. The program does not have WinSock/SLIP capability.
Comments	This crippled unregistered version is limited to 2,400 bps. Registered users get additional features, including higher modem speeds. The package seems to be a nice one, but the registration costs are a little steep.

WinQVT

Primary purpose	Mail (send and receive), Usenet newsreader, Telnet, ftp file transfers, FTP/RCP server, network printer, and SMTP server
Filename	QVTWS398.ZIP or QVTW3983.ZIP (WinSocket versions)
Note: Separate packet driver and Windows NT versions are available from the biochemistry location under different filenames. This site can be difficult to access.	
File size	390,960 bytes
Latest version	3.98 (December 1994)
Available from	biochemistry.cwru.edu: gopher/pub/qvtnet ftp.cica.indiana.edu: /pub/pc/win3/winsock (or mirrors)
Status	Shareware: $40; students $20. Registered users receive a complete set of fonts, an 85-page user manual, and upgrades for one year.
Documentation	Installation instructions and on-line help are included
Features	VT52/VT102/VT220 terminal emulation; SMTP/POP3 send and receive mail, with polling (timed background mail checking); and capability to operate as a server for ftp. A basic SMTP server daemon has been added in this new version, permitting direct receipt of mail for network users who are always logged on.
Comments	WinQVT requires, at minimum, a 386 processor. The package is full-featured, and this upgrade is welcome for the bug fixes and feature enhancements it provides.

WinVN

Primary purpose	Mail (send only) and Usenet newsreader
Filename	WV16_93_11.ZIP
File size	261,848 bytes
Latest version	0.93.11 (December 1994)
Available from	ftp.ksc.nasa.gov: /pub/winvn/win3
Status	Public domain
Documentation	Installation instructions and on-line help included
Features	A threaded newsreader with the capability to send (but not receive) mail, using SMTP or MAPI, and built-in uudecoding, which is especially useful and convenient for downloading and viewing pictures
Comments	*Recommended.* WinVN is a relatively popular (and at times controversial) newsreader that is getting intensive development effort.

Miscellaneous

More specifically, this section offers a little bit of this and a little bit of that. One suggestion: If you've just received the bill from your Internet provider and you're having serious breathing problems, you may want to look at a new program in this section called SLIP db.

NCSA Audible Collage for Microsoft Windows

Primary purpose	Multiplatform collaboration tool
Filename	COL_12B1.ZIP
File size	203,546 bytes
Latest version	1.2 beta 1 (December 1993)
Available from	ftp.cica.indiana.edu: /pub/pc/win3/winsock (or mirrors)
Status	No mention of any charges
Documentation	Installation and start-up instructions
Comments	Collage is a whiteboard program that enables users to collaborate and share data across the three supported platforms: X Windows workstations, Apple Macintosh systems, and Windows systems. This program's documentation says, "You must have a Macintosh or an X Windows workstation running a server in order to use the network collaboration capabilities." Interesting.

Panda

Primary purpose	Mostly a mail program and newsreader for now
Filename	WINPANDA.ZIP
File size	244,842 bytes
Latest version	May 1994
Available from	chop.isca.uiowa.edu: /pub/panda
Status	No mention of any charges
Documentation	Almost nothing is included with the package, but logging on as **public** with the default configuration enables you to retrieve some basic information from an Iowa server.
Comments	Panda is a multipurpose, customized program being developed at the University of Iowa for campus network use. The program will include Gopher, Usenet, Mail, ftp, and so on. The current version does not retain configuration-setting changes between sessions and is somewhat rough and unstable at this point. Panda is a good example of some of the development work taking place in one of the universities; the program is of passing interest only.

SLIP db

Primary purpose	SLIP cost-accounting database (connection time and cost log)
Filename	SLIPDB10.ZIP
File size	426,014 bytes
Latest version	1.01 (September 1994)
Available from	ollc.mta.ca: /pub/slip ftp.cica.indiana.edu: /pub/pc/win3/winsock
Status	Shareware: $30 Canadian
Documentation	Start-up instructions and on-line help
Features	Automated installation. SLIP db records the date and time of each connection and disconnection from your Internet service provider; it then calculates elapsed time and figures out a cost based on a per-minute charge. The program has a browse mode that enables you to see a log of your calls, print a report, and delete records.
Comments	SLIP db is a good, all-purpose SLIP bean counter. The program is specifically designed to work with a SLIP dialup connection such as is provided by Trumpet WinSock.

Tcpmeter

Primary purpose	Graphical display of data flow
Filename	TCPMETER.EXE
File size	19,200 bytes
Latest version	October 1994
Available from	ftp.trumpet.com.au: /ftp/pub/beta/tcpmeter
Status	No information
Documentation	None
Comments	This program is from Peter Tattam, the Trumpet WinSock author. Tcpmeter provides a chart-recorder-type graphical readout of data flow. Received bytes per second are shown from the top down in green, and send bytes per second are shown from the bottom up in red. Clicking the right and left mouse buttons increases or decreases the vertical display scale from the default 1K per second. I'm not really sure about the intended use for this program, but it may be useful for monitoring the effective data-transfer rates while WinSock or other settings are being adjusted. The graphics are kind of neat. I believe that this program is designed to work only with Trumpet WinSock.

UpTime for Windows 3.1

Primary purpose	Connection-time log
Filename	UPTIME.ZIP
File size	3,337 bytes
Latest version	1.0 (October 1994)
Available from	ftp.cica.indiana.edu: /pub/pc/win3/util (or mirrors)
Status	Copyrighted, but no mention of any charges for use
Documentation	Basic start-up and use information
Comments	This program — a simple utility designed to track session logon time — is intended primarily for use with a dialup SLIP connection but is not limited to that. You must have the Visual Basic module VBRUN300.DLL (not included) installed on your system. It is included with many other programs and widely available from many locations.

WINAPPS

Primary purpose	Comprehensive client start-up package
Filename	WINAPPS.ZIP

(continued)

WINAPPS (continued)

File size	131,516 bytes
Latest version	N/A (most of these applications date from mid- to late 1993)
Available from	bode.ee.ualberta.ca: /pub/dos/win3/winsock
Status	Shareware, but no mention of any cost for use
Documentation	None
Features	The package includes ftp, Ping, telnet, Archie, Hopcheck, and Chat clients.
Comments	These applications are basic examples of simple WinSock clients that no longer are of any real interest, although the clients still are usable and this file still is available at many sites.

WINAPPS2

Primary purpose	Comprehensive client start-up package
Filename	WINAPPS2.ZIP
File size	123,743 bytes
Latest version	2.0 Rev A, released October 1994 to coincide with the release of the new Trumpet WinSock version 2.0. Individual clients range in date from 1993 to the present. Early versions were included in the original WINAPPS package (described in the preceding table).
Available from	ftp.trumpet.com.au: /ftp/pub/winsock ftp.cica.indiana.edu: /pub/pc/win3/winsock
Status	Shareware: no mention of any charges for use, but not to be resold or distributed for sale
Documentation	Negligible
Features	The package includes Ping, telnet, Archie, Chat, and viewer clients. The telnet client has been available separately for a while and is listed in the "Telnet" section later in this chapter.
Comments	WINAPPS2 is a basic starter package from Peter Tattam, the Trumpet WinSock author. An ftp client is, surprisingly, absent.

Windows Socket RCP client

Primary purpose	RCP client
Filename	WRCP09.ZIP
File size	55,676 bytes
Latest version	0.9 beta (November 1994)
Available from	stoner.eps.mcgill.ca: /pub/windows/winsock
Status	Freeware

Documentation	Basic installation and start-up instructions
Comments	The author is Steve McCauley.

Windows Sockets Net Watch

Primary purpose	Host checker
Filename	WS_WATCH.ZIP
File size	34,779 bytes
Latest version	Alpha 7 (December 1994)
Available from	ftp.usma.edu: /pub/msdos/winsock.files
Status	May be freely distributed and used but not sold
Documentation	Basic start-up instructions
Features	Lookup, Finger, and whois tools now added
Comments	The purpose of this program is to make active checks on hosts that are listed in its database file. This program is designed to work on any WinSock DLL, but it works much better on one that supports raw sockets. Released by John Junod, this program is something for network geeks to play with. This experimental program requires Microsoft's Win32s version 1.2. It also works well with Windows 95 and Windows NT 3.5.

WinLab and NetProto

Primary purpose	Advanced image processing and photo retouching with file-transfer module
Filename	WLABV30B.ZIP
File size	855,660 bytes
Latest version	3.0 (October 1994)
Available from	hp750.dibe.unige.it: /pub/phd (primary site: Italy) ftp.cica.indiana.edu: /pub/pc/win3/desktop (or mirrors)
Status	Shareware WinLab: 120.000 lire ($80 U.S.) NetProto: 30.000 lire ($20 U.S.)
Documentation	Start-up instructions and on-line help
Comments	The package contains an image processor (WinLab) and has the capability to remotely send or receive documents (NetProto) from another machine (also running NetProto) through the use of WinSock. This program is fully functional but is still a beta release. A commercial version is being developed.

WinTAR (Windows Tape Archive)

Primary purpose	Network tape-drive archiving program
Filename	WTAR122U.ZIP
File size	135,319 bytes
Latest version	1.22 (October 1994)
Available from	ftp.cica.indiana.edu: /pub/pc/win3/winsock (or mirrors)
Status	Shareware: single-copy registration $20 U.S., $25 Canadian. Volume discounts are available.
Documentation	All instructions included in on-line help
Comments	This program uses WinSock to connect through a network to access a tape drive to archive files. WinTAR can create or open files and can control the tape-drive mechanism. The program is not limited to tape drives; it also can archive to a local hard drive or floppy disk. WinTAR has a colorful toolbar.

Miscellaneous Non-WinSock

The general-purpose items listed in this section — viewers, decoders, and so on — often are used in conjunction with WinSock applications and are listed here for convenience.

CyberCom

Primary purpose	Windows replacement serial-port communications driver
Filename	CYBERC.ZIP or CYBERDRV.ZIP ***Note:*** Despite the different names, these files have identical content. The ZIP files were created with different compression ratios, which adds to the illusion that these files are different files that can be found in various locations.
File size	8,237 or 7,766 bytes, respectively
Latest version	1.1.0.0P (November 1993)
Available from	Try disabuse.demon.co.uk: /pub/ibmpc/windows/cybercom
Status	No charge for noncommercial use
Documentation	Simple installation instructions. When the driver is installed, its use is transparent.
Comments	CyberCom is a replacement for the standard Windows driver (COMM.DRV) that permits data transfers up to 115 kbps if you have a 16550 serial port chip and operate Windows 3.1 in enhanced mode. Now that 28-kbps modems are readily available, this driver (from CyberSoft Corporation) is one way to overcome the limitation of the standard Windows 3.1 driver. CyberCom is a relatively basic product. If you want to spend a little money, you can purchase apparently better drivers.

Note: Several commercial communications software packages, such as WinFax Pro, sometimes include similar replacement drivers for optional installation. A replacement driver is of no value if you have a slower modem and is not necessary if you have Windows for Workgroups (WFW) 3.11 installed. To find out whether you have a 16550 serial port, exit from Windows and run the DOS command MSD.

Fix16550 Device Driver

Primary purpose	To fix problems with AMI BIOS and 16550 UARTs
Filename	FIX16550.ZIP
File size	3,493 bytes
Latest version	1.01 (October 1993)
Available from	ftp.sogang.ac.kr: /msdos/sysutil
Status	Shareware: $10
Documentation	Basic information and instructions. The driver is relatively simple to install.
Comments	This device driver was written to overcome a problem that occurred in systems with an AMI BIOS combined with a 16550 UART serial port chip. Under certain circumstances and on some systems, a failure may occur after a soft reset when the system becomes unable to recognize the serial COM port, necessitating a hard restart to clear up the problem. This driver fixes that problem and should be installed only if you have specifically experienced the problem. As a secondary feature, this driver can be installed to enable COM3 and COM4 capability on older systems that lack these ports (mostly older 286 and 386 machines from certain manufacturers).

LView and LView Pro

Primary purpose	Graphic-image viewers
Filename	LVIEW31.ZIP and LVIEWP1A.ZIP (both 16-bit software)
File size	224,210 and 304,843 bytes, respectively
Latest version	LView: 3.1 (September 1993) LView Pro: 1.0A (January 1995)
Available from	oak.oakland.edu: /pub3/win3/graphics (both versions)
Status	LView: Freeware LView Pro: Shareware. Single registration $30 plus shipping.
Documentation	On-line help is included. The Pro version on-line help includes some good information about the JPEG format, suitability, and compression capabilities as well as speed-test results comparing the 16- and 32-bit versions of this program.

(continued)

LView and LView Pro	***(continued)***
Features	The Pro version is a graphics viewer capable of handling a wide range of popular formats: BMP/DIB/GIF/JPG/TGA/TIFF/PCX/PBM/PGM/PPM. This version supports both GIF87a and GIF89a variations. The freeware version is more limited.
Comments	*Recommended.* LView is a popular graphics viewer used primarily to view GIF and JPG picture formats, which are commonly found on the Internet. For most casual users, little difference exists between the two versions, although the Pro version now handles more file formats. The most significant advantage of the Pro version is that if you choose to register it, you can receive a 32-bit version for Windows 3.1 (if you have Win32s installed) or Windows NT systems; this version should be faster than the 16-bit version. The author, Leonardo Haddad Loureiro, is very active in continuing to develop this program (the Pro version).

MPEGPLAY

Primary purpose	Moving-picture player, MPEG (.MPG) format
Filename	MPEGW32H.ZIP

Note: You also should retrieve a FAQ.TXT file in the same directory. This file supplies some more information about potential installation and viewing problems, the MPEG format, and so on.

File size	641,988 bytes
Latest version	1.65 (September 1994)
Available from	decel.ecel.uwa.edu.au: /users/michael
Status	Shareware: single user $25, site license $50
Documentation	Installation instructions and on-line help are included, as well as some interesting technical information and history on the MPEG format.
Features	Supports the Microsoft WinG™ Windows gaming library
Comments	MPEGPLAY is a good MPEG player for Mosaic. The unregistered version is crippled and will not play MPEGs larger than 1MB. A sample video, ROCKET.MPG, is included.

Note: MPEGPLAY is a 32-bit player. You must have Win32s Version 1.15a or higher installed before you attempt to install or use this product. (See the listing for Win32s later in this section.)

UU (DOS)

Primary purpose	Uudecoder
Filename	UU33.ZIP

File size	31,165 bytes
Note: Unzipped, the program is only 8,917 bytes; the rest is documentation.	
Latest version	3.3 (November 1994)
Available from	ftp.io.com: /pub/usr/zboray/coding wuarchive.wustl.edu: /pub/MSDOS_UPLOADS/uucode
Status	Freeware
Documentation	Very extensive
Features	This program can be used on machines as slow as 8086 and 8088 models and with DOS versions as early as 2.0.
Comments	*Recommended.* UU, by Ben Jos Walbeehm, is one of the best uudecoders money can't buy — a very compact, very fast DOS program that can sort through and decode files that were uuencoded by a variety of other packages. The program can deal with many uuencode variations and glitches. As much as I hate DOS, the capability to go into a directory in which I have downloaded a large number of encoded files, type **uu *.***, and watch UU finish spitting out the viewable files in seconds makes this program indispensable. UU is great for chomping through Trumpet News archive folders (.MFL) and for decoding and putting together coded files and pictures that have been archived from newsgroups.

WIN32s (non OLE version)

Primary purpose	32-bit enhancement for Windows 3.1
Filename	PW1118.EXE
File size	1,244,633 bytes
Latest version	1.20 (October 1994)
Available from	ftp.microsoft.com: softlib/MSLFILES
Status	Distributed free to licensed users of Windows 3.1 or Windows for Workgroups 3.11
Documentation	Minimal
Comments	This Microsoft program adds an extension to Windows 3.1, enabling it to run some of the 32-bit programs that are beginning to appear (such as all recent releases of Mosaic *except* the latest alpha 8 version). As a bonus, the program includes a 32-bit game called Freecell. Being able to play the game confirms that the upgrade has been successfully installed. Version 1.20 has a simpler automated installation process and automatically removes any unnecessary files from previous versions it finds during installation. You must have, at minimum, a 386 processor (32-bit capability). One disadvantage of Win32s is the additional burden it places on a system's resources — a potential problem on lower-powered (processor and RAM) machines.

(continued)

WIN32s (non OLE version) (continued)	
Note:	If you ever need to remove Win32s from your system, the procedure is described in Microsoft document Q120486, dated September 29, 1994. This document should be available from ftp.microsoft.com: /developr/win32dk/kb/Q120/4/86.txt.

WIN32s (OLE version)	
Primary purpose	32-bit enhancement to Windows 3.1
Filename	w32sole.exe
File size	2,240,650 bytes
Latest version	1.20 with OLE (September 1994)
Available from	ftp.ncsa.uiuc.edu: /Web/Mosaic/Windows This is in the same location as the corresponding new version of Mosaic, and so both can be conveniently downloaded at the same time. For modem users, it might be a good idea to begin these downloads at the beginning of your lunch hour.
Status	Distributed free to licensed users of Windows 3.1 or Windows For Workgroups 3.11
Documentation	Negligible
Comments	Because the new version of Mosaic is now an OLE-compatible application, Mosaic users must have this version, Win32s 1.20 with OLE, installed on their system first before trying to install or use this new Mosaic version alpha 8. The regular Win32s version 1.20 is no longer adequate. This self-extracting file should be placed in a temporary directory and exploded. The install.bat file that is created then must be run, and finally setup.exe on "disk1" can be run to begin the installation. Installation was smooth for me; it overwrote the existing non-OLE 1.20 version I had just installed a month or two earlier.

NFS Clients

Ha! Fooled you — there *aren't* any true WinSock NFS (Network File System) clients. The current WinSock 1.1 specification apparently doesn't support NFS. These products won't exist, therefore, until the spec is updated (I haven't a clue when) and the new compliant products begin to appear. The best interim solution is to try to find an NFS client that is specific to your TCP/IP stack. The information about NFS in this section is condensed from a variety of newsgroup postings by People Who Know About These Things. The section lists some good possibilities for specific systems.

XFS (16-bit)

Primary purpose	NFS client
Filename	XFS186.ZIP
File size	163,390 bytes
Latest version	1.8 (September 1994)
Available from	lwfws1.uni-paderborn.de: /pub/xfs oak.oakland.edu: /SimTel/msdos/nfs
Status	Shareware: educational users $15, business users $25. Site licenses are available.
Documentation	Start-up documentation
Comments	XFS is a Network File System (NFS) client implementation for PCs running MS-DOS. The product works with most recent versions of MS-DOS and is compatible with Trumpet WinSock but must be loaded first. XFS also can be used with Microsoft Windows for Workgroups, Microsoft LAN Manager, and Novell NetWare IPX and ODI.

XFS32 (32-bit)

Primary purpose	NFS client
Filename	XFS32-11.ZIP
File size	101,477 bytes
Latest version	1.01 (September 1994)
Available from	lwfws1.uni-paderborn.de: /pub/xfs oak.oakland.edu: /SimTel/msdos/nfs
Status	Shareware: educational users $15, business users $25. Site licenses are available.
Documentation	Start-up documentation and on-line help
Comments	XFS32 is an NFS client for PCs running MS-DOS, Microsoft Windows for Workgroups (WFW), and Microsoft TCP/IP-32.

Ph Clients

Ph clients are used to access CSO name servers, which contain a database used primarily for the storage and retrieval of telephone and e-mail directory information. Huh? In other words, Ph is similar to an electronic phone book.

Ph is another protocol similar to Finger. Ph clients are designed to access sites running a CSO server to obtain e-mail addresses. If, for example, you had only a person's name and location but needed his exact e-mail address and a CSO server was operating at that site, you could query that server to obtain the necessary information. The database also can be used to store other general information, such as weather data, and can be used for security purposes to validate users. Ph clients are increasingly being incorporated as components of other WinSock packages, such as mail programs and WWW browsers. CSO was the acronym for the University of Illinois Computing Services Office, which developed this database system. (CCSO stands for Computer and Communications Services Office, formerly known as CSO.)

IRL CCSO Phone Windows Client

Primary purpose	CCSO Windows Ph client
Filename	IRLPHWIN.ZIP or IRLPH23.ZIP
File size	399,110 bytes (both)
Latest version	2.3.2 beta (September 1994)
Available from	auck.irl.cri.nz: /pub/phone
Status	Freeware
Documentation	Start-up instructions and on-line help included
Features	The program contains both 16- and 32-bit execution files (your choice), although for the 32-bit version, you must have Microsoft's Win32s extension installed (and the latest version, 1.15a; see the "Miscellaneous Non-WinSock" section later in this chapter for more information).
Comments	This program is by Graeme Campbell.

PHWIN

Primary purpose	CCSO Windows Ph client
Filename	PHWIN22.ZIP
File size	119,378 bytes

Note: If you are downloading this program from another location, watch the file size. For some strange reason, useless fragments about 5K in size appear under this filename in many locations.

Latest version	2.2 beta (November 1993)
Available from	Try ftp.cac.psu.edu: /pub/access/test
Status	Freeware
Documentation	Start-up instructions and on-line help included
Comments	This program, by Graeme Campbell, appears to be an early version of the IRL CCSO Phone Windows Client, listed earlier in this section.

Ping

Do you remember those old World War II movies, with the crew of the submarine huddled over the sonar, watching the echoes coming back? Ping is sort of the computer equivalent of sonar. Ping clients are used to provide echolike checks of servers to confirm that a good connection exists. A Ping client sends data packets to a host, which (if it supports Ping, and most hosts do) bounces back a reply packet. Packets are numbered so that any dropout can be identified and the quality of the connection can be determined. If nothing comes back, no connection exists. If you have a good connection, you can go ahead and launch the torpedoes.

WSNWUTIL

Primary purpose	Echo, Ping, and ftp clients; Echo server
Filename	WSNWUTIL.ZIP
File size	162,674 bytes
Latest version	December 15, 1994
Available from	rmii.com: /pub2/mclouden (latest version)
	ftp.cica.indiana.edu: /pub/pc/win3/winsock (or mirrors)
Status	Freeware (limited); cannot be sold
Documentation	Installation instructions and on-line help
Comments	Previously called WSNWDEMO, this new release does not include the Finger client. This product is interesting and worth looking at. WSNWUTIL is being actively developed by its author, Mark Clouden.

WS Ping (Windows Sockets Ping client)

Primary purpose	Ping client
Filename	WS_PING.ZIP
File size	60,496 bytes
Latest version	Release 1 (October 1994)
Note: Older versions may be floating around other locations with the same filename, so match by file size to identify the version.	
Available from	ftp.usma.edu: /pub/msdos/winsock.files
Status	Public domain
Documentation	Almost none
Comments	WS Ping is from John Junod; source code is included. The program does not work with Microsoft TCP/IP-32 and Windows NT.

Telephone Dialers

Never got that archaic dialing script for Trumpet to work properly? At least you have other options. Be forewarned that, as good as many of these dialers are, they can't always anticipate all the logon quirks of the various Internet service providers. Be prepared to try more than one package. The good news is that some significant improvements are being made in some of the products.

Dialer

Primary purpose	Telephone dialer
Filename	DIALEXE.ZIP
File size	31,072 bytes
Latest version	2.0a (May 1994)
Available from	disabuse.demon.co.uk: /pub/ibmpc/windows/utilities
Status	No indication of any charges for use
Documentation	No start-up instructions or on-line help
Comments	Dialer has an easy-to-create logon script.

GoSlip!

Primary purpose	Telephone dialer
Filename	GOSLIP2.ZIP
File size	1,237,954 bytes
Latest version	2.0 alpha 2 (October 1994)
Available from	ftp.cica.indiana.edu: /pub/pc/win3/winsock (or mirrors)
Status	Free for noncommercial use
Documentation	Negligible
Features	Automatic logon with easy-to-use scripts, automated setup, and support for multiple configurations. Configuration options, scripts, and application-launch controls can be tweaked while the system is running.
Comments	The preceding version of this program was an impressive Windows dialer with an easy-to-use scripting capability. This major new revision of the program aims to add many features, including direct handling of dynamic (randomly assigned when you log on each time) IP addresses. In alpha release at the moment, primarily for testing purposes, GoSlip! is difficult to use and buggy and is best avoided unless you are interested in helping with testing. This program is promising and will be worth looking at when the final version becomes available. The preceding version still may be available at a number of sites under the filename GOSLIP11.ZIP. The old version was very functional and stable, but the fact that it could not handle dynamic IPs limited its appeal.

NetDial

Primary purpose	Telephone dialer
Filename	ND250S.ZIP
File size	640,958 bytes
Latest version	2.50 (November 1994)
Available from	oak.oakland.edu: /pub3/win3/winsock disabuse.demon.co.uk: /pub/ibmpc/winsock/apps/netdial
Status	Shareware: $20
Documentation	Installation instructions and on-line help included
Features	Automatic logon with easy-to-use scripts; support for as many as five separate configurations; redialing up to 99 times; support for modem speeds up to 256 kbps; capability to run minimized, with audible notification on connect; and automated installation. The program now includes a connection-logging capability that keeps track of on-line time. In the new version, an optional carriage-return kick occurs during logon, which some host systems require.
Comments	*Recommended.* A major new upgrade now supports dynamic IP addresses (randomly assigned when you log on each time). NetDial requires, at minimum, a 386 processor and a 100 percent Hayes-compatible modem. NetDial is a well-designed, easy-to-use program. The biggest nuisance is that because of the many recent changes being made, the upgrades are not always compatible with previous versions; therefore, the user may have to create a new INI file, including new scripts, with every installation. At least a minor version change seems to occur every few weeks. On the positive side, NetDial is the first dialer I have been able to get working properly with the dynamic IP from my Internet provider. The script did, however, take a certain amount of trial and error combined with a careful reading of the corresponding help-file documentation.

WAIS Dialer

Primary purpose	Telephone dialer
Comments	This dialer is included with the new version of USGS WinWAIS and now is automatically installed as a stand-alone SLIP dialer with its own Windows icon. The program is specifically designed to work with Trumpet WinSock. WAIS Dialer is a simple-to-use program with a manual script that provides maximum flexibility with time delays and time-outs. Maximum modem speed is 19,200 kbps. For file information and other details, see the listing for USGS WinWAIS.

Telnet

For many users, nothing has provided more frustration than the search for a good, freely available Telnet program (the Holy Grail). Fortunately, over the past few months, some good, new programs have appeared. In addition, most programs listed in this section continue to be worked on and improved by their authors. A unique solution comes from David Yon, whose COMt program provides the usually powerful Telnet functions of a commercial communications program with access to the Internet.

COMt: the Telnet Modem

Primary purpose	Modem Telnet interface utility
Filename	COMT.ZIP
File size	113,692 bytes
Latest version	1.03 (October 1994)
Available from	ftp.std.com: /customers/software/rfdmail
Status	Shareware: $15.95
Documentation	Installation instructions and on-line help included
Features	COMt is a relatively flexible package, enabling you to connect by using IP addresses or host names. You can choose terminal-type options, baud-rate options, serial-port number, and so on. The product has limited support for transparent TCP/IP access to modem pools, as well as automated installation.
Comments	According to the developer of this programs, ". . . solution to under-powered Windows Telnet client programs. COMt allows you to use your favorite Windows communications program (that is, Procomm Plus for Windows, Crosstalk for Windows, etc.) to communicate over TCP/IP. COMt does this by installing itself ahead of the standard Windows COMM driver (COMM.DRV) and intercepts accesses to the COM ports of your choosing, routing them to TCP/IP. Requests to access other ports are passed on to the original COMM driver, allowing you to continue to use those devices." In other words, COMt acts as an interface that permits the terminal emulators in your commercial communications package to access the Internet. The program is compatible with Trumpet WinSock. The latest version works with CompuServe's WinCIM Version 1.3, although it does not work with Reflections (HP). COMt, which comes from the same company that produces RFD Mail, is proving to be popular.

EWAN

Primary purpose	Telnet (terminal emulator)
Filename	EWAN105.ZIP

File size	252,802 bytes
Latest version	1.05 (December 1994)
Available from	ftp.lysator.liu.se: /pub/msdos/windows
Status	Freeware
Documentation	Simple start-up instructions and on-line help
Features	ANSI/VT52/VT100 emulation with automated installation. Each stored site can have a customized configuration associated with it.
Comments	Released a few months ago, EWAN continues to be improved by its author and has developed a strong following. ANSI capability was added recently. If you have problems with tiny windows in versions 1.02 or 1.03, try changing to a larger default font; window size is determined by font size! A short description of how to create emulations for EWAN (for current Version 1.03) is available in a Windows Write format through the WWW at http://www.lysator.liu.se/~zander/ewan.html.

NCSA WinTel

Primary purpose	Telnet (terminal emulator)
Filename	WINTELB3.ZIP
File size	55,834 bytes
Latest version	Unsupported beta 3 (1993)
Available from	ftp.cica.indiana.edu: /pub/pc/win3/winsock (or mirrors)
Status	No charge for use
Documentation	Minimal; no on-line help
Comments	Not supported; not currently under development

QWS3270 EXTRA

Primary purpose	Telnet (terminal emulator)
Filename	QWS3270.ZIP

Note: If you are downloading the program from other locations, match the file date or size to ensure that you are getting the latest version. Each new release continues to be circulated under the same filename, making the different releases hard to distinguish.

File size	Freeware version: 73,365 bytes
	Shareware version: 102,873 bytes
Latest version	Freeware (limited): 3.2e (October 1994)
	Shareware: 2.0 (November 1994)

(continued)

QWS3270 EXTRA ***(continued)***

Available from	Freeware: ftp.ccs.queensu.ca: /pub/msdos/tcpip Shareware: ftp.cica.indiana.edu: /pub/pc/win3/winsock (or mirrors)
Status	Freeware Shareware: $35
Documentation	Setup instructions and on-line help
Features	Support for IBM 3270 and Tektronix 4010 terminals; 64-character type-ahead buffer; full customized keyboard; and support for about a dozen foreign-language character-translation sets, including German, Danish, Dutch, French, and Swedish
Comments	Both the freeware and enhanced (EXTRA) shareware versions have been circulated with the same filename; the files can be distinguished only by file size (without unzipping). The freeware version is being supported (bug fixes and minor enhancements) only for Queens University faculty members and students and is up to Version 3.2. The shareware EXTRA version started at 1.0 and now is up to 2.0. For the best features, get the newest shareware version, which is being actively developed by its author.

Tektel

Primary purpose	Telnet (terminal emulator)
Filename	TEKTEL1B.ZIP
File size	56,826 bytes
Latest version	1b (June 1994)
Available from	ftp.cica.indiana.edu: /pub/pc/win3/winsock (or mirrors)
Status	Public domain
Documentation	Limited; no on-line help
Features	Tektronix T4010 terminal emulation
Comments	The program is written in Visual Basic and requires VBRUN300.DLL, which is not included but is widely available (and often bundled with other programs).

Trumpet Telnet

Primary purpose	Telnet (terminal emulator)
Filename	TTEL0_07.ZIP
File size	29,639 bytes
Latest version	0.07 alpha (September 1994)

Available from	ftp.trumpet.com.au: /ftp/pub/beta/trmptel
Status	Currently copyright freeware, but eventually will be shareware
Documentation	None
Features	A basic VT100, now with cut-and-paste and font control
Comments	Trumpet Telnet is from Peter Tattam.

UW Term

Primary purpose	Telnet (terminal emulator)
Filename	See "Comments"
File size	Approximately 20 files, 1,261,000 bytes
Latest version	0.97g (November 1994)
Available from	ftphost.cac.washington.edu: /pub/winsock/uwterm_0.97g
Status	Freeware
Documentation	Good, but no on-line help
Features	VT52/VT100/VT200 emulation, automated installation, adjustable colors and fonts, save-and-restore capability for configurations, and automated login. Multiple terminals can be active simultaneously.
Comments	This program is available only as a cluster of files in a directory, all of which you should download. Some of the files (such as VBRUN300.DLL) may create duplicates on your system and can be deleted after installation if you already have an existing equivalent version in a path directory. The program is slightly customized for intended use at the University of Washington, and outside use is not supported by the author.

Note: According to the author, this program does not work properly with Trumpet WinSock 1.0a or the newer Trumpet 1.0b beta 6. No information is available about compatibility with more recent Trumpet releases, such as 2.0.

VT-220 for Workgroups

Primary purpose	Telnet (terminal emulator)
Filename	VT220.EXE
File size	552,388 bytes
Latest version	1.5 (May 1994)
Available from	bode.ee.ualberta.ca: /pub/dos/win3/winsock
Status	Demo copy provided for evaluation purposes only
Documentation	Negligible; no on-line help
Features	VT52/VT100/VT220 terminal emulation and automated setup
Comments	For the latest price and other information, send e-mail to sales@dart.com (Dart Communications).

YAWTEL

Primary purpose	Telnet (terminal emulator)
Filename	YAWTEL02.ZIP
File size	12,024 bytes
Latest version	0.2 beta (July 1994)
Available from	ftp.cica.indiana.edu: /pub/pc/win3/winsock (or mirrors)
Status	No charge for now, while the product is being developed
Documentation	Negligible; no on-line help in this early version
Features	VT100 emulation
Comments	This package was designed with Mosaic in mind. Use caution: This program is being released for testing purposes and apparently is at a very early stage in development. You can expect the program to be buggy. The author will appreciate feedback.

Note: For more Telnet information, see WinQVT in the "Mail and News" section and see CSMRLW and UNIBOL/Desktop Terminal in the "Commercial Demo Packages" section, both earlier in this chapter.

TCP/IP

TCP/IP stands for Transmission Control Protocol/Internet Protocol. This networking standard is used by the Internet for the transfer of data packets. It's a standard that essentially allows two computers to talk to each other.

Microsoft TCP/IP-32 for Windows for Workgroups 3.11

Primary purpose	TCP/IP networking package
Filename	WFWT32.EXE
File size	Approximately 678,000 bytes
Latest version	3.11a (November 1994)
Available from	ftp.microsoft.com: /peropsys/windows/public/tcpip
Status	No charge
Documentation	Primitive, but little documentation is required. The program installs as a protocol in Network Setup.
Comments	The program, which is for network users, runs only under Windows for Workgroups. The package includes the Microsoft WinSock and a few clients, such as telnet, Ping, and ftp. This update has just been released to fix bugs.

Time Synchronizers

Is your PC's clock always wrong? Are you too lazy to bother resetting it? Here's the solution! The packages listed in this section can access your local Internet server (and other servers); compare the server's time setting with that of your PC; and report the difference or, if you choose, do an automatic update for you. Features and operation vary somewhat from package to package. If you are not satisfied with the accuracy of your local server, an atomic clock is available for access at time-A.timefreq.bldrdoc.gov (132.163.135.130).

NTTardis (Windows NT version)

Primary purpose	Time synchronizer
Filename	NTTARDIS.ZIP
File size	53,795 bytes
Latest version	1.0 (September 1994)
Available from	ftp.cica.indiana.edu: /pub/pc/win3/nt (or mirrors)
Status	Shareware: $20
Documentation	Start-up documentation
Features	The Tardis Server for Windows NT implements RFC 868 (TCP only; no UDP). The program acts as both an RFC 868 server and client — that is, it can get the time from a time server that has the correct time and then make the correct time available to local clients. The program can run in the background, checking at defined intervals, and contains a maximum adjustment filter.
Comments	Other than the fact that both packages come from Demon country across the ocean and have similar names, this package has nothing in common with Tardis, the Windows 3.1 version (described in the following listing). The programs appear to have different authors.

Tardis

Primary purpose	Time synchronizer
Filename	TARDISV2.ZIP
File size	36,684 bytes
Latest version	2.0 (November 1994)
Available from	ftp.cica.indiana.edu: /pub/pc/win3/winsock (or mirrors)
Status	Shareware: individual user $20, site license $40
Documentation	Start-up instructions and on-line help included
Features	Can run in the background, checking at defined intervals; contains a maximum adjustment filter
Comments	The latest version of Tardis is noticeably improved from the first release. I was particularly impressed by the author's simple solution for the time-zone problem this time around. Authors of similar programs should emulate (that is, steal) this idea.

Timesync

Primary purpose	Time synchronizer
Filename	TSYNC1_8.ZIP
File size	399,725 bytes
Latest version	1.8 (July 1994)
Available from	ftphost.cac.washington.edu: /pub/winsock
Status	Public domain
Documentation	Setup instructions
Features	Automated setup
Comments	Timesync is a simple WinSock application that sets your PC's clock to match the time on a remote host. The remote host must provide the UNIX time service on port 37 (Timesync does not use NTP). This program should make the time setting accurate at least to within one second.

Windows Time Client

Primary purpose	Time synchronizer
Filename	WSTIM101.ZIP
File size	86,527 bytes
Latest version	1.01 (August 1994)
Available from	sunsite.unc.edu: /pub/micro/pc-stuff/ms-windows/winsock/apps ftp.cica.indiana.edu: /pub/pc/win3/winsock wuarchive.wustl.edu: /pub/MSDOS_UPLOADS/winsock
Status	Freeware; all source code included
Documentation	Start-up instructions and on-line help included
Features	The last five time servers accessed are added to the host menu for easy access. The program can modify the local system's time or simply report the time returned from the time server. TCP or UDP connection option.
Comments	Windows Time Client has been tested only on Trumpet WinSock, but it should work on most stacks. The program is fast and simple to use, and it should be accurate to within one second.

WinSNTP

Primary purpose	Time synchronizer
Filename	WSNTP15F.ZIP
File size	157,926 bytes

Latest version	1.5f (November 1994)
Available from	sunsite.unc.edu: /pub/micro/pc-stuff/ms-windows/winsock/apps louie.udel.edu: /pub/ntp
Status	Shareware: $25
Documentation	Start-up instructions and on-line help included
Features	The program can operate over a wide range of different network connections, ranging from SLIP to high-speed local-area networks. WinSNTP can periodically poll the NTP server to keep the PC clock accurate within a configurable limit. The program can handle changes in daylight savings time.
Comments	This program, an implementation of the Simple Network Time Protocol (SNTP), is designed to keep a computer clock synchronized to the correct time with a high degree of accuracy for critical applications. WinSNTP requires access to an NTP server. A 32-bit Windows NT version is under development.

WAIS (Wide Area Information Service)

The Wide Area Information Service (WAIS) project — started by Thinking Machines, Apple Computer, and Dow Jones News Retrieval — now is being operated by the Clearinghouse for Networked Information Discovery and Retrieval. About 300 servers are available worldwide as part of the network. WAIS is an information-search system that has not become very popular.

ElNet WinWAIS

Primary purpose	WAIS search client
Filename	EWAIS204.ZIP
File size	1,451,068 bytes
Latest version	2.04 (June 1994)
Available from	ftp.einet.net: /einet/pc
Status	Shareware; $35 after 30-day evaluation period
Documentation	Start-up instructions and some on-line help included
Features	Automated installation procedure; two graphics viewers (gfxVIEW and winECJ) included. The program can be configured so that you can use your own viewers.
Comments	This is the largest of the WAIS clients, due partly to the graphics viewers that are included.

USGS WinWAIS (U.S. Geological Survey WAIS for Windows)

Primary purpose	WAIS search client
Filename	WWAIS24.EXE
File size	591,071 bytes
Latest version	2.4 (March 1994)
Available from	wais.com: /pub/freeware/dos
Status	Freeware
Documentation	Start-up instructions and on-line help included, in addition to basic instructions and examples on how to use the program
Features	Automated installation procedure; includes a separate (optional) SLIP dialer and a VT100 telnet application
Comments	No graphics viewers are included in the program. See the listing for the separate SLIP dialer, WAIS Dialer, in the "Telephone Dialers" section earlier in this chapter.

WAIS Manager

Primary purpose	WAIS search client
Filename	WAISMAN3.ZIP
File size	851,085 bytes
Latest version	3.1 (June 1993)
Available from	ftp.cnidr.org: /pub/nidr.tools/wais/pc/windows
Status	Free for noncommercial purposes
Documentation	Includes start-up instructions and on-line help
Comments	If you are using the DOS program PKUNZIP, use the -d option when you unzip this file to create proper subdirectories (for example, pkunzip -d waisman3.zip). According to a recent newsgroup posting, this program no longer is supported by its author.

Whois

Whois clients use the whois protocol for looking up people, hosts, and organizations in the database kept by the Network Information Center (NIC) at SRI International or at other whois servers. The information available is limited.

WinWhois

Primary purpose	Whois identification
Filename	WINWHOIS.ZIP
File size	37,877 bytes
Latest version	1.1 (September 1994)
Available from	Try ftp.sunet.se: /pub/pc/windows/winsock/apps/winwhois
Status	Copyrighted, but no mention of any charges
Documentation	Minimal. A brief explanation of the protocol and how to use it is included, but there are no installation instructions or on-line help. You can obtain some additional information from the default server by performing a whois search on the word *help.*
Features	This version has a history feature, which saves in an INI file as many as the last ten servers that were looked up.
Comments	This package is a simple one, although a little more documentation would be nice.

WinWhois 32 (Windows NT version)

Primary purpose	Whois identification
Filename	WHOIS32.ZIP
File size	24,656 bytes
Latest version	Beta version 1 (May 1994)
Available from	ftp.cica.indiana.edu: /pub/pc/win3/winsock (or mirrors)
Status	Copyrighted, but no mention of any charges
Documentation	Minimal
Comments	This program is a 32-bit version of WinWhois for Windows NT, created by Larry Kahn. The program appears to work with regular Windows 3.1 with a Win32s upgrade.

World Wide Web Browsers

Less than a year before this book was published, the only Web browsers available were Cello (feature-poor) and Mosaic (bug-rich). Since then, we have seen the release of a limited demo version of Air Mosaic and free versions of Netscape, WinWeb, and other programs. Each newcomer has its fans and its critics, and none is ideal. Users have choices that we lacked before, and competition will provide a rapid evolution of features. From a user's point of view, it's similar to going to an ice-cream store and one day finding, to your surprise, that rather than just vanilla, the store has different, wonderful flavors. It may still be ice cream, but it's different and it's better.

Curiously enough, the large number of WWW browsers that are freely available on the Internet is discouraging many companies from developing and offering their own packages. After all, what's the point in spending money to develop a product that your competitors are giving away for free? This is the ultimate buyer's market. Netscape Communications (formerly Mosaic Netscape) has wisely chosen to make most of its money on the more controllable server side of the business; other companies may use similar strategies. Incidentally, Netscape is a good choice if you're looking for your first browser; despite its many problems, it is undoubtedly the most popular WWW browser currently in use.

Cello

Primary purpose	World Wide Web (WWW) browser
Filename	CELLO.ZIP
Note:	Watch out for older versions that have the same filename. Match the file size if you are downloading the program from other locations.
File size	328,429 bytes
Latest version	1.01a (March 1994)
Available from	ftp.law.cornell.edu: /pub/lii/cello
Status	No charge for noncommercial use
Documentation	Installation instructions and on-line help included
Comments	Cello is a basic WWW viewer, much easier to run than Mosaic, although it doesn't have all the features, such as support for in-line pictures. What Cello does have is fewer bugs, and it is much less demanding on your system's resources.

InternetWorks Lite

Primary purpose	WWW browser
Filename	NETLITE.EXE
File size	1,529,647 bytes
Latest version	Beta 4 (December 1994)
Available from	ftp.booklink.com: /lite
Status	Demo preview version. A full commercial version, with working mail, news, and a directory, is available for $99 from Booklink (which has been purchased by America Online).
Documentation	Start-up instructions and on-line help
Features	Automated installation. Multitasking support with separate windows created for each activity.
Comments	The browser's background color (which will be white on most machines) is tied to Windows desktop settings and is not separately adjustable. Similar to Mosaic, Netscape text is displayed first, enabling you to begin reading immediately while the graphics are then retrieved. The default pages that are provided are primarily menu-driven and easy to use. This demo version works with SLIP only — there is no PPP support.

NCSA Mosaic (16-bit)

Primary purpose	WWW browser
Filename	WMOS20A2.ZIP
File size	243,749 bytes
Latest version	2.0 alpha 2 (March 1994)
Available from	ftp.ncsa.uiuc.edu: /Web/Mosaic/Windows/old
Status	No charge for noncommercial use
Documentation	Good
Comments	This program, which is the regular 16-bit version, is the final release for a 16-bit Windows 3.1 version. No additional development is planned for this version. NCSA Mosaic is not compatible with Windows for Workgroups 3.11. See the following listing for the 32-bit version.

NCSA Mosaic (32-bit)

Primary purpose	WWW browser
Filename	MOS20A8.ZIP
File size	955,546 bytes
Latest version	2.0 alpha 8 (December 1994)
Available from	ftp.ncsa.uiuc.edu: /Web/Mosaic/Windows
Status	No charge for noncommercial use
Documentation	Installation and setup instructions are included. On-line help is precisely that — downloaded from the NCSA server as required and, therefore, available to you only when you are logged on.
Features	Has added tables, a number of new tags, and a stand-alone mode that does not require a winsock.dll on your system
Comments	This new version requires a special OLE-compatible version of Win32s that must be installed on your system before installing this newer version of Mosaic. Details about this program are in the "Miscellaneous Non-WinSock" section earlier in this chapter. Fortunately, your existing .INI file is retained with this installation so that you don't have to reedit all over again to add viewers.

Note: If you get one of the following errors when you try to run this new version of Mosaic:

"Win32s. Initialization of dll failed. Process is terminating abnormally"

or

"Unexpected DOS error 21"

change the international settings of Windows (with the Control Panel) to show language "English (American)" and *not* Finnish or Swedish or Norwegian or any other foreign-language setting.

Netscape ("Mozilla")

Primary purpose	WWW browser
Filename	NS16-100.EXE
File size	706,929 bytes
Latest version	1.0N (December 1994)
Available from	ftp.mcom.com: /pub/netscape/windows ftp.digital.com: /pub/net/infosys/netscape stones.com: /pub/netscape
Status	Free for use by students or employees in nonprofit companies. All others may use this program for only an evaluation period before paying the registration fee.
Documentation	Minimal with the package. Most of the information is available on-line from the home site.
Features	Features document interaction (work on a document) before the entire document is downloaded. Capable of accessing multiple servers simultaneously. Optimized to run on 14.4 kbps modems. Internal support for JPEG image format. The ability to use Netscape server/client software to securely send credit card information over the Internet will help to speed the commercialization and development of the Internet.
Comments	Netscape has many features that are bound to be popular. Netscape is perhaps unique among browsers in not being able to vary the background gray color. This package has become controversial because its developers have implemented some advanced HTML (HyperText Markup Language) capabilities, such as text flowing around images, control over font sizes, and centering. Unfortunately, these features are not part of the current HTML standard and will not necessarily be part of the next standards update. Documents specifically created with these features, although pleasing to view on Netscape, will not be properly displayed on the numerous other browsers. This program, incidentally, was written from scratch by the developers, some of whom were part of the original NCSA Mosaic development team. The choice of Mosaic Netscape as the initial name was unfortunate and incorrectly implied a connection with the NCSA Mosaic browser. The company name has since been changed to Netscape Communications Corporation.

Note: A commercial version of this program will be released soon. Although the code is essentially the same, the commercial version will have a printed manual and technical support. MCI Communications will offer a version of the Netscape browser through its recently announced Internet service.

SETMOS

Primary purpose	Configuration setup utility for NCSA Mosaic
Filename	SMOSAIC.ZIP
File size	349,321 bytes
Note: The program itself is very small, but the ZIP file contains the obligatory VBRUN300.DLL standard Visual Basic file. You probably have at least half a dozen duplicates of this file scattered across your system if you have installed any number of shareware packages.	
Latest version	1.2 alpha (September 1994)
Available from	ftp.cica.indiana.edu: /pub/pc/win3/winsock (or mirrors)
Status	Nothing stated
Documentation	Negligible
Features	Automated installation
Comments	This program is designed to simplify the traditionally cumbersome process of configuring the MOSAIC.INI file with all the necessary viewers and connection information. The information you enter in a simple window is fed back and used to update the corresponding sections of MOSAIC.INI automatically. Although this program is very straightforward, the lack of documentation is disconcerting initially. The author, Rod Potter, suggests that you use the official Mosaic documentation to understand and determine your settings. This program represents a good idea that is relatively well executed.

SlipKnot

Note: This program is not a WinSock program; it operates on the UNIX shell.	
Primary purpose	WWW browser
Filename	SLNOT100.ZIP
File size	1,193,552 bytes
Latest version	1.0 (November 1994)
Available from	oak.oakland.edu: /SimTel/win3/internet
Status	Shareware: $29 U.S., Canada, Japan, and western Europe; $20 elsewhere. Ten percent of all fees is donated to refugee relief.
Documentation	Start-up information and on-line help
Features	As many as five different documents can be displayed on-screen simultaneously. You can ask for the retrieval of many documents, and these requests are queued up to be activated one by one. For functionality reasons, only X and Y protocol downloads are supported, and not Z. You are allowed to switch

(continued)

SlipKnot (continued)

	between WWW and your UNIX terminal session (except when downloading documents). You can choose not to retrieve the pictures embedded inside documents, thereby speeding the downloading process significantly. Then, if you change your mind, you can ask SlipKnot to get the same document with the pictures.
Comments	This is an interesting and innovative program — a WWW browser that uses Windows, but not WinSock or SLIP. SlipKnot, released by MicroMind, is designed for modem users who have ordinary dialup UNIX shell accounts. The program requires a 386 processor or better and at least 4MB of RAM. In addition, your service provider must have certain software on the server (Lynx, for example). SlipKnot has not yet been tested on Windows NT. The current version does not support some features (such as Forms and Authentication) and does not currently access Gopher. This version is the first release, and some problems exist, but nonetheless it is a unique and welcome addition to the browser ranks.

WinWeb

Primary purpose	WWW browser
Filename	WINWEB.ZIP
File size	598,834 bytes
Latest version	1.0A2.1.1 (November 1994)
Available from	ftp.einet.net: /einet/pc/winweb
Status	No charge for noncommercial use
Documentation	Somewhat weak. On-line help is provided for, but none is included with the current version.
Features	The latest version supports the capability to load local documents and read them off-line; the only requirement is a WINSOCK.DLL file that the program can locate (Trumpet WinSock, for example).
Comments	WinWeb is a new addition to the ranks of WWW browsers. The program is easy to install and should run well even on less powerful machines that have only 4MB of RAM. The flexible cache can adjust automatically to use any additional memory that is available. The current version of WinWeb does not contain any way to launch Telnet or WAIS clients.

X.500 (DUA) Clients

The help file in WaX500 says, "X.500 is an international standard for providing on-line directory services. The easiest way to think about X.500 is as a worldwide, distributed, electronic telephone book. The X.500 directory can contain information about people, organizations, documents, and just about anything else. At the present time, there is a pilot worldwide X.500 directory in which the information available is mostly about people and organizations."

piXie

Primary purpose	X.500 DUA (directory user agent)
Filename	PIXIE22B.ZIP
File size	194,165 bytes
Latest version	2.2b (January 1994)
Available from	Try ns.uab.es: /pub/msdos/x500
Status	Free for noncommercial purposes
Documentation	Relatively comprehensive, with on-line help
Comments	The program should work with OS/2 and Windows NT.

Swix

Primary purpose	X.500 DUA
Filename	SWIX21.EXE
File size	223,955 bytes
Latest version	2.1 (November 1994)
Available from	ftp.umu.se: /pub/pc/swix
Status	Public domain
Documentation	Installation instructions and on-line help included
Comments	A good program that continues to be developed

WaX500

Primary purpose	X.500 DUA
Filename	WAXR103.ZIP
File size	189,664 bytes
Latest version	1.03 (August 1994)
Available from	terminator.rs.itd.umich.edu: /x500/wax500
Status	Copyrighted
Documentation	Start-up instructions and on-line help included
Comments	A Mac version is available from the same site.

WDUA32 (Windows Directory User Agent)

Primary purpose	X.500 DUA
Filename	WDUAINST.EXE
File size	718,961 bytes
Latest version	Release 2.0B (June 1994)
Available from	naic.nasa.gov: /software/windows-dua
Status	Not stated
Documentation	Start-up documentation and on-line help
Features	Automated installation
Comments	Both 16- and 32-bit versions are included.

Additional Information

The following sections serve as appendixes for this chapter. Included are sections about recommended Internet applications, handling errors, and documentation resources.

Getting started

Unfortunately, little information about WinSock and SLIP is available on the Internet, and even less of it is easy to understand for someone just starting. Most documents are strongly oriented toward the networking side of the business or are aimed at systems professionals. The best exceptions I've seen are the following two documents. In a similar vein, people looking for a quick way to get up and running with the key Internet functions can use the two omnibus installation kits listed after the two document listings.

- *"Personal Internet Access Using SLIP or PPP: How You Use It, How It Works."* For a thorough, basic, nontechnical explanation of SLIP and SLIP applications, this document, by Frank Hecker, is highly recommended. The document is included in Chapter 12.
- *"Windows and TCP/IP for Internet Access."* This document, by Harry M. Kriz, provides a good explanation of the services available on the Internet; technical details of connecting a PC to the Internet, including an explanation of WinSock; and a review of several basic client applications, with installation instructions. The document includes information about both modem and network-based connections. The file — WTCPIP06.ASC — is available by ftp from the following site:

```
nebula.lib.vt.edu in directory /pub/windows/winsock
```

A hypertext version also is available on the Web at the following location:

```
http://learning.lib.vt.edu/wintcpip/wintcpip.html
```

- *Scientist-Friendly MS Windows Internet Kit.* To provide an easier introduction to WinSock software clients, a few efforts have been made to supply a "bundle" of the major client packages in an easy-to-install format with detailed instructions. One of these bundles is the Scientist-Friendly MS Windows Internet Kit, available by ftp from the following site:

  ```
  sol.dmp.csiro.au: /pub/internet/all
  ```

  The kit contains two files: INTERNET.EXE (2,181,885 bytes), which contains all the programs; and INSTALL.TXT (12,834 bytes), which has the installation instructions and should be read first. The package includes Trumpet WinSock; WINQVT; NCSA Mosaic (WWW client); HGOPHER; WINTRUMPET (newsreader; WS_FTP; TRMPTEL (terminal emulator); and some miscellaneous accessories, such as preinstalled Mosaic viewers. All the programs are shareware or freeware.

  The programs in this package are fine programs of their type but are not necessarily the latest versions. The programs were chosen primarily for reliability and ease of installation. Basic Windows and Internet knowledge is required. For anyone who is just getting started, this package is worth considering.

- *Internet SLIP Starter Kit.* This starter kit, put together by Jean van Eeden, contains Trumpet WinSock, WS_FTP, WSARCHIE, WINTRUMPET (newsreader), HOPCHKW, NCSA Mosaic (WWW browser), PINGW, FINGER, EUDORA14 (mail), and EWAN (terminal emulator). All the programs are shareware or freeware packages, with installation instructions included. Again, these programs are not necessarily the latest versions; they were chosen for reliability and ease of installation. The kit includes a copy of Harry M. Kriz's document "Windows and TCP/IP for Internet Access," described earlier in this section.

  The kit is available from the following site:

  ```
  aztec.co.za: /pub/win3/Slip_Starter_Kit
  ```

  The kit consists of two files: README (5,430 bytes) and STARTER2.EXE (1,426,082 bytes).

FAQ lists

One of the friendlier aspects of the Internet is the existence of frequently asked questions (FAQ) documents, which are not only invaluable guides for newcomers but also sources of reference information for everyone about a huge range of Internet-related topics. People looking for more information about WinSock may want to examine the following FAQ documents. Unfortunately, the documents tend to be very technical and not very helpful for beginners. "'Demon' Documentation" is somewhat more helpful, although more oriented toward users in Great Britain. If you're already up and running, and if you have WWW access, "WinSock Application FAQ/List" enables you to obtain additional software and information and to expand your capabilities.

- *"comp.protocols.tcp-ip.ibmpc Frequently Asked Questions (FAQ)."* This document, by Bernard Aboba, is very well done, although it's somewhat technical and oriented toward professionals. The document is mostly a TCP/IP FAQ, with extensive coverage of currently available TCP/IP networking software, but WinSock is covered in several sections. The document, last updated in October 1994, is available at the following site:

  ```
  FTP: ftp.netcom.com /pub/mailcom/ibmtcp/ibmtcp.zip (79,454 bytes)
  WWW: http://www.zilker.net/users/internaut/update.html (approximately 219
  kbytes)
  ```

- *"Frequently Asked Questions about Windows Sockets Version 1.1."* Fairly technical and oriented toward professionals, this FAQ was put together by Mark Towfiq and is available from the following site:

  ```
  sunsite.unc.edu: /pub/micro/pc-stuff/ms-windows/winsock
  ```

  The filename is just FAQ (15,317 bytes). The last update occurred in December 1993.

- *"'Demon' Documentation."* "Demon" is the nickname of a large Internet site located in Britain. Some of the documentation available at that site is worth a look. Be forewarned, though: The information sometimes is customized with unique Demon references. Most documents are updated regularly.

  The site address is `disabuse.demon.co.uk`. The following documents are available:

  `/pub/doc/os/windows.txt` (how to set up Windows software for the Internet, 31,438 bytes)

  `/pub/doc/general/dis-meta.faq` (contains references to other documents and books, 38,134 bytes)

  `/pub/doc/os/winmos.txt` (configuration of Mosaic for Windows, 17,072 bytes)

  `/pub/doc/os/wintcp.txt` (advanced configurations for Windows-software TCP/IP and dialing, 7,598 bytes)

- *"WinSock Application FAQ/List."* This document is a regularly updated listing of WinSock applications available for ftp. In the document — a more broadly based listing than mine — Craig Larsen covers client, daemon, and miscellaneous WinSock software; he also provides file information, source information, and comments. If you go the e-mail route, you receive a return e-mail copy of the document. The WWW access is particularly recommended, however, because it enables you to retrieve the software being described.

  The document is available in the following ways:

  E-mail: `info@LCS.com`. Subject: **FAQS** (put nothing in the letter body)

  WWW URL: `http://www.LCS.com/faqhtml.html`

Trumpet WinSock

The previous release of Trumpet WinSock — 1.0a — is available from several sites under a couple of names, as in the following examples:

`disabuse.demon.co.uk: /pub/ibmpc/winsock/stacks/trumpwsk`

TWSK10A.ZIP (120,569 bytes)

`ftp.cica.indiana.edu /pub/pc/win3/winsock`

WINSOCK.ZIP (120,569 bytes)

Apparently because of some bugs in this version, some WinSock clients do not work properly work with this version. The 1.0a release has been around for a while, however, and it has proved to be fairly durable and widely popular for establishing a SLIP connection.

The newest version of Trumpet WinSock is 2.0b, released in November 1994. The program is available from many sites, including the following:

`ftp.trumpet.com.au: /ftp/pub/winsock`

TWSK20B.ZIP (179,015 bytes)

`disabuse.demon.co.uk: /pub/ibmpc/winsock/stacks/trumpwsk`

TWSK20B.ZIP (179,015 bytes)

The first is an Australian site that is the primary release location, but that site sometimes is difficult to access and generally can handle only 20 connections at a time. The greatest advantage of the most recent version of the program is that it now has functioning PPP capability, if your server supports it.

This latest full release contains improvements in stability and operability. Worth noting are the addition of PPP support (but no CHAP or LQP yet) and firewall support for SOCKS 4.2. Keep in mind, though, that this version is new and relatively unproved.

The shareware version has a registration cost of $25.

An alternative means of obtaining a SLIP/PPP connection is Chameleon Sampler, described in the "Commercial Demo Packages" section earlier in this chapter.

Optimum Trumpet settings

Considerable discussion and controversy have taken place about the optimum settings for Trumpet WinSock to maximize data-transfer speed. Some efforts have been made to calculate the (theoretically) best settings, but the results tend to be at odds with real-world observations. The best information I've seen was posted recently to newsgroup `alt.winsock` by Keith Rowland. Rowland conducted a series of experiments, with the following results:

Transfer Speeds at Different Trumpet Settings with Different File Types

Trumpet Settings			*300K ZIP*		*330K DRV*		*200K TEXT*	
MSS	***MTU***	***RWIN***	***UL***	***DL***	***UL***	***DL***	***UL***	***DL***
200	240	800	1.32	2.69	2.39	2.43	2.07	—
512	552	2,048	1.63	1.58	4.27	3.64	3.10	2.91
984	1,024	2,952	1.63	1.59	4.26	3.51	3.19	2.75
1,024	1,064	4,096	1.63	1.48	3.92	4.16	3.20	2.99
1,460	1,500	8.192	—	1.47	3.97	—	—	—

Speeds are in kilobytes per second (kbps).

UL = upload speed
DL = download speed
ZIP = ZIP-compressed file
DRV = driver executing on type file
MTU = maximum transmission unit
RWIN = TCP receive window
MSS = TCP maximum segment size

Rowland's conclusion was that *for his particular situation,* the 512/552/2,048 and 984/1,024/2,952 values are best. These numbers are not presented here as a recommendation that these settings are best for everyone; rather, they indicate what you should do to determine your optimum settings. You may obtain different results with different hardware and software. Your results also may vary depending on network traffic, the servers you commonly access, your hardware setup, and your software configurations.

Popular WinSock source locations

Several Internet sites carry a fair amount of Windows and WinSock software, including most of the packages listed previously (but not always the latest versions). You can access these sites and download the software through ftp. The most significant site is CICA. Following is the information you need in order to access this site:

Host	`ftp.cica.indiana.edu`
IP number	129.79.26.27
Directory	`/pub/pc/win3/winsock`
Gopher access	`gopher.cica.indiana.edu`
WWW URL	`http://www.cica.indiana.edu`

Comments CICA is a major source of Windows software in general and often is difficult to log in to because of its popularity. Downloading the various README files is the best place to begin to identify what's available and in which directories, if you are interested in other areas.

Several other locations *mirror* (carry a copy of) the CICA directories and files. The following sites often are easier to access than CICA:

U.S. sites

```
mrcnext.cso.uiuc.edu [128.174.201.12]
wuarchive.wustl.edu [128.252.135.4]
gatekeeper.dec.com [16.1.0.2]
ftp.cdrom.com [192.153.46.2]
polecat.law.indiana.edu [129.79.131.170]
ftp.marcam.com [198.102.216.30]
```

Non-U.S. sites

```
ftp.cc.monash.edu.au [130.194.1.106] (Australia)
nic.funet.fi [128.214.6.100] (Finland)
ftp.uni-paderborn.de [131.234.2.32] (Germany)
ftp.uni-stuttgart.de [129.69.8.13] (Germany)
ftp.uni-koeln.de [134.95.100.208] (Germany)
ftp.uni-regensburg.de [132.199.1.17] (Germany)
ftp.iij.ad.jp [192.244.176.50] (Japan)
ftp.nectec.or.th [192.150.251.33] (Thailand)
ftp.technion.ac.il [132.68.1.10] (Israel)
nic.switch.ch [130.59.1.40] (Switzerland)
src.doc.ic.ac.uk [146.169.17.5] (UK)
ntu.ac.sg [155.69.1.5] (Singapore)
nctuccca.edu.tw [192.83.166.10] (Taiwan)
ftp.cyf-kr.edu.pl [149.156.1.8] (Poland)
```

TIA — The Internet Adapter

As stated in the introduction of this chapter, to use Windows packages on the Internet, you need a special SLIP connection from an Internet provider. Many providers charge extra for this type of connection, and a few do not offer it at all. Now an alternative is available: a commercial software package, developed by Cyberspace Development, Inc., that operates on a user's UNIX shell account and emulates a SLIP account. This innovative product is called TIA, The Internet Adapter, and it has been very controversial.

Major advantages of TIA

- TIA operates through the basic UNIX shell account, providing the user with SLIP access without the need to pay surcharges for a true SLIP account. TIA also provides access where SLIP accounts are not available or are very expensive. TIA is a low-cost package.

- Although users may have some problems setting up TIA and getting it to work, it seems to work well and has generated strong support among many of its users.

Major disadvantages of TIA

- TIA increases the burden on the provider's server more than a SLIP or straight UNIX shell account would, although to what degree is arguable (and is being argued). Although system administrators use this statement against TIA, supporters of TIA feel that the real truth lies in the following item.
- The use of TIA deprives providers of the incremental revenue gained from selling SLIP account upgrades.
- TIA currently is not compatible with some minor WinSock packages, such as Ping and CU-SeeMe. Neither does TIA currently support PPP connections (although this feature is being worked on).
- To keep costs low, technical support is available only for licensed sites, not for individual users (although they do receive bug fixes when those fixes are issued).
- Because TIA is not a true SLIP connection, when logging on, the user does not receive an IP number; therefore, operating a remote server is impossible. (A permanent, nonfunctional dummy number is used to satisfy client applications.)

Considerable documentation on TIA, including a FAQ, is available at the following site:

```
FTP: marketplace.com: /tia
WWW: http://marketplace.com/0/tia/tiahome.html
```

This location is also accessible by Gopher. TIA operating software is available from the same location, although you need a license code to actually use it. Free evaluation licenses, good for 14 days, are available. If you later decide to buy, single-user licenses cost only $25. Host and site licenses also are available. As a first step, you should talk to your Internet service provider to get the provider's approval to use TIA.

Growstub error

People who use the Microsoft mouse with driver version 9.01 receive a "growstub error" message when they boot up Mosaic. The error apparently is caused by a conflict between Microsoft's Win32s 32-bit software extension program and the Microsoft mouse driver. It's just one of those cases in which the left hand doesn't know what the right hand is doing.

Anyway, the solution is to upgrade to the version 9.01b mouse driver, available by ftp at the following site:

```
ftp.microsoft.com: /softlib/mslfiles/hd1061.exe
```

This file includes a new POINTER.DLL, which fixes the problem.

An alternative solution, according to Microsoft, is to remove `pointer.exe` from the `load=` line in the WIN.INI file and then restart Windows. Disabling POINTER.DLL also deactivates the advanced features of the mouse driver: magnify, snap-to, screen wrap, and locate.

Error: "Unhandled Exception 0xc0000005"

Widespread reports have appeared about a problem with Version 1.15 of the Win32s 32-bit extension when Version 2.0a7 of NCSA Mosaic is launched. The result is an error message: `Unhandled Exception 0xC0000005`.

Until recently, the solution that seemed to work for most people was to copy (copy, not move) file CTL3DV2.DLL from the windows/system directory to windows/system/win32s and then rename this new file CTL3D32.DLL.

Concern about creating this dummy file, which someday may affect other programs that really need it, has led to a change in advice from the NCSA Mosaic group. The current recommendation is that you obtain the real CTL3D32.DLL from the NCSA ftp server and install it in your windows/system/win32s directory. This file is available at the following location:

`ftp.ncsa.uiuc.edu: /Web/Mosaic/Windows`

Eudora documentation

The Eudora mail package, from Qualcomm, Inc., is one of the better and more popular Internet mail readers currently available. Although the registered version comes with full documentation, the basic free version contains almost nothing. Fortunately, most of its features are relatively intuitive. If necessary, however, some supplementary manuals are available through the Internet:

A *new* Windows version of the manual (currently 376,851 bytes) is finally available by ftp from Qualcomm, Inc.:

`ftp.qualcomm.com: /quest/windows/eudora/documentation/14manual.exe`

A third-party HTML version manual for the PC and Mac versions is accessible through the WWW from the following site:

`http://www.soc.staffs.ac.uk/eudora/contents.html`

Mark Branigan, of the Staffordshire University School of Computing, has done an excellent job of setting up this site. The text is applicable to both Windows and Mac versions, but the graphics shots are all Windows. The manual covers versions 1.4.2 and 1.4.3b1.

North Americans can use the mirror site:

`http://www.csos.orst.edu/slip/highway/docs/eudora/contents.html`

A variation of the preceding Staffordshire manual is also available. Leopoldo Saggin revised an older version of the previous item, bringing it up-to-date with Eudora Version 1.42b16. His version is available through the WWW from the following site:

`http://cribil.bio.unipd.it/html/eudora/contents.html`

This Italian site can be difficult to access (it's slow) from North America.

Pentium serial-port problems

Occasional postings report strange problems with communications software on Pentium machines. If you are using a Pentium-based machine with a 16550 UART chip and Windows for Workgroups, and if the system hangs when you use the serial communications port, consult Microsoft Product Support Applications. The document "WG101: Updated serial.386 driver for Windows for Workgroups" provides a replacement serial driver for Windows for Workgroups. The product note and new driver are available at the following address:

```
ftp.microsoft.com: /softlib/msfiles/wg1001.exe
```

The product note is dated March 1994, so the problem is likely to occur only for users running older versions of WFW.

SLIP versus PPP

The most recent version 2.0 of Trumpet WinSock offers additional support for the PPP protocol. In addition, Microsoft has indicated stronger future support for PPP than for SLIP. These events have generated widespread interest in the PPP protocol.

What is PPP, and why is it better than SLIP (or is it)? Some people have unrealistic expectations that PPP must be faster than SLIP to have picked up this support. It is important to begin with the understanding that SLIP and PPP are protocols for handling the transmission of packetized data through a serial connection between two devices. The following table summarizes some of the differences between the two protocols:

	SLIP	***PPP***
Compression	None originally. Compressed SLIP (CSLIP) was added later as an option that both the client and host must support. Use of CSLIP requires manual intervention and configuration, but this procedure must be used only one time for the same client and host.	Yes. Automatically negotiated as part of the connection process.
Connection configuration	IP settings must be made manually, or else a separate program (such as a dialer login script) must be run to configure these settings. This is mostly a problem with servers using dynamic IP allocation.	IP configuration is part of the connection process and is transparent to the user. PPP software will be more complex than SLIP as a result.
Error detection	None. SLIP is vulnerable to noisy lines, although error-correcting modems on each end of a connection usually cover for this deficiency, and the user is not affected.	PPP has built-in error detection

Industry support	Almost none.	Although Microsoft, out of necessity, plans to support both clients in upcoming releases, only a PPP server has been implemented in Windows NT 3.5 (Daytona).
Protocol handling	SLIP handles IP only.	PPP offers multiprotocol handling, including IP and IPX.
Speed	See PPP column.	In the few actual tests that compared SLIP and PPP, no significant difference existed either way. A PPP frame does contain additional protocol overhead (some for error correction), which theoretically could result in slightly slower transmission.
Standards	SLIP is a de facto standard only; it is not an Internet standard (not controlled protocol, or reviewed by any standards group). In the early 1980s, someone used it; then other people used it; today, many people use it.	PPP is an official Internet-standard.

CSLIP = Compressed SLIP (also known as header compression and Van Jacobson compression)
IP = Internet protocol
IPX = Internetwork packet exchange (Novell networking stack)
PPP = Point-to-point protocol
SLIP = Serial-line Internet protocol

One point to keep in mind is that your connection choice — SLIP or PPP — will have no effect on your WinSock applications. Your current WinSock programs will function normally, no matter which connection method you use.

Chapter 32
Macintosh Internet Applications

by Art Kerns

Using a Macintosh and a SLIP or PPP Internet connection is perhaps the easiest way for the average person to start using the Internet. There's no need to memorize long lists of cryptic commands; most of the programs have a similar look and feel, so that learning a new application is easy; and from a user's standpoint, it is fairly easy to get up and running. Although not quite as many Internet programs are available for the Mac as for other computers, you can find a number of excellent applications that are extremely well written and well supported — if you know where to look.

Usually, the first places to check are the Mac archives at Stanford and the University of Michigan. The ftp addresses of the Internet communications directories in these archives are:

```
ftp://sumex-aim.stanford.edu/info-mac/comm/tcp/
ftp://mac.archive.umich.edu/mac/util/comm/
```

The best part about the programs in these directories is that all of them are shareware or freeware, which means that you can try them for free before officially registering your copy and paying for the package. All the programs mentioned here are readily available on the Internet, and you'll find that they are generally as good as — and quite often superior to — commercially available products. Unless your needs are very specific or very unusual, you should be able to find the software that you need for free and to make sure that it does what you need before you buy it. Unless you already know that you are an exceptional case, don't even think about buying any communications software until you've seen what you can get off the Internet.

Internet services usually are characterized by something called a *client/server relationship*. A great deal of information is stored on a computer that is running a *server* program, and remote computers that want to retrieve the information use *client* programs. A single computer can be either a client or a server or both, but most users on the Internet are retrieving information rather than providing it. If this is true for you, you are interested only in client software.

The Macintosh is not really designed to be a server: it is designed to interact with one user, not with hundreds or thousands of remote computers. Large servers are relatively expensive machines that have only one purpose: to be network servers. As a result, most of the Macintosh Internet software consists of client applications.

If you want to run a server that will provide text and some data to a relatively small group of people, your Macintosh should do just fine. If, however, you want to run a very popular server, used by hundreds or thousands of people around the world on a regular basis, you probably will be better off if you look at some other options.

Also remember that for traffic and security reasons, some network configurations do not allow users to set up servers that can be accessed by the outside world. If your server program seems to be working fine but people outside your network can't connect to it, ask your local administrators for further help.

Getting Your Mac on the Internet

Most Internet applications require that a program called MacTCP be installed on your computer and properly configured. MacTCP enables your Macintosh computer to use the TCP/IP network protocol, which enables your computer to exchange information with other types of computers and to connect it to the Internet. MacTCP is required whether you are using SLIP, PPP, ARA, or a direct connection to interface with the Internet.

This chapter assumes that you already have your Mac hooked up to the Internet and that MacTCP is properly configured for your specific connection. For more information on how to find and set up the MacTCP program, read Chapter 14, which discusses how to connect your Macintosh to the Internet. The Macintosh Internet applications described in this chapter will not be useful until you have properly installed MacTCP and have an Internet provider.

Mac Internet Software

Following are my personal recommendations for specific applications that fill a certain niche within the Internet. These are the programs that I find to be the easiest and most fun to use, as well as the most suitable for a person who is just starting to use the Internet. From each area of the Internet, I picked one program that I found to be powerful and particularly easy to use.

This chapter does not provide detailed instructions on how to use these programs; all the programs are very well documented, and you should look at a specific application's documentation for in-depth instruction on how to use it.

No single program will do everything that you need (although the World Wide Web browsers are beginning to come close), but all of them do something useful. The programs are well written and well supported, and you can try all of them for free before registering them.

Once again, keep in mind that all these choices are personal preferences; numerous other programs do similar things and may be more appropriate for your particular needs. Plenty of people are happily using programs that are just as good as — and possibly even better than — the programs described in this chapter. Some of these alternative programs are listed at the end of each section. Look around, and don't be afraid to try new programs.

Finally, it is important to make sure that you try the latest version of whatever Internet software you are using. A great deal of development is going on in the area of Mac Internet applications, and the newest versions of your favorite applications usually have useful new features (and often have fewer bugs). The newest versions allow you to switch between Internet applications easily, and they have significantly improved performance. Of course, you also should remember that newer isn't always better. Remember to try the new version for a while before you drag the old one into the Trash; sometimes, the older version actually performs better for your needs.

FTP client applications

	Memory	*Size*	*Cost*	*Version*	*Year*
Fetch	293KB	1.2MB	$25	2.1.2	1994

The first program that you will need is a useful program called Fetch. The Fetch application allows you to retrieve any other programs that you want quickly and easily by using *ftp*, the Internet's standard file-transfer protocol. Ftp enables you to take a file from a remote computer and save that file on your own computer. If you already have a copy of Fetch, the first thing that you should retrieve is the latest version of the program. If you don't already have Fetch, you are going to have to do a little work to find it.

The easiest place to find Fetch is on the Internet. Both the Stanford and UMich archives (addresses are at the beginning of the chapter) have a copy in their communications directories. If you already have an Archie or Gopher program, you can use that program to retrieve Fetch. NCSA Telnet also has ftp capabilities. If you have an e-mail program, such as Eudora, that allows you to decode binary files easily, you can access the Stanford Mac archives through e-mail. (For details on how to do this, see the chapter on connecting your Macintosh to the Internet.)

America Online and some other on-line services now offer ftp access. If you are having trouble finding Fetch by any other method, you may have to use one of these commercial on-line services. Some, like America Online, offer a free trial period that will give you plenty of time to get Fetch and a few other programs without paying a cent.

If you don't have any programs that will allow you to get Fetch over the Internet, and if you don't want to use a commercial service to find it, you are on your own. You will have to find someone with the program who will make you a copy, or you'll have to find a book or disk that contains the application. *The Internet Starter Kit for Macintosh*, written by Adam Engst, includes the MacTCP program as well as Fetch. (Hayden Books, 1994, ISBN 1-56830-064-6).

This may seem like a lot of trouble to go through to get one program. Don't worry — nearly everyone who has a Mac connected to the Internet will have this program and can give you a copy. It seems like a hassle now, but this will be the last time that you have to go through this sort of trouble. When you have Fetch, you can do everything easily and electronically from your computer.

Fetch is very easy to set up and use. Because you already have configured MacTCP with the information that you need to connect with the Internet, Fetch does not need any addresses or numbers. Using the Customize menu, you can do a few things to customize Fetch, such as entering a default password and turning on or off some specific functions, but these settings are not necessary when you start using the program. If Fetch loads properly and displays a window titled "Open Connection," you are ready to go.

If you have used ftp before, you should have no problems using Fetch. If you haven't used ftp, just think of it as being a fancy Copy command that enables you to copy a file from a remote computer to your desktop. Connecting to an ftp server is as easy as clicking Open Connection and filling in the necessary information. Most public servers allow you to log in by using *anonymous* as your user name and your e-mail address as your password. When you are connected, you can navigate through the folders and files just as you would through a normal directory residing on your hard drive. When you find the file or folder that you want to retrieve, highlight the filename by clicking it, and then click the Get button.

Fetch uses helper applications to decompress and decrypt retrieved files (information on helper applications appears in its own section later in this chapter). If you want to change the helper applications that Fetch uses, choose the Suffix Mapping and Post Processing options from the Customize menu.

You also can set various other personal preferences by choosing the Preferences option from the Customize menu. For example, to save text files in a particular format (such as Microsoft Word), pull down the Customize menu and choose Preferences; then pull down the Topic menu and choose Downloading. You now should see a dialog box that allows you to choose downloading options. Pulling down the Edit Text With menu enables you to choose the word processor that you want to use.

Fetch also supports shortcuts and bookmarks. A *shortcut* is a frequently used ftp site, the folder you want to go to on that site, and your name and password. Fetch comes with several useful shortcuts already defined, including the Stanford, UMich, and Apple archives. You can create your own shortcuts by using the Customize menu. You can use existing shortcuts directly from the Open Connection dialog box by choosing a specific shortcut from the Shortcuts pulldown menu.

Bookmarks are similar to shortcuts, but they save a specific place within an ftp site. If you find a directory within a site that you might want to come back to later, you can save your place by saving a bookmark. To create a bookmark, choose Save Bookmark from the File menu or simply press ⌘-S. If you ever need to return to that location, you can return quickly and easily by opening the bookmark; choose Open Bookmark from the File menu or press ⌘-O.

One final tip for using Fetch involves the difference between receiving a text file and receiving a binary file. The main Fetch dialog box, which enables you to Put and Get files, has three options: Automatic, Text, and Binary. By default, Fetch uses the Automatic method to determine what type of file you are downloading. The program makes its best guess as to whether you are getting a text or binary file, and it then decodes and saves the file as that type. If you are having no problem receiving a file but are having trouble using the file, try getting the file again with Fetch and manually setting the transfer type to Text or Binary (whichever is appropriate). Sometimes, files simply won't decode no matter what you do; in such a case, your best bet is to try to find the file somewhere else.

Other Macintosh ftp client applications include the following:

	Memory	*Size*	*Cost*	*Version*	*Year*
Xfer It	512KB	527KB	$10	1.5b4	1992

FTP server applications

	Memory	*Size*	*Cost*	*Version*	*Year*
FTPd	313KB	629KB	$10	2.3.0	1994

Running an ftp server enables your desktop Mac to share some of its programs and files with the rest of the Internet. Instead of simply retrieving information from other computers, a server provides its own information to others. Because the Macintosh was designed with a single user in mind, it is not well suited to be a server; as a result, all types of Mac servers tend to be slow. If you need to share your files with a relatively few people and don't want to invest in a dedicated server, using your Macintosh is a reasonable solution.

Always remember that running a server carries a certain security risk. Although most servers do their best to limit the amount of information that can be accessed through them, improperly configuring the server software could make all the files on your computer — and all the files in any computer on a connected network — available to millions of people around the world.

FTPd is the easiest-to-use and most powerful ftp server application for the Mac. The program generally is considered to be great, but slow (although this shortcoming probably has more to do with the Mac itself than with the program). I have not used this program extensively, but it seems to be extremely easy to set up and run. Read the Quick Start file that comes with the program, and then run FTPd Setup to configure the system. Within minutes, you should have a working server.

If all that you need is a small ftp server that runs from your desktop, FTPd is a steal at $10. Keep in mind, however, that the performance will deteriorate rapidly as more users connect and retrieve information; keep the maximum number of users low, and try to limit use of the server as much as possible.

FTPd also can be configured as a Gopher server application and will run nicely in the background so that you can continue to use your Macintosh for other things. FTPd is an all-around great program.

Archie applications

	Memory	Size	Cost	Version	Year
Anarchie	250KB	1MB	$10	1.3.1	1994

An archie application enables you to search for a program throughout the Internet. If you know a filename or part of a filename, archie automatically searches the Internet for the file. When you need to find a specific file but don't know where that file may be, Archie is a possible solution. Anarchie is a Macintosh application that enables you to use Archie painlessly.

Anarchie is very simple to use. To start an Archie search, simply choose the Archie option from the File menu. A dialog box prompts you for the string to find. In the Find box, simply type the name (or part of the name) of whatever file you are looking for — for example, **anarchie, fetch, homer**, and so on. You can choose the Archie server to use by changing the entry in the Server box, or use one of Anarchie's built-in server preferences by clicking the arrow to the right of this text box.

When you finish, simply click the Find button, and let Anarchie do all the work for you. Anarchie will inform you of its progress and alert you when the search is complete.

Anarchie allows multiple searches at the same time. Anarchie also works in the background, meaning that you can start using another program while Anarchie continues its search.

Anarchie's biggest drawback is its speed — not a flaw in the Anarchie program itself, but in the Archie search. If Anarchie doesn't seem to be giving you any results, the problem may not be with your Anarchie configuration but with the server that you are using. At peak hours, which are generally the normal weekday business hours of the country where the machine is located, most servers are very, very slow. Using Gopher or the World Wide Web to find applications yourself may be quicker. If you have to use Archie, try to find a server that isn't heavily used, or conduct your searches in the off hours.

Other Macintosh Archie client applications include the following:

	Memory	Size	Cost	Version	Year
Archie	384KB	102KB	$10	1.0	1992

Gopher applications

	Memory	Size	Cost	Version	Year
Turbo-Gopher	700KB	350KB	free	1.0.8b4	1994

Gopher provides a means of looking for programs or information on the Internet. Unlike an Archie search, a Gopher search is not automated. The user finds what he is looking for by choosing a subject from a hierarchical menu, which leads to another menu and another subject choice, and so on until the user narrows down the information to the point at which he finds what he's looking for. Gopher is useful if you have a general idea of the type of file you are looking for but don't know its filename or where it is located. Don't worry — you can't break anything and won't get in trouble for looking at anything that is publicly accessible.

The TurboGopher application implements this process by displaying a menu that looks similar to a standard Macintosh file-selection dialog box. Performing a gopher search is as easy as double-clicking the menu item that you want to see and waiting for the next menu of choices to appear.

TurboGopher is fast and easy to use. Menu options that lead to other menus are displayed as folders; files are displayed as files; searches are displayed as boxes with a question mark. Overall operation is very smooth and easy to follow, especially if you are familiar with the way that the gopher system is set up. Experiment a little and see what's out there.

Like the Fetch application, TurboGopher allows you to set bookmarks, which serve to mark your place. Later, you can call up that bookmark and return to wherever you were when you set it, eliminating the need to search through everything every time.

TurboGopher cannot directly display pictures, sounds, and some text files, so it uses helper applications that do all the work. To configure these applications, choose Options from the Setup menu. See the Helper Applications section for more information on what helpers are, which ones to use, and how to use them, see "Helper applications," later in this chapter.

Other Macintosh Gopher client applications include the following:

	Memory	*Size*	*Cost*	*Version*	*Year*
GopherApp	1MB	1MB	free	2.2b43	1993
Mac-Gopher	512KB	468KB	free	0.5b14	1992
Sextant	512KB	306KB	free	1.0	1993

IRC applications

	Memory	*Size*	*Cost*	*Version*	*Year*
Homer	1MB	2MB	$25	0.93.4	1994

Homer represents a unique way of implementing a unique Internet service. The Internet Relay Chat (IRC) is perhaps the least regulated and least standardized service of the Internet, and Homer is a reflection of this disorganization. The IRC allows for real-time chats among multiple users. The users are spread across channels, each of which is devoted to a certain topic or group of people. When a user joins a channel, she can talk to everyone else on the channel by typing her short message and sending it. Likewise, she can see the messages that everyone else is sending.

The greatest advantage of the IRC is the fact that it happens in real time; other people see what you type seconds after you type it. This capability has proved to be useful in emergency situations, such as earthquakes or hurricanes, in which many people from around the world wanted up-to-date information on what was happening. Usually, though, the IRC is a place where people socialize and discuss whatever interests them at the moment.

Homer's graphic interface and documentation fall somewhat short of Macintosh standards but, when used regularly, make a lot of sense. Still, Homer is far from being the easy-to-use, portable type of application for which the Mac is known. With this fact in mind, experiment with Homer before trying to do anything serious (assuming that any serious applications of the IRC exist).

If you have a tendency to irritate people or to be easily irritated, keep in mind that Homer has some serious security shortcomings. With a few keystrokes, a person can make Homer play extremely irritating sounds, and you can do little or nothing about it. Even if you set the sound-volume level at zero and turn off all of Homer's sound preferences, some sounds will get through. Remember this fact before you start something that you can't stop.

The feature that Homer is most sorely missing is script support, which activates certain automated, complicated features. Sometimes, these features do useful things; at other times, they are used maliciously. As mentioned earlier, malice can be a problem, and the lack of an easy way for Homer users to retaliate makes them all the more tempting as targets.

One final problem with Homer is its speed and reliability. Homer can be slow and has a tendency to freeze up. This problem is not necessarily with Homer but with the IRC in general. One solution is to disable the automated channel list fetcher, which will eliminate the worst of the pauses.

Despite its nonstandard interface, security problems, and reliability shortcomings, Homer is a decent IRC client for the casual Mac user. Serious users are advised to stick with a UNIX client applications.

Another Macintosh Internet Relay Chat client applications is the following:

	Memory	***Size***	***Cost***	***Version***	***Year***
IRCle	192KB	221KB	free	1.5.1	1992

Usenet news applications

	Memory	Size	Cost	Version	Year
News-Watcher	1.2MB	900KB	free	2.0b22	1994
News-hopper	1.5MB	876KB	$90	1.0 demo	1994

Usenet news provides a service similar to electronic bulletin boards. People post their thoughts and opinions on a particular topic, and other people around the world respond in similar fashion. The discussions are broken into subjects, called *newsgroups*, that try to focus the discussion on a particular topic. Some newsgroups are extremely informative and helpful; others are devoted to gossip, insults, and even threats. Most newsgroups fall somewhere in between. To get a feel for a group and its participants, be sure to read some of the messages in a newsgroup before you post your own. If a list of frequently asked questions (FAQs) is posted, be sure to read it before you ask a question that has been asked hundreds of times before.

Depending on your needs, Usenet news can be a helpful resource or a fun way to waste some time. Many people who start using the service soon find themselves spending more time reading news than they originally intended.

NewsWatcher is a feature-packed, easy-to-use news reader for the Macintosh. The program is available only for the Mac, and many people have commented that it is the best reason to use a Macintosh on the Internet.

NewsWatcher is *threaded*, meaning that articles within a newsgroup are grouped according to subject so that you can read related articles at the same time. The program keeps track of what newsgroups you are interested in and what messages within those groups you've already read. The excellent user documentation explains the use of keyboard shortcuts, which allow you to execute common actions by pressing one key, as well as nearly everything else you would want to know about setting up and using the program. NewsWatcher also allows you to save your group list to disk, making it an ideal news reader for a lab in which many people will be using the same news program.

Perhaps the best feature of NewsWatcher is its excellent support for included binary files. Some newsgroups allow users to post programs, pictures, and sounds in something called *uuencoded format*, which encodes binary files in a text format. The usual way to decode these files is to cut the text from one or more news messages, paste the text into a text editor, and then run a uudecoding program on the resulting text file.

Needless to say, this process is tedious at best. NewsWatcher eliminates all this trouble. If a uuencoded file is included in the message, NewsWatcher displays a file icon in the upper-right corner of the message window. Clicking the file icon automatically collects the information and sends it to a uudecoding helper program, which automatically does all the necessary decoding. This procedure simplifies the process considerably: All you have to do to retrieve such a file is click the file icon and specify a filename. If you use uuencoded files on even an irregular basis, this feature alone makes NewsWatcher worth using.

Newer versions of NewsWatcher allow you to Fetch a file or to use MacWeb to see a World Wide Web page simply by holding down the ⌘ key and clicking an ftp address or Web URL address enclosed within a message. Did someone mention a new Web page or some publicly available software that you are interested in? You don't have to manually cut out the address and paste it into another program — NewsWatcher automatically does that for you. In the future, you can expect a seamless interface between NewsWatcher for News, Fetch for ftp, Eudora for e-mail, and MacWeb and Netscape for World Wide Web information.

NewsWatcher is missing some features. All these features are scheduled to be added eventually, but the author has so many new features to support that it could be a while before they are implemented. The first feature is something called a *kill file*, which enables you to ignore, or "kill", any messages related to a particular subject or person. If you are tired of certain topics or certain people, you can add them to your kill file and never see anything related to them again. Obviously, this capability is useful but not absolutely necessary. Because NewsWatcher doesn't force you to read every message, you can simply skip any messages with subjects or authors that don't interest you.

The other feature is the capability to edit e-mail sent from NewsWatcher with an e-mail program such as Eudora. Currently, the mail that you send from within NewsWatcher is not saved along with your other e-mail — a frustrating situation if you like to keep copies of all your old mail by subject. The temporary fix for this problem is to tell NewsWatcher to send a copy of all messages to your e-mail address; you can set this option in the Preferences menu. This is only a quick fix, though, because NewsWatcher still sends the mail itself, and you have to process the mail when you receive it.

One feature that the author of NewsWatcher does not intend to implement is off-line reading. Users who are charged by the amount of time they spend connected to a network do not want to browse through hundreds or thousands of messages while they are still on-line and being charged. An off-line news reader allows a user to retrieve all new articles in certain areas and then read and reply to those messages later, when the user is not connected to the network.

One off-line reader that has been receiving a great deal of praise from users is Newshopper, a demo of which is available on all the usual Macintosh archive sites. A full-fledged version costs about $90, but users have stated that this money is quickly made back in saved connection charges. If you are being charged for your connection time, you may want to check out this program.

Some other news readers implement these features and others. Many people prefer NewsWatcher for its ease of use and binary support; others feel just as strongly about other programs. Give all the programs a try before you settle on one. The programs are geared to different types of people, and one of them may be a perfect fit for your needs.

Other Macintosh Usenet news applications include the following:

	Memory	Size	Cost	Version	Year
InterNews	750KB	1.1MB	$25	1.0.4	1994
News-fetcher	750KB	384KB	free	0.4.5	1994
News-grazer	256KB	179KB	free	1.0	1994
Nuntius	1MB	808KB	free	1.2	1994
The News	1.3MB	612KB	$25	2.3	1994

Telnet applications

	Memory	Size	Cost	Version	Year
NCSA/ BYU Telnet	554KB	553KB	free	2.5	1992

Telnet is a simple protocol that allows a user to connect to a remote machine. This protocol enables you to connect to a UNIX-based computer and essentially use your Macintosh as a terminal. This way, you can use a remote account from your desktop Mac. Even if you don't need to use another machine, telnet is one of the least complicated Internet protocols and often is useful for testing a network connection.

The NCSA/BYU Telnet application is easy to use, complete, and free; it is, therefore, strongly recommended for your Macintosh telnet needs. This program also enables you to use FTP, although Fetch has many more features and is much easier to use.

Other Macintosh telnet applications include the following:

	Mem	Size	Cost	Vers	Year
Comet	600k	1.1MB	free	3.0.7	1994

World Wide Web browser (client) applications

	Memory	Size	Cost	Version	Year
MacWeb	700KB	500KB	free	1.00 A2	1994
NCSA Mosaic	2MB	2MB	free	2.0.0 A8	1994
Netscape	2MB	1.1MB	free	0.9b	1994

The World Wide Web (WWW) is the fastest-growing segment of the Internet and is increasingly becoming the most popular, and its use of point-and-click methods of navigating graphics and text seamlessly makes it ideally suited for the Macintosh. The introduction of two excellent new WWW Macintosh clients, in addition to the standard NCSA Mosaic, is a reflection of the Web's newfound popularity. Because the World Wide Web and the programs associated with it are changing so rapidly, I've chosen to discuss all three major browsers instead of choosing just one. Each program is useful in a particular way; all of them are still evolving and changing. Be sure to try all three browsers before settling on one.

As mentioned before, NCSA Mosaic has been and continues to be the standard for the Web across many platforms. Mosaic is filled with features and implements every Web standard to the letter. Unfortunately, these capabilities come at the price of speed and size; Mosaic generally tends to be slow and to use a great deal of memory and disk space. Mosaic also has a disturbing tendency to crash when you try to cancel a request. Newer alpha releases have been faster but still use considerable memory and are subject to crashes.

MacWeb, the second major Web client application released for the Macintosh, currently is in a beta version. This program's strengths are its size and speed; it requires considerably less memory than Mosaic does and is noticeably faster. MacWeb also is less likely to crash, although crashes still happen.

MacWeb is without question the best Mac client available if you are short on memory or running other communications programs simultaneously. Another very handy feature is the ability to choose between displaying a selection and saving it to disk. This feature enables you to save the inline pictures that the Web client displays, which none of the other client applications can do easily. MacWeb eventually will be released as a commercial product.

Netscape, the newest addition to the World Wide Web, is in its preliminary beta release. Netscape has two big advantages: it's very fast, and it has many fun graphics features. The only real disadvantage of the program is that it is not yet completely compatible with all the forms and documents that you will run across — something to be expected, however, in a beta release. The program also uses a great deal of memory. Although Netscape can run with 2 megs of available memory, it really prefers to have about 4. Netscape probably will end up becoming the most feature-filled and fun product, but MacWeb will remain the most compact of the three. Netscape eventually will be released as a commercial product.

The biggest problems with the World Wide Web usually involve its lack of speed. You can greatly increase the speed of all three programs by turning off the automatic display of images. The application then displays a small icon where the inline picture should be, and you can click that icon if you really want to see the picture. This capability is especially useful in graphics-intensive sites, which can take several minutes to load on a slow connection if you display all the pictures all the time. Another easy solution is to increase the configured buffer size. When you move from one page to another, the old pages are saved in memory so that if you go right back to them, you won't need to resend all of that information over the Internet. By increasing the buffer size, you increase the amount of information that can be saved in this buffer, which eliminates the need to constantly resend data that you had already received earlier.

Sometimes, a Web program tells you that it doesn't have enough memory to load the helper application that is needed to display pictures and movies or to play a sound. Because Web programs grab all the memory they can when they start, even if they don't need it, you may want to load an important helper application first. If you know that you are going to be using one of these programs when you start, this practice increases speed — and saves you from having to buy more memory.

World Wide Web server applications

	Memory	*Size*	*Cost*	*Version*	*Year*
MacHTTP	512KB	2MB	$100	2.0	1994

A World Wide Web server application enables your computer to provide information in the form of hypertext Web pages to the rest of the world. This information could be as simple as a short page that contains your picture and some brief information about yourself or as complicated as an interactive multiuser information system. The Macintosh is not well suited to do the job of a heavily used server. If you are interested in providing a few pages of text and images that will be used by a limited number of people, your Mac is quite sufficient. As you add more users and more information, however, performance will deteriorate. Using your Mac as a server certainly is worth a try if you want to avoid buying another machine, but be advised that if your server becomes popular, you may encounter performance problems.

MacHTTP is the only World Wide Web server available for the Macintosh. The program is extremely easy to set up and can be configured easily for a variety of uses. Interestingly, the easiest way to set up the program is to run it and then use a Web browser application to read the on-line documentation; the procedure for doing this is contained in the Quick Start Guide file.

You configure MacHTTP through the MacHTTP.config file. If you start to run into performance problems, try changing the values of MAXUSERS, PIG_DELAY, and DUMP_BUF_SIZE. Reducing the maximum number of users obviously will make the connection faster for those users who connect. PIG_DELAY sets the amount of processing time that MacHTTP uses; smaller values make it run in the background less noticeably, and larger values increase the amount of time that your computer sets aside for MacHTTP. DUMP_BUF_SIZE determines how much information is sent at any time. The value should be smaller if you have many users accessing small amounts of data and larger if you have a few users who are retrieving images or sounds.

A great deal of work has gone into this product, and it most likely will continue to improve. At $100, MacHTTP is somewhat expensive, but the author is extremely reasonable, offering discounts for noncommercial use and for people who can't afford the full price. If you want to run a small Web server from your desktop Mac, MacHTTP certainly is worth the minimal effort of trying it.

Helper applications

	Memory	Size	Cost	Version	Use
JPEGView	600KB	400KB	free	3.0	JPEG and GIF images
Simple Player	300KB	145KB	free	1.0a1	QuickTime movies
Sparkle	600KB	204KB	free	1.6	MPEG movies
StuffIt Expander	384KB	77KB	free	3.0.1	sit and cpt archives
uuUndo	275KB	85KB	free	1.0b4	uuencoded files

Helper applications are stand-alone programs that also can be controlled by another program currently being used. For example, when a World Wide Web client application wants to display certain types of pictures or movies that it is not capable of displaying, it simply calls the helper application, which does the job. This capability makes the Web client simpler and easier to use, and it allows the user to choose the program that he wants to use to view the picture or movie. The same idea is used in playing sounds, compressing data, and performing other common actions.

In the future, many Internet applications will call one another to handle specific tasks. For example, your news program will allow you to send mail with your e-mail program, directly download a file from an ftp site mentioned in a news article, or go to a World Wide Web page. You already can do some of these things; you soon will be able to do the others.

All the helper applications listed at the beginning of this section perform particular functions. JPEGView shows GIF and JPEG pictures; Simple Player shows QuickTime movies; Sparkle shows MPEG animation; and StuffIt and uuUndo decompress and decode files that you have retrieved. Other programs perform similar functions, but I have found these programs to be the most useful and reliable of the bunch. All the programs are well written, and all of them are free.

You also can use these programs as stand-alone applications. For instructions on how to configure a certain program to use one of these applications automatically, you should check that Internet program's documentation. Many Internet programs come preconfigured to use these helper applications, so if you are having no trouble playing sounds or seeing pictures, you don't need to worry about finding or configuring these applications.

Other useful Internet applications

	Memory	Size	Cost	Version	Year
Finger	100KB	417KB	$5	1.5.0	1992
Talk	196KB	170KB	$5	1.1.1	1993
MacTCP Watch	196KB	230KB	free	1.1.2	1993
MacTCP Switch	50KB	26KB	free	1.0	1993
Network Time	n/a	587KB	$5	2.0.1	1993

In addition to full-blown Internet applications, you may find several small communications utilities to be useful on your computer. Finger and Talk implement two commonly used UNIX commands on your Mac, allowing remote users to "finger" your computer, which gives them information about the computer and its users, or to "talk," which allows two users to have a real-time chat.

MacTCP Watch is useful if you are having problems with your Internet connection. The program monitors all communications activity and allows you to do simple things like "pinging" another computer, which will tell you whether you can connect with that machine. If you can successfully ping another machine on your network, you know that your computer is properly connected to that network. If you can ping a machine on another network connected to the Internet, you know that your network is connected to the Internet. If you know that your machine is properly connected, you can check the status of other remote machines by pinging them.

MacTCP Switch enables a single computer to use different MacTCP configurations. This program may be useful if you have a portable computer that sometimes is connected to the office network and at other times is remotely connected to a network with a SLIP/PPP connection. MacTCP Switch enables you to switch between the two setups without having to manually change the configuration each time.

Network Time synchronizes the time on your computer with the rest of the network. This program is useful for ensuring that your clock is correct. Network Time also is useful if you want to guarantee that all computers on your network are properly synchronized — important for some applications and security configurations.

Art Kerns is an engineer with Qualcomm, Inc., of San Diego, where he is working on the Globalstar satellite phone system. He also has experience designing and programming real-time physics simulations for the Macintosh, including the HMWBS projectile simulator.

Chapter 33

Installing the Shareware Disks

Unlike the disks in other SECRETS books, these disks don't contain a lot of software programs, because the Net itself is usually the best place to get the latest versions of software.

Disk 1: Windows software and Scripts

WINZIP shareware archiver version 5.6 (WINZIP56.EXE)

WINZIP requires Windows 3.1 or later. It's shareware, with a $29 payment due to the author. Payment options are explained in the program.

To install WINZIP, follow these steps:

1. Insert disk in disk drive.
2. From Program Manager or File Manager, run A:WINZIP56.
3. The program prompts you for a location into which to temporarily place installation files. Accept the suggestion or edit the directory, then press Enter.
4. WINZIP setup program runs; prompts for location into which to permanently install WINZIP. Accept suggesion or edit directory, press Enter.
5. Setup uncompresses and installs files; information and setup screens follow. Press Enter at each menu to accept defaults.

WINCODE freeware encoder/decoder version 2.6.1 (WNCOD261.ZIP)

Requires Windows 3.1 or later. The program is freeware, so no payment is required. A help file and e-mail support is available for a $5.00 payment to the author.

To install WINCODE, follow these steps:

1. Unzip the archive WNCOD261 into a temporary directory such as \TEMP (WINZIP can do this automatically); run WINZIP, open WNCOD261, and click on Install.

2. Run the "snappy install" program INSTALL.EXE. If you're using WINZIP Install, it's run automatically after a screen that lets you decide if you want the option of uninstalling. If you're not using WINZIP, run INSTALL.EXE from the Windows Program Manager or File Manager.
3. Answer the installation program's questions; press Enter at each menu to accept the defaults.

Other files on Disk 1

ZIMM.TXT	PGP public key for and description of Phil Zimmerman Defense Fund. See Chapter 5, "Internet Privacy and Security."
OFFLINE	Directory containing scripts from Chapter 26, "Network News."
WAIS	Directory containing WAIS user scripts from Chapter 24, "Using WAIS."

Disk 2: E-mail mailing lists

This disk contains two very large files, each of which is a directory of on-line mailing lists. The files are uncompressed ASCII text.

Windows users should note that the files are far too big for the standard Notepad text editor, but Write can handle them without trouble.

LISTSERV.TXT	Complete listing as of February 1995 of all LISTSERV mailing lists on all hosts connected into the LISTSERV system.
MAILLIST.TXT	December 1994 edition of Publicly Accessible Mailing Lists compiled by Stephanie da Silva.

Index

Symbols

* (asterisk) with IRC commands, 516–517
^ (caret) character, with IRC commands, 516–517
, (comma) with IRC, 524
.newsrc file, 731–732, 739, 749, 761–762
.nn/init file, 738
40-bit codes encryption technique, 135

A

Accent speech-synthesizer card, 185
Acceptable Use Policies (AUP), 84
access provider, organization network connections, 271–272
accounts, shell, 272
acquiring PGP, 152–153
addresses
  alan@ingress.com (Alan Chung), 801
  alt.bigfoot, 43
  alt.cascade, 43–44
  alt.flame, 43
  alt.irc.recovery (recovery service), 16
  alt.security.pgp, 116
  alt.shenanigans, 43–44
  bentley4@slb.com (Michael Bentley), 833–847
  bind-request@uunet.uu.net (BIND), 252
  biz.books.technical, bookstore and publisher ads, 95
  biz.comp.hardware, commercial hardware info, 96
  biz.general (business operations and offerings), 96
  biz.misc, miscellaneous commercial information, 96
  biz.oreilly.announce, computer book announcements, 96
  cbk@ingress.com (Charles Kaplan), 801
  cert-advisory-request@cert.org, 95
  chip@tct.com (Chip Salzenberg), 49
  cix.org, Commercial Internet Exchange (CIX), 98
  com-priv-request@psi.com, 95
  comp.infosystems.*, 287
  comp.mail.sendmail (DNS newsgroup), 252
  comp.newprod (newsgroup), 51
  comp.os.limux.help, 287
  comp.os.ms-windows.networking.tcp-ip (newsgroup), 287
  comp.os.msdos.mail-news (newsgroup), 287
  comp.protocols.tcp-ip, DNS newsgroup, 252
  comp.protocols.tcp-ip.domains, DNS newsgroup, 252
  comp.protocols.tcp-ip.ibmpc (newsgroup), 287
  comp.protocols.tcpip.domains (BIND software), 244
  comp.sys.next.marketplace, Usenet marketplace, 101
  comp.sys.novell, 287
  cybersight.com/cgi-bin/cs/s?main.gmm, 97
  deeryan@virtuoso.com, 781–797
  dns-errors-request@pop.psu.edu (DNS), 252
  doug+@osu.edu (Doug Stevenson), 418–419
  dsacks@news.primenet.com (Dennis Sacks), 637–668
  dws@ora.com (Sanderson, David W.), 207–211
  emv@msen.com (Edward Vielmetti), 56–64
  falk@sun.com (David Falk), 151–159
  fedix.fie.com, Federal Information Exchange Inc., 98
  free-market@ar.com, Internet Free-Market, 95
  ftp.ibm.net, Internet Connection upgrade, 390
  ftp.trumpet.com.au, Trumpet WinSock, 282–283
  ftp://ftp.std.com/pub/ibb/ibb.html, 97
  ftp://newdev.harvard.edu/pub/okipkt/okipkt.com, 281
  ftp://nimbus.anu.edu.au/pub/tridge/samba (Samba), 286
  ftp://sunsite.unc.edu/pub/Linux, Linux, 276
  ftp://tsx-11.mit.edu/pub/linux, Linux, 276
  gopher-news, 833
  gopher.lib.umich.edu, 94
  gopher.msen.com, Internet Business Pages, 98
  gopher.ntia.doc.gov, 98
  gopher.ora.com, O'Reilly & Associates Publishers, 99
  gopher.std.com/periodicals/TRADEWINDS, 99
  gopher.tmn.com, Safety and the Arts, 197
  gopher.town.hall.org, Federal Acquisition Regs, 98
  gopher://infoeagle.bc.edu, Boston College, 296
  handicap.shel.isc-br.com, Handicap BBS, 197
  hecker@access.digex.net (Frank Hecker), 301–337, 453
  HENZE@LDB.han.de, (Stephan Henze), 442
  hickman@cleo.bc.edu, (Thomas Hickman), 290–297
  houston.forsale, marketplace newsgroup, 100
  http://biomed.nus.sg/people/commmenu.html, 96
  http://catalog.savvy.com, Catalog Mart, 97
  http://crow.acns.nwu.edu:8082/hyplan.html, 531–561
  http://cyteria.netaxs.com, 97
  http://garnet.acns.fsu.edu/~chofack/article.html, 98
  http://http2.sils.umich.edu/-lou/chhome.htm, 94
  http://marketplace.com, MarketPlace.com, 98
  http://rs600.adm.fau.edu/faahr/netiquette.html, 96
  http://urth.ascu.buffalo.edu/irc/WWW/ircdocs.htm, 19

http://www.access.digex.net/~hecker/, 301–337
http://www.blackbox.com, Black Box On-Line Catalog, 96
http://www.cc.gatech.edu/gvu/user_surveys/, 97
http://www.commerce.net/information/help/find.html, 96
http://www.directory.net, 98
http://www.directory.net, Commercial Sites Index, 96
http://www.dns.net/dnsrd (DNS), 252
http://www.eunet.ch/werbal/experiments/, 98
http://www.gems.com:80/, 97
http://www.hello-direct.com/hd/home.html, 97
http://www.hot.presence.com/hot/, 97
http://www.hotwired.com/, HotWired, 97
http://www.lib.umich.edu/chhome.html, 94
http://www.mall2000.com, Mall 2000, 97
http://www.past.com/, CyberNaut Rest Stop, 97
http://www.portal.com/~skip/ayli.html, 96
http://www.rtd.com/people/rawn/business.html, 96
http://www.service.com/onourserver.html, 97
http://www.sofcom.com.au, Sofcom Home Shopping, 98
http://www.trinet.com/course.html, 97
http://www.trinet.com/kcomputing/drawing.html, 97
http://www.trinet.com/tgp/, The Gray Pages, 96
http://www.wiltel.com/ritim/ritim/html, 98
http://www.xmission.com/~americom/, Americom, 91
inet-secrets@ii.com, (Nancy McGough), 409–427, 673, 687–702
info-rama@wired.com, Wired magazine, 91
info@aol.com, 81
info@compuserve.com, 81
info@delphi.com, 81
info@netcom.com, 81
info@well.com, 81
info@world.std.com, 81
IP, 216, 271, 307, 312
iron.nttc.edu, National Technology Transfer Center, 99
jacker@nwu.edu (Jack Graham), 531–561
jallan@tenet.edu (Jim Allan M.S.), 181–206
jaym@iecc.com (Jay Maynard), 100–107
jfurr@acpub.duke.edu (Joel Furr), 27
joe@galcit.caltech.edu, 562–573
jtbell@presby.edu (Jon Bell), 725, 766–780
Kcd@tenet.edu (K.C. Dignan Ph.D.), 181–206
kinnaman@world.std.com (Dave Kinnaman, MS, MA), 77–99, 181–206
leestral@mcs.com (Lee Stral), 591–607
leroux@vdl2.ca (Philippe Le Roux), 5–26
listporc@cni.org, 95
listproc@einet.net, Internet Marketing, 95
listserv@scns.com, High Tech Marketing Comm, 95
listserv@uriacc.uri.edu, Telecommunications/Info, 95
lynn.alexander@excalibur.org (Lynn L. Alexander), 469–502
margy@iecc.com (Margaret Levine Young), 725, 749–780
mfriley@WPLEDU (Margaret F. Riley), 503–507
mi.forsale, Usenet marketplace, 101
mike@ingress.com (Michael Y.C. Hur), 801
mikeryan@virtuoso.com, 781–797
misc.forsale.non-computer, Usenet marketplace, 101
mjr@tis.com (Marcus J. Ranum), 160–179
mramey@u.washington.edu (Mike Ramey), 673
mvanheyn@cs.indiana.edu (Marc VanHeyningen), 418
netannounce@deshaw.com (Mark Moraes), 49
news.groups (newsgroup), 54
NORA/HARLEQUIN marriage, 20–22
ocl@gih.co.uk, (Olivier M.J. Crepin-Leblond), 815–832
ooblick@intercon.com (Mikki Barry), 108–113
phl@cyways.com (Peter H. Lemieux), 269–288
pine-fau@docserver.cac.washington.edu, 669
pkware.inc@mixcom.com, PKWARE, 90
postmaster@anytown.edu (postmaster), 44
ram@iecc.com (Raphael Manfredi), 703
randolph@air.org (Randolph Chung), 849–864
rec.bicycles.marketplace, Usenet marketplace, 101
reinhold@world.std.com (Arnold G, Reinhold), 115–159
rfabian@interlog.com (Bob Fabian), 456–468
ric@ingress.com (Richard Chung), 801
ripem.msu.edu (SecureEdit program), 125
ronda@panix.com (Ronda Hauben), 65–67
rs.internic.net (InterNIC Registration Services), 87, 98
sarah@tuna.uchicago.edu (Sarah Hulburt), 574–589
sct@po.cwru.edu (Stephen Trier), 339, 631–636
shop.net, Internet Shopping Network, 98
sirrah@cg57.esnet.com, (Stuart Harris), 509–529
smileys, 211
soda.berkeley.edu, 197
spaf@cs.purdue.edu (Gene Spafford), 49
support@pkware.com, PKWARE, 90
taylor@netcom.com (Dave Taylor), 710–723
telnet bounced.e-mail.net (Match-Maker), 17
telnet Chat.hotwired.com (Wired Cafe), 17

tsipple@vnet.ibm.com (Timothy Sipples), 387–405
una.hh.lib.umich.edu/ intdirsstacks, 94
val-dor.cc.buffalo.edu (CODI), 196
verve@cyberwerks.com (Eric S. Theise, Ph.D), 608–630
warnock@clark.net (Archie Warnock), 637–668
wohler@newt.com (Bill Wohler), 737–748
wuarchive.wustl.edu (smileys), 211
WWW links, 577–578
Zimmerman defense fund, 135
administrators
Gopher server, 842–846
newsgroup, 728
server, 560
Advertising in the Internet, listproc@cni.org, 95
advice, whom to ask, 121–122
AIX 3.2 operating system, 226–227
AIX 3.2.5 operating system, 231
alan@ingress.com, Alan Chung, 801
Alex gopher, 578–579
Alex text catalogue, 489
Alexander, Lynn L, lynn.alexander @excalibur.org, 469–502
aliases
domain name, 274
IRC, 520–523
Allan, Jim M.S., jallan@tenet.edu, 181–206
alt.bigfoot, 43
alt.cascade, 43–44
alt.flame, 43
alt.irc.recovery (recovery service), 16
alt.security.pgp (encryption ideas), 116
alt.shenanigans, 43–44
alternative keyboards, keyboard/ mouse disability, 190
AlterNet, 217
America Online, 80, 217
Americom (http://www.xmission .com/~americom/), 91
Amiga operating system, graphical gopher clients, 627
angry young men (AYM), 32–33
animated text strings, 423–424
Ann Hemyng Candy, Inc.'s Chocolate Factory, 498
anonymity, 29–30
anonymous FTP, 321
online retrieval instructions, 454
OS2/Warp resources, 402
anonymous remailers, 145
ANSnet, 217
Apartment Relocation Service, http://cyteria.netaxs.com, 97
Apple
MacTCP software, 309–310
networking software, 370
Remote Access connection, 353–354
application-embedded encryption, 129
application-level gateways, 165, 175
applications, Macintosh Internet, 941–955
applied cryptography, 116
archetypes, 32–46
angry young men, 32–33
clueless people, 34–35
complainers, 32–33
conspiracy theorists, 38–40
control freaks, 35–38
curmudgeons, 41
demogogues, 41–42
fanatics, 42–43
flamers, 43–44
general weirdos, 40–41
loons, 41
net personalities, 45–46
newbies, 34–35
terrorists, 43–44
Archie, 470
applications, Macintosh, 946
gopher server, 603–604
mail servers, 438–439
firewalls, 177
history, 608
archives guide, 477
archives, directory structure, 351–352
Argus Internet Tools and Resources Guide, The, 499
Arlene Rinaldi's netiquette, 96
ARPANET, 5, 217, 219
art, ASCII, 423
ARTFL text database, 580–582
search form, 583
articles
anatomy of, 729–730
crossposting, 733–734
posting test, 733
redirecting follow-ups, 734–735
Arts & Farces, 501
As you like it Electronic book-reader for Windows, 96
ASCII (American Standard Code for Information Interchange), 51, 60, 443
ASCII art, signature/finger files, 423
ASK forms, Gopher servers, 593–594
AskERIC, 502
asterisk (*) character, with IRC commands, 516–517
AT&T 3B15 minicomputer, 8
AT&T 800 directory, 490
atomic clock, 919
AUP (Acceptable Use Policies), 84
European providers, 823–824
authentication, 118
automatic signature instructions, UNIX, 410–417

B

B News software, 65–66
B&R Samizdat Express, PLEASE COPY THIS DISK catalog, 498–499
back doors, IRC, 527
backfinger script, 421–422
backup hardware, 802–803
bang sings (!), Usenet, 217
Baroudi, Carol, 298–299
Barr, David, 244–245
barriers, net, 29–32
BARRNet, 217
Barry, Mikki, ooblick@intercon .com, 108–113
bastion host, 163, 168
BAT alternative disability keyboard, 190
BBS, 16–17
deferred dialogue, 16
development of, 16–17
handles, 18
Internet connections, 17
Match-Maker, telnet bounced .e-mail.net, 17
Milk Rounds, 16
multiline, 17
overview, 108–109
publication responsibilities and liabilities, 110–112
switched telephone network, 17

system administrator, 17
Wired Cafe, telnet Chat.hotwired.com, 17
Bell, Jon, jtbell@presby.edu, 725, 766–780
Bentley, Michael, bentley4@slb.com, 833–847
Berkeley Software Design (BSD), network server software, 277
Bern, Jochen, 414
Bill of Rights and Responsibilities for the Electronic Community of Learners, 202
BIND (Berkeley Internet Name Domain), 217, 222–223
software, comp.protocols .tcip.domains, 244
bind-request@uunet.uu.net, 252
biographies, WWW, 577
BITFTP mail server, 437–438
BITNET, 58, 217
BITNET network, LISTSERV mailing lists, 430–432
bits, creating random, 144
biz.books.technical (bookstore and publisher advertising), 95
biz.comp.hardware (commercial hardware information), 96
biz.general (business operations and offerings), 96
biz.misc (miscellaneous commercial information), 96
biz.oreilly.announce (computer book product announcements), 96
Black Box On-Line Catalog, http:// www.blackbox.com, 96
book reviews, WWW, 576–577
bookmarks, 470
Gopher servers, 597–598
search strategies, 463–464
books
disability access, 195
firewalls, 178
on-line, 582–587
parts, 1–2
readers, 1
bookstore, publisher advertising, biz.books.technical, 95
Boolean
connectors, 470
operators, IRC, 523
search, WAIS, 640
Boston College, network information system, 295–296
Braille Blazer (DOS/Windows/ Mac) software, 188
Braille translators, 187–188
broadcast address, organization network, 271
broadcast model, 109–110
browsers, HTML, 543–544
business marketing, 77–82
acceptable tactics, 84–91
Acceptable Use Policies, 84
ad formats/limitations, 102
address naming conventions, 81
books and periodicals, 94
buying and selling marketplace items, 102–104
cardinal rule, 86
cash transactions, 92
discussion lists, 94–95
e-mail hot lines, 81
e-mail signature, 87
employee net training, 87
finalizing marketplace transactions, 104–106
finding specific marketplace items, 102
For Discussion of Marketing, 95
Free-Market discussion list, 83–84
freeware/shareware, 89–91
global base, 86
gopher sites, 98–99
handling bad deals, 106
hardware requirements, 79–80, 93
Inet-Marketing discussion list, 82–83
information providing, 86
information resources, 93–99
inquiry response time, 87
Internet cultural norms, 82–84
Internet do's/don'ts, 85–89
ISP customer service literature, 81
limiting message distribution, 101–102
logistical options, 91–93
marketplace groups, 100
message topics, 85
mission, 77–81
net access, 93
net monitoring, 88
newsgroup rules, 86
online documents, 94
periodicals/books, 94
product endorsements, 87
promotional/operational strategies, 77–78
provider pricing information sources, 81
registering a domain name, 87
selecting marketplace group, 101
service providers, 80–81
shipping considerations, 105
skilled people, 79
software resources, 93
strategic niche, 80, 90
teaser announcements, 85
technical options, 91–93
things to avoid, 88–89
Usenet hierarchy, 100
Usenet newsgroups, 95–96
World Wide Web indexes/lists, 96
World Wide Web sites, 96–98
business operations/offerings, biz.general, 96
Business Vision (DOS/Windows) software, 186

C

C News software, 65–76
C.O.D. (collect on delivery), 104
cable companies, providers, 805
caches, DNS, 225, 235
canonicalization, 230
Capstone encryption technique, 136–139
Captain, 5
caret (^) character, with IRC commands, 516–517
CARL (Colorado Alliance of Research Libraries), 480–482
casual busybodies, 119
Catalog Mart, http:// catalog.savvy.com, 97
catalogs, PLEASE COPY THIS DISK, 498–499
catalogues, Alex, 489
cbk@ingress.com, Charles Kaplan, 801
CCITT, 824
Central Point, System Consultant, 279
CERFNET, 217
CERN httpd server software, 554–556
CERT Computer Security Mailing List, 95
cert-advisory-request@cert.org (CERT Computer Security), 95

CGI (Common Gateways Interface), 856–862
  applications
    passing parameters, 857–858
    sample, 858–860
    setting up, 856–857
  scripts, 856–862
    capabilities, 861
channels, IRC, 510
characters
  * (asterisk) with IRC commands, 516–517
  ^ (caret) with IRC commands, 516–517
  ISO 6937/2, 444–452
  non-English, 443–452
chatlines
  addictions of, 15–16
  as social tool, 9–12
  e-mail, 22–23
  electronic meetings, 10–12
  falling in digital love, 12–14
  genesis of, 6–7
  learning by osmosis, 15
Chung, Alan, alan@ingress.com, 801
Chung, Randolph, randolph@air.org, 849–864
Chung, Richard, ric@ingress.com, 801
CIA, the, 499
Cipher Block Chaining (CBC), 130
cix.org, Commercial Internet Exchange (CIX), 98
Class-B network, organizations, 271
Class-C network, organizations, 271
clearinghouse for subject-oriented Internet resource guides, 94, 475–477
client programs, 941
client/server relationship, 941
Clipper, 136–139
closed mailing list, 429–430
CloseView software, Macintosh, 184
clueless people, 34–35
CNIDR, 651
CODI, val-dor.cc.buffalo.edu, 196
com-priv-request@psi.com, Communications/Privacy Discussion, 95
comma (,) with IRC, 524
commands
  IRC
    / (forward slash) with, 511
    /ALIAS, 520–523
    /BIND, 519–520
    /BYE, 511
    /CTCP command, 513
    /EXEC, 513
    /FLUSH, 511
    /HELP, 511
    /IGNORE, 512
    /JOIN, 510
    /LIST, 510
    /NICK (nickname up to nine characters), 510
    /SET, 515
    /SET BEEP MAX, 512
    /SET BEEP OFF, 512
    /SET CLOCK_ALARM, 515
    /SET HOLD_MODE, 511
    /SET INDENT ON, 515
    /SET LOG ON/OFF, 515
    /SET LOGFILE, 515
    /SET MAIL 2, 512
    /SET NOVICE OFF, 512
    /SET REALNAME, 514
    /SET SEND_IGNORE_MSG ON, 512
    /SET SHOW_CHANNEL_NAMES ON, 515
    /SET SHOW_WHO_HOPCOUNT ON, 515
    /SET STATUS_FORMAT, 515
    /SET USER_INFORMATION, 514
    /SET VERBOSE_CTCP ON, 514
    /WHOIS, 513
  Trn, 751
  UNIX
    PING, 261
    ROUTE, 262
  UQWK software, 785
CommerceNet Find Page, 96
commercial
  demo packages, 872–876
  hardware information, biz.comp.hardware, 96
Commercial Internet Exchange (CIX), cix.org, 98
Commercial OnLine Newspaper Services, 502
Commercial Sites Index, http://www.directory.net, 96
common carrier model, 109–110
Common Sense and Cryptography, 115–150
Communications Act, Title II, 110
communications software
  from the net, 357–358, 941–955
  Pentium machines, 938
Communications/Privacy Discussion, com-priv-request@psi.com, 95
comp.infosystems.* (newsgroup), 287
comp.infosystems.gopher (newsgroup), 833
comp.mail.sendmail (DNS newsgroup), 252
comp.newprod (newsgroup), 51
comp.os.linux.help (newsgroup), 287
comp.os.ms-windows.networking.tcp-ip (newsgroup), 287
comp.os.msdos.mail-news (newsgroup), 287
comp.protocols.tcp-ip (DNS newsgroup), 252
comp.protocols.tcp-ip.domains (DNS newsgroup), 252
comp.protocols.tcp-ip.ibmpc (newsgroup), 287
comp.protocols.tcpip.domains (BIND software), 244
comp.sys.next.marketplace (Usenet marketplace), 101
comp.sys.novell (newsgroup), 287
complainers, 32–33
Complete Home Page Directory, The, 498
components, firewalls, 162–166
Compressed SLIP (CSLIP), 303
compression
  files, 355
  formats, Macintosh, 356
  programs, Macintosh, Stuffit, 356
CompuServe, 80, 217
computer book product announcements, biz.oreilly.announce, 96
computer-access technology, 182
computers
  as morphological analyzer, 575
  AT&T 3B15, 8
  disability access means, 182–183
  Goupil G4, 8
  host, 270
  provider requirements, 801–802
  router, 270
conferences, disability, 201
configuring, WWW server, 851–852

conspiracy theorists, 38–40
control freaks, 35–38
control-key combinations, IRC, 519–520
conversion utilities, Macintosh, 355–356
COPS software (UNIX system), 267
Copyright and Intellectual Property Forum, 95
Cornucopia of Disability Information (CODI), 196
Crack software (UNIX system), 267
Crepin-Leblond, Olivier M.J. (ocl@gih.co.uk), 815–832
Cripta Plus, 140
Crynwr Software, Russell Nelson, 278–279
Crypt, encryption technique, 129
crypto-communication facts, 145
cryptographic smart cards, 139–140
CSLIP (compressed SLIP), TCP/IP header compression, 345–346
CSNET, 217
CSO (Computing Services Office) phone directory, 604
CSU/DSU units, provider requirements, 804
CTCP (client-to-client protocol), IRC, 514
Ctrl-K (Kill) keyboard shortcut, 44
culture
  barriers, 29–32
  freedom, 29–32
  Internet, 27–48
  petri dish, 27–29
curmudgeons, 41
CyberNaut Rest Stop, http://www.past.com/, 97
CyberSight, 474
  http://cybersight.com/cgi-bin/cs/s?main.gmm, 97
Cyberspace Development, Inc., 380, 386, 935
Cyteria Swimming Pool Management, http://cyteria.netaxs.com, 97

D

da Silva, Stephanie, 434
DANTE, 821
data carrying signals, 127
data-remnants, 124–125
data
  amount to be protected, 119
  availability besides codebreaking, 122–128
  consequences of being compromised, 121
  erasing technique, 125
  how long sensitive, 119
  legal obligation to protect, 121
  number sharing, 119
  other ways to steal, 122–128
  protecting, 118
  protecting from whom, 119
  remanence, 124–125
  safety at origin/destination, 119
  security threat classification schemes, 120–121
database
  ARTFL, 580–582
  Physician's GenRx, 491
  WAIS, 653
DCC (direct client connection), IRC, 525–526
DDN NIC, 818
DDS (Digital Data Service), 258
DecTalk speech-synthesizer card, 185
dedicated
  cook-bot, IRC, 524
  line, UNIX system, 257–258
  router, versus host computer, 270
  SLIP, UNIX system, 257
deeryan@virtuoso.com, Dee Ryan, 781–797
deferred dialogue, 16
degaussers, security, 126
Delphi, 80
demogogues, 41–42
derfing, 112
DES (data encryption standard), 129–131
design decisions, firewalls, 161, 174
Desqview/X software suite, 285
Deutsch, Peter (Archie), 608
diagnostic tools, 876–877
DIALOG, 498
dialup SLIP, UNIX system, 257
digests
  LISTSERV mailing list, 431–432
  mailing list, 430
Digital Agora, 7
digital audiotape (DAT) technology, 124
Digital Data Service (DDS), 258
digital
  love, 12–14
  relationships, survival guide, 25
  signatures/authentication, 140–150
Dignan, K.C., Ph.D, kcd@tenet.edu, 181–206
directories, electronic, 929–930
disability
  Bill of Rights, 202
  book list, 195
  computer-access technology, 182
  defining, 181–182
  e-mail considerations, 192
  ERIC clearinghouses, 198–199
  future Internet access, 191–192
  general information sources, 199–200
  Internet resources, 196–199
  keyboard/mouse, 188–190
  organizations/conferences, 201
  print, 182–188
  secrets, 182
  sound, 191
  state technology-related assistance, 194
  Technology-Related Assistance Act, 194
  Usenet newsgroups, 197–198
  vendors/products, 192–194
disabled persons, Internet access, 181–206
discussion lists
  Advertising in the Internet, 95
  business marketing, 94–95
  CERT Computer Security Mailing List, 95
  Communications and Privacy, 95
  Copyright and Intellectual Property Forum, 95
  High Tech Marketing Communications, 95
  Internet Marketing, 95
  subscribing/unsubscribing, 94
  Telecommunications/Information Marketing, 95
disk compression programs, security, 125
disks, installing shareware, 957–958
distance-insensitive pricing, frame relay, 258
DNS (Domain Name System), 215–253
  /etc/named.boot file, 227–229

/etc/resolv.conf file, 226
adding/deleting hosts file, 241
additional resources, 252
BIND (Berkeley Internet Name Domain), 217, 222–223
cache file, 235
caches, 225
debugging output, 242
domain name interpretations, 219–222
domain name registration form, 246–250
domain nameservers, 215, 227–230
domains, 217, 223–226
dotted-octet notation, 216
e-mail resources, 252
explained, 218–219
forward lookup file, 232–233
FQDN (fully qualified domain name), 220
hierarchical naming scheme, 218
historical reading, 251
hostnames, 321–322
hostnames/IP addresses, 216
hosts file, 216
introduction, 215–216
iterative versus recursive name requests, 225–226
loopback file, 235–236
maintenance, 240–242
Matrix, 217
MX resource record, 230–231
name resolution, 223–226
named daemon, 222–223, 227–230
named data file resource records, 236–240
named data files, 227, 231–232
nameservers, 215, 218
namespace, 228
namespace dump, 241
namespace refresh, 240–241
newsgroups, 252
original implementation (JEEVES), 217
origins, 216–217
primary master nameserver, 221
primary server, 227
provider registration requirements, 804
redundant servers, 225
references, 253
resolvers, 226–227
resolving problems with provider, 244
reverse lookup file, 233–234
RFC 1034, 236
root servers, 250
second-level domains, 218
secondary server, 227
sendmail, 230–231
sendmail.cf file, 231
servers, 225–226
subdomains, 218
TCP/IP, 216
TCP/IP speedups, 344–345
tools, 245–246
troubleshooting problems, 242–243
working with firewalls, 175–176
workings of, 222–223
zone transfer, 221, 228
zones, 223–226
DNS database files, 231–232
DNS newsgroup
comp.mail.sendmail, 252
comp.protocols.tcp-ip, 252
comp.protocols.tcp-ip.domains, 252
dns-errors-request@pop.psu.edu (DNS), 252
documents, online business marketing, 94
domain names
aliases, 274
organization network, 272–274
registration form, 246–250
registering, 87
value of, 273
domain nameservers, DNS, 215, 227–230
domains, 217
DNS, 223–226
DOS/Windows Client Kit (Novell), 279
dotted decimal format, IP address, 271
dotted-octet notation, 216
doug+@osu.edu (Doug Stevenson), 418–419
Doupnik, Joe, SIS_PKT9.DOS (NDIS shim), 284
Dragon Dictate (DOS) software, 189
Drawing for Course address, 97
drivers
monolithic IPX, 278
packet, 278–279
Drool, interactive dog game address, 97
dsacks@news.primenet.com (Dennis Sacks), 637–668
dual-homed gateway, 163, 167–168
Dubois public key, 159
Dunlap, Kevin, 217
Duxbury (DOS/Mac) Braille translator software, 187
Dyer, Jim, 413–416

E

e-mail, 429–442
Archie by mail, 438–439
business marketing signature, 87
disability considerations, 192
DNS resources, 252
encounters, 22–23
FAQ archive, 442
filter software, 695–698, 717–722
filtering, 687–702
ftp by mail, 435–438
Gopher by mail, 439–440
hot lines, 81
InfoBot, 442
information sources, 701–702
Interest-Groups list of lists, 485
ISO 6937/2 terminal, 451
Listproc mailing lists, 433
LISTSERV mailing lists, 430–432
mail auto-responders, 710–723
mail folder strategies, 687–688
mail servers, 434–442
Mailagent software, 703–710
mailing lists, 429–430
mailing lists, installing, 958
MajorDomo mailing lists, 433
managing, 669–723
naming incoming mail folders, 687–688
offline newsreaders, 782–783
online FAQ, 700–701
Procmail software, 688–694, 722–723
publicly addressable mailing list file, 434
reading incoming-mail folders, 688
SLIP/PPP account, 304, 314–319
WAIS by mail, 441
WWW by mail, 440–441
e-mail gateway, UNIX system, 257
E-Page Systems, 502
EARN, 819
EBCDIC, 51
EBONE (European BackBONE), 821
EDS Shadow Patent Office, 496
Edupage newsletter, 484

EFF Extended (Big Dummy's) Guide, 474–475
electronic
  authentication, 18
  directory, 929–930
  phone book, 6
  signature, necessary, 142
  signatures, 141, 152
Electronic Code Book, 130
Ellsworth, J.H. (The Internet Business Book), 97
Elm software
  organization header, 426
  signature instructions, 412
ElNet Galaxy, 473
Emacs Mail Mode software, signature instructions, 414–415
Embot software, 710–717
  capabilities, 713–716
  commands, 713–714
  evolutionary path, 716
  installing, 711–713
  overview, 710–711
  shareware license, 717
  sources, 711–713
Emtage, Alan (Archie), 608
encryption, 115–159
  exporting software, 117
  foreign countries, 116
  learning about, 116
  why needed, 116–118
encryption security tips, 150
encryption software, exporting, 117
encryption techniques
  40-bit codes, 135
  application-embedded encryption, 129
  Capstone, 136–139
  Clipper, 136–139
  Crypt, 129
  DES, 129–131
  Electronic Code Book, 130
  hardware based, 136–139
  IDEA, 131
  one-time pads, 143
  PCMIA, 139–140
  PGP, 134–135
  private-key encryption, 130
  public-key cryptography, 130, 151
  RC2, 135
  RC4, 135
  RIPEM, 133–134
  rot13, 129
  RSA, 132–133
  Skipjack, 136–139
  Tessera, 138
  Triple DES, 131
  which to use, 128–140
EPMB (European Multi-Protocol Backbone), 821
ERIC (Educational Resources Information Center), 198–199
errors
  Macintosh TIA, 386
  unhandled exception 0xc0000005, 937
Ethernet
  maximum segment size, 283
  maximum transmission unit (MTU), 283
  receive window, 283
Eudora software (Qualcomm), 314–319, 699–700
  documentation, 937
EUnet, 821
EuropaNET, 821
European Internet provider, 815–832
European NII, 818
EurOpen (European Forum for Open Systems), 821
Explore OnNet for Windows software, 327
extinct users, 46

F

Fabian, Bob, rfabian@interlog.com, 456–468
Falk, Deward, falk@sun.com, 151–159
fanatics, 42–43
FAQ (Frequently Asked Questions), 19, 335, 796–797, 931–932
  lists, 931–932
  Macintosh TIA, 380–384
FAQ archive mail server, 442
FBI, opinion on cryptography, 138
FCC
  regulations pertaining to Usenet, 109–110
  republication standard, 110
Federal Acquisition Regulations, gopher.town.hall.org, 98
Federal Information Exchange Inc., fedix.fie.com, 98
FedWorld, 501
Feminist Web Page, 500
Fetch software, 321
FidoNet, 217
file compression, Macintosh, 355
file extensions, compressions, 356
file formats, Macintosh, 355–356
file references
  Macintosh TIA, 363–364
  parts, 363
file serves, 293
File-search protocols, 877–881
File-transfer protocols (FTP), 877–881
filename, file reference, 363
files
  .newsrc, 731–732, 739, 749, 761–762
  .nn/init, 738
  /etc/hosts, 216
  /etc/named.boot, 227–229
  /etc/resolv.conf, 226
  /etc/syslog.con, UNIX system, 266
  cache, 235
  copying, 363
  deleting, 125
  DNS database, 231–232
  FAQ, 796–797
  finger, 422–423
  forward lookup, 232–233
  GIF, 543–544
  global kill, 735, 774
  hostalias, 344
  hosts, 216, 241
  HOSTS.TXT, 216–217
  kill, 735–736, 744, 762–764, 774–778
  local kill, 735, 774
  loopback, 235–236
  MSD.EXE (MS-DOS), 279
  named data, 227, 231–232
  NET.CFG, 279–281
  newsgroup kill, 735, 774
  ODIPKT.COM, 281
  PROTOCOL.INI, 284
  publicly addressable mailing list, 434
  reverse lookup, 233–234
  sendmail.cf, 231
  shar, 756–757
  signature, 422–423, 730–731
  TCPMAN.EXE, 282
  TELNET.CFG, 342
  uuencoded, Trn program, 756
  WIN.INI, 282
  WINPKT.COM, 282

WINSOCK.DLL, 282
Filter software, 717–722
commands, 720–722
configuration/setup, 719–720
files setup, 697
language, 717–719
online help, 698
setting up, 695
testing files, 695–696
testing setup, 696–697
tracking incoming mail, 698
troubleshooting, 697–698
finger daemon, 417–418
finger files
ASCII art, 423
conventions, 422–423
Finger programs, 881–883
finger URL, 418–419
finger
adding information, 419–420
changing default information: chfn, 419
finding out who fingers you, 420
firewalls, 177
locations, 422
testing, 420
UNIX instructions, 417–422
firewalls, 123, 160–179
application-level gateway, 165, 175
Archie, 177
bastion host, 163, 168
books, 178
breaching, 161–162
can't protect against, 173
components, 162–166
corporation, 841
design decisions, 161, 174
dual-homed gateway, 163, 167–168
Finger, 177
Gopher, 177
hybrid gateways, 165–166, 169–170
level of compromise, 161–162
making DNS work, 175–176
making FTP work, 176
observations, 171
online information, 178–179
packet-screening tools, 175
protection against, 173
proxy servers, 175
related tools, 170
screened subnet, 164, 168–169
screened-host gateway, 164, 168
screening router, 163, 16–167
security questions, 165–166
Telnet, 177
using on the Internet, 173–179
UNIX system, 266
Whois, 177
why to use, 160–161
X Windows, 177–178
First Amendment protections, Usenet, 109–110
fizjm@halina.univ.gda.pl (Janusz J. Miodzianowski), 443–452
flame war, 44, 84, 109
flamers, 43–44
flaming, 31–32
flea market, virtual, 100–107
folklore, Internet, 27–48
For the Discussion of Marketing, 95
forms, ARTFL text database search, 583
forms
ASK, Gopher servers, 593–594
domain name registration, 246–250
forums, 8
WWW, 576
forward lookup file, DNS, 232–233
forwarders, 175–176
FQDN (fully qualified domain name), 220, 409
FRAD (frame relay access device), 258
frame relay, 258
distance-insensitive pricing, 258
frame relay access device (FRAD), 258
France Telecom, electronic phonebook, 7–12
Free Drawing for Course address, 97
free interactive dog game, Drool address, 97
Free Software Foundation, 276
Free-Market discussion list, 83–84
free-market@ar.com (Internet Free-Market Discussion), 95
freedom, net, 29–32
FreeWAIS software, 651–652
freeware, 89–91
FTP (File Transfer Protocols), 470, 809
addresses, Macintosh applications, 941
client applications, Macintosh 943–945
firewalls, 176
server applications, Macintosh, 945
servers, 293
sites
offline newsreaders, 797
search strategies, 465
smileys, 211
SLIP/PPP account, 321–322
software, packet driver specification, 278
FTP by mail, online retrieval instructions, 454–455
ftp URLs (Uniform Resource Locator), 363
ftp.ibm.net (Internet Connection), 390
ftp.trumpet.com.au (Trumpet WinSock), 282–283
ftp://ftp.std.com/pub/ibb/ibb.html, 97
ftp://mac.archive.umich.edu/mac/util/comm/, 357, 941
ftp://newdev.harvard.edu/pub/okipkt/okipkt.com (ODIPKT.COM), 281
ftp://nimbus.anu.edu.au/pub/tridge/samba (Samba), 286
ftp://rs.internic.net/templates/domain-templates.txt, 246
ftp://sumex-aim.stanford.edu/info-mac/comm/tcp/, 357, 941
ftp://sunsite.unc.edu/pub/Linux (Linux), 276
ftp://tsx-11.mit.edu/pub/linux (Linux), 276
FTPMAIL mail server, 435–437
full-service connection, 270
full-time dedicated telecommunications circuits, 270
Furr, Joel, jfurr@acpub.duke.edu, 27

G

games (MUDs), 883–885
games (other), 885–886
Gates, Bill, 817
gateways
application-level, 165, 175
dual-homed, 163, 167–168
hybrid, 165–166, 169–170
proxy, 165, 175
screened-host, 164, 168
Georgia Institute of Technology's Web User Survey, 97

GetAllMessages UNIX script, 788
GetMail UNIX script, 788
GetMessages UNIX script, 789
GetSummary UNIX script, 788–789
GIF files, using with HTML, 543–544
Global Electronic Marketing Service address, 97
global kill file, 735
GN server, 631–636
  Access denied message, 631
  access to, 635–636
  File does not exist message, 631
  GNUzip utility, 635
  gz file extension, 635
  hardware requirements, 633
  menu files, 631–633
  mkcache, 632–633
  mkmenu, 633
  overview, 631–634
  philosophy, 634
  search capabilities, 634–635
  switching from University of Minnesota gopher, 632
GN server software, 557
GNUS software, signature instructions, 416
Gopher, 470, 810–811
  All the gopher servers in the World listing, 833–834
  applications, Macintosh, 946–947
  disability access resources, 196–199
  firewalls, 177
  history of, 608–610
  mail servers, 439–440
  overview, 833–834
  SLIP/PPP account, 306
  SLIP/PPP account access, 322–323
  types, 835
Gopher client, *see* Gopher servers
Gopher Jewels, 478–479
Gopher Jewels Law Resources, 493–494
Gopher servers, 293–294, 590–594
  administration, 842–846
  Archie, 603–604
  ASK forms, 593–594
  bookmarks, 597–598
  browsing, 594–598
  content administration, 841
  CSO phone directory, 604
  designing, 837–840
  establishing, 837–841
  finding people on, 604
  firewalls, 841
  future interfaces, 630
  Gopher+ enhancements, 592–594
  home Gopher menu, 594
  installing, 840
  Jughead, 601–602
  locating new resources, 598–599
  mailing lists, 606–607
  menu items, 592
  overview, 610–612
  registering, 841
  running, 841–846
  search engines, 599–604
  selecting, 613–627
  subject-oriented, 595–596
  turning off directory caching, 842
  user support, 846–847
  types, 611–612
  University of Minnesota, 594–595
  UofM DOS: PC_Client, 617
  Usenet newsgroups, 607
  Veronica, 599–601, 627–629
  WAIS (wide-area information services), 602
  Washington and Lee University (WLU), 595
  WWW links, 604–606
Gopher sites, 98–99, 503–506
  search strategies, 465–466
Gopher+, 836–837
Gopher+ server, 590–594
  types, 612
gopher-news-request@boombox.micro.umn.edu, 833
gopher.msen.com (Internet Business Pages), 98
gopher.ntia.doc.gov, 98
gopher.ora.com (O'Reilly & Associates Publishers), 99
gopher.std.com/periodicals/TRADEWINDS, 99
gopher.tmn.com (Safety and the Arts), 197
gopher.town.hall.org (Federal Acquisition Regulations), 98
gopher://infoeagle.bc.edu, Boston College, 26
GopherApp++/2.2b43 software, 619–620
GOPHERJEWELS mailing list, 606–607
GOPHERJEWELS-TALK mailing list, 607
Gophers, 886–889
  Alex, 578–579
  Wiretap, 579–580
  WWW, 578–587
  WWW library, 577
Gopherspace, 833
Goupil G4 microcomputer, 8
government security agencies, 120
government, electronic signature system, 141
Graham, Jack
  http://crow.acns.nwu.edu:8082/hyplan.html, 531–561
  jacker@nwu.edu, 531–561
graphical interfaces, HTML, 544–546
Gray Pages, The, http://www.trinet.com/tgp/, 96
GRETEL, 6–7, 11–12
GriefNet, 492
groups, marketplace, 100
growstub error, 936
guides
  Net-Letter, 484
  The Internet Press, 484
gurus, development of, 15

H

hackers, 120
Hall, Adrian, 20
Handicap BBS, handicap.shel.isc-br.com, 197
HandiCode (DOS/Windows) software, 189
HandiWord (DOS/Windows) software, 190
hardware-based cryptographic products, 136–139
hardware requirements
  backups, 802–803
  business marketing, 79–80, 93
  organization network server, 275–277
  providers, 801–804
  SLIP/PPP accounts, 308–310
Harris, David (Pegasus Mail for Windows), 287
Harris, Stuart, sirrah@cg57.esnet.com, 509–529
Harvest, 489–490
hashing function, 140
Hauben, Ronda, ronda@panix.com, 65–67
header compression, TCP/IP, 345–346

headers, Organization, 424–426
Health Headlines newsletter, 491–492
Health Science Resources on Bitnet/Internet, 490–491
Hecker, Frank
  hecker@access.digex.net, 301–337, 453
  http://www.access.digex.net/~hecker/, 301–337
Heelan, Bill (Archie), 608
Helldiver Packet View 1.01B newsreader, 795
Heller vs. Bianco, defamation suit, 111
Hello Direct Tools for Telecommunication address, 97
Helper applications, Macintosh 954
Henze, Stephan, HENZE@LDB.han.de, 442
HGopher 2.4 software, 624–625
Hgopher software, 322
Hickman, Thomas, hickman@cleo.bc.edu, 290–297
hierarchy
  Domain Name System (DNS), 215–253
  newsgroups, 726–727
  Usenet, 100
High Tech Marketing Communications, listserv@scns.com, 95
Hildebrand, Garret, 215–253
Ho, Thomas (Favorite Electronic Commerce WWW Resources), 96
Hobbes' Internet Timeline v1.2, 497
Hoffman, Ron, 298–299
host computer
  finger daemon, 417–418
  versus dedicated router, 270
Host Information1, Macintosh software, 369–370
Host lookup programs, 889–890
host name, file references, 363
HOSTALIAS environment variable, UNIX, 344–345
hostalias files, TCP/IP, 344
hostnames
  DNS, 216, 321–322
  organization network, 273
hosts file, DNS, 216, 241
HOSTS.TXT file, 216–217
Hot Hot Hot Online, http://www.hot.presence.com/hot/, 97
hot lines, e-mail, 81
HotWired, http://www.hotwired.com/, 97
houston.forsale (marketplace newsgroup), 100
HTML (Hypertext Markup Language), 470, 531–546
  anchor tags, 538–539
  authoring, 853
  browser designing, 543–544
  check boxes, 565–566
  "click-here" syndrome, 545
  definition tags, 534–535
  design pitfalls, 542–546
  documents, WWW tips, 862–863
  FORM tag, 563
  format tags, 535–538
  forms setup, 563–570
  graphical interfaces, 544–546
  graphics tags, 540
  hidden elements, 567–568
  image maps, 572–573
  in-line image netiquette, 543
  invoke media tags, 539
  layout tags, 535
  line-mode browsers, 544
  link ethics, 545–546
  link tags, 538–542
  linking to other media, 540
  links to other Internet resources, 541–542
  list tags, 536–537
  Mozilla effect, 544
  netiquette, 542
  nonstandard tags, 545
  opening/closing tags, 535
  overview, 534–542
  radio buttons, 565–566
  reset button, 567
  script output, 571–572
  selection menus, 566–567
  SGML (Standard Generalized Markup Language), 534
  style tags, 537–538
  submit button, 567
  tags in, 532–542
  tenplate, 542
  text input, 563–565
  troubleshooting, 558–559
  Web Psychic page, 568–570
http: (hypertext transfer protocol), 470
HTTP (Hypertext Transfer Protocol) servers, 547–557
  custom, 548–557
  custom versus established, 559–561
  established, 547–548
http://biomed.nus.sg/people/commmenu.html, 96
http://catalog.savvy.com (Catalog Mart), 97
http://cybersight.com/cgi-bin/cs/s?main.gmm (Cybersight), 97
http://cyteria.netaxs.com, Apartment Relocation Service, 97
http://garnet.acns.fsu.edu/~chofack/article.html, 98
http://marketplace.com (MarketPlace.com), 98
http://rs600.adm.fau.edu/faahr/netiquette.html, 96
http://urth.ascu.buffalo.edu/irc/WWW/ircdocs.htm, 19
http://ww.missouri.edu/internet-advertising-guide.html, 97
http://www.access.digex.net/~hecker/ (Frank Hecker), 301–337
http://www.blackbox.com, Black Box On-Line Catalog, 96
http://www.cc.gatech.edu/gvu/user_surveys/, 97
http://www.commerce.net/information/help/find.html, 96
http://www.directory.net (Commercial Sites Index), 96
http://www.dns.net/dnsrd (DNS), 252
http://www.eunet.ch/werbal/experiments/, 98
http://www.gems.com:80/, 97
http://www.hello-direct.com/hd/home.html, 97
http://www.hot.presence.com/hot/ (Hot Hot Hot Online), 97
http://www.hotwired.com/ (HotWired), 97
http://www.mall2000.com (Mall 2000), 97

http://www.past.com/, CyberNaut Rest Stop, 97
http://www.portal.com/~skip/ayli.html, 96
http://www.rtd.com/people/rawn/business.html, 96
http://www.service.com/onourserver.html, 97
http://www.sofcom.com.au (Sofcom Home Shopping), 98
http://www.trinet.com/course.html, 97
http://www.trinet.com/kcomputing/drawing.html, 97
http://www.trinet.com/tgp/ (The Gray Pages), 96
http://www.wiltel.com/ritim/ritim/html, 98
http://www.xmission.com/~americom/ (Americom), 91
http://www.directory.net (Open Market Directory of Commerce), 98
HTTPD (Hypertext Transfer Protocol Daemon), 849
Hulburt, Sarah, sarah@tuna.uchicago.edu, 574–589
Human-Computer Interaction (HCI) Launching Pad, 475
Hunt, Craig, TCP/IP Network Administration, 277
Hur, Michael Y.C., mike@ingress.com, 801
hybrid gateways, 165–166, 169–170
Hyper-G, 891
hypermedia, 470, 863
hypertext, 470
  WWW, 532
HyperWAIS for Mac software, 643
hytelnet, 470–472

I

IBM Global Network, registering through OS2/Warp, 389–392
IBM
  OS/2 Warp, 387–405
  OS/2 Warp software, 309
IDEA (international data encryption algorithm), 131
image maps
  creating, 854
  HTML, 572–573
IMAP (Internet message access protocol), 670
IN A resource record, 238
IN CNAME resource record, 238
IN HINFO resource record, 237
IN MX resource record, 238–239
IN NS resource record, named data file, 237
IN PTR resource record, 239
IN SOA resource record, named data file, 236–237
in-line image, HTML, 543
INCONFIG program, UNIX system, 260
indexes
  WAIS, 653–658
  World Wide Web, 96
industrial spies, 120
Inet-Marketing discussion list, 82–83
inet-secrets@ii.com, Nancy McGough, 409–427, 673, 687–702
info-bots, IRC, 523–524
info-rama@wired.com (Wired magazine), 91
Infobahn, 816
InfoBot mail server, 442
information redundancy, 183
Information Superhighway, 816
InfoSeek search service, 488–489
INITs, turning off, 371
InLarge software, Macintosh, 184
installation
  Embot, 711–713
  NetWare LAN TCP/IP, 279–283
  network TCP/IP, 283–284
  OS2/Warp, 388–389
  Pine, 683–685
  UQWK software, 783
  US software, 785
  WAIS server, 659–660
  workstation TCP/IP, 277–279
Intellikeys alternative disability keyboard, 190
INTER-LINKS, 474
InterCon Systems Corporation, InterSLIP, 309
Interest-Groups list of lists, 485
interfaces, versus shell accounts, 806–807
international data encryption algorithm (IDEA), 131
Internet
  Acceptable Use Policies, 84–91
  advertising taboos, 82–84
  BBS connections, 17
  business marketing, 77–82
  connection types/comparative costs, 255–256
  culture, 27–48
  development of, 17–23
  disability access resources, 196–199
  disabled persons access, 181–206
  e-mail, 429–442
  economic model, 458
  firewalls, 173–179
  flame war, 84
  folklore, 27–48
  foundations of, 5–6
  full-service connection, 270
  future disability access, 191–192
  future uses, 24–25
  linking an organization network to, 269–288
  Macintosh, 349–362, 942
  Macintosh applications, 941–955
  non-English character support, 443–452
  online retrieval instructions, 453–455
  PC LAN connections, 277–284
  profile agents, 24–25
  resource locations, 469–502
  search strategies, 456–468
  society, 27–32
  spam message, 83
  text on, 574–589
Internet Adapter (TIA) software, 330, 935–936
Internet Advertising Resource Guide address, 97
Internet applications, Macintosh, 955
Internet Book Information Center (IBIC), 501
Internet Business Book, The address, 97
Internet Business Center (IBC), The, 500
Internet Business Pages, gopher.msen.com, 98
Internet Business Training Course address, 97
Internet Chameleon software (NetManage), 308

Internet Chameleon TCP/IP for Windows software, 327–328
Internet Connection software upgrade, ftp.ibm.net, 390
Internet Distribution Services address, 97
Internet Free-Market Discussion, free-market@ar.com, 95
Internet in a Box software, 328
Internet Mail Access Protocol (IMAP), 275
Internet Marketing, listproc@einet.net, 95
Internet Press, The, 484
Internet providers, 801–814
  European, 815–832
Internet Relay Chat (IRC), 19–22
Internet Resources Meta-Index, 474
Internet server
  see also servers
  organization network setup, 275–277
  service requirements, 275–276
Internet service provider (ISP), 80–81
Internet Shopping Network, shop.net, 98
Internet suites software, 285–287
Internet-on-a-Disk, 499
InternetWorks software, 328
InterNIC (Internet Network Information Center), 218, 818
  Information Services, Scout Report, 456
  Registration Services, rs.internic.net, 87, 98
InterSLIP scripts, 372–373
InterSLIP software (InterCon Systems Corporation), 309
  installing, 371–376
  settings, 375–376
Introduction to the Internet for Commercial Organizations, 96
IP (Internet Protocol), 216
IP address, 271, 307, 312, 216
  dotted decimal format, 271
  dotted-octet notation, 216
IP network number, provider requirements, 804
ipforwarding, 168
IPX/SPX protocol, 278
IRC (Internet Relay Chat), 19–22, 509–529, 809–810
  applications, Macintosh, 947–948
  OS2/Warp resources, 403
  * (asterisk) character with commands, 516–517
  ^ (caret) character with commands, 516–517
  , (comma) with, 524
  / (forward slash) with commands, 511
  /ALIAS commands, 520–523
  /BIND command, 519–520
  /BYE command, 511
  /CTCP command, 513
  /EXEC command, 513
  /FLUSH command, 511
  /HELP command, 511
  /IGNORE command, 512
  /JOIN command, 510
  /LIST command, 510
  /NICK (nickname up to nine characters) command, 510
  /ON command features, 516–519
  /SET BEEP MAX command, 512
  /SET BEEP OFF command, 512
  /SET CLOCK_ALARM, 515
  /SET commands, 515
  /SET HOLD_MODE command, 511
  /SET HOLD_MODE OFF command, 511
  /SET INDENT ON command, 515
  /SET LOG ON/OFF command, 515
  /SET LOGFILE command, 515
  /SET MAIL 2 command, 512
  /SET NOVICE OFF command, 512
  /SET REALNAME command, 514
  /SET SEND_IGNORE_MSG ON command, 512
  /SET SHOW_CHANNEL_NAMES ON command, 515
  /SET SHOW_WHO_HOPCOUNT ON command, 515
  /SET STATUS_FORMAT command, 515
  /SET USER_INFORMATION command, 514
  /SET VERBOSE_CTCP ON command, 514
  /WHOIS command, 513
  aliases, 520–523
  arithmetical operators, 523
  back doors, 527
  basic commands, 510–511
  Boolean operators, 523
  channels, 19, 510
  cleaning up your screen, 516–519
  control-key bindings, 519–520
  control-key combinations, 519–520
  CTCP (client-to-client protocol) setup, 514
  DCC (direct client connection), 525–526
  dedicated cook-bot, 524
  establishing identity, 510
  event trapping with /ON command, 517–519
  FAQs, 19
  Homer Friend List, 526
  http://urth.ascu.buffalo.edu/irc/WWW/ircdocs.htm, 19
  info-bots, 523–524
  interconnected servers, 19
  joining multiple channels, 512
  lastlogs, 520
  mail notification levels, 512
  mouse (point-and-click) with, 510
  NORA/HARLEQUIN marriage address, 20–22
  on-screen help, 511
  overview, 509–510
  real names, 514
  reverse-scrolling, 511–513
  screen configurations, 515–516
  screen control, 516–519
  script writer standard parameters, 522
  scripts, 526–528
  scroll speed, 511
  security holes, 527
  sleuthing, 513
  status bar, 511
  taking chances, 509–510
  transparent robots, 524
  Trojan horses, 527
  writing aliases, 520–523
  WSIRC war mode, 526–527
  WWW access, 529
iron.nttc.edu (National Technology Transfer Center), 99
IRS (Internal Revenue Service), 500
ISDN (Integrated Services Digital Network), 258, 805
  phone line, 324
ISO 6937/2 characters, 444–452

ISO 6937/2 terminal
 adapting applications to, 449–452
 e-mail, 451
 entering UNIX commands, 450
 keyboard, 446–447
 line printer, 452
 passwords, 450
 software availability, 452
 talk service, 451–452
 Telnet, 449–450
 terminals, 446–449
 text editor, 450–451
 transmission, 445
 video interrupt handler, 448
ISP (Internet service provider), 80–81

J

Jacobson compression, 345
Jaws (DOS/Windows) software, 186
jaym@iecc.com (Jay Maynard), 100–107
JEEVES, original DNS implementation, 217
joe@galcit.caltech.edu (Joe Cates), 562–573
Joel's Hierarchical Subject Index, 473
Jones, Alun (WFTPD.EXE), 286
journals, WWW, 576
jtbell@presby.edu (Jon Bell), 725, 766–780
Jughead, 470
 gopher server, 601–602
 gopher searches, 629–630
Juhasz, Robert (XFS), 281

K

Kahle, Brewster (WAIS), 652
Kaplan, Charles, cbk@ingress.com, 801
Kasperowski, Richard, 415
Katz, Philip (PKZIP), 90
Kaufmann, Matt, 415
Ke:nx software, Macintosh, 189
Kerberos authentication protocol, 312
kernel variable, modifying, 168
key escrow, 136
keyboard/mouse disability, 188–190
 alternative keyboards, 190
 Morse code, 189
 operating system tools, 188–190
 user access, 188–190
 word prediction software, 190
keyboarding injury, soda.berkeley.edu, 197
keyboards
 disability alternatives, 190
 ISO 6937/2, 446
Keynote Gold speech-synthesizer card, 185
kill files, 44, 735–736, 744
 editing Trn program, 764
 global, 774
 local, 774
 newsgroup, 774
 Trn program, 762–764, 774–778
Kinnaman, Dave M.S. M.A., kinnaman@world.std.com, 77–99, 181–206
Kirch, Olaf, Linux Network Administration, 276
Knowledge One, 500
Kriguer, Marc, 423–424

L

Lagarde, Dr. Francois, 8
LAN (local area network), 274
Lanciani, Dan (ODIPKT.COM), 281
Landaret, Michel, 7
languages
 HTML (Hypertext Markup Language), 532–546
 SGML (Standard Generalized Markup Language), 534
LANtastic software, 278
large networks, 290–299
lastlogs, IRC, 520
Lawrence, David, 53
laws, European providers, 825–826
Le Roux, Philippe, leroux@vdl2.ca, 5–26
leestral@mcs.com, Lee Stral, 591–607
legal defense fund, Phil Zimmerman, 158
Legal List, The, 492–493
Lemieux, Peter H., phl@cyways.com, 269–288
Levine, John R., 699
library Gophers, WWW, 577
line printer, ISO 6937/2 terminal, 452
line-mode browsers, HTML, 544
link-level data compression, 804
links, WWW, 532
Linux software, 276
 ftp://tsx-11.mit.edu/pub/linux, 276
Listproc mailing lists, 433
listproc@cni.org (Advertising in the Internet), 95
listproc@cni.org (Copyright and Intellectual Property Forum), 95
listproc@einet.net (Internet Marketing), 95
lists
 Interest-Groups list of lists, 485
 LISTSERV mailing, 430–432, 485–488
 World Wide Web, 96
LISTSERV mailing lists, 430–432, 485–488
 getting digests, 431–432
 listing subscribers, 432
 lists listing, 432
 subscribing/unsubscribing, 431
 turning mail on/off, 431–432
listserv@nervm.nerdc.ufl.edu, Marketing, 95
listserv@scns.com (High Tech Marketing Communications), 95
listserv@uriacc.uri.edu (Telecommunications/ Information), 95
local area network (LAN), 274
Local IR, 819
local kill files, 735
local networks, Macintosh, 351–352
loons, 41
loopback file, DNS, 235–236
love, Internet, 12–14
lurking, 30
Lynn.Alexander@excalibur.org (Lynn L. Alexander), 469–502

M

M.I.T., Kerberos authentication protocol, 312
Mac Internet software, 942–955
MacBinary, 355
MacGopher 0.5b14 software, 621–622
MacGzip/unzip program, Macintosh, 356
MacHTTP server software, 549–550

Macintosh
  Apple Remote Access connection, 353–354
  Archie applications, 946
  clean up startup, 371
  connect to local network, 351–352
  connecting to Internet, 349–362
  connecting to remote network, 352–354
  conversion utilities, 355–356
  custom HTTP server, 548–550
  file formats, 355–356
  FTP client applications, 943–945
  FTP server applications, 945
  getting on the Internet, 942
  Gopher applications, 946–947
  graphical gopher clients, 617–622, 625–627
  helper applications, 954
  information sources, 358–362
  Internet applications, 941–955
  Internet information, 358–362
  IRC applications, 947–948
  MacBinary, 355
  MacTCP, 367
  mailing lists, 359–360
  NNTP server, 378
  PPP connection, 353
  rebooting, 376
  SecureEdit program, 125
  SLIP connection, 352–353
  software 357–358
  software archives, 357
  starting up on Internet, 376–377
  Stuffit collection, 356
  Telnet, 376–377
  Telnet applications, 951
  TIA (The Internet Adapter), 363–386, 365
  troubleshooting Internet connection, 354–355
  Usenet news applications, 949–951
  Usenet newsgroups, 360–361
  virus checking, 371
  World Wide Web, 361–362, 364
    browser applications, 951–953
    server applications, 953
Macintosh Keyboard, alternative disability keyboard, 190
Macintosh software
  Archie applications, 946
  CloseView, 184
  Disinfectant, 371
  Gopher, 946–947
  Helper, 954
  Host Information1, 369–370
  InLarge, 184
  InterSLIP, 371–376
  IRC, 947–948
  Ke:nx, 189
  MacTCP, installing, 371–376
  networking, 370
  OutSpoken, 186–187
  SecureEdit, 125
  Stufffit, 356
  Telepathic, 190
  Telnet, 951
  TIA trial information, 368
  Usenet news, 949–951
  Voice Navigator II, 189
Macintosh TIA, 364–365
  -p option, 379
  .tia file, 380
  basic requirements, 365–366
  errors, 386
  frequently asked questions (FAQs), 360–384
  getting trial version, 368
  hardware cable, 366
  MacTCP, 367
  quickie shell, 379
  reading mail, 377
  reading news, 377
  right connections, 366
  shell accounts and SLIPS, 365
  software to use with, 367
  testing connections, 366
  troubleshooting, 384–385
  use file references, 363–364
MacPPP software, 309
MacTCP program, 309–310, 350–351, 367, 942
  installing, 351, 371–376
  settings, 373–374
MacWAIS software, 643–650
magazines, WEBster, 484
Magic (DOS/Windows) software, 184
Magic Deluxe (DOS/Windows) software, 184
magnetic media, 125
  secure disposal, 126
mail accessories, 891–895
mail folders
  naming, 687–688
  reading incoming, 688
mail programs, 891–895
mail servers, 429, 434–442
  Archie, 438–439
  BITFTP, 437–438
  FAQ archive, 442
  FTPMAIL, 435–437
  Gopher, 439–440
  InfoBot, 442
  WAIS, 441
  WWW, 440–441
mail
  reading, with Macintosh TIA, 377,
  signature instructions, 413
mail/newsreader programs, 895–899
Mailagent software, 703–710
  locking, 709
  message safety issues, 708
  references, 709
  setting up, 703–705
  supported folder types, 709
  tracking incoming mail, 706–707
  troubleshooting, 705–706
  using, 706–707
mailers, 409
  organization header, 424
mailing lists, 429–430
  C+Health, 491
  closed, 429–430
  digests, 430
  Gopher servers, 606–607
  GOPHERJEWELS, 606–607
  GOPHERJEWELS-TALK, 607
  information searches, 485–488
  installing, 958
  joining, 429
  Listproc, 433
  LISTSERV, 430–432, 485–488
  Macintosh, 359–360
  MajorDomo, 433
  manually maintained, 430
  moderated, 429–430
  Net-happenings, 483
  New-List, 485
  Pine, 671–672
  publicly addressable, 434
  unmoderated open, 429–430
maintenance, DNS, 240–242
Mall 2000, http://www.mall2000.com, 97
Manfredi, Raphael, ram@iecc.com, 703
manually maintained mailing list, 430
marketing, 77
  see also business marketing
Marketing and Sales address, 98
Marketing Resources address, 98
marketplace groups, 100

marketplace
  ad formats/limitations, 102
  buying/selling items, 102–104
  finalizing transactions, 104–106
  handling bad deals, 106
  shipping considerations, 105
  Usenet, 100–107
MarketPlace.com, http://marketplace.com, 98
Massachusetts Institute of Technology (MITnet), 298–299
Match-Maker, telnet bounced .e-mail.net, 17
Matrix, 217
maximum segment size, 283
maximum transmission unit (MTU), 283, 341
Maxwell, Robert, 8
Maynard, Jay, jaym@iecc.com, 100–107
McGough, Nancy, inet-secrets@ii .com, 409–427, 673, 687–702
McManus, Dorothy, 20
MegaDots (DOS) Braille translator software, 187
menus, Gopher, 592
Merel, Peter, 20
messages, signing, 152
metaculture, 27
mfriley@WPLEDU (Margaret F. Riley), 503
MH and Emacs mh-e software, signature instructions, 415–416
mi.forsale (Usenet marketplace), 101
Microsoft Keyboard, alternative disability keyboard, 190
Microsoft, Windows 95 software, 309
mike@ingress.com, Michael Y.C. Hur, 801
mikeryan@virtuoso.com, Mike Ryan, 781–797
Milk Rounds, 16
MIME (multipurpose Internet mail extensions), 670
Minitel, 6
  3615 phone line, 8
  as social chatline, 9–12
Miodzianowski, Janusz J., fizjm@halina.univ.gda.pl, 443–452
misc.forsale.non-computer (Usenet marketplace), 101
miscellaneous commercial information, biz.misc, 96
MITnet network, 298–299
mjr@tis.com (Marcus J. Ranum), 160–179
Mockapetris, Paul, 217
modems
  provider requirements, 803
  V.34 protocol, 271
moderated
  mailing list, 429–430
  newsgroups, 728
monolithic
  drivers, network operating systems, 278
  IPX driver, 278
monopolies, European providers, 824–825
Monster Board, The, 499
Moraes, Mark, netannounce @deshaw.com, 49–76
morphological analyzer, 575
Morse code, keyboard/mouse disability solution, 188–190
Mosaic software (NCSA), 24, 287, 322
  error unhandled exception Oxc0000005, 937
  growstub error, 936
  mouse, 936
Mother-of-all BBSs, The, 475
mouse, and Mosaic, 936
Mozilla (Mosaic Communications' Web client Netscape), 544
mramey@u.washington.edu (Mike Ramey), 673
MSD.EXE file (MS-DOS), 279
MUA (mail user agent), 409, 687
MUD (Multiuser Dungeon), 24, 810
  SLIP/PPP account, 322
mvanheyn@cs.indiana.edu, (Marc VanHeyningen), 418
MX resource record, DNS, 230–231
mythical users, 46

N

NACSIM, 126
name requests, iterative versus recursive, 225–226
name resolution, DNS, 223–226
name-place area code lookup, 91
named daemon, 227–230
  debugging output, 242
  DNS, 222–223
  namespace dump, 241
  namespace refresh, 240–241
named data files
  DNS, 227, 231–232
  resource records, 236–240
nameservers
  DNS, 215, 218, 227–230
  primary master, 221
namespace, DNS, 228
National Capital Area Public Access Network Inc. (CapAcess), 301
National Center for Supercomputing Applications (NCSA), 323
National Security Agency (NSA), 116–117
National Semiconductor, 140
National Technology Transfer Center, iron.nttc.edu, 99
National Telecommunications and Information Administration, 98
Native Language Support (NLS), 443
NCSA (National Center for Supercomputer Applications), 449
NCSA httpd for Windows server software, 550–551
NCSA httpd server software, 551–553
NCSA Mosaic software, 287, 322
NCSA WinHTTPD ServerV1.4, 851
NEARNET, 217
Nelson, Russell (Crynwr Software), 278–279
net
  see also Internet
  culture, 27–32
  personalities, 45–46
  privacy, 151–159
  terrorism, 106
Net-happenings mailing list, 483
Net-Letter Guide, 484
NET.CFG file, 279–281
NetBEUI operating system, 278
NetBIOS operating system, 278
netcom, 80
NetCruiser software, 330
Netfind, 472
netiquette
  Arlene Rinaldi, 96
  WWW, 542–543

NetManage
ChameleonNFS software, 286
Internet Chameleon software, 308
Netscape software, 24, 287
bookmark system, 24
viewpoint sharing, 24
NETSTAT, UNIX system, 261
NetWare LAN, TCP/IP installation, 279–283
NetWare operating system, 278
Network Device Interface Specification (NDIS), 278
Network Information Center (NIC), 216
Network News (NNTP) server, 275
Network News Transfer Protocol (NNTP), 392, 808–809
networks
BITNET, 430–432
centralized support environment, 290
centralized versus distributed management, 290–299
Class-B, 271
Class-C, 271
component testing, 299
design plan, 298
desktop solutions, 292
diagnostic tools, 299
distributed support environment, 290
end users, 290
file servers, 293
ftp servers, 293
gopher-based information systems, 293–294
hardware selection issues, 291
information system needs, 294–295
information systems, 292–294
large, 290–299
management information systems, 292
management issues, 290–291
managing large, 290–299
MITnet, 298–299
MTU (maximum transmission unit), 341
news, 725–797
OS2/Warp connections, 404–405
peer-to-peer, 278
quality issues, 298
scalable solutions, 298
software selection issues, 291
spare parts, 299
TCP/IP installation, 283–284
technical support issues, 291–292
topology issues, 299
vendor relations, 299
wire management systems, 299
WWW information systems, 294
Neutral Access Networks, 821
New-List mailing list, 485
newbies, 34–35
treatment of, 31
news administrator, 728
news messages, Organization header, 424
news, reading, with Macintosh TIA, 377,
newsgroup kill files, 735–736
newsgroups
alphabetizing, 732–733
alt.irc.recovery (recovery service), 16
article analysis, 729–730
article distributions, 733
buying/selling personal property, 100–107
comp.infosystems.*, 287
comp.infosystems.gopher, 833
comp.newprod, 51
comp.os.limux.help, 287
comp.os.ms-windows .networking.tcp-ip, 287
comp.os.msdos.mail-news, 287
comp.protocols.tcp-ip.ibmpc, 287
comp.sys.novell, 287
crossposting articles, 733–734
DNS, 252
fans, 42–43
guidelines, 53–54, 63
hierarchy, 726–727
kill files, 735–736
listing, 728–729
Macintosh, 360–361
moderated, 728
news.groups, 54
offline newsreaders, 796
OS2/Warp, 401–402
Pine, 671–672
posting test articles, 733
redirecting follow-up articles, 734–735
search strategies, 465
signature discussion, 424
unsubscribing, 732
Usenet, 95–96, 100, 674–675
Usenet creation, 53–54, 62–63
Usenet disability, 197–198
Usenet Gopher, 607
newsletters
Edupage, 484
Health Headlines, 491–492
Internet-on-a-Disk, 499
Repetitive Strain Injury, 491
newsreaders, 790–795
Helldiver Packet Viewer 1.01B, 795
offline, 781–797
NewsWatcher server address settings, 378
NewsWerthy newsreader, 795
NeXT software, 627
NFS clients 908–909
NFS server software, 286
NFSNET, 217
NIC (Network Information Center), 216, 813
NII (National Information Infrastructure), 815–818
advertising industry's view, 817
computer manufacturer's view, 816
consumer electronics manufacturer's view, 817
entertainment/media industry's view, 817
European, 818
retailing industry's view, 817
software publisher's view, 816
telecommunication corporation's view, 816
nn
additional information, 747–748
appending signature to articles/ replies, 746
article previews, 741
article searches, 745
automatic post save, 746
catching up, 741–742
automatically, 741
interactively, 741–742
command line options, 744
configuring, 738–739
consolidated menus, 746–747
discussions, 743
e-mail replies, 743
group order, 747
kill files, 744
killing articles, 744
newsgroup listing, 747
.newsrc file, 739

.nn/init file, 738
on-line help, 739
overview, 737–738
quitting, 742
reading mode, 741
reading news, 739–742
responding to articles, 743
saving articles, 742–743
seeing first article in a thread, 746
selection mode, 740
subscribing/unsubscribing to newsgroups, 742
using a mailer to send mail, 745
nn software
Organization header, 426
signature instructions, 416
NNTP (Network News Transport Protocol), 392, 808–809
Nolo Press Self-Help Law Center, 495
non-English characters, Internet support, 443–452
non-WinSock applications, 904–908
NFS clients, 908–909
Ph clients, 909–910
Northam, Mike, 416
Novell NetWare operating system, 278
Novell, DOS/Windows Client Kit, 279
NSA (National Security Agency), 46, 116–117
preferred crypto standard, 137
TEMPEST, 126
NSFNET (National Science Foundation NET), 84–85
NTIA, 816

O

O'Reilly & Associates Publishers, gopher.ora.com, 99
ocl@gih.co.uk (Olivier M.J. Crepin-Leblond), 815–832
ODIPKT.COM, ftp://newdev.harvard.edu/pub/okipkt/odipkt.com, 281
offline newsreaders, 781–797
advantages, 781
disadvantages, 781
e-mail, 783
FAQ files, 796–797
ftp sites, 797
newsgroups, 796
NewsWerthy, 795
Offliner, 795
packet formats, 782–783
packet handling, 782–783
PaperBoy, 794–795
requirements, 782
retrieving/downloading messages, 783–784
sending messages, 784–785
UNOR, 794
uses, 781
Yarn, 790–794
Offliner newsreader, 795
online mailing lists, 958
online information, firewalls, 178–179
on-screen help, IRC, 511
one-time pads
encryption technique, 143–144
problems, 143–144
Online Computer Library Center (OGLC), 500
Online Writing Lab (OWL), 497–498
Ontario Institute for Studies in Education Gopher, The, 498
ooblick@intercon.com (Mikki Barry), 108–113
Open Datalink Interface (ODI) specification, 278
Open Market's Directory of Commerce address, 98
operating systems
AIX 3.2, 226–227
AIX 3.2.5, 231
Amiga, 627
monolithic drivers, 278
NetBEUI, 278
NetBIOS, 278
Novell NetWare, 278
operators, IRC
arithmetical, 523
Boolean, 523
Organization header, 424–426
organization network
access provider connection, 271–272
aliases, 274
broadcast address, 271
Class-B network, 271
Class-C network, 271
connection requirements, 270
domain name registration, 272–274
hostname, 273
Internet server setup, 275–277
IP address, 271
linking to the Internet, 269–288
overview, 269–270
PC LANS connections, 277–284
server hardware requirements, 275–277
service provider domain names, 273
shell accounts, 272
subnet mask, 271
TCP/IP on NetWare LANs, 279–283
TCP/IP transport software, 286
organizations, disability, 201
OS/2 graphical gopher clients, 627
OS/2 Warp software (IBM), 309, 331, 387–405
anonymous ftp resources, 402
BonusPak, 387
ftp (file transfer protocol), 396–398
FTPPM, 397–398
gopher, 398–399
gopher resources, 402
IBM Global Network registration, 389–392
IBM Web Explorer, 399–400
installing, 388–389
Internet Connection
additions, 403
applications, 392–400
registration, 389–392
settings, 391–392
Internet rate information, 390–391
Internet Relay Chat (IRC), 403
Multimedia Viewer, 388
multitasking feature, 388
network card use, 404–405
newsgroups, 401
NewsReader/2, 392–394
overview, 387–388
Person to Person, 387
preemptive multitasking feature, 388
price, 388
registration information, 391
resources, 401–403
REXX programming language, 403
technical support, 390–391
Telnet, 395–396
Telnet 3270, 395–396
third-party dialup providers, 403–404

Timeout Warning dialog box, 400–401
Ultimedia Mail/2 Lite, 394–395
Video IN, 387–388
Web Explorer, 390
World Wide Web resources, 402
OutSpoken software, Macintosh, 186–187

P

packet drivers, 278–279
packet screening tools, firewalls, 175
packets
QWK, 782
SOUP, 782
TCP/IP, 340
pages, 470
WWW, 466
PaperBoy newsreader, 794–795
parameters, passing CGI applications, 857
pass phrase, choosing, 147–148
passwords, 140–150
creating random, 148–150
good, 146
ISO 6937/2 terminal, 450
pass phrase, 147–148
poor, 146–147
selection, 122
sending on the net, 380
SLIP/PPP account, 311–312
writing down, 148
path, file reference, 363
PC LANS, connecting to Internet, 277–284
PC newsreaders, 790–795
PC Tools for Windows software, 279
PCMCIA
cryptographic smart cards, 139–140
PC Card slots, 140
slots, 138
peer-to-peer network, 278
Pegasus Mail for Windows (David Harris), 287
Pentium machines, serial port problems, 938
people, types on net, 32–46
Persona Card, 140
personal identification number (PIN), 311
Personal NetWare software, 278
personal property, buying/selling, 100–107
petri-dish, 27–29
PGP (pretty good privacy), 151
acquiring, 152–153
digital signatures, 152
encryption technique, 134–135
legal notes, 158
setting up, 154–157
Ph clients, 909–910
phl@cyways.com (Peter H. Lemieux), 269–288
physical theft, 123–124
Physician's GenRx database, 491
pico, text editor, 409, 687
Pine software, 275, 669–723
/user/spool/mail, 684
abort message, 679–680
appending signatures to mail, 674
as noninteractive shell script, 677
BASE 64 encoding, 682
Berkeley Mail conversions, 685
blind carbon copy header field, 672
configuration information, 683
configuring, 683–685
content-length header, 682
conversions, 683–685
deciphering MIME-aware mail program attachments, 685
documentation availability, 671
dual mailbox access, 681
eliminating @host.domain from local address, 678–679
Elm aliases conversions, 685
folder locks, 680–681
header definitions, 677
IMAP, 670
installation, 683–685
ispell spelling checker, 673–674
locked, will override in seconds message, 681–682
Macintosh communications software support, 684
mail check forcing, 677
mailing lists, 671–672
message filtering, 675–676
MIME, 670
news postings, 675
newsgroups, 671–672
on-line FAQ, 686
organization header, 425–426
overview, 669
pasting address into message text, 675
PC communications software support, 684
Pico composer, 673–674
platform support, 671
POP server incompatibilities, 683
print to ANSI print option, 684
reading ROT13-encoded messages, 678
reading Usenet newsgroups, 674–675
references, 685
sending messages without showing all names, 672
signature-at-bottom variable, 411
signature instructions, 411–412
sources, 670
Tenex mailbox, 683
terminal support, 684
troubleshooting problems, 679–685
user tips, 672–679
pine-faq@docserver.cac.washington.edu, 669
PING command, UNIX system, 261
Ping programs, 911
PKWARE, 90
PKZIP, 90
Planet Earth Home Page, 473
PLEASE COPY THIS DISK catalog, 498–499
Plexus server software, 557
PNLInfoBrowser 1.05 software, 625–627
Point-to-Point Protocol (PPP), 166, 270, 303, 807–808, 826
book and software bundles, 331–334
commercial Internet packages, 326–331
dedicated Internet connection, 324–325
electronic mail, 304, 314–319
file transfer using FTP, 305
FTP access, 321–322
Gopher, 306
Gopher access, 322–333
hardware requirements, 308–310
Internet access basics, 313–314
Internet connection, 310–313
introduction to, 301–303
IP address, 307, 312
ISDN lines, 324
Macintosh, 353

MUD (Multi-User Dungeons), 322
offline mail, 795–796
online information, 334–337
overview, 303
passwords, 311–312
POP3 mail server, 316
reasons for using, 302–303
remote login using telnet, 304
service providers, 310–313
software requirements, 308–310
telnet access, 322
Usenet news, 305, 319–321
user ID, 311–312
uses, 304–306
WWW (World Wide Web), 306
PoP (Point of Presence), 822
POP (post-office protocol), 275, 316, 670
POP3 mail server, 316
Post Office Protocol (POP), 275, 316, 670
postmaster@anytown.edu (postmaster), 44
POTS line, 323
POWERLan software, 278
PPP connection, Macintosh, 353
PPP vs SLIP, 938–939
Prestel, 5
primary master nameserver, 221
primary server, 227
print disability, 182–188
Braille translators, 187–188
language disability, 186–187
print is too small to read, 184
screen-magnification programs, 184
screen-review software, 185–186
speech-synthesizer cards, 185
types of, 182–183
user cannot read printout, 187–188
user cannot see the screen, 184–186
privacy, 115–180
on the net, 151–159
setting up PGP, 154–157
private-key encryption, 130
Procmail software, 688–694, 722–723
files setup, 690–691
online help, 694
setting up, 688–691
test recipe, 693
testing files, 689–690
testing setup, 690
tracking incoming mail, 693–694
troubleshooting, 692–693
products/vendors, disability, 192–194
profile agents, 24–25
programmers, TCP/IP, 339
programs see software
PROJECT DA-CLOD, 474
pros, 45
protocol suite, 51
PROTOCOL.INI file, 284
protocols
CTCP (client-to-client), IRC, 514
file references, 363
IMAP (Internet message access protocol), 670
IPX/SPX, 278
Kerberos authentication, 312
POP (post-office protocol), 670
PPP, 166
UUCP, 51
V.34 modem, 271
providers
backup hardware, 802–803
basic services, 806–811
cable companies, 805
contacts, 813–814
cost considerations, 812
CSU/DSU units, 804
DNS registration, 804
European
Acceptable Use Policies (AUP), 823–824
address classes, 819
allocation procedures, 820
considerations, 822–826
DANTE, 821
EBONE, 821
EPMB, 821
EUnet, 821
EuropaNET, 821
EurOpen, 821
fundamentals, 818–826
future outlook, 830–832
IP address allocation, 819–820
language issues, 822–823
large providers, 829–830
laws, 825–826
monopolies, 824–825
Neutral Access Networks, 821
overview, 821
players, 818–819
PoP distance, 822
provision of service, 826–830
registration, 819–820
RIPE NCC funding, 819
small providers, 826–829
FTP, 809
games/MUDs, 810
gopher, 810–811
hardware requirements, 801–804
Internet, 801–814
Internet Relay Chat (IRC), 809–810
IP network number, 804
ISDN adapters, 805
link-level data compression, 804
logistics, 812
market issues, 811–812
modem requirements, 803
network feeds, 804–805
network news, 808–809
NNTP (network News transfer protocol), 808–809
PPP/SLIP, 807–808
router vendors, 813–814
routers, 804
security issues, 805–806
serial lines versus high-speed lines, 804–805
shell accounts versus interfaces, 806–807
support issues, 811
telnet, 809
terminal server requirements, 803
TIA, 808
WWW, 810–811
X Windows, 807–808
proxy gateways, 165, 175
proxy servers, 175
PSInet, 217
public-key cryptography, 130, 151
publications
content responsibilities/liabilities, 110–112
WWW, 531–561
publicly addressable mailing list file, 434
publishers, WWW, 531–561
punctuation, smileys as, 208–209
Qualcomm, Eudora, 314–319
Quarterdeck
Desqview/X software suite, 285
Manifest, 279
QWK packet, 782

R

ram@iecc.com (Raphael Manfredi), 703
Ramey, Mike, mramey@u.washington.edu, 673
randolph@air.org, (Chung, Randolph), 849–864

random bits, creating, 144
random passwords/keys, 148–150
random strings, overwriting files, 125
Ranum, Marcus, mjr@tis.com, 160–179
Rapport NORA-MINC, 5
RARE, 818
rare users, 46
RC2 encryption technique, 135
RC4 encryption technique, 135
readers, book, 1
rec.arts.comics, 45
rec.bicycles.marketplace, Usenet marketplace, 101
receive window, TCP/IP, 341–342
recovery service, alt.irc.recovery, 16
redundant servers, DNS, 225
references
  DNS, 253
  parts, 363
  WinSock, 930–931
registration form, domain name, 246–250
regular expression, 687
regulations, Technology-Related Assistance Act, 194
Reinhold, Arnold G. reinhold@world.std.com, 115–159
remailers, anonymous, 145
remote access servers, 311
remote networks, Macintosh, 352–354
Repetitive Strain Injury newsletter, 491
republication standard, 110
resolvers, DNS, 226–227
resource records
  address to name:, IN PTR, 239
  alias: IN CNAME, 238
  host information: IN HINFO, 237
  mail exchange: IN MX, 238–239
  name to address: IN A, 238
  named data file, 236–240
  nameserver: IN NS, 237
  start of origin: IN SOA, 236–237
resources
  Gopher servers, 598–599
  locating on the Internet, 469–502
  Macintosh, 359–362
retransmission time-out, TCP/IP, 343
reverse lookup file, DNS, 233–234
rfabian@interlog.com (Bob Fabian), 456–468
RFC (Request for Comments), 409
RFC 1034, 215, 217, 236
RFC 1035, 215, 218
RFC 1521 (MIME), 670
ric@ingress.com (Richard Chung), 801
Riley, Margaret F., mfriley@WPI.EDU, 503–507
Rinaldi, Arlene (netiquette), 96
Riordan's Internet Privacy Enhanced Mail (RIPEM), 133–134
RIPE NCC, 818–820
RIPEM encryption technique, 133–134
ripem.msu.edu (SecureEdit program), 125
Rivers, Ron, 135
root servers, DNS, 250
Rosenbaum, Janet, 421–422
rot13 code, 754–755
rot13 encryption technique, 129
ROUTE command, UNIX, 262
router controversy, 270
routers, provider requirements, 804
rs.internic.net (InterNIC Registration Services), 87, 98
RSA Data Security Inc., 132, 135
RSA encryption technique, 132–133
rules of behavior, 29–32
Ryan, Dee, deeryan@virtuoso.com, 781–797
Ryan, Mike, mikeryan@virtuoso.com, 781–797

S

Sacks, Dennis, dsacks@news.primenet.com, 637–668
safes, 124
Safety and the Arts, gopher.tmn.com, 197
Salmon, Andras, 252
Salzenberg, Chip, chip@tct.com, 49–76
Samba software, ftp://nimbus.anu.edu.au/pub/tridge/samba, 286
Sanderson, David W., dws@ora.com, 207–211
sarah@tuna.uchicago.edu (Sarah Hulburt), 574–589
Scarecrow's ASCII Art Archives, 501
Scout Report, Internet search strategies, 456
Screen Power (DOS) software, 187
screen savers, 122
screen-review software, 185–186
ScreenDoors alternative disability keyboard, 190
screened subnet, 164, 168–169
screened-host gateway, 164, 168
screening router, 163, 166–167
script writers, IRC standard parameters, 522
scripts
  backfinger, 421–422
  CGI, 856–862
  IRC, 526–528
  UNIX, 787–790
  writing, 860–861
  WWW, 562–563
sct@po.cwru.edu (Stephen Trier), 339, 631–636
search forms, ARTFL text database, 583
search strategies
  access tools, 461–464
  access types, 458–459
  bookmarks, 463–464
  ftp site, 465
  gopher site, 465–466
  limits, 456–458
  necessary limits, 456–458
  newsgroups, 465
  Scout Report, 456
  source types, 459–461
  Web pages, 466
  Yahoo, 457
search utilities, 469–502
  Alex text catalogue, 489
  archives guide, 477
  AT&T 800 directory, 490
  C+Health mailing list, 491
  CARI, 480–482
  CyberSight, 474
  DIALOG, 498
  EDS Shadow Patent Office, 496
  Edupage newsletter, 484
  EFF Extended (Big Dummy's) Guide, 474–475
  Gopher Jewels, 478–479
  Gopher Jewels Law Resources, 493–494
  GriefNet, 492
  Harvest, 489–490
  HCI Launching Pad, 475
  Health Headlines newsletter, 491–492
  Health Science Resources Bitnet/Internet, 490

InfoSeek site, 488–489
INTER-LINKS, 474
Interest-Groups list of lists, 485
Internet Resources Meta-Index, 475
Joel's Hierarchical Subject Index, 473
Legal List, The, 492–493
library resources, 479–483
LISTSERV mailing lists, 485–488
Net-happenings mailing list, 483
Net-Letter Guide, 484
Netfind, 472
New-List mailing list, 485
Nolo Press Self-Help Law Center, 495
Physician's GenRx database, 491
Planet Earth Home Page, 473
PROJECT DA-CLOD, 474
Repetitive Strain Injury newsletter, 491
Special Internet Connections, 474
Sto's Internet Patent Search System, 495
subject-oriented clearinghouse, 475–477
The Complete Home Page Directory, 498
The Internet Press, 484
The Mother-of-all BBS, 475
Town Hall U.S. Patent & Trademark Office, 496
type/location searches, 477–479
UnCover, 482–483
WEBster e-mail magazine, 484
West's Legal Directory, 494–495
WWW, 472–477
WWW virtual library: listing, 473
WWW virtual library: subject catalog, 473
Yahoo, 473
searches, WAIS, 639–640
second-level domains, DNS, 218
secondary server, 227
SecureEdit program, Macintosh, 125
security, 115–180
digital signatures/ authentication, 140–150
holes, IRC, 527
one-time pads, 143–144
plans, choosing, 118–128
provider issues, 805–806
tips, 150
UNIX system, 266–267
using firewalls, 160–161
security problems
data-carrying signals, 127
data remnants, 124–125
degaussers, 126
digital audiotape threat, 124
erasing data, 125
file deletion, 125
Macintosh, SecureEdit program, 125
magnetic media, 125
media disposal, 126
password selection, 122
passwords, 140–150
physical theft, 123–124
safes, 124
shielded room, 128
TEMPEST, 126–128
terminals, unattended, 122
traffic analysis, 123
Trojan horses, 122–123
unattended terminals, 122
unauthorized entry via Internet, 123
virtual memory, 125
viruses, 122–123
security questions, 118–128
amount of data, 119
consequences of compromised data, 121
data protecting, 118
how else is data accessible, 122–128
legal obligation to protect data, 121
length of time data is sensitive, 118
number of people sharing information, 119
protect data from whom, 119–121
safety of data at origin or destination, 119
threat classification schemes, 120–121
whom to trust for advice, 121–122
segment size, setting TCI/IP, 340–341
selecting articles, 744
send window, TCP/IP, 342
sendmail
canonicalization, 230
DNS, 230–231
sendmail.cf file, 231
SendMessages, UNIX script, 789–790
Serial Line Internet Protocol (SLIP), 303
server administrators, responsibilities, 560
server programs, 941
custom versus established, 559–561
DNS, 225–226
DNS root, 250
file, 293
FTP (File Transfer Protocol), 293
GN, 631–636
Gopher, 293–294, 590–594, 833–847
Gopher+, 590–594
HTTP, 547–557
mail, 429
Network News (NNTP), 275
NFS, 286
POP3 mail, 316
primary, 227
redundant DNS, 225
remote access, 311
secondary, 227
service requirements, 275–276
terminal, 803
Usenet, 293
WAIS, 659–665
WWW, 294
WWW on Windows, 843–863
Service Mèdical (SM), 7–8
as social chatline, 9–12
AT&T 3B15 minicomputer, 8
Goupil G4 computer, 8
service providers, 310–313, 806–811
America Online, 80
choosing, 80–81
CompuServe, 80
customer support, 244
Delphi, 80
netcom, 80
organization network domain names, 273
publication liabilities, 110–112
publication responsibilities, 110–112
SLIP/PPP, 310–313
The Well, 80
settings, MacTCP, 373–374
SFgate software, 663–665
SGML (Standard Generalized Markup Language), 534
shar files, Trn program, 756–757
shareware, 89–91
shareware disks, installing, 957–958

shell account, 302
  organization network, 272
  versus interfaces, 806–807
shells, Macintosh TIA, 379
shims
  ODIPKT.COM file, 281
  packet driver emulation, 278
  SIS_PKT9.DOS (Joe Doupnik), 284
shop.net (Internet Shopping Network), 98
signature file, 730–731
  ASCII art, 423
  conventions, 422–423
signatures
  see also automatic signature
  electronic, 152
  e-mail, 87
  instructions, troubleshooting problems, 417
  newsgroups, 424
  testing, 411
signing messages, 152
Simple Mail Transport Protocol (SMTP), 275
Sipples, Timothy, tsipple@vnet.ibm.com, 387–405
sirrah@cg57.esnet.com (Stuart Harris), 509–529
sites
  Gopher, 98–99, 503–506
  InfoSeek, 488–489
  World Wide Web, 96–98
  WWW, 506–507
Skipjack encryption technique, 136–139
SLIP (Serial Line Internet Protocol), 270, 364, 807–808, 826
  book and software bundles, 331–334
  commercial Internet packages, 326–331
  dedicated Internet connection, 324–325
  electronic mail, 304, 314–319
  file transfer using FTP, 305
  FTP access, 321–322
  Gopher, 306
  Gopher access, 322–333
  hardware requirements, 308–310
  Internet access basics, 313–314
  Internet connection, 310–313
  introduction to, 301–303
  IP address, 307, 312
  ISDN lines, 324
  logging in, 310–313
  Macintosh, 352–353
  MUD (Multi-User Dungeons), 322
  offline mail, 795–796
  on-line information, 334–337
  overview, 303
  passwords, 311–312
  POP3 mail server, 316
  reasons for using, 302–303
  references, 930–931
  remote login using telnet, 304
  service providers, 310–313
  software requirements, 308–310
  telnet access, 322
  Usenet news, 305, 319–321
  user ID, 311–312
  uses, 304–306
  WWW (World Wide Web), 306
SLIP vs PPP, 938–939
smileys, 207–211
  as punctuation, 208–209
  collection, 210–211
  how many, 208
  how to get more, 210–211
  list of new, 209–210
  why use, 207
SMTP (Simple Mail Transfer Protocol), 315
Social Security Administration, 497
soda.berkeley.edu (Keyboarding Injury), 197
Sofcom Home Shopping, http://www.sofcom.com.au, 98
software
  B News, 65–66
  BIND, 222–223, 244
  Braille Blazer (DOS/Windows/Mac), 188
  business marketing, 93
  Business Vision (DOS/Windows), 186
  C News, 65–76
  CERN httpd server, 554–556
  ChameleonNFS (NetManage), 286
  CloseView (Macintosh), 184
  communication programs, 868–872
  COPS (UNIX system), 267
  Crack (UNIX system), 267
  demo packages, 872–876
  Desqview/X (Quarterdeck), 285
  diagnostic tools, 876–877
  DOS/Windows Client Kit (Novell), 279
  Dragon Dictate (DOS), 189
  Duxbury (DOS/Mac), 187
  Elm, 412, 426
  Emacs Mail Mode, 414–415
  Embot, 710–717
  Eudora (Qualcomm), 314–319, 699–700
  Explore OnNet for Windows, 327
  Fetch, 321
  file-search protocols, 877–881
  file-transfer protocols, 877–881
  filter, 695–698
  Finger programs, 881–883
  FreeWAIS (CNIDR), 651–652
  FreeWAIS-sf, 652
  FTP sites, 862
  games (MUDs), 883–885
  games (other), 885–886
  GN server, 557
  GNUS, 416
  GopherApp++/2.2b43, 619–620
  gophers, 886–889
  HandiCode (DOS/Windows), 189
  HandiWord (DOS/Windows), 190
  Helldiver Packet View 1.10B newsreader, 795
  Hgopher, 322
  HGopher 2.4, 624–625
  host lookup programs, 889–890
  Hyper-G, 891
  HyperWAIS for Mac, 643
  InLarge (Macintosh), 184
  Internet Adapter (TIA), 330
  Internet Chameleon (NetManage), 308
  Internet Chameleon TCP/IP for Windows, 327–328
  Internet in a Box, 328
  Internet suites, 285–287
  InternetWorks, 328
  InterSLIP (InterCon Systems Corporation), 309
  Jaws (DOS/Windows), 186
  Ke:nx (Macintosh), 189
  keyboard/mouse disability, 188–190
  LANtastic, 278
  MacGopher 0.5b14, 621–622
  MacHTTP server, 549–550
  Macintosh communication applications, 941–955
  Macintosh Internet, 942–955
  MacPPP, 309
  MacTCP (Apple), 309–310, 367

MacWAIS, 643–650
Magic (DOS/Windows), 184
Magic Deluxe (DOS/Windows), 184
mail accessories, 891–895
mail programs, 891–895
mail/newsreaders, 895–899
Mailagent, 703–710
Manifest, 279
MegaDots (DOS), 187
MH and Emacs mh-e, 415–416
Miscellaneous, 899–904
NCSA httpd for Windows server, 550–551
NCSA Mosaic, 287, 322
NDSA httpd server, 551–553
NetCruiser, 330
Netscape, 287
NetWare, 278
network server, 277
NewsWerthy newsreader, 795
NeXT, 627
NFS clients, 908–909
NFS server, 286
nn, 416, 426, 737–748
non-Winsock applications, 904–908
Offliner, 795
operating system and TCP/IP transport, 286
OS/2 Warp (IBM), 309, 331, 387–405
OutSpoken (Macintosh), 186–187
packet driver, 279
PaperBoy newsreader, 794–795
PC Tools for Windows, 279
Pegasus Mail for Windows (David Harris), 287
Personal NetWare, 278
Ph clients, 909–910
Pine, 275, 411–412, 425–426, 660–723
Ping programs, 911
PKZIP, 90
Plexus server, 557
PNLInfoBrowser 1.05, 625–627
POWERLan, 278
print disability, 184–188
Procmail, 688–694, 722–723
Screen Power (DOS), 187
screen-review, 185–186
SFgate, 663–665
shareware/freeware, 89–91
SLIP/PPP, 308–310
SoundProof (DOS) software, 187
SUN OpenWindows Mail Tool, 414
SuperHighway Access for Windows, 329
Swais, 641
System Consultant (PC Tools), 279
TCP/Connect II, 329
TCP/IP, 918
Telepathic (Macintosh), 190
telephone dialers, 912–913
Telnet, 914–918
TIA, 935–936
time synchronizers, 919–921
to use with Macintosh TIA, 367
Tripwire (UNIX system), 267
Trumpet WinSock, 282–283, 308–310, 329, 342, 933–934
TurboGopher, 322
TurboGopher 2.0b5, 617–619
UNOR newsreader, 794
UQWK, 782–785
US, 785–786
Usenet, 52, 60
Usenet readers, 895–899
VersaPoint (DOS/Windows/ Mac) Braille translator, 188
Vocal Eyes (DOS) software, 187
Voice Navigator II (Macintosh), 189
WAIS, 921–922
Waisq, 641–642
waissearch, 641–642
WAIStation for Mac, 643
WFTPD.EXE (Alun Jones), 286
Whois programs, 922–923
Windows 95 (Microsoft), 309
Windows for Workgroups, 278
WinGopher Complete, 329
WinPAC Complete, 329
WinSock, 281–282, 867–939
WinVision (DOS/Windows), 186
WinWAIS, 643
WN server, 557
Word Scholar (DOS), 187
WS_FTP, 321
WSGopher, 464
WSGopher 1.2, 622–624
WWW browsers, 923, 928
X Window, 627
X.500 (DUA) clients, 929–930
Xwais, 640–641
Yarn newsreader, 790–794
ZDist, 666
ZoomText (DOS/Windows), 184
ZoomText Plus (DOS/Windows), 184
sound disability, 191
Sounding Board speech-synthesizer card, 185
SoundProof (DOS) software, 187
SOUP packet, 782
source locations
  Macintosh, 358–362
  WinSock applications, 934–935
Spafford, Gene, Spaf@cs.purdue .edu, 49–76
spam message, 83
spamming, 101
Special Internet Connections, 474
speech-synthesizer cards, 185
Spencer, Henry (Usenet News), 65–67
standards, character, 443–452
Stanford, Macintosh communication applications, 357, 941
Stevenson, Doug, doug+@osu.edu, 418–419
Sto's Internet Patent Search System, 495
stopwatch, timing TCP/IP improvements, 339
Stral, Lee, leestral@mcs.com, 591–607
Stuffit program, Macintosh, 356
subdomains, DNS, 218
subject-oriented Gophers, 595–596
subnet mask, organization network, 271
suites, Internet, 285–287
Sun Microsystems, network server packages, 277
SUN OpenWindows Mail Tool signature instructions, 414
SuperHighway Access for Windows software, 329
support@pkware.com (PKWARE), 90
Swais software, 641
system administrators, Usenet, 52, 61–62, 109

T

tactical invasive posting, 44
tags, HTML, 532–533
talk, ISO 6937/2 terminal, 451–452
Tattam, Peter, Trumpet WinSock, 282, 308, 310

Taylor, Dave, taylor@netcom.com, 710–723
TCP wrappers, UNIX system, 267
TCP/Connect II software, 329
TCP/IP (Transmission Control Protocol/Internet Protocol, 216, 307
  Domain Name Service (DNS), 344–345
  header compression, 345
  HOSTALIAS environment variable, 344–345
  hostalias files, 344
  local size setting, 341
  maximum transmission unit (MTU), 341
  NetWare LAN installation, 279–283
  network installation, 283–284
  overview, 340
  packets, 340
  programmers, 339
  programs, 918
  receive window, 341–342
  retransmission time-out, 343
  segment size setting, 340–341
  send window, 342
  SLIPping to speed, 345–346
  TELNET.CFG file, 342
  time-outs, 343
  timing with stopwatch, 339
  transport software, 286
  tuning, 339–347
  workstation installation, 277–279
TCP/IP stack, 278
TCPMAN.EXE file, 282
Technology-Related Assistance Act, 194
Telebit Corporation, 813
Telecommunications and Information Marketing address, 95, 98
telematics, 5
Telepathic software, Macintosh, 190
telephone dialers, 912–913
Telequip Corporation, 140
Telidon, 5
Telnet program, 470, 809, 914–918
  applications, Macintosh 951
  firewalls, 177
  ISO 6937/2 terminal, 449–450
  Macintosh, 376–377
  SLIP/PPP account, 322
  SLIP/PPP remote login, 304
TELNET.CFG file, 342
TEMPEST (transient electromagnetic pulse emanation standard) 126, 128
TEMPEST servers
  measures to defeat, 127–128
  security problems, 126–128
  shielded room to defeat, 128
templates, HTML, 542
Tenex mailbox, Pine, 683
TERENA, 819
terminal servers, provider requirements, 803
terminals
  ISO 6937/2, 446–449
  unattended, 122
terrorism
  detecting, 44–45
  Net, 106
terrorists, 43–44
Tessera, Clipper encryption cards, 138
text
  available online types, 575–577
  defining online, 574–575
  how computer reads, 575
  Internet, 574–589
  morphological analyzer, 575
  online advantages, 580
  online problems, 579–580
  rare books online, 582–587
  WWW, 532
text editor, ISO 6937/2 terminal, 450–451
text strings, animated, 423–424
The Codebreakers, 116
The Well, 80
Theise, Eric S., Ph.D., verve@cyberwerks.com, 608–630
Thinking about Firewalls, 160–172
Thomas Ho's Favorite Electronic Commerce WWW Resources, 96
thousand pound gorilla, 46
threaded newsreader (Trn), 749–780
TIA
  trial version, Macintosh software, 368
  Macintosh, 363–386, 808
time synchronizers, 919–921
time-outs, TCP/IP, 343
tips, security, 150
tools
  DNS, 245–246
  firewall, 170, 175
Torvalds, Linus, 276
Town Hall U.S. Patent & Trademark Office, 496
TRACEROUTE, UNIX system, 261–262
Tradewinds Internet, gopher.std.com/periodicals/TRADEWINDS, 99
traffic analysis, 123
transient electromagnetic pulse emanation standard, TEMPEST 126, 128
Transpac (X-25 network), 6
transparent robots, IRC, 524
Tridgell, Andrew (Samba), 286
Trier, Stephen, sct@po.cwru.edu, 339, 631–636
Triple DES encryption technique, 131
Tripwire software (UNIX system), 267
Trn
  adding/deleting newsgroups, 760–762
  article response with follow-up article, 759–760
  article searches by people or subject, 771–773
  canceling kill commands, 764
  canceling or superseding articles, 770
  changing default editor, 769
  commands, 751
  decoding binary data, 756–757
  e-mail article response, 758–759
  editing kill file, 764
  follow-up article, 759–760
  global kill file, 774
  information searches, 770
  initial start-up, 749
  junking threads automatically, 776
  kill file, 762–764, 774–778
  killing articles, 762–763
  local kill file, 774
  newsgroup kill file, 774
  newsgroups searches, 770–771
  .newsrc file, 749
  .newsrc file editing, 761–762
  options, 779–780
  overview, 749
  quitting, 764
  reading articles, 768
  reading news, 753–754
  reordering newsgroups, 762
  resources, 778–779

responding to articles, 758–760
rot13 code, 754–755
running, 749–750
saving articles, 755–756
security issues, 757
selecting
articles by thread, 751–753
newsgroups, 750–751
threads automatically, 775
selecting/junking articles
automatically, 774–775
with search commands, 776–777
setting options, 779–780
signatures, 769
text searches, 755, 774
thread-selection menu formats, 766–767
tips and tricks, 766–780
using, 750
uuencoded data, 756
Trojan horses, 122–123
IRC, 527
troublemakers, 43–45
troubleshooting
DNS problems, 242–243
Macintosh Internet connection, 354–355
Macintosh TIA, 384–385
Trumpet Winsock software (Peter Tattam), 308, 310, 329, 933–934
ftp.trumpet.com.au, 282–283
receive window parameters, 342
optimum settings, 933–934
Trusted Information Systems, Inc, 160
tsipple@vnet.ibm.com (Timothy Sipples), 387–405
TurboGopher 2.0b5 software, 617–619
TurboGopher software, 322
types
Gopher, 611–612, 835
Gopher+, 612

U

U.S. National Information Infrastructure plan, 815–817
unattended terminals, 122
unauthorized entry via Internet, 123
UnCover software, 482–483
Uniform Resource Locator (URL), 96
University of Illinois Urbana-Champaign, 323
University of Michigan, Macintosh communication applications, 357, 941
University of Minnesota, 322–323
Mother of All Gophers, 594–595
UNIX
automatic signature instructions, 410–417
backfinger script, 421–422
custom HTTP server, 548, 551–556
entering commands in ISO 6937/2 terminal, 450
finger instructions, 417–422
ftp command, 363
HOSTALIAS environment variable, 344–345
Listproc mailing lists, 433
ORGANIZATION environment variable, 425
University of Minnesota Gopher server, 613–616
UNIX scripts, 787–790
GetAllMessages, 788
GetMail, 788
GetMessages, 789
GetSummary, 788–789
SendMessages, 789–790
UNIX system
/etc/syslog.conf file, 266
configuration samples, 263–266
connecting to the Internet, 255–267
connection types/comparative costs, 255–256
COPS software, 267
Crack software, 267
debugging, 260
dedicated line, 257–258
dedicated SLIP, 257
dialup SLIP, 257
e-mail gateway, 257
frame relay, 258
hardware configuration, 258–259
INCONFIG program, 260
ISDN dialup service, 258
monitoring activities, 267
NETSTAT, 261
PING command, 261
ROUTE command, 262
security concerns, 266–267
software configuration, 259–260
TCP wrappers, 267
TRACEROUTE, 261–262
Tripwire software, 267
unmoderated open mailing list, 429–430
UNOR newsreader, 794
UofM DOS: PC_Client server, 617
UofM UNIX Gopher server
accessing other servers, 616
advanced features, 615
basic features, 614–615
bookmarks, 615
copying information, 615–616
printing files, 616
Veronica features, 616
UQWK software, 782–785
commands, 785
installation, 783
reading/posting messages, 787
retrieving/downloading messages, 783–784
sending messages, 784–785
URL (Uniform Resource Locator), 96, 409, 453–455, 470
finger, 418–419
ftp: (ftp server), 453
gopher: (Gopher server), 453
http: (WWW server), 453
online retrieval instructions, 453–455
US software, 785–786
getting selected articles, 786
installing, 785
running, 786
summary file, 785–786
Usenet, 29, 49–76
active newsgroup listings, 53
ad formats/limitations, 102
advertising on, 58
alphabetizing newsgroups, 732–733
article analysis, 729–730
article distributions, 733
articles, 725
author responsibilities, 111–112
B News software, 65–66
BITNET parts, 58
buying/selling marketplace items, 102–104
buying/selling online, 100–107
C News software, 65–76
censorship problems, 109
control of, 61–62
derfing, 112
diversity, 52, 61
expired articles, 726

falsehoods, 49–52, 56–60
FCC regulations, 109–110
finalizing marketplace transactions, 104–106
finding specific marketplace items, 102
First Amendment protections, 109–110
getting known in groups, 31
Gopher newsgroups, 607
group structure, 61
hierarchy, 100
Internet differences, 59
interview with Henry Spencer, 65–76
kill files, 735–736
limiting message distribution, 101–102
marketplace users, 101–102
moderated newsgroups, 728
naming conventions, 61
news administrator, 728
news.groups newsgroup, 54
newsgroup
  appeals, 54–55, 63
  creation, 53–54, 62–63
  guidelines, 53–54, 63
  hierarchy, 726–727
  listing, 728–729
newsgroups, 95–96, 197–198, 360–361, 674–675, 725
newsgroups' recommendations, 727–728
.newsrc file, 731–732
operating systems, 51, 59–60
organization of, 56–57
origination, 51, 59
overview, 109, 725–726
periodic postings, 53, 62
posting test articles, 733
propagation of, 53, 62
providers, 57–58
publication responsibilities and liabilities, 110–112
readers, 895–899
redirecting follow-up articles, 734–735
rot13 code, 754–755
servers, 293
second opinion, 56–64
signature file, 730–731
software support, 52, 60
spamming, 101
system administrator, 52, 61–62, 109
truisms, 52–56, 60–64
unsubscribing to newsgroups, 732
upstream/downstream sites, 52
UUNET, 53
words to live by, 55, 63–64
Usenet bang signs (!), 217
Usenet News, 217, 293
  applications, Macintosh, 949–951
  Henry Spencer, 65–76
  SLIP/PPP account, 305, 319–321
Usenet newsgroups, 95–96, 725
  disability, 197–198
  Macintosh, 360–361
  reading with Pine, 674–675
user ID, SLIP/PPP account, 311–312
users
  extinct, 46
  mythical, 46
  rare, 46
using firewalls on the Internet, 173–179
utilities, search, 469–502
UUCP (UNIX-to-UNIX Copy) protocol, 51, 53, 59, 826
UUCP mail network, 217
uuencoded files
  security warning, 757
  Trn program, 756
UUNET, 53

V.34 modem protocol, 271
val-dor.cc.buffalo.edu (CODI), 196
VanHeyningen, Marc, mvanheyn@cs.indiana.edu, 418
VaxVMS, University of Minnesota Gopher server, 613–616
vendors, router, 813–814
vendors/products, disability, 192–194
Veronica, 470
  gopher server, 599–601
  gopher searches, 627–629
VersaPoint (DOS/Windows/Mac) Braille translator software, 188
verve@cyberwerks.com (Eric S. Theise, Ph.D), 608–630
ViaCrypt products, 135, 153
video interrupt handler, ISO 6937/2, 448
Vielmetti, Edward, emv@msen.com, 56–64
virtual flea market, 100–107
virtual memory, security, 125
virus protection programs, 122
viruses, 122–123
Vixie, Paul, 244
Vocal Eyes (DOS) software, 187
Voice Navigator II software, Macintosh, 189
VVV, 5

WAIS (wide area information servers), 470, 637–668, 921–922
  articles/books, 667–668
  Boolean indexer, 655–656
  Boolean search, 640
  clients, 638–639
  companies/organizations, 666
  database catalogs/descriptions, 655
  database management, 660–661
  detail indexing, 658
  distributions, 651–652
  document indexing, 653–658
  document types, 655
  Essence, 665
  fielded searches with WAIS-sf, 657
  FreeWAIS (CNIDR), 651–652
  FreeWAIS-sf, 652
  function, 638
  future enhancements, 665–666
  gopher server, 602
  Harvest, 665
  HyperWAIS for Mac, 643
  indexer command line options, 654
  indexing, 653–658
  installing, 659–660
  MacWAIS, 643–650
  mail servers, 441
  multiple data types, 656–657
  origin of, 637
  relevance feedback, 640
  resources, 666–668
  scoring algorithm search, 639
  searches, 639–640
  server configuration, 660–661
  server security issues, 662–663
  server usage statistics, 661–662
  servers, 659–665

setting hit numbers, 640
SFgate, 663–665
software, 667
Swais, 641
synonym indexing, 657
WAIS-sf fielded searches, 657
Waisq, 641–642
waissearch, 641–642
WAIStation for Mac, 643
WinWAIS, 643
World Wide Web gateways, 650, 663–665
Xwais, 640–641
ZDist, 666
Waisq software, 641–642
waissearch software, 641–642
WAIStation for Mac software, 643
Warnock, Archie, warnock@clark.net, 637–668
Washington and Lee University (WLU) gopher, 595
web of trust, 141
WEBster e-mail magazine, 484
weirdos, 40–41
Werbal Phantasy Detergent Cleany address, 98
Wesson, Rick (Free-Market discussion list), 83–84
West's Legal Directory, 494–495
WFTPD.EXE software, Alun Jones, 286
Wheet, Lori, 20
White House, 496–497
Whois programs, 922–923
firewalls, 177
WIN.INI file, 282
WINCODE, installing, 957–958
Windows 95 software (Microsoft), 309
Windows for Workgroups software, 278
Windows HTTP, 850
Windows sockets interface, 851
Windows
custom HTTP server, 548, 550–551
graphical gopher clients, 622–627
WWW server, 849–864
WinGopher Complete software, 329
WinHTTPD, 849
WinPAC Complete software, 329
WINPKT.COM file, 282
Winsock (Windows Sockets) applications, 281–282, 851, 867–939
bugs, 868
Chat programs, 868–872
commercial demo packages, 872–876
diagnostic tools, 876–877
Eudora documentation, 937
getting started, 930–931
file-search protocols, 877–881
file-transfer protocols, 877–881
Finger programs, 881–883
games (MUDs), 883–885
games (other), 885–886
Gophers, 886–889
host lookup programs, 889–890
Hyper-G, 891
IRC programs, 868–872
mail accessories, 891–895
mail programs, 891–895
mail/newsreaders, 895–899
miscellaneous, 899–904
Mosaic and MS mouse, 936
personal communication programs, 868–872
Ping, 911
source locations, 934–935
TCP/IP, 918
telephone dialers, 912–913
Telnet, 914–918
TIA, 935–936
time synchronizers, 919–921
Trumpet WinSock, 933–934
Usenet readers, 895–899
WAIS, 921–922
Whois, 922–923
World Wide Web browsers, 923–928
X.500 (DUA) clients, 929–930
WINSOCK.DLL file, 282
WinVision (DOS/Windows) software, 186
WinWAIS software, 643
WINZIP, installing, 957
Wired Cafe, telnet Chat.hotwired.com, 17
Wired magazine, info-rama @wired.com, 91
Wiretap gopher, 579–580
WN server software, 557
Wohler, Bill, wohler@newt.com, 737–748
WOO (webbed Moo), 863
Word Scholar (DOS) software, 187
workstations
TCP/IP installation, 277–279
TCP/IP stack, 278
World Wide Web (WWW), 24, 470, 810–811
address links, 577–578
archives guide, 477
ARTFL text database, 580–582
available online text types, 575–577
biographies, 577
book reviews, 576–577
browser applications, Macintosh, 951–953
browsers, 923–928
browsing, 472–477
custom versus established servers, 559–561
CyberSight, 474
defining online text, 574–575
DNS resources, 252
document ownership identification, 546–547
EFF Extended (Big Dummy's) Guide, 474–475
ElNet Galaxy, 473
forums, 576
future, 863
gateways, WAIS, 650, 663–665
gopher links, 604–606
Gophers, 578–587
handling form results, 570–572
home pages for WinHTTPD, 862
how computers read text, 575
HTML (Hypertext Markup Language), 531–546
check boxes, 565–566
forms setup, 563–570
hidden elements, 567–588
radio buttons, 565–566
reset button, 567
selection menus, 566–567
submit button, 567
tags, 532–542
text input, 563–565
HTTP servers, 547–557
Human-Computer Interaction (HCI) Launching Pad, 475
image maps, 572–573
indexes/lists, 96
INTER-LINKS, 474
interactive features, 562–573
Internet Resources Meta-Index, 474
introduction, 531–542

IRC access, 529
Joel's Hierarchical Subject Index, 473
journals, 576
library Gophers, 577
link ethics, 545–546
links, 532
Macintosh, 361–362, 364
Mosaic, 24
Mozilla effect, 544
NAME links, 547
navigational aids, 546
netiquette, 542–543
Netscape, 24
nonstandard tags, 545
online text problems, 579–580
online retrieval instructions, 454
page additions, 546–547
pages, 466, 854
parsing form results, 571
Planet Earth Home Page, 473
PROJECT DA-CLOD, 474
publicizing pages, 561
publishing information on, 531–561
rare books online, 582–587
references, 570
script output, 571–572
scripts, 562–563
searching by type or location, 477–479
server administrator responsibilities, 560
server applications, Macintosh, 953
servers, 294
SGML (Standard Generalized Markup Language), 534
sites, 96–98, 506–507
SLIP/PPP account, 306
SLIP/PPP account access, 322–323
Special Internet Connections, 474
text, 574–589
text/hypertext, 532
The Mother-of-all BBS, 475
tips for HTML documents, 862–863
troubleshooting, 557–559
URL (Uniform Resource Locator), 453–455
virtual library: listing, 474
virtual library: subject catalog, 473
Web Psychic page, 568–570
"whats new?" pages, 547
Yahoo, 457, 473
WS_FTP software, 321
WSGopher 1.2 software, 622–624
WSGopher software, 464
WWW mail servers, 440–441
WWW server, Windows, 849–864
applications to help run, 852–853
CGI scripts, 856–862
configuring, 851–852
creating imagemaps, 854–856
dressing up pages, 854–861
FTP for software, 862
hardware requirements, 850
HTML authoring, 853
references, 862
resources, 862
sample CGI application, 858–860
software requirements, 850
tips for setting up, 852–853
writing scripts, 860–861

X Window software, 627, 807–808
firewalls, 177–178
X.500 (DUA) clients, 929–930
Xwais software, 640–641

Yahoo, 473
Internet search strategies, 457
Yanoff, Scott, Special Internet Connections, 474
Yarn newsreader, 790–794
installation/setup, 791–792
running, 792–793
uses, 793–794
Young, Margaret Levine, margy@iecc.com, 725, 749–780

Z

ZDist software, 666
Zimmermann, Phillip, 134–135, 151
legal defense fund, 158–159
zone transfer, DNS, 221, 228
zones, DNS, 223–226
ZoomText (DOS/Windows) software, 184
ZoomText Plus (DOS/Windows) software, 184

IDG BOOKS WORLDWIDE LICENSE AGREEMENT

Important — read carefully before opening the software packet(s). This is a legal agreement between you (either an individual or an entity) and IDG Books Worldwide, Inc. (IDG). By opening the accompanying sealed packet(s) containing the software disk(s), you acknowledge that you have read and accept the following IDG License Agreement. If you do not agree and do not want to be bound by the terms of this Agreement, promptly return the book and the unopened software packet(s) to the place you obtained them for a full refund.

1. License. This License Agreement (Agreement) permits you to use one copy of the enclosed Software program(s) on a single computer. The Software is in "use" on a computer when it is loaded into temporary memory (i.e., RAM) or installed into permanent memory (e.g., hard disk, CD-ROM, or other storage device) of that computer.

2. Copyright. The entire contents of this disk(s) and the compilation of the Software are copyrighted and protected by both United States copyright laws and international treaty provisions. The individual programs on the disk(s) are copyrighted by the authors of each program respectively. Each program has its own use permissions and limitations. You may only (a) make one copy of the Software for backup or archival purposes, or (b) transfer the Software to a single hard disk, provided that you keep the original for backup or archival purposes. To use each program, you must follow the individual requirements and restrictions detailed for each in Chapter 33 of this Book. Do not use a program if you do not want to follow its Licensing Agreement. None of the material on this disk(s) or listed in this Book may ever be distributed, in original or modified form, for commercial purposes.

3. Other Restrictions. You may not rent or lease the Software. You may transfer the Software and user documentation on a permanent basis provided you retain no copies and the recipient agrees to the terms of this Agreement. You may not reverse engineer, decompile, or disassemble the Software except to the extent that the foregoing restriction is expressly prohibited by applicable law. If the Software is an update or has been updated, any transfer must include the most recent update and all prior versions.

4. Limited Warranty. IDG Warrants that the Software and disk(s) are free from defects in materials and workmanship for a period of sixty (60) days from the date of purchase of this Book. If IDG receives notification within the warranty period of defects in material or workmanship, IDG will replace the defective disk(s). IDG's entire liability and your exclusive remedy shall be limited to replacement of the Software, which is returned to IDG with a copy of your receipt. This Limited Warranty is void if failure of the Software has resulted from accident, abuse, or misapplication. Any replacement Software will be warranted for the remainder of the original warranty period or thirty (30) days, whichever is longer.

5. No Other Warranties. To the maximum extent permitted by applicable law, IDG and the author disclaim all other warranties, express or implied, including but not limited to implied warranties of merchantability and fitness for a particular purpose, with respect to the Software, the programs, the source code contained therein and/or the techniques described in this Book. This limited warranty gives you specific legal rights. You may have others which vary from state/jurisdiction to state/jurisdiction.

6. No Liability For Consequential Damages. To the extent permitted by applicable law, in no event shall IDG or the author be liable for any damages whatsoever (including without limitation, damages for loss of business profits, business interruption, loss of business information, or any other pecuniary loss) arising out of the use of or inability to use the Book or the Software, even if IDG has been advised of the possibility of such damages. Because some states/jurisdictions do not allow the exclusion or limitation of liability for consequential or incidental damages, the above limitation may not apply to you.

Alternate Disk Format Available.

The enclosed disks are in 3 1/2" 1.44MB, high-density format. If you have a different size drive, or a low-density drive, and you cannot arrange to transfer the data to the disk size you need, you can obtain the program's 3-1/2" 720K low-density disks by writing to the following address:

IDG Books Disk Fulfillment Department
Attn: *Internet SECRETS*
IDG Books Worldwide
7260 Shadeland Station
Suite 100
Indianapolis, IN 46256

or call 800-762-2974. Please specify the size of disk you need, and please allow 3 to 4 weeks for delivery.

IDG BOOKS WORLDWIDE REGISTRATION CARD

RETURN THIS REGISTRATION CARD FOR FREE CATALOG

Title of this book: Internet SECRETS

My overall rating of this book: ❑ Very good [1] ❑ Good [2] ❑ Satisfactory [3] ❑ Fair [4] ❑ Poor [5]

How I first heard about this book:

❑ Found in bookstore; name: [6] ❑ Book review: [7]

❑ Advertisement: [8] ❑ Catalog: [9]

❑ Word of mouth; heard about book from friend, co-worker, etc.: [10] ❑ Other: [11]

What I liked most about this book:

What I would change, add, delete, etc., in future editions of this book:

Other comments:

Number of computer books I purchase in a year: ❑ 1 [12] ❑ 2-5 [13] ❑ 6-10 [14] ❑ More than 10 [15]

I would characterize my computer skills as: ❑ Beginner [16] ❑ Intermediate [17] ❑ Advanced [18] ❑ Professional [19]

I use ❑ DOS [20] ❑ Windows [21] ❑ OS/2 [22] ❑ Unix [23] ❑ Macintosh [24] ❑ Other: [25]________________ (please specify)

I would be interested in new books on the following subjects:
(please check all that apply, and use the spaces provided to identify specific software)

❑ Word processing: [26] ❑ Spreadsheets: [27]

❑ Data bases: [28] ❑ Desktop publishing: [29]

❑ File Utilities: [30] ❑ Money management: [31]

❑ Networking: [32] ❑ Programming languages: [33]

❑ Other: [34]

I use a PC at (please check all that apply): ❑ home [35] ❑ work [36] ❑ school [37] ❑ other: [38] ________________

The disks I prefer to use are ❑ 5.25 [39] ❑ 3.5 [40] ❑ other: [41]________________

I have a CD ROM: ❑ yes [42] ❑ no [43]

I plan to buy or upgrade computer hardware this year: ❑ yes [44] ❑ no [45]

I plan to buy or upgrade computer software this year: ❑ yes [46] ❑ no [47]

Name: Business title: [48] Type of Business: [49]

Address (❑ home [50] ❑ work [51]/Company name:)

Street/Suite#

City [52]/State [53]/Zipcode [54]: Country [55]

❑ **I liked this book!** You may quote me by name in future IDG Books Worldwide promotional materials.

My daytime phone number is ________________

IDG BOOKS ®

THE WORLD OF COMPUTER KNOWLEDGE

Please keep me informed about IDG's World of Computer Knowledge. Send me the latest IDG Books catalog.

NO POSTAGE
NECESSARY
IF MAILED
IN THE
UNITED STATES

BUSINESS REPLY MAIL

FIRST CLASS MAIL PERMIT NO. 2605 FOSTER CITY, CALIFORNIA

IDG Books Worldwide
919 E Hillsdale Blvd, STE 400
Foster City, CA 94404-9691